International Finance

International Finance

Theory into Practice

Piet Sercu

Princeton University Press
Princeton and Oxford

ISBN: 978-0-691-13667-7 (alk. paper)

Library of Congress Control Number: 2008941943

British Library Cataloging-in-Publication Data is available

This book has been composed in LucidaBright using TEX
Typeset and copyedited by T&T Productions Ltd, London

Printed on acid-free paper ∞

press.princeton.edu

Printed in the United States of America

10 9 8 7 6 5 4 3 2 1

Contents

Preface

About This Book

Updating *International Financial Markets and the Firm*, the 1995 forerunner to this book by me and Raman Uppal, was something that we had wanted to do for a long time. By 2004, Raman and I reluctantly agreed that a text full of Italian lira or German marks, and where traders still had a full two minutes to respond to market makers' quotes, might sooner or later get outdated. Starting the revision itself turned out to be much more difficult than agreeing on the principle, though. In the end Raman, being so much busier and more rational than I am, preferred to bow out. How right he was. Still, now that the effort has become a sunk cost, forever bygone, I find that episodes where I sincerely curse the book (and myself and Princeton University Press) are becoming fewer and farther between. Actually, there are now several passages I almost like.

The book targets finance students, or at least students that want a genuine finance text, not an international-management or -strategy text with a finance slant nor an international monetary economics text with some corporate applications. There is a continued bias in favor of financial markets and economic logic; the aim is to provide students with a coherent picture of international markets and selected topics in multinational corporate finance. Sure, during everyday practice later on, this framework will then get amended and corrected and qualified; but the feeling of fundamental coherence will remain, I hope.

This book is still more analytical than the modal text in the field. But there is less math than in the Sercu–Uppal book, and it is brought in differently. Many of the appendixes are gone or have been much shortened. While in *International Financial Markets* we had every theorem or proof followed by an example, now the example comes first whenever possible. If so, the proof is often even omitted, or turned into a do-it-yourself assignment. In fact, a third innovation is that, at least in the chapters or sections that are sufficiently analytical rather than just factual, the reader is invited to prove or verify claims and solve analogous problems. The required level of math is surely not prohibitive; anybody who has finished a good finance course should be able to master these do-it-yourself assignments.

Every part, except the first, now has its own introductory case, which is intended to stimulate the reader's appetite and which can be a source of assignments. The cases usually cover issues from most chapters in the part.

A fifth change is that the part on exchange-rate pricing is much reduced. The chapters on exchange-rate theories, predictability, and forward bias are now shrunk to one (admittedly long) chapter. And, lastly, three wholly new chapters have been added: two on international stock markets—especially cross listing with the associated corporate-governance issues—and one on Value-at-Risk.

Typically, a preface like this one continues with a discussion and motivation of the book's content. But my feeling is that most readers—and surely students—skip prefaces anyway. Since the motivation of the structure is quite relevant, that material is now merged into the general introduction, chapter 1.

How to Use This Book

The text contains material for about two courses. One possibility is to take the second part, International Financial Markets, as one course, and group the more business-finance oriented material (Exchange Risk, Exposure, and Risk Management (part III) and Long-Term Financing and Investments (part IV)) as a second. Fixed-income markets, which are now in part III, could be included in the markets/instruments course, as they were in the 1995 book; and the whole package could also duplicate as an introductory derivatives course, along with the apocryphal chapter that is available on my website. I myself run two courses of unequal length—this is Europe—covering, respectively, parts II and III (instruments and risk management) and part IV (stocks, bonds, and capital budgeting).

For a single course one could focus, in part II, on spot (chapter 3) and forwards (chapters 4 and 5), and then continue with the chapters on the relevance of hedging and exposure (chapters 12 and 13), to finish with capital budgeting (chapter 21); this shortlist can be complemented by a few chapters of your liking.

About the Author

Piet Sercu is Professor of International Finance at the Katholieke Universiteit Leuven. He holds the degrees of Business Engineer, Master of Business Administration, and Doctor in Applied Economics from K.U.Leuven. He taught at the Flemish Business School in Brussels (1980–86), before returning to Leuven, where he currently teaches the International Business Finance courses in the Masters and Advanced Masters programs. He also held Visiting Professor appointments at New York University, Cornell University, the University of British Columbia, the London Business School, and Université Libre de Bruxelles. He taught shorter finance courses in Helsinki, Bandung (Indonesia), Leningrad, and India (as a UNDP expert and, in 1994, as a fellow of the European Indian Cooperation and Exchange Programme), and regularly teaches executive courses. He held the 1996/97 Francqui Chair at the Facultés Universitaires Notre-Dame de la Paix at Namur, and the 2000/04 PricewaterhouseCoopers Chair on Value and Risk at K.U.Leuven, together with Marleen Willekens. Until 2000, he organized and taught doctoral courses in the European Doctoral Education Network, as part of the Finance faculty of the European Institute for

Advanced Studies in Management. He was the 1994 Vice-President and 1995 President of the European Finance Association, won the 1999 Western Finance Association award for Corporate Finance (with Xueping Wu and Charley Park) and was Hanken Fellow in 2002.

His early research focused on international asset pricing with real exchange risk and inflation risk. He also did some work on corporate takeover models and lending but has recently returned to international finance and hedging. He has published in the *Journal of Finance*, *Journal of Banking & Finance*, *Journal of International Money and Finance*, *European Economic Review*, and other journals. He is on the editorial boards of the *European Financial Management Journal* and the *Journal for International Financial Markets, Institutions & Money*.

Piet Sercu and Raman Uppal jointly won the 1995 Sanwa Prize for a monograph in international finance, *Exchange Rate Volatility, Trade, and Capital Flows under Alternative Currency Regimes*, published by Cambridge University Press in 2000 and 2006. They have also produced *International Financial Markets and the Firm* (International Thomson Publishers, Cincinnati, OH, and London, 1995), the forerunner to this book. There are also a number of joint academic articles.

About the Foundation Jeanne Devos

All of the royalties paid on sales of this book are being donated directly to the Foundation Jeanne Devos, a charity. Jeanne Devos works in Mumbai where, in 1985, she set up the National Domestic Workers Movement to improve the lot of domestic workers, mostly illiterate, lower-caste women, girls, and children. She received an honorary doctorate at K.U.Leuven as well as the Harvard Leadership Prize. You can find more information on www.ndwm.org or on www.jeannedevos.org. Any additional help is highly appreciated.

Acknowledgments

There are many individuals who played an important role in the production of this book. First and foremost I thank Raman Uppal, not only for his invaluable contribution to the first book but also for the discussions about how to structure a new version, for translating the text parts of the old manuscript into LaTeX, and for setting up a master file system to produce the whole. Thanks also to the former and current doctoral students or assistants who read earlier drafts of the first and second books and who suggested several improvements: Badrinath, Thi Ngoc Tuan Bui, Katelijne Carbonez, Cédric de Ville de Goyet, Kathy Dehoperé, Marian Kane, Fang Liu, Rosanne Vanpée, Tom Vinaimont, and Xueping Wu. Marian, especially, did lots of work on the exercises. Professor Martina Vandebroek occasionally helped with spreadsheets and graphs, at which she Excels; she, Fang Liu, and Badrinath provided the empirical results for chapters 10 and 11. I also want to thank Richard Baggaley at Princeton University Press (U.K.) for his unflagging support despite my multiply missed deadlines and for securing the Jeanne Devos Foundation a generous royalty, and Jon Wainwright at T&T Productions Ltd, London, who was the perfect counterweight to my overly relaxed attitude toward tables, references, and the English language in general. Many thanks, lastly, to colleagues who read drafts and provided comments, some of them at Princeton's request but some even of own their free will: Hu Shengmei, Karen Lewis, Bernard Dumas, Stan Standaert, Charles van Wymeersch, and an anonymous (but wholly positive) referee reporting to Princeton University Press. Of course, I remain responsible for all remaining errors. Comments and feedback from readers about errors, presentation, and content are very welcome: do email me at piet.sercu@econ.kuleuven.be.

I dedicate this book to my parents, Jan Sercu and the late Térèse Reynaert, and to my wife Rita and children Maarten and Jorinde, who have patiently put up with my inattentive absentmindedness during the time it has taken to complete this project and, come to think of it, most of the time before and since.

International Finance

PART I

Introduction and Motivation for International Finance

1

Why Does the Existence of Borders Matter for Finance?

Almost tautologically, international finance selects from the broad field of finance those issues that have to do with the existence of many distinct countries. The fact that the world is organized into more or less independent entities instead of a single global state complicates a chief financial officer's (CFO's) life in many ways—ways that matter far more than does the existence of provinces or states or *Landen* or *départements* within a country. Below, we discuss

- the existence of national currencies and, hence, the issue of exchange rates and exchange risk;
- the segmentation of goods markets along predominantly national lines; in combination with price stickiness, this makes most exchange-rate changes "real";
- the existence of separate judicial systems, which further complicates the already big issue of credit risk, and has given rise to private-justice solutions;
- the sovereign autonomy of countries, which adds political risks to standard commercial credit risks;
- the existence of separate and occasionally incompatible tax systems, giving rise to issues of double and triple taxation.

We review these items in section 1.1. Other issues or sources of problems, such as differences in legal systems, investor protection, corporate governance, and accounting systems, are not discussed in much depth, not because they are irrelevant but for the simple reasons that there is too much heterogeneity across countries and I have no expertise in them. Still, in chapters 17 and 18 there are sections that should create a basic awareness in these issues, so that the reader can then critically look at the local regulation and see its relative strengths and weaknesses.

The above list includes some of the extra issues a CFO in an international company needs to handle when doing the standard tasks of funding, evaluation, and risk management (section 1.2). The outline of how we will work our way through all this material follows in section 1.3.

1.1 Key Issues in International Business Finance

1.1.1 Exchange-Rate Risk

Why do most countries have their own money? One disarmingly simple reason is that printing bank notes is profitable, obviously, and even the minting of coins is usually a positive net present value (NPV) business. In the West, at least since the days of the Greeks and Romans, governments have been involved as monopoly producers of coins or at least as receivers of a royalty ("seignorage") from the use of the official logo. More recently, the ascent of paper money, where profit margins are almost too good to be true, has led to official monopolies virtually everywhere. One reason why money production is not handed over to the United Nations (UN) or the International Monetary Fund (IMF) or World Bank is that governments dislike giving up their monopoly rents. For instance, the shareholders of the European Central Bank (ECB) are the individual euro countries, not the European Union (EU) itself; that is, the countries have given up their monetary independence, but *not* their seignorage. In addition, having one's own money is a matter of national pride too: most Britons or Danes would not even dream of surrendering their beloved pound sterling or crown for, of all things, a European currency. Lastly, a country with its own money can adopt a monetary policy of its own, tailored to the local situation. Giving up a local policy was a big issue at the time the introduction of a common European currency was being debated.[1]

If money had intrinsic value (e.g., a silver content), if that intrinsic value were stable and immediately obvious to anybody, and if coins could be de-minted into silver and silver re-minted into coins at no cost and without any delay, then the value of a German joachimsthaler relative to a Dutch florin and a Spanish real would all be based on their relative silver content, and would be stable. But in practice many sovereigns were cheating with the silver content of their currencies, and got away with it in the short run. Also, there are costs in identifying a coin's true intrinsic value and in converting Indian coins, say, into

---

[1] Following a national monetary policy assumes that prices for goods and services are sticky, that is, they do not adjust quickly when money supply or the exchange rate are being changed. (If prices fully and immediately react, monetary policy would not have any "real" effects.) Small open economies do face the problem that local prices adjust too fast to the level of the countries that surround them. So it is not a coincidence that Monaco, San Marino, Andorra, and the Vatican do not bother to create their own currencies. Not-so-tiny Luxembourg similarly formed a monetary union with Belgium in 1922. Those two then fixed their rate to the DEM and NLG with a 1% band in 1982. For more countries that gave up, or never had, their own money, see Wikipedia's article on monetary union. See section 2.5.2 for a discussion of fixed exchange rates and currency boards, and countries that give up monetary policy but not seignorage.

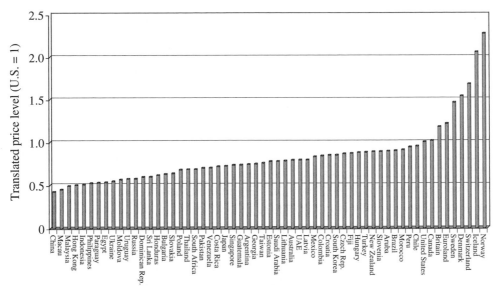

Figure 1.1. Relative prices of the Big Mac across the world, based on data from the *Economist*, May 26, 2006.

Moroccan ones. Finds of hoards dating from Roman or medieval times reveal astounding differences in the silver content of various coins with the same denomination. For instance, among *solidus* pieces from various mints and of many vintages, some have silver contents that are twice that of other solidus coins found in the same hoard. In short, intrinsic value never did nail down the market value in a precise way, not even in the days when coins really were made of silver, and as a result exchange rates have always fluctuated. Since the advent of paper money and electronic money, of course, intrinsic value no longer exists: the idea that paper money was convertible into gold coins lost all credibility after World War I. After World War II, governments for some time controlled the exchange rates, but largely threw in the towel in 1973–74. Since then, exchange rates are based on relative trust, a fickle good, and the resulting exchange-rate risk is a fact of life for all major currency pairs.

Exchange risk often implies that there is *contractual exposure*: there is uncertainty about the value of any asset or liability that expires at some future point in time and is denominated in foreign currency. But exchange risk also affects a company's financial health via another channel—an interaction, in fact, with another international issue: segmentation of consumer-goods markets.

1.1.2 Segmentation of Consumer-Goods Markets

While there are true world markets—and, therefore, world prices—for commodities, many consumer goods are really priced locally, and for traditional services international influence is virtually absent. Unlike corporate buyers of say oil or corn or aluminum, private consumers do not bother to shop around internationally for the best prices: the amounts at stake are too small, and the transportation cost and hassle and delay from international trade would be prohibitive anyway. Distributors, who are better placed for international shopping around, prefer to pocket the resulting quasi-rents themselves rather than passing them on to consumers. For traditional services, international trade is not even an option. So prices are not homogenized internationally even after conversion into a common currency. One strong empirical regularity is that, internationally, prices rise with GDP per capita. In figure 1.1, for instance, you see prices of the Big Mac in various countries, relative to the U.S. price. Obviously, developed countries lead this list, with growth countries showing up as less expensive by the *Economist*'s Big Mac standard. The ratio of Big Mac prices in Switzerland to those in China is 3.80. In early 2006, Norway was more than five times as expensive as China; and two years before, the gap between Iceland and South Africa was equally wide.

Within a country, by contrast, there is less of this price heterogeneity. For example, price differences between "twin" towns that face each other across the borders between the United States and Canada or between the United States and Mexico are many times larger than differences between East- and West-Coast towns within the United States. One likely reason that contributes to more homogeneous pricing within a country is that distributors are typically organized nationally. Of course, the absence of hassle with customs and international shippers and foreign indirect tax administrations also helps.

A second observation is that prices tend to be sticky. Companies prefer to avoid price increases, because the harm done to sales is not easily reversed: consumers are resentful, or they just write off the company as "too expensive" and do not even notice when prices come down again. Price decreases, on the other hand, risk setting off price wars, and so on.

Now look at the combined picture of (i) price stickiness, (ii) lack of international price arbitrage in consumption-goods markets, and (iii) exchange-rate fluctuations. The result is *real exchange risk*. Barring cases of hyperinflation, short-run exchange-rate fluctuations have little or nothing to do with the internal prices in the countries that are involved. So the appreciation of a currency is not systematically accompanied by falling prices abroad or soaring prices at home so as to keep goods prices similar in both countries. As a result, appreciation or depreciation can make a country less attractive as a place to produce and export from or as a market to export to. They therefore affect the market values and competitiveness of companies and economies, that is, *economic exposure*. For instance, the soaring USD in the Reagan years has meant the end of many a U.S. company's export business, and the rise of the DEM in the 1970s forced Volkswagen to become a multicountry producer.

Real exchange risk also affects asset values in a more subtle way. Depending on where they live, investors from different countries realize different real returns from one given asset if the real exchange-rate changes. Thus, one of the fundamental assumptions of, for example, the capital asset pricing model (CAPM)—that investors all agree on the returns and risks of all assets—becomes untenable. While this may sound like a very theoretical issue, it becomes more important once you start thinking about capital budgeting. For instance, a U.S. firm may be considering an investment in South Africa, starting from projected cash flows in South African rand (SAR). How to proceed? Should the managers discount them using a SAR discount rate, the way a local investor would presumably do it, and then convert the present value into USD using the current spot rate? Or should they do it the U.S. way: use expected future spot rates to convert the data into expected USD cash flows, to be discounted at a USD rate? Should both approaches lead to the same answer? *Can* they, in fact?

Exchange risk is the issue that takes up more space than any other separate topic in this book. Its importance can be seen from the fact that so many instruments exist that help us cope with this type of uncertainty: forward contracts, currency futures and options, and swaps. You need to understand all these instruments, their interconnections, their uses and limitations, and their risks.

1.1.3 Credit Risk

If a domestic customer does not pay, you resort to legal redress, and the courts enforce the ruling. Internationally, one problem is that at least two legal systems are involved, and they may contradict each other. Usually, therefore, the contract will stipulate what court will rule and on the basis of what law—say Scottish law in a New York court (I did not make this up). Even then, the new issue is that this court cannot enforce its ruling outside its own jurisdiction.

This has given rise to private-contract solutions: we seek guarantees from specialized financial institutions (banks, factors, insurance companies) that (i) are better placed to deal with the credit risks we shifted toward them, and (ii) have an incentive to honor their own undertakings because they need to preserve a reputation and safeguard relations with fellow banks, etc. So you need to understand where these perhaps Byzantine-sounding payment options (such as D/A, D/P, L/C[2] without or with confirmation, factoring, and so on) come from, and why and where they make sense.

1.1.4 Political Risk

Governments that decide or rule as sovereigns, having in mind the interest of their country (or claiming to have this in mind), cannot be sued in court as long as what they do is constitutional. Still, these decisions can hurt a company. One example is imposing currency controls, that is, blocking some or all exchange contracts, so that the money you have in a foreign bank account gets stuck

---

[2] Documents against acceptance, documents against payment, and letter of credit.

there, that is, *transfer risk*. You need to know how you can react pro- and retroactively. You also need to know how this risk must be taken into account in international capital budgeting. If and when your foreign-earned cash flow gets stuck abroad, it is obviously worth less than its nominal converted value because you cannot spend the money freely where and how you want—but how does one estimate the probabilities of this happening at various dates, and how does one predict the size of the value loss?

Another political risk is expropriation or nationalization, overtly or by stealth. While governments can also expropriate locally owned companies (like banks, as in France in 1981), foreign companies in the "strategic" sectors (energy, transportation, mining and extraction, and, flatteringly, finance) are especially vulnerable: most of them were expropriated or had to sell to locals in the 1970s. The 2006 Bolivian example, where President Evo Morales announced that "The state recovers title, possession and total and absolute control over [our oil and gas] resources" (*Economist*, May 4, 2006), also has to do with such a sector. Again, one issue for the finance staff is how to factor this into NPV calculations.

1.1.5 Capital-Market Segmentation Issues, Including Aspects of Corporate Governance

A truly international stock and bond market does not exist. First, while stocks and bonds of big corporations do get traded in many places and are held by investors all over the world, mid-size or small-cap companies are largely one-country instruments. Second, portfolios of individual and institutional investors exhibit strong home bias—that is, heavy overweighting of local stocks relative to foreign stocks—even regarding their holdings of shares in large corporations. A third aspect of fragmentation in stock markets is that we see no genuine international stock exchanges (in the sense of institutions where organized trading of shares takes place); instead, we have a lot of local *bourses*. A company that wants its shares to be held in many places gets a listing on two or three or more exchanges (*dual* or *multiple listings*; *cross listing*): being traded in relatively international places like London or New York is not enough, apparently, to generate worldwide shareholdership. How come?

The three phenomena might be related, and caused by the problem of asymmetric information and investor protection. Valuing a stock is more difficult than valuing a bond, even a corporate bond, and the scope for misrepresentation is huge, as the railroad and dot-com bubbles have shown. All countries have set up some legislation and regulation to reduce the risks for investors, but there are enormous differences in the amount of information, certification, and vetting required for an initial public offering (IPO). All countries think, or claim to think, that other countries are fools by imposing so much/little regulation. The scope for establishing a common world standard in the foreseeable future is nil. Pending this, there can be no single world market for stocks.

The same holds for disclosure requirements once the stock has been launched, and the whole issue of corporate governance. The big issue here is how to avoid managers self-dealing or otherwise siphoning off cash that ought to belong to the shareholders. Good governance systems contain checks and balances: separation of the jobs of chairman of the board of directors and chief executive officer (CEO); a sufficient presence of independent directors on the board; an audit committee that closely watches the accounts; comprehensive information provision for investors; a willingness, among the board members, to fire poorly performing CEOs, perhaps on the basis of preset performance criteria; a board that can be fired by the assembly general meeting in one shot (as opposed to staggered boards, where every year only one fifth comes up for (re)election, for example); and an annual general meeting that can formulate binding instructions for the board and the CEO. Good governance also requires good information provision, with detailed financial statements accompanied by all kinds of qualitative information.

But governance is not just a matter of corporate policies: it can, and ideally must, be complemented by adequately functioning institutions in the country. For instance, how active and independent are auditors, analysts (and, occasionally, newspaper reporters)? Is a periodic evaluation of the company's financial health by its house bank(s), each time loans are rolled over or extended, a good substitute for outside scrutiny? Are minority shareholders well protected, legally? How stringent are the disclosure and certification requirements, and are they enforced? Are there active large shareholders, like pension funds, that follow the company's performance and put pressure on management teams they are unhappy with? Is there an active market for corporate officers, so that good managers get rewarded and (especially) vice versa? Is there an active acquisition market where poorly performing companies get taken over and reorganized? Again, on all these counts there are huge differences across countries, which makes it impossible to set up one world stock market. The Organisation for Economic Co-operation and Development (OECD) has been unable to come up with a common stance even on something as fundamental as accounting standards. In 2006, Telenet, my internet provider, had to prepare three sets of accounts: Belgium's generally accepted accounting principles (GAAP), U.S. GAAP, and International Financial Reporting Standards (IFRS). Even though in the United States its shares are only sold to large private investors rather than the general public, Telenet still had to create a special type of security for the U.S. markets.

In short, markets are differentiated by regulation and legal environment. In addition, companies occasionally issue two types of shares: those available for residents of their home country, and unrestricted stocks that can be held internationally. Some countries even impose this by law. China is a prominent example, but the list used to include Korea, Taiwan, and Finland, Sweden, and Norway. Typically, only a small fraction of the shares was open to nonresidents. Other legislation that occasionally still fragments markets includes the following: a prohibition to hold foreign exchange (forex); restrictions or prohibitions on purchases of forex, especially for financial (i.e., investment) purposes; caps on the percentage of mutual funds or pension funds invested abroad, or minima for domestic investments; dual exchange rates that penalize financial transactions relative to commercial ones; taxes on deposits by non-residents; requirements to invest at zero interest rates at home, proportionally with foreign investments or even with imports, and so on.

In OECD countries or newly industrialized countries, these types of restrictions are now mostly gone. In December 2006, Thailand imposed some new regulations in order to discourage inflows—usually the objective is to stop outflows—but hastily reversed them after the Bangkok stock market crashed by 15%; this example goes to show that this type of restriction is simply *not done* anymore. But some countries, like Chile, never lifted them altogether, while in other countries the bureaucratic hassle still strongly discourages (India) or virtually prohibits (Russia) capital exports.

There are two repercussions for corporate finance. One is via the share-holders. Specifically, in countries with serious restrictions on outward invest-ments, the investment menu is restricted and different from the opportu-nity set available to luckier investors elsewhere. This then has implications for the way one works with the CAPM: companies in a walled-off country have to define the market portfolio in a strictly local way, while others may want to go all the way to the world-market version of the market portfolio. So companies' discount rates are affected and, therefore, their direct invest-ment decisions. Another corporate-finance implication is that a company that wants to issue shares abroad cannot simply go to some "international" mar-ket: rather, it has to select a country and, often, a segment (an exchange—which exchange? which board?—or the over-the-counter market or the private-investors segment), carefully weighting the costs and benefits of its choices. An important part of the costs and benefits has to do with the corporate-governance and disclosure ramifications of the country and market segment one chooses.

1.1.6 International Tax Issues

Fiscal authorities are understandably creative when thinking up excuses to tax. For instance, they typically want to touch all residents for a share in their income, whether that income is domestic or foreign in origin; but they typically also insist on taxing anybody making money inside the territory, whether the earner is a resident or not. So an Icelandic professor making money in Luxem-bourg as visiting faculty would be taxed by both Luxembourg—she did make money there—and Iceland—she is a resident there.

In corporate examples things get even worse. When an Icelandic corporation sets up shop in Luxembourg, the subsidiary is taxed there on its profits: it is a resident of Luxembourg, after all. But when that company then pays a dividend to its parent, both Luxembourg and Iceland may want to tax the parent company again: the parent makes money in Luxembourg, but is a resident in Iceland.

Fortunately, legislators everywhere agree that double or triple taxation may be somewhat overdoing things, so they advocate neutrality. But, as we shall see, there is no agreement as to how a "neutral" system can be defined, let alone how it is to be implemented. This makes life for the CFO complicated. But it also makes life exciting, because of the loopholes and clever combinations ("treaty shopping") that can substantially affect the tax burden.

1.2 What Is on the International CFO's Desk?

This book is a text on international finance. Thus, it does not address issues of multinational corporate strategy, and the discussion of international macroeconomics is kept to a minimum. Within the finance discipline, it addresses only the problems caused by the existence of many countries, as described in the preceding section.

One way to further describe the material is to think about the tasks assigned to an international financial manager. These tasks include asset valuation, international funding, the hedging of exchange risk, and management of other risks. We hasten to add that these functions cannot be viewed in isolation, as will become clear as we proceed.

1.2.1 Valuation

One task of an international finance officer is the valuation of projects with cash flows that are risk free in terms of the foreign currency. For example, the manager may need to evaluate a large export order with a price fixed in foreign currency and payable at a (known) future date. The future cash flow is risky in terms of the domestic currency because the future exchange rate is uncertain. Just as one would do with a domestic project with cash flows that are risky in terms of the domestic currency, this export project should be subject to an NPV analysis. Thus, the manager needs to know how to compute present values when the source of risk is the uncertainty about the future exchange rate. Valuation becomes even more complicated in the case of foreign direct investment (FDI), where the cash flows are random even in terms of the foreign currency. The issues to be dealt with now are how to discount cash flows subject to both business risk and exchange risk, how to deal with tax complications and political risks inherent in FDI, and how to determine the cost of capital depending on whether or not the home and foreign capital markets are segmented.

1.2.2 Funding

A second task is, of course, funding the project. A standard financing problem is whether the firm should issue equity, debt, or equity-linked debt (such as convertible bonds). If bonds are issued or a loan is taken out, the standard questions are what the optimal maturity is, and whether the terms offered by a bank or a group of banks are attractive or not. In an international setting, the additional issue to be considered is whether the bond or loan should be denominated in home currency or in another one, whether or when there are any tax issues in this choice, how the risk can be quantified when it is correlated with other risks, and so on.

If funding is done in the stock markets, the issue is whether to issue stocks locally or to get a secondary listing elsewhere, or perhaps even move the company's primary listing abroad. The targeted foreign market may be better organized, have more analysts who know and understand your business, and give access to deep-pocketed investors who, being well-diversified already, are happy with lower expected returns than the current shareholders. But there are important corporate-governance issues as well, as we saw: getting a listing in a tough place is like receiving a certificate of good behavior and making a strong commitment to behave well in future too. So the mere fact of getting such a listing can lift the value of the company as a whole. There are, of course, costs: publishing different accounts and reports to meet diverging accounting and disclosure rules can be cumbersome and expensive, and listing costs are not trivial either. Because of the corporate-governance issues, cross listings are not purely technical decisions that belong to the CFO's competence: the whole board of directors should be involved.

1.2.3 Hedging and, More Generally, Risk Management

Another of the financial manager's tasks is usually to reduce risks, like exchange risk, that arise from corporate decisions. For example, a manager who has accepted a large order from a customer, with a price fixed in foreign currency and payable at some (known) future point in time, may need to find a way to hedge the resulting exposure to exchange rates.

There are, however, many other sources of uncertainty besides exchange rates. Some are also "market" risks: uncertainties stemming from interest rates, for instance, or commodity prices, or, for some companies, stock market gyrations. Exchange risk cannot be hedged in isolation, for the simple reason that market risks tend to be correlated. As a result, many companies want to track the remaining uncertainties of their entire portfolio of activities and contracts. This is usually summarized in a number called *Value-at-Risk* (VaR), the maximum loss that can be sustained with a given probability (say, 1%) over a given horizon (say, one day), taking into account the correlations between the market risks.

1.2.4 Interrelations between Risk Management, Funding, and Valuation

While the above taxonomy of CFO assignments is logical, it does not offer a good structure for a textbook. One reason is that valuation, hedging, and funding are interrelated. For instance, a firm may be unwilling to accept a positive-NPV export contract (valuation) unless the currency risk can be hedged. Also, the funding issue cannot be viewed in isolation from the hedging issue. For example, a Finnish corporation that considers borrowing in yen should not make that decision without pondering how this loan would affect the firm's total risk. That is, the decision to borrow yen may be unacceptable unless a suitable hedge is available. In another example, a German firm that has large and steady dollar revenues from exports might prefer to borrow USD because such a loan provides not just funding, but also risk reduction. In short, project evaluation, funding, and hedging have to be considered together.

But risks do not stop at market risks. There are credit risks, political risks, operational risks, reputation risks, and so on, and these also interact with the more financial issues. For instance, the evaluation of an export project should obviously take into account the default risk. Similarly, NPV computations for FDI projects should account for the risk that foreign cash flows may be blocked or that the foreign business may be expropriated.

1.3 Overview of this Book

In the preceding section, we discussed the key issues in international finance on the basis of managerial functions. As I pointed out, this is not a convenient way to arrange the text because the functions are all interlinked. Instead, we proceed as follows. We begin with an introductory chapter on the history of the international monetary system. The remainder of this textbook, then, is divided into three parts: part II on international financial markets and instruments; part III on exchange-rate risk, exposure, and risk management; and part IV on long-term financing and investment decisions. In most of the chapters except the next one, the focus is on corporate financial issues, such as risk management and funding and capital budgeting. Let us briefly review the contents of each part.

1.3.1 Part I: Motivation and Background Matter

After the present motivational chapter, we go over some background material: how is money created, how is it paid internationally, what is the role of governments in exchange markets, and what does the balance of payments mean for a country?

1.3.2 Part II: International Financial Markets

Part II of the book describes the currency market in its widest sense, that is, including all its satellites or derivatives. Chapter 3 describes spot markets. Forward markets, where price and quantity are contracted now but delivery and payment take place at a known future moment, are introduced in chapter 4, in a perfect-markets setting. Chapter 5 shows how and when to use contracts in reality: for arbitrage, taking into account costs; for hedging; for speculation; and for shopping-around and structured-finance applications including, especially, swaps. Currency futures and modern currency swaps, both of which are closely related to forward transactions, are discussed in chapters 6 and 7, respectively. Chapter 8 introduces currency options and shows how these options can be used to hedge against (or, alternatively, speculate on) foreign exchange risk. How currency options are priced is explained in chapter 9; we mostly use the so-called binomial approach but also link it to the famous Black–Merton–Scholes model.

At any instant, the market value of a forward, futures, or options contract depends on the prevailing spot rate (and, if the contract is not yet at the end of its life, also on the domestic and foreign interest rates). This dependence on the future spot rate means that all these contracts can be used to hedge the exchange-rate risk to which the firm is exposed. The dependence of these contracts on the future spot rate also means that their current market values can be expressed, by relatively simple arbitrage arguments, as functions of the current spot rate and of the domestic and foreign interest rate. Throughout this part of the text, a unified approach based on arbitrage-free pricing is used to value these assets, whose payoffs are dependent on the exchange rate.

1.3.3 Part III: Exchange Risk, Exposure, and Risk Management

This parts opens with a discussion of the behavior and predictability of nominal and real exchange rates (chapters 10 and 11). We conclude that exchange rates are hard to explain, let alone predict, and that most of the nominal uncertainty is also real, thus affecting the long-term value of a company.

This may sound like a good excuse to hedge. Yet one could argue that (i) hedging is a standard financial transaction, (ii) in efficient markets, financial transactions are zero-NPV deals, and (iii) hedging, therefore, does not add value. In chapter 12 we show the way out of this fallacy: hedging does add value if it does more than just increase or decrease the firm's bank account, that is, if and when it affects the firm's operations. Given that firms may want to hedge, the next issue is how much to hedge: what is the size of the exposure (chapter 13)? We distinguish between contractual, operational, and accounting exposures. Value-at-Risk is reviewed in chapter 14. Chapter 15 concludes this part with a description and critical discussion of the various ways to insure credit risks and transfer risks in international trade.

1.3.4   Part IV: Long-Term Financing and Investment Decisions

The prime sources for long-term financing are the markets for fixed-interest instruments (bank loans, bonds) and stocks. We review the international aspects of these in chapters 16 and in 17 and 18, respectively, including the fascinating issue of cross listing and corporate governance. Expected returns on stocks provide one key input of investment analysis, so in chapter 19 we consider the CAPM and the adjustments to be made to take into account real exchange risk. The other inputs into NPV computations are expected cash flows, and these are typically quite similar to what one would see in domestic projects. There is one special issue here: international taxes (chapter 20). In chapter 21 we see how to do the actual NPV, extending the usual two-step approach—NPV followed by adjusted NPV to take into account the aspects of financing relevant in imperfect markets—to a three-step version to separately handle intra- and extra-company financial arrangements. We conclude with an analysis of joint-venture projects, where NPV is mixed with the issue of designing a fair profit-sharing contract (chapter 22).

Here we go then.

2

International Finance:
Institutional Background

Before we can learn about topics such as currency futures and options, currency swaps, the behavior of exchange rates, the measurement of exchange risk, and valuation of real and financial assets in the presence of this risk, we need to understand a much more fundamental issue: namely, money. All of us are aware that money exists and that it is quite useful. Still, a review of why it exists and how it is created is crucial to understanding some of the finer points of international finance, such as how the ownership of money is transferred across countries, how a central bank's balance sheet is maintained, how money from one country can be exchanged for money from another, and so on. Government policy with respect to the exchange rate (the price at which this buying and selling of currencies occurs) is also an important institutional aspect.

This chapter is structured as follows. First, we explain how money gradually evolved from a commodity with an intrinsic value to fiduciary money whose value is based on trust, and how the role of banks has changed accordingly. In section 2.2 we consider international banking transactions. This then leads to our discussion, in section 2.3, about international banking (often still called eurobanking). The emergence of the international bond market is also explained in that section. We then turn to two more macro-oriented issues: the balance of payments and its relation to exchange transactions (section 2.4), and the relation of government policy to the exchange rate (section 2.5).

2.1 Money and Banking: A Brief Review

In this section, we first review the role of money. We then look back a few millennia and explain how money has evolved over time from a bulky, commodity-type physical object into its current form, a record in a bank's electronic memory.

Figure 2.1. Baroque open-market policies. (Fresco, probably by J. M. Rottmayr (1656–1730), in the cupola of the Karlskirche, Vienna. Author's photo.)

2.1.1 The Roles of Money

Money has to do with buying and selling. The need for money arises in any economy in which economic units (for example, households, tribes, or fiefdoms) start to trade with each other. Pure, moneyless barter is inconvenient. To make a deal, a hungry blacksmith does not want to wander around until he meets a farmer whose horse has lost a shoe. The blacksmith would rather compensate the farmer for the food by giving him something called money. The advantage of paying in money rather than in horseshoes is that the farmer can then spend the money on other things if and when the need arises, and on any goods he chooses. Thus, trade and exchange with money are much easier, and the costs of searching for someone who needs exactly what you are selling at a particular point in time are greatly reduced if the buying and the selling bits can be separated.

Three conditions are needed for money to be a successful least-cost medium of exchange. First, it must be storable; the farmer would not like the unspent money to evaporate or rot. Second, it must have a stable purchasing power; the farmer would not like to discover that his hoard of money can buy a far smaller amount of goods than he had anticipated. This, in turn, requires that the stock of outstanding money must not rise substantially faster than the volume of transactions. Third, money must be easy to handle. Once these conditions are met, money can fulfill its role as the *least-cost medium of exchange.* When prices are expressed in units of money, money also acts as a *unit of account* or *numéraire.* Finally, money can also be lent and borrowed, which allows one to transfer purchasing power over time in a low-risk fashion.

2.1.2 How Money Is Created

In this section we trace the development of money from commodities and metal coins in early economies to privately issued money and, more recently, to official currency notes issued by the central bank of a country, or even electronic claims representing the right to withdraw currency notes.

2.1.2.1 Official Metal Coins

In relatively primitive economies, standard commodities played the role of money. In prehistoric Europe, domestic animals were used as unit of account. In fact, the Latin word for money, *pecunia*, simply derives from *pecus*, cattle. Also the ancient Greek silver *talanton* ("weight") betrays its links to the old practice of using domestic animals as money: the original talent had the shape of a sheepskin, and it was about as heavy as a good-sized lamb—one slave could carry just one *talanton.*

Only cowboys, at best, would think of herds of cattle as being easy to handle. The ascent as a medium of exchange of one particular class of commodities, namely precious metals, occurred because for a given amount of purchasing power, precious metals are far less bulky and easier to transport than cattle. Second, precious metals do not rust. And third, production was and is sufficiently costly to ensure that the stock of rare metal does not grow much faster than the economy as a whole, thus ruling out sudden inflation due to a rapidly expanding money stock.

Early gold and silver money was defined by its weight. The *as*, early Rome's basic currency unit, actually served as weight unit too: it was a cast piece of bronze weighing about $\frac{1}{3}$ kg. Likewise, almost all medieval European states had a pound or a *libra*, *livre*, or a *lira* unit of account, referring to 330–500 g of silver (see panel 2.1 and table 2.1). (Also *mark* was originally a weight—about $\frac{1}{4}$ kg—as was *peso*, from the Latin *pensum*, meaning weight.) What is striking is that the current value of the British or Irish or Maltese pound, not to mention the Turkish or late Italian lira, is not anywhere near the value of 370 g of silver. This *debasing* of the currency started quite early. One problem was that people reduced the true precious-metal content by melting down their coins, adding some cheap metal, and reminting the alloy.[1] To stop this practice—or, cynics might say, to monopolize it—the local lord, or seigneur, of the fiefdom installed an official mint to which people could bring precious metals for minting. The seigneur then imprinted his quality stamp on the coins in return for a commission or tax, the *seignorage*. This was one way that governments earned money. Later, governments made the issuing of coins their sole monopoly. This allowed them to become poachers themselves and reduce the gold or

---

[1] A related problem with precious metal coins was coin clipping: people scratched off part of the gold or silver around the edge, which reduced the intrinsic value of the coin but may have passed unnoticed. The ribs or other decorations that can still be seen on the rims of modern coins were originally meant to make coin clipping easier to detect.

In 1158, England's King Henry II fixed the financial pound on the basis of the weight standard of the French city of Troyes (Troy, in English) in the county of Champagne, then a leading European trading center. (In France, the leading currency was the *livre Tournois* (the Tournois pound)—20 *sols*, each consisting of 12 *deniers*—from Tours; its rival had been the livre Parisis—20 *sols*, each consisting of 15 *deniers*).

The *troy pound* (5760 gr.) consisted, Roman style, of 12 *troy ounces* (480 gr.), each worth 20 *pennyweights* (24 gr.). There was a 16 ounce *pound avoirdupois* too, fixed at 7000 gr. by Henry VIII, but that was for regular weighting. The *troy mark* was 8 troy ounces or 160d. and the *crown* was worth one-quarter pound or five shillings or 60d. The *troy ounce* is still being used nowadays for precious metals; it is 31.103 476 8 g.

Sterling is not an indication of weight but of quality for silver; it derives, like the old French *esterlin*, from Easterling, the name for a member of the German *Hansa*, a league of trading cities. Cynics might conclude that "pound sterling" means "a French coin of German quality," but you did not hear *me* say this.

Like the mark, the pound was originally just a unit of account: while there were shilling coins (silver) and crown coins (silver and gold), there was no silver pound coin as that would have been inconveniently bulky and heavy. Henry VII first minted gold pounds in 1489. Its weight was 0.5 troy ounce, 23kt (96% pure), soon lowered to 22kt (92%) under Henry VIII. This coin was dubbed *sovereign* because it showed the king on the obverse.

The *guinea* originally referred to new pound coins (1663), made of gold from the Gulf of Guinea (Ghana, the Gold Coast). The new, unworn coins traded at a premium over the old. With gold appreciating relative to silver, the gold-based guineas and sovereigns further rose against the silver-based shilling (up to 30s. per guinea). By the twentieth century, the guinea had become just a unit of account meaning 21s., and since 1967 it has just been a hoity-toity synonym for pound; English barristers, for instance, say guinea when they mean pound. The English (and Irish and Scottish) pound went metric in 1967; at that time, Australia and New Zealand introduced their dollars (initially worth 0.5 pounds).

Panel 2.1. How British is the pound sterling?

silver value of their own coins. France's King Philippe Le Bel (Philip the Fair) was known in Flanders as, among other things, *Flup de munteschroder* (Flup the coinscratcher). The official minting monopoly meant that the rulers could produce a coin at a cost below its purchasing power and make a substantial profit—still called *seignorage* in a broader sense. Debasing another country's currency was not uncommon either: it was just part of economic warfare. For example, Philip the Bold, first duke of Burgundy, minted low-alloy replicas of the English *noble* and used them to pay for imports from England.[2]

This debasing—see parts (a) and (b) of table 2.1—threatened the stability of the money's purchasing power. Fluctuations in purchasing power also arose when the gold and silver mines were exhausted, when Germany opened new silver mines in Joachimsthal and started coining *joachimsthalers* or *thalers*, or when Spain imported huge amounts of gold and silver into Europe from its colonies.

---

[2] During World War II, the German "Operation Bernhard" similarly attempted to counterfeit various denominations between £5 and £50 producing 500,000 notes each month in 1943. The original military plan was to parachute the money on Britain in an attempt to destabilize the British economy, but economists pointed out that it was more profitable to use the notes to make payments throughout Europe. Why give the *seignorage* away, indeed?

Table 2.1.   A family tree of floundering currencies.

(a) Ancient

Name	Original parity	Wikis
as, pl. aeres	*aes* = bronze	Republican Rome; related words: öre, øre (= metal, ore)
sesterce	2.5 *as*	Republican Rome
denarius	4 *sesterce*	Republican Rome, silver; see *denier*
solidus	gold (4.5 g)	Rome, 309 C.E.; called *numisma* in Byzantium

Until 270 B.C.E., the Roman *as*, a cast bronze piece, also doubled as a 1 lb. weight (ca. 325 g—Roman ounces were copied by medieval Europe, but Rome used a 12 oz. not a 16 oz. pound). Then, weight and coin became disjointed, with the coin falling by $\frac{11}{12}$ to 1 *uncia* of weight in a mere 60 years. By 23 B.C.E. it had become a small copper coin. In 270 C.E. its purchasing power was zip, and the coin was abandoned. Rome's *denarius* (10 *as*, later 16 *as*), which still survives as *dinar* in many countries in the Mediterranean or the Middle East, started off as a 4.75 g silver coin. It was still 93% pure (4.5 g) under Emperor Nero. Two hundred years later, in 215 C.E., it was down to 50% silver, and by 260 C.E. to 2.5%.

(b) Charlemagne (ca. 800 C.E.) and medieval

Name	Original parity	Wikis
denier (d.)	silver (1.55 g)	*dinaro, dinero, dinheiro, dinar*
solidus (s.)	12 *deniers*	*solde, solt, sol, sou, suelva, shilling*; *gros, grosschen, grote*
libra (£)	20s., 240d.	*livre, lira*, pound

The *denarius* was revived by Charlemagne (ca. 800 C.E.) and contained about 1.55 g of silver, a pennyweight or *denier*; 12 *deniers* made one (European, not ancient Roman) *solidus*. *Solidus*, of course meaning "strong," is at the origin of the French *sou* and, after translation, the French *gros* or the German *Groschen* or the Flemish *grote*. Tellingly, both *sou* and *Grosschen* are now bywords for worthless coins. The French *livre Tournois* was often called *franc* after its inscription "FRANCORUM REX," king of the Franks.

2.1.2.2   *Privately Issued Paper Money*

Another drawback of precious-metal money was that carrying huge amounts of gold from Italy to Scotland, for example, was rather cumbersome and risky. Traders therefore deposited money with international bankers (who often started off as goldsmiths), and used the receipts, or later also bills of exchange and promissory notes, to pay each other.[3] The receipts and bills were convertible into the underlying coins *at sight* (that is, whenever presented to the bank),

---

[3] A bill of exchange is a summary of the invoice; it is written (drawn) by the seller (drawer) and presented to the customer (drawee), who is asked to accept the bill (that is, acknowledge the existence of the debt by countersigning it) and to return it to the drawer. A promissory note, in contrast, is an "I owe you" note rather than a "you owe me" note; that is, it is written by the customer rather than by the seller. Bills and promissory notes can be sold to investors or can be used to pay off other debts.

Table 2.1. *Continued.*

(c) Late medieval and modern

Name	Original parity	Wikis
real	1.25s.	Spanish (= Royal). Survives in Saudi Arabia, Yemen, Oman, Iran, Quatar (Ri(y)al); resurrected in Brazil
half crown	2.5s.	U.K. coin until 1967; became quarter dollar in New Zealand and Australia
crown	5s.	survives in Scandinavia or pre-1967 U.K.
florin	4 flemish s.	Dutch Republic, gold; copied after Firenze (Florence)
thaler	2.5 florins	German, silver; aliases: daler, daalder, tolar, or dollar; England (e.g., Macbeth, act 1, scene 1): 1 dollar = 10s.
peso	1 *thaler*	Spain, Latin America
piaster	1 *thaler*	France; Louisiana; now $\frac{1}{100}$ Middle East £, dinar, or lira
écu	3 £*Tournois*	French, gold or silver; *escudo* (PT), *scudo* (IT)
euro	1 ECU	ECU itself originally worth 1 EUA, code for 1 USD

The *thaler* was the first world currency, especially in its Austrian, French, and Spanish versions (Maria Theresa (M-T) dollar, *piaster*, *peso*). The silver M-T dollar still circulates in the Arabian peninsula. Because of its parity, 2.5 florins, the *thaler* was denoted in the same way as the old *sesterce* (2.5 *as*): IIS in Roman numerals ("II" for "2" and "S" for "semi"), compressed into "$" (and thence "$"). The value of the 1958 USD was copied into the European Unit of Account (EUA)— the old European Community bookkeeping unit—and thence into the ECU and the EUR.

and were as good as gold as long as the issuer was creditworthy.[4] Note that a merchant who pays with a promissory note that remains in circulation for years before being cashed in, obtains an interest-free loan. By rolling over the notes, the merchant earns quite an advantage. This is *seignorage* (income from creating money) under a new guise.

Banks themselves then started issuing bills on a regular basis. Early bank notes were rather similar to the modern traveler's check—they were printed and issued by a private bank, in standard denominations, and were convertible at sight into the underlying, official coins. But bankers knew that, on average, only a small fraction of the circulating notes was actually cashed in; most of them remained in circulation for quite some time. This meant that, on the basis of one coin, a bank could issue notes for a much larger total value. Let us see how such an issuing bank's balance sheet is built up and how it creates money.

---

[4] This practice started about 1,000 years ago in Italy and went on until the nineteenth century. You can still find references to this practice in Thomas Mann's novel, *Buddenbrooks*, which is set in nineteenth-century northern Germany.

Table 2.2. Balance sheet of an issuing bank: day 1.

Assets		Liabilities		
Silver coins (owner's input)	120	Equity		120
Gold (A's deposit)	100	Notes issued	to A	100
Domestic credit (loan to B)	200		to B	200
Credit to the government (loan to G)	150		to G	150
Foreign credit (loan to F)	70		to F	70
(dollar T-bills)	100		to X	100
Total assets	740	Total notes issued		740

Once you understand the following example, it becomes easier to understand how modern central banks work.

Example 2.1. Consider a bank that issues its own notes. On the bank's opening day, the following five transactions take place:

- A merchant, A, deposits 100 golden crowns in exchange for bank notes. The notes become the bank's liabilities, since they are essentially promissory notes that can be cashed in for true money (gold coins). The merchant's coins go into the bank's vault and are part of its assets.

- Another merchant, B, asks for a loan of 200 crowns. The bank issues bank notes (a liability, since the borrower can cash in the notes for coins), and accepts a promissory note (or any similar claim) signed by B as the offsetting asset.

- The government, G, asks for a loan of 150 crowns. The bank hands over bank notes (that are, again, part of the bank's liabilities), and accepts a Treasury bill (T-bill) or a government bond as the corresponding asset.

- A foreign merchant, F, wants to borrow 70 crowns. The bank issues notes, and it accepts a claim on the foreign trader as the corresponding asset.

- A local exporter, X, wants to convert dollar bank notes into crown bank notes worth 100 crowns. The bank issues crown bank notes (a liability), and it uses the dollar notes to buy foreign T-bills.

By the end of the day, the bank's balance sheet looks like table 2.2. For completeness, I have added 120 crowns of silver initially brought in by the owner/shareholder: there always needs to be some equity.

Table 2.2 shows how bank notes are created, and how an issuing bank's balance sheet is being built up. The issuing bank's own bank notes are the liability side of its balance sheet.[5] On the asset side we find (i) international reserves or "reserves of foreign exchange" (gold and silver, plus claims on foreigners or governments of foreign countries), (ii) claims on the domestic

---

[5] A "note" often means an "I owe you" document; in the United States, 1- to 10-year bonds are called notes, for instance; and we all know about promissory notes (PNs). So "bank note" literally means bank debt.

Figure 2.2. Bank notes: echoes from the past. Two new notes and an old one. (a) The Barbados dollar note still reassures the holder that this note is "legal tender for the payment of any amount," that is, cannot be refused as a means of payment. (b) This particular Hong Kong dollar note is issued by HSBC, a private bank, and still bears the message that the general manager (of HSBC) "promises to pay the bearer on demand at its Office here" the amount of ten dollars (in coins). (c) I will translate the 1910 German note bit by bit: *Ein Tausend Mark* (one thousand marks) *zahlt die Reichsbankhauptkasse* (the central teller of the *Reichsbank* pays) *in Berlin* (in Berlin) *ohne legitimationsprüfung* (without proof of legitimation) *dem Einlieferer dieser Banknote* (to the deliverer of this bank note).

private sector, and (iii) claims on the domestic government. Note also that most of the money it created is *lent* to the economy, not given away. So by refusing to roll over the loans, the bank can shrink the money supply back to the original size. Even the money brought into circulation as a payment for assets bought from the private sector or the government, as in the above foreign exchange example, can be retired: just sell back the asset into the open market and take payment in notes. This mechanism, as we shall see, is still the basis of monetary policy.

Since the production cost of bank notes was quite low, private banks earned a large seignorage. The risk, of course, was that holders of the notes would lose confidence in the issuer, in which case there would be a run on the bank, with many people simultaneously trying to convert their notes into coins. In the United States, for instance, there were widespread runs on banks as late as 1907. John Pierpont Morgan, a New York banker, helped solve the crisis by shipping in a then gigantic USD 100 million (100m) worth of gold from Europe. As recently as 2007, there was a run on an English bank, inaptly named Northern Rock—the first such run since 1866.

To avert such crises in confidence (and probably also to regain the seignorage), most governments then assigned the production of bank notes to a government institution, or at least a semiofficial institution, the central bank.[6]

---

[6] There are exceptions: in Hong Kong, for instance, notes are still issued by three private banks (Standard Chartered, HSBC, and Bank of China). But even there, these banks are closely supervised by the currency board. In Belgium, the central bank is a listed company, part-owned by the government, by the commercial banks, and by the public.

2.1.2.3   Official Paper Money and the Central Bank

Initially, the official bank notes were still convertible at sight into true money—that is, into the coins issued by the mint or the treasury. For instance, until the mid 1900s, most bank notes still said that the note was "payable on sight" (although the 1910 reichsmark note ominously added that you had to see the Berlin head office for that purpose). Indian rupee bank notes still show a payable-at-sight phrase: "I [the governor of the central bank] promise to pay to the bearer the sum of x rupees." So do British pounds. Still, for all practical purposes, the central bank's notes have become as good as (or even better than) the treasury's coins, and have become the true underlying money in the eyes of the population. In many countries, coins are no longer legal tender above certain amounts. For instance, the seller of a house cannot be forced to accept payment of the full amount in coins. Thus, money has become a fiduciary instrument. Unlike cattle or gold, modern money has basically no intrinsic worth of its own, nor is the value of modern money based on a right to convert bank notes into gold. Rather, the value of money is based on the trust of the people, who believe that money will have a reasonably stable purchasing power.[7]

One difference between a modern central bank and the private issuing banks of old is that the modern bank notes are no longer convertible into gold. If many central banks still hold gold, the reason is that they think of it as a good investment. Other differences between a modern central bank and a private issuing bank include the following:

- A central bank no longer deals directly with the public. Its customers are commercial banks, foreign central banks, and the government. Commercial banks, in fact, act as liaisons between the public and the central bank. For instance, commercial banks can borrow from the central bank by rediscounting commercial paper (i.e., by passing on to the central bank loans they extended to private companies), or by selling to the central bank the foreign currency they bought from the private sector.

- When a central bank buys a domestic or foreign asset from a commercial bank, it no longer pays entirely in the form of bank notes. Commercial banks demand notes only to the extent that their own customers demand actual currency; most of the payment for the asset the commercial bank sold is credited to its account with the central bank, where it is still payable at sight. One result is that the central bank's liabilities consist not only of bank notes, but also of commercial banks' deposits into their account with the central bank. This liability side (bank notes circulating plus central bank deposits) is called the country's *monetary*

---

[7] Israel's experience in the 1970s illustrates this point: when inflation came close to 1,000% per year, people started expressing prices in USD rather than in Israeli pounds. The pound was no longer a trustworthy currency, nor was it a convenient numéraire because prices expressed in pounds had to be changed every day. Similar breakdowns occurred in Germany after World War II, when Lucky Strike cigarettes and chocolate bars became the effective currency.

SDRs are internationally created funds. They were invented toward the end of the fixed-rate era (1944–74), in an attempt to create an alternative international currency next to the beleaguered USD, with the seignorage going to the IMF member states rather than to the United States. The original SDR was at par with the USD. One difference with the USD is that the original SDR was issued by the IMF rather than by the Federal Reserve. Another difference is that the SDR is a purely electronic currency; an SDR deposit cannot be cashed in for SDR bank notes or coins. Central banks can make payments to each other in SDRs, or convert SDRs into other currencies and vice versa at the going market value of the SDR. When in the 1970s the USD plunged relative to the DEM and JPY, the SDR was redefined as a basket of sixteen currencies. This definition was rather cumbersome, so after some time the basket was again redefined, this time in terms of just five currencies: USD 0.54, DEM 0.46, JPY 34, FRF 0.74, and GBP 0.071. Since the introduction of the EUR, the marks and francs have not been replaced by euros, so the SDR now consists of just USD, GBP, and JPY.

The changes in the SDR composition did not help to make the SDR popular. And in many countries, politicians hated surrendering seignorage to the UN in the first place, disingenuously arguing that the IMF's money was inflationary.

Panel 2.2. The special drawing right (SDR).

base or M_0. The monetary base is still the basis for money creation by commercial banks, in the sense that it provides the backing for the electronic money the commercial banks are issuing—as we shall see in the next section.

A minor change is that the bank's reserves also include special drawing rights (SDRs) held with the IMF[8] (see panel 2.2). But the amounts are tiny, at best.

2.1.2.4 Privately Issued Electronic Money

The official monopoly on the printing of bank notes did not mean that private banks lost all seignorage. Any private bank knows from experience that its borrowers rarely take up the full amount of a loan as notes or coins. Rather, customers tend to leave most of their borrowed funds in a *checking account* (also called a *sight account* or *current account*, in Europe), and make payments by check (United States) or bank transfer (Europe). In short, *loans make deposits*.

Example 2.2. Shengmei gets a car loan from her bank. She almost surely will not withdraw the money in cash, but will pay for the car by check or bank transfer. The car dealer will likewise keep most of the money in a bank account; and if and when

---

[8] The International Monetary Fund (IMF) was created as part of the 1944 Bretton Woods Agreement with the mission of providing short-term financing to deserving central banks that wanted to intervene in exchange markets. (Bretton Woods is a ski resort in New England, where the Allies met to hammer out a postwar financial infrastructure.) It is funded by the participating countries. Since the demise of the fixed-rate exchange-rate system and the near-disappearance of intervention, the IMF has become a general lender to governments, often making loans conditional on changes in economic policy and even general policies about institutions. Lately, the Fund (and the World Bank) has been losing business because most countries can nowadays borrow directly themselves.

How does a central bank stop bank runs? At the very least, a commercial bank can always immediately draw down, in cash, all of its deposits of money kept with the central bank. Slightly more generously, the central bank is willing to lend money to a beleaguered commercial bank. But this safeguard should not be abused. An orthodox central bank will not waste taxpayers' money on banks that chose risky assets, so last-resort lending is only possible for short periods (one day at a time) and if the private bank can post excellent security. In addition, many central banks would charge a penalty interest rate so as to make the prospect of such refinancing really a last-resort option.

That, at least, is the Anglo-Saxon theory of last-resort lending. In practice, the indirect cost of letting a commercial bank go belly-up are so high that central banks often dance around the official rules and seek other solutions. Japan's central bank would kindly ask other private banks to take over a sickly colleague, for instance. Many European central banks, and now also the European Central Bank, lend on the basis of subprime assets too; they just take a bigger haircut. In England there was a genuine bank run, with long rows of people queuing up outside the troubled Northern Rock bank, in the fall of 2007—the early months of the "subprime" crisis. When Northern Rock had run out of prime (i.e., first-class solid) assets, the Bank of England also relaxed its lending rules and took second-rate collateral instead. The Treasury (Britain's ministry of finance), in addition, guaranteed all customer deposits with the bank to stop the run. In the end, Northern Rock was entirely taken over by the government.

In general, any sizable bank can probably bet that central banks and/or governments will step in no matter how ineptly the bank was run (the "too big to fail" guarantee): given the web of interbank OTC contracts, an individual failure would have "domino effects," to use the standard phrase, and ruin the credibility and perhaps solvability of all other banks. Japan even flooded its economy with money, bringing down interest rates to near-zero levels, for a bewildering fifteen years so as to nurse back to health the country's commercial banks, badly hurt by the real-estate crash of 1990.

Another first, in the subprime crisis, is that the Federal Reserve even extended its safety net to noncommercial banks (including notably Bear Sterns, an investment bank) and to bond dealers. This probably means they will now be supervised more closely. Lastly, the duration of last-resort lending was extended from days to a few weeks and even a few months.

Panel 2.3. Last-resort lending: putting practice into theory.

the money is spent (to pay wages and suppliers and taxes and so on) it will mostly be via checks or transfers, not cash. The new holders will likewise keep most of the money in their bank accounts, etc.

The *loans make deposits* principle means that private banks can (and do) extend loans for a much larger volume than the amount of base money that they keep in their vaults or with the central bank. So today, private banks create electronic money (loans recorded in the bank's computer) rather than physical money (bank notes). The ratio between the total amount of money (monetary base plus checking-account money, M_1) and the monetary base (M_0) is the *money multiplier.*

This mechanism again creates the possibility of runs on commercial banks if deposit-holders want to convert all of their sight deposits into notes and coins. A recent example was the minor run on Hong Kong banks after the 1987 stock market crash, or the run on Northern Rock, an English bank hit by the "subprime" crisis, in 2007. To avert runs and enhance credibility, private banks in many countries must meet *reserve requirements*: they must keep

Figure 2.3. Hyperinflation in 1946: a one-billion milpengö bank note from Hungary. One milpengö is already a million pengös, so this note stands for 10^{15} pengös.

a minimum fraction of the customers' deposits in coins or bank notes, or, more conveniently, in a non-interest-bearing account with the central bank. The central bank also agrees to act as *lender of last resort*, that is, to provide liquidity to private banks in case of a run (see panel 2.3).

This whole section is neatly summarized in the following formula:

$$\text{Money supply} = M_1 = m\,M_0 = m \times (D + G + \text{RFX}), \qquad (2.1)$$

where m is the money multiplier, M_0 is the money base (notes and commercial banks' deposits with the central bank), D is credit to the domestic private sector, G is credit to the government, RFX is the reserves of foreign exchange (including gold), and $M_0 = D + G + \text{RFX}$ (equality of the central bank's assets and liabilities).

Equation (2.1) says that the total money supply depends on the money multiplier and the monetary base, which, in turn, consists of domestic credit, credit to the government, and foreign reserves. The equation is also useful in explaining how monetary policy works, which is the topic of the next section.

2.1.2.5 Monetary Policy

Even though central banks generously leave most of the money creation to commercial banks, they still control the process. This control is exerted by the central bank's power over the monetary base and over the money multiplier.

Intervention in the foreign-exchange markets. Central banks can influence the monetary base by buying or selling foreign exchange (changing RFX in equation (2.1)). This expansion of the central bank's asset side is accompanied by an expansion of the liability side (domestic money supply): the central bank pays in notes (or it credits the commercial banks' accounts with the central bank) for the foreign exchange it buys from the commercial banks. Thus, any change in RFX leads to an identical change in M_0, which then affects the amount of money that private banks can create on the basis of M_0.

Open-market policy. Likewise, central banks can influence the monetary base by restricting or expanding the amount of credit they give to the government or the private sector (that is, change D and G in equation (2.1)). Open-market policy works in the same way as interventions in the foreign exchange market: the central bank pays in notes (or it credits the commercial banks' accounts with the central bank) for the T-bills or commercial paper it buys from the government or from the private banks.

Reserve requirements. Alternatively, the central bank can curb money creation by commercial banks by changing the reserve requirements (changing the upper bound on the multiplier m in equation (2.1)). If banks have to hold more base money per unit of electronic money, the total amount of loans they can extend with a given amount of base money becomes smaller. Around 1990, for instance, India stepped up the reserve requirements to a staggering 50% in order to bring inflation back to single-digit levels. A 50% reserve requirement means that the money multiplier can be at most 2.

Credit controls. The most direct way to control M_1 is to impose limits on the amounts that private banks can lend.

Having examined what money is and how it is created, we now turn to its more international aspects.

2.2 The International Payment Mechanism

In this section, we explain how transactions involving the exchange of foreign currency are made, while discussing the effects these transactions have on the money supply.

2.2.1 Some Basic Principles

Recall that money mainly changes hands (or bank accounts) when one is buying or selling goods, services, or assets. A special problem arises if the buyer and seller live in countries that have different currencies: then at least one of the parties has to handle a foreign currency. As long as currencies are defined by their weight in gold or silver and are freely minted, this creates no special problem. An ounce of gold is an ounce of gold everywhere, and currencies minted in various countries freely circulated elsewhere, traded approximately on the basis of their intrinsic value (see the story of the guinea in panel 2.1). So, basically, any trade imbalance was settled in gold or silver (which were themselves also physical goods), and this happened by physically transporting the coins.

Today, things are not that easy. If the invoice is in the exporter's currency, the importer often has to buy the currency of the exporter, or the exporter can agree to be paid in foreign currency, and then exchange the foreign money for domestic currency herself. If payment is in bank notes, the notes can still simply be handed over, but most international payments are by check or bank transfer. The following example shows how such payments take place.

Example 2.3. Assume that a U.S. importer, USM, pays by check in his own currency, USD 1m, to a U.K. exporter, UKX. Writing the check, of course, means that the U.S. importer has a checking account with a U.S. bank (USB). By definition, money on that account is convertible into dollar notes and coins. One possible scenario is that the U.K. exporter also has a checking account with a U.S. bank. We shall assume that this is the same bank as the U.S. importer's bank, USB. (If this is not the case, think of USB as the consolidation of all U.S. banks.) UKX deposits the check into her account with USB, and can cash in that amount at any time. Clearly, the U.S. money supply is not affected; there is only a transfer of ownership of electronic money from the U.S. importer to the U.K. exporter.

In the modified example below, we see what happens if the U.K. exporter does not have an account in the United States, but, as in the previous example, still decides not to sell the USD yet.

Example 2.4. The U.K. exporter deposits the check into a USD checking account he or she holds with the London bank. The U.K. bank, UKB, records in its books that it owes the exporter USD 1m (a liability), and that it has received a check. UKB will then deposit the check into its account with USB, because this is where the money can be cashed in; thus, the UKB's asset now is a USD 1m claim on USB. The difference from the previous example is that, after this transaction, the U.K. exporter has a USD claim not on a U.S. bank, but on a U.K. bank, which, in turn, holds a claim on a U.S. bank. The U.K. bank acts as a front between the owner of the funds (UKX) and the bank where the money is ultimately held (USB).

The fact that the U.K. exporter now has a USD claim not on a U.S. bank but on a U.K. bank (which, in turn, holds a claim on a U.S. bank) makes a difference. The London bank is not a U.S. bank: that is, it has no USD reserves deposited with the U.S. central bank (the Federal Reserve), nor can it call on the Federal Reserve as a lender of last resort. This U.K. bank will, understandably, not give the exporter the right to convert the USD deposit into USD notes and coins at sight (that is, without prior notice and without costs). In that sense, the London USD checking account is not a sight account in the strict sense. If the exporter asks for dollar notes, the London bank could possibly cash in USD 1m from its U.S. account and have the notes flown over, which would be expensive, or the London bank could buy USD dollar notes from somebody else in the United Kingdom, if that is cheaper. The implication is that USD held on a *non-U.S.* bank account will generally have a different price (or exchange rate) than USD notes, as you probably noticed from your bank's posted exchange rates or from your newspaper.

There is also seignorage associated with having a currency that is used internationally. Recall how local merchants, when paying with promissory notes that were not immediately cashed in, effectively obtained interest-free loans.

Table 2.3. Netting: and example.

		To			Gross out	Net
		A	B	C	(row sum)	out
From	A	—	40	15	55	10
	B	30	—	60	90	15
	C	15	35	—	50	—
Gross in (column sum)		45	75	75	195	
Net in		—	—	25		25

The same still happens internationally: a small country, whose currency is not used anywhere else, has to pay for its imports by exporting goods, or by selling assets.[9] In contrast, a large country like the United States, which has a widely accepted currency, can pay in its own money and still expect that this money will remain in circulation among international traders for many years before it is cashed in for goods or for assets. This becomes an interest-free loan, with an unstated time to maturity, from the rest of the world to the United States.

2.2.2 Domestic Interbank Transfers: Real-Time Gross Settlement versus Periodic Netting

If you want to transfer money to another business electronically, you move money from your bank account to the other's bank account. Cash payments remain possible but are becoming quite rare, except for small (or illegal) transactions. True, if you buy and sell a lot to each other all the time, you and the other firm may open a mutual *current account*. This functions like a booklet where you jot down all transactions that increase or decrease your net debt to the other party. But entries into such a current account are not payments. Rather, they help you keep track of how much the actual net payment will be at the moment you really make the transfer (in cash, or via a bank account) at end of the day, or week, or month, or quarter.

In the same vein, commercial banks ("depository institutions") within one country typically transfer money to each other via their central bank rather than in cash. All banks have an account with their central bank,[10] showing how much money they can withdraw in cash if they would want to. So to make a payment, the sending bank S instructs the central bank to transfer money from S's account into the account of the receiving bank, R. Banks may do some netting via a bilateral or multilateral netting system, but the final net payment is via their accounts with the central bank.

---

[9] The country can also borrow, but when the loan matures, it still has to pay with money earned from exports or from the sale of assets. The interest on the loan is the price it pays for postponing the real payment.

[10] This is by definition: a bank is a bank from country X if it has an account with the central bank of country X. The bank may be foreign-owned, but that is another issue entirely.

Traditionally, banks did set up a netting/clearing system among each other—often, but not always, in cooperation with the central bank—and then made or received the net payments once a day. This daily settlement typically happens toward the end of the working day. Let us consider a simple example, which looks at the wire transfers between banks.[11] Table 2.3 shows a simple example with three banks; the matrix shows how much bank X (= {A, B, C}) has to transfer to bank Y because of payment instructions from its customers. The row sums tell us, for each bank, the total amount of outgoing payment instructions, while the column sums provide us with the incoming ones. The difference of the "total out" and the "total in" gives us the "net out" (if positive) or the "net in" (if negative). By netting the payments, the volume of transfers is substantially reduced, from 195 to 25 in this example. This allows banks to work with far smaller balances in their central bank account: you cannot make payments exceeding what is in your bank account, so each bank would have needed larger central bank balances if the gross payments had been due rather than the net ones.[12]

So far so good. But big players with big amounts due may want their money faster. Also, when they deposit a check or a bill into their account they do not like being credited tentatively ("with the usual reservation"), they appreciate *finality* of payments. For big amounts, since the mid 1990s central banks have usually offered a system where transfers are executed immediately rather than bottled up until the next daily settlement. And of course, if there is no waiting at all, then there cannot be any netting either. Hence the name *real-time gross settlement* (RTGS). Often, committees must have spent a lot of time finding a clever acronym, like CHAPS (United Kingdom), SPOT (Portugal), HERMES (Germany), ELLIPS (Belgium), IRIS (Ireland), DEBES (Denmark). The United States chose *Fedwire*. The European Central Bank has its TARGET supersystem, which links the RTGS programs of each EU central bank (whether an EMU member or not) provided the payment is in euros. Each of these systems typically provides the option of intraday borrowing, per hour. (Traditionally, lending or borrowing was per day, of course, given that payments were only done once a day.)

The above relates to interbank transfers within one country. These are just one step in a transfer from company X to person Y, and the other steps can

---

[11] By wire transfers we mean payments initiated by the payor. Some payments are set in motion by the beneficiary or payee, at least as far as the bank is concerned: checks, promissory notes, trade bills, and acceptances (i.e., accepted bills) are all handed in to a bank by the payee, not the payor. Drawbacks of such payee-driven systems are the mail float (the delay between the moment the check (etc.) is sent by the payor and the moment it is received by the payee and then sent to a bank), plus the risk of tampering by the beneficiary. Payor-driven systems, long popular in many European countries, are nowadays fully electronic (PC banking, internet banking, XML (Extensible Markup Language) instructions to banks). Checks remain popular in the United States, mainly for retail payments. European countries typically also have a *giro* transfer service, run by the post office, but most of these lose market share.

[12] Recall that the money on the central bank account, being pseudo-cash, does not earn interest; so it is costly to have large balances like that. True, the bank can borrow "central bank funds" from another bank, but borrowing is costly too, and netting still means that less is to be borrowed.

occur fairly independently of the interbank part. For instance, if you deposit a check into your bank account, the amount is usually credited "with the usual reservations," with same-day or first- or second-working-day value— long before your bank actually receives the payment from the writer's bank, that is.[13]

2.2.3 International Payments

Let us now consider international payments. One extra problem is that the sending and receiving banks, S and R*, are no longer members of the same clearing organization. (We use an asterisk to indicate "foreign.") The traditional solution is to work with *correspondent banks*. If banks S* and S have agreed to act as correspondents for each other, they have a current-account relationship, with a liability account called *loro* ("theirs") or *vostro* ("yours") and an asset account called *nostro* ("ours"). So S sends the payment instruction to S*, which then makes the payment to R* via the foreign central bank's clearing system. The current account is then settled quite rarely, say once a quarter or whenever the balance becomes too big. The main point of postponed settlement of the loro/nostro accounts is of course a kind of netting over time. The way the party with the surplus receives a genuine payment for the net remaining balance— since transfers via the central bank are not possible between S and S*—is to spend the balance: simply buy securities or withdraw cash. Correspondent banking is slow and expensive, especially with payee-driven payments: a check has to be sent abroad, from S to S*, and then to R*, and each has to handle and record it, etc.

There are international wire (or bank-transfer) systems too. Europe's postal banks have set up *Eurogiro*, which delivers fifth-day value as the default option: the beneficiary can withdraw cash the fifth working day after the payment is initiated. Second-day value is available, at a price, as well as quasi-immediate value, via Western Union, a U.S. telephone/telegraph company that has been offering fast wiring services for ages. The most important player, however, is the Society of Worldwide Interbank Telecommunication (SWIFT). SWIFT was set up as a cooperative, after World War II, by JP Morgan, near Brussels (BE), and later transferred to a consortium of banks. SWIFT transmits messages between banks, well over ten million of them per day, for a small fee; any free cash flow remaining after SWIFT has paid its expenses is then paid out to the shareholding banks. Payments via SWIFT mean same-day value. Other services offered by SWIFT (and Eurogiro) include the option to have a local check

---

[13] This is one reason why such payments are so expensive, in terms of bank fees. The other reasons have to do with the costs of the handling, mailing, recording, etc., of pieces of paper.

In Euroland, the Single European Payments Area (SEPA) directive stipulates that by 2012 interbank payments cannot take more than one day; an older rule also said that inter-Euroland crossborder transfers cannot cost more than domestic ones. At this stage, there are still national clearers, though. The London-based European Bankers Association has set up an international structure, EBA Clearing, but it operates on a strictly members-only basis.

printed out in the beneficiary's country, by SWIFT or Eurogiro; that check is then immediately delivered to the debtor's bank, thus avoiding mail float.

2.3 International ("Euro") Money and Bond Markets

In the previous section, we mentioned that one can deposit a USD check into a sight account with a bank located outside the United States. One can, however, also make a *time deposit* by depositing the USD with a U.K. bank for, say, three months. In return for interest income, the owner of these funds then transfers the right to use the money during that period to the U.K. bank. This is an example of a "eurodollar" transaction, in the sense that the dollar is deposited in Europe, outside the dollar's home turf.

In this textbook, money and capital markets are called *international* if the currency of denomination is not the official currency of the country where the transaction takes place. The traditional name for international markets, still frequently used, is euromarkets—euromoney and eurobond markets, for example—and especially eurodollars. This name made sense initially, since the only international markets in those days were those for dollars in Europe (including the United Kingdom). The terminology became more artificial when the term was applied not just to eurodollars but also to other currencies. Deutsche Marks deposited in Paris were then, somewhat confusingly, called euro-DMs. Things became quite problematic when the European Union coined its new common currency, the euro: a euro-deposit in London (outside Euroland) would then, bewilderingly, be called a euro-euro. There have been calls to use the prefix *xeno-* to indicate such extranational transactions, but this has not caught on. For this reason we use the term "international" where others might still use "euro-." Another candidate term might have been "offshore," but this word has a connotation of "exempt from domestic tax rules," like a ship in international waters—which is not what we have in mind here.

Example 2.5. A Norwegian investor may deposit USD with a bank located outside the United States, perhaps in Oslo or in London. This deposit is then considered an international deposit. (USD deposits with an *international banking facility*, a U.S. banking institution that is deemed to be outside the United States as far as banking regulations are concerned, are also considered to be not U.S.) In contrast, if the USD deposit is made in the United States, the transaction is a domestic deposit.

Such international markets have long antecedents. In many European trading centers, bankers have been accepting deposits and trading commercial paper denominated in many different currencies since the Middle Ages (see figure 2.4). The prefix euro- was first used for USD deposits and loans made in Paris and especially London after World War II when the USD replaced the GBP as the leading international currency. Later, such international markets also emerged for other currencies.

In Bruges, the main trading center in the Low Countries (Benelux) until the late 1400s, exchange transactions and discounting and trading of bills took place on a little square in front of two inns, Ter Beurse (picture) and De Oude Beurs, named after the innkeeper, Van der Beurze (beurs means purse)—hence the continental words börse, beurs, bourse, bolsa, borsa, and so on, for organized capital markets. Bruges's Beurs was rather informal by current standards, but it drew up a rulebook in 1309, including the opening and closing bell still found in the NYSE. The first truly organized exchange in the West, with fixed opening hours, rules, members, and such, was the Beurs of Antwerp in 1531; commercial paper and T-bills were traded in the afternoon while commodity forwards and options were traded in the morning. One of the Beurs's members was Lord Thomas Gresham—yes, the Gresham of good and bad money—who soon convinced Elizabeth I to build a similar bursa in London, 1565. (She later changed its name, by decree, into Royal Exchange. Do read Gresham's CV on Wikipedia, incidentally: the SEC would jail him, nowadays.) Rotterdam and Amsterdam followed in 1595 and 1613, respectively. Amsterdam's addition was the anonymous joint-stock company and the corporate bond (the Dutch United East India Company issued shares and bonds in 1603). (Author's photo.)

Figure 2.4. Bourse, börse, borsa, beurs, bolsa, exchange.

Banks accept deposits in order to relend them: international deposits must also be accompanied by international loans. The development of international money and loan markets was followed by the opening of markets for securities, the first of which was the international bond market. A more recent phenomenon is the international commercial paper market; an international equity market is also emerging. We shall discuss these markets in chapters 16–18.

There are many reasons why some investors preferred to make their USD deposits outside the United States, as well as why there was (and is) so much USD borrowing outside the United States. One of these reasons was that the international markets were less regulated than the United States market. There has been substantial deregulation everywhere, but for a long time the absence of reserve requirements, deposit insurance, transaction taxes, withholding taxes, etc., made international transactions cheaper than similar transactions in many domestic money markets. Also, it was comparatively easy to evade income taxes on income from international deposits, which further increased the attractiveness of this market. These factors have allowed the emergence of a market for large, wholesale deals, at interest spreads that are narrower than the spreads that typically prevail in domestic markets. A detailed discussion of these and other explanations for the success of eurocurrency markets is provided in chapter 16.

One thing is certain, however: in order for many dollars to end up in the hands of non-U.S. companies and individuals, the United States must have had a long and persistent deficit on its current account. This brings us to the next topic, the balance of payments.

2.4 What Is the Balance of Payments?

In this section, we explain the balance of payments accounts and its subaccounts, along with the accounting convention used to record transactions in these accounts.

2.4.1 Definition and Principles Underlying the Balance of Payments

The balance of payments (BOP) account is a statistical record of the flow of all financial transactions between the residents of one country and the rest of the world over a given period of time (usually one year). Transactions are grouped in "source" and "use" tables. If you are familiar with basic accounting, you can think of each transaction being recorded twice, like under double-entry accounting: once as a source and once as a use.

- **Sources** get a *plus* sign (credit). The source side of a deal tells us where we obtained the money in the international transactions. We could have earned some (goods or services sold, or income from labor or capital or real estate), we could have sold assets, we may have borrowed, or (note this!) we could have depleted our bank account. Some money or assets might even have been brought along by immigrants.

- **Uses** get a *minus* sign (debit). The use side of a deal tells us what we did with the money. We may have bought goods or services; we could have paid foreign workers or investors or landlords; perhaps we purchased assets or lent money internationally, or gave it away as development aid; or (note again!) we may have added money to our bank account.

There is an account for each possible source and use. It is customary to group these accounts into the following groups and subgroups; do read the list shown in table 2.4 and the resulting BOP, table 2.5.[14] Most entries are pretty obvious—except perhaps for changes in financial items, and primarily so for liquidities, where it is very tempting to think of the entries in terms of corporate balance sheets rather than sources/uses. It is probably worth spelling out the likely source of confusion.

Note, indeed, from the definition, that the balance of payments, being mostly a record of the *flow* of payments over a period of time, does not describe the country's *stock* of foreign assets and liabilities; in that sense, it is not at all like a company's balance sheet. Rather, just like a corporation's sources-and-uses statement, the BOP analyzes and explains changes in consecutive assets-and-liabilities statements. Yet, when we see an entry like "CAD liquidities: +10m" or "securities: −5m" we are likely think of changes in balance-sheet items and we would therefore misinterpret the sign. BOP entries are nothing like

---

[14] I use "KFA," not "CFA," for the net "capital and financial transactions" account to avoid confusion with the C in "CA," current account; "K" is often used for "capital" in microeconomics or international economics.

Table 2.4. Classification of various international sources and uses of funds.

- **The current account** (or group of accounts, really):
    - "merchandise": goods sold (+) or bought (−) internationally
    - "services": services sold (+) or bought (−) internationally, including consulting, insurance, and so on
    - "income":
        * from labor: wages earned (+) or paid (−) internationally
        * from capital: interest or dividends earned (+) or paid (−) internationally
    - unilateral income transfers, inward (+) or outward (−): repatriated wages, etc.
- **The capital and financial account** (really, a group of accounts, again):
    - "capital account": unilateral transfers like aid received (+) or granted (−), assets brought in or taken out by immigrants
    - "financial account": tradable assets, or contractual assets or liabilities with similar effects as traded assets:
        * private transactions:
            - FDI: inward (+) or outward (−)
            - securities sold (+) or bought (−) internationally
            - derivatives sold (+) or bought (−) internationally
            - loans received (+) or granted (−) internationally
            - changes in liquidities
            - other
        * central-bank transactions (similar)
- **Statistical discrepancies**

---

balance-sheet items or changes therein. The above entries mean that, of all the money that we used in international payments, 10m was obtained out of our bank accounts (source, +) and 5m was used (−) to buy securities. The signs for sources and uses are opposite to those of changes in the balance sheet.

Example 2.6. If countries had balance sheets like companies have, a decrease in the balance-sheet item "securities" would have meant a sale of assets (ΔAssets < 0), but this is a source of cash (+). Or, in another example, if a company uses 5m to buy securities, this purchase is booked as a use (−) for the "securities" line in a sources-and-uses table, but the corresponding balance-sheet position goes up, not down. Do not mix these things up.

Note also that the BOP is related to the exchange market, but far less than is sometimes claimed. Within Euroland, countries still make euro payments

Table 2.5. The balance of payments: new definition.

(a) Sources	(b) Uses	Balance = (a) − (b)
1. Current transactions		
+ Exports of goods	− Imports of goods	= Merchandise balance
+ Exports of services	− Imports of services	= "Invisibles" balance
+ Factor income received	− Factor income paid	= Net factor
+ Labor	− Labor	income received
+ Capital	− Capital	
+ Unilateral, inc.	− Unilateral, inc.	= Unilateral, inc.
transfers IN	transfers OUT	transfers balance
	Subtotal	= Current account balance =: CA
2. Capital and financial (C&F) transactions		
+ Unilateral asset	− Unilateral asset	= Capital account
transfers OUT	transfers IN	(new definition!)
+ Private sales of assets	− Private purchases of assets	
+ Inward FDI	− Outward FDI	= Net private
+ Shares, bonds sold	− Shares, bonds bought	sales of assets
+ Derivatives sold	− Derivatives bought	(formerly =: KA)
+ Other assets sold	− Other assets bought	
+ Central bank's	− Central bank's	= Net central bank
sales of assets	purchases of assets	asset sales =: $-\Delta$RFX
	Subtotal	= C&F account balance =: KFA
3. Statistical discrepancy		
+ (Unrecorded inflows)[a]	− (Unrecorded outflows)[a]	= Net errors and omissions = E&O
Grand total		CA + KFA + E&O = 0

[a]Only net errors and omissions are observable.

to each other, all of them recorded in the BOP, even if there is no exchange transaction. Or one Australian can exchange pounds for dollars with a fellow Australian; here, there is an exchange transaction but no international payment. Likewise, a Japanese company holding dollars can pay for imports from the United States without making an exchange transaction, even though there will be a double entry into the BOP. There is only a very close link between the BOP and the exchange market under what one might call the late 1940s' scenario: every country has its own currency, and residents of country X only hold their own currency, never any foreign one.[15] In that setting, every international transfer is an exchange transaction too. But the emergence of international money accounts has considerably weakened the link between the balance of payments and the exchange market.

A further implication of the BOP definition is that every "source" must be "used" somewhere, which means that every entry must have a counterpart. In other words, if you hear or read that a certain country has a balance-of-payments deficit, it must be referring to some subtotal in the BOP, some sub-group of accounts rather than the whole BOP account. Thus, when you hear about a deficit, you should always ask yourself to which subaccount of the BOP reference is being made. Old texts occasionally refer to a net excess credit booked by the central bank as "the surplus on the balance of payment." In books or the printed press, the term "balance" may refer not to the sources-and-uses table as a whole, but to one of the net surpluses or deficits (that is, the result of credits minus debits) for a subgroup indicated in table 2.5. For example, one often uses the term *merchandise balance* or *trade balance* for net exports of goods, *invisibles balance* for net exports of services, and *current-account balance* for the sum of the above plus net inward income transfers. But hasty writers may very well say "BOP surplus" when they mean "trade surplus" or "current-account surplus." Newspapers and the like can be amazingly sloppy about this, contradicting themselves as if there were no tomorrow.

> **DIY Problem 2.1.** A "training" question on www.fxcm.com (November 2006) was "What happens to the USD if the U.S. trade deficit widens due to Japanese sell off of U.S. treasuries?"
>
> - Why is this gobbledygook? (Do be gentle.)
> - What might they really have meant?
> - What additional information would you need to answer the question?

In table 2.6 we show a few examples of how the omniscient statistician in the sky would record various transactions. We dissect each deal into its two legs (source, use) and indicate the account where each half belongs.

> **DIY Problem 2.2.** Read the three examples worked out for you in table 2.6, then complete the three remaining ones.

2.4.2 Some Nitty-Gritty

There are a few technical details to be added.

---

[15] The postwar years, when in many countries privately held balances of foreign exchange (and, in some places, even gold) was illegal, represented a very bad dip in a long tradition of open markets. Especially in the Victorian age and the early 1900s we had a truly global financial market, which has come back only in the late 1980s.

Table 2.6. Six records in Canada's theoretical BOP.

	Transaction	Use (−) or source (+)	Credit	Debit
1.	StarDucks Canada, a Canadian firm, imports CAD 100m worth of coffee from Ghana AraCoff...	Current (−), (merchandise)		−100m
	...and pays for it by transferring CAD 100m from its account at CIBC (a Canadian bank) to AraCoff's account with the Bank of Nova Scotia	Financial (+), (CAD liquidities)	+100m	
2.	StarDucks uses the services of Accra Stevedoring, worth 10m...	Current (−), (services)		−10m
	...and pays for it by transferring USD 7.5m (CAD 10m, after translation) from its account at CIBC to Stevedoring's account with CIBC	Financial (+), (USD liquidities)	+10m	
3.	The University of Brunswick at Colomba (UBC) sells 15m worth of bonds to a London broker	Financial (+), (securities)		−15m
	...and receives CAD 15m into its account at Brunswick Bank, from the broker's account with Bank of Toronto	Financial (−), (CAD liquidities)	+15m	
4.	A professor at UBC tenders 10m shares in an acquired Canadian firm, valued at CAD 77m, to a U.S. acquirer...			
	...and receives 2m shares of the acquirer in return			
5.	StarDucks exports 1m worth of coffee mugs to the Dutch Antilles...			
	...in return for a trade bill accepted by the customer, payable 90 days			
6.	A customer of StarDucks, however, pays the CAD 1m 75 days early...			
	...and StarDucks sends back the trade bill			

Accruals versus cash accounting. The examples work on what accountants would define as an accruals basis: exports or imports are recorded when the invoice is sent, not when the payment is being done. In practice, the BOP is put together by the central bank, which uses information from commercial banks on actual payments. Thus, a real-world BOP would not show transaction 5 (StarDucks exporting mugs, payment 90 days), as the central bank would not be aware of that contract; instead, records 5 and 6 would show up in a merged version (exports +1m, liquidities −1m) when the payment occurs.

Economically, however, showing record 5 would have made sense. By comparing customs data with central-bank data one can get an impression of the size of the change in internationally outstanding accounts receivable (A/Rs) or accounts payable (A/Ps).

CIF versus FOB.   Imports are usually booked at a value *cost, insurance, freights* (CIF), so in reality they include an "invisibles" or service component. Exports, in contrast, are usually valued *free on board* (FOB), not including freight and insurance. This is one reason for not focusing on the merchandise balance on its own. The current account makes much more sense as it contains the sum of goods and services trade; misclassifications *à la* CIF/FOB do not matter if we look at the total, and even apart from this there is no good reason why the merchandise subtotal would be intrinsically more crucial than the invisibles one.

FDI versus portfolio investments.   If shares in an existing firm are bought, it is deemed to be *direct investment* if the investor acquires a controlling share or at least participates in the management of the firm. *Portfolio investment*, on the other hand, refers to a transaction in which securities are held purely as a financial investment. For clerks in statistical offices it is often difficult to distinguish between direct investment and portfolio investment and, typically, the classification is made on the basis of the proportion of the firm held by the investor. The cutoff level of ownership beyond which an investment is classified as direct investment varies between countries but is usually around 10%.

Foreigners versus nonresidents.   We talked about international transactions without stating precisely what was meant by this. They could be defined by using a nationality criterion: any deal between a national and a foreigner would be recorded even if no goods or assets cross borders (because the foreigner lives here, or the national lives abroad). Alternatively, the criterion could be on the basis of residence not nationality. The choice is linked to how one views the other national accounts: does gross product refer to all value added by residents (gross domestic product) or by nationals (gross national product)?

Old versus new definitions.   The definitions we used were implemented as of the second half of the 1990s, but if you check older books or statistics, these are likely to use different meanings. First, all unilateral transfers used to be part of the current account; now, unilateral capital transfers (such as assets brought by immigrants, or development-aid grants, or debt forgiven) have been moved into the capital account, which is a subtotal of the capital and financial account. For generous countries like Norway, moving development aid—a use, therefore a minus—out of the current account has a big positive impact on the current-account balance, but it does not reflect any real change: there is an offsetting hole in the financial account. Second, central bank deals used to be reported separately, rather than alongside the non-central-bank players (which coincides mostly with the private sector). Third, in the old terminology one said "capital account" for what is now called the non-central-bank part of the "financial account"; do not get confused. Lastly (and most trivially), one now uses "statistical discrepancies" for what used to be called, too honestly perhaps, "net errors and omissions." We have not yet discussed this one, so here goes.

2.4.3 Statistical Discrepancy: Errors and Omissions

The last item in the BOP is the statistical discrepancy. Since any sources-and-uses statement must balance by definition, the foreign exchange transactions in the current account and those in the capital account should sum to zero. That is,

$$CA + KFA = 0. \tag{2.2}$$

This says that if you spent more than you earned (CA $<$ 0), then you must either have borrowed or sold some of the family silver (KFA $>$ 0). (Remind yourself how selling assets means a +.) In practice, there is a problem with measuring all transactions accurately. KFA contains the change in the reserves, and it is reasonable to assume that, in most countries, there is little error in that item. However, the measurement of the other items can be quite difficult and errors can occur easily. Commercial banks do not ask for details when the amounts involved in international payments are small; as a result, the central bank has to guess what the small deals were used for, or just book them as "unknown." It is also a safe bet that at least some of the reported deals misstate the purpose, for instance for tax reasons. And, of course, there is no foolproof way to detect international payments in cash. Nor can the central bank double-check its export and import data with the customs data. One reason is that the timing of recognition differs, with the bank using a cash basis and customs an accruals basis; and also, of course, customs do not know everything correctly. It is generally believed that the errors on the KFA are larger than those on the CA.

Thus, in terms of statistically recorded transactions, equation (2.2) generally does not hold as an equality. So when we work with estimated CA and KFA numbers—indicated, below, by the hat over the symbols—the item errors and omissions (E&O) must be added to the left-hand side to get an equality relationship:

$$\widehat{CA} + \widehat{KFA} + E\&O = 0. \tag{2.3}$$

The E&O term can be surprisingly large, sometimes of the same magnitude as the $\widehat{CA}$ and $\widehat{KFA}$. Thus, one needs to be very careful when reading these accounts and very cautious in interpreting the data from the BOP.

Throughout the rest of our discussion of the BOP, we shall think in terms of the more relevant true (hatless) exports of goods, services, and assets rather than the recorded (hatted) figures; thus, equation (2.2) holds as an equality by definition of "true" numbers. In the next section, equation (2.2) is used to analyze the relationship between a country's fiscal policy and its BOP accounts.

2.4.4   Where Do Current Account Surpluses or Deficits Come From?

A deficit on the CA means that the country as a whole is spending more abroad (buying goods and services, or giving money away) than it is earning from abroad. By looking at the rest of the national accounts we can see who is responsible and to what extent for the overall deficit, the private sector or the government. There is a direct link between the CA and the private-sector and government surplus or deficit. The equation, to be derived below, is as follows:

$$CA = \underbrace{[S_p - I_p]}_{\text{Private surplus}} + \underbrace{[Tx - C_g - I_g]}_{\text{G's surplus}}, \qquad (2.4)$$

where S_p is private-sector savings, I_p is private-sector real investments, Tx is the government's tax revenue, C_g is government consumption (spending other than investment), and I_g is the government's real investments.

The first bracketed term is the private-sector free cash flow, savings minus real investment. The second one is the surplus on the government budget: tax income minus government spending.[16] Thus, if both the private sector and the government have a surplus, the country as a whole is in surplus, meaning that the current account must be in surplus too—and vice versa.

> **Example 2.7.** In Japan, where since the mid 1990s the government has been running big deficits, the CA remained positive because the private-sector surplus was so huge.[17]

> **Example 2.8. Q.** Suppose you were Groucho Marx, the President of Freedonia, and you lowered taxes while increasing government spending, in a country going through an investment boom but with virtually no savings. What would be your prediction regarding the current account?
>
> **A.** You predict overspending for both the private sector and the government. The aggregate overspending will show up in a current-account deficit which must be financed by a capital-account surplus. Thus, Freedonia must borrow (e.g., sell bonds to foreigners), or dispose of shares in domestic or foreign companies, or sell other assets (like its famous Stonefeller Center, its renowned NGN Studios, or its beloved Kreissler Corporation).

For the intellectually ambitious reader, here is the story behind equation (2.4). One macro accounting relation looks at total availability of goods (and services, but let's keep it short) and their destination. Goods are made available

---

[16] The surplus is usually negative; so *minus* the surplus is called the deficit.

[17] In fact, the government was spending so much *because* the private sector refused to spend. The government's objective was to let the country's yen roll locally rather than disappear abroad. (A large CA surplus necessarily means a large capital outflow, remember?)

by local production (with final net output Y) or imports (M). What is available can be consumed (C), or invested in machinery or research (I), or exported (X). Where appropriate we add a subscript "p" (for private) or "g" (government). Thus,

$$\underbrace{Y}_{\text{Output}} = \underbrace{C_{\text{p}} + C_{\text{g}} + I_{\text{p}} + I_{\text{g}}}_{\text{(Local) "absorption"}} + \underbrace{X - M}_{\text{Net } X}. \qquad (2.5)$$

This equation focuses on the goods side of production and tells us where the goods that were produced or imported ended up: in the consumers' stomachs, or as machines in the factories, or abroad. But selling goods also generates income or, more precisely, value added. Thus, the next equation dissects the income side into various destinations: private-sector income can be spent in private consumption, or saved (S_{p}), or surrendered to the tax man (Tx), or transferred to foreigners as interest or dividends or wages or repatriation of income (Tr):

$$Y = C_{\text{p}} + S_{\text{p}} + \text{Tr} + \text{Tx}. \qquad (2.6)$$

Combining both equations we get

$$C_{\text{g}} + I_{\text{p}} + I_{\text{g}} + X - M \overset{(2.5)}{=} Y - C_{\text{p}} \overset{(2.6)}{=} S_{\text{p}} + \text{Tr} + \text{Tx} \qquad (2.7)$$

or

$$\left. \begin{aligned} X - M - \text{Tr} &= [S_{\text{p}} - I_{\text{p}}] + [\text{Tx} - C_{\text{g}} - I_{\text{g}}], \\ \Rightarrow \quad \text{CA} &= [S_{\text{p}} - I_{\text{p}}] + [\text{Tx} - C_{\text{g}} - I_{\text{g}}], \end{aligned} \right\} \qquad (2.8)$$

which finishes the proof.

2.4.5 The Net International Investment Account

As described above, the BOP is an account that keeps track of the flow of foreign exchange into and out of the country. To measure the result of these cumulative inflows and outflows, we have the *net international investment* (NII) account, or the *net external assets* account. The NII account tries to measure the net ownership of foreign assets. That is, the NII account is designed to measure a country's stock of international assets and liabilities—somewhat like a company's statement of assets and liabilities, except that the NII account omits domestic assets owned by residents.

Example 2.9. Here we compare the BOP and the NII account. Suppose that you keep two accounts. The first account keeps track of your income and expenditures during the year. This account informs you about the inflow (sources) and outflow (uses) of funds each year and is analogous to a nation's BOP account. The second account shows you how much money you have accumulated at the bank and (assuming you have no other assets) your net asset position. In itself, this account represents your solvency at a given point in time. This second account is analogous to the NII account. The NII account is what we should look at in order to judge the ability of a country to meet its international debts without having to sell locally owned domestic assets. Thus, while the BOP tells us whether a country's asset portfolio is getting better or worse, the NII account tells us how good or how bad things actually are, in an absolute, cumulative sense, at a given point in time.

We now consider an example at the level of a country, rather than an individual.

Example 2.10. We must look at stock versus flow information from the BOP and the NII account. Suppose that a country has been running a current-account deficit of USD 20 billion for each of the last three years, but its NII account has a positive balance of USD 1,000 billion. Then, even though the current-account balance in the BOP accounts reflects a deficit, given the large positive balance in the NII account, this current-account deficit is not a problem—at least, not at this time.

There is obviously a link between the BOP and the NII account; increases in the amount of foreign assets owned add to the NII account. That is, the combined balance on the current and capital accounts leads to a change in the net asset position of the country. This change is reflected in the NII account. Recall, however, that transactions in the current account and capital account are not recorded perfectly. For example, unrepatriated earnings are not recorded in the current account, nor are changes in the market values of foreign assets (arising from either a change in the local value of these assets or a change in the exchange rate). Thus, the true NII account may change in a way not fully explained by the official BOP statistics.

Example 2.11. There may be large differences between the estimated net asset position of a country and the NII account computed from the BOP. In 1992, the NII account balance for the United Kingdom was reported as GBP 60 billion. However, the true mid-1992 net asset figure was estimated by one source as somewhere between GBP 80 and 100 billion.

A CA deficit and a deterioration in the NII account balance are traditionally viewed as bad news for the country and its currency, so they may lead to government action. This is especially true if the government wants to maintain a constant exchange rate and feels that it is threatened by a deficit.

Example 2.12. Q. Go back to Groucho Marx's Freedonian CA deficit. What would be your prediction regarding the NII account and the strength of the Freedonian crown (FDK)?

A. If the CA deficit goes on, Freedonia's NII account, which was hugely positive in the 1960s, will go into the red (i.e., the country's foreign-held debts exceed its foreign assets). Foreigners may be very happy to buy the Freedonian assets if there is a stock-market bubble going on, but absent this they will be prepared to buy more and more Freedonian assets only if the price falls. A drop in the value of the FDK is one way to achieve this.

This brings us to the last topic of this chapter: exchange-rate regimes.

2.5 Exchange-Rate Regimes

We have seen how money is created and how it is transferred from one owner to another owner in a different country. In the examples we considered, money was transferred as a payment for goods, but very often this entails an exchange transaction: the importer buys the exporter's currency and pays, or the importer pays in her own currency but the exporter then converts this money into her own money. Exchange transactions are, per definition, also needed when somebody wants to shift investments from one currency to another. The price that one pays for one unit of the foreign currency, in such a transaction, is the exchange rate. This rate depends on the supply and demand for the foreign currency. Very often governments instruct their central banks to influence the supply and demand for a currency.

Government intervention in the exchange markets occurs through the buying and selling of foreign currency by a country's central bank. In section 2.1.2.5 we noted that such intervention affects the country's monetary base and, hence, its money supply. Yet influencing the money supply is usually not the primary purpose of intervention in the foreign exchange market. Instead, the main purpose of intervention is to control or at least influence the exchange rate. Thus, the central bank buys foreign exchange when the exchange rate (the market price of foreign currency) is too low, and it sells foreign exchange when the exchange rate is too high. Many central banks intervene on the basis of policy objectives and rules formulated by the government. Loosely, a country's exchange-rate regime can be defined as the set of rules that its central bank follows when buying and selling in the interbank market. These rules can vary greatly. We shall discuss them briefly in reviewing postwar international monetary history.

2.5.1 Fixed Exchange Rates Relative to Gold

Before World War I, most countries had an official gold parity; that is, they fixed the price of gold in terms of their own currency. (This, in fact, refers to the old principle that gold was the true currency.) After World War II, only the USD had a fixed gold parity, officially USD 35 per troy ounce of fine gold with intervention points at 34.8 and 35.2.

"You shall not crucify mankind upon a cross of gold," was how the 1896 U.S. Democratic presidential candidate, William Jennings Bryan, famously expressed his sentiments about the gold standard (www.tntech.edu/history/crosgold.html). As the dollar was convertible into gold, the ratio of outstanding dollars to gold reserves needed to remain credible in order to prevent runs on the gold stock. For example, an individual feels confident that he or she will be able to effectively exchange USD notes into gold when the number of USD notes exceeds their gold backing by only 2 to 1. If, however, the number of dollars exceeds their gold backing by 100 to 1, it is obvious that if, in a period

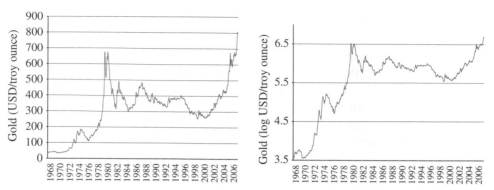

Figure 2.5. The gold price, 1968–2007. The plot shows the monthly average of the daily fixings in the London market ("free" market, during Bretton Woods: the "official" market, open only to central banks, had a fixed price till 1973). I first plot the price and then the log price, which helps you see where the rates of return (as opposed to absolute price rises) were the biggest. Thus, percentage-wise the rise 1977–80 was much more pronounced than the 1998–2007 hike. The 1980 peak was also spectacular in the sense that if corrected for general (CPI) inflation, it amounts to about USD 1,000, a price level that reappeared only in 2008. (*Source:* Underlying data are from DataStream.)

of uncertainty, a small fraction of USD notes is converted into gold, then the remaining USD notes will have no gold backing left. If the USD-to-gold ratio is high, the slightest scare is sufficient to send people flying to the bank, trying to be ahead of the others. Such a stampede then achieves the very event the investors are afraid of: the bank runs out of gold. Thus, to avert panic, the U.S. central bank (the Federal Reserve) has to make sure that the money stock does not grow faster than the stock of gold. However, there is also a limit to the value of transactions that can take place in, for example, one month, with a given amount of dollars in circulation. For this reason, a limit on the stock of dollars also imposes a limit on the value of transactions made in dollars; maintaining a credible gold backing ultimately creates the risk of slowing down economic activity in the United States and international trade, two domains where USD are used as the medium of exchange. The necessity of choosing between economic growth and credibility is often called the *Triffin Dilemma*, after the professor at Yale University who again pointed out the problem in the early 1960s.

The United States did not restrict the supply of dollars after World War II. Internally, this was no problem, because U.S. residents were no longer allowed to convert dollars (or any other currency) into gold. Externally, there was a problem, though: the Vietnam War and the Great Society Program created a government deficit, leading to a CA shortfall, financed by large-scale transfers of dollars to foreigners. Unlike U.S. residents, these non-U.S. investors and central banks *could* always buy or sell gold (at USD 35) in the London gold pool, where the Federal Reserve stabilized the USD gold price by using the pooled gold stocks of the central banks of most Western nations. Decreased credibility led to minor runs on gold, which further decreased credibility, which led to more runs on the gold stock. The U.S. Federal Reserve, which had held about two thirds of the world's gold stock in the late 1940s, soon saw its reserves dwindle. In the mid 1960s, the official gold market had to be closed to all private investors, while central banks were expected to avoid buying gold from the Federal Reserve. (France, notably, did not oblige.) In 1971, the official gold price was raised from USD/oz. 35 to 38, but that did not avert the ultimate collapse of the system. In 1972, the U.S. government gave up all pretense that the USD was convertible into gold at a fixed rate. The gold price soared, and has mostly been in the range of USD 300–600 ever since (figure 2.5). In the most recent decade (1998–2007), the low was about USD 250 (mid 1999), the high at the end (800+), part of a general commodities boom that is commonly ascribed to China's demand—even though I think hedge funds helped too. In early 2008, the price went over the USD 1,000 mark.

Besides the Triffin Dilemma, the gold standard suffered from the fact that gold has industrial uses and is expensive to mine. From that perspective, the use of gold as the basis for a financial system is a waste of scarce resources. Finally, some politicians objected to allowing major—but politically incorrect—gold producers like South Africa and the USSR cheap access to USD, while others resented the crucial role and seignorage gains this system granted to the United States.

2.5.2 Fixed Exchange Rates vis-à-vis a Single Currency

Under a fixed exchange-rate regime, the government wants to guarantee a virtually constant price for a particular foreign currency, and instructs the central bank to buy or sell as soon as the exchange rate deviates by $x\%$ from that constant rate. The target exchange rate is called the country's *official parity*.

This system was strongly recommended under the Bretton Woods Agreement, signed in 1945 by the major Western nations. For instance, between 1949 and 1967, the United Kingdom set the central parity with respect to the USD at USD/GBP 2.8, and instructed the Bank of England (BoE) to intervene whenever the pound's value rose to 2.821 or dropped to 2.779. Thus, the intervention points were set by the government at 0.75% on each side of the official parity. As long as the BoE did not run out of USD, it would sell USD when the dollar became too expensive. If the dollar became too cheap, the BoE would buy. Likewise, Germany set the central parity at DEM/USD 4, and the Bundesbank would always make sure that the USD stayed in the range DEM/USD 3.97–4.03.

Note that the United States did not declare an official parity with respect to any other currency; the Federal Reserve was never under any obligation to intervene in the exchange markets. Note also that there was no official parity (and hence no intervention) for non-USD rates either, for example DEM/GBP. There are, of course, implicit, indirect bounds on what the DEM/GBP rate can be: if there are limits on how expensive the USD can be in terms of DEM, and limits on how expensive GBP can be in terms of USD, there is obviously an implied limit on how expensive or cheap GBP can become in terms of DEM.

Fixed exchange rates work satisfactorily only as long as the countries maintain their competitiveness, but this requires similar economic policies. To see this, note that the United Kingdom could not possibly have 100% inflation and still maintain the exchange rate if its trading partners have near-zero inflation: with a stable exchange rate, the U.K.'s exporters would have to quit foreign markets, and British firms selling in the United Kingdom would likewise be wiped out by foreign producers. In short, fixed rates require similar inflation rates across countries, which, in turn, requires coordination of economic policy. There was very little policy coordination in the period following World War II, however, and this ultimately led to the demise of the fixed-rate system. As of the early 1960s, the comparatively high inflation rate in the United Kingdom meant that GBP became manifestly overvalued (U.K. producers could no longer compete at USD/GBP 2.8), while DEM was undervalued (German producers could undercut anyone anywhere, at DEM/USD 4). Also, international trade and exchange, heavily restricted immediately after the war, were gradually liberalized. With everyone free to buy and sell foreign exchange, and with a rapidly growing volume of international transactions, the BoE had to buy more and more GBP (that is, sell USD) if it wanted to support the value of GBP. Likewise, the Bundesbank had to buy more and more USD to support the price of the USD and to keep down the price of DEM. As a result, the BoE frequently ran out of USD while supporting GBP, and the Bundesbank accumulated too many USD.

Often, the Bundesbank lent USD to the BoE (under a swap arrangement; for more details, see chapter 7), or the United Kingdom borrowed USD from the International Monetary Fund, but these were only meant to be solutions to temporary problems. The idea, under the Bretton Woods Agreement, was that *structural misalignments* should be corrected by changes in the official parities (re- or devaluations). But this did not work very well. For one thing, the difference between a structural problem and a temporary problem was never defined. Moreover, devaluations were perceived by politicians as a sign of defeat, while revaluations were also unpopular because they hurt exporters. Nor did the IMF have the supranational power to impose parity adjustments on member countries. The result was that parity adjustments were postponed too long. As we have argued in the preceding section, the USD/gold parity had also become unrealistic by that time. The combined effect of disequilibrium exchange rates and gold prices led to the collapse of the system of fixed parities in 1972. Since that year, the currencies of the major OECD countries have floated with respect to the USD.

Some countries still maintain fixed exchange rates, with narrowish intervention bands, relative to one currency. A supposedly foolproof way of guaranteeing such a fixed rate is having a *currency board* instead of a central bank.

Figure 2.6. A bank note printed by a colonial currency board. The colonial central bank for the Congo, Rwanda, and Urundi (now Burundi) used to exchange local francs for Belgian francs and vice versa. After independence (mid 1960), Congo's currency board (*conseil monétaire*) initially just printed a reference to the Republic of the Congo on the old colonial notes. The Dutch at the bottom means "one thousand francs payable at sight" ("duizend frank betaalbaar op zicht") and "the counterfeiter is punished by forced labor" ("de namaker wordt met strafdienst gestraft").

The roots of this system were in the colonial period, where a local institution issued a local currency but was not allowed to pursue an active monetary policy; rather, it just exchanged, say, Belgian francs into Congolese francs or vice versa, one to one, and issued no extra Congolese francs via any other means (figure 2.6). In a modern currency board, the idea is similarly that (i) the board can issue local currency only if agents freely want to obtain it in exchange for hard currency, and (ii) the board has to take back local currency in exchange for hard currency if investors prefer so. From rule (i), all local currency should be fully backed by hard currency, so rule (ii) should pose no problems. Monetary policy is to be passive, just determined by the economy's demands—a libertarian's wet dream. It should also be fully immune to speculative attacks.

In reality, the above predictions can be confounded. Argentina set up a currency board regime in 1991 (choosing, perhaps ominously, April 1 as the starting date), under which the Argentine peso was pegged one for one to the U.S. dollar. On January 6, 2002, the system collapsed ignominiously. How was this possible? First, in modern practice the 100% coverage only relates to M_0: the currency board only deals with commercial banks, not with the general public, and lets M_0 wax and wane if and when the commercials banks demand more or less local currency. But the commercial banks themselves can (and do) create far more money on their own, and this extra is not fully backed by foreign exchange (forex) reserves. So, speculative attacks are still possible, with investors starting a run on their banks to convert their electronic pesos into cash pesos (and those, hopefully, into dollars), a demand that commercial banks cannot possibly meet. In the end, Argentina's government froze all peso deposits. Second, a credible board should make risk-free hard-currency investments only, which rules out government financing. Nor should the board act as

Table 2.7. Exchange-rate regimes and anchors of monetary policy, 2004.

No separate currency as legal tender (40)	
Another country's money is legal tender	Ecuador, El Salvador, Kiribati, Marshall Island, Micronesia, Palau, Panama, San Marino
East Caribbean currency union	Antigua and Barbuda, Dominica, Grenada, Saint Kitts and Nevis, Saint Lucia, Saint Vincent and the Grenadines
West African Economic and Monetary Union	Benin, Burkina Faso, Ivory Coast, Guinea-Bissau, Mali, Niger, Senegal, Togo
Central African Economic and Monetary Community	Cameroon, Central African Republic, Chad, Republic of the Congo (Brazzaville), Equatorial Guinea, Gabon
Euro area	Austria, Belgium, Finland, France, Germany, Greece, Ireland, Italy, Luxembourg, Netherlands, Portugal, Spain

Currency board arrangements (7)
Argentina, Bosnia-Herzegovina, Brunei, Hong Kong (People's Republic of China), Djibouti, Estonia, Lithuania

Other fixed peg or de facto fixed (40)	
Against single currency (30)	Aruba, Bahamas, Bahrain, Bangladesh, Barbados, Belize, Bhutan, Cape Verde, People's Republic of China (mainland), Comoros, Iran, Jordan, Lebanon, Lesotho, Macedonia (FYR), Malaysia, Maldives, Namibia, Nepal, Netherlands Antilles, Oman, Qatar, Saudi Arabia, Sudan, Suriname, Swaziland, Syria, Turkmenistan, United Arab Emirates, Zimbabwe
Against basket (10)	Botswana, Fiji, Kuwait, Latvia, Libya, Malta, Morocco, Samoa, Seychelles, Vanuatu

Pegged with band (5)	
ERM II (1)	Denmark
Other (4)	Cyprus, Egypt, Hungary, Tonga

Crawling peg (4)
Bolivia, Costa Rica, Nicaragua, Solomon Islands

Crawling peg with band (6)
Belarus, Honduras, Israel, Romania, Uruguay, Venezuela

lender of last resort or overseer of the commercial banks: that would conflict with its supposed fully passive monetary stance. But Argentina's board did act as lender of last resort during the Mexican crisis (1995), and was allowed (and expected) to invest in government bonds rather than just hard currency. So, even M_0 was not fully covered, with the backing occasionally falling as low as 83%. Third, even if the board had been able to defend the exchange rate, ultimately the decision to maintain or cancel the system still remained a political issue. The rate can turn out to be less attractive than politicians first

Table 2.7. *Continued.*

Managed float (40)	
Monetary aggregate target (11)	Ghana, Guinea, Guyana, Indonesia, Jamaica, Mauritius, Mongolia, Sao Tome and Principe, Slovenia, Sri Lanka, Tunisia
Inflation target (1)	Thailand
Monetary program (19)	Azerbaijan, Cambodia, Croatia, Ethiopia, Iraq, Kazakhstan, Kenya, Kyrgyzstan, Laos, Mauritania, Nigeria, Pakistan, Russia, Rwanda, Trinidad and Tobago, Ukraine, Vietnam, Yugoslavia, Zambia
Other (12)	Algeria, Angola, Burundi, Dominican Republic, Eritrea, Guatemala, India, Union of Myanmar, Paraguay, Singapore, Slovakia, Uzbekistan
Independent float (41)	
Monetary aggregate target (7)	Gambia, Malawi, Peru, the Philippines, Sierra Leone, Turkey, Yemen
Inflation target (15)	Australia, Brazil, Canada, Chile, Colombia, Czech Republic, Iceland, Korea, Mexico, New Zealand, Norway, Poland, South Africa, Sweden, United Kingdom
Monetary program (10)	Albania, Armenia, Congo (Democratic Republic), Georgia, Madagascar, Moldova, Mozambique, Tajikistan, Tanzania, Uganda
Other (8)	Afghanistan, Haiti, Japan, Liberia, Papua New Guinea, Somalia, Switzerland, United States

From the IMF (www.imf.org/external/np/mfd/er/2003/eng/0603.htm). Note the date, June 2003. Since then, most notably, the yuan became a floater and Euroland expanded to encompass Slovenia (2007) and Cyprus and Malta (2008). Slovakia joins in 2009.

thought. For instance, after Argentina's huge neighbor and competitor, Brazil, devalued massively in 1999 and the USD had risen against the yen and the European currencies, the peso had a much harder time, and politicians had second thoughts about the one-to-one fixed rate. Also, when the speculative attacks came, interest rates rose to 40–60% as investors dumped peso commercial paper and bonds. This was very costly to the government, which was running huge deficits. So, in the end, the politicians pulled the plug.

This does not mean a currency board cannot work: the Baltic states' experience with the system was much more positive, for instance, and so is Hong Kong's. But you should remember that even this safe-looking regime requires a responsible fiscal policy, and needs a bit of luck—no bad external shocks, notably.

In table 2.7 we see that, in December 2003, eight countries had a currency board. The table shows that, apart from the eight currency-board cases, thirty countries went for a traditional fixed-rate regime vis-à-vis one currency, and five had a fixed-rate-with-band regime. In addition, fourteen countries use a CFA (Communauté Financière Africaine) franc, which is basically fixed vis-à-vis the euro.[18] All in all, this means that sixty-nine countries still have fixed rates. The major OECD countries, however, have adopted different exchange-rate regimes. In the following sections, we discuss fixed rates as they relate to a basket, multilateral intervention points (notably, the European Union's Exchange Rate Mechanism), and dirty floating.

2.5.3 Fixed Exchange Rates Relative to a Basket

After 1973–74, some countries unilaterally defined a target parity for a portfolio or basket of currencies with intervention points around that target. Table 2.7 mentions ten countries that have pegged their currencies to a basket. One such basket is the SDR (panel 2.2). At one time, Sweden, Norway, and Finland pegged their currencies to another existing basket, the ECU, which is described in section 2.5.4. Some countries go for a basket of their own rather than taking an existing combination like the SDR. At one time, this group contained Australia, Sweden, Norway, and Finland. Before explaining how a basket regime works, we must consider how a basket is constructed.

Example 2.13. Suppose that since the election of President Groucho Marx the composition of Freedonia's trade has been fairly stable: about 60% of trade is with Euroland and 40% with the United States. Thus, Freedonia can create a basket with these approximate weights for, respectively, the EUR and the USD, and tie its crown (the FDK) to that basket. Suppose the rates are currently FDK/EUR 3 and FDK/USD 2.5, and that the government finds these rates acceptable. To define the basket, it would have to find a number (n_E) of EUR and a number (n_D) of USD such that the EUR has a weight of 60%:

$$\frac{n_E \times 3}{n_E \times 3 + n_D \times 2.5} = 0.6. \tag{2.9}$$

Arbitrarily setting $n_D = 1$, we find $n_E = 1.25$. Thus, President Marx defines the basket as containing USD 1 and EUR 1.25.[19]

Now that we understand how a basket is constructed, let us see how it is used in the central bank's intervention policy. The idea is that the basket should always be worth roughly its target level, FDK 6.25, and not deviate by more than 5%, for example. This implies intervention points of 5.9375–6.5625. At any given moment, the central bank can compute the spot value of the basket. If the basket hits or approaches an intervention point, the central bank intervenes: if the basket is too expensive, the central bank sells USD and/or EUR and buys crowns, and vice versa.

---

[18] The CFA used to be managed by the Banque de France; nowadays, the French Treasury guarantees the rate and provides a credit line to the two CFA central banks.

[19] To verify that the weight of the EUR is 60%, first compute the basket's current value. At the going exchange rates, FDK/EUR 3 and FDK/USD 2.5, one unit of the basket is worth

$$\text{EUR } 1.25 \times 3 + \text{USD } 1 \times 2.5 = \text{FDK } 6.25,$$

such that the euro's weight is indeed $[1.25 \times 3]/6.25 = 0.6$.

The earliest antecedent of the European Union was the *European Community for Coal and Steel* (ECCS), which started off as a six-country group in 1954 (Benelux (Belgium, the Netherlands, and Luxembourg), France, Germany, and Italy) meant to control Germany's "strategic" coal and steel production under the (thin) guise of a joint management of all six countries' coal and steel sectors. In 1957, the six then signed the *Euratom* Treaty and the Treaty of Rome; both became effective in 1958. The Rome Treaty founded the *European Economic Community* (EEC), which was a customs union topped up with a common agricultural policy and free movement of capital and labor.

The ECCS, Euratom, and the EEC were soon merged into the European Community (EC). The United Kingdom, Ireland, and Denmark joined the EC in 1973, Greece in 1981, and Portugal and Spain in 1986. In 1993, the EC became the *European Union* (EU), by adding plans for a monetary union, a common foreign policy, and police and judicial cooperation. Sweden, Finland, and Austria joined in 1995. The number of members rose from fifteen to twenty-five in 2004, with the Czech Republic, Cyprus, Estonia, Hungary, Latvia, Lithuania, Malta, Poland, Slovakia, and Slovenia all joining, and to twenty-seven in 2007 (Bulgaria and Romania).

Panel 2.4. Europe: economic community, community, or union?

Example 2.14. If, for instance, the EUR is trading at FDK/EUR 3.2 and the USD at FDK/USD 2.2, the basket is worth $1.25 \times 3.2 + 1 \times 2.2 = 6.2$. This is well within the admissible band (5.9375–6.5625). If the USD then appreciates to FDK/USD 2.5, the basket's value increases to $1.25 \times 3.2 + 1 \times 2.5 = 6.5$. This is dangerously close to the upper bound, and the Freedonian central bank will probably already be in the market to support the crown.

2.5.4 The 1979–93 Exchange Rate Mechanism of the European Monetary System

The purpose of the European Union's (on the EU, see panel 2.4) initial Exchange Rate Mechanism (ERM) was to restrict the fluctuations of the currencies of the ERM member states relative to each other without, however, restricting the fluctuations of these currencies relative to outside currencies like the USD and the JPY. For this reason, a similar, earlier system was called "the snake." (Picture the member currencies as contained within the skin of a snake, which, as a whole, floats relative to other currencies like the USD and the JPY.) The United Kingdom joined the system as late as 1991, along with (briefly) Italy, and dropped out in 1992. Greece joined only in the late 1990s, as a prequel to the adoption of the EUR. The ERM was the key part of the European Monetary System (EMS), itself a forerunner of the European Monetary Union (EMU).

The ERM was built around a basket of all EU currencies, called the European Currency Unit or ECU.[20] Still, the role of the ECU is different from the role a basket plays in the system described in section 2.5.3, as we shall see. Here is an outline of how the system worked:

---

[20] Note that, not coincidentally, "ecu" is also the name of an ancient French gold coin—a cousin of the escudo (from Latin, *scutum*).

- Politicians and experts thrashed out a set of weights based on the members' GDP and share in total trade. At the then-prevailing exchange rates they then constructed a basket that had the same initial value as the European Unit of Account (EUA), a bookkeeping unit for payments among the EC and its member states.[21]

- Each currency had an official target exchange rate against the ECU. The initial levels were just the values of the EUA in each currency, inherited from the days of "the snake." From all these, a full grid of cross-rates between all member countries was computed. For example, if Belgium has BEF/ECU 40 and Germany DEM/ECU 2, the implied "cross" target rate is 20 BEF/DEM.

- Unlike in a pure basket system, intervention was not based on the value of the basket but on each of the bilateral cross-rates. True, one also watched, for each currency, the relative deviation between the actual and target value of the ECU, from which a daily "divergence indicator" was extracted. But this was just a measure of health, not a signal for actual intervention.

- The system was more cooperative than Bretton Woods. First, *both* central banks undertook to maintain, by standard intervention, the actual bilateral rates within a $\pm 2.25\%$ band around the bilateral target parity.[22] Second, governments and central bankers met periodically to coordinate economic policies. Third, de- or revaluations had to be negotiated multilaterally rather than decreed unilaterally.

- Any candidate member had to be able to show respectable records on inflation and interest rates, and a stable exchange-rate history against the ECU, covering two years prior to application.

The early ERM went through fairly frequent realignments. However, by 1990–91, the system seemed very stable, with converging inflation rates across member states. When, in 1990, even Margaret Thatcher admitted that it was not totally inconceivable that the United Kingdom might at some point consider pondering the option of replacing the GBP by some form of common currency, the market went delirious. The euphoria was, however, premature. On September 15, 1992, Finland, which was not a member but had unilaterally pegged its FinMark to the ECU, gave in to continued pressure and abandoned its target rate. Speculation then turned to Sweden, which soon gave up its own unilateral link to the ECU too, and then to the weaker ERM members. In a matter of hours the peseta (ESP) devalued, the lira and pound dropped out of the ERM,

---

[21] The EUA had started off at par with the USD, and became a basket of the (then nine) member currencies in the 1970s. So the similarity in the values of the EUR and USD is not a coincidence.

[22] Still, the central bank with the weak currency had to pay back, sooner or later, all the money spent in interventions by the central bank with the strong money. So the undertaking by (notably) Germany to intervene was not a blank check but just an unlimited credit line to its fellow central banks. A currency could, therefore, still be brought to its knees by speculators if its government thought debts were running up too high.

and Spain, Portugal, and Ireland reimposed capital controls. George Soros—or his mutual funds—made a billion dollars. But the Banque de France and the Bundesbank were able to successfully defend the FRF/DEM rate, and quiet gradually returned to the markets—until the summer of 1993.

The cause of the currency turmoil during the summer of 1993 was a disagreement about economic policy. The Bundesbank wanted to stamp out inflation (caused by German unification) with a strict monetary policy and high interest rates. Many other countries, including France, preferred to lower interest rates in order to get their economies out of recession. This led to speculation that France might devalue, so as to be able to lower its interest rates. Enormous interventions followed. In the end, the ERM admissible band was widened from 2.25% to 15% each side, which meant a virtual suspension of the ERM. By early 1994, most currencies had returned to rates within or close to the old 2.25% band, and Soros had lost the better part of the billion dollars he had gained in 1992. Still, the message of the 1992–93 turmoil is that the credibility of the system is vital for its survival, and that the only 100% credible regime is one with just a single currency.

2.5.4.1 European Monetary Union and the Euro

The Maastricht Treaty, signed a few months before the 1992 ERM catastrophe, contained, among other things, an EMU plan. To qualify for membership of the Union, a country had to meet the (in)famous *Maastricht criteria*. These included total independence of the central bank from the government, an inflation rate and short-term interest rate that were close to the average for the best performers, a government deficit not exceeding 3% of GDP, and a government debt not exceeding 60% of GDP (or at least showing considerable progress toward that target). Many governments may have been secretly happy with the tough norms: painful policy measures could now be blamed on "Maastricht" or "Brussels,"[23] a practice which also made the EU quite unpopular in some quarters. The United Kingdom and Denmark, feeling that too much sovereign power would be lost by EMU membership, obtained the right to opt out of the common currency. The European Central Bank (ECB) would be totally independent of politics, and its first aim would be to keep average inflation below 2%; growth and employment were explicitly labeled as secondary. Monetary policy was to be decided by the ECB's board (on which all governors of the national central banks sit, plus the ECB governor and some other ECB top people); the national central banks became mere local implementors. Lastly, a

---

[23] Maastricht (the Netherlands) was the venue for the meeting that led to the Treaty, but has no permanent EU institutions. Brussels (Belgium) is home to the EU Commission and the Council of Ministers. The Parliament has its ten to twelve annual plenary meetings in Strasbourg (France), on the French–German border, but spends most of its time in Brussels too. The European Court and the European Investment Bank are in Luxembourg, and the European Central Bank is in Frankfurt (Germany).

Table 2.8. The twelve early EUR countries and conversion rates.

Currency	Abbreviation	Rate
Austrian schilling	ATS	13.7603
Belgian franc	BEF	40.3399
Dutch gulden	NLG	2.20371
Finnish markka	FIM	5.94573
French franc	FRF	6.55957
German mark	DEM	1.95583
Irish pound	IEP	1936.27
Italian lira	ITL	0.787564
Luxembourg franc	LUF	40.3399
Portuguese escudo	PTE	200.482
Spanish peseta	ESP	166.386
Greek drachma	GRD	340.750
Slovenian tolar	SIT	239.640
Cypriot pound	CYP	0.585274
Maltese lira	MTL	0.429300

"growth and stability pact" made the 3% limit on government deficits a permanent rule rather than just an initial prerequisite for membership. A country in breach of the rule could be warned, censored, or even fined, but any such countermeasures would be a political decision, not an automatism.

In the fall of 1996 the name of the common currency, the euro (EUR), was agreed upon, and soon thereafter the list of qualifying countries. Greece did not qualify yet (it has joined since, though), the two opt-outs did not want to join, and Sweden said no via a referendum; so, in early 1999 the EMU started with an eleven-country Euroland plus Greece in the antechamber. In the period 1999–2001, rates remained irrevocably fixed, and all interbank finance transactions were expressed in euros rather than the old currencies, as were stock-market prices; but retail transactions, and payments with physical money, remained as before. In 2002 the common currency was finally introduced,[24] physically and in all bank-to-customer relations. The process went off quite smoothly, with hindsight. The 2% inflation cap has proved hard to meet, however, and is often criticized as economically harmful;[25] nowadays the 2% figure is a target rather than a cap. Also, the 3% deficit rule has been enforced unevenly: Portugal was fined, but Greece was let off the hook when it admitted that its books had been cooked (by a previous government, of course). When France and Germany then went into the red, the rule was readily modified:

---

[24] San Marino and the Vatican, which gave up their liras, and Monaco, which gave up its franc, also introduced the euro in 2002.

[25] One argument is that inflation is overstated in the first place, as the official figure tends to ignore creeping improvements in the quality of goods. Also, moderate inflation allows relative prices or wages in problem industries to fall without need of decreases in nominal terms. (Nominal wage drops are even less popular than real wage drops.)

the new version is softer in that it says that, "averaged over the entire business cycle," budget deficits cannot exceed 3%; but the new rule is also tougher in that it requires surpluses in boom periods. The "toughening" was again applied unevenly: France, Germany, and Italy seemed to go unpunished for taking a very long time to get their act together. In 2007 the freshly elected president of France, Sarkozy, immediately traveled to Brussels to explain the necessity of even more deficits and to ask the Council's pardon. He got it, of course.

Denmark has an ERM-type relation with the euro ("ERM II"), and so have many of the 2005 entrants, notably the Estonian kroon (EEK), the Latvian lats (LVL), the Lithuanian litas (LTL), and the Slovak koruna (SKK). Four other former ERM II countries have already joined: Slovenia, the first of the "new" European members, in 2007; Cyprus and Malta in 2008; and Slovakia in 2009. There have been no big speculative attacks on any of the ERM links, except for a few heady days in the credit-crunchy fall of 2008 (the Baltics and Hungary). In principle, all of the remaining "new" ERM II members are candidates for EMU membership.[26]

The EUR started at USD 1.17 in 1999, then ignominiously sank to 0.80, but in 2004 rose back above par, even going beyond 1.35 early 2005. Most of that was a weakening of the USD rather than a strengthening of the EUR. There are no compelling simple explanations for these swings. Perhaps it was just U.S. hedge funds piling into forex as they did into commodities, and fears that Asian central banks would sooner or later dump their huge dollar balances. The even worse fall of the USD, at the end of 2007 and in early 2008, to below EUR 0.67 (USD/EUR 1.50) and even below CAD 1 probably reflected an increasing lack of confidence in U.S. assets. (Remember that a country with a CA deficit is a net seller of assets not of goods.) U.S. banks were deeper in the subprime-mortgage mess than their overseas colleagues; and big investors, fed up with depreciating dollar assets, effectively started divesting them. However, the sudden weakening of the euro in the fall of 2008, along with the simultaneously crashing oil and commodity prices, suggests that the "deleveraging" (the reduction of speculative positions) by U.S. investors like hedge funds has been a major force behind the price swings.

2.5.5 Other Exchange-Rate Systems

Some countries have an unofficial target rate, and unofficial intervention points, with respect to a single currency or a basket. For example, the Swiss franc and, before EMS membership, the Austrian schilling were kept fairly stable with respect to the DEM. The intervention rates were never explicitly announced—and obviously changed over time.

---

[26] The GBP and the SEK float, as do the Czech koruna (CZK), the Gibraltar pound (GIP), the Hungarian forint (HUF), and the Polish zloty (PLN). Since two successful ERM II years are a prerequisite for EUR membership, these three "new-Europe" floaters are not trying very hard to join.

The central banks of the Group of Five (G5), later expanded to G8,[27] meet twice a year to discuss exchange-rate targets for the three main currency blocks (USD, JPY, and EUR). Central banks occasionally intervened in the USD/DEM and USD/JPY market on a unilateral or coordinated basis ("*dirty floating*"), but there seems to be little of that going on nowadays.

Other countries, including many Latin American countries, have experimented with a *crawling peg* system, where the official parity is revised fairly frequently. This sometimes happens semiautomatically, on the basis of a formula involving, for instance, inflation and balance-of-payments data. In table 2.7, ten countries officially follow this system.

The remaining countries, eighty-one in table 2.7 (plus, for external purposes, the twelve Euroland countries), are floaters. About half of them professedly disregard the exchange rate and only look at internal indicators as a basis for monetary policy. The "*managed float*" countries combine internal and external indicators without, however, committing to a fixed value or fixed formula.

*   *   *

The above should have equipped you with enough background insights to start the real stuff. We begin with the currency market and its satellites.

TEST YOUR UNDERSTANDING

Quiz Questions

True–False Questions

1. If a country has a BOP deficit, the total of all BOP subaccounts is negative.

2. The current account is a record of all trade in goods and services, while the capital account is a record of direct and portfolio investment and unilateral transfers.

---

[27] G5 consisted of the United States, Japan, Germany, France, and the United Kingdom. Later, Canada and Italy were invited too (G7). Even more recently, Russia has been asked, first as an observer (G7$\frac{1}{2}$, according to some cynics). A notable meeting was the G5 1985 "Plaza Agreement," where the G5 publicly agreed that the USD should decrease in value. This is often viewed as having provided an important impetus to the drop in the USD after its unprecedented rise in the early 1980s. Recently, Gx meetings have been prominent mostly by their lack of visibility.

G6 is an unrelated group: it refers to a club of six major players in the Doha round (a WTO negotiation forum): Australia, Brazil, the EU (whose external trade policy is a supranational matter, implemented by the Commission), India, Japan, and the United States.

3. When the U.S. private sector purchases more goods or makes more investments abroad than foreigners purchase or invest in the United States during a year, the Federal Reserve (the U.S. central bank) must make up for the shortfall.

4. All errors and omissions in the BOP are a result of black market transactions.

5. When a corporation purchases a company abroad, and the value of the firm appreciates over time, the NII account and the capital account of the BOP is updated to reflect this change.

6. The BOP theory of exchange-rate determination says that most changes in the exchange rate are due to the arrival of new information about the future.

7. Under a fixed exchange-rate regime, if a country's private sector sells abroad more than it purchases, the central bank must sell foreign exchange.

8. BOP theory is flawed because it assumes that investors only invest in risk-free domestic and foreign assets.

Multiple-Choice Questions

For the following three questions, assume that Antarctica is the home country, and its currency is the Antarctica dollar (AAD), and Greenland is the foreign country and its currency is the Greenland crown (GRK). Choose the correct answer.

1. All else being equal, an increase in income in Greenland leads to:
   (a) An increase in consumption in Antarctica, and therefore an increase in imports, resulting in an appreciation of the AAD.
   (b) A decrease in consumption in Antarctica, and therefore an increase in exports, resulting in a depreciation of the AAD.
   (c) An increase in consumption in Greenland, and therefore an increase in imports, resulting in an appreciation of the AAD.
   (d) An increase in consumption in Greenland, and therefore an increase in imports, resulting in a depreciation of the AAD.

2. All else being equal, a decrease in the interest rate r^* in Greenland leads to:
   (a) Decreased demand for assets in Greenland, and therefore a depreciation of the GRK.
   (b) Decreased demand for assets in Greenland, and therefore a depreciation of the AAD.
   (c) An increase in consumption in Greenland, and therefore an increase in imports, resulting in an appreciation of the GRK.
   (d) An increase in consumption in Antarctica, and therefore an increase in exports, resulting in a depreciation of the AAD.

3. All else being equal, a decrease in prices in Greenland leads to:

   (a) An increase in exports to Antarctica, and therefore an appreciation of the AAD.

   (b) An increase in exports to Antarctica, and therefore a depreciation of the AAD.

   (c) An increase in consumption in Greenland, and therefore an increase in imports, resulting in an appreciation of the AAD.

   (d) A decrease in consumption in Greenland, and therefore a decrease in imports, resulting in a depreciation of the AAD.

Additional Quiz Questions

1. The German subsidiary of a Canadian firm (that is, the subsidiary is owned by the Canadian firm) is sold to a German firm. The Canadian firm invests the funds obtained from the sale in Frankfurt. How is the transaction recorded in the Canadian BOP?

2. The BOP of Timbuktu showed the following entries for 1988: a capital account surplus of 50, a deficit in the services account of 15, and a trade deficit of 45. The change in the official reserves was zero. What was the balance of unilateral transfers for Timbuktu?

3. If the central bank sets an exchange rate that undervalues the foreign currency—and the flows of goods and capital adjust simultaneously—what will be the impact on the following:

   (a) RFX (increase/decrease);
   (b) BOP (surplus/deficit).

4. If the current account balance has a surplus of USD 2 billion and the official settlements balance (RFX) has a deficit of USD 5 billion, what is the balance of the capital account?

5. A British importer purchases goods from a French company and obtains a trade credit for the full value of the shipment (equal to GBP 100). How should this transaction be recorded in the BOP of the United Kingdom?

6. Numenor, a country on the Atlantis continent, has a government deficit of 40 billion while private investment exceeds private savings by 10 billion. What is Timbuktu's current account balance if its exchange rate is fixed?

Applications

1. Antarctica uses a system of fixed exchange rates, its current-account deficit is USD 6 billion, and its capital account balance is USD 4 billion. Based on this information, answer the following questions.

   (a) What is the change in the official foreign exchange reserves of Antarctica?

   (b) What is the gap between the income of Antarctica and its expenditure on domestic output?

(c) If there is only one other country in the world, Greenland, can you estimate the current account balance of Greenland?

2. The data below are taken from the BOP of Switzerland. Based on these data, decide whether the following statement is true or false and explain your answer.

> From 1979 to 1982, foreigners have been net issuers of SF-denominated bonds in the Swiss capital markets.

Capital account	1979	1980	1981	1982
Portfolio investment				
(in billions of dollars)	−11.8	−11.8	−11.9	−32.2

3. A company in Philadelphia purchases machinery from a Canadian company for USD 150 and receives one-year's trade credit. The machinery is transported to Philadelphia by a Canadian trucking company that charges the U.S. company USD 10. The U.S. company insures the shipment with a U.S. insurance company and pays a premium of USD 3. After delivering the machinery to Philadelphia, the Canadian truck continues its trip to Houston, where it picks up microcomputers sold by a Texan company to a Mexican company. This shipment, which is worth USD 170, is insured by a U.S. insurance company for a premium of USD 4. No trade credit is given to the Mexican company. Compute the BOP for the United States and assume that Canadian and Mexican companies maintain dollar deposits in New York.

4. Suppose that you are an analyst for the central bank of Zanzibar. Decide how the BOP accounts are affected by the following.

(a) A budget deficit financed by foreign borrowing.
(b) An import quota for foreign cars.
(c) A purchase of a new embassy in Luxembourg.
(d) A grain embargo.

5. The following data are taken from the balance of payments of Freedonia (currency FDK):

Capital account	1995	1996	1997	1998
Portfolio investment				
(in billions of dollars)	+2.9	−6.9	−5.4	−8.7

Is the following statement consistent with the data shown above?

> After 1995, foreigners issued FDK-denominated bonds in the Freedonian capital market in order to take advantage of the favorable interest rate differential with respect to the U.S. capital market.

6. The following passage is from an article that appeared in a newspaper: "Last year, the U.S. demand for capital to fund the federal deficit and to finance private investment in buildings and equipment exceeded net domestic savings by about USD 100 billion." What can we infer about the magnitude of the U.S. current-account deficit?

7. The following passage is from an article that appeared in an old news-paper. Which account of the German BOP is the article talking about?

    FRANKFURT, West Germany: West Germany's balance of payments, which measures all flows of funds into and out of the country, was in surplus by the current equivalent of USD 210.3 million in February, up from the year-earlier surplus of USD 206.4 million, but sharply lower than January's surplus of USD 10.04 billion, the central bank said January's large surplus was caused in part by heavy central-bank intervention in support of the French franc prior to the realignment of the European Monetary System at mid-month.

8. You have been hired by the IMF to design a program to improve the current account balance. How should your program influence the following variables (increase/decrease):

    (a) taxes;
    (b) government spending;
    (c) private savings.

9. The BOP of the United States in 1982 and 1984 is given below. Is it correct to state, as it has often been done, that the deterioration of the current account was primarily financed by sales of U.S. Treasury securities to foreigners?

U.S. balance of payments (billions of dollars)

	1982	1984
Trade account	−36	−108
Service account	35	17
Unilateral transfer	−8	−11
Current account	−9	−102
Changes in U.S. assets abroad (private) of which:	−108	−16
Portfolio	−8	−5
Bank-reported	−111	−7
Direct investment	6	−6
Other	5	2
Changes in foreign assets in U.S. (private) of which:	92	91
U.S. Treasury security	7	22
Other	85	69
Private capital	−16	75
Official settlements	−8	−3
Statistical discrepancy	33	30

10. Venizio had a government surplus of 15 billion in the year 1988. In addition, private after-tax savings exceeded private investment spending by 10 billion. What was the current account balance of Venizio in 1988?

PART II

Currency Markets

About This Part

This part describes the currency market in its widest sense, that is, the exchange market plus all its satellites. In chapter 3, we describe spot markets. Forward markets, where price and quantity are contracted now but delivery and payment take place at a known future moment, are introduced in chapter 4, in a perfect-markets setting. Chapter 5 shows how and when to use contracts in reality: for arbitrage, taking into account costs; for hedging; for speculation; and for shopping around and structured finance applications including, especially, swaps. Currency futures and modern currency swaps, both of which are closely related to forward transactions, are discussed in chapters 6 and 7, respectively. Chapter 8 introduces currency options and explains how these options can be used to hedge against (or, alternatively, speculate on) foreign exchange risk. How one can price currency options is explained in chapter 9; we mostly use the so-called binomial approach but also link it to the famous Black–Merton–Scholes model.

At any instant, the market value of a forward, futures, or options contract depends on the prevailing spot rate (and, if the contract is not yet at the end of its life, also on the domestic and foreign interest rates). This dependence on the future spot rate means that these contracts can be used to hedge the exchange-rate risk to which the firm is exposed. The dependence of these contracts on the future spot rate also means that their current market values can be expressed, by relatively simple arbitrage arguments, as functions of the current spot rate and of the domestic and foreign interest rates. Throughout this part of the text, a unified approach based on arbitrage-free pricing is used to value these assets whose payoffs are dependent on the exchange rate.

Brabant Bus Company

Holland's Brabant Bus Company NV (BBC) considers selling buses to the San Antonio Transit Authority (SATA) in the Caribbean. The proposed order is worth USD 12.5m (2.5m down and four annual payments of 2.5m each). This represents three months of production, so it is a sizable order by BBC's standards. Given the spot exchange rate of EUR/USD 1.2000–1.2005 and a variable production cost of EUR 13.6m spread over three months, the contract provides a profit margin of $[12.5\text{m} \times 1.2 - 13.6\text{m}]/13.6\text{m} = 10\%$—"still a sound percentage, kind of" in the sales manager's words. Also, the personnel manager sides with the sales manager: "BBC simply needs the deal to keep the factories going; laying off workers is something to be avoided at all reasonable costs," he argues. "And in this instance, there is a 10% profit rather than a cost."

The accounting department, however, raises the issue of exchange risk. BBC's accounting policy is to mark-to-market all foreign currency balance-sheet items every quarter, on the basis of the current exchange rate. "This is the only sound procedure," the accounting manager reminds his colleagues. "The current rate is close to the best possible forecast of the future rate, so there is no point in hiding one's head in the sand and continuing to use historic exchange rates to value A/R or A/P." Given this procedure, the fluctuations in the EUR value of the USD 10m A/R in the balance sheet would substantially influence the quarterly earnings. Next to this translation risk, there would also be a transaction risk: the actual realized value of the USD flows are rather uncertain.

The sales manager replies that a 10% profit margin is more than enough to absorb the transaction risk. "And hedging the exposure of the A/R is easy," he continues. "It suffices to borrow USD 10m, amortized in four slices of USD 2.5m each, to offset the exposure of the A/R. At any reporting date, the exchange rate effects on the loan balance (a liability) and on the remaining A/R (an asset) will cancel out, thus leaving BBC unexposed."

The finance manager, however, dislikes the USD-loan proposal. It is true that BBC needs a loan to finance the production outlays (EUR 13.6m). However, if BBC were to take up a USD loan, it would mean forgoing the attractive EUR financing provided by the Benelux Export Bank (BEB). (BEB is a fictitious Benelux joint-government agency that provides soft financing for, among others, long-term export contracts outside the EU. BEB loans are almost 2% cheaper than commercial bank loans, but BEB extends EUR loans only.) "It would be foolish to forgo this gorgeous interest subsidy," the finance manager concludes, "so we cannot borrow USD. This means that we have to use forward contracts to hedge the transaction risk." The sales manager disagrees. "This is too costly: the average forward rate that BBC can obtain is EUR/USD 1.117, which is 7% below the current spot rate. This would wipe out two thirds of the deal's profit," he snorts, "and swaps have the same effect. Finally, neither forward contracts nor swaps would eliminate the balance-sheet risk."

But the finance manager has other worries too. While BBC has an excellent credit rating, the prospective customer is definitely less creditworthy, and the country San Antonio itself is rumored to be close to asking for a debt rescheduling. In fact, given the maturities and risks, not a single European bank is willing to guarantee SATA's four payments for fees less than 5% upfront (calculated as a percentage of the cumulative receivable amount, USD 10m); that is, a bank guarantee would eliminate half of the profit. An alternative is credit insurance. In fact, BBC already has an overall credit insurance contract with BeneLloyds, and could obtain 90% insurance against commercial and political risk for an annual fee of 2% per annum, calculated on the beginning-of-period outstanding insured USD balance (the 100%, that is) and payable at the beginning of each year.

Issues

If the material is new to you, you probably already have questions about the nature of the instruments that were brought up: spot hedging via loans, forwards, options, and swaps. All these instruments are introduced in this part. (Other items, like credit insurance and letters of credit will come up in part III.) Here, then, is a list of calculations or issues you should be able to solve in a few minutes after working your way through this part. The necessary data are listed on the next page.

Q1. Discuss the sales manager's suggestion to hedge the exposure by a 10m USD loan amortized in four equal payments.

- What is wrong with the proposal?
- How can you solve this problem using a USD loan?

(*Hint.* Even after reading the entire part, this question may be somewhat tricky; so if you don't see the answer immediately, don't worry—just move to the next question, which may in fact give you ideas about how to solve the present one.)

Q2. Ignore the subsidized loan for a moment, as well as the default risk. Suppose BBC wants to fully hedge all projected USD cash inflows. Should it

- borrow USD at 6.5% and convert spot, or
- hedge forward each payment, and borrow EUR at 3.45%, or
- swap the USD annuity into an EUR annuity, and again borrow EUR against this EUR income (at 3.45%)?

Q3. There manifestly is default risk, in this case. How would this risk change your answer to the previous question?

Q4. Some people may claim that a risky export proposal like the present one is like submitting a bid in an international tender—there is a substantial probability that the money will not come in. Therefore, these people may say, BBC should hedge using options rather than unconditional contracts like forward contracts or loans or swaps. What is your opinion?

Q5. The acceptance or rejection of the order is obviously an NPV problem. In computing the true NPV (before subsidies), should BBC

- convert the USD flows into EUR forward (or swap them), and discount at 3.45%, or
- convert the USD flows into EUR forward (or swap them), and discount at the subsidized rate, 1.5%, or
- discount the USD flows at 6.5%, and convert spot, or
- discount the USD flows at 9%, and convert spot?

(*Hint.* Think of the real-world transactions that would correspond to the above suggestions, and consider whether all risks are taken care of if the transactions were actually made. Note also that you are asked to discuss the merits and shortcomings of the procedures rather than compute the numerical outcomes of the proposed procedures.)

Q6. We have a borrowing rate for USD payments promised by SATA, and it includes a premium for default. Is there a way to obtain a translation or conversion of this credit-risk premium into EUR? Can you use it in this example?

Q7. If you take out insurance, which would you prefer: the letter of credit (bank guarantee) or credit insurance?

Q8. In proper NPV calculations, the subsidies are taken into account only after computing the "true" NPV (which you did in Q5). What is the "adjusted" NPV including the subsidy and after proper incorporation of risk considerations? Should BBC accept the order?

Q9. What should we think about this hedging business? Is there a good reason why BBC should worry about it at all? Sure, adverse movements could wipe out the profits, but might not profits equally well double if the dollar appreciates?

In answering the questions, use the following data:

- For four-year constant-annuity loans (and loans that have almost constant annuities), BBC can borrow (xeno-)USD at 6.5%, EUR at 3.45% from its house bank, or EUR at 1.5% from BEB.
- SATA can borrow (xeno-)USD at 9.0% for maturities up to four years.
- Swap rates for four-year constant-annuity loans are 3% (in EUR) or 6% (USD).
- Four-year annuity factors, i.e., $a(\text{four years}, R) = \sum_{t=1}^{4}(1 + R)^{-t}$, are as follows:

R (%)	1.5	3	3.45	6	6.5	9
$a(4, R)$	3.854 384	3.717 098	3.677 443	3.465 106	3.425 799	3.239 720

- BBC can sell forward at the following long-term rates (in euros per dollar):

Maturity	(spot)	$T = t + 1$	$t + 2$	$t + 3$	$t + 4$
Rate	(1.200)	1.166	1.132	1.100	1.070

3

Spot Markets for Foreign Currency

In this chapter, we study the mechanics of the spot exchange market. Section 3.1 explains the various ways in which exchange rates can be quoted, and section 3.2 how the exchange markets themselves operate. Section 3.3 then considers exchange transactions in greater detail, focusing on bid and ask rates (that is, the rates at which a bank buys and sells). This also gives us an opportunity to learn about arbitrage. Specifically, in the third section, we shall already apply arbitrage arguments to the simplest possible problem, the relation between rates quoted by different banks for the same currency. Understanding this simple application now will make it easier to digest more complicated versions of similar arguments later. One such application already occurs in section 3.4, where we use arbitrage arguments to explain how exchange rates quoted by, for example, German banks (against EUR) relate to rates offered by New Zealand banks (against the NZD).

The chapter ends with the concepts of, and empirical evidence on, "purchasing power parity" (PPP) rates and real exchange rates. The conclusion of that part will be that exchange rates can make or break an exporting company, not just because of capital losses on foreign-currency-denominated receivables but possibly also because of a loss of competitiveness. Exchange risk even interferes with capital market equilibrium and the CAPM. These findings motivate the attention given to exchange rates in this book.

3.1 Exchange Rates

As we begin exploring exchange rates, we first provide a definition. We then describe the convention used to quote exchange rates throughout this book, as well as the conventions used in the exchange market. Finally, we explain how exchange rates are quoted in the presence of bid–ask spreads.

3.1.1 Definition of Exchange Rates

An exchange rate is the amount of a currency that one needs in order to buy one unit of another currency, or it is the amount of a currency that one receives when selling one unit of another currency. An example of an exchange rate quote is 0.8 USD per CAD (which we will usually denote as "USD/CAD 0.8"): you can, for instance, buy a CAD by paying USD 0.80.

In the above, we have combined currency names following the conventions in physics: EUR/USD means euros per dollar just as "km/h" means kilometers per hour. This is the most logical convention. For instance, if you exchange 3m dollars into euros at a rate of 0.8 euros per dollar, the result is 2.4m euros—a number of euros. This fits with our notation:

$$\text{USD } 3\text{m} \times \text{EUR/USD } 0.8 = \text{EUR } 2.4\text{m}. \tag{3.1}$$

This may seem self-evident. The reason why we bring this up is that the pros do it differently. In the convention typically adopted by traders, bankers, and journalists, EUR/USD is not the dimension of the quote but the name of the exchange rate: it is the *value* of the euro, *expressed* in dollars, not its dimension. That is, the pros write "EUR/USD = 1.2345," whereas we write "S_t = USD/EUR 1.2345." The dimension the trader asks for is USD/EUR, the inverse of what they write—but they do not mean a dimension, they mean a name.[1] In all our examples *we* use dimensions. The "name" notation pops up occasionally in press clippings or in pictures of trading screens, etc., and should not be a problem. To harden yourself, stare at the following entries for a full minute:

Currency name	Value
EUR/USD	USD/EUR 0.75
EUR/GBP	GBP/EUR 0.60
USD/CHF	CHF/USD 1.05

The telltale difference is that the dimension is immediately followed (or, occasionally, preceded) by the number. If there is no number, or if there is an "=" or "is" or "equals," etc., between the ratio and the number, it must be the name of a rate. Sometimes practitioners drop the slash in the name and write EURUSD or EUR:USD instead of EUR/USD, which makes more sense.

It is even more crucial that you understand how exchange rates are quoted. While the notation is occasionally confusing—are we using dimensions or names?—there could be even more confusion as to which currency should be used as the numéraire. While you are familiar with the idea of buying goods and services, you may be less used to buying money with money. With exchange transactions, you need to agree which money is being bought or sold. There would be no ambiguity if one of the currencies were your home currency. A purchase then means that you obtained foreign currency and paid in home currency, the way you would do it with your other purchases too; and a sale

---

[1] It is sometimes whispered that the trader notation comes from a kind of pseudo-math like "EUR 1 = USD 1.2345," where one then "divides both sides by USD." The mind boggles. This is like denoting a speed as "1 h = 100 km" instead of $v = 100$ km/h.

means that you delivered foreign currency and received home currency. If neither currency is your home currency, then you need to establish which of the two acts as the home currency.

Example 3.1. In a Paris bank, a tourist hands over USD 1,000 to the bank clerk and receives CAD 1,250 in return. This event would be described differently depending on whether the person is a U.S. tourist, a Canadian, or a Frenchman:

- The U.S. tourist would view this as a purchase of CAD 1,250 at a total cost of USD 1,000, implying a unit price of [USD 1,000]/[CAD 1.250] = USD/CAD 0.8.
- The Canadian would think of this transaction as a sale of USD 1,000 for CAD 1,250, implying a unit price of [CAD 1,250]/[USD 1,000] = CAD/USD 1.25.
- The Frenchman would regard this as an exchange of two foreign currencies, and would be at a loss if he were asked which of these is being sold and which bought.

Among pros, the currency in which the price is expressed is called the *quoting currency*, and the currency whose price is being quoted is called the *base currency* or *reference currency*. We avoid the terms, except in the next two lines. We have just noted that pros denote a rate as base/quoting (or, better, base:quoting) while its dimensions are quoting/base. A different issue is whether the quoting currency is the home or the foreign one.

3.1.2 Our Convention: Home Currency per Unit of Foreign Currency

Once we agree which country is, or acts as, the home country, we can agree to quote exchange rates as the price in units of home currency (HC) per unit of foreign currency (FC). That is, we quote the rate as HC/FC throughout this text, meaning that one unit of FC is worth N HC units (dimension HC/FC). As we shall see, some people do it differently and state that, with one unit of home currency, they can buy $M = 1/N$ units of foreign currency (FC/HC). We adopt the HC/FC convention because it is the most natural one. It is the convention we use when buying goods. For example, we say "the price is five dollars per umbrella" (HC/umbrella), not "with one dollar you can buy one-fifth of an umbrella" (umbrellas per unit of home currency).

Example 3.2.

1. A quote like USD/EUR 1.25 is an American's natural quote for the EUR; it is the USD price an American gets or pays per EUR. For Germans or other Eurolanders, a quote as EUR/USD (euros per dollar) is the more natural one.
2. A quote like USD/CAD 0.75 is an American's natural quote for the CAD, since the CAD is the currency in the denominator: a price in USD per CAD.

Expressing prices in HC is the convention for not just umbrellas but also for financial assets. Thus, standard finance results hold: the current market value is the expected future value (including interest earned), discounted at a rate that takes into account the risk. Under the alternative quotation, confusingly, the current value would be determined by the inverse of the expected inverse of future value, multiplied by unity plus the required return. (If you just felt you had to read this sentence twice, you may want to consider reading technical note 3.1 at the end of the chapter instead.)

The direct (HC/FC) quoting convention used to be standard in continental Europe, and is called the "direct" quote, or the "right" quote. In the United States, a price with dimension USD/FC is called "American terms." The alternative is called the "indirect" or "left" quote or, in the United States, "European terms." Let's see who uses which and why.

3.1.3 The Indirect Quoting Convention

One group of people using mostly indirect quotes are professional traders in the United States. Between 1944 and the mid 1980s, each and every exchange deal went through the USD; even when a German needed to buy CHF, the DEM would first be converted into USD and these dollars were then exchanged for CHF. Naturally, when New York traders talk to, say, their German counterparts, both must talk the same language, quotewise; otherwise too much time would be wasted inverting each other's rates all the time. Both Germans and Americans actually preferred to quote in terms of DEM/USD rather than USD/DEM, for the simple reason that the official parities, set by the German government, were expressed in DEM/USD.[2] More generally, U.S. professionals use the exchange-rate convention as quoted in the other country. Thus, for countries that quote directly themselves, like Japan, New York traders would talk JPY/USD. But in the case of countries that quote indirectly themselves, like the United Kingdom, the pros would also use USD/GBP. Thus, U.S. pros use indirect quotes for countries that themselves quote directly, and direct quotes for countries that themselves quote indirectly.

As already hinted at, in the United Kingdom one uses the reverse quote, the number of foreign units that can be bought with one pound, or FC/HC. Some former British or Commonwealth countries (e.g., Australia and New Zealand) and, until 1979, Ireland do likewise.[3] One reason is that, before World War I, the pound was the world's reserve currency and played the role taken over by the dollar after World War II. In addition, until 1967 the GBP was still severely nondecimal—one pound consisted of twenty shilling, each worth twelve pence[4]—while currencies not based on the pound had gone decimal long before. It is much easier to multiply or divide by a decimal number, say

---

[2] Recall from the previous chapter that, until 1972, countries declared an official parity in relation to the USD, say DEM/USD 4. Intervention kept the actual rates between an upper and lower bound expressed, likewise, in DEM/USD.

[3] Canada and South Africa went off the pound ages ago, which is why they quote differently.

[4] Recall there also was a dollar (10s.), a crown (5s.), and a guinea, worth 21s. in the end; and in Elizabethan times many wages were expressed in marks (13s.4d., i.e., 160d.). But by modern times most prices were in pounds, shillings, and pence.

Table 3.1. Key exchange rates: pros' notation, dimensions, and nicknames.

Symbol	Currency pair	Dimension	Trading terminology
USDJPY	U.S. dollar, in Japanese yen	JPY/USD	Dollar yen
USDCHF	U.S. dollar, in Swiss francs	CHF/USD	Dollar Swiss or Swissy
USDCAD	U.S. dollar, in Canadian dollars	CAD/USD	Dollar Canada
USDZAR	U.S. dollar, in South African rand	ZAR/USD	Dollar ZAR or South African rand
GBPUSD	British pound, in U.S. dollars	USD/GBP	Cable
GBPCHF*	British pound, in Swiss francs	CHF/GBP	Sterling Swiss
GBPJPY*	British pound, in Japanese yen	JPY/GBP	Sterling yen
AUDUSD	Australian dollar, in U.S. dollars	USD/AUD	Australian dollar
NZDUSD	New Zealand dollar, in U.S. dollars	USD/NZD	New Zealand dollar or Kiwi
EURUSD	Euro, in U.S. dollars	USD/EUR	Euro
EURGBP*	Euro, in British pounds	GBP/EUR	Euro sterling
EURJPY*	Euro, in Japanese yen	JPY/EUR	Euro yen
EURCHF*	Euro, in Swiss francs	CHF/EUR	Euro Swiss
CHFJPY*	Swiss franc, in Japanese yen	JPY/CHF	Swiss yen
GLDUSD	Gold, in U.S. dollars per troy ounce	USD/ozXAU	Gold
SLVUSD	Silver, in U.S. dollars per troy ounce	USD/ozXAG	Silver

*Cross rate, from the U.S. perspective. Most names should be obvious, except perhaps CHF (*Confederatio Helvetica*, Latin for Switzerland—the way a four-language country solves a political conundrum). The ZAR, the South African rand, is not to be confused with SAR, the Saudi riyal. GLD and SLV are unorthodox: the official codes as used by, for example, Swift are XAU and XAG, with X signalling a nonstandard currency (also like the CFA franc and the ecu of old), and the Latin *aurum* and *argentum*. "Cable" for USDGBP refers to the fact that it is about bank-account money, with payment instructions wired by telegram cable rather than sent by surface mail. There was a time when telegraphy was cutting-edge technology.

FC/GBP 0.792 08, than with a number like £1/s5/d3 (one pound, five shillings, three pence). So everyone preferred to talk FC units per pound.

A third (and more recent) class of people using the indirect quote are the Eurolanders, who always quote rates as USD/EUR or JPY/EUR even though they traditionally quoted directly (as DEM/USD). Cynics conjecture that the Europeans may have coveted the reserve-currency status associated with an indirect quote. Another possible reason is that, initially, the euro was foreign to all existing currencies. For example, to Germans the euro was introduced as worth 2 DEM, so they would quite naturally introduce it to Americans and Japanese as being worth 1.20 USD or 110 JPY. When, eventually, the euro had become the home currency, the habit simply stuck.

Example 3.3. Have a look at table 3.1, showing the most important rates in the way they are always quoted by pros. The primary rates are in non-U.S. currencies except for the GBP, NZD, and AUD, or for the EUR; you know why. Cross rates for the EUR are in non-EUR currencies, and likewise for the GBP.

Table 3.2. Sample spot exchange rate quotes. (From the *Wall Street Journal Europe*, which sensibly shows both the natural and indirect quotes.)

AMERICAS	Per euro	In euros	Per U.S. dollar	In U.S. dollars	EUROPE	Per euro	In euros	Per U.S. dollar	In U.S. dollars
Argentino peso-a	3.9628	0.2523	3.0838	0.3243	Euro zone euro	1	1	0.7782	1.2851
Brazil real	2.9588	0.3380	2.3025	0.4343	Czech Rep koruna-b	28.260	0.0354	21.992	0.0455
Canada dollar	1.438	0.7073	1.1002	0.9089	Denmark krone	7.4576	0.1341	5.8034	0.1723
Chile peso	683.07	0.001464	531.55	0.001881	Hungary forint	262.82	0.003805	204.52	0.004890
Columbia peso	3186.28	0.0003138	2479.50	0.0004033	Malta lira	0.4294	2.3288	0.3342	2.9926
Ecuador US dollar-f	1.2850	0.7782	1	1	Norway krone	7.800	0.1282	6.0698	0.1648
Mexico peso-a	14.5307	0.0688	11.3075	0.0884	Poland zloty	3.9369	0.2540	3.0637	0.3264
Peru sol	4.2368	0.2360	3.2970	0.3033	Russia ruble-d	34.669	0.02884	26.979	0.03707
Uruguay peso-e	30.841	0.0324	24.000	0.0417	Slovak Rep koruna	37.7856	0.02647	29.4040	0.03401
U.S. Dollar	1.2850	0.7782	1	1	Sweden krona	9.2662	0.1079	7.2108	0.1387
Venezuala bolivar	2759.39	0.000362	2147.30	0.000466	Switzerland franc	1.5604	0.6109	1.2103	0.8262
...	...	...	...	...	...	...	...	...	...

a—floating rate b—commercial rate c—government rate d—Russian Central Bank rate f—Special Drawing Rights from the International Monetary Fund; based on exchange rates for U.S., British and Japanese currencies.
Note: Based on trading among banks in amounts of $1million and more, as quoted by Reuters

Example 3.4. Look at the *Wall Street Journal Europe* excerpt in table 3.2, conveniently showing both quotes; the value in USD or EUR of one unit of the third ("foreign") currency, and the value of 1 USD or EUR in units of that third ("foreign") currency. The natural quote for Americans or Europeans would be the first one, but U.S. traders and Eurolanders may use the other quote. Take a minute to look at table 3.2 and see if you understand the exchange rates as quoted.

Q1. What is the dollar equivalent of one euro, according to the quotes in the *Wall Street Journal*?

A1. If your answer is USD 1.285, you are correct.

Q2. Determine the amount of Peruvian soles per EUR.

A2. If you answered 4.2368 soles per EUR, you are right.

3.1.4 Bid and Ask Rates

When you deal with foreign currency, you will discover that you pay a higher price at the time of purchase than when you sell one currency for another. For example, for dollar–rouble deals the currency booth in your hotel will quote two numbers, say RUB/USD 35–36. This means that if you sell USD for RUB, you receive RUB 35, while if you wish to buy USD you will have to pay RUB 36. The rate at which the bank will buy a currency from you is called the *bid* rate: they bid (i.e., they announce that they are willing to pay) 35 per dollar; and the rate at which the bank will sell a currency to you is the *ask* rate (they ask 36 per dollar). It is, initially, safer not to think about the meaning of bidding and asking because the words refer to the bank's view, not yours. Just remember that *you* buy at the bank's ask rate, and *you* sell at the bank's bid rate. The bid is the lower quote, and ask is the higher one. The ask comes higher in the alphabet—use any trick that works, until you get used to it.

Indeed, if exchange rates are being quoted with the currency of interest—the currency you are buying or selling—in the denominator, then the ask rate will be higher than the bid rate. Obviously, it could not be the other way around: with a bid rate above the ask rate you would be able to make huge risk-free profits by buying at the ask and immediately reselling at the assumedly higher bid. No bank will allow you to buy low and then immediately resell at a profit without taking any risk, because your sure gains would obviously mean sure losses for the bank. In theory, there could still be room for a situation "bid rate = ask rate" (which offers no such arbitrage opportunities). Yet the real-world situation is invariably "bid rate < ask rate": banks want to make some money from foreign-currency transactions.

Another way to think of this difference between the ask and the bid rates is that the difference contains the bank's commission for exchanging currencies. The difference between the buying and selling rates is called the *spread*, and you can think of the bank's implicit commission as being equal to half the spread. The following example explains why the commission is half of the spread rather than the spread itself.

Example 3.5. Suppose that you can buy CAD at RUB/CAD 38.6 and sell at RUB/CAD 38.0. With these rates, you can think of a purchase as occurring at the midpoint rate (RUB/CAD 38.3), grossed up with a commission of 0.30. Likewise, a sale can be thought of as a sale at the midpoint, 38.3, from which the bank withholds a commission of 0.30. Thus, the equivalent commission per one-way transaction is the difference between the bid (or ask) and the midpoint rate, that is, half the spread. (The spread itself would be the cost of a round-trip deal—buy and then sell.)

To get an idea of whether your house bank charges a low commission, you can ask for a two-way quote to see if the spread is small. If this is the case, you probably do not have to check with other banks. However, for large transactions, you should also compare the spot quotes given by different banks. (This will be examined further in section 3.3, especially section 3.3.3.) We discuss the determinants of spreads later, after we have described the market microstructure.

3.1.5 Primary Rates versus Cross Rates

As of 1945 and until well into the 1980s, all exchange rates in the wholesale segment were against the USD. They were and are called *primary rates*, while any rate not involving the USD would be called a *cross rate* and would traditionally be regarded as just implied by the primary rates. You will find an example for midpoint rates in table 3.3. The primary rates are in the first column (FC/USD) or the bottom line (USD/FC).[5] The rest of the table is obtained

---

[5] Many newspapers give currency j the jth row and the jth column instead of the $(N - j)$th row and the jth column, but the layout is not crucial. The orientation of the empty diagonal (or the unit diagonal, as other tables might show it) is the sign to watch.

Table 3.3. Cross rates as in the *Wall Street Journal Europe.*

Cross rates U.S. dollar and euro foreign-exchange rates in global trading

	USD	GBP	CHF	SEK	RUB	NOK	JPY	ILS	*EUR*	DKK	CDN	AUD
Australia	1.3253	2.4818	1.0915	0.1838	0.0491	0.2183	0.0118	0.2934	*1.7031*	0.2284	1.2046	—
Canada	1.1002	2.0603	0.9061	0.1526	0.0408	0.1813	0.0098	0.2436	*1.4038*	0.1896	—	0.8302
Denmark	5.8034	10.867	4.7794	0.8048	0.2151	0.9561	0.0518	1.2847	*7.4576*	—	5.2748	4.3789
Euro	*0.7782*	*1.4573*	*0.6409*	*0.1079*	*0.0288*	*0.1282*	*0.0069*	*0.1723*	—	*0.1341*	*0.7073*	*0.5872*
Israel	4.5173	8.4592	3.7202	0.6265	0.1674	0.7442	0.0403	—	*5.8049*	0.7784	4.1058	3.4085
Japan	112.11	209.93	92.325	15.547	4.1553	18.469	—	24.817	*144.06*	19.317	101.90	84.589
Norway	6.0698	11.367	4.9988	0.8418	0.2250	—	0.0541	1.3437	*7.8000*	1.0459	5.5170	4.5800
Russia	26.978	50.521	22.218	3.7414	—	4.4448	0.2407	5.9724	*34.669*	4.6488	24.521	20.357
Sweden	7.2108	13.503	5.385	—	0.2673	1.1880	0.0643	1.5963	*9.2662*	1.2425	6.5541	5.4409
Switzerland	1.2145	2.2739	—	0.1684	0.0405	0.2000	0.108	0.2688	*1.5604*	0.2092	1.1037	0.9162
U.K.	0.5340	—	0.4398	0.0741	0.0198	0.0880	0.0048	0.1182	*0.6862*	0.0920	0.4854	0.4029
U.S.	—	1.8726	82.236	0.1387	0.0371	0.1648	0.0089	0.2214	*1.2850*	0.1723	0.9089	0.7546

The numbers in the "EUR" column, for instance, show the values of the euro in other currencies (that is, the EUR acts as FC), while those in the "EUR" row show the values of the other currencies in euros (that is, the EUR acts as HC).

by division or multiplication: GBP/EUR = GBP/USD × USD/EUR, for example. Each of the resulting new rows or columns is a set of quotes in HC/FC (row) or FC/HC (column). With 12 currencies you have 144 entries, of which 12 are on the information-free diagonal, and half of the remaining 132 are just the inverses of the others.

We have a whole section on the relation between primary and cross rates in the presence of spreads, so at this stage we just consider why, among pros, there were until the 1980s just primary rates. There were several reasons:

- Official parities were against the USD; there was no official parity (in the sense of being defended by any central bank) for rates against other currencies.

- The USD market had the lowest spreads, so all real-world transactions would effectively be done via the dollar anyway. That is, pounds were converted into marks by buying dollars first and then exchanging these for marks, for example, because that was the cheapest way to do so (see below). The cross-rate would just be the rate implied by the two primary rates used in the transaction.

- In pre-electronic days it would be quite laborious to keep track of, say, a 30×30 matrix of cross rates with 435 distinct meaningful entries, making sure all cross rates are consistent with the primary ones all the time. So rather than quoting cross rates all the time, banks just showed primary quotes and then computed cross rates if and when needed.

By the 1980s desktop computers were ubiquitous and, for many pairs of "big" currencies the volume of cross transactions had become large enough to make direct cross exchanges competitive compared with exchanges via the USD. Official exchange rates were gone in many cases, or in the ERM case had become multilateral. So we now see explicit quotes for some of the cross rates. Look at figure 3.4 to see what rates have active multilateral electronic markets—a good indication of there being a reasonable volume. Note also that for some new EU members the market against the EUR works well while the market against the USD lacks liquidity; that is, for these countries the rate against the euro is economically the key one, even though Americans would regard it as just a cross rate.

3.1.6 Inverting Exchange Rates in the Presence of Spreads

The next issue is how a pair of quotes for one currency can be translated into a pair of quotes for a different currency. The rule is that the inverse of a bid quote is an ask quote, and vice versa. To conceptualize this, consider the following illustration.

Example 3.6. An Indian investor wants to convert her CAD into USD and contacts her house bank, Standard Chartered. Being neither American nor Canadian, the bank has no natural preference for either currency and might quote the exchange rate as either USD/CAD or CAD/USD. The Indian bank would make sure that its potential quotes are perfectly compatible. If it quotes from a Canadian viewpoint, the bank gives a CAD/USD quote (which says how many CAD the investor must pay for 1 USD, for instance, CAD/USD 1.5). If it uses the U.S. perspective, the bank gives a USD/CAD quote, which says how many USD the U.S. investor gets for 1 CAD, 0.666 67.

The bank's alternative ways of quoting will be fully compatible if

$$S_{\mathrm{bid},t}^{\mathrm{CAD/USD}} = \frac{1}{S_{\mathrm{ask},t}^{\mathrm{USD/CAD}}}, \tag{3.2}$$

$$S_{\mathrm{ask},t}^{\mathrm{CAD/USD}} = \frac{1}{S_{\mathrm{bid},t}^{\mathrm{USD/CAD}}}. \tag{3.3}$$

To fully understand this, recall that what looks like buying (at the ask) to a U.S. resident looks like selling to a Canadian, at the Canadian's bid. Alternatively, recall that the ask is the higher of the two quotes. But if you invert two numbers, the inverse of the larger number will, of course, be smaller than the inverse of the smaller number. Because the inverse of a larger number is a smaller number, the inverse ask must become the bid, and vice versa.

Example 3.7. Suppose that you read the following quote on the Reuters screen: USD/CAD 1.000–1.005.

Q1. What is the bank's buying and selling rate for CAD?

A1. The bank's buying rate for CAD is USD 1.000 and its selling rate is USD 1.005; that is, *you* sell CAD at USD 1.000 and buy at 1.005.

Q2. What, therefore, are the bank's buying and selling rates for USD (in CAD)?

A2. The bank's buying rate or bid for USD is 1/1.005 = CAD/USD 0.995 025 (probably rounded to 0.9950) and the selling rate or ask is 1/1.000 = 1.000; that is, wearing your Canadian hat, *you* sell USD at CAD 0.9950 and buy at 1.000.

One corollary is that in countries like the United Kingdom, where the reverse or indirect quote is used, the rate relevant when you buy is the lower of the two, while the higher quote is the relevant rate when you sell. Thus, it is important to be aware of what the foreign currency is, and what convention is being used for quoting the exchange rate. Again, it is always easier and more convenient to have the foreign currency in the denominator. That way the usual logic will work: banks buy low and sell high.

3.2 Major Markets for Foreign Exchange

In this section, we describe the size and structure of the exchange market and the types of transactions one can make in this market.

3.2.1 How Exchange Markets Work

The foreign exchange market is not an organized market. Stock markets or futures markets are: they have fixed opening hours, a more or less centralized mechanism to match supply and demand, standardized contracts, an official publication channel for data on volumes and prices, and a specific location or one designated group of computers running everything. In contrast, the exchange market consists of a wholesale tier, which is an informal network of about 500 banks and currency brokerages that deal with each other and with large corporations, and a retail tier, where you and I buy and sell foreign exchange. At any point in time, wholesale exchange markets on at least one continent are active, so that the worldwide exchange market is open twenty-four hours a day (see figure 3.1). Until the mid 1990s, most interbank dealing was done over the telephone; most conversations were tape-recorded, and later confirmed by mail, telex, or fax. Reuters, which was already omnipresent with its information screens, and EBS[6] have now built computer networks which allow direct trading and which now largely replace the phone market. The way the computer systems are used depends on the role the bank wants to play. We make a distinction between deals via (i) market makers, (ii) auction platforms, or (iii) brokers.

---

[6] Electronic Broking Services (EBS) was created by a partnership of the world's largest foreign exchange market-making banks. Over approximately USD 150 billion in spot foreign exchange transaction and hundreds of tonnes of gold and silver are traded every day over the EBS Spot Dealing System. It was created in 1990 to challenge Reuters's threatened monopoly in interbank spot foreign exchange and provide effective competition. ICAP Plc, the world's largest broker of transactions between banks, agreed in 2006 to buy EBS.

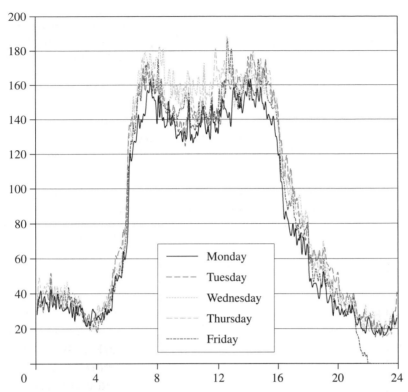

Figure 3.1. Trader activity over the day. Graph courtesy of Luc Bauwens, Université Catholique de Louvain. The graph shows, per 5 min interval over 24 hours, the evolution of the average number of indicative quotes entered into the Reuters FX/FX pages. Time is GMT in summer, GMT+1 in winter; that is, European time is $t + 2$ h, London +1, New York -4 h; Sydney and Tokyo time are at $t + 10$ and $t + 9$ h, respectively. Below I describe working days as 8:00–17:00, but many a trader starts earlier and/or works later. At 0:00, when the morning shift in Sydney has been up and running for about two hours and Tokyo for one hour, Hong Kong starts up, to be followed by Singapore in one hour and Bahrain in three hours. Between 6:00 and 8:00 the Far East bows out but Western Europe takes over: first the continent (6:00 GMT), then London (7:00); activity soars. A minor dip follows around the European noon but activity recovers again in the afternoon, peaking when New York takes over (12:00) and Europeans close their positions (15:00 on the continent, 16:00 in London). New York does less and less as time passes. By 22:00 Sydney is starting up, and Tokyo is preparing breakfast.

3.2.1.1 Market Making

Many players in the wholesale market act as market makers. If a market-making credit agreement between two banks has been signed, either party undertakes to provide a *two-way* quote (bid and ask) when solicited by the other party, without even knowing whether that other party intends to buy, or rather sell. Such a quote is *binding*: market makers undertake to effectively buy or sell at the price that was indicated.

A *Reuters* conversation   An EBS broking screen

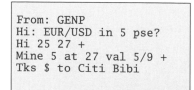

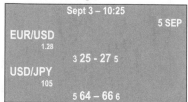

Figure 3.2. A Reuters conversation and an EBS broking window. In the Reuters conversation window, GENP is an abbreviated name (Jenpi, Jean-Pierre); he asks for a quote for EUR in USD for quantity 5m (dollars); pse is GENP's code for "please." The counterparty answers by keying in the small numbers, and Jenpi replies he buys 5 (million) at the ask, 27, for value date September 5. The counterpart closes with "Thanks, I'll send the dollars to your correspondent, Citibank. Bye bye." The second picture shows part of an EBS broking screen. On top, the current date and time. Next line: the spot delivery date, September 5. For two currencies you then see in small font the "big" figure (the part of the quote that is usually omitted) and in big font the "small" quotes: bid and ask, each preceded/followed by the quantity available, in millions. Thus, somebody bids 1.2825 for 3 million dollars, another party offers 5 million dollars at 1.2827.

Example 3.8. Deutsche may ask Hong Kong and Shanghai for a quote of EUR against USD. HSBC must then provide a bid and an ask without knowing the direction of Deutsche's possible trade; and if Deutsche replies with "I buy 10 million" then HSBC must sell that quantity at the price they quoted.

Of course there are limits to the market makers' commitments to their quotes. First, potential customers should decide almost immediately whether to buy ("mine"), or to sell ("yours"), or not to deal; they cannot invoke a quote made, say, three minutes ago. Second, if the intended transaction exceeds a mutually agreed level, laid down in the prior credit agreement—say USD 25m—market makers can refuse. For larger transactions, the trader asking for a quote should reveal immediately what the size of the transaction will be. Third, the credit agreement also provides a limit to the total amount of open contracts that can be outstanding between the two banks at any moment;[7] if the limit is reached, no more deals are allowed.

Transactions via binding two-way quotes are typically concluded on computers, by means of chatting windows (more grandly called "conversations"). Bank A's trader X clicks his conversation window with trader Y at bank B—there may be up to 64 such windows open at any given point of time—and might type in, for instance, PLS EUR/USD, meaning "please provide a quote for the EUR, in USD." Player A can also mention the quantity, in millions. The millions are omitted—that is, 5 means five million—and the quantity bears on the currency in the denominator, traditionally the USD or the GBP. B's trader may answer, for instance, 13–16, meaning that (the last two digits of) her bid and ask are 13 and 16. (Traders never waste time by mentioning the leading

---

[7] Exchange transactions are settled with a delay of at least two days, so each contract remains outstanding for at least two days; many live much longer. See section 3.2.3.

numbers: everybody knows what these are. Only the "small" numbers are mentioned.) The first party can let the offer lapse; if not, he answers MINE or YOURS, mentions the quantity if not already indicated, and hits the SEND key. The deal is done, and both traders now pass on the information to their "back office," which enters the data into the information systems. The back offices will also check with each other to see whether the inputs match; with the logs of the conversations, disputes are of course far less likely than before, when everything went by phone and when traders handed down hand-scribbled "tickets" to the accountants who then checked with each other via telexes. Voice deals still exist, but they are getting rarer.

3.2.1.2 Implications of Market Making for the Size of the Bid–Ask Spread and the Maximum Order Size

Normally, the lower the volume in a particular market, the higher the spread. Also, during holidays, weekends, or lunch breaks, spreads widen. Spreads are also higher during periods of uncertainty, including at the open and close of the market each day. Maximum order quantities for normal quotes follow a similar pattern: a market maker is prepared to handle large lots if the market is liquid (thick) or the volatility low.

All these phenomena are explained by the risk of market making. Notably, if a customer has "hit" a market maker, the latter normally wants to get rid of that new position quickly. But in a thin or volatile market, the price may already have moved against the market maker before he or she was able to close out; thus, the market maker wants a bigger commission as compensation for the risk, and puts a lower cap on the size of the deals that can be executed at this spread. For the same reason, quotes for an unusually large position are wide too: getting rid of a very large amount takes more time, during which anything could happen. At the retail end of the market, in contrast, the spread increases for smaller transactions. This is because 100 small transactions, each for USD 100,000, cost more time and effort than one big transaction of USD 10m.

For high-volume currencies like the USD/EUR, the difference between one market-maker's own bid and ask is often as low as three basis points (in a quote of four or five digits, like 1.2345 or 0.9876), and the difference between the best bid (across all market makers) and the best ask (also across all market makers) may be just two or one or, occasionally, zero basis points. See section 3.3.2 for more information on quoting behavior.

Table 3.3 shows the minimum and maximum amounts quoted by an internet dealer;[8] they are smaller than interbank (and spreads are bigger than interbank), but you can still notice how the maximum amounts and the spreads relate to each other, presumably both reflecting liquidity and volatility.

---

[8] "Size of 1.0 lot" (about 1m USD) shows the minimum, which is clearly targeting players out of the interbank league (where the lot size is 1m) but still above the micro-investor's league. "Instant execution" is the maximum amount you can buy or sell at the trader's regular quotes.

Ticker	Size of 1.0 lot	Instant execution	Spread	Limit and stop levels	March 9, 2007 rate (in pips)	Spread (‰)
EURUSD	EUR 100,000	up to 10M	2 pips	2 pips	13,115	1.5
GBPUSD	GBP 100,000	up to 10M	3 pips	3 pips	19,319	1.6
EURCHF	EUR 100,000	up to 5M	3 pips	3 pips	16,163	1.9
EURJPY	EUR 100,000	up to 10M	3 pips	3 pips	15,489	1.9
USDJPY	USD 100,000	up to 10M	3 pips	3 pips	11,810	2.5
GBPCHF	GBP 100,000	up to 5M	7 pips	7 pips	23,810	2.9
EURGBP	EUR 100,000	up to 5M	2 pips	2 pips	6,788	2.9
GBPJPY	GBP 100,000	up to 5M	7 pips	7 pips	22,817	3.1
USDCHF	USD 100,000	up to 10M	4 pips	4 pips	12,325	3.2
USDCAD	USD 100,000	up to 5M	4 pips	4 pips	11,735	3.4
AUDUSD	AUD 100,000	up to 5M	3 pips	3 pips	7,802	3.8
CHFJPY	CHF 100,000	up to 5M	4 pips	4 pips	9,583	4.2
EURCAD	EUR 100,000	up to 3M	8 pips	8 pips	15,389	5.2
NZDUSD	NZD 100,000	up to 2M	5 pips	5 pips	9,583	5.2
USDSGD	USD 100,000	up to 1M	8 pips	8 pips	15,267	5.2
EURAUD	EUR 100,000	up to 5M	10 pips	10 pips	16,810	5.9

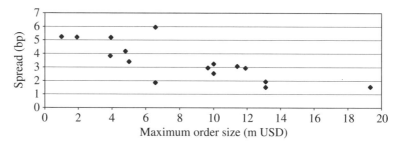

Figure 3.3. Order limits and spreads for various rates, semi-professional. The table shows conditions for various currencies from a particular internet broker. The minimum and maximum quantities are not interbank, but still aim at semi-professionals or perhaps day traders rather than pop and mom investors, the hardcore retail. The spread and the tick size for limit and stop levels are likewise wider than interbank. Do note how the spread varies depending on liquidity and the level of the rate, and on how the maximum order size (imperfectly) relates to the spread (graph). *Source:* www.alpari.co.uk/en/cspec/ for columns 1–5; the *Wall Street Journal Europe*, March 12, 2007, for column 6; spread in basis points has been added. Data have been rearranged by increasing relative spread. For the graph the order sizes have been converted from reference currency (the FC in the quote) to USD.

3.2.1.3 *Auctioning Off through a Broking System*

All the above was about market making. Beside these purely bilateral deals—the successors to bilateral phone conversations—there nowadays are increasingly many semi-multilateral deals. If a trader actively wants to buy, or sell, she may enter a limit order into EBS's or Reuters's limit-order book rather than calling a number of market makers or waiting until someone else calls her. This is comparable to you offering, say, a used car for sale on eBay rather than calling various car dealers or posting a sign on your door and then waiting until someone rings your bell. For instance, bank A may have EUR 30m for

BIS is commonly described as the bank of the central banks. It was first set up after World War I to act as a payment agent distributing the German and Austrian war reparation payments. After World War II it ran the European Payment Union (EPU), serving as a netting institute for payments among EPU members. By netting the international payments, the volume of actual payments was reduced, which alleviated the problems of dollar shortages in the first years after the war. Currently, the BIS is still the bank of the central bankers: all central banks have accounts there, in various currencies, and can route their payments to each other via the BIS. But nowadays the BIS mainly serves as a talking club for central bankers and regulators. One of its missions is to gather data on exchange markets, euro and OTC markets, new financial instruments, bank lending to sovereign borrowers, and so on. Another mission is to provide a forum where regulators coordinate the capital adequacy rules that they impose on financial institutions. The Basel I rules covered credit risk—in a crude way, perhaps, but it was a useful first step; the recent Basel II rules refine Basel I and add market-price risks; see the chapter on Value-at-Risk.

Panel 3.1. The Bank of International Settlements (BIS).

3.2.2 Markets by Location and by Currency

Every three years, in April, the Bank of International Settlements (panel 3.1) makes a survey of the over-the-counter (OTC) markets, including forex. At the latest count, April 2007, the daily volume of trading on the exchange market and its satellites—futures, options, and swaps—was estimated at more than USD 3.2 trillion. This is over 45 times the daily volume of international trade in goods and services, 80 times the United States's daily GDP, 230 times Japan's GDP, and 400 times Germany's GDP, and 7,500 times the world's official development-aid budget.[10] The major markets were, in order of importance, London, New York, Tokyo, and Frankfurt (the European Central Bank's home base). London leads clearly, easily beating even New York, Tokyo, and Singapore taken together, and still increasing its market share. Frankfurt is a fast riser but from a low base.

The most important markets, per currency, are the USD/EUR and the USD/JPY markets; together they represent almost half of the world's trading volume. Add in the GBP, and the transactions involving just the top four moneys represent two thirds of all business. The USD still leads: in 88% of transactions it takes one of the sides (down from 90% in 2004), while the EUR is one of the two currencies in less than 40% (up from 35%) of that volume—and the bulk of that is USD/EUR trade.

3.2.3 Markets by Delivery Date

The exchange market consists of two core segments: the spot exchange market and the forward exchange market.

The *spot* market is the exchange market for quasi-immediate payment (in home currency) and delivery (of foreign currency). For most of this text we shall denote this spot rate by S_t, with t referring to current time. In practice,

---

[10] All data are from the CIA Factbook. Trade and aid, 2004; GDP, early 2007 estimates for 2006.

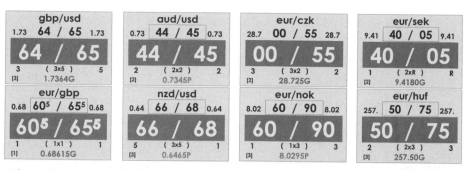

Figure 3.4. A panel of Reuters broking windows. The entries should by now be obvious, except the bottom line, which shows the last trade (quantity and price).

sale and want at least USD/EUR 1.3007 for them—an ask price. The bank posts this info, for instance, on Reuters's "3000" system. Reuters's window, at any moment, then shows the best bid across all "buy" limit orders, and the best ask among all "sell" limit orders outstanding at that moment. For instance, on Reuters's 3000 screen a line EUR/USD 10–11 3xR means that the highest bid posted at that very moment is 10, the lowest ask 11, and that the quantities for these limit orders are, respectively, 3 and "a number exceeding 50" (= R).[9] You see the EBS counterpart of Reuters 3000 in figure 3.2. Any party interested in one of these offers can then click on the quote they like (either the bid or ask) and specify the quantity taken. Or another bank may enter a limit order that is automatically matched, wholly or partly, with an already outstanding limit order. Reuters's computer then informs the IT systems of both banks of the transactions that were concluded so that no more human intervention with "tickets" and telexes and faxes is needed (*straight through processing* (STP)).

The decision by an FX trader whether to use EBS or Reuters Dealing 3000 (also known as D2) is driven largely by currency pair. In practice, EBS is used mainly for EUR/USD, USD/JPY, EUR/JPY, USD/CHF, and EUR/CHF, and Reuters D2 is used for all other interbank currency pairs. Have a look at table 3.4 to see who leads where. In these multilateral electronic dealing systems, the spread for EUR/USD is typically one pip, that is, one hundredth of a USD cent. (Online currency brokers targeting private investors typically offer a two-pip spread; just feed "foreign exchange" into your Web search engine to find these brokers.) For other exchange rates spreads are often wider.

Note that the advent of these multilateral systems has made the market somewhat more like an organized market: there is centralization of buy and sell orders into one matching mechanism, there are membership rules (not anyone can log on to the program), rules about orders, etc. But the exchange market is still fully private, whereas many exchanges are semi-official institutions that are heavily regulated and need, at least, a license.

---

[9] The quotes are, again, "small numbers" and the quantities mean millions of dollars. Remember also that, for traders, EUR/USD means "the value of the euro in dollars."

Table 3.4. EBS versus Reuters D2: who leads, who follows, who fails.

	Primary		Other cross rates			Cross against EUR		
	EBS	Reut.		EBS	Reut.		EBS	Reut.
EUR/USD	+	+/−	AUD/JPY		−	EUR/AUD		−
AUD/USD	+/−	+	AUD/NZD		+/−	EUR/CAD		−
GBP/USD	+/−	+	CHF/JPY	−		EUR/CHF	+	+/−
NZD/USD		+	GBP/JPY		−	EUR/CZK	−	+
USD/CAD	+/−	+				EUR/DKK	−	+
USD/CHF	+	+/−				EUR/GBP	+/−	+
USD/CZK		−				EUR/HUF	−	+
USD/DKK		−				EUR/ISK		+
USD/HKG	−	+				EUR/JPY	+	+/−
USD/HUF		−				EUR/NOK	−	+
USD/ILS		+				EUR/NZD		+/−
USD/INR		+				EUR/PLN	−	+
USD/ISK		−				EUR/RON		−
USD/JPY	+	+/−				EUR/SEK	−	+
USD/MXN	−	+				EUR/SKK		+
USD/NOK		−				EUR/TRY		−
USD/PLN	−	+				EUR/ZAR		+/−
USD/RON		−						
USD/RUB		+						
USD/SAR		+						
USD/SEK		−						
USD/SGD	−	+						
USD/THB		+						
USD/TRY		+						
USD/ZAR		+						

+, Primary liquidity source; +/−, supported, but liquidity not good or not stable; −, supported but not used in practice. Rates are expressed following the "name" convention, not the dimensions. *Source:* www.londonfx.co.uk/autobrok.html, accessed February 2007.

3.2.1.4 Brokers

One last way of shopping around in foreign exchange markets is through currency brokers. In the telephone-market days, brokers used to do the go-between stuff that nowadays is handled via limit-order books: on behalf of a bank or company, the broker would call many market makers and identify the best counterpart. Roughly half of the transaction volume in the exchange market used to occur through brokers. Nowadays, brokers are mainly used for unusually large transactions, or "structured" deals involving, say, options next to spot and/or forward; for bread-and-butter deals their role is much reduced.

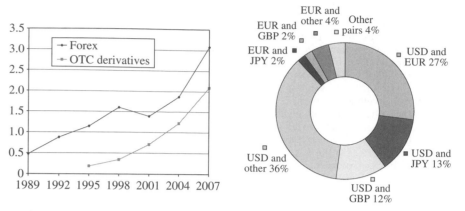

Figure 3.5. Forex turnover, daily, billions of USD, and market shares of currency pairs. *Source:* BIS, *Triennial Central Bank Survey of Foreign Exchange and Derivatives Market Activity in April 2007*, Preliminary Global Results, September 2007.

"quasi-immediate" means "right now" only when you buy or sell notes or coins. (This section of the market is marginal.) For electronic money (that is, money that will be at your disposal in some bank account), delivery is in two working days for most currencies ("$t+2$"), and one day between Canada and the United States or between Mexico and the United States ("$t+1$"). Thus, if you buy AUD 2m today, at AUD/EUR 2, the AUD 2m will be in your account two working days from now, and the EUR 1m will likewise be in the counterpart's account two days from now. The two-day delay is largely a tradition from the past, when accounts were kept by hand. The hour of settlement depends on the country, but tends to be close to noon. Thus, the EUR side of an EUR/USD transaction is settled in Europe about six hours before the USD leg of the deal is settled in New York.[11]

The *forward* market is the exchange market for payment and delivery of foreign currency at some future date, say, three months from now. For example, supposing today is January 3, you could ask your bank to quote you an exchange rate to sell dollars for pounds for a date in March, say March 5, and the transaction would be settled on that date in March, at the rate agreed upon on January 3 (irrespective of the spot rate prevailing on March 5). The forward market, in fact, consists of as many subsegments as there are delivery dates, and each subsegment has its own price. We shall denote this forward rate by $F_{t,T}$, with T referring to the future delivery date. (Forward rates and their uses will be discussed in great detail in chapters 4 and 5.)

The most active forward markets are for 30, 90, 180, 270, and 360 days, but nowadays bankers routinely quote rates up to ten years forward, and occasionally even beyond ten years. Note that months are indicated as 30 days.

---

[11] This leads to the risk that, between the two settlement times, one party may file for bankruptcy or be declared bankrupt. This is called "Herstatt risk," after a small German bank that pulled off this feat on June 26, 1974. Nowadays, regulators close down banks *outside* working hours.

Table 3.5. Market shares. Percentage for foreign exchange trading.

	U.K.	U.S.	Japan	Singapore	Other
1998	32.5	17.9	6.9	7.1	35.6
2001	31.2	15.7	9.1	6.2	37.8
2004	31.3	19.2	8.3	5.2	36.0
2007	34.1	16.6	6.0	5.8	37.5

Source: BIS, *Triennial Central Bank Survey of Foreign Exchange and Derivatives Market Activity in April 2007*, Preliminary Global Results, September 2007.

In principle, a 30-day contract is settled one month later than a spot contract, and a 180-day forward contract is settled six months later than a spot contract—each time including the two-day initial-delay convention.[12]

Example 3.9. A 180-day contract signed on March 2 works as follows. Assuming that March 4 is a working day, spot settlement would have been on March 4. For a 180-day forward deal, the settlement date would be moved by six months to, in principle, September 4, or the first working day thereafter if a holiday. The actual number of calendar days is at least (2+)184 days: there are four 31-day months in the March–September window.

The above holds for standard dates, But you can always obtain a price for a "*broken date*" (i.e., a nonstandard maturity), too. For instance, on April 20 you can stipulate settlement on November 19 or any other desired date.

Worldwide, spot transactions represent less than 50% of the total foreign-exchange market volume. The forward market together with the closely related swap market (see chapter 7) make up over 50% of the volume. About 3% of total trade consists of currency-futures contracts (a variant of forward contracts traded in secondary markets—see chapter 6) and currency options (see chapter 8).

After this digression on the meaning of exchange rates and their relation to real quantities, we now return to the operations of the spot exchange market. We want to introduce one of the cornerstones of finance theory: the law of one price.

3.3 The Law of One Price for Spot Exchange Quotes

In frictionless markets, two securities that have identical cash flows must have the same price. This is called the law of one price. There are two mechanisms that enforce this law. The first one is called *arbitrage* and the second one could be called *shopping around*. We explain these two concepts below.

Suppose that two assets or portfolios with identical cash flows do not have the same price. Then any holder of the overpriced asset could simultaneously

---

[12] Further details of settlement rules are provided in Grabbe (1995).

In a short sale you hope to be able to buy low and sell high, but with the selling preceding the buying, unlike in a long position. Thus, a short seller hopes to make money from falling prices rather than from rising prices.

In markets with delivery a few working days later, you can always go short for a few hours: sell "naked" in the morning, for instance, and then buy later within the same day so as to be able to deliver n days later.

For longer horizons one needs more. In the case of securities, short selling then requires borrowing a security for, say, a month and selling it now; at the end of the month you then buy back the number of securities you borrowed and restitute them to the asset lender, including dividends if any were paid out during that period.

For currencies, longer-term short selling can be done by just borrowing forex and selling it, hoping to be able to buy back the forex (including interest) later at a lower price. If there is a forward market, lastly, going short is even easier: promise to deliver on a future date at a price that is fixed now. If prices have dropped by then, as you hope, you will be able to close out (buy spot) cheaply and make money on the forward deal.

Panel 3.2.   What is short selling?

sell this asset and buy the cheaper asset instead, thus netting the price difference without taking on any additional risk. If one does not hold the overpriced asset, one could still take advantage of this mispricing by short selling (panel 3.2) the overpriced asset and covering this with the purchase of the cheaper security. For example, you sell an overpriced asset at 1.2135 and buy a perfect substitute at 1.2133, netting 0.0002 per unit right now and no net cash flow at T. Such transactions are called arbitrage. These arbitrage transactions generate an excess supply of the overpriced asset and an excess demand for the underpriced asset, moving the prices of these two assets toward each other. In frictionless markets, this process stops only when the two prices are identical. Note that apart from the arbitrage gain, an arbitrage transaction does not lead to a change in the net position of the arbitrageur; that is, it yields a sure profit without requiring any additional investment.

The second mechanism that enforces the law of one price is shopping around. Here, in contrast to arbitrage, investors do intend to make particular changes in their portfolios. Shopping around has to do with the fact that, when choosing between different ways of making given investments, clever investors choose the most advantageous way of doing so. Therefore, when choosing between assets with identical cash flows, investors buy the underpriced assets rather than the more expensive ones. Likewise, when choosing which assets to sell, investors sell the overpriced ones rather than the ones that are relatively cheap. This demand for the underpriced assets and supply of the overpriced ones again leads to a reduction in the difference between the prices of these two securities.

Although the arbitrage and shopping-around mechanisms both tend to enforce the law of one price, there are two differences between these mechanisms.

- First, an arbitrage transaction is a round-trip transaction. That is, you buy and sell, thus ending up with the same position with which you started.

As arbitrage requires a two-way transaction, its influence stops as soon as the price difference is down to the *sum* of the transaction costs (buying and selling). In contrast, in shopping around one wishes to make a particular transaction, and the issue is which of the two assets is cheaper to trade.[13] As a result, the influence of shopping around can go on as long as the price difference exceeds the *difference* of the two transactions costs.[14]

- Second, arbitrage is a strong force because it does not require any capital and can, therefore, generate enormous volumes. In contrast, shopping around can be a price-equalizing mechanism only if there are investors who wish to make that particular transaction. This exogenously triggered volume, if any, is always finite and may be exhausted before it has actually equalized the prices.

In this section, we apply these arguments to spot rates quoted for the same currencies by different market makers. In a perfect exchange market with zero spreads, arbitrage implies that the rate quoted by bank X must equal the rate quoted by bank Y: there can be only one price for a given currency—otherwise, there is an arbitrage opportunity.

Example 3.10. If Citibank quotes DEM/USD 1.6500, while Morgan Chase quotes DEM/USD 1.6501, both at zero spreads, then there are two possibilities:

- There is an arbitrage opportunity. You can buy cheap USD from Citibank and immediately sell to Morgan Chase, netting DEM 0.0001 per USD. You will, of course, make as many USD transactions as you can. So will everybody else. The effect of this massive trading is that either Citibank or Morgan Chase, or both, will have to change their quotes so as to stop the rapid accumulation of long or short positions. That is, situations with arbitrage profits are inconsistent with equilibrium, and are eliminated very rapidly.

- There is also a shopping-around pressure. All buyers of USD will buy from Citibank, and all sellers will deal with Morgan Chase.

The only way to avoid such trading imbalances is if both banks quote the same rate.[15]

What we now want to figure out is how arbitrage works when there are bid–ask spreads. The point is that, because of arbitrage, the rates cannot be

---

[13] Accordingly, Deardorff (1979) refers to standard arbitrage as *two-way arbitrage* and to shopping around as *one-way arbitrage*.

[14] Denote by P_U and k_U the price and transaction cost when dealing in the underpriced asset, and denote by P_O and k_O the counterparts for the overpriced asset. The advantage of buying the cheap asset rather than the expensive one remains positive as long as $P_U + k_U < P_O + k_O$; that is, as along as $P_O - P_U > k_U - k_O$. In contrast, the advantage of buying the cheap asset and selling the expensive one remains positive as long as $P_O - k_O - (P_U + k_U) > 0$, that is, as long as $P_O - P_U > k_O + k_U$: you pay both costs instead of replacing one by another.

[15] This is often put as "by arbitrage, the quotes must be the same" or "arbitrage means that the quotes must be the same." Phrases like these actually mean that to rule out arbitrage opportunities, the quotes must be the same.

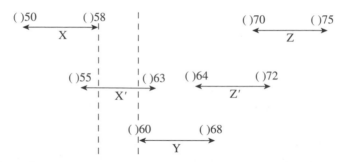

Figure 3.6. Arbitrage and shopping-around opportunities across market makers.

systematically different; and if the quotes do differ temporarily, they cannot differ by too much.

3.3.1 Arbitrage across Competing Market Makers

Suppose bank X quotes you INR/NZD 20.150–20.158 while bank Y quotes INR/NZD 20.160–20.168. If you see such quotes, you can make money easily: just buy NZD from bank X at INR 20.158, immediately resell it to bank Y at INR 20.160, and pocket a profit worth INR 0.002 for each NZD. Note two crucial ingredients: (1) you are not taking any risk, and (2) you are not investing any capital since the purchase is immediately reversed and both transactions are settled on the same day. The fact that you immediately reverse the transaction explains why this is called arbitrage.

   If such quotes are found in the exchange market (or elsewhere, for that matter), large trades by a few alert dealers would immediately force prices back into line. The original quotes would not be equilibrium quotes. In equilibrium, the arbitrage argument says that you cannot make money without investing capital and without taking risk. Graphically, any empty space between the two quotes would correspond to an arbitrage profit. Thus, the no-arbitrage condition says that any two banks' quotes should not be separated by empty space; that is, they should overlap by at least one point, like the quotes X′ and Y in figure 3.6.

3.3.2 Shopping Around across Competing Market Makers

Shopping-around activity implies that small differences like those between the pair (X′,Y) in figure 3.6 will not persist for very long. Rather, the two quotes will sometimes be the same, and, if at other times one bank is more expensive, then this would say very little about what the situation will be five minutes later. To see this, suppose that bank X′ quotes INR/NZD 20.55–20.63, while bank Y quotes INR/NZD 20.60–20.68. In such a situation, all buyers of NZD will, of course, prefer to deal with bank X′, which has the lower ask rate (20.63 instead of 20.68), while all sellers will now deal with bank Y, which has the better bid rate (20.60 instead of 20.55). It is conceivable that these banks actually want this to happen, for instance, if bank X' has an excess of foreign currency (long), and bank Y is short of forex and wants to replenish its FC inventory. But we would not expect this to be a long-run phenomenon. It is true that very often a bank may want one type of transaction only, but situations like that must change very rapidly because otherwise that bank's position would become unacceptably large and risky.

Example 3.11. Suppose you see five banks quoting EUR against USD, as follows:

Citibank	USD/EUR	1.3450–52
Bank of America	USD/EUR	1.3450–52
Continental Bank	USD/EUR	1.34<u>51</u>–53
Deutsche Bank	USD/EUR	1.3450–52
Banca da Roma	USD/EUR	1.3449–<u>51</u>

Q1. Which bank(s) is (are) keen on buying EUR? Keen on selling EUR? Not interested in dealing?

A1. Continental, with its high bid, is quite attractive to sellers, so this trader clearly wants to buy—for example, to fill a short position or because she expects a rise. Roma, in contrast, judging by its low ask, is quite attractive to buyers, so their trader clearly wants to sell—maybe to move an unwanted long position, or in anticipation of a fall in the rate. The others are just twiddling thumbs: as things stand, they are unwilling to match Continental's or Roma's rates, and they hope that things will soon be better.

Q2. Why does Continental raise both its bid and its ask, rather than just its bid?

A2. Apparently it wants not just to attract sellers but also to scare off buyers. Similarly, Roma does not just fancy buyers, but does not want any sellers at all.

Q3. If we were to look at these banks' quotes every five minutes, would we always expect to see the same pattern, i.e., Continental quoting higher and Roma lower than the majority?

A3. Of course not: as soon as their desired positions are reached, they will return to the fold. Thus, the top and bottom positions are picked by a particular bank for only a brief period, and move randomly across the list of banks.

3.3.3 Triangular Arbitrage

Now that we know how exchange rates are quoted and what arbitrage means, let us look at the relationships that exist between spot rates quoted in various currencies. The forces that support these linkages are again arbitrage and shopping around. For our purposes, we can ignore the many market makers: when we talk about bid and ask, we now mean the *market quote*, that is, the best bid across all market makers, and the best ask. The new issue is how these market quotes in various currencies are linked.

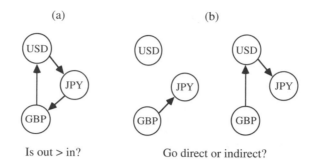

Figure 3.7. (a) Triangular arbitrage (do I make money doing this?) and (b) triangular shopping around (which of the two gives me the best price?).

- Someone engaging in triangular *arbitrage* tries to make money by sequentially buying and selling various currencies, ending with the original currency. For instance, you could convert AUD into USD, and then immediately convert the USD into GBP and the GBP back into AUD, with the hope of ending up with more AUD than you started out with. The no-arbitrage condition says that you should not make a profit from such activities. Actually, when there are transaction costs or commissions, you are likely to end up with a loss. The potential loss is due to commissions, notably the bid–ask spread. Thus, in this context, arbitrage implies that the set of exchange rates quoted against various base currencies should be such that you cannot make any risk-free instantaneous profits after paying transaction costs.

- *Shopping around* is the search for the best way to achieve a desired conversion. For instance, an Australian investor who wants to buy GBP may buy directly, or may first convert AUD into USD and then convert these USD into GBP. Shopping around implies that the direct AUD/GBP market can survive only if its quotes are no worse than the implied rates from the indirect transaction.

In the case of perfect markets, the regular arbitrage and shopping-around arguments lead to the same conclusion. We illustrate this in the following example (and figure 3.7 shows the difference between arbitrage and shopping around).

Example 3.12. Suppose 1 GBP buys USD 1.5, while 1 USD buys AUD 1.6; therefore, if we directly convert GBP into AUD, 1 GBP should buy $1.5 \times 1.6 = 2.4$ AUD. With this AUD/GBP rate and assuming a zero spread,

- nobody can make a free-lunch profit by any sequence of transactions, and
- everyone is indifferent between direct conversions between two currencies and indirect, triangular transactions.

Below, we see what the implications of arbitrage and shopping around are when there are bid–ask spreads. In order to simplify matters, we shall first show how to compute the implied rates from an indirect route. We shall call these implied rates the *synthetic* rates. Having identified these synthetic rates, we can then invoke the same mechanisms that enforce the law of one price as when we studied the relationship between the quotes made by various market makers.

3.3.3.1 Computing Synthetic Cross Rates

In general, a synthetic version of a contract is a combination of two or more other transactions that achieves the same objective as the original contract. That is, the combination of the two or more contracts *replicates* the outcome of the original contract. We shall use the notion of replication repeatedly in this textbook. For now, consider a simple spot transaction: a Japanese investor wants to convert JPY into GBP.

- The investor can use the direct market and buy GBP against JPY. We will call this the original contract.
- Alternatively, the investor can first buy USD with JPY, and then immediately exchange the USD for GBP. This is a combination of two contracts. It replicates the original contract since, by combining the two transactions, the investor initially pays JPY, and ultimately ends up with GBP. Thus, this is a synthetic way of achieving the original transaction.

Note that the synthetic contract may be the more efficient way to deal, since the USD market has a lot of volume (or depth) in every country, and therefore has smaller spreads. (This is why the USD is involved in 90% of the trades.) Let us see how the synthetic JPY/GBP rates can be computed.

Example 3.13. What are the synthetic JPY/GBP rates, bid and ask, if the quotes are JPY/USD 101.07–101.20 and USD/GBP 1.3840–1.3850?

Step 1: multiply or divide? The dimension of the rate we are looking for is JPY/GBP. Because the dimensions of the two quotes given to us are USD/GBP and JPY/USD, the way to obtain the synthetic rate is to multiply the rates, as follows:

$$[JPY/GBP] = [JPY/USD] \times [USD/GBP]. \qquad (3.4)$$

Note that on the right-hand side of the equation, the USD in the denominator of the first quote cancels out the USD in the numerator of the second quote, leaving us with the desired JPY/GBP number.

Step 2: bids or asks? The first quote is the natural quote for a Japanese agent, the second one takes the USD as the base. Consider the synthetic ask (relevant for buying GBP from a JPY position). Starting from JPY we buy USD, so we need the ask; and with the USD we buy GBP, so we again need ask. Thus,

$$\text{Synthetic } S_{t,\text{ask}}^{\text{JPY/GBP}} = S_{t,\text{ask}}^{\text{JPY/USD}} \times S_{t,\text{ask}}^{\text{USD/GBP}}$$
$$= 101.20 \times 1.3850 = 140.16. \qquad (3.5)$$

By a similar argument, we can obtain the rate at which we can synthetically convert GBP into USD and these into JPY:

$$\text{Synthetic } S_{t,\text{bid}}^{\text{JPY/GBP}} = S_{t,\text{bid}}^{\text{JPY/USD}} \times S_{t,\text{bid}}^{\text{USD/GBP}}$$
$$= 101.07 \times 1.3840 = 139.88. \tag{3.6}$$

This example is the first instance of the law of the worst possible combination, or the rip-off rule. You already know that, for any single transaction, the bank gives you the worst rate from your point of view (this is how the bank makes money). It follows that if you make a sequence of transactions, you will inevitably get the worst possible cumulative outcome. This law of the worst possible combination is the first fundamental law of real-world capital markets. In our example, this law works as follows:

- Note that we are computing a product. The synthetic ask rate for the GBP (the higher rate, the one at which you buy) turns out to be the highest possible product of the two exchange rates: we multiply the two high rates, ask times ask. Note, finally, that if the purpose is to buy forex, then a high rate is also an unfavorable rate. In short, we buy at the worst rate, the highest possible combined rate.

- We see that, likewise, the synthetic bid rate for the GBP (the lower rate, the one at which you sell) turns out to be the lowest possible product of the two exchange rates: we multiply the two low rates, bid times bid. Note also that if the purpose is to sell forex, then a low rate is also an unfavorable rate. In short, we sell at the worst rate, the lowest possible combined rate.

Let us look at another example. The data are the same except that the British quotes are now direct and not indirect.

DIY Problem 3.1. The JPY/GBP synthetic bid and ask rates, if the quotes are JPY/USD 101.07–101.20 and GBP/USD 0.722 02–0.722 54, are

$$\left.\begin{array}{l} \text{Synthetic } S_{t,\text{bid}}^{\text{JPY/GBP}} = \dfrac{S_{t,\text{bid}}^{\text{JPY/USD}}}{S_{t,\text{ask}}^{\text{GBP/USD}}} = 139.88, \\[3mm] \text{Synthetic } S_{t,\text{ask}}^{\text{JPY/GBP}} = \dfrac{S_{t,\text{ask}}^{\text{JPY/USD}}}{S_{t,\text{bid}}^{\text{GBP/USD}}} = 140.16. \end{array}\right\} \tag{3.7}$$

- Derive this solution from the previous one, invoking our earlier results on inverse rates, equations (3.2) and (3.3).
- Verify that you get the above answer also if you first think of the dimensions and then apply the law of the worst possible combination.

Figure 3.8 shows the spreadsheet set up by one particular trader to help him shop around.

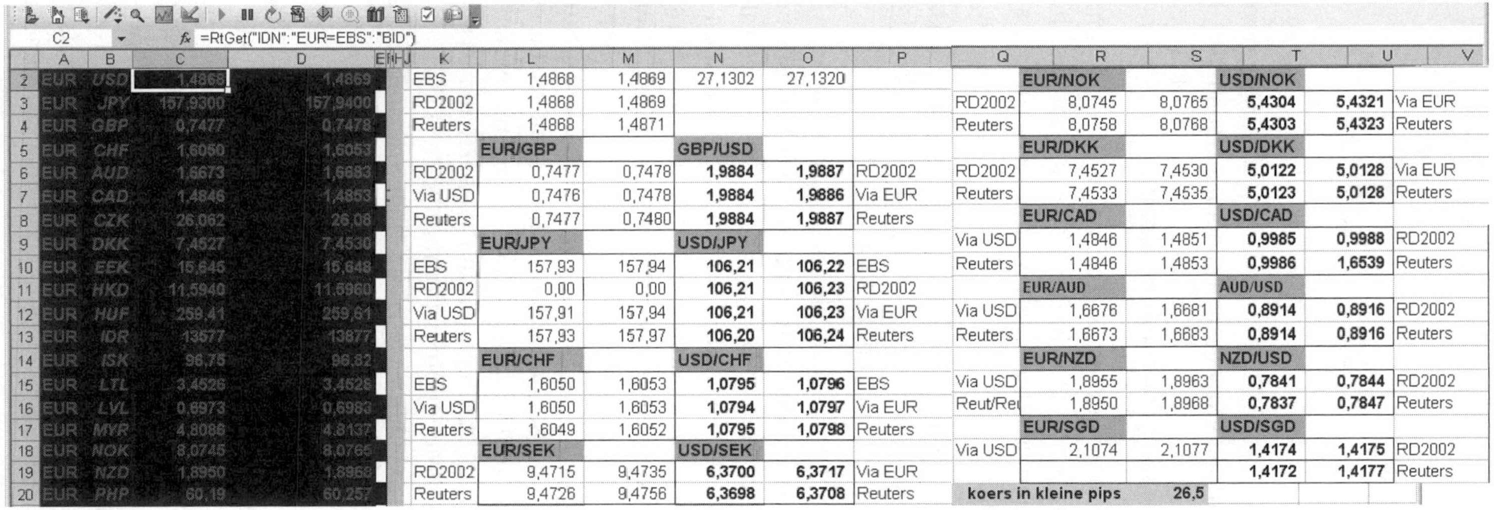

C2   `=RtGet("IDN":"EUR=EBS":"BID")`

Currency list (columns A–D):

A	B	C	D
EUR	USD	1,4868	1,4869
EUR	JPY	157,9300	157,9400
EUR	GBP	0,7477	0,7478
EUR	CHF	1,6050	1,6053
EUR	AUD	1,6673	1,6683
EUR	CAD	1,4846	1,4853
EUR	CZK	26,062	28,08
EUR	DKK	7,4527	7,4530
EUR	EEK	16,646	16,648
EUR	HKD	11,5940	11,5960
EUR	HUF	259,41	259,61
EUR	IDR	13877	13877
EUR	ISK	96,75	96,82
EUR	LTL	3,4526	3,4526
EUR	LVL	0,6963	0,6963
EUR	MYR	4,8086	4,8137
EUR	NOK	8,0745	8,0765
EUR	NZD	1,8950	1,8950
EUR	PHP	60,19	60,257

Left quote grid (columns K–P):

K	L	M	N	O	P
EBS	1,4868	1,4869	27,1302	27,1320	
RD2002	1,4868	1,4869			
Reuters	1,4868	1,4871			
EUR/GBP			**GBP/USD**		
RD2002	0,7477	0,7478	1,9884	1,9887	RD2002
Via USD	0,7476	0,7478	1,9886	1,9886	Via EUR
Reuters	0,7477	0,7480	1,9887	1,9887	Reuters
EUR/JPY			**USD/JPY**		
EBS	157,93	157,94	106,21	106,22	EBS
RD2002	0,00	0,00	106,21	106,23	RD2002
Via USD	157,91	157,94	106,21	106,23	Via EUR
Reuters	157,93	157,97	106,20	106,24	Reuters
EUR/CHF			**USD/CHF**		
EBS	1,6050	1,6053	1,0795	1,0796	EBS
Via USD	1,6050	1,6053	1,0794	1,0797	Via EUR
Reuters	1,6049	1,6052	1,0795	1,0798	Reuters
EUR/SEK			**USD/SEK**		
RD2002	9,4715	9,4735	6,3700	6,3717	Via EUR
Reuters	9,4726	9,4756	6,3698	6,3708	Reuters

Right quote grid (columns Q–V):

Q	R	S	T	U	V
	EUR/NOK		**USD/NOK**		
RD2002	8,0745	8,0765	5,4304	5,4321	Via EUR
Reuters	8,0758	8,0768	5,4303	5,4323	Reuters
	EUR/DKK		**USD/DKK**		
RD2002	7,4527	7,4530	5,0122	5,0128	Via EUR
Reuters	7,4533	7,4535	5,0123	5,0128	Reuters
	EUR/CAD		**USD/CAD**		
Via USD	1,4846	1,4851	0,9985	0,9988	RD2002
Reuters	1,4846	1,4853	0,9986	1,6539	Reuters
	EUR/AUD		**AUD/USD**		
Via USD	1,6676	1,6681	0,8914	0,8916	RD2002
Reuters	1,6673	1,6683	0,8914	0,8916	Reuters
	EUR/NZD		**NZD/USD**		
Via USD	1,8955	1,8963	0,7841	0,7844	RD2002
Reut/Rel	1,8950	1,8968	0,7837	0,7847	Reuters
	EUR/SGD		**USD/SGD**		
Via USD	2,1074	2,1077	1,4174	1,4175	RD2002
			1,4172	1,4177	Reuters
koers in kleine pips			26,5		

Figure 3.8. A dealer's shopping-around spreadsheet. Courtesy of Paul Goossens, dealer at KBC Brussels. Paul's spreadsheet shows the best quotes from EBS's broking screens, from Reuters Dealing 2002, and the indirect quotes (via USD or EUR). The latter are obviously rounded. Check how the indirect quotes are always wider at one side at least. (With only two pips between the best direct quotes, and with rounding of the synthetic quotes, one side must always seem to match.) The wider quotes labeled Reuters are the indicative, nonbinding ones from the Reuters FX/FX pages; they mean nothing except that some banks are willing to quote. See how Paul's sheet gets the EUR/USD quote from EBS into the darker parts of the spreadsheet. Cell 1 is selected; spot the underlying command =RtGet("IDN":"EUR=EBS":"BID") in the enter function box above the spreadsheet. From the imported data in the black part, synthetic rates are computed.

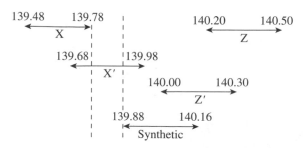

Figure 3.9. Triangular arbitrage and shopping around.

3.3.3.2 Triangular Arbitrage with Transactions Costs

Now that we understand synthetic quotes, we can derive bounds imposed by arbitrage and shopping around on quotes in the wholesale market. Just think of the direct quotes as the quotes from bank X, and think of the synthetic quotes as the quotes from bank Y.

- *Arbitrage* then says that the two bid–ask quotes should overlap by at least one point; otherwise, you can buy cheap in the direct market and sell at a profit in the synthetic market or vice versa.

- *Shopping around* implies that if a bank skews its quotes so as to be (very) attractive at (only) one side, then it will attract a lot of business very fast; thus, this skewing cannot be persistent. But when we talk about market quotes (the best bid, and the best ask, across all market makers) rather than the quotes by an individual dealer, the force is even stronger. Individually, a market maker may very well want to make one of its quotes unappealing for some time, as we saw. But if there are many market makers it would be quite unlikely that, across all market makers, even the best direct quote would still be unappealing against the synthetic one, for that would mean that among all the competing market makers there is not a single one that is interested in that particular type of deal. Thus, instances where a direct quote is dominated by a synthetic one at one side should be rare and short-lived, and the more so the higher the number of market makers.

- The above assumes that the direct market has enough volume. Indeed, with a very thin market, the spread required to make market making sustainable may be too wide to allow the direct market to compete on both sides with the synthetic market via a heavily traded vehicle currency (like the USD or the EUR). The volume and depth of the wholesale market for dollars relative to almost any other currency is so large (and the spreads, therefore, so small) that a substantial part of the nondollar transactions are, in fact, still executed by way of the dollar. Direct cross deals emerged as of the mid 1980s only, and are still confined to heavy-volume currency pairs.

As a final note, in the retail markets most customers have no direct access to cross rates, and bank clerks occasionally compute cross rates even where the actual transaction could be executed very differently. A Japanese bank, for instance, would post quotes for JPY/GBP and JPY/EUR rates for its retail customers, but typically not for GBP/EUR. Should a retail customer sell EUR and buy GBP, the clerk would actually compute the synthetic rates we have just derived, as if the customer first went from EUR to JPY and then to GBP, even if in the bank's trading room the actual conversion may be done directly from EUR into GBP. Unless you have an account with a Euroland or U.K. bank, or enough clout with your home bank, you would have little choice but to accept the large spread implied by such synthetic rates.

This finishes our tour of the workings of the exchange markets. We continue the chapter with some wise advice on the merits and shortcomings of using exchange rates to translate foreign amounts of money. This brings us to the twin concepts of "PPP" and "real" exchange rates, key issues for understanding the relevance of currency risk.

3.4 Translating FC Figures: Nominal Rates, PPP Rates, and Deviations from PPP

Obviously, when you exchange an FC amount into HC or vice versa, you will use the exchange rate relevant at the moment. But actual transactions like this are not the sole conceivable purpose for such a conversion; rather, the purpose may just be *translation*, that is, to have an idea what an FC amount means in a unit that you are more familiar with, the HC. For instance, if a resident of Vanuatu tells you she is making 1m vatus a month, most people would not have a clue whether they should be impressed or not. In a case like this we do not want to actually exchange any vatus into our own HC; we would simply like to translate an FC number into a unit that is more meaningful to us.

The most commonly used solution is to resort to the market exchange rate to make the translation. The result is an improvement on the FC amount in the sense that you know what you would be able to do with this converted amount if you consumed it here, at home. But your objective may be to have a feel for what the FC amount would mean to a resident of the foreign country, that is, if the money is consumed there, not here. Both questions—the purchasing power of some amount of money in your home country, and the purchasing power abroad—provide the same answer if prices abroad and at home are on average the same once they have been converted into the same currency. This situation is known as (absolute) purchasing power parity (APPP). As we will illustrate below, APPP does not hold in reality, with deviations becoming more important the more different the two countries are in terms of location or economic development.

3.4.1 The PPP Rate

To have a more reliable feel for what a given amount of foreign money really means locally, one needs for each country a number called the price level, which we denote by Π (at home, and in HC), and Π^* (abroad, and in FC), respectively. A price level is an absolute amount of currency—not an index number—needed to buy a standard consumption bundle. Computing price levels for different countries makes sense only if the consumption bundle whose cost is being measured is the same across countries. In a simple economy in which fast food is the only commodity, the bundle may be one soda, one burger, one fries (medium), a salad, and a coffee—let's call this the BigMeal. We simply jot down the prices of the components abroad and at home, and tot them up into price levels for BigMeals.

Any differences in price levels, after conversion into a common currency, would make a simple conversion of an FC amount into the HC rather misleading if translated price levels are very different.

Example 3.14. You often chat with a friend living in the Republic of Freedonia, where, since the presidency of Groucho Marx, the currency is the Freedonian crown (FDK). Let S_t = USD/FDK 0.010. You earn USD 50 per unit of time, your Freedonian friend 2,000 FDK. What does that income really mean if the standard consumption bundle, our BigMeal, costs USD 5 here and FDK 250 in Freedonia?

- At the spot rate of USD/FDK 0.010, your friend seems to earn only 2,000 × 0.010 = USD 20, suggesting that she is 60% worse off than you.

- But this ignores price differences. What you "really" earn is 50/5 = 10 BigMeals, while your friend makes 2000/250 = 8 BigMeals. That is, your friend is "really" almost as well off as you are.

3.4.1.1 What Is the PPP Rate?

To buy eight BigMeals at home, you would need $8 \times 5 =$ USD 40. So one way to summarize the situation is that FDK 2,000 means as much to your friend abroad as USD 40 means here, to you. The USD 40 is called the translation of FDK 2,000 using the PPP rate rather than the nominal rate, and the implied PPP rate is the $40/2,000 = 0.020$ USD per FDK, the ratio of the two price levels.

Let us generalize. Suppose you want to have a feel for what an FC amount Y^* "really" means to a foreigner. The question can be made more precise as follows. Give me an HC amount $\hat{Y}$ such that its purchasing power here, $\hat{Y}/\Pi_t$, equals the purchasing power abroad of the original amount, Y^*/Π_t^*:

$$\text{Find } \hat{Y} \text{ such that } \frac{\hat{Y}}{\Pi_t} = \frac{Y^*}{\Pi_t^*}$$

$$\implies \quad \hat{Y} = \frac{\Pi_t}{\Pi_t^*} Y^* = \hat{S}_t^{\text{PPP}} Y^*, \quad \text{where } \hat{S}_t^{\text{PPP}} \overset{\text{def}}{=} \frac{\Pi_t}{\Pi_t^*}. \tag{3.8}$$

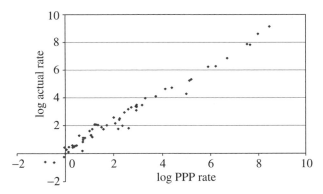

Figure 3.10. Log PPP versus log actual rates, HC/USD.
Source: Based on data from the *Economist*, May 26, 2006.

So we can always compute the PPP rate as the ratio of the two price levels. For example, your friend's foreign amount (FDK 2,000) could have been translated at the PPP rate, 5/250 = 0.020, which would have told you immediately that her income buys as much (in Freedonia) as USD 40 buys here.

Example 3.15. At the end of 2006, the CIA Factbook assessed Russia's 2005 GDP at 1.589 USD trillion using the PPP rate, and at 740.7 billion using the nominal official rate (www.cia.gov/cia/publications/factbook/geos/rs.html). What is the explanation for this? Are prices lower in Russia than in the United States, or is it the reverse?

For China, the figures were USD 8.883 trillion (PPP) and USD 2.225 trillion (official exchange rate), a ratio of about four to one instead of Russia's two to one. Which country, then, has the lower price level?

DIY Problem 3.2. Check that the PPP rate has dimension HC/FC.

The IMF and the World Bank, for instance, often use PPP rates rather than the regular ("nominal") rate to translate foreign GDPs or incomes or government budgets. Newspapers and magazines have also begun to adopt this approach. Lastly, the PPP rate also serves as a benchmark for the nominal rate. Many economists feel that, in the long run, the nominal rate for two similar economies should loosely fluctuate around the PPP rate, and never wander off very far above or below it. Let us see how well this theory fares, empirically.

3.4.1.2 PPP in Reality

In table 3.6 we take the *Economist*'s favorite consumption bundle, the Big Mac, and we compute PPP rates for 59 countries—once in USD (a New Yorker should get 0.295 dollars to be as happy as a Beijinger with one extra yuan) and once in non-U.S. currency (a Beijinger should get 3.39 yuan to be as happy as a New Yorker with one extra dollar). You see that countries where the Big Mac has a high local price have, of course, low PPP rates but also tend to have low actual

Table 3.6. PPP rates based on Big Mac prices from the *Economist*, May 26, 2006.

	Currency	Local price	Actual value of $	PPP rate of $	Real rate of $	Actual value in $	PPP rate in $	Real rate in $
China	yuan	10.5	8.03	3.39	2.371	0.125	0.295	0.422
Macau	pacata	11.1	7.99	3.58	2.231	0.125	0.279	0.448
Malaysia	ringgit	5.5	3.63	1.77	2.046	0.275	0.564	0.489
Hong Kong	dollar	12	7.75	3.87	2.002	0.129	0.258	0.499
Indonesia	rupia	14600	9325	4709.68	1.980	0.000	0.000	0.505
Philippines	peso	85	52.6	27.42	1.918	0.019	0.036	0.521
Paraguay	guarani	9000	5505	2903.23	1.896	0.000	0.000	0.527
Egypt	pound	9.5	5.77	3.06	1.883	0.173	0.326	0.531
Ukraine	hryvna	8.5	5.05	2.74	1.842	0.198	0.365	0.543
Moldava	leu	23	13.2	7.42	1.779	0.076	0.135	0.562
Uruguay	peso	42.3	23.9	13.65	1.752	0.042	0.073	0.571
Russia	ruble	48	27.1	15.48	1.750	0.037	0.065	0.571
Dominican Rep	peso	60	32.6	19.35	1.684	0.031	0.052	0.594
Sri Lanka	rupee	190	103	61.29	1.681	0.010	0.016	0.595
Honduras	lempira	35.95	18.9	11.60	1.630	0.053	0.086	0.614
Bulgaria	lev	2.99	1.54	0.96	1.597	0.649	1.037	0.626
Slovakia	koruna	58	29.5	18.71	1.577	0.034	0.053	0.634
Poland	zloty	6.5	3.1	2.10	1.478	0.323	0.477	0.676
Thailand	baht	60	28.4	19.35	1.467	0.035	0.052	0.682
South Africa	rand	13.95	6.6	4.50	1.467	0.152	0.222	0.682
Pakistan	rupee	130	60.1	41.94	1.433	0.017	0.024	0.698
Venezuela	bolivar	5701	2630	1839.03	1.430	0.000	0.001	0.699
Costa Rica	colon	1130	510	364.52	1.399	0.002	0.003	0.715
Japan	yen	250	112	80.65	1.389	0.009	0.012	0.720
Singapore	dollar	3.6	1.59	1.16	1.369	0.629	0.861	0.730
Guatemala	quetzal	17.25	7.59	5.56	1.364	0.132	0.180	0.733
Argentina	peso	7	3.06	2.26	1.355	0.327	0.443	0.738
Georgia	lari	4.15	1.8	1.34	1.345	0.556	0.747	0.744
Taiwan	dollar	75	32.1	24.19	1.327	0.031	0.041	0.754
Estonia	kroon	29.5	12.3	9.52	1.293	0.081	0.105	0.774
Saudi Arabia	riyal	9	3.75	2.90	1.292	0.267	0.344	0.774
Lithuania	litas	6.5	2.69	2.10	1.283	0.372	0.477	0.779
Australia	dollar	3.25	1.33	1.05	1.269	0.752	0.954	0.788
UAE	dirham	9	3.67	2.90	1.264	0.272	0.344	0.791
Latvia	lats	1.35	0.55	0.44	1.263	1.818	2.296	0.792
Mexico	peso	29	11.3	9.35	1.208	0.088	0.107	0.828
Colombia	peso	6500	2504	2096.77	1.194	0.000	0.000	0.837
Croatia	kuna	15	5.72	4.84	1.182	0.175	0.207	0.846
South Korea	won	2500	952	806.45	1.180	0.001	0.001	0.847

exchange rates. Figure 3.10 shows this graphically. To "shrink" the outliers and give the smaller numbers more space, we plot the log of the actual against the log of the PPP rate. (This explains why there are negative rates: numbers below unity produce negative logs.) There is obviously a very strong link.

DIY Problem 3.3. Knowing that the Big Mac costs 3.10 in the United States and 155 in Freedonia, and that the spot rate is 100 crowns per dollar, complete Freedonia's PPP rates in the table:

	Currency	Local price	Actual value of $	PPP rate of $	Real rate of $	Actual value in $	PPP rate in $	Real rate in $
Freedonia	korona	155	100					

Table 3.6. *Continued.*

	Currency	Local price	Actual value of $	PPP rate of $	Real rate of $	Actual value in $	PPP rate in $	Real rate in $
Czech Rep	koruna	59.05	22.1	19.05	1.160	0.045	0.052	0.862
Fiji	dollar	4.65	1.73	1.50	1.153	0.578	0.667	0.867
Hungary	forint	560	206	180.65	1.140	0.005	0.006	0.877
Turkey	lire	4.2	1.54	1.35	1.137	0.649	0.738	0.880
New Zealand	dollar	4.45	1.62	1.44	1.129	0.617	0.697	0.886
Slovenia	tolar	520	189	167.74	1.127	0.005	0.006	0.888
Aruba	florin	4.95	1.79	1.60	1.121	0.559	0.626	0.892
Brazil	real	6.4	2.3	2.06	1.114	0.435	0.484	0.898
Morocco	dirham	24.5	8.71	7.90	1.102	0.115	0.127	0.907
Peru	new sol	9.5	3.26	3.06	1.064	0.307	0.326	0.940
Chile	peso	1560	530	503.23	1.053	0.002	0.002	0.949
United states	dollar	3.1	1	1.00	1.000	1.000	1.000	1.000
Canada	dollar	3.52	1.12	1.14	0.986	0.893	0.881	1.014
Britain	pound	1.94	0.532	0.63	0.850	1.880	1.598	1.176
Euroland	euro	2.94	0.781	0.95	0.824	1.280	1.054	1.214
Sweden	krona	33	7.28	10.65	0.684	0.137	0.094	1.462
Denmark	krone	27.75	5.82	8.95	0.650	0.172	0.112	1.538
Switzerland	franc	6.3	1.21	2.03	0.595	0.826	0.492	1.680
Iceland	kronur	459	72	148.06	0.486	0.014	0.007	2.056
Norway	kroner	43	6.1	13.87	0.440	0.164	0.072	2.274

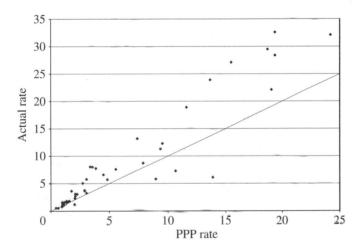

Figure 3.11. PPP versus actual rates, HC/USD.
Source: Based on data from the *Economist*, May 26, 2006.

But a closer look at the table reveals big relative deviations, which are hard to spot from a log graph dominated by outliers. Kicking out the twenty highest cases so as to be able to forgo logs, this time, we get figure 3.11. Note how the observations tend to be above the equality line (where actual = PPP): the dollar tends to be too expensive, by Big Mac PPP standards. Yet there are also important deviations below the 45° line, where the slope of the ray through the dot is even below 0.5 in one case. The slope of this ray is called the *real exchange rate*, to which we now turn.

3.4.2   Commodity Price Parity

A concept used in textbooks is commodity price parity (CPP). It is said to hold when translated prices for an individual good are equalized across two countries:

$$\text{CPP holds if } P_{j,t} = S_t \times P_{j,t}^*, \tag{3.9}$$

with j referring to an individual good, and P_j (P_j^*) referring to its price at home, in HC (abroad, in FC). In fact, all the Big Mac evidence shown thus far is about CPP rather than PPP, a distinction that the *Economist* tends to gloss over.

CPP would hold if trading were costless and instantaneous. Obviously, in reality it does not work across the board; for commodities it is not too bad an approximation (within the bounds created by transportation costs and the like), but for consumer goods it is essentially a joke.

PPP in the true sense—i.e., for a bundle of goods—would clearly hold if CPP held for every individual good, or if deviations from CPP washed out after averaging across many goods. As we have seen, this is not really the case; apparently, too many deviations from CPP turn out to be in the same direction, suggesting there is a common force behind them. Forget CPP.

3.4.3   The Real Exchange Rate and (Deviations from) Absolute PPP

The real exchange rate (RER) is a measure of how far the nominal rate differs from the PPP rate: it is simply the nominal exchange rate divided by the PPP counterpart.

Example 3.16. In our Freedonian story, the nominal rate was 0.010 USD/FDK while the PPP rate was 0.020 USD/FDK; thus, the real rate was 0.5, which is a large deviation from unity, but not uncommon between two very different economies.

The real rate is a dimensionless number: [HC/FC] divided by [HC/FC]. In a way, it simply tells us what the ratio is of the *translated* price levels:

$$\text{RER}_t \overset{\text{def}}{=} \frac{S_t}{\hat{S}_t^{\text{PPP}}} \tag{3.10}$$

$$= \frac{S_t \times \Pi_t^*}{\Pi_t}, \quad \text{from (3.8).} \tag{3.11}$$

Again, in the example one can find the RER for the FDK against the USD by translating into USD the foreign price of the BigMeal, FDK $250 \times 0.010 =$ USD 2.5, and divide it by the domestic price level, 5, which gets us $2.5/5 = 0.5$. Thus, the RER rate tells you how much cheaper (if RER < 1) or more expensive (if RER > 1) the foreign country is. A country with a below-unity real rate would be a nice place to spend your domestic income, or could be an attractive base to export from, but may not be the best place to export to. These are very different questions than the one answered by the PPP rate.

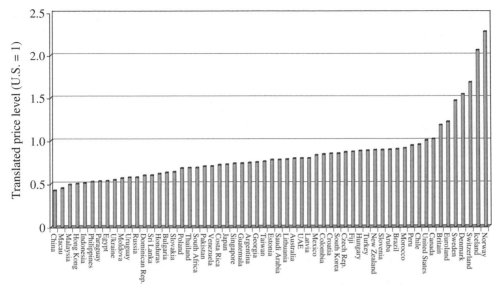

Figure 3.12. Relative prices of the Big Mac across the world, based on data from the *Economist*, May 26, 2006.

Obviously, if the real rate equals unity, both countries have the same price level. If that is true, Absolute PPP is said to hold:

$$\text{Absolute PPP holds if } \text{RER}_t = 1 \Leftrightarrow S_t = S_t^{\text{PPP}} \Leftrightarrow S_t \times \Pi_t^* = \Pi_t. \qquad (3.12)$$

In figure 3.12, and in table 3.6 the countries have been ranked on the basis of the real rate. Two observations stand out. First, there is a five-to-one ratio between the most and least expensive countries, Norway and China. So deviations from PPP are big. Second, there is a system to it, to some extent: undervalued currencies tend to be developing ones, and overvalued ones developed. (The fact that thus USD is not top is anomalous, in this view. The long-lasting deficit in its current account may be one reason.) The (imperfect but strong) relation between real rate and degree of economic development is discussed in chapter 10.

DIY Problem 3.4. Norway is most expensive. In figure 3.11, identify the dot that corresponds to Norway.

3.4.4 The Change in the Real Rate and (Deviations from) Relative PPP

For most of the time since the 1980s, Japan has had a real rate above unity: it was a more expensive place to spend a dollar than the United States or Europe. Sometimes one is interested in whether a country's situation has worsened or improved. That is, has the real rate increased or decreased (as distinct from the issue of whether its level is above unity or not)?

To measure this, one can simply compute the RER's percentage change. Not surprisingly, the percentage change in the RER is determined by the percentage changes in the spot rate and the price levels—the inflation rates.

Example 3.17. Q. Suppose that five years ago the FDK traded at USD/FDK 0.012, and the price levels were USD 4 in the United States and FDK 250 abroad. (So, with current price levels being 5 and 250, respectively, inflation was 25% in the United States and zero in Freedonia.) Recalling that the current RER is $250 \times 0.010/5 = 0.5$, how much has the RER changed since then?

A. The old RER was $250 \times 0.012/4 = 0.75$; so the rate changed by $(0.50-0.75)/0.75 = -0.33$, that is, -33%. There was real depreciation of the crown—that is, Freedonia became cheaper over time—because the FDK went down *and* because inflation in Freedonia was lower than in the United States.

Below, we first show the general relation between the percentage change in the RER and the changes in the nominal rate, and then a first-order approximation that is occasionally used:

$$\text{Percentage change in the RER} = (1 + s_{t_0,t}) \frac{1 + \text{infl}^*_{t_0,t}}{1 + \text{infl}_{t_0,t}} - 1 \qquad (3.13)$$

$$\approx s_{t_0,t} + [\text{infl}^*_{t_0,t} - \text{infl}_{t_0,t}], \qquad (3.14)$$

where $s_{t_0,t}$ is the simple percentage change in the spot rate S between times t_0 and t while $\text{infl}_{t_0,t}$ and $\text{infl}^*_{t_0,t}$ denote inflation at home and abroad, respectively, over the same time window. The first-order approximation works well if both inflation rates are low. This is not the case in our Freedonian example.

Example 3.18. In our above story, foreign inflation was zero, U.S. inflation 25%, and the exchange-rate changed by minus one sixth; so the RER changes by

$$\left(1 - \frac{1}{6}\right) \frac{1 + 0.00}{1 + 0.25} - 1 = 0.666\,67 - 1 = -\frac{1}{3},$$

as computed directly before. In contrast, the first-order approximation would have predicted a change of $-\frac{1}{6} - 0.25 = -41.67\%$ rather than -33.33%. The error is nontrivial because, in this example, two numbers—the U.S. inflation rate and the change in the exchange rate—are far from zero.

If the RER is constant, whatever the level, then relative PPP (RPPP) is said to hold; and the percentage change in the RER is a standard measure of deviations from RPPP. An RPPP deviation is most often resorted to if the RER itself cannot be computed because price-level data are missing. If, indeed, absolute price levels for identical bundles are not available, there is no way of computing which of the two countries is the cheaper. But one can still have an idea whether the RER went up or down if one estimates the inflation rates from the standard consumption price indices (CPIs) rather than the price levels. A CPI is a relative number vis-à-vis a base period, and the consumption bundle is

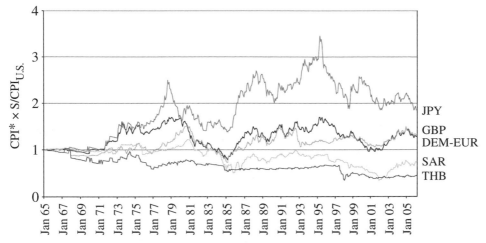

Figure 3.13. [Actual rate]/[RPPP rate] against the USD, 1965 = 1.00.
Source: Underlying data are from DataStream.

typically tailored to the country's own consumption pattern rather than being a common, internationally representative bundle of goods. Still, in most cases this makes little difference to the inflation rates.

The RPPP rate relative to some chosen base period t_0 is the level of the current rate that keeps the RER at the same level as in the base period:

$$[\text{RPPP rate vis-à-vis } t_0] = S_t^{\text{RPPP},t_0}$$

$$= S_{t_0} \frac{1 + \text{infl}_{t_0,t}}{1 + \text{infl}^*_{t_0,t}}; \qquad (3.15)$$

$$\text{Relative real rate vis-à-vis } t_0 = \frac{S_t}{S_t^{\text{RPPP},t_0}}$$

$$= \frac{S_t}{S_{t_0}} \frac{1 + \text{infl}^*_{t_0,t}}{1 + \text{infl}_{t_0,t}}, \qquad (3.16)$$

which is unity plus the change in the real rate except that we use each country's CPI inflation (or some similar index) rather than the change in the absolute price of an internationally common basket. In pre-EUR days, the EC or EU ministers of the ERM[16] countries used the RPPP norm when devaluations were negotiated. They went back to the time of the last realignment, and corrected that base-period level for the accumulated inflation differential since then, as in equation (3.15). But the main use of the RPPP for business is that it tells us whether a country has become cheaper, or more expensive, relative to another one. Cheapening countries are good if they are your production centers or your favorite holiday resort, but bad if they are the markets where you sell your output.

---

[16] The Exchange Rate Mechanism—the arrangement that kept members' cross rates stable. See chapter 2.

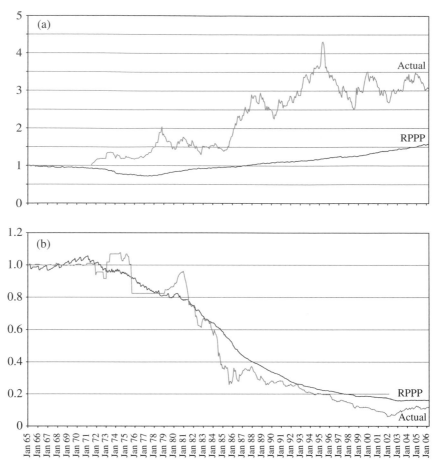

Figure 3.14.   RPPP versus actual rates against USD, 1965 = 1.00. (a) JPY RPPP versus actual; (b) SAR RPPP versus actual. *Source:* Underlying data are from DataStream.

For this reason, deviations from RPPP are important. Are they large? Figure 3.13 shows time-series data, taking January 1965 as the base period, on relative real rates against USD, for the DEM-EUR, JPY, GBP, SAR, and THB. We note four facts.

(i) First, there are huge swings in the medium run, with the real rate appreciating by 50% and then going back—and occasionally even doubling or halving—in a matter of years, not decades. Imagine being caught in this as an exporter.

(ii) Second, in the short run there is lots of inertia: once the rate is above its mean, it tends to stay there for years. Statistical analysis shows that the average half-life is three to five years, meaning that it takes three to five years, on average, for a deviation to shrink to half its original size. Thus, when you get into a bad patch, you can expect that this will be a matter of years rather than weeks or months.

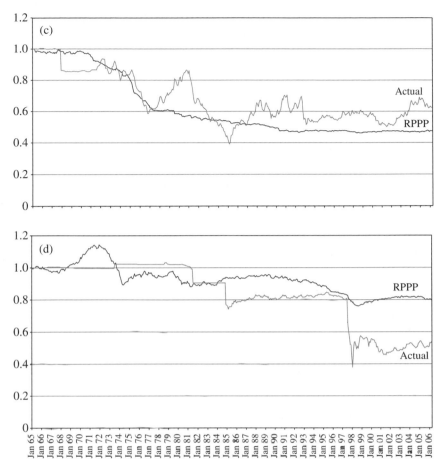

Figure 3.14. *Continued.* (c) GBP RPPP versus actual; (d) THB RPPP versus actual.

(iii) Third, when we look at the RPPP rates and the actual ones separately (figure 3.14), we see that, almost always, in the short run most of the variation in the real rate stems from the nominal rate; the RPPP rate is usually smooth relative to the actual, except of course under a fixed-exchange-rate regime (see graphs) and in hyperinflation cases (not shown). The fall, rise, and fall of the USD against the DEM under presidents Carter and Reagan had nothing to do with inflation. In a way, that's good, because there are good hedge instruments against swings in nominal rates. Hedging nominal rates, in the short run, almost stabilizes the real rate too.

(iv) Even though deviations between actual and RPPP rates are huge, there often does seem to be a link, in the long run. As a result, the long-run variability of the inflation-corrected rate is somewhat lower than that in the nominal rate.

(v) A last fact, impossible to infer from the graphs but to be substantiated in chapter 10, is that changes in both nominal and real exchange rates seem hard to predict.

Should you care? If exchange risk just led to capital gains and losses on assets or liabilities denominated in FC, most (but not all) firms would be able to shrug it off as a nuisance, perhaps, but no more than that. However, there is more: real-rate moves may also make your production sites uncompetitive or your export markets unprofitable, and it is harder for a firm to shrug this off. Another implication worth mentioning is that when two investors from different countries hold the same asset, they will nevertheless realize different real returns if the real exchange rate is changing—which it does all the time. Thus, exchange risk undermines one of the basic assumptions of the CAPM, namely that investors all agree on expected returns and risks. These implications explain why exchange risk gets so much attention in this text.

3.5 CFO's Summary

In this chapter, we have seen how spot markets work. From the treasurer's point of view, one immediately interesting aspect is the possibility for arbitrage and shopping around.

- Arbitrage consists of buying and immediately reselling (or vice versa), thus taking no risk and engaging no capital. One could try to do this across market makers (for one particular exchange rate) or in a triangular way. In practice, the likelihood of corporate treasurers finding such a riskless profit opportunity is tiny. Arbitrage by traders in the wholesale market eliminates this possibility almost as quickly as it arises. In addition, most firms deal in the retail market, where spreads are relatively wide.

- Shopping around consists of finding the best route for a particular transaction. In contrast to arbitrage, shopping around may work—not in the sense of creating large profits, but in the sense of saving on commissions or getting marginally better rates. It is generally worth calling a few banks for the best rate when you need to make a large transaction. And it may pay to compute a triangular cross rate, especially through routes that involve heavily traded currencies like the USD or the EUR. Doing such a computation could enable corporate treasurers to find cheaper routes for undertaking transactions as compared with direct routes.

The spot rate is, by definition, the right number to use if you need to do an actual transaction. But for other purposes, other exchange-rate concepts are quite useful:

- The PPP rate is the ratio of the two price levels. Translating foreign income numbers or investment budgets at this rate tells you what the foreign figures really mean to locals, but expressed in terms that are familiar to you.

- The *real exchange rate* (or the deviation from absolute PPP) is the ratio of the *translated* price levels. It tells you which country is more expensive. This is relevant if you want to evaluate a country as a destination for exports, or a source of imports, or a place to live or produce.

- Both the above concepts require data on price levels, which are not available for all countries. One often makes do with the *deviation from RPPP* relative to a given base period, which estimates to what extent the real exchange rate has changed since then.

There is a clear, but imperfect, relation between actual rates and PPP rates: countries that have gone through high-inflation episodes and, thus, ended up with high nominal prices for all goods, pay high nominal prices for currencies too. But the relation is far from one to one: real rates can be five to one (Norway against China, for instance, in the Big Mac data set). There is also a lot of variability over time, making countries more attractive or unattractive as production centers or markets. Most of that variability comes from the nominal exchange rate: inflation contributes little, except for hyperinflation episodes (with inflation rates measured in 100s or 1,000s per month). Thus, currency risk affects contractual cash flows fixed in FC but also the operations of a firm. It even messes up the CAPM because real exchange risk means that investors from different countries no longer perceive asset returns and risks in the same way.

What are the implications for the CFO? You should remember, first, that variations in the real exchange rate are long-memory events and can be vast. So they can have a big impact on how and where you should produce, and may even force you to change your fundamental strategy. All this comes on top of a shorter-run effect, of course: variations in exchange rates cause capital gains and losses on FC-denominated contractual claims and liabilities.

Your instinctive reaction may be that the firm should try to reduce the impact of these changes. This may be too fast, though: we first need to determine whether any such "hedging" policy really adds value. To be able to answer this question, we need to understand how the hedge instruments work: forwards, futures, swaps, and options. A good knowledge of these derivatives is, of course, also required to make an informed choice among the available hedge instruments. This is what the remainder of part II is about. We begin with forward markets.

3.6 Technical Notes

Technical note 3.1 (what is wrong with the FC/HC convention, in a text-book?). In the text just below example 3.2 we claimed that using the FC/HC convention would mean all the familiar formulas from finance would have to be abandoned. Here is this message in math. Let r^* denote the risk-free interest rate earned on FC, and $\tilde{S}_1$ the (random) future value, in HC of one unit of FC. If you buy one unit of FC, you will have $1 + r^*$ units of them next period, worth $\tilde{S}_1(1 + r^*)$ in HC. Standard finance theory then says that the current price, S_0, should be the future value discounted at a rate $E(\tilde{r}_S)$ that takes into account this risk of $\tilde{S}_1$:

$$S_0 = \frac{E(\tilde{S}_1)(1 + r^*)}{1 + E(\tilde{r}_S)}. \qquad (3.17)$$

This looks quite normal and well-behaved. Now look at what would happen if we had used the inverse rate, $X := S^{-1}$, and if we wanted a theory about how X_0 is set. First substitute $X = S^{-1}$ into the equation and then solve for X_0:

$$\frac{1}{X_0} = \frac{E(1/\tilde{X}_1)(1 + r^*)}{1 + E(\tilde{r}_S)} \quad \Longrightarrow \quad X_0 = \frac{1 + E(\tilde{r}_S)}{E(1/\tilde{X}_1)(1 + r^*)}.$$

All connection with finance is gone. Confusingly, the discount rate is on top, and the expectation is below, and the expectation is about the inverse of X. Clearly, this makes no sense in a finance textbook.

TEST YOUR UNDERSTANDING

Quiz Questions

1. Using the following vocabulary, complete the text: forward; market maker or broker; shopping around; spot; arbitrage; retail; wholesale.

   When trading on the foreign exchange markets, the Bank of Brownsville deals with a (a) on the (b) tier, while an individual uses the (c) tier. If the bank must immediately deliver EUR 2 million to a customer, it purchases them on the (d) market. However, if a customer needs the EUR in three months, the bank buys them on the (e) market. In order to purchase the EUR as cheaply as possible, the bank will look at all quotes it is offered to see if there is an opportunity for (f). If the bank finds that the quotes of two market makers are completely incompatible, it can also make a risk-free profit using (g).

2. From a Canadian's point of view, which of each pair of quotes is the direct quote? Which is the indirect quote?

   (a) CAD/GBP 2.31; GBP/CAD 0.43.
   (b) USD/CAD 0.84; CAD/USD 1.18.
   (c) CAD/EUR 1.54; EUR/CAD 0.65.

3. You are given the following spot quote: EUR/GBP 1.5015–1.5040.

   (a) The above quote is for which currency?
   (b) What is the bid price for EUR in terms of GBP?

4. You read in your newspaper that yesterday's spot quote was CAD/GBP 2.3134–2.3180.

   (a) This is a quote for which currency?
   (b) What is the ask rate for CAD?
   (c) What is the bid rate for GBP?

5. A bank quotes the following rates. Compute the EUR/JPY bid cross -rate (that is, the bank's rate for buying JPY).

	Bid	Ask
EUR/CAD	0.64	0.645
CAD/JPY	0.01	0.012

6. A bank quotes the following rates: CHF/USD 2.5110–2.5140 and JPY/USD 245–246. What is the minimum JPY/CHF bid and the maximum ask cross rate that the bank would quote?

7. A bank is currently quoting the spot rates of EUR/USD 1.3043–1.3053 and NOK/USD 6.15–6.30. What is the lower bound on the bank's bid rate for the NOK in terms of EUR?

8. Suppose that an umbrella costs USD 20 in Atlanta, and the USD/CAD exchange is 0.84. How many CAD do you need to buy the umbrella in Atlanta?

9. Given the bid–ask quotes for JPY/GBP 220–240, at what rate will:

   (a) Mr. Smith purchase GBP?
   (b) Mr. Brown sell GBP?
   (c) Mrs. Green purchase JPY?
   (d) Mrs. Jones sell JPY?

True–False Questions

Indicate the correct statement(s).

1. CPP says that you can make a risk-free profit by buying and selling goods across countries.

2. CPP implies causality. It states that foreign prices are determined by domestic prices and other factors such as production costs, competitive conditions, money supplies, and inflation rates.

3. In order for a firm not to be affected by real exchange risk, CPP must hold not only for the goods a firm produces but also for all production inputs, and for the prices of complementary and substitute goods.

4. The equilibrium exchange rate suggested by the absolute purchasing power parity hypothesis depends on the relative relationship between the prices of a representative consumption bundle in the currencies of two countries.

5. Your purchasing power is the number of representative consumption bundles that you can buy.

6. The real effective exchange rate is the price of an average foreign consumption bundle in units of domestic currency.

7. Relative PPP shows how a consumer's purchasing power changes over time.

8. Absolute PPP may hold even when relative PPP does not because absolute PPP looks at levels at a specific point in time, and levels are always comparable regardless of the composition of the consumption bundle.

9. Given the empirical evidence on the correlation between the nominal and real exchange rate, it is possible to use the nominal financial instruments to hedge real exchange risk.

10. PPP is based on the idea that the demand for a country's currency is derived from the demand for that country's goods as well as the currency itself.

Multiple-Choice Questions

Choose the correct answer(s).

1. CPP may not hold because:

    (a) the prices for individual goods are sticky;
    (b) transaction costs increase the bounds on deviations from CPP, making it more difficult to arbitrage away price differences;
    (c) quotas and voluntary export restraints limit the ability to arbitrage across goods markets;
    (d) parallel imports lead to two different prices for the same good;
    (e) the prices of tradable goods fluctuate too much, which makes it difficult to take advantage of arbitrage opportunities.

2. Absolute PPP may not hold when:

    (a) the prices of individual goods in the consumption bundle consistently deviate from CPP across two countries;
    (b) the consumption bundles of different countries are not the same;
    (c) the prices for individual goods are sticky;
    (d) there are tariffs, quotas, and voluntary export restraints;
    (e) competition is perfect.

3. Relative PPP is relevant because:

    (a) empirical tests have shown that absolute PPP is always violated, while relative PPP is a good predictor of short-term exchange-rate exposure;
    (b) consumption bundles are not always comparable across countries;

(c) price levels are not stationary over time;

(d) investors care about the real return on their international portfolio investments;

(e) investors care about the nominal return on their international portfolio investments.

Applications

1. You have just graduated from the University of Florida and are leaving on a whirlwind tour to see some friends. You wish to spend USD 1,000 each in Germany, New Zealand, and Great Britain (USD 3,000 in total). Your bank offers you the following bid-ask quotes: USD/EUR 1.304–1.305, USD/NZD 0.67–0.69, and USD/GBP 1.90–1.95.

   (a) If you accept these quotes, how many EUR, NZD, and GBP do you have at departure?

   (b) If you return with EUR 300, NZD 1,000, and GBP 75, and the exchange rates are unchanged, how many USD do you have?

   (c) Suppose that instead of selling your remaining EUR 300 once you return home, you want to sell them in Great Britain. At the train station, you are offered GBP/EUR 0.66–0.68, while a bank three blocks from the station offers GBP/EUR 0.665–0.675. At what rate are you willing to sell your EUR 300? How many GBP will you receive?

2. Abitibi Bank quotes JPY/EUR 155-165, and Bathurst Bank quotes EUR/JPY 0.0059–0.0063.

   (a) Are these quotes identical?

   (b) If not, is there a possibility for shopping around or arbitrage?

   (c) If there is an arbitrage opportunity, how would you profit from it?

The following spot rates against the GBP are taken from the *Financial Times* of Friday, February 2, 2007. Use the quotes to answer the questions in applications 3–5 below.

Country	Code	Midpoint	Change	Spread
Czech Rep.	CZK	42.7945	+0.1868	616–273
Denmark	DKK	11.30929	+0.0289	065–119
Euro area	EUR	1.5172	+0.0039	168–175
Norway	NOK	12.3321	+0.0394	263–379
Russia	RUB	52.1528	−0.0368	376–679
Switzerland	CHF	2.4531	+0.0040	522–540
Turkey	TRY	2.7656	−0.0050	614–698

Note. Bid-ask spreads show only the last three decimal places. When the ask seems to be smaller then the bid, add 1,000.

3. What are the bid-ask quotes for:

    (a) CZK/GBP?

    (b) DKK/GBP?

    (c) EUR/GBP?

    (d) NOK/GBP?

4. What are the bid-ask quotes for:

    (a) GBP/CZK?

    (b) GBP/DKK?

    (c) GBP/EUR?

    (d) GBP/NOK?

5. What are the cross bid-ask rates for:

    (a) RUB/CHF?

    (b) NOK/TRY?

    (c) DKK/EUR?

    (d) CZK/CHF?

6. In figure 2.5 I showed plots of the gold price and mentioned that if we had corrected for inflation, then the 1980 price would be seen to be much above the current peak: obviously, the small percentage price rise of gold, between 1980 and 2007, must have been way below the percentage rise of the U.S. CPI.

    (a) In the above we presumably use U.S. CPI rate to deflate the USD prices. But can this result be generalized to all countries? Is this conclusion necessarily also valid for Japanese or German investors? Why (not)?

    (b) If you think the result does not necessarily hold true elsewhere, what would you bet with respect to a hyperinflator like Zimbabwe? If inflation is much higher, then the real price of gold must have fallen even more—or am I wrong in this?

    (c) What would guarantee identical real price paths in all countries: APPP, RPPP, or what?

4

Understanding Forward
Exchange Rates for Currency

In this chapter, we discuss forward contracts in perfect financial markets. Specifically, we assume that there are no transaction costs; there are no taxes, or at least they are nondiscriminatory: there is but one overall income number, with all capital gains and interest earned being taxable and all capital losses and interest paid deductible; there is no default risk; and people act as price takers in free and open markets for currency and loans or deposits. Most of the implications of market imperfections will be discussed in later chapters; in this chapter we provide the fundamental insights that will only need to be mildly qualified later.

In section 4.1, we describe the characteristics of a forward contract and how forward rates are quoted in the market. In section 4.2, we show, with a simple diagram, the relationship between the money markets, spot markets, and forward markets. Using the mechanisms that enforce the law of one price, section 4.3 then presents the covered interest parity theorem. Two ostensibly unconnected issues are dealt with in section 4.4: how do we determine the market value of an outstanding forward contract, and how does the forward price relate to the expected future spot price. We wrap up in section 4.5.

4.1 Introduction to Forward Contracts

4.1.1 Basics

Recall, from the first chapter, the definition of a forward contract. Like a spot transaction, a forward contract stipulates how many units of foreign currency are to be bought or sold and at what exchange rate. The difference with a spot deal, of course, is that delivery and payment for a forward contract take place in the future (for example, one month from now) rather than one or two working days from now, as in a spot contract. The rate that is used for all contracts initiated at time t and maturing at some future moment T is called the time-t forward rate for delivery date T. We denote it as $F_{t,T}$.

Table 4.1. Spot and forward quotes, mid-market rates in Toronto at noon. *Source: Globe and Mail.*

	Outright		Swap rate Premium or discount, in cents	
	CAD per USD	USD per CAD	CAD per USD	USD per CAD
U.S. Canada spot	1.3211	0.7569		
1 month forward	1.3218	0.7565	+0.07	−0.05
2 months forward	1.3224	0.7562	+0.13	−0.07
3 months forward	1.3229	0.7559	+0.18	−0.10
6 months forward	1.3246	0.7549	+0.35	−0.20
12 months forward	1.3266	0.7538	+0.55	−0.31
3 years forward	1.3316	0.7510	+1.05	−0.59
5 years forward	1.3579	0.7364	+3.68	−0.05
7 years forward	1.3921	0.7183	+7.10	−3.86
10 years forward	1.4546	0.6875	+13.36	−6.94

Like spot markets, forward markets are not organized exchanges, but over-the-counter (OTC) markets, where banks act as market makers or look for counterparts via electronic auction systems or brokers. The most active forward markets are the markets for 30 and 90 days, and contracts for 180, 270, and 360 days are also quite common. Bankers nowadays quote rates up to ten years forward, and occasionally even beyond that, but the very-long-term markets are quite thin. Recall, lastly, that any multiple of 30 days means that, relative to a spot contract, one extra calendar month has to be added to the spot delivery date, and that the delivery date must be a working day. Thus, if day $[t + 2$ plus n months] is not a working day, we may move forward to the nearest working day, unless this would make us change months, in which case we would move back.

Example 4.1. A 180-day contract signed on Thursday, March 2, 2006, is normally settled on September 6. Why? The initiation day being a Thursday, the "spot" settlement date is Monday, March 6. Add 6 months; September 6, being a working day (Wednesday), is then the settlement date.

4.1.2 Market Conventions for Quoting Forward Rates

Forward exchange rates can be quoted in two ways. The most natural and simple quote is to give the actual rate, sometimes called the *outright* rate. This convention is used in, for instance, the *Wall Street Journal*, the *Frankfurter Allgemeine*, and the Canadian *Globe and Mail*. The *Globe and Mail* is one of the few newspapers also quoting long-term rates, as table 4.1 shows.

In table 4.1, the CAD/USD forward rate exceeds the spot rate for all maturities. Traders would say that the USD trades *at a premium*. Obviously, if the CAD/USD rate is at a premium, the USD/CAD forward rates must be below the USD/CAD spot rate; that is, the CAD must trade *at a discount*.

The second way of expressing a forward rate is to quote the difference between the outright forward rate and the spot rate—that is, quote the premium or discount. A forward rate quoted this way is called a swap rate.[1] Antwerp's *De Tijd*, or the London *Financial Times*, for example, used to follow this convention. Since both newspapers actually showed bid and ask quotes, we will postpone actual excerpts from these newspapers until the next chapter, where spreads are taken into consideration. The rightmost two columns in table 4.1 shows how the *Globe and Mail* quotes would have looked in swap-rate form. In that table, the sign of the swap rate is indicated by a plus or a minus sign. The *Financial Times* used to denote the sign as pm (premium) or dis (discount).

The origin of the term swap rate is the swap contract. In the context of the forward market, a swap contract is a spot contract immediately combined with a forward contract in the opposite direction.

Example 4.2. To invest in the U.S. stock market for a few months, a Portuguese investor buys USD 100,000 at EUR/USD 1.10. In order to reduce the exchange risk, she immediately sells forward USD 100,000 for 90 days, at EUR/USD 1.101. The combined spot and forward contract—in opposite directions—is a swap contract. The swap rate, EUR/USD 0.1 (cent), is the difference between the rate at which the investor buys and the rate at which she sells.

To emphasize the difference between a stand-alone forward contract and a swap contract, a stand-alone forward contract is sometimes called an outright contract. Thus, the two quoting conventions described above have their roots in the two types of contracts. Today, the outright rate and the swap rate are simply ways of quoting, used whether or not you combine the forward trade with a reverse spot trade.[2]

One key result of this chapter is that there is a one-to-one link between the swap rate and the interest rates for the two currencies. To explain this relation, we first show how the spot market and the forward market are linked to each other by the money markets for each of the two currencies. But first we need to agree on a convention for denoting risk-free returns.

4.1.2.1 Our Convention for Expressing Risk-Free Returns

We adopt the following terminology: the (effective) risk-free (rate of) return is the simple percentage difference between the initial, time-t value and the final, time-T value of a nominally risk-free asset over that holding period.

---

[1] Confusingly, the terms swap contract and swap rate can have other meanings, as we shall explain in chapter 7.

[2] Sometimes, the swap rate is called the cost of the swap, but to financial economists that is a very dubious concept: at the moment the contract is initiated, both the spot and the forward part are zero-NPV deals, that is, their market value is zero. So the swap rate is not the cost of the swap in the same way a stock price measures the cost of a stock. It is more like an accounting concept of cost, in the style of the interest being the cost of a loan.

Example 4.3. Suppose that you deposit CLP 100,000 for four years and that the deposit will be worth CLP 121,000 at maturity. The four-year effective (rate of) return is

$$r_{t,T} = \frac{121{,}000 - 100{,}000}{100{,}000} = 0.21 = 21\%. \qquad (4.1)$$

You can also invest for nine months. Suppose that the value of this deposit after nine months is 104,200. Then the nine-month effective return is

$$r_{t,T} = \frac{104{,}200 - 100{,}000}{100{,}000} = 0.042 = 4.2\%. \qquad (4.2)$$

Of course, at any moment in time, the rate of return you can get depends on the time to maturity, which equals $T - t = 4$ years in the first example. Thus, as in the above examples, we always equip the rate of return, r, with two subscripts: $r_{t,T}$. In addition, we need to distinguish between the domestic and the foreign rate of return. We do this by denoting the domestic and the foreign returns by $r_{t,T}$ and $r_{t,T}^*$, respectively.

It is important to understand that the above returns, 21% for four years and 4.2% for nine months, are not expressed on an annual basis. This is a deviation from actual practice: bankers always quote rates that are expressed on an annual basis. We shall call such a *per annum (p.a.)* percentage an *interest rate*. If the time to maturity of the investment or loan is less than one year, your banker will typically quote you a simple p.a. interest rate. Given the simple p.a. interest rate, you can then compute the effective return as

$$r_{t,T} = [\text{time to maturity, in years}]$$
$$\times [\text{simple p.a. interest rate for that maturity}]. \qquad (4.3)$$

Example 4.4. Suppose that the p.a. simple interest rate for a three-month investment is 10%. The time to maturity, $T - t$, is $\frac{1}{4}$ of a year. The effective return is then

$$r_{t,T} = \tfrac{1}{4} \times 0.10 = 0.025. \qquad (4.4)$$

The convention we adopt in this text is to express all formulas in terms of effective returns, that is, simple percentage differences between end values and initial values. One alternative would be to express returns in terms of *per annum* simple interest rates—that is, we could have written, for instance, $(T-t)R_{t,T}$ (where capital R would be the simple interest on a p.a. basis) instead of $r_{t,T}$. Unfortunately, all formulas would then look more complicated. Worse, there are many other ways of quoting an interest rate in p.a. terms, such as interest with annual, or monthly, or weekly, or even daily compounding; or banker's discount; or continuously compounded interest. To keep from having to present each formula in many versions (depending on whether you start from a simple rate, or a compound rate, etc.), we assume that you have already done your homework and have computed the effective return from your p.a.

interest rate. Appendix 4.6 shows how effective returns can be computed if the p.a. rate you start from is not a simple interest rate. That appendix also shows how returns should *not* be computed.

Thus, in this section, we will consider four related markets: the spot market, the forward market, and the home and foreign money markets. One crucial insight we want to convey is that any transaction in one of these markets can be replicated by a combination of transactions in the other three. Let us look at the details.

4.2 The Relation between Exchange and Money Markets

We have already seen how, using the spot market, one type of currency can be transformed into another at time t. For instance, you pay home currency to a bank and you receive foreign currency. Think of one wad of HC bank notes being exchanged for another wad of FC notes. Or even better, since spot deals are settled on the second working day, think of a spot transaction as an exchange of two checks that will clear two working days from now. From now, we denote the amounts by *HC* and *FC*. To make clear that we mean amounts, not names, they are written as mathematical symbols (in an italic font), not as HC and FC, our notation for names of the currencies. Another notational difference between currency names and amounts is that *HC* and *FC* always get a time subscript. To emphasize the fact that, in the above example, the amounts are delivered (almost) immediately, we add the t (current time) subscript: you pay an amount HC_t in home currency and you receive an amount FC_t of foreign currency.

By analogy to our exchange-of-checks idea for a spot deal, then, we can picture a forward contract as an exchange of two promissory notes, with face values HC_T and FC_T, respectively.

Example 4.5. Suppose you sell forward USD 100,000 at EUR/USD 0.75 for December 31. (Note that the quote defines the euro as the HC.) Then

- you commit to deliver USD 100,000, which is similar to signing a promissory note (PN) with face value FC_T = USD 100,000 on December 31 and handing it over to the bank;

- the bank promises to pay you EUR 75,000, which is similar to giving you a signed PN with face value HC_T = EUR 75,000 for that date.

Intimately linked to the exchange markets are the money markets for the home and foreign countries, that is, the markets for short-term deposits and loans. A HC deposit of GBP 1m "spot"[3] for one year at 4% means that you pay

---

[3] A spot deposit or loan starts the second working day. For one-day deposits, one can also define the starting date as today ("overnight") or tomorrow ("tomorrow/next"), but this must then be made explicit. In all our examples, the deals are spot—the default option in real life, too.

an amount of GBP 1m to the bank now, and the bank pays you an amount GBP 1.04m at time T. This is similar to handing over the spot money amount of $HC_t = 1$m in return for a PN with face value $HC_T = 1.04$m. Likewise, if you borrow GBP 10m at 6% over one year, this is tantamount to you receiving a check with face value $HC_t = $ GBP 10m in return for a promissory note with face value $HC_T = $ GBP 10.6m.

4.2.1 Graphical Representation of Chains of Transactions: An Example

For the remainder of this section, we take the Chilean peso (CLP) as our home currency and the Norwegian crown (NOK) as the foreign one. Suppose that the spot rate is $S_t = $ CLP/NOK 100, the four-year forward rate is $F_{t,T} = $ CLP/NOK 110, the effective CLP four-year risk-free rate of return is $r_{t,T} = 21\%$, and the NOK one is $r_{t,T}^* = 10\%$. Very often we will discuss sequences of deals, or combinations of deals. Consider, for example, a Chilean investor who has CLP 100,000 to invest. He goes for an NOK deposit "swapped into CLP," that is, an NOK deposit combined with a spot purchase and a forward sale. Let us see what the final outcome is.

Example 4.6. The investor converts his CLP 100,000 into an amount NOK_t, deposits this for four years, and sells forward the proceeds NOK_T in order to obtain a risk-free amount of CLP four years from now. The outcome is computed as follows:

1. Buy spot NOK: the input given to the bank is CLP 100,000, so the output of the spot deal, received from the bank, is $100,000 \times 1/100 = 1,000$ crowns.

2. Invest these NOK at 10%: the input into the money market operation is $NOK_t = 1,000$, so after four years you will receive from the bank an output equal to $1,000 \times 1.10 = 1,100$ crowns.

3. This future NOK outcome is already being sold forward at t; that is, right now you immediately cover or hedge the NOK deposit in the forward market so as to make its time-T value risk free rather than contingent on the time-T spot rate. The input for this transaction is $NOK_T = 1,100$, and the output in CLP at time T will be $1,100 \times 110 = 121,000$.

There is nothing difficult about this, except perhaps that by the time you finish reading step 3 you have already half forgotten the previous steps. We need a way to make clear at one glance what this deal is about, how it relates to other deals, and what the alternatives are. One step in the right direction is to adopt the following notation:

$$
\begin{array}{cccc}
\text{Buy spot:} & & \text{Deposit:} & \text{Sell forward:} \\
\times 1/100 & & \times 1.10 & \times 110 \\
HC_t = 100,000 \overset{\displaystyle\rightharpoonup}{} & FC_t = 1,000 \overset{\displaystyle\rightharpoonup}{} & FC_T = 1,100 \overset{\displaystyle\rightharpoonup}{} & HC_T = 121,000.
\end{array}
$$

So the arrows show how you go from a spot CLP position into a spot NOK one (the spot deal), and so on. We can further improve upon this by arranging the amounts in a diagram, where each kind of position has a fixed location. There

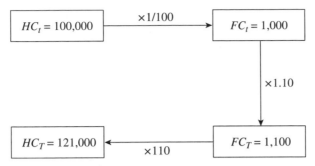

Figure 4.1. Spot/forward/money market diagram: example 4.6.

are four kinds of money in play: foreign and domestic, each coming in a day-t and a day-T version. Let us show these on a diagram, with HC on the left and FC on the right, and with time t on top and time T below. Figure 4.1 shows the result for the above example.

We can now generalize. Suppose the spot rate is still CLP/NOK 100, the four-year forward rate is CLP/NOK 110, the CLP risk-free rate is 21% effective, and the NOK rate is 10%. The diagram in figure 4.2 summarizes all transactions open to the treasurer. It is to be read as follows:

- Any "t"-subscripted symbol HC_t (FC_t) refers to an *amount* of spot money; and any "T"-subscripted symbol HC_T (FC_T) refers to a T-dated known amount of money, e.g., promised under a PN, A/P, A/R, or deposit, or forward contract.

- Any possible transaction (spot or forward sale or purchase; home or foreign money-market deal) is shown as an arrow. A transaction is characterized by two numbers: (a) your position before the transaction, an input amount you surrender to the bank, and (b) your position after the transaction, the output amount you receive from the bank. The arrow starts from the (a) part and ends at the (b) part. For example,

  — a move $HC_t \rightarrow FC_t$ refers to *buying* FC—spot (see "t");
  — a move $FC_T \rightarrow HC_T$ refers to *selling* FC—forward (see "T");
  — a move $HC_t \rightarrow HC_T$ refers to *investing* or *lending* HC;
  — a move $FC_T \rightarrow FC_t$ refers to *borrowing* against an FC income—e.g., discounting an FC PN.

- Next to each arrow we write the factor by which its "input" amount has to be multiplied to compute the "output" amount. Again, "input" is what you give to the bank (at either t or T), "output" is what you receive from it.

4.2.2 The General Spot/Forward/Money Market Diagram

To use the diagram, first identify the starting position. This is where you have money right now, such as FC_T (a customer will pay you FC in future, or a

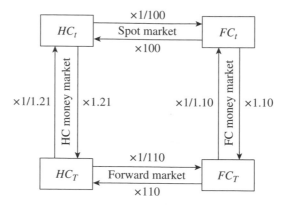

Figure 4.2.   Spot/forward/money market diagram: the general picture.

deposit will expire). Then determine the desired end point, such as HC_T (you want future HC instead; that is, you want to eliminate the exchange risk). Third, determine by which route you want to go from START to END. Lastly, follow the chosen route, sequentially multiplying the starting amount by all the numbers you see along the path.

Example 4.7. In example 4.6, the path is $HC_t \rightarrow FC_t \rightarrow FC_T \rightarrow HC_T$, and the end outcome, starting from $HC_t = 100{,}000$, is immediately computed as

$$HC_T = 100{,}000 \times \frac{1}{100} \times 1.10 \times 110 = 121{,}000. \tag{4.5}$$

The alert reader will already have noted that this is a synthetic HC deposit, constructed out of an FC deposit and a swap, and that (here) it has exactly the same return as the direct solution. Indeed, the alternative route, $HC_t \rightarrow HC_T$, yields $100{,}000 \times 1.21 = 121{,}000$. (In *im*perfect markets this equivalence of both paths will no longer be generally true, as we shall see in the next chapter.)

Example 4.8. Suppose that a customer of yours will pay NOK 6.5m at time T, four years from now, but you need cash pesos to pay your suppliers and workers. You decide to sell forward, and take out a CLP loan with a time-T value that, including interest, exactly matches the proceeds of the forward sale. How much can you borrow on the basis of this invoice without taking any exchange risk?
    The path chosen is $FC_T (= \text{NOK } 6{,}500{,}000) \rightarrow HC_T \rightarrow HC_t$, and it yields

$$6.5\text{m} \times 110 \times \frac{1}{1.21} = \text{CLP } 590{,}909{,}090.91. \tag{4.6}$$

The clever reader will again eagerly point out that there is an alternative: borrow NOK against the future inflow (that is, borrow such that the loan cum interest is serviced by the NOK inflow), and convert the proceeds of the loan into CLP. Again, in our assumedly perfect market, the outcome is identical: $6.5\text{m}/1.10 \times 100 = \text{CLP } 590{,}909{,}090.91$. Thus, the diagram allows us to quickly understand the purpose and see the outcome of a sequence of transactions.

It also shows there are always two routes that lead from a given starting point to a given end point—a useful insight for shopping-around purposes. The advantage of using the diagram will be even more marked when we add bid–ask spreads in all markets (next chapter) or when we study forward forwards or forward rate agreements and their relationship to forward contracts (appendix 4.7),[4] or when we explain forward forward swaps (chapter 5).

4.3 The Law of One Price and Covered Interest Parity

The sequences of transactions that can be undertaken in the exchange and money markets, as summarized in figure 4.2, can be classified into two types.

1. You could do a sequence of transactions that forms a round-trip. In terms of figure 4.2, a round-trip means that you start in a particular box, and then make four transactions that bring you back to the starting point. For example, you may consider the sequence $HC_T \rightarrow HC_t \rightarrow FC_t \rightarrow FC_T \rightarrow HC_T$. In terms of the underlying transactions, this means that you borrow CLP, convert the proceeds of the CLP loan into NOK, and invest these NOK; the proceeds of the investment are then immediately sold forward, back into CLP. The question that interests you is whether the CLP proceeds of the forward sale are more than enough to pay off the original CLP loan. If so, you have identified a way to make a sure profit without using any of your own capital. Thus, the idea behind a round-trip transaction is *arbitrage*, as defined in chapter 3.

2. Alternatively, you could consider a sequence of transactions where you end up in a box that is not the same as the box from which you start. The two examples 4.7 and 4.8 describe such non-round-trip sequences. Trips like that have an economic rationale. In the first example, for instance, the investor wants to invest CLP, and the question here is whether the swapped NOK investment ($CLP_t \rightarrow NOK_t \rightarrow NOK_T \rightarrow CLP_T$) yields more than a direct CLP investment ($CLP_t \rightarrow CLP_T$). Using the terminology of chapter 3, this would be an example of *shopping around* for the best alternative.

In what follows, we want to establish the following two key results:

1. To rule out arbitrage in perfect markets, the following equality must hold:

$$F_{t,T} = S_t \frac{1 + r_{t,T}}{1 + r_{t,T}^*}. \tag{4.7}$$

(In *im*perfect markets, this sharp equality will be watered down to a zone of admissible values, but the zone is quite narrow.)

---

[4] Forward forwards (FFs) and forward rate agreements (FRAs) are contracts that fix the interest rate for a deposit or loan that will be made (say) six months from now, for (say) three months. This can be viewed as a six-month forward deal on a (then) three-month interest rate. See the appendix on forward interest rates.

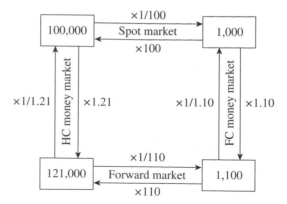

Figure 4.3.   Spot/forward/money market diagram: arbitrage computations.

2. If equation (4.7) holds, shopping-around computations are a waste of time since the two routes that lead from a given initial position A to a desired end position B produce exactly the same. Stated positively, shopping around can (and will) be useful only because of imperfections.

4.3.1   Arbitrage and Covered Interest Parity

In this section, we use an arbitrage argument to verify equation (4.7), a relationship called the *covered interest parity* (CIP) theorem. The theorem is evidently satisfied in our example:

$$110 = F_{t,T} = S_t \frac{1 + r_{t,T}}{1 + r_{t,T}^*} = 100\frac{1.21}{1.10} = 110. \tag{4.8}$$

Arbitrage, we know, means full-circle round-trips through the diagram. There are two ways to go around the entire diagram: clockwise and counterclockwise. Follow the trips on figure 4.3, where the symbols for amounts have been replaced by the specific numbers used in the numerical examples. We should not make any profit if the rate is 110, and we should make free money as soon as the rate does deviate.

Clockwise round-trip. The starting point of a round-trip is evidently immaterial, but let us commence with an HC loan: this makes it eminently clear that no own capital is being used. Also the starting amount is immaterial, so let us pick an amount that produces conveniently round numbers all around: we write a PN with face value $CLP_T = 121{,}000$. We discount this,[5] and convert the proceeds of this loan into crowns, which are invested. At the same moment we already sell forward the future crown balance. The final outcome is

$$121{,}000 \times \frac{1}{1.21} \times \frac{1}{100} \times 1.10 \times 110 = 121{,}000. \tag{4.9}$$

---

[5] Discounting a PN or a T-bill or a trade bill not only means computing its PV; it often means borrowing against the claim. In practice, under such a loan the borrower would typically also cede the claim to the financier, as security. This lowers the lender's risk and makes the loan cheaper.

So we break even exactly: the forward sale nets us exactly what we need to pay back the loan.

DIY Problem 4.1. Show, similarly, that the counterclockwise round-trip also exactly breaks even. For your convenience, start by writing a PN with face value $NOK_T = 1,100$. What is the path? What is the outcome?

What if $F_{t,T}$ is too low, say 109? If one price is too low relative to another price (or set of other prices), we can make money by *buying* at this too-low rate. The trip where we buy forward is the counterclockwise one. We start as before, except for the new price in the last step:

$$1,100 \times \frac{1}{1.10} \times 100 \times 1.21 \times \frac{1}{109} = 1110.09 > 1,100. \qquad (4.10)$$

So the forward purchase nets us 1110.09 pesos, 10.09 more than the 1,100 we need to pay back the loan.

DIY Problem 4.2. What if $F_{t,T}$ is too high, say 111? Indicate the path and calculate the arbitrage profit.

DIY Problem 4.3. To generalize these numerical results, we now start with PNs with face value 1, and replace all rates by their symbols. One no-arb condition is that the proceeds of the clockwise trip should not exceed the starting amount, unity. Explain how this leads to the following expression:

$$\frac{1}{1 + r_{t,T}} \times \frac{1}{S_t} \times (1 + r_{t,T}^*) \times F_{t,T} \leqslant 1. \qquad (4.11)$$

This produces an inequality constraint,

$$F_{t,T} \leqslant S_t \frac{1 + r_{t,T}}{1 + r_{t,T}^*}.$$

Write the no-arbitrage-profit condition for the counterclockwise trip and express it as another inequality constraint. Lastly, derive the CIP.

4.3.2 (The Pointlessness of) Shopping Around

The diagram in figure 4.2 also tells us that any non-round-trip sequence of transactions can be routed two ways. For instance, you can go directly from CLP_t to CLP_T, or you can go via NOK_t and NOK_T. In two earlier examples, 4.7 and 4.8, we already illustrated our claim that, in perfect markets where CIP holds, both ways to implement a trip produce exactly the same outcome. It is simple to show that this holds for all of the ten other possible trips one could think of in this diagram; but it would also be so tedious that we leave this as an exercise to any nonbeliever in the audience. It would also be a bit pointless, because in reality shopping around does matter. As we show in the next chapter, the route you choose for your trip may matter because of

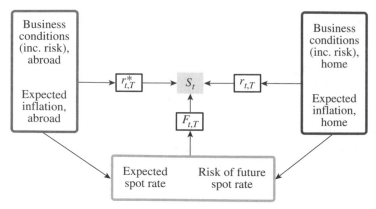

Figure 4.4. Appending underlying stories to the variables in CIP.

imperfections like bid–ask spreads, taxes (if asymmetric), information costs (if leading to inconsistent risk spreads asked by home and foreign banks), and legal subtleties associated with swaps.

4.3.3 Infrequently Asked Questions on CIP

Before we move on to new challenges such as the market value of a forward contract and the relation of the forward rate to expected future spot rates, a few crucial comments are in order. We first talk about causality, then about why pros always quote the swap rate rather than the outright, and lastly about taxes.

4.3.3.1 *Covered Interest Parity and Causality*

As we have seen, in perfect markets the forward rate is linked to the spot rate by pure arbitrage. Such an arbitrage argument, however, does not imply any causality. CIP is merely an application of the law of one price, and the statement that two perfect substitutes should have the same price does not tell us where that "one price" comes from. Stated differently, showing $F_{t,T}$ as the left-hand-side variable (as we did in equation (4.7)) does not imply that the forward rate is a "dependent" variable, determined by the spot rate and the two interest rates. Rather, what covered interest parity says is that the four variables (the spot rate, the forward rate, and the two interest rates) are determined jointly, and that the equilibrium outcome should satisfy equation (4.7). The fact that the spot market represents less than 50% of the total turnover likewise suggests that the forward market is not just an appendage to the spot market. Thus, it is impossible to say, either in theory or in practice, which is the tail and which is the dog, here.

Although CIP itself does not say which term causes which, many economists and practitioners do have theories about one or more terms that appear in the CIP theorem. One such theory is the Fisher equation, which says that interest rates reflect expected inflation and the real return that investors require.

Another theory suggests that the forward rate reflects the market's expectation about the (unknown) future spot rate, $\tilde{S}_T$.[6] We shall argue in section 4.4 that the latter theory is true in a risk-adjusted sense. In short, while there is no causality in CIP itself, one can append stories and theories to items in the formula. Then CIP becomes an ingredient in a richer economic model with causality relations galore—but S, F, r, and r^* would all be endogenous, determined by outside forces and circumstances. Figure 4.4 outlines a plausible causal story of how interest rates and the forward rate are set and, together, imply the spot rate.

4.3.3.2 CIP and the Swap Rate

When the forward rate exceeds the spot rate, the foreign currency is said to be *at a premium*. Otherwise, the currency is *at a discount* ($F_{t,T} < S_t$), or *at par* ($F_{t,T} = S_t$). In this text, we often use the word premium irrespective of its sign; that is, we treat the discount as a negative premium. From (4.7), the sign of the premium uniquely depends on the sign of $r_{t,T} - r_{t,T}^*$:

$$[\text{Swap rate}]_{t,T} \stackrel{\text{def}}{=} F_{t,T} - S_t$$

$$= S_t \left[\frac{1 + r_{t,T}}{1 + r_{t,T}^*} - 1 \right]$$

$$= S_t \left[\frac{1 + r_{t,T}}{1 + r_{t,T}^*} - \frac{1 + r_{t,T}^*}{1 + r_{t,T}^*} \right]$$

$$= S_t \left[\frac{r_{t,T} - r_{t,T}^*}{1 + r_{t,T}^*} \right]; \tag{4.12}$$

$$\Longrightarrow \quad \frac{\partial \cdot}{\partial S_t} = \left[\frac{r_{t,T} - r_{t,T}^*}{1 + r_{t,T}^*} \right] \approx r_{t,T} - r_{t,T}^*. \tag{4.13}$$

Thus, a higher domestic return means that the forward rate is at a premium, and vice versa. To a close approximation (with low foreign interest rates and/or short maturities), the percentage swap rate is simply the effective return differential.

To remember this easily, think of the following. If there were a pronounced premium, we would tend to believe that this signals an expected appreciation for the foreign currency.[7] That is, the foreign currency is "strong." But strong currencies are also associated with low interest rates: it is the weak money that has to offer a high rate to shore up its current value. In short, a positive forward premium goes together with a low interest rate because both are traditionally associated with a strong currency.

---

[6] We use a tilde (˜) above a symbol to indicate that the variable is random or uncertain.

[7] Empirically, the strength of a currency is predicted by the swap rate only in the case of pronounced premia. When interest rates are quite similar and expectations rather diffuse, as is typically the case among OECD mainstream countries, the effects of risk premia and transaction costs appear to swamp any expectation effect. See chapter 10.

A second corollary from the CIP theorem is that, whenever the spot rate changes, all forward rates must change in lockstep. In old, precomputer days, this was quite a burden to traders/market makers, who would have to manually recompute all their forward quotes. Fortunately, traders soon noticed that the swap rate is relatively insensitive to changes in the spot rate. That is, when you quote a spot rate and a swap rate, then you make only a small error if you do not change the swap rate every time S changes.

Example 4.9. Let the p.a. simple interest rates be 4 and 3% (HC and FC, respectively). If S_t changes from 100 to 100.5—a huge change—the theoretical one-month forward changes too, and so does the swap rate, but the latter effect is minute:

	Spot	Forward	Swap rate
$Level_0$	100.0	$100.0 \times \frac{1.003\,333}{1.002\,500} = 100.0831$	0.0831
$Level_1$	100.5	$100.5 \times \frac{1.003\,333}{1.002\,500} = 100.5835$	0.0835
Change	0.5	0.5004	0.0004

The rule of thumb of not updating the swap rate all the time used to work reasonably well because, in the olden days, interest rates were low[8] and rather similar across currencies (the gold standard, remember?), and maturities short. This makes the fraction on the right-hand side of (4.12) a very small number. In addition, interest rates used to vary far less often than spot exchange rates. Nowadays, of course, computers make it very easy to adjust all rates simultaneously without creating arbitrage opportunities, so we no longer need the trick with the swap rates. But while the motivation for using swap rates is gone, the habit has stuck.

DIY Problem 4.4. Use the numbers of example 4.9 to numerically evaluate the partial derivative in equation (4.13):

$$\frac{\partial (F_{t,T} - S_t)}{\partial S_t} = \left[\frac{r_{t,T} - r_{t,T}^*}{1 + r_{t,T}^*} \right] \approx r_{t,T} - r_{t,T}^*.$$

Check whether this is a small number, when interest rates are low (and rather similar across currencies) and maturities short. (If so, it means that the swap rate hardly changes when the spot rate moves.) Also check that the analytical result matches the calculations in the example.

We now bring up an issue we have been utterly silent about thus far: taxes.

---

[8] During the Napoleonic Wars, for instance, the United Kingdom issued perpetual (!) debt (the consolidated war debt, or *consol*) with an interest rate of 3.25%. Toward the end of the nineteenth century, Belgium issued perpetual debt with a 2.75% coupon (to pay off a Dutch toll on ships plying for Antwerp). Rates crept up in the inflationary 1970s to, in some countries, 20% short term or 15% long term around 1982. They then fell slowly to quite low levels, as a result of falling inflation, lower government deficits, and, in the first years of the twenty-first century, high uncertainty and a recession—the "flight for safety" effect.

Table 4.2. HC and swapped FC investments with nondiscriminatory taxes.

	Invest CLP 100		Invest NOK 1 and hedge	
Initial investment		100	$1 \times 100 =$	100
Final value	$100 \times 1.21 =$	121	$[1 \times 1.10] \times 110 =$	121
Income		21		21
Interest		21	$[1 \times 0.10] \times 110 =$	11
Capital gain		0	$110 - 100 =$	10
Taxable		21		21
Tax (33.33%)		7		7
After-tax income		14		14

4.3.3.3 CIP: Capital Gains versus Interest Income, and Taxes

When comparing the direct and synthetic HC deposits, in example 4.7, we ignored taxes. This, we now show, is fine as long as the tax law does not discriminate between interest income and capital gains.

The first point you should be aware of is that, by going for a swapped FC deposit instead of an HC one, the total return is in principle unaffected but the relative weight of the interest and capital-gain components is changed. Consider our Chilean investor who compares an investment in NOK to one in CLP. Given the spot rate of 100, we consider investments of 100 CLP or 1 NOK. In table 4.2 you see that the CLP investment yields interest income only, while the NOK deposit earns interest (10 pence, exchanged at the forward rate 110) and a capital gain (you buy the principal at 100, and sell later at 110). But in both cases, total income is 21. (This is indeed the origin of the name CIP: the return, covered, is the same.)

DIY Problem 4.5. Verify that the expression below follows almost immediately from CIP, equation (4.7):

$$F_{t,T} r_{t,T}^* + (F_{t,T} - S_t) = S_t r_{t,T}. \tag{4.14}$$

Then trace each symbol in the formula to the numbers we used in the numerical example. Identify the interest on the peso and crown deposits, and the capital gain or loss.

So we know that total pretax income is the same in both cases. If all income is equally taxable, the tax is the same too, and so must be the after-tax income. It also follows that if, because of, for example, spreads, there is a small advantage to, say, the peso investment, then taxes will reduce the gain but not eliminate it. That is, if pesos would yield more before taxes, then they would also yield more after taxes.

In most countries, corporate taxes are neutral between interest income and capital gains, especially short-term capital gains. But there are exceptions. The United Kingdom used to treat capital gains on FC loans differently from capital losses and interest received. Under personal taxation, taxation of capital gains is far from universal, and/or long-term capital gains often receive beneficial treatment. In cases like this, the ranking of outcomes on the basis of after-tax returns could be very different from the ranking on pretax outcomes. Beware!

4.4 The Market Value of an Outstanding Forward Contract

In this and the next section, we discuss the market value of a forward contract at its inception, during its life, and at expiration. As is the case for any asset or portfolio, the market value of a forward contract is the price at which it can be bought or sold in a normally functioning market. The focus, in this section, is on the value of a forward contract that was written in the past but that has not yet matured. For instance, one year ago (at time t_0), we may have bought a five-year forward contract for NOK at $F_{t_0,T} = $ CLP/NOK 115. This means that we now have an outstanding four-year contract, initiated at the rate of CLP/NOK 115. This outstanding contract differs from a newly signed four-year forward purchase because the latter would have been initiated at the now-prevailing four-year forward rate, CLP/NOK 110. The question then is, how should we value the outstanding forward contract?

This value may be relevant for a number of reasons. At the theoretical level, the market value of a forward contract comes in quite handy in the theory of options, as we shall see later on. In day-to-day business, the value of an outstanding contract can be relevant in, for example, the following circumstances:

- If we want to negotiate early settlement of the contract, for instance to stop losses on a speculative position, or because the underlying position that was being hedged has disappeared.
- If there is default and the injured party wants to file a claim.
- If a firm wishes to "mark to market" the book value of its foreign-exchange positions in its financial reports.

4.4.1 A General Formula

Let us agree that, unless otherwise specified, "a contract" refers to a forward purchase of one unit of foreign currency. (This is the standard convention in futures markets.) Today, at time t, we are considering a contract that was signed in the past, at time t_0, for delivery of one unit of foreign currency to you at T, against payment of the initially agreed-upon forward rate, $F_{t_0,T}$. Recall the convention that we have adopted for indicating time: the current date is always denoted by t, the initiation date by t_0, the future (maturity) date by T, and we have, of course, $t_0 \leqslant t \leqslant T$.

The way to value an outstanding contract is to interpret it as a simple portfolio that contains an FC-denominated PN with face value 1 as an asset, and an HC-denominated PN with face value $F_{t_0,T}$ as a liability. Valuing an HC PN is easy: just discount the face value at the risk-free rate. For the FC PN, we first compute its PV in FC (by discounting at r^*), and then translate this FC value into HC via the spot price.

Example 4.10. Consider a contract that has four years to go, signed in the past at a historic forward price of 115. What is the market value if $S_t = 100$, $r_{t,T} = 21\%$, and $r_{t,T}^* = 10\%$?

- The asset leg is like holding a PN of FC 1, now worth $\text{PV}^* = 1/1.10 = 0.909\,09$ NOK and, therefore, $0.909\,090\,9 \times 100 = 90.909$ CLP.
- The liability leg is like having written a PN of HC 115, now worth CLP $115/1.21 = 95.041$.
- The net value now is therefore CLP $90.909 - 95.041 = -4.132$.

The generalization is as follows:

$$
\begin{bmatrix} \text{Market value} \\ \text{of forward} \\ \text{purchase} \\ \text{at } F_{t_0,T} \end{bmatrix} = \underbrace{\overbrace{\frac{1}{1+r_{t,T}^*}}^{\substack{\text{PV}^* \text{ of} \\ \text{asset, FC1}}} \times S_t}_{\substack{\text{Translated value} \\ \text{of FC asset}}} - \underbrace{\frac{F_{t_0,T}}{1+r_{t,T}}}_{\substack{\text{PV of HC} \\ \text{liability}}}.
\tag{4.15}
$$

There is a slightly different version that is occasionally more useful: the value is the discounted difference between the current and the historic forward rates. To find this version, multiply and divide the first term on the right of (4.15) by $(1 + r_{t,T})$, and use CIP:

$$
\begin{bmatrix} \text{Market value} \\ \text{of forward} \\ \text{purchase} \\ \text{at } F_{t_0,T} \end{bmatrix} = \frac{1}{1+r_{t,T}} \underbrace{\frac{1+r_{t,T}}{1+r_{t,T}^*} S_t}_{=F_{t,T} \ (\text{CIP})} - \frac{F_{t_0,T}}{1+r_{t,T}}
$$

$$
= \frac{F_{t,T} - F_{t_0,T}}{1+r_{t,T}}.
\tag{4.16}
$$

Example 4.11. Go back to example 4.10. Knowing that the current forward rate is 110, we immediately find a value of $(110 - 115)/1.21 = -4.132$ CLP for a contract with historic rate 115.

One way to interpret this variant is to note that, relative to a new contract, we are overpaying by CLP 5: last year we committed to paying 115, while we would have got away with 110 if we had signed right now. This "loss," however, is dated four years from now, so its PV is discounted at the risk-free rate.

The skeptical reader may object that this "loss" is very fleeting: its value changes every second; how is it, then, that we can discount at the risk-free rate? One answer is that the value changes continuously because interest rates and (especially) the spot rate are in constant motion, but that does not invalidate the claim that we can always value each PN using the risk-free rates and the spot exchange rate prevailing at that moment. Relatedly, the future loss relative to market conditions at t can effectively be locked in at no cost, by selling forward for the same date.

Example 4.12. Consider a contract that has four years to go, signed in the past at a historic forward price of 115, for speculative purposes. Right now you see there is a loss, and you want to close out to avoid any further red ink. One way is to sell forward HC 1 at the current forward rate, 110. On the common expiry date of the old and new contracts, we then just net the loss of $115 - 110 = 5$:

	HC flows at T	FC flows at T
Old contract: buy at $F_{t_0,T} = 115$	-115	1
New contract: sell at $F_{t_0,T} = 110$	110	-1
Net flow	-5	0

But because this loss is only realized within four years, its PV is found by discounting. Discounting can be at the risk-free rate since, as we see, the locked-in loss is risk free.

We can now use the result in equation (4.15) to determine the value of a forward contract in two special cases: at its inception and at its maturity.

4.4.2 Corollary 1: The Value of a Forward Contract at Expiration

At its expiration time, the market value of a purchase contract equals the difference between the spot rate that prevails at time T—the value of what you get—and the forward rate $F_{t_0,T}$ that you agreed to pay:

$$\begin{bmatrix} \text{Expiration value of} \\ \text{a forward contract} \\ \text{with rate } F_{t_0,T} \end{bmatrix} = S_T - F_{t_0,T}. \qquad (4.17)$$

Equation (4.17) can be derived formally from equation (4.15), using the fact that the effective return on a deposit or loan with zero time to maturity is zero (that is, $r_{T,T} = 0 = r^*_{T,T}$). The result in (4.17) is quite obvious, as the following example shows.

Example 4.13.

- You bought forward, at time t_0, 1 NOK at CLP/NOK 115. At expiry, T, the NOK spot rate turns out to be CLP/NOK 123, so you pay 115 for something you can immediately resell at 123. The net value is therefore $123 - 115 = 8$.
- As above, except that S_T turns out to be CLP/NOK 110. You have to pay 115 for something worth only 110. The net value is therefore $110 - 115 = -5$: you would be willing to *pay* 5 to get out of this contract.

The value of a unit forward sale contract is of course just the negative of the value of the forward purchase: forward deals are zero-sum games. The seller

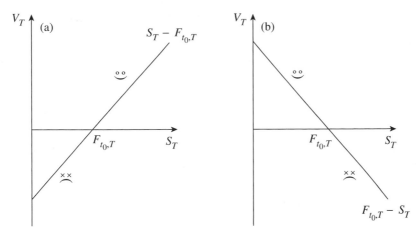

Figure 4.5. The value of a forward purchase or sales contract at expiry: (a) buy forward; (b) sell forward.

wins if the spot value turns out to be below the contracted forward price, and loses if the spot value turns out to be above. Figure 4.5 pictures the formulas, with smileys and frownies indicating the positive and negative parts.

Equation (4.17) can be used to formally show how hedging works. Suppose that you have to pay one unit of foreign currency at some future time T. The foreign currency debt is risky because the cash flow at time T, in home currency, will be equal to minus the future spot rate—and, at time t, this future spot rate is uncertain, a characteristic we stress by adding a tilde ($\tilde{}$) over the variable. By adding a forward purchase, the combined cash flow becomes risk free, as the following bit of arcane math shows:

$$
\begin{array}{lc}
\text{Cash flow from amortizing the debt at expiration:} & -\tilde{S}_T \\
\text{Value of the forward purchase at expiration:} & \underline{\tilde{S}_T - F_{t_0,T}} \\
\text{Combined cash flow:} & -F_{t_0,T}
\end{array}
\tag{4.18}
$$

Putting this into words, we say that hedging the foreign-currency debt with a forward purchase transforms the risky debt into a risk-free debt, with a known outflow $-F_{t_0,T}$. We shall use this result repeatedly in chapter 5 (on uses of forward contracts), in chapter 9 when we discuss option pricing, and in chapter 13, where we analyze exposure and risk management.

Make sure you realize that the hedged liability may make you worse off, *ex post*, than the unhedged one. Buying at a preset rate, $F_{t,T}$, gives that great warm feeling, *ex post*, if the spot rate S_T turns out to be quite high; but it hurts if the spot rate turns out to be quite cheap. The same conclusion was already implicit in (4.17): the value of the contract at expiry can be of either sign. This raises the question of whether hedging is really so good as it is sometimes cracked up to be. We return to the economics of hedging in chapter 12.

4.4.3 Corollary 2: The Value of a Forward Contract at Inception

The value at expiry, above, was probably so obvious that it is, in a way, just a means of proving that the general valuation formula (4.15) makes sense. The same holds for the next special case: the value at inception, i.e., the time the contract is initiated or signed. At inception, the market value *must* be zero. We know this because (a) when we sign a forward contract, we have to pay nothing, and (b) hard-nosed bankers would never give away a positive-value contract for free, nor accept a negative-value contract at a zero price. To show the (initial) zero-value property formally, we use the general value formula (4.16) and consider the special case where $t_0 = t$, implying that $F_{t_0,T} = F_{t,T}$ (that is, the contract we are valuing is new). Obviously,

$$\begin{bmatrix} \text{Initial value of a} \\ \text{forward contract} \\ \text{with rate } F_{t,T} \end{bmatrix} = \frac{F_{t,T} - F_{t,T}}{1 + r_{t,T}} = 0. \tag{4.19}$$

The value of a forward contract is zero at the moment it is signed because the contract can be replicated at zero cost. Notably, if a bank tried to charge you money for a contract at the equilibrium (CIP) forward rate, you would refuse, and create a synthetic forward contract through the spot and money markets.

Example 4.14. Let $S_t = 100$, $r^*_{t,T} = 0.10$, $r_{t,T} = 0.21$, $F_{t,T} = 110$; but a bank wants to charge you a commission of 3 for a forward purchase. You would shrug dismissively and immediately construct a synthetic forward contract at 110 at a zero cost:

- write a PN to the amount of HC 110, discount it;
- convert the proceeds, $110/1.21 = 90.909\,090$, into FC, giving you FC $0.909\,09$;
- invest at 10% to get HC1 at T.

Thus, you can replicate a forward purchase contract under which your payment at T amounts to 110, just as in the genuine, direct forward contract, but it does not cost you anything now.

4.4.4 Corollary 3: The Forward Rate and the Risk-Adjusted Expected Future Spot Rate

The zero-value property of forward contracts discussed above has another, and quite fundamental, interpretation. Suppose that the CLP/NOK four-year forward rate equals 110, implying that you can exchange one future NOK for 110 future CLP and vice versa without any up-front cash flow. This must mean that the market perceives these amounts as being *equivalent* (that is, having the same value). If this were not so, there would have been an up-front compensation to make up for the difference in value.

Since any forward contract has a zero value, the present values of CLP 1 four years and NOK 110 four years must be equal anywhere; that is, the equivalence of these amounts holds for any investor or hedger anywhere. However, the equivalence property takes on a special meaning if we pick the CLP (which is the currency in which our forward rate is expressed) as the home currency: in that particular numéraire, the CLP amount is risk free, or certain. In terms of CLP, we can write the equal-value property as

$$PV_t(\tilde{S}_T) = PV_t(F_{t,T}), \tag{4.20}$$

where $PV_t(\cdot)$ is the present-value operator. In a way, equation (4.20) is just the zero-value property: the PV of the uncertain future cash inflow $\tilde{S}_T$ generated by the contract cancels out against the PV of the known future outflow, $F_{t,T}$. We can lose or gain, but these prospects balance out in present-value terms, from our time-t viewpoint. But the related, second interpretation stems from the fact that, in home currency, the forward price on the right-hand side of equation (4.20) is a risk-free, known number, whereas the future spot rate on the left is uncertain. That is, at time t an amount of $F_{t,T}$ pesos payable at T is not just *equivalent* to one unit of foreign currency payable at T; this amount of future home currency is also a *certain*, risk-free amount. For this reason, we shall say that, in home currency, the forward rate is the time-t *certainty equivalent* of the future spot rate, $\tilde{S}_T$.

Example 4.15. In our earlier CLP/NOK examples, the certainty equivalent of one Norwegian crown four years out is CLP 110. You can offer the market a sure CLP 110 at T and get 1 crown (with risky value $\tilde{S}_T$) in return; but equally well you can offer the market 1 crown (with risky value $\tilde{S}_T$) and get a sure CLP 110 in return.

The notion of the certainty equivalent deserves some elaboration. Many introductory finance books discuss the concept of an investor's subjective certainty equivalent of a risky income. This is defined as the single known amount of income that is equally attractive as the entire risky distribution.

Example 4.16. Suppose that you are indifferent between, on the one hand, a lottery ticket that pays out with equal probabilities either USD 100m or nothing and, on the other hand, a sure USD 35m. Then your personal certainty equivalent of the risky lottery is USD 35m. You are indifferent between 35m for sure and the risky cash flow from the lottery.

Another way of saying this is that, when valuing the lottery ticket, you have marked down its expected value, USD 50m, by USD 15, because the lottery is risky. Thus, we can conclude that your personal certainty equivalent, USD 35m, is the expected value of the lottery ticket corrected for risk.[9]

---

[9] When we say that investors are risk averse, we mean they do not like symmetric risk for their entire wealth. The amounts in the example are so huge that they would represent almost the entire wealth of most readers; so in that case, risk aversion guarantees that the risk adjustment is downward. But for small investments with, for instance, lots of right skewness, one observes upward adjustments: real-world lottery players, for instance, are willing to pay more than the expected value because, when stakes are small, right-skewness can give quite a kick.

In the example, the risk adjustment is quite subjective. A *market* certainty equivalent, by analogy, is the single known amount that the market considers to be as valuable as the entire risky distribution. And market certainty equivalents are, of course, what matter if we want to price assets, or if we want to make managerial decisions that maximize the market value of the firm. We have just argued that the (CLP) market certainty equivalent of the future CLP/NOK spot rate must be the current CLP/NOK forward rate. Stated differently, the market's time-t expectation of the time-T CLP/NOK spot rate, corrected for risk, is revealed in the CLP/NOK forward rate, $F_{t,T}$. Let us express this formally as

$$\text{CEQ}_t(\tilde{S}_T) = F_{t,T}, \tag{4.21}$$

where $\text{CEQ}_t(\cdot)$ is called the *certainty-equivalent* operator.

A certainty-equivalent operator is similar to an ordinary expectations operator, $E_t(\cdot)$, except that it is a risk-adjusted expectation rather than an ordinary expected value. (There are good theories as to how the risk-adjusted and the "physical" densities are related, but they are beyond the scope of this text.) Like $E_t(\cdot)$, $\text{CEQ}_t(\cdot)$ is also a conditional expectation, that is, the best possible forecast given the information available at time t. We use a subscript "t" to emphasize this link with the information available at time t.

To make the market's risk-adjustment a bit less abstract, assume the CAPM holds. Then we could work out the left-hand side of (4.20) in the standard way: the PV of a risky cash flow $\tilde{S}_T$ equals its expectation, discounted at the risk-adjusted rate. The risk-adjusted discount rate, in turn, consists of the risk-free rate plus a risk premium $\text{RP}_{t,T}(\beta_S)$, which depends on market circumstances and the risk of the asset to be priced, β_S. Working out the right-hand side of (4.20) is straightforward: the PV of a risk-free flow F is F discounted at the risk-free rate r. Thus, we can flesh out (4.20) into

$$\frac{E_t(\tilde{S}_T)}{1 + r_{t,T} + \text{RP}_{t,T}(\beta_S)} = \frac{F_{t,T}}{1 + r_{t,T}}. \tag{4.22}$$

After a minor rearrangement (line 1, below), we can then use the notation CEQ as in (4.21), to conclude that

$$F_{t,T} = E_t(\tilde{S}_T) \frac{1 + r_{t,T}}{1 + r_{t,T} + \text{RP}_{t,T}},$$

$$\implies \quad \text{CEQ}_t(\tilde{S}_T) = E_t(\tilde{S}_T) \frac{1 + r_{t,T}}{1 + r_{t,T} + \text{RP}_{t,T}} \tag{4.23}$$

$$\approx E_t(\tilde{S}_T) \frac{1}{1 + \text{RP}_{t,T}}. \tag{4.24}$$

The last line is only an approximation of the true relation (4.23). We add it to merely show why the fraction on the right-hand side of (4.23) is called the risk adjustment.

Example 4.17. Suppose your finance professor offers you a 1% share in the next-year royalties from his finance textbook, with an expected value, next year, of USD 3,450,000. Given the high risk (☺), the market would discount this at 10%—3 risk free plus a 7 risk premium. The CEQ would be

$$CEQ = 3,450,000 \frac{1.03}{1.10} = 3,450,000 \times 0.936\,363\,636 = 3,090,000. \quad (4.25)$$

Thus, the market would be indifferent between this proposition and USD 3,090,000 for sure. You could unload either of these in the market at a common PV,

$$\frac{3,450,000}{1.10} = 3,000,000 = \frac{3,090,000}{1.03}. \quad (4.26)$$

The risk-adjusted expected value plays a crucial role in the theory of international finance. As we shall see in the remainder of this chapter and later in the book, the risk-adjusted expectation has many important implications for asset pricing as well as for corporate financial decisions.

4.4.5 Implications for Spot Values; the Role of Interest Rates

In principle, we can see the spot value as the expected future value of the investment—including interest earned—corrected for risk and then discounted at the appropriate risk-free rate. In this subsection we consider the role of interest rates and changes therein, hoping to clear up any confusion that might exist in your mind. Notably, we have noted that a forward discount, i.e., a relatively high foreign risk-free rate, signals a weak currency. Yet we see central banks increase interest rates when their currencies are under pressure, and the result is often an appreciation of the spot value. How can increasing the interest rate, a sign of weakness, strengthen the currency?

The relation to watch is, familiarly,

$$S_t = \frac{CEQ_t(\tilde{S}_T)(1 + r^*_{t,T})}{1 + r_{t,T}}. \quad (4.27)$$

We also need to be clear about what is changing, here, and what is held constant. Let us use an example to guide our thoughts.

Example 4.18. Assume that the CAD (home currency) and GBP risk-free interest rates, $r_{t,T}$ and $r^*_{t,T}$, are both equal to 5% p.a. Then, from equation (4.27), initially no change in S is expected, after risk adjustments: the spot rate is set to be equal to the certainty-equivalent future value. Now assume that bad news about the British (foreign) economy suddenly leads to a downward revision of the expected next-year spot rate from, say, CAD/GBP 2 to 1.9. From equation (4.27), if interest rates remain unchanged, the current spot rate would immediately react by dropping from 2 to 1.9, too. Exchange rates, like any other financial price, anticipate the future.

Now if the Bank of England does not like this drop in the value of the GBP, it can prop up the current exchange rate by increasing the British interest rate. To do this, the U.K. interest rate will need to be increased from 5% to over 10.5%, so that S_t equals CAD/GBP 2, even though $\text{CEQ}_t(\tilde{S}_T)$ equals 1.9:

$$\frac{1.9 \times 1.105\,26}{1.05} = 2. \tag{4.28}$$

Thus, the higher U.K. interest rate does strengthen the current GBP spot rate, all else being equal.

But this still means that the currency is weak, in the sense that the GBP is still expected to drop toward 1.9, after risk adjustment, in the future. Actually, in this story the pound strengthens now so that it can become weak afterward. So there is no contradiction, since "strengthening" has to do with the immediate spot rate (which perks up as soon as the U.K. interest rate is raised, holding the CEQ constant), while "weakening" refers to the expected movements in the future.

A second comment is that, in the example, the interest-rate hike merely postpones the fall of the pound to a risk-adjusted 1.9. In this respect, however, this partial analysis may be incomplete, because a change in interest rates may also affect expectations. For instance, if the market believes that an increase in the British interest rate also heralds a stricter monetary policy, this would increase the expected future spot rate, and reinforce the effect of the higher foreign interest rate. Thus, the BoE would get away with a lower rise in the U.K. interest rate than in the first version of the story.

Of course, if expectations change in the opposite direction, the current spot rate may decrease even when the foreign interest rate is increased. For example, if the foreign interest rate rises by a smaller amount than was expected by the market, this may then lead to a downward revision of the expected future exchange rate and, ultimately, a drop in the spot value.

Example 4.19. Suppose that the current interest rates are equal to 5% p.a. in both Canada (the home country) and the United Kingdom, and the current and expected exchange rates are CAD/GBP 2. The BoE now increases its interest rate to 5.25% p.a. in an attempt to stem further rises in U.K. inflation. It is quite possible that this increase in interest rates is interpreted by the market as a negative signal about the future state of the U.K. economy (the BoE wants to slow things down) or as insufficient to stop inflation. So the market may revise expectations about the CAD/GBP exchange rate from 2 to 1.95. Thus, the change in the interest rate is insufficient to match the drop in the expected exchange rate. Instead of appreciating, the current exchange rate drops to CAD/GBP $1.95 \times 1.0525/1.05 = 1.955$.

Note the difference between the two examples. In the first, there was a drop in expectations that was perfectly offset by the interest rate, for the time being, that is: the drop is just being postponed, by assumption. In the second example the interest rate change came first, and then led to a revision of expectations. So we need to be careful about expectations too when the role of interest rates is being discussed.

Let us now return to more corporate-finance-style issues.

4.4.6 Implications for the Valuation of Foreign-Currency Assets or Liabilities

The certainty-equivalent interpretation of the forward rate implies that, for the purpose of corporate decision making, one can use the forward rate to translate foreign-currency-denominated claims or liabilities into one's domestic currency without much ado. Indeed, identifying the true expectation and then correcting for risk would just be reinventing the wheel: the market has already done this for you, and has put the results on the Reuters screen. This makes your life much more simple. Rather than having to tackle a valuation problem involving a risky cash flow—the left-hand side of equation (4.22)—we can simply work with the right-hand side, where the cash flow is risk free. With risk-free cash flows, it suffices to use the observable domestic risk-free rate for discounting purposes.

Example 4.20. If the domestic CLP risk-free return is 21%, effective for four years, and the four-year forward rate is CLP/NOK 110, then the (risk-adjusted) economic value of an NOK 5,000 four-year zero-coupon bond can be found as

$$\frac{\text{NOK } 5{,}000 \times \text{CLP/NOK } 110}{1.21} = \text{CLP } 454{,}545.45, \qquad (4.29)$$

without any fussing and worrying about expectations or risk premia.

As illustrated in the example, the expected spot rate is not needed in order to value this position, and discounting can be done at the risk-free rate of return. In contrast, if you had tried to value the position using the left-hand side of equation (4.22), you would probably have had to discount the expected future spot rate at some risk-adjusted rate. Thus, the first problem would have been to estimate the expected future spot rate. Unlike the forward rate, this expectation is not provided in the newspapers or on the Reuters screens. Second, you would have had to use some asset-pricing theory like the international CAPM to calculate a risk-adjusted discount rate that we use on the left-hand side of equation (4.22). In this second step, you would run into problems of estimating the model parameters, not to mention the issue of whether the CAPM is an appropriate model. In short, the forward rate simplifies decision making considerably. We shall use this concept time and again throughout this text.

4.4.7 Implication for the Relevance of Hedging

In this mercifully short last section before the wrap-up, we briefly touch upon the implications of the zero initial value for the relevance of hedging, that is, using financial instruments to reduce or even entirely eliminate the impact of exchange rates on the cash flow. Forward contracts are a prime instrument for this purpose: if one contractually fixes the rates at which future exchanges will be made, then the future spot rate no longer affects your bank account—at least not for those transactions.

The zero-value property has been invoked by some (including me, when *very* young) as implying that such hedging does not add value, or more precisely that any value effects must stem from market imperfections. This is wrong, but it took me some time to figure out exactly what was wrong.

The argument views the firm as a bunch of cash-flow-generating activities, to which a hedge is added. The cash flow triggered by the hedge is some positive or negative multiple of $\tilde{S}_T - F_{t,T}$, and its PV is zero the moment the hedge contract is signed. True, its value will become nonzero one instant later, but we have no clue whether this new value will be positive or negative; so our knowledge that the zero-value property is short-lived is of no use for hedging decisions. But does zero initial value mean that the hedge is (literally) worthless? There can be, and will be, a value effect if the firm's other cash flows are affected. For instance, the chances that adverse currency movements wipe out so much capital that R&D investments must be cut, or that banks increase their risk spreads on loans, or that customers desert the company, or that the best employees leave like rats from a sinking ship—the chances that all these bad things happen should be lower, after hedging. Perhaps the firm is so well off that the probability of painful bad luck—bad luck that affects operations, not just the bank account—is already zero. If so, count your blessings: hedging will probably not add any value. But many firms are not in such a comfortable position. To them hedging adds value because it improves the future cash-flow prospects from other activities. We return to this in chapter 12.

4.5 CFO's Summary

In this chapter, we have analyzed forward contracts in a perfect market. We have discovered that forward contracts are essentially packaged deals, that is, transactions that are equivalent to a combination of a loan in one currency, a spot transaction, and a deposit in the other currency. In this sense, the forward contract is a distant forerunner of financial engineering. We have also seen how exchange markets and money markets are interlinked and can be used for arbitrage transactions and for identifying and comparing the two ways to make a particular transaction.

In perfect markets, it does not matter whether one uses forward contracts as opposed to their money-market replications. This holds for any possible transaction and its replication. For instance, a German firm will neither win nor lose if it replaces an EUR deposit by a swapped USD deposit since, from interest rate parity, the two are equivalent. Or, more precisely, *if* it matters, it is because of market imperfections like spreads, or because the firm's other cash flows are affected too, but not because of the pure exchange of an FC cash flow by one in HC. We turn to market imperfections in the next chapter, and to the relevance of hedging in chapter 12.

We have also found that the value of a forward contract is zero. This means that, everything else being the same, our German firm will not win or lose if it replaces an EUR deposit by an *uncovered* USD deposit. Again, a big word of caution is in order, here, because the "everything else being the same" clause is crucial. The above statement is perfectly true about the pure PV of two isolated cash flows, one in EUR and one in USD. But if the firm is so levered, the USD deposit is so large, and the EUR/USD so volatile that the investment could send the firm into receivership, then the dollar deposit would still not be a good idea—not because of the deposit per se, but because of the repercussions it could have on the firm's legal fees and interest costs and asset values. In short, the deposit's cash flows can have interactions with the company's other business, and these interactions might affect the firm's value.

A last crucial insight is that the forward rate is the market certainty equivalent, that is, the market's expectation corrected for any risks it thinks to be relevant. This insight can save a company a lot of time. It is also fundamental for the purpose of asset pricing. For cash flows with a known FC component, the logic is of course straightforward: (a) an asset with a known FC flow C_T^* is easy to hedge: sell forward C_T^* units of FC; (b) the hedged asset is easy to value: $(C_T^* \times F_{t,T})/(1 + r_{t,T})$; and (c) the unhedged asset must have the same value because the hedge itself has zero initial value and because a risk-free FC amount C_T^* cannot be affected by the hedge. Interestingly, under some distributional assumptions we can also apply the logic to cash flows that are highly nonlinear functions of the future exchange rate. We return to this issue in chapter 9.

Forward currency contracts have been around for centuries. A more recent instrument is the forward or futures contract on interest rates. Since forward interest contracts are not intrinsically "international" and many readers may already know them from other sources, I relegate them to appendixes, but if they are new to you, be warned that we are going to use them later on. A key insight is that interest rates (spot and forward interest rates, and "yields at par") are all linked by arbitrage. Forward interest rates in various currencies are likewise linked through the forward markets.

4.6 Appendix: Interest Rates, Returns, and Bond Yields

4.6.1 Links between Interest Rates and Effective Returns

We have defined the effective (rate of) return as the percentage difference between the initial (time-t) value and the maturity (time-T) value of a nominally risk-free asset over a certain holding period. For instance, suppose you deposit CLP 100,000 for six months, and the deposit is worth CLP 105,000 at maturity.

The six-month effective return is

$$r_{t,T} = \frac{105{,}000 - 100{,}000}{100{,}000} = 0.05 = 5\%. \tag{4.30}$$

In reality, bankers never quote effective rates of returns; they quote interest rates. An interest rate is an annualized return, that is, a return extrapolated to a twelve-month horizon. In the text, we emphasize this by adding an explicit per annum (or p.a.) qualification whenever we mention an interest rate. However, annualization can be done in many ways. It is also true that, for any system, there is a corresponding way to de-annualize the interest rate into the effective return—the number you need.

1. Annualization can be "simple" (i.e., linear): 5% for six months is extrapolated linearly, to 10% p.a. A simple interest rate is the standard method for term deposits and straight loans when the time to maturity is less than one year. Conversely, the effective return is computed from the quoted simple interest rate as

$$1 + r_{t,T} = 1 + (T - t) \times [\text{simple interest rate}]. \tag{4.31}$$

Example 4.21. Let $(T - t) = 0.5$ years and let the simple interest rate be 10% p.a. Then

$$1 + r_{t,T} = 1 + \tfrac{1}{2} \times 0.10 = 1.05. \tag{4.32}$$

2. Annualization can also be compounded, with a hypothetical reinvestment of the interest. Using this convention, an increase from 100 to 105 in six months would lead to a constant-growth-extrapolated value of $105 \times 1.05 = 110.25$ after another six months. Thus, under this convention, 5% over six months corresponds to 10.25% p.a. Conversely, the return is computed from the quoted compound interest rate as

$$1 + r_{t,T} = (1 + [\text{compound interest rate}])^{T-t}. \tag{4.33}$$

Example 4.22. Let $(T - t) = 0.5$ years and let the compound interest rate be 10.25% p.a.; then

$$1 + r_{t,T} = 1.1025^{1/2} = \sqrt{1.1025} = 1.05. \tag{4.34}$$

Compound interest is the standard method for zero-coupon loans and investments (without interim interest payments) exceeding one year.

3. Banks may also compound the interest every quarter, every month, or even every day. The result is an odd mixture of linear and exponential methods. If the interest rate for a six-month investment is i p.a., compounded m times per year, the bank awards you i/m per subperiod of $1/m$ year. For instance, the p.a. interest rate may be $i = 6\%$, compounded four times per year. This means you get $\tfrac{6}{4} = 1.5\%$ per quarter. Your investment has a maturity of six months, which corresponds to two capitalization periods of one quarter each. After compounding over these two quarters, an initial investment of 100 grows to

$100 \times (1.015)^2 = 103.0225$, implying an effective rate of return of 3.0225%. Thus, the effective return is computed from the quoted interest rate as

$$1 + r_{t,T} = \left(1 + \frac{[\text{quoted interest rate}]}{m}\right)^{(T-t)m}. \tag{4.35}$$

Example 4.23. Let $(T - t) = 0.5$ years and let the compound interest rate be 9.878% with quarterly compounding; then

$$1 + r_{t,T} = (1 + 0.098\,781 \times \tfrac{1}{4})^{1/2 \times 4} = 1.05. \tag{4.36}$$

You may wonder why this Byzantine mixture of linear and exponential is used at all. In the real world it is used when the bank has a good reason to understate the effective interest rate. This is generally the case for loans. For deposits, the reason may be that the quoted rate is capped (by law, like the United States's former Regulations Q and M, or because of a cartel agreement among banks). In finance theory, the mixture of linear and exponential is popular in its limit form: the continuously compounded rate.

4. In the theoretical literature, the frequency of compounding is often carried to the limit ("continuous compounding," i.e., $m \to \infty$). From your basic math course, you may remember that

$$\lim_{m \to \infty} \left(1 + \frac{x}{m}\right)^m = e^x, \tag{4.37}$$

where e ≈ 2.718 is the base of the natural (naperian) logarithm. Conversely, the return is computed from the quoted interest rate ρ as

$$1 + r_{t,T} = \lim_{m \to \infty} \left(1 + \frac{\rho}{m}\right)^{(T-t)m} = e^{\rho(T-t)}. \tag{4.38}$$

Example 4.24. Let $(T - t) = 0.5$ years and assume that the continuously compounded interest rate equals 9.758 03%. Then

$$1 + r_{t,T} = e^{0.097\,580\,3/2} = 1.05. \tag{4.39}$$

Note the following link between the continuously and the annually compounded rates i and ρ:

$$(1 + i) = e^{\ln(1+i)} \quad \Rightarrow \quad (1 + i)^{T-t} = e^{\ln(1+i)\cdot(T-t)} \quad \Rightarrow \quad \ln(1 + i) = \rho. \tag{4.40}$$

5. Bankers' discount is yet another way of annualizing a return. This is often used when the present value is to be computed for T-bills, promissory notes, and so on—instruments where the time-T value (or "face value") is the known variable, not the PV as in the case of a deposit or a loan. Suppose the time-T value is 100, the time to maturity is 0.5 years, and the p.a. discount rate is 5%. The PV will then be computed as

$$\text{PV} = 100 \times (1 - 0.05/2) = 97.5. \tag{4.41}$$

Conversely, the return is found from the quoted bankers' discount rate as

$$1 + r_{t,T} = \frac{1}{1 - (T - t) \times [\text{bankers' discount rate}]}. \qquad (4.42)$$

Example 4.25. Let $(T - t) = 0.5$ years and let the p.a. bankers' discount rate be 9.5238%. Then

$$1 + r_{t,T} = \frac{1}{1 - \frac{1}{2} \times 0.095238} = 1.05. \qquad (4.43)$$

In summary, there are many ways in which a bank can tell its customer that the effective return is, for instance, 5%. It should be obvious that what matters is the effective return, not the stated p.a. interest rate or the method used to annualize the effective return. For this reason, in most of this text, we use effective returns. This allows us to simply write $(1 + r_{t,T})$. If we had used annualized interest rates, all formulas would look somewhat more complicated, and would consist of many versions, one for each possible way of quoting a rate.

4.6.2 Common Pitfalls in Computing Effective Returns

To conclude this appendix we describe the most common mistakes when computing effective returns. The first is forgetting to de-annualize the return. Always convert the bank's quoted interest rate into the effective return over the period $(T - t)$. *And* use the correct formula.

Example 4.26. Let $T - t = 0.75$ years. What are the effective rates of return when a banker quotes a 4% p.a. rate, to be understood as, alternatively, (1) simple interest, (2) standard compound interest, (3) interest compounded quarterly, (4) interest compounded monthly, (5) interest compounded daily, (6) interest compounded a million times a year, (7) interest compounded continuously, and (8) bankers' discount rate?

Convention	Formula	Result $(1 + r)$
Simple	$1 + \frac{3}{4} \times 0.04$	1.030 000 000
Compound, $M = 1$	$(1 + 0.04)^{3/4}$	1.029 852 445
Compound, $M = 4$	$(1 + 0.04/4)^{4 \times 3/4}$	1.030 301 000
Compound, $M = 12$	$(1 + 0.04/12)^{12 \times 3/4}$	1.030 403 127
Compound, $M = 360$	$(1 + 0.04/360)^{360 \times 3/4}$	1.030 452 817
Compound, $M = 1,000,000$	$(1 + 0.04/10^6)^{10^6 \times 3/4}$	1.030 454 533
Continuous compounding	$e^{0.04 \times 3/4}$	1.030 454 533
Banker's discount	$1/(1 - \frac{3}{4} \times 0.04)$	1.030 927 835

Second, it is important to remember that there is an interest rate (or a discount rate) for every maturity $(T - t)$. For instance, if you make a twelve-month deposit, the p.a. rate offered is likely to differ from the p.a. rate on a six-month deposit. Students sometimes forget this, because basic finance courses occasionally assume, for expository purposes, that the p.a. compound interest rate is the same for all maturities. Thus, there is a second pitfall to be avoided—using the wrong rate for a given maturity.

The third pitfall is confusing an interest rate with an internal rate of return on a complex investment. Recall that the return is the simple percentage difference between the maturity value and the initial value. This assumes that there is only one future cash flow. But many investments and loans carry numerous future cash flows, like quarterly interest payments and gradual amortizations of the principal. We shall discuss interest rates on multiple-payment instruments in the next appendix. For now, simply remember that the interest rate on, say, a five-year loan with annual interest payments should not be confused with the interest rate on a five-year instrument with no intermediate interest payments (zero-coupon bond).

Example 4.27. If a newspaper says the 10-year bond rate is 6%, this means that a bond with an annual coupon of 6% can be issued at par. That is, the 6% is a "yield at par" on bullet bonds with annual coupons. What we need, in this chapter, are zero-coupon rates rather than yields at par.

4.7 Appendix: The Forward Forward and the Forward Rate Agreement

4.7.1 Forward Contracts on Interest Rates

You may know that loans often contain options on interest rates (caps and floors; see chapter 16). Besides interest-rate options, there are also forward contracts on interest rates. Such forward contracts come in two guises: the forward forward (FF) contract and the forward rate agreement (FRA).

An FF contract is just a forward deposit or loan: it fixes an interest rate today (time t) for a deposit or loan starting at a future time T_1 ($> t$) and expiring at T_2 ($> T_1$).

Example 4.28. Consider a six-to-nine-month FF contract for 10m Brazilian real at 10% p.a. (simple interest). This contract guarantees that the return on a three-month deposit of BRR 10m, to be made six months from now, will be 10%/4 = 2.5%. At time T_1 (six months from now), the BRR 10m will be deposited, and the principal plus the agreed-upon interest of 2.5% will be received at time T_2 (nine months from now).

A more recent, and more popular, variant is the FRA. Under an FRA, the deposit is *notional*—that is, the contract is about a hypothetical deposit rather than an actual deposit. Instead of effectively making the deposit, the holder of the contract will settle the gain or loss in cash, and pay or receive the present value of the difference between the contracted forward interest rate and market rate that is actually prevailing at time T_1.

Example 4.29. Consider a nine-to-twelve-month CAD 5m notional deposit at a forward interest rate of 4% p.a. (that is, a forward return of 1% effective). If the Interbank Offer Rate after nine months (T_1) turns out to be 3.6% p.a. (implying a return of 0.9%), the FRA has a positive value equal to the difference between the promised interest (1% on CAD 5m) and the interest in the absence of the FRA, 0.9% on CAD 5m. Thus, the investor will receive the present value of this contract, which amounts to

$$\text{Market value of FRA} = \frac{5m \times (0.01 - 0.009)}{1.009}$$
$$= 4{,}955.40. \tag{4.44}$$

In practice, the reference interest rate on which the cash settlement is based is computed as an average of many banks' quotes, two days before T_1. The contract stipulates how many banks will be called, from what list, and how the averaging is done. In the early 1980s, FRAs were quoted for short-term maturities only. Currently, quotes extend up to ten years.

4.7.2 Why FRAs Exist

Like any forward contract, an FRA can be used either for hedging or for speculation purposes. Hedging may be desirable in order to facilitate budget projections in an enterprise or to reduce uncertainty and the associated costs of financial distress. Banks, for example, use FRAs, along with T-bill futures and bond futures, to reduce maturity mismatches between their assets and liabilities. For instance, a bank with an average duration of three months on the liability side and twelve months on the asset side can use a three-to-twelve month FRA to eliminate most of the interest-rate risk. An FRA can, of course, serve as a speculative instrument too.

As we shall show in the next paragraph, FFs (or FRAs) can be replicated from term deposits and loans. For financial institutions, and even for other firms, FRAs and interest futures are preferred over such synthetic FRAs in the sense that they do not inflate the balance sheet.

Example 4.30. Suppose that you need a three-to-six month forward loan for JPY 1b. Replication would mean that you borrow (somewhat less than) JPY 1b for six months and invest the proceeds for three months, until you actually need the money. Thus, your balance sheet would have increased by JPY 1b, without any increase in profits or cash flows compared with the case where you used an FF or an FRA.

The drawback of using an FF or FRA is that there is no organized secondary market. However, as in the case of forward contracts on foreign currency, long-term FRA contracts are sometimes collateralized or periodically recontracted. This reduces credit risk. Thus, a fairly active over-the-counter market for FRAs is emerging.

4.7.3 The Valuation of FFs (or FRAs)

We now discuss the pricing of FFs (or FRAs—both have the same value). How should one value an outstanding contract, and how should the market set the normal forward interest rate at a given point in time? In this section, we adopt the following notation: t_0 is the date on which the contract was initiated; t ($\geqslant t_0$) is the moment the contract is valued; T_1 is the expiration date of the forward contract (that is, the date that the gains or losses on the FRA are settled, and the date when the notional deposit starts); T_2 ($> T_1$) is the expiration date of the notional deposit; $r^{\text{f}}_{t_0,T_1,T_2}$ is the effective return between T_1 and T_2, without annualization, promised on the notional deposit at the date the FRA was signed, t_0.

First consider a numerical example.

DIY Problem 4.6. Consider an FF under which you will deposit JPY 1b in nine months and receive 1.005b in twelve. The effective risk-free rates for these maturities are $r_{t,T_1} = 0.6\%$ and $r_{t,T_2} = 0.81$, respectively. Value each of the PNs that replicate the two legs of the FF. Compute the net value.

The generalization is obvious. Below, we take a notional deposit amount of 1 (at T_1):

$$\text{PV, at } t, \text{ of a unit FF} = \underbrace{\frac{\text{Promised inflow at } T_2}{1 + r_{t,T_2}}}_{\text{``Asset'' PN}} - \underbrace{\frac{\text{Promised outflow at } T_1}{1 + r_{t,T_1}}}_{\text{``Liability'' PN}}$$

$$= \frac{1 + r^{\text{f}}_{t_0,T_1,T_2}}{1 + r_{t,T_2}} - \frac{1}{1 + r_{t,T_1}}. \tag{4.45}$$

In one special case we can consider the expiry moment ($t = T_1$).

DIY Problem 4.7. Derive, from this general formula, our earlier cash-settlement equation,

$$\text{PV, at } T_1, \text{ of a unit FF} = \frac{r^{\text{f}}_{t_0,T_1,T_2} - r_{T_1,T_2}}{1 + r_{T_1,T_2}}. \tag{4.46}$$

The other special case worth considering is the value at initiation ($t_0 = t$). We know that this value must be zero, as for any standard forward contract, so this provides a way to relate the forward rate to the two spot rates, all at t.

DIY Problem 4.8. Derive, from the general formula, the relation between the time-t spot and forward rates:

$$(1 + r_{t,T_1})(1 + r^{\text{f}}_{t,T_1,T_2}) = 1 + r_{t,T_2}; \tag{4.47}$$

$$\Longleftrightarrow \quad r^{\text{f}}_{t,T_1,T_2} = \frac{1 + r_{t,T_2}}{1 + r_{t,T_1}} - 1. \tag{4.48}$$

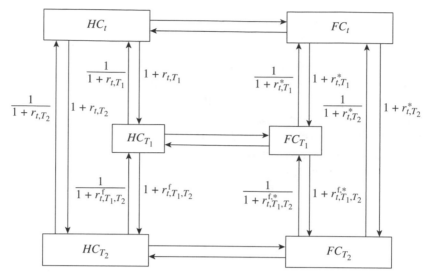

Figure 4.6.   Spot and forward money markets (with international links).

The left-hand side of the first equality, equation (4.47), has an obvious interpretation: it shows the gross return from a synthetic deposit started right now (t) and expiring at T_2, made not directly but replicated by making a t-to-T_1 spot deposit which is rolled over (i.e., reinvested, here including the interest earned) via a T_1-to-T_2 forward deposit. So the money is contractually committed for the total t-to-T_2 period, and the total return is fixed right now—two ingredients that also characterize a t-to-T_2 deposit. In that light, equation (4.47) just says that the direct and the synthetic t-to-T_2 deposits should have the same return.

As in the case of currency forwards, no causality is implied by our way of expressing equation (4.48). The three rates are set jointly and have to satisfy equation (4.48), and that is all. As in the body of this chapter, one could argue that causality, if there is any, may run from the forward interest rate toward the spot rate because the forward rate reflects the risk-adjusted expectations about the future interest rate. We shall use equation (4.48) when we discuss eurocurrency futures, in the appendix to chapter 6.

There is an obvious no-arbitrage version of this. In figure 4.6 we combine two of our familiar spot-forward currency diagrams, one for future date T_1 and the other for date T_2. The focus, this time, is not on the exchange markets, so the horizontal lines that refer to currency deals are made thinner. The forward deposits and loans are shown as transactions that transform T_1-dated money into T_2 money (the deposit) or vice versa (the loan), and the multiplication factors needed to compute the output from a transaction, shown next to the arrows, are $(1 + r^{\mathrm{f}})$ and $1/(1 + r^{\mathrm{f}})$, respectively. This diagram shows that every spot or forward money-market deal can be replicated, which helps you in shopping-around problems. The diagram also helps identifying the no-arb constraints.

DIY Problem 4.9. We have already shown how to replicate the t-to-T_2 deposit. In the table below, add the replications for the other transactions and check that they generate the gross returns shown in the rightmost column.

Replicand	Replication	Output value
t-to-T_2 deposit	Spot deposit t to T_1, rolled over forward T_1 to T_2	$(1 + r_{t,T_1})(1 + r^{\mathrm{f}}_{t,T_1,T_2})$
Forward deposit T_1 to T_2		$\dfrac{1 + r_{t,T_2}}{1 + r_{t,T_1}}$
Spot deposit t to T_1		$\dfrac{1 + r_{t,T_2}}{1 + r^{\mathrm{f}}_{t,T_1,T_2}}$
t-to-T_2 loan		$\dfrac{1}{(1 + r_{t,T_1})(1 + r^{\mathrm{f}}_{t,T_1,T_2})}$
Forward loan T_1 to T_2		$\dfrac{1 + r_{t,T_1}}{1 + r_{t,T_2}}$
Spot loan t to T_1		$\dfrac{1 + r^{\mathrm{f}}_{t,T_1,T_2}}{1 + r_{t,T_2}}$

The output value is computed for input value equal to unity.

But the diagram shows not just the replication possibilities: there are also two no-arb constraints inside each money market, corresponding to, respectively, the clockwise and counterclockwise round-trips. You start, for instance, in the time-T_2 box, issuing a PN note dated T_2. You discount it immediately and make a synthetic deposit t to T_2. The constraint is that the proceeds of this deposit be no higher than 1, the amount you owe to the holder of the PN:

$$HC_{T_2} \quad \rightarrow \quad HC_t \quad \rightarrow \quad HC_{T_1} \quad \rightarrow \quad HC_{T_2}$$

$$1 \times \frac{1}{1 + r_{t,T_2}} \times (1 + r_{t,T_1}) \times (1 + r^{\mathrm{f}}_{t,T_1,T_2}) \leqslant 1. \qquad (4.49)$$

DIY Problem 4.10. Identify the other no-arb trip in the home money market and write the corresponding constraint. Combine it with constraint (4.49) and check that you get back equation (4.47).

To seasoned arbitrageurs like you, it is easy to add bid and ask superscripts to the rates of return (and to the exchange rates, while you are at it). The no-arb constraints are still [synthetic bid] $\leqslant$ [ask] and [bid] $\leqslant$ [synthetic ask], with the synthetics computed from the worst-possible-combination versions of the perfect-market replication that you have just worked out yourself.

Before we move to other markets, there is another set of no-arb constraints and shopping-around opportunities to be discussed, namely those created via international linkages rather than relations within each money market. Remember, one can replicate a currency-X spot deposit or loan by swapping a currency-Y spot deposit or loan into currency X. Well, the same holds for forward deposits and loans. For instance, in the few years when USD or GBP had FRA markets but minor European currencies had not (yet), pros replicated the missing FRAs by swapping USD or GBP FRAs into, say, NLG via a forward-forward currency swap, in or out. Such swaps are described in chapter 5, and consist of a currency forward in one direction combined with a second currency forward in the other direction. In short, when the starting date of a deposit or loan is not spot but n days forward, we just replace the spot leg of the swap by the appropriate forward leg.

4.7.4 Forward Interest Rates as the Core of the Term Structure(s)

Remember that forward exchange rates, being the risk-adjusted expectations, are central in any theory of exchange rates. In the same way, forward interest rates can be viewed as the core of every theory of interest rates. The standard *expectations theory* hypothesizes that forward interest rates are equal to expected future spot rates, and Hicks added a *risk premium*, arguing—to use a post-Hicksian terminology—that the beta risk of a bond is higher the longer its time to maturity. Modern versions would rather state everything in terms of PN prices rather than interest rates, but would agree with the basic intuition of the old theories: forward rates reflect expectations corrected for risks.

Various theories or models differ as to how expectations evolve and risk premia are set, but once the forward rates are set, the entire term structure follows. We illustrate this with a numerical example, and meanwhile introduce you to the various interest-rate concepts: spot rates, yields at par for bullet bonds, and other yields at par.

We start with the first row in table 4.3, which shows a set of forward rates. For simplicity of notation, current time t is taken to be zero, so that a one-period forward rate looks like $r^f_{0,n-1,n}$ rather than the more laborious $r^f_{t,t+n-1,t+n}$. For some reason—mainly expectations, one would presume—there is a strong "hump" in the forward rates: they peak at the three-to-four year horizon. (A period is of unspecified length, in the theories; but let us agree they are years.[10]) The initial spot rate and the forward rate with starting date 0 are, of course, the same. Below we show you the formulas to be used in a spreadsheet to generate all possible term structures (TSs).

The TS of spot rates is obtained in two steps. First we cumulate the forward rates into effective spot rates, using equation (4.47):

$$1 + r_{0,n} = \prod_{j=1}^{n} (1 + r^f_{0,j-1,j}). \tag{4.50}$$

The rate on the left-hand side is the effective rate we have always used in this book. But for the theory of term structures it is useful to convert the effective

---

[10] For this reason the only nonarbitrary theory is one that works with continuous time, where a period lasts dt years. But for introductory courses this has obvious drawbacks.

Table 4.3. Term structures and their linkages.

	Rate or PV factor for various n						
	$n = 1$	$n = 2$	$n = 3$	$n = 4$	$n = 5$	$n = 6$	$n = 7$
Forward rate per period, $r^{\mathrm{f}}_{0,n-1,n}$	0.0300	0.0350	0.0380	0.0400	0.0360	0.0300	0.0200
$1 + r^{\mathrm{f}}_{0,n-1,n}$	1.0300	1.0350	1.0380	1.0400	1.0360	1.0300	1.0200
$1 + r_{0,n} = \prod_{j=1}^{n}(1 + r^{\mathrm{f}}_{0,j-1,j})$	1.0300	1.0661	1.1066	1.1508	1.1923	1.2280	1.2526
$\bar{r}_{0,n} = (1 + r_{0,n})^{1/n} - 1$	0.0300	0.0325	0.0343	0.0357	0.0358	0.0348	0.0327
$\mathrm{PV}_{0,n} = \dfrac{1}{1 + r_{0,n}}$	0.9709	0.9380	0.9037	0.8689	0.8387	0.8143	0.7984
PV annuity, $a_{0,n} = \sum_{j=1}^{n} \mathrm{PV}_{0,j}$	0.9709	1.9089	2.8126	3.6816	4.5203	5.3346	6.1330
$R_{0,n} : \dfrac{1 - (1 + R_{0,n})^{-n}}{R_{0,n}} = a_{0,n}$	0.0300	0.0316	0.0330	0.0340	0.0346	0.0347	0.0342
$c_{0,n} = \dfrac{1 - \mathrm{PV}_{0,n}}{a_{0,n}}$	0.0300	0.0325	0.0342	0.0356	0.0357	0.0348	0.0329

Starting with an assumed set of forward rates, I compute the set of "spot" zero-coupon rates (lines 3 and 4) and present value factors (line 5). This allows us to find the PV of a constant unit annuity (line 6) and the corresponding yield. Finally, I compute the yield at par for a bullet bond. The math is described in the text.

rate to a per-period rate, which we denote by $\bar{r}$. The computation is

$$1 + \bar{r}_{0,n} := (1 + r_{0,n})^{1/n}. \qquad (4.51)$$

The spot rates are the yields to maturity on zero-coupon bonds expiring at n. Note how the per-period gross rates are rolling geometric averages—numerically close to simple averages—of all gross forward rates between times 0 and n.[11] See how the strong hump is very much flattened out by the rolling-averaging, and the peak pushed to $n = 5$ instead of $n = 4$ for the forward rates. A second alternative way to work with the effective rate is to compute the PV of one unit of HC payable at time n,

$$\mathrm{PV}_{0,n} = \frac{1}{1 + r_{0,n}}. \qquad (4.52)$$

The TS of yields for constant-annuity cash flows is a different TS. It is not as popular as the TS of yields at par for bullet loans (see below), but it is convenient to look at this one first. Any yield or *internal rate of return* is the compound "flat" rate that equates a discounted stream of known future cash flows C_j to an observed present value:

$$y : \frac{C_1}{1 + y} + \frac{C_2}{(1 + y)^2} + \cdots + \frac{C_n}{(1 + y)^n} = \text{observed PV}. \qquad (4.53)$$

---

[11] A gross rate is $1 + r$, r being the net rate we always use in this text.

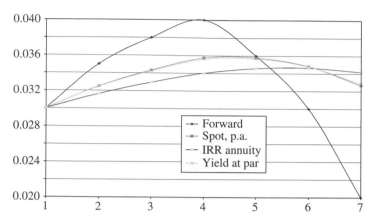

Figure 4.7. Term structures: forward, spot, and two types of yields.

Here we look at the special case $C_j = 1$, $\forall j$, the constant unit-cash-flow stream, the right-hand side of the above equation. Let us first find the PV of the constant stream. Since we already know the PV of a single unit payment made at n, the PV of a stream paid out at times $1, \ldots, n$ is simply the sum. This special PV is denoted as $a_{0,n}$, from "annuity." We compute its value for various n as

$$a_{0,n} = \sum_{j=1}^{n} PV_{0,j}. \tag{4.54}$$

Next we find the yield that equates this PV to the discounted cash flows. When the cash flows all equal unity, the left-hand side of equation (4.53) is equal to $(1 - (1 + y)^{-n})/y$, but the y that solves the constraint must still be found numerically, using, for example, a spreadsheet tool. In the table the result is found under the label $R_{0,n}$. Note how this yield is an analytically nontraceable mixture of all spot rates. The hump is flattened out even more, and its peak pushed back one more period.

The TS of yields at par for bullet loans is defined as a yield that sets the PV of a bullet loan equal to par. But it is known that to get a unit value the yield must be set equal to the coupon rate. So we can now rephrase the question as follows: how do we set the coupon rate c such that the PVs of the coupons and the principal sum to unity?

$$c_{0,n}: \quad \underbrace{c_{0,n} \times a_{0,n}}_{\substack{\text{PV of} \\ \text{coupons}}} + \underbrace{PV_{0,n} \times 1}_{\substack{\text{PV of} \\ \text{amortization}}} = 1 \quad \Longrightarrow \quad c_{0,n} = \frac{1 - PV_{0,n}}{a_{0,n}}. \tag{4.55}$$

Again, this is numerically much closer to the spot rates than the yield on constant-annuity loans, and the reason is obviously that the bullet loan is closer to a zero-coupon loan—especially in an example where, as in ours, interest rates are generally low. In figure 4.7, which shows the four TSs graphically, those for swap and spot rates overlap almost perfectly.

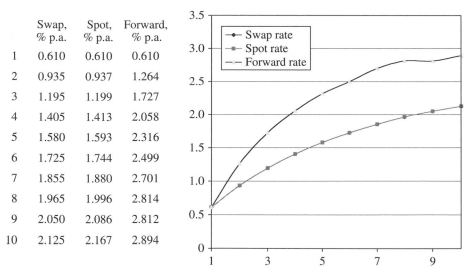

	Swap, % p.a.	Spot, % p.a.	Forward, % p.a.
1	0.610	0.610	0.610
2	0.935	0.937	1.264
3	1.195	1.199	1.727
4	1.405	1.413	2.058
5	1.580	1.593	2.316
6	1.725	1.744	2.499
7	1.855	1.880	2.701
8	1.965	1.996	2.814
9	2.050	2.086	2.812
10	2.125	2.167	2.894

Figure 4.8. Extracting spot and forward rates from the JPY swap rates. Swap and spot are so close, in these figures, that on the graph you can no longer spot the difference; you need to look at the numbers.

This illustrates how the TS of forward rates contains all information for pricing, so that TS theories are basically theories about forward rates. It also gives you a feeling about how swap dealers set their long-term interest rates, which are yields-at-par for bullet bonds. As we do here, they construct them from spot rates. These spot rates, in turn, are obtained from PV factors extracted, via regression analysis, from bond prices in the secondary market. You can, of course, reverse-engineer all this and extract PV factors from swap rates, and thence forward rates. Then you may ask the question of whether there seem to be good reasons for the forward rate to behave as it appears to do, and perhaps invest or disinvest accordingly. For instance, in figure 4.8 we have taken the JPY swap rates from chapter 7 and extracted spot and forward rates. Spot rates are familiarly close to swap rates (yields at par for bullet bonds) but the forward rate, equally familiar, moves much faster than the spot rate (a rolling average). So one can ask the question, how do these forward rates compare with your expectations about future spot rates?

A second insight you should remember is that there is no such thing as "the" TS. Academics first think of the TS of spot rates or forward rates (and are precise about that). But practitioners first think about the TS of yields at par for bullet bonds, the numbers one sees in the newspaper or that are quoted by swap dealers (who call them swap rates). Many traditional practitioners would apply the yield-at-par rates for any instrument, whether it is a bullet loan or not. This can imply serious errors and inconsistencies.

Yields are funny. Even if we just consider bullet bonds, there is still a yield for every *total* time to maturity n. So in the situation depicted in table 4.3 a coupon paid at time 1 would be discounted at 3% if it is part of a one-period bond, 3.25% if it is part of a two-period bond, 3.42% if it is part of a three-period bond, and so on. It is much more logical to work with a discount rate for every payment horizon, regardless of what bond pays out the money, rather than a discount rate for every bond, regardless of the date of the payment.

TEST YOUR UNDERSTANDING

Quiz Questions

1. Which of the following statements are correct?

   (a) A forward purchase contract can be replicated by borrowing foreign currency, converting it to domestic currency, and investing the domestic currency.

   (b) A forward purchase contract can be replicated by borrowing domestic currency, converting it to foreign currency, and investing the foreign currency.

   (c) A forward sale contract can be replicated by borrowing foreign currency, converting it to domestic currency, and investing the domestic currency.

   (d) A forward sale contract can be replicated by borrowing domestic currency, converting it to foreign currency, and investing the foreign currency.

   (e) In a perfect market you could forbid forward markets (on the basis of antigambling laws, for instance), and nobody would give a fig.

   (f) The spot rate and the interest rate determine the forward price.

   (g) No, the forward determines the spot.

   (h) No, the forward and the spot and the foreign interest rate determine the domestic interest rate.

   (i) No, there are just four products that are so closely related that their prices cannot be set independently.

2. What is wrong with the following statements?

   (a) The forward is the expected future spot rate.

   (b) The sign of the forward premium tells you nothing about the strength of a currency; it just reflects the difference of the interest rates.

   (c) The difference of the interest rates tells you nothing about the strength of a currency; it just reflects the forward premium or discount.

   (d) The forward rate is a risk-adjusted expectation but the spot rate is independent of expectations.

   (e) A certainty equivalent tends to be above the risk-adjusted expectation because of the risk correction.

   (f) A risk-adjusted expectation is always below the true expectation because we do not like risk.

(g) A risk-adjusted expectation can be close to, or above, the true expectation. In that case the whole world would hold very little of that currency, or would even short it.

(h) Adding a zero-value contract cannot change the value of the firm; therefore a forward hedge cannot make the shareholders better off.

Applications

1. Check analytically the equivalence of the two alternative ways to do the following trips:

   (a) Financing of international trade: you currently hold an FC claim on a customer payable at T, but you want cash HC instead.

   (b) Domestic deposits: you currently hold spot HC and you want to park that money in HC, risk free.

   (c) You want to borrow HC for three months.

   (d) Immunizing an HC dent: you want to set aside some of your cash HC so as to take care of a future FC debt.

   (e) Borrowing FC: you want to borrow FC but a friend tells you that swapping an HC loan is much cheaper

2. You hold a set of forward contracts on EUR, against USD (= HC). Below I show you the forward prices in the contract; the current forward prices (if available) or at least the current spot rate and interest rates (if no forward is available for this time to maturity). Compute the fair value of the contracts.

   (a) Purchased: EUR 1m 60 days (remaining). Historic rate: 1.350; current rate for same date: 1.500; risk-free rates (simple per annum): 3% in USD, 4% in EUR.

   (b) Purchased: EUR 2.5m 75 days (remaining). Historic rate: 1.300; current spot rate: 1.5025; risk-free rates (simple per annum): 3% in USD, 4% in EUR.

   (c) Sold: EUR 0.75m 180 days (remaining). Historic rate: 1.400; current rate for same date: 1.495; risk-free rates (simple per annum): 3% in USD, 4% in EUR.

3. Sixty-day interest rates (simple, p.a.) are 3% at home (USD) and 4% abroad (EUR). The spot rate moves from 1.000 to 1.001.

   (a) What is the return differential and what is the corresponding prediction of the change in the forward rate?

   (b) What is the actual change in the forward rate?

   (c) What is the predicted change in the swap rate computed from the return differential?

   (d) What is the actual change in the swap rate?

4. Sixty-day interest rates (simple, p.a.) are 3% at home (USD) and 4% abroad (EUR). The spot rate is 1.250.

   (a) Check that investing EUR 1m, hedged, returns as much as USD 1.25m

   (b) Check that if taxes are neutral and the tax rate is 30%, the after-tax returns are also equal. (Yes, this *is* trivial.)

(c) How much of the income from swapped EUR is legally interest income and how much is capital gain or loss?

(d) If you do not have to pay taxes on capital gains and cannot deduct capital losses, would you still be indifferent between USD deposits and swapped EUR?

5. Sixty-day interest rates (simple, p.a.) are 3% at home (USD) and 4% abroad (EUR). The spot rate is 1.250.

   (a) Check that borrowing EUR 1m (= current proceeds, not future debt), hedged, costs as much as borrowing USD 1.25m

   (b) Check that if taxes are neutral, and the tax rate is 30%, the after-tax costs are also equal. (Yes, this *is* trivial.)

   (c) How much of the costs of borrowing swapped EUR is legally interest paid and how much is capital gain or loss?

   (d) If you do not have to pay taxes on capital gains and cannot deduct capital losses, would you still be indifferent between USD loans and swapped EUR?

6. Groucho Marx, as Governor of Freedonia's central bank, has problems. He sees the value of his currency, the FDK, under constant attack from Rosor, a wealthy mutual-fund manager. Apparently, Rosor believes that the FDK will soon devalue from GBP 1.000 to 0.950.

   (a) Currently, both GBP and FDK interest rates are 6% p.a. By how much should Groucho change the one-year interest rate so as to stabilize the spot rate even if Rosor expects a spot rate of 0.950 in one year? Ignore the risk premium, that is, take 0.950 to be the certainty equivalent.

   (b) If the interest-rate hike also affects Rosor's expectations about the future spot rate, in which direction would this be? Taking into account this second-round effect as well, would Groucho have to increase the rate by more than your first calculation, or by less?

5

Using Forwards for International Financial Management

In this chapter, we discuss the five main purposes for which forward contracts are used: arbitrage (or potential arbitrage), hedging, speculation, shopping around, and valuation. These provide the topics of sections 5.2 to 5.6, respectively. But first we need to spend some time on practical issues: the quotation method, and the provisions for default risk (section 5.1).

5.1 Practical Aspects of Forwards in Real-World Markets

5.1.1 Quoting Forward Rates with Bid–Ask Spreads

With bid–ask spreads, a forward rate can still be quoted "outright" (that is, as an absolute number), or as a swap rate. The outright quotes look like spot quotes in that they immediately give us the level of the forward bid and ask rates; for instance, the rates may be CAD/USD (180 days) 1.1875–1.1895. Swap rates, on the other hand, show the numbers that are to be added to or subtracted from the spot bid and ask rates in order to obtain the forward quotes. One ought to be careful in interpreting such quotes, and make sure that the correct number is added to or subtracted from the spot bid or ask rate.

Example 5.1. Most papers nowadays show outright rates, but Antwerp's *De Tijd* used to publish swap rates until late 2005. Table 5.1 shows an example, to which I have added a column of midpoint swap rates and Libor 30-day interest rates (simple, p.a.). Swap rates are quoted in foreign currency since the quotes against the euro are conventionally in FC units; and they are in basis points, i.e., hundredths of cents.

To compute the outright forward rates from these quotes, one adds the first swap rate to the spot bid rate, and the second swap rate to the spot ask rate. The excerpt shows the midpoint spot rate rather than the bid–ask quotes. Suppose, however, that the bid and ask spot rates are (1.17)74–78 for the USD. Then the

Termijnkoersen										Bron: Dexia		*LIBOR*	
	1 maand		2 maand		3 maaand		6 maand		12 maand			*Spot rate*	*30d*
Amerikaanse dollar	19.20	19.28	37.30	37.50	58.82	59.07	115.00	115.60	229.60	231.00		*1.1776*	*4.20*
Australische dollar	46.00	46.60	84.20	85.10	128.00	130.00	239.00	242.00	464.00	468.00		*1.5988*	*5.55*
Brits pond	13.40	13.60	24.20	24.50	36.50	36.80	65.70	66.40	121.00	123.00		*0.6846*	*4.81*
...													
Japanse Yen	-29.10	-28.80	-57.20	-56.80	-89.10	-88.60	-177.00	-176.00	-370.00	-366.00		*139.7800*	*0.03*
Nieuw-Zeelandse dollar	80.10	81.10	148.00	149.00	226.00	228.00	425.00	429.00	818.00	829.00		*1.7035*	*7.48*
...													
Zweedse Kroon	-52.10	-47.80	-132.00	-126.00	-189.00	-181.00	-372.00	-356.00	-655.00	-607.00		*9.5162*	*1.60*
Zwitserse frank	-21.40	-21.10	-39.70	-38.90	-60.00	-59.70	-114.00	-111.00	-211.00	-205.00		*1.5491*	*0.80*
eur													*2.335*

Figure 5.1. Swap quotes, bid and ask, from *De Tijd*.

outright forward rates, one month, are computed as follows:

$$\text{Bid:} \quad 1.1774 + 0.000\,192\,0 = \text{USD/EUR } 1.177\,592\,0,$$

$$\text{Ask:} \quad 1.1778 + 0.000\,192\,8 = \text{USD/EUR } 1.177\,992\,8.$$

DIY Problem 5.1. Check the interest rates, and note which ones are higher than the EUR one. Figure out which forward rates should be above par and which below. Verify that the signs of the swap rates are correct, especially once you remember that the EUR is the FC (also for the GBP quote).

Note from the example that whenever we observe a premium we always add the smaller of the two swap rates to the spot bid rate, and the larger swap rate to the spot ask rate. As a result, the forward spread is wider than the spot spread (figure 5.2). Likewise, in case of a discount, the number we subtract from the spot bid rate is larger, in absolute value, than the number we subtract from the spot ask rate; and this again produces a wider spread in the forward market than in the spot market (figure 5.2). Finally, note that the difference between the swap rates becomes larger the longer the contract's time to maturity. This illustrates the *second law of imperfect exchange markets*: the forward spread is always larger than the spot spread, and increases with the time to maturity.

One explanation of this empirical regularity is that the longer the maturity, the lower the transaction volume; and in thin markets, spreads tend to be high. A second reason is that, over short periods, things generally do not change much, but a lot can happen over long periods. Thus, a bank may be confident that the customer will still be sound in 30 days, but feel far less certain about the customer's creditworthiness in five years. In addition, the exchange rate can change far more over five years than over 30 days; so the further off the maturity date, the larger the potential loss if and when default happens and the bank is forced to close out, i.e., reverse, the forward contract it had signed with the customer at t_0.[1] Thus, banks build a default-risk premium into their

---

[1] Note that the exchange risk is only relevant if and when the customer defaults. Normally, a bank closes its position soon after the initial deal is signed, but this close-out position unexpectedly turns out to be an open one if and when the customer's promised deal evaporates. In short, exchange risk only arises as an interaction with default risk.

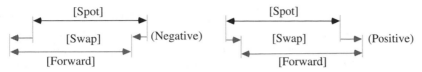

Figure 5.2. The bid–ask spread in a forward is wider than in a spot. For negative swap rates the bid is the bigger one, in absolute terms, while for positive swap rates the ask is the bigger one. This is equivalent to observing a larger total bid–ask spread in the forward market.

spreads, which, therefore, goes up with time to maturity. Later on we will see by how much the spreads can go up maximally with time to maturity.

The second law keeps you from getting irretrievably lost when confronted with bid–ask swap quotes, because the convention of quoting is by no means uniform internationally. Sometimes the sign of the swap rate (+ versus −; or p versus d) is entirely omitted, because the pros all know the sign already. Or sometimes the swap rates are quoted, regardless of sign, as "small number–big number," followed by p (for premium) or d (for discount). When in doubt, just test which combination generates the bigger spread.

Let us now address weightier matters: how is credit risk handled?

5.1.2 Provisions for Default

Forward dealers happily quote forward rates based on interbank interest rates, even if their counterpart is much more risky than a bank. Shouldn't they build risk spreads into the interest rates, as they do when they lend money? The answer is no (or, at most, not much): while the bank's risk under a forward contract is not entirely absent, it is still far lower than under a loan contract. Banks have, in effect, come up with various solutions that partially solve the problem of default risk.

The right of offset. First and foremost, a forward contract has an unwritten but time-hallowed clause saying that if one party defaults, then the other party cannot be forced to complete its own part of the deal; moreover, if that other party still sustains losses, the defaulting party remains liable for these losses. Thus, if the customer defaults, the bank that sold FC forward can now dispose of this amount in the spot market (rather than delivering it to the defaulting customer) and keep the revenue. There is still a potential loss if and to the extent that this revenue (S_T) is below the amount promised ($F_{t_0,T}$), but even if nothing of this can be recouped in the bankruptcy court the maximum loss is ($F_{t_0,T} - S_T$), not $F_{t_0,T}$.[2]

---

[2] To obtain a security with the same credit risk for a synthetic forward contract, the bank would have to insist that the customer hold the deposit part of its synthetic contract in an escrow account, to be released only after the customer's loan is paid back. The forward contract is definitely the simpler way to achieve this security, which is one reason why an outright contract is more attractive than its synthetic version.

Example 5.2. Citibank has sold forward JPY 100m at USD/JPY 0.0115 to Fab4 Inc., a rock band, to cover the expenses of their upcoming tour; but on the due date Citi discovers they have declared bankruptcy. Since bankers are traditionally careful (really), Citi had bought forward the yen it owed Fab4. Given the bankruptcy, Citi has no choice but to sell these JPY 100m spot at, say, $S_T = 0.0109$. The default has cost Citi $100m \times (0.0115 - 0.0109) = USD\ 60,000$. In contrast, if Fab4 had promised JPY 100m in repayment of a loan, Citi might have lost the full $100m \times 0.0115 = USD\ 1.15m$. Since, under the forward contract, Citi can revoke its own obligation the net loss is always smaller, and could even turn into a gain.

Interbank: credit agreements. In the interbank market, the players deal only with banks and corporations that are well-known to one another and have signed credit agreements for (spot and) forward trading, that is, agreements that they will freely buy and sell to each other. Even there, credit limits are set per bank to limit default risk.

Firms: credit agreements or security. Likewise, corporations can buy or sell forward if they are well-known customers with a credit agreement providing—within limits—for spot and forward trades, probably alongside other things like overdraft facilities and envelopes for discounting of bills or for letters of credit. The alternative is to ask for margin. For unknown or risky customers, the margin may be as high as 100%.

Example 5.3. Expecting a depreciation of the pound sterling, Burton Freedman wants to sell forward GBP 1m for six months. The 180-day forward rate is USD/GBP 1.5. The bank, worried about the contingency that the pound may actually go up, asks for 25% margin. This means that Mr. Freedman has to deposit $1m \times USD/GBP\ 1.5 \times 0.25 = USD\ 375,000$ with the bank, which remains with the bank until he has paid for the GBP. The interest earned on the deposit is Mr. Freedman's. This way, the bank is covered against the combined contingency of the GBP rising by up to 25% *and* Mr. Freedman defaulting on the contract.

Restricted use. Even within an agreed credit line, "speculative" forward positions are frowned upon, unless a lot of margin is posted. Banks see forwards as hedging devices for their customers, not as speculative instruments.

Short lives. Maturities go up to 10 years, but in actual fact the life of most forward contracts is short: most contracts have maturities of less than one year, and longer-term contracts are entered into only with customers that have excellent credit ratings. To hedge long-term exposures one then needs to roll over short-term forward contracts. For example, the corporation can engage in three consecutive one-year contracts if a single three-year contract is not available.

Example 5.4. At time 0, an Indian company wants to buy forward USD 1m for three years. Suppose that the bank gives it a three-year forward contract at $F_{0,3} = INR/USD\ 40$. Suppose the bank's worst nightmares come true: the spot rate goes down all the time, say, to 38, 36, and 34 at times 1, 2, and 3, respectively. If, at time 3, the company defaults, the bank is stuck with USD 1m worth INR 34m rather than the contracted value, 40m. Thus, the bank has a loss of $(F_{0,3} - S_3) = $ INR 6m.

Suppose instead that, at $t = 0$, the bank gave a one-year contract at the rate $F_{0,1} = 40.3$. After one year, the customer pays INR 40.3m for the currency, takes delivery of the USD 1m, and sells these (spot) at $S_1 = 38$. After verification of the company's current creditworthiness, the bank now gives it a new one-year contract at, say, $F_{1,2} = 37.2$. At time $t = 2$, the customer takes the second loss. If it is still creditworthy, the customer will get a third one-year forward contract at, say, $F_{2,3} = 35.9$. If there is default at time 3, the bank's loss on the third contract is just 1.9m rather than the 6m it would have lost with the three-year contract.

From the bank's point of view, the main advantage of the alternative of rolling over short-term contracts is that losses do not accumulate. The uncertainty, at time 0, about the spot rate one year out is far smaller than the uncertainty about the rate three years out. Thus, *ex ante* the worst possible loss on a three-year contract exceeds the worst possible loss on a one-year contract. In addition, the probability of default increases with the time horizon—in the course of three years, a lot more bad things can happen to a firm than in one year, *ex ante*—and also with the size of the loss. For these three reasons, the bank's expected losses from default are larger the longer the maturity of the forward contract.

The example also demonstrates that rolling over is an imperfect substitute to a single three-year forward contract. First, there are interim losses or gains, creating a time-value risk. For instance, the hedger does not know at what interest rates he or she will be able to finance the interim losses or invest the interim gains. Second, the hedger does not know to what extent the forward rates will deviate from the spot rates at the rollover dates: these future forward premia depend on the (unknown) future interest rates in both currencies. Third, the total cumulative cash flow, realized by the hedger over the three consecutive contracts, depends on the time path of the spot rates between time 1 and time 3.

$$* \quad * \quad *$$

All this has given you enough background for a discussion of how and when forward contracts are used in practice. Among the many uses to which forward contracts may be put, the first we bring up is arbitrage, or at least the potential of arbitrage: this keeps spot, forward, and interest rates in line.

5.2 Using Forward Contracts (1): Arbitrage

One question to be answered is to what extent interest rate parity still holds in the presence of spreads. A useful first step in this analysis is to determine the synthetic forward rates.

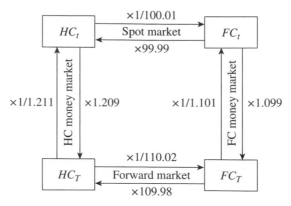

Figure 5.3. Spot/forward/money market diagram with bid–ask spreads.

5.2.1 Synthetic Forward Rates

It should not come as a surprise to you that, in the presence of spreads, the synthetic forward rates are the worst possible combinations of the basic perfect-markets formula. We can immediately see this when we do the two trips on the diagram in figure 5.3. These figures are familiar from the last chapter, but now we use bid rates that are slightly below the formerly unique exchange or interest rates, and ask rates slightly above these old values. What are the synthetic rates?

Synthetic bid. The synthetic-sale trip is $FC_T \to FC_t \to HC_t \to HC_T$, and it yields

$$HC_T = FC_T \times \frac{1}{1.101} \times 99.99 \times 1.209, \qquad (5.1)$$

$$\implies \quad \text{synthetic } F_{t,T}^{\text{bid}} = \frac{HC_T}{FC_T} = 99.99 \frac{1.209}{1.101} = 109.798. \qquad (5.2)$$

Synthetic ask. The synthetic-purchase trip is $HC_T \to HC_t \to FC_t \to FC_T$, and it yields

$$FC_T = HC_T \times \frac{1}{1.211} \times \frac{1}{100.01} \times 1.099, \qquad (5.3)$$

$$\implies \quad \text{synthetic } F_{t,T}^{\text{ask}} = \frac{HC_T}{FC_T} = 100.01 \frac{1.211}{1.099} = 110.202. \qquad (5.4)$$

We see that, in computing the synthetic bid rate, we retain the basic CIP formula but add the *bid* or *ask* qualifiers that generate the lowest possible combination: *bid × bid / ask*. Likewise, in computing the synthetic ask rate we pick the highest possible combination: *ask × ask / bid*. In short,

$$\text{synthetic } [F_{t,T}^{\text{bid}}, F_{t,T}^{\text{ask}}] = \left[S_t^{\text{bid}} \frac{1 + r_{t,T}^{\text{bid}}}{1 + r_{t,T}^{*\text{ask}}}, S_t^{\text{ask}} \frac{1 + r_{t,T}^{\text{ask}}}{1 + r_{t,T}^{*\text{bid}}} \right]. \qquad (5.5)$$

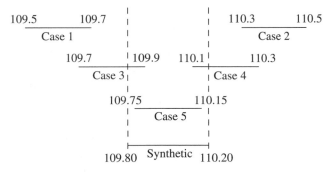

Figure 5.4. Synthetic and actual forward rates: some conceivable combinations.

5.2.2 Implications of Arbitrage and Shopping Around

In figure 5.4, we illustrate the by-now familiar implications of the arbitrage and shopping-around mechanisms.

1. Arbitrage ensures that the synthetic and actual quotes can never be so far apart that there is empty space between them. Thus, given the synthetic quotes 109.8–110.2, we can rule out case 1: we would have been able to buy directly at 109.7 and sell synthetically at 109.8. Likewise, situations like case 2 should vanish immediately (if they occur at all): we would have been able to buy synthetically at 110.2 and sell at 110.3 in the direct market.

2. The usual shopping-around logic means that, in situations like case 3 and case 4, there would be no customers in the direct market on one side.

   - If there were only one market maker, competing against the synthetic market, case 3 or case 4 could occur if—and as long as—that market maker has excess inventory (case 3) or a shortage (case 4). These situations should alternate with case 5.

   - But the more market makers there are, the less likely it is that not a *single* one of them would be interested in buying.[3] Likewise, with many market makers, situations where none of them wants to sell become very improbable. Thus, cases 3 and 4 should be rare and short-lived, unless there are very few market makers.

3. With many market makers, then, case 5 should be the typical situation: the direct market dominates the synthetic one at both sides.

5.2.3 Back to the Second Law

How wide is the zone of admissible prices? The example has a spread of 0.4% between the two worst combinations, but that cannot be realistic at all possible

---

[3] In case 3, for instance, 109.7 is by definition the best bid; all other market makers must have been quoting even lower if 109.7 is the best bid.

maturities $T - t$. Let us first trace the ingredients behind the computations of the synthetic rates in (5.2) and (5.4). The spot bid–ask spread is, in the example, 0.02 pesos wide, which is about 0.02%. In the $(1 + r)^*$ part of the formula, multiplying by 1.211 instead of 1.209 makes a difference of +0.17% ($1.211/1.209 = 1.0017$), and the choice of $(1 + r^*)$ has an impact of +0.18%. Add all this up (the effect of compounding these percentages is tiny) and we get the 0.40% spread in the earlier calculations.

In the example, about 0.35 of this 0.40% comes from interest spreads. Bid–ask spreads in money markets fluctuate over time and vary across currencies, but they rise fast with time to maturity. For example, the *Wall Street Journal Europe*, January 25, 2005, mentions a eurodollar spread of just 0.01% p.a. for 30 days and 0.04% p.a. for 180 days, implying effective spreads of less than one-tenth of a basis point for 30 days and 2 basis points for 180 days. So at the one-month end, interest spreads for both currencies add little to the spread between the worst combinations, but at 180 days most of that spread already comes from money markets. For currencies with smaller markets, spot spreads are higher but so are money-market spreads, so it is hard to come up with a general statement. Still, synthetic spreads do rise fast with time to maturity.

The widening of the spread between the worst combinations does give banks room to also widen the bid–ask spread on their actual quotes. As we already argued, there are good economic reasons why equilibrium spreads would go up with the horizon: markets are thinning, and the compound risk of default and exchange losses increases.[4] All this, then, explains the second law: banks have not only the room to widen the spreads with time to maturity but also an economic reason to do so.

This finishes our discussion of arbitrage and the law of one price. The second usage to which forward contracts are put is hedging, as discussed in the next section.

5.3 Using Forward Contracts (2): Hedging Contractual Exposure

The issue in this section is how to measure and hedge contractual exposure from a particular transaction. There is said to be contractual exposure when the firm has signed contracts that ensure a known inflow or outflow of FC on a well-defined date. There are other exposures too, as discussed in chapter 13; but contractual exposure is the most obvious type, and the most easily hedged.

We describe how to measure the exposure from a single transaction, how to add up the contractual exposures from different contracts if these contracts mature on the same date and are denominated in the same currency, and how

---

[4] Note that the risk is compound: a risk on a risk. The simple exchange risk under normal circumstances (i.e., assuming no failure) is hedged by closing out in the forward or, if necessary, synthetically. Exchange risk pops back up only if there is default and the bank unexpectedly needs to reverse its earlier hedge.

the resulting net transaction can be hedged. Of course, a firm typically has many contracts denominated in a given foreign currency and these contracts may have different maturity dates. In such a case, it is sometimes inefficient to hedge individually the transactions for each particular date. In section 17.3, we show how one can define an aggregate measure of the firm's exposure to foreign-currency-denominated contracts that have different maturity dates, and how one can hedge this exposure with a single transaction.

5.3.1 Measuring Exposure from Transactions on a Particular Date

By exposure we usually mean a number that tells us by what multiple the HC value of an asset or cash flow changes when the exchange rate moves by ΔS, everything else being equal. We denote this multiple by $B^*_{t,T}$:

$$B^*_{t,T} = \frac{\Delta \tilde{V}_T}{\Delta \tilde{S}_T}. \tag{5.6}$$

Note that the deltas are for constant T, and remember that T is a known future date. That is, we are not relating a change in S over time to a change in V over time; rather, we compare two possible situations or scenarios for a future time T that differ as far as S is concerned. In continuous-math terms, we might have in mind a partial derivative. In sci-fi terms, we are comparing two closely related parallel universes, each having its own S_T. Economists, more grandly, talk about comparative statics.

This is the general definition, and it may look rather otherworldly. To reassure you, in the case of contractual exposure $B^*_{t,T}$ is simply the FC value of the contract at maturity.

Example 5.5. Assume that your firm (located in the United States) has an A/R next month of JPY 1m. Then, for a given change in the USD/JPY exchange rate, the impact on the USD value of the cash flows from this A/R is 1m times larger. For example, if the future exchange rate turns out to be USD/JPY 0.0103 instead of the expected 0.0100, then the USD value of the A/R changes from USD 10,000 to 10,300. Thus, the exposure of the firm is

$$B^*_{t,T} = \frac{10,300 - 10,000}{0.0103 - 0.0100} = 1,000,000. \tag{5.7}$$

To the mathematically gifted, this must have been obvious all along: if the cash flow amounts to a known number of FC units C^*, then its HC value equals $V_T = C^* \times S_T$, implying that the derivative $\partial V_T / \partial S_T$ or the relative difference $\Delta V_T / \Delta S_T$ both equal C^*, the FC cash flow. A point to remember, though, is that while exposure *might* be a number described in a contract or found in an accounting system, it generally is not. We will get back to this when we talk about option pricing and hedging, or operations exposure, or hedging with futures.

An ongoing firm is likely to have many contracts outstanding, with varying maturity dates and denominated in different foreign currencies. One can measure the exposure for each given future day by summing the outstanding contractual foreign-currency cash flows for a particular currency and date as illustrated in example 5.6. Most items on the list are obvious except, perhaps, the long-term purchase and sales agreements for goods and services, with FC-denominated prices for the items bought or sold. By these we mean the contracts for goods or services that have not yet given rise to delivery and invoicing of goods and, therefore, are not yet in the accounting system. Don't forget these! More generally, contracts do not necessarily show up in the accounting system, notably when no goods have been delivered yet or no money-market transaction has yet been made.

The net sum of all of the contractual inflows and outflows then gives us the firm's net exposure—an amount of net foreign currency inflows or outflows for a particular date and currency, arising from contracts outstanding today.

Example 5.6. Suppose that a U.S. firm, Whyran Cabels, Inc., has the following AUD commitments (where AUD is the foreign currency):

1. A/R: AUD 100,000 next month and AUD 2,200,000 two months from now.
2. Expiring deposits: AUD 3,000,000 next month.
3. A/P: AUD 2,300,000 next month and AUD 1,000,000 two months from now.
4. Loan due: AUD 2,300,000 two months from now.

We can measure the exposure to the AUD at the one- and two-month maturities as shown below (commercial contracts are in roman, financial in italic):

Item	30 days		60 days	
	In	Out	In	Out
(a) A/R	100,000	—	2,200,000	—
(b) Commodity sales contracts	0	—	0	—
(c) *Expiring deposits*	3,000,000	—	0	—
(d) *Forward purchases*	0	—	0	—
(e) *Inflows from forward loans in FC*	0	—	0	—
(f) A/P	—	2,300,000	—	1,000,000
(g) Commodity purchase contracts:	—	0	—	0
(h) *Loan due*	—	0	—	2,300,000
(i) *Forward sales*	—	0	—	0
(j) *Outflows for forward deposits in FC*	—	0	—	0
Net flow	+800,000		−1,100,000	

Thus, the net exposure to the AUD one month from now is AUD 800,000 and two months from now is AUD −1,100,000.

Note that from a contractual-exposure point of view, the future exchange rate would not matter if the net future cash flows were zero, that is, if future FC-denominated inflows and outflows exactly canceled each other out. This, of course, is what traditional hedging is about, where one designs a hedge whose cash flows exactly offset those from the contract being hedged. Thus, if one could match every contractual foreign currency inflow with a corresponding outflow of the same maturity and amount, then the net contractual exposure would be zero. However, perfect matching of commercial contracts (sales and purchases, as reflected in A/R and A/P and the long-term contracts) is difficult. For example, exporters often have foreign sales that vastly exceed their imports. An alternative method for avoiding contractual exposure would be to denominate all contracts in one's domestic currency. However, factors such as the counterparty's preferences, their market power, and their company policy may limit a firm's ability to denominate foreign sales and purchases in its own home currency or in a desirable third currency. Given that a firm faces contractual exposure, one needs to find out how this exposure can be hedged. Fortunately, one can use financial contracts to hedge the net contractual exposure. This is the topic of the next section.

5.3.2 Hedging Contractual Exposure from Transactions on a Particular Date

5.3.2.1 One-to-One Perfect Hedging

A company may very well dislike being exposed to exchange risk arising from contractual exposure. (Sound economic reasons for this are discussed in chapter 12.) If so, the firm could easily eliminate this exposure using the financial instruments analyzed thus far: forward contracts, loans and deposits, and spot deals. Perfect hedging means that one takes on a position that exactly offsets the existing exposure, and with contractual exposure this is easily done.

Example 5.7. We have seen, in example 5.5, that holding a JPY T-bill with a time T face value of JPY 1,000,000 creates an exposure of JPY +1,000,000. Thus, to hedge this exposure, one can sell forward the amount JPY 1,000,000 for maturity T.

In the above, the purpose is just to hedge. If the firm also needs cash (in HC), it could then borrow against the future HC income from the hedge. Alternatively, the familiar spot-forward diagram tells us, one could short spot foreign exchange, that is, borrow the present value of JPY 1,000,000, and convert the proceeds into USD, the home currency. At maturity, one would then use the cash flows from the JPY T-bill to service the loan; as a result, there is no more uncommitted JPY cash left, so that no spot sale will be needed anymore, meaning that exposure is now zero.

Example 5.8. To hedge its net exposure as computed in example 5.6, Whyran Cabels could hedge the one-month exposure with a 30-day forward sale of AUD 800,000, and the two-month exposure by a 60-day forward purchase of AUD 1,100,000.

5.3.2.2 Issue #1: Are Imperfect Hedges Worse?

Forward contracts, or FC loans and deposits, allow you to hedge the exposure to exchange rates perfectly. There are alternatives. Futures may be cheaper, but are less flexible as far as amount and expiry date are concerned, thus introducing noise into the hedge; also, futures exist for heavily traded exchange rates only. Options are "imperfect" hedges in the sense that they do not entirely eliminate uncertainty about future cash flows; rather, as explained in chapter 8, options remove the downside risk of an unfavorable change in the exchange rate, while leaving open the possibility of gains from a favorable move in the exchange rates. This may sound fabulous, until one remembers there will be a price to be paid, too, for that advantage.

> **Example 5.9.** Whyran Cabels could buy a 30-day put option (an option to *sell* AUD 800,000 at a stated price) and a 60-day call option (an option to *buy* AUD 1,100,000 at a stated price). Buying these options provides a lower bound or floor on the firm's inflows from the AUD 800,000 asset, and an upper bound or cap on its outflows from the AUD 1,100,000 liability.

If one is willing to accept imperfect hedging with downside risk, then one could also cross-hedge contractual exposure by offsetting a position in one currency with a position (in the opposite direction) in another currency that is highly correlated with the first. For example, a British firm that has an A/R of CAD 120,000 and an A/P of USD 100,000 may consider itself more or less hedged against contractual exposure given that, from a GBP perspective, movements in the USD and the CAD are highly correlated and the long positions roughly balance the short ones. Similarly, if an Indian firm exports goods to Euroland countries, and imports machinery from Switzerland and Sweden, there is substantial neutralization across these currencies given that the movements in these currencies are highly correlated and the firm's positions have opposite signs.

5.3.2.3 Issue #2: Credit Risk

So far, we have limited our discussion to contractual exposure, and ignored credit risk. The risk of default, if nontrivial, creates the following dilemma:

- If you leave the foreign currency A/R unhedged (open) and the debtor does pay, you will be worse off if the exchange rate turns out to be unexpectedly low. This is just the familiar exchange risk.

- On the other hand, if you do hedge but the debtor defaults, you are still obliged to deliver foreign exchange to settle the forward contract. As soon as you hear about the default, you know that this forward contract, originally meant to be a hedge, has become an open (quasi-speculative) position. So you probably want to *reverse* the hedge, that is, close out by adding a reverse forward.[5] But by that time the erstwhile hedge contract may have a negative value, in which case reversing the deal leads to a loss.

---

[5] You could also close out with a combination of money- and spot-market deals, or negotiate an early settlement with your banker, but this necessarily produces essentially the same cash flows as those from closing out forward. Lastly, you could leave the position open until the end,

When there is default on the hedged FC, the lowest-risk option is indeed to *reverse* the original hedge position. For instance, if an A/R was hedged by a forward sale and if the exposure suddenly evaporates, you immediately buy the same amount for the same date. But there is about a 50% chance that this would be at a loss, the new forward rate being above the old one. This risk, arising when a hedged exposure disappears, is called *reverse risk*.

Example 5.10. Suppose you had hedged a promised RUR 10m inflow at a forward rate of 0.033 EUR/RUR. Now you hear the customer is defaulting. So now you want to buy forward RUR 10m to neutralize the initial sale, but you soon discover that, by now, the forward rate for the same date has risen to 0.038. So if you reverse the position under these conditions, you are stuck with a loss of $10m \times (0.038 - 0.033) =$ EUR 50,000.

If the default risk is substantial, one can eliminate it, at a cost,[6] by obtaining bank guarantees or by buying insurance from private or government credit-insurance companies. Foreign trade credit insurance instruments that allow one to hedge against credit risk are discussed in chapter 15.

Credit risk means that contractual forex flows are not necessarily risk free. But this is just the tip of the iceberg: in reality, the dividing line between contractual (or, rather, known) and risky is fuzzy and gradual in many other ways. We return to this when we discuss operations exposure in chapter 13.

5.3.2.4 Issue #3: Hedging of Pooled Cash Flows—Interest Risk

We have already seen how one should aggregate the exposure from transactions that have the same maturity date and that are denominated in the same currency. Typically, however, a firm will have exposures with a great many different maturities. Computing and hedging the contractual exposure for each day separately is rather inefficient; rather, the treasurer would probably prefer to group the FC amounts into time buckets, say, months for horizons up to two years, quarters for horizons between two and five years, and years thereafter. Then only one contract would be used to hedge the entire bucket.

Example 5.11. There are two obvious potential savings from grouping various exposures over time:

- If there are changes in sign of the flows in the bucket, *netting over time* saves money. Suppose that on day 135 you have an inflow of SEK 1.8m and on the next day an outflow of SEK 1.0m. Rather than taking out two forward hedges for a total gross face value of SEK 2.8m, it would be more sensible to sell

---

and then buy spot currency to deliver as promised under the forward contract. The problem with this avenue is that the worst possible losses become bigger; so early termination of some form is usually preferred.

[6] Accounting-wise this is a cost; but if the premium paid is worth the expected loss, the NPV of this deal would be low or zero.

forward just SEK 0.8m for day 135, and keep the remaining SEK 1m inflow to settle the debt the next day. You would save the extra half-spread on SEK 2m.

- *Scale economies in transaction costs.* Even if there are no changes in sign—for example, if the firm is a pure exporter—the total commission cost of doing one weekly deal of SEK 500,000 will be lower than the cost of doing five daily deals of about SEK 100,000.

One should be aware that if pooling over time is carried too far, a degree of interest-rate risk is introduced. Suppose, to keep things simple, that Whyran Cabels faces an inflow of SEK 100m at the beginning of year $t + 5$, and one of SEK 50m at the end of that year. They could hedge this by selling forward SEK 150 dated July 1. Interest risk creeps in here because the SEK 100m that arrives on January 2 will earn interest for six months, while Whyran will have to borrow about SEK 50m because they sold forward the SEK 50m for a day predating the actual inflow. If the horizon is substantial and the potential amount of interest at play becomes nontrivial, the company can hedge the interest-rate risk by forward deposits and loans. The example that follows assumes you know these instruments; if not, skip the example or return to appendix 4.7 first.

Example 5.12. Suppose the forward interest rates 5×5.5 years are 3.50–3.55% p.a., and the forward interest rates 5.5×6 years are 3.75–3.80% p.a.[7] Then Whyran Cabels can do the following:

1. Arrange a deposit of SEK 100m, 5 against 5.5 years, at the bid rate of 3.5% p.a., that is, 1.75% effective over six months. This will guarantee an SEK inflow of 101.75m on July 1.

2. Arrange a loan with final value SEK 50m, 5.5 against 6 years at the ask rate of 3.8% p.a., that is, 1.9% effective over six months. The proceeds of the loan, on July 1, will be 50m/1.019 = 49,067,713.44.

3. Sell forward the combined proceeds of the deposit (SEK 101.75m) and the loan (SEK 49.07m) for July 1.

5.3.2.5 Issue #4: Value Hedging versus Cash-Flow Hedging?

An extreme form of grouping occurs if the company hedges all its exposures by one single position. One simple strategy would be the following:

- Compute the PV, in forex, of all FC contracts. Call this PV_c^* ("c" for contract).

- Add an FC position in the bond or forward market with PV_h^* ("h" for hedge).

- The naive full hedge solution would then be to set $PV_h^* = -PV_c^*$.

---

[7] See the appendix to chapter 4 on forward interest rates.

Example 5.13. Suppose the spot interest rates are 3.4% p.a. compound for five years and 3.45% p.a. compound for six years. Then, assuming these are the company's only FC positions, Whyran Cabels can hedge its five- and six-year SEK debts as follows:

1. Compute $PV_c^* = 100m/1.034^5 + 50m/1.0345^6 = 125.4m$ SEK.
2. Arrange a loan with the same PV. If the loan is for one year and the one-year interest rate is 3%, the face value is $125.4 \times 1.03 = 129.2m$.

The reasoning behind this hedging rule is that if the spot exchange rate moves, the effect on the PVs of the contractual position and the hedge position will balance out, thus leaving the firm's total PV unaffected. It is, however, important to realize that this argument assumes that the FC PVs of the hedge and contractual positions are not changing, or at least that any changes in these PV^*s are identical. However, foreign interest rates can change, and these shifts are likely to differ across the time-to-maturity spectrum. And even if the shifts were identical for all interest rates, the PV of the five- and six-year items would still change by far more than the one-year position. Thus, PV hedging may again induce a big interest-rate risk. This is why the full hedge with just PV-matching was called "naive," above.

This can be solved by throwing in an interest-risk management program. But maturity mismatches can also lead to severe liquidity problems if short-term losses are realized while the offsetting gains remain, for the time being, unrealized. A simpler solution would accordingly be to abandon the PV-hedging policy. If every single exposure is hedged by a hedge for the same date, then the impact of interest-rate changes is the same for PV_h^* and PV_c^*. This would still be approximately true if exposures are grouped into buckets that are not too wide, and if the hedge has a similar time to maturity.[8] This is why, in example 5.12, we hedged the five- and six-year loan by a position at 5.5 years. In fact, since the five-year flow is much larger than the six-year flow (100m versus 50m), the hedge horizon should perhaps be closer to five years than to six. For example, one could go for a duration-matched hedge, the one that protects the company against small, parallel shifts in the term structure.[9]

Example 5.14. Assuming the same data, Whyran Cabels can do the following:

1. Compute

$$PV_c^* = \frac{100m}{1.034^5} + \frac{50m}{1.0345^6} = 125.4m \text{ SEK.}$$

---

[8] Also, group inflows and outflows into separate buckets before you compute durations. (Durations for portfolios with positive and negative positions with similar times to maturity can lead to absurdly large numbers, because of leverage.) Then add a hedge on the side with the smaller PV, in absolute size.

[9] If duration is not a familiar concept, close your eyes and think of England; then skip the example.

2. Compute the duration:

$$\frac{100\text{m}/1.034^5}{125.4\text{m}} \times \frac{5}{1.034} + \frac{50\text{m}/1.0345^6}{125.4\text{m}} \times \frac{6}{1.0345} = 5.15 \text{ years}$$

(5 years, 54 days).

3. Arrange a loan with the same PV and duration. If five- and six-year rates move by the same (smallish) amount, then the effect of a shift in the term structure will equally affect the hedge instrument and the hedged positions.

As a final note, we add that complete value hedging, where the company takes one single position per currency to cover all the risks related to that currency regardless of their time to maturity, is mostly a textbook concept, even in financial companies. What does happen is hedging of net exposures that expire at dates that are close to each other; few CFOs are venturing to go any further. The complexity of the interest hedge and the need to continuously update the interest and currency positions are obvious issues. Also, bear in mind that even if the PVs of the combined exposures and of the hedge could be kept in perfect agreement, there is still the problem that the expiry dates do not match. Cash losses may be matched by capital gains, but the latter are unrealized and unrealizable, implying that there could be serious liquidity problems. Another issue with company-value hedging is that even "contractual" exposures are never *quite* certain, as we have already noted; moreover, most cash flows foreseen for a few months out are not contractual anyway, and uncertainties about noncontractual foreseen flows are often deemed to be too high to make hedging safe or reliable to managers. We return to the issues associated with noncontractual cash flows in chapter 13. Value hedging, in short, mainly exists in academic papers, where the managers and bankers have already read the article and therefore are as well informed as the author of the article assumes them to be. In reality, value hedging is confined to a few, very simple, well-understood structures like risk-free forex positions or derivatives rather than being applied to the company as a whole.

This finishes our discussion of the second way companies and individuals use forward contracts, hedging. Later on in this book we will discuss other applications of hedging, including hedging of operating exposure (chapter 13) and hedging for the purpose of managing and pricing of derivatives (chapters 8, 9, and 14). The third possible application of forward contracts is speculation, as discussed in the next section.

5.4 Using Forward Contracts (3): Speculation

What is speculation? One possible definition is that a speculator takes a position in currencies (or commodities or whatever) for purely financial reasons, not because she needs the asset or wants to hedge another position. In that sense, speculators are the agents that pick up the positive or negative net position, long minus short, left by all hedgers taken together. The forward contracts must be priced such that total net demand by hedgers and speculators is zero.

On reflection, however, almost all investments are for purely financial reasons, so by that definition almost all investors are speculators. So while this is a perfectly valid definition, it does not necessarily match what the average person has in mind when hearing the word speculation. Many people would say that speculation involves risk-seeking, in contrast to hedging, where risk is reduced rather than sought. Again, we should refine this: even buying the market portfolio involves taking risk, so by that standard most investors are again speculators. Perhaps, then, the crucial element that distinguishes speculation from ordinary investment is the giving up of diversification, that is, taking positions that deviate substantially from weights chosen by the average investor in a comparable position.

If this is what we mean by speculation, the question arises whether such speculation can be rational for risk-averse investors. Shouldn't normal investors diversify rather than putting an unusual amount of money into a few assets? The answer is that speculation, or underdiversification, can be rational provided there is a sufficient expected return that justifies giving up diversification. Extra expected returns arise from buying underpriced assets or short selling overpriced assets. But the underdiversified speculator must realize that, by deeming some assets to be under- or overpriced, her or his opinion is necessarily in disagreement with the market's. Indeed, if the entire market had concurred that asset X is underpriced and asset Y overvalued, then you would not find any counterparts to trade at these rates, and prices would already be moving so as to eliminate the mispricing. In short, an underdiversified speculator thinks that (a) she or he spots mispricing which the market, foolishly, has not yet noticed, (b) the market will soon see the error of its ways and come around to the speculator's view, and (c) the gains from that hoped-for price adjustment justify the underdiversification resulting from big positions in the mispriced assets.

In this section we discuss speculation on the spot rate, the forward rate, and the swap rate. In the examples, we take speculation to mean intentional underdiversification.

5.4.1 Speculating on the Future Spot Rate

Example 5.15. Suppose Milton Freedman is more optimistic about the euro than the market (see figure 5.5(a)). As we know, the profit from buying forward will be $\tilde{S}_T - F_{t,T}$. Almost tautologically, the market thinks that the expected profit, after a bit of risk adjustment, is zero, otherwise the forward price would already have moved. But Milton thinks that, in reality, there is more of the probability mass to the right of $F_{t,T}$, and less to the left, than the market realizes. Since the potential for

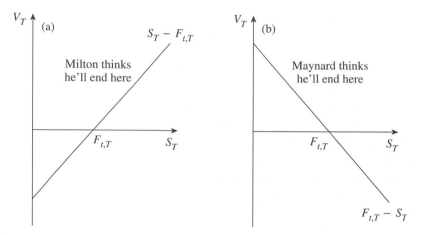

Figure 5.5.   Speculating in the spot market: (a) buy forward; (b) sell forward.

profit is underestimated and the room for losses overrated, Milton thinks a forward purchase is a good deal, warranting a big position.

Example 5.16. Suppose Maynard Keenes is less optimistic than the market about the dollar (see figure 5.5(b)). The profit from selling forward will be $F_{t,T} - \tilde{S}_T$ with a risk-adjusted expectation of zero, according to the market. But Maynard knows more than the market (or at least he thinks he does): depreciations are more probable, and appreciations less likely, than the market perceives. Betting on depreciations, Maynard sells forward.

In both cases, the speculator thinks that the chances of ending in the red are overrated and the chances of making a profit underrated.[10] Note also that the forward position is closed out at the end by a spot transaction: at time T, Milton has to sell spot to realize the gain he hopefully made; and Maynard must buy spot at T because under the initial forward contract he has promised to deliver. In hedge applications, in contrast, no spot deal is needed because there already is a commercial contract which generates an in- or outflow at T.

Of course, speculation can also be done in the spot market. Relative to buying spot, a forward purchase has the additional feature of automatic leverage: it is like buying an FC deposit already financed by an HC loan. Likewise, one alternative to selling forward is to borrow FC and sell the proceeds spot; but the extra feature in the forward sale is that the foreign currency is automatically borrowed. Here, the leverage is in FC. In either case, the leverage is good, at the private level, in the sense that positions can be bigger; but of course the risk increases correspondingly. The leverage also allows more people to speculate. This is, socially, a good thing if these extra players really do know more than the market does: then speculators are pushing prices in the right

---

[10] To the purists: yes, the argument is sloppy, I should talk about partial expectations, not chances of profits. But you all know what I mean.

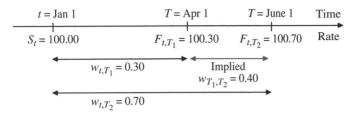

Figure 5.6. Speculating on a rise in the swap rate.

direction. And even if their opinions are, on average, no better than the other players, speculators would still help: the larger the number of people allowed to vote on a price, the smaller the average error.

5.4.2 Speculating on the Forward Rate or on the Swap Rate

Suppose that—at time t, as usual—you want to speculate not on a future spot rate $\tilde{S}_T$ but on a future forward rate: you think that, by time T_1, the forward rate for delivery at T_2 will have gone up relative to the current level. So we speculate on $\tilde{F}_{T_1,T_2}$ instead of $\tilde{S}_{T_1}$. For example (see figure 5.6), current time may be January and the current rate for delivery on June 1 (= T_2) may be 100.7, but you feel pretty confident that, by April 1 (=T_1), the rate for delivery in early June will be higher than that. You would

- buy forward now (at t) for delivery on June 1, and
- early April, close out—that is, sell forward for June 1—at a rate that right now (in January) is still unknown.

This way, in April you will lock in a cash flow of $\tilde{F}_{T_1,T_2} - F_{t,T_2}$, which will then be realized at the end of June. For example, if in April the June rate turns out to be 101.6, up from 100.7, you make $101.6 - 100.7 = 0.9$ per currency unit; or if, against your expectations, the rate falls to 100.1, you lose 0.6 per currency unit. The general net result, in short, will be $\tilde{F}_{T_1,T_2} - F_{t,T_2}$, locked in at T_1 and realized at T_2.

Of course, speculating on a drop in the forward rather than a rise works in reverse: you would sell forward now (at t) for delivery in June, and in April you would then close out and lock in the time-1 gain (or loss), $F_{t,T_2} - \tilde{F}_{T_1,T_2}$ to be realized at T_2.

Note that this boils down to speculation on the sum of the spot rate and the swap rate. Most of the uncertainty originates from the spot rate, however. So what would you do if you wanted to speculate on just the swap rate, not obscured by the spot exchange rate? And what exactly is the underlying bet?

The nature of the bet would be different. If you simply speculate on a rise in the spot rate, you bet on a difference between the current (risk-adjusted) expectation and the subsequent realization. If you speculate on the future swap rate, in contrast, you are placing a bet on future revisions of the expectation. Consider the example in figure 5.6. On January 1, the swap rate for delivery on April 1 is 0.30, implying that the risk-adjusted expected rise is 0.30 over that horizon. On the same date, the six-month swap rate is 0.70, implying a risk-adjusted expected rise by 0.70 over six months. Implicit in these numbers is a risk-adjusted expected rise of $0.70 - 0.30 = 0.40$ between April 1 and June 30. Suppose that you feel pretty certain that, by April 1, the market will revise its expected three-month rise upward. Your bet is that, on April 1, the three-month swap rate will exceed 0.40.

How would you do it? The answer, as we verify in the next example, is as follows:

- you speculate on a rise of the entire forward rate (spot plus swap), as before;

- but you immediately also hedge away the spot-rate risk component by a forward sale for delivery in April, leaving you with exposure to just the swap rate;

- you gain if and to the extent that the future swap rate exceeds the difference between the current swap rates (June–April).

To explain this via an example, let us again consider a bet that the swap rate will rise.

Example 5.17. Current data:

Spot	Date T_i	Forward	Swap rate
100	April 1	100.3	0.3
id	June 30	100.7	0.7
Spread June–April		0.4	0.4

The table below lists the two ingredients in the combined strategy (the speculative bet on a fire in the forward rate, and the spot hedge) and, for each of these, the actions undertaken now and in April, plus the payoffs. The payoff of the first component is the difference between the April forward (for delivery in June) and the initial one, 100.07; the April rate is immediately written as $\tilde{S}_{\text{Apr}} + \tilde{w}_{\text{Apr-Jun}}$, where $\tilde{w}$ is the swap rate:

Ingredient	Action at t	Action at T_1 (Apr)	Payoff at expiry
Bet on F_{Apr} ↑	Buy forward Jun	Sell forward Jun	$[\tilde{S}_{\text{Apr}} + \tilde{w}_{\text{Apr-Jun}}] - 100.7$
Hedge S_{Apr}	Sell forward Apr	Buy spot	$100.3 - \tilde{S}_{\text{Apr}}$
Combined:	Forward-forward swap "out"	Spot-forward swap "in"	$\tilde{w}_{\text{Apr-Jun}} - [100.7 - 100.3]$ $= \tilde{w}_{\text{Apr-Jun}} - [0.7 - 0.3]$

We see that the ultimate profit is the realized swap rate in excess of the difference of the original ones, $0.7 - 0.3 = 0.4$.

An interesting reinterpretation is obtained if we look at the "actions" in the example's table not row by row as we have done so far, but column by column (that is, by date).

- Start with the future actions (those planned for April). Clearly, what we will do in April is a spot-forward swap: we will buy spot and simultaneously sell forward. (This is called a swap "*in*" because the transaction for the nearest date, the spot one, takes us into the FC.)

- What we do right now, at *t*, is not dissimilar: we sell forward for one date and simultaneously buy forward for another. This is called a *forward-forward swap*, and this particular one is called "*out*" because the transaction for the nearest date is a sale, which takes us out of the FC.

Thus, instead of saying that we bet on a rise in the April forward rate and hedge the April spot component, we could equally well say that we now do a forward-forward swap, April against June, and that on April 1 we reverse this with a spot-forward swap.

5.5 Using Forward Contracts (4): Minimizing the Impact of Market Imperfections

In the previous chapter we discovered that, in perfect markets, shopping around is pointless: the two ways to achieve a given trip produce exactly the same output. Among the imperfections we introduce in this section are (a) bid–ask spreads, (b) asymmetric taxes, (c) information asymmetries leading to inconsistent default-risk spreads, and (d) legal restrictions. Each of them makes the treasurer's life far more interesting than we might have surmised in the previous chapter.

5.5.1 Shopping Around to Minimize Transaction Costs

This type of problem is easily solved by using the spot/forward/money-markets diagram. A safe way to proceed is as follows.

1. Identify your current position; this is where your trip starts.

2. Identify your desired end position.

3. Calculate the outputs for each of the two routes that lead from your START to your END.

4. Choose by applying the "more is better" rule: more output for a given level of input is always desirable.

Example 5.18. Ms. Takeshita, treasurer of the Himeji Golf & Country Club (HG&CC), often faces problems like the following:

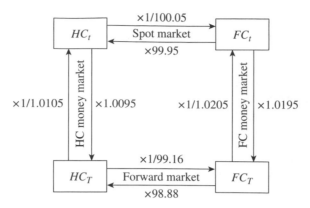

Figure 5.7. Spot/forward/money market diagram: Ms. Takeshita's data.

- A foreign customer has promised a large amount of USD (= FC), but today the club needs JPY cash to pay its workers and suppliers and does not like the exchange risk either. Should the club borrow dollars or yen?

- The next day there are excess JPY liquidities that should be parked, risk free. Should HG&CC go for a yen deposit or a swapped dollar one?

- Two days later the club wants to earmark part of its JPY cash to settle a USD liability expiring in six months. Should they keep yen and buy forward or move into dollars right away?

- One week later, HG&CC receives USD from a customer, and orders new irons payable in USD 180 days. Should the current USD be deposited and used later on to settle the invoice?

On her laptop she sees the following data:

Spot	JPY/USD 99.95 − 100.05 (spread 0.10)	180d	JPY/USD 98.88 − 99.16 (spread 0.18)
JPY, 180d	1.90 − 2.10% p.a., simple (0.95 − 1.05% effective)	USD, 180d	3.90 − 4.10% p.a., simple (1.95 − 2.05% effective)

Having taken this course, Ms. Takeshita organizes the data into the familiar diagram (figure 5.7) and sets to work. Her calculations, which take her (or her computer) a mere 90 seconds, are neatly summarized in table 5.1.

Note how all computations start with one unit. The true amounts are all missing from the calculations and even from the data, thus forcing you to focus on the route. In practice, once you have found the best route, you can then rescale everything to the desired size. For instance, in application 1, if the future FC income is USD 1.235m, the output is proportionally higher too.

In this context, let me point out a mistake frequently made in solving problems like application 3. Assume the liability is USD 785,235. We have just found that the best way to move spot yen into future dollars is via the forward market, and the output per JPY input is 0.010 189 905. We can easily calculate the

Table 5.1. Ms. Takeshita's calculations.

Problem; start, end	Alternatives and output
Finance FC-denominated A/R (FC_T to HC_t)	* Via FC_t: $\frac{1}{1.0205} \times 99.95 = 97.942\,185$ ♥♥ * Via HC_T: $98.88 \times \frac{1}{1.0105} = 97.852\,548$
HC deposit (HC_t to HC_T)	* Direct: $1.009\,500$ ♥♥ * Synthetic: $\frac{1}{100.05} \times 1.0195 \times 98.88 = 1.007\,577\,8$
Invest in FC (HC_t to FC_T)	* Via FC_t: $\frac{1}{100.05} \times 1.0195 = 0.010\,189\,905$ ♥♥ * Via HC_T: $1.0095 \times \frac{1}{99.16} = 0.010\,180\,51$
Park FC (FC_t to FC_T)	* Direct: 1.0195 ♥♥ * Synthetic: $99.95 \times 1.0095 \times \frac{1}{99.16} = 1.017\,542\,60$

required investment by rescaling the whole operation, in rule-of-three style:

(1) time-t input JPY

           1   produces time-T output of USD $0.001\,018\,9905$;

(2) time-t input JPY

$$\frac{1}{0.001\,018\,9905}$$ produces time-T output of USD 1;

(3) time-t input JPY

$$\frac{785,235}{0.001\,018\,9905}$$ produces time-T output of USD $785,235$;

$\Longrightarrow$ (short version) $JPY_t = \dfrac{785,235}{0.010\,189\,905} = 77,060,090.$ (5.8)

This seems easy enough. What can (and often does) go wrong is that you mix up computational inputs and outputs with financial inputs and outputs. In computations or math, the term input refers to the data and the term output to the result of the exercise. Financially, however, we have defined input as what you feed into the financial system and output as what you get out of it. Sometimes the mathematical and the financial definitions coincide, but not always. In application 3, we exchange spot yen for future dollars, so the financial input is JPY_t and the output USD_T. But for the computations, the data is $USD_T = 785.235$ and the result is $JPY_t = 776,841.15$. If you are hasty, you risk thinking that the trip you need to make is from data (the mathematical input, future dollar) to result (the mathematical output, spot yen), while the actual money flow is in the other direction. Because of the mistake, you go through the graph the wrong way, using borrowing not lending rates of return and bid exchange rates instead of ask. In short, it is tempting to work back from the end point (USD_T) to the starting point: how much HC_t is needed for this? If you are really good, you will remember that going from financial output to financial input means going "against" the arrows, and choosing on the basis of a "less is better" rule (less input for a given output is better). But if you are new to this, it may be safer to start by provisionally setting $HC_t = 1$, then identifying the route that delivers most output (FC_T), and finally rescaling the winning trip such that the end output reaches the desired level.

A second comment is that, in the second and fourth problems, the direct deposits yield more than the synthetic ones. This is what one would expect, at least if the rates are close to interbank rates. But if the problem is retail, a small FC deposit may earn substantially less than the wholesale rate (which starts at USD 1m or thereabouts), and under these circumstances the direct solution may be dominated by the indirect alternative.

Example 5.19. Suppose that the HG&CC holds a lot of JPY so that it gets interbank rates for these; but its USD deposits are small. If the rate she gets on USD were less than 3.58% p.a., Ms. Takeshita would be better off moving her USD into the JPY market for six months.

On the basis of the above, one would expect that, in the wholesale market, swapping of deposits or loans should be very rare: a three-transaction trip should not be cheaper than the direct solution. But this conjecture looks at bid–ask costs only. In practice, we see that swaps are often used, despite their relatively high transaction cost, if there is another advantage: fiscal, legal, or in terms of credit-risk spreads. We start with the tax issue.

5.5.2 Swapping for Tax Reasons

In the previous chapter we saw that swapped FC deposits and loans should yield substantially the same rate before tax, and therefore also after tax if the system is neutral. But in many countries, under personal taxation, capital gains are tax exempt and capital losses are not deductible while interest income is taxed. A swapped FC deposit in a strong currency then offers an extra tax advantage: part of the income is paid out as a capital gain and is, therefore, not taxed. In table 5.2, we go back to an example from the previous chapter and add the computations for the case where capital gains/losses are not part of taxable income. The swapped NOK deposit now offers a CLP 3.33 extra because of the tax saved on the CLP 10 capital gain.

If this is the tax rule, the implications for a deposit are as follows:

1. if the FC risk-free rate is above the domestic rate, the HC deposit does best;

2. when there are many candidate foreign currencies, the lower the FC interest rate, the higher the forward premium, so the bigger the capital gain and therefore the larger the tax advantage.

DIY Problem 5.2. What are the rules for a loan instead of a deposit?

Table 5.2. HC and swapped FC investments if only interest is taxed.

	Invest CLP 100	Invest NOK 1 and hedge
Initial investment	100.00	$1 \times 100 = 100.00$
Final value	$100 \times 1.21 = 121.00$	$[1 \times 1.10] \times 110 = 121.00$
Income	21.00	21.00
Interest	21.00	$[1 \times 0.10] \times 110 = 11.00$
Capgain	0	$110 - 100 = 10.00$
Neutral taxes, 33.33%		
Taxable	21.00	21.00
Tax (33.33%)	7.00	7.00
After-tax income	14.00	14.00
Only interest is taxed, 33.33%		
Taxable	21.00	11.00
Tax (33.33%)	7.00	3.67
After-tax income	14.00	17.33

You should have found that if the tax rule also holds for loans, then one would like to borrow in a weak currency, one that delivers an untaxed capital gain that is paid for, in risk-adjusted expectations terms, by a matching but tax-deductible interest fee.

Note, finally, that there could be other tax asymmetries—for instance, capital losses being treated differently from capital gains. In that case the optimal investment rules are very different. Connoisseurs will see that in that case the tax asymmetry works like a currency option—a financial instrument whose payoff depends on the future spot rate in different ways depending on whether S_T is above or below some critical number. To analyze this we need a different way of thinking to that we have used previously.

DIY Problem 5.3. (For this do-it-yourself assignment you do need to know the basics of option pricing.) Suppose there is a tax rule that says that corporations can deduct capital losses on long-term loans from their taxable income but they need not add capital gains to taxable income. Explain why this is different from the case above. Then show that, in this case, there is always an incentive to borrow *unhedged* FC regardless of the interest rates. (*Hint.* Reexpress the effect of this tax rule in terms of the payoff from an option.) Finally, show that, when choosing among many FCs, you would go for the highest-volatility one, holding constant the interest rates.

5.5.3 Swapping for Information-Cost Reasons

Until now we have ignored credit risk. In reality even AAA borrowers pay a credit-risk spread on top of the risk-free rate. If a firm compares HC and FC borrowing, it is quite conceivable that the credit-risk spread on the FC loan is incompatible with the one on the HC alternative. For instance, if both loans are offered by the same bank, the credit analyst may have been sloppy, or may simply not have read this section of the textbook on how to translate risk spreads. Or, more seriously, the FC loan offer may originate from a foreign bank which has little information, knows it has little information, and therefore asks a stiff spread just in case.[11] The rule is then that a spot-forward swap allows the company to switch the currency of borrowing while preserving the nice spread available in another currency.

Example 5.20. Don Diego Cortes can borrow CLP for four years at 23% effective, 2% above the risk-free rate; and he can borrow NOK at 12%, also 2% above the risk-free rate. Being an avid reader of this textbook, he knows that the difference between the two risk-free rates reflect the market's opinion on the two currencies; no value is created or destroyed, everything else being the same, if one switches one risk-free loan for another, both at the risk-free rates. But the risk spreads are different: one *can* pay too much, here, and Don Diego especially feels that 2% in a strong currency (NOK) is not attractive relative to 2% extra on the peso.

If, for some exogenous reason, Don Diego prefers NOK over CLP, the solution is to borrow CLP and swap into NOK:

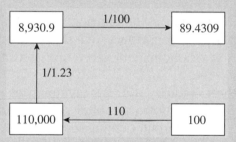

If FC_T is set at 100,000, then a direct loan at 12% produces $FC_t = 100{,}000/1.12 = 89{,}285.71$; but the swapped peso loan ($FC_T \rightarrow HC_T \rightarrow HC_t \rightarrow FC_t$) yields $(100{,}000 \times 110/1.23)/100 = 89{,}430.90$. Stated differently, Don Diego can borrow synthetic NOK @ $(100{,}000 - 89{,}430.90)/89{,}430.90 = 11.81\%$ instead of 12%.

One message is that, when comparing corporate loans in different currencies, one should look at risk spreads, not total interest rates. Second, when comparing spreads we should also take into account the strength of the currency. For example, 2% in a strong currency is worse than 2% in a weak one. We show, below, that the strength of the currency is adequately taken care of by comparing the PVs of the risk spreads, each computed at the currency's own risk-free rate: a 2% risk spread in a low-interest-rate currency then has a higher PV than a 2% spread in a high-rate currency. A related point, relevant for credit managers who need to translate a risk spread from HC to FC, is that

---

[11] Banks hate uncertainty. When they face an unfamiliar customer, they particularly fear *adverse selection*. That is, if the bank adds too stiff a credit-risk premium, the customer will refuse, leaving the bank no worse off; but if the bank asks too little, the borrower will jump at it, leaving the bank with a bad deal. In short, unfamiliar customers too often mean bad deals.

two spreads are equivalent if their PVs are identical. Note that these results hold for zero-coupon loans; the version for bullet loans with annual interest follows in chapter 7.

Example 5.21.

- Don Diego can immediately note that, for the CLP alternative, the discounted spread is $0.02/1.21 = 1.652\,89\%$, better than the NOK PV of $0.02/1.10 = 1.818\,18\%$.

- Don Diego's banker can compute that, when quoting an NOK spread that is compatible with the 2% asked on CLP loans, he can ask only 1.81%:

$$\frac{0.02}{1.21} = \frac{0.0181}{1.10} = 0.016\,528\,9. \tag{5.9}$$

This, as we saw before, is exactly the rate that Don Diego got when borrowing CLP and swapping.

DIY Problem 5.4. Here is a proof without words. Add the words, i.e., explain the proof to a friend who is obviously not as bright as you are. We denote the risk spreads by ρ and ρ^*, respectively:

$$\text{Swapped HC loan yields } \begin{matrix} \text{more} \\ \text{the same} \\ \text{less} \end{matrix} \text{ if } \quad \frac{F_{t,T}}{1+r+\rho} \times \frac{1}{S_t} \gtreqless \frac{1}{1+r^*+\rho^*}$$

$$\Updownarrow$$

$$\frac{1+r}{1+r^*}\frac{1}{1+r+\rho} \gtreqless \frac{1}{1+r^*+\rho^*}$$

$$\Updownarrow$$

$$\frac{1+r}{1+r+\rho} \gtreqless \frac{1+r^*}{1+r^*+\rho^*}$$

$$\Updownarrow$$

$$\frac{1+r+\rho}{1+r} \lesseqgtr \frac{1+r^*+\rho^*}{1+r^*}$$

$$\Updownarrow$$

$$\frac{\rho}{1+r} \gtreqless \frac{\rho^*}{1+r^*}. \tag{5.10}$$

5.5.4 Swapping for Legal Reasons: Replicating Back-to-Back Loans

In the examples thus far, we have used the swap to change the effective denomination of a deposit or a loan. We now discuss reasons for working with a stand-alone swap. The main use of this contract is that it offers all the features of back-to-back loans (that is, two mutual loans that serve as security for each other), but without mentioning the words loan, interest, or security. We proceed in three steps. First, we explain when and why back-to-back loans may make sense. We then establish, via an example, the economic equivalence of a swap and two back-to-back loans. Lastly, we list the legal advantages from choosing the swap representation of the contract over the direct back-to-back loan.

5.5.4.1 Why Back-to-Back Loans May Make Sense

The most obvious reason for a back-to-back-like structure is providing security to the lender.

Example 5.22. During the Bretton Woods period (1945–72), central banks often extended loans to each other. For example, to support the GBP exchange rate, the Bank of England (BoE) would buy GBP and sell USD. On occasion it would run out of USD. Hoping that the pressure on the GBP (and the corresponding scarcity of USD reserves) was temporary, the BoE would borrow USD from, say, the Bundesbank (Buba), the central bank of Germany. The Buba would ask for some form of security for such a loan. In a classical short-term swap deal, the guarantee was in the form of an equivalent amount of GBP to be deposited with the Buba by the BoE. Barring default, on the expiration day the USD and the GBP would each be returned, with interest, to the respective owners. If either party defaulted, the other was automatically exonerated of its own obligations and could sue the defaulting party for any remaining losses.

Example 5.23. The central bank of the former Soviet Union often used gold as security for hard-currency loans obtained from Western banks, but repeatedly failed to pay back the loans. For the Western counterparty, the risk was limited to the face value of the loan minus the market value of the gold. The Soviet Union always made good this loss.

Example 5.24. Companies often post bonds or T-bills or other tradable securities as guarantee to a loan. One way to view this is that the borrower lends the bonds to the bank, which in return then lends money to the company. The bank can confiscate the bonds and sell them off if the company fails to pay back the loan.

Other applications are of the pure back-to-back loan type: a customer lends money to the bank, which in turn lends money back to the customer and uses the deposit as security for the loan. One motivation may be money laundering.

Example 5.25. After a long and successful career in the speakeasy business, Al-C wants to retire and spend his hard-won wealth at leisure. Fearing questions from the tax authorities, he deposits his money in the Jamaica office of a big bank, and then borrows back the same amount from the New York office of that bank. The deposit serves as security for the loan: if Al is unexpectedly taken out, the bank confiscates the deposit in lieu of repayment of the loan. And when questioned by the tax inspectors as to the source of the money he spends so freely, Al can prove it is all borrowed money.[12]

Another motivation is avoidance of exchange restrictions or other costs of moving money across borders. Back-to-back loans (or parallel loans) were often

---

[12] The example lacks credibility because the tax man's next question would be *why* the bank lent so much to Al. So this can only be done on a small scale, by persons or companies that could have borrowed such amounts without the guaranteeing deposit.

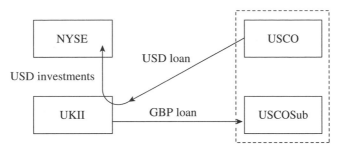

Figure 5.8. The parallel loan: example 1.

inspired by the investment dollar premium that existed in the United Kingdom from the late sixties to the mid seventies and made it expensive for companies to buy dollars for foreign investments.[13] Back-to-back loans, promoted and arranged by U.K. merchant banks, were a way to avoid this investment dollar premium.

Example 5.26. Suppose a U.K. institutional investor (UKII) wants to invest in the NYSE. The trick is to find a foreign company (say, USCO) that wants to extend a loan to its U.K. subsidiary. The USCO, rather than lending to its U.K. subsidiary, lends USD to UKII. Thus, the UKII borrows USD and pays them back later, which means that it does not have to buy USD initially and that there is no subsequent sale of USD. In short, the investment dollar premium is avoided. The second leg of the contract is that UKII lends GBP to USCO's subsidiary, so that USCO's objectives are also satisfied. The expected gains from avoiding the implicit tax can then be divided among the parties. The flow of the principal amounts of the reciprocal loans is shown in figure 5.8.

As it stands, the design of the back-to-back loan would be perfect if there were no default risk. Suppose, however, that USCO's subsidiary defaults on its GBP loan from the UKII. If no precautions had been taken, UKII would still have to service the USD loan from USCO, even though USCO's subsidiary did not pay back its own loans. Writing a right-of-offset clause into each of the separate loan contracts solves this problem. If USCO's subsidiary defaults, then UKII can suspend its payments to USCO, and sue for its remaining losses (if any)— and vice versa, of course. Thus, the right of offset in the back-to-back loan is one element that makes this contract similar to mutually secured loans. The similarity becomes even stronger if you consolidate USCO with its subsidiary and view them as economically a single entity—see the dashed-line box in the

---

[13] In those years, the United Kingdom had a two-tier exchange rate. Commercial USD (for payments on current account, like international trade and insurance fees) were available without constraints, but financial USD (for investment) were rationed and auctioned off at premia above the commercial rate. These premia, of course, varied over time and thus were an additional source of risk to investors. In addition, the law said that when repatriating USD investments, a U.K. investor had to sell 25% of his financial USD in the commercial market; the premium lost was an additional tax on foreign investment. In summary, there was quite a cost attached to foreign investment by U.K. investors.

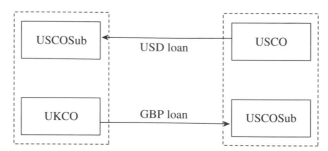

Figure 5.9. The parallel loan: example 2.

figure. Then, there is clearly a reciprocal loan between USCO and UKII, with a right of offset.

Example 5.27. If USCO also faced capital export controls (for example, Nixon's "voluntary" and, later, mandatory controls on foreign direct investment), there would be no way to export USD to the U.K. counterpart. Suppose that there was also a U.K. multinational that wanted to lend money to its U.S. subsidiary, if it were not for the cost of the investment dollar premium. The parallel loan solves these companies' joint problem, as shown in figure 5.9. (The diagram shows the direction of the initial principal amounts.) USCO lends UKCO dollars in the United States, without exporting a dime, while UKCO lends pounds to USCO's subsidiary in the United Kingdom (and, therefore, is making no foreign investment either).

Thus, no money crosses borders, but each firm has achieved its goal. UKCO's subsidiary has obtained USD, and USCO's subsidiary has obtained GBP, and the parents have financed the capital injections. This parallel loan replicates the reciprocal loan inherent in the short-term swap when we consolidate the parents with their subsidiaries (see the dashed boxes). In addition, the parallel loan typically has a right-of-offset clause that limits the potential losses if one of the parties defaults on its obligations.

Example 5.28. Suppose you have left Zimbabwe, where you lived most of your life, but you are not allowed to take out the Zimbabwe dollars you accumulated during your career. What you can do is try to find someone who, puzzlingly, wants to invest money in Zimbabwe, and to convince that party to lend his pounds to you in London, while you undertake to finance his Zimbabwe investment. (One occasionally sees such proposals in the small-ad sections of the *Times* or the *Economist*.) Both parties would feel far safer if there is also a right-of-offset clause in the loans.

Now that we understand why people might want mutually secured loans, we turn to the link between these contracts and swaps.

5.5.4.2 *The Economic Equivalence between Back-to-Back Loans and Spot-Forward Swaps*

Let us go back to the USD loan from Buba to BoE, and add some specific figures. We then summarize the contract in a table.

Example 5.29. The little table below shows this deal from BoE's point of view: the USD loan in the second column, the GBP deposit in the third. (Ignore the fourth column for the time being.) The rows show for each contract the promised payments at t and T, assuming a dollar loan of 100m, a spot rate of USD/GBP 2.5, and an effective six-month rate of 3% on dollars and 5% on pounds. Outflows, from BoE's point of view, are indicated by the "⟨" and "⟩" signs around the amounts.

	USD 100m borrowed at 3%	GBP 40m lent at 5%	
t	USD 100.0m	⟨GBP 40.0m⟩	= spot purchase of USD 100m @ 2.5
T	⟨USD 103.0m⟩	GBP 42.0m	= forward sale of USD 103m @ 2.4523

The funny thing is that if one looks at the table by date (i.e., row by row) rather than by contract (i.e., column by column), one sees for date t a spot conversion of USD 100m into GBP, at the spot rate of 2.5. For the end date, there is a promised exchange of USD 103m for GBP 42m, which sounds very much like a forward deal. Even the implied forward rate is the normal forward rate, as one can see by tracing back the numbers behind that rate:

$$2.4523 = \frac{103}{42} = \frac{100}{40}\frac{1.03}{1.05} = S_t \frac{1 + r_{\text{USD}}}{1 + r_{\text{GBP}}} = F. \tag{5.11}$$

Thus, depending on one's preferences, the promised cash flows can be laid down either in two loan contracts that serve as security for each other or in a spot contract plus an inverse forward deal—a spot-forward swap. But the similarity goes beyond the promised cash flows: even in the event of default the two stories still have the same implication. If, say, BoE defaults, then under the two-loans legal structure Buba will invoke the security clause, sell the promised GBP 42m in the market rather than give them to BoE, and sue if there is any remaining loss. Under the swap contract, if BoE defaults, Buba will invoke the right-of-offset clause, sell the promised GBP 42m in the market rather than give them to BoE, and sue if there is any remaining loss. Thus, the two contract structures are, economically, perfect substitutes. But lawyers see lots of legal differences, and many of these make the swap version more attractive than the mutual-loan version.

5.5.4.3 Legal Advantages of the Swap Contract

Simplicity. Legally speaking, structuring the contract as a spot-forward transaction is simpler than the double-loan contract described earlier.

Example 5.30. In a repurchase order (repo) or repurchase agreement, an investor in need of short-term financing sells low-risk assets (like T-bills) to a lender, and buys them back under a short-term forward contract. This is another example of a swap contract (a spot sale reversed in the forward market). In terms of cash flows, this is equivalent to taking out a secured loan. Because of the virtual absence of risk, the interest rate implicit between the spot and forward prices is lower than an

Figure 5.10.   A bank betraying its pawnshop roots. (Author's picture.)

ordinary offer rate and differs from the lending rate by a very small spread, called the bank's "haircut." In the case of default, the bank's situation is quite comfortable because it is already legally the owner of the T-bills.

Repo lending is a fancy name for what is done in pawnshops. In fact, banking and pawning used to be one and the same. In Germany, a repo is called a *Lombard* (and the repo rate is called the Lombard rate), after the north Italian bankers who introduced such lending during the Renaissance; in Dutch, *lommerd* just means pawnshop. The Catholic Church, incensed at the high rates charged, then started its own Lombard houses with more reasonable rates. These institutions were often called *Mons Pietatis*, Mount(ain) of Mercy; some still exist nowadays and a few have grown into big modern banks. The oldest surviving bank, Monte dei Paschi de Siena (1472), is one of these. Figure 5.10 shows a Spanish example.

We know, from chapter 2, that central banks can steer the money supply upward by lending money to commercial banks or downward by refusing to roll over old loans to banks. Nowadays these loans typically take the form of repos. In many countries the repo rate has become the main beacon for short-term interest rates.

In short, simplicity and efficiency is one advantage of a swap contract over a secured or back-to-back loan. To lawyers, who do not necessarily view simplicity as a plus, the main attractions are that the words security, interest, and loan/deposit are not mentioned at all.

The term *security* is not used. If the contract involves private firms rather than two central banks, the firm's shareholders need not be explicitly informed about the implicit right-of-offset clause in a swap because a forward contract is not even in the balance sheet (see below). In contrast, if there had been two loans, the financial statements would have had to contain explicit warnings about the mutual-security clause.[14] In some countries, the clause must

---

[14] Anybody involved with the firm has the right to know what assets have been pledged as security: this would mean that the firm's assets are of no use to the ordinary claimant if and when the firm defaults on its obligations.

even be officially registered with the commercial court or some similar institution. Providing security may also be contractually forbidden if the company has already issued bonds or taken up loans with the status of *senior* bonds or loans: giving new security would then weaken the position of the existing senior claimants. Bond covenants may also restrict the firm's ability to provide new security. All these problems are avoided by choosing the swap version of the contract.

The term *interest* is not used. Similarly, the word interest is also never mentioned in a swap contract; there is only an implied capital gain. This can be useful for tax purposes, as we saw earlier. In the example below, the reason is religious objections against interest.

Example 5.31. In the Middle Ages, the Catholic Church prohibited the payment of interest; swap-like contracts were used to disguise loans. Eldridge and Maltby (1991) describe a three-year forward sale for wool, signed in 1276 between the Cistercian abbey of St. Mary of the Fountains (in the north of England) and a Florentine merchant. The big "margin" deposited by the merchant was, in fact, a disguised loan to the abbey, serviced by deliveries of wool later on. The forward prices were not stated explicitly, because the implied interest would have been made too easy to spot.

The term *loan* or *deposit* is not used. A parallel loan would have shown up on both the asset and liability sides of the balance sheet. In contrast, a forward deal is off-balance-sheet.[15] This has several advantages: (i) it does not inflate debt, so it leaves unaffected the debt/equity ratio or other measures of leverage; (ii) it does not inflate total assets, so it leaves unaffected the profit/total-assets ratio. Under the old BIS rules ("Basel I"), capital requirements on swaps were less exacting than those on separate loans and deposits (see panel 5.1).

A more shady application of disguising one's lending and borrowing arose when a finance minister decided to speculate with taxpayers' money, and used swaps for the purpose.

Example 5.32. At one EC Council meeting in the mid 1980s, even Margaret Thatcher, caught off guard, was provoked into saying that she could not entirely exclude the possibility that the United Kingdom might ever think of discussing the option of joining a common European currency. Belgium's then finance minister, Mr. Maystadt, concluded that the advent of the common currency was a matter of a few years and that it would be introduced at the official parities, without any interim realignments. From these views—which, it later turned out, were both wrong—it

---

[15] This accounting rule is not unreasonable. There is indeed a difference between a swap and two separate contracts (one asset and one liability). In the case of the swap, default on the liability wipes out the asset. For that reason, accountants think it would be misleading to show the swap contract as if it consisted of a standard separate asset and liability. The inconsistency is, however, that once an asset has been pledged as security, it remains on the balance sheet *except* for forwards, futures, swaps, etc.

followed that the huge interest differential between lira and marks had become virtually an arbitrage opportunity. Thus, speculation was justified: one should borrow in a low-interest currency, like DEM, and invest the proceeds in a high-interest one, like ITL (the "carry trade"). Still, the country's rule books stated that the finance ministry could borrow only to finance the state's budget deficit. The minister therefore signed a huge long-term swap contract instead, arguing that, since the law did not mention swaps, their use was unrestricted.

The whole deal blew up in his face when the ERM collapsed in 1992 and the ITL lost one third of its value.

This has brought us to the end of our list of possible uses of forward contracts. We close the chapter with a related management application, where we are not strictly using the forward contract but rather the forward rate as a useful piece of information, notably in the case of valuation for management accounting purposes. This is discussed in the next section.[16]

5.6 Using the Forward Rate in Commercial, Financial, and Accounting Decisions

5.6.1 The Forward Rate as the Intelligent Accountant's Guide

Suppose a Canadian exporter sells goods in New Zealand, on an NZD 2.5m invoice. This transaction has to be entered into the accounts,[17] and as the exporter's books are CAD-based, the accountants need to translate the amount into CAD. In this context, many accountants fall for the following fallacy: "if we sell NZD 2.5m worth of goods, and 1 NZD is worth CAD 0.9, then we sell CAD 2.25m worth of goods." So these accountants would naturally use the spot rate to convert FC A/R or A/P into HC.

Why is this a fallacy? What is wrong with the argument is that it is glossing over timing issues. True, if we sell our wares today *and* get paid second working day *and* we convert the NZD spot into CAD right now, we will get CAD 2.25m in our bank account on day $t + 2$. But almost all real-world deals involve a credit period. So the above story should be modified: today we sell, and we will receive NZD 2.5m in, say, 45 days. At what rate we will convert this amount into CAD depends on whether we sell forward or not. This is how a finance person worth her salt would think:

- If we do sell forward, then it would look natural to book the invoice at the forward-based value. After all, if we sell NZD 2.5m worth of goods

---

[16] Of course there are more exchange-rate related issues in accounting than those we discuss here, but they are not directly related to the forward rate; we relegate those to chapter 13.

[17] In traditional accounting this is done as soon as the invoice has been sent or received. Under IFRS, this can be done as soon as there is a firm commitment. More precisely, the firm commitment is then entered initially at a zero value but can and must be updated when the invoice arrives or leaves and at any intervening reporting date. See chapter 13 for more.

The Bank for International Settlements of Basel, Switzerland, has no power to impose rules on banks anywhere. However, the BIS deserves credit for bringing together the regulatory bodies from most OECD countries in a committee called the BIS Committee, or the Basel Committee, or the Cooke Committee (after the committee's chairman), to create a common set of rules. The objective of establishing a common set of rules was to level the field for fair competition.

Under the original agreement the general capital requirement was 8%, meaning that the bank's long-term funding had to be at least 8% of its assets. For some assets and for off-balance-sheet positions with a right of offset, the risk was deemed to be less than the risk of a standard loan to a company, and the capital ratio was correspondingly lowered. For instance, a loan to any (!?) government or bank was assumed to have zero credit risk, and did not require any long-term capital. The rule was crude but was deemed to be better than no rule at all.

This is now called Basel I. The more recent Basel II rules have replaced the 8% rule for credit risks by a system of ratings—external whenever possible, internal otherwise—and have added Value-at-Risk (chapter 13) to cover market risks.

Panel 5.1. Capital adequacy rules v 1.0 (Basel I).

and we know we will receive CAD 0.88 per NZD, one would logically book this at CAD $2.5 \times 0.88 = 2.2$m.

- If we do not sell forward, we do not yet know what the exact CAD proceeds will be. So we have to settle for some kind of expected value or equivalent value, for the time being. Since we know that hedging does not change the economic value (at the moment of hedging, at least), we should use the same valuation procedure as if we had hedged—the forward rate, that is. So we still book this as a CAD 2.20m sale even if there is no hedging.

Many accountants would howl in protest. For instance, they might say, if one converts the NZD 2.5m at the forward rate, then the CAD accounting entry would depend on whether the credit period is 30 days or 60 or 90, etc. This is true. But there is nothing very wrong with it. The root of this problem is that accountants are *always* booking face values, not corrected in any way for time value. If they had used PVs everywhere, nobody would have a problem with the finding that an invoice's present value depends on how long one has to wait for the money.

This, of course, might be hard to grasp for some of the accountants. If so, at this point you take advantage of his confusion and ask him whether, if valuation for reporting purposes is done at the spot rate, there is a way to actually lock in that accounting value—that is, make sure you actually get the book value of CAD 2.25m. The only truthful answer of course is that there is no way to do this. You can then subtly point out that there *is* a way to lock in the accounting value of 2.20m: hedge forward. Giving no quarter, you then ask whether the spot rate takes into account expected exchange-rate changes and risks. Of course not, the accountant would bristle: in accounting, there surely is no room for subjective terms like "expectations" and "risk adjustments." The spot rate, he would add, is objective, as any valuation standard should be. You can then subtly point out that the forward rate is actually the risk-adjusted expectation, and that it is a market-set number and not a subjective opinion. At this point your scorecard for the competing translation procedures looks as follows:

Criterion	Convert at S_t	Convert at $F_{t,T}$
Can be locked in at no cost?	No	Yes
Takes into account expected changes?	No	Yes
Takes into account risks?	No	Yes
Objective?	Yes	Yes
Understandable to accountants?	Yes	Hmm

The accountant's last stand might be that valuation at 0.88 instead of 0.90 lowers sales and therefore profits; and more profit is good. This is an easy one. First, for other currencies there might be a forward premium rather than a discount; and for A/P a discount would increase operating income rather than decreasing it. So there is no general rule as to which valuation approach would favor sales and lower costs. Second, you point out, total profits are unaffected by the valuation rule: the only thing that is affected is the way profits are split up into operating income and financial items.

Example 5.33. Suppose, for instance, that our Canadian firm does not hedge the NZD 2.5m, and at T the spot rate turns out to be 0.92. Suppose also that the cost of goods sold is CAD 1.5m. Then profits amount to $2.5m \times 0.92 - 1.5m = 2.3m - 1.5m = 0.8m$ regardless of what you did with the A/R.

True, the operating profit does depend on the initial valuation of the A/R, but there is an offsetting effect in the capital gain/loss when the accounting value is confronted with the amount actually received:[18]

	Using $S_t = 0.90$		Using $F_t = 0.88$	
• At t:				
A/R	2,250		2,200	
COGS		1,500		1,500
Operating income		750		700
• At T:				
Bank	2,300		2,300	
A/R		2,250		2,200
Capital gain/loss		50		100

---

[18] Note that while what I show in the table looks like accounting entries to the untrained eye, it violates all kinds of accounting rules and conventions. For instance, one does not immediately calculate and recognize the profit when a sale is made. Still, you can interpret it as a CEO's secret private calculations of profits and losses from this transaction; and it does convey the gist of what accountants ultimately do with this deal.

5.6.2 The Forward Rate as the Intelligent Salesperson's Guide

For similar reasons, the forward rate should also be used as the planning equivalent in commercial decisions. Let us use the same data as before, except that the production cost is 2,210. If the "spot" valuation convention is followed, a neophyte sales officer may think that this is a profitable deal. It is not: the equivalent HC amount of NZD 2.5m is $2.5m \times 0.88 = 2{,}200$, not 2,250 as the spot translation would seem to have implied.

Some cerebrally underendowed employees may think that the valuation difference is the cost of hedging, but you should know better by now. The acid test again is that the value 2,200 can be locked in at no cost, while you would have had to pay about 50 (minus a small PV-ing correction) for a nonstandard forward contract (sell NZD 2,500 at 0.90 instead of at the market forward rate, 0.88). That is, locking in a value of 2,250 would cost you 50 at T, implying that the true future value is 2,200.

5.6.3 The Forward Rate as the Intelligent CFO's Guide

Lastly, in taking financing decisions we can always use the forward rate to produce certainty equivalents for FC-denominated service payments. The principle has been explained before. The CEQ idea or, equivalently, the zero-initial-value property of a forward deal implies that no value is added or lost by replacing a loan by another one in a different currency.

Two remarks are in order. First, the above statement ignores credit risks, as we have shown: while no value is gained or lost when adding a swap, value *is* gained when an unnecessarily high-risk spread is replaced by a better one. We should also look at various fees and transaction costs, and possible nonneutralities in the tax law. All these issues make the CFO's life far more interesting than it would have been in a perfect world. Second, when stressing the CEQ property, we also assume that the market knows what it is doing. Some CFOs may disagree, or at least disagree some of the time, and turn to speculation. Others may agree that the market rates are fair but still have a preference for an FC loan, for instance because it hedges other FC income. So even if in terms of market values nothing would be gained or lost, there can still be a preference for a particular currency.

But when swaps are possible, the ultimate currency of borrowing can be separated from the currency in which the original bank loan is taken up. Thus, we first choose on the basis of costs. Then we ask the question of whether the currency of the cheapest loan is also the currency we desire to borrow in. If so, then we are already happy. If not, then (i) a cheap HC loan can be swapped into FC if desired, e.g., to hedge other income or to speculate, or (ii) a cheap FC loan can be hedged, if desired. Thus, in the presence of swap and forward markets it is always useful to split the discussion of, say, what currency to borrow from what bank, into two parts: (i) What are the various transaction costs, risk spreads, and tax effects? (ii) Do we want to change the currency of lowest-cost solution by adding a swap or a forward?

How would we sum up costs and spreads and so on? Here is an example. We calculate all costs in PV terms, using the risk-free rate of the appropriate currency.[19]

Example 5.34. Suppose you have three offers for a loan, one year. You need EUR 1m or, at $S_t = 1.333$, USD 1.333m if you borrow USD. Below, I list the interest rate asked, stated as swap plus spread, and the up-front fee on the loan—a fixed amount and a percentage cost. How would you chose?

- Bank A: EUR at 3% (Libor) + 1.0%; up-front EUR 1,000 + 0.50%.
- Bank B: EUR at 3% (Libor) + 0.5%; up-front EUR 2,000 + 0.75%.
- Bank C: USD at 4% (Libor) + 0.9%; up-front USD 1,000 + 0.50%.

The computations are straightforward:

	Amount	PV risk spread	Up-front	Total
A	EUR 1m	$\dfrac{1m \times 0.010}{1.03} = 9{,}708.7$	$1{,}000 + 5{,}000.0 = 6{,}000$	15,708.7
B	EUR 1m	$\dfrac{1m \times 0.005}{1.03} = 4{,}854.4$	$2{,}000 + 7{,}500.0 = 9{,}500$	14,354.4
C	USD 1.333m	$\begin{aligned}\dfrac{1.333m \times 0.009}{1.04 \times 1.333}\\ = 8{,}653.8\end{aligned}$	$\begin{aligned}\dfrac{1{,}000 + 1.333m \times 0.005}{1.333}\\ = 5{,}750.2\end{aligned}$	14,404.0

So the second loan is best. The issue of whether or not to speculate then boils down to whether you are keen on selling a large amount of USD 360 days, for instance to speculate on a falling USD or to hedge other USD income.

5.7 CFO's Summary

This concluding section has two distinct parts. First I want to simply review the main ideas you should remember from this chapter. The second item is a bird's-eye view of the currency markets and their players.

5.7.1 Key Ideas for Arbitrageurs, Hedgers, and Speculators

We opened this chapter with a discussion of bid–ask spreads. Any transaction or sequence of transactions ("trip") that is not a round-trip (not a pure arbitrage transaction) can still be made through two different routes. In imperfect

---

[19] Discounting at the risk-free rate is not 100% correct: when we want to find the PV, to the borrower or lender, of a series of payments, we should take a rate that includes default risk. (The procedure with discounting at the risk-free rate, above, was derived to find equivalent payment streams from the swap dealer's point of view, who has a much safer position than the lender.) But in the presence of up-front fees it is no longer very obvious what the rate on the loan is, and the error from using the swap rate instead is small. A more in-depth discussion follows in chapter 16.

markets—and, notably, with positive spreads—it is a near certainty that one route will be cheaper than the other, and, therefore, it generally pays to compare the two ways of implementing a "trip." The route chosen matters because, with spreads, it is mathematically impossible that for every single trip the two routes end up with exactly the same result. Equality of outcomes may hold, by a fluke, for at most one trip. And even if the difference between the outcomes of the two routes is small in the wholesale market, that difference can be more important in the retail market, where costs are invariably higher.

But there is more to be taken into consideration than spreads. Differential taxation of capital gains/losses and interest income/cost provides another reason why two routes are likely to produce different outcomes. For most corporate transactions, however, taxes may not matter, since interest and short-term capital gains (like forward premia received or paid) typically receive the same tax treatment. Lastly, information asymmetries can induce incompatibilities between the risk spreads asked by different banks; and, if the loans also differ by currency, one can go for the best spread and then switch to the most attractive currency via a swap. Recall that the attractiveness of a loan is mainly determined by its (PV-ed) risk spread, not the total interest rate.

A second implication of bid–ask spreads relates to the cost of hedging. In chapter 4, we argued that, in perfect markets, hedging has no impact on the value of the firm unless it affects the firm's operating decisions. In the presence of spreads, however, this needs a minor qualification. If a firm keeps a net foreign exchange position open, it will have to pay transaction costs on the spot sale of these funds, when the position expires. If the firm does hedge, in contrast, it will have to pay the cost in the forward market. Since spreads in the forward markets are higher, the extra cost represents the cost of the hedging operation. But we know that the cost of a single transaction can be approximated as half the bid–ask spread, so the cost of hedging is the extra half-spread, which at short maturities remains of the order of a fraction of 1%. Not zero, in short, but surely not prohibitive.

Forward contracts are often used as a hedge. Remember that there may be an alternative hedge, especially if the hedge is combined with a loan or deposit. Also, show some restraint when a single contract is to be used for hedging many exposures pooled over a wide time horizon. An extreme strategy is to hedge all exposures, duly PV-ed, by one hedge. Such a strategy involves interest-rate risk and may also cause severe liquidity problems if the gains are unrealized while the losses are to be settled in immediate cash. It is safer and simpler to stay reasonably close to the matching of cash flows rather than hedging the entire exposed present value via a single contract.

Speculation is a third possible application. Recall that, as an underdiversified speculator, you implicitly pretend to be cleverer than the market as a whole (which, if true, probably means that reading this book is a waste of time). Speculation can be done on the spot rate, the forward rate, or the difference of the two, the swap rate. One can execute this last strategy by forward-forward and spot-forward swaps, but upon scrutiny this turns out to be just speculation on the forward rate, with the spot-rate component in that forward rate simply hedged away.

Swaps can also offer the same advantages as secured loans or back-to-back loans with, in addition, all the legal advantages of never mentioning the words security, interest, or loan. They have been the fastest-growing section of the exchange market since their emergence from semi-obscurity in the 1980s. We return to the modern currency swap in chapter 7.

Lastly, it is recommended that you use forward rates to value contractual obligations expressed in FC. Standard practice is to use the current spot rate, but there is no way to lock in the current spot rate for a future payment; relatedly, that spot rate is not the risk-adjusted expectation or certainty equivalent of the future spot rate either. But remember that total profits are unaffected: the only impact is on the division of profits into operational versus financial income. So as long as you remember that a premium or discount is not the cost of hedging in any economically meaningful way, little harm is done by using the wrong rate.

This ends the "review" part of this concluding section. At this stage you know enough about spot and forward markets to understand the global picture. Let us consider this, too.

5.7.2 The Economic Roles of Arbitrageurs, Hedgers, and Speculators

This is the second of two chapters on forward markets. One thing you should remember from these, it is hoped, is the fact that spot, money, and forward markets are one intertwined cluster. Traditionally, players in these markets are categorized as hedgers, speculators, or arbitrageurs. For current purposes, we shall define speculation widely, including all pure financial deals, whether they are based on perceived mispricing or not. Likewise, let us temporarily broaden arbitrage to include not just strict arbitrage but also shopping around: both help enforcing the law of one price. Let us now see how these markets and these players interact to arrive at an equilibrium.

The role of hedgers is obvious. In agricultural markets, for instance, soy farmers want to have some certainty about the sales value of their next crop, so they sell forward part or all of the expected harvest. Manufacturers that need soy as inputs likewise are interested in some degree of certainty about their costs and could buy forward. Similarly, in currency markets, companies with long positions want to sell forward, and players with short positions want to buy. But if hedgers were the only players, the market might often be pretty thin, implying that the market-clearing price could occasionally be rather weird. That is where speculators and arbitrageurs come in.

The role of arbitrageurs, notably, is to make sure that a shock in one market gets immediately spread over all related markets, thus dampening its impact. For instance, if excess sales by hedgers would require a sharp drop in the forward rate to clear the market, then CIP means that the spot rate will feel the pressure too; and if the spot rate moves, all other forward rates start adjusting too. What happens, in principle, is that arbitrageurs rush in and buy, thus making up for the (by assumption) "missing" demand from hedge-buyers; these arbitrageurs then close out synthetically, via spot and money markets or via other forward currency and forward money markets. So instead of a sharp price drop in one segment, we might see a tiny drop in all related markets, or even no drop at all. In fact, the hedgers themselves probably do some of the "arbitrage" work (in the wider sense), since their shopping-around calculations would normally already divert part of the selling toward spot markets if forward rates drop too deep relative to spot prices.

This role of spreading the pressure works for any shock, of course, not just the forward disequilibrium we just used as an example. Suppose, for instance, that a central bank starts selling dollars for euros in a massive way. This would in a first instance affect the spot value: market makers see a constant flow of sell orders coming, which clogs up their books—so they lower their quotes to discourage the seller(s?) and attract new buyers. But, at constant interest rates, all forward rates would also start moving, thus also similarly influencing players in forward markets: there is less supply, and more demand, for these slightly cheaper forward dollars. The pressure can even be borne by other currencies too. For instance, suppose the market sees the change in the USD/EUR rate as a dollar problem; that is, they see no good reason why the EUR/JPY rate would change, for instance, or the EUR/GBP rate, etc. Part of the pressure is diverted to yen and pound spot markets and thence to all yen and pound forward markets too, and so on. Spreading pressure helps to dampen the impact the initial spot sales wave would have had if there had been an isolated market.

The above looks at the markets as a self-centered system where hedgers place orders for exogenous reasons and where market makers just react to order flow. The role of speculators, then, is to link prices to the rest of the world. Notably, the forward price is also a risk-adjusted expected future value. So when the forward dollar depreciates while investors see no good arguments why it should, they would start buying forward, thus limiting the deviation between the forward value and the expected future value.[20] Again, this "speculative" function is a role that can also be assumed by a "hedger"; for instance, if the forward is already pretty low relative to expectations, potential hedgers of long positions may have second thoughts and decide not to sell forward after all, while players with short positions would see the extra expected gain as a nice boon that might tilt the balance in favor of hedging.

If hedgers also function as arbitrageurs (when shopping around) or as speculators (when judging the expected cost of closing out), does that mean that

---

[20] If they take big positions, then they also assume more risk, so the risk correction may go up, too. This explains why, even at constant expectations, the forward rate may move. The point is that the discrepancy should be limited, though.

the usual trichotomy of players is misleading? Well, hedgers *are* special, or distinct: they start from a long or short position that has been dictated by others, like the sales or procurement departments, and they have to deal with this optimally. Speculators do not have such an exogenous motivation. But both will look at expected deviations between forward prices and expected future spot rates—"speculation"—and both will do their trades in the most economical way, thus spreading shocks into related markets—"arbitrage." So speculation and arbitrage are roles, or functions, that should be assumed by all sapient humans, including hedgers.

We are now ready to move to two related instruments—younger cousins, in fact, to forward contracts: futures and swaps.

TEST YOUR UNDERSTANDING

Quiz Questions

1. Which of the following are risks that arise when you hedge by buying a forward contract in imperfect financial markets?

    (a) Credit risk: the risk that the counterpart to a forward contract defaults.

    (b) Hedging risk: the risk that you are not able to find a counterpart for your forward contract if you want to close out early.

    (c) Reverse risk: the risk that results from a sudden unhedged position because the counterpart to your forward contract defaults.

    (d) Spot rate risk: the risk that the spot rate has changed once you have signed a forward contract.

2. Which of the following statements are true?

    (a) Margin is a payment to the bank to compensate it for taking on credit risk.

    (b) If you hold a forward purchase contract for JPY that you wish to reverse, and the JPY has increased in value, you owe the bank the discounted difference between the current forward rate and the historic forward rate, that is, the market value.

    (c) If the balance in your margin account is not sufficient to cover the losses on your forward contract and you fail to post additional margin, the bank must speculate in order to recover the losses.

3. Which of the following statements are correct?

(a) A forward purchase contract can be replicated by: borrowing foreign currency, converting it to domestic currency, and investing the domestic currency.

(b) A forward purchase contract can be replicated by: borrowing domestic currency, converting it to foreign currency, and investing the foreign currency.

(c) A forward sale contract can be replicated by: borrowing foreign currency, converting it to domestic currency, and investing the domestic currency.

(d) A forward sale contract can be replicated by: borrowing domestic currency, converting it to foreign currency, and investing the foreign currency.

4. The following spot and forward rates are in units of THB/FC. The forward spread is quoted in centimes.

	Spot	1 month	3 months	6 months	12 months
1 BRL	18.20–18.30	+0.6 +0.8	+2.1 +2.7	+3.8 +4.9	+6.9 +9.1
1 DKK	5.95–6.01	−0.1 −0.2	−0.3 −0.1	−0.7 −0.3	−0.9 +0.1
1 CHF	24.08–24.24	+3.3 +3.7	+9.9 +10.8	+19.3 +21.1	+36.2 +39.7
100 JPY	33.38–33.52	+9.5 +9.9	+28.9 +30.0	+55.2 +57.5	+99.0 +105.0
1 EUR	39.56–39.79	−1.7 −1.0	−3.4 −1.8	−5.8 −2.9	−10.5 −5.2

Choose the correct answer.

(i) The one-month forward bid–ask quotes for CHF are:

    (a) 27.387–27.942

    (b) 25.078–24.357

    (c) 24.113–24.277

    (d) 24.410–24.610

(ii) The three-month forward bid–ask quotes for EUR are:

    (a) 39.526–39.772

    (b) 36.167–37.992

    (c) 39.641–40.158

    (d) 39.397–39.699

(iii) The six-month forward bid–ask quotes for JPY are:

    (a) 38.902–39.273

    (b) 88.584–91.025

    (c) 33.686–33.827

    (d) 33.932–34.095

(iv) The twelve-month forward bid–ask quotes for BRL are:

    (a) 18.731–19.352

    (b) 25.113–27.404

    (c) 17.305–17.716

    (d) 18.279–18.391

5. Suppose that you are quoted the following NZD/FC spot and forward rates:

	Spot bid–ask	3-month forward bid–ask	P.a. 3-month euro interest	6-month forward bid–ask	P.a. 6-month euro interest
NZD			5.65–5.90		5.47-5.82
USD	0.5791–0.5835	0.5821–0.5867	3.63–3.88	0.5839–0.5895	3.94–4.19
EUR	0.5120–0.5159	0.5103–0.5142	6.08–6.33	0.5101–0.5146	5.60–6.25
DKK	3.3890–3.4150	3.3350–3.4410	6.05–6.30	3.3720–3.4110	5.93–6.18
CAD	0.5973–0.6033	0.5987–0.6025	1.71–1.96	0.5023–0.5099	2.47–2.75
GBP	0.3924–0.3954	0.3933–0.3989	5.09–5.34	0.3929–0.3001	5.10–5.35

(a) What are the three-month synthetic-forward NZD/USD bid–ask rates?

(b) What are the six-month synthetic-forward NZD/EUR bid–ask rates?

(c) What are the six-month synthetic-forward NZD/DKK bid–ask rates?

(d) What are the three-month synthetic-forward NZD/CAD bid–ask rates?

(e) In (a)–(d), are there any arbitrage opportunities? What about least cost dealing at the synthetic rate?

6. True or false: occasionally arbitrage bounds are violated using domestic ("on-shore") interest rates because

(a) offshore or euromarkets are perfect markets while "on-shore" markets are imperfect;

(b) offshore or euromarkets are efficient markets while "on-shore" markets are inefficient.

Applications

1. Michael Milkem, an ambitious MBA student from Anchorage, Alaska, is looking for free lunches on the foreign exchange markets. Keeping his eyes glued to his Reuters screen until the wee small hours, he spots the following quotes in Tokyo:

Exchange rate: spot	NZD/USD	1.59–1.60	JPY/USD	100–101
	NZD/GBP	2.25–2.26	JPY/GBP	150–152
180-day forward	NZD/USD	1.615–1.626	JPY/USD	97.96–98.42
	NZD/GBP	2.265–2.274	JPY/GBP	146.93–149.19
Interest rates (simple, p.a.)	USD	5–5.25%	JPY	3–3.25%
180 days	NZD	8–8.25%	GBP	7–7.25%

Given the above quotes, can Michael find any arbitrage opportunities?

2. U.S.-based Polyglot Industries will send its employee Jack Pundit to study Danish on an intensive training course in Copenhagen. Jack will need DKK 10,000 at $t = 3$ months when classes begin, and DKK 6,000 at $t = 6$ months, $t = 9$ months, and $t = 12$ months to cover his tuition and living expenses. The exchange rates and p.a. interest rates are as follows:

DKK/USD	Exchange rate	P.a. interest rate USD	P.a. interest rate DKK
Spot	5.820–5.830		
90 days	5.765–5.770	3.82–4.07	8.09–8.35
180 days	5.713–5.720	3.94–4.19	8.00–8.26
270 days	5.660–5.680	4.13–4.38	7.99–8.24
360 days	5.640–5.670	4.50–4.75	7.83–8.09

Polyglot wants to lock in the DKK value of Jack's expenses. Is the company indifferent between buying DKK forward and investing in DKK for each time period that he should receive his allowance?

3. Check analytically that a money-market hedge replicates an outright forward transaction. Analyze, for instance, a forward sale of DKK 1 against NZD.

Applications 4–6 use the following time-0 data for two fictitious currencies, the Walloon franc (WAF) and the Flemish yen (FLY), on January 1, 2000. The initial spot rate is 1 WAF/FLY, and the interest rates (p.a., simple) are as follows:

	Interest rates FLY	WAF	Swap rate WAF/FLY
180 days	5%	10.125%	0.025
360 days	5%	10.250%	0.050

4. On June 1, 2000, the FLY has depreciated to WAF 0.90, but the six-month interest rates have not changed. In early 2001, the FLY is back at par. Compute the gain or loss (and the cumulative gain or loss) on two consecutive 180-day forward sales (the first one is signed on January 1, 2000), when you start with a FLY 500,000 forward sale. First do the computations without increasing the size of the forward contract. Then verify how the results are affected if you do increase the contract size, at the rollover date, by a factor $1 + r^*_{T_1,T_2}$, that is, from FLY 500,000 to FLY 512,500.

5. Repeat the previous exercise, except that after six months the exchange rate is at WAF/FLY 1, not 0.9.

6. Compare the analyses in applications 4 and 5 with a rolled-over money-market hedge. That is, what would have been the result if you had borrowed WAF for six months (with conversion and investment of FLY—the money-market replication of a six-month forward sale), and then rolled over (that is, renewed) the WAF loan and the FLY deposit, principal plus interest?

6

The Market for Currency Futures

In part I we first studied interest rate parity (or covered interest parity) in perfect markets, but we soon introduced transaction costs and other market imperfections that make life more exciting. But spreads, taxes, and information costs are not the only practical issues that can arise in this context. In this chapter, we start from two other problems connected to forwards: default risk, and absence of a secondary market. We discuss how they are handled (or not handled) in forward markets—traditionally by rationing and up-front collateralizing, nowadays also by periodic recontracting or variable collateralizing. This is the material for section 6.1.

We then describe in section 6.2 the institutional aspects of futures contracts. A crucial feature is that futures contracts address the problem of default risk in their own way: daily marking to market. This is similar to daily recontracting of a forward contract, except that the undiscounted change in the futures price is paid out in cash. In section 6.3, we then trace the implications of daily marking to market for futures prices. Especially, we show that the interim cash flows from marking to market create interest-rate risk, which affects the futures prices. In section 6.4 we address the question how to hedge with futures contracts. We conclude, in section 6.5, by describing the advantages and disadvantages of using futures compared with forward contracts. In the appendix we digress on interest-rate futures—not strictly an international-finance contract, but one that is close to the FRAs discussed in chapter 4, which, you will remember, are closely related to currency forwards and forward-forward swaps.

6.1 Handling Default Risk in Forward Markets: Old and New Tricks

Futures contracts are designed to minimize the problems arising from default risk and to facilitate liquidity in secondary dealing. The best way to understand these contracts is to compare them with forward markets, where these problems also arise. When asked for forward contracts, bankers of course do worry about default by their customers, and, as we shall see, the credit-risk problem also makes it difficult to organize a secondary market for standard forward contracts. The old ways of handling default risk are rationing (that is, refusing shady customers) and asking for up-front collateral. More recent techniques are periodic recontracting and variable collateralizing.

6.1.1 Default Risk and Illiquidity of Forward Contracts

As we saw in part I, a forward contract has two "legs": on the maturity date of the contract, the bank promises to pay a known amount of one currency, and the customer promises to pay a known amount of another currency. Each of these legs can be replicated by a money-market position—at least in terms of promises, that is, or as long as there is no default. However, it is important to understand that, from a bank's point of view, the credit risk present in a forward contract is of a different nature to the credit risk present in a loan. Specifically, the implicit loan and the deposit are tied to each other by the *right of offset*. The right of offset allows the bank to withhold its promised payment without being in breach of contract, should the customer default. That is, if the customer fails to deliver foreign currency (worth $\tilde{S}_T$), the bank can withhold its promised payment $F_{t_0,T}$. The bank's net opportunity loss is then $\tilde{S}_T - F_{t_0,T}$, not $\tilde{S}_T$. Likewise, if a customer bought forward but fails to pay, the bank refuses to deliver and instead sells the currency spot to the firstcomer; so what is at stake is again the difference between the price obtained in the cash market ($\tilde{S}_T$) and the one originally promised by the customer ($F_{t_0,T}$).

Example 6.1. Company C bought forward USD 1m against EUR. The bank, which has to deliver USD 1m, bought that amount in the interbank market to hedge its position. If company C defaults, the bank has the right to withhold the delivery of the USD 1m. However, the bank still has to take delivery of (and pay for) the USD it had agreed to buy in the interbank market at a price $F_{t_0,T}$. Having received the (now unwanted) USD, the bank has no choice but to sell these USD in the spot market. Given default by C, the bank therefore has a risky cash flow of ($\tilde{S}_T - F_{t_0,T}$).

The second problem with forward contracts is the lack of secondary markets. Suppose you wish to get rid of an outstanding forward contract. For instance, you have a customer who promised to pay you foreign currency three months from now and, accordingly, you sold forward the foreign currency revenue to hedge the A/R. Now you discover that your customer is bankrupt. In such a situation, you probably do not want to hold the outstanding hedge contract for another three months because the default has turned this forward position from a hedge into an open ("speculative") position. So you probably want to liquidate your forward position. Similarly, a speculator would often like to terminate a previous engagement before it matures, whether to cut her losses or to lock in her gains.

Whatever your motive for getting out early, "selling" the original forward contract is difficult. There is no organized market where you can auction off your contract: rather, you have to go beg your banker to agree on an early settlement in cash. One reason why there is no organized market is that each contract is tailor-made in terms of its maturity and contract amount, and not many people are likely to be specifically interested in your contract. Also, for your contract you probably had to provide extra security to cover default risk (see below). This means that your bank may not want you to be replaced by somebody else as a counterparty, unless comparable security is arranged (a hassle!) or you yourself guarantee the payment (dangerous!). Thus, the problem of illiquidity is partly explained by the credit-risk problem.

Example 6.2. Suppose a Spanish wine merchant receives an order for ten casks of 1938 Amontillado, worth USD 1,234,567.89 and payable in 90 days, from a (then) rich American, Don Bump. The Spanish merchant hedges this transaction by selling the USD forward. However, after 35 days, Don Bump goes bankrupt (again) and will obviously be unable to pay for the wine. The exporter would like to get out of the forward contract, but it is not easy to find someone else who also wants to sell forward exactly USD 1,234,567.89 for 55 days from the current date. In addition, the wine merchant would have to convince his banker that the new counterparty is at least as creditworthy as himself.

6.1.2 Standard Ways of Reducing Default Risk in the Forward Market

As you might remember from the preceding chapter, banks have come up with various solutions that partially solve the problem of default risk: the right of offset; credit lines (when dealing with banks), or credit agreements and security (when dealing with other customers); restricted applications; and shorter lives, with an option to roll over if all goes well.

From that discussion, we see that the problem of credit risk is more or less solved by restricting access to the forward market, by requiring margins and pledges, and by limiting the maturities of forward contracts. But the second problem—illiquidity arising from the absence of secondary markets—is not addressed. One can negotiate an early (premature) settlement with the original counterparty of the forward contract. But this is a question of negotiation, not a built-in right for the holder of the contract. Also, one cannot rely on an immediately observable market price to determine the value of the outstanding contract. Rather, one has to compute the bounds on the fair value (using the law of the worst possible combination), and negotiate some price within these bounds. Thus, the early settlement of forward contracts is rather inconvenient. As a result, and in contrast to futures contracts, virtually all forward contracts remain outstanding until they expire, and actual delivery and payment is the rule rather than the exception. Closing out, if done at all, is often via adding a reverse contract, as we have seen. While this works out well enough most of the time, a long and a short do not add up to a zero position if there is default.

Example 6.3. Some time ago you bought USD 15m forward from Herstatt & Franklin, your favorite bank, but you have just closed out by selling to it, same amount and same date. You think you are out; however, if prior to T H&F has gone into receivership, then you have a problem. One of the two contracts probably has a negative value to you and the other a positive one. Then the bank's receivers will make you pay for the one with the negative value. For the contract with a positive value, though, you can only file a claim with the receivers, and *maybe* you will see some of your money some day.

6.1.3 Reducing Default Risk by Variable Collateral or Periodic Recontracting

As we saw in the previous section, one often needs to post margin when a forward contract is bought or sold. The margin may consist of an interest-earning term deposit or of securities (like stocks or bonds). Note that posting margin is very different from paying something to the bank. A payment is made to settle a debt, or to become the owner of a commodity or a financial asset. Whatever the reason for the payment, the bank that receives a payment becomes the owner of the money. In contrast, margin that is posted still belongs to the customer; the bank or broker merely has the right to seize the collateral if and only if the customer defaults.

The required margin can be quite high because the bank is willing to take only a small chance that the contract's expiration value, if negative, is not covered by the margin. In about half of the cases, the collateral will turn out to have been unnecessary because there is roughly a 50% chance that $\tilde{S}_T - F_{t_0,T}$ will end up being positive. There are two ways to reduce the need for margin.

Variable collateral. Under this system, the bank requests two kinds of margin. First, there is a small but permanent margin, say, the amount that almost surely covers the worst possible one-day drop in the market value of the forward contract. If the market value of the contract becomes negative, the bank then asks for additional collateral in order to cover at least the drop in the current market value of the forward contract. If the customer fails to put up the additional margin, the bank seizes all margin put up in the past—including the initial safety margin—and closes out the outstanding contract in the forward market. Obviously, under such a system the amount of collateral that has to be put up is far smaller, on average, than what is required if a single, large, initial margin has to be posted. The reason is that, under this system, collateral is called for only when needed, and only to the extent that it is needed at that time.

Periodic recontracting. Under this system, the new market value of yesterday's contract is computed every day. The party that ends up with a negative value then buys back the contract from the counterparty, and both sign a new contract at the day's new price. If the loser fails to settle the value of

Table 6.1. Forward contracts with variable collateral or daily recontracting.

Time	Data	Variable collateral	Periodic recontracting
0	$F_{0,3} = 40$ $r_{0,3} = 3\%$	Smitha buys forward USD 1m at $F_{0,3} = 40$	Smitha buys forward USD 1m at $F_{0,3} = 40$
1	$F_{1,3} = 38$ $r_{1,3} = 2\%$	Market value of old contract is $$\frac{38m - 40m}{1.02} = -1.961m$$ Smitha puts up T-bills worth at least 1.961m	Market value of old contract is $$\frac{38m - 40m}{1.02} = -1.961m$$ Smitha buys back the old contract for 1.961m and signs a new contract at $F_{1,3} = 38$.
2	$F_{1,3} = 36$ $r_{2,3} = 1\%$	Market value of old contract is $$\frac{36m - 40m}{1.01} = -3.960m$$ Smitha increases the T-bills put up to at least 3.960m	Market value of old contract is $$\frac{36m - 38m}{1.01} = -1.980m$$ Smitha buys back the old contract for 1.980m and signs a new contract at $F_{2,3} = 36$.
3	$F_{3,3} = S_3$ $= 34$ $r_{3,3} = 0\%$	Smitha pays the promised INR 40m for the USD 1m, and gets back her T-bills	Smitha pays the promised INR 36m for the USD 1m
Total paid:		INR 40m	(Adjusted for time value) Time 3: 36m Time 2: $1.980 \times 1.01 =$ 2m <u>Time 1: $1.961 \times 1.02 =$ 2m</u> Total: 40m

yesterday's contract, the bank seizes the initial margin, and closes out the contract in the forward market. Under this system, only a small amount of margin is needed, since the collateral only has to cover a one-day change in the market value.

It is useful to spell out the cash flows, because this will help you understand what futures contracts are and why they differ from recontracted forwards.

Example 6.4. Suppose that, at time 0, Smitha Steel has bought forward USD against INR for delivery at time 3. In table 6.1 we describe the implications under the systems of variable collateral and periodic contracting, respectively. We ignore the initial margin, since it is the same in both cases. All amounts are in INR. The example assumes that the forward rate always goes down, as this is the possibility that Smitha's bank worries about.

With variable collateral, nothing is changed relative to a standard contract (except that collateral is asked for only as and when needed): Smitha has temporarily moved some assets from her own safe to her bank's, and pays INR 40m at time 3. With recontracting, in contrast, there are three genuine payments, one per day, but by design their time-value-corrected final value is still equal to INR 40m at time 3. To see this, just consider the total paid, at time 3, when the interim losses are financed by loans which are paid back at time 3:

$$\text{Time 1: pay} \quad \underbrace{(40 - 38)/1.02}_{1.961 \text{ borrowed}} \times 1.02 = 40 - 38 = 2$$

$$\text{Time 2: pay} \quad \underbrace{(38 - 36)/1.01}_{1.98 \text{ borrowed}} \times 1.01 = 38 - 36 = 2$$

$$\text{Time 3: pay} \quad \underline{36}$$

$$\text{Total: pay} \quad 40$$

So the discounting, which is part of the market value calculations that are behind the recontracting payments, also means that, after taking into account time value, the recontracting cancels out: it can be "undone" by financing any losses via loans, or by depositing any gains, thus shifting all cash flows back to time $T = 3$.

> **DIY Problem 6.1.** Given a sequence $\{F_{1,4}, F_{2,4}, F_{3,4}, F_{4,4} = S_4\}$, write in algebraic form the cash flows from daily recontracting, and show that if all losses are financed by loans and all gains are deposited until time $T = 4$, you pay, all in all, $F_{1,4}$.

The system of variable collateral is used in many stock exchanges in continental Europe. Somewhat confusingly, these contracts are sometimes called futures contracts; in reality, they are collateralized forward contracts. "Futures" just sounds cooler than forwards, though.

This finishes our discussion of credit risks in forward contracts. We now see how this is handled in futures markets, and how secondary dealing has been organized.

6.2 How Futures Contracts Differ from Forward Markets

A currency futures contract has the following key characteristics: (i) it has zero initial vale; (ii) it stipulates delivery of a known number of forex units on a known future date T; and (iii) the HC payment for the forex is a known amount $f_{t,T}$, paid later.

The only news here, relative to a forward contract, is the last word—the vague term "later" rather than the precise expression "at T." In fact, we can be more specific about the timing of the payments: of the total, which is $f_{t,T}$, the part $f_{t,T} - \tilde{S}_T$ is paid gradually during the life of the contract via daily marked-to-market payments, and the remainder, $\tilde{S}_T$, is paid at maturity. Note that the pattern of the payments over time is *ex ante* unknown: we only know the grand total that we will pay, the no-time-value-correction sum.

We show how this marked-to-market system is a somewhat primitive version of the daily recontracting system we discussed in the previous section. So it is a way to mitigate the problem of default risk. Given that this problem is largely solved, futures contracts can be transferred among investors with minimal problems. We will see how this is done: with standardized contracts, in organized markets, and with the clearing corporation as the central counterpart. We will use the following jargon: "buying a contract" means engaging in a purchase transaction—going long forex, that is, you will get forex and pay HC; and a futures price is per unit of currency, even though the contract is always for a multiple of FC units.

6.2.1 Marking to Market

Recall that when a forward contract is recontracted every day, the buyer receives a daily cash flow equal to the *discounted* change in the forward price. Thus, rising prices mean cash inflows for the buyer, and falling prices mean cash outflows. (The signs are reversed when the seller's point of view is taken.) Also, as the interim payments are based on the discounted forward price, the total amount paid is still equivalent to paying the initially contracted rate, $F_{t_0,T}$, at the contract's expiration date.

A futures contract works quite similarly, except that the discounting is omitted. So the daily payments are equal to the undiscounted changes in the futures prices. The reasons for this simplification are not hard to guess: it made sense at the time futures were designed, the mid 1800s. (i) Futures contracts had short lives, and interest rates were low (this was the days of the gold standard), so discounting made no huge difference. (ii) Discounting means smaller payments; this is welcome when the payment is an outflow (as in our Smitha example), but it is bad news when we face inflows. So if price rises are roughly as probable as price falls, on average it made no difference, people felt. And (iii), painfully, in the 1800s discounting would have to be done by longhand division rather than electronically. For these reasons people simply dropped it. As we shall see, the argument that "it all washes out as price rises are as probable as falls" is not quite true, but the effect is indeed minimal.

So in practice we have daily cash flows that, for the buyer, are equal to $f_{t,T} - f_{t-1,T}$, with the final payment, $f_{T,T} = S_T$, taking place after the last trading day. The last trading day is two working days before delivery, as in spot markets. So the last-trading-day futures price must be equal to the contemporaneous spot rate. As a result, after all the marked-to-market payments have been made, the buyer is left with a spot contract.

Example 6.5. In the Smitha Steel example, suppose the rates were futures prices rather than forward ones. Then the cash flows would have been $-2, -2, -2$ (= the last marking to market), and -34 (the spot payment, $f_{3,3} = S_3$). Below, I detail this, and compare it with a marked-to-market forward contract:

Price (rate, r)	40 (0.03)	38 (0.02)	36 (0.01)	34 (0.00)
Futures	—	$38 - 40 = -2.000$	$36 - 38 = -2.000$	$34 - 36 = -2.000$ and then buy at 34
Fwd, mk2mk	—	$\dfrac{38 - 40}{1.02} = -1.961$	$\dfrac{36 - 38}{1.01} = -1.980$	buy at 36

Thus, ignoring time value, the cumulative payments from the buyer are equal to 40 units of home currency.

The cash flows to the seller are the reverse. In fact, what happens is that the buyer pays the seller if prices go down and receives money from the seller if prices go up. In short, good news (rising prices for the buyer, falling prices for the seller) means an immediate inflow, and bad news an immediate outflow. These daily payments from "winner" to "loser" occur through accounts the customers hold with their brokers, and they are transmitted from the loser to the winner through brokers, *clearing members*, and the clearing corporation. The *settlement price*, upon which the daily marked-to-market cash flows are based, is in principle equal to the day's closing price or close price. However, futures exchanges want to make sure that the settlement price is not manipulated, or they may want a more up-to-date price if the last transaction took place too long before the close. One way to ensure this is to base the settlement price not on the actual last trade price but on the average of the transaction prices in the last half hour of trading or, if there is no trading, the average of the market makers' quotes (LIFFE).

Suppose, lastly, that somewhere in the middle of the second trading day, the day where the price drops from 38 to 36, Smitha sells her contract at a forward price 37.5. The total marking to market for day 2 is still $36 - 38 = -2$; but now this will be split into $37.5 - 38 = -0.5$ for Smitha, and $36 - 37.5 = -1.5$ for the (then unsuspecting) new holder.

Marking to market is the most crucial difference between forward and futures contracts. It means that if an investor defaults, the "gain" from defaulting is simply the avoidance of a one-day marked-to-market outflow: all previous losses have already been settled in cash. This implies the following.

- Compared with a forward contract, the incentive to default on a futures contract is smaller. By defaulting on the marked-to-market payment, one only avoids a payment equal to that day's price change. In contrast, in the case of a forward contract, defaulting means that the investor saves the amount lost over the entire life of the contract.

Example 6.6. Investor A bought EUR 1m at $f_{t_0,T} = $ USD/EUR 0.96. By the last day of trading but one, the futures price has drifted down to a level of

USD/EUR 0.89. So investor A has already paid, cumulatively, $1m \times (0.96 - 0.89) = $ USD 70,000 as marked-to-market cash flows. If, on the last day of trading, the price moves down by another ten points, then, by defaulting, investor A only avoids the additional payment of $1m \times 0.001 = $ USD 1,000. In contrast, if this had been a forward contract, the savings from defaulting would have been the entire price drop between t_0 and T, that is, $1m \times (F_{t_0,T} - S_T) = 1m \times (0.96 - 0.889) = $ USD 71,000.

- From the point of view of the clearing house, the counterpart of the above statement is that if an investor nevertheless fails to make the required margin payment, the loss to the clearing house is simply the day's price change.

In practice, the savings from defaulting on a futures contract (and the clearing house's loss if there is default) are even smaller than the above statement suggests because of a second characteristic of futures markets—the margin requirements.

6.2.2 Margin Requirements

To reduce even the incentive of evading today's losses, the buyer or seller also has to put up initial security that almost surely covers a one-day loss. This is true security in the sense that one earns interest on it.[1] The general idea behind the margin requirements is that the margin paid should cover virtually all of the one-day risk. This, of course, further reduces both one's incentive to default as well as the loss to the clearing house if there is default.

Margin also means limit, or line. In that sense, two margins have to be watched when trading in futures markets, *initial margin* and *maintenance margin*. Indeed, in theory every gain or loss is immediately settled in cash, but this may mean frequent, small payments, which are costly and inconvenient. So in practice losses are allowed to accumulate to certain levels before a *margin call* (a request for payment) is issued. These small losses are simply deducted from the initial margin until a lower bound, the maintenance margin, is reached. At this stage, a margin call is issued, requesting the investor to bring the margin back up to the initial level.

Example 6.7. The initial margin on a GBP 62,500 contract may be USD 3,000, and the maintenance margin USD 2,400. The initial USD 3,000 margin is the initial *equity* in your account. The buyer's equity increases (decreases) when prices rise (fall), that is, when marked-to-market gains or losses are credited or debited to your account. As long as the investor's losses do not sum to more than USD 600 (that is, as long

---

[1] The marked-to-market payments are often called margin payments. This term is a bit misleading if "paying margin" is interpreted as "posting additional security": if the payments really were security, the payer would still be entitled to the normal interest on the money put up. In reality there are no interest payments on the marked-to-market payments, so economically these are final payments not security postings—unlike the initial margin, which is genuine security.

What went wrong in the Barings case, and can it happen again? Both the futures exchanges and Barings (and possibly many other firms, in those days) made a number of mistakes:

Internal organizational problems. Nick Leeson headed both the dealing room (front office) and the accounting interface (back office). Also, he came from the back office. So he could bend the rules, key in misleading records, and funnel cash between various accounts. Also, there was no middle office (risk management) and there were no enforced position limits.

Gullible greed in London. Barings's HQ thought Nick was making huge profits and did not want to slaughter the goose with the golden eggs, so they kept sending money which they thought was just security postings.

Failing oversight. Both the Osaka and Singapore futures exchanges were worried about the size of Nick's positions, and they talked about it to each other, but in the end did nothing.

These mistakes are unlikely to be made again any time soon in any well-run firm. That is, the next catastrophe will again be of a totally unexpected nature.

That, at least, is what we all thought. Yet in January 2008 it transpired that Jérôme Kerviel at France's Société Générale had built a secret portfolio of stock futures for a notional value of EUR 50b—more than the bank's own market value of equity then, 36b—on which the realized loss turned out to be 4.9b. Of the total loss, his lawyers objected, almost two thirds was due to a panic liquidation by SG after discovering a 1.7b proper loss by Kerviel himself.

Before becoming a trader he had worked in IT in the middle office, where he had figured out five passwords and identified some loopholes. For instance, SG checked the position limits only every three days; so just before the checks, Kerviel simply reduced the net exposures by fictitious trades. (Checks should be random and frequent, and limits should look not just at the net but also at the gross positions.) Worse, SG was blamed for ignoring no fewer than 75 danger signals (including "does not take up his holidays" and "sweats a lot," alongside, more seriously, worried questions from futures exchanges). Like Barings before, SG preferred to look the other way because Kerviel had posted a profit of 1.4b in 2006 (on a maximum position of 125m!).

Panel 6.1. Leeson's lessons on the end of Barings.

as the investor's equity does not fall below the maintenance margin, USD 2,400), no margin call will be issued to her. If her equity, however, falls below USD 2,400, she must immediately add *variation margin* to restore her equity to USD 3,000.

Failure to make the margin payment is interpreted as an order to liquidate the position. That is, if you bought and cannot pay, your contract will be put up for sale at the next opening, as if you had ordered to sell the contract; and if you were short, your contract will likewise be closed out the next day as if you had ordered to buy. This way, the exchange finds a new party that steps into your shoes. The loss or gain on this last deal is yours, and is added to or subtracted from the margin.

Example 6.8. When Nick Leeson had gambled his employer, the then 233-year-old Barings bank, into ruin he had accumulated losses of GBP 800m, more than Barings's entire equity. But the Singapore Exchange lost "only" 50m. Barings London had sent Nick about 500m for marked-to-market payments (thinking these were deposits or something like that), and Nick had "borrowed" about 250m from other customers' accounts to pay even more margin without telling London. So the SME was already covered for about GBP 750m. The balance was lost when Nick's huge open positions were liquidated at short notice and when the initial margin proved totally inadequate to cover the losses caused by the massive price pressure.

6.2.3 Organized Markets

As we saw, forward contracts are not really traded; they are simply initiated in the over-the-counter market (typically with the client's bank) and held until maturity. In the forward market, market makers quote prices but there is no organized way of centralizing demand and supply. The only mechanisms that tend to equalize the prices quoted by different market makers are arbitrage and least-cost dealing; and, as traders are in permanent contact with only a few market makers, price equalization is imperfect. Nor is there any public information about when a transaction took place, and at what price.

In contrast, futures are traded on organized exchanges, with specific rules about the terms of the contracts, and with an active secondary market. Futures prices are the result of a centralized, organized matching of demand and supply. One method of organizing this matching of orders is the *open outcry* system, where floor members are physically present in a trading pit and auction off their orders by shouting them out. U.S. exchanges traditionally work like this; so did London's LIFFE and Paris's MATIF.[2] You can see open outcry trading in the Ackroyd–Murphy movie *Trading Places*. Another method, traditionally used in some continental exchanges (including Germany's DTB and Belgium's Belfox, now part of Eurex and Euronext, respectively) is to centralize the limit orders in a computerized *public limit-order book*.[3] Brokers sit before their screens, and can add or delete their orders, or fill a limit order posted on the screen. Computerized trading, whether *price-driven* (i.e., with market makers) or *order-driven* (with a limit-order book), is gradually replacing the chaotic, opaque, open-outcry system.

6.2.4 Standardized Contracts

Each forward contract is unique in terms of size, and the expiry date can be chosen freely. This is convenient for hedgers who mean to hold the contract until maturity, but not very handy if secondary markets are to be organized:

---

[2] LIFFE is the London International Financial Futures Exchange (where, since the merger with the London Traded Options Exchange, options are also traded). MATIF is the Marché à Terme International de France (the International Futures Market of France). Both are now part of Euronext, which has grouped all its futures and options business in London, under Euronext LIFFE.

[3] DTB is the Deutsche Termin Börse. Belfox is the Belgian Futures and Options Exchange. A limit order is an order to buy an indicated number of currency units at a price no higher than a given level, or to sell an indicated number of currency units at a price no lower than a given level. The limit orders submitted by an individual reveal the individual's supply and demand curve for the currency. By aggregating all limit orders across investors, the market supply and demand curves are obtained. The market opens with a call, that is, with a computer-determined price that equates demand and supply as closely as possible. Afterwards, the computer screens display the first few unfilled orders on each side (purchase and sell orders), and brokers can respond to these, or cancel their own orders, or add new orders as customer orders come in.

Table 6.2. Contract sizes at some futures exchanges.

Rate	At	Contract size (FC)	Other exchanges
USD/GBP	IMM	62,500	PBOT, LIFFE, SIMEX, MACE
USD/EUR	IMM	125,000	LIFFE, PBOT, SIMEX, MACE, FINEX
EUR/USD	OM-S	50,000	EUREX
USD/CHF	IMM	125,000	LIFFE, MACE, PBOT
USD/AUD	IMM	100,000	PBOT, EUREX
NZD/USD	NZFE	50,000	
USD/NZD	NZFE	100,000	
USD/JPY	IMM	12,500,000	LIFFE, TIFFE, MACE, PBOT, SIMEX
USD/CAD	IMM	100,000	PBOT, MACE

Key: EUREX, European Exchange (comprising the former German DTB and the former Swiss SFX); IMM-International Money Market (Merc, Chicago); LIFFE, London International Financial Futures Exchange; MACE, MidAmerican Commodity Exchange; NZFE, New Zealand Futures Exchange. OM-S, OptionsMarkned Stockholm; PBOT, Philadelphia Board of Trade; SIMEX, Singapore International Money Exchange; TCBOT, Twin Cities Board of Trade (St. Paul/Minneapolis); TIFFE, Tokyo International Financial Futures Exchange. *Source:* Data from Sercu and Uppal (1995).

for every single trade, new terms and conditions would have to be keyed in and new interest rates dug up.

To facilitate secondary trading, all futures contracts are standardized by contract size (see table 6.2 for some examples) and expiration dates. This means that the futures market is not as fragmented—by too wide a variety of expiration dates and contract sizes—as the forward market. Although standardization in itself does not guarantee a high volume, it does facilitate the emergence of a deep, liquid market.

Expiration dates traditionally were the third Wednesdays of March, June, September, or December, or the first business day after such a Wednesday. Nowadays, longer-lived contracts and—for the nearer dates—a wider range of expiry dates are offered, but most of the interest is still for the shortest-lived contracts. Actual delivery takes place on the second business day after the expiration date. When a contract has come to expiry, trade in a distant-date contract is added. For instance, in the old March–June–September–December cycle, the year starts with March, June, and September contracts, but come the end of March, one opens trade for a December contract and so on.

6.2.5 The Clearing Corporation

Formally, futures contracts are not initiated directly between individuals (or corporations) A and B. Rather, each party has a contract with the futures clearing corporation or clearing house. For instance, a sale from A to B is structured as a sale by A to the clearing house, and then a sale by the clearing house to B. Thus, even if B defaults, A is not concerned (unless the clearing house also

FUTURES PRICES [...] CURRENCY								
						Lifetime		Open
	Open	High	Low	Settle	Change	High	Low	Interest
JAPAN YEN	**(CME)**	–	**12.5**	**million yen**	**;**	**$ per yen**	**(.00)**	
Sept	.9458	.9466	.9386	.9389	– .0046	.9540	.7945	73,221
Dec	.9425	.9470	.9393	.9396	– .0049	.9529	.7970	3,455
Mr94				.9417	– .0051	.9490	.8700	318
Est vol 28,844; vol Wed 36,595; open int 77,028, + 1.820								

Figure 6.1. WSJ information on currency futures.

goes bankrupt). The clearing corporation levies a small tax on all transactions, and thus has reserves that should cover losses from default.

The clearing house thus guarantees payment or delivery. In addition, it effectively "clears" offsetting trades: if A buys from B and then some time later sells to C, the clearing house cancels out both of A's contracts, and only the clearing house's contracts with B and C remain outstanding. Player A is effectively exonerated of all obligations. In contrast, as we saw, a forward purchase by A from B and a forward sale by A to C remain separate contracts that are not cleared: if B fails to deliver to A, A has to suffer the loss and cannot invoke B's default to escape its (A's) obligations to C.

6.2.6 How Futures Prices Are Reported

Figure 6.1 contains an excerpt from the *Wall Street Journal*, showing information on yen futures trading at the International Money Market (IMM) of the Chicago Mercantile Exchange (CME). The heading, JAPAN YEN, shows the size of the contract (12.5m yen) and somewhat obscurely tries to say that the prices are expressed in USD cents. The June 1993 contract had expired more than a month before, so the three contracts being traded on July 29, 1993, are the September and December 1993 contracts, and the March 1994 contracts. In each row, the first four prices relate to trading on Thursday, July 29—the price at the start of trading (open), the highest and lowest transaction prices during the day, and the settlement price ("Settle"), which is representative of the transaction prices around the close.

The settlement price is the basis of marking to market. The column, "Change," contains the change of today's settlement price relative to yesterday. For instance, on Thursday, July 29, the settlement price of the September contract dropped by 0.0046 cents, implying that a holder of a purchase contract has lost $12.5m \times (0.0046/100) = $ USD 575 per contract and that a seller has made USD 575 per contract. The next two columns show the highest and lowest prices that have been observed during the life of the contract. For the March contract, the "High–Low" range is narrower than for the older contracts, since the March contract has been trading for little more than a month. "Open interest" refers to the number of outstanding contracts. Notice how most of the trading is in the nearest-maturity contract. Open interest in the March 1994 contract is minimal, and there was not even any trading that day. (There are no open, high, or low data.) The settlement price for the March 1994 contract has been set by the CME on the basis of bid–ask quotes.

The line below the price information gives an estimate of the volume traded that day and the previous day (Wednesday). Also shown are the totals of open interest across the three contracts, and the change in open interest relative to the day before.

*   *   *

This finishes our review of how futures differ from forwards. From a theoretical perspective, the main difference is the marking to market, or, if you wish, the omission of discounting in the daily recontracting. In the next section we see whether this has an impact on the pricing and, if so, in what direction.

6.3 Effect of Marking to Market on Futures Prices

We saw that the absence of discounting in the daily recontracting has been waved aside as unimportant, *ex ante* at least, if price rises and price drops are equally unlikely. Is this a good argument? In this section we show that the claim is correct if price changes are independent of the time path of interest rates; this is not quite true, but is close enough for most purposes.

Recall that if a corporation hedges a foreign-currency inflow using a forward contract, there are no cash flows until the maturity date, T; and, at T, the money paid by the debtor is delivered to the bank in exchange for a known amount of home currency. In contrast, if hedging is done in the futures markets, there are daily cash flows. As we saw at the beginning of this chapter, interim cash flows do not affect pricing if these cash flows are equal to the discounted price change, as is the case with a forward contract that is recontracted periodically. The reason is that, with daily recontracting, one can "undo" without cost the effects of recontracting by investing all inflows until time T and by financing all outflows by a loan expiring at T. The question we now address is whether the price will be affected if we drop the discounting of the price changes, that is, if we go from forward markets to futures markets. We will develop our argument in three steps, and illustrate each step by using an example. For simplicity, we assume that next period there are only two possible futures prices and that investors are risk neutral. All these simplifying assumptions can easily be relaxed without affecting the final conclusion.

Let there be three dates ($t = 0$, $t = 1$, and $t = T = 2$, the maturity date), and let the initial forward rate be $F_{0,2} = \text{USD } 100$. Let there be only two possible time-1 forward prices, 105 and 95, and let these be equally probable. We want to verify the conjecture that $f_{t,2} = F_{t,2}$. This is easily seen to be true at time 1: since as of that date there are no more extra marked-to-market cash flows relative to forward contracts, futures and forward prices must be the same at time $T - 1$. The issue is whether this also holds for earlier dates, or *the* earlier

Table 6.3. HC cash flows assuming that $F_{0,2} = f_{0.2}$.

$F_{1,2}$	HC cash flow: futures		HC cash flow: forward		Difference	
	Time 1	Time 2	Time 1	Time 2	Time 1	Time 2
105	$105 - 100 = +5$	$(\tilde{S}_2 - 105) - \tilde{S}_2 = -105$	0	-100	$+5$	-5
95	$95 - 100 = -5$	$(\tilde{S}_2 - 95) - \tilde{S}_2 = -95$	0	-100	-5	$+5$

Table 6.4. HC net time value (NTV) effect at $t = 2$ assuming that $F_{0,2} = f_{0.2}$.

State	Case 1		Case 2		Case 3	
	r	NTV at $t = 2$	r	NTV at $t = 2$	r	NTV at $t = 2$
Up	0	$5 \times 1.00 - 5 = 0.00$	0.10	$5 \times 1.10 - 5 = 0.50$	0	$5 \times 1.08 - 5 = 0.40$
Down	0	$-5 \times 1.00 + 5 = 0.00$	0.10	$-5 \times 1.10 + 5 = -0.50$	0	$-5 \times 1.12 + 5 = -0.60$
$E(\cdot)$		0.00		0.00		-0.10

date, in our case. The answer must be based on the difference of the cash flows between the two contracts (table 6.3):

- The buyer of the forward contract simply pays 100 at time 2. This is shown under the columns "HC cash flow: forward" in table 6.3.

- The buyer of the futures contract pays 5 or receives 5, depending on the price change at time 1. The balance is then paid at time $T = 2$, partly as the last marked-to-market payment and partly as the HC leg of a spot purchase. Thus, the buyer will receive/pay the cash flows shown under the columns "HC cash flow: futures"—either -5 and -95 or $+5$ and -105.

- The columns labeled "Difference" show the cash flows for the futures contract relative to the cash flow of the forward contract.

We see that the futures is like a forward except that the buyer also gets a zero-interest loan of 5 in the upstate, and must make a zero-interest deposit of 5 in the downstate. Whether this zero-rate money-market operation makes a difference depends on interest rates. In table 6.4 we look at three cases: a zero interest rate in both the upstate and the downstate, a 10% interest rate in both the upstate and the downstate, and lastly an 8% rate in the upstate and a 12% one in the downstate.

- In the zero-rate case you of course do not mind receiving a zero-rate loan in the upstate, but you do not think this is valuable either: everybody can get that for free, by assumption. Nor do you mind the forced deposit at zero percent in the downstate: you can borrow the amount for free from a bank anyway. In short, the marked-to-market flows do not add or destroy any value when interest rates are zero. It follows that the conjecture $F = f$ is acceptable.

- For a 10% interest rate you positively love receiving a zero-rate loan: you can invest that money and earn 0.50 on it at time 2. In contrast, now you do mind the forced deposit at zero percent: you lose 0.50 interest on it. But if the up- and down-scenarios are equally probable, a risk-neutral investor still does not really mind, *ex ante*: the expected time-value effect remains zero. It follows that the conjecture $F = f$ is still acceptable when the risk-free rate is a positive constant.

- In the third case you still like the zero-rate loan, but the gain is lower: at time 2 you make just 8% on the 5, or 0.40. Likewise, you still mind the forced deposit at zero percent, but now you lose 0.60 time value on it since the interest rate is higher, 12%. And if, *ex ante*, the up- and down-scenarios are equally probable, a risk-neutral agent now dislikes the zero-rate operations: the expected time value effect is now negative. It follows that the conjecture $F = f$ is no longer acceptable when the risk-free rate is higher in the downstate.

The example is quite special, but the basic logic holds under very general circumstances as it is based on a simple syllogism:

Fact 1. Unexpectedly low interest rates tend to go with rising asset prices, while unexpectedly high interest rates tend to go with falling prices.

Fact 2. To the futures buyer, rising prices are like receiving a zero-interest loan, relative to a forward contract, while falling prices mean zero-interest lending (you have to pay money to the clearing house).

Therefore, the time-value game is not fair: you get the free loan when rates tend to be low, while you are forced to lend for free when rates tend to be high.

Stated differently, money received from marking to market is, more often than not, reinvested at low rates, while intermediate losses are, on average, financed at high rates. Thus, the financing or reinvestment of intermediary cash flows is not an actuarially fair game. If futures and forward prices were identical, a buyer of a futures contract would, therefore, be worse off than a buyer of a forward contract. It follows that, to induce investors to hold futures contracts, futures prices must be lower than forward prices.[4]

The above argument is irrefutable, and contradicts the gut feeling of the 1800s that discounting made no difference, on average. But how important is the effect? In practice, the empirical relationship between exchange rates

---

[4] If the correlation were positive rather than negative, then marking to market would be an advantage to the buyer of a futures contract; as a result, the buyer would bid up the futures price above the forward price. Finally, if the correlation were zero, futures and forward prices would be the same.

and short-term interest rates is not very strong. Moreover, simulations by, for example, French (1983) and Cornell and Reinganum (1981) have shown that even when the interest rate is negatively correlated with the futures price, the price difference between the forward and the theoretical futures price remains very small—at least for short-term contracts on assets other than T-bills and bonds. Thus, for practical purposes, one can determine prices of futures contracts almost as if they were forward contracts.

6.4   Hedging with Futures Contracts

In this section, we see how one can use futures to hedge a given position. Because of its low cost even for small orders, a hedger may prefer the currency futures market over the forward market. There are, however, problems that arise with hedging in the futures market.

- The contract size is fixed and is unlikely to exactly match the position to be hedged.

- The expiration dates of the futures contract rarely match those for the currency inflows/outflows that the contract is meant to hedge.

- The choice of underlying assets in the futures market is limited, and the currency one wishes to hedge may not have a futures contract.

That is, whereas in the forward market we can tailor the amount, the date, and the currency to a given exposed position, this is not always possible in the futures market. An imperfect hedge is called a *cross-hedge* when the currencies do not match, and is called a *delta-hedge* if the maturities do not match. When the mismatches arise simultaneously, we call this a *cross-and-delta-hedge*.

Example 6.9. Suppose that, on January 1, a U.S. exporter wants to hedge an SEK 9,000,000 inflow due on March 1 ($= T_1$). In the forward market, the exporter could simply sell that amount for March 1. In the futures market, hedging is less than perfect:

- There is no USD/SEK contract; the closest available hedge is the USD/EUR futures contract.
- The closest possible expiration date is, say, March 20 (T_2).
- The contract size is EUR 125,000. At the current spot rate of, say, SEK/EUR 9.3, this means SEK 1,162,500 per contract.

So assuming, unrealistically, a constant SEK/EUR cross rate, the hedger would have to sell eight contracts to approximately hedge the SEK 9,000,000: $8 \times 1,162,500 = 9.3$m. But the more difficult question is how to deal with the cross-rate uncertainty and the maturity mismatch. This is the topic of this section.

As we shall see, sometimes it is better to hedge with a portfolio of futures contracts written on different sources of risks rather than with only one type of futures contract. For example, theoretically there is an interest-rate risk in both SEK and USD because the dates of hedge and exposure do not match, so one could consider taking futures positions in not just EUR currency but also in EUR and USD interest rates, and perhaps even SEK interest rates. However, in order to simplify the exposition, we first consider the case where only one type of futures contract is being used to hedge a given position.

6.4.1 The Generic Problem and Its Theoretical Solution

The problems of currency mismatch and maturity mismatch mean that, at best, only an approximate hedge can be constructed when hedging with futures. The standard rule is to look for a futures position that minimizes the variance of the hedged cash flow. Initially, we shall assume the following:

(i) There is one unit of foreign currency e ("exposure") to be received at time T_1, for instance, one Swedish krona is to be converted into USD, the HC.

(ii) A futures contract is available for a "related" currency h ("hedge")—for instance, the EUR—with an expiration date T_2 ($\geqslant T_1$).

(iii) The size of the futures contract is one unit of foreign currency h (for instance, 1 EUR).

(iv) Contracts are infinitely divisible; that is, one can buy any fraction of the unit contract.

Items (i) and (iii) are easily corrected. Item (iv) means we will ignore the fixed-contract-size problem. The reason is that nothing can be done about it except finding a theoretical optimum and then rounding to the nearest integer.

Let us show the currency names as superscripts, parenthesized so as to avoid any possible confusion with exponents. Denote the number of contracts sold by β.[5] The total cash flow generated by the futures contracts between times t and T_1 is then given by the size of the position, $-\beta$, multiplied by the change in the futures price between times t and T_1. (True, this ignores time-value effects, but we cannot be too choosy: the hedge is approximate anyway.) It follows that the hedged cash flow equals

$$\text{Cash flow at time } T_1 = \tilde{S}^{(e)}_{T_1} - \beta \times (\tilde{f}^{(h)}_{T_1,T_2} - f^{(h)}_{t,T_2}). \tag{6.1}$$

The standard approach is to choose β so as to make the variance of the hedged cash flow as small as possible. But we already know the solution. If we had written the problem as one of minimizing $\text{var}(\tilde{\epsilon})$, where $\tilde{\epsilon} := \tilde{y} - \beta\tilde{x}$, you

---

[5] Beta should get a time subscript, as should the variance and covariance in the solution. But the notation is already cluttered enough.

would immediately have recognized this to be a "regression" problem, with the usual regression beta as the solution:

$$\beta = \text{the slope coefficient from } \tilde{S}_{T_1}^{(e)} = \alpha + \beta \tilde{f}_{T_1,T_2}^{(h)} + \tilde{\epsilon}$$

$$= \frac{\text{cov}(\tilde{f}_{T_1,T_2}^{(h)}, \tilde{S}_{T_1}^{(e)})}{\text{var}(\tilde{f}_{T_1,T_2}^{(h)})}. \tag{6.2}$$

DIY Problem 6.2. Formally derive this result. First write out the variance of the hedged cash flow for a given β, using the fact that the (known) current futures price does not add to the variance. Then find the value for β that minimizes the variance of the remaining risk.

We now look at a number of special cases.

6.4.2   Case 1: The Perfect Match

There is a perfect match if the futures contract expires at T_1 (that is, $T_2 = T_1$) and $e = h$. For example, assume there is an SEK contract with exactly the same date as your exposure. The convergence property means that $\tilde{f}_{T_1,T_2}^{(e)} = S_{T_1}^{(e)}$: on the last day of trading an SEK futures price exactly equals the spot rate at the same moment because both stipulate delivery at $t + 2$. Thus, in this special case of a perfect match, equation (6.2) tells us we should regress the variable upon itself. There is of course no need to actually do so: in that regression, the slope coefficient (and the R^2) can only be unity. So you sell forward one for one: if the exposure is B units of forex, you sell B units. In short, this is standard hedging where nothing needs to be estimated.

But one is usually not that lucky.

6.4.3   Case 2: The Currency-Mismatch Hedge or Cross-Hedge

We now consider a case where the futures contract matches the maturity of the foreign-currency inflow but not the currency ($h \neq e$). For instance, the U.S. exporter's SEK inflow is hedged using an EUR future. We can use the convergence property $f_{T_1,T_1} = S_{T_1}$ to specify the hedge ratio as

$$\beta = \frac{\text{cov}(\tilde{S}_{T_1}^{(e)}, \tilde{S}_{T_1}^{(h)})}{\text{var}(\tilde{S}_{T_1}^{(h)})} \tag{6.3}$$

$$= \text{the slope coefficient in } \tilde{S}_{T_1}^{(e)} = \alpha + \beta \tilde{S}_{T_1}^{(h)} + \tilde{\epsilon}. \tag{6.4}$$

This measure of linear exposure will come up again and again in this book, most prominently in chapter 9 on option pricing and hedging and in chapter 13, where we quantify operating exposure. Recall that exposure holds the time constant, and compares possible future scenarios. Similarly, our regression is, in principle, forward looking: it should be run across a representative number of (probability-weighted) possible future scenarios. This is not easy, so you may want to run the regression on past data instead. Then, one assumption is that β is constant, so that the past is a good guide to the future. For technical and statistical reasons that are beyond the scope of this chapter, one should not regress levels of exchange rates on levels if the data are time series. A regression between changes of the variables, in contrast, would be statistically more acceptable:

$$\text{Regress } \Delta S_t^{(e)} = \alpha' + \beta \, \Delta S_t^{(h)} + \tilde{\epsilon}_t', \tag{6.5}$$

where, this time, deltas refer to changes over time. Many researchers would still be unhappy with this, and actually prefer to work with a regression in percentage changes: in a long time series with much variation in the level of S, it is hard to believe that the distribution of ΔS is constant. If you run a regression between percentages, you need to transform the slope γ from an elasticity into a partial derivative:[6]

$$\text{Regress } \tilde{s}_t^{(e)} = \alpha'' + \gamma \, \tilde{s}_t^{(h)} + \tilde{\epsilon}_t'' \text{ and use } \beta = \gamma \, \frac{S_t^{(h)}}{S_t^{(e)}} \tag{6.6}$$

$$= \gamma \, S_t^{(h/e)}, \tag{6.7}$$

where $S^{(h/e)}$ is the cross rate, which in our example is the value of 1 SEK in EUR, which is euros per crown or, generally, h/e. The assumption is then that γ, not β, is constant.

Practitioners often use a rule of thumb that superficially fits in with this solution. Suppose you do not actually run this regression and, instead, just guess that the gamma equals unity. For instance, our U.S. trader expects that every percentage in the EUR (against the USD) on average leads to a similar change in the USD value of the SEK. Then the hedge ratio would simply be set equal to the cross rate:

$$\text{Rule of thumb for cross hedge: } \gamma = 1 \text{ so } \beta = S_t^{(h/e)}. \tag{6.8}$$

Example 6.10. The current spot rates are 1.201 for the EUR and 0.133 for the SEK. The quick-and-dirty hedge ratio would be set equal to the cross rate, the value of 1 SEK in EUR, which equals $0.133/1.201 = 0.111$. The reason is that you think that percentage changes in the two currencies will be similar ($\gamma = 1$), but since the EUR is worth about nine kronar now, 1 EUR would change by as much as would nine kronar. Therefore, one euro shorted would hedge about 9 SEK. In other words, 0.111 euros per SEK will do.

Suppose, alternatively, that you prefer to run a regression between monthly percentage changes on SEK and EUR, and the slope is 0.96 with an R^2 of 0.864. Also, the current spot rates are 1.201 for the EUR and 0.133 for the SEK. Then

$$\text{Regression-based hedge ratio} = 0.96 \times 0.111 = 0.106.$$

That is, you would lower your hedge ratio.

---

[6] In terms of a regression of y on x, the exposure is written as $\Delta y/\Delta x$. An elasticity equals $e = (\Delta y/\Delta x) \times (x/y)$, so $\Delta y/\Delta x = e \times (y/x)$.

The rule of thumb is almost surely biased, which is bad, but has one big advantage: it has zero sampling error. Let us explain each statement. First, the assumption of unit gammas across the board does not make sense, statistically. For example, if it *were* true, then the reverse regression, between EUR and SEK rather than the inverse, would also produce a unit gamma, but this is mathematically possible only when there is no noise. It is easy to show that the product of the two gammas—the one from y on x and the one from x on y—is the R^2, which is surely a number below unity; so one expects at least one of the two gammas to be below unity, and normally both will be below unity.[7]

But while the drawback of the rule of thumb is a bias, it has the advantage of no sampling error. If you actually run regressions, then the estimated sample will randomly deviate, depending on sampling coincidences, even if nothing structural has changed. Now from the point of view of the user, sampling error is as bad as bias. For instance, if the true gamma (known to the great statistician in the sky only) is 0.95, then the error introduced by an estimated gamma of 0.90 is as bad as the bias introduced by the rule-of-thumb value, unity. Likewise, hedging with a unit gamma would be as bad as hedging with an estimated gamma that equals, with equal probability, 1.00 or 0.90. So it all depends on squared bias versus estimation variance. Experiments (Sercu and Wu 2000) show that the rule of thumb does better than the regression-based hedge if the relation between i and j is close, which is the case for the USD/SEK and USD/EUR rates. When the link between the two variables becomes lower, sampling-error variance increases but so does the bias, and in fact bias tends to become the worse of the two evils.

6.4.4 Case 3: The Delta-Hedge

Suppose now that there is an SEK contract, but for the wrong date instead of for the wrong currency. Our money comes in on February 15, while the contract expires on March 20, for example. So our futures contract will still have a 35-day life remaining when it is liquidated. In principle, we would have to regress possible spot values for the SEK on the corresponding 35-day futures price of the SEK. One problem is that we do not have time-series data on 35-day futures: the real-world data have a daily changing maturity.

There are two ways out, both connected to IRP. Since futures are almost indistinguishable from forwards, we know that

$$\tilde{f}^{(e)}_{T_1,T_2} \approx \tilde{S}^{(e)}_{T_1} \frac{1 + \tilde{r}_{T_1,T_2}}{1 + \tilde{r}^{(e)}_{T_1,T_2}}, \tag{6.9}$$

---

[7] Technically, the rule of thumb is based on the assumption that no change in the relative values is expected: $E_t(\Delta y/y) = E_t(\Delta x/x)$. This says that if you regress *expected* changes of y on *expected* changes of x, then the slope equals unity. But if you run that regression using realized changes instead of expectations, the *un*expected change in x causes an "errors-in-variables bias" that forces the coefficient toward zero. This bias is attenuated by correlation between the unexpected components in x and y.

where the risk-free rates r now get tildes because we do not yet know what they will be on February 15. So one way to solve the ever-changing-maturity problem in the data is to construct forward rates from spot and interest data, probably using 30-day p.a. rates to approximate the 35 p.a. data.[8] The other way out is to use a rule of thumb. Inverting equation (6.9), we get

$$\tilde{S}_{T_1}^{(e)} = \frac{1 + \tilde{r}_{T_1,T_2}^{(e)}}{1 + \tilde{r}_{T_1,T_2}} \tilde{f}_{T_1,T_2}^{(e)}. \tag{6.10}$$

The rule of thumb then follows under a not very harmful assumption, namely that there is no uncertainty about the interest rates. For instance, suppose you knew that the ratio $(1 + r^{(e)})/(1 + r)$ for a 35-day contract would be 1.005 on February 15. Then equation (6.9) would specialize into

$$\tilde{S}_{T_1}^{(e)} = 1.005 \tilde{f}_{T_1,T_2}^{(e)}, \tag{6.11}$$

which tells us immediately that the forward-looking regression coefficient of $S^{(e)}$ on $f^{(e)}$ is 1.005. So the rule of thumb for the delta hedge is to set the hedge ratio equal to the forecasted ratio $(1 + r^{(e)})/(1 + r)$ for a 35-day contract for February 15. Experiments show that it hardly matters how you implement this: take the current 35-day rates or forecasts implicit on forward interest rates (if available). Also, since the regression (if you run it) has a very high R^2, the bias is tiny and the rule of thumb does quite well.

6.4.5 Case 4: The Cross-and-Delta-Hedge

Now combine the problems: we use an EUR contract expiring on March 20 to hedge SEK that come forth on February 15. In principle we have to regress possible SEK spot rates on 35-day EUR futures.

The rule of thumb is a combination of the two preceding ones: set the hedge ratio equal to the current cross rate times the forecast ratio $(1 + r^{(e)})/(1 + r)$. Again, the rule of thumb does quite well when the currencies i and j are closely related and the R^2, therefore, are high.

6.4.6 Adjusting for the Sizes of the Spot Exposure and the Futures Contract

Thus far, we have assumed that the exposure was one unit of currency j, and that the size of one futures contract is one unit of foreign currency i. If the exposure is a larger number, say n_{S_j}, then the number of contracts one needs to sell obviously goes up proportionally, while if the size of the futures contract is n_{f_i} rather than unity, the number of futures contracts goes down proportionally. Thus, the generalized result is as follows: the number of

---

[8] This would also solve synchronization problems in data: spot and interest rates are observed at the same time, while the futures prices may be from a different database and observed at a different time of the day.

contracts to be sold in order to hedge n_{S_j} units of currency j using a futures contract with size n_{f_i} units of currency i is given by

$$\text{Hedge ratio} = \frac{n_{S_j}}{n_{f_i}} \beta, \tag{6.12}$$

where β can be regression-based or a rule-of-thumb number.

Example 6.11. Suppose that you consider hedging an SEK 2.17m inflow using EUR futures with a contract size of EUR 125,000. A regression based on 52 points of weekly data produces the following output:

$$\Delta S_{[USD/SEK]} = 0.003 + 0.105 \Delta f_{[USD/EUR]} \tag{6.13}$$

with an R^2 of 0.83 and a t-statistic of 15.62. Then:

- In light of the high t-statistic, we are sure that there actually is a correlation between the USD/SEK spot rate and the USD/SEK futures price.

- Assuming all correlation between the two currencies is purely contemporaneous, hedging reduces the total uncertainty about the position being hedged by an estimated 83%. If the horizon is more than one week and if there are lead/lag reactions between the currencies, this estimate is probably too pessimistic.

- The regression-based estimate for the number of contracts to be sold is

$$\text{Hedge ratio} = \frac{2,170,000}{125,000} \times 0.105 = 1.822, \tag{6.14}$$

or, after rounding, two contracts.

6.4.7 More About Regression-Based Hedges

When implementing a regression-based hedge you need to think about a number of items:

Estimation error. Novices think of a regression coefficient as a sophisticated number computed by clever people. Old hands dejectedly look at the error margin, conveniently calculated for you by the computer program, and then wail in even more despair when they remember that the calculated margin is almost surely too optimistic: the real world is never so clean as our computers assume.

Errors in the regressor. If you use futures data, there is a problem of bid–ask noise (you would probably like to have the midpoint rate, but the last traded price is either a bid or an ask—you do not know which), changing maturities, jumps in the basis when the data from an expiring short contract are followed by prices from a three-month one, and synchronization problems between spot and forward prices. So if you use futures transaction data, there is an errors-in-variables problem that biases the β estimate toward zero.

Many of these problems can be solved by using forward prices computed from midpoint spot and money-market rates for the desired maturity $T_2 - T_1$.

Lead/lag reactions and the intervalling effect. The SEK tends to stay close to the EUR, from a USD perspective. But this means that if the EUR appreciates, for example, and the SEK does not entirely follow during the same period, then there typically is some catching-up going on in the next period. This means that the correlation between changes in the euro and the krona is not purely contemporaneous.

This gives rise to the *intervalling effect*. The beta computed from, say, five-minute changes is quite low, but the estimates tend to increase if one goes to hourly, daily, weekly, and monthly intervals. This is because the longer the interval, the more of the lagged reaction is captured within the interval.

Example 6.12. Suppose that "in the long run" every percentage change in the EUR means an equal change in the SEK's value, but only three quarters of that takes place the same day, with the rest taking place the next day, on average. Then your estimated y from daily data would be more like 0.75 than 1.00 as your computer overlooks the noncontemporaneous linkages. But if you work with weekly data (five trading days), then for four of the days the lagged effect is included in the same week and picked up by the covariance; only 0.25 of the last-day effect is missed, out of five days' effects, causing a bias of just $0.25/5 = 0.05$. Obviously, with monthly data the problem is even smaller.

The intervalling effect means that, ideally, the interval in your regression should be equal to your hedging horizon, otherwise the beta tends to be way too low. This can be implemented in three ways. First, you could take *nonoverlapping holding periods*. The problem is that this often leaves you with too few useful observations. For instance, if your horizon $T_2 - T_1$ equals three months and you think that data older than five years are no longer relevant, you have just a pitiful twenty quarterly observations. Second, you could use *overlapping observation periods*. For example, you work with 13-week periods, the first covering weeks 1–13, the next weeks 2–14, etc. This leaves you more useful information; but remember that the usual R^2 and t-statistics are no longer reliable because of the overlap created between the observations. Third, you could use a clever *nonstandard regression* technique that tries to capture the relevant lead/lag effects. Examples are the instrumental-variables estimators by Scholes and Williams (1977) or Sercu et al. (2008), or the multivariate-based beta by Dimson (1979), or an error-correction model like that in Kroner and Sultan (1993).

6.4.8 Hedging with Futures Using Contracts on More than One Currency

Occasionally one uses more than one futures contract to hedge. For instance, a U.S. hedger exposed to NOK may want to use EUR and GBP contracts to get as close as possible to the missing NOK contract. In principle, the solution is to regress NOK spot prices on EUR *and* GBP futures prices, and use the multiple regression coefficients as hedge ratios. Rules of thumb do not exist here. If one uses actual regression of past time-series data, one would of course resort to first changes (ΔS, etc.) or percentage changes.

This finishes our discussion of how to adjust the size of the hedge position for maturity and currency mismatches. In the appendix we digress on interest-rate futures—not strictly an international-finance contract, but one that is close to the FRAs discussed in an appendix to chapter 4, which, you will remember, are closely related to currency forwards and forward-forward swaps. We conclude with a discussion of how forwards and futures can coexist. Clearly, each must have its own important strengths, otherwise one of them would have driven out the other.

6.5   The CFO's Conclusion: Pros and Cons of Futures Contracts Relative to Forward Contracts

Now that we understand the differences between futures and forwards, let us compare the advantages and disadvantages of using futures rather than forwards. The advantages of using futures include:

- Because of the institutional arrangements in futures markets, the default risk of futures contracts is low. As a consequence, relatively unknown players without an established reputation or without the ability to put up substantial margin can trade in futures markets. This is especially relevant for speculators who are not interested in actual delivery at maturity.

- Because of standardization, futures markets have low transaction costs; commissions in futures markets tend to be lower than in forward markets, especially for small lot sizes. Remember that to get wholesale conditions in the forward market, one needs to deal in millions of USD, while in the futures section 100,000 or thereabouts suffices.

- Given the liquidity of the secondary market for futures, futures positions can be closed out early with greater ease than forward contracts.

Clearly, there are also drawbacks to futures contracts, otherwise, forward markets would have disappeared entirely:

- One drawback is the standardization of the futures contract. A credit-worthy hedger has to choose between an imperfect but cheap hedge in the futures markets and a more expensive but exact hedge in the forward market. The standardization of the futures contracts means that one will rarely be able to find a contract of exactly the right size or the exact same maturity as that of the underlying position to be hedged.

- Futures contracts exist only for a few high-turnover exchange rates. This is because futures markets cannot survive without large trading volumes. Thus, for most exchange rates, a hedger has to choose between forward contracts or money-market hedges, or a cross-hedge in the futures markets. A cross-hedge is less effective because the relationship between the currency one is exposed to and the currency used as a hedge instrument is obscured by cross-rate risk.

- Also, marking to market may create ruin risk for a hedger. A firm that expects to receive EUR 100m nine months from now faces no inflows or outflows when it hedges in the forward market. In contrast, the daily marking to market of a futures contract can create severe short-term cash flow problems. It is not obvious that interim cash outflows can always be easily financed.

- Assuming that financing of the interim cash flows is easy, marking to market still creates interest-rate risk. The daily cash flows must be financed or deposited in the money markets at interest rates that are not known when the hedge is set up. This risk is not present in forward hedging. The correlation between futures prices and interest rates is typically rather low, implying that the interest-rate risk is small *on average*; but in an individual investment the *ex post* effect can be larger.

- Lastly, futures markets are available only for short maturities. Maturities rarely exceed eleven months, and the markets are often thin for maturities exceeding six months. In contrast, forward contracts are readily available for maturities of up to one year, and today the quotes for forward contracts extend up to ten years and more.

We see that the competing instruments—forwards and futures—appear to cater to two different clienteles. As a general rule, forward markets are used primarily by corporate hedgers, while futures markets tend to be preferred by speculators. But remember, this is a general rule, not an exact law.

6.6 Appendix: Eurocurrency Futures Contracts

Eurocurrency futures contracts can be used to hedge or to speculate on interest-rate risk, in contrast to currency futures, which allow one to hedge (or speculate on) exchange risk. That is, eurocurrency futures are the futures-style counterparts of FF contracts and FRAs, in the same way as futures contracts on currencies relate to currency forward contracts.

The first traded eurocurrency futures contract was the eurodollar contract traded at the International Money Market on the Chicago Mercantile Exchange (CME), now working on a merger with its archrival commodity exchange, the Chicago Board of Trade (CBOT). Eurodollar futures were also quickly introduced on the London International Financial Futures Exchange (LIFFE), now

Table 6.5. Some interest-futures markets.

	Underlying	Exchange	Contract size*	Longest**
AUD	90-day accepted bills	SFX	500,000	3y
BEF	3-month Bibor	BELFOX	25,000,000	9m
CAD	Canadian B/A	ME	1,000,000	2y
DEM	3-month Libor	LIFFE, MATIF, DTB	1,000,000	9m
EIP	3-month Dibor	IFOX	100,000	9m
BRC	Domestic CD	BM&F	10,000	11m
GBP	3-month euro–sterling	LIFFE	500,000	9m
JPY	3-month Libor	TIFFE, SIMEX	1,000,000	9m
FRF	3-month Pibor	MATIF	5,000,000	9m
NZD	90-day accepted bills	NZFE	500,000	2y
USD	3-month Libor	CME, SIMEX, LIFFE, TIFFE	1,000,000	2y
USD	1-month Libor	CME, CBOT	3,000,000	2y
USD	30-day Federal funds	CBOT	5,000,000	2y

*At first exchange listed. Contract size at other exchanges may differ. **Life of longest contract, at first exchange listed; m = month, y = year. *Key:* SFX: Sidney Futures Exchange; BELFOX: Belgian Futures and Options Exchange; ME: Montreal Exchange; LIFFE: London International Financial Futures Exchange; MATIF: Marché à Terme International de France; DTB: Deutsche TerminBörse; IFOX: Irish Futures and Options Exchange; BM&F: Bolsa y Mercantil y de Futuros (Saõ Paulo); TIFFE: Tokyo International Financial Futures Exchange; SIMEX: Singapore Monetary Exchange; NZFE: New Zealand Futures Exchange; CME: Chicago Mercantile Exchange (includes IMM); CBOT: Chicago Board of Trade.

part of Euronext, and the Singapore Monetary Exchange (SIMEX). Currently, most financial centers of countries with a well-developed capital market have a contract written on the local interbank interest rate—for instance, the EUR contract that used to be traded on the *Marché à Terme International de France* (MATIF) in Paris, now part of Euronext's LIFFE CONNECT. As can be seen from table 6.5, many exchanges also trade a few foreign contracts—for instance, JPY in SIMEX. (The list is just a sample; no completeness is intended.)

Many of the European futures contracts are in effect collateralized forward contracts, where the investor puts up more collateral (securities or interest-bearing deposits) if the price evolution is unfavorable, rather than making a true payment. As was explained in section 6.1, a collateralized forward contract is not subject to interest-rate risk.

Let us now see how a eurocurrency futures contract works. A useful first analogy is to think of such a contract as similar to a futures contract on a CD, where the expiration day, T_1, of the futures contract precedes the maturity date, T_2, of the CD by, typically, three months. (The three-month money-market rate is widely viewed as the representative short-term rate.) Thus, such a futures contract serves to lock in a three-month interest rate at time T_1.

Example 6.13. Suppose that in January you agree to buy, in mid March, a CD that expires in mid June. The maturity value of the CD is 100, and the price you agree to pay is 99. This means that the return you will realize on the CD during the last three months of its life is $(100 - 99)/99 = 1.0101\%$, or 4.0404% simple interest on a yearly basis. Thus, this forward contract is analogous to signing an FRA at 4.0404% p.a. for three months, starting mid March.

In the example, we described the futures contract as if it were a forward contract. If there is marking to market, the interest-rate risk stemming from the uncertain marked-to-market cash flows will affect the pricing. Another complication with futures is that the quoted price is often different from the effective price, as we discuss below. Still, it helps to have the above example in mind to keep from getting lost in the institutional details. We first derive how forward prices on T-bills or CDs are set, and how they are linked to the forward interest rate. We then discuss the practical problems with such a system of quotation and explain how this has led to a modern futures quote, an animal that differs substantially from the forward price on a T-bill or CD.

6.6.1 The Forward Price on a CD

The forward price on a CD is just the face value (1, most often quoted as 100%) discounted at the forward rate of return, $r^{\mathrm{f}}_{t,T_1,T_2}$. To understand this property, consider a forward contract that expires at T_1 and whose underlying asset is a euro-CD maturing at T_2 ($> T_1$). Since the euro-CD has no coupons, its current spot price is

$$V_t = \frac{1}{1 + r_{t,T_2}}, \tag{6.15}$$

where, as always in this textbook, r_{t,T_2} denotes an effective return, not a p.a. interest rate. The CD's forward price at t for delivery at T_1 is this spot value grossed up with the effective interest between t and T_1 (line 1, below), and the combination of the two spot rates then gives us the link with the forward rate:

$$
\begin{aligned}
V^{\mathrm{f}}_{t,T_1,T_2} &= V_t \,(1 + r_{t,T_1}) \\
&= \frac{1 + r_{t,T_1}}{1 + r_{t,T_2}} \qquad \text{(see (6.15))} \\
&= \frac{1}{1 + r^{\mathrm{f}}_{t,T_1,T_2}} \qquad \text{(see (4.48)).} \tag{6.16}
\end{aligned}
$$

Example 6.14. Consider a six-month forward on a nine-month bill with face value USD 1. Let the p.a. interest rates be 4% for nine months and 3.9% for six months. Then $r_{t,T_2} = (9/12) \times 4\% = 0.03$, so that the spot price (quoted as a percentage) is equal to

$$V_t = \frac{100\%}{1.03} = 97.087\,377\%. \tag{6.17}$$

Also, $r_{t,T_1} = (6/12) \times 3.9\% = 0.0195$; thus, the forward price today is

$$V^{\mathrm{f}}_{t,T_1,T_2} = 97.087\,377 \times 1.0195 = 98.980\,583\%. \tag{6.18}$$

Alternatively, we can compute the six-month forward price on a nine-month T-bill via the forward rate of return:

$$1 + r^f_{t,T_1,T_2} = \frac{1.03}{1.0195} = 1.010\,299\,166$$

$$\Rightarrow \quad V^f_{t,T_1,T_2} = \frac{1}{1.010\,299\,166} = 98.980\,583\%.$$

For some time, interest rate futures markets in Sydney were based on this system of forward prices for CDs. Although the system is perfectly logical, traders and investors are not fond of quoting prices in this way. One reason is that traders and dealers are more familiar with p.a. interest rates than with forward prices for deposits or CDs. The process of translating the forward interest rate into a forward price is somewhat laborious: equation (6.16) tells us that the unfortunate trader has to divide the p.a. forward rate by four, add unity, and take the inverse to compute the normal forward price as the basis for trading. A second problem is that real-world interest rates are typically rounded to one basis point (0.01%). Thus, unless forward prices are also rounded, marking to market will result in odd amounts. These very practical considerations lead to a more user-friendly manner of quoting prices for futures on CDs.

6.6.2 Modern Eurodollar Futures Quotes

To make life easier for the traders, rather than quoting a true futures price, most exchanges quote three-month eurodollar futures contract prices as follows:

$$\text{Quote} = 100 - [\text{per annum forward interest rate}], \qquad (6.19)$$

and base the marking to market on *one quarter* of the change in the quote.

Before we explain the marked-to-market rule, let us first consider the quotation rule given in equation (6.19). This quote decreases when the forward interest rate increases—just as a true forward price on a T-bill—and the long side of the contract is still defined as the one that wins when the quote goes up, the normal convention in futures or forward markets. However, one major advantage of this price-quoting convention is that a trader or investor can make instant decisions on the basis of available forward interest quotes, without any additional computations.

Example 6.15. Let the p.a. forward interest rate be 4.1% p.a. for a three-month deposit starting at T_1. The true forward price would have been computed as

$$V^f_{t,T_1,T_2} = \frac{1}{1 + (1/4) \times 0.041} = 98.985\,300 \approx 98.99. \qquad (6.20)$$

In contrast, the eurodollar forward quote can be found immediately as $100\% - 4.1\% = 95.9\%$.

06/06/06		Open	Sett	Change	High	Low	Est.Vol	Open int
Euribor 3m*	Jun	96.97	96.96	-0.01	96.98	96.96	98.491	553.392
Euribor 3m*	Sep	96.69	96.69	-1.01	96.70	96.68	107.380	582.722
Euribor 3m*	Dec	96.49	96.48	-0.02	96.50	96.47	110.900	608.862
Euribor 3m*	Mar	96.39	96.37	-0.03	96.40	96.36	95.601	487.298
Euribor 3m*	Jun	96.30	96.29	-0.03	96.32	96.28	86.201	414.737
. .								. . .
Euroswiss 3m*	Jun	98.48	98.47	-0.01	98.48	98.46	8.045	75.781
. . .								. . .
Sterling 3m*	Jun	95.27	95.26	-0.02	95.27	95.26	15,291	416,929
. . .								. . .
Eurodollar 3m#	Jun	94.68	94.67	-0.01	94.69	94.66	117,026	1297,150
. . .								. . .
FedFnds 30d+	Jun	94.970	94.965	-0.005	94.970	94.965	1,078	107,907
. . .								. . .
Euroyen 3m±	Jun	99.655	99.650	-0.020	99.665	99.650	15.364	586.998
. . .								. . .

Contracts are based on volumes traded in 2004   Sources: * LIFFE # CME + CBOT ± TIFFE

Figure 6.2. Interest-rate futures as reported by the *Financial Times*.

The second advantage of the "100 minus interest" way of quoting is that such quotes are, automatically, multiples of one basis point because interest rates are multiples of one basis point. With a standard contract size of USD 1m, one tick (equal to 1/100th of a percent) in the interest rate leads to a tick of 1m × 0.0001 = USD 100 dollars in the underlying quote (no odd amounts here). Note that, since marking to market is based on one quarter of the change in the quote, a one-tick change in the interest rate leads to a USD 25 change in the required margin.

To understand why marking to market is based on one quarter of the change of the quote, go back to the correct forward price, equation (6.16). The idea is to undo the fact that the change in the quote (equation (6.19)) is about four times the change in the correct forward price (equation (6.16)). To understand this, note that $T_2 - T_1$ corresponds to three months ($\frac{1}{4}$ year). Thus, as a first-order approximation,

$$\frac{1}{1 + r^f} \approx 1 - r^f = 1 - \tfrac{1}{4} \times (4r^f) = 1 - \tfrac{1}{4} \times \text{[p.a. forward interest rate]}. \quad (6.21)$$

Thus, the change in the true forward price is about one quarter of the change in the futures quote. To bring marking to market FF more or less in line with normal (price-based) contracts, the changes in the quote (or in the p.a. forward interest rate) must be divided by four. If this were not done, a USD 1m contract would, in fact, hedge a deposit of roughly USD 4m, which would have been very confusing for novice buyers and sellers.

Example 6.16. Suppose that you hold a five-month, USD 1m CD and you want to hedge this position against interest-rate risk two months from now. If, two months from now, the three-month interest rate drops from 4% to 3.9%, the market value of your deposit increases from $1m/(1 + \tfrac{1}{4} \times 0.04) = 990,099.01$ to $1m/(1 + \tfrac{1}{4} \times 0.039) = 990,344.14$, a gain of USD 245.13. The price quoted for a futures contract would change by 0.1% or, on a USD 1m contract, by USD 1,000.

Marking to market, however, is one quarter of that, or USD 250. So the marked-to-market cash flows on the eurodollar futures contract would reasonably match the 245.13 dollar change in the deposit's market value.

The pros and cons of interest futures, as compared with FRAs, are the same as for any other futures contract. The main advantage is an active secondary market, where the contract can be liquidated at any moment and there are lowish entry barriers because of the efficient way of handling security: ask for cash only if and when it is needed. But that cannot be the end of the story. FRAs also have some advantages over T-bill futures and bond futures, and these advantages are similar to those of forward exchange contracts over currency futures contracts, as discussed in chapter 6.

- FFs or FRAs are pure forward contracts, which means that there is no marking to market. It follows that, by using FFs or FRAs, one avoids the additional interest-rate risk that arises from marking to market.

- In the absence of marking to market, there is no ruin risk. The firm need not worry about potential cash outflows that may lead to liquidity problems and insolvency.

- In the absence of marking to market, there is an exact arbitrage relationship between spot rates and forward rates; hence these contracts are easy to value. In contrast, the pricing of a futures-style contract is more difficult because of interest-rate risk—covariance between market values and the interest-rate evolution, which in the case of interest derivatives is, of course, stronger than for futures on currency or stocks of commodities.

- FRAs are tailor-made, over-the-counter instruments and are, therefore, more flexible than (standardized) futures contracts. Hedgers with small exposures may not like a contract of USD 1m, and if three-month futures are used to hedge against a change in the four-month or nine-month interest rate, the hedge is, at best, imperfect.

- The menu of underlyings is quite limited: three-month rates, and (in the bond market, which we have not discussed) medium-term bonds.

For these reasons, FFs and FRAs are better suited for arbitrage or hedging than are futures.

6.7 Technical Notes

Technical note 6.1 (why gammas are below unity). Technically, the rule of thumb of setting y equal to unity is supposedly based on the assumption that no change in the relative values is expected. So if the percentage changes in the SEK and EUR spot rates are denoted by y and x, respectively, then the trader's feeling is that $E_t(\tilde{y}) = E_t(\tilde{x})$. But this is an unconditional statement.

A regression is a conditional statement: what do we expect about $\tilde{y}$ for a given value of x. Suppose, for instance, that both $\tilde{x}$ and $\tilde{y}$ have an unconditional mean of zero. Then in the regression $y = a + bx + e$ the slope b can indeed be unity—but it can also be 0.5, or zero, or -1 for that matter. Indeed, if $y = a + bx + e$ holds, then $\mathrm{E}(\tilde{y}) = a + b\mathrm{E}(\tilde{x}) + 0$ follows, and since the expectations are zero, the only constraint is that a must be zero; the slope b can still be anything.

Thus, conditional and unconditional expectations are different animals. In our case,

$$\mathrm{E}_t(\tilde{s}_T^{\mathrm{SEK}}) = \mathrm{E}_t(\tilde{s}_T^{\mathrm{EUR}}) \text{ does not imply } \mathrm{E}_t(\tilde{s}_T^{\mathrm{SEK}} \mid s_T^{\mathrm{EUR}}) = s_T^{\mathrm{EUR}}, \qquad (6.22)$$

even though the reverse statement does hold:

$$\mathrm{E}_t(\tilde{s}_T^{\mathrm{SEK}} \mid s_T^{\mathrm{EUR}}) = s_T^{\mathrm{EUR}} \text{ does imply } \mathrm{E}_t(\tilde{s}_T^{\mathrm{SEK}}) = \mathrm{E}_t(\tilde{s}_T^{\mathrm{EUR}}). \qquad (6.23)$$

The above uses statistics to make the point, which may fail to impress many readers; so let us also think of the economics. Exchange rates in our currency threesome can move because there is news about the United States, or about Euroland, or about Sweden. A lot of world news has implications for all three, but some news is purely local—for instance, housing starts in Sweden may be below what pundits had expected while things are fine elsewhere.

Suppose the USD/EUR rate increases. This could be because of relatively bad news about the United States or relatively good news about Euroland. If the source is pure dollar news, then the USD/SEK rate would also go up by a similar percentage, as there is no reason for the EUR/SEK rate to change: it's the dollar that falls, not the euro that rises. But if, in contrast, the source is pure euro news, then the appreciation of the USD/EUR rate is because the euro rises not because the dollar falls, meaning that the USD/SEK rate would not budge. To sum up, in our stylized story,

(i) if there's dollar news, then

$$\mathrm{E}_t(\tilde{s}_T^{\mathrm{SEK}} \mid s_T^{\mathrm{EUR}}) = s_T^{\mathrm{EUR}}$$

(the crown rises as much as the euro),

(ii) if there's euro news, then

$$\mathrm{E}_t(\tilde{s}_T^{\mathrm{SEK}} \mid s_T^{\mathrm{EUR}}) = 0$$

(the crown does not follow the euro),

and since we don't know whether the news will be about the United States or about Euroland, gamma must be between unity (case (i)) and zero (case (ii)). Where exactly gamma is depends on the relative probabilities of either type of news, and also about how earth-shattering it is. For instance, if both types of news are equally likely but European news merely raises eyebrows while U.S. news causes heart attacks, the first scenario would dominate the distribution and gamma would be closer to unity than to zero.

TEST YOUR UNDERSTANDING

Quiz Questions

1. For each pair shown below, which of the two describes a forward contract? Which describes a futures contract?

    (a) Standardized/made to order.
    (b) Interest-rate risk/no interest-rate risk.
    (c) Ruin risk/no ruin risk.
    (d) Short maturities/even shorter maturities.
    (e) No secondary market/liquid secondary market.
    (f) For hedgers/speculators.
    (g) More expensive/less expensive.
    (h) No credit risk/credit risk.
    (i) Organized market/no organized market,

2. Match the vocabulary below with the following statements.

(1)	Organized market	(11)	Maintenance margin
(2)	Standardized contract	(12)	Margin call
(3)	Standardized expiration	(13)	Variation margin
(4)	Clearing corporation	(14)	Open interest
(5)	Daily recontracting	(15)	Interest-rate risk
(6)	Marking to market	(16)	Cross-hedge
(7)	Convergence	(17)	Delta-hedge
(8)	Settlement price	(18)	Delta-cross-hedge
(9)	Default risk of a future	(19)	Ruin risk
(10)	Initial margin		

    (a) Daily payment of the change in a forward or futures price.
    (b) The collateral deposited as a guarantee when a futures position is opened.
    (c) Daily payment of the discounted change in a forward price.
    (d) The minimum level of collateral on deposit as a guarantee for a futures position.
    (e) A hedge on a currency for which no futures contracts exist and for an expiration other than what the buyer or seller of the contract desires.
    (f) An additional deposit of collateral for a margin account that has fallen below its maintenance level.
    (g) A contract for a standardized number of units of a good to be delivered at a standardized date.
    (h) A hedge on foreign currency accounts receivable or accounts payable that is due on a day other than the third Wednesday of March, June, September, or December.
    (i) The number of outstanding contracts for a given type of futures.

Table 6.6. Excerpt of futures prices from the *Wall Street Journal*.

	Open	High	Low	Settle	Change	Lifetime High	Lifetime Low	Open interest
JAPAN YEN (CME): 12.5 million yen; $ per yen (.00)								
June	0.9432	0.9460	0.9427	0.9459	+0.0007	0.9945	0.8540	48.189
Sept	0.9482	0.9513	0.9482	0.9510	+0.0007	0.9900	0.8942	1,782
Dec	0.9550	0.9610	0.9547	0.9566	+0.0008	0.9810	0.9525	384

Est. vol. 13,640; vol. Fri 15,017; open int. 50,355, +414

	Open	High	Low	Settle	Change	Lifetime High	Lifetime Low	Open interest
UNITED STATES DOLLAR (CME): 125,000 dollars; $ per dollar								
June	0.5855	0.5893	0.5847	0.5888	+0.0018	0.6162	0.5607	87,662
Sept	0.5840	0.5874	0.5830	0.5871	+0.0018	0.6130	0.5600	2,645
Dec	0.5830	0.5860	0.5830	0.5864	+0.0018	0.5910	0.5590	114

Est. vol. 40,488; vol. Fri 43,717; open int. 90,412, −1,231

	Open	High	Low	Settle	Change	Lifetime High	Lifetime Low	Open interest
UNITED KINGDOM POUND (CME): 100,000 pounds; $ per pound								
June	0.7296	0.7329	0.7296	0.7313	+0.0021	0.7805	0.7290	43,132
Sept	0.7293	0.7310	0.7290	0.7297	+0.0018	0.7740	0.7276	962
Dec	0.7294	0.7295	0.7285	0.7282	+0.0016	0.7670	0.7270	640

Est. vol. 5,389; vol. Fri 4,248; open int. 44,905, −1,331

(j) The one-day futures price change.

(k) A proxy for the closing price used to ensure that a futures price is not manipulated.

(l) Generally, the last Wednesday of March, June, September, or December.

(m) Organization that acts as a "go-between" for buyers and sellers of futures contracts.

(n) The risk that the interim cash flows must be invested or borrowed at an unfavorable interest rate.

(o) A hedge on a currency for which no futures contract exists.

(p) The risk that the price of a futures contract drops (rises) so far that the purchaser (seller) has severe short-term cash-flow problems due to marking to market.

(q) The property whereby the futures equals the spot price at expiration.

(r) Centralized market (either an exchange or a computer system) where supply and demand are matched.

Table 6.6 is an excerpt of futures prices from the *Wall Street Journal* of Tuesday, February 22, 2007. Use this table to answer questions 3–6.

3. What is the CME contract size for:

    (a) Japanese yen?

    (b) U.S. dollar?

    (c) U.K. pound?

4. What is the open interest for the September contract for:

    (a) Japanese yen?
    (b) U.S. dollar?
    (c) U.K. pound?

5. What are the daily high, low, and settlement prices for the December contract for:

    (a) Japanese yen?
    (b) U.S. dollar?
    (c) U.K. pound?

6. What is the day's cash flow from marking to market for the holder of a:

    (a) JPY June contract?
    (b) USD June contract?
    (c) GBP June contract?

7. What statements are correct? If you disagree with one or more of them, please put them right.

    (a) Margin is a payment to the bank to compensate it for taking on credit risk.
    (b) If you hold a forward purchase contract for JPY that you wish to reverse, and the JPY has increased in value, you owe the bank the discounted difference between the current forward rate and the historic forward rate, that is, the market value.
    (c) If the balance in your margin account is not sufficient to cover the losses on your forward contract and you fail to post additional margin, the bank must speculate in order to recover the losses.
    (d) Under the system of daily recontracting, the value of an outstanding forward contract is recomputed every day. If the forward rate for GBP/NZD drops each day for ten days until the forward contract expires, the purchaser of NZD forward must pay the forward seller of NZD the market value of the contract for each of those ten days. If the purchaser cannot pay, the bank seizes his or her margin.

Applications

1. Innovative Bicycle Makers must hedge an accounts payable of MYR 100,000 due in 90 days for bike tires purchased in Malaysia. Suppose that the GBP/MYR forward rates and the GBP effective returns are as follows:

Time	$t = 0$	$t = 1$	$t = 2$	$t = 3$
Forward rate	4	4.2	3.9	4
Effective return	12%	8.5%	4%	0%

    (a) What are IBM's cash flows given a variable-collateral margin account?
    (b) What are IBM's cash flows given periodic contracting?

2. On the morning of Monday, August 21, you purchased a futures contract for 1 unit of CHF at a rate of USD/CHF 0.7. The subsequent settlement prices are shown in the table below.

    (a) What are the daily cash flows from marking to market?
    (b) What is the cumulative total cash flow from marking to market (ignoring discounting)?
    (c) Is the total cash flow greater than, less than, or equal to the difference between the price of your original futures contract and the price of the same futures contract on August 30?

August	21	22	23	24	25	28	29	30
Futures rate	0.71	0.70	0.72	0.71	0.69	0.68	0.66	0.63

3. On November 15, you sold ten futures contracts for 100,000 CAD each at a rate of USD/CAD 0.75. The subsequent settlement prices are shown in the table below.

    (a) What are the daily cash flows from marking to market?
    (b) What is the total cash flow from marking to market (ignoring discounting)?
    (c) If you deposit USD 75,000 into your margin account, and your broker requires USD 50,000 as maintenance margin, when will you receive a margin call and how much will you have to deposit?

November	16	17	18	19	20	23	24	25
Futures rate	0.74	0.73	0.74	0.76	0.77	0.78	0.79	0.81

4. On the morning of December 6, you purchased a futures contract for 1 EUR at a rate of INR/EUR 55. The following table gives the subsequent settlement prices and the p.a. bid–ask interest rates on an INR investment made until December 10.

    (a) What are the daily cash flows from marking to market?
    (b) What is the total cash flow from marking to market (ignoring discounting)?
    (c) If you must finance your losses and invest your gains from marking to market, what is the value of the total cash flows on December 10?

December	6	7	8	9	10
Futures price	56	57	54	52	55
Bid-ask interest rates, INR, % p.a.	12.00–12.25	11.50–11.75	13.00–13.25	13.50–13.75	NA

5. You want to hedge the EUR value of a CAD 1m inflow using futures contracts. On Germany's exchange there is a futures contract for USD 100,000 at EUR/USD 1.5.

(a) Your assistant runs a bunch of regressions:

   (i) $\Delta S_{[EUR/CAD]} = \alpha_1 + \beta_1 \Delta f_{[USD/EUR]}$.
   (ii) $\Delta S_{[EUR/CAD]} = \alpha_2 + \beta_2 \Delta f_{[EUR/USD]}$.
   (iii) $\Delta S_{[CAD/EUR]} = \alpha_3 + \beta_3 \Delta f_{[EUR/USD]}$.
   (iv) $\Delta S_{[CAD/EUR]} = \alpha_4 + \beta_4 \Delta f_{[USD/EUR]}$.

Which regression is relevant to you?

(b) If the relevant β were 0.83, how many contracts do you buy? Sell?

6. In the previous question, we assumed that there was a USD futures contract in Germany with a fixed number of USD (100,000 units) and a variable EUR/USD price. What if there is no German futures exchange? Then you would have to go to a U.S. exchange, where the number of EUR per contract is fixed (at, say, 125,000), rather than the number of USD. How many USD/EUR contracts will you buy?

7. A German exporter wants to hedge an outflow of NZD 1m. She decides to hedge the risk with an EUR/USD contract and an EUR/AUD contract. The regression output is, with t-statistics in parentheses and $R^2 = 0.59$, as follows:

$$\Delta S_{[EUR/NZD]} = a + \underbrace{0.15 \Delta f_{[EUR/USD]}}_{(1.57)} + \underbrace{0.7 \Delta f_{[EUR/AUD]}}_{(17.2)}.$$

(a) How will you hedge if you use both contracts, and if a USD contract is for USD 50,000 and the AUD contract for AUD 75,000?

(b) Should you use the USD contract, in view of the low t-statistic? Or should we only use the AUD contract?

7

Markets for Currency Swaps

As already discussed in chapter 5, the choice of the currency of borrowing may be difficult; for instance, the currency that offers the lowest PV-ed risk spread may not be the most attractive one from the risk-management point of view. We also know how a firm can nevertheless have its cake and eat it: one can borrow in the low-cost denomination and then swap that loan into the desired currency. The case we looked at was the simplest possible loan, with just one single future payment, standing for interest and principal. In that case we (i) convert the up-front inflow via a spot transaction from the currency of borrowing into the desired one, and (ii) convert the future outflow in the forward market, thus again replacing the currency of the loan's original outflow by the desired one.

But most loans with a life exceeding one year are, of course, multi-payment: interest is typically due at least once a year, and often even twice or four times; and also the principal can be amortized gradually rather than in one shot at the end. To swap such a loan, one would need as many forward hedges as there are future payments. The modern currency swap provides an answer to this: in one contract the two parties agree upon not just the spot conversion in one direction, but also the reverse conversions for all future service payments. The contract is typically set up such that the time pattern of the final payments corresponds to the time pattern of the original. For example, if the original loan is a bullet loan with a fixed interest rate, then the swapped package can also be of the bullet type and with a constant coupon. That last feature would not be achievable with a set of forward contracts: if the original loan has a constant coupon, then the converted coupons will vary depending on their due dates because the forward rates that we use for the conversion depend on the due date. With modern swaps we can even transform a currency-A *floating-rate* loan into a fixed-rate loan in currency B, something which cannot be done with simple forward contracts since the future service payments are not even known yet. So modern swaps are a general and flexible device to change one loan, chosen perhaps because of its low cost, into another loan that for some reason is viewed as more desirable. The second loan could be different from the original one in terms of currency or interest payments (fixed versus floating), or both. And these are just the plain-vanilla cases; many ad hoc structures can be arranged at the customer's request.

This chapter is structured as follows. In the first section, we consider a landmark deal between two highly respected companies, the currency swap between IBM and the World Bank negotiated in 1981 (commonly viewed as the mother of modern swaps) and we indicate the subsequent evolution of the swap into a standard, off-the-shelf product. We then show, in section 7.2, how the modern currency swap works, and why such deals exist. An even more popular variant of currency swap is the interest-rate swap or fixed-for-floating-rate swap, which we discuss in section 7.3. Section 7.4 discusses a combination of the currency swap and the interest swap, called the fixed-for-floating currency swap or circus swap. Section 7.5 concludes this chapter.

7.1 How the Modern Swap Came About

From chapter 5 we know how spot-forward swaps can be used to transform one zero-coupon loan into a zero-coupon loan in a different currency. Swaps can also be used in themselves, as a package of back-to-back loans. The problem is that many of the applications are somewhat shady: shirking taxes, avoiding currency controls, not to mention laundering money. For this reason, back-to-back and parallel loans or spot-forward swaps were for a long time viewed as not entirely respectable. In 1981 all that changed. Two quite-above-board companies, IBM and the World Bank (WB), set up a contract which was quite clever and had a respectable economic purpose: avoiding transaction costs. There was a tax advantage too, but this was almost by accident.

The IBM–WB swap was a bilateral deal, very much tailor-made. But rapidly the swap became a standardized product offered routinely by banks. This evolution is depicted after our description of the IBM–WB deal.

7.1.1 The Grandfather Tailor-made Swap: IBM–WB

In 1981, IBM wanted to get rid of its outstanding DEM- and CHF-denominated callable debt because the USD had appreciated considerably and the DEM and CHF interest rates had also gone up. As a result of these two changes, the market value of IBM's foreign debt, expressed in terms of DEM and CHF, was below its face value, and the gap between market value and book value was even wider in terms of USD. IBM wanted to lock in this capital gain by replacing the DEM and CHF debt by new USD debt. However, in order to do this, IBM would have to incur many costs:

- IBM would have to buy DEM and CHF currency, thus incurring transaction costs in the spot market. In 1981 this was not yet the puny item it has become by now.

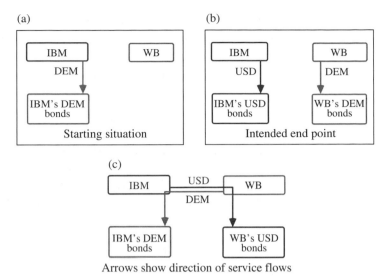

Figure 7.1. The IBM–WB swap: (a) the initial situation; (b) the originally intended final situation; (c) how the essence of the desired solution was realized, at a lower cost.

- Much more importantly, IBM's loans were indeed callable (that is, IBM could amortize them early), but at a price above par. So IBM would have to fork out more than the DEM and CHF face value rather the economic value of the straight-bond component, which was below par. Calling would be like exercising an out-of-the-money option.

  Finance theorists will happily point out that hedging the debt would be the obvious solution: borrow dollars and invest them in DEM and CHF assets that match the outstanding debt, thus neutralizing any possible re-appreciation of these currencies without any need to actually withdraw the old bonds. But CFOs will unhappily note that, in conventional accounting terms, this would double the debt.

- IBM would have to pay a capital-gains tax on the difference between the (dollar) book value and the price it paid to redeem the bonds.

- Lastly, IBM would have to issue new USD bonds to finance the redemption of its CHF and DEM debt. In those days, a bond issue costed at least a few percentages of the nominal value.

The WB, on the other hand, wanted to borrow DEM and CHF to lend to its customers. Its charter indeed said that, currency by currency, its assets should be matched by its liabilities. Clearly, issuing new CHF and DEM bonds would have entailed issuing costs.

To sum up, IBM wants to *withdraw* CHF and DEM bonds (at a rather high cost) while WB wants to *issue* CHF and DEM bonds (also at a cost) (see figure 7.1). To avoid all of these expenses, IBM and WB agreed the following:

- The WB would not borrow CHF and DEM, but would borrow USD instead. With the proceeds, it would buy spot CHF and DEM needed to make loans to its customers.

- The WB undertook to take over the servicing of IBM's outstanding DEM and CHF loans, while IBM promised to service the WB's (new) USD loan.

This way, each party achieved its objective. IBM has effectively traded (or swapped) its DEM and CHF obligations for USD obligations: its DEM–CHF debt is taken care of by WB, economically, and IBM now services USD bonds. The WB, on the other hand, has an obligation to deliver DEM and CHF, which is what WB needed. One obvious joint saving of the swap was the cost of issuing new WB bonds in DEM and CHF, and redeeming the old IBM loans in DEM and CHF. Also, the recognition of IBM's capital gain was postponed because the old bonds were not redeemed early. Another saving was that the WB could issue USD bonds at a lower risk spread than IBM.[1]

Of course, the amounts to be exchanged had to be acceptable to both parties. The present value of IBM's USD payments to the WB should, therefore, be equal to the present value of the DEM and CHF inflows received from the WB.

Example 7.1. Assume, for simplicity, that IBM has an outstanding DEM debt with a face value of DEM 100m and a book value of USD 60m (based on the historic USD/DEM rate of 0.6), maturing after five years and carrying a 5% annual coupon. Assume the current five-year DEM interest rate is 10% and the DEM now trades at USD/DEM 0.4. In DEM, IBM's existing debt would have a present value of[2]

$$\text{DEM } 100\text{m} \times [1 + (0.05 - 0.1) \times a(10\%, 5 \text{ years})] = \text{DEM } 81.05\text{m}, \qquad (7.1)$$

where $a(r, n)$ is the present value of an n-year unit annuity discounted at a rate r:

$$a(r, n) \overset{\text{def}}{=} \sum_{t=1}^{n} \frac{1}{(1+r)^t} = \frac{1 - (1+r)^{-n}}{r}. \qquad (7.2)$$

At the current spot rate of USD/DEM 0.4, WB's undertaking to service this debt is worth $81.05 \times 0.4 = \text{USD } 32.42\text{m}$.

The equal-value principle requires that IBM's undertaking have the same present value. Thus, the USD loan (issued at the then-prevailing rate for five years) must have a present value of USD 32.42m.

As we have argued, one purpose of the entire IBM–WB deal was to avoid transaction costs. A nice by-product, in terms of taxes, was that IBM locked in its capital gain on its foreign currency debt without immediately realizing the profit. Let us quantify some of these elements using the above figures. If IBM had called its DEM debt at 102% of its DEM par value, the cost of withdrawing the debt would have been $10\text{m} \times 1.02 \times \text{USD/DEM } 0.4 = \text{USD } 4.08\text{m}$, thus

---

[1] Critical economists would rightly object that this is a saving only to the extent that the difference in the risk spreads was irrational.

[2] See technical note 7.1 if the formula is new to you.

realizing a taxable capital gain of USD 6m − 4.08 = USD 1.92m. In contrast, under the swap, the DEM debt remains in IBM's books for another five years. That is, in accounting terms, the capital gain will be realized only when, five years later, IBM pays the swap principal (USD 3.242m) to the WB and receives DEM 10m to redeem its DEM debt. In short, the swap also allowed IBM to defer its capital gains taxes.

7.1.2 Subsequent Evolution of the Swap Market

We know that a forward contract is like an exchange of two initially equivalent promissory notes, one in HC and one in FC. In the IBM–WB deal we see, instead, something like an exchange of two bonds (or at least cash-flow patterns that correspond to bond servicing schedules). This differs from the forward contract in the sense that there is not just an exchange of two main amounts at the end, but also interim interest is being paid to each other at regular dates. But the principle of initial equivalence of the two "legs" of the deal is maintained.

One feature that has changed nowadays, relative to the IBM–WB example, is that almost invariably a reverse spot exchange is added. One reason is that very often the purpose of the swap is to transform a loan taken up in currency X into one expressed in currency Y; and to do that, one also needs the immediate currency-Y inflow beside the future outflows.

DIY Problem 7.1. Suppose you want to borrow GBP, but what you actually do is borrow USD and swap, the way we saw in chapter 5. So part of the deal is that you promise the swap dealer a stream of GBP; the swap dealer in return then pays you USD with which you can service your bank loan. But all this only delivers you the future-GBP-outflow part of the desired loan. To also get the immediate-GBP-inflow part, you convert the USD proceeds of the bank loan into pounds.

A second reason for adding the spot deal is that the exchange of time-t PVs simplifies the negotiation process. One has indeed to realize that swaps are typically add-ons to biggish loans; and taking up a big loan is a much rarer and slower decision than, say, a spot or forward transaction that has to do with trade transactions. Since negotiations take hours or days, and since the spot rate is moving all the time, one would have to continuously change one leg of the swap to maintain initial equivalence of the future payments. By throwing in an exchange of the spot PVs, this problem is much reduced. The idea is that one can still get zero initial value for the swap as a whole if the *net* PV of each leg separately is zero—the PV of the future payments minus the initial flow in the opposite direction.

Example 7.2. Suppose that, at the beginning of the negotiations, a U.S. company promises to send to a Dutch company a stream of USD corresponding to a bullet loan with notional value USD 50m at 4% payable annually. Suppose the normal yield rate for this type of bond is 4%, so that PV_{USD} = USD 50m. Company B promises a stream of EUR in return. On the basis of S_t = USD/EUR 1.25 and an EUR interest rate of 4.5%, the EUR payments would mirror the service payments for an EUR 40m loan at 4.5%. This way, the PVs of the EUR and USD streams are identical, resulting in a zero total value of the contract.

But if one hour later the spot rate is 1.26, the calculations would have to be revised. This revision would become unnecessary if the contract also stipulates an initial exchange of EUR 40m for USD 50m. Then, to the U.S. company, the appreciation of the EUR increases the USD PV of the incoming future euros but also increases by the same factor the USD value of the EUR amount the company needs to fork out immediately. Thus, the net value of the EUR leg remains zero as long as interest rates do not change.

Once the up-front exchange of the principals has been added, one could do with approximate equivalence of the two notional amounts. An approximate equivalence is still important because the two loans also serve as security for each other. If one side were far smaller than the other, the security provision would be unacceptably asymmetric.

A second major change, relative to the IBM–WB example, is that contracts are now standardized. The early swaps were carefully negotiated between two parties, with large teams of financial economists and lawyers in attendance, to calculate the gains and to arrive at a fair division of the gains. Inevitably, then, one huge initial problem was to find a counterparty with complementary objectives. In forward markets, we know that banks act as intermediaries. If company A buys forward, the bank agrees, and afterward solicits a sale from someone else by skewing its bids (chapter 3), or the bank closes out in the spot and money markets (synthetic sale). This is exactly how things have become in the swap markets too. A company signs a swap agreement with a bank, which may keep this contract "on its book" (i.e., open) for a while, until new contracts have brought the overall book closer to neutrality. If the risk is too large, the bank can always hedge in the bond and spot markets (synthetic swap). This hedging was easiest in the USD interest-rate swap market, where the two notional loans that constitute the swap are expressed in the same currency but have different interest forms—typically, one leg fixed-rate and the other floating-rate. Given that there is a huge market for similar fixed- and floating-rate bonds outstanding, swap dealers could easily close out in the bond market. Also, a lively secondary market for swaps has emerged.

We are now ready to have a closer look at the how swaps are set up. We begin with "fixed-for-fixed" currency swaps, that is, swaps with fixed coupons in each leg.

7.2 The Fixed-for-Fixed Currency Swaps

7.2.1 Motivations for Undertaking a Currency Swap

The reasons for using swaps are essentially those mentioned for spot-forward swaps (chapter 5). Generally, the point is to avoid unnecessary costs generated by market imperfections, primarily information costs that lead to excessive risk spreads asked by uninformed banks. The IBM–WB case was mainly a transaction-cost motivated structure. Also the advantages of off-balance-sheet reporting remain valid, at least when a swap is compared with its synthetic version (borrow in one currency and invest in another).

Also, transactions in the style of the Bundesbank–BoE example 5.22 are still being used. In 2008, for instance, the major central banks opened gigantic swap lines to each other so that, for instance, the ECB or the Bank of Japan would always be able to lend USD (borrowed from the Fed) to local players, even outside the Fed's usual business hours. By way of security, they simultaneously lent their own currencies to the central bank whose currency they were borrowing.

An extreme form of market imperfection arose in one particular instance: in the early 1980s, the French car manufacturer Renault wanted to borrow yen and use the proceeds to redeem outstanding USD debt, but found that in those days the yen bond market was quasi-closed to foreign borrowers. So Renault swapped its USD loan with Yamaichi Securities for JPY debt. This example is discussed in section 7.4, below.

7.2.2 Characteristics of the Modern Currency Swap

In many ways, the modern fixed-for-fixed currency swap is simply a long-term version of the classical spot-forward swap. A fixed-for-fixed currency swap can be defined as a transaction where two parties exchange, at the time of the contract's initiation, two principals denominated in different currencies but with (roughly) the same market value, and return these principals to each other when the contract expires. In addition, they periodically pay a normal interest to each other on the amounts borrowed. The deal is structured as a single contract, with a right of offset. The features of a fixed-for-fixed currency swap are described in more detail below.

7.2.2.1 Swap Rates

In a fixed-for-fixed currency swap, the interest payments for each currency are based on the currency's "swap (interest) rate" for the swap's maturity. These swap rates are simply yields at par for near-riskless bonds with the same maturity as the swap.[3] In practice, the swap rates are close to the long-term offshore rates on high-quality sovereign loans, that is, loans by governments. For the following reasons, it is appropriate to use near-risk-free rates to compute the interest on the amounts swapped even if the counterparty in the contract is not an AAA company:

---

[3] The N-year yield at par is the coupon that has to be assigned to an N-year bond in order to give it a market value equal to the par value (the principal). If the parties want a cash-flow pattern that differs from the single-amortization ("bullet") loan, the swap dealer is usually willing to design a contract that deviates from the standard form, but at a different swap rate. See the subsection on nonbullet loans, later in this section.

06/06/06	Euro-C bid	Euro-C ask	£ Stlg bid	£ Stlg ask	SwFr bid	SwFr ask	US $ bid	US $ ask	Yen bid	Yen ask
1 year	3.42	3.45	4.96	4.99	1.91	1.97	5.46	5.49	0.60	0.62
2 year	3.64	3.67	5.03	5.07	2.26	2.34	5.41	5.43	0.92	0.95
3 year	3.77	3.80	5.08	5.12	2.46	2.54	5.41	5.43	1.18	1.21
4 year	3.86	3.89	5.09	5.14	2.59	2.67	5.42	5.45	1.39	1.42
5 year	3.93	3.96	5.09	5.14	2.69	2.77	5.45	5.47	1.56	1.60
6 year	3.99	4.02	5.09	5.14	2.78	2.86	5.46	5.50	1.71	1.74
7 year	4.05	4.08	5.08	5.12	2.85	2.93	5.49	5.51	1.84	1.87
8 year	4.10	4.13	5.06	5.11	2.91	2.99	5.51	5.54	1.95	1.98
9 year	4.15	4.18	5.04	5.09	2.97	3.05	5.53	5.56	2.04	2.06
10 year	4.20	4.23	5.01	5.07	3.02	3.10	5.55	5.58	2.11	2.14
12 year	4.28	4.31	4.96	5.03	3.08	3.18	5.58	5.62	2.24	2.27
15 year	4.38	4.41	4.88	4.97	3.17	3.27	5.63	5.66	2.38	2.41
20 year	4.47	4.50	4.75	4.88	3.26	3.36	5.66	5.69	2.54	2.57
25 year	4.51	4.54	4.64	4.77	3.27	3.37	5.66	5.70	2.63	2.66
30 year	4.52	4.55	4.56	4.69	3.26	3.36	5.66	5.69	2.67	2.70

Bid and ask rates are as of close of London business. US $ is quoted annual money actual/360 basis against 3-month Libor, pound and yen quoted on a semiannual actual/365 basis against 6-month Libor, euro/Swiss franc rate quoted on annual bond 30/360 basis against 6-month Euribor Libor with the exception of the 1-year rate, which is quoted against 3-month Euribor/Libor.

Source: ICAP plc.

Figure 7.2.   Swap rates as quoted in the *Financial Times*.

- The bank's risks in case of default are limited because of the right-of-offset clause. In unusually risky cases, the contract parties also have to post margin.

- The probability of default is small. This is because the customers are screened; small or low-grade companies get no chance, or have to post initial margin.

- In addition, many swap contracts have a *credit trigger* clause, stating that if the customer's credit rating is revised downward, the financial institution can terminate the swap, and settle for the swap's market value at that moment. Thus, the bank has an opportunity to terminate the contract long before default actually occurs, unless the company goes straight from AA to failure, Enron-style.

- Finally, because of the right of offset, the uncertainty about the bank's inflows is the same as the uncertainty about the bank's outflows. The fact that the uncertainties are the same implies that the corrections for risk virtually cancel out. That is, it hardly matters whether or not one adds a similar (and small) default risk premium to the risk-free rates when one discounts the two cash-flow streams. The effect of adding a small risk premium when valuing one "leg" of the swap will essentially cancel out against the effect of adding a similar risk premium in the valuation of the other leg.

Look at the rates in figure 7.2. Sterling has a one-year swap rate of 4.96–4.99. Elsewhere in the same copy of the *Financial Times*, I found the following one-year rates: interbank sterling 4.875–4.968 75, BBA sterling 4.656 25, sterling CD 4.906 25–4.9375, local authority departments 4.875–4.9375. Thus, the swap rate is close to a risk-free rate. There *is* a small risk premium, but it is so low that for all practical purposes you can think of the swap rate as the risk-free rate, the same way Libor is called risk free.

The key to the *Financial Times* table mentions another detail: a swap rate is quoted against a particular floating rate. This is from the fact that the busiest section of the swap market is the interest swap, fixed versus floating or vice versa. In principle it should not matter exactly what the floating-rate part is: since investors can freely choose between, say, three-, six-, or nine-month Libor, the three should be equivalent. In practice, differences in, for example, liquidity may cause the swap rate to differ, in a minor way, depending on what the floating-rate part is.

7.2.2.2 Costs

The swapping bank charges a small annual commission of, say, USD 200 on a USD 1m swap, for each payment to be made. Most often this fee is built into the interest rates, which would raise or lower the quoted rate by a few basis points.

Example 7.3. Suppose that the seven-year yields at par are 3.17% on USD and 3.9% on EUR. The swap dealer quotes USD 3.15–3.19% and EUR 3.88–3.92%. If your swap contract is one where you "borrow" EUR and "lend" USD, you would then pay 3.95% on the EUR and receive 3.13% on the USD.

Alternatively—but rarely—the series of future commissions, one per payment, might be replaced by a single up-front fee with a comparable present value. It is useful for you to calculate this to have an idea of the overall cost. For a ten-year USD 1m swap at 3% annually that has a USD 200 commission per payment, the equivalent up-front commission would be about $200 \times a(3\%, 10 \text{ years}) = 200 \times 8.530\,203 =$ USD 1,706, or 0.17% of the face value.

Thus, although the swap remains a zero-value contract, the customer has to pay a small commission. (You can tell the difference between a price and a commission because the commission is always paid, whether one goes long or short; in contrast, the price is paid if one buys, and is received if one sells.) The commissions in the swap are small because the costs of bonding and monitoring are low—as we saw, default risk is minimal anyway—and because the amounts are large. (A typical interbank swap transaction is for a few million USD, and the Reuters swap-dealing network requires minimally USD 10m; for corporations, swaps can be smaller but contracts below USD 1m are rare.) Familiarly, the swap spread also depends on liquidity. Deep markets like USD, EUR, and JPY, in figure 7.2, have spreads of 3bp or thereabouts, but for CHF and GBP the margin is wider, rising to 10bp at the far end of the maturity spectrum.

Table 7.1. Fixed-for-fixed currency swap: the interim solution.

	Loan JPY 1,000 borrowed at 1%	Swap		Combined
		JPY 1,000 lent at 0.6%	USD 10m borrowed at 3%	
Principal at t	JPY 1,000m	⟨JPY 1,000m⟩	USD 10m	USD 10m
Interest (p.a.)	⟨JPY 10m⟩	JPY 6m	⟨USD 0.3m⟩	⟨JPY 4m⟩ ⟨USD 0.3m⟩
Principal at T	⟨JPY 1,000m⟩	JPY 1,000m	⟨USD 10m⟩	⟨USD 10m⟩

7.2.2.3 How to Handle and Compare Risk Spreads

Suppose a Japanese company wants to borrow cheaply in JPY (= HC) from its house bank, at 1% for seven years, bullet, and then swap the loan into USD. The swap rates quoted are 0.6% on JPY and 3% on USD. In table 7.1 the second column shows the original loan (JPY at 1%), the next two columns show the twin legs of the swap, and the final column shows the combined cash flow (loan and swap). The version we show first is, actually, rarely applied in practice; we use it mainly as an interim step because it helps to explain the advantage of the swap as well as the logic of the ultimate solution. The spot rate being about JPY/USD 100, we work with notional principals of JPY 1,000 and USD 10m. So the company

- borrows JPY 1,000m from the house bank at 1% (the actual loan rate),
- "relends" these JPY 1,000m to the swap dealer, at 0.6% (the JPY swap rate),
- ... who in return "lends" USD 10m to the firm at 3% (the USD swap rate).

This is summarized in table 7.1. Note how the company borrows, ultimately, USD 10m, with an annual interest payment consisting of the USD risk-free rate (3%) plus a risk spread which is, literally, the risk spread on a JPY loan from the house bank: 1% − 0.6% = 0.4% on JPY 1,000m.[4]

The above solution is still somewhat inelegant because the company pays part of its annual interest payments in JPY, an undesirable feature if it basically wants a USD loan. There are two simple solutions:

- either replace the seven annual JPY 4m payments by an equivalent up-front fee, which is of course their PV,

$$\text{Equivalent up-front fee} = 4\text{m} \times a(0.6\%, 7 \text{ years})$$
$$= 4\text{m} \times 6.834\,979 = \text{JPY } 27.339\,917\text{m}, \quad (7.3)$$

---

[4] Note that, since these two amounts are in different currencies with a stochastic future exchange rate, there is no way to amalgamate them into one number or one percentage. That is, 3% in USD and 0.4% in JPY is not 3.4%.

Table 7.2. Fixed-for-fixed currency swap: marked-up USD rate.

	Loan JPY 1,000 borrowed at 1%	Swap		Combined
		JPY 1,000 lent at 1%	USD 10m borrowed at 3.438 823%	
Principal at t	JPY 1,000m	⟨JPY 1,000m⟩	USD 10m	USD 10m
Interest (p.a.)	⟨JPY 10m⟩	JPY 10m	⟨USD 343,882.30⟩	⟨USD 343,882.30⟩
Principal at T	⟨JPY 1,000m⟩	JPY 1,000m	⟨USD 10m⟩	⟨USD 10m⟩

- or replace it by an equivalent USD annuity,

$$\text{Find } X^* \text{ such that } \underbrace{S_t \times X^* \times a(3\%, 7 \text{ years})}_{\text{USD PV of annuity } X^*} = \underbrace{4m \times a(0.6\%, 7 \text{ years})}_{\text{JPY PV of annuity 4m}}$$

$$\implies X^* = \frac{4m}{S_t} \frac{a(0.6\%, 7 \text{ years})}{a(3\%, 7 \text{ years})}$$

$$= \frac{4m}{100} \frac{6.834\,979}{6.230\,282} = \text{USD } 43{,}882.30m. \qquad (7.4)$$

Technically, we ask the swap dealer to pay us 1% (our borrowing rate) on the yen instead of 0.6% (the swap rate), and in return we increase the dollar interest paid to the swap dealer by the equivalent amount. Table 7.2 summarizes the modified solution.

The second solution immediately allows us to discover whether the swapped loan is more attractive than a direct USD loan (an alternative we have not yet looked at). The translated risk spread equivalent to the 0.4% charged by the Japanese house bank, as a percentage of the USD 10m borrowed, amounts to $43{,}882.30/10m = 0.438\,823\%$. Let us denote the risk spreads by ρ and ρ^*, as in chapter 5, and let us use s and s^* to refer to the swap rates. You can check that the generalized equivalence condition is

$$\rho^* \overset{\text{equiv}}{=} \rho \frac{a(s,n)}{a(s^*,n)} \quad \Leftrightarrow \quad \underbrace{\rho^* \times a(s^*,n)}_{\text{PV of FC risk spread}} \overset{\text{equiv}}{=} \underbrace{\rho \times a(s,n)}_{\text{PV of HC risk spread}}. \qquad (7.5)$$

Thus, a borrower gains from the swap if the spread quoted for a direct loan is higher than this translated HC risk spread, the HC figure projected into a different interest-rate environment via the adjustment $\times a(s,n)/a(s^*,n)$. Similarly, a credit analyst working for a bank can use the formula to consistently translate the borrower's HC risk spread into FC. The solution is a straightforward generalization of the one for simple spot-forward swaps in chapter 5: an FC risk spread ρ^* is equivalent to an HC ρ if their PVs are the same. The only change is that, of course, the PV-ing now involves annuities rather than a single payment: in a bullet loan, the risk premium is paid many times, not just once. Note also that for nonbullet loans the above formula no longer works, because the risk-spread payments (in amounts, not percentages) are then no

Table 7.3. Replicating a constant-annuity loan from bullet loans.

	Interest payments on loan maturing in year...			Amortization payments on loan maturing in year...			
	1	2	3	1	2	3	Sum
Year 1	41.985	52.901	65.421	839.694	0	0	1,000
Year 2	0	52.901	65.421	0	881.679	0	1,000
Year 3	0	0	65.421	0	0	934.579	1,000

Key: The loans are 839.694 for one year, 881.679 for two years, and 934.579 for three— just believe me, or read figure 7.3. The annual interest payments are 5% (one-year loan), 6% (two), or 7% (three), and each loan is amortized on the promised dates. The total combined service schedule is exactly 1,000 every year.

longer constant. The equal-PV rule for equivalence would still hold, but the computations would be messier.

Also the intuition as to why and when a translated risk spread exceeds the original one remains the same as before. In risk-adjusted terms, the yen is the strong currency here, as we can infer from its lower interest rate. So a strip of 0.4% payments in USD cannot be as good as a series of 0.4% in yen, the strong currency. The above formula tells us how the strength of the currencies, as embodied in their interest rates, has to be used in the translation process: taking into account the relative annuity factors, one needs to offer 0.438 823% in USD to be in balance with 0.4% in yen.

7.2.2.4 Nonbullet Loans

Standard swap-rate quotes are for bullet loans. Any other package is replicated as a combination of bullet loans with different times to maturity, and for each component the appropriate swap rate holds.

Example 7.4. Assume the swap rates for 1, 2, and 3 years are 5, 6, and 7%, respectively. We want to create a three-year constant-annuity loan, with three payments worth 1,000 each. The tools we have are three bullet loans: a one-year specimen with face value V_1 (to be determined); a two-year loan with face value V_2; and a three-year loan with face value V_3.

Finding the replication requires solving a simple linear system. In the case of a constant-annuity loan, the rule is that $V_t = V_{t+1}/(1+s_t)$, with a "dummy" V_4 defined as the annuity itself—that is, $V_3 = 1,000/1.07 = 934.579$, $V_2 = 934.579/1.06 = 881.678$, and $V_1 = 881.679/1.05 = 839.694$. Table 7.3 verifies that this indeed produces a combined cash flow for the three loans together of 1,000 every year, and figure 7.3 shows you how you get these numbers.

This way, the swap dealer has also found that the PV of the three-year annuity is 934.58 + 881.68 + 839.69 = 2,655.95. Spreadsheet aficionados will readily confirm that this corresponds to an IRR of 6.347%. This would then be the swap dealer's rate for three-year constant-annuity loans. As you can see, this

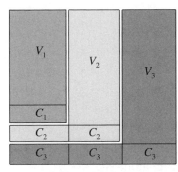

$$V_3 + C_3 = 1{,}000,$$
$$V_3(1 + s_3) = 1{,}000 \implies V_3,$$
$$V_2 + C_2 + C_3 = 1{,}000,$$
$$V_2(1 + s_2) + V_3 s_3 = 1{,}000 \implies V_2,$$
$$V_1 + C_1 + C_2 + C_3 = 1{,}000,$$
$$V_1(1 + s_1) + V_2 s_2 + V_3 s_3 = 1{,}000 \implies V_1,$$
$$V_3 = 934.58, \quad V_2 = 881.68, \quad V_1 = 839.69.$$

Key. A service schedule amounting to three times 1,000 is arranged as follows:

- We begin with year 3. In that year, only the 3-year loan is still alive, and its total service cost including 7% interest must be 1,000. So the requirement is to find V_3 such that $V_3 \times 1.07 = 1{,}000$, that is, $V_3 = 1{,}000/1.07 = 934.579$. The balance is interest on the 3-year bullet loan.

- Of the total 1,000 paid in year 2, the same 934.579 is available, after paying the interest in the 3-year bullet loan, for principal and coupon of the 2-year bullet loan: $V_3 = V_2 \times 1.06$. So $V_2 = V_3/1.06 = 881.678$, etc.

Figure 7.3. Replicating a constant-annuity loan from bullet loans.

is neither the three-year rate nor the two- or one-year rate for bullet loans, but a complicated mixture of all three. But this is the swap dealer's problem: the user can just work with the swap rate given to her for the particular type of loan at hand.

7.2.2.5 *Valuing an Outstanding Fixed-for-Fixed Currency Swap*

The last issue that we discuss in the section on fixed-for-fixed currency swaps is the valuation of such a swap after its inception. An assessment of the market value of a swap is required for the purpose of true and fair reporting to shareholders and overseeing authorities, or when the contract is terminated prematurely (by negotiation, or by default, or by the credit trigger clause).

Just as a forward contract, the fixed-for-fixed currency swap acquires a nonzero value as soon as the interest rates change, or as the spot rate changes. Since a swap is like a portfolio of (a) a loan and (b) an investment in long-term deposits (or in bonds), we can always value a swap as the difference between the market value of the loan and the market value of the investment.

Example 7.5. Two years ago, a bank swapped a company loan (asset) of USD 100m for GBP 50m for seven years, at the swap rates of 4% on the USD leg and 5% on the GBP leg. This reflected the long-term interest rates and the spot rate of USD/GBP 2 prevailing when the contract was signed. Now the five-year USD swap rate is 2.5%, the five-year GBP swap rate is 4%, and the spot rate is USD/GBP 1.7. The procedure suggested by the International Swap Dealers Association is to value the swap by applying the traditional bond valuation formula to each of the swap's legs. Thus, the company's USD outflows are valued as

$$PV_{USD} = 100m \times [1 + (0.04 - 0.025) \times a(2.5\%, 5 \text{ years})]$$
$$= USD\ 106,968,742.74, \tag{7.6}$$

while its GBP inflows are worth

$$PV_{GBP} = 50m \times [1 + (0.05 - 0.04) \times a(4\%, 5 \text{ years})]$$
$$= GBP\ 52,225,911.17. \tag{7.7}$$

At the spot rate of USD/GBP 1.7, these GBP inflows are worth USD 88,784,048.98. The contract has therefore become a net liability, with value USD 88,784,048.98 − 106,968,742.74 = −USD 18,184,693.76.

This finishes our discussion of the fixed-for-fixed currency swap. We now turn to other types of swaps, the most important of which is the interest-rate swap or coupon swap.

7.3   Interest-Rate Swaps

In an interest-rate swap, there is still an exchange of the service payments on two distinct loans. However, the two loans involved now differ not by currency, but by the method used to determine the interest payment (for instance, floating rate versus fixed rate). Because both underlying loans are in the same currency, there is no initial exchange of principals and no final amortization. In that sense, the two loans are *notional* (fictitious or theoretical). The only cash flows that are swapped are the interest streams on each of the notional loans. In short, parties A and B simply agree to pay/receive the difference between two interest streams on the notional loan amounts.

The standard interest swap is the fixed-for-floating swap or coupon swap. The base swap is rarer. We discuss each of them in turn.

7.3.1   Coupon Swaps (Fixed-for-Floating)

We now describe the characteristics of a fixed-for-floating swap and how one can value such a financial contract.

7.3.1.1   Characteristics of the Fixed-for-Floating Swap

In our discussion of the fixed-for-fixed currency swap, we saw that, in terms of the risk spread above the risk-free rate, a firm often has a comparative advantage in one currency but may prefer to borrow in another currency. The firm can retain its favorable risk spread and still change the loan's currency of denomination by borrowing in the most favorable market and swapping the loan into the preferred currency. The same holds for the fixed-for-floating swap except that, instead of a preferred currency, the firm now has a preferred type of interest payment. For instance, the firm may have a preference for financing at a fixed rate, but the risk spread in the floating-rate market may be lower. To retain its advantage of a lower spread in the floating-rate market, the firm can borrow at a floating rate, and swap the loan into a fixed-rate loan using a fixed-for-floating swap.

Because the swap contract is almost risk free, the interest rates used in the swap contract are (near) risk-free rates. For the floating-rate leg of the swap, the rate is traditionally Libor or a similar money market rate, while the relevant interest rate for the fixed-rate leg is the same as the *N*-year swap rate used in fixed-for-fixed currency swaps. In fact, traditionally, the fixed swap rate was *defined* as the rate which the swap dealer thought to be as good as Libor, that is, which she or he was willing to take as the fixed-rate leg in a fixed-for-floating or floating-for-fixed swap. Also, Libor in currency X is also defined as acceptable against Libor in currency Y, which in turn must be acceptable against currency-Y fixed.

Example 7.6. An AA Irish company wants to borrow NZD to finance (and partially hedge) its direct investment in New Zealand. Because the company is better known in London than in Auckland, it decides to tap the euro–NZD market rather than the loan market in New Zealand. As NZD interest rates are rather volatile, the company prefers fixed-rate loans. But eurobanks, which are funded on a very short-term basis, dislike fixed-rate loans, which means that the company would have to tap bond market. The company's alternatives are the following:

- A euro–NZD fixed-rate bond issue would be possible only at 7%, which represents a hefty 2% spread above the NZD swap rate of 5%.

- From a London bank, the Irish company can get an NZD floating-rate bank loan at Libor + 1%.

The company can keep the lower spread required in the floating-rate market and still pay a fixed rate by borrowing NZD at the NZD Libor + 1%, and swapping this into a fixed-rate NZD loan at the 5% swap rate. The payment streams, per NZD, are summarized in table 7.4. To help you see the link between the payments under the swap contract and the underlying notional loans, we have added the theoretical principals at initiation and at maturity. In practice, the principals will not be exchanged. We see that this company borrows foreign currency at the NZD risk-free fixed rate (5%) plus the spread of 1% it can obtain in the "best" market (the floating-rate eurobank-loan market). Therefore, the company pays 6% fixed rather than the 7% that would have been required in the bond market.

Having done the number crunching, let's talk economics now: how it is possible that the bond market requires 2%, by way of risk spread, when banks are happy with 1%? One reason is that banks are quite good at credit analysis, while Swiss dentists—still a nontrivial part of the bond-market clientele—are not trained analysts. Also, the amounts at stake for a bank do justify a thorough analysis, while the 10,000 dollars invested by the Swiss dentists are too small for this. Furthermore, our Irish company will be happy to privately provide

Table 7.4. Fixed-for-floating swap.

	Loan NZD 1 borrowed at Libor + 1%	Swap		
		NZD 1 lent at Libor %	NZD 1m borrowed at 5%	Combined
Principal at t	NZD1	⟨NZD 1⟩	NZD 1	NZD 1
Interest (p.a.)	⟨Libor + 1%⟩	Libor %	⟨5%⟩	⟨5% + 1% = 6%⟩
Principal at T	⟨NZD 1⟩	NZD 1	⟨NZD 1⟩	⟨NZD 1⟩

information to its bank that it would not dream of publishing in a prospectus. In short, the bank knows more, and knows better what the information means.

The swap dealer, who has to find a new party with (roughly) the opposite wants as our AA company, might then talk to an institutional investor, like an insurance company. They like long-duration deals. So everybody is happy. The insurance company gets a long-run fixed-rate investment and the firm the long-run fixed-rate funding, but the credit analysis and the first-line default risk are left to the credit specialist, the bank.

From the above discussion, it is obvious that the potential advantages of the coupon swap are similar to the ones mentioned in the case of the fixed-for-fixed currency swap. What remains to be discussed is how to determine the value of the fixed-for-floating swap.

7.3.1.2 Valuing a Fixed-for-Floating Swap

We have seen that in a fixed-for-floating swap without default risk, the incoming stream is the service schedule of a risk-free floating-rate loan, and the outgoing stream is the service schedule of a traditional risk-free fixed-rate loan (and vice versa for the other contract party). The fixed-rate payment stream is easily valued by discounting the known cash flows using the prevailing swap rate for the remaining time to maturity. The question now is how should one value the floating-rate part for which the future payments are not known in advance.

Let us study the value of a series of floating-rate cash inflows. This series of (as yet unknown) inflows must have the same market value as a short-term deposit where the principal amount is reinvested periodically. The reason for this equivalence is that the cash flows are the same, as the example will show. To buy such a series of deposits we need to buy only the currently outstanding deposit. No extra money is needed to redeposit the maturing principals later on.

Example 7.7. Suppose that you want to replicate a risk-free USD 10,000 floating-rate bond with semiannual interest payments equal to the six-month T-bill rate, the first of which is due within four months. At the last reset date, the six-month T-bill rate

Figure 7.4. Crucial dates for valuing a floating-rate note.

was 3% p.a.; thus, the next interest payment equals $10{,}000 \times (1/2) \times 3\% = $ USD 150. The current four-month rate of return is 0.9% (or 2.7% p.a., simple interest).

The above floating-rate bond can be replicated by "buying" USD 10,150 due three months from now at a present value cost of USD $10/1.009 = $ USD 10,059.46. After four months, you withdraw USD 150 to replicate the bond's first coupon, and you redeposit the remaining 10,000 at the then-prevailing six-month return. When this investment expires, you again withdraw the interest and redeposit the 10,000 at the then-prevailing rate, and you continue to do so until the bond expires. Notice that the future payoffs of the rolled-over deposit are identical to the payoffs of the floating rate bond. The cost to you was only the initial USD 10,059.46. Then, by arbitrage, the floating rate bond is also worth 10,194.

The general expression for the value of a floating-rate bond is

$$\text{Value of a risk-free floating-rate bond} = [\text{Face value}] \times \frac{1 + r_{t_0, T_1}}{1 + r_{t, T_1}}, \qquad (7.8)$$

where t_0 is the last reset date, T_1 is the next reset date, t is the present date (the valuation date, with $t_0 < t < T_1$), r_{t_0, T_1} is the coupon effectively payable at T_1, r_{t, T_1} is the effective current return until time T_1.

The current market value of a coupon swap then equals the difference between the market value of the loan that underlies the incoming stream and the market value of the loan that underlies the outgoing stream.

Example 7.8. Some time ago, a South African company speculated on a drop in fixed-rate interest rates, and swapped ZAR 10m at 7%, semiannual and fixed, for ZAR 10m at the six-month ZAR Libor. That is, the contract stipulates that, every six months, the firm pays the six-month ZAR Libor rate (divided by two) on a notional ZAR 10m, and receives $7/2 = 3.5\%$ on the same notional amount. Suppose that ZAR medium-term interest rates have fallen substantially below 7%. The company reckons it has made a nice profit on its swap contract, and wants to lock in the gain by selling the swap. Current conditions are as follows:

- The swap has five years and two months left until maturity.
- The current five-year ZAR swap rate (for semiannual payments) is 5% p.a., or 2.5% every six months.
- The ZAR Libor rate, set four months ago for the current six-month period, is 4% p.a.
- The current two-month ZAR Libor is 3.5% p.a.

To value the (incoming) ZAR cash flows, note that there are eleven remaining interest payments at 3.5% each, the first of which is due two months from now. Discounted at $5/2 = 2.5\%$ per half-year, the value is

$$PV^{fix} = 10m \times [1 + (0.035 - 0.025) \times a(2.5\%, 11)] \times 1.025^{2/3}$$
$$= ZAR\ 11,133,193, \tag{7.9}$$
$$PV^{flo} = 10m \times \frac{1 + (1/2) \times 0.04}{1 + (2/12) \times 0.035} = ZAR\ 10,041,425. \tag{7.10}$$

So the value of the fixed-rate leg exceeds the value of the floating-rate leg by

$$ZAR\ 11,133,193 - 10,041,425 = ZAR\ 1,691,768. \tag{7.11}$$

This is what the company should receive for its swap contract.

7.3.2 Base Swaps

Under a base swap, the parties swap two streams of floating-rate interest payments where each stream is determined by a different base rate. For example, a Libor-based revolving loan can be swapped for a U.S. T-bill-based revolving loan. The spread between these two money-market rates is called the TED spread (treasury–eurodollar spread). The TED spread is nonzero because T-bills and euro-CDs are not perfect substitutes in terms of political risk[5] and default risk. TED swaps can be used either to speculate on changes in the TED spread or to hedge a swap book containing contracts with different base rates.

Example 7.9. The U.S. office of a major bank has signed a fixed-for-floating swap based on the USD T-bill rate, while the London office has signed a floating-for-fixed swap based on USD Libor. This bank now has the USD T-bill rate as an income stream and the USD Libor rate as an outgoing stream. To cover the TED-spread risk, it can swap its T-bill income stream for a Libor income stream using a base swap. The counterparty to this swap may be a speculator or simply another swap dealer who faces the opposite problem.

7.4 Cross-Currency Swaps

The cross-currency swap, or circus swap, is a currency swap combined with an interest-rate swap (floating versus fixed rate), in the sense that the loans on which the service schedules are based differ by currency *and* type of interest payment. An early example is the Renault–Yamaichi swap already mentioned in section 7.2. The historic background for the swap is as follows:

- Renault, a French car producer, wanted to get rid of its USD floating rate debt, and wanted to borrow fixed-rate JPY instead. The snag was that,

---

[5] Dollar deposits in London cannot be blocked by the U.S. government, which is attractive to some parties. This is no longer a major issue.

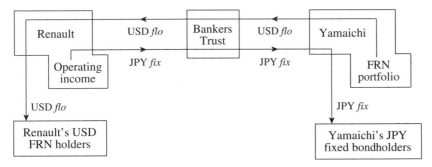

Figure 7.5. Renault's 1981 circus swap.

because of Japanese regulations at the time, Renault was not permitted to borrow in the Japanese market.

- Simultaneously, Yamaichi Securities was being encouraged by Japan's Ministry of Finance to buy USD assets.[6] It could have bought, for instance, Renault's USD floating rate notes but was unwilling to take the exchange risk.

With the help of Bankers Trust, an investment bank, Renault convinced Yamaichi to borrow fixed-rate JPY and to buy floating-rate USD notes of similar rating and conditions as Renault's notes. As illustrated in figure 7.5, Yamaichi was to hand over the USD service income from the USD investment to Renault, who would use the floating-rate USD interest stream to service its own floating-rate notes. As compensation, Renault undertook to service Yamaichi's equivalent fixed-rate yen loan, and pay a spread to both Bankers Trust and Yamaichi.

The advantages of the swap to each party were:

- Renault was able to access the JPY capital market and get rid of its USD liability. (A more obvious solution would have been to borrow JPY and retire the USD floating-rate notes with the proceeds. However, the first part of this transaction was not legally possible and the second part would have been expensive in terms of transaction costs or call premia.)

- Yamaichi earned a commission. In addition, it now held USD assets (which was politically desirable) but these assets were fully hedged against exchange risk by the swap.

- Bankers Trust earned a commission on all of the payments that passed through its hands, plus a fee for arranging the deal.

The swap is also memorable because, even though it came quite soon after IBM–WB, it was already much more modern: it was not negotiated directly between two companies, but set up by Bankers Trust. Relatedly, there was no direct swap contract between Renault and Yamaichi, but two contracts (the

---

[6] Japan wanted to show it was doing its bit to help finance the U.S. deficit and also help "recycle the petrodollars," a big issue after the second oil shock, in the early 1980s.

Table 7.5. Swaps: overview.

Preferred loan is:		Direct loan with best spread is:	
		Fixed rate	Floating rate
Fixed rate	Same currency	(Do not swap)	Do interest swap
	Other currency	Fix–fix currency swap	Do circus swap
Floating rate	Same currency	Do interest swap	(Do not swap)
	Other currency	Do circus swap	Flo–flo currency swap

double swap, as it was then called): Renault versus Bankers Trust, and Bankers Trust versus Yamaichi. This way, Bankers Trust took over the counterparty risk from Renault and Yamaichi, or, to be more precise, replaced the original counterparty risk by the risk that Bankers Trust itself may get into trouble.[7]

7.5 CFO's Summary

The interest paid on any loan can be decomposed into the risk-free rate plus a spread that reflects the credit risk of the borrower. Swaps allow a company to borrow in the market where it can obtain the lowest spread, and then exchange the risk-free component of the loan's service payments for the risk-free component of another loan. This is useful if the other loan is preferred in terms of its currency of denomination or in terms of the way the periodic interest payments are determined (fixed or floating), as shown in figure 7.5. The use of risk-free rates within the swap is justified because the right of offset and the credit trigger eliminate virtually all risk from the swap, even though the company's ordinary loans remain risky. If desired, the original loan's risk-spread payments can also be swapped into the desired currency without altering their PV.

The difference between the spreads asked in different market segments usually reflects an information asymmetry—for instance, the firm's house bank often offers the best spreads because it is less afraid of adverse selection—but may also reflect an interest subsidy. Another advantage is that the swap contract is a single contract, and is therefore likely to be cheaper than its replicating portfolio (borrowing in one market, converting the proceeds into another currency, and investing the resulting amount in another market). Other potential advantages include tax savings, or access to otherwise unavailable loans, or advantages of off-balance-sheet reporting.

Depending on the combination of the preferred type of loan and the cheapest available loan, one could use a fixed-for-fixed swap, a fixed-for-floating swap, or a circus swap. Each of these swaps can also be used to speculate on changes in interest rates or exchange rates. Likewise, base swaps are used to hedge against, or to speculate on, changes in the TED spread.

---

[7] Bankers Trust *did* get into trouble, and was taken over by Deutsche Bank. Also Yamaichi sank ignominiously and was absorbed by Nomura, Japan's largest broker and investment bank.

These four swaps are just the most common types; in fact, many more exotic swap-like contracts are offered. Thus, swaps have become increasingly popular with financial institutions and large corporations. All of these swaps are based on the principle of initial equivalence of the two legs of the contract. Thus, like forward contracts on exchange rates or currencies, the initial value of a swap is zero. To compute the market value of such a contract after inception, we just value each leg in light of the prevailing exchange and interest rates.

7.6 Technical Notes

Technical note 7.1 (the value of a bond as a function of its yield to maturity). The valuation formula is derived as follows. Let the face value be 1, the coupon c per period, and the first coupon due exactly 1 period from now. (The yield is denoted by R, not r, because an annualized, compound yield on a coupon bond should not be confused with an effective simple return on a zero-coupon bond.) We start with (almost) a definition. Use the annuity formula; add and subtract 1; divide and multiply by R; and rearrange:

$$
\begin{aligned}
\text{PV} &= \sum_{t=1}^{n} \frac{c}{(1+R)^t} + \frac{1}{(1+R)^n} \\
&= c \frac{1 - (1+R)^{-n}}{R} + (1+R)^{-n} \\
&= c \frac{1 - (1+R)^{-n}}{R} + (1+R)^{-n} - 1 + 1 \\
&= c \frac{1 - (1+R)^{-n}}{R} + R \frac{(1+R)^{-n} - 1}{R} + 1 \\
&= (c - R) \frac{1 - (1+R)^{-n}}{R} + 1 = (c - R)\, a(n, R) + 1. \quad (7.12)
\end{aligned}
$$

If the time to the next coupon is $1 - f$ rather than unity, the PV rises by a factor $(1+R)^f$.

TEST YOUR UNDERSTANDING

Quiz Questions

1. How does a fixed-for-fixed currency swap differ from a spot contract combined with a forward contract in the opposite direction?

2. Describe some predecessors to the currency swap, and discuss the differences with the modern swap contract.

3. What are the reasons why swaps may be useful for companies who want to borrow?

4. How are swaps valued in general? How does one value the floating-rate leg (if any), and why?

Applications

1. The modern long-term currency swap can be viewed as:

    (a) a spot sale and a forward purchase;

    (b) a combination of forward contracts, each of them having zero initial market value;

    (c) a combination of forward contracts, each of them having, generally, a nonzero initial market value but with a zero initial market value for all of them taken together;

    (d) a spot transaction and a combination of forward contracts, each of them having, generally, a nonzero initial market value but with a zero initial market value for all of them taken together.

2. The swap rate for a long-term swap is:

    (a) the risk-free rate plus the spread usually paid by the borrower;

    (b) the risk-free rate plus a spread that depends on the security offered on the loan;

    (c) close to the risk-free rate, because the risk to the financial institution is very low;

    (d) the average difference between the spot rate and forward rates for each of the maturities.

3. The general effect of a swap is:

    (a) to replace the entire service payment schedule on a given loan by a new service payment schedule on an initially equivalent loan of another type (for instance, another currency, or another type of interest);

    (b) to replace the risk-free component of the service payment schedule on a given loan by a risk-free component of the service payment schedule on an initially equivalent loan of another type (for instance, another currency or another type of interest);

    (c) to change the currency of a loan;

    (d) to obtain a spot conversion at an attractive exchange rate.

4. You borrow USD 1m for six months, and you lend EUR 1.5m—an initially equivalent amount—for six months, at p.a. rates of 6% and 8%, respectively, with a right of offset. What are the equivalent spot and forward transactions?

5. Your firm has USD debt outstanding with a nominal value of USD 1m and a coupon of 9%, payable annually. The first interest payment is due three months from now, and there are five more interest payments afterward.

    (a) If the yield at par on bonds with similar risk and time to maturity is 8%, what is the market value of this bond in USD? In yen (at $S_t = $ JPY/USD 100)?

(b) Suppose that you want to exchange the service payments on this USD bond for the service payments of a 5.25-year JPY loan at the going yield, for this risk class, of 4%. What should be the terms of the JPY loan?

6. You borrow NOK 100m at 10% for seven years, and you swap the loan into NZD at a spot rate of NOK/NZD 4 and the seven-year swap rates of 7% (NZD) and 8% (NOK). What are the payments on the loan, on the swap, and on the combination of them? Is there a gain if you could have borrowed NZD at 9%?

7. Use the same data as in the previous exercise, except that you now swap the loan into floating rate (at Libor). What are the payments on the loan, on the swap, and on the combination of them? Is there a gain if you could have borrowed EUR at Libor + 1%?

8. You can borrow CAD at 8%, which is 2% above the swap rate, or at CAD Libor + 1%. If you want to borrow at a fixed rate, what is the best way, direct or synthetic (that is, using a floating-rate loan and a swap)?

9. You have an outstanding fixed-for-fixed NOK/NZD swap for NOK 100m, based on a historic spot rate of NOK/NZD 4 and initial seven-year swap rates of 7% (NZD) and 8% (NOK). The swap now has three years to go, and the current rates at NOK/NZD 4.5, 6% (NZD three years), and 5% (NOK three years). What is the market value of the swap contract?

10. Use the same data as in the previous exercise, except that now the NZD leg is a floating rate. The rate has just been reset. What is the market value of the swap?

8

Currency Options (1): Concepts and Uses

So far we have studied three contracts whose payoffs are contingent on the future spot rate(s): foreign-currency forward contracts, futures contracts, and swaps. The payoffs from these instruments are linear in the future spot rate. That is, if you buy any of these instruments and the underlying exchange rate increases, you gain proportionally, and when the rate decreases, you lose money proportionally. In other words, the payoff of these instruments is symmetric (except, of course, for the sign): a unit drop in the exchange rate has the opposite effect on the contract's cash flow as a unit rise in the exchange rate. However, one would often rather not have this symmetric payoff. In many situations, one would like to make money when the price of the instrument goes up, but not lose money if the price goes down. Options are instruments that permit investors to achieve such asymmetric, nonlinear payoffs.

Options are somewhat harder to understand than forward contracts, and the pricing of options is also more complicated. On the other hand, a good understanding of these issues is valuable because options, compared with forwards or futures, are instruments that are much more flexible for hedging or for speculating, and because option pricing theory has valuable applications in other fields, like investment analysis. We devote two chapters to the discussion of options. In this chapter, we describe the features of currency option contracts (section 8.1), the markets in which they are traded (section 8.2), and their applications—arbitrage, hedging, and speculation (sections 8.3–8.5). In the next chapter, we show how one can price options in a discrete setting and how this leads to the famous Black–Scholes formula for the valuation of options.

8.1 An Introduction to Currency Options

In this section, we describe call and put options and explain the difference between European- and American-style options. We also see how one can interpret the decision to buy an option as a decision to buy insurance, and the price paid for the option as an insurance premium.

8.1.1 Call Options

A *call* (or *call option*) is a contract that gives the *holder* the right to buy a stated number of units of the *"underlying" asset* at a given price (which is called the *exercise price* or *strike price* or simply *strike*) from the counterparty (called the *writer* of the option). In the case of a *European-style* option, this right can be exercised at a given expiry moment T—say, Wednesday between 15:50 and 16:00—while for an *American-style* option it can be exercised at any time until the expiry moment. The names European- and American-style have nothing to do with where they are traded: both types are used all over the world.

Depending on the underlying asset on which the option is written, a call can be an option on a stock, a stock market index, a currency, a commodity, a bond, or an interest rate, or even a futures contract or a swap (*swaption*). In this chapter, we will mainly consider options on foreign currency.

8.1.1.1 A European-Style Call

Example 8.1. Suppose that you buy a call option on 1 NZD at GBP/NZD 0.50 expiring on June 30. You, as the buyer or owner of the right, are the holder of the option. You are "*long the call.*" The counterparty, who grants you this right, is the seller or writer of the call; he has an obligation to deliver 1 NZD to you at 50 cents if you want him to (that is, if you exercise the option). He is "*short the call.*" The exercise price is GBP/NZD 0.50. Thus, if the spot rate at time T turns out to be GBP/NZD 0.55 or 0.60, you will exercise your right and buy NZD at GBP/NZD 0.50, and thus save NZD 0.05 or 0.10, respectively. Of course, if $\tilde{S}_T$ is less than 0.50, you will not exercise the option: there is no point buying NZD from the writer at GBP/NZD 0.50 if you can obtain NZD for a lower price in the spot market.

If your option is a call on NZD 12,500 at GBP/NZD 0.50, the writer may have to deliver NZD 12,500 to you at 50 cents each. For a contract size of NZD 12,500, this means that if and when you decide to exercise your call option, you will pay GBP $12,500 \times 0.50 =$ GBP 6,250 for the NZD 12,500, irrespective of the spot price at that moment. If the then-prevailing spot price is 0.60, you will have saved GBP $12,500 \times (0.60 - 0.50) =$ GBP 1,250.

To summarize, a call option allows you to obtain only the "nice" part of the forward purchase, the part with the positive sign. Denoting the strike price or exercise price by X, then under a forward purchase you would have paid X for the foreign currency whether you liked it or not, that is, whether or not X is a good price, relative to S_T. With a call, in contrast, you pay *no more than* X, and possibly less than X, notably when the spot rate turns out to be a bad price relative to the strike.

This has a straightforward implication for the *expiry value*. Recall that the expiry value of a forward purchase equals the money saved by buying one unit at X instead of at S_T. Similarly, the expiry value is the money saved because of owning (and judiciously exercising) the option:

- if the spot rate ends above X (and you exercise: buy at X), you save $S_T - X$;

Table 8.1. Expiry values of a European call and put at strike 0.50.

If $S_T =$	0.45	0.46	0.47	0.48	0.49	0.50	0.51	0.52	0.53	0.54	0.55
then $C_T =$	0	0	0	0	0	0	0.01	0.02	0.03	0.04	0.05
and $P_T =$	0.05	0.04	0.03	0.02	0.01	0	0	0	0	0	0

- if the spot rate ends below X (and you forget about the option), you save nothing.

The second outcome makes the difference relative to the forward purchase: having bought forward, we have to purchase and pay even if the deal turns out to be a bad one.

This way of reasoning is applied for a range of possible exchange rates at expiry in table 8.1 for a call with strike price 0.50 (or "*struck at 0.50*"[1]). The resulting call value is zero for rates below 0.50, and becomes positive if and to the extent that the rate exceeds 0.50. In the familiar graph, whenever a comparable forward purchase would have produced a negative expiry value, the call option ends worthless—you can walk away, you do not have to buy if you do not like it. This is shown in figure 8.1.

There are standard mathematical and notational conventions for relations like this. One can write the two possible outcomes explicitly, along with the condition under which each value holds. Alternatively, one writes it as a Max function, where $\text{Max}(a, b)$ means "the greater of a or b"; so $\text{Max}(S_T - X, 0)$ again means "$S_T - X$ (as in the forward purchase) but with the negative part replaced by zero." The third notation is $(S_T - X)$ with a "+" subscript, again meaning "if positive; otherwise zero":

$$\tilde{C}_T = \begin{cases} \tilde{S}_T - X & \text{if } \tilde{S}_T > X \\ 0 & \text{otherwise} \end{cases}$$
$$= \text{Max}(\tilde{S}_T - X, 0)$$
$$= (\tilde{S}_T - X)_+.$$

For a European-style call option, the current market price is based solely on the final payoff $(\tilde{S}_T - X)_+$. In the next chapter we shall show that the current value of a European-style option is the risk-adjusted expected value of this final payoff, discounted back to the present. Things are different for American-style calls.

8.1.1.2   An American-Style Call

An *American-style option* can be exercised at any time τ prior to T. Thus, a writer is not sure what the American option's effective life is going to be, which makes its valuation more complicated. For rational *early exercise* (prior to T), the immediate payoff or *value dead*, $(S_\tau - X)$, must meet two conditions.

---

[1] Pros will express the strike in cents, and say "struck at 50."

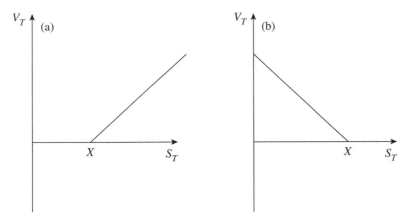

Figure 8.1. Expiry values of calls and puts, long: (a) call, long; (b) put, long.

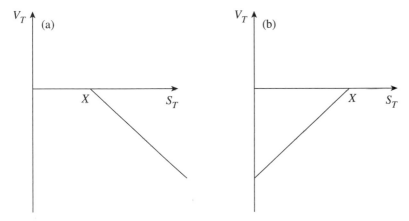

Figure 8.2. Expiry values of calls and puts, short: (a) call, short; (b) put, short.

The first is obvious: the value dead must be positive. The second condition is more subtle: the value dead must not be below the market value of the option (the *value alive*), which is the PV of possible later exercise in more propitious circumstances. If the value alive is indeed too large, you had better wait—or you sell to others who obviously do think it is better to wait.

Example 8.2. Suppose that you have an American call option to buy 1 unit of NZD at X = GBP/NZD 0.50. Currently, NZD trades at 0.48. You will not exercise early: there is no point in paying GBP 0.50 if an NZD can be bought spot for GBP 0.48. (This does not mean that the option is worthless. Exercise may still become profitable later on.)

Suppose that, a few weeks later, the NZD has appreciated to 0.52. It might make sense to exercise early and earn 2 cents on the NZD. But if the market price of the option at that moment is 3 cents, there is no point in exercising early. Exercising nets the holder only 2 cents, while selling the option yields 3 cents.

8.1.2 Put Options

As we saw, a European-style call option gives you the nice part of a forward purchase contract. Likewise, you might be interested in contracts that give you just the nice part of a forward sale—the right to sell at a prespecified price when the currency trades below that price, without the obligation to sell at X when the currency is worth more. With such an option, you obtain no less than X per unit of foreign currency, and possibly more than X. In contrast, with a forward sale you always get X, even if, with hindsight, you do not like this price. A *right* to sell at X, without any obligation to do so, is called a *put option* or *put*.

Example 8.3. You may buy the right to sell NZD 125,000 at a strike price of 0.50 (GBP/NZD) on July 30. When exercised, this put will mean the delivery of NZD 125,000 at GBP 0.50 per NZD (that is, GBP 62,500 for all of the NZD 125,000). Of course, if at maturity S_T is more than 0.50, you will not exercise the option.

Table 8.1 shows the outcomes for some possible realizations of $\tilde{S}_T$. So the expiration value of a European-style put (or an American-style one, if still alive) is

$$
\tilde{P}_T = \begin{cases} X - \tilde{S}_T & \text{if } X > \tilde{S}_T \\ 0 & \text{otherwise} \end{cases}
$$
$$
= \text{Max}(X - \tilde{S}_T, 0)
$$
$$
= (X - \tilde{S}_T)_+ .
$$

This was for European-style sell options. The holder of an American-style put may also exercise at any moment τ prior to T. By analogy to what holds for calls, the following two conditions must be met for early exercise of puts to be rational: (i) the immediate exercise value of the put, $(X - S_\tau)$, must be positive, and (ii) the put option's market value (*alive*) must be no higher than the value from immediate exercise, otherwise it would be better to sell the option than to exercise it.

8.1.3 Option Premiums and Option Writing

A firm that faces a future outflow of NZD might buy a call option on NZD with strike price X. The ensuing right to buy NZD at X means that this firm will pay no more than X per NZD. Thus, buying a call is like taking out an insurance contract against the risk of high exchange rates. Likewise, a firm that expects to receive future NZD might acquire a put option on NZD—the right to sell at X ensures that this firm gets no less than X for its NZD. Thus, buying a put is like taking out an insurance contract against low exchange rates. As in any insurance contract, the insured party will pay an insurance premium to the insurer (the *writer* of the option). The price of an option is, not coincidentally, often called the *option premium* and acquiring an option contract is called buying an option. As with ordinary insurance contracts, the option premium is usually paid up-front.

Insurance companies are willing to sell insurance policies because they receive a premium that covers the discounted expected costs and because they can diversify most of the risks. Likewise, option writers sell options because they receive a premium that covers the discounted expected exercise value of the claim and because they can diversify or hedge most of the risks. In the case of options, risk reduction is obtained not just by writing both puts and calls, but also by cleverly taking positions in forward contracts, or futures, or deposits and loans so as to offset most of the remaining risks. We shall explain how this is done in the next chapter.

8.1.4   European-Style Puts and Calls as Chopped-Up Forwards

The four graphs in figures 8.1 and 8.2 allow you to see that European-style puts and calls are basically bits and pieces of forward contracts:

- Buying a call corresponds to the favorable part of a forward purchase since you (gladly) buy at X when $\tilde{S}_T > X$.

- Selling a call corresponds to the bad part of a forward sale since you are forced to sell at X when $\tilde{S}_T > X$, thus incurring a loss.

- Buying a put corresponds to the favorable part of a forward sale since you (gladly) sell at X when $\tilde{S}_T < X$

- Selling a put corresponds to the bad part of a forward purchase since you are forced to buy at X when $\tilde{S}_T < X$, thus incurring a loss.

To phrase this even more concisely: the long positions are the upper halves of forwards while the shorts the negative parts, and puts are active at rates below X while calls wake up for rates above X. Of course, we can also see this in reverse: puts and calls (short and long) can be reassembled into forward purchases or sales. This, as we shall see, implies that the values of these contracts must be related.

8.1.5   Jargon: Moneyness, Intrinsic Value, and Time Value

An option is said to be *in the money* (ITM) if immediate exercise generates a positive cash flow. If the spot rate equals the strike price, the option is said to be *at the money* (ATM). Otherwise, the option is *out of the money* (OTM). An option with a strike price that differs substantially from the current spot rate is called *deep in the money*, or *deep out of the money*. The term *around the money* is used to indicate that the strike price is close to the spot rate. In the above, "the money" refers to the spot rate; occasionally, however, one hears about *at the forward* options (meaning $X = F_{t,T}$).

The *intrinsic value* is the option's value if you had to make the exercise decision right now. For options that are in the money, the intrinsic value is $(S_t - X)$ for calls and $(X - S_t)$ for puts. For out-of-the-money options, the holder will not exercise immediately, and so the intrinsic value is zero.

Example 8.4. For a call on NZD with strike price X = US cents/NZD 43, the intrinsic value is

- 5 cents if the spot rate is 48 cents,
- 0 if the spot rate is US cents/NZD 40 (or any other rate $\leqslant 43$).

For a put option at X = US cents/NZD 43, by analogy, the intrinsic value is

- 3 cents when the spot rate is 40,
- 0 when the spot rate is US cents/NZD 48 (or any other rate $\geqslant 43$).

In short, the intrinsic value of a call at time t is $\text{Max}(S_t - X, 0)$ or $(S_t - X)_+$, and for a put it is $\text{Max}(X - S_t, 0)$ or $(X - S_t)_+$. These look like the expiry-value expressions, except of course that they are about current premia related to the current spot rate, not premia and spot rates at expiry.

Even an out-of-the-money option should usually have a positive price, however small. This is because there is nearly always a positive probability that the exchange-rate changes in the favorable direction and the option moves back into the money before it expires. Clearly, immediate exercise of an out-of-the-money option cannot be the buyer's motivation, so such an option's market value is based entirely on the chance of profitable exercise at a later date. In options-speak, the option premium in this case is said to be pure *time value*.[2]

A similar reasoning applies to in-the-money options. When the NZD trades at 42.5, a put with strike price 43 has a positive immediate exercise value of 0.5. However, there may be a consensus in the market that the (uncertain) prospects of possible later exercise are worth even more than immediate exercise. The option would then trade above its intrinsic value of 0.5 cents, say at 0.55. The excess of the premium over the intrinsic value—0.05 in the above example—is generally called the *time value* of the option. Thus, we can always decompose an observed market price of an option into the intrinsic value and a residual time value:

$$\text{Option value} = \text{Intrinsic value} + \text{Time value}. \qquad (8.1)$$

We have already discovered that an American option should not be exercised early when its market price exceeds the early exercise value. In our new terminology, we can rephrase this as follows: early exercise of an in-the-money option is not rational if the option has a positive time value. Early exercise

---

[2] This should not be confused with the standard meaning of time value—the compensation for pure waiting without any change in risk. The terminology is quite unfortunate, but too standard to change now.

would mean that you receive only the intrinsic value and throw away the time value.

Perhaps you are wondering whether time value can be negative. This issue will crop up when we talk about arbitrage applications. But first we need some institutional information.

8.2 Institutional Aspects of Options Markets

Whereas futures contracts are traded only on organized exchanges and forward contracts only over the counter, options are available both in over-the-counter markets (*OTC options*) and on organized exchanges (*traded options*).

8.2.1 Traded Options

An organized option exchange, like a futures market, has an organized secondary market, with a clearing house as a guarantor. The clearing house also clears offsetting contracts: if an investor bought an option some time ago and now sells it to someone else, his or her net obligation is zero. Another idea that option exchanges have borrowed from futures markets is standardization:

Expiration dates. Originally, all options expired on the third Wednesday of March, June, September, or December, and only the contracts with the three nearest expiration dates were traded. Nowadays this basic scheme, borrowed from futures markets, is often completed by extra short-lived options at the near end (e.g., one, two, and three months at LIFFE) and long-lived options at the far end (up to three years at LIFFE). Early exercise is possible until the last Saturday of the option's life.

Contract sizes. At PBOT (Philadelphia, the first currency-option exchange), one NZD option contract gives the right to buy or sell NZD 62,500, a yen contract JPY 6,250,000, and so on. LIFFE offers USD 10,000 contracts (see figure 8.3) while the Eurex contracts mentioned in the *Neue Zürcher Zeitung* extract (figure 8.4) are for USD 100,000. One cannot trade fractions of contracts.

Exercise prices. The PBOT strike prices must be multiples of 1 USD cent (for NZD, EUR, or CAD options), of 5 cents for GBP options, and multiples of 0.01 cent for JPY options. With respect to the exercise prices being offered, options exchanges ensure that there are always contracts available with strike prices around the prevailing spot rate. Thus, as time elapses and the spot rate changes, options at different strike prices become available.

OTC traded options prices are shown daily in the financial press. The top part of figure 8.4 gives you an example of how a column from the *Neue Zürcher Zeitung* looks; they are pretty much the same across newspapers.

US DOLLAR / EURO OPTIONS

Underlying:

Codes and classification			
Mnemo	DEX	MEP	AMS
Exercise type	European	Unit	€

US Dollar / Euro Options

Unit of trading	100
Contract size	USD 10.000
Expiry months	1) Initial lifetime: 1, 2, and 3 months Cycle: all months 2) Initial lifetime: 6, 9 and 12 months Cycle: March, June, September and December 3) Initial lifetime: 3 years Cycle: September
Quotation	Euros per USD 100
Minimum price movement (tick size and value)	EUR 0.01 (= EUR 1 per contract)
Last trading day	Trading in expiring currency derivatives have the EuroFX rate as their settlement basis and ends at 13.00 Amsterdam time on the third Friday of the expiry month, provided this is a business day. If it is not, the previous business day will be the last day of trading.
Settlement	EuroFX rate contracts: Cash settlement, based on the value of the Euro / US Dollar rate set by EuroFX at 13.00 Amsterdam time. For DEX, the inverse value of the EuroFX Euro / US Dollar rate is used and rounded off to four decimal places.
Trading hours	9.00 – 17.25 Amsterdam time
Clearing	LCH.Clearnet S.A.
Option style	European style. Holders of long positions are not entitled to exercise their options before the exercise date.
Exercise	European
Last update	21/12/04

- **Trading Platform:** LIFFE CONNECT ®
- **Wholesale Service:** Prof Trade Facility

Figure 8.3.   Contract data for EUR/USD option (DEX) at LIFFE.
Source: www.euronext.com, accessed January 2007.

Example 8.5. The exchange rate is denoted by using the traders' convention, so "$/Fr" means "value of the (US) dollar in (Swiss) francs." The *Kassamittelkurs* in the header refers to the midpoint spot price for the exchange rate itself, at the time the options exchange closed; also shown is the contract size, and the units in which the option prices are expressed (Swiss centimes—*Rappen*, in Swiss German— or eurocents per unit of FC). Thus, at the close, you could buy a call on USD (100,000 per contract) that expires in September and with strike price of 1.2000 (CHF/USD), at 0.0260 CHF/USD. If you buy one contract, you pay $100,000 \times 0.0260 = $ CHF 2,600. Similarly, a June put with strike price 1.2750 is traded at 9.80 CHF/USD, which means CHF 9,800 per contract.

DIY Problem 8.1. Why is the June put so much more expensive than the September call? Using just your common sense, identify two obvious reasons. (*Hint.* Look at prices in the same column, and at prices in the same row.)

DEVISENOPTIONEN

Strike		Call			Strike		Put		
	Sep	Dez	Mar	Jun		Sep	Dez	Mar	Jun
$/Fr		Kassamittelkurs: **1.2235**						100,000 $; Rp/$	
1.2000	2.60	3.06	3.41	3.65	1.2000	0.62	2.23	3.56	4.71
1.2250	1.07	1.90	2.34	2.66	1.2250	1.59	3.53	4.97	6.18
1.2500	0.41	1.12	1.57	1.91	1.2250	3.42	5.23	6.67	7.89
1.2750	0.25	0.67	1.05	1.37	1.2750	5.57	7.27	8.62	9.80
€/Fr		Kassamittelkurs: **1.5781**						100,000€; Rp/€	
1.5750	2.60	3.06	3.41	3.65	1.5750	0.62	2.23	3.56	4.71
1.6000	0.23	0.37	0.47	0.53	1.6000	2.62	3.39	4.10	4.74
1.6250	0.22	0.25	0.30	0.34	1.6250	5.09	5.75	6.41	7.01
1.6500	0.21	0.23	0.26	0.27	1.6500	7.85	8.22	8.84	9.41
€/$		Kassamittelkurs: **1.2917**						100,000 $; Cent/$	
1.2750	2.74	4.01	5.12	6.02	1.2750	0.58	1.49	2.08	2.55
1.3000	1.02	2.61	3.73	4.66	1.3000	3.52	1.03	4.48	4.85
1.3250	0.42	1.63	2.66	6.54	1.3250	3.52	4.03	4.48	4.85
1.3500	0.26	1.01	1.87	2.66	1.3500	5.84	5.87	6.11	6.36

Quelle: UBS

Figure 8.4. Option prices in the *Neue Zürcher Zeitung.*

Currency Options	Call	Put
USD	3.0	2.1
CHF	0.5	0.6

At-the-money options, expressed as a percentage of the face value.

Figure 8.5. OTC ATM option prices in *De Tijd.*

8.2.2 Over-the-Counter Markets

Over-the-counter (OTC) options are written by financial institutions. These OTC options are more liquid than forward contracts: at any moment, the holder can sell them back to the original writer, who quotes two-way prices. Like forward contracts, OTC options are tailor-made. In the OTC market, you can pick a particular expiration date, contract size, and strike price. As a consequence, the bid–ask spread in the OTC market is higher than in the traded-options market. This sounds like the forward market, but there is one difference: while forwards come in all sizes, OTC options are wholesale-size only—a million USD or equivalent.

In OTC markets, most of the options are written at a strike price equal to the spot price of that moment ("at-the-money options"). Prices of at-the-money options are sometimes published as percentages of the underlying value. Figure 8.5 gives information on OTC options on USD, CHF, etc., against EUR, as published in Antwerp's *De Tijd* (translated from Dutch).

Example 8.6. In this example, an at-the-money call on 1 USD is trading at 3% of the face value. Thus, with a spot value of EUR/USD 0.832 48, this call costs 0.832 48 × 0.03 = EUR 0.024 974 4. Therefore, an at-the-money call contract on USD 1m would cost EUR 2,497.44.

The percentage notation is convenient because when spot rates change, at-the-money option prices remain proportional to the spot rate if, at least, the interest rates and the degree of uncertainty about the future exchange rate evolution are unchanged.

All the above relates to regular options—"cash" options on "cash" forex. There are also futures-style options on cash, and options on futures, and the combination. Let us consider these before we go on.

8.3 An Aside: Futures-Style Options on Futures

In this section we describe options on currency futures, forward-style options, and futures-style options on currency or on currency futures. These instruments sound more exotic than "cash" options, but are quite similar once you have figured out what they mean. They have been designed to facilitate both speculation and arbitrage across markets.

8.3.1 Options on Currency Futures

A call on a currency futures contract with strike price X gives the holder the right to establish, without additional cost, a long position in a currency futures contract with futures price X, while the writer must take the short side of the futures contract. Like any other futures contract that is initiated (or changes hands) at that time, this newly created futures contract is marked to market at the end of each day, starting with the day of exercising.

> **Example 8.7.** Think of a June NZD 62,500 futures contract currently trading at price 60 (cents/NZD). If you exercise a call with strike price 50 cents, you become the holder of an NZD 62,500 futures contract with a futures price of 50 cents (0.5 GBP/NZD). This contract, like any outstanding futures contract, can be sold immediately, and such a sales transaction then triggers a marked-to-market cash flow of $62,500 \times (0.60 - 0.50) = $ USD 6,250. If you hold on to the contract, the marking to market in the evening will be against 0.50, not the current price 0.60, so you still get $62,500 \times (0.60 - 0.50) = $ USD 6,250 extra, relative to an ordinary investors who buys at the current market price.

Thus, this option on a futures contract differs from an option on NZD itself ("on the cash") in the sense that its expiry value equals the difference between the strike and the *futures* price that prevails at the time of exercise of the option. If an option on a futures is a European-style option that expires on the same day as the futures contract, then the option on futures and on spot will have the same value. This is because at maturity the future price and the spot are the same, $\tilde{f}_{T,T} = \tilde{S}_T$ (convergence property); thus, an option on the "cash" and an option on a maturing futures contract produce the same payoff. However, if the expiration times of the option and the futures contract do not coincide, the payoffs from a standard call, $\mathrm{Max}(\tilde{S}_T - X, 0)$, and an option on the futures, $\mathrm{Max}(\tilde{f}_{T,T2} - X, 0)$, are no longer the same. The difference between the two payoffs is the basis, which is to some extent unpredictable. Therefore, when expiration times of the option and the futures contract differ, an option on the futures will be priced differently from an option on the cash.

Options on futures are attractive to professional option writers, who often hedge their risks in the futures markets. Such a futures hedge absorbs less cash than a spot hedge. Thus, if one is hedging in the futures market, it is more convenient to create options on the same underlying instruments.

8.3.2 Forward-Style Options

Long before the introduction of modern options in the 1980s, options were already traded in the Paris and Brussels forward stock markets. There was one difference, though: the premium is paid at expiry rather than at the time of initiation. Thus, such a *"premium affair"* was a forward-style option, that is, a forward contract on a modern (European-style) option. The buyer of such a forward-style option receives the option at T and, at that time, also pays the initially agreed-upon price. Immediately after receiving the option (and paying for it), the holder then decides whether or not to exercise the option. Here is a quaint example.

Example 8.8. You conclude a premium affair purchase on ten Petrofina stocks at $X = F_{t,T} = $ BEF 15,400 per share for a premium of BEF 380 per share. At time T, say two weeks later, you pay the option writer BEF $10 \times 380 = $ BEF 3,800, regardless of the stock's value. If, at T, the stock trades above 15,400, you also exercise the option and buy the ten stocks at 15,400.

Logically, then, the premium must be set equal to the price of a regular European-style option, grossed up with the normal time value, $r_{t,T}$.

8.3.3 Futures-Style Options

Futures-style options were first introduced on the London International Financial Futures Exchange (LIFFE). They are basically futures contracts where the underlying asset is the option. Thus, they differ from premium affairs in the same way that futures contracts differ from forward transactions. As we saw, with a premium affair, the entire premium is paid at expiry (T). In contrast, the payment for a futures-style option is partly in the form of daily marking to market, and the balance is paid at expiry. That is, when buying a futures-style option, you simply pay an initial margin (in interest-earning cash or by posting securities), and the agreed-upon price is paid later on—with a cash outflow each time the option price drops, a cash inflow each time the option price rises, and a final purchase at the expiry value of the option. The effect of marking to market is to reduce the risk of default relative to premium affairs.

Example 8.9. Suppose that you buy ten futures-style option contracts, each of size NOK 62,500 and with two days to go, at a premium of USD 0.021. In table 8.2, we

Table 8.2. A futures-style option.

Day	Price of option	Cash flows		
0	0.021	—		
1	0.030	Marking to market:		
		USD $10 \times 62{,}500 \times (0.030 - 0.021)$	=	USD 5,625
2	0.035	Marking to market:		
		USD $10 \times 62{,}500 \times (0.035 - 0.03)$	=	USD 3,125
		Buying the option:		
		$(-)($USD $10 \times 62{,}500) \times 0.035$	=	$(-)$USD 21,875
		Total: USD $10 \times 62{,}500 \times 0.021$	=	$(-)$USD 13,125

show the cash flows that arise when, one day later, the futures price of the option is 0.030 and when, at maturity, the price is 0.035 (which must be the intrinsic value of the option, as the option matures on day two). There are two marked-to-market *in*flows of 0.9 and 0.5 cents each (per NOK), and at the end you pay the exercises value, 3.5 cents. Thus, as with an ordinary futures contract, the buyer of a futures-style option pays, all in all, the initial price, $3.5 - 0.9 - 0.5 = 2.1$ cents per NOK. Of course, this crude summation ignores time value.

Futures being close to forwards, and forwards differing from cash contracts just with regard to timing of the payment of the premium, futures-style option premia should be equal to cash prices corrected for time value. So we do not need a separate pricing model for them.

A futures-style option is attractive to speculators. Consider an investor who thinks that calls are underpriced. He or she could buy a standard call (paying the premium) and hope to sell it later at a profit. However, the initial outlay required is even smaller if a futures-style option is bought. The hoped-for gain will then come in the form of inflows from marking to market until the time that the option position is reversed.

8.3.4 Futures-Style Options on Futures

Another financial claim is the futures-style option on a futures contract. When exercised, the option creates a long position in a futures contract with price X (which will trigger an immediate marked-to-market cash flow), but the agreed-upon option premium is paid "later on," partly through marking to market and partly at T through the final purchase of the option. The *Deutsche Terminbörse*, renamed Eurex since its merger with its Swiss counterpart, started futures-style options on futures contracts.

This option combines the advantages of options on futures and of futures-style options. Little capital is needed to open a position, and hedging the option in the futures market is easier when the instrument is written on the futures contract rather than on the cash. A futures-style option on futures, with futures and options expiring on the same date T, also facilitates arbitrage between European-style puts and calls, as we shall see when we discuss a relation called put–call parity.

All this should have provided enough background for a review of how options can be used. We discuss hedging and speculation, but first and foremost arbitrage applications.

8.4   Using Options (1): Arbitrage

There is an arbitrage opportunity if one can obtain, at a zero initial cost, a cash flow that is positive with a strictly positive chance, and never worse than zero. There is also an arbitrage opportunity if one can obtain, at a negative initial cost, a cash flow that is never worse than zero. Any such arb opportunity should be jumped at. Sadly, then, they disappear fast.

Let us denote American-style premia by C_t^{Am} and P_t^{Am}, reserving C_t and P_t for European-style options. Let us interpret the "comparable" forward contract as one with the same underlying, expiry day, and strike price. Let us also agree that all options are nondegenerate, in the sense that there is always some uncertainty about whether there will be exercising or not. Below we review some of the more obvious arbitrage applications you may be watching out for.[3] We start with calls.

1. Option premia are nonnegative. This is, of course, because the final payoff is, at worst, zero. If there is a positive chance of ending in the money, the option price should be positive too. This holds for puts and calls, whether European- or American-style:[4]

$$C_t > 0, \quad C_t^{\mathrm{Am}} > 0 \quad \text{and} \quad P_t > 0, \quad P_t^{\mathrm{Am}} > 0. \tag{8.2}$$

2. American-style options are worth no less than European-style ones. This is because they provide all the rights of European-style options plus the extra right of early exercise. This extra right can never have negative implications, and there is usually a positive probability that it may be used profitably.[5] Thus,

$$C_t^{\mathrm{Am}} \geqslant C_t > 0 \quad \text{and} \quad P_t^{\mathrm{Am}} \geqslant P_t > 0. \tag{8.3}$$

3. A European-style call is worth more than the comparable forward purchase. This is because, in the call, the possible negative payoff from a forward purchase is missing. The right to walk away from the option can never have

---

[3] Merton (1973) lists, all in all, twenty-three no-arbitrage bounds on option prices.

[4] For degenerate options with zero chance of ending in the money, the $\geqslant$ relations become equalities, and vice versa: zero option prices imply zero chance of returning into the money.

[5] The extra right has zero value if it is fully known that there is no rational early exercise. A famous case is the zero-interest currency or the nondividend-paying stock (see below). But even when the current interest rate is (close to) zero, there is still never 100% certainty that it will not go up later in the option's life.

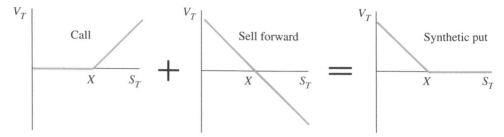

Figure 8.6.   Arbitraging with an underpriced call.

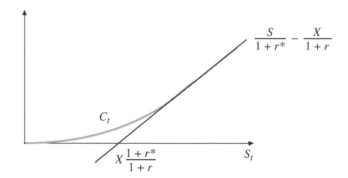

Figure 8.7.   Current call price as a function of the current spot rate.

negative implications, and there is usually a positive probability that it may be used profitably.[6] Thus,

$$C_t > \frac{S_t}{1 + r_{t,T}^*} - \frac{X}{1 + r_{t,T}}. \qquad (8.4)$$

Example 8.10. Suppose $X = 43.785$ cents, $S_t = 48$ cents, and $r_{t,T} = 0.02 = r_{t,T}^*$. Then a forward contract stipulating purchase at $X = 0.43785$ can be replicated at a cost $48/1.02 - 43.785/1.02 = 4.13235$ cents. (The first part, $0.48/1.02$, is the value of the FC PN, the second part the PV-ed HC bit of the replication). If you could buy a call at, say, 3.5 cents, you would pay less for a product that never pays out less and perhaps pays out strictly more. This represents an arb opportunity: you would sell the overpriced for 4.13 and buy the underpriced for 3.5, thus netting a positive inflow of 0.63 now *and* a nonnegative extra cash flow later.

As figure 8.6 shows, buying the call and selling forward means we are creating a synthetic put. If the call violates the lower bound, the cost of the synthetic put is negative, thus generating an arb opportunity.

Reassembling this along with earlier results we get

$$C_t^{\mathrm{Am}} \geqslant C_t > \mathrm{Max} \left(\frac{S_t}{1 + r_{t,T}^*} - \frac{X}{1 + r_{t,T}}, 0 \right). \qquad (8.5)$$

---

[6] The extra right has zero value in the degenerate case where it is fully known that there will be exercise; then the call is de facto a forward purchase.

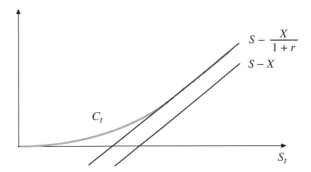

Figure 8.8. Current call price as a function of the current spot rate when $r = 0$.

The option price approaches the zero bound when the option is far OTM. ("Far" has to be read in statistical terms: many standard deviations.) The option price is close to the comparable-forward-purchase bound when the option is far ITM—so far that exercise has become almost certain and the call has become almost a forward purchase. In that case, the lower bound is quite high, of course. For more in-between cases, one expects the call price so be some smooth function of the current spot rate: it starts from its zero asymptote and slowly rises toward its comparable forward bound, as in figure 8.7.[7]

4. An American-style call is worth at least its intrinsic value.

Example 8.11. Suppose $X = 43$ (cents), $S_t = 48.785$ (cents), implying an intrinsic value of 5.785 cents. If the American-style option were trading at 4 cents, you could buy it and immediately exercise, thus netting 1.785 cent at no risk.

Thus,

$$C_t^{\text{Am}} \geqslant \text{Max}(S_t - X, 0) \stackrel{\text{def}}{=} \text{Intrinsic value.} \tag{8.6}$$

Note that there is no *strict* inequality. There can indeed be equality—notably if (and only if) there is a consensus in the market that early exercise is rational, or at maturity if the option is in the money.

There is an exciting implication for early exercise of American-style calls. Suppose the foreign rate of return is zero, as for the JPY in the early 2000s or for a nondividend-paying stock. Figure 8.8 shows that, in this case, bound (8.5) is tighter than bound (8.6): if the intrinsic value is positive, it is always below the value of the comparable forward contract. Now, the latter is a lower bound for American-style calls. The implication is that the value of an American-style call on a zero-interest currency can never fall as low as the intrinsic value. There is always time value—except at T, when $r_{T,T}^*$ drops to zero too. Thus, the call will never be exercised early, and the America-style call on a zero-interest currency is priced like its European-style counterpart.

We can quickly find the analogs of the last two constraints for puts.

---

[7] Such a smooth function is reasonable, but it cannot be proved in perfect generality. There may be strange distributions of S that induce jumpy option prices.

5. A European-style put is worth more than the related forward sale. Again, the right to walk away from the option can never pay off negative amounts, and there is a positive probability that it may add value.[8] So

$$P_t > \frac{X}{1 + r_{t,T}} - \frac{S_t}{1 + r^*_{t,T}}. \tag{8.7}$$

Reassembling this along with earlier results we get

$$P_t^{\text{Am}} \geqslant P_t > \text{Max}\left(\frac{X}{1 + r_{t,T}} - \frac{S_t}{1 + r^*_{t,T}}, 0\right). \tag{8.8}$$

In figure 8.9, we show how you would arbitrage in case of violation. Buying the (assumedly underpriced) put and selling forward means we are creating a synthetic call, and if the put violates the lower bound, the cost of the synthetic call is negative, thus generating an arb opportunity.

6. An American-style put is worth at least its intrinsic value. Otherwise you would buy one and immediately exercise. Thus,

$$P_t^{\text{Am}} \geqslant \text{Max}(X - S_t, 0) \stackrel{\text{def}}{=} \text{Intrinsic value}, \tag{8.9}$$

with an equality if (and only if) there is a consensus in the market that early exercise is rational, or at maturity if the option is in the money.

DIY Problem 8.2. Suppose the domestic rate of return is zero, as for the JPY in the early 2000s. Show that, in this case, bound (8.8) is tighter than bound (8.9), that is, bound (8.8) ensures that the put price never drops to its intrinsic value as long as the foreign return is positive. Show that this implies that the put should never be exercised early.

7. Put–call parity for European-style options. We have seen that you can create synthetic puts from calls and forwards, and synthetic calls from puts and forwards. We have just noted that, until now, the prices of these synthetic options should be positive, otherwise there is something wrong. But we can do more: the prices of synthetic options should also equal those of the directly traded options, otherwise there would still be an arb opportunity.

Formally, one way to get at the relation is to note that a portfolio consisting of a call and a short put always makes you buy, at time T: the call allows you to (happily) buy when $S_T \geqslant X$, and the short put forces you to (sulkily) buy when $S_T < X$. You can check this from figure 8.10, or from table 8.1, or from the one line of math below:

$$\underbrace{(\tilde{S}_T - X)_+}_{\text{Payoff E call}} - \underbrace{(X - \tilde{S}_T)_+}_{\text{Payoff E put}} = (\tilde{S}_T - X)_+ + (\tilde{S}_T - X)_- = \underbrace{\tilde{S}_T - X}_{\substack{\text{Payoff} \\ \text{forward} \\ \text{purchase}}}. \tag{8.10}$$

---

[8] The extra right has zero value in the degenerate case where it is fully known that there will be exercise; then the put is de facto a forward sale.

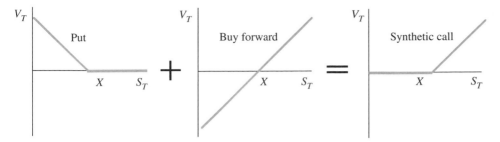

Figure 8.9. Arbitraging with an underpriced put.

The above says that one can reconstruct or replicate the future payoff from a forward purchase using European-style puts and calls. But, familiarly, if two portfolios have the same future payoff they must fetch the same price now, otherwise there would be an arbitrage opportunity. This equality is called *put–call parity*:

$$C_t - P_t = \frac{S_t}{1 + r_{t,T}^*} - \frac{X}{1 + r_{t,T}}. \tag{8.11}$$

Thus, if one type of option is too expensive relative to the other prices, you can start to arbitrage. For instance, if puts are in high demand because of a sudden panic, you can buy synthetic puts and then write the put itself.

Example 8.12. Suppose $X = 43.785$ cents, $S_t = 48$ cents, and $r_{t,T} = 0.02 = r_{t,T}^*$. Then a forward contract stipulating purchase at $X = 0.43785$ can be replicated at a cost $48/1.02 - 43.785/1.02 = 4.13235$ cents. Suppose that calls sell for 9 cents and puts for 6. Then put–call parity is violated: $9.00 - 6.00 \neq 4.13$. The put is too expensive, or the call too cheap, or both. So you buy the call at a cost of 9 and sell the forward contract for 4.13.[9] This means you hold a synthetic put at a cost of $9.00 - 4.13 = 4.87$. Then you sell a regular put to somebody else at 6. There is no risk because the synthetic put neutralizes the written put. So the only effect is that your bank account went up by $6.00 - 4.87 = 1.13$.

DIY Problem 8.3. Show, from put–call parity, the following results:

- bound (8.4) is implied by put–call parity and the positiveness of put prices;
- bound (8.7) is implied by put–call parity and the positiveness of call prices;
- at-the-forward puts and calls have the same value;
- at-the-money (ATM) calls are worth more than ATM puts if $r_{t,T}^* < r_{t,T}$;
- ATM calls are worth less than ATM puts if $r_{t,T} > r_{t,T}^*$.

(A simple way to remember these last results is as follows. If $r_{t,T}^* > r_{t,T}$, then the forward is below par: the risk-adjusted expectation is that the FC will fall. This means that the PV of the upward potential—the ATM call price—is

---

[9] You would actually replicate it: borrow the PV of FC1 and lend the PV of HC X.

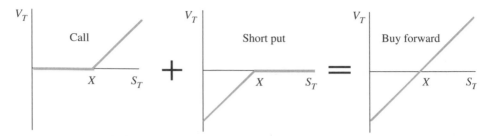

Figure 8.10. Call − put = forward. *Key:* Options being chopped-up forwards, you can combine a call and a written put into a replica of a forward purchase: via the call you (happily) buy when $S_T > X$, while via the written put you are forced to buy when $S_T < X$. The forward purchase itself is, of course, a portfolio of PNs. More generally, from the set of {put, call, FC PN, HC PN}, each subset of three instruments replicates the fourth instrument (see figures 8.6 and 8.9).

smaller than the PV of the downward potential—the ATM put price. Likewise, for a strong currency we have $r_{t,T}^* < r_{t,T}$ (a low foreign rate), and strong means that the ATM call—the upward potential—is worth more than the downward potential—the ATM put.)

8. Put–call parity for futures-style options on futures. Recall that forward-style options prices are equal to cash option prices increased by $r_{t,T}\%$ time value to correct for the delay in the payment. Recall also that futures prices are almost indistinguishable from forwards. If we add the superscript "f" to the usual P or C symbols to denote futures-style put and call prices, we get the following:

$$P_t^{\text{f}} = P_t \times (1 + r_{t,T}), \qquad\qquad (8.12)$$

$$C_t^{\text{f}} = C_t \times (1 + r_{t,T}). \qquad\qquad (8.13)$$

Now let us take the standard put–call parity equation for cash options, as repeated below, and multiply both sides by $(1 + r_{t,T})$ (line 2). Then we use the above relations for futures-style option prices as well as covered interest parity. We end up with a very simple parity relation between futures-style option premia, the current futures price, and the strike:

$$C_t - P_t = \frac{S_t}{1 + r_{t,T}^*} - \frac{X}{1 + r_{t,T}} \qquad ((8.11)\text{ repeated}),$$

$$\Longrightarrow \quad (C_t - P_t)(1 + r_{t,T}) = S_t \frac{1 + r_{t,T}}{1 + r_{t,T}^*} - X,$$

$$\Longrightarrow \quad C_t^{\text{f}} - P_t^{\text{f}} = f_{t,T} - X. \qquad\qquad (8.14)$$

For time-pressed traders, this is quite convenient as a no-arb relation, because no discounting is necessary; they can see at a glance whether prices are in line with each other. This simplicity is one (marginal) reason why Eurex and others prefer these options over the cash version.

Example 8.13. Suppose that you observe $f_{t,T} = 35$ and a price of 3 for a futures-style call on a futures contract at $X = 33$. The futures-style put price on a futures contract at $X = 33$ must equal 1, in order to satisfy the no-arbitrage condition $3 - P_t^f = 35 - 33$. If the actual futures-style put price differs from unity, arbitrage will take place until the prices of calls, puts, and futures are back in line.

This ends our (selective) review of arbitrage relations in options markets. Let us summarize some key results in this section as follows.

- With a market for European-style puts and calls, we can synthetically create forward contracts. Conversely, combining forward contracts and calls, we can replicate puts; and, from forward contracts and puts, we can synthetically create calls. Of course, forward contracts themselves are simply positions in domestic and foreign T-bills or PNs.

- From a practical perspective, this means that brokers (who trade at very low costs) will arbitrage between the direct (market) prices of options or T-bills and the prices for synthetic European-style options or T-bills. This is similar to the arbitrage arguments used in earlier chapters. The result of this arbitrage is put–call parity, equation (8.11).

- From a theoretical perspective, the implication is that there is no need for two option-pricing models—one for puts and one for calls. Put–call parity tells us that if we have a call-pricing model, the put-pricing model is implied.

8.5 Using Options (2): Hedging

In this and the next section, we study applications of options other than arbitrage, and we discuss their potential advantages relative to forward or futures contracts. The key advantage of an option is that, to the holder, it provides only the favorable part of the payoff of a comparable forward contract. Still, it would be unwise to go all dewy-eyed about options now. There are no free lunches: while the initial market value of a forward contract at $F_{t,T}$ is zero, an at-the-forward option has a positive price. More generally, the price of an option is always higher than the market value of the comparable forward contract, since the downside of the forward contract is eliminated in the case of options. A second advantage of options is they are more flexible instruments than forward contracts, whether they are used to hedge or to speculate on exchange-rate changes. This means that they can be used in cases where forward hedges make less sense or occasionally even no sense at all, as we shall see.

8.5.1 Hedging the Risk of a Loss without Eliminating Possible Gains

Options can be used to hedge long and short positions in foreign currency. We provide a few examples using the point of view of a U.S. corporation (USCO).

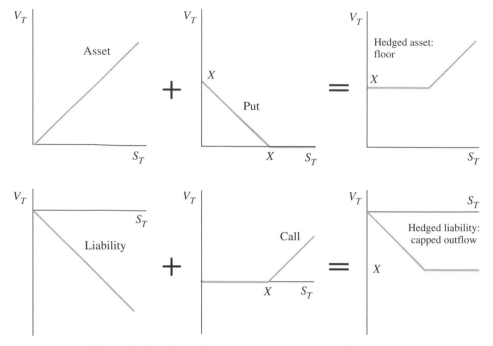

Figure 8.11. Hedging an asset or liability with options.

Example 8.14. Suppose that USCO has issued CHF promissory notes (thus, USCO is short foreign exchange). To hedge its position, the firm buys a call on CHF at $X =$ USD/CHF 0.8 expiring at the same date as the promissory notes. Then, the USD cost of paying back the CHF debt cannot be higher than USD/CHF 0.8, but it might be lower:

- If, at time T, the CHF trades above 0.8, USCO exercises its call and buys at 0.8.
- If $\tilde{S}_T < 0.8$, USCO simply buys its CHF spot and lets the call expire unexercised.

In contrast, if USCO had used a forward purchase at $F_{t,T} =$ USD/CHF 0.8, then it could not benefit from a possible lower value of the CHF. Bear in mind, though, that the forward purchase is free; the call is not.

So the downside risk on a foreign currency outflow can be hedged by a call: you get a floor on the value (see figure 8.11). The put option, by analogy, hedges the downside risk of a foreign currency inflow: the outflow is capped. This is shown in the figure and illustrated below.

Example 8.15. Suppose UKCO holds NZD assets (UKCO is long foreign exchange). To hedge itself, the firm buys a put on NZD at $X =$ GBP/NZD 0.4 expiring at the same date as the NZD asset. Then the USD proceeds from selling the NZD cannot be lower than GBP/NZD 0.4, but they might be higher:

- If, at time T, the NZD trades below 0.4, UKCO exercises its put and sells at 0.4.

- If $\tilde{S}_T > 0.4$, UKCO simply sells its NZD spot, and lets the put expire unexercised.

In contrast, if USCO had used a forward sale at $F_{t,T}$ = GBP/NZD 0.4, then it could not benefit from a possible higher value of the NZD. But remember that the forward purchase is free; the put is not.

8.5.2 Hedging Positions with Quantity Risk

In the above examples, we used options to hedge an assumedly risk-free cash flow denominated in foreign currency. One can also use options to hedge foreign currency cash flows that are not certain, that is, foreign currency cash flows that are conditional on other events. It is often claimed—not very convincingly, as we shall see—that options work better here. But let us first see what we are talking about. Examples where inflows or outflows may be uncertain include the following:

International tenders. The potential foreign exchange inflows may not materialize, notably when the firm contending for the contract loses the deal to another bidder. Thus, if this firm loses the contest but has already sold the potential foreign revenues forward, it is still obliged to fulfill the forward contract and therefore bears the *reverse risk*: it may need to reverse (close out) the contract early, and if so there might be a loss.

FC A/R with substantial default risk. If you hedge forward and the debtor does not pay, you again face a reverse risk.

International "deductible" reinsurance. AXA, a French insurance company, may reinsure its fire risk for the year 2008 with a Lloyd's syndicate, in the sense that all damage above a threshold (or *deductible*) of, say, EUR 100m will be covered by the London reinsurer. Clearly, the Lloyd's syndicate is exposed since it might have to pay out EUR if (and to the extent that) the insurance losses exceed EUR 100m. However, forward coverage is difficult. AXA's losses may not exceed EUR 100m; and, if they do, the extent by which the threshold is exceeded is uncertain.

Risky portfolio investment. If a Finnish investor covers the exchange risk of a U.S. stock portfolio position worth USD 100,000 by selling this amount forward, he or she may end up being overinsured (and short USD) if the U.S. stock market declines and her portfolio is worth only USD 75,000.

In each of the above examples, options are more flexible hedging devices than forwards and futures in the sense that the holder cannot be forced to exercise. This, brochures by banks would gush, is nice: if the expected flow does not materialize, there is no reverse risk because you do not *have* to deliver. Exercising is a right, not an obligation. Note, however, that options do not hedge perfectly the cash flows described in the examples above. The instrument is basically unsuited for this type of risk: its value is contingent on

Table 8.3. Options and forwards as hedges in an international tender.

Hedge strategy	$\tilde{S}_T$ outcome classes	Outcome of tender: Win the contract	Fail to win contract
Sell forward	$\tilde{S}_T \geqslant 0.80$	$\tilde{S}_T + (0.80 - \tilde{S}_T) = 0.80$	$0 + (0.80 - \tilde{S}_T) \leqslant 0$
	$\tilde{S}_T < 0.80$	$\tilde{S}_T + (0.80 - \tilde{S}_T) = 0.80$	$0 + (0.80 - \tilde{S}_T) > 0$
Buy a put	$\tilde{S}_T \geqslant 0.80$: Do not exercise	$\tilde{S}_T + 0 \geqslant 0.80$	0
	$\tilde{S}_T < 0.80$: Exercise	$\tilde{S}_T + (0.80 - \tilde{S}_T) = 0.80$	$0 + (0.80 - \tilde{S}_T) > 0$

the exchange rate, while the foreign cash flow is contingent on another event. Since an option's value has nothing to do with this other event, the hedge is far from perfect. If an option is purchased to hedge such a contingent cash flow, the exchange rate still affects the total cash flows because the company will rationally exercise an in-the-money option regardless of whether the other event was favorable or unfavorable.

Example 8.16. A Portuguese company submitted a CAD 1b bid in a tender to construct a hospital in Toronto. First, consider a hedge using a forward sale at $F_{t,T} =$ EUR/CAD 0.80. The firm's corresponding time-T cash flows, shown in the upper part of table 8.3, are derived as follows: if the company wins the contract, it earns CAD 1b, which is worth EUR $\tilde{S}_T$, while its forex revenue from the tender is zero if the contract is awarded to a competitor. The cash flows from the forward sale are $(0.80 - \tilde{S}_T)$, regardless of the outcome of the tender. Thus, the firm receives a combined cash flow of EUR 0.80 if it is awarded the contract, but has an unwanted open forward position if the contract goes to a competitor (implying reverse risk). This unwanted position leads to losses in the event that $\tilde{S}_T > 0.80$.

Hedging with a put option, on the other hand, generates the cash flows shown in the lower part of the table. The cash flows from the put option are $\mathrm{Max}(0.80 - \tilde{S}_T, 0)$, regardless of the outcome of the tender. We see that, even when an option is used to hedge the risk, the future spot rate still affects the cash flows because the company will exercise an ITM put even if it does not win the contract.

In the example, the put is a "good" hedge in the sense that it avoids having two bad events occur at the same time—not being awarded the contract *and* losing money on the forward sale (the uppermost cell in the column "Fail to win the contract"). However, it is not a perfect hedge. A "perfect" hedge (in the sense of eliminating all uncertainty) would be a forward contract conditional on the other source of uncertainty. In the tender example, this would be a conditional forward contract that becomes void if you lose the tender contract. Some government export agencies and banks do provide such *tender-to-contract* forward contracts (and even tender-to-contract options).

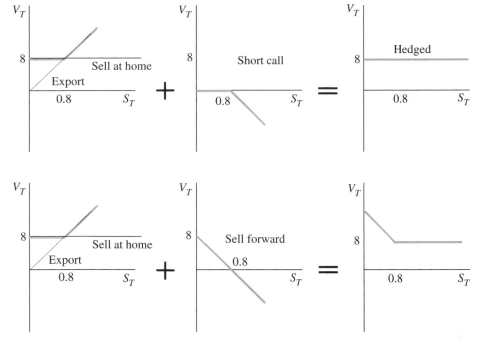

Figure 8.12. Boulinger du Clos's exposure to the dollar.

8.5.3 Hedging Nonlinear Exposure

The expiration values of the foreign currency debts and claims considered in section 8.5.1 were linear in the exchange rate; that is, they could be represented as straight lines on a diagram that plotted their home currency value against the future spot rate, $\tilde{S}_T$. The effect of unexpected exchange-rate changes on your financial affairs may not be that simple, though. In some cases, the cash flow you wish to hedge may be a nonlinear function of the exchange rate. In this case, a linear instrument like a forward contract is not an appropriate hedging tool. Options are often better suited to hedge nonlinear exposures because of their asymmetric payoff profiles.

Example 8.17. A French exporter of champagne, Boulinger du Clos Reims, expects to export 100,000 bottles to the United States next year, at USD 10 per bottle, net of costs. Alternatively, she can sell this wine at home, at EUR 8 per bottle, net. Thus, if the dollar is trading below EUR/USD 0.8, she would choose not to export at all, but would sell her wares at home. Her problem is that she needs cash now. Borrowing EUR is risky because, with her existing financial commitments, she may go bankrupt if she does not earn some extra cash from exports.

Selling a call option on USD 1m—100,000 bottles $\times$ 10 USD/bottle—with a strike price EUR/USD 0.8 and a market value of, for example, EUR 0.1 per USD will solve two problems for the French exporter. First, it brings in immediate cash, EUR 0.1 per USD or 1m$\times$0.1 = EUR 100,000 altogether. Second, it makes the exporter's cash flows independent of the exchange rate. To understand why there is no exchange-rate risk, we analyze how the original (unhedged) sales revenue depends on the exchange rate:

- If the rate is below EUR/USD 0.8, each bottle is sold at home for a price of EUR 8; thus, the entire inventory is worth $100,000 \times 8 = $ EUR 800,000.
- For higher rates, a bottle is worth EUR $[10 \times \tilde{S}_T]$, since it would be exported and sold at USD 10 net; thus, with high exchange rates, the inventory is worth EUR $100,000 \times 10 \times \tilde{S}_T$.

The payoff schedule is shown in figure 8.12, on the left, as the kinked thicker line. The alert reader will already have noticed that this schedule is the same as the profile for an EUR 800,000 T-bill plus a call on USD 1m, struck at $X = 0.8$. Thus, selling a call contract on USD 1m with the same strike price, $X = $ EUR/USD 0.8, offsets the exchange risk of the inventory value exactly. The new profile, after writing the call option, is shown as the straight flat line—a fully hedged result.

In contrast, suppose Ms. Boulinger borrowed EUR 100,000 instead of issuing options for the same value, and suppose she hedged the expected sales revenue by selling forward USD 1m. Hedging with a forward sale would only have changed the payoff schedule from a "gain when $\tilde{S}_T$ is high" profile to a "gain if $\tilde{S}_T$ is low" picture, rather than eliminating the uncertainty created by exchange risk. That is, rather than being in trouble when there are no exports, Ms. Boulinger would be in trouble when there are exports.[10] This is shown in the lower part of the figure.

Thus, the firm's option to export is similar to a call; and writing a call against the potential export revenue means that we "sell" the uncertain future gains for immediate cash.

By analogy, your customer's option to buy imported goods is like you being the writer of a put.

Example 8.18. The unimaginatively named Danish wool trader DanskWool faces potential competition from Australia. If there are no imports from Australia, the Danish price of wool will be DKK 100 per unit, and DanskWool's inventory will be worth DKK 100 per unit. Australian competitors sell at a roughly fixed net price of AUD 25 (including expenses like transportation costs and tariffs). The Australians will enter the Danish market as soon as the exchange rate drops below DKK/AUD 4, and then DanskWool will have to lower prices in step with the competitors' translated DKK price, $25 \times \tilde{S}_T$. The trader's position can be summarized as follows:

- for $\tilde{S}_T < 4$, one unit of wool will be worth $25 \times \tilde{S}_T$;
- for $\tilde{S}_T \geqslant 4$, the value of wool is DKK 100.

If you plot this payoff as we did in the previous example, you will discover that one unit of wool is like a DKK 100 bond, minus a put on AUD 25 (that is, you implicitly wrote a put on AUD 25) with strike price $X = 4$. Thus, buying a similar put should

---

[10] Recall that the first solution brings in cash from selling the put—more than the cash you would get from selling forward at 0.80 if 0.80 is not the current forward. (Why?) This extra cash for the first solution is not shown in the picture.

Table 8.4. DanskWool's exposure to the Australian dollar.

$\tilde{S}_T =$	3	3.2	3.4	3.6	3.8	4	4.2	4.4	4.6	4.8	5
Wool price	75	80	85	90	95	100	100	100	100	100	100
25 puts on AUD	25	20	15	10	5	0	0	0	0	0	0
Wool + puts	100	100	100	100	100	100	100	100	100	100	100

eliminate the exposure. Table 8.4 shows the relevant figures in a table rather than in a graph. The bottom line shows that the portfolio of inventory and puts has a combined value that is independent of the future spot rate, $\tilde{S}_T$. That is, the exposure to the exchange rate is perfectly hedged.

From the above examples, we see that nonlinearities in the firm's future cash-flow schedule may stem from competitive threats or price pressures that become active for only a certain range of exchange rates. The examples are artificially simple, in the sense that perfect price takership holds—the champagne exporter can sell any desired amount at an exogenous market price—and there is no other uncertainty. In chapter 13, entirely devoted to exposure modeling and measurement, we shall, however, argue that, in general, the HC cash flow from foreign operations is unlikely to be proportional to the spot rate if the exchange rates affect your business via things like competitive threats or price pressures. That is, there is usually a nonlinear relation between exchange rates and HC cash flow, even though the relation is rarely as simple as the examples we have looked at here. But even then, options are useful, as we shall see, because a portfolio of options with different strikes and quantities can produce an arbitrarily close piecewise linear approximation to any nonlinear relation you can think of.

In the next example, the source of the nonlinearity is a financial contract.

Example 8.19. A U.S. company issued bonds giving the holder, at maturity T, the choice between USD 10,000 or NZD 20,000. If the holder is a U.S. investor, he or she would most naturally view such a bond as a USD 10,000 bond plus a call on NZD 20,000 at $X = $ USD/NZD 0.5. That is, the investor gets paid USD 10,000, but has the right to exchange the USD 10,000 for NZD 20,000. The option (the right to choose) is clearly with the bondholder—thus, the issuing company has written the option. The company can hedge against potential losses by buying a call that offsets the implicit call it has written.

DIY Problem 8.4. Show that you can also look at this as an NZD 20,000 bond plus a put, held by the bondholder, on NZD 20,000 at $X = 0.5$. Then link the two descriptions of the bond via put–call parity.

The more general statement is that any nonlinear payoff function of S_T can always be approximated by a piecewise-linear function, which in turn can be perfectly replicated by a portfolio of options. Figure 8.13 shows you a smooth

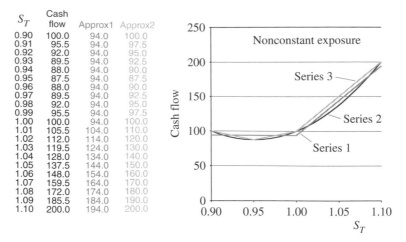

S_T	Cash flow	Approx1	Approx2
0.90	100.0	94.0	100.0
0.91	95.5	94.0	97.5
0.92	92.0	94.0	95.0
0.93	89.5	94.0	92.5
0.94	88.0	94.0	90.0
0.95	87.5	94.0	87.5
0.96	88.0	94.0	90.0
0.97	89.5	94.0	92.5
0.98	92.0	94.0	95.0
0.99	95.5	94.0	97.5
1.00	100.0	94.0	100.0
1.01	105.5	104.0	110.0
1.02	112.0	114.0	120.0
1.03	119.5	124.0	130.0
1.04	128.0	134.0	140.0
1.05	137.5	144.0	150.0
1.06	148.0	154.0	160.0
1.07	159.5	164.0	170.0
1.08	172.0	174.0	180.0
1.09	185.5	184.0	190.0
1.10	200.0	194.0	200.0

Figure 8.13. Approximating a nonlinear function using options.

function and two alternative piecewise-linear approximations, one with just one kink and one with two kinks. Finding the replicating option positions is easy enough from the tabulated versions of the graph.

DIY Problem 8.5. Show that the one-kink version can be replicated by (i) an HC PN with face value 94, and (ii) a call on FC 1,000 with $X = 1$.
  Show that the two-kink version can be replicated by (i) an HC PN with face value 100; (ii) an FC loan with future value FC 250; (iii) a call on FC 250 with $X = 0.95$; and (iv) a call on FC 750 with $X = 1.00$.

8.6 Using Options (3): Speculation

In all of the applications considered so far, the objective has been to reduce the uncertainty arising from changes in the exchange rate. Options can also be used to speculate in exchange markets. Recall that we have defined this as follows: someone acts as a speculator if (i) he or she disagrees with the market's perceived probability distribution function for an asset's future value, and (ii) he or she is willing to back up the dissident opinion with money (that is, buying the "underpriced" asset and selling, or short selling, the "overpriced" asset). The alleged mispricing provides enough extra expected return to justify giving up diversification.

8.6.1 Speculating on the Direction of Changes

Buying puts (calls) is a convenient way of speculating on decreases (increases) in the exchange rate. Options require only a limited investment and imply, in the worst case, the loss of the premium paid up-front. It should be added, in fairness, that the probability of losing the premium is typically quite high. In fact, for an at-the-money option, the probability of losing the entire investment is approximately 50%—and most investors would not describe an investment as low-risk if it has a 50% chance of total loss of value. But selling or buying forward is even worse: with about a 50% chance it can lead to losses that can be quite big rather than limited to the premium paid. In addition, as we saw in the preceding chapter, a speculative uncovered forward transaction is likely to absorb substantial financial resources in the form of margin that must be posted.

Put writing can also be used to speculate on a rise in the exchange rate, and call writing is a way to speculate on a depreciation. In each case, the writer collects the premium up-front and hopes that the option will expire unexercised. Misleadingly, such strategies are often said to "generate income" or "increase the return on the portfolio." In fact, writing options is issuing a liability, like risky debt—debt which, with about 50% probability, will trigger cash outflows at a later date, depending on what the exchange rate turns out to be at maturity. Obviously, when a company issues debt it would not call the proceeds "income" in the sense of being parts of profits. Rather, the proceeds should be on the balance sheet, booked against the liabilities that were issued. This is also the way you should think about options: put them among the liabilities, and do not book any profit until the options have expired.

But options are especially popular for speculation on risk.

8.6.2 Speculating on Changes in Volatility

In the above, the speculator essentially disagreed with the market's expectations about the currency's future value as reflected in the current spot and forward rate. It is, however, possible to agree about the expected value but disagree about the standard deviation (volatility) of the time-T exchange rate. That is, one might think that the market underestimates by how much the exchange rate may move—whether up or down. To capitalize on this belief, a strategy is needed that pays off when the exchange rate moves by a large amount irrespectively of whether the movement is up or down. The option strategy that allows one to speculate on the volatility of the exchange rate is to go long both the call and the put. This option strategy is called a *straddle* if both options have the same strike price, or a *vertical combination* (or *strangle*) if the call's strike price is different from the exercise price of the put.

The logic of the straddle is obvious from its payoff diagram in figure 8.14. The holder makes large gains for any large change in S_T, whether it be positive or negative. Of course, the speculator has to pay the premia for the put and for the call. However, since the market thinks that the movement of S_T is likely to be small, the price charged for the options is quite low, in the speculator's opinion. In short, the investor thinks that puts as well as calls are undervalued and, accordingly, buys both of them.

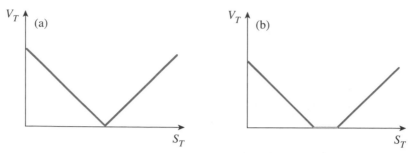

Figure 8.14. Straddles and strangles: (a) long straddle; (b) long strangle.

Example 8.20. Assume that the future exchange rate $\tilde{S}_T$ can take on the possible values shown below, together with the corresponding values of a put and a call at $X = 10$. We then specify two probability distributions—one as viewed by the market, and one that reflects your beliefs. The two distributions have the same mean, $E(\tilde{S}_T = 10.00)$, but yours (subscript "u") has a higher variance than the one viewed by the market (subscript "m"):

If	$\tilde{S}_T =$	9	9.5	10	10.5	11
then	$\tilde{C}_T =$	0	0	0	0.5	1
and	$\tilde{P}_T =$	1	0.5	0	0	0
Pr_m		0.0	0.2	0.6	0.2	0.0
Pr_u		0.1	0.2	0.4	0.2	0.1

We compute the expected expiration value of each option over each set of probabilities by simply multiplying each possible (nonzero) payoff by its probability and summing. The market's expectation and your view of the payoff from the call and the put are, respectively:

$$E_m(\tilde{C}_T) = 0.0 \times 0.2 + 0.0 \times 0.6 + 0.5 \times 0.2 = 0.10,$$

$$E_u(\tilde{C}_T) = 0.0 \times 0.1 + 0.0 \times 0.2 + 0.0 \times 0.4 + 0.5 \times 0.2 + 1.0 \times 0.1 = 0.20,$$

$$E_m(\tilde{P}_T) = 0.5 \times 0.2 + 0.0 \times 0.6 + 0.0 \times 0.2 = 0.10,$$

$$E_u(\tilde{P}_T) = 1.0 \times 0.1 + 0.5 \times 0.2 + 0.0 \times 0.4 + 0.0 \times 0.2 + 0.0 \times 0.1 = 0.20.$$

Your expectations of the expiration values are higher because you assign larger probabilities to extreme payoffs, and because extreme payoffs on the upward (downward) side add value to the call (put). True, the options can end much farther out of the money too, but that does not matter: a "big" zero is still just a zero. That is, the value effect comes from the asymmetry, the convexity, and this holds for both puts and calls. Therefore, you believe that the market underprices both options. You buy both a put and a call option because you do not know about the direction of the price change. With a put and a call, you gain whichever way the spot rate moves, as long as the change is sufficiently large. Or you could hold the option until the market realizes that uncertainty is indeed higher, at which point the options' market values should rise; then you cash in.

By analogy, you short both the call and the put if you think that the market overestimates the volatility, and therefore overprices all options. In that case, your strategy would be to write both options (the short straddle or the short vertical combination). Thus, options markets allow one to speculate on volatility, that is, on the likely absolute size of exchange-rate movements, rather than just on the likely directions of changes. Speculation on volatility is not possible using forward contracts.

8.7 CFO's Summary

We first briefly review the key topics and results; then we proceed to the issue of whether options are really as expensive an many managers seem to think.

One important insight is that a currency option, being the right to buy or sell a known amount of foreign currency at an agreed-upon price, is a much more flexible instrument than a forward or futures contract. The payoffs of various "European-style" option positions (long or short the call, long or short the put) can be viewed as the favorable or unfavorable parts of the payoffs from forward positions. Specifically, option writers take on the negative-payoff part of a forward transaction, while the holders obtain the positive part of the payoff. Puts give the payoffs when the spot rate is below the strike price, while calls represent the payoffs when $\tilde{S}_T$ is above X. One implication of this is that forward contracts can always be used to convert a European-style call into a European-style put, and vice versa. This replication argument leads to the conclusion that the prices of both types of European-style options must be related (put–call parity).

Obviously, in order to convince the writer of an option to take over the unfavorable side of a forward contract, the holder has to pay the writer an up-front premium. Once an option has been bought, it can always be sold in the secondary market. Its market price can never drop below zero. Nor can the price drop below the value of a comparable forward contract. The holder of the option is prepared to pay the premium because the option acts as an insurance contract; that is, one can obtain insurance against the possible depreciation of a foreign currency by buying a put, while a call option offers insurance against a possible appreciation. Thus, when options are used to hedge linear exposures, they eliminate the possibility of a loss but not the potential gain, and when options are used as speculation devices, they limit the potential for losses. Options are also more appropriate when the exposure to be hedged is nonlinear, or when the objective is to speculate on the absolute size of exchange-rate changes. American-style options, lastly, can also be exercised before their expiration dates, which adds to the flexibility of the hedging or speculative strategy.

Are options too expensive for the advantage they offer? There is a fairly widespread view among managers that this is the case. Much of that, I think, is based on misunderstandings. Let us see why.

One possible response is to think of the most expensive option, one that is very deep in the money. Such an option is de facto almost a forward contract, and nobody would think that this would be mispriced or outrageous.

Example 8.21. Suppose a Slovenian firm has a USD receivable of 1m, 90 days. The standard deviation over that horizon might be 10%, so a 30% ITM option is deep in the money. Let the spot rate be EUR/USD 0.80 and the effective rates 1% (EUR) and 1.2% (USD), respectively. A put struck at $X = 0.80 \times 1.30 = 1.04$ would be worth approximately

$$P_t \approx \text{PV}(1.04 - \tilde{S}_T) = \frac{1.04}{1.01} - \frac{0.80}{1.012} = 0.239\,189. \qquad (8.15)$$

This is expensive compared with a regular forward contract, which is free. But a regular forward sale is at $F_{t,T} = 0.80 \times 1.01/1.012 = 0.798\,419$, not 1.04, and any sane manager should see that the premium paid is a fair compensation for the extra received 90 days from now.

But the critical CFO may fail to be convinced by the above example: it has no meaningful uncertainty, and perhaps the perceived overcharging is about the uncertainty—the chance that the option will die out of the money and the probability-weighted expected value in the money. It surely is a fact that, for an ATM option, there is a roughly 50% chance that the option will expire unused. Does that mean that the premium paid was wasted? Most companies do take fire insurance, where the chance that the premium was paid "in vain" is much higher than 50%; yet, when on December 31 the CFO notes that the plant has not burned down, the typical reaction is not that "we were unlucky again—paid insurance for nothing." Why does one feel differently about options, all the more since for ordinary insurance contracts the "load" (the extra paid over and above the expected payoff) is much larger than for options? Of course, part of the answer is that a major fire is not just a financial loss: it affects operations, it puts at risk the customer base, and so on. But if you feel that forex losses, if any, are just minor financial items without impact on the operations, then this is an argument that hedging per se adds no value, as we have seen; it is not an argument against hedging per se, and surely not an argument against hedging with options instead of forwards.

Perhaps the reason why options are considered expensive is the bid–ask spread. This is, percentage-wise, way above what you see in forward markets, but there are good reasons. First, in option markets the spread is measured as a percentage of the premium rather than of the strike. If the commission plus half the spread for a retail forward contract of USD 100,000 is EUR 125, this is 1/8th of 1%. But in the above example of the deep-ITM option, the option's midpoint price would be $100,000 \times 0.239 = 23,900$ euros, and the same commission would already seem to amount to $125/23,900 = 0.52\%$.

Recall also that this is a very expensive option, being deep ITM; as a fraction of a much cheaper ATM option premium, the percentage would become a few times larger again. In addition, a regular around-the-money option needs to be hedged dynamically, and in reality such hedging is always imperfect and, therefore, risky; in contrast, a forward can be hedged statically and perfectly. So a bank may be justified in not being happy with just an EUR 125 fee. For small transactions, bid–asks are of the order of percentages, not basis points as in forex markets, for all these reasons. But, I repeat, this is still small beer to what your fire, car, or health insurer is charging.

Lastly, the feeling that options are expensive just reflects a lack of insight in the pricing and, therefore, a feeling that the bank may be ripping you off. A nice ploy may be to ask for bid *and* ask prices, and judge the spread. An alternative is to try and understand option pricing. See the next chapter. There surely is, occasionally, a lack of basic insight. Here is an example based on a mail I received from a friend in East Asia, one of whose customers was entirely overlooking the effect of time on time value.

Example 8.22.

To: piet.sercu@econ.kuleuven.be
Subject: Option value
From: boooooooo
Date: Thu, 13 Jul 2006 16:49:51 +0800

Dear Piet,
For the past few days, one of clients called me asked me about option value on the valuation report we provided upon their request. It was not easy to make him understand because he hardly knows about derivatives. It was an OTC European call option whose strike price is 15,000 and expires 9 months later starting from 16 Nov, 2005. The spot price was 10,000 at 31 Dec, 2005, but had risen to 12,000 by 30 Jun, 2006. Using B-S I valued the option at a lower price than initially. The client asked me why the value has decreased in absolute amount even though the price has risen by 2,000. The client's logic was that the option value should be increased in absolute amount because the price has risen and therefore the probability to exercise the option has increased. He had entirely overlooked time value.

The option-savvy reader will have noted that time to maturity has shrunk from 7.5 months to 1.5, which means that the conditional variance of $\ln \tilde{S}_T$ shrinks to one fifth of the original value, *ceteris paribus*. Thus the effective volatility drops to $\sqrt{1/5} = 0.447$ of its original value. The result is that the option is now more standard deviations OTM than originally. To show this I use, below, an original effective sigma of 25%, but you can check that any other number preserves the ranking of the standardized log *moneyness*:

$$\frac{\ln 10{,}000 - \ln 15{,}000}{0.25} = -1.62 \text{ (old) versus now,} \tag{8.16}$$

$$\frac{\ln 12{,}000 - \ln 15{,}000}{0.447 \times 0.25} = -2.00. \tag{8.17}$$

So the chance of ending ITM is down. Of course, this is not the sole determinant of value, but it is a big one.

Mistakes like the one above will be avoided if we understand basic option pricing. So that is what we will turn to in the next chapter.

TEST YOUR UNDERSTANDING

Quiz Questions

True–False Questions

1. The only difference between European-style and American-style options is that European-style options are traded only in Europe while American options are traded only in the USD.

2. The buyer of an option has an obligation to purchase the underlying asset in the case of a call, or sell in the case of a put, while the seller of an option has the right to deliver in the case of a call, or take delivery in the case of a put.

3. A put offers the holder of an asset protection from drops in the underlying asset's value, while a call provides protection from an increase in the underlying asset's price.

4. The intrinsic value of a call is its risk-adjusted expected value.

5. The immediate exercise value of an option is its value alive.

6. If a call's strike price exceeds the spot rate, the call is in the money.

7. If an in-the-money put has positive value, its value is based purely on time value.

8. A European-style call will always be at least as valuable as a comparable American call.

9. An option is always at least as valuable as the comparable forward contract.

10. Put–call parity implies that puts and calls written at the forward rate will have different values because, if the foreign interest rate exceeds the domestic rate, the forward rate is at a discount; therefore, the exchange rate is expected to depreciate, making the put more valuable.

11. Speculators disagree with the market's probability distribution function for an asset's value; that is, they sell assets that the market perceives as overvalued and buy assets that the market perceives as undervalued.

Multiple-Choice Questions

The exercises below assume that the put and the call both have a strike price equal to *X*, a domestic T-bill has a face value equal to *X*, and both a foreign T-bill and forward contract pay off one unit of foreign currency at expiration. All instruments expire on the same date.

1. A forward sale can be replicated by:
   (a) selling a put and buying a call;
   (b) selling a foreign T-bill and buying a domestic T-bill;
   (c) buying a put and selling a call;
   (d) both (b) and (c);
   (e) all of the above.

2. A put can be replicated by:
   (a) buying a call and selling foreign currency forward;
   (b) buying a foreign T-bill and selling a call;
   (c) buying a domestic T-bill, selling a foreign T-bill, and buying a call;
   (d) both (a) and (c);
   (e) all of the above.

3. A call can be replicated by:
   (a) buying foreign currency forward and buying a put;
   (b) buying a foreign T-bill and selling a put;
   (c) buying a put, selling a domestic T-bill, and buying a foreign T-bill;
   (d) all of the above;
   (e) none of the above.

Additional Quiz Questions

Use the data in table 8.5 to answer questions 1–4.

1. What is the last quote for an April call option on GBP with a strike price of 155?

2. What is the last quote for a May put option on NZD with a strike price of 58?

3. What is the last quote for a June put option on JPY with a strike price of 93½?

4. For the options below, what is the intrinsic value? Is the intrinsic value greater than, less than, or equal to the option premium?
   (a) June call on GBP with a strike price of 150.
   (b) May put on GBP with a strike price of 147½.
   (c) April call on NZD with a strike price of 59.
   (d) June put on NZD with a strike price of 59.
   (e) May call on JPY with a strike price of 93.
   (f) May put on JPY with a strike price of 94.

Table 8.5. Data from the *Wall Street Journal* of Tuesday, March 22, 1994.

Option and underlying	Strike price	Call–Last Apr	May	Jun	Put–Last Apr	May	Jun
31,250 British pounds–cents per unit							
148.61	147½	r	r	r	0.95	1.80	r
148.61	150	0.60	r	1.85	r	r	r
148.61	155	0.07	r	0.57	r	r	r
148.61	157½	0.03	r	r	r	r	r
62,500 New Zealand dollars–cents per unit							
59.04	58	1.08	r	r	0.35	0.65	0.90
59.04	58½	0.79	r	1.35	0.46	r	1.13
59.04	59	0.51	0.80	1.02	0.80	1.10	1.40
59.04	59½	0.35	r	r	r	r	r
6,250,000 Japanese yen–100ths of a cent per unit							
94.18	93	r	r	r	r	r	1.29
94.18	93½	r	r	r	0.72	r	r
94.18	94	r	r	r	r	1.41	1.68
94.18	94½	0.81	r	r	1.12	r	r

r, not traded; s, no option offered; last is premium (purchase price).

5. You hold a foreign exchange asset that you have hedged with a put. Show graphically how the put limits the potential losses created by low exchange rates, without eliminating the potential gains from high rates.

6. You have covered a foreign exchange debt using a call. Show graphically how the call limits the potential losses created by high exchange rates, without eliminating the potential gains from low rates.

7. Assume that the contracts discussed below are described with the GBP as the home currency and that the option's expiration date matches the expiration date of the cash flow to be hedged. Illustrate how the exchange rate affects the GBP value of:

   (a) an NZD 500,000 accounts receivable and a purchase of ten puts each worth NZD 50,000 with a strike price of GBP/NZD 0.42;

   (b) a JPY 10,000,000 accounts payable and a purchase of ten calls each worth JPY 1,000,000 with a strike price of GBP/JPY 0.0067.

Applications

1. The Danish wool trader in section 8.5.3 faces potential competition from Australian producers.

   (a) Graphically analyze the value of the trader's inventory as a function of the future spot price.

   (b) Explain why a put on AUD eliminates the dependence of the inventory's value on the exchange rate for DKK/AUD.

2. The U.K. firm Egress Import-Export Ltd sells its goods at home for P_b when the value of the EUR is low. As the value of the EUR increases, it starts exporting its goods at the foreign price (net of costs) P_a, netting it $P_a \times \tilde{S}_T$.

   (a) Illustrate the value of Egress's goods as a function of the future spot price.

   (b) How can Egress eliminate its exposure to the EUR (that is, sell its potential EUR profits)?

3. The Thailand Plettery Steel Company has a debt of NZD 100,000, which is repayable in twelve months. Plettery's controller Jane Due is having trouble sleeping at night knowing that the debt is unhedged. The current THB/NZD exchange rate is 20, and p.a. interest rates are 21% on THB and 10% on NZD. Jane is considering a forward hedge (at $F_{t,T} = 20 \times 1.21/1.10 = 22$), but a friend tells her that he recently bought a call on NZD 100,000 with $X = 20$, and is willing to sell it to her at the historic cost, THB 1 per NZD or THB 100,000 for the total contract. What should she do?

4. Assume that the interest rates are 21% and 10% p.a. in Thailand and Switzerland, respectively. Consider a call and a put at $X = $ THB/CHF 21.

   (a) What is the lower bound for European-style options with lives equal to $T-t = $ one year, six months, three months, one month, when $S_T = 18, 20, 22, 24$, respectively?

   (b) If $S_T = 20$, $r_{t,T} = 0.21$, $r_{t,T}^* = 0.10$, a one-year call with $X = $ THB/NZD 20 priced at 1 is undervalued. Show that, with this call price, we can buy a synthetic put at a negative price.

5. A charitable organization has issued a bond that gives the holder the option to cash in the principal as either USD 10,000 or NZD 20,000. This asset can be viewed as a USD 10,000 bond plus a call on NZD_T 20,000 at $X = 0.5$ GBP/NZD.

   (a) Can the bond also be viewed as an NZD bond plus an option?

   (b) Explain how the two equivalent views are just an application of put–call parity.

   (c) The strike price, $X = $ GBP/NZD, is the natural way of quoting a rate for a U.S. investor. But buying NZD 20,000 at GBP/NZD 0.5 is the same as selling USD 10,000 at $X' = $ NZD/USD 2. This way of expressing the transaction makes more sense to a German investor. Restate the conditions of the bonds using this NZD/USD strike price, and give two possible interpretations of the option from a German investor's point of view.

6. The software giant Kludge Systems has issued a bond that gives the holder the choice between USD_T 10,000, NZD_T 20,000, and GBP_T 5,000. Can Kludge's bond be replicated using simple options?

7. You have purchased a zero-coupon EUR bond that gives you the choice between EUR 100,000 at $T_2 = 2$ or EUR 90,000 at $T_1 = 1$.

   (a) What options (put and/or call) are implicit in this bond? (*Hint.* There are two correct descriptions.)

   (b) Show that the two equivalent views of this instrument are an application of put–call parity.

8. The lower bound on a nondegenerate American-style put (that is, a put where there is still some uncertainty about whether $\tilde{S}_T > X$ or not) is

$$P_t^{\text{Am}} > P_t > \frac{X}{1 + r_{t,T}} - \frac{S_t}{1 + r_{t,T}^*}.$$

Assume that $S_T = 0$ and $r_{t,T} = 0$. Common sense says that you should exercise the put, since the exchange rate cannot fall any further. Yet the bound $P_t > X$ says that the put should trade above its intrinsic value. Where is the fallacy?

9. A *cylinder* option on the sale of foreign currency is a contract defined as follows:

   • If $\tilde{S}_T < X_1$, you sell foreign exchange at X_1, the floor.

   • If $\tilde{S}_T > X_2$, where $X_2 > X_1$, you sell at X_2, the cap.

   • If $X_1 \leqslant \tilde{S}_T \leqslant X_2$, you sell at $\tilde{S}_T$.

This contract restricts the uncertainty about the futures sales price to the range $X_1 \leqslant \tilde{S}_T \leqslant X_2$.

For instance, Barrel Imports has a sales contract to sell CAD against USD:

   • at $X_1 = $ USD/CAD 0.80 if the CAD trades below 0.80;

   • at $X_2 = $ USD/CAD 0.90 if the CAD trades above 0.90;

   • the spot rate if that rate is between 0.80 and 0.90.

   (a) Show the payoff of the contract graphically.

   (b) Show that it can be viewed as a combination of European-style options.

   (c) Illustrate the value of a foreign currency claim hedged with such a contract.

9

Currency Options (2): Hedging and Valuation

In the preceding chapter we described options and their possible applications. We know that the buyer of an option has to pay a premium, but we have not yet explained how this premium is set, nor how one can judge whether or not a quoted price is fair, nor how the writer can keep the risk of selling options within bounds. In this chapter we address these issues. We adopt a relatively simple approach, the *binomial option-pricing model* as developed by Cox et al. (1979) on the basis of ideas by, for example, Sharpe (1978). But toward the end we do link the results to the model of Black, Merton, and Scholes (Black and Scholes 1973; Merton 1973) as it was applied to currency options by Garman and Kohlhagen (1983) and Grabbe (1983). For completeness I also mention a curiously ignored paper by Samuelson and Merton (1969) that already contained the familiar BMS formula, and related work by Rubinstein (1976) and Brennan (1979), which is utility-based. This works in discrete time (like the binomial model) but with prices drawn from a continuous distribution (as in the continuous time model).

In the binomial option-pricing model, time is discrete rather than continuous, and asset prices are drawn from a very restricted discrete scale. Specifically, the model assumes that, given the current level of the exchange rate, there are only two possible values for the exchange rate next period: "up" and "down." The exchange rate cannot stay constant. The one-period binomial model, attributed to Sharpe (1978) and Rendleman and Bartter (1980), was later extended by Cox et al. (1979) to a multiperiod setting capable of valuing options on dividend-paying stocks and American stock options.

This binomial assumption may appear rather restrictive. However, the distribution of the total return (after many of these binomial price changes) becomes close to bell-shaped, and the binomial option-pricing model converges to the celebrated Black–Merton–Scholes option-pricing model. In this sense, the binomial model gives us an understanding of what goes on in the more complicated Black–Merton–Scholes model for European options. Even better, the binomial approach is much more accessible in the sense that simple math suffices and it is relatively easy to interpret all results. This is one reason why we do most of our analysis of currency option pricing with the simple binomial model.

This approach is also used to value more complex derivative financial contracts than European-style options, and even real (operating) options that arise in capital-budgeting problems. Analytical solutions are rare except for very basic options, so most of the time we need numerical techniques. The binomial model allows you to do that yourself, with just a spreadsheet; no need to hire outsiders or get acquainted with special software to solve partial differential equations. In short, the binomial model is useful not only as a way of understanding the Black–Merton–Scholes model for simple European-style options, but also in itself, as an accessible model for the pricing of complex options.

We will take the model to a general n-period version. Cox et al. then take the limit for $n \to \infty$ and arrive at the Black–Merton–Scholes equation. We will omit that step, but we still look at that famous equation and we figure out where the terms come from and how they relate to the binomial model. In this way you can understand the BMS model without having to suffer the agony of going through the formal proof.

The structure of this chapter is as follows. In section 9.1 we present, from various angles, the no-arbitrage arguments underlying the binomial approach in the context of valuing a call option one period before maturity. We also interpret the binomial approach as one based on risk-adjusted expected values. In section 9.2, we introduce our notation and the assumptions underlying the multiperiod binomial model. Section 9.3 then extends the single-period-call pricing model to multiple periods, and in section 9.4 we indicate how this approach ultimately leads to the Black–Merton–Scholes valuation formula. How the binomial model can be used to value European contingent claims other than calls is the issue of section 9.5; we notably consider other European-style options and American-style variants.

9.1 The Logic of Binomial Option Pricing: One-Period Problems

Binomial option pricing can be explained from two points of view, using either a replication approach or a hedging approach. Both the replication and the hedging can be done either in forward markets or in spot markets (using domestic and foreign money-market positions). Since you are familiar with forward contracts and since using forwards simplifies the math and the logic substantially, we shall focus on replication and hedging in the forward market. We then conclude this section with an interpretation of option pricing in terms of risk-adjusted probabilities and certainty equivalents of the future spot exchange rate.

Both the hedging and the replication approaches are illustrated by the following numerical example. Consider a call on 1 USD against Sri Lanka rupees, the home currency, with strike price X = LKR/USD 105. The current (time-0) spot rate is S_0 = LKR/USD 100. Assume the domestic (LKR) risk-free return is

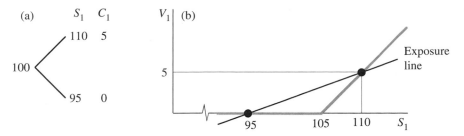

Figure 9.1. Valuing a call struck at 105: binomial model. (a) The (very simple) event three. (b) The two possible outcomes ($S = 95$, $V = 0$) and ($S = 110$, $V = 5$) are shown on the graph. These are the sole possible outcomes, and it does not matter whether they are viewed as points on the standard kinked payoff schedule for a call option or as points on the line through them.

5% per period and the USD risk-free return is 3.9604%. With these data, the one-period forward rate is LKR/USD 101:

$$F_{0,1} = S_0 \frac{1 + r_{0,1}}{1 + r_{0,1}^*} = 100 \frac{1.05}{1.039\,604} = 101. \tag{9.1}$$

We assume that from the current spot rate, the exchange rate can "branch out" either to the up-level 110 or to the down-level 95 at time 1.[1] Immediately after this change in the spot rate, the call expires. In figure 9.1, we show the binomial tree for the spot price changes—a tree that, in a single-period model, has only two branches. We also include the expiration values of the call that correspond to each of the possible time-1 exchange rates.

An equally useful way to show the possible pairs of exchange rates and call values is to plot the future call values against the corresponding future exchange rates (figure 9.1(b)). The graph shows the two possible outcomes as two points, through which we have drawn a straight line (labeled "Exposure line"). The slope of this line, which we call the option's exposure, can be computed as

$$\text{Exposure} = B_0 = \frac{5 - 0}{110 - 95} = \frac{5}{15} = \frac{1}{3}. \tag{9.2}$$

B gets a time subscript because it will change over the option's life as soon as we go to more periods. Exposure measures the relative sensitivity of the future call price with respect to the future exchange rate. In this sense, it is related to the notion of a (partial) derivative of C_1 with respect to S_1, holding constant all other data.

9.1.1 The Replication Approach

In this section, we show how the payoff of an option can be replicated in the forward market. We then invoke the law of one price—two assets or portfolios

---

[1] Typically, the up- and down-levels are taken to be each other's inverse, like ×1.1 for up and ×1/1.1 for down. This is just for computational speed and mathematical convenience, though; the binomial logic works for any pair of future rates. We take numbers that are easy to handle.

Figure 9.2. Replicating the call. In a two-situation world, replicating the call is the same as replicating the linear payoff that runs through these two points, which is easily done.

with the same payoff must have the same price—to infer the price of the option from the value of the replicating portfolio.

As indicated in figure 9.2, the payoff from the call—[5 if $S_1 = 110$] and [0 if $S_1 = 95$]—can be replicated by a forward purchase of 1/3 USD and an LKR PN with time-1 face value 2. To verify this numerically, simply compute the payoffs at time $T = 1$ from this portfolio in each of the two possible exchange-rate "states":

- if $S_1 = 95$, the portfolio pays off $(1/3) \times (95 - 101) + 2 = 0$, and
- if $S_1 = 110$, the portfolio pays off $(1/3) \times (110 - 101) + 2 = 5$,

which are indeed identical to the payoffs of the call in each of the two possible states. To rule out arbitrage opportunities between two items with identical payoffs, the call must command the same price as the replicating portfolio. Now the time-0 cost of the replica is just the initial value of the PN: while in principle we need to add the time-0 cost of the forward position, that particular expense item amounts to zero. The initial cost of the replica can then be calculated as LKR $2/1.05$ = LKR 1.905, so that we must have $C_0 = 1.905$ too.

9.1.2 The Forward Hedging Approach

We have just seen how the call, in a binomial world, has the same payoffs as a forward purchase of USD 1/3 and an LKR PN worth LKR 20 at time 1. More generally, we choose a risk-free investment and a forward position such that

$$\text{Forwards} + \text{PN} = \text{Call}.$$

The hedged version of the binomial model tells the story slightly differently. It rearranges the above into

$$\text{Call} - \text{Forwards} = \text{PN},$$

meaning that we can make the call risk free. This is convenient because, at the moment of hedging, the hedged and unhedged versions have the same market value and because a risk-free portfolio is easy to price. In short, we resort to a trick already pointed out in chapter 4: valuing the hedged asset instead of the unhedged one.

The above two equations show that the replication and hedge stories are two sides of the same coin. This is why we see the same numbers pop up in

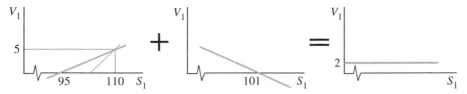

Figure 9.3. Hedging the call. In a two-situation world, hedging the call is the same as hedging the linear payoff that runs through these two points, which is easily done.

both stories. You should detect this in the following do-it-yourself exercise: the hedged call is worth 2 no matter what the rate does.

DIY Problem 9.1. So we should be able to hedge the call by selling forward 1/3 units of foreign currency. We verify this numerically: what is the hedged call worth if $S_1 = 95$ and if $S_1 = 110$?

Thus, the call's payoff has become risk free. The hedging procedure is shown in figure 9.3. The graph reproduces the call's exposure line with, as we know, a slope of 1/3. The forward sale of 1/3 of foreign currency is represented by its payoff line with slope $-1/3$, and zero expiration value if $S_1 = F_{0,1} = 101$.[2] Of course, the portfolio with the call and the forward hedge is risk free, since their slopes, $+1/3$ and $-1/3$, offset each other.

If the portfolio containing the call and the forward contract is paying a risk-free 2, in an arbitrage-free market this portfolio must be priced exactly like an LKR PN with future value 2, that is, at LKR 2/1.05 = LKR 1.905. Finally, at time 0 the call must be worth the same as its hedged version, because the initial market value of the forward hedge is zero. We conclude again that $C_0 = 1.905$.

9.1.3 The Risk-Adjusted Probability Interpretation

If the valuation of the option had been asked as a class assignment, the first question that would have come up almost surely would have been, "What is the probability of the up outcome?" Then, perhaps, "What is the beta?" or, more generally, "How do we find the required return?" These are indeed the questions that need to be answered if one values the call as an expected future value discounted at an appropriate rate. Apparently, however, we do not need that information to value the call: it must be worth 1.905, as we have just shown. The truth is that this value does rely on probabilities and risk correction, but implicitly so. In this section we want to make this explicit. Notably, we will interpret the binomial arbitrage approach as one that implicitly computes the call's risk-adjusted expected payoff (or certainty equivalent) from a risk-adjusted probability hidden in the forward rate and incorporates both the

---

[2] It does not matter that, in our binomial example, S_1 will never actually be 101. What matters is that the payoff is $-(1/3) \times [110 - 101]$ if the spot exchange rate goes up and $-(1/3) \times [95 - 101]$ if the exchange rate goes down. A line with slope $-1/3$ that crosses the S_T-axis at $S_T = 101$ produces these payoffs.

true probabilities and the required risk correction. The call's current value is then obtained by discounting the certainty-equivalent payoff at the risk-free rate. Let us see how this works.

We know from chapter 4 that the forward rate is a risk-adjusted expectation. In a binomial model, a regular expectation of the spot rate would be computed from the (true) probability p of the exchange rate moving up as follows:

$$E_0(\tilde{S}_1) = p\, S_{1,\text{up}} + (1-p)\, S_{1,\text{down}}. \tag{9.3}$$

Since the only parameter in a binomial model is the probability of a price rise, the only way we can adjust for risk is by correcting that probability p. That is, a risk-adjusted expected value must be based on a risk-adjusted probability of an "up." Let us denote this risk-adjusted probability by q. By definition, then, the certainty-equivalent value of the future spot rate, $\text{CEQ}_0(\tilde{S}_1)$ is

$$\text{CEQ}_0(\tilde{S}_1) = q\, S_{1,\text{up}} + (1-q)\, S_{1,\text{down}}. \tag{9.4}$$

While it may be very interesting to know how q relates to p and to possibly other relevant variables, we do not need to understand all this if our purpose is to price options; all we need is a number. And, in fact, once we observe the forward rate, we can infer the risk-adjusted probability q that was implicitly used by the market. In our example, the forward rate is 101, so the implied risk-adjusted probability is

$$
\begin{aligned}
q:\quad 101 &= q \times 110 + (1-q) \times 95 \\
&= 95 + q \times (110 - 95),
\end{aligned}
$$

$$\implies\quad q = \frac{101 - 95}{110 - 95} = 0.40. \tag{9.5}$$

DIY Problem 9.2. How does this q react to differences in forward prices? Compute the q if the forward rate had been lower or higher:

If $F_{0,1} = \ldots$	96.5	99.5	102.5	105.5	108.5
then $q = \ldots$					

Let us return to the example where q equals 0.40. The next logical step is that the risk-adjusted probability of observing $[S_1 = 110]$ is also the risk-adjusted probability that the call will end up worth 5: $[S_1 = 110]$ and $[C_1 = 5]$ are one and the same event, in the sense that $C_1 = 5$ if and only if $S_1 = 110$. Similarly, the downstate event $[S_1 = 95]$ is the same as the event $[C_1 = 0]$. In short, the risk-adjusted probabilities for the asset should also be valid for the call. So the risk-adjusted expected value of the call must be

$$\text{CEQ}_0(\tilde{C}_1) = 0.4 \times 5 + (1 - 0.4) \times 0 = 2. \tag{9.6}$$

This number should ring a bell. This 2 is indeed the value of the hedged call. Since hedging costs you nothing, the call's payoff and the hedged call's payoff are equivalent (in the sense of having the same value): you can switch from either to the other at no cost. So our guess that the q-weighted expected value is a CEQ turns out to be correct.

So we now have the call's expected future value, corrected for risk. (Note how clever this is: by using the forward rate as our source of information, we use all risks that the market thinks are relevant. This not only saves time but also avoids any errors that would have been made if we had chosen a model and estimated its parameters.) The present value is then obtained by discounting this risk-adjusted expected value at the risk-free rate:

$$C_0 = \frac{2}{1.05} = 1.905. \tag{9.7}$$

We conclude that a one-period call option can be valued in three steps:

(i) Extract the risk-adjusted distribution from the forward rate.

(ii) Compute the risk-adjusted expected value of the call, $CEQ_0(\tilde{C}_1)$.

(iii) Discount this CEQ at the risk-free rate.

In short,

$$C_t = \frac{q_t \times C_{t+1,\text{up}} + (1 - q_t)C_{t+1,\text{down}}}{1 + r_{t,t+1}}, \tag{9.8}$$

where

$$q_t = \frac{F_{0,1} - S_{t+1,\text{down}}}{S_{t+1,\text{up}} - S_{t+1,\text{down}}}.$$

The intellectually curious reader can find the (short) formal proof in technical note 9.1.

9.1.4 American-Style Options

All our results have been about European-style options. You might think that, in a one-period setting, there is no room for early exercise. But that is not quite true: an American-style option can also be exercised at time 0. Let us see how this can be handled.

Let us make the LKR/USD call at $X = 105$ American-style. The only additional choice an American-style option offers, in a one-period problem, is whether to exercise now (*kill the option*) or do it later. We have all the elements for that decision:

- Value *dead*: if we exercise now, we get the intrinsic value, which is zero.
- Value *alive*: the PV of possible later exercise, we know, is 1.905.

So we wait. This option is worth 1.905 just like the European one.

So with American options we always compare the values dead and alive, and then choose the value-maximizing strategy.

Two closing remarks are in order. First, we can compare the value alive to the intrinsic value instead of the value dead, as many textbook prescribe. True, the value dead can be negative while the intrinsic value never is, by definition; but in a case with negative value dead the market value is still zero or positive, so it does not matter whether you compare it with the value dead or the intrinsic value. The second remark is that the value alive is the PV of later exercise. But note that "later" and "at expiration" are no longer the same as soon as we leave the one-period framework: if the option gets far enough ITM later in its life, it could still be exercised early at that moment, which would affect its value then and also, therefore, all earlier PVs. In short, in a multiperiod setting the value alive is not usually the same as the value of the European option; this would be true only in two-date problems like the one above.

Multiperiod hedging and pricing is the topic of the following sections. Our first task is to introduce our general notation and assumptions.

9.2 Notation and Assumptions for the Multiperiod Binomial Model

9.2.1 The Standard Version of the Binomial Model

In a multiperiod extension of the binomial model, we shall use two additional assumptions, the first of which relates to the risk-free interest rates.

Assumption 9.1. *The risk-free one-period rates of return on both currencies are constant.*

For simplicity of notation, we therefore drop the cumbersome time subscripts used in the preceding chapters. That is, we simply write r and r^* rather than $r_{t,t+1}$ and $r^*_{t,t+1}$.

The next assumption has to do with the size of the up and down movements. We assume that the up-moves are always by the same percentage, and similarly for the down-moves. That is, the "tree" of possible future exchange rates is *multiplicative* rather than *additive*. The (multiplicative) up factor, u, will denote unity plus the percentage change upward; in our previous example, u was 1.1 (such that $S_{1,\text{up}} = 100 \times 1.1 = 110$). The (multiplicative) down factor, d, likewise denotes unity plus the return in the downstate; in the example, d was 0.95 (such that the price $S_{1,\text{down}} = 1,000 \times 0.95 = 95$).

Assumption 9.2. *The multiplication factors u and d that drive the jumps are constant over time.*

The assumption of constant interest rates is also present in the Black–Merton–Scholes model, and the assumption of constant multiplicative u and d corresponds to the Black–Merton–Scholes assumptions of (i) no sudden devaluations or revaluations or other discontinuities in the exchange rate process, and (ii) a constant variance of the period-by-period percentage changes in the exchange rate. It has two further implications, derived below: q is constant, and $\tilde{S}_n$ approaches a lognormal.

Implication 9.3. *The risk-adjusted probability, q, is constant over time.*

In the short proof below we start from our earlier solution for q, equation (9.5); then we feed into that formula the covered interest parity relation, and we write the up- and down-rates as S_0 times u or d; lastly, we simplify:

$$q = \frac{F - S_{1,\text{down}}}{S_{1,\text{up}} - S_{1,\text{down}}} \tag{9.9}$$

$$= \frac{1}{S_0 u - S_0 d}\left(S_0 \frac{1+r}{1+r^*} - S_0 d\right)$$

$$= \frac{1}{u - d}\left(\frac{1+r}{1+r^*} - d\right). \tag{9.10}$$

In a generalized version we should have added time subscripts to q, r, r^*, u, and d; but if the terms on the right-hand side are all constants, then so is q. This of course speeds up the calculations in numerical applications, and increases the chances of finding reasonably digestible analytical solutions.

Actually, we know more about q than that it is constant.

Proposition 9.4. *In an arb-free world, q is strictly between 0 and 1.*

To see this, start from another no-arb result: in equilibrium we must have

$$S_{1,\text{down}} < F_{0,1} < S_{1,\text{up}}. \tag{9.11}$$

For instance, if the two possible exchange rates are 95 and 110, the forward rate must be somewhere in-between. We show this by contradiction. If the forward rate were below 95—say, 94.5—we would all buy forward gigantic uncovered amounts at 94.5, and, at time 1, sell the FC for at least 95 (and, with a bit of luck, even 110). Likewise, if the forward rate were above 110—say, 111—we would all sell forward enormous uncovered amounts at 111, and, at time 1, buy the promised FC for no more than 110 (and, with a bit of luck, even 95). Either situation would represent an arb opportunity. Thus, the relations in (9.11) must indeed hold.[3]

The implication of relation (9.11) is that q is always between 0 and 1, as one would expect from a probability, even a risk-adjusted one. This can be seen immediately from equation (9.9): its numerator is strictly positive, and smaller than its denominator (which itself is of course positive).

Assumption 9.2 has another corollary.

Implication 9.5. *The distribution of all possible exchange rates after a large number of small jumps is lognormal.*

To see this, first think of a somewhat simpler conceivable binomial random walk, the *additive process*. In that case, every jump is a constant amount added or subtracted—say, 10 cents up or down instead of 10% up and down from

---

[3] In a binomial model, strict equality of F to the up or down value is possible if and only if that value will materialize with certainty. For instance, $F = 95$ must signal that there is zero chance to observe $S_1 = 110$, otherwise there would be an arb opportunity. By ruling out the equalities we assume that there is genuine uncertainty.

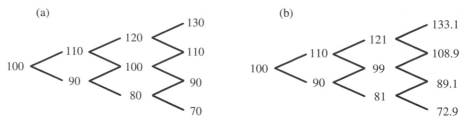

Figure 9.4. The (a) additive and (b) multiplicative process.

the previous value (figure 9.4). Think of a large number of small jumps. The final value then equals the initial value plus n changes, each of which is an independent random drawing always from the same distribution:

$$\tilde{S}_n - S_0 = \tilde{\Delta}_1 + \tilde{\Delta}_2 + \cdots + \tilde{\Delta}_n, \quad \text{where } \tilde{\Delta}_i = \begin{cases} U & \text{with chance } p, \\ D & \text{with chance } 1-p. \end{cases} \tag{9.12}$$

The central limit theorem (CLT) then says that the distribution of the right-hand side, being the sum of many small i.i.d. random variables, approaches a Gaussian or normal.

Now think of the *multiplicative process* instead. In that case we are compounding multiplicative changes:

$$\tilde{S}_n = S_0 \times \tilde{x}_1 \times \tilde{x}_2 \times \cdots \times \tilde{x}_n, \quad \text{where } \tilde{x}_i = \begin{cases} u & \text{with chance } p, \\ d & \text{with chance } 1-p. \end{cases} \tag{9.13}$$

The CLT does not apply to this expression because the theorem is about sums not products; but we can easily transform our expression into sums by taking logs on both sides:

$$\ln \tilde{S}_n = \ln S_0 + \ln \tilde{x}_1 + \ln \tilde{x}_2 + \cdots + \ln \tilde{x}_n,$$

$$\text{where } \ln \tilde{x}_i = \begin{cases} \ln u & \text{with chance } p, \\ \ln d & \text{with chance } 1-p. \end{cases} \tag{9.14}$$

Thus, the *log* of $\tilde{S}_n$ equals the initial log-value plus a sum of many small i.i.d. changes. This makes the log of $\tilde{S}_n$ normally distributed. A variable whose log is normal is called *lognormal*. Thus, additive processes lead to normality, multiplicative ones to lognormality.

9.2.2   Does the Model Make Sense?

Why does the literature prefer lognormals over normals? One reason is that, while the assumption of a constant distribution of percentage changes is far from realistic, the alternative of constant additive changes in cents is even worse. A jump by one cent up or down from a level $S = 10$ is very different from a similar change if the level has drifted down to $S = 0.5$ or up to 100. If we have to choose between the two, we prefer the percentage story.

A second (and closely related) point is that the additive can drift to zero or even below zero, which makes little sense for stocks[4] and none whatsoever for exchange rates. Third, the inverse of an exchange rate is also an exchange rate—the FC value of HC 1. Now if you invert all numbers in the additive tree of figure 9.4, the resulting tree is no longer additive; so this introduces a disconcerting asymmetry into the model: if the USD/EUR rate is normal, the EUR/USD rate is not. In contrast, the log of an inverse is just minus the log of the original: $\ln(1/S_n) = -\ln S_n$. So if $\ln \tilde{S}_n$ is normal, then so is $-\ln \tilde{S}_n$. If the USD/EUR rate is lognormal, then so is the EUR/USD rate.

DIY Problem 9.3. Show that the inverse of a normal is so *ab*normal that its expected value is undefined. (*Hint.* The expected value of the inverse is computed, in principle, by listing all possible values, inverting them, and then computing their probability-weighted sum. But one of the possible values is ... , and its inverse is ... , so ....)

Still, the choice between lognormals and normals is rather like identifying the lesser of two evils. Even the multiplicative process is far from perfect. First, in reality, there is mean reversion toward the PPP rate: one cannot imagine one country becoming infinitely more expensive than another. So exchange rates are not quite the aimlessly drifting variables one gets from the binomial. True, in the short run—and especially when the current PPP deviation is not outrageous—the mean-reversion feature is very weak. But one should not really trust the model for the pricing of long-run options or long-run real options,[5] an application of option theory to investment analysis, where horizons are years rather than months or weeks: the standard model would substantially overestimate the uncertainty about faraway exchange rates and, therefore, overprice all options.

The second issue concerns the other "i" of i.i.d.—identical distributions. Mean reversion induces changes in the expected percentage change, but this is a minor problem in the short run, as we said. The worse problem has to do with volatility. In reality, uncertainty is not constant: it changes over time, with a big random component but with traces of autocorrelation and mean reversion. This feature is entirely overlooked in the standard model. The implication is that the basic hedging policy, as shown above and extended below, only provides coverage against unexpected changes in the exchange rate at constant volatility, but not against changes in volatility.

Example 9.6. After the 1985 G5 meeting, where joint efforts were announced to bring down the dollar, the dollar initially remained stable. But option prices nevertheless all went through the roof: the market felt very uncertain about what would

---

[4] At a pinch we could think of unlimited-liability shares as the ultimate underlying processes, and treat limited-liability shares as derivatives.

[5] "Real options" refer to operational flexibility in real investments, like the options to postpone, expand, shrink, mothball, or close down early. In capital budgeting (NPV analysis), valuing these options might be quite important.

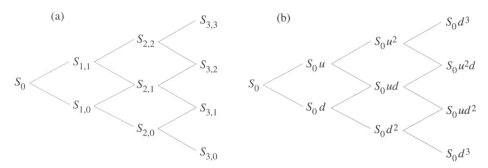

Figure 9.5.   Notation for the binomial tree.

happen next. All option writers that had applied just the standard delta hedge and thought they were immunized lost badly.

Better models, where risk is also risky, are available nowadays; but the basic version remains very valuable to our understanding of the logic of this way of pricing. This is why we proceed with the i.i.d. case.

9.2.3   Further Notation

Lastly, let us introduce the notation for the exchange rate process. In this chapter, we give the exchange rate process, $\tilde{S}$, two subscripts. The first one is a time subscript and shows the number of periods (or price changes) since time 0, while the second one shows how many of these changes were "up." A three-period process is shown in figure 9.5. For example, to get to node (1,1)— every place where the tree is branching out is called a *node*—the exchange rate must increase. Thus $S_{1,1}$ equals S_0 times the up factor. To reach node (2,2), the exchange rate has to rise again, so that its value at node (2,2) equals $S_{1,1} \times u = (S_0 \times u) \times u = S_0 u^2$. Note also that an "up" followed by a "down" leads to the same value as a "down" followed by an "up." For example, if, starting from S_0, the exchange rate increases first (to $S_0 \times u$) and then falls (to $S_0 \times u \times d$), the time-2 level is the same as it would be if the exchange rate had first decreased (to $S_0 \times d$) and then increased (to $S_0 \times d \times u$). That is, the tree is *recombining*.

DIY Problem 9.4.

- Suppose that the rate jumps five times. The initial rate is 100, u is 1.01, and d equals 0.99. Compute the six possible rates by letting j, the number of ups, go from 0 to 5.
- Suppose the initial rate is S_0, the number of jumps n, of which j were up and $n - j$ down. Write $\tilde{S}_n$ as a function of S_0, n and $\tilde{j}$: $S_{n,j} = \ \ldots \ $.

One implication of the fact that there are two ways to get to node (2,1) is the probability of the outcome $[\tilde{S}_2 = S_{2,1}]$ is higher than the probability that $\tilde{S}_2$

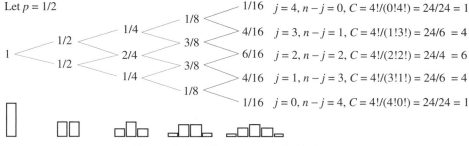

Let $p = 1/2$

1/8 ⟶ 1/16 $j = 4, n - j = 0, C = 4!/(0!4!) = 24/24 = 1$

4/16 $j = 3, n - j = 1, C = 4!/(1!3!) = 24/6 = 4$

6/16 $j = 2, n - j = 2, C = 4!/(2!2!) = 24/4 = 6$

4/16 $j = 1, n - j = 3, C = 4!/(3!1!) = 24/6 = 4$

1/16 $j = 0, n - j = 4, C = 4!/(4!0!) = 24/24 = 1$

Figure 9.6. The emerging bell-shape.

assumes one of the extreme values. More generally, the central values in the tree are always the more likely outcomes because more paths end centrally than deep in the tails.

Example 9.7. To get to node (3,2) we need two up changes and one down. The exchange rate at node (3,2) accordingly is $S_{3,2} = S_0 u^2 d$. There are three ways to arrive at this node: the drop could come at time 1, or at time 2, or at time 3. In contrast, there is only one way to arrive at node (3,3): we need three consecutive rises.

DIY Problem 9.5. How many ways are there to end in $S_{3,1}$? $S_{3,0}$? What is the probability of ending in $S_{3,j}, j = 0, \ldots, 3$, if the probability of an up is 0.5?

The relative popularity of the central outcomes is, of course, the reason why, if you let the branching-out process go on for many periods, the resulting distribution for the time-n value of the exchange rate becomes reasonably bell-shaped, whether normal or lognormal. You can verify this by reviewing your statistics textbook, and examining how the probabilities evolve with an increasing number of steps. For example, if the probability of an up equals 0.5, the probabilities evolve as shown in figure 9.6. With only four changes, a bell-shaped distribution is already emerging.

Thus, the multiperiod binomial model quickly gets us very close to the bell-shaped distributions observed in practice. But how does one set the factors u and d?

9.2.4 How to Choose u and d

In a nutshell, u and d are chosen so as to match a target standard deviation for the change in the log exchange rate over the option's life. For instance, you may feel that the standard deviation over three months is 0.05 (5%).[6] How to set u and d to achieve this amount of risk at the end of the tree? Of course, the answer to this question depends very much on n, the number of periods into which the three-month horizon is subdivided. Nowadays one chooses $n = 100$

---

[6] Recall that the change of a log is reasonably close to a simple percentage change, unless changes are really big. So it makes sense to think of standard deviations as a percentage.

or more, but that decision depends on the speed of your computer, the time pressure, and the degree of closeness to BMS (the limit for $n \to \infty$) you want.

The target volatility, 5% over one quarter, is usually expressed as an annualized figure, called *volatility*. A year is four quarters; an annual change is the sum of four quarterly changes; and the variance of a sum of four i.i.d. changes is four times the variance of one single quarterly change. Thus, taking square roots, the p.a. volatility is $\sqrt{4} = 2$ times the target volatility, meaning 10%. So we want to phrase the question as: how do we set u and d such that it generates an effective standard deviation of

$$\hat{\sigma} := \text{Target standard deviation} = \sigma_{\text{p.a.}} \times \sqrt{T - t}? \qquad (9.15)$$

Example 9.8. Suppose you have in mind a standard deviation of 6%, effective, over four months (1/3 year). This is annualized into $0.06 \times \sqrt{3} = 10.39\%$. Conversely, when you quote a volatility of 10.39% 120 days, you mean an effective standard deviation $\hat{\sigma}$ of $0.1039 \times \sqrt{1/3} = 0.06$.

Having chosen n, $T - t$, and the volatility, we need to set u and d. For computational speed and analytical convenience one chooses $d = 1/u$, so that after an up-and-down episode the rate is back at the same value as two changes ago. For a large n, one then sets the change of the log as the target volatility times $\sqrt{1/n}$. (The details of the derivation are in technical note 9.2.) This means that the u factor becomes

$$u = e^{\hat{\sigma} \times \sqrt{1/n}}$$

$$= e^{\sigma_{\text{p.a.}} \times \sqrt{(T-t)/n}}$$

$$= e^{\sigma_{\text{p.a.}} \times \sqrt{h}}, \qquad (9.16)$$

where $h := (T - t)/n$, the length of one subperiod, in years.

Example 9.9. For example, with $n = 120$ subperiods over one quarter (i.e., $T - t = 0.25$), h equals $0.002\,083\,3$, and for a volatility of 0.10 one sets

$$u = e^{\sqrt{0.002\,083\,3} \times 0.10} = 1.004\,574\,787$$

and

$$d = 1/1.004\,574\,787 = 0.995\,446\,046.$$

While convenient for computers, such numbers are very awkward to read, and would slow us down if the objective were to understand the logic. So in the next section we continue using big, easy-to-read changes of 10% up or down.

9.3 Stepwise Multiperiod Binomial Option Pricing

The obvious drawback of the one-period model is that it assumes that the exchange rate can take one of only two possible values at expiration. This is a rather simplistic view and an undesirable feature of the single-period model. We would prefer a richer distribution, one that has many possible values at maturity and is close to bell-shaped.

We have already found that if there are two changes, there are already three possible exchange rates at the end, and that the middle outcome is more probable than the extreme outcomes. After 30 changes, there will be 31 possible exchange rates at the end, and the probabilities will be approximately bell-shaped. Thus, if we wanted to price a one-month option, we would be much closer to reality if, instead of modeling the time-T exchange rate as the result of a single, big change, we model it as the result of 30 small, daily changes. Of course, if we increase the number of subperiods into which the one-month life of the option is divided, we must also shrink the factors u and d toward unity; otherwise, the variance of the exchange rate at expiration would no longer match reality. Likewise, the risk-free rate of return per subperiod must be rescaled, for instance, from a monthly rate to a daily rate.

In this section, we first show how to extend the one-period binomial model to such a multiperiod setting. In the numerical examples, we omit the adjustments to the u, d, r, and r^* parameters that should be made if we divide a given option's life into more and more periods. Working with familiar numbers is easier, and helps us focus on the logic of the pricing approach. The two-period examples we present below should be interpreted as going from a one-month valuation problem (with one single, big change in the exchange rate) to a two-month problem (with two consecutive, big changes in the exchange rate). The second enrichment, in this section, is a discussion of American-style options and early exercise.

9.3.1 Dynamic Hedging or Replication: A European-Style Option

We will illustrate the logic (and other results in this chapter) using the tree shown in figure 9.7. (Ignore for the moment the reverse tree added on the right of the figure.) The exchange rate process starts at $S_0 = 100$, and has $u = 1.10$ and $d = 0.9$. We will further assume $1 + r = 1.05$, and in order to obtain a convenient forward rate of 102, we will set $1 + r^* = 1.029\,411\,8$. Another crucial number is q, computed as

$$q = \frac{1.02 - 0.90}{1.10 - 0.90} = \frac{0.12}{0.20} = 0.6. \tag{9.17}$$

Let us consider a numerical example for a call, assuming that there are two price jumps before the option expires. We use the now familiar tree, on the left in the figure, and consider a call with $X = 95$ that expires at the end of the second period. You can easily verify that, when plotting the three possible time-2 call values against the corresponding asset prices, the three points are no longer on one single line. That is, at time 0, we can no longer hedge or replicate the call using only one (two-period) forward contract. Therefore, we need to introduce a new assumption.

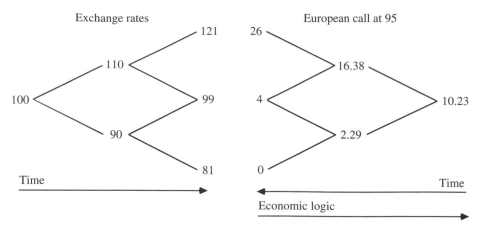

Figure 9.7. Valuing a European-style call, two periods.

Assumption 9.10. *At any discrete moment in the model, investors can trade and adjust their portfolios of home currency and foreign currency loans.*

The above assumption corresponds to the Black–Merton–Scholes assumption that trading can be done continuously. As a result of assumption 9.10, we can now use a dynamic hedge, that is, a series of one-period hedges that are revised each period. To see this, note that at time 1 the one-period valuation approach will still work. For instance, if at time 1 the exchange rate is 110, then there are only two possible values that the exchange rate can take at maturity: 121 and 99. Thus, if at time 1 the rate is 110, then we can easily hedge or replicate, and, if we can hedge or replicate, we can use the easy-to-remember risk-adjusted valuation formula to value the call at node $(1,1)$. For a European call, we use our result $q = 0.6$, and we immediately find the call price at node $(1,1)$ using equations (9.6) and (9.7):

$$C_{1,1} = \frac{26 \times 0.60 + 4 \times 0.40}{1.05} = \frac{17.2}{1.05} = 16.38. \qquad (9.18)$$

Likewise, if at time 1 the exchange rate has moved down to $S_{1,0} = 90$, then there are only two possible exchange rates at expiration, implying that a linear hedge or replication is possible; thus, we know the call will then be valued as

$$C_{1,1} = \frac{4 \times 0.60 + 0 \times 0.40}{1.05} = \frac{2.40}{1.05} = 2.29. \qquad (9.19)$$

We still have to find the value of the option at time 0. But the above calculations have reduced the problem to just one more two-point problem. Indeed, at time 0, there only two possible values for the exchange rate at time 1: S_1 is either 110 or 90, and we have just identified each of the corresponding call prices: $C_1 = 16.38$ if $S_1 = 110$ and $C_1 = 2.28$ if $S_1 = 90$. Thus, we now have to solve a one-period, two-outcome problem—and two points can be hedged (or replicated) linearly, implying a risk-adjusted expectation valuation relationship. Thus, the price at time 0 must be

$$C_0 = \frac{16.38 \times 0.60 + 2.29 \times 0.40}{1.05} = \frac{10.74}{1.05} = 10.23. \qquad (9.20)$$

In terms of the hedging model, this stepwise valuation implicitly uses a hedge that looks only one period ahead. That is, every period we select a hedge that offsets the uncertainty of the option's value one period ahead. The size of the required hedge, the option's delta, changes all of the time because it depends on moneyness (i.e., on the evolution of the exchange rate) and time to maturity.

Example 9.11. Suppose that we hold a currency-option bond and that we want to hedge the call option that is implicit in it. The bond and the implicit call option expire in two periods. To hedge the call, we determine its exposure, B_t, to the exchange rate one period ahead, and then take out a one-period forward contract of size B_t. At the end of the first period, we reassess the exposure, and take out a new forward contract. The new contract hedges the next change in the exchange rate. Its payoff, combined with the payoff from the first hedge and with the option itself, then gives us the overall hedged value.

For simplicity, we assume that the call that is attached to the bond, in the above example, has the same terms and conditions as the option we have just analyzed. We can compute the deltas in our two-period problem as follows. The initial delta is

$$B_0 = \frac{16.38 - 2.29}{110 - 90} = 0.705. \qquad (9.21)$$

Therefore, at time 0, we sell forward 0.705 units of foreign currency, and lock in the certainty equivalent of the option, $C_0(1 + r) = 10.23 \times 1.05 = 10.74$ without risk.

- Up: $16.38 - 0.705 \times (110 - 102) = 10.74$.
- Down: $2.29 - 0.705 \times (90 - 102) = 10.74$.

This, you will recall, is why the option is initially worth $10.74/1.05$.

The next hedge depends on which way the exchange rate has moved. If the rate went up to node $(1,1)$, the option moved deep into the money. Accordingly, to hedge the option we now need to sell forward a greater amount:

$$B_{1,1} = \frac{26 - 4}{121 - 99} = 1. \qquad (9.22)$$

This is a borderline case: we sell the full unit of FC because we are fully certain that the option we hold will end in the money. The hedge again works.

- Up: $26 - 1 \times (121 - 112.2) = 17.2$ at $t = 2$.
- Down: $4 - 1 \times (81 - 91.8) = 17.2$ at $t = 2$.

This is, of course, the option value at node (1,1) times 1.05. (The option value is the hedged future value, discounted, remember?) Adding in the payoff from the hedge that was set up at time 0, we get a total of

$$17.2 + \underbrace{[-0.705 \times (110 - 102)]}_{\text{Hedge's payoff at } t = 1} \underbrace{\times 1.05}_{\text{Carry to } t = 2} = 17.2 - 5.95 = 11.28 \quad \text{at } t = 2.$$

(9.23)

If, at time 1, we see the rate went down to node (1,0), in contrast, then the option is now fairly out of the money and becomes less sensitive to the exchange rate. You should be able to calculate exposure and locked-in value.

> **DIY Problem 9.6.** First calculate the exposure:
>
> $$B_{1,0} = \frac{}{} = 0.222. \tag{9.24}$$
>
> Therefore, after a down-move we sell forward 0.222 units of foreign currency, and lock in the certainty equivalent of the option.
>
> - Up: = 2.40.
> - Down: = 2.40.
>
> This is, again, the option value at node (1,0) times 1.05.

Adding in the payoff from the hedge that was set up at time 0, we get a total of

$$2.40 + \underbrace{[-0.705 \times (90 - 102)]}_{\text{Hedge's payoff at } t = 1} \underbrace{\times 1.05}_{\text{Carry to } t = 2} = 2.40 + 8.88 = 11.28 \quad \text{at } t = 2.$$

(9.25)

You can verify that the all-in hedged value at time 2, 11.28 regardless of the path, is the option's initial value times 1.05^2.

Thus, we start the hedge at time 0 with 0.705 units sold forward. The time-1 hedge will be to sell forward either 1 or 0.222 units of foreign currency, depending on whether the exchange rate moves up or down. This is called *dynamic hedging*. A *static hedge*, in the sense of a forward position initiated at time 0 and held till time 2, cannot work because the two-period forward contract has a payoff that is linear in $\tilde{S}_2$, while there are three final possible call values which are not linear in $\tilde{S}_2$. The three points (S_2, C_2) cannot be captured by one single line.

9.3.2   What Can Go Wrong?

The above shows how beautifully hedging works. The caveat we want to add at this stage is that this is true only within the assumptions of the model. In reality, everything can go horribly wrong, as the financial collapse that started off as the "subprime" crisis has shown.

The item that probably wreaks most havoc is volatility in the volatility. In the above we assumed a constant $\pm 10\%$ volatility. What if, at time 1, this is unexpectedly changed?

Example 9.12. Suppose that, at the up node $(1,1)$, volatility unexpectedly goes to $\pm 20\%$. What is the option price? We first need to recompute q:

$$q_{1,1} = \frac{1.02 - 0.80}{1.20 - 0.80} = 0.55.$$

Then the new price and hedge ratio follow:

$$C_{1,1} = \frac{26 \times 0.55 + 0}{1.05} = 19.36 \quad \text{and} \quad B_{1,1} = \frac{26 - 0}{120 - 80} = 0.65.$$

The new hedge set up at node $(1,1)$ will be different. More problematically, our initial time-0 hedge was meant to offset a price change from 10.23 to 16.38 should the rate move up—but the actual price went much higher. Our initial hedge would not have worked.

DIY Problem 9.7. Suppose that, at the down node $(1,0)$, volatility unexpectedly goes to $\pm 5\%$. What is the option price and the hedge at node $(1,0)$?

- $q_{1,0} = \ldots$
- $C_{1,0} = \ldots$
- $B_{1,0} = \ldots$

How do we handle this? First note that if the changes are fully known in advance, we can build this into our valuation and hedging. If it is known that the option price, at the first jump, goes to 19.36 or 0.00 instead of 16.38 and 2.29, we would compute the initial hedge ratio or exposure as

$$B_0 = \frac{19.36 - 0}{110 - 90} = 0.97, \tag{9.26}$$

instead of 0.77; and we would price the option not at 10.23 but at

$$C_0 = \frac{19.36 \times 0.60 + 0}{1.05} = 11.06. \tag{9.27}$$

More generally, if the u, d, r, and r^* variables are not constant but still binomial (in the sense that there are only two possible next-step scenarios) and predictable (the scenarios are fully known), then calculations would be slower but essentially unaltered.

If the changes in the variables are random, some serious thinking is needed. First, how will we build trees? Can the new uncertainty be hedged? If not, is it priced or can we treat it as if investors were risk-neutral? All this is beyond the scope of this introductory text, but definitely worth pondering for any professional option writer.

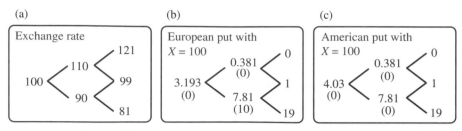

Figure 9.8. Pricing an American put: $u = 1.1$, $d = 0.9$, $r = 5\%$, $(1 + r)/(1 + r^*) = 1.02$, $q = 0.60$.

9.3.3 American-Style Options

Hoping that the example has pared down your confidence in the standard model to a healthier level, we now return to it and consider how early exercise can be handled. You have already guessed how it works: we work stepwise backward from the expiry values, as before, but (i) the market price is the maximum of the values dead and alive, or equivalently the maximum of value alive and intrinsic value, and (ii) the value alive is usually not the PV of exercise at the boundary but of optimal exercise, which is a matter of calculation.

An example will help. We take the familiar tree, reproduced in figure 9.8(a). In (b) you see the resulting tree of European prices—this time for a put struck at 100—and also the intrinsic values, in parentheses. How to proceed? At time 1, "exercise later" can only mean "exercise at expiration," so we can use the European-style prices as the values alive for time 1. Then we need to look at three nodes:

Node (1,1). In this node the choices are as follows.

- PV of later exercise (0 or 1): 0.381.
- Value of immediate exercise: 0.

So we wait, and the market price is 0.381, as for the European option.

Node (1,0). Now the choices are as follows.

- PV of later exercise (0 or 19): 7.81.
- Value of immediate exercise: 10.

So we exercise, and the market price is 10, more than the European-style premium.

Node (0). We now choose between the following.

- PV of later exercise (0 or 1 at time 2, or 10 at time 1):

$$P_0^{\text{alive}} = \frac{0.381 \times 0.60 + 10 \times 0.40}{1.05} = 4.03.$$

- Value of immediate exercise: 0.

So we wait, and the market price is 4.03.

Note how at node 0 the option's value alive is no longer the value of the European option, because the future has changed: we will exercise early if the rate moves ITM. As a result, the initial option premium exceeds the value of the European put: we might exercise early, at time 1.

This finishes our presentation of the binomial model as a practical pricing tool. You may be left wondering how all this leads to the Black–Merton–Scholes equation. That model is indeed an equation, not a numerical exercise with many stepwise calculations. So in the next section we look at the model more analytically and discover how it connects to the Black–Merton–Scholes (BMS) model.

9.4 Toward Black–Merton–Scholes (European Options)

Recall that the multiperiod model is used primarily to break down the life of a given option into a large number of subperiods, and model the exchange rate at maturity as the result of many small, random price changes. Pricing is equally piecemeal: we compute step by step, conditional on some time-t price and assuming that the future prices will be rationally computed in a similar way. In this section, we show how, for a European-style option, the multiperiod pricing model with a large number of steps (n) approaches a Black–Merton–Scholes type solution involving standard normal probabilities. We first write the general n-period binomial model in a "shortcut" version, where we just compute one single $\mathrm{CEQ}_0(\tilde{C}_n)$ for the entire distribution of final values and conditional just on the time-0 price. Then we show how the model can be rewritten as an expression involving two binomial probabilities. Lastly, we indicate why these probabilities become standard-normal probabilities when the number of steps or subperiods is large. To close this section, we show the links between the final valuation expression, the exposure, and the delta or hedge ratio. Readers scared by the math should still read that last subsection.

9.4.1 A Shortcut for European Options

In the above subsection, we have solved a two-period valuation problem by breaking it up into a sequence of one-period problems, each of which can be solved by using the one-period risk-adjusted expectations approach. You can already guess that any multiperiod problem can be solved by using such a recursive approach. We could write a computer program that calculates the $n + 1$ possible time-n expiration values (*boundary conditions*, in options-speak). From these expiration values, the program would then derive the n possible call prices, in each of the n nodes of time $n - 1$. Working backward, we would then compute the $n - 1$ possible call prices in time $n - 2$, and so on, until we ultimately reach the (unique) price at time zero.

For European options, it is not strictly necessary to value the call recursively by explicitly computing all of the call's future prices at each node. We can obtain a one-shot valuation formula that leads straight from the nth-period payoffs to the time-0 price. Let us verify this in the numerical example from the preceding subsection.

Step one is to compute the (risk-adjusted) chances of getting to each of the three possible final nodes:

- Probability of ending at node (2,2): $\text{Pr}_2 = q^2 = 0.6^2 = 0.36$.
- Probability of ending at node (2,1): $\text{Pr}_1 = 2q(1-q) = 2 \times 0.6 \times 0.4 = 0.48$.
- Probability of ending at node (2,0): $\text{Pr}_0 = (1-q)^2 = 0.4^2 = 0.16$.

Step two is to compute the CEQ of $\tilde{C}_2$ at time zero, computed the way one would obtain an expectation conditional on initial information:

$$\text{CEQ}_0(\tilde{C}_2) = 26 \times 0.36 + 4 \times 0.48 + 0 \times 0.16 = 11.28.$$

DIY Problem 9.8. Go back to the previous section and find where we have seen this number before. Then have a healthy "of course" experience.

Step three is to discount the CEQ at the two-period risk-free rate:

$$C_0 = \frac{\text{CEQ}_0(\tilde{C}_2)}{(1+r)^2} = \frac{11.28}{1.05^2} = 10.23.$$

DIY Problem 9.9. How do we know that the two-period risk-free rate is 5% per period? We have assumed a constant one-period rate, but does that imply that the two-period rate is 10.25% (5% per period, a flat term structure)?

In figure 9.9 the step-by-step valuation is summarized for a new problem: a put not a call, and three periods instead of two. We first roll out the three-period tree, starting from the current level (100) and going rightward. Option pricing starts at the rightmost end, with the boundary conditions (for a put, this time), and then works its way back to the present as follows:

$$C_{2,2} = \frac{0.00 \times 0.6 + 0.00 \times 0.4}{1.05} = 0.00,$$

$$C_{2,1} = \frac{0.00 \times 0.6 + 10.9 \times 0.4}{1.05} = 4.152,$$

$$C_{2,0} = \frac{10.0 \times 0.6 + 27.1 \times 0.4}{1.05} = 16.55,$$

$$C_{1,1} = \frac{0.000 \times 0.6 + 4.152 \times 0.4}{1.05} = 1.582,$$

$$C_{1,0} = \frac{4.152 \times 0.6 + 16.55 \times 0.4}{1.05} = 8,678,$$

$$C_0 = \frac{1.582 \times 0.6 + 8,678 \times 0.4}{1.05} = 4.210.$$

But the one-shot approach also works here.

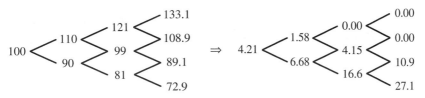

Figure 9.9. Valuing a three-period put.

DIY Problem 9.10. Denote the (risk-adjusted) probabilities for each of the four possible final values by $\Pr_j$. Compute

- $\Pr_3 = \ldots$
- $\Pr_2 = \ldots$
- $\Pr_1 = \ldots$
- $\Pr_0 = \ldots$
- The (risk-adjusted) chance of ending in the money is …
- $C_0 = \dfrac{\underline{\quad} \times \underline{\quad} + \underline{\quad} \times \underline{\quad} + \underline{\quad} \times \underline{\quad} + \underline{\quad} \times \underline{\quad}}{\underline{}} = 4.21.$

9.4.2 The General Formula

In general, then, the option price is the discounted value of the CEQ of the final values. Denoting the probability of j up-jumps out of a total n jumps by $\Pr_j$, the formula is

$$C_0 = \frac{C_{n,0}\Pr_0 + C_{n,1}\Pr_1 + \cdots + C_{n,n}\Pr_n}{(1+r)^n} = \frac{\sum_{j=0}^{n} C_{n,j}\Pr_j}{(1+r)^n}. \tag{9.28}$$

The next step is to drill down into how the expiry values $C_{n,j}$ were calculated: $C_{n,j} = (S_{n,j} - X)_+$. The in-the-moneyness condition $(\cdot)_+$ can be expressed as a condition on j: we figure out how many jumps, out of a total of n, have to be "up" for the call to end ITM.[7] For instance, in figure 9.9, a call struck at 100 ends in the money if there are at least two rises. We denote this required number of ups by a. So we restrict the sum to ITM outcomes (line 1, below); we then split the sum of differences $S_n - X$ into a difference of sums (line 2), putting the X up-front in the second sum:

$$C_0 = \frac{\sum_{j=a}^{n}(S_{n,j} - X)\Pr_j}{(1+r)^n}, \quad \text{where } a: \tilde{j} \geq a \Leftrightarrow \tilde{S}_{n,j} \geq X, \tag{9.29}$$

$$= \frac{\sum_{j=a}^{n} S_{n,j}\Pr_j}{(1+r)^n} - \frac{X}{(1+r)^n}\sum_{j=a}^{n}\Pr_j. \tag{9.30}$$

---

[7] If we had written an integral, we would have written the sum as an integral over all values of S_n from X to infinity. But we have a sum, and it is written in terms of j, not S_n. So moneyness is expressed as a condition on j not S_n. This is just a technicality—no worries.

Example 9.13. Consider a call struck at 100 in the three-period tree of figure 9.9. The ITM outcomes are $j = \{2, 3\}$ corresponding to $S_n = \{133.1, 109.9\} > 100$. That is, $a = 2$. The call is valued as

$$C_0 = \frac{(133.1 - 100) \times 0.216 + (108.9 - 100) \times 0.432}{1.05^3}$$

$$= \frac{[133.1 \times 0.216 + 108.9 \times 0.432]}{1.05^3} - \frac{100}{1.05^3} \times [0.216 + 0.432]$$

$$= \frac{59.46}{1.05^3} - \underbrace{86.383}_{\text{Price PN}} \times \underbrace{0.648}_{\Pr(S_n > X)} . \tag{9.31}$$

Note the second sum in equation (9.30) or in the example. Up-front in this second term we have the strike price, discounted. This is one of the terms that shows up in the comparable-forward-purchase valuation—FC PN minus HC PN—which in turn is a lower bound of the call premium. Unlike in the comparable-forward-purchase formula, here this HC PN price is followed by a sum of probabilities. This sum of probabilities has a nice economic interpretation: it measures the total chance that j will be larger than a, meaning the total chance that S_n will end above X. (All probabilities are risk-adjusted, of course.)

The FC PV part of the comparable-forward-purchase formula can also be brought out, notably from the first sum in equation (9.30). This requires two tricks. First, write $S_{n,j}$ as $S_0 u^j d^{n-j}$. Second, bring in the foreign interest rate by writing

$$\frac{1}{(1 + r)^n} = \frac{1}{(1 + r^*)^n} \left(\frac{1 + r^*}{1 + r} \right)^n . \tag{9.32}$$

You can see that, this way, a term $S_0/(1 + r^*)^n$ can be factored out of the first sum of equation (9.30). The beauty is that the sum next to it, after tedious manipulations (technical note 9.3), can be written as a binomial probability too.[8] Specifically, equation (9.30) ends up as

$$C_0 = \underbrace{\frac{S_0}{(1 + r^*)^n} \sum_{j=a}^{n} \pi_j}_{\text{FC PN}} - \underbrace{\frac{X}{(1 + r)^n} \sum_{j=a}^{n} \Pr_j}_{\text{HC PN}} . \tag{9.33}$$

Binomial cumulative probabilities can be computed explicitly, but you should remember that, for mid or large sample sizes n, such a probability is well approximated by a cumulative normal. So now we at least understand why in the BMS formula we see the underlying asset price (the FC PN) followed by a probability, and the discounted strike followed by another probability:

$$\sum_{j=a}^{n} \pi_j \to N(d_1) \quad \text{and} \quad \sum_{j=a}^{n} \Pr_j \to N(d_2), \tag{9.34}$$

---

[8] While the probabilities $\Pr_j$ have an economic interpretation, the other ones, the π_js, are just a mathematical result. Sorry.

where

$$d_1 = \frac{\ln(F_{0,T}/X) + \frac{1}{2}\hat{\sigma}^2}{\hat{\sigma}} \quad \text{and} \quad d_2 = \frac{\ln(F_{0,T}/X) - \frac{1}{2}\hat{\sigma}^2}{\hat{\sigma}}.$$

So

$$C_0 = \underbrace{\frac{S_0}{1 + r_{0,T}^*}}_{\text{FC PN}} N(d_1) - \underbrace{\frac{X}{1 + r_{0,T}}}_{\text{HC PN}} N(d_2). \tag{9.35}$$

This insight was the purpose of our efforts. If you care to walk an extra mile you can also read technical note 9.4 and find out exactly where d_1 and d_2, the arguments of the BMS normal probabilities, come from.

9.4.3 The Delta of an Option

Equation (9.33) or (9.35) tells us that the option has the same price as a portfolio containing the following two positions:

- a fraction $\sum_{j=a}^{n} \pi_j$ or $N(d_1)$ of an FC PN with face value unity, and
- a fraction $\sum_{j=a}^{n} \text{Pr}_j$ or $N(d_2)$ of an HC PN with face value X.

But the portfolio is not just one that has the same value as the option: being a replicating portfolio it also behaves in the same way, at least in the short run. So the above still describes how to set up a replicating portfolio in an n-period model. True, we see no forward contract, here, but a forward contract itself is a portfolio of the HC and FC PNs. So here we see the formula taken to its most basic level.

The number of foreign currency units one needs in order to replicate the option is called the option's delta or hedge ratio. This last term reflects the familiar fact that hedging and replication are simply two sides of the same coin. If one can replicate an option by buying and investing δ_0 units of foreign exchange (partly financed by a loan in home currency), then one can hedge the option by borrowing δ_0 units of foreign exchange for one period—hence, the hedge-ratio terminology.

We have just described the replica or hedge in terms of PNs, the instruments that also underly the comparable forward contract; but you might as well hedge or replicate using deposits or forward contracts. The required size of the positions—in PNs, spot deposits, or forward/futures contracts expiring at T—can be read off from the three ways to write the first item in the portfolio[9] (see table 9.1).

9.5 CFO's Summary

In this chapter, we have seen how to value currency options when the underlying asset, the exchange rate, is approximated by a binomial process. The valuation method we have studied is based on arbitrage arguments. One way to

---

[9] For the forward version, use CIP to see that $F/(1 + r) = S/(1 + r^*)$.

Table 9.1.

Version of formula	Hedge instrument	Unit price	Size of position
$C_0 = \dfrac{S_0}{1 + r_{0,T}^*} N(d_1) - \cdots$	FC PN expiring at T	$\dfrac{S_0}{1 + r_{0,T}^*}$	$N(d_1)$
$C_0 = S_0 \dfrac{N(d_1)}{1 + r_{0,T}^*} - \cdots$	FC spot deposit	S_0	$\dfrac{N(d_1)}{1 + r_{0,T}^*}$
$C_0 = F_{0,T} \dfrac{N(d_1)}{1 + r_{0,T}} - \cdots$	Forward expiring at T	$F_{0,T}$	$\dfrac{N(d_1)}{1 + r_{0,T}}$

value options is to build a portfolio that contains some domestic PNs and forward contracts and that exactly replicates the short-run price evolution of the option; thus, the law of one price implies that the option must have the same value as the replicating portfolio. A closely related approach to option valuation is to hedge the option against short-term exchange-rate changes. Since the resulting portfolio is risk free, it is easily valued by discounting the known next-period value at the risk-free rate. Both approaches also have an appealing economic interpretation: option prices can be thought of as risk-adjusted expected future values discounted at the risk-free rate, where the information required to compute the risk-adjustment is implicit in the forward premium.

Hedging or replication works only in the short run (one period ahead, in the binomial model). That is, with a linear instrument like the forward contract, we can replicate or hedge only the short-run price movements of the option. The reason is that the sensitivity of the option's value to the exchange rate is not constant. Rather, the exposure of the option is changing, depending on how far in-the-money or out-of-the-money the option is, and the length of the option's remaining life. To track the option in the longer run, we need to adjust the forward positions dynamically. We described how the hedge ratios can be computed.

The applications of this binomial model stretch beyond the realm of financial assets. For instance, this binomial approach can be used to value investments that contain "operational" or "real" options, such as the option to close down a plant or the option to reenter a market in light of the exchange rate prospects.

One should not forget the model's weaknesses, though. While it uses a no-arb approach, it is not nearly as robust as, say, covered interest parity. CIP just assumes perfect markets, and in reality the interbank spreads are so tiny that the CIP formula does quite well. The binomial model, in contrast, also assumes that the exchange rate is a log random walk that always behaves the same way. In reality, exchange rates exhibit mean reversion—weak in the short run, but sufficiently noticeable when the horizon is several years. Worse, even in the short run the volatility is fluctuating, so that delta hedging does not immunize the writer nearly as well as she might hope. Pricing and especially hedging should be based on more complete models. That is the bad news. The good news is that the logic of these generalized models is quite similar to the one expounded here; so you should learn quickly if that were necessary.

*   *   *

We have now finished our discussion of exchange markets in the wider sense, including derivatives. Among the possible applications of these derivatives, hedging turned out to be a popular and respectable one. So it is time to move on to a more fundamental issue: does hedging pay at all? The economics of exchange risk, exposure, and hedging are the central theme of the next part.

9.6 Technical Notes

Technical note 9.1 (the replication approach: formal proof). For any portfolio containing a risk-free PN with face value V_1 and a position in the forward market of size B_0, the future value equals

$$\text{Value at time } 1 = V_1 + B_0 (\tilde{S}_1 - F_{0,1}). \tag{9.36}$$

We want to set V_1 and B_0 such that the portfolio's future value matches the call's value in both the upstate and the downstate:

$$B_0, V_1: \quad V_1 + B_0 (S_{1,\text{up}} - F_{0,1}) = C_{1,\text{up}}, \tag{9.37}$$

$$V_1 + B_0 (S_{1,\text{down}} - F_{0,1}) = C_{1,\text{down}}. \tag{9.38}$$

Subtracting equation (9.37) from (9.38) we find the condition that identifies B_0:

$$B_0 (S_{1,\text{up}} - S_{1,\text{down}}) = C_{1,\text{up}} - C_{1,\text{down}}, \tag{9.39}$$

$$\implies \quad B_0 = \frac{C_{1,\text{up}} - C_{1,\text{down}}}{S_{1,\text{up}} - S_{1,\text{down}}}, \tag{9.40}$$

which is, of course, just the exposure of the option. Finding V_1 is done as follows. We first solve equation (9.38) for V_1 and rearrange, and next we substitute the solution for B_0 into that expression. For the sake of interpretation we then regroup so as to bring out a term relabeled q, which will turn out to be the risk-adjusted probability:

$$V_1 = C_{1,\text{down}} - B_0 (S_{1,\text{down}} - F_{0,1})$$

$$= C_{1,\text{down}} + B_0 (F_{0,1} - S_{1,\text{down}})$$

$$= C_{1,\text{down}} + \frac{C_{1,\text{up}} - C_{1,\text{down}}}{S_{1,\text{up}} - S_{1,\text{down}}} (F_{0,1} - S_{1,\text{up}})$$

$$= C_{1,\text{down}} + (C_{1,\text{up}} - C_{1,\text{down}}) \underbrace{\frac{F_{0,1} - S_{1,\text{down}}}{S_{1,\text{up}} - S_{1,\text{down}}}}_{=q}$$

$$= q\, C_{1,\text{up}} + (1 - q)\, C_{1,\text{down}}. \tag{9.41}$$

This identifies the ingredients of the replicating portfolio. To finish the valuation of the call we note that it must be worth as much as its replica, and the cost of the replicating portfolio is just the cost of the risk-free investment: the hedge part has zero initial value. The cost of an investment with face value V_1 is $V_1/(1 + r_{0,1})$. We sum this up as

$$C_0 = \frac{V_1}{1 + r_{0,1}} = \frac{q\, C_{1,\text{up}} + (1 - q)\, C_{1,\text{down}}}{1 + r_{0,1}}, \tag{9.42}$$

where

$$q = \frac{F_{0,1} - S_{1,\text{down}}}{S_{1,\text{up}} - S_{1,\text{down}}}.$$

The first equality means that V_1 must be the CEQ, and the second equality then means that q must be the risk-adjusted probability.

Technical note 9.2 (setting u and d). The shortest route is to assume that $p = 0.5$.[10] We denote the one-step change in $s := \ln S$ by $\pm\Delta$. Below we first find the one-step variance, then the variance over n i.i.d. steps, and finally the standard deviation over n i.i.d. steps, each time as a function of Δ. This last standard deviation is our target, expressed on an effective (not annualized) basis:

$$\text{var}_t(\tilde{s}_{t+1}) = \tfrac{1}{2}(+\Delta)^2 + \tfrac{1}{2}(-\Delta)^2 = \Delta^2,$$

$$\implies \quad \text{var}_t(\tilde{s}_{t+n}) = n\Delta^2,$$

$$\implies \quad \hat{\sigma} := \text{std}_t(\tilde{s}_{t+n}) = \sqrt{n}\,\Delta. \tag{9.43}$$

Normally, the target effective standard deviation is expressed as the (p.a.) volatility times $\sqrt{T - t}$. Thus, we need to set Δ such that

$$\sqrt{n}\,\Delta = \sigma_{\text{p.a.}}\sqrt{T - t},$$

$$\implies \quad \Delta = \sigma_{\text{p.a.}}\sqrt{(T - t)/n}. \tag{9.44}$$

Recall that Δ is the change of the log:

$$\ln S_i = \ln S_{i-1} \pm \Delta,$$

$$\implies \quad S_i = S_{i-1}e^{\pm\Delta}$$

$$= S_{i-1}e^{\pm\sigma_{\text{p.a.}}\sqrt{(T-t)/n}},$$

$$\implies \quad u = e^{+\sigma_{\text{p.a.}}\sqrt{(T-t)/n}}, \tag{9.45}$$

$$d = e^{-\sigma_{\text{p.a.}}\sqrt{(T-t)/n}}. \tag{9.46}$$

---

[10] We could have started more generally and then taken limits for shorter and shorter periods, which leads to the same final result. The intuition is that, for shorter and shorter periods, p approaches 0.5 anyway.

Technical note 9.3 (the partial-mean term in the n-period binomial formula).
We rewrite $S_{n,j}\mathrm{Pr}_j/(1+r)^n$ using $S_{n,j} = S_0\,u^j d^{n-j}$ and multiplying and dividing by $(1+r^*)^n$ (line 1, below). Next we temporarily adopt a more convenient notation $\varrho := (1+r^*)/(1+r)$ and write $\varrho^n = \varrho^j \varrho^{n-j}$. In line 3 we use $\mathrm{Pr}_j = C_j^n q^j (1-q)^{n-j}$,[11] and we group all items with the same exponents:

$$\frac{S_{n,j}}{(1+r)^n}\mathrm{Pr}_j = \frac{S_0}{(1+r^*)^n}\left(\frac{1+r^*}{1+r}\right)^n u^j d^{n-j}\mathrm{Pr}_j$$

$$= \frac{S_0}{(1+r^*)^n}\varrho^j u^j \varrho^{n-j} d^{n-j}\mathrm{Pr}_j$$

$$= \frac{S_0}{(1+r^*)^n}C_j^n [\varrho\, u\, q]^j [\varrho\, d\,(1-q)]^{n-j}. \tag{9.47}$$

We now want to show that the term inside the second set of square brackets equals minus the term inside the first set: $\varrho\, d\,(1-q) = 1 - \varrho\, u\, q$. Actually, we rewrite each of the sides of this interim *demonstrandum* into a common expression, as follows:

$$1 - \varrho\, u\, q = 1 - \varrho\, u\frac{\varrho^{-1} - d}{u - d}$$

$$= \frac{u - d - u + \varrho du}{u - d}$$

$$= d\frac{-1 + \varrho u}{u - d}, \tag{9.48}$$

while

$$\varrho\, d\,(1-q) = \varrho\, d\frac{u - d - \varrho^{-1} + d}{u - d}$$

$$= d\frac{\varrho u - 1}{u - d}. \tag{9.49}$$

Denote $\varrho\, u\, q$ by ϕ. We end with

$$\frac{S_{n,j}}{(1+r)^n}\mathrm{Pr}_j = \frac{S_0}{(1+r^*)^n}C_j^n \underbrace{[\varrho\, u\, q]}_{=:\phi}{}^j \underbrace{[\varrho\, d\,(1-q)]}_{= 1-\phi}{}^{n-j}$$

$$= \frac{S_0}{(1+r^*)^n}\underbrace{C_j^n \phi^j (1-\phi)^{n-j}}_{=:\pi_j}. \tag{9.50}$$

As indicated in the last line, the final expression has all the properties of the probability of observing j up-moves out of n moves if the chance of an up is ϕ. This pseudo-probability is denoted by π_j in the text.

Technical note 9.4 (from binomial probabilities to normal ones). When n is large and the probability q around 0.50, then j becomes roughly normal (with mean nq and variance $nq(1-q)$). This explains why in the BMS formula

---

[11] C_j^n stands for $\binom{n}{j} = n!/[j!\,(n-j)!]$, the number of paths that have j ups out of n jumps.

the discounted strike price is followed by a cumulative *normal* probability that can be read from a standard normal table. In this section we want to add more insight as to why the arguments of the cumulative normals are what they are. We start by identifying the true probabilities and then add the correction for risk.

In the limit, when n is at infinity, the grid for possible final exchange rates has become continuous and the rate itself lognormal. What is the chance that $\tilde{S}_T \geqslant X$? This is the type of exercise we are familiar with from introductory statistics: we standardize the problem. Denoting the effective mean and standard deviation for $\ln \tilde{S}_n$ by $\mu_{0,T}$ and $\hat{\sigma}$, respectively, we rewrite the condition $[\tilde{S}_T \geqslant X]$ as an equivalent condition on a standardized normal: take logs, subtract the mean, and divide by the standard deviation:

$$\tilde{S}_T \geqslant X \Leftrightarrow \underbrace{\frac{\ln \tilde{S}_T - \mu_{0,T}}{\hat{\sigma}}}_{\text{A unit normal } \tilde{z}} \geqslant \underbrace{\frac{\ln X - \mu_{0,T}}{\hat{\sigma}}}_{\text{A given value } z} . \tag{9.51}$$

Example 9.14. Let $\ln \tilde{S}_T$ have effective mean 2 and standard deviation 0.06. What is the chance of ending in the money if $X = 7.50$? We rewrite the question as one on a unit normal and read off the answer from a standard normal table:

$$\Pr(\tilde{S}_T \geqslant 7.50) = \Pr\left(\frac{\ln \tilde{S}_T - 2}{0.06} \geqslant \frac{\ln 7.5 - 2}{0.06}\right)$$
$$= \Pr(\tilde{z} \geqslant 0.248)$$
$$= 0.40. \tag{9.52}$$

There is one notational issue: it has become customary, in this literature, to express probabilities as chances that $\tilde{z} \leqslant z$, not $\tilde{z} \geqslant z$ as we just did. But that is easy: $\Pr(\tilde{z} \leqslant z) = \Pr(\tilde{z} \geqslant -z)$ because of the symmetry of the unit normal. For example, the chance that a unit normal $\tilde{z}$ turns out to be above 0.248 is the same as the probability that a unit normal is below -0.248. We conclude that

$$\Pr(\tilde{S}_T \geqslant X) = N(d_2'), \quad \text{where } d_2' = \frac{\mu_{0,T} - \ln X}{\hat{\sigma}}, \tag{9.53}$$

with $N(d_2')$ denoting the chance that a unit normal will turn out to be less than or equal to d_2'.

Let us now do the risk correction. We have seen that, in the binomial model, going from the true probability p to the risk-adjusted one, q, is the same as replacing $E_0(\tilde{S}_T)$ by $F_{0,T}$. We need to do the same operation here, but all we see is the expectation of the log of $\tilde{S}_T$, not the expectation of $\tilde{S}_T$ itself. There must be a link, of course, and in technical note 9.5 this relation is identified as

$$E(\tilde{S}_T) = e^{\mu_{0,T} + \hat{\sigma}^2/2}. \tag{9.54}$$

To bring out the mean in d_2', we therefore rearrange it as shown below. We then replace the expectation by the forward rate to get d_2', the risk-corrected version of d_2':

$$
d_2' = \frac{\mu_{0,T} - \ln X}{\hat{\sigma}} = \frac{[\mu_{0,T} + \frac{1}{2}\hat{\sigma}^2] - \frac{1}{2}\hat{\sigma}^2 - \ln X}{\hat{\sigma}}
$$

$$
= \frac{\ln E_0(\tilde{S}_T) - \frac{1}{2}\hat{\sigma}^2 - \ln X}{\hat{\sigma}}
$$

$$
= \frac{\ln(E_0(\tilde{S}_T)/X) - \frac{1}{2}\hat{\sigma}^2}{\hat{\sigma}},
$$

$$
\implies \quad d_2 = \frac{\ln(F_{0,T}/X) - \frac{1}{2}\hat{\sigma}^2}{\hat{\sigma}}. \tag{9.55}
$$

We need to do something similar with the first term. It is convenient to go back to the version that appeared in the first sum in (9.30) and take limits. The discrete sum becomes an integral and the condition $j \geqslant a$ becomes $\tilde{S}_T \geqslant X$:

$$
\sum_{j=a}^{n} S_{n,j} \text{Pr}_j \rightarrow \int_X^{\infty} S_T f(\mu_{0,T}, \hat{\sigma}) \, dS_T. \tag{9.56}
$$

The integral is like computing an expected value, except that we only consider values in the domain $[X, \infty[$ instead of all possible values; so it is called the *partial mean*. In technical note 9.5 we show that, for a lognormal, such a partial mean equals

$$
\int_X^{\infty} S_T f(\mu_{0,T}, \hat{\sigma}) = E_0(\tilde{S}_T) \int_X^{\infty} f(\mu_{0,T} + \hat{\sigma}^2, \hat{\sigma}). \tag{9.57}
$$

So we take the expectation—or, after risk-correction, the forward rate—and multiply it by a kind of probability, computed as if the mean were $\mu_{0,T} + \hat{\sigma}^2$ not $\mu_{0,T}$. But this means that, for that integral, we can fall back on our earlier work, except for the shift in the mean: adding $\hat{\sigma}^2$ turns the term $-\frac{1}{2}\hat{\sigma}^2$ into $+\frac{1}{2}\hat{\sigma}^2$:

$$
\int_X^{\infty} S_T f(\mu_{0,T}, \hat{\sigma}) = E_0(\tilde{S}_T) N(d_1'), \tag{9.58}
$$

where

$$
d_1' = \frac{\ln(E_0(\tilde{S}_T)/X) + \frac{1}{2}\hat{\sigma}^2}{\hat{\sigma}}.
$$

So the risk-adjusted version becomes

$$
\sum_{j=a}^{n} S_{n,j} \text{Pr}_j \rightarrow F_{0,T} N(d_1), \tag{9.59}
$$

where

$$
d_1 = \frac{\ln(F_{0,T}/X) + \frac{1}{2}\hat{\sigma}^2}{\hat{\sigma}}.
$$

The final call formula can be written, depending on your preference, as

$$C_0 = \frac{F_{t,T}}{1 + r_{t,T}} N(d_1) - \frac{X}{1 + r_{t,T}} N(d_2) \qquad (9.60)$$

$$= \frac{S_t}{1 + r_{t,T}^*} N(d_1) - \frac{X}{1 + r_{t,T}} N(d_2). \qquad (9.61)$$

The discounting operations are usually written via continuously compounded p.a. rates rather than effective rates (as we have done here), and the effective standard deviation is expressed via its p.a. volatility, as shown before. But this is cosmetic, not essential.

The put price can be obtained by analogous means, or via put–call parity:

$$P_0 = C_0 - \left(\frac{S_t}{1 + r_{t,T}^*} - \frac{X}{1 + r_{t,T}} \right)$$

$$= \frac{X}{1 + r_{t,T}} [1 - N(d_2)] - \frac{S_t}{1 + r_{t,T}^*} [1 - N(d_1)]$$

$$= \frac{X}{1 + r_{t,T}} N(-d_2) - \frac{S_t}{1 + r_{t,T}^*} N(-d_1). \qquad (9.62)$$

Technical note 9.5 (the expectation of the exponential of a normal and similar problems). Consider the problem of identifying $E(e^{a\tilde{y}})$, where $\tilde{y}$ is Gaussian:

$$E(e^{a\tilde{y}}) = k \int_{-\infty}^{+\infty} e^{ay} \exp\left(-\frac{1}{2} \left(\frac{y - m}{s} \right)^2 \right) dy, \qquad (9.63)$$

with $k = 1/(s\sqrt{2\pi})$. (Statisticians call $E(e^{a\tilde{y}})$ the *moment-generating function* of $\tilde{y}$'s distribution.) The arguments of the exponentials can be grouped and rearranged:

$$ay - \frac{1}{2} \left(\frac{y - m}{s} \right)^2$$

$$= -\frac{1}{2} \frac{-2as^2 y + (y^2 - 2my + m^2)}{s^2}$$

$$= -\frac{1}{2} \frac{y^2 - 2(m + as^2)y + m^2}{s^2}$$

$$= -\frac{1}{2} \frac{y^2 - 2(m + as^2)y + m^2 + (2mas^2 + a^2 s^4) - (2mas^2 + a^2 s^4)}{s^2}$$

$$= -\frac{1}{2} \frac{y^2 - 2(m + as^2)y + (m + as^2)^2 - (2mas^2 + a^2 s^4)}{s^2}$$

$$= -\frac{1}{2} \frac{(y - (m + as^2))^2}{s^2} + a(m + \tfrac{1}{2}as^2),$$

$$\Longrightarrow \quad k \int e^{ay} \exp\left(-\frac{1}{2} \left(\frac{y - m}{s} \right)^2 \right) dy$$

$$= e^{a(m + as^2/2)} \int k \exp\left(-\frac{1}{2} \left(\frac{y - (m + as^2)}{s} \right)^2 \right) dy, \qquad (9.64)$$

where the new integrand is a normal density with mean $m + a\,s^2$ and variance s^2. Since the area under any density equals unity it then follows that

$$E(e^{a\tilde{y}}) = e^{a(m+as^2/2)} \int_{-\infty}^{+\infty} k \exp\left(-\frac{1}{2}\left(\frac{y-(m+as^2)}{s}\right)^2\right)dy$$

$$= e^{a(m+as^2/2)}. \tag{9.65}$$

Corollary 9.15 (the expected value of a lognormal). *Let $\tilde{y} = \ln \tilde{y}$ be normal with mean μ and variance σ. Then*

$$E(\tilde{y}) = E(e^{\ln \tilde{y}}) = E(e^{\tilde{y}}) = e^{\mu+\sigma^2/2}. \tag{9.66}$$

Corollary 9.16 (the partial mean of a lognormal). *Let $y = \ln Y$ be normal with mean μ and variance σ. The partial mean of $\tilde{y}$ between A and B is*

$$\int_A^B Yk \exp\left(-\frac{1}{2}\left(\frac{y-m}{s}\right)^2\right)dy = e^{\mu+\sigma^2/2}\int_A^B k \exp\left(-\frac{1}{2}\left(\frac{y-(\mu+\sigma^2)}{s}\right)^2\right)dy$$

$$= E(\tilde{y})\int_A^B k \exp\left(-\frac{1}{2}\left(\frac{y-(\mu+\sigma^2)}{s}\right)^2\right)dy. \tag{9.67}$$

So one takes the regular mean $E(\tilde{y})$ and multiplies it by a kind of probability that $\tilde{y}$ falls between A and B, except that this pseudo-probability is not computed from the true density (centered around μ), but from a shifted one with mean $\mu + \sigma^2$.

TEST YOUR UNDERSTANDING

Quiz Questions

True–False Questions

1. An option's exposure is the sensitivity of a change in the price of the underlying asset to a change in the option's price.
2. The binomial model uses the risk-adjusted probability q as the certainty equivalent for the unknown (true) probability p.
3. The factor u is the risk-adjusted probability of an upward change in the exchange rate.
4. Dynamic hedging assumes that at any discrete moment investors can readjust their portfolio holdings.
5. The delta or exposure of an option is constant.

6. The delta or hedge ratio is the number of calls one needs in order to replicate foreign currency.

7. The probability π is a cumulative probability while

$$\left(\sum_{j=a}^{n} \right) \binom{x}{y} q^j (1-q)^{n-j}$$

is a probability for a single drawing.

8. The value of an American option should always be greater than or equal to its intrinsic value.

Multiple-Choice Questions

1. The replication approach to valuing a call option means:

   (a) that the payoffs of the call and its underlying asset are always identical;

   (b) buying forward a number of units of the underlying asset such that the payoffs of the option and the forward purchase are identical;

   (c) buying forward a number of units of the underlying asset such that the payoffs of the option and the forward purchase are identical up to a known amount, which is then replicated in the money market;

   (d) selling the call and buying forward a number of units of the underlying asset such that the payoffs are equal to zero.

2. The forward hedging approach to valuing a call option means:

   (a) buying the call and selling forward a number of units of the underlying asset such that the payoffs are equal to the value of a domestic T-bill;

   (b) buying forward a number of units of the underlying asset such that the payoffs of the option and the forward purchase are identical;

   (c) buying the call and selling forward a number of units of the underlying asset such that the payoffs are identical;

   (d) selling the call and buying forward a number of units of the underlying asset such that the payoffs are equal to zero.

3. To compute the certainty equivalent of the future payoff you need:

   (a) the true probability p;

   (b) the risk-adjusted probability q;

   (c) the expected probability $E(p)$;

   (d) the implied probability of p.

4. As the number of periods in the binomial model increases,

   (a) the resulting probability distribution of the future spot rate becomes bell-shaped;

   (b) the resulting probability distribution of the call price becomes bell-shaped;

   (c) the greater the likelihood that the exchange rate will become negative because price changes are additive;

   (d) the risk-adjusted expected probability q decreases.

Additional Quiz Questions

1. If $S_0 = 100$ and the spot rate can increase by 6% or decrease by 3%, what is the spot rate at node:
   (a) (3,3)?
   (b) (3,2)?
   (c) (3,1)?
   (d) (3,0)?

2. Suppose that the current EUR/GBP spot rate is 0.6, the effective risk-free rates of return are $r = 6\%$ and $r^* = 8\%$, and the spot rate will either increase to 0.62 or decrease to 0.57 at time 1.
   (a) What is the risk-adjusted probability of an increase in the spot rate? Of a decrease?
   (b) What is the risk-adjusted expected value of the European call with a strike price of 0.59?
   (c) What is the time-0 value of the call?
   (d) What is the factor $u(d)$ by which the spot rate increases? Decreases?
   (e) What is the option's exposure?
   (f) Would the option's value change if it were American?

3. Repeat the question above using a put with the same strike price, instead of a call.

Applications

1. In the one-period example in section 7.1.2, how could you make risk-free money if the call were valued at 10 rather than at 1.905?

2. In the same example, how would you change your answer if you discovered that the probability of "up" was 0.1, so that the exchange rate looked grossly overvalued?

3. For the two-period call example in section 7.6:
   (a) Show the tree of European call values if $X = 90$.
   (b) Compare this with the call's intrinsic values at each node.
   (c) Check whether there is a chance of early exercise if the option were American.

4. Consider a one-period call option on the British pound. Suppose that the current exchange rate is USD/GBP 2, the exercise price is USD/GBP 1.9, the one-period risk-free rate on the USD is 5%, and the one-period risk-free rate on the GBP is 10%. Suppose that the spot rate can either go up by a factor of 1.1 (to USD/GBP 2.2) or down by 0.9 (to USD/GBP 1.8).
   (a) Write down the two equations that show how one can replicate the cash flow from the option by investing in the foreign currency and borrowing domestically. What is the value of the call option, using the replication approach?
   (b) Compute the risk-neutral probabilities and use these to value the above call option.

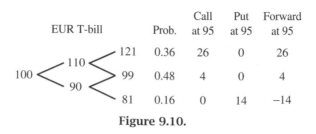

| | EUR T-bill | | | Call | Put | Forward |
			Prob.	at 95	at 95	at 95
		121	0.36	26	0	26
		99	0.48	4	0	4
		81	0.16	0	14	−14

Figure 9.10.

5. Suppose that the current spot rate is $S_0 =$ USD/GBP 2 and that the one-period interest rates today are $r = 5\%$ and $r^* = 10\%$. Also, you are given that in the next period the spot rate will either be USD/GBP 2.2 or USD/GBP 1.8.

   (a) What is the value today of a one-period put option on the GBP that has a strike price of USD/GBP 1.9?

   (b) Suppose that you already hold this put option. If you wish to hedge the payoff from the put, so that the net payoff of your portfolio is independent of the exchange rate, how many additional units of the spot should you buy/sell?

6. In this exercise, we numerically verify that the probabilities derived for European calls also work for other contracts by (i) valuing the contracts starting from the value of a call, and (ii) by checking whether a risk-adjusted probability evaluation provides the same answer.

   Consider the example used in section 7.4. The data used were $u = 1.1$, $d = 0.9$, $(1 + r) = 1.05$, $(1 + r^*) = 1.029\,411\,8$, $S_0 = 100$; for our call, $X = 95$. The tree, including the (risk-adjusted) probabilities for time 2, is reproduced in figure 9.10; for the time being, ignore the columns added to the right.

   (a) Compute the call value using the binomial model.

   (b) Compute the two-period forward rate directly (using interest rate parity), and indirectly (using our risk-adjusted probabilities, that is, as $CEQ_0(\tilde{S}_2)$).

   (c) Compute the present value of an "old" forward purchase struck at $F_{t0,2} = 95$ directly (using the formula in chapter 3) and indirectly (using q).

   (d) Value a European put with $X = 95$ directly (using put–call parity) and indirectly (using q).

7. Consider a four-month call option on the British pound. Suppose that the current exchange rate is USD/GBP 1.6, the exercise price is USD/GBP 1.6, the risk-free rate on the USD is 8% p.a., the risk-free rate on GBP is 11% p.a., and the volatility of the spot rate (and the forward rate) is 10%. Using the results in section 9.2.4, translate the volatility into an up and down factor (u and d). Then solve the following problems:

   (a) What is the value that you would be willing to pay for this American call option if you used the one-period binomial approach to value it?

   (b) What would you be willing to pay for this option if the volatility were 14.1%?

8. Suppose that the spot rate is USD/CAD 0.75 and the volatility of this exchange rate is 4% p.a. The risk-free rate in the United States is 7% p.a. and in Canada it is 9% p.a. Suppose that the exercise price is CAD 0.75 and the American put option matures in nine months.

   (a) Find the value of this option using the one-period binomial approach.
   (b) Find the value of this option using the two-period binomial approach.

9. A foreign currency put option is equivalent to a position in the foreign currency T-bill and a certain amount of borrowing/lending of the home currency. Is your replicating position in the foreign currency T-bill long or short? Why? Do you borrow or lend the home currency? Why?

10. Show that $CEQ_t(\tilde{F}_{T_1,T_2}) = F_{t,T_2}$.

11. What happens to the value of an option when both S_0 and X change by the same factor, holding u, d, r, and r^* constant?

PART III

Exchange Risk, Exposure, and Risk Management

About This Part

This part focuses on the economics of exchange risk and hedging. To set the scene, we look into the question of whether exchange-rate changes are easy to understand and predict (chapters 10 and 11). If so, there would not be much of a problem: all predicted changes would be already built into contracts, and there would be no bad surprises. Unfortunately, it turns out that exchange-rate movements are hard to predict; worse, even *ex post* they are hard to understand and explain.

We saw in chapter 3 that real exchange rates can move a lot and that this is important to firms. Coupled with the finding that most of the change comes from the nominal rate and that this part is hard to predict, it seems obvious that hedging is a good idea. We have to qualify, upon reflection: our conclusion in chapter 12 is that hedging adds value if and only if it affects the company's real operations, not just its bank account.

Given that there are many channels through which the decision whether to hedge or not may affect operations, we conclude that hedging should often be relevant. The next question is to determine the size of the forward hedge. What is the amount at stake? Chapter 13 reviews the various exposure concepts. Chapter 14 shows how to quantify the remaining unhedged risks as part of all market-related risks. We conclude with a review of ways to handle credit risk and transfer risk in international trade.

The case that follows brings up most of the issues.

Danish Weaving Machines

This is Copenhagen, in the late afternoon of December 31, 2005. Amid the din of popping champagne corks, you (a trainee) and three regulars (Peter, Paul, and Mary) are still working hard. This very evening your firm, Danish Weaving Machines (DWM), has to submit its bid for an international tender for the delivery of a piece of fully automated weaving equipment. The customer, Taiwan Weaving Amalgamated (TWA), has invited bids in the currency of the bidder (DKK for your firm). There is only one serious competitor, France's *Équipements de Tissage* (ET). Due to a combination of luck and intelligence work involving, among less unspeakable things, a rather expensive lunch in Paris, you know that ET has submitted a bid of EUR 2.8m. TWA will make up its mind on April 1, 2006, and will look at the price only (your and ET's equipment are embarrassingly similar). Production and delivery take a few weeks, payment would be by a banker's acceptance payable on sight and drawn on TWA's bank, First National of Taiwan, under a D/A documentary credit opened by First National via an L/C confirmed by your bank, Handelsbanken. The production cost would be DKK 18m. How should you set your price?

That looks easy to Peter: "For two months in a row, the EUR has been at the bottom of the ERM band (at DKK/EUR 7.5), and it cannot go any deeper. So we set our price at DKK 20.999, somewhat below ET's price (EUR 2.8m × 7.5 = 21m). This leaves us a nice, sure profit of DKK 2.999." Paul disagrees. "You must be out of your mind," he shouts. "It's decidedly on the cards that the DKK will revalue soon; and bankers tell me that if and when there is a realignment, then by a time-honored ERM rule it will be by the cumulative inflation differential since the last realignment, that is, about 8%, to DKK/EUR 6.9. Just look at these forward exchange rates in the afternoon issue of *Børsen*:

spot	30d	60d	90d	180d	360d
7.50	7.30	7.25	7.20	7.15	7.10

If that's not half-predicting a lower EUR rate, I'll eat my hat." (Knowing Paul's hat quite well, the others look awed.) "If there is a realignment, ET would win hands down. So we should set our price at DKK 19.319," Paul concludes, "somewhat below EUR 2.8m × 6.9 = 19.32, so that we win whatever happens. This still leaves us a profit of DKK 1.319m. This profit, unlike Peter's figure, is really safe; and 1.319m in the hand is better than 2.999m in the bush."

Mary is less than fully supportive: "Proverbs are for nitwits. What's 'a' bird anyway? What about two humongous birds in the bush versus a tiny, scruffy specimen in the hand? That is, how do you know that the PV of the risky but potentially high-payoff bid is lower than the PV of the risk-free one? You haven't even stated what the probabilities of a devaluation are. Nor have you explained how you set the discount rate as a function of the uncertainty, and how you defined the risk."

A thoughtful silence follows (apart from the continuous popping of champagne corks, elsewhere in the office). Fortunately for Peter, Paul, and Mary, at this very moment the managing director comes in and takes them on his one-horse open sleigh to *Ensemble*, a (then) Michelin-starred restaurant on Tordenskjoldsgade, thus leaving you, the trainee, with the problem. You have to fax TWA tonight, and the wrong decision will end your career at DWM.

Issues

1. What occult meanings and dark messages might be hidden in the cryptic phrase "payment would be by a banker's acceptance payable on sight and drawn on TWA's bank, First National of Taiwan, under a D/A documentary credit opened by First National via an L/C confirmed by your bank, Handelsbanken"?

Read chapter 15 to find out. For current purposes, take this as meaning you get paid upon shipment of the machines. Using this interpretation, think of the issues raised by the following questions 2-9.

2. Suppose you want to reduce the uncertainty about the exchange-rate change. Is there any theory or type of information that would help reduce the uncertainty, or at least come up with a probability?

   Read chapter 10 to find out.

3. What kind of exposure is there if we submit the high DKK price, and if we submit the low price: contractual, operating, or accounting exposure?

4. Can one determine the size of the exposure, and, if so, what is the hedged value?

   Read chapter 13 to find out about these two questions.

5. In choosing between the two alternatives, could any additional considerations play a role, or do we have enough information for the decision?

6. Suppose the optimal decision involves exchange risk. Does it make a difference whether you actually hedge, or is computing a hedged value as a tool in decision making all that matters?

7. Suppose that you read the Call for Tenders again, and, lo and behold, it says (in rather small print) that submitting an EUR bid is allowed.

   Your first reaction is that this does not help, since in the presence of a forward market any bid in EUR can be hedged into a DKK bid and vice versa. Then you realize that this hunch is clearly incorrect. Why? What was wrong with your initial hunch?

   Read chapter 12 to find out about questions 5-7.

8. What would the exposure be if you submit a price in EUR, say 2.799 85? Does a hedged value exists and, if so, what is it? Would you use this option to quote an EUR price?

9. What does TWA gain by adding the EUR option to the Call for Tenders?

10

Do We Know What Makes Forex Markets Tick?

In chapter 3, we had a first quick look at exchange rates, both nominal and real (relative to a base period). We saw that there are significant deviations from purchasing power parity. The real exchange rate is not equal to unity, as some economists hold (or held); and while deviations are quite persistent in the short run, the real rate fluctuates a lot in the longer run. Moreover, we saw that the nominal rate is responsible for most of the variability in the real rate. Lastly, neither the nominal nor the real rate seem to follow smooth paths with lots of predictability: there is not a lot of momentum (which would have allowed us to extrapolate past changes), nor is there a lot of mean reversion (which would have allowed us to predict a fast return to a putative normal level, after a shock). Yet all that was based on graphs and impressions; and the preliminary diagnosis of poor predictability was just univariate, that is, it referred to information from the same time series. In this chapter we present a more numerical picture of these and similar facts. We also ask two related questions. First, to what extent can one understand or explain, after the fact, what went on in the exchange markets? For instance, do formal models have anything to say about the yo-yoing of the USD, or can one hardly go beyond vague and hard-to-test statements like confidence and sentiment and so on? Second, can we predict exchange-rate changes using variables other than the time series of past spot data?

The two questions are distinct. For instance, there might be momentum—that is, a rise tends to be followed by another (but usually weaker) rise, and similarly for price drops—which would mean there is some predictability; but we may still be unable to understand why there is momentum, and what makes markets change direction if and when that happens. Or it may be that exchange rates look like random walks because the underlying factors behave that way too; for example, if changes in the values of currencies were driven by the current account, and if the current account itself changed sign unpredictably, then we would have an explanation but no forecasting potential.

For readers with a craving for neat and tidy insights, these twin chapters will not make happy reading. Exchange rates behave very much like random walks, and the standard theories fail to explain anything meaningful. Not surprisingly, then, standard theories fail even more signally to predict movements, except in the very long run, the one in which we will all be dead if Keynes is right about long runs. Also, technical models, which try to forecast on the basis of past price patterns, do less than splendidly. Even specialists, or self-proclaimed specialists, have a poor record, except maybe central banks.

We proceed as follows. First, we show you a battery of standard descriptive statistics—means, standard deviations, skewness and kurtosis, autocorrelations, and the like—about nominal exchange rates: their levels, their percentage changes, and the squares of these percentage changes. We try to see what it all means.

To find out whether a theory explains any of this, we then show the same statistics about two time series: (i) the rate as predicted by the theory, and (ii) the movements of the actual rate that are not explained by the theory under consideration. For instance, to see what PPP achieves, we look at the statistical properties of the relative PPP forecast $\hat{S}^{\text{PPP}}$, and then at those of $S/\hat{S}^{\text{PPP}}$, the real exchange rates. If PPP does well as a theory, its forecast $\hat{S}^{\text{PPP}}$ should behave in a similar way to the observed rate, and in the real rate there should be little variation left. Besides PPP we also consider the monetary model. For more recent competitors—approaches based on the real-business-cycle model and the Taylor rule—we review the literature.

The next chapter moves on to what could be called implicit predictors. One is the forward rate. If risk-adjusted expectations are close to true expectations, then any predictability of the exchange-rate change would be picked up by the forward premium. So even if we do not understand quite how and why the market sets the forward premium, we might still be able to use it in our planning, thus free-riding on the market's hoped-for superior information and/or insights. In another bid to see whether real-world humans might not be cleverer than econometricians, we look at the forecasts or buy/sell recommendations by self-styled experts, or at the behavior of individuals like traders—or institutions like central banks—who could plausibly be experts.

The main text only looks at the usefulness, or lack thereof, of a model. More details about the derivation of the model itself or about the test are presented as technical notes at the end of the chapter. Most of the results discussed here are illustrated on the basis of the same, recent, database. We do refer to findings by others too, of course; but in our survey of this vast area of research, we do not attempt to be complete; instead, we look at some representative studies and broadly summarize the results of a class of many empirical tests. (Apologies to the many colleagues I have omitted to mention.)

From the above, you may have gathered that this chapter uses more statistics than the rest of the book. If your background in statistics is weak, just try to understand the conclusions. If you know some general statistics but little about the specific issues in time series analysis, a useful investment may be to read an introductory textbook. If, lastly, you have had some exposure to time series analysis but you need to dust it off, you may want to glance at the first two technical notes, which review some statistical concepts that are used in this chapter. You surely should do so if you do not quite remember the meaning of conditional moment, unconditional moment, stationary variables, trending, autocorrelation, unit-root processes (with an infinite unconditional mean and variance), random walk, martingale, studying changes of I(1) variables, cointegration (technical note 10.1), and mean, variance, skewness, excess kurtosis, tests on autocorrelation estimates (Q, DF/ADF), half-life (technical note 10.2). If you know all that, you may still be curious about terms like strict versus covariance stationarity, trend, characteristic equation of an autocorrelation spectrum. If so, read the technical notes for your education. Then proceed to the main results.

All statistical results are based on the same data set, covering seven countries and, thus, six currency pairs against the USD. Three countries have been mainstream Western economies during the period from 1970 until the present day: Germany (DE; DEM spliced together with EUR, as of 2003), the United Kingdom, and Japan (JP). Four more countries were chosen for being important mezzanine economies and also for having good data coverage: India (IN), Brazil (BR), South Africa (ZA), and Thailand (THB); not all have good data readily accessible, though. The OECD group is occasionally referred to, in this chapter, as the mature economies, and the second trio as the emerging-market (EM) group. Data are mostly from the IMF's International Financial Statistics database, now part of Thomson DataStream. All data start in 1970 unless otherwise indicated, and end in July 2007. All data are monthly except for the (shorter) daily spot-rate files. For the monetary model we have used quarterly observations. Jumps in series due to monetary reforms (BR) are avoided by rescaling.[1]

We start with a description of the spot data.

10.1 The Behavior of Spot Exchange Rates

10.1.1 Why Levels of (Log) Exchange Rates Have Bad Statistical Properties

Any statistician would, naturally, first study the properties of the variable in the form in which they are usually encountered in real life. In the case of exchange rates, etc., this is the level of the rate, not the change or percentage

---

[1] In 1967, the *novo cruzeiro* (BRB) replaced 1,000 old ones (BRZ). In 1986 the *cruzado* (BRC) replaced 1,000 no-longer-new *cruzeiros*—only to be exchanged 1,000 to 1, in 1989, for the *novo crusado* (BRN). The latter was renamed *cruzeiro* (BRE) in 1990. In 1993 1,000 of these were replaced by the *cruzeiro real* (BRR); the name harks back to the colonial *real* (pl., *reis*) and later *mil reis*. In 1994 2,750 of these became the current *real* (BRL), initially worth USD 1.

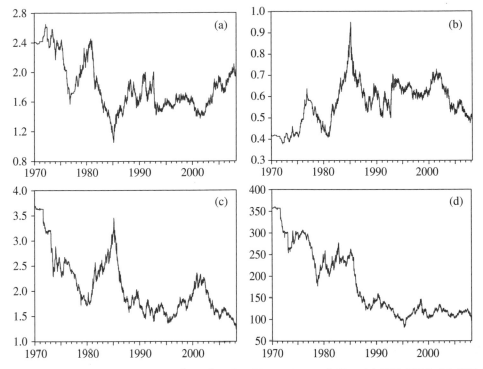

Figure 10.1. Exchange rates: plots for the GBP, DEM, and JPY. (a) USD/GBP, (b) GBP/USD, (c) DEM/USD, (d) JPY/USD. *Key:* Rates are in the market's standard units, that is, in HC/USD (rates for the USD as foreign currency) except for GBP, which is in USD/GBP (the GBP as foreign currency). The pound is also shown the other way. *Source:* Underlying data are from DataStream. Graphs kindly provided by Liu Fang.

change. Figures 10.1 and 10.2 show these data, but we want more than just to look at pictures: we want to find out the crucial properties, as summarized by statistical parameters. Upon hearing the data are a time series, a seasoned economist would not first check the "moments" (mean, variance, skewness, kurtosis), but the autocorrelation spectrum: this contains information that tells us whether the sample moments are of any use at all.

An economist would probably also study logs rather than the raw numbers. By taking logs the values below unity are extended (all the way to $-\infty$) while the big ones are reined in, and the more so the bigger they are:

S	0.00001	0.0001	0.001	0.01	0.1	1	10	100	1,000	10,000	100,000
$\ln S$	-11.51	-9.21	-6.91	-4.61	-2.30	0.00	2.30	4.61	6.91	9.21	11.51

Why or when is the log transformation useful? First, in a series with lots of variation as to the levels, taking logs de-exponentializes the effects of growth. Many economic series grow steadily over time, so on a long-term graph there is hardly any visible change at low levels while wild jumps take place at high levels. After taking logs we see more balanced patterns, where every millimeter on the graph means the same *percentage* growth everywhere, whether we are

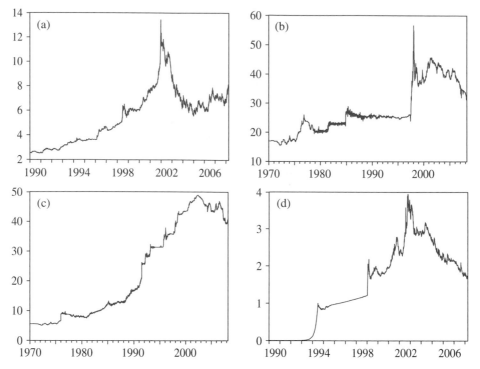

Figure 10.2. Exchange rates: plots for the ZAR, THB, BRL, and INR. (a) ZAR/USD, (b) THB/USD, (c) INR/USD, (d) BRL/USD. *Key:* Rates are in the market's standard units, that is, HC/USD (rates for the USD as foreign currency). For Brazil, the earliest years refer to the cruzeiro, replaced by the crusado at 1,000 to 1 in 1993. In 1994, 2,750 crusado's became one real. All numbers underlying the graph are in real. So the 1990 numbers, for instance, are the then-used cruzeiro rates divided by 2,750,000. *Source:* Underlying data are from DataStream. Graphs kindly provided by Liu Fang.

at the low or the high end of the range. This is useful if you think that a change from 100 to 110 is as important as a change from 1,000 to 1,100. Figure 10.3 illustrates this. Second, taking logs makes things more symmetric up versus down. After all, most economic numbers are nonnegative, so they can drop by no more than 100%; but they can rise by 200% or 400%. So if you feel that a drop from 100 to 50 is as momentous as a rise from 100 to 200, logs will do that for you: $\ln 100 - \ln 50 = 0.693$ while $\ln 100 - \ln 200 = -0.693$. Third, by (almost) the same token, in the case of exchange rates the distribution is not essentially affected whether we use FC/HC or HC/FC: $\ln 1/S = -\ln S$.

Let us turn to the statistical results. When studying descriptions of $\ln S$, we should pay particular attention to the following:

• The "simple" first-order autocorrelation coefficient $\rho_{1,S}$, derived from the simple regression

$$\ln S_t = \rho_{1,S} \ln S_{t-1} + e_t,$$

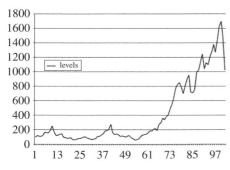
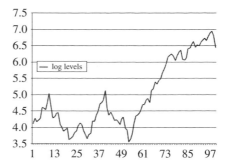

Figure 10.3. Levels versus logs. *Key:* The level graph was generated by my computer as a unit-root process with a drift. Taking logs, changes at low levels become relatively more pronounced while changes at high levels get downsized. Specifically, equal percentage rises now look equally big everywhere, and so do equal percentage falls.

> where a unit value indicates a wandering process without any long-run attractor value (i.e., no unconditional expectation and a fortiori no unconditional variance).

- The Box–Ljung statistic (a test of whether the true ρs might all be zero, with a low value for Q meaning the ρs tend to be low).

- The augmented Dickey–Fuller (ADF) coefficient b in

$$\ln S_t - \ln S_{t-1} = a + b \ln S_{t-1} + c\, t + \sum_{l=1}^{L} \rho_{l,\Delta S}[\ln S_{t-l} - \ln S_{t-l-1}] + e_t'',$$

> which offers a test of whether the process $\ln S$ might be wandering around without having any long-term unconditional expected value to which it keeps being attracted. A simple version is derived in the next section, and a generalization in a technical note, but it should be obvious that a sufficiently negative b means that such an attractor probably exists while a slightly negative b means there might very well be no such thing as an unconditional attractor. Indeed, when b is negative, unusually high exchange rates are then followed by drops, and unusually low exchange rates are followed by rises, but when b equals zero we simply have aimless wandering behavior.

We look at daily series (with a shorter coverage) and at monthly versions starting in 1970.

The autocorrelation coefficients in table 10.1 are all large. For daily data, there is virtually no trace of mean reversion. In fact, each and every estimated ρ for the daily data is rounded to 1.00, i.e., falls between 0.995 and 1.005. Of the ADFs, only one (Brazil's) is far enough below zero to convincingly reject the martingale. Do glance at the Qs, too: these would be absurdly large numbers if a true unconditional mean and variance did exist. All this evidence in favor of a unit root means there is no point in looking at the estimated moments (means, variances, skewness, kurtosis).

In the monthly data there are occasional traces of mean reversion. Now twenty-four out of thirty-five $\hat{\rho}$s are below 0.995, and eight are even below 0.975. Yet the lowest number is still 0.92, and the ADFs remain unimpressed by all these below-unity autocorrelations: only the real's logs are again diagnosed as almost surely not a martingale.

We conclude that the series are close to martingales. If they had been perfect martingales, this would have meant that sample moments from mean to kurtosis are pointless, and that standard statistical tools are of no use. Here we do have traces of mean reversion, implying that moments and standard statistics might possibly work in infinite samples. But we have a finite one, and we have no idea about the reliability of moments and so on in a sample of a mere thirty-five years, and we are not even sure there would be mean reversion in an infinite sample. Thus, we resort to differenced data, that is, changes in the logs rather than levels of logs.

10.1.2   Changes in Log Rates: Findings

10.1.2.1   Interpreting Changes in Logs

Changes in logs (sometimes called "continuously compounded returns") are closely related to percentage changes. The relationship the best and brightest may remember from chapter 8 is that the log-change return is the log of the gross simple return (unity plus the simple return):

$$\underbrace{\ln S_T - \ln S_t}_{\substack{\text{Continuously} \\ \text{compounded} \\ \text{return}}} = \ln\left(\frac{S_T}{S_t}\right) = \ln\left(1 + \underbrace{\frac{S_T}{S_t} - 1}_{\substack{\text{Simple} \\ \text{return}}}\right). \qquad (10.1)$$

But the relation does not stop at there being an exact link. In fact, log changes are numerically similar to percentage changes, at least when not too large. In standard calculus, this reflects the property $d\ln x = dx/x$: for absolutely tiny changes, the log change equals the percentage change. True, negative returns are stretched out and positive ones pulled back, but that effect is strong only for big changes:

$(\Delta S)/S$	-0.9	-0.50	-0.100	$-0.010\,00$	$-0.001\,000\,0$	0
$\Delta\ln S$	-4.6	-0.69	-0.105	$-0.010\,05$	$-0.001\,000\,5$	0

$(\Delta S)/S$	$0.001\,000\,0$	$0.010\,00$	0.100	0.50	1.0
$\Delta\ln S$	$0.000\,999\,5$	$0.009\,95$	0.095	0.41	0.69

Given that we have short intervals, changes in logs are essentially percentage changes or, loosely speaking, "returns." (The language is loose because the true return from holding forex normally includes the foreign interest, which we do not consider here.) Relative to regular simple returns, these continuous-compounding returns have the advantage that they are additive over time: the two-period return is the sum of two one-period returns. To demonstrate this,

Table 10.1. Descriptive statistics on spot rates (1): logs of levels.

Daily logs of levels

	Nobs	Moments				Autocorrelations for the variable itself							Autocorrelations among squares					
		avg	var	skw	krt	ρ_1	ρ_2	ρ_3	ρ_4	ρ_5	Q	ADF	ρ_1	ρ_2	ρ_3	ρ_4	ρ_5	Q
GBP	9650	0.57	0.03	0.41	-0.32	1.00	1.00	1.00	1.00	1.00	48 111	-2.11	1.00	1.00	1.00	1.00	1.00	48 111
DEM	9650	0.69	0.06	0.55	-0.61	1.00	1.00	1.00	1.00	1.00	48 171	-2.00	1.00	1.00	1.00	1.00	1.00	48 171
JPY	9650	5.10	0.16	0.36	-1.40	1.00	1.00	1.00	1.00	1.00	48 237	-1.71	1.00	1.00	1.00	1.00	1.00	48 237
ZAR	9650	0.85	0.77	0.00	-1.40	1.00	1.00	1.00	1.00	1.00	48 262	-0.60	1.00	1.00	1.00	1.00	1.00	48 262
THB	7040	3.40	0.06	0.51	-1.34	1.00	1.00	1.00	1.00	1.00	35 164	-1.82	1.00	1.00	1.00	1.00	1.00	35 164
BRL	4163	-0.19	4.10	-2.35	4.51	1.00	1.00	1.00	1.00	1.00	20 837	-5.92	1.00	1.00	1.00	1.00	1.00	20 837
INR	9114	2.97	0.49	0.00	-1.69	1.00	1.00	1.00	1.00	1.00	45 415	-0.70	1.00	1.00	1.00	1.00	1.00	45 406

Monthly logs of levels

	Nobs	Moments				Autocorrelations for the variable itself							Autocorrelations among squares					
		avg	var	skw	krt	ρ_1	ρ_2	ρ_3	ρ_4	ρ_5	Q	ADF	ρ_1	ρ_2	ρ_3	ρ_4	ρ_5	Q
GBP	444	0.57	0.03	0.41	-0.34	0.99	0.97	0.95	0.94	0.92	2046	-2.14	0.99	0.97	0.95	0.94	0.92	2046
DEM	444	0.69	0.06	0.54	-0.60	0.99	0.98	0.97	0.96	0.95	2112	-2.04	0.99	0.98	0.97	0.96	0.95	2112
JPY	444	5.10	0.16	0.36	-1.40	1.00	0.99	0.99	0.98	0.98	2194	-1.71	1.00	0.99	0.99	0.98	0.98	2194
ZAR	444	0.85	0.77	0.00	-1.40	1.00	1.00	1.00	1.00	0.99	2229	-0.63	1.00	1.00	1.00	1.00	0.99	2229
THB	324	3.40	0.06	0.52	-1.34	0.99	0.98	0.97	0.96	0.95	1553	-1.50	0.99	0.98	0.97	0.96	0.95	1553
BRL	192	-0.19	4.11	-2.38	4.68	1.00	0.99	0.99	0.98	0.97	955	-4.55	1.00	0.99	0.99	0.98	0.97	955
INR	420	2.97	0.49	-0.01	-1.70	1.00	1.00	1.00	1.00	1.00	2118	-1.03	1.00	1.00	1.00	1.00	1.00	2119

Key: Nobs, number of observations; avg, average; var, variance; skw, skewness; krt, (excess) kurtosis; ρ_l, autocorrelation coefficient for lag l; Q, Box–Ljung statistic on the sum of the ρs, against the null of a zero sum; ADF, augmented Dickey–Fuller statistic for the null of no mean reversion (i.e., a unit root). See the technical notes for definitions. The critical values for the ADF with an intercept, at 5% (1%), are −2.88 (−3.45), and those for the Box–Ljung $\chi^2(5)$ are 11 (15). Table kindly provided by R. H. Badrinath.

we consider the return over the two-period interval between $t-1$ and $t+1$, then add-and-subtract $\ln S_t$, and immediately discover the two one-period returns:

$$\overbrace{\ln S_{t+1} - \ln S_{t-1}}^{\text{2-period return}} = \underbrace{\ln S_{t+1} - \ln S_t}_{\text{2nd-period return}} + \underbrace{\ln S_t - \ln S_{t-1}}_{\text{1st-period return}}. \qquad (10.2)$$

This additivity implies that means and variances of log-change returns are easily annualized. The example reminds you how we did this in chapter 9 (option pricing).

Example 10.1. If the expected return next month is 1% and its variance 0.0025, we figure out what would be the outcome if we had twelve such months in a row, assuming independence:

- The expected value of a sum of twelve monthly returns, each with mean 1%, would be 12%.
- The variance of a sum of twelve independent monthly returns, each with variance 0.0025, would be $12 \times 0.0025 = 0.03$, i.e., an annualized standard deviation (*volatility*) of $\sqrt{0.03} = 17.3\%$.

This is just an annualization: we do not really believe that all monthly returns are i.i.d. It is like saying you now drive at 60 km/hr even though you know that, over the next hour, your speed will change all the time.

As an aside, log changes do have one big imperfection, which explains why they have not always and everywhere replaced simple returns. Notably, the log change of a portfolio (the portfolio return) is not a weighted average of the log changes of the component assets. Simple returns do have that additivity-across-assets property. That is why simple returns are used in portfolio theory and in related empirical work while log-change returns are the preferred variant for time series analysis.

10.1.2.2 Interpreting Autocorrelations in Returns

Being experienced statisticians, we will again first look at the autocorrelations. Now, in a reasonably efficient market, speculative returns cannot be unit-root, or even remotely like unit-root: (i) in a properly functioning market, deviations from the market's expected return must be totally unpredictable, and (ii) these unexpected deviations represent most of the variation over time, dwarfing the contribution of changes in expected returns over time. Given that we know that returns are not unit-root, our interest is no longer in how close the ρs are to unity. Rather, we want to know how close they are to zero and what we can infer from them about how markets think. The issue is how predictable percentage changes are, and the most popular statistic is the first-order ρ.

We will assume, as of now, that ρ_1 is sufficiently close to zero so as to make the return well-behaved, like having an unconditional mean and variance. If the first-order ρ is the only one that matters, then the condition is that ρ be strictly below unity and above -1.[2] But even when the unconditional moments for the returns are meaningful numbers, a nonzero ρ still means that the conditional moments are not constant, and most noticeably so the expected value. For convenience, let us denote log changes (or "returns") by $\tilde{s}_{t,t+1} := \ln \tilde{S}_{t+1} - \ln S_t$. Then the first-order autocorrelation model means that, upon observing the last-period return, we update the unconditional forecast $E(\tilde{s})$ as follows:

$$E_t(\tilde{s}_{t,t+1} \mid s_{t-1,t}) - E(\tilde{s}) = \rho_1 [s_{t-1,t} - E(\tilde{s})]. \tag{10.3}$$

Example 10.2. Suppose that $\rho_1 = 0.10$. If in the long run the currency is appreciating by 0.1% per month but last month the currency fell by 5%, then our forecast for this month is no longer the unconditional 0.1% but

$$0.001 + 0.10 \times (-0.05 - 0.001) = 0.001 - 0.0051 = -0.0041 = -0.41\%.$$

What could be behind a nonzero ρ_1? We first discuss positive ρ_1s and then negative ones.

Positive autocorrelation. If $0 < \rho_1 < 1$, any above-average value of $\tilde{s}$ tends to be followed by a value that is still above the mean ("momentum"), but typically less so than its forerunner ("regression toward the mean" for returns).

Positive autocorrelation in returns, if observed, could be consistent with many explanations. Our discussion is based on equation (11.18) in technical note 11.2, which states that the expected exchange-rate return equals (approximately) the forward premium plus the risk premium—the normal expected return over and above the risk-free rate for an asset of this risk. So the realized return equals this normal expected return plus a noise term:

$$\tilde{s}_{t,t+1} \equiv E_t(\tilde{s}_{t,t+1}) + \tilde{\epsilon}_{t,t+1}$$
$$\approx FP_{t,t+1} + RP_{t,t+1} + \tilde{\epsilon}_{t,t+1}. \tag{10.4}$$

In light of this, the autocorrelation could come from any of the three terms on the right:

Slow changes in forward premia. Forward premia are highly autocorrelated, approaching unit-root behavior. That is, when the premium rises, most or all of that rise is persistent rather than temporary. Long episodes of high premia, everything else being the same, then logically mean long episodes of above-average returns and vice versa, i.e., autocorrelation in the returns.

Waves in the risk premium. Positive autocorrelation could result from slow changes in risk or in the degree of risk aversion in the market. Waves of

---

[2] If $\rho_1 = -1$, we get a contradiction similar to the one when $\rho_1 = 1$ if we conjecture that the unconditional variance exists: if $x_t = -x_{t-1} + e_t$, then $\text{var}(x) = \text{var}(x) + \text{var}(e)$?! So ρ_1s of $+1$ and -1 both mean that (means and) variances are infinite, i.e., not defined. Note that when higher-order autocorrelations also play a role (over and above the first-order part), then we should look at the sum of all nonzero partial autocorrelations, not just the first one, before we dare make any statements about whether the process might be stationary or not.

higher risk or higher risk aversion could lead to higher expected returns for fairly long periods, which again means that above-average returns would tend to be followed by more above-average returns.

While theoretically correct, these are not powerful explanations. As we shall see in section 11.1, the link between forward premia and exchange-rate changes is empirically very poor. So either the variability in the forward premium must be trivial relative to that in ϵ or movements in the forward premium must tend to be offset by opposite changes in the risk premium, so that their sum hardly moves over time.[3] This last line of thinking means we ought to model the risk premium separately; but, as we shall see, attempts to do so have been largely unsuccessful. This gets us to the third possible source of momentum:

Inefficiencies. The error term in equation (10.4) should be truly unpredictable if markets are efficient: unexpected changes should be, er, unexpected, i.e., unpredictable. So only inefficiencies could lead to positive autocorrelation (momentum or continuation) in the error term. Here are a couple of examples:

Bandwagon effects. When an increase in the spot rates has been observed, following an exogenous event, investors think that more increases will follow. Thus, they start buying the foreign currency too, "before it is too late," which reinforces the initial increase, and so on—the same way a rolling bandwagon gains momentum each time a new passenger jumps on board.

Slow dissemination of information. At first, only well-informed players trade on good (or bad) news, and force a price change; then other groups gradually obtain the same information, trade on it, and induce more price changes in the same direction, and so on.

Negative autocorrelation. If, instead, ρ_1 turns out to be negative but above minus unity, then the interpretation is that an above-average observation tends to be followed by one that is below the mean—but with a smaller deviation, in absolute terms. Since the mean is close to zero, this boils down to saying that price rises or drops tend to be partly undone in the next period, with $|\rho|$ telling us how much of the original price change is wiped out in the next period.

Negative autocorrelation cannot stem from the forward premia (which are positively autocorrelated); they are unlikely to come from risk premia: risks are not commonly thought of as flipping their signs in the short run; so inefficiencies are the more likely explanation. Notably, any negative autocorrelation would point at a tendency for the market to overreact to new information: any

---

[3] I just list the mathematical possibilities. Finding an economic reason why this would be the case is quite another kettle of fish.

Table 10.2. Descriptive statistics on the spot rate (2): changes of logs.

Daily logs changes

| | | Moments | | | | Autocorrelations for the variable itself | | | | | | | Autocorrelations among squares | | | | | |
	Nobs	avg (%²)	var (%²)	skw	krt	ρ_1	ρ_2	ρ_3	ρ_4	ρ_5	Q	ADF	ρ_1	ρ_2	ρ_3	ρ_4	ρ_5	Q
GBP	9649	-0.19	0.33	-0.12	4.41	0.03	0.01	-0.01	0.01	0.03	23	-42.09	0.11	0.13	0.12	0.13	0.11	698
DEM	9649	-1.04	0.40	-0.03	4.67	0.01	0.00	0.00	0.01	0.01	4	-96.99	0.16	0.13	0.07	0.05	0.08	548
JPY	9649	-1.19	0.40	-0.82	11.84	0.01	0.02	0.00	0.00	0.01	8	-1.72	0.09	0.07	0.04	0.03	0.04	167
ZAR	9649	2.35	0.69	1.04	62.56	-0.01	-0.02	-0.01	0.01	-0.01	5	-23.89	0.07	0.06	0.04	0.04	0.12	254
THB	7039	0.52	0.40	3.68	132.80	-0.16	0.08	-0.14	0.12	0.00	452	-13.74	0.28	0.22	0.20	0.22	0.24	1918
BRL	4162	20.20	1.65	3.60	88.92	-0.03	0.16	0.11	0.12	0.10	270	-4.48	0.48	0.25	0.01	0.01	0.00	1203
INR	9100	1.78	0.22	118.01	3.38	-0.13	0.06	-0.02	-0.01	-0.02	188	-68.44	0.11	0.27	0.02	0.01	0.02	811

Monthly log changes

| | | Moments | | | | Autocorrelations for the variable itself | | | | | | | Autocorrelations among squares | | | | | |
	Nobs	avg (%)	var (%)	skw	krt	ρ_1	ρ_2	ρ_3	ρ_4	ρ_5	Q	ADF	ρ_1	ρ_2	ρ_3	ρ_4	ρ_5	Q
GBP	443	-0.04	0.08	2.19	-0.19	0.07	0.01	0.01	0.01	0.02	3	-19.44	0.19	0.02	0.00	0.10	0.08	23
DEM	443	-0.23	0.10	0.95	0.03	0.05	0.07	0.01	-0.02	0.00	4	-19.94	0.12	0.03	0.00	0.09	0.03	11
JPY	443	-0.26	0.10	2.03	-0.55	0.04	0.06	0.06	0.01	-0.03	4	-20.13	0.06	0.07	-0.02	0.02	0.10	8
ZAR	443	0.51	0.16	6.95	1.10	0.04	0.06	0.09	-0.03	-0.10	11	-20.22	0.20	0.04	0.11	0.10	0.17	42
THB	323	0.11	0.09	26.36	1.56	0.12	-0.05	0.09	-0.07	0.09	13	-7.02	0.26	0.22	0.17	0.10	0.20	63
BRL	191	4.28	1.27	2.35	1.69	0.67	0.64	0.61	0.59	0.58	376	-2.53	0.64	0.64	0.57	0.50	0.48	318
INR	419	0.38	0.04	25.25	2.77	0.06	0.09	0.05	0.05	0.04	8	-4.21	0.00	0.00	0.01	0.00	0.00	0

Key: Nobs, number of observations; avg, average; var, variance; skw, skewness; krt, (excess) kurtosis; ρ_l, autocorrelation coefficient for lag l; Q, Box-Ljung statistic on the sum of the ρs, against the null of a zero sum; ADF, augmented Dickey-Fuller statistic for the null of no mean reversion (i.e, a unit root). See the technical notes for definitions. The critical values for the ADF with an intercept, at 5% (1%), are −2.88 (−3.45), and those for the Box-Ljung $\chi^2(5)$ are 11 (15). Table kindly provided by R. H. Badrinath.

change would then generally be corrected afterward. This view is implicit in the term "technical correction," popularly used by the press: a price drop makes the asset more attractive, so demand increases, which forces the price back up.

All this should help you make sense of autocorrelation coefficients in returns. Provided that autocorrelations are sufficiently low, the regular moments also make sense now, as do autocorrelations for squared returns. Autocorrelations for squared returns are very close to autocorrelations in squared unexpected returns, since expected returns have but a small variability. So these autocorrelations in squared returns signal either continuation or oscillation in variance:

$$\text{If} \qquad\qquad \epsilon^2_{t,t+1} = \gamma + \delta\epsilon^2_{t-1,t} + \nu,$$

$$\text{then} \qquad E_t(\epsilon^2_{t,t+1} \mid \epsilon_{t-1,t}) = \gamma + \delta\epsilon^2_{t-1,t},$$

$$\text{i.e.,} \qquad \text{var}_t(\epsilon_{t,t+1} \mid \epsilon_{t-1,t}) = \gamma + \delta\epsilon^2_{t-1,t}. \qquad (10.5)$$

So following a big change (in absolute terms), the variance for the next period would be updated in the positive sense, if δ is positive. (Negative δs, which would induce oscillation in the variance rather than continuation, are harder to imagine.) We have a closer look at this class of "autoregressive conditional heteroskedasticity" (ARCH) models in chapter 14 when we discuss Value-at-Risk models.

Let us now see what the actual numbers are.

10.1.2.3 Findings

Table 10.2 summarizes the tests. Here is the tale.

Autocorrelation. Are log returns possibly unit-root variables, like martingales or other footloose processes? That is, are autocorrelations statistically far from unity? Under the hypothesis of reasonably efficient markets and fairly stable expected returns we expect total asset returns to be closer to white noise than to martingales. Even though, in our tests, we omit the interest component from the returns, these expectations are not generally confounded: all the ADFs now comfortably reject the martingale for returns, except the real at the monthly frequency.

Let us now see how close the autocorrelations are to zero. In that respect there are differences across currencies and frequencies. The OECD currencies and the ZAR have essentially zero autocorrelations at the daily level. True, the pound has a significant Q, but this does not necessarily mean a lot. In a large sample (almost 10,000 data), even an autocorrelation of 0.03 is statistically convincing; economically, though, it is meaningless: such an autocorrelation means that, upon seeing yesterday's return, we can reduce the uncertainty about today's coming return by a mere $R^2 = 0.03^2 = 0.0009$, i.e., 0.09%. For the baht, rupee, and real there is some zigzagging, with overreaction at the first lag and continuation at the second.[4] The coefficients are also economically large. But they could be largely due to one or two outlier reversals. For instance, the huge spike in the baht exchange rate in figure 10.2 means a big positive return, largely undone by a big negative one the next day. This huge negative cross product is responsible for most of the negative autocorrelation. That is, the "overreaction" signaled by the negative ρ_1 does not necessarily mean systematic overreaction; one huge correction suffices.

At the monthly level, in contrast, there is general evidence of momentum. For the first three currencies, the individual ρs are not significant (with 444 observations, the standard error is 0.0475); and even taken together the four coefficients $\rho_1, \ldots, \rho_4$ do not reject the pure martingale for prices, as the Qs show. The ZAR, THB, and INR are border cases. The real, finally, showed extremely heavy autocorrelation even for returns, even to the extent that the ADF does not rule out a martingale (?!). This can be traced back to the subperiod of hyperinflation, where the USD appreciated by huge percentages for months in a row.

Given that means and variances do seem to exist, for returns, we can now fruitfully study the moments too.

Unconditional moments. The *means* are negative for OECD countries (the USD fell), and positive for the EMs. These averages, in percent, are small except for the real, where the USD appreciated strongly. Equally sensibly, the *variances* are smallest for the INR, a managed rate, and largest for the BRL. For the OECD countries, *skewness* is close to zero, but for the EMs the skewness was more pronounced, and positive. Since the EM rates are in HC/USD, this means that the biggest moves were mainly positive, i.e., rises in the dollar. *Kurtosis*, finally, is generally excessive (relative to the normal), but far more so for the EMs. At the monthly level there seems to have been a bit of a central-limit effect, though: both skewness and kurtosis are far less abnormal. Brazil's kurtosis is even quite low, but with such massive autocorrelation the estimated moments may behave quite unexpectedly.

Conditional heteroskedasticity. Recall that the ρs for returns tell us that, especially for daily returns for EMs, conditional expectations are not constant. Similarly, the autocorrelations for squared returns can tell us whether uncertainty comes in waves. At both the daily and monthly frequency, Qs are significant for all currencies, the ρs economically meaningful, and the echoes in risk often go back several periods. We conclude, unsurprisingly, that variance is unstable over time.

---

[4] This is not strange: if $r_t = -0.15 r_{t-1} + e_t$, then the first-order link in itself already induces a second-order link of $(-0.15)^2 = 0.062$. The fact that the actual ρ_2 is higher than ρ_1^2 means that there is a positive direct effect from day $t-2$ over and above the compounded one-day effects.

10.1.3 Concluding Discussion

Before moving on, let us review what a few other authors have found in studies more ambitious than ours, and let us put all this into an economic context.

The findings of near-unit-root behavior has triggered a lot of research because, for exchange rates, it is a priori a rather implausible story. There are two elements in the argument:

- Real exchange rates, for one, cannot go wandering off aimlessly: no country can become a hundred times more expensive than its neighbor. Now the real rate is the difference between the nominal and the PPP rate; given that for most countries the PPP rate moves very sluggishly, we would be surprised if the mean reversion we expect in real rates is not showing up in nominal rates too.

- Nor would predictability in exchange rates mean that markets are inefficient. The reason is that expected appreciation or depreciation is just part of the investor's total return; the second part, foreign interest income, can perfectly reconcile predictability in the capital gains/losses with rationality. For example, if a currency is unusually undervalued by PPP standards and, therefore, would be expected to appreciate, then its interest rate should be lower too, making the total return no higher and no lower than what risk would justify.

So why do we fail to see much of that mean reversion? Like in the literature on real exchange rates (where much more research has been done), the answer may very well be that the basic tests lack statistical power. Remember that, when the null hypothesis is that there is a unit-root, failure to reject this hypothesis does not prove that there *is* a unit root; rather, it just means that there *might be* a unit root. More precisely, the observed deviations from what the null predicts were not large enough to be near impossible under the null; but failing to prove that H_0 is wrong is a far cry from proving that H_0 is right. If you observe an $\hat{\rho}_1$ of 0.95 and if the ADF accepts the null of a unit root, then the true ρ_1 may be 1.00—but it might also be 0.95, and quite possibly even 0.90 and all values in-between. Now if the test lacks power, deviations from what one expects under the null can become very large before one concludes the null is almost surely wrong. Thus, failures to reject probably cover many cases where in reality there was no unit root, but the evidence was not compelling enough to make this glaringly obvious even to congenitally agnostic statisticians. How can we improve power?

Longer data periods. One way to gain power is to add more data, preferably in the form of longer periods, not higher observation frequencies. Lothian and Taylor (1996) study two hundred years of annual USD/GBP and FRF/GBP data and find clear mean reversion. Still, one wonders how relevant data from the gold-standard era are if one's purpose is to understand the current float.

Multivariate tests. The other way to add power is to work with multivariate tests: combine time series and cross-sections into a single estimation round. Sweeney (2006) puts the data through seemingly unrelated regressions (SURs). This technique estimates many equations simultaneously rather than one by one, and tries to exploit any cross-series correlations between errors to obtain extra precision. Sweeney concludes that there is mean reversion:

> SUR tests on panels of Group-of-Ten nominal rates frequently reject the null of unit roots in favor of mean reversion for various samples over the current float, the first such results in the literature. Second, in out-of-sample forecasts, mean-reversion models tend to beat random walks. Third, asset-pricing model tests support the joint hypothesis of mean reversion and exchange-market efficiency.

Cleverer models. One can also gain power by adopting a nonlinear model. The standard error-correction models, including the ADF test, are all log-linear models, in that the expected percentage change is supposed to be proportional to the initial percentage deviation between the actual rate and its supposed attractor (here, a long-run mean):

$$E_t(\tilde{s}_{t,t+1}) = \kappa \left[E(\ln \tilde{S}) - \ln S_t \right] + \cdots . \tag{10.6}$$

Yet it is increasingly clear in many areas of economics that small deviations between an observed variable and its equilibrium value are largely ignored by the market, while bigger and bigger deviations do lead to faster and faster adjustment. That is, κ should not be modeled as a constant; instead, it should be allowed to be small when the disequilibrium is small in the absolute sense, and approach unity when the disequilibrium is huge. If κ is a function of $\ln S_t - E(\ln \tilde{S})$, the model becomes nonlinear in the logs. We will see applications of this type in the next section.

Alternatively or complementarily, one can try to filter out noise. Lisi and Medio (1997) combine this with a nonlinear model. Filtering is done via a multichannel version of singular spectrum analysis—don't ask—adapted to a nonlinear dynamics context. "Filtered data are then used to perform an out-of-sample, short-term prediction, by means of a nonlinear (locally linear) method. This method is applied to exchange-rate series of the major currencies and the predictions thus obtained are shown to outperform neatly those derived from the [random walk hypothesis]."

Changing the question. From the above, the unit-root diagnosis may be due to too few data and overly simple statistics. Yet one cannot help thinking that if it takes such arcane techniques and such long histories to discover mean reversion, then its practical relevance in the short run must be minimal. Maybe we are even asking the wrong question. Remember that if mean reversion is weak, then to statistically establish that property one needs data that cover a long period. But using a long period may undermine the test, because the models considered thus far assume a constant unconditional mean as the attractor, which may be palpably inappropriate in the long run.

> **Example 10.3.** In 1958 France's president De Gaulle introduced the *nouveau* (= new) *franc* at 100 times the *ancien franc*'s value, or, to me, ten Belgian francs. Decades later the FRF was down to BEF 7 and even 6. There was no hope that this would be reversed, since France had been inflating much faster than Belgium. No government would willingly strangle the country's entire open sector (exporting and import-substituting) by a huge revaluation away from the equilibrium rate.[5]
>   Likewise, the GBP used to be worth BEF 140 and then sank to 45 (in 1992) to settle at about 60. There is no good economic reason for the rate to return to its old value.

So if the attractor is the PPP rate and if that rate has long memory, reversion to the PPP rate would land us with a unit-root nominal rate too. So perhaps it is time that we looked at the PPP model.

10.2   The PPP Theory and the Behavior of the Real Exchange Rate

Recall, from chapter 3, that the PPP rate is the notional exchange rate that would equalize the price levels Π internationally:

$$\hat{S}_t^{\mathrm{PPP}} = \frac{\Pi_t}{\Pi_t^*}. \tag{10.7}$$

As early as the Renaissance, scholars at the University of Salamanca claimed that exchange rates tended to equalize prices across countries. In 1918 the Swedish economist Gustav Cassel (1866–1945) rediscovered the idea, and coined the term "purchasing power parity." To test this hypothesis two questions need to be answered first, one practical and one conceptual.

10.2.1   Issues with PPP Tests

10.2.1.1   *What If We Don't Really Have Long Time Series of Frequent Price-Level Data?*

The practical problem is that data on absolute price levels are patchy, at best.[6] The World Bank and the OECD computed them every ten years or so as of the 1980s, for a cross section of fifty countries, using a relatively narrow bundle of goods. The IMF produced a bigger study in 2007, covering most of the IMF's (then) 185 members and a bundle of 3,000 goods. For years without price-level data, proxies can be constructed by updating the latest available figure

---

[5] Going back to BEF/FRF 10 would be OK only if France's price level also dropped by 60% relative to its main trading partners, but that would be a long and painful struggle which no politician would ever attempt, not even for *la gloire*.
[6] Recall that price levels tell us the total cost, in local currency units, of a given bundle of goods. Indices, by contrast, use different bundles tailored to local tastes and express the cost relative to the cost in a base year rather than as an absolute cost figure.

via inflation rates obtained from local CPIs. But there certainly is no monthly figure for true price levels in most countries.

In academic research, the standard alternative is to use CPIs as second-best proxies. The assumption is that CPIs are proportional to price levels:

$$\left.\begin{array}{l} \Pi_t \approx k\,I_t \\ \Pi_t^* \approx k^*\,I_t^* \end{array}\right\} \quad\Longrightarrow\quad \hat{S}_t^{\mathrm{PPP}} \approx \frac{k\,I_t}{k^*\,I_t^*} =: \alpha\frac{I_t}{I_t^*}. \tag{10.8}$$

Note that, in the absence of good price-level data, the ks cannot be identified and their ratio α must be estimated from the data. For instance, one can set α such that it fits the first observation, or such that the average deviation over the entire sample is zero; but then one is really testing relative PPP not absolute PPP. Stated differently, we cannot verify how far the real rate deviates from unity, only to what extent it drifts off from its initial or average level. With just CPIs, there is simply no way to find out whether a country is cheaper, on average, than another.

Incidentally, the IMF's 2007 survey revived other qualms about PPP-rate proxies. Notably, questions were raised about including goods into the "world representative bundle" that, in some countries, are not even available, let alone consumed by most agents.[7] In addition, prices can be very heterogeneous even inside a country. China's coastal cities, for instance, are very different from Tibet, and so is Hong Kong relative to most of continental China. To solve the latter problem, in the IMF study the "special administrative zones" (SARs), Hong Kong and Macau, are reported separately from the rest of China; but it's not so easy to treat the coast as separate from inland China. In 2007, the IMF's 60% upward revision of China's and India's price levels, which meant a 40% cut in their GDPs (computed at the PPP rates), understandably raised eyebrows, and was said by some to be the result of giving too much weight to city prices.

10.2.1.2 What If the Indices Contain Many Nontradables? The Balassa–Samuelson Effect

The second issue concerns the existence of nontradables, that is, goods that cannot be shipped (like real estate) or for which the trading cost would be so high that they are de facto never traded (like haircuts).[8] Can one hope for any

---

[7] In welfare economics and so on, differences in preferences are handled by defining country-specific bundles, scaled in such a way that one unit of the bundles provides the same level of utility everywhere. For instance, if investors have Cobb–Douglas preferences $c_0^a\,c_1^{1-a}$ at home and $c_0^b\,c_1^{1-b}$ abroad, then the bundles would be defined as combinations that (i) are on the indifference curve $c_0^a\,c_1^{1-a} = 1$ at home and $c_0^b\,c_1^{1-b} = 1$ abroad, and (ii) are utility-maximizing given the relative prices in the country. Note that, when tastes differ across countries, APPP would generally not hold even in perfect commodity markets. In practice, of course, there is no way to operationalize the same-utility criterion as we do not know utility functions well enough.

[8] Every rule has its exception. Mobutu Sese Seko Nkuku Nbengdu Wa Za Banga, the less than universally lamented late dictator of the Kongo (Zaire), used to have a barber flown over from New York to Kinshasa, first class, once a month. Still, most agents would think the cost of doing so excessive.

commodity-price-parity effect for these? At first sight, it seems reasonable to say that in countries where tradables are cheap the nontradables prices are also low. But Balassa (1964) and Samuelson (1964) pointed out that the relative price of tradables and nontradables differs vastly across countries, and that the differences are strongly related to the productivity of labor and hence to real GDP per capita. Here are the details.

Balassa and Samuelson assume that there is a nontradable good (denoted, below, as good 0) in each country, and one perfectly tradable good (good 1). The real exchange rate can always be written as a function of the relative prices of the nontraded good abroad and at home. Below we start from the definition of the real exchange rate, and specify the function, for simplicity, as weighted averages of the prices of tradables and nontradables.[9] For a less cluttered view, I omit the time-t subscripts in all variables. In the second line I factor out the tradable-goods prices, and in the third I use the property of perfect tradables: their exchange-adjusted prices are identical, or $SP_1^* = P_1$,

$$S_t \frac{\Pi^*(P_0^*, P_1^*)}{\Pi(P_0, P_1)} = S_t \frac{w^* P_0^* + (1 - w^*)P_1^*}{w P_0 + (1 - w)P_1}$$

$$= S_t \frac{P_1^*}{P_1} \times \frac{w^*[P_0^*/P_1^*] + (1 - w^*)}{w[P_0/P_1] + (1 - w)}$$

$$= \frac{w^*[P_0^*/P_1^*] + (1 - w^*)}{w[P_0/P_1] + (1 - w)}. \tag{10.9}$$

In this equation, the real exchange rate is determined by the relative prices of nontradables versus tradables: how many widgets do I need to give up for a haircut? Now tradables are essentially industrial goods, Balassa and Samuelson argue, while nontradables heavily overlap with services. The Balassa–Samuelson proposition is then that APPP will not hold: the poorer country will be cheaper, on average, because services are cheaper.

Below, we arbitrarily assume that the home country is more developed than the foreign one. The argument then proceeds as follows. In the developed home country with its capital-intensive industries, productivity of labor is high, and so, therefore, are wages, relative to the price of industrial goods. For example, the home wage per hour may amount to six widgets, the foreign one just two. But in the service industries, technologies are much more similar across countries; say, one needs half an hour per haircut in either country. So to keep a barber at home from taking a job in the tradables industry, the price of a haircut at home must be high, like three times the price of a widget, while, abroad, paying the barber the equivalent of one widget is enough. Or, stated from the macro point if view, if labor is productive in the industrial sector, then the half-hour spent clipping someone's coiffure is costly in terms of

---

[9] This would work as a first-order approximation for the case of identical Cobb–Douglas preferences, in which case the price level should really be measured by $\Pi = a^a(1-a)^{1-a}c_0^a c_1^{t-a}$. The purpose, here, is just to give you the gist of the argument.

widgets that could have been produced during that time: while P_0^*/P_1^* equals unity abroad, the relative cost is three at home. Thus, if the price indices have the same weights, the real rate for the developing country is below unity. That conclusion holds a fortiori if, realistically, $w > w^*$ (that is, if the richer country (home) also consumes more services).

Example 10.4. If the productive labor force at home is paid an hourly wage equivalent to six widgets at home while labor abroad earns just the value of two widgets, then a half-hour haircut must cost three widgets at home and one abroad. So the real rate is calculated as follows:

$$\text{Real rate} = \frac{w^* \times 1 + (1 - w^*)}{w \times 3 + (1 - w)},$$

$$\text{if } w = 0.5 = w^*: \quad \text{real rate} = \frac{0.5 + 0.5}{1.5 + 0.5} = 0.50. \tag{10.10}$$

This explains what many readers may have experienced already when traveling: richer countries tend to be more expensive. One implication is that the old practice of translating GDP per capita numbers at nominal rates systematically overstates real income disparities. Returning to our earlier practical issue—having to use CPIs for lack of true price-level data—the implication is that we will probably miss a lot of deviations from absolute PPP. But that cannot be helped.

10.2.2 Computations and Findings

Since there is no standard quote, in trading rooms, for PPP rates, we now adopt the same quote method for all countries. Specifically, we look at rates from the U.S. point of view, in USD per FC corrected for inflation differences, for example. First we work with graphs. We download CPIs and compute ratios I_t/I_t^* for all months 1970–2007. We then fix the constant α such that the mean of $\alpha I_t/I_t^*$ matches the mean of the actual rates over the first decade, 1970–79. Thus, by construction the actual and PPP series do match fairly well over the first ten years; the question is whether they still stay close to each other in the twenty-six subsequent years. Matching over an entire decade is less subject to sample coincidences than matching just the first date (as we did in chapter 3), and less biased in favor of PPP than making the averages match over the entire sample.

The picture that emerges from figures 10.4 and 10.5 is quite similar to the one we guessed at in chapter 3: for every country, (i) RPPP rates are much smoother and more predictable than actual spot rates; and (ii) the time paths of the two series are rather loosely connected, at best. It is in fact hard to gauge how much of a link there is between actual rates and the RPPP predictions. The pound should have lost a lot of value but somehow it hasn't: it is still close to the rate in 1970 (or in the days of Shakespeare, for that matter). But if you had not seen the last five years, you would say the two paths are

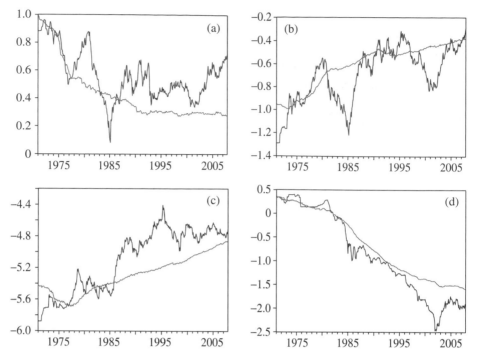

Figure 10.4. Exchange rates and inflation: plots for the GBP, DEM, and JPY. (a) USD/GBP, (b) USD/DEM, (c) USD/JPY, (d) USD/ZAR. *Key:* Rates are logs of USD/FC (natural U.S. quotes). The RPPP rates are computed from CPIs and rescaled such that their average over the first ten years matches that of the corresponding actual exchange rate. *Source:* Underlying data are from DataStream. Graphs kindly provided by Fang Liu.

fairly closely linked. The DEM and JPY serendipitously end close to their RPPP predictions, but in the meantime there were enormous deviations. The ZAR is like a textbook example, and might fool many a student—until you start seeing the scale of the deviations: in 2002, the difference between the logs of the two rates is over one unit large, which, in standard numbers, means a deviation of more than 2.5 to 1 ($e^1 \approx 2.7$). Thus, in 2002 the rand was all of a sudden worth less than 40% of its RPPP value versus 1970–80. The baht is a case to be studiously avoided by PPP teachers. The rupee, next, should have dived, RPPP says, and it duly did—but by far more than predicted. Brazil, finally, looks like another example that would set a PPP believer's hair on fire—until, again, you start noticing the scale of the deviations: there is a good fit in the hyperinflation days, but basically nothing after that, with big differences of up to 1 for logs, i.e., more than 2.5 to 1 in standard numbers. The second graph for Brazil, where the hyperinflation period is left out, shows this quite clearly.

From the graphs I would conclude that there is "often" a "meaningful, long-run" link—but do note how I hedge my words: my tendency to see links might just be the result of my strong a priori opinion in favor of the PPP logic. So let us turn to more cold-hearted numbers.

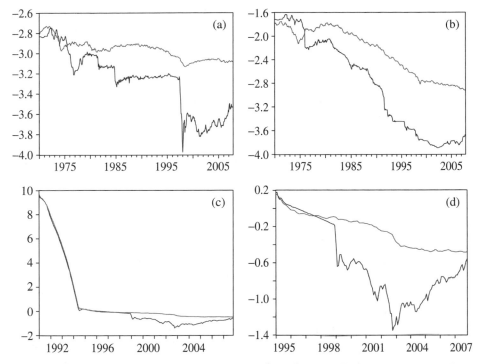

Figure 10.5. Exchange rates and inflation: plots for the ZAR, THB, BRL, and INR. (a) USD/THB, (b) USD/INR, (c) USD/BRL, (d) USD/BRL. *Key:* Rates are logs of USD/FC (natural U.S. quotes). The RPPP rates are computed from CPIs and rescaled such that their average over the first ten years matches that of the corresponding actual exchange rate. *Source:* Underlying data are from DataStream. Graphs kindly provided by Fang Liu.

The same conclusions emerge when we let the numbers speak. Table 10.3 applies the by-now familiar array of tests to the log of the RPPP rate, and then to the log real rate, i.e., the difference between the log actual and the log RPPP one.

If PPP works well, the RPPP rate would behave very much like the actual rate as described in the previous section. In terms of persistence this is certainly true. Specifically, when comparing the RPPP rates with the S statistics (the top half of table 10.3 versus the bottom half of table 10.1) we see very similar values for the first-order correlations and the ADFs, and even slightly higher values for the Box–Ljungs on the sum of the correlations. (Make sure you compare with the monthly, not the daily, spot data in table 10.1.) Thus, RPPP rates are very close to unit root. On more a priori grounds this is quite plausible: unlike for a real or nominal rate (where, I argued, unit-root properties are hard to imagine in the long run), it does seem acceptable that the RPPP rate has no tendency to revert. Once a country has inflated, it may want to lower its inflation rate but never goes to the lengths of actually lowering its absolute prices by persistent deflation. Once prices have gone up they stay up.

In light of this prior and the sample evidence, I happily accept unit-root characteristics for the RPPP rate. This makes a study of the moments of that time series rather pointless. The next question is whether this explains the behavior of the nominal rate, in the sense that the two time series never wander off very far from each other. More formally, the question is whether the log of the real rate—which is the difference of the two martingales or almost-martingales—is a much more finite-variance process, as it should be, according to Cassel:

$$\text{Long-run RPPP:} \quad \ln S = \ln \hat{S}^{\text{RPPP}} + \epsilon, \quad \text{where var}(\epsilon) < \infty. \tag{10.11}$$

Table 10.3 shows the necessary information. What we actually see is that the first-order correlations are not all that much lower than those we saw in the previous section, on the raw spot rates. Instead of mostly 1.00–0.99 the ρs are now falling slowly from an average of 0.99 at lag one to 0.92 at lag five. Of course, in light of that, the Qs must also fall; and they do. But the ADFs are actually closer to zero (the population value for a unit-root process) than what we saw in the case of raw spot rates. Thus, unexpectedly to Cassel & Cy, even the real rate is close to unit-root.

If so, then autocorrelations between changes must be close to zero. To check this we also produce statistics on the changes in the logs of the PPP rate and the real rate. Table 10.4 summarizes the results. Here are some striking observations:

- Changes in RPPP rates—inflation differences across the two countries, basically—are only mildly autocorrelated. What looks like an easily predictable path is not actually more predictable than the real rate: in reality, it just has lower volatility. One exception is the real, where there was strong persistence in the inflation differences and where even the ADF does not reject martingale behavior. Yet that finding probably reflects just the (long past) period of hyperinflation; how relevant it is nowadays is dubious.

- The variability of the log changes in the RPPP rate is quite small relative to that of the actual rate of the real rate—with the single exception of, again, the real.

- Moments for changes in log real rates are close to their nominal counterparts, and the same holds for autocorrelations. The single exception is, once more, the real, where the real rate's returns had lower variance than the nominal rate's returns.

In short, the main driver of a real rate is the nominal rate, not the PPP rate. Or, stated differently, the RPPP rate has small variability and explains virtually nothing about the nominal rate. Only for a hyperinflator like (at one point) Brazil does the inflation differential explain away much of nominal-rate changes. To disappoint the incurable optimists: this does not mean that

Table 10.3. Descriptive statistics on the scaled RPPP rate and the real rate (1): log levels.

Log RPPP rates

	Moments					Autocorrelations for the variable itself							Autocorrelations among squares					
	Nobs	avg	var	skw	krt	ρ_1	ρ_2	ρ_3	ρ_4	ρ_5	Q	ADF	ρ_1	ρ_2	ρ_3	ρ_4	ρ_5	Q
GBP	443	0.41	0.04	1.49	1.10	1.00	1.00	1.00	1.00	1.00	2229	-3.70	1.00	1.00	1.00	1.00	0.99	2227
DEM	443	-0.64	0.03	-0.84	-0.67	1.00	1.00	1.00	1.00	1.00	2235	-2.41	1.00	1.00	1.00	1.00	1.00	2234
JPY	443	-5.36	0.05	0.09	-0.99	1.00	1.00	1.00	1.00	1.00	2233	-0.05	1.00	1.00	1.00	1.00	1.00	2233
ZAR	443	-0.64	0.47	0.09	-1.61	1.00	1.00	1.00	1.00	1.00	2238	-0.80	1.00	1.00	1.00	1.00	1.00	2237
THB	323	-3.35	0.00	-0.17	-1.54	1.00	0.99	0.99	0.99	0.98	1608	-0.61	1.00	0.99	0.99	0.99	0.98	1609
BRL	215	6.32	12.29	1.69	1.31	1.00	1.00	0.99	0.99	0.99	1087	-3.84	1.00	1.00	0.99	0.99	0.98	1081
INR	441	-2.50	0.15	-0.29	-1.50	1.00	1.00	1.00	1.00	1.00	2221	0.12	1.00	1.00	1.00	1.00	1.00	2222

Log of actual over RPPP rates

	Moments					Autocorrelations for the variable itself							Autocorrelations among squares					
	Nobs	avg	var	skw	krt	ρ_1	ρ_2	ρ_3	ρ_4	ρ_5	Q	ADF	ρ_1	ρ_2	ρ_3	ρ_4	ρ_5	Q
GBP	443	0.16	0.02	-0.15	-0.20	0.98	0.95	0.93	0.91	0.88	1940	-2.15	0.97	0.93	0.89	0.85	0.81	1777
DEM	443	-0.05	0.03	-0.62	-0.15	0.98	0.96	0.94	0.91	0.89	1969	-2.22	0.97	0.94	0.91	0.87	0.83	1841
JPY	443	0.26	0.06	-0.33	-0.26	0.99	0.98	0.97	0.95	0.94	2094	-2.70	0.98	0.96	0.93	0.91	0.89	1953
ZAR	443	-0.21	0.06	-0.85	0.50	0.99	0.97	0.96	0.94	0.92	2041	-2.21	0.98	0.95	0.92	0.88	0.85	1885
THB	316	-0.05	0.03	-0.43	-1.01	0.99	0.97	0.95	0.94	0.92	1495	-1.77	0.93	0.87	0.83	0.80	0.79	1174
BRL	191	-5.09	0.07	-0.28	-0.69	0.97	0.95	0.93	0.91	0.89	854	-1.21	0.97	0.95	0.93	0.91	0.89	849
INR	417	-0.44	0.11	0.29	-1.37	1.00	1.00	0.99	0.99	0.99	2077	-2.10	1.00	0.99	0.99	0.98	0.98	2064

Key: The RPPP rates are computed from CPIs and rescaled such that their average over the first ten years matches that of the corresponding actual exchange rate. Nobs, number of observations; avg, average; var, variance; skw, skewness; krt, (excess) kurtosis; ρ_l, autocorrelation coefficient for lag l; Q, Box–Ljung statistic on the sum of the ρs, against the null of a zero sum; ADF, augmented Dickey–Fuller statistic for the null of no mean reversion (i.e., a unit root). See the technical notes for definitions. For an ADF test with an intercept, in a sample of the size of ours, the critical values at the 5% and 1% significance level are about -2.88 and -3.45, respectively, and those for Box–Ljung are about 11 and 15. Table kindly provided by R. H. Badrinath.

Table 10.4. Descriptive statistics on the RPPP rate and the real rate (2): changes in logs.

Changes in log RPPP rates

	Nobs	Moments				Autocorrelations for the variable itself							Autocorrelations among squares					
		avg (%)	var (%)	skw	krt	ρ_1	ρ_2	ρ_3	ρ_4	ρ_5	Q	ADF	ρ_1	ρ_2	ρ_3	ρ_4	ρ_5	Q
GBP	442	−0.16	0.00	−1.96	7.99	0.27	0.10	0.07	0.02	0.06	42.7	−3.27	0.29	0.07	0.09	0.05	0.00	136.56
DEM	442	0.13	0.00	−0.20	2.17	0.22	0.18	0.15	0.08	0.15	58.7	−3.07	0.14	0.04	0.17	0.05	0.02	23.93
JPY	442	0.13	0.00	−1.19	3.70	0.17	−0.07	0.03	0.08	0.18	33.3	−2.59	0.24	0.13	0.20	0.17	0.16	77.27
ZAR	442	−0.44	0.01	−0.47	0.77	0.07	0.12	0.23	0.04	0.12	40.4	−3.03	0.04	0.15	0.08	0.01	0.02	14.28
THB	322	−0.04	0.00	−0.48	1.61	0.26	−0.08	0.00	−0.05	0.07	26.6	−3.73	0.00	0.02	−0.01	0.09	0.10	5.73
BRL	214	−5.86	1.18	−2.41	7.83	0.85	0.81	0.77	0.71	0.67	641.6	−1.61	0.42	0.42	0.36	0.29	0.24	136.56
INR	440	−0.26	0.01	0.22	1.16	0.49	0.25	0.13	0.04	−0.13	148.8	−4.87	0.30	0.22	0.08	0.11	0.12	77.33

Changes in log of actual over RPPP rates

	Nobs	Moments				Autocorrelations for the variable itself							Autocorrelations among squares					
		avg (%)	var (%)	skw	krt	ρ_1	ρ_2	ρ_3	ρ_4	ρ_5	Q	ADF	ρ_1	ρ_2	ρ_3	ρ_4	ρ_5	Q
GBP	442	0.13	0.09	−0.20	2.03	0.07	0.01	0.00	0.00	0.02	2.53	−19.48	0.19	0.00	0.02	0.10	0.08	23.09
DEM	442	0.10	0.10	−0.06	0.97	0.04	0.07	0.01	−0.03	0.01	3.51	−20.13	0.12	0.03	0.00	0.08	0.05	10.21
JPY	442	0.14	0.11	0.47	1.99	0.07	0.05	0.05	0.00	−0.01	4.49	−19.62	0.06	0.05	−0.01	0.03	0.10	7.50
ZAR	442	−0.07	0.16	−0.92	6.42	0.04	0.04	0.09	−0.06	−0.10	11.20	−5.37	0.23	0.04	0.10	0.14	0.22	59.64
THB	315	−0.09	0.10	−1.32	25.89	0.10	−0.08	0.07	−0.08	0.08	11.09	−7.22	0.23	0.21	0.14	0.08	0.18	52.06
BRL	190	0.12	0.37	−2.50	21.80	−0.07	−0.05	0.03	0.02	0.07	2.80	−5.54	0.05	0.18	0.00	−0.01	−0.02	7.17
INR	416	−0.13	0.05	−1.73	12.44	0.12	0.07	0.08	0.03	0.01	11.74	−5.29	0.00	0.00	0.01	0.02	0.00	0.24

Key: Nobs, number of observations; avg, average; var, variance; skw, skewness; krt, (excess) kurtosis; ρ_l, autocorrelation coefficient for lag l; Q, Box-Ljung statistic on the sum of the ρs, against the null of a zero sum; ADF, augmented Dickey-Fuller statistic for the null of no mean reversion (i.e., a unit root). See the technical notes for definitions. For an ADF test with an intercept, in a sample of the size of ours, the critical values at the 5% and 1% significance level are about −2.88 and −3.45, respectively, and those for Box-Ljung are about 11 and 15. Table kindly provided by R. H. Badrinath.

Brazil's real rate had low volatility; in fact, the opposite is true. Explaining a large fraction of an enormous nominal variability does not mean that the unexplained part is smaller than for sedate currencies.

10.2.3 Concluding Discussion

Before moving on, let us again review what a few other authors have found when they dug deeper into this issue, and what it all means economically. As before, we will note that the disappointing results may be due to short periods, simplistic models, or inefficient tests. But even these consoling thoughts cannot hide the fact that reversion to the PPP rate must be a pretty poor force; so we will also discuss the economics behind this.

10.2.3.1 PPP Tests: Statistical Issues

The earliest study of long memory in real rates was probably by Roll (1979). In fact, he proposed and tested what he called "*ex ante* PPP": RPPP holds, period by period, in terms of expectations not realizations. Avowedly prompted by a referee, Adler and Dumas (1983) note that *ex ante* PPP implies that the real rate is a random walk. Adler and Lehmann (1983) and Sercu (1983) then test for random walks, and found ρ_1s amazingly close to unity for the levels (Sercu) and to zero for the changes (Adler and Lehman). Abuaf and Jorion (1990) added the then newish ADF tests; using monthly postwar data they could not reject the random walk. All this seems to put PPP theory to rest. But the picture is no longer quite as bleak because better tests have come up. We discuss, sequentially, longer periods, nonlinear models, and multivariate estimation.

Covering long periods. Abuaf and Jorion were more successful when using one century of annual data collected by Kim Moon. They found half-lives of about three to five years—still not suggesting a dazzling speed of reversal, though. In their study of two hundred years of history for the USD/GBP and FRF/GBP rates, Lothian and Taylor (1996) find similarly clear reversion in the real rate. Half-lives are estimated at three to six years and a simple autoregressive model has an in-sample R^2 of 60–80%. Again, you might be right in wondering whether old data say much about the present and the future, and what the quality of really ancient price-index data might have been. But a companion paper, by Lothian (1997), surely raises the power issue by showing how, in random simulations with artificial data that have identical sample characteristics to the two-hundred-year sample standard, unit-root tests have extremely low power over sample sizes corresponding to the recent float. A twenty-year sample has virtually no chance of statistically establishing the mean reversion, and even fifty years does not suffice. Thus, the length of the time period is a big issue.

Multivariate estimation. Running the regressions simultaneously and exploiting links between them provides an alternative way to add power. Jorion and

Sweeney (1996) used a constrained multivariate framework, and provided the strongest evidence ever, at that time, that real exchange rates were mean reverting even over just twenty years (1973–93). The approach also works out-of-sample: forecasts that the rate will return toward the mean do far better than no-change forecasts, especially at long horizons. In addition, forecasting works much better than when a univariate (equation-by-equation) approach is adopted.

Nonlinear adjustments. A popular variant of a model with a variable adjustment speed, of the type already alluded to before, is the exponential smooth transition autoregressive (ESTAR) model. Its adjustment speed κ depends on how large the deviation from the equilibrium value is. Denote the log deviation from RPPP by $\Delta := \ln S_t - \ln(I_t/I_t^*)$. Suppose the long-run mean value of Δ is μ. (This may be the scaling factor in an RPPP equation; but it may also contain a genuine long-run deviation from APPP, for instance a Balassa–Samuelson effect.) Consider the function

$$f(\Delta) = \exp\left(-\left(\frac{\Delta - \mu}{\lambda}\right)^2\right). \tag{10.12}$$

This is the Gaussian density function up to a multiplicative constant; so $f(\cdot)$ is a bell-shaped function in Δ. It reaches a peak value of unity when Δ equals μ,[10] it curves down toward zero when $|\Delta| \to \infty$, and the width of the bell is steered by λ, the same way the standard deviation achieves this in a Gaussian bell. In the ESTAR model, one uses these properties by setting the adjustment speed equal to

$$\kappa(\Delta) = 1 - \exp\left(-\left(\frac{\Delta - \mu}{\lambda}\right)^2\right), \tag{10.13}$$

a function that converges to unity when $|\Delta| \to \infty$, and dips smoothly to zero when $|\Delta| \to 0$. The parameters μ and λ are estimated via nonlinear regression. Successful applications of the model were reported by, for example, Taylor et al. (2001) and Kilian and Taylor (2003). Using this model, Kilian and Taylor (2003) also report significant predictability of exchange rates at horizons of two to three years, but not at shorter horizons.

De Grauwe and Grimaldi (2001) test two PPP and quantity-theory propositions: when money supply doubles, then everything else being the same both the level of local prices and the value of foreign currencies should rise proportionally. (We will return to this in the next section.) Using a sample of one hundred countries over a thirty-year period they find that "the evidence in favour of these propositions is weak for the low inflation countries and very strong for the high inflation countries." One possible explanation is that the asymmetry has to do with productivity shocks and transaction costs. Again the story is that big signals—here, large inflation differences—are not ignored by

---

[10] Recall that EXP(0)=1. A normal distribution has no such fixed height since it includes a scaling factor $1/\sqrt{\pi\sigma^2}$, which pulls down the peak the wider the density.

the markets. Stated differently, by looking at orthodox OECD samples we may have been looking at samples where the signals were too weak to be relevant.

The weak OECD signals might also have been too noisy to be relevant. When prices are really soaring, the same monetary factor dominates the evolution of any price index, no matter what its coverage and construction is. But in a low-inflation environment, reported differences in inflation across countries may be mostly noise, perhaps because the index contains irrelevant goods or because the inflation differences stem from international inconsistencies in the weighting of the indices. This brings us to the last item.

Choice of indices. Xu (2003) finds that mean reversion is much stronger when traded-goods price indices (TPIs) are used, compared with wholesale price indices (WPIs), and a fortiori consumer price indices (CPIs). CPIs contain a lot of services, while WPIs mostly refer to manufactured goods, but not all of them are tradable.

It will probably not come as a surprise that PPP seems to do better the lower the weight of nontradables in the indices. Some economists have said that this practice reduces PPP to an uninteresting truism. This is not the case, I think: many "tradables" are not really traded in free, open markets, as we shall see, so long-run price parity for items that some academic or government clerk deems to be tradable is far from a foregone conclusion. Anyway, even if PPP between TPIs were really a truism, the businessman could not care less: if it allows better forecasts, even an uninteresting truism becomes fascinating. And better forecasts are exactly what the TPI-based variant provides.

10.2.3.2 PPP Tests: Economic Issues

From the above, there probably is mean reversion in the real rate, after all; and this mean reversion allows you to outclass the no-change forecast, at least for horizons of a few years. Still, the young economist or MBA might wonder how come the force is so weak. Most of the considerations below have to do with imperfections in the market for tradables, which make price-equalizing arbitrage difficult or impossible. But we begin with an argument that would work even with perfect arbitrage.

Relative price effects. Recall that we should be using price-level data—the cost of a given, common bundle of goods and services—but we actually rely on CPIs that reflect inflation in country-specific bundles. If one economy consumes lots of services and a second, less developed, country consumes far more basic goods, these different weights are reflected in the two CPIs.

These differences in CPI construction matter because for most of postwar history, service prices have tended to inflate faster than those of manufactured goods, reflecting slower growth in productivity and higher income elasticity for services; and food prices have been rising even more slowly, until quite recently. So even if, internationally, there were parity for each individual good and service, the service-hungry country would still report a higher overall inflation rate than the other one, after translation, because the CPIs are made differently.

Example 10.5. Suppose the United States gives weight 0.75 to services, and China 0.40. If, over ten years, inflation amounts to 50% for services against 20% for goods in both countries (after translation), then we would see

$$\text{U.S. inflation} = 0.75 \times 0.50 + 0.25 \times 0.20 = 0.425,$$
$$\text{China's inflation} = 0.40 \times 0.50 + 0.60 \times 0.20 = 0.320.$$

So there would seem to be a 10% deviation from RPPP even though each good is assumed to be priced the same in both countries.

Note that this is not the Balassa–Samuelson effect. The Balassa–Samuelson story is about nontradables with different prices across countries, while in the relative-price story we see developed countries inflate faster even if services are perfectly tradable and technologies are the same across countries. But a second reason why we see such weak links between price levels is indeed the existence of nontradables.

Nontraded goods. Many goods are essentially nontradable. For example, the price of goods such as housing or services (theater tickets, haircuts, or masters degrees) can differ enormously across countries because it is very difficult, almost impossible, to trade these goods.

The existence of nontradables might cause deviations from APPP if productivities differ across countries. But we are actually using CPIs, so we test, at best, RPPP. If services and other nontradables follow the same inflation rate as tradables, the existence of nontradables would still not cause any persistent RPPP deviations. But the rise in service prices could be drastically different across countries, even after translation, because of divergent economic growth.

Economic development. Although it is hard to imagine for youngsters, Japan in the 1960s was a simple country that specialized in imitations of Western products and cheap tin toys. So in the last fifty years the country has moved from the status of an emerging market to a very productive economy. Following Balassa–Samuelson, the real value of the yen should have risen, with Japan's service prices soaring from very cheap to very expensive. This rise in the real value of the yen should not be reversible, that is, it ought to be a long-run phenomenon. The same of course holds for all countries that catch up with the West: we should see a long-run rise in the real rates.

The remainder of the possible explanations of the observed persistence of RPPP deviations focus on why even for goods that are tradable (or that look as if they should be tradable) we see large, persistent price differences across countries.

Transaction costs. Tariffs, transportation costs, insurance fees, and other such costs, mean that if arbitrage transactions are to occur, a deviation from

CPP[11] must be sufficiently large to offset these costs. Thus, in the presence of such costs, commodity arbitrage, at best, restricts the deviations from CPP to within a band defined by transaction costs. CPP itself becomes a pipe dream.

Example 10.6. Let the price of this book in the United States be USD 65 and the spot exchange rate be USD/GBP 2.0. Now, the CPP hypothesis would propose a U.K. price of GBP 32.5. Suppose, however, that the book is selling in the United Kingdom at GBP 35. Then, in perfect markets, you could make USD 5 in (before-cost) arbitrage profits by buying the book in the United States and selling it in the United Kingdom (or British readers would save GBP 2.5 by buying from the United States). However, if the shipping and insurance costs for exporting the book from one country to another are USD 7, then you have no incentive to arbitrage or shop around as we just described.

Thus, in this case, the price of the book in the United Kingdom could be as high as (USD 65 + 7)/2 = GBP 36 before you would start exporting to the United Kingdom, and as low as (USD 65 − 7)/2 = GBP 29 before you would consider importing this book from the United Kingdom.

Now if such direct costs were all there was to it, PPP deviations could never have achieved the amplitudes and persistence we see in reality. In reality, commodity arbitrage as we have just described it is rarely possible because most goods are not easily traded (i.e., they are not commodities in the narrow sense), and they are often not tradable at all.

Nontariff barriers. In the presence of quotas, "voluntary" export restrictions, and other such barriers to trade, it is impossible to import more units once the import ceiling has been reached. Artificial technical restrictions similarly prevent trade.

Nonpecuniary costs. For most goods that prima facie ought to be tradable, direct cash expenses are not the sole consideration when weighing local purchases versus imports. Delays are one additional consideration. Referring to our earlier example on this textbook: if the first class, tomorrow, starts with a quiz that counts toward the final grade, you will buy locally even if Amazon can get it to you "within three weeks" at a saving of one pound. Hassle is another cost. For most goods, there is no such Amazon-like institution that simplifies international shopping around. So when buying, say, a hairdryer, few people will bother trying to find out prices in other countries: the likely savings are not worth the hassle.

When buying big-ticket items like cars, savings can indeed be quite significant. Still, most people would not know how to ship an automobile across the ocean, clear it through customs, and have it inspected for conformity with local regulations. Clearly, also, most people don't bother to find out. It's not just an issue of hassle: part of the reason is that an imported car (or any

---

[11] Recall, from chapter 3, that commodity price parity is the equivalent of APPP for an individual good j: $P_{j,t} = S_t P_{j,t}^*$.

imported durable) is not quite the same as a locally bought one in terms of after-sales service, warranty, and so on. In addition, you may fear that, when you bring in your car for repairs, the local dealer will regard you as a mean, devious backstabber who deserves to be taught a lesson.

The upshot of all the above is that the consumer rarely does the shopping around that could force prices back in line across countries. Even within the EU's supposedly unified markets there are 30–40% price differences for identical cars. The EU Commission has been issuing dark warnings to the producers for decades not to restrict trade, and has tried to prise open the dealership networks and stimulate "parallel" imports, but it has achieved preciously little, thus far.

To close the discussion we ask why the international producers and distributors themselves do not keep prices aligned, or why professional arbitrageurs do not step into what seems to be a hole in the market.

Price rigging. Most goods are not commodities (in the sense of goods that can be produced by many different suppliers and for which an open market exists). For manufactured goods, intracompany trade is the rule nowadays. Multinationals control worldwide distribution, and they set local prices so as to maximize profits. For example, exclusive dealerships lead to segmented markets across which one cannot arbitrage. Similarly, manufacturers make parallel imports difficult so that they can profit from price discrimination. Moreover, optimal prices for most manufactured goods tend to be quite sticky.

- When the currency of a market where a multinational sells is appreciating, the exporter is typically reluctant to pass on the change to the consumer. That would indeed mean lowering sales prices, i.e., starting a price war. It is usually better to stick to the cosy implicit cartel and keep prices close to those of the local producers.

- When the currency depreciates, multinationals are equally loath to pass on the change to the consumers, i.e., raise the sales price in the export market: the exporter would lose market share, which means that their investments in distribution and brand awareness would perish worthlessly and might have to be rebuilt, expensively, later on if and when the exchange rate reverts.

So local prices do not change even when there have been huge moves in the currency markets.

> **Example 10.7.** In the late 1980s, when the USD depreciated against the Japanese yen, CPP would have suggested that Japanese firms increase the USD prices of their goods. Given that many of the Japanese firms compete against only a small number of American firms (in the automobile and computer industry, for instance), instead of increasing their prices in the United States and thus losing market share, the Japanese firms decided to maintain their USD prices and suffer a reduction in profits.

Entry costs for professional arbitrageurs. You might still wonder why professional importers do not step in to import cars and the like in the customers' stead, and split the gains with them. The problem is that the setup cost is high: you would need to build not just a distribution network, but often also a maintenance and support network. The entry cost is even more of a problem because there is substantial uncertainty about future deviations from CPP and because the investments are mostly perishable. Will you really invest millions if the chances are that, in a few years, the price difference will be much smaller or might even have reversed and if, in that case, virtually nothing of the original investment could be recouped?

Krugman (1989) has insightfully added that the current float has been a killjoy for arbitrageurs. The larger the uncertainty about the future deviations from CPP, the larger the current deviation must be before you would consider incurring a big, irreversible entry cost to exploit the price gap. Thus, volatility is to some extent self-perpetuating since it discourages the arbitrage trade that otherwise constrains exchange rates.[12]

One message from this section surely is that the PPP force is weak in the short run, and that deviations from PPP can be very high before they trigger trade adjustments. Within this wide zone of acceptable exchange rates, the currencies then behave like financial assets. This point was already known to Keynes, who famously said that the value of the pound is set in the Stock Exchange not in the goods markets. The monetary model, which we discuss next, is much more of a financial theory, as are most models developed since.

10.3 Exchange Rates and Economic Policy Fundamentals

Since PPP, new models have come up that try to relate the exchange rate to "fundamentals" other than prices. Since most of this literature is macro, economic policy variables are especially sought after. The idea is that these might explain the price levels themselves, as in the original monetary model, and/or deviations from PPP, as in some second-generation versions of the monetary model and in the newer approaches. These models also claim to be more financial in nature, trying to price the exchange rate as discounted expectations. The most common starting point is either of the two equations below. The first is

---

[12] The argument echoes a result from option theory. When the underlying is more volatile, an option is worth more. Thus, for an American-style option early exercise tends to be postponed until the option is quite deep into the money. To see the link with our problem, you need to realize that setting up an arb network at an irreversible cost X is just an example of exercising an option on an asset (the network) and paying the strike price X. Also, the cash flow from running the business is a convex function in the exchange rate: export profits rise without limit when the FC keeps appreciating, but at the downside the option to quit means that cash flows ultimately stop falling when the FC keeps sinking. Flexibility in the pricing policy would add even more convexity to the cash flow function (chapter 13).

familiar from chapter 3; the second is an approximation of the first:

$$S_t = \frac{E_t(\tilde{S}_{t+1})(1 + r^*_{t,t+1})}{1 + r_{t,t+1} + RP_{t,t+1}}, \tag{10.14}$$

$$\implies \quad \ln S_t \approx E_t(\ln \tilde{S}_{t+1}) + \ln(1 + r^*_{t,t+1}) - \ln(1 + r_{t,t+1}) - RP_{t,t+1}. \tag{10.15}$$

Purists will disapprovingly note the approximation in the second line—equating, shockingly, $\ln[E(\tilde{S})]$ to $E[\ln(\tilde{S})]$ and taking the risk premium out of the log of the required return. But objecting to that is a losing battle, I have realized by now: macroeconomists' regrettable tolerance for approximations is a fact one has to learn to live with, along with death and taxes. Another problem is that the risk premium is unobservable; the typical "solution" is to assume it away, which lands us with, approximately, the uncovered interest parity (UIP) hypothesis (chapter 3). The new problem is that, empirically, the interest differential basically does not seem to be related to the future spot rate, as we will see in the next chapter: in reality, either the market seems to be unable to predict exchange-rate changes or the risk premium totally obscures that prediction. But, again, macroeconomists happily close their eyes to this minor imperfection and use UIP regardless.

We start with the grandfather model, the monetary approach, and then proceed to the real-business-cycle and Taylor-rule models.

10.3.1 The Monetary Approach to the Exchange Rate

The monetary approach to the exchange rate, or the asset approach—forex is regarded as an asset, not a relative price—combines the quantity theory of money with long-run PPP. Readers with a scholarly bent can find the derivation in technical note 10.3. In the most finance-oriented version, the approach is viewed as providing a theory about the market's expectations about the future spot rate; the current value is then obtained by discounting, taking into account the foreign interest earned.

The model says that, everything else being the same and in the long run, the spot rate converges to the PPP rate, which, in turn, reflects monetary policies and real activities. Our notation is L_s for money supply, Y for the real volume of transactions per period, and v for the velocity of the money. Here is the monetarist prediction:

$$\hat{S}^{\mathrm{mon}} = \frac{v}{v^*} \frac{L_s}{L_s^*} \frac{Y^*}{Y}. \tag{10.16}$$

Monetarists take the velocities to be constant or, at most, mildly fluctuating in line with interest rates. Given the velocities, the PPP prediction about the spot value of a foreign currency rises, ceteris paribus, if

- money supply abroad grows at a relatively slower rate, or
- real growth is relatively higher abroad.

The first prediction sounds uncontroversial, but the second one probably deserves some comment. The official version of the model relies on PPP and the quantity theory of prices, so the way real activity officially affects the exchange rate is via money demand and prices: more real activity requires more real money, but more real money, at constant nominal money supply and velocity, can only be obtained by falling prices—which then affect the PPP rate. Earthlings may have doubts about the argument; but to many the idea that booming economies have strong currencies does have an intuitive appeal regardless of the mechanism allegedly behind it.

Even hardcore monetarists would regard the above equilibrium rate as just a long-run attractor. In fact, all of the above are long-term equilibrium relations: no sane person believes that any change in money supply is instantaneously absorbed by a leap in prices; and PPP is also, at best, a long-run relation only. So we need to specify the link between the long-run value and the current exchange rate. Moreover, this must be done in a realistic setting.[13] One approach is to regard the vs, Πs, and Ys as current expectations about long-run values. These then determine the market's long-run expected exchange rate. The current spot rate, lastly, would be linked to the expected future value via the two countries' long-term interest rates, as suggested by UIP—basically equation (10.14) with a zero risk premium:

$$S_t = \frac{1 + r_{t,T}^*}{1 + r_{t,T}} \frac{v^*}{v} \frac{L_s}{L_s^*} \frac{Y^*}{Y}, \quad \text{where } T - t \text{ is "the long run."} \tag{10.17}$$

On this view, any rumor that has implications about long-run inflation rates and economic health would set the current exchange rate in motion. In addition, long-interest-rate changes would affect the spot rate. The Dornbusch variant, for instance, predicted that following a monetary expansion the domestic interest rate initially falls. The combined effect of the higher long-run expected value of the FC and the initial fall in the domestic interest rate is that the FC rises above its long-run level ("overshooting"), until domestic interest rates pick up as inflation actually starts to rise. Ultimately, the deviation from PPP peters out.

What is qualitatively interesting about this view is that, unlike the primitive PPP models, this story tells us why the exchange rate is moving all the time: because expectations do so too, as do interest rates. And the view that good

---

[13] In the model as it was written up originally, money supply changed once and forever, and the question was how that monetary shock would affect the long-run value of the spot rate and what its (interest-rate-driven) time path thither would be. So we need to adapt this to a world with ever-changing vs, Πs, and Ys.

Frankel (1979) brings in an intertemporal dimension in a totally different way. He assumed that the model holds contemporaneously and that the velocities can be written as $v = e^{\kappa R}$ (at home) and $v^* = e^{\kappa R^*}$ (abroad), so that v/v^* equals $e^{\kappa(R-R^*)}$. He then assumes unbiased expectations so that the interest differential predicts the expected rate of appreciation of the spot rate. For our purposes this is not interesting since if the model holds contemporaneously we have the perfect answer already: we do not need expectations.

news about the economy (Y) strengthens its currency, as does a higher interest rate, is surely popular.

Example 10.8. The very morning I typed up the above paragraph, on January 8, 2007, *De Morgen*, citing *De Volkskrant*, wrote that the recent weakening of the pound from its traditional level of EUR/GBP 1.5 to about 1.35 reflected reports of "a weakening of the British economy ... after almost a decade of feast years, ... disappointing Christmas sales, ... cooling of the residential market—pronounced drop of real-estate prices in December for the U.K." The expectation was that the BoE would cut its interest rates, "a reversal of the pound's traditional role as the harbor of choice for investors seeking higher yields. The official rate was lowered from 5.75 percent to 5.5, the first reduction in two years." The ECB, in contrast, was pondering a rate hike in light of inflation fears.

The model may sound appealing, by and large, but there are conceptual criticisms even before we take it to the data. The link between expectations and present value ignores risk, for instance. Empirically, exchange rates react more to short-term interest rates than to long-term ones. The empiricist may further object that, as it stands, the model remains untestable until the long-run expectations are somehow made visible.

One way to make the model testable is to heroically assume that long-run expectations are functions of just the current levels (Markov processes). Then the log exchange rate is explained by the interest rate and the current money supplies and real activities—the velocities are assumed to be constant, by and large—and the same relation holds between changes in $\ln S$ and in the fundamentals. All coefficients should be close to unity, and the predictions should be better than the martingale model. These regressions in levels and changes were famously run by Meese and Rogoff (1983), with disastrous consequences for the model.

10.3.2 Computations and Findings

We again have a look at some graphs to judge how strong the link between actual and model rates is. We download quarterly M_1, M_3, and real GDP data, and compute ratios $[L_t Y_t^*]/[L_t^* Y_t]$ for, ideally, all quarters in the period 1970–2007. The data availability turns out to be much poorer here, though, so for most countries we now have far fewer observations. (For the case of India we divided the annual GDPs by four to be able to add some early years.) We then fix the constant ω such that the mean of $\omega[L_t Y_t^*]/[L_t^* Y_t]$ matches the mean of the actual rates over the first decade, 1970–79. Again, by construction the actual and monetary model series do match fairly well over the first ten years, so the real question is whether they still stay close to each other in the subsequent years. In judging the results, remember that the model rates are not estimated by regression, but computed in the same a priori way as a PPP shadow rate, before.

Table 10.5. Descriptive statistics on the monetary model of the exchange rate (1): logs of levels, quarterly.

Actual spot rate, log

	Nobs	Moments				Autocorrelations for the variable itself							Autocorrelations among squares					
		avg	var	skw	krt	ρ_1	ρ_2	ρ_3	ρ_4	ρ_5	Q	ADF	ρ_1	ρ_2	ρ_3	ρ_4	ρ_5	Q
GBP	77	0.49	0.01	0.30	2.30	0.78	0.64	0.48	0.39	0.28	94.1	−2.73	0.53	0.36	0.05	−0.02	−0.07	60.8
DEM	144	−0.73	0.06	−0.60	2.44	0.93	0.87	0.80	0.73	0.64	444.4	−2.65	0.89	0.78	0.69	0.60	0.51	384.3
JPY	137	−5.10	0.15	−0.29	1.51	0.96	0.92	0.88	0.84	0.80	530.9	−1.42	0.87	0.78	0.70	0.62	0.53	385.0
ZAR	136	−0.76	0.77	−0.13	1.64	0.97	0.94	0.92	0.89	0.86	606.4	−0.56	0.97	0.95	0.92	0.88	0.85	617.8
THB	45	−3.54	0.05	0.50	1.45	0.91	0.83	0.73	0.66	0.59	148.3	−1.14	0.77	0.70	0.65	0.53	0.45	117.0
BRL	44	0.89	9.04	1.77	4.73	0.88	0.77	0.66	0.55	0.44	126.6	−3.01	0.84	0.67	0.51	0.37	0.25	94.5
INR	146	−3.82	0.00	−0.03	1.80	0.85	0.69	0.58	0.46	0.34	44.6	−1.81	0.63	0.27	0.03	−0.18	−0.42	43.7

Log of actual over proposed attractor, $(\omega M Y^* / M^* Y)$

	Nobs	Moments				Autocorrelations for the variable itself							Autocorrelations among squares					
		avg	var	skw	krt	ρ_1	ρ_2	ρ_3	ρ_4	ρ_5	Q	ADF	ρ_1	ρ_2	ρ_3	ρ_4	ρ_5	Q
GBP	77	−0.03	0.01	0.60	2.33	0.88	0.79	0.72	0.65	0.59	236.6	−2.72	0.66	0.55	0.27	0.16	−0.04	69.8
DEM	144	0.23	0.09	−0.17	2.06	0.95	0.91	0.85	0.79	0.73	508.2	−2.06	0.92	0.82	0.73	0.61	0.51	408.3
JPY	137	0.79	0.97	0.18	2.52	0.94	0.91	0.91	0.91	0.85	590.1	−1.89	0.72	0.61	0.64	0.67	0.43	330.8
ZAR	136	−0.90	0.60	−0.14	1.69	0.97	0.94	0.92	0.89	0.86	606.9	−0.66	0.97	0.94	0.90	0.86	0.82	599.0
THB	45	−0.25	0.10	−0.06	1.61	0.93	0.85	0.80	0.77	0.70	179.1	−0.28	0.69	0.38	0.26	0.25	0.05	39.7
BRL	44	−0.77	1.27	1.54	6.39	0.76	0.55	0.39	0.16	−0.02	66.5	−5.21	0.69	0.37	0.19	0.04	−0.04	35.8
INR	146	0.03	0.00	0.02	2.79	0.64	0.34	0.47	0.62	0.28	23.5	−1.58	0.33	−0.28	−0.11	0.12	−0.09	7.3

Key: Quarterly data. Nobs, number of observations; avg, average; var, variance; skw, skewness; krt, (excess) kurtosis; ρ_l, autocorrelation coefficient for lag l; Q, Box–Ljung statistic on the sum of the ρs, against the null of a zero sum; ADF, augmented Dickey-Fuller statistic for the null of no mean reversion (i.e., a unit root). See the technical notes for definitions. The constant ω in the attractor is set so as to equalize the means of attractor and actual rate over the first ten years. Table kindly provided by Fang Liu.

Table 10.6. Descriptive statistics on the monetary model of the exchange rate (1): changes of logs, quarterly.

Actual spot rate, change of log

		Moments				Autocorrelations for the variable itself							Autocorrelations among squares					
	Nobs	avg	var	skw	krt	ρ_1	ρ_2	ρ_3	ρ_4	ρ_5	Q	ADF	ρ_1	ρ_2	ρ_3	ρ_4	ρ_5	Q
GBP	76	0.18	0.28	−1.00	7.46	−0.12	−0.03	−0.09	0.01	−0.12	1.8	−9.40	0.06	0.04	0.00	−0.05	−0.02	2.2
DEM	143	0.56	0.30	−0.23	2.75	0.06	0.09	0.10	0.07	−0.07	4.7	−12.29	−0.03	0.11	0.08	0.04	0.00	1.8
JPY	136	0.75	0.38	0.50	3.46	0.04	−0.12	0.17	0.02	−0.15	13.2	−11.41	−0.01	0.04	−0.05	−0.04	0.00	1.7
ZAR	135	−1.49	0.45	−0.08	5.50	0.07	−0.03	0.18	0.12	−0.04	11.2	−12.04	0.29	0.14	0.17	0.13	0.11	12.3
THB	44	−0.83	0.40	−1.05	7.43	0.07	0.19	−0.30	0.03	−0.16	11.3	−6.00	0.57	0.48	0.30	0.03	0.06	45.7
BRL	43	−16.95	9.63	−1.42	3.78	0.83	0.69	0.56	0.47	0.40	111.3	−2.31	0.76	0.53	0.38	0.29	0.22	60.2
INR	145	−0.12	0.04	−0.36	3.18	0.07	0.11	−0.09	0.02	0.22	5.4	−3.19	0.19	−0.27	−0.15	0.08	0.23	5.6

Change of log of actual over proposed attractor

		Moments				Autocorrelations for the variable itself							Autocorrelations among squares					
	Nobs	avg	var	skw	krt	ρ_1	ρ_2	ρ_3	ρ_4	ρ_5	Q	ADF	ρ_1	ρ_2	ρ_3	ρ_4	ρ_5	Q
GBP	76	−0.15	0.29	−1.15	7.51	−0.12	−0.03	−0.10	0.02	−0.12	1.8	−9.43	0.04	0.03	0.00	−0.04	−0.02	1.3
DEM	143	0.52	0.35	0.00	2.67	0.10	0.11	0.13	0.08	−0.05	7.5	−11.86	−0.09	0.14	0.07	0.07	−0.03	4.6
JPY	136	1.45	7.03	1.42	6.61	−0.09	−0.41	−0.13	0.76	−0.10	195.1	−12.57	0.08	0.25	0.11	0.84	0.05	138.3
ZAR	135	−1.28	0.46	−0.05	5.51	0.06	−0.03	0.19	0.12	−0.05	11.0	−12.10	0.30	0.15	0.17	0.13	0.11	13.1
THB	44	−0.60	0.89	−0.01	5.22	0.07	−0.23	−0.19	0.42	0.03	51.3	−5.85	−0.08	−0.04	0.30	−0.04	−0.11	0.8
BRL	43	−7.15	27.88	2.92	17.05	−0.08	−0.09	0.43	−0.06	−0.02	3.2	−8.89	0.08	0.08	0.31	0.01	0.01	2.1
INR	145	0.01	0.24	−0.55	2.47	−0.02	−0.72	0.14	0.69	−0.17	22.3	−4.60	−0.48	0.27	−0.22	0.15	−0.24	3.2

Key: Quarterly data. Nobs, number of observations; avg, average; var, variance; skw, skewness; krt, (excess) kurtosis; ρ_l, autocorrelation coefficient for lag l; Q, Box-Ljung statistic on the sum of the ρs, against the null of a zero sum; ADF, augmented Dickey-Fuller statistic for the null of no mean reversion (i.e., a unit root). See the technical notes for definitions. The constant ω in the attractor is set so as to equalize the means of attractor and actual rate over the first ten years. For the changes of logs, mean and variance are in percent. Table kindly provided by Fang Liu.

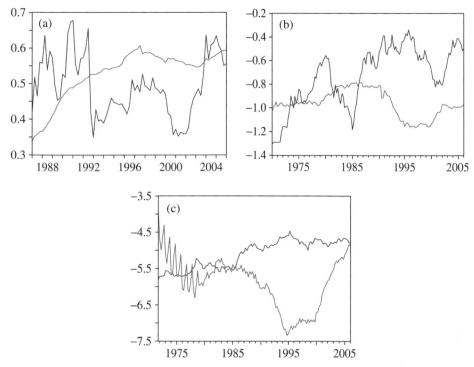

Figure 10.6. Exchange rates, money supply, and real growth: plots for the GBP, DEM, and JPY. (a) USD/GBP, (b) USD/DEM, (c) USD/JPY. *Key:* Rates are logs of USD/FC (natural U.S. quotes). The theoretical attractors are computed from CPIs and rescaled such that their average over the first ten years matches that of the corresponding actual exchange rate. The actual rate is the jumpy one for GBP and DEM, while for the JPY it is the one with the relatively steady path. *Source:* Underlying data are from DataStream. Graph kindly provided by Fang Liu.

Figures 10.6 and 10.7 show the results. Compared with the actual rates, the model predictions are—I weigh my words—bizarre. There does not seem to be a clear link for any of the OECD countries. Among the EMs there seems to be one success story, the real and its forerunners. But even in that case there is less than initially meets the eye. First, it is relatively easy to explain the effects of hyperinflation. Second, note that even for the hyperinflation period the log changes for the predicted and actual rates are off by about 3, i.e., a multiplicative factor of $e^3 \approx 20$. All this suggests that there is something fundamentally wrong with the model. It could be the assumption of constant velocities, or the assumption that expectations about the future are based on current levels, or the myth of PPP—probably all of the above.

Let us now let the numbers speak. Table 10.5 provides the by-now familiar statistics on the log of the actual rate, and then on the log of the ratio [actual rate]/[model rate]. We first note that in quarterly actual rates the autocorrelations are lower than in daily and monthly data: the mean ρ_1 is 0.82, for instance, against 0.99 (daily) and 0.97 (monthly). So there could be mean

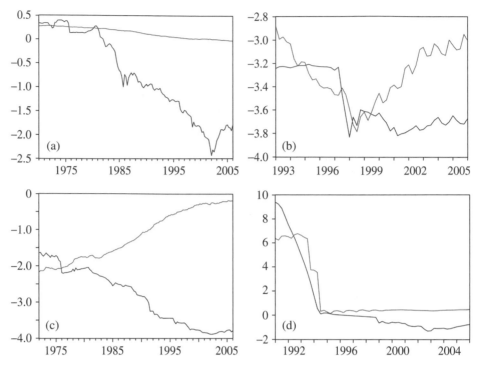

Figure 10.7. Exchange rates, money supply, and real growth: plots for the ZAR, THB, BRL, and INR. (a) USD/ZAR, (b) USD/THB, (c) USD/INR, (d) USD/BRL. *Key:* Rates are in USD/FC (natural U.S. quotes). The theoretical attractors are computed from CPIs and rescaled such that their average over the first ten years matches that of the corresponding actual exchange rate; for the BRL we took five years. The model rate is the almost-flat one for the ZAR, the V-line pattern for the THB, the rising one for the INR, and the almost-step-function for the BRL. *Source:* Underlying data are from DataStream. Graph kindly provided by Fang Liu.

reversion in the longer run. But that is just a conjecture: the ADF remains insignificant, perhaps because the samples are smaller. What is of interest here is also whether actual rates are explained by the monetary model. That does not seem to be the case. In table 10.5, the variances of the deviations are not below the variances of the originals, and the autocorrelations are not lower. (If the model had done well, the actual rate would have been attracted to the model's level, implying a lower autocorrelation for the deviations.) Only one of the ADFs rejects a unit root for the deviations—BRL, as you might have guessed. Nor is the model any good at explaining changes in actual rates. After "stripping out" changes in the model's prediction, variance is invariably up rather than down (as we would expect if the model had worked), and in the ADFs there is no sign of more mean reversion. So as we had guessed from the graphs, there is no link between actual and model numbers—or at least there is no trace of it in these data. Might other models of fundamentals do better?

10.3.3 Real Business Cycle Models

The monetary model is just one of the theories about the fundamentals. A briefly popular model with some similarity to the monetary approach was the real-business-cycle model. It starts from a rather arcane theory that the exchange rate should be the ratio of the marginal utility of nominal spending abroad versus that at home. The marginal utility of nominal spending then depends on the marginal utility of real spending and on inflation. For a simple utility function featuring something called constant relative risk aversion, lastly, the marginal utility of real spending depends on time preference and real consumption.

Interestingly, the model says that when a country's consumption is rising relative to another's, its exchange rate should fall. The logic is that if one country does well, the marginal utility of its representative consumer falls relative to that in the other country. The currency of the lucky country, therefore, must fall. Via this mechanism, the rich country's windfall is spread internationally: its falling exchange rate enables less-lucky countries to import from the lands of plenty.

The predicted negative link between a country's consumption and its exchange rate is the opposite of what current folklore or the monetary approach says, if one is at least willing to gloss over the difference between consumption and economic activity. The model's prediction is more in line with the neo-Keynesian way of thinking. In this view, a booming economy imports more, and the current-account deficit then depresses the country's currency.

The model with equal relative risk aversions and time preferences was tested as an exact theory and, of course, rejected (Backus and Smith 1993). Apte et al. (1994) treat the model as a long-run attractor and allow for differences across countries. They find that their generalized real-business-cycle model does better than PPP; but this, we know, is a low standard, and there is no out-of-sample forecasting.

10.3.4 Taylor Rule Models

Another strand that links the exchange rate to fundamentals is via the so-called Taylor rule. This modern monetary policy rule, proposed by John Taylor (1993),[14] stipulates how much the central bank should change the nominal interest rate in response to divergences of log actual GDP (y) from log potential GDP ($\bar{y}$) and divergences of actual rates of inflation (π) from a target rate of inflation ($\bar{\pi}$). Below, I write the risk-free rate in its a continuous-compounding form, and (arbitrarily) for the foreign country (see the asterisks). On the right-hand side you see, first, the classic Fisher rule: the nominal rate is the sum of the equilibrium desirable real rate (RR) plus expected inflation; but Taylor

---

[14] Another Taylor, Mark, pops up repeatedly in the review of empirical work, and one Stephen Taylor will be cited for his trading-rule tests. But the rule's Taylor is John.

recommends deviations proportional to how much inflation and real activity are above target:

$$\ln(1 + r^*_{t,t+1}) = \underbrace{\pi^*_t + RR^*_t}_{\text{Fisher rule}} + \underbrace{a^*_\pi(\pi^*_t - \bar{\pi}^*_t) + a^*_y(y^*_t - \bar{y}^*_t)}_{\text{Corrective monetary policy}}. \qquad (10.18)$$

This is the version for a closed economy, or for a central bank that benignly neglects exchange-rate issues (the United States). In a smaller open economy where the central bank does have an exchange-rate target, the interest rate should also take into account the deviation between the current exchange rate and its target value:

$$\ln(1 + r_{t,t+1}) = \pi_t + RR_t + a_\pi(\pi_t - \bar{\pi}_t) + a_y(y_t - \bar{y}_t) + a_s(\ln \bar{S}_t - \ln S_t). \quad (10.19)$$

We can now plug the Taylor-rule equations into, typically, equation (10.15). Various versions differ as to how they model the risk premium (zero, all too often) and the real rates (equal, perhaps); whether the as are internationally the same (yes, typically); and whether and how they further amend the Taylor rules. Technical note 10.4 explains how one can turn the above equations into an exchange-rate pricing model.

This class of models, however fashionable, suffers from the weakness that, in reality, the key UIP relation (10.15) with a zero risk premium, does not work at all; and if we do allow a risk premium, its real-world effect appears to be to neutralize the movements of the forward premium, as we will see in the next chapter. That is, for mainstream, well-behaved currencies the interest differentials do not predict exchange-rate changes. Thus, if empirically the models built from that equation appear to work, then it is not via the proposed logic.

The reason I still bring up this model is because it helps Engel and West (2005) to explain the Meese and Rogoff (1983) "disconnect" puzzle. The current rate in the Taylor model (and, in fact, a variant of the monetary model) can always be written as a function of current and future fundamentals, from here to eternity. The future fundamentals come up with exponentially decaying weights the further away they are. If the decay is very slow, though, Engel and West show that the resulting spot rate will be a unit-root process provided at least one of the variables in the Taylor rule is. Engel and West provide empirical support for the slow-decay condition. A nice additional insight is that if the spot rate relates to future fundamentals, it should predict them; this notion also gets some guarded support from Engel and West.

10.3.5 Concluding Discussion

Our simple exploratory tests of the monetary model were not an unqualified success. This, of course, is not a new finding. As already mentioned, Meese and Rogoff (1983) tested the monetary model and, disastrously, found that the martingale model (or the no-change forecast) did better than the model's prediction. This lack of connection with fundamentals, called the "disconnect" puzzle, has not really been solved by the subsequent models.

Many articles claim breakthroughs or at least partial successes, which are then often denied by others. A comprehensive study by Cheung et al. (2005) concludes that "the results do not point to any given model/specification combination as being very successful. On the other hand ... it may be that one model will do well for one exchange rate, and not for another." Earlier surveys by Frankel and Rose (1994) and Hopper (1997) are equally pessimistic. The latter concludes that "exchange rates don't seem to be affected by economic fundamentals in the short run. Being able to predict money supplies, central bank policies, or other supposed influences does not help forecast the exchange rate." Frankel and Rose largely concur:

> Exchange rates are difficult to forecast at short- to medium-term horizons. There is a bit of explanatory power to monetary models such as the Dornbusch "overshooting" theory, in the form of reaction to "news" and in forecasts at long-run horizons. Nevertheless, at short horizons, a driftless random walk characterizes exchange rates better than standard models based on observable macroeconomic fundamentals.

Note the speck of hope about the Dornbusch variant. But Faust and Rogers (2003) criticize even this cautiously optimistic result and conclude that "the overshooting cannot be driven by Dornbusch's mechanism."

Might nonlinearities be the explanation? Not as far as we can see, say Meese and Rose (1991). They consider five theoretical models of exchange-rate determination, and examine nonlinearities using a variety of parametric and nonparametric techniques. They find that "the poor explanatory power of the models considered cannot be attributed to nonlinearities arising from time-deformation or improper functional form." But one can think of other nonlinearities. De Grauwe and Grimaldi (2001) find that in a sample of high-inflation countries the QTM and PPP effects that underpin the monetary model are very much present. Altavilla and De Grauwe (2006) arrive at the following conclusion.

> Linear models tend to outperform at short forecast horizons especially when deviations from long-term equilibrium are small. In contrast, nonlinear models with more elaborate mean-reverting components dominate at longer horizons especially when deviations from long-term equilibrium are large. The results also suggest that combining different forecasting procedures generally produces more accurate forecasts than can be attained from a single model.

In the mid 1990s the view that the bad results were due to short horizons gained ground. Mark (1995) and Mark and Choi (1997), for instance, concluded that for horizons of one to four years there was a lot of predictability (Mark and Choi 1997):

Fixed-effects regressions employing differentials in productivity, real interest rates, and per capita income display some predictive power but fundamentals based on simple monetary models are generally more accurate and significant.

Starry-eyed economists even murmured about R^2s of 75%, no less. But the conclusion that long-term forecasts do better than the martingale's no-change forecast may have been based on faulty statistics. Cheung and Chinn (1998) find that the twin time series of long-run forecasts and realizations never exhibit the one-to-one cointegration relation one would expect, and too often exhibit no cointegration whatsoever. Berkowitz and Giorgianni (2001) find that the "standard assumption of a stationary error-correction term between exchange rates and fundamentals biases the results in favor of predictive power." To obtain reliable tests, critical values should be based on the more stringent null that there is no cointegration or that exchange rates and fundamentals are generated by vector autoregressions with no integration restrictions.

Other reported successes may just have been luck, or selective publishing policies. (Editors of journals do not like negative results unless they upset conventional wisdom; so the rare reports of successful forecasts are looked upon kindly.) Mark (1995), for instance, finds long-horizon exchange rate predictability for the DEM and JPY; but Faust et al. (2003) observe that shifting the data period two years up or down destroys the results. Bad macro data may be another cause, the same authors report: "Approximately one-third of the improved forecasting performance over a random walk is eventually undone by data revisions."

There are other possible explanations beside statistical weaknesses. Politics is missing, say Blomberg and Hess (1997): "by including political variables that capture party-specific, election-specific and candidate-specific characteristics ... our political model outperforms the random walk in out-of-sample forecasting at 1–12 month horizons for the pound/dollar, mark/dollar, pound/mark and the trade-weighted dollar, mark and pound exchange rates." Frankel and Rose (1994) think that speculative bubbles have played a role; it's all sentiment, Hopper (1997) concludes. Finally, Evans and Lyons (2005) propose to make better use of micro-based models.

10.4 Conclusion

Whatever the explanation, few readers would call our search for a good predictive theory of exchange rates an unmitigated success, thus far. In academic papers, a statement that "this model does not much worse than the no-change forecast" are quite common. The mood is not upbeat. "Among rational economists, the debate is over whether the glass is 5% full or 95% empty," Rogoff says (the *Economist*, November 24, 2007, p. 81).

Perhaps the models are too simple, though; in reality, the indicators watched by analysts are many, and the list changes over time. In the 1970s and early 1980s the current account was the main number everyone watched; then "confidence in the economy" took over, alongside interest rates; and right now nobody seems to know—except that there are too many dollars in foreign hands and far too many banks, in far too many countries, are in a bad shape. The models discussed so far do not mention these items, nor events like the Iran hostages crisis (under President Carter), or the Amsterdam Treaty, or the fall of the Iron Curtain, or China's entry into the WTO with, as a result, an explosion in its traditional current account surplus.

If real-world traders use many diffuse indicators and weight them differently over time, then simple, single-minded models like PPP or the monetary approach are bound to fail. But perhaps the forward rate would be the way out. Being the certainty equivalent of the future spot rate, the forward rate should be a combination of expectations and risk corrections. With luck, the risk correction might be constant or small, and then the forward rate would tell us a lot about the market's expectations. Being ignorant amateurs ourselves, we would still not know how the market formed its expectations, but at least we would know whether they saw things coming or not. In addition, we would be able to free-ride on the market's superior insights and simply copy the forward rate into our corporate plans.

The next chapter explores this avenue. Since it is so closely connected to this one, I postpone the usual CFO's summary until then.

10.5 Technical Notes

Technical note 10.1 (fundamental notions about time series).

Conditional versus unconditional moments. Imagine a Martian who will shortly be dropped onto our planet on a date that will be chosen in a totally random way by a time-travel machine. Suppose that just before landing, the Martian has to fill out an Immigration and Customs Declaration Form which includes, among other items, the following questions:

Enter your guess about tomorrow's price, in USD, of one Troy ounce of gold:

Enter your guess about the CPI for Botswana next month:

Enter your guess about the weight of the first Earthling you will meet:

These are questions about *unconditional* distributions: the Martian does not know the previous level of the gold price, for instance, and the prospects for gold production and demand; the Martian does not know the current level of the CPI and the recent inflation rates; nor does the Martian know whether the Earthling will be male or female, tall or short, well-fed or starving.

If the Martian had known this extra information, her forecast would have been much more precise. These would have been *conditional* predictions. Of course, a conditional forecast changes very much depending on how much you know about the item to be predicted. In some cases you might wonder whether an unconditional question makes sense at all. This is what this technical note is about.

Stationary distributions. For the weight of an Earthling, the question does not sound nonsensical. There *is* an average weight for humans, and it is probably fairly stable in the reasonably short run (the type of horizon we would use in actual practice); so the unconditional mean can be estimated, and the estimate would become more precise the more data we use—not only cross-sectionally but also longitudinally, i.e., in the time dimension.

A process is called *strictly stationary* if its unconditional distribution is not changing over time. A somewhat weaker definition is *covariance stationarity* (or *weak-sense* or *wide-sense stationarity*): first and second unconditional moments are assumed to exist and the autocovariance for a given lag is constant.[15] An example comes up shortly. We could also think of a process where there is a trend over time, for instance, income growing by 1% per year: that is, the log of income growing according to

$$\ln Y_t = \ln Y_0 + \ln(1.01) \cdot t + e_t. \qquad (10.20)$$

Clearly, once you have removed the trend, you are back in the standard case. One example of such a *trend-stationary* process would be if e_t is i.i.d. with mean zero. But e could be richer than i.i.d. For instance, the log of income could have *autocorrelated noise* around the trend: once we are above the trend in a given period, that gain would tend to disappear slowly over time rather than being already gone next time, on average, as the i.i.d. case would hold. For instance, one could think of

$$x_t = \underbrace{(A + B \cdot t)}_{\text{Trend}} + \rho_1 \underbrace{[x_{t-1} - (A + B \cdot (t - 1))]}_{\text{Previous deviation from trend}} + e_t. \qquad (10.21)$$

If ρ_1 is positive and less than unity, then according to this equation the variable is trending—see the "$(A + B \cdot t)$" bit; but if it happens to be n units above the trend, then on average the next observation will still be $\rho_1 n$ units above the trend; that, at least, is what the "$+\rho_1[x_{t-1} - (A + B \cdot (t - 1))]$" bit is telling us. So, on average, deviations take time to disappear instead of vanishing overnight. In addition, this is just "on average": every period, there is a new noise event—the "$+e_t$" bit—which, with about a 50% chance, might widen the

---

[15] The lth-order autocovariance of x is $\text{cov}(x, x_{-l})$, where x_{-l} denotes the vector of lagged observations x_{t-l}.

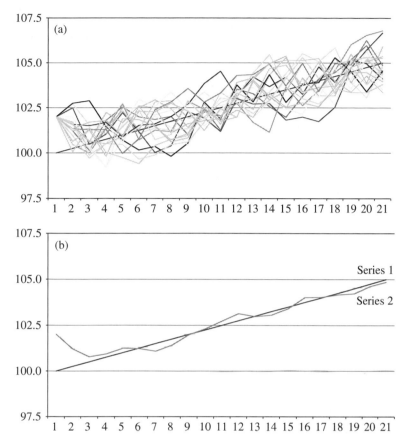

Figure 10.8. A trend-stationary process. *Key:* The process is wandering around a line $x_t = 99.75 + 0.75 \cdot t$, with time starting from 1. Every period, half of the previous *ex post* deviation is corrected and a new random error is then added:

$$x_t = \underbrace{[99.75 + 0.25 \cdot t]}_{\text{Trend}} + 0.5 \underbrace{[x_{t-1} - (99.75 + 0.25 \cdot (t-1))]}_{\text{Previous deviation from trend}} + \tilde{u}_t,$$

with $\tilde{u}$ uniform on $[-1.5, +1.5]$. Initially, x is at 102, 2 units above its trend, 100. I generate twenty possible subsequent paths. In (b) I show the average of these twenty possible paths. It approaches the trend line, but in a wobbly fashion and with over- and undershooting. If I had computed twenty million possible paths rather than just twenty, the new average path would have smoothly approached the trend line. That, of course, would just be the expectation at time 1; the realization can be far off: see (a).

distance again. Still, crucially, in this trend-stationary case, if one waits long enough any off-trend realizations would still be expected to dwindle away, *on average*, however slowly.

This is true on average, that is, for the expectation. There is no claim that the realized variable will be closer to the trend, n periods from now: the statement is just about the mean of all possible future realized values. In figure 10.8 I try to illustrate this. The process for $t = 1, 2, \ldots, 19, 20$ is

$$x_t = [99.75 + 0.25 \cdot t] + 0.5 [x_{t-1} - (99.75 + 0.25 \cdot (t-1))] + \tilde{u},$$

with $\tilde{u}$ uniform on $[-1.5, +1.5]$. Initially, x is at 102, 2 units above its contemporaneous trend value, 100. I generate twenty possible subsequent paths.
Obviously, only a fool would claim that the process *will* return to the trend line.
All one can say is that the average of all possible paths will tend to converge
toward the trend. In the second graph I show the average of the twenty possible paths. It approaches the trend line, but in a wobbly fashion and with over-
and undershooting. If I had computed twenty million possible paths rather
than just twenty, the new average path would have smoothly approached the
trend line. That is all that is being claimed.

Another impression we have from the graph is that the realized paths all
stay in a (fuzzy) zone around the trend. They cannot go wandering off to $+\infty$
or $-\infty$ because the persistence (autocorrelation) of errors is not very high. But
one could think of processes that do not return to a trend, or to a flat line, as
the next subsection tells.

The martingale and the random walk. At the other extreme of stationarity is
the *unit-root process*. We postpone a precise definition and start with a familiar
example, the standard binomial process. Suppose, for instance, that we flip
coins at time t, and add/subtract one tick to/from x_{t-1} if heads/tails shows
up. Then

$$x_t = x_{t-1} + e_t, \quad \text{where } e_t = \begin{cases} +1, & p = \frac{1}{2}, \\ -1, & p = \frac{1}{2}. \end{cases} \tag{10.22}$$

The errors could be more complicated than that—for instance, they could
be uniform on $[-\frac{1}{2}, +\frac{1}{2}]$, or we could modify the standard deviation of the
changes. Any such process with independent mean-zero changes is called a
martingale. If the changes are normals instead of binomials or uniforms or
whatever, then the martingale is specified to be a *random walk*. Obviously, any
martingale x can and will wander aimlessly; there is no tendency to return to
some unconditional expected value. Figure 10.9 shows three realizations with
$N = 3,200$ observations and with changes that are uniform i.i.d.s between $-\frac{1}{2}$
and $+\frac{1}{2}$. There is no similarity across the three trial graphs. Studying one will
not help you understand another, nor does studying the first half help you
understand the second half.

The long graph below the three is just the stretched version of the third
trial. Note, for fun, how the path displays many patterns that our order-craving
brains may want to see in there, like long bear and bull markets and, at shorter
distance, "channels" and "support lines" and "flags" and "banners." It's all
in the observer's brain, though: in this graph there are no patterns and no
predictability.

Let us see the implication for our statistically challenged extraterrestrial.
Our Martian may gather all the statistics (s)he may want, and still learn nothing useful. In table 10.7 I show sample variances computed from five different
runs of my little spreadsheet program. In each time series I first compute the

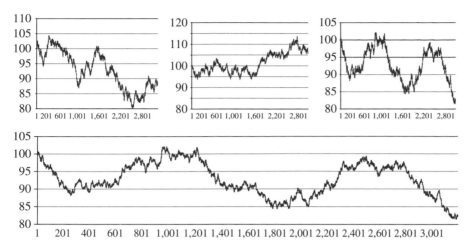

Figure 10.9. Three sample paths ($N = 3,200$) of a martingale with uniformly distributed $(0,1)$ changes starting from $x_0 = 100$.

Table 10.7. Sample variances computed from six sample paths ($N = 3,200$) of a martingale with uniform $(0,1)$ changes starting from $x_0 = 100$.

N	Path 1	Path 2	Path 3	Path 4	Path 5	Path 6
100	0.43	2.22	2.05	0.88	1.15	2.22
200	0.90	7.31	1.40	0.81	0.90	2.21
400	2.71	11.02	1.09	5.55	0.93	2.22
800	10.74	9.57	1.81	7.49	4.99	19.75
1,600	47.28	14.16	5.05	10.13	13.07	24.61
3,200	34.14	21.32	31.46	16.50	69.95	28.20

The table shows sample variances computed from five different runs of a little spreadsheet program that generates martingales. From each of the five series each I compute the sample variance for the first 100 observations, then the first 200, and so on, all the way up to 3,200.

sample variance for the first 100 observations, then the first 200, and so on, all the way up to 3,200. Means and variances differ bewilderingly across samples for given N, for instance, and they do not tend to stabilize around a putative limit value as the sample size increases. Look at the values for 800 observations. This is a big sample, to most statisticians, so the variance estimates should be quite precise; yet, they differ unrecognizably across columns. The only clear phenomenon is that the sample variance goes up, unevenly, with N rather than stabilizing around a limit value. This is worrying: the definition of the unconditional population variance is, loosely speaking, "the estimate one would obtain from an infinite sample." So if that estimate is always rising in N, the unconditional population variance is infinite, i.e., not defined. This is not surprising, since the unconditional mean is not defined either. If $E(\tilde{x})$ is not defined, how then could $E[\tilde{x} - E(\tilde{x})]^2$ be?

The conclusion is that, for the random walk, neither the mean nor the variance "exists" in an unconditional sense. All one can do is make conditional forecasts, like the expected value and variance given the current level and given a forecasting horizon. We consider the conditions under which the first two moments do exist in the next subsection.

Unit-root processes. We can generalize the binomial martingale somewhat and make the noise, e, less simplistic; and we can add a constant (the "drift") to generate an upward or downward trend:

$$x_t = a + x_{t-1} + e_t, \quad \text{where } \mathrm{E}(e_t) = 0. \tag{10.23}$$

The process would be an aimless random path added to a time trend; that is, it would not exhibit any tendency to return to the time trend once it is off it. An uninformed Martian would have absolutely no clue about what to answer if she faced a question about such a variable.

These are examples of a unit-root process, or a process integrated of order unity. Unit root refers to the *autocorrelation spectrum*. The variable x follows an *autocorrelated process of order p* if

$$x_t = a + \rho_1 x_{t-1} + \rho_2 x_{t-2} + \rho_3 x_{t-3} + \cdots + \rho_p x_{t-p} + e_t. \tag{10.24}$$

We want to discover the conditions on the *spectrum*—the set of autocorrelation coefficients—under which the mean and the variance exist in an unconditional sense. Let us initially focus on the case $p = 2$. Assuming that the unconditional mean and variance do exist, these would be computed as

$$\mathrm{E}(x) = a + \rho_1 \mathrm{E}(x) + \rho_2 \mathrm{E}(x),$$
$$\implies \quad a = (1 - \rho_1 - \rho_2)\mathrm{E}(x),$$
$$x_t = (1 - \rho_1 - \rho_2)\mathrm{E}(x) + \rho_1 x_{t-1} + \rho_2 x_{t-2} + e_t, \tag{10.25}$$
$$\mathrm{var}(x) = \rho_1^2 \,\mathrm{var}(x) + 2\rho_1\rho_2 \,\mathrm{var}(x) + \rho_2^2 \,\mathrm{var}(x) + \mathrm{var}(e)$$
$$= (\rho_1^2 + 2\rho_1\rho_2 + \rho_2^2)\,\mathrm{var}(x) + \mathrm{var}(e). \tag{10.26}$$

Equation (10.25) tells us that, to conditionally forecast x_1, one should attach a weight $(1 - \rho_1 - \rho_2)$ to the unconditional mean, and then weights ρ_1 and ρ_2 to the preceding two observations. Note, crucially, that if $(1 - \rho_1 - \rho_2)$ equals zero, the weight given to the unconditional mean is zero. That would mean that x is not at all attracted to any long-run mean or, stated differently, that there is no such thing as an unconditional mean. The statistically astute reader may then wonder about the variance too: how can we define an unconditional variance if the unconditional expectation does not exist? In effect, if $(1 - \rho_1 - \rho_2) = 0$, i.e., $\rho_2 = (1 - \rho_1)$, then equation (10.26) tells us that the variance is

$$\mathrm{var}(x) = [\rho_1^2 + 2\rho_1(1 - \rho_1) + (1 - \rho_1)^2]\,\mathrm{var}(x) + \mathrm{var}(e)$$
$$= [\rho_1 + (1 - \rho_1)]^2\,\mathrm{var}(x) + \mathrm{var}(e)$$
$$= \mathrm{var}(x) + \mathrm{var}(e). \tag{10.27}$$

If var(e) is strictly positive, the above result makes no sense unless var(x) = ∞ (the unconditional variance does not exist). Thus, when $\rho_1 + \rho_2 = 1$, x has no mean and no variance in the unconditional meaning. The generalization to a process of any order $p \geq 1$ is as follows:[16]

$$\text{Unit root, i.e., } \sum_{l=1}^{p} \rho_l = 1 \quad \Longrightarrow \quad \text{the unconditional E and var are not defined.}$$

(10.28)

For completeness, let me add that an infinite mean is sufficient to have an infinite variance, but not necessary: the variance can be infinite even if the mean is not. Thus, there are cases where $\sum_{l=1}^{p} \rho_l$ is below unity and the variance still does not exist.

Handling unit roots: differentiate the "integrated" process. If we have a unit-root process, we can compute first differences to get better-behaved numbers. This is easiest to see for the first-order process—changes are pure i.i.d. noise:

$$\text{If } x_t = x_{t-1} + e_t \text{ (i.e., } x \text{ is unit-root), then } x_t - x_{t-1} = e_t. \quad (10.29)$$

Thus, changes are i.i.d., the statistician's wet dream. This readily extends to the second-order case:

$$\text{If } x_t = \rho_1 x_{t-1} + \rho_2 x_{t-2} + e_t \text{ and } \rho_1 = 1 - \rho_2 \text{ (i.e., } x \text{ is unit-root),}$$
$$\text{then } x_t = x_{t-1} - \rho_2(x_{t-1} - x_{t-2}) + e_t,$$
$$\text{i.e., } x_t - x_{t-1} = -\rho_2(x_{t-1} - x_{t-2}) + e_t. \quad (10.30)$$

So we have a first-order process for the changes, where the ρ_2-in-levels becomes the (minus) ρ_1-in-changes. If, in levels, ρ_1 is positive, then we have $\rho_2 = 1 - \rho_1 < 1$, that is, the first-order autocorrelation for changes is negative but not below -1.

   If a variable needs to be first-differenced to become well-behaved, we say it is integrated once ("I(1)"), with "integrated" meaning the opposite of "differenced." Many variables in economics and finance are close to integrated of order unity. Some empiricists believe that even inflation is I(1); if so, then the log CPI would be I(2): we would have to differentiate twice, i.e., study changes in inflation rates, to have well-behaved numbers.[17]

Cointegration: error-correction models. Two processes x_1 and x_2 are said to be *cointegrated* if (i) each of them is I(1), i.e., has a unit root, but (ii) there exists a linear combination which is I(0): $a x_1 + b x_2 = e$ with var(e) $< \infty$.

---

[16] The term unit root refers to the so-called *characteristic equation* of an autocorrelated process: $m^p + m^{p-1}\rho_1 + m^{p-2}\rho_2 + \cdots + \rho_p = 0$. A unit-root case is said to arise if one of the roots (solutions) of this polynomial is $m = 1$.

[17] I personally think that when ADFs do not reject a unit root, the cause is too small a sample. Inflation rates do return to acceptable levels even after hyperinflation—perhaps even especially after hyperinflation. The same holds for interest rates and interest differentials or forward premia: they often have a long memory but the notion that they are really I(1) defies common sense.

For example, if the forward premium is stationary, then $\ln F$ and $\ln S$ are cointegrated with *cointegration vector* $\{a, b\} = \{1, -1\}$. The cointegration vector can be determined up to a scalar only; for instance, for spot and forward rates the vectors $\{100, -100\}$ or $\{-2, 2\}$ will also do—if the swap rate is stationary, then so is 100 times the swap rate, or minus twice the swap rate. Likewise, if $a\,x_1 + b\,x_2$ has finite variance, then so has $x_1 + (b/a)\,x_2$.

The cointegration vector may be known a priori in the sense that other relative values do not make sense a priori. For instance, PPP would say that $\ln S$, $\ln I$, and $\ln I^*$ are linked by $\ln S - \ln I + \ln I^* = e$, e having finite variance. That is, PPP says that the cointegrating vector is proportional to $\{1, -1, 1\}$. One can then estimate the vector and test the hypothesis. For instance, the estimates may be that the linear combination $\ln S - 1.5 \ln I + \ln I^*$ has finite variance. That would be very puzzling in the sense that then the PPP deviation itself, $\ln S - \ln I + \ln I^*$, would have infinite variance.[18] If I were the researcher who got this result, I would ascribe the result to some flaw in the data or the test. In other cases, one just estimates the relation without any precise priors, and one takes any estimate as reasonable or acceptable.

If two variables are cointegrated, then one can refine the ADF-type relations into a twin-error correction model (VECM or vector ECM) like

$$\Delta x_1 = -\kappa_1 (x_1 - c\,x_2) + \cdots \quad \text{and} \quad \Delta x_2 = -\kappa_2 (x_2 - x_1/c) + \cdots . \quad (10.31)$$

If they are not cointegrated, then we have a nonstationary regressor in the ECM, which rubbishes the usual confidence levels for t-statistics in the same way, qualitatively, as in the ADF test (see the next technical note).

Technical note 10.2 (standard test statistics on levels and changes).

Moments. The first moment is the mean, which estimates the expected value:

$$\bar{x} := \frac{\sum_{j=1}^{N} x_j}{N} = \hat{E}(x). \quad (10.32)$$

The second "central" moment estimates the variance:[19]

$$\overline{(x - \bar{x})^2} := \frac{\sum_{j=1}^{N} (x_j - \bar{x})^2}{N}$$
$$\approx \hat{E}[x - E(x)]^2. \quad (10.33)$$

The third, central, standardized moment estimates the skewness:

$$\frac{\overline{(x - \bar{x})^3}}{[\widehat{std}(x)]^3} := \frac{\sum_{j=1}^{N} (x_j - \bar{x})^3 / N}{[\widehat{std}(x)]^3}. \quad (10.34)$$

---

[18] The PPP deviation would be $e + 0.5 \ln I$ with, so the tests want us to believe, e having finite and $\ln I$ infinite variance.

[19] This is the large-sample version. Remember that in smaller samples the division is by $N - 1$ not N because the sample mean always overfits the data: typically, $(x_j - \bar{x})^2 < (x_j - E(x))^2$. Hence the need for correction.

If the distribution is symmetric, the true skewness is zero. If the coefficient is negative, then there are big negative outliers, that is, the left tail is relatively stretched. If the coefficient is positive, then there are big positive outliers, that is, the right tail is the stretched one. Lastly, the fourth, central, standardized moment estimates the peak and tail thicknesses relative to the Gaussian:

$$\frac{\overline{(x - \bar{x})^4}}{[\widehat{\mathrm{std}}(x)]^4} := \frac{\sum_{j=1}^{N}(x_j - \bar{x})^4/N}{[\widehat{\mathrm{std}}(x)]^4}. \tag{10.35}$$

For the normal, this *raw kurtosis* statistic equals 3. For this reason, one often already subtracts 3 from the raw kurtosis; this is called the *excess kurtosis*. Others subtract 3 and just name the result *kurtosis*. In short, make sure you know what you are talking about.

Larger values signal that there are too many events close to the mean and too many extreme events, at the expense of the events at in-between distances from the mean, at the flanks of the density graph; t-distributions, including the Cauchy, are examples of such *leptocurtic* distributions. A smaller value indicates tails that are too short and central peaks that are too low—thick flanks, that is; the extreme example of such a *platycurtic* distribution is the uniform or rectangular one.

Simple autocorrelations, and tests thereon. The *simple autocorrelation coefficient* for lag l is the simple regression coefficient of x_t on x_{t-l}, as in[20]

$$x_t = a + \rho_1 x_{t-l} + e_{t|l} \Rightarrow x_t - \mathrm{E}(x) = \rho_1(x_{t-l} - \mathrm{E}(x)) + e_{t|l} \text{ if } \mathrm{E}(x) \text{ exists. } \tag{10.36}$$

The partial correlation is the regression coefficient from a multiple regression involving all lags from 1 to L, that is,

$$x_t = a + \rho_1 x_{t-1} + \rho_2 x_{t-2} + \cdots + \rho_L x_{t-L} + e_{t|1,\dots,L}. \tag{10.37}$$

If the true autocorrelations for all orders are zero, the sample ρ_l for lag l has a standard estimation error of $\sqrt{N - l - 1}$. This can be used to test the null hypothesis about a single estimate. To test whether all estimates might simultaneously equal zero, one uses the *Box–Ljung* or *Ljung–Box* "Q" statistic,

$$Q := \frac{T(T + 2)}{T - L} \sum_{l=1}^{L} \rho_l^2, \tag{10.38}$$

which under the null has a $\chi^2(L)$ distribution. The *Box–Pierce* original version had T instead of the fraction but does not do well in small samples.

The other null that may be of interest is the unit-root one, which for the first-order case means $\rho_1 = 1$. If the estimate is close to, say, 0.95, how do we know the true value might not be +1? Or if the first- and second-order partial ρs sum to 0.97, might this come from a nonstationary process? The augmented

---

[20] A correlation coefficient is defined as $\mathrm{cov}(x, x(-1))/[\mathrm{std}(x) \cdot \mathrm{std}(x(-1))]$, but if x is not unit root, then $\mathrm{std}(x) = \mathrm{std}(x(-1))$ so correlation coefficients and regression coefficients are the same, in principle. In small samples, there might be a minor difference.

Dickey–Fuller test offers a way to judge the acceptability of a unit root (the null hypothesis) against the alternative that the process is a stationary pth-order autocorrelated process. To understand the test, take the case $p = 2$ with, for completeness, a drift and a deterministic time trend:

$$x_t = a + bt + \rho_1 x_{t-1} + \rho_2 x_{t-2} + \epsilon_t. \tag{10.39}$$

Subtract x_{t-1} from both sides (line 1, below) and then add/subtract $\rho_2 x_{t-1}$:

$$
\begin{aligned}
x_t - x_{t-1} &= a + bt + (\rho_1 - 1)x_{t-1} \qquad\qquad + \qquad\qquad \rho_2 x_{t-2} + \epsilon_t \\
&= a + bt + (\rho_1 - 1)x_{t-1} + \rho_2 x_{t-1} - \rho_2 x_{t-1} + \rho_2 x_{t-2} + \epsilon_t \\
&= a + bt + \underbrace{(\rho_1 + \rho_2 - 1)}_{=c}x_{t-1} \underbrace{-\rho_2}_{=+d}(x_{t-1} - x_{t-2}) + \epsilon_t,
\end{aligned}
$$

$$\implies \quad \Delta x_t = a + bt + cx_{t-1} + d\Delta x_{t-1} + \epsilon_t. \tag{10.40}$$

So if we regress changes in x on the past level and on past changes (for as many lags as is necessary), the first coefficient, b, provides an estimate of $\sum_{l=1}^{p} \rho_l - 1$, and is zero when the process has a unit root. Thus, a small value means that the process might be nonstationary, while sufficiently negative values mean that the process probably is stationary. The original Dickey–Fuller test only considered first-order processes (i.e., $\rho_2 = 0$), possibly with drift and/or a deterministic time trend; the higher-order version is called the "augmented" test. The test focuses on b's t-ratio rather than b's value; the critical values depend on the order and the (non)existence of drift and trend, but they are always substantially larger than the usual critical z or t scores when x is nonstationary. Your statistics software should tell you whether the test is significant at the usual levels, and should give hints as to how many lags should be included or whether a drift is needed.

You might have guessed much of this without the formal derivation, just by looking at the test equation. If there is momentum with mean reversion, then b is negative: a positive deviation from the mean tends to be followed by negative changes. The first term, $b[x'_{t-1} - E(x')]$, would then be called the error-correction term, with $[x'_{t-1} - E(x')]$ being the error and b the speed of correction. In contrast, for a unit-root process (see the preceding technical note), the mean does not exist; one can compute a sample mean (and your computer will happily do so), but that sample mean does not function as an attractor. So in that case, b equals zero in an infinite sample and should be close to zero in a finite one. Because a unit-root regressor does not meet the assumptions of ordinary statistics, including the assumption that $\text{var}(x)$ exists, under the null $H_0 : b = 0$ the t-ratio for b is not the usual one.

If b is significantly negative, we conclude that the hypothesis $H_0 : b = 0$ is almost surely untrue. If b is not significantly negative, the hypothesis might be true, that is, the process might be unit root; but it could also be what it seems to be: a highly autocorrelated (or "long memory") process with very weak mean reversion.

Half-life. For a first-order process, the one-period-ahead forecast is

$$E_{t-1}[x_t - E(x)] = \rho[x_{t-1} - E(x)]. \tag{10.41}$$

What about a two-period prediction? Below, we first write what our one-step prediction will be next period, when x_t will be known. We then see what we can already say now—before x_t is known—about x_{t+1}: we just use our prediction rule about x_t. Here goes:

$$E_t[x_{t+1} - E(x)] = \rho[x_t - E(x)],$$
$$\implies \quad E_t[x_{t+1} - E(x)] = \rho E_t[x_t - E(x)]$$
$$= \rho \times \rho[x_t - E(x)] \quad \text{from equation (10.41)}$$
$$= \rho^2[x_t - E(x)]. \tag{10.42}$$

Iterating again and again, we get

$$E_t[x_{t+n} - E(x)] = \rho^n[x_t - E(x)]. \tag{10.43}$$

Thus, when $1 < \rho < 0$, the variable is expected to return to its mean exponentially—meaning, here, in ever-smaller steps, not ever-bigger ones.

What is the half-life? That is, how long should we wait, on average, before the currently observed deviation from the mean gets halved? The requirement is as follows:

$$\text{Find } n \text{ such that } E_t[x_{t+n} - E(x)] = \tfrac{1}{2}[x_{t-1} - E(x)],$$
$$\Updownarrow \text{ equation (10.43)}$$
$$\rho^n = \tfrac{1}{2},$$
$$n \ln(\rho) = \ln(\tfrac{1}{2}),$$
$$n = \frac{\ln(\tfrac{1}{2})}{\ln(\rho)}. \tag{10.44}$$

Autocorrelation for squared returns. For stationary variables it also makes sense to compute autocorrelations for squared de-meaned returns, as in the regressions

$$(x_t - \bar{x})^2 = \kappa_0 + \kappa_l(x_{t-l} - \bar{x})^2 + e. \tag{10.45}$$

κ_0 is an unconditional component in the variance. Positive coefficients κ_1 indicate that uncertainty comes in waves: an unusually big squared return for date $t - 1$ also tends to go with unusually big returns today. Multiple models would look like

$$(x_t - \bar{x})^2 = \kappa_0 + \kappa_1(x_{t-l} - \bar{x})^2 + \kappa_2(x_{t-2} - \bar{x})^2 + \cdots + e. \tag{10.46}$$

Taking expectations, we find the unconditional variance on the left and following each kappa:

$$E(x_t - \bar{x})^2 = \kappa_0 + \kappa_1 E(x_{t-1} - \bar{x})^2 + \kappa_2 E(x_{t-2} - \bar{x})^2 + \cdots,$$
$$\text{i.e., } \operatorname{var}(x) = \kappa_0 + (\kappa_1 + \kappa_2 + \cdots)\operatorname{var}(x)$$
$$= \frac{\kappa_0}{1 - \kappa_1 - \kappa_2 - \cdots}. \tag{10.47}$$

So when variance waxes and wanes in waves, we need $\sum_{l=1}^{p} \kappa_l < 1$, otherwise the variance is undefined.

Technical note 10.3 (the monetary approach to the exchange rate). The monetary approach is based on two building blocks: purchasing power parity (PPP) as a long-run attractor for the exchange rate, and the quantity theory of money (QTM) as a theory about the price levels in the PPP equation.

We use the following notation to denote the variables relevant for the home country: Π is the price level, Y the real output, L the stock of money held by the public, and v is the velocity of the money. The velocity is defined as the number of times the money stock is turned over in a given period:

$$v := \frac{Y \cdot \Pi}{L}. \tag{10.48}$$

As usual, the foreign counterparts are asterisked versions of these. The above definition can be turned into the beginning of a theory by assuming that v is constant or, at most, exogenously defined by the payments technology and the interest rate. In addition, real activity Y is not influenced by monetary policy, hardcore monetarists would claim. In that view, we can turn equation (10.48) into a theory of the price level:

$$\Pi = v \frac{L}{Y}. \tag{10.49}$$

Thus, uncontroversially, at constant velocity, prices rise when money supply is increasing faster than real activity. And doubling the velocity has the same effect as doubling the money stock.

A similar equation holds abroad. Finally, we add the PPP ingredient:

$$\begin{aligned}
\hat{S}^{\text{PPP}} &= \frac{\Pi}{\Pi^*} \\
&= \frac{vL/Y}{v^*L_d^*/Y^*} \\
&= \frac{v}{v^*} \frac{L}{L_s^*} \frac{Y^*}{Y}.
\end{aligned} \tag{10.50}$$

Thus, the PPP prediction about the spot value of a foreign currency rises, ceteris paribus,

- if the money supply grows slower abroad (less inflation abroad),
- real activity grows faster abroad (more demand for foreign money, causing prices to fall abroad).

Technical note 10.4 (the asset view of exchange rates). We start from the asset pricing model (10.15), into which we plug the Taylor rules (10.18) and (10.19):

$$\begin{aligned}
\ln S_t = \text{E}_t \ln S_{t+1} &- [\pi_t + RR_t + a_\pi(\pi_t - \bar{\pi}_t) + a_y(y_t - \bar{y}_t) + a_s(\ln \bar{S}_t - \ln S_t)] \\
&- RP_t + [\pi_t^* + RR_t^* + a_{\pi^*}^*(\pi_t^* - \bar{\pi}_t^*) + a_y^*(y_t^* - \bar{y}_t^*)],
\end{aligned}$$

$$(1 + a_s) \ln S_t = E_t \ln S_{t+1} - [\pi_t + RR_t + a_\pi(\pi_t - \bar{\pi}_t) + a_y(y_t - \bar{y}_t) + a_s \ln \bar{S}_t]$$
$$- RP_t + [\pi_t^* + RR_t^* + a_{\pi^*}^*(\pi_t^* - \bar{\pi}_t^*) + a_y^*(y_t^* - \bar{y}_t^*)],$$

$$\implies \quad \ln S_t = \frac{E_t \ln S_{t+1}}{1 + a_s} - \frac{\pi_t + RR_t + a_\pi(\pi_t - \bar{\pi}_t) + a_y(y_t - \bar{y}_t) + a_s \ln \bar{S}_t}{1 + a_s}$$
$$- \frac{RP_t}{1 + a_s} + \frac{\pi_t^* + RR_t^* + a_{\pi^*}^*(\pi_t^* - \bar{\pi}_t^*) + a_y^*(y_t^* - \bar{y}_t^*)}{1 + a_s}.$$

The target rate $\bar{S}$ could be an official parity or, in a float model, the PPP rate—you name it. You can simplify by getting rid of the real interest rates; for instance, assume that they are equal.

For ease of manipulation, let us compress the right-hand side into

$$\ln S_t = \frac{E_t \ln S_{t+1}}{1 + a_s} + \frac{A'X_t}{1 + a_s}. \tag{10.51}$$

Now a_s is not a discount rate, but it has the mathematical appearance of one; actually, in the macro literature one unblushingly and unabashedly calls the first term the discounted expectation. To get rid of the expectation, you can use the equation to specify next period's expectation and then substitute it, and so on and so forth. We do so below. In the last line we split $A'X_{t+i}$ into $a_s \ln \bar{S}_{t+i}$ and the rest, denoted as BY_{t+i}:

$$E_t \ln S_{t+1} = \frac{E_t \ln S_{t+2}}{1 + a_s} + \frac{E_t A'X_{t+1}}{1 + a_s},$$

$$E_t \ln S_{t+i} = \frac{E_t \ln S_{t+i+1}}{1 + a_s} + \frac{E_t A'X_{t+i}}{1 + a_s},$$

$$\implies \quad \ln S_t = \frac{E_t \ln S_{t+2}}{(1 + a_s)^2} + \frac{E_t A'X_{t+1}}{(1 + a_s)^2} + \frac{A'X_t}{1 + a_s}$$

$$= \frac{E_t \ln S_{t+3}}{(1 + a_s)^3} + \frac{E_t A'X_{t+2}}{(1 + a_s)^3} + \frac{E_t A'X_{t+1}}{(1 + a_s)^2} + \frac{A'X_t}{1 + a_s}$$

$$\vdots$$

$$= \underbrace{\frac{E_t \ln \bar{S}_{t+n}}{(1 + a_s)^\infty}}_{=0 \text{ (no bubbles)}} + \sum_{i=1}^{\infty} \frac{E_t A'X_{t+i}}{(1 + a_s)^i}$$

$$= a_s \sum_{i=1}^{\infty} \frac{\ln \bar{S}_{t+i}}{(1 + a_s)^i} + \sum_{i=1}^{\infty} \frac{E_t B'Y_{t+i}}{(1 + a_s)^i}. \tag{10.52}$$

Similar models can be built out of the monetary model by specifying the velocity to be a function of the interest rate, notably $v = v_0 e^{a_r \ln(1+r)}$: if $a_r = a_r^*$, the ratio of the two theoretical price levels will contain the interest differential, which will allow you to use UIP, equation (10.15). The point in doing so is less obvious as the monetary model itself already provides us with the level of the exchange rate; all one achieves is to replace the interest differential (in the v/v^* part) by an infinite series of expected future exchange rates.

11

Do Forex Markets Themselves See What Is Coming?

In the preceding chapter we concluded that academics have a hard time understanding exchange markets beyond long-term PPP effects. But perhaps the models take themselves too seriously. They all assume highly streamlined agents who are concerned only about wealth and, more crucially, all agree about how the exchange rate ought to be priced—invariably by a simple formula—and what the input data into the formula should be. In reality things are more complex. Markets use more than a few variables, and do not have a formal equation in mind. So pricing really is a black-box process, badly understood by academics.

But perhaps markets themselves are much cleverer: they presumably know better why which variable matters at what time, and they think much more multi-dimensionally. So this time we look at the forward rate (hoping that the market-expectations component in it may reveal a lot), at forecasts by specialists, and at trading results by central bankers and traders, which, if successful, would mean that these parties at least know how to predict markets.

11.1 The Forward Rate as a Black-Box Predictor

In this section we first explain how one can test the predictive performance of the forward rate. We then show our (dismal) results and discuss the literature.

11.1.1 How to Verify the Forward Rate's Performance as a Predictor

The early literature on the forecasting performance of the forward rate ignored risk premia, perhaps because it started as part of macroeconomics rather than as part of finance and asset pricing. Thus, this literature centered on the uncovered interest parity (UIP) hypothesis we discussed in chapter 3 and used in chapter 10. You can read technical note 11.1 on this train of thought, and discover how it led to the test equation:

$$\text{If } RP = 0, \text{ then } \tilde{s}_{t,t+1} \approx FP_{t,t+1} + \tilde{\epsilon}_{t+1}, \text{ where } E_t(\tilde{\epsilon}_{t+1}) = 0, \tag{11.1}$$

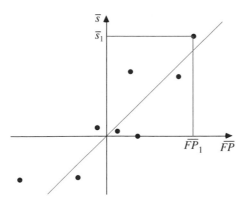

Figure 11.1. Plotting mean realized changes and forward premia for various currencies. *Key:* For every currency, the time-series mean of the realized change is plotted against the time-series mean of forward premia. We get as many dots as there are exchange rates in the database. The dots should be randomly scattered around a 45° line.

where $FP_{t,t+1}$ denotes the forward premium, $\ln(F_{t,t+1}/S_t)$, or its CIP counterpart, $\ln(1 + r_{t,t+1})/(1 + r^*_{t,t+1})$. The derivation in the technical note uses simple percentages, as required by asset pricing theory; in keeping with most of the empirical literature I here replace them by their log-change counterparts, which is entirely pointless but, fortunately, also largely harmless.[1]

The hypothesis has a number of testable implications.

1. Currency-by-currency means tests. We can compute a time series of *ex post* forecast errors, and test whether its average rejects the hypothesis that errors have zero expectation:

$$\text{If} \qquad E_t(\epsilon_{t,T}) = 0, \tag{11.2}$$

$$\text{then} \qquad E(\epsilon) = 0 \iff E(\overline{FP}) = E(\tilde{s}). \tag{11.3}$$

Thus, if every week or month or whatever the conditional expected error is zero, then the expectation is zero unconditionally too. So we can compute a time series of errors ϵ_t, and test whether its mean deviates significantly from zero.

2. Cross-currency patterns in currency-by-currency means. We can compute, for every currency j, the mean realized change $\bar{s}_j$ and the mean forward premium $\overline{FP}_j$. When we plot all these pairs $(\bar{s}_j, \overline{FP}_j)$, they should all be statistically close to a 45° line (figure 11.1).

---

[1] The basic hypothesis is $E_t(\tilde{S}_{t+1}) = F_{t,t+1}$. One problem with this hypothesis is that if it holds for, say, the USD/EUR rate, then it cannot hold for the inverse, the EUR/USD rate: $E_t(\tilde{S}_{t+1}) = F_{t,t+1}$ rules out $E_t(1/\tilde{S}_{t+1}) = 1/F_{t,t+1}$ (the "Siegel paradox"). To "solve the paradox," many researchers then test the hypothesis $E_t(\ln \tilde{S}_{t+1}) = \ln F_{t,t+1}$, instead. This is free of a Siegel problem, but the new problem is that there is no way to transform the basic hypothesis, $E_t(\tilde{S}_{t+1}) = F_{t,t+1}$, into $E_t(\ln \tilde{S}_{t+1}) = \ln F_{t,t+1}$ except as a (pointless) empirical approximation. Instead of "solving the Siegel paradox," the log version just sweeps the paradox under the carpet: the only way the paradox can be solved is by adding back into the basic test equation the inflation adjustments and risk premium that were unjustifiably thrown out. But that is beyond the scope of this textbook.

Unlike the preceding test, this looks at many means at the same time and provides a visual picture, but like that test it is still an "unconditional" test. As such, it could leave many inefficiencies undetected. Suppose, for instance, that the market absurdly believes that the coming month's change will be the same as the one that was just observed.[2] Then the market would set $FP_{t,t+1}$ equal to the past change, $s_{t-1,t}$, while in reality $E_t(\tilde{s}_{t,t+1})$ must always be much closer to the unconditional expected value. Yet our means test would not detect this systematic error: if $FP_{t,t+1} = s_{t-1,t}$ while $s_{t-1,t} \neq E_t(\tilde{s}_{t,t+1})$, then we still have unconditional unbiasedness, $E(\overline{FP}) = E(\tilde{s})$, even though at every moment the forward rate badly misses the conditional expectation. The sample averages, $\bar{s}$ and $\overline{FP}$, would still be very close despite the glaring inefficiency we just assumed.

3. Currency-by-currency regression tests. From the above, we have to relate each forward premium to the specific realized change that was supposedly predicted by the premium. All this gets lost if one computes time-series averages.

Fama (1984) and Cumby and Obstfeld (1984) came up with such a test. They regress realized changes $s_{t,t+1}$ on the premium $FP_{t,t+1}$ and test for a unit slope. Indeed, in the regression

$$E_t(\tilde{s}_{t,t+1}) = \gamma_0 + \gamma_1 FP_{t,t+1}, \tag{11.4}$$

we should have $\gamma_1 = 1$ and $\gamma_0 = 0$ if unbiased expectations hold. The picture is the same as figure 11.1, except that the units of observations are not time-series averages of changes and premia for many currencies, but a great many individual pairs of period-by-period changes and premia for one currency.

4. Evaluation of trading rules. The period-by-period matching of expectations and interest differentials can also be tested by checking how well one would have done when following a trading rule that tries to exploit possible deviations from UIP.

- One possible rule takes the interest rate as its signal: in true carry-trade style, every month one borrows in the currency with the lowest possible interest rate to invest the proceeds in the money with the highest interest rate. If interest differentials compensate for expected exchange-rate changes, then on average such carry-trades are neither profitable nor unprofitable.

- Another possible rule takes expected exchange-rate changes as its clue. For instance, ERM currencies that have recently fallen are bought and vice versa, in a gamble on the negative autocorrelation that must (and does) exist for currencies with an admissible-band regime. According to UIP, expected appreciations should be met by lower interest rates and vice versa.

---

[2] This is absurd because it would mean that returns are believed to be unit-root processes while they must in fact be close to zero-ρ variables.

	avg s	avg FP	s FP	t	prob
ats	−14.20	−31.30	17.10	0.83	0.41
bef	−4.80	−11.20	6.40	0.31	0.75
cad	−1.60	−8.60	7.00	0.26	0.80
chf	−19.70	−48.00	28.30	1.20	0.23
dem	−16.80	−34.80	18.00	0.88	0.38
dkk	−3.80	0.75	−4.55	−0.22	0.83
esp	21.50	28.99	−7.49	−0.39	0.70
frf	6.05	−3.20	9.25	0.45	0.65
iep	−2.10	5.45	−7.55	−0.43	0.67
itl	18.90	23.90	−5.00	−0.24	0.81
jpy	−23.50	−47.20	23.70	0.84	0.40
nok	−0.60	2.41	−3.01	−0.16	0.87
nlg	−13.80	−30.20	16.40	0.82	0.41
pte	56.31	65.35	−9.04	−0.44	0.66
sek	−0.40	1.57	−1.97	−0.10	0.92
usd	−14.40	−18.40	4.00	0.14	0.89

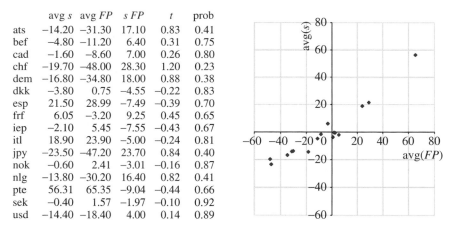

Figure 11.2. Unconditional tests of UIP. The regression representation of the plotted data is $s = 3.37 + 0.64FP$, (1.47), (0.05), $R^2 = 0.92$. *Key:* I test the equality of mean monthly exchange-rate changes and one-monthly forward premia against the GBP (quoted as HC/GBP, U.K. style), 1977–96. All means (and their differences) are expressed as basis points, i.e., percentages of percentages. The plot on the right visualizes the means. Means and t-tests kindly provided by Martina Vandebroek.

11.1.2 Statistical Analysis of Forecast Errors: Computations and Findings

In this chapter I use three different databases that colleagues had on their hard disks. One was provided by Lieven De Moor and contains five-weekly observations on one-month changes and forward premia for 17 currencies against the GBP, 1977–96. The period is set to match that of Huisman et al. (1998). The other contains weekly data for one-week contracts against the DEM, 23 years, provided by Martina Vandebroek, who, in addition, did most of the data analysis on both sets. The third set is from Fang Liu, who also processed it. It has 24 years of weekly observations on (overlapping) monthly contracts for the DEM. All data are originally from DataStream.

11.1.2.1 *Unconditional Tests*

Let us consider the means tests. Standard t-tests in the first sample (monthly, 1977–96, 19 currencies) always accept the null of equality of average premia and average rates of change in the spot value. Figure 11.2 shows the means and their t-tests as a table, and a scatter plot of the means of s and FP. The picture shows a clear link between forward premia and exchange-rate changes, on average. Using a simple standard t-test, the mean expected excess return is never significantly nonzero. The R^2 of a simple regression across all means is an impressive 0.92, and the slope is 0.64. If the standard errors are to be trusted (a big if), this is definitely above zero. Sadly, it would also be definitely below unity.

When we do the same test in the weekly data against the DEM we find a very similar picture. Across ten currencies and thirteen years we find an OLS slope coefficient y_1 below 0.60, a near-zero (and statistically insignificant) intercept y_0, and an R^2 of 0.42. Note that the below-unity slope means that a 1% forward premium on average means less than 1% of appreciation. This means that strong currencies are bad investments, on average, and weak ones good investments. To see this we consider the total return from being long forex, $\tilde{s} + r^*$, in excess of the home return, r:

$$\text{If} \qquad\qquad \tilde{s} \approx 0.6 \times (r - r^*) + \tilde{\epsilon},$$

$$\text{then} \quad \tilde{s} + r^* - r \approx 0.6 \times (r - r^*) + (r^* - r)$$

$$= -0.4 \times (r - r^*) \begin{cases} > 0 & \text{when } r - r^* < 0 \text{ (FC weak)}, \\ < 0 & \text{when } r - r^* > 0 \text{ (FC strong)}. \end{cases}$$

$$(11.5)$$

The last equation tells us that carry trade—borrow low-interest currencies and lend high-rate ones—pays, on average. This fits in with what the average layman would think to be a normal risk premium: weak currencies are risky, strong ones are not. This feeling is neatly reflected in a comment I noticed two days after I first drafted this paragraph: "riskier currencies have lost ground to the relative security of the Japanese yen and the Swiss franc" (the *Economist*, January 26, 2008, p. 68). When discussing the carry trade, the *Economist* is fond of likening the strategy to "picking up pennies in front of a steamroller": a risky game that only fools will play. Whether that notion of risk agrees with what finance theory thinks about it—a covariance with the market as a whole, for instance—remains to be seen. It certainly fits in with the more humdrum notions of risk like career perspectives. In fact, the most influential investors now play not with their own money but with that of their customers or employers. These professional portfolio managers do not necessarily look for the best return, but for the best track record. The big, strong currencies do look safe and respectable. Paraphrasing the old saying about IBM's computers, one could state that "nobody ever got fired for buying CHF." Getting fired for buying Turkish lira is much easier to imagine. In the stock market there is a similar aversion to very small-capitalization stocks or to shares that have done badly in the recent past ("fallen angels"): investors do not like them, so they are priced with big returns.

At this stage you know that, on average, a forward premium predicts a (smaller) rise and a forward discount a (smaller) fall. Yet that interim conclusion gets badly shaken when we consider time-series regression.

11.1.2.2 Time-Series Regression Tests

When we run simple OLS regressions, with the monthly database against the GBP, the result is disastrous. In table 11.1 I just show the slopes from samples 1 and 3. The average in sample 1 is not the +1 that UIP predicts, nor the

Table 11.1. Simple Cumby–Obstfeld/Fama regression coefficients:
$$E_t(\tilde{s}_{t,t+1}) = y_0 + y_1 FP_{t,t+1}.$$

Monthly observations, one-month contracts for GBP, 1977–96							
ATS	BEF	CAD	CHF	DEM	DKK	ESP	FRF
−1.52	−1.21	−4.98	−1.24	−1.08	−0.90	0.22	−0.61

IEP	ITL	JPY	NOK	NLG	PTE	SEK	USD	Mean
0.35	−1.38	−5.11	0.01	−1.97	0.71	−2.68	−2.79	−1.50

Weekly observations, one-month contracts for DEM, 1976–98							
ATS	BEF	DKK	FRF	NLG	ITL	ESP	IEP	Mean
0.11	0.25	0.15	0.78	−0.66	0.16	0.91	0.15	0.23

Key: Monthly percentage exchange-rate changes are regressed on one-month forward premia. The base currency is the GBP, and we use OLS. Table kindly provided by Martina Vandebroek.

0.50–0.60 that unconditional tests would suggest, but −1.50 (yes, *minus* 1.5). Only two slope estimates are positive, and none exceeds unity. In sample 3, which has overlapping weekly observations on one-month contracts (instead of nonoverlapping monthly observations) and a few extra years, the results are better behaved: just one slope is estimated to be negative, and the average is positive; yet, that mean gets no higher than 0.23.

The R^2s, it must be added, are abysmal, like −1 or +5%. This may mean that there is basically nothing to predict. Everyone knows what the really strong currencies are, and the weak ones. But it may be hard to say when a weak currency is even weaker than usual and vice versa; similarly, it may be far from clear at what times a strong currency's appreciation is more likely than usual and vice versa. If there is nothing to predict in the statistical sense (that is, if conditional means are always very close to unconditional ones), then fluctuations in forward premia must reflect fluctuations in risk, or random fluctuations that are too small to be arbitraged away. If that is true, we cannot but get the terrible regression results we saw.

That is why we turn to the second DEM sample, sample 2. These data allow us to also study intra-ERM rates at a shorter horizon (one week, not one month), and these are unusual in that there *is* very strong predictability in the exchange-rate changes. Specifically, at the daily and weekly level, ERM rates have negatively autocorrelated changes. This should not be surprising: if a currency has to stay within a band, then a fall would more often be followed by a rise than by another fall, and a rise would be less likely to be continued and more likely to be undone by a subsequent fall. True, a currency that is near the bottom may devalue instead of returning toward the middle, but empirically the mean reversion dominates.

The ten exchange rates against the DEM are mostly European, including four core ERM currencies (BEF, DKK, FRF, NLG) and three intermittently or informally associated with the ERM (CHF, ITL, and, as the weakest affiliate, GBP).[3] To verify whether the findings are indeed typical for European exchange rates we also include three major outside currencies (USD, JPY, CAD). Table 11.2 shows the first-order autocorrelations from standard regression (where all observations have equal weight) and GARCH, where high-uncertainty days get less weight. The four ERM currencies have strong negative ρs (-0.22 on average; the extreme is -0.48) while for the non-ERM rates they seem more like white noise, as in the preceding chapter. The autocorrelation weakened during the wild period 1992III–1993IV (the collapse of the system in September 1992, and the long attack on the FRF in 1993, culminating in the widening of the band to $\pm 16\%$ each side). In the last period, the autocorrelations came back, even though they were less spectacular than before (-0.22 on average versus -0.27 before the crisis period), as one would expect with a much wider band.

Given that there is a fair amount of predictability, one would expect that interest rates would reflect this. Yet we see none of this in table 11.3. In that table we show results on the merged version of the Fama/Cumby–Obstfeld regression and the autocorrelation equation:

$$\tilde{s}_{t,t+1} = y_0 + y_1 FP_{t,t+1} + \kappa_1 s_{t-1,t} + \tilde{\epsilon}_{t,t+1}. \qquad (11.6)$$

As before, we hope for a unit y_1; in addition, the κs should be zero: all predictability should already be captured by the interest differential.

Example 11.1. Suppose that last week the franc fell by 0.25% and that $\rho_1 = -0.4$. If this is the only useful information there is, one would expect a rise by $-0.4 \times -0.25\% = 0.10\%$ this week, and the franc should now pay 0.10% less, in terms of effective returns over this week.

In reality, the premium could be different from that, because the premium could take into account other information (like where in the band the currency is, how long it has been there, and many other items) and thus become a superior forecaster that subsumes the information from past changes. In short, when the regression includes the forward premium and when this premium equals the best possible forecast, then κ_1 should equal zero: FP should be a better predictor than the ρs_{t-1} from the pyre autocorrelation model.

We use OLS and two system estimators, full information maximum likelihood (FIML) assuming normality and constant moments, and generalized method of moments (GMM), using all ten forward premia and ten lagged changes as instruments. Estimates are provided for the entire data set and for each of the three subperiods defined before, except for GMM for which the

---

[3] Although the Swiss central bank denies intervention, the CHF is widely seen as informally linked to the DEM and, now, the euro. The ITL was an ERM member but with an unusually wide band. The GBP unilaterally tracked the ECU in 1990–91 as a prelude to formal ERM membership, in the spring of 1992, but dropped out in September 1992.

Table 11.2. First-order autocorrelations, weekly: $E_{t-1}(\tilde{s}_t) = \kappa_0 + \rho_1 \tilde{s}_{t-1}$.

	Autocorrelation coefficients ρ_1 for individual currencies										Averages	
	BEF	DKK	FRF	NLG	CHF	ITL	GBP	JPY	CAD	USD	ERM	Other
	Total period (1985/6–1998/3), $\sigma(\rho) = 0.039$											
OLS	*–0.28	*–0.15	*–0.17	*–0.48	–0.03	0.11	0.01	–0.01	0.01	0.02	–0.22	0.03
GARCH	*–0.38	*–0.22	*–0.11	*–0.44	–0.00	–0.01	0.01	–0.01	0.04	0.01	–0.23	0.01
	Early ERM (tight band, 1985/6–1992/8), $\sigma(\rho) = 0.052$											
OLS	*–0.36	*–0.30	*–0.13	*–0.51	–0.03	0.03	0.00	–0.03	0.03	0.01	–0.26	–0.01
GARCH	*–0.39	*–0.28	*–0.17	*–0.52	0.02	0.12	–0.01	–0.04	0.00	–0.01	–0.27	0.01
	September 92 to end 93 (turbulence, 1992/9–1993/12), $\sigma(\rho) = 0.12$											
OLS	0.02	0.01	*–0.24	*–0.45	0.02	0.13	0.04	0.02	–0.08	0.08	–0.13	0.04
GARCH	–0.21	0.01	*–0.26	*–0.32	–0.00	0.13	0.07	0.08	–0.21	0.04	–0.16	–0.02
	Late ERM (wide band, 1994/1–1998/3), $\sigma(\rho) = 0.066$											
OLS	*–0.39	–0.09	*–0.17	*–0.26	–0.08	0.11	–0.03	–0.13	0.09	–0.01	–0.20	0.01
GARCH	*–0.42	*–0.18	*–0.16	*–0.26	–0.05	–0.08	–0.03	–0.13	0.11	–0.01	–0.21	–0.03

Key: The variables s_t are weekly percentage changes in the exchange rate against the DEM. Autocorrelations are estimated by using OLS and GARCH(1,1) specifications for the variance. The averages shown are for the first and second sets of five currencies, respectively, labeled somewhat inaccurately "ERM" and "other." Standard deviations are shown in the panel headers, and an asterisk denotes significance at the 1% level (one-sided).

Table 11.3. Cumby-Obstfeld/Fama tests of UIP. $E_t(\tilde{s}_{t,t+1}) = \gamma_0 + \gamma_1 FP_{t,t+1} + \kappa_1 s_{t-1,t} + \tilde{e}_{t,t+1}$.

(a) COF slope coefficient (γ_1)

	Coefficients for individual currencies										Central values	
	BEF	NLG	DKK	FRF	ITL	CHF	GBP	JPY	CAD	USD	Avg	Med
Total period (1985/6–1998/3)												
OLS	−0.05	−0.18	0.38	0.69	1.17	−0.33	2.07	0.30	0.26	2.75	0.71	0.34
FIML	−0.34	−0.36	0.17	0.46	0.32	−0.33	0.97	−1.06	−0.48	1.95	0.13	−0.08
GMM	−0.11	−0.59	0.27	0.38	0.53	−0.38	1.57	−0.56	0.10	2.08	0.33	0.18
Early ERM (tight band, 1985/6–1992/8)												
OLS	−0.37	−0.33	−0.21	1.71	0.38	−0.44	0.80	−3.96	−1.90	−0.42	−0.47	−0.35
FIML	−0.58	−0.67	−0.28	1.49	0.17	−0.28	−0.62	−4.42	−1.48	−0.96	−0.76	−0.60
GMM	−0.46	−0.75	−0.17	1.33	0.28	−0.41	0.93	−4.52	−1.37	0.30	−0.49	−0.29
September 92 to end 94 (turbulence, 1992/9–1993/12)												
OLS	1.74	2.48	0.89	−2.42	9.31	−12.53	3.44	57.92	9.06	63.30	13.32	2.96
FIML	0.57	−0.62	−0.04	−3.78	7.13	−3.81	5.35	19.29	−5.43	12.10	3.08	0.27
Late ERM (wide band, 1994/1–1998/3)												
OLS	−1.11	−1.55	−4.31	−2.35	−5.52	−3.90	−7.23	−19.06	−2.66	−7.20	−5.49	−4.10
FIML	−2.18	−1.85	−4.18	−2.22	−4.15	−2.71	−1.74	−23.64	−5.08	0.31	−4.74	−2.47
GMM	0.07	−1.63	−4.28	−2.12	−5.30	−3.57	−6.80	−17.82	−2.58	−6.79	−5.08	−3.92

Key: The regressands s_t are weekly percentage changes in the exchange rate against the DEM, the regressors are the beginning-of-period one-week forward premium (FP_t) and the lagged change. The estimation methods are OLS, FIML (normality, constant moments), and GMM (2×10 instruments). The p values are two-sided and based on the Lagrange multiplier test. The two central values shown in the rightmost columns are the mean and the median for κ_1. Table kindly provided by Martina Vandebroek.

Table 11.3. *Continued.*

(b) Autoregression coefficient (κ_1)

	Coefficients for individual currencies										Averages	
	BEF	NLG	DKK	FRF	ITL	CHF	GBP	JPY	CAD	USD	ERM	Other
Total period (1985/6–1998/4), $\sigma(\kappa_2) = 0.039$												
OLS	*−0.28	*−0.48	*−0.16	*−0.18	*0.10	−0.04	0.01	0.01	−0.01	0.02	−0.20	0.00
FIML	*−0.29	*−0.43	*−0.17	*−0.21	0.08	−0.03	0.02	0.02	−0.01	0.02	−0.20	0.00
GMM	*−0.28	*−0.45	*−0.16	*−0.17	0.09	−0.02	0.01	0.00	−0.01	0.02	−0.19	0.00
Early ERM (tight band, 1985/6–1992/8), $\sigma(\kappa_2) = 0.052$												
OLS	*−0.35	*−0.51	*−0.30	*−0.14	−0.03	−0.03	0.00	−0.05	0.03	−0.01	−0.27	−0.01
FIML	*−0.35	*−0.46	*−0.29	*−0.12	0.01	−0.03	0.04	−0.02	0.04	0.02	−0.24	0.01
GMM	*−0.33	*−0.48	*−0.29	*−0.14	−0.03	−0.04	0.02	−0.03	0.04	0.02	−0.26	0.00
September 92 to end 93 (turbulence, 1992/9–1993/12), $\sigma(\kappa_2) = 0.12$												
OLS	0.01	*−0.44	−0.05	−0.22	−0.09	−0.03	0.06	−0.12	0.03	0.08	−0.16	0.01
FIML	−0.13	*−0.39	−0.09	*−0.31	−0.06	0.05	0.08	−0.04	−0.04	0.05	−0.20	0.02
Late ERM (wide band, 1994/1–1998/3), $\sigma(\kappa_2) = 0.066$												
OLS	*−0.39	*−0.27	*−0.14	*−0.18	0.09	−0.09	−0.05	0.09	−0.14	−0.02	−0.18	−0.04
FIML	*−0.37	*−0.25	*−0.16	*−0.16	0.05	−0.10	−0.02	0.07	−0.09	0.01	−0.18	−0.02
GMM	*−0.39	*−0.26	*−0.13	*−0.18	0.09	−0.09	−0.05	0.08	−0.13	−0.02	−0.18	−0.04

Key: The two central values shown in the rightmost columns are the means of κ_2 for the ERM core currencies (BEF, NLG, DKK, FRF, CHF, the latter an informal member) and the non-ERM ones, respectively.

second subperiod is too short. Since the forward premium is almost a unit-root process, the regular t-tests vastly overstate the significance.[4] But there is no unit-root problem with the lagged S; the standard deviation for its coefficient, κ_1, is given in the header of each panel in the table.

In terms of the slope coefficient for the forward premium, the picture is qualitatively no better than in the rest of the literature despite the predictability we have just documented. True, in table 11.3(a) there are some promising averages: at 0.71, the mean OLS slope for the forward premium is rather good. But the median slopes are already substantially lower than the simple averages, and the two system estimators tend to come up with much lower slopes. Note also that the promising average comes from the supposedly unpredictable USD, GBP, and ITL, not from the predictable core-ERM members. Upon closer inspection, the positive equation-by-equation slopes are entirely due to the tumultuous middle period, where the size of the estimates is, in fact, bizarre. In the larger subsamples ((a)(ii) and (iv)), negative slopes dominate, and the recent figures are worse than the early ones. The evidence from the second sample is, in short, not reassuring: DEM-based test results do not provide any better support for UIP, and neither is there improvement over time.

While we observe no clear difference between intra-European versus other rates in (a), there is a sharp divide in (b), where ERM members still show massive negative first-order autocorrelation. The standard t-test for this variable is reliable, and most coefficients remain significant even though the forward premium has been added as a regressor. Also algebraically the κ_1s in table 11.3 are strikingly similar to the ρ_1s in a simple autoregression (not shown). Thus, forward premia do not at all pick up the predictability inherent in the negative autocorrelation of s. The significance of the lagged changes is puzzling: the predictability was easy to spot, there are statistical doubts about the significance, and it is hard to imagine a risk premium that always mirrors the lagged changes.

In this second sample you see how sensitive the estimated slopes are to the estimation method, subperiod, and currency. Samples 1 and 3 had already shown how the adding of observations can change the picture for a constant methodology. Relative to the general literature, the first sample produced uncommonly bad results, the second one uncommonly good ones. On average they behave roughly as most other researchers found. Froot and Thaler (1990) consider the Fama/Cumby–Obstfeld regression equation and, on the basis of over seventy-five studies, estimate that the value of the estimated slope coefficient, β, is approximately -0.8. Perhaps that is too pessimistic; but the conclusion is that the coefficient is definitely below unity.

There are two implications. The first should be of interest for traders: the carry trade, applied dynamically, should be even more profitable than a static

---

[4] We did compute (two-sided) probabilities against H_0: $\kappa_1 = 1$ from the Lagrange multiplier test, a statistic which fares much better in the Bekaert and Hodrick (2001) experiments on UIP tests. Many of the FIML and GMM estimators reject the null when the OLS does not.

one. When a strong currency's forward premium is unusually positive, there surely is no similar rise in the expected spot rate. In fact, for all we know (which is not a lot), there may be no expected rise at all, and perhaps even an expected fall. Likewise, when a weak currency's forward premium is unusually negative, the weak currency may actually rise, on average, or not fall; but there surely is no expected fall that exactly balances the interest advantage. We already had this result across currencies; now we know it holds, and perhaps holds even more, within each time series separately. So you could change lending and borrowing depending on how forward premia compare with their average.

The second implication is about the possible source of these results. From the bit of math in technical note 11.2, the interested reader may conclude the following. If the below-unity slopes are due to a missing variable—for instance, a risk premium—then

- the variable's covariance with the forward premium is negative;
- that covariance is even larger than the variance of the forward premium; and
- the variability of the missing variable exceeds that of the expected changes.

What the missing variable might be is not at all clear. Maybe it is just an inefficiency or a behavioral bias. We return to the issue when we close this section on forward bias.

11.1.3 Trading Rules

11.1.3.1 Trading Rules Based on the Forward Bias: The Carry Trade

Note that negative y_1 coefficients in the regression tests predict that the carry trade works, provided that the intercept is zero. If the forward premium is positive, the expected change in the spot rate is negative, so we should borrow such currencies: we pay little interest, and we can rationally expect a depreciation. Similarly, if the forward premium is negative, the expected change is positive, so we should borrow such currencies and cash in both the high interest fees and an expected capital gain. But note the proviso of a zero intercept. While, empirically, intercepts are typically insignificant, they are hard to estimate with a lot of precision.

Fortunately, it is possible to avoid regression and directly test the profitable-carry-trade prediction. Robinson and Warburton (1980), and later Bell and Kettell (1983), have tested UIP using the interest differential rather than the forward premium. As we know, UIP suggests that the capital gain on the exchange rate should be equal to the interest rate differential. This is equivalent to saying that the total return on a foreign risk-free investment (the sum of capital gains and interest income) should be equal to the return from the domestic bond, as discussed in chapter 4. *Ex post*, we would expect deviations from the equality between returns from the domestic bond and returns from the foreign bond. However, in the absence of a risk premium, these deviations should be random, that is, totally unsystematic and unpredictable on the basis of available information. To verify this conclusion, four alternative investment strategies are tested. These strategies require the following actions at the beginning of every month:

(i) Invest in the currency with the highest nominal interest rate.

(ii) Invest in the currency with the highest real interest rate, based on recent inflation as measured by the consumer price index.

(iii) Invest in the currency with the highest real interest rate, based on recent inflation as measured by the wholesale price index.

(iv) Invest in the currency with the highest real interest rate corrected for "competitiveness" as measured by the International Monetary Fund's unit production cost index.

For each of these strategies, the average return over the sample period is computed. The results are that the average total returns (including foreign interest) differ significantly across strategies, and that these strategies tend to do better than the passive strategy of buying one currency and holding it until the end of the period (buy-and-hold). More precisely, interest rate differentials tend to overcompensate for expected depreciations—in the sense that high-interest currencies typically provide the highest total returns.

Similarly, Thomas (1986) finds that trading using futures contracts instead of forwards and investing in currencies with high interest rates yields positive returns. Taylor (1992) also finds that simple trading rules, based on moving averages of futures prices, can generate positive returns. There have been many more trading-rule tests, but they typically start from expected returns rather than from interest rates. Many of these forecasts rely on chartism, that is, technical trading rules that just rely on past prices and returns.

11.1.3.2 Trading Rules Based on the Technical Exchange-Rate Forecasts

There is absolutely nothing wrong with exchange rates being partly predictable. The true questions are (i) how much of that predictability is picked up by interest differences—all of it, as UIP suggests?—and (ii) if some excess returns remain after taking into account interest, is this an inefficiency or a rational equilibrium outcome? At this stage we still look at the first question only, focusing more particularly on chartist trading rules.

Chartism is popular among traders. Lui and Mole (1998) sum up the findings of their survey as follows:

> ... >85% of respondents rely on both fundamental and technical analyses for predicting future rate movements at different time horizons. At shorter horizons, there exists a skew toward reliance on technical analysis as opposed to

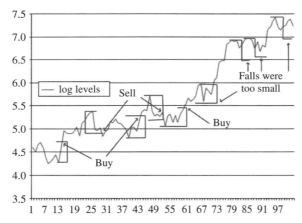

Figure 11.3. The Alexander filter. *Key:* If the trader is long, then if the price falls by more than a preset distance ("filter") from what looks like a peak, she sells. Likewise, if the trader is out of the market, then if the price rises by more than the filter from what looks like a trough, she buys. Some changes toward the end of the graph are big but do not meet the filter size.

> fundamental analysis, but the skew becomes steadily reversed as the length of horizon considered is extended. Technical analysis is considered slightly more useful in forecasting trends than fundamental analysis, but significantly more useful in predicting turning points. Interest rate-related news is found to be a relatively important fundamental factor in exchange rate forecasting, while moving average and/or other trend-following systems are the most useful technical technique.

One such trend-following rule, popular in the academic literature, is known as the Alexander filter. Alexander (1961) tested whether stock market movements tend to persist over time. If increases tend to be followed by more increases, then a policy of buying after observing an x% rise from a low would, on average, generate profits; and if price drops tend to be followed by more decreases, then selling after observing an x% fall from a "high" would again pay, on average, as shown in figure 11.3. The percentage x used to decide when to buy or sell is called the size of the filter. The filter is meant to detect significant changes as opposed to meaningless noise generated by accidental fluctuations in supply and demand.

Sweeney (1986, 1988) finds statistically significant returns, before transaction costs, from using the Alexander filter in the exchange market. This confirms the weak persistence of movements found in early runs tests and autocorrelation tests. They exceed the risk premium if, at least, risk on the "in" days is the same as on the "out" days. Gernaey (1988), in contrast, tests 584 different trading rules,[5] and finds that not even 10% of the rules produced

---

[5] This includes variants of the same basic rule. For instance, in a moving-average rule there is a signal when the path of the short-term moving-average crosses that of the long(er)-run average. So one could try with a short window of 5, 10, 20, or 30 days and a long window of 40, 60, 120, 180, 240—which produces 20 rules.

profits that are significant at the 10% level before transaction costs, and that only 0.3% of the rules are profitable after accounting for transaction costs. Curcio and Goodhart (1991) test whether decision-makers' performance improved depending on whether they did or did not use a popular chartist package marketed by a London firm. They conclude that the software does not make any difference. Interestingly, pros make similar profits as students, with or without the software. Stephen Taylor (1992) concludes that technical trading rules do help: even simple moving-averages combined with ARIMA models generate so much extra money that it is unlikely to be just a risk premium. (Recall that Lui and Mole had explicitly mentioned moving averages as the most popular rule, among traders.) Similar conclusions are obtained in a subsequent paper (Taylor 1994) and in a piece with Allen. Similar results from daily data are from Levich and Thomas (1993) and Surajaras and Sweeney (1992). For weekly data see Kho (1996). Okunev and White (2003) use monthly data. Intraday data, in contrast, do not seem to work (see Neely and Weller 2003; Raj 2000).

Neely et al. (1997) explore (successfully, they claim) nonconventional search methods. They also claim "economically significant out-of-sample excess returns to those rules for each of six exchange rates over the period 1981–95. Further, when the dollar/deutsche mark rules are allowed to determine trades in the other markets, there is significant improvement." Their results are beta-adjusted, with bootstrap significance tests. Gençay (1999) likewise recommends nonlinear methods (computationally slow but reliable, he says) and concludes that "simple technical rules provide significant forecast improvements for the current returns over the random walk model." Chang and Osler (1999) focus on the head-and-shoulders pattern; they conclude that "the rule is profitable, but not efficient, since it is dominated by simpler trading rules." Sercu et al. (forthcoming) find very large and consistent profits, adjusted for unknown but constant risk, from betting on reversals inside the ERM band.

Recently, there are, it seems, more articles claiming to find profits than the reverse. There may be less there than meets the eye: (i) journals have a bias against negative results (like "rule x does not work"), especially if the negative finding contradicts a fundamental paradigm like market efficiency; and (ii) if scores of researchers across the globe keep mining the same data for profitable rules, such examples must sooner or later turn up on a per chance, *ex post* basis; the issue is whether they persist.

What to believe, then? The answer may very well be that technical trading does work, but in a modest way: really blatant profits are unlikely to remain undiscovered for a long time. Markets cannot be perfectly efficient, otherwise watching prices would no longer be worthwhile, which would immediately lead to inefficiencies (Grossman and Stiglitz 1980); so the only sustainable equilibrium is one where the analysts and traders earn their banks just enough money to justify their wages. Thus, remember also that it does take time and resources to watch the charts all the time. Most CFOs do not bother. One reason is that predictability is typically a short-term phenomenon. It may be exploitable when setting up a hedge policy for contractual exposures; but many exposures, and many decisions, involve long-run horizons.

11.1.4 The Forward Bias: Concluding Discussion

The bad performance of the forward rate is often regarded as one of big puzzles in international finance, along with, for example, the disconnect puzzle or the strong home bias in investors' portfolios. Let us see what explanations have been tried and what the results of additional tests, if any, are.

11.1.4.1 An Orthodox Risk Premium

One interpretation of the low γ_1s is that there is a missing variable that correlates with the forward premium, and a prime candidate is a risk premium.[6] Early tests took the then standard model, the CAPM, in its one-country or world version (see chapter 19). In that case, the risk premium is $\beta \operatorname{E}(\tilde{r}_m - r)$ with $\operatorname{E}(\tilde{r}_m)$ the expected return on the market portfolio and β the beta of the exchange rate.[7] In practice, one can regress excess returns on forex on the market and see whether this explains the nonnegative mean. The CAPM indeed says that the expected excess return on a risky asset j equal the asset's beta times the expected excess return on the market portfolio:[8]

$$\operatorname{E}(\tilde{r}_j - r_0) = \overbrace{\beta_j \operatorname{E}(\tilde{r}_m - r_0)}^{RP} \text{ with } \beta_j \text{ as in } \tilde{r}_j - r_0 = \alpha_j + \beta_j (\tilde{r}_m - r_0) + \epsilon_j. \quad (11.7)$$

Our risky asset is the FC, whose excess return is

$$[\text{Return on FC}] - r_0 = [(1 + \tilde{s})(1 + r_0^*) - 1] - r_0 \approx \tilde{s} + r_0^* - r_0$$
$$= \tilde{s} - \underbrace{(r_0 - r_0^*)}_{\approx FP}. \quad (11.8)$$

In practice, beta risk does not noticeably dent the mean return from the carry trade or from technical trading rules.

A more state-of-the-art approach is based on a generalization of the CAPM. In a less restrictive version of the model, the risk premium comes from covariance with changes in marginal utility, which in turn depend on consumption growth and inflation. This can be built into the model used in the real-business-cycle theory, where the exchange rate itself is the ratio of the two countries' marginal utilities. Finally, it can be shown that the risk-free rates, in this setting, are the expected value of minus the growth in marginal utility.

---

[6] Frankel and Engel (1984), Domowitz and Hakkio (1985), Hodrick and Srivastava (1986), Hodrick (1987, 1989), Cumby (1987), Mark (1988), Engel (1995), Hollifield and Uppal (1997), Mark and Wu (1997), Backus et al. (2001), and Chinn and Frankel (2002) all fail to explain the forward puzzle well; but see Bansal (1997) for a dissident view.

[7] The beta of an asset is the slope coefficient obtained when regressing the asset's return onto the market return.

[8] To avoid confusion I denote the risky asset's return by $\tilde{r}_j$ and the risk-free one (asset 0) by r_0. I also drop time subscripts: three subscripts would be too much of a good thing.

Clearly, this can all be used in a coherent theory of how the interest differential might co-move with the risk premium; after all, everything here derives from marginal utilities.

Hollifield and Uppal (1997) explore these links in the context of a general-equilibrium model originally developed by Dumas (1992) and Uppal (1993). They do find that the risk premium is negatively correlated with the forward premium, but not nearly enough to explain why the Fama y_1s are so far below unity. Bansal (1997), using the consumption CAPM (a variant closely related to the marginal-utility model), proves that the risk premium should not only be negatively related with the forward premium, but also nonlinearly so, in a way that if one ignores it, y_1 changes sign depending on the sign of *FP*. He does find that pattern in USD rates in the 1980s and early 1990s, but others have been less lucky when they change the period or reference currency.

Lustig and Verdelhan (2007) think that the carry-trade gains do fit in with orthodox risk definitions. There is, they say, a curious asymmetry: high-interest-rate currencies depreciate on average when domestic consumption growth is low and low-interest-rate currencies appreciate under the same conditions, so low-interest-rate currencies provide domestic investors with a hedge against domestic aggregate consumption growth risk. Yet, in the underlying theory (discussed, in chapter 11, under the real-business-cycle header) currencies should not behave differently depending on the interest rate, so the empirical regularity lacks a good foundation. Let us wait for review tests in a few years to see whether the regularity survives. Also, the Lustig–Verdelhan phenomenon can explain the long run only, not the short-term gyrations of the rates.

In general, indeed, the success of trading rules, and especially the speed with which expected returns seem to vary, is hard to reconcile with risk premia. With the notable exception of the carry trade, most trading rules identify brief periods in which one is recommended to be long or short, alternating with periods where no position is to be sought. If this is to be explained by a fluctuating risk premium, then the risk must be changing at short notice, going from positive or negative to zero and back in a matter of days. This required pattern seems very far from the usual view of risk premia, which under normal circumstances change only slowly. For these and related reasons, the risk premium is not the sole missing variable and probably not the main such variable.

11.1.4.2 Markets Need Time to Learn about New Policies

One explanation for the forward bias is that it is the result of investors making errors in forming expectations. According to this view, there is either no risk premium or the premium does not change over time; instead, very often the exchange rate increases when investors had expected the currency to depreciate and accordingly had set the forward rate below par. Likewise, when the investors expect the currency to appreciate and set a positive forward premium, then on average the exchange rate decreases. We need to explain how such errors in expectations can arise even in efficient markets.

The hypothesis that even clever investors make errors in forming expectations relies on the assumption that it takes time for investors to learn about market conditions. Thus, the effect of changes in monetary policy or in exchange-rate policy may not be immediately reflected in market prices. Lewis (1989) finds that slow learning by market participants about changes in U.S. monetary policy could potentially explain about half of the forward rate bias. The problem with this explanation is that one needs to explain why this bias persists, that is, why investors do not eventually learn about how such events affect exchange rates. For a permanent bias, one would need the rules of the game to change all the time and in all countries, and the investors always and everywhere to be wrong-footed—a strange story.

11.1.4.3 Dark Matter Theories: Peso Risks, Overreaction, and Career Risks

Another explanation that has been advanced to explain the forward bias is that of the "peso problem."[9] According to this view, for long periods of time investors may assign a small but positive probability to certain relatively infrequent events (such as a devaluation, a change of monetary policy, a change of exchange-rate regime, a war, or some other major event) which may never materialize in a limited sample period. The expectation of such an extreme event will be reflected in today's forward exchange rate. However, because of the infrequent occurrence of such an event, the econometrician may never get a chance to actually observe such an event. So the researcher would conclude the market was wrong all the time.

Peso risk could obviously explain why the mean observed change might differ from the mean premium, but one would need a story with changing risks if one wanted to explain covariances. A plausible mechanism is as follows. When bad news about the foreign currency hits the market, the spot rate drops. But the concomitant selling of short-term FC paper (or, for the short sellers, the borrowing in FC) also pushes up the foreign interest rate, thus seemingly foretelling a further drop—or, if you wish, slowing down the immediate drop. The bad news considered here is a rise in the chance of a peso catastrophe. But if, as is likely, the peso event then fails to materialize, the peaking forward premium tends to be followed by a recovery in the spot rate, producing the negative regression coefficients.

One problem with this view is that peso risks are logically associated with controlled exchange rates. The 1992 collapse of the ERM, for instance, was a huge event for the FIM, SEK, GBP, and ITL, involving value losses of up to one

---

[9] The term refers to the Mexican peso, which for a long period of time was traded at a large discount, but was not devalued for years. So the market was always wrong, it seemed. Then, one day, the peso's value dropped significantly.

third. For floating rates, in contrast, one wonders what the huge peso event might be if there is no system of interventions or exchange restrictions that keep the accumulating tensions bottled up for a long time. Yet most of the empirical evidence on too-low y_1s comes from floating rates.

If one accordingly rejects the peso view as implausible for floating rates, then it may seem that we are only inches away from the overreaction hypothesis. On this view, the huge change fails to materialize not because its probability is low, but because it exists only in the minds of the traders. People are subject to bouts of panic or overoptimism, causing soon-corrected movements in spot rates accompanied by changes in interest rates in the opposite direction.

Overreactions are one form of inefficiency. Liu and Sercu (2008) propose a variant where traders do act rationally. Their starting point is that the market is dominated by professional investors (traders or portfolio managers), not individuals playing with their own stakes. For a professional, the ultimate decision criterion is the portfolio manager's career and remuneration prospects. This is not the same as the return on the portfolio to be managed because PV-ed remunerations and reputation are not linear in the portfolio return, and also depend on how and when any losses have occurred. Imagine, again, bad news about a foreign currency, immediately showing up in a falling spot rate and a falling forward premium (rising foreign money-market rates). The manager may play it safe and liquidate the foreign positions, thus risking missing a recovery; or she may act contrarian and stay long, risking a further drop in the spot rate. In making the choice she will note that a cash loss looks worse than an opportunity loss, in general. But a cash loss from being contrarian (when there has been a clear and publicly observable bad initial signal) looks much worse than an opportunity loss from missing a rally—especially if, judging by the initial forward premium, the rally was deemed to be the less likely event. Any cash loss from going against the flow will be met with the comment that the trader "should have seen it coming," but the opportunity loss from following the consensus signal will not. In short, when bad news hits the market, professional investors head for the exit even if there is an expected gain from the subsequent recovery, because the expected gain from the recovery is counterbalanced by a dark matter, the potential damage to the professional investor's career if expectations turn out to be wrong. In the stock market this is known as the "fallen angel" effect: stocks that did badly are shunned by portfolio managers and, therefore, generate high returns (see Ikenberry et al. 1995).

If high interest rates are viewed as one of the danger signals, then forward discounts are associated with career risk premia, that is, higher expected returns. Liu and Sercu (2008) observe the predicted pattern in European rates against the DEM. But the mechanism seems to require a fixed-rate regime, where a "good" position is easily identifiable: Liu and Sercu (2008) find that the predicted pattern is absent in floating rates against the USD, but does show up in the HKD/USD rate. Commonsensically, the fallen-angel effect also seems to require a strong currency as a basis; for rates against the ITL (instead of the DEM), the pattern again disappears. Thus, the hypothesis fails to explain many cases.

11.1.4.4 "There's Nothing to Predict, or Profits Are Way Too Risky"

Recall that Froot and Thaler, on the basis of over seventy-five studies, estimate that the value of the estimated Fama/Cumby–Obstfeld slope coefficient, y_1, is approximately -1. They also find, however, that the average residual standard error is equal to 36% p.a. This implies that, by borrowing in the low-interest-rate currency and investing in a currency with an interest rate that is 1% higher, the total expected return is 2% p.a. (The interest rate differential is 1%, and the fact that y_1 is assumed to be -1 implies that a 1% forward premium yields an expected capital gain of another 1%.) Thus, the predicted return on USD 500, invested for one year, is equal to USD $500 \times 0.02 =$ USD 10. However, the standard error of this expected return is USD $500 \times 0.36 =$ USD 180 p.a. This implies that an investor would make, on average, USD 10 p.a. but, allowing for the returns to vary two standard deviations, the investor could reasonably expect a return as high as USD 370 or as low as $(-)$USD 350. This much variability in the return is not attractive for the investor, given that the expected return is only USD 10, and when the investor allows for transaction costs, such an investment is even less attractive.

Sercu et al. (forthcoming) beg to differ. In their trading rules based on ERM mean reversion, profits are substantial, averaging 14% p.a., and low risk. Sharpe ratios are extremely high, and strategies never produced losses in any two-year subperiod. Sercu et al. reject regular risk premia, peso effects, and hedging pressure as sufficient explanations.

11.1.4.5 Transaction Costs; "Extreme Support"

Huisman et al. (1998) start from the idea that if markets are subject to transaction costs, uncovered interest arbitrage cannot perfectly align expected exchange rates and forward premia. Most of the time, they argue, expectations of exchange-rate changes are probably so small that this friction-induced noise between expectations and premia largely obscures the theoretical parity between the two. However, there may be occasions where the market does expect unusually large changes; and if the impact of friction is essentially unaffected by the size of the expected change, then in these instances the signal-to-noise ratio must be relatively favorable. Highly positive or negative forward premia should therefore be better predictors than small premia. Cast in familiar statistical terms: the Fama regression suffers from an errors-in-the-regressor-type bias toward zero, and for a given variance of the noise term this bias can be reduced by constructing a subsample where the variance of the regressor is larger. Huisman et al. test this model using panel techniques with a cross-currency constraint that ensures numéraire-invariance of the estimates. They report that large-variance observations generate y_1 regression coefficients close to unity, and even substantially above unity if the definition of "large variance" is very strict.

Sercu and Vandebroek (2005) point out that the above tests reveal something about the missing variable: for such results, the expectation signal needs to be thicker-tailed than the missing variable. Transaction costs may produce the right sort of bias: it is (i) bounded (i.e., it has no tails at all), (ii) wide (i.e., it may generate betas below 1/2), and (iii) U-distributed, which makes an "extreme" sample quite effective. They derive theoretical and numerical results in the direction of what Huisman et al. observe. Liu and Sercu (2008) observe the Huisman et al. effect in a more recent sample of floating rates against the USD, but not in the ERM data. Sercu and Vinaimont (2006) do not note it either in rates for the ECU, and when Martina Vandebroek looked at sample 1 for me, she was unable to find any such effect either.

11.1.4.6 Statistical Flaws in the Tests

Lastly, there may be statistical problems with most tests. One issue is that the *FP* regressor is so autocorrelated that, often, the unit-root hypothesis is not rejected. This casts doubt on the reliability of the usual standard errors and significance tests. Roll and Yan (2000) show that the true confidence bounds for y_1 are way beyond the conventional numbers produced by standard regression coefficients, so that in many cases one can, in reality, not reject the hypothesis of a unit slope. Most tests since then have taken this into account. Still, this leaves unexplained why the observed deviations are so predominantly downward; if there were no bias, then estimates above unity should be as frequent as estimates below unity.

*   *   *

To conclude: the forward rate is a more than dubious predictor of the future spot rate, for reasons that are far from clear. So we continue our quest for predictability and turn our attention to specialists.

11.2 Forecasts by Specialists

In the first few sections of this chapter, we discussed the performance of various economic models that try to predict the exchange rate based on information about the fundamentals in the economy. Our initial illusions, if any, were largely dashed. We then asked whether, even if we do not know what markets will do, maybe the markets themselves do know. As far as we can judge from forward rates, they do not. But there is still hope: perhaps the best and brightest of the players do see what is coming. Accordingly, the first issue, in this section, is whether central bankers seem to be successful at foreseeing the spot rate. After all, they have information about monetary policy that is not available to private investors; they can afford to take a long-run, bird's-eye view; and, having been in the game for centuries, they may also be quite experienced at reading the market's mind. We then evaluate the record of professional forecasters and, finally, of traders in predicting the future spot rate.

11.2.1 Forecasts Implied by Central Bank Interventions

Central banks claim that they "lean against the wind" but do not "go against the market": they supposedly intervene in currency markets to maintain an orderly market and to smooth out excessive swings in exchange rates but they do not try to move the exchange rate away from its fundamental value. If they succeed in pulling this off, central banks must be quite good at predicting exchange rates: the central bank then buys if it knows that the current low price of foreign currency is a temporary aberration that will soon be reversed, and it likewise sells to speed up the drop of the currency that it knows is imminent anyway.

Milton Friedman once remarked that if central bankers were really successful in distinguishing excessive swings from fundamental trends, they should be hugely profitable. Indeed, they would start buying when the exchange rate is below its equilibrium value, and they would start selling when the exchange rate is above its equilibrium value. However, when Taylor (1982) measured profits from intervention, he found that seven central banks out of eight actually made substantial losses from currency trading. In three cases, these losses could not even remotely be ascribed to chance. In short, the results from Taylor's study seem to suggest that either central banks are bad at outguessing the market, or they actually go against the market (at the taxpayers' expense). However, some of these results were sensitive to the time period of the study. For example, if Taylor's study is extended by two years, the central banks actually make a modest profit from their currency trading.

The Taylor paper soon triggered a flood of studies conducted by the central banks themselves; these are more precise since the banks have the exact details about timing and amounts while Taylor only has weekly totals for interventions. De Nederlandsche Bank applied Taylor's methodology to its interventions in the currency markets and found that it made money on its spot market interventions, but lost money when it intervened in the forward market (Fase and Huijser 1989). The Bank of Canada studied its profitability and effectiveness over the period 1975–88 (Murray et al. 1990). They concluded that the government's trading in the currency market had been profitable and that this trading had tended to be stabilizing in the sense that the actions of the central bank helped move the exchange rate closer to its long-run equilibrium value and helped reduce its short-term volatility. However, despite this record of profitability over the 1975–88 period, the Bank of Canada incurred substantial losses during other periods. Fischer (2003), at the Swiss National Bank, concludes that "the SNB foreign exchange interventions were profitable when considering the 1986–95 period." (The year 1995, in case you are suspicious about the age of the sample period, is when the SNB stopped intervening; and before 1986 its interventions were not published.) Leahy (1995), at the Federal Reserve, concludes that "U.S. intervention since the beginning of generalized floating in 1973 has earned profits for the U.S. monetary authorities. ... it is unlikely the profits are merely the outcome of chance or a normal return to bearing time-invariant risk."

Meanwhile, back in academia, many studies were applying Taylor-like computations to data from various periods and countries. Sweeney (1997) sums up the literature:

> Estimates of central bank intervention losses or profits vary widely; some estimates find substantial losses, others profits. In most cases, estimated profits are not risk-adjusted, and risk adjustment can have large effects. Furthermore, profit estimates involve variables integrated of order one, and because of this test-statistics may have nonstandard distributions; few studies take this into account. Estimates of risk-adjusted profits for the U.S. Fed and the Swedish Riksbank, with allowances for possible nonstandard distributions, suggest that neither made losses and might have made significant profits.

But when he (and a coauthor) actually published their results on the Federal Reserve and the Riksbank, the wording was more careful. Sweeney (2000), studying the Federal Reserve, tries to adjust for foreign-exchange risk premia—via betas—and finds that "profits appear economically and statistically significant, whether risk premia are modeled as time-constant or as appreciation's market beta depending on Fed intervention." But, he adds, "the estimates are sensitive to the method of risk adjustment and to the periods used." Sjöö and Sweeney (2000, 2001) consider Sweden's Riksbank. Their summary is even more hedged around with caveats:

> Estimated profits can be quite sensitive as to whether rates of return are risk-adjusted or not, and how the risk-adjustment is done. ... Results, on daily data, support the view that Riksbank intervention did not make risk-adjusted losses over the period 1986–1990. The results might be challenged as arising from inappropriate risk adjustment.

In a 2007 sequel, Sweeney explores the risk-premium issue:

> Fed foreign-currency sales cause economically and statistically significant increases in the systematic risk premium in appreciation and thus in the dollar's expected appreciation rate, the direction the Fed desires. ... Even successful intervention to strengthen the dollar may be costly; by increasing the dollar's systematic risk, intervention reduces the attractiveness of U.S. relative to foreign investments.

To sum this up: central banks probably make some money in the long run, but whether this exceeds the risk premium is far less clear; and there is certainly lots of variability in the short run. So even privileged players have a hard time predicting rates. So let us see how ordinary earthlings do.

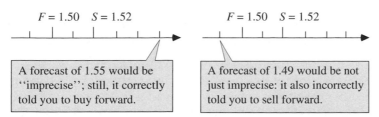

Figure 11.4. Is MSE a good performance criterion? *Key:* The forward rate "predicted" 1.50 and the outcome was 1.52. In both examples of specialist's forecasts, 1.55 or 1.49, the *ex post* squared error is 0.03^2; still you'd be happy in the first case, unhappy in the second.

11.2.2 Evaluating the Performance of Professional Traders and Forecasters

In this subsection we discuss two groups from the private end of the financial sector: professional forecasting services and traders.

Specialized forecasters jumped into a new hole in the market when Bretton-Woods collapsed and most currencies started floating. After the first few years of floating rates, Goodman (1979) surveyed the predictions made by these self-styled specialists. He makes a distinction between econometric services, which use economic models such as the ones described in the above sections to predict exchange rates, and services using technical (chartist) models to predict the spot rate. Goodman concludes that, while the first group is not very good at predicting the spot rate, the technical forecasters do somewhat better. The conclusions of Goodman's yearly reviews published by *Euromoney* as of 1979 are similar, except that even the technical predictors' records appear to deteriorate over time. In the end, even this subgroup's success rate was down to 50/50. *Euromoney* discontinued the series, so we have no more recent results.

Levich (1980a,b), in a comprehensive survey, concludes that forecasting services (econometric and judgmental) do poorly when the mean square error (MSE) is used as the criterion for testing the accuracy of forecasts relative to the MSE for the forward rate.[10] However, he finds that they may have some ability to predict whether the future spot rate will be greater than or smaller than the current forward rate—the information needed to make the correct hedging decision and to undertake the correct speculative position, as explained below.

Example 11.2. To see why the direction of forecast (relative to the forward rate) may be at least as important as the absolute or squared error, suppose that the current three-month forward rate is USD/EUR 1.50 and the realized rate then turns out to be 1.52. Then the forward's squared error is 0.02^2. We contrast this with

---

[10] If the forecast is $\hat{S}_t$ and the realization S_t, the MSE is defined as the mean of the squared errors, $\sum_{t=t_1}^{t_n} (\hat{S}_t - S_t)^2 / n$.

two possible earlier forecasts, each equally bad in terms of squared error (0.03^2, notably) but one still being a good forecast, on reflection (see figure 11.4):

- Suppose first that the forecast was 1.55. This implies a worse squared error (at 0.03^2) than that of the forward rate, but you would still be happy with the forecast because it was correct in predicting that a forward purchase would make you money. True, you hoped for 0.05, but you still got 0.02.

- Suppose, alternatively, that the forecast was 1.49. This is an equally bad square error (at 0.03^2), but now you would be unhappy with the forecast because it was incorrect in predicting that a sale would make you money. You hoped for 0.01 from selling, but you actually made −0.02.

Levich finds that the relative number of correct signals for some forecasting services significantly exceeds 50%. Thus, it seems that some forecasters have some skill in predicting the direction of change in the spot. Levich's significance tests, however, ignore the dependence between the test results. If a U.S. forecaster was lucky predicting the DEM, he or she almost surely would have been lucky forecasting the related currencies, such as the CHF, NLG, and FRF. Thus, the evidence is hard to interpret. Moreover, when Levich (1983) did the same study a few years later, he found that the forecasting services that performed well in the first study were not the same as those that did well in the updated survey. Thus, it seems that no service can consistently predict the future spot rate relative to the forward.

Another group of specialists is the body of traders that work for banks all over the globe. A 1995 survey of Hong Kong traders reveals (Lui and Mole 1998) that, like professional forecasters, they use both chartism and fundamental models. Traders are paid well, there are many of them, the infrastructure they need is costly, and their operating expenses are high. Doesn't that mean that they must make money for their employers too, and, by implication, that trades are not the zero-NPV deals that they should be, in efficient markets? Not necessarily. Banks do make a lot of money from their trading rooms, but few banks bother to separate profits from intermediation—humdrum bid–ask income when customer orders are executed—from gains from "proprietary trading," i.e., the buying and selling for the bank's own account. There is one study that tries to do so: Lyons (1998) tracks all trades by one trader from a big U.S. bank for a whole week. His conclusions are mixed.

The trader does make pots of money: "he averages $100,000 profit per day (on volumes of $1 billion per day). By comparison, equity dealers average about $10,000 profit per day (on volumes of roughly $10 million per day)." Extreme positions are cut quite quickly: the half-life for the dealer's net position is only 10 minutes, against 1 week for equity specialists. But most, or actually more than most, of the money seems to come from intermediation. As Lyons does not know what trades are speculative or not, his evidence here is circumstantial but credible: (i) after a purchase (sale), prices do not rise (fall) in any way that a statistician can detect, suggesting that there is no predictive power; and (ii) when Lyons recalculates the dealer's profits using midpoint prices rather than bids and asks, thus stripping out all bid–ask income, there is a small loss. In addition, "speculative profits are much more volatile than profits from intermediation. Nevertheless, our findings are consistent with those from the much lower-frequency analysis of Ammer and Brunner (1997)." These conclusions are also consistent with the boom–bust cycles that the trading business seems to go through, with banks firing entire brigades of them after suffering big losses and then, after some time, succumb to hope and optimism again.

To summarize the literature on the performance of forecasters of exchange rates, the evidence suggests that predictions based on fundamental variables do not seem to be accurate. In view of our earlier direct evidence on these models, this may not be surprising. Technical forecasters, at least for short-term forecasts, may to do better, though their record is not unambiguous either. The performance by traders is largely unknown: Lyons studied just one trader at one bank for one week, hardly a representative sample. Still, that evidence does not suggest that traders have a way to predict currency movements.

11.3 CFO's Summary

This discussion covers both the present chapter and the preceding one. Remember that we first studied formal models. Spot rates behaved very much like random walks (with some drift, and with weak traces of mean reversion). Real rates hardly do better: even though there is a long-run PPP effect, it is basically irrelevant when the horizon is six months, for instance. Models that try to link rates to economic policy basically fail to predict; they actually do worse than the no-change forecast. But, we hoped, maybe that just reflects the crudeness of formal models. Perhaps reality is too complex to be captured by equations involving just a few variables obtained from ceteris-paribus theories. But we see that forward rates, or central banks, or traders do not much better. Forward rates may even ignore predictabilities detectable with auto-correlations or simple technical trading rules. What sense can we make of all this?

The apparent incomprehensibility of exchange markets seems hard to square with the daily comments by journalists and analysts. Hopper (1997) comes up with an excellent picture of CFOs' daily experience when reading the financial pages or talking to bankers:

> Readers of the financial press are familiar with the gyrations of the currency market. No matter which way currencies zig or zag, it seems there is always an analyst with a quotable, ready explanation. Either interest rates are rising faster than expected in some country, or the trade balance is up or down, or central banks are tightening or loosening their monetary policies.

Theme of the Week - January 6, 2008 to January 11, 2008

Euro Gains vs Dollar on Hawkish Trichet and Dovish Bernanke: The pair climbed 100 pips following the hawkish tone of Trichet's conference. The pair then extended those gains after Fed Chairman Bernanke, in a speech, said that the FOMC was ready to lower rates to offset "downside risk to growth" fueling speculation of a 50 basis point cut in the next meeting.

German Data Weakens Euro: Fundamental reports out of Germany showed retail sales declining by 1.3% and industrial production falling 0.9% in November. The news undershot forecasts of increases to both indicators and caused the Euro to weaken.

Pound Falters Prior to BOE Announcement: The Pound fell during Wednesday's trading session following data showing consumer confidence is at a 10 month low.

« Previous Week's Recap   **Next Week's Outlook »**

Sunday, January 06

Region	EST	Indicator	Actual	Forecasted	Previous
NZ	4:45pm	⊞ Trade Balance	-0.65B	-0.47B	-0.72B ℝ
JPN	6:50pm	⊞ Monetary Base y/y	0.4%		1.0%

Monday, January 07 | Market Highlights

Region	EST	Indicator	Actual	Forecasted	Previous
				Video Recap	Nilsson's Commentary
SWZ	1:45am	⊞ Unemployment Rate	2.6%	2.6%	2.6%
EMU	4:30am	⊞ Sentix Investor Confidence	8.2	10.5	11.9
EMU	5:00am	⊞ Producer Price Index m/m	0.8%	0.7%	0.7% ℝ
EMU	5:00am	⊞ Consumer Confidence	-9	-8	-8
EMU	5:00am	⊞ Economic Sentiment Indicator	104.7	104.3	104.8
EMU	5:00am	⊞ Industrial Confidence	2	2	3
EMU	5:00am	⊞ Business Climate Indicator	0.92	0.90	1.04
EMU	5:00am	⊞ Unemployment Rate	7.2%	7.2%	7.2%
AUS	5:30pm	⊞ Construction PMI	59.2		53.2
UK	7:01pm	⊞ BRC Retail Sales y/y	0.3%	0.8%	1.2%
AUS	7:30pm	⊞ Building Approvals	8.9%	0.0%	-3.6% ℝ

Tuesday, January 08 | Market Highlights

Region	EST	Indicator	Actual	Forecasted	Previous
				Video Recap	Nilsson's Commentary
UK	3:00am	⊞ House Prices m/m (Halifax Bank of Scotland)	1.3%	0.5%	-1.3%
EMU	5:00am	⊞ Retail Sales m/m	-0.5%	0.4%	-0.7%
GER	6:00am	⊞ Factory Orders m/m	3.4%	-1.6%	4.0%
USA	10:00am	⊞ Pending Home Sales m/m	-2.6%	-0.7%	3.7% ℝ
USA	3:00pm	⊞ Consumer Credit m/m	15.4B	7.5B	2.0B ℝ
UK	7:01pm	⊞ Consumer Confidence Index (NCCI)	85	85	86
AUS	7:30pm	⊞ Retail Sales m/m	0.8%	0.5%	0.3% ℝ
NZ	9:00pm	⊞ Commodity Price Index (ANZ)	0.0%		0.8%

Figure 11.5. Cues for day traders: January 6–11, 2008, part 1.
Source: www.cmsfx.com on January 12, 2008.

What variables are the pundits watching? The Hong Kong survey referred to above mentioned first and foremost the interest rate, and it is considered to be positively correlated with the currency's value. (This ties in with theory if, at least, the interest rate hike does not come along with a drop in the risk-adjusted expected future value. What is strange, we know by now, is that after

GER	2:00am	⊞ Trade Balance	19.3B	17.5B	18.9B ℝ
GER	2:00am	⊞ Retail Sales m/m	-1.3%	1.3%	-2.3% ℝ
EMU	5:00am	⊞ Gross Domestic Product	0.8%	0.7%	0.7%
UK	5:30am	⊞ BRC Shop Price Index y/y	1.0%		1.1%
GER	6:00am	⊞ Industrial Production m/m	-0.9%	0.3%	0.1% ℝ
CAN	8:15am	⊞ Housing Starts	188K	220K	228K
UK	10:30am	⊞ Leading Index	-0.3%		0.2%
AUS	7:30pm	⊞ Trade Balance	-2.3B	-2.5B	-2.9B ℝ

Thursday, January 10 | Market Highlights

Region	EST	Indicator	Actual	Video Recap Forecasted	Nilsson's Commentary Previous
JPN	12:00am	⊞ Leading Index	10.0	10.0	18.2
UK	4:30am	⊞ Trade Balance	£-7.4B	£-7.2B	£-7.4B ℝ
UK	7:00am	⊞ BOE Interest Rate Statement	5.50%	5.50%	5.50%
EMU	7:45am	⊞ ECB Interest Rate Statement	4.0%	4.0%	4.0%
EMU	8:30am	⊞ ECB President Trichet Speaks			
USA	8:30am	⊞ Jobless Claims	332K	340K	337K ℝ
CAN	8:30am	⊞ Building Permits	-9.9%	-1.9%	6.8%
CAN	8:30am	⊞ New Housing Price Index	0.5%	0.2%	0.1%
USA	10:00am	⊞ Wholesale Inventories	0.6%	0.4%	0.0%
USA	1:00pm	⊞ Fed Chairman Bernanke Speaks			
JPN	6:50pm	⊞ M2+CD Money Supply y/y	2.1%	2.0%	2.0%

Friday, January 11

Region	EST	Indicator	Actual	Forecasted	Previous
JPN	12:00am	⊞ Eco Watchers Survey	36.6	39.0	38.8
GER	2:00am	⊞ Wholesale Price Index m/m	-0.5%	0.5%	1.0%
UK	4:30am	⊞ Industrial Production	-0.1%	0.1%	0.4%
UK	4:30am	⊞ Manufacturing Production	-0.1%	0.1%	0.3%
CAN	7:00am	⊞ Employment Change	-18.7K	15.0K	42.6K
CAN	7:00am	⊞ Unemployment Rate	5.9%	5.9%	5.9%
CAN	8:30am	⊞ Trade Balance	3.7B	3.2B	3.3B
USA	8:30am	⊞ Trade Balance	-63.1B	-59.5B	-57.8B
USA	8:30am	⊞ Import Prices	0.0%	0.0%	2.7%
USA	12:45pm	Fed Governor Mishkin Speaks			

Figure 11.6. Cues for day traders: January 6–11, 2008, part 2.
Source: www.cmsfx.com on January 12, 2008.

the hike the currency does not typically slide back.) Other popular cues can be identified from the page from a website for day traders shown in figure 11.5. In table 11.4 I group the cues into six main categories, and count the number of times each comes up. Note that the frequencies not only depend on the website's perception about the traders' interests, but also on the frequency of official releases and, of course, on the number of statistics that fit into a particular category. Having said that, the picture surely is one where a lot of attention is paid to economic activity (observed and expected). But the balance of payments is there too, and prices, and even money supply.

There is no shortage of variables, in short. But there are about as many good-news items as bad-news ones. How do the pundits know what matters most? In

Table 11.4. Cues for day traders: summary.

Interest rates		3
Economic activity (observed)		24
Employment	5	
Construction, housing	7	
Retail sales, consumer credit	6	
Industrial production, inventories, orders, GDP	5	
Commodity prices	1	
Expectations, confidence, sentiment		10
Trade balance		6
Money supply		2
CPI, WPI, or TPI		4

Key: Summary of themes in figures 11.5 and 11.6.

reality, on many days neither the newspaper writers nor the professionals they talk to have any good view of why rates are moving in a particular direction. On such bad days, a four-step procedure is adopted:

(i) Check what direction the market moved that day.

(ii) Run down the list of currently accepted possible explanations, and tick any item on which there was news that would explain the move; carefully ignore any news that would have pointed the other way.

(iii) If unsuccessful at step (ii), run down the list of conventional stories, and selectively cite elements from the current situation, even if the situation has not changed, that is, if there was no news on that front. For instance, "the EUR again suffered from the rigidity of Old Europe's labor markets." "The dollar came under pressure because it still pays less interest than the EUR and GBP, while the U.S. current-account deficit remains negative."

(iv) Write a cogent, simple, and unhesitating comment.

As my colleague Paul De Grauwe likes to say, these explanations occasionally even start leading their own life. If one factor is suddenly brought into the limelight, analysts and investors start looking at this new variable, and its impact becomes a self-fulfilling prophecy. This, incidentally, is not just a currency-market story: stock market analysts have the same problems, and often guess explanations. But for currency markets there is far less structure in the pricing. There are no underlying dividends or cash flows to forecast and discount, and there is not even a consensus model. In the end, pricing is often just sentiment, Hopper (1997) concurs.

Evans (2002) criticizes another feature of the academic approach: the myth of homogeneous expectations. In reality, agents have heterogeneous beliefs and heterogeneous motivations and clues for trading. Instead of coming up with a single equilibrium price, this heterogeneous-information structure permits the existence of an equilibrium distribution of transaction prices at a point in time. I develop and estimate a model of the price distribution using data from the deutsche mark/dollar market that produces two striking results: (1) Much of the short-term volatility in exchange rates comes from sampling the heterogeneous trading decisions of dealers in a distribution that, under normal market conditions, changes comparatively slowly; (2) public news is rarely the predominant source of exchange-rate movements over *any* horizon.

All this is just about explaining past prices. Things get even worse when professionals start making predictions. Hopper continues as follows:

Whatever the explanations, the underlying belief is that exchange rates are affected by fundamental economic forces, such as money supplies, interest rates, real output levels, or the trade balance, which, if well forecasted, give the forecaster an advantage in predicting the exchange rate. ... It is all too common to encounter private-sector foreign exchange economists who tell very cogent stories designed to buttress their short-term forecasts for the values of currencies. These stories are often based on plausible economic assumptions or models. These economists hope that market participants will act on their forecasts and trade currencies.

(Note that this skeptical view comes from someone who worked for a New York investment bank at the time his survey was published, after a job at the Federal Reserve.) In reality, there are the little problems that (i) we have a hard time forecasting the fundamentals—and we need to predict all of them correctly, not just a few; (ii) we do not know very well how the fundamentals will affect the exchange rate, especially as there are so many of them; and (iii) we do not know to what extent our expectations about the forecasts and our opinion on their impact are shared by the rest of the market. If other players fully agree with you about the foreseeable fundamentals and about their implications for S, then all those predictions and insights should already be in the price right now, which makes the exercise pointless. If the rest of the market does not share your view, in contrast, the successful forecaster must have either secret information, a rare event when news is about the macro economy, or superior insights. Superior insights are logically not impossible, but you cannot count on high R^2s too: even if you are right in principle in your train of thought, there are many other considerations and influences that may swamp or overturn your ingenious ceteris paribus prediction. Thus, the failure of economists to predict exchange rates (or stock prices, etc.) does not mean, or may not mean, that they are no good at their jobs; rather, it could be that there are too many economists already that are up to scratch, so that it becomes quite difficult for an individual to beat the pack.

All the above is about unpredictability. But that is not the only puzzling finding in these two chapters. The second finding is the bias in the forward rate. Does that mean that we should not use $F_{t,T}$ in valuation or planning applications? To answer this, we should settle the question of whether the bias or excess return is an inefficiency or, instead, a characteristic of a logical equilibrium. It is true that formal models of risk premia fail to explain the excess return. Yet that may say more about the models than about the markets: models might be way too stylized and tunnel-visioned, and the estimates probably miss crucial aspects of the real-world data-generating process. It would be conceited, in short, to conclude that if academics do not understand reality, then reality is wrong. For the remainder of this book, therefore, I humbly stick to the old rule: the forward rate is the expected future spot rate corrected for any risks the market thinks are relevant. If we want to maximize shareholder wealth, we should also accept the market's way of pricing.

The near unpredictability of exchange rates has obvious implications for business. One is that capital losses on short-term contractual exposures are about as likely as capital gains, and you really cannot tell the difference *ex ante*. Similarly, it is anybody's guess whether your overseas plant will enjoy a better competitive position or not, one year on, relative to what we see now.[11] One implication of real-rate changes being largely unpredictable is that you cannot prepare an operational response. Preemptively shifting production or sourcing to another location, or expanding output capacities, is difficult and costly, and if the chances of being right are closer to 50/50 than to 90/10, most CEOs would understandably hesitate. All this seems to suggest that financial hedges would be quite useful. Whether—or when—this is true is the topic of the next chapter, though.

TEST YOUR UNDERSTANDING

Quiz Questions

True-False Questions

1. Technical forecasting models analyze microeconomic variables in an attempt to forecast future changes in the exchange rate.

2. Fundamental analysis models analyze macroeconomic variables in an attempt to forecast future changes in the exchange rate.

---

[11] Note that the statement is about the next change relative to the current situation, not about the next level of the nominal or real exchange rate. I did not say that if Freedonia is quite cheap today, there is about a 50% chance that it will be expensive next year relative to the rest of the world. What I did say is that if Freedonia is quite attractive in terms of production costs today, then on average this will persist next year, with, in fact, almost a 50% chance that the country's position would improve even more.

3. By a "technical correction," one means that investors underreact to bad news so that the exchange rate does not drop as low as it should. This means that demand must fall further, in order to correctly value a foreign currency in terms of the home currency.

4. If the exchange rate bottoms out (that is, it hits a low point but begins to rise again), and then increases again by $x\%$, we can make substantial (and low-risk) profits by buying foreign currency—even when paying "retail" bid–ask spreads.

5. Because we cannot make significant profits from predicting the exchange rate based on past information, the exchange markets are weak-form efficient.

6. Runs tests have confirmed that positive changes in the exchange rate tend to be followed by positive changes, and negative changes by negative changes. This is consistent with the conclusions from autocorrelation tests.

7. The results from runs tests and autocorrelation tests provide unambiguous evidence that the foreign exchange market is inefficient.

8. Central bankers are able to forecast the future spot rate because they have inside information.

9. Central bankers are manifestly able to forecast the future spot rate because they have inside information, but they cannot forecast the current forward rate because they cannot know the future risk-free rates of return.

Multiple-Choice Questions

Choose the correct answer(s).

1. Technical analysis:
   (a) has been proved to be utterly useless as a way of predicting exchange rates;
   (b) relies on statistical and econometric models rather than on trading rules;
   (c) is solely based on a forecaster's sentiments about the exchange rate markets;
   (d) can only work when there is weak-form market efficiency;
   (e) provides evidence of semi-strong-form inefficiency (when technical analysis works, that is);
   (f) is none of the above.

2. Fundamental analysis:
   (a) has been proved to be of little value as a way of predicting exchange rates;
   (b) relies on macroeconomic variables like inflation, interest rates, and real economic output;
   (c) may rely on a forecaster's sentiments about the exchange rate markets rather than solely on a formal, quantitative model;
   (d) can only work when there is weak-form market efficiency;
   (e) provides evidence of semi-strong-form inefficiency (when fundamental analysis works, that is).

Technical note 11.1 (the "risk-neutrality" story: unbiased expectations).
One of the oldest hypotheses in international finance is that the forward rate
predicts the future spot rate. This would be trivially true under certainty.

Example 11.3. If everybody knows for certain that, one year from now, the euro
and the dollar will be at par, then the forward rate must be unity otherwise there
would be arbitrage gains.

So, in general,

$$\text{Under certainty: } F_{t,T} = S_T. \tag{11.9}$$

The simplest way to introduce uncertainty is to assume risk neutrality. Risk-
neutral investors, economists would argue, just base everything on expected
values. Thus, denoting the market's expectations by E^m, we have

$$\text{"Risk neutrality": } F_{t,T} = E_t^m(\tilde{S}_T). \tag{11.10}$$

This is the "unbiased expectations" hypothesis.[12]

You may wonder what the above quotation marks mean. There are, in fact,
a few conceptual problems with the claim. First, investors are not really risk
neutral. But, economists often reply, exchange risk may be diversifiable; and
if so, the claim would still be OK. Well, that is a big *if*: how can a risk that
changes the competitiveness of entire countries be diversifiable? The second
problem is that even risk-neutral people should still care about expected real
values not nominal values. To make things worse, investors from different
countries use different real units, and the relative value of these real units—
the real exchange rate—is changing stochastically all the time. This makes
it questionable whether supposedly risk-neutral investors with different real
units can still come to an agreement. Also the Siegel paradox (that is, the
fact that the assumption $E_t(\tilde{S}_T) = F_{t,T}$ rules out a similar situation abroad,
$E_t(\tilde{S}_T^{-1}) = F_{t,T}^{-1}$) tells us that the unbiased expectations story can never be more
than an approximation.

There is also a technical-statistical issue with testing the hypothesis in its
present form, but one that is easier to solve. For empirical purposes, working with time series of speculative prices (like S or F) causes lots of problems because they behave too much like random walks—processes for which
the notion of an unconditional expected value makes no sense. This, it can
be shown, invalidates crucial parts of standard statistical theory. The common reaction among statisticians is to study changes of variables instead, or

---

[12] It is also called "uncovered interest parity" because it predicts that an FC deposit earns as
much, on average, as an HC one:

$$E_t^m(\tilde{S}_T) = S_t \frac{1 + r_{t,T}}{1 + r_{t,T}^*} \quad \Longrightarrow \quad (1 + r_{t,T}^*) \frac{E_t^m(\tilde{S}_T)}{S_t} = 1 + r_{t,T}.$$

The left-hand side shows the expected payoff if HC1 is converted into FC (you get $1/S_t$ units of
FC), then immediately invested at $r_{t,T}^*$, and finally converted at $\tilde{S}_T$. The right-hand side of course
shows the payoff if the HC1 is invested at home instead.

percentage changes or the like. For instance, the notion of an unconditional expected value for percentage changes in spot rates and for percentage forward premia does make sense, even though forward premia are still uncannily persistent. To bring out percentages, I divide through, on both sides, by S_t, and then I make the link with two percentage changes. Notably, let $\tilde{s}$ denote the percentage change in the spot rate and FP the percentage forward premium. Then the market's expected percentage change in the spot rate must be the percentage forward premium:

$$\text{If} \qquad F_{t,T} = \mathrm{E}_t^{\mathrm{m}}(\tilde{S}_T),$$

$$\text{then} \qquad \frac{F_{t,T}}{S_t} = \frac{\mathrm{E}_t^{\mathrm{m}}(\tilde{S}_T)}{S_t},$$

$$\text{i.e.,} \qquad 1 + FP = 1 + \mathrm{E}_t^{\mathrm{m}}(\tilde{s}_{t,T}),$$

$$FP = \mathrm{E}_t^{\mathrm{m}}(\tilde{s}_{t,T}). \tag{11.11}$$

This may look nice, but it is still useless because the market's expectation is not observable. What we do see is the realized change, and it differs from the market's prior expectation by a forecast error. Let us denote the error by ϵ. Then

$$\tilde{s}_{t,T} = \mathrm{E}_t^{\mathrm{m}}(\tilde{s}_{t,T}) + \epsilon_{t,T}. \tag{11.12}$$

Taking expectations conditional on the market's information and insights, the expected value of epsilon must be zero, tautologically:

$$\mathrm{E}_t^{\mathrm{m}}(\tilde{s}_{t,T}) = \mathrm{E}_t^{\mathrm{m}}(\tilde{s}_{t,T}) + \mathrm{E}_t^{\mathrm{m}}(\epsilon_{t,T}) \;\Rightarrow\; \mathrm{E}_t^{\mathrm{m}}(\epsilon_{t,T}) = 0$$

$$\Longrightarrow \quad \text{(From equation (11.11))} \quad \tilde{s}_{t,T} = FP + \epsilon_{t,T} \text{ with } \mathrm{E}_t^{\mathrm{m}}(\epsilon_{t,T}) = 0. \tag{11.13}$$

Now the market may *think* that its forecast error is unpredictable, but to cleverer people, or to investors who know more, the market may be predictably wrong. So to close the argument, we add another ingredient, market efficiency: investors always use all available information, and they use it correctly. If this holds, then the market's expectations are also the best possible expectations—the true expectations, if you like:

$$\text{Efficient markets: } \mathrm{E}_t^{\mathrm{m}}(\cdot) = \mathrm{E}_t(\cdot), \tag{11.14}$$

$$\Longrightarrow \quad \tilde{s}_{t,T} = FP + \epsilon_{t,T} \text{ with } \mathrm{E}_t(\epsilon_{t,T}) = 0. \tag{11.15}$$

Thus, any test of unbiased expectations is also a test of market efficiency. The market may think it is unbiased but if its expectations are systematically wrong the researcher will reject the proposition.

Technical note 11.2 (possible effects of risk premia on the Fama/Cumby–Obstfeld test). We now show that, with risk aversion, a risk premium must be added on the right-hand side, and that this risk premium is, to a first-order approximation, the same as the one we encountered in chapter 5, where we spelled out the difference between expectations and CEQs. Even though the risk premium is not observable, we can infer some of its properties from estimated betas.

In principle, as we have known since chapter 5, the forward rate is a certainty equivalent, which in turn can be related to three other numbers: the expected value, the required return, and the risk-free rate. Below, I first show the relation as I wrote it in chapter 5. (Recall that $E_t(\tilde{r}_{\tilde{s},t,T})$ refers to the return expected by the market, in equilibrium, on an investment with the same risk as $\tilde{S}$.) In line two, I move the risk correction to the right-hand side. Next, I write the expected return as the risk-free rate plus a risk premium, RP. In line three, I take a first-order approximation to the fraction.[13] Here goes:

$$E_t(\tilde{S}_T)\frac{1 + r_{t,T}}{1 + E_t(\tilde{r}_{\tilde{s},t,T})} = F_{t,T},$$

$$\implies \quad E_t(\tilde{S}_T) = F_{t,T}\frac{1 + E_t(\tilde{r}_{\tilde{s},t,T})}{1 + r_{t,T}}$$

$$= F_{t,T}\frac{1 + r_{t,T} + RP}{1 + r_{t,T}}$$

$$\approx F_{t,T}(1 + RP). \tag{11.16}$$

Now we again restate the above in terms of percentage changes in S and percentage forward premia:

$$\frac{E_t(\tilde{S}_T)}{S_t} = \frac{F_{t,T}}{S_t}(1 + RP),$$

$$\implies \quad 1 + E_t(\tilde{s}_{t,T}) = (1 + FP)(1 + RP),$$

$$\implies \quad E_t(\tilde{s}_{t,T}) = 1 + FP + RP + FP \times RP - 1 \tag{11.17}$$

$$\approx FP + RP. \tag{11.18}$$

The last line uses the fact that a product of two percentages is empirically less important. Thus, the effect of risk aversion is that there is a missing variable in the standard regression test.

Let us see how this affects the Fama/Cumby–Obstfeld regression. In that regression we compute the slope as $\text{cov}(\tilde{s}, FP)/\text{var}(FP)$, where we now think that $\tilde{s} = FP + RP + \epsilon$. Below, we first substitute this relation into the beta formula. In line two, we interpret $\text{cov}(FP, FP)$ as $\text{var}(FP)$, and we note that if ϵ is unpredictable white noise, it cannot be correlated with a variable that is observed at the beginning of the period:

$$\beta = \frac{\text{cov}(FP + RP + \epsilon, FP)}{\text{var}(FP)} = \overbrace{\frac{\text{cov}(FP, FP)}{\text{var}(FP)}}^{=\text{var}(FP)} + \frac{\text{cov}(RP, FP)}{\text{var}(FP)} + \overbrace{\frac{\text{cov}(\epsilon, FP)}{\text{var}(FP)}}^{=0\ (\text{eff. mkts})}$$

$$= 1 + \frac{\text{cov}(RP, FP)}{\text{var}(FP)}. \tag{11.19}$$

---

[13] Linear approximations can be quite dangerous if they are introduced at the beginning of a theory, that is, when a lot of subsequent stuff is built upon it. Here we do it to derive an equation that is immediately tested; second-order effects are likely to be less crucial in such a case.

Thus, the estimate of beta tells us something about the sign of the correlation between the risk premium and the forward premium:

$$\beta \gtreqless 1 \iff \text{cov}(RP, FP) \gtreqless 0. \tag{11.20}$$

We also immediately infer how negative the covariance must be, relative to the variance of the risk premium, before turning the beta into a negative number:

$$\beta \gtreqless 0 \iff \text{cov}(RP, FP) \gtreqless -\text{var}(FP). \tag{11.21}$$

Fama came up with one more clever interpretation, saying something about the variability over time of the risk premium versus that of the period-by-period conditional expectations about $\tilde{s}$. To bring out these expectations—denoted, for compactness, as E_s, below—in $\text{cov}(\tilde{s}, FP)/\text{var}(FP)$, he substitutes $FP = E_s - RP$ and $\tilde{s} = E_s + \epsilon$. Again, epsilon is uncorrelated with FP, RP, and E_s, so we can immediately drop it from the covariances. Thus,

$$\begin{aligned}
\beta &= \frac{\text{cov}(E_s, E_s - RP)}{\text{var}(E_s - RP)} \\
&= \frac{\text{cov}(E_s, E_s) - \text{cov}(E_s, RP)}{\text{var}(E_s) - 2\,\text{cov}(E_s, RP) + \text{var}(RP)} \\
&= \frac{\text{var}(E_s) - \text{cov}(E_s, RP)}{\text{var}(E_s) - 2\,\text{cov}(E_s, RP) + \text{var}(RP)}.
\end{aligned} \tag{11.22}$$

The implication is that we can infer which of the two determinants of FP, E_s, or RP has the higher variability over time:

$$\beta \gtreqless \tfrac{1}{2} \iff \text{var}(E_s) \gtreqless \text{var}(RP). \tag{11.23}$$

Think of a currency like the rouble. It went through periods of pronounced and generally acknowledged weakness, notably during the hyperinflation days; then it strengthened and stabilized. Thus, the variability over time in the expectations was large. Alternatively, think of mainstream Western currencies where there was rarely very much to predict. Assuming, heroically, the same variability over time for the risk premia, Fama would predict a higher beta for the rouble than for the Western currencies. Of course, the variability over time of the risk premium for the rouble was probably higher too. Still, the message is that a low beta might mean that there was virtually nothing to predict.

12

(When) Should a Firm
Hedge Its Exchange Risk?

From chapters 3 and especially 10 and 11 you may, I hope, remember that (i) deviations from purchasing power parity are sufficiently large and persistent so as to expose firms to real exchange-rate risk, and (ii) it is difficult to predict exchange rates. In earlier chapters we have already described how forward or spot contracts can be used to reduce or even eliminate the effect of unexpected exchange-rate changes on the firm's cash flows. We have not yet discussed the relevance of doing so. Thus, the central question that we address in this chapter is: do firms add value when hedging their foreign exchange risk?

A key element in the discussion will be the zero-initial-value property of a forward contract: when the hedge is set up, its net asset value is zero. In light of this we can rephrase the question as follows: how can adding a zero-value contract increase the value of the firm? We will argue that hedging does add value if its effect is not just to add a gain or loss on the hedge but also to change something else in the firm, like decreasing the chances of financial distress. But there is a second question we need to address too, namely: if the hedge does add value, cannot the shareholders do the hedging if the firm does not? To this question we will answer that there are many good reasons why homemade hedging is not a perfect substitute for corporate hedging. The bottom line of this chapter is, however, not that hedging adds value (full stop): rather, we would say that there are circumstances under which hedging helps, but these circumstances surely do not apply to all firms all of the time.

In the first section of this chapter, we describe how and when hedging may achieve more than just adding a gain or loss on a forward or spot contract. In section 12.2, we dismiss some bad reasons that lesser human beings occasionally advance in favor of, or against, hedging and some FAQs, starting with the issue of whether companies cannot simply leave hedging to the shareholders. Our conclusions are presented in section 12.3.

12.1 The Effect of Corporate Hedging May Not Just Be "Additive"

Hedging affects, quite possibly, the expected future cash flows of the firm, and it surely affects risk. How can we simultaneously take these two aspects into account? A finance person would immediately point out one excellent summary measure of the expected-value and risk effects of hedging: look at its net effect on present value. So in this chapter we adopt the Modigliani–Miller-style point of view that financial decisions should be rated on the basis of their impact on the company's market value.

In this light, then, one way to focus the discussion is to raise the zero-initial-value property of a forward contract: when the hedge is set up, its net asset value is zero. So we can rephrase the question as follows: how can adding a zero-value contract increase the value of the firm? One innocent answer would be that the zero-value property is a short-lived affair: almost immediately after being signed, the contract's value has already changed. But the reply to this red herring is that one cannot even predict whether the value change will be for better or for worse. So, again, how can a contract add value if, roughly speaking, the chance that it acquires a negative value is 50%?[1]

The serious answer is that the zero-value property applies to the cash flows generated by a stand-alone forward contract: $PV_t(\tilde{S}_T - F_{t,T}) = 0$. But the effect of hedging may very well be that the firm's other cash flows—anything that has to do with investing and producing and marketing and servicing debt, etc.—are affected by the hedge operation too. If (and only if) that is the case, hedging adds value—not because its own cash flow $\tilde{S}_T - F_{t,T}$ would have a positive net value in itself, we repeat, but because that cash flow has by assumption beneficial side effects on the firm's existing or future business. So the added value, if any, stems from a useful interaction between the hedge's cash flow and the other cash flows of the firm.[2]

This gets us to the real question: how can hedging interact with the firm's other cash flows? Below, we discuss (i) reduction of financial-distress costs, both *ex post* and *ex ante*; (ii) reduction of agency costs; (iii) lower expected taxes; and (iv) less noise in the profit figures.

---

[1] A variant of the above puzzle runs as follows. In an efficient market, the argument says, the gain from hedging or from any forward deal must have zero expected value, so that on average hedging does not help. This version of the puzzle is factually wrong: the forward rate is a biased predictor of the future spot rate, implying that $E(\tilde{S}_T - F_{t,T}) \neq 0$. Also, the claim confines the effect of hedging to a purely additive one; but we already know that any value from hedging must stem not from $(\tilde{S}_T - F_{t,T})$, but rather from interactions with other cash flows. Lastly, the argument focuses on expectations, ignoring risks. One should look at PV instead.

[2] This echoes an argument that may be familiar from the Modigliani–Miller (MM) literature: one of the sufficient conditions for the irrelevance of the company's debt or payout policy is that the firm's "investments"—operations, really—are not affected. This assumption rules out interactions between the debt or payout decisions and the other cash flows. Many post-MM arguments question precisely this assumption—most prominently, Jensen's "free cash flow" theory and MM's tax theory.

12.1.1 Corporate Hedging Reduces Costs of Bankruptcy and Financial Distress

The most obvious route through which hedging can affect the firm's prosperity is by decreasing its risk of financial distress. A firm is said to be in financial distress when its income is not sufficient to cover its fixed expenses, including financial obligations. The state of financial distress can lead to bankruptcy, which of course involves direct costs from reorganization or liquidation and the like. Large, uncovered exposures, combined with adverse exchange-rate movements, may send a firm into insolvency and bankruptcy or may at least contribute to such an outcome.

Example 12.1. In 1992, Rederi AB Slite, a Swedish shipping company that ran a ferry between Sweden and Finland for the Viking Lines, should have taken delivery of a very large ship. She had been ordered some years before from Meyer Werft in Papenburg, Germany. At the time of signing the purchase contract, Slite had decided not to hedge the DEM outflow because the SEK was tied to a basket in which the DEM had a large weight, and because the DEM was at a substantial forward premium relative to the SEK. However, by September 1992, Sweden had been forced to abandon the link between the SEK and the DEM, which had appreciated substantially against the SEK by the end of 1992. As a consequence of the appreciation of the DEM, Slite could no longer afford the ship (which was already painted in Viking's red and white colors). So Meyer Werft kept it and soon managed to charter it to Viking Line's rival, Silja Line, which repainted it (mostly white), named it Silja Europe, and put it on the—you guessed it—Stockholm–Helsinki line.[3] A few months later, Slite keeled over and went bankrupt.

Outright bankruptcy is costly because of the costs associated with liquidation. In the absence of these costs, Slite's shareholders would simply have lost control of the firm to the bondholders and banks, who would have either carried on the business as before or sold their ownership rights to others who, in turn, would have gone on running the firm as before. That is, in the absence of what Miller and Modigliani call bankruptcy costs, the event of insolvency would not have affected the value of the firm as a whole. In reality, of course, bankruptcy is costly; and the cost includes not only the fees paid to receivers, lawyers, assessors, and courts, but also the potential end of operations, loss of clientele and reputation, and therefore liquidation at fire-sale rather than going-concern prices.

Example 12.2. In 2006, a company called Schefenacker that made mirrors for Mercedes and BMW and the like got in trouble and had to go through a reorganization. Bondholders lost over half of their stake, and Mr. Schefenacker himself surrendered three quarter of his shares to debtors in lieu of repayment. The company

---

[3] Adding insult to injury, the world's first floating McDonald's restaurant was located onboard the Silja Europa from its maiden trip until 1996, Wikipedia tells us. But in 1996 the McDonald's was closed down and replaced by Silja Line's own hamburger restaurant.

even moved its headquarters to the United Kingdom so as to be able to restructure under English law. Only the legal advisors were radiant, coming out EUR 40m the richer, which was almost 10% of the company's original debt.

In the same year, British Energy was an even greater bringer of joy and happiness to the legal crowd: with debts of GBP 1.2b (plus liabilities for taking care of spent nuclear fuel and decommissioning power stations) it paid GBP 121m for legal advice related to its restructuring (*Economist*, December 15, 2007, p. 67). Even in a relatively simple case like Northern Rock's, the English bank that skirted failure in the 2007–8 subprime mess, Deringer (a London law firm) made USD 20m from advice to the bank, Slaughter & May made USD 6m from advice to the Treasury, and Clifford Chance Linklaters made undisclosed amounts from working for third parties (*Economist*, March 15, 2008, p. 78).

Costs of restructuring are soaring because financial structures are more complex now. Instead of, for example, three levels (senior, unsecured, and subordinated—once viewed as quite Byzantine), we now see, for example, first-lien senior/second-lien senior/mezzanine/senior subordinated/junior subordinated. In each of these "classes" a majority has to approve the deal, giving each such class a veto right and, thus, endless possibilities of wrangling and blackmailing.

Example 12.3. Another car-parts maker, Meridian Automotive System of Michigan, took twenty months to reorganize. First-lien lenders had to yield part of their rightful takings to second-lien colleagues, which meant that seniority no longer meant seniority. In the case of yet another car-parts firm, American Remanufacturers, second-lien lenders vetoed a proposal by first-lien lenders to refinance. Rather than paying them off, the first-lien group upped sticks and let the firm go bankrupt; neither class got anything, in the end. The two groups of lien holders "just shot each other," one lawyer said. Unusually (and disappointingly for the lawyers), the whole thing took just eleven days (*Economist*, March 15, 2008, p. 78).

But even before a firm actually goes bankrupt, the mere potential of future financial distress can affect the operations and the value of the firm significantly. Thus, if hedging can reduce the volatility of the firm's cash flows, and hence the likelihood of the firm being in financial distress, hedging increases the firm's current value. Let us consider three specific links between the financial state of a firm and its real operations.

The product market and reorganization costs. Many firms sell products for which after-sales service is needed. The firms typically offer product warranties. A buyer's decision to purchase such products depends on his or her confidence in the firm's after-sales service. These firms sell more and must, therefore, be worth more the lower the probability of their going out of business. Hedging, by reducing the volatility of cash flows, decreases the probability of (coming uncomfortably close to) bankruptcy.

Example 12.4. When the U.S. computer manufacturer Wang got into financial problems, one of Wang's customers noted that, "Before the really bad news, we were looking at Wang fairly seriously [but] their present financial condition means that I'd have a hard time convincing the vice president in charge of purchasing. At some point we'd have to ask 'How do we know that in three years you won't be in Chapter 11 [bankruptcy]'?" (Rawls and Smithson 1990, p. 11).

The labor market and wage costs. Risk-averse employees are likely to demand higher wages if their future job prospects are very uncertain. In the event of bankruptcy, a forced change of job generally entails monetary and/or nonmonetary losses to employees. Thus, the employees want to protect themselves by requiring higher wages when working for a firm that is more likely to be in financial distress. If they do not get the risk premium, they quit—and especially the best ones, who can easily start elsewhere. This does *not* sound good.

The goods markets and purchasing costs. Risk-averse suppliers are similarly likely to demand cash upon delivery or, if they want to avoid even the risk of useless truck rides, cash before delivery. Trade credit would now be possible only in return for a big markup for default risk. Again, this is not a pleasant surprise.

The capital market and refinancing costs. Loan covenants can trigger early repayment if the firm's income falls below a stated level, or credit lines can be canceled and outstanding credits called if there is a material deterioration in the firm's creditworthiness. To the extent that refinancing is difficult or costly when things do not look bright, it is wise for the firm to reduce income volatility by hedging. Costs associated with refinancing include not just an increased risk spread but also the hassle and distraction of transacting and negotiating, new restrictions on management, additional monitoring and reporting, and so on.

Financial distress costs are not the only link between hedging and the firm's operations. Following Jensen (1986), one could argue that another link arises via agency costs.

12.1.2 Hedging Reduces Agency Costs

Agency costs are the costs that arise from the conflicts of interest between shareholders, bondholders, and the managers of the firm. We will argue that these agency costs can affect the firm's wage bill, its choice of investment projects, and its borrowing costs. Hedging, by reducing the volatility of a firm's cash flows, can reduce the conflict of interests between different claimants to the firm's cash flows and can increase the firm's debt capacity and reduce its cost of capital.

One conflict is that between the managers of the firm and the shareholders. The source of the problem is that, through their wages and bonus plans, the wealth of the managers depends to a large extent on the performance of the firm. Since managers cannot sell forward part of their lifetime future wages in order to diversify, the only way that they can reduce the risk to their human wealth is to hedge the exposure by creating negatively correlated cash flows through positions in the foreign exchange, commodity futures, and interest futures markets. As argued below, "homemade" hedging (by shareholders or, here, by managers) is not a good substitute for corporate hedging because personal hedging is expensive and difficult. In addition, there is likely to be a maturity mismatch between the hedge and the exposed human wealth, which creates a ruin–risk problem similar to the one mentioned in connection with marking to market in futures markets (see chapter 6). The reason for the mismatch is that affordable forward contracts are likely to have short maturities, while the wages that are exposed are realized in the longer run. The maturity mismatch between the short-term hedge and the long-term exposure becomes a problem when the value of human wealth goes up. Then, the short-term hedge triggers immediate cash outflows, while the benefits in terms of wages will not be realized until much later. That is, the personal hedge creates liquidity problems and, in the limit, may lead to personal insolvency.

For the above reasons, managers dislike hedging on a personal basis and would rather the firm hedge instead. If the firm does not hedge, managers can react in two ways. First, they are likely to insist on higher wages, as a premium for the extra risk they have to bear. Second, if the firm has investment opportunities that are very risky, the managers may refuse to undertake such projects even if they have a positive net present value. As the shareholders have imperfect information about the firm's investment opportunities or the management's diligence and motives, there is little they can do about these actions of the managers. Thus, the shareholders are better off if the firm hedges its exposures: this will automatically also hedge the managers' exposures, and therefore make them look more kindly on the once-risky projects as well as their own pay checks.

Another example of agency costs is the conflict that arises between shareholders and bondholders in the choice of investment projects. This conflict arises because bondholders get (at most) a fixed return on their investment, while shareholders receive the cash left over after bondholders have been paid off. That is, the shareholders have a call option on the value of the firm, with the face value of the firm's debt as the option's strike price. The value of an option increases when the volatility of the underlying asset increases. (If this last bit is new to you, you did not properly read chapter 8 on options.) Thus, in the case of a levered firm that is close to financial distress, shareholders may have an incentive to undertake very risky projects even if the project's net present value is negative. This *overinvestment problem* (Jensen and Meckling 1976) arises if, due to increased uncertainty, the value of equity (the option on the future value of the firm as a whole) increases even though the current value of the firm as a whole goes down.

Example 12.5. A company has assets worth 60, currently invested risk free, and debt with face value 50. For simplicity, assume risk neutrality and a zero risk-free rate. An investment opportunity arises where the investment would be 60, and the proceeds either 100 or 0 with equal probability. Therefore, the NPV is $(100 + 0)/2 - 60 = -10$. But the shareholders might nevertheless be tempted by this plan because it would distribute more than enough wealth away from the bondholders and toward themselves:

Decision	Future outcome		Resulting PV
Do not invest	$V_1 = 60$: Bonds 50		Bonds 50
	Stocks 10		Stocks 10
			Total = 60
Invest	Lucky: $V_1 = 100$	Unlucky: $V_1 = 0$	
	Bonds 50	Bonds 0	Bonds 25
	Stocks 50	Stocks 0	Stocks 25
			Total = 50

Obviously, if the shareholders are sufficiently ruthless to undertake this investment, the bondholders are worse off. Similarly, when a firm is close to bankruptcy, shareholders may have an incentive not to take on risk-reducing projects, even if these projects have a positive net present value. This *"debt overhang" underinvestment problem* (Myers 1977) occurs if the current value of the firm goes up when the project is undertaken but the value of the option on the firm (the equity) goes down.

Bondholders, of course, recognize and anticipate these potential conflicts of interest and, therefore, adjust the terms of their loan appropriately. One way is to increase the interest charged on the loan. Another is to impose restrictions on management (the bond covenant), which requires costly monitoring by a trustee, slows down management, and may inadvertently even prevent good investments. Thus, if by hedging one reduces the variability of the firm's cash flows, one also reduces the potential for conflicts of interest associated with financial distress, and one thereby avoids the above extra costs of borrowing.

12.1.3 Hedging Reduces Expected Taxes

Hedging reduces expected cash flows if taxes are convex rather than linear functions of income. One example of a convex tax function is a progressive tax schedule, where the tax rate increases with income. In this case, smoothing the income stream will imply a lower average tax burden.

Example 12.6. Suppose that if income is USD 100, you pay USD 45 in taxes, while if income is USD 50, you pay only USD 20 in taxes. The expected tax when the earnings are USD 50 without risk then equals USD 20, while the expected tax is USD 22.5 when earnings are, with equal probability, either USD 100 or 0.

It may be argued that most countries' corporate tax rate schedules are, for all practical applications, flat. However, a more subtle type of convexity is created by the fact that, when profits are negative, taxes are usually not proportionally negative. In some countries, there are negative corporate taxes, but the amount refunded is limited to the taxes paid in the recent past. Such a rule is called *carry-back*: this year's losses are deducted from profits made in preceding years, implying that the taxes paid on these past profits are recuperated. Still, carry-back is limited to the profits made in only a few recent years, which means that negative taxes on losses are limited, too. In other countries, there is no carry-back at all. All one can do is deduct this year's losses from potential future profits (*carry-forward*), which at best postpones the negative tax on this year's losses.

Example 12.7. In Belgium, firms are not allowed to carry back losses. If a particular Belgian firm's profits are either EUR 35m or EUR 15m with equal probability, the expected profit is EUR 25m and the expected tax (at 30%) is EUR 7.5m. In contrast, if its profits are either EUR 100m or −EUR 50m with equal probability, the expected profit is still EUR 25m but now the expected tax is (EUR 100m × 0.3 + EUR 0)/2 = EUR 15m. It is true that the potential EUR 50m loss can be carried forward and deducted from subsequent profits, but these later tax savings are uncertain, and even if they were certain, there would still be the loss-of-time value.

Now consider a case where a firm is allowed to carry back its losses. Even in this case, excessive variability of income can affect the tax liability if the current losses are larger than the profits against which they can be set off. In the United States, for instance, there is a three-year carry-back provision. Suppose that a particular firm's profits in the last three years amounted to USD 30m. If, for the next year, its profits are either USD 35m or USD 15m with equal probability, the expected profit is USD 25m and the expected tax (at 30%) is USD 7.5m. In contrast, if its profits are either USD 100m or −USD 50m with equal probability, the expected profit is still USD 25m but the potential loss now exceeds the profits made in the past three years. This means that in case of losses, the firm can recuperate the taxes paid on the USD 30m recent profits (that is, there is a negative tax of USD 30m × 30% = USD 9m), and the remaining USD 20m "unused" losses can be carried forward. Thus, the expected tax is [(USD 100m × 0.3) + (−USD 30m × 0.3)]/2 = USD 10.5m rather than USD 7.5m. It is true that the unused losses of USD 20m can be deducted from subsequent profits, but these later tax savings are uncertain, and even if they were certain, there would still be a loss-of-time value.

While the convex-taxes argument in favor of hedging is logically unassailable, you will probably agree that quantitatively this looks like a less important effect than the earlier ones (and especially financial distress), unless losses cannot be carried back or forward—for instance, because the company is not likely to survive anyway.

12.1.4   Hedging May Also Provide Better Information for Internal Decision Making

Multidivisional multinationals need to know the operational profitability of their divisions. By having each division hedge its cash flows, a multinational knows each division's operating profitability without the noise introduced by unexpected exchange-rate changes. This may lead to better decision making and may, thus, lead to an increase in expected cash flows.

Of course, the same information can be obtained in different ways, and the alternatives may be cheaper. The firm could request that all divisions keep track of their contractual exposure at every moment, and could compute afterward how profitable each division would have been if it had actually hedged. Nowadays, this just requires some programming. Another alternative, similar in spirit, is to shift all exchange risk toward a reinvoicing center. Under such an arrangement, a Canadian production unit, for instance, sells its output to a reinvoicing center on a CAD invoice, while a Portuguese marketing subsidiary buys these products from the center on an EUR invoice. In terms of information per subsidiary, this achieves the same objective as the subsidiary-by-subsidiary hedging policy. The corporation may then decide, on other grounds, whether or not the reinvoicing center should hedge the corporation's overall exposure.[4]

Actual hedging entails a (small) cost, but as-if-hedged financial reporting is not costless either, and the corporation's operations may be too small to justify the fixed costs of a reinvoicing center. Thus, the bottom line is that the choice between actual hedging and as-if-hedged financial reporting or reinvoicing will depend on the circumstances.

12.1.5   Hedged Results May Better Show Management's Quality to Shareholders and Please Wall Street

This argument is very close to the previous one: without exchange-rate-induced noise, one better sees the effect of management's decisions. The difference is that now the audience targeted by the clearer picture is the outside shareholder, not headquarters. Thus, the effect on value is more direct, and informal

---

[4] If the reinvoicing center is instructed to hedge its exposure, this is likely to be cheaper than a policy where each subsidiary hedges its own exposures. First, the reinvoicing center can economize on hedging costs because it can "net" (clear) offsetting exposures. Second, there are likely to be benefits from specialization and scale economies. Third, the reinvoicing center is often located in a tax haven and simultaneously serves to reduce (or at least postpone) taxation on part of the group's profits.

solutions like pro forma as-if-hedged financial statements would be confusing or not credible.

A related argument is that analysts and investment bankers like stable profits, as this makes prediction and valuation easier. A hedging policy would contribute to that.

We conclude with a review of some open issues.

12.2 FAQs about Hedging

12.2.1 FAQ1: Why Can't Firms Leave Hedging to the Shareholders: Homemade Hedging?

Fans of the original Miller and Modigliani article may remember that the options of homemade leveraging (or unleveraging) and homemade dividends play a big role in the argument. So we likewise ask the question, here, whether the firm cannot simply leave the hedging to the shareholders. There are many arguments saying that homemade hedging will not do, or not do as well as corporate hedging:

- The existence of financial-distress costs or agency costs is the most fundamental reason why "homemade" hedging is an imperfect substitute for corporate hedging. In reality, no individual shareholder can buy a contract that perfectly hedges against the costs of financial distress, like the loss of value when customers vote with their feet or employees flee. The problem, in short, is that the homemade hedge just produces the final cash flow $\tilde{S}_T - F_{t,T}$, and not the interactions with the firm's other business that provide the true advantage from hedging.

- But even if hedging were purely additive, homemade hedging would not do as well as corporate hedging:

  — One reason is that, in the real world, shareholders have far less information than the managers about the firm's exposure. If shareholders have very imprecise knowledge of the firm's exposure, "homemade" hedging will be far less effective than corporate hedging.

  — Because of economies of scale, firms can obtain better terms for forward or money-market hedging than the individual shareholder. Thus, shareholders may value financial transactions undertaken for them by the firm.

  — Short-selling constraints can provide an additional reason why hedging is better undertaken by the firm rather than left to individual shareholders. In idealized markets, investors can easily borrow (or sell forward) any currency that they choose. However, in financial markets, personal borrowing in foreign currencies is not easy, and forward positions require substantial margin or else are discouraged by banks. It is true that going short is easy in futures markets; but the size of the futures contracts, however modest, may still be too large for shareholders with small positions in exposed equity. Moreover, for many currencies, there simply are no futures markets.

Thus, corporations have better hedging opportunities than individual shareholders, which again means that "homemade" financial decisions are a poor substitute for corporate decisions.

12.2.2 FAQ2: Does Hedging Make the Currency of Invoicing Irrelevant?

Does it matter whether prices are quoted in terms of the home currency or the foreign currency?

- The traditionalists state that someone must bear the exchange risk. Either you invoice in HC, in which case the foreign customer bears the exchange risk, or you invoice in FC, in which case you bear the exchange risk.

- The radical young Turks believe that, with the existence of a forward market, there is no problem.

Example 12.8. Giovanni wants to buy his Carina GTI directly from Japan and calls Mr. Toyota. We could envision two ways to set (and pay) the price:

- In story 1, Mr. Toyota asks for JPY 2m in 60 days. Giovanni agrees and immediately hedges at JPY/EUR 125 in 60 days. Thus, Giovanni's cost is locked in at 2m/125 = EUR 16,000 in 60 days.

- Alternatively, Mr. Toyota could ask for EUR 16,000 in 60 days. If Giovanni agrees, Mr. Toyota immediately hedges at JPY/EUR 125 in 60 days, and locks in an inflow of $16,000 \times 125 = $ JPY 2m in 60 days.

So the currency of invoicing, in the young Turks' view, merely shifts the hedging from seller to buyer, or vice versa. Finally, it does not matter which party hedges since, at a given point in time, each party can buy the foreign currency at the same rate.

While the above point of view is correct, you should realize that the example has two special features that are surely not always present. Notably, in the Toyota example the buyer and the seller are effectively able to hedge at the same moment and at the same rates. Conversely, the invoicing currency may matter as soon as (i) there is a time lag between the moment a price is offered by the exporter and the moment the customer decides to actually buy the goods, or (ii) the cost of hedging differs depending on who hedges. We illustrate these situations in the examples below. The first one focuses on the delay between the price offer and the customer's decision, the second one about differential costs.

Example 12.9. The currency of invoicing matters when you publish a list of prices that are valid for, say, six months. The problem here stems from the fact that there is a lag between the time that the FC prices are announced and the time the customer purchases an item. Since you do not know the timing and volume of future sales, you cannot hedge perfectly if you list prices denominated in foreign currency. Not hedging until you do know, on the other hand, may mean that by that time the rate has changed against you.

Example 12.10. The Argentina sales branch of a Brazilian stationery distributor instructs its customers to pay in BRL. Since the orders are frequent, and usually small, the Argentinean customers pay substantial implicit commissions whenever they purchase BRL. It would be cheaper if the exporter let them pay in peso (ARS) and converted the total sales revenue into reals once a day or once a week.

In situations like this, one can still hedge approximately if sales are fairly steady and predictable. Many companies hedge all expected positions within a twelve-month horizon, and adjust their forward positions whenever sales forecasts are revised. However, in other cases, the time lag between the exporter's price offer and the importer's purchase decision may imply substantial sales uncertainty. In perfect markets, even this risk should be hedgeable at a low cost. In practice, the cost of hedging may very well depend on the currency in which prices are expressed.

Example 12.11. Here we consider an international tender, characterized by a time delay and a differential cost of hedging. Suppose that a Canadian hospital invites bids for a scanner.

Buyer's currency. In an international tender, suppliers are usually invited to submit bids in the buyer's currency (CAD, in this case). A foreign contender's dilemma is whether or not to hedge, considering that:

- Forward hedging may leave the contender with an uncovered, risky forward position. Specifically, if the contract is not awarded to him, the bidding firm would then have to reverse: it would have to buy CAD spot—or forward, if the contract is reversed earlier—just to be able to deliver them, as stipulated in the forward contract. The rate at which such a time T purchase will be made is uncertain and can surely lead to losses.

- Not hedging at all means that if the contender does make the winning bid, the CAD inflow is risky.

Thus, whether or not the contender hedges, there is a potential risky cash flow in CAD. It is true that banks offer conditional hedges, that is, contracts that become standard forward contracts (or standard options) when the potential supplier wins the tender but are void otherwise. However, these products are very much tailored to specific situations. The bank must assess and monitor the probability that a particular contender makes the winning bid, which makes such a contract expensive in terms of commissions. Thus, hedging is costly when bids are to be expressed in the customer's currency.

Supplier's currency. The alternative is that the buyer invites bids in the suppliers' own currencies. Indeed, the buyer can easily wait until all bids have been submitted, then translate them into CAD_T—using the prevailing forward rates—and, at the very same moment she notifies the lucky winner, lock in the best price by means of a standard forward contract. In this way, all risk and all unnecessary bid–ask spreads in hedging disappear. To illustrate this, suppose that the Canadian hospital's procurement manager receives three bids in three different currencies, shown in column (a) below. She looks up the forward rates CAD_T/FC_T shown in column (b), and extracts the following CAD_T equivalent bid prices:

Supplier	Price	Forward rate	CAD cost hedged
Oetker & Kölner, Bonn	EUR 120,000	CAD/EUR 1.65	CAD 198,000
Johnson Kleinwortsz, PA	USD 150,000	CAD/USD 1.35	CAD 195,000
Marcheix, Dubois & Fils, Québec	CAD 200,000		CAD 200,000

If price is the only consideration, she accepts the U.S. offer, and immediately buys forward USD. Thus, when prices are to be submitted in the supplier's currency, a standard (and therefore cheap) forward hedge will suffice.

What this example shows, again, is that the currency of invoicing matters if the cost of hedging is not independent of the way prices are quoted. The Canadian hospital can use a cheap, standard contract if prices are submitted in the contending suppliers' home currencies. In contrast, with bids to be submitted in CAD, hedging is difficult and expensive for the bidders—because they are unsure about being awarded the contract. The solution in this case is to let the suppliers quote bids in their own currency. The general message to remember is that the option to hedge forward does not make the currency of invoicing irrelevant.

12.2.3 FAQ3: "My Accountant Tells Me That Hedging Has Cost Me 2.17m. So How Can You Call This a Zero-Cost Option?"

Your accountant may have meant one of at least three things. First, she may have calculated that if you had not hedged, you would have raked in an extra 2.17m. Stated differently, the *ex post* sum of all the gains/losses $(\tilde{S}_T - F_{t,T})$ was −2.17m. This is indeed sad. But this is hindsight. All you can use, for decision-making purposes, is a PV criterion. And this brings us irrevocably back to the diagnosis that, in light of the zero-NPV property of $(\tilde{S}_T - F_{t,T})$, value stems from positive interactions, if any. The *ex post* value is just good or bad luck and is useless for decision making.

Alternatively, your accountant may have meant that the accounts show an *ex ante* cost of 2.17m. This concept is based on the not-infrequent (but misleading) practice of using spot rates to convert FC A/Rs or A/Ps into HC. If one then hedges, the actual cash flow differs from the book value, and the accountant hilariously calls this the cost of hedging. If, at the moment of booking the invoice, translation had been done at the forward rate, hedging would have entailed no accounting cost nor gain whatsoever.

Example 12.12. Recall our example in chapter 5 of a Canadian firm that exports NZD 2.5m worth of goods. We were discussing an accounting issue: should we translate the A/R at the spot rate or at the forward? In that example we compared translation at the spot rate (0.90) and at the forward (0.88), and then looked at the outcome if the firm had not hedged. Now we assume the firm does hedge. The cost of goods sold being CAD 1.5m, profits then amount to $2.5m \times 0.88 - 1.5m = 2.2m - 1.5m = 0.7m$. But the operating profit depends on the initial valuation of the A/R, and the balance (if any) is called the cost/benefit of hedging:[5]

	Using $S_t = 0.90$		Using $F_t = 0.88$	
• At t:				
A/R	2,250		2,200	
COGS		1,500		1,500
Operating income		750		700
• At T:				
Bank	2,200		2,200	
Hedging cost (D) or gain (C)	50		—	
A/R		2,250		2,200

Which view is true? We know that hedging is free, in principle, so booking the forward premium as a cost or gain makes no sense. That accounting definition is a pure construct, based on the flawed practice of translating at the spot rate (see chapter 4).

Of course, you could shrug off this accounting convention as irrelevant. There is indeed nothing wrong with writing weird things in books: the entire SF literature thrives on it. The only problem is that some people might actually believe this is a genuine cost in the same way as, for example, the gas or oil bill is a genuine cost. This risk arises especially among people that have no clue as to what accounting is about and simply believe a cost must be bad, otherwise it would be called a benefit.

In reality, there are in fact costs of hedging: there might be an up-front commission of a few euros, and the bid–ask spread in the forward rate is always somewhat wider than in the spot. But these transaction costs have nothing to do with the forward premium, and they amount to only a few basis points.

---

[5] In the old example, without hedging, there was a random capital gain. Here the effect is predictable, so accountants would call this a cost or benefit from hedging rather than a capital gain. Both are financial (i.e., nonoperating) items.

12.2.4 FAQ4: "Doesn't Spot Hedging Affect the Interest Tax Shield, as Interest Rates Are So Different Across Currencies?"

The last fallacy to be discussed is that hedging matters because it affects the interest tax shields. The issue is most often raised when the hedging alternative being considered is a money-market hedge rather than a forward transaction. Suppose, for instance, that a Russian company has accounts receivable denominated in Swiss francs, and that the firm needs to borrow in order to finance its operations. CHF interest rates are much lower than RUR interest rates—say 6% as compared with 20%. If it borrows in RUR, the firm has a tax shield of 20%, and can reduce its taxes correspondingly. If it borrows in CHF, the loan also acts as a hedge, but the tax shield is a mere 6%. Thus, the argument concludes, the currency of borrowing affects the tax shields and, ultimately, the value of the firm.

As already pointed out in chapter 4, the logical error in this argument is that it overlooks the fact that the taxes are affected not only by the interest paid, but (in the case of foreign currency borrowing) also by the capital gain or loss when the foreign currency depreciates or appreciates during the loan's life. Once this capital gain or loss is also taken into consideration, it is easily proved that, in PV terms, the currency of borrowing does not affect the current value of the firm even when there are taxes, as long as the tax on capital gains equals the tax on interest. Only when there is some form of tax discrimination may hedging affect the PV-ed tax shield.

Example 12.13. The United Kingdom used to have a rule that stated that exchange losses on long-term loans were deductible but capital gains were tax free. Given the risk-adjusted expectation that the AUD or NZD would depreciate relative to the GBP, a U.K. company had an incentive to borrow in, for instance, NZD or AUD. The expected capital gain would be tax-free, while the (then) high interest payments would be fully tax deductible. Here there is a tax effect because taxes are discriminatory.

12.3 CFO's Summary

In the opening chapter of part II we argued that there are deviations from PPP. These deviations can be very large at any given point in time, and they also tend to persist over time. It typically takes three years before the distance between the actual spot rate and the PPP prediction is reduced by half. Moreover, it is difficult to predict exchange rates. All of this implies that firms that sell goods abroad, or import goods, or firms that compete with foreign firms or may have to compete with foreign producers in the future are exposed to real exchange-rate risk. In this chapter, we have argued that it may be important that firms hedge this risk.

The Miller–Modigliani (1958) theorems state that financial policies, such as a firm's hedging strategy, cannot increase the value of a firm. However, this result is true only in perfect markets and if the firm's other cash flows are utterly unaffected by the financial decision at hand. Given the presence of convex tax schedules, costs of financial distress, and agency costs, hedging exchange risk can increase the value of a firm through its effect on future expected cash flows and the firm's borrowing costs. For a well-capitalized and profitable firm those considerations may carry little weight, and we do see many such firms happily ignoring exchange risk.

Not all companies are that lucky, though. For them, hedging adds value. But many comfortably rich companies have hedging policies too, often implemented by a reinvoicing center. Their view is that hedging may add little intrinsic value, but it is a low-cost option with some collateral attractions. For instance, managers like to reduce the risk of not meeting their numbers, Wall Street analysts appreciate predictability, and HQ strategists prefer not to be distracted by items that have nothing to do with the division's own decisions. Also, strategists may argue that the decision *not* to hedge is not very different from a decision to speculate. There is nothing intrinsically wrong with speculation, but a firm's expertise is likely to be in its own business, not in speculating on foreign exchange. Thus, even thick-walleted companies often hedge their exposure.

TEST YOUR UNDERSTANDING

Quiz Questions

True–False Questions

1. In perfect markets, a manager's decision to hedge a firm's cash flows is irrelevant because there is no exchange-rate risk.

2. In perfect markets, a manager's decision to hedge a firm's cash flows is irrelevant because the shareholders can hedge exchange risk themselves.

3. If a large firm keeps track of the exposure of each of its divisions, the firm has better information about each division, and is therefore better able to make decisions.

4. If a firm does not have a hedging policy, the managers may insist on higher wages to compensate them for the risk they bear because part of their lifetime future wealth is exposed to exchange-rate risk.

5. If the firm does not have a hedging policy, the managers may refuse to undertake risky projects even when they have a positive net present value.

6. The risk-adjusted expected future tax savings from borrowing in your local currency always equals the present value of the expected tax savings from borrowing in a foreign currency.

7. The cost of hedging is roughly half of the difference between the forward premium and the spot exchange rate.

8. A reinvoicing center assumes the exchange-rate risk of the various subsidiaries of a multinational corporation if it allows each subsidiary to purchase or sell in its "home" currency.

Valid–Invalid Questions

Determine which statements below are valid reasons for the manager of a firm to hedge exchange-rate risk and which are not.

1. The manager should use hedging in order to minimize the volatility of the cash flows and therefore the probability of bankruptcy even though the expected return on the firm's stock will also be reduced.

2. Firms may benefit from economies of scale when hedging in forward or money markets, while individual shareholders may not.

3. The chance of financial distress is greater when a firm's cash flows are highly variable, and financial distress is costly in imperfect markets.

4. Shareholders do not have sufficient information about a firm's exposure.

5. Risk-averse employees demand a risk premium when the volatility of a firm's cash flows is high.

6. Short selling is often difficult or impossible for individual shareholders.

7. Hedging a foreign currency inflow is beneficial when the forward rate is at a premium, because it is profitable and therefore desirable. In contrast, such hedging is not desirable when the forward rate is at a discount.

8. Since a forward contract always has a zero value, it never affects the value of the firm—but it is desirable because it reduces the variability of the cash flows.

9. Hedging reduces agency costs by reducing the variability of the firm's cash flows. Hedging means that the manager bears less personal income risk, making the manager more likely to accept risky projects with a positive net present value.

10. Hedging is desirable for firms that operate in a flat-tax-rate environment because income smoothing means that they can expect to pay less tax.

11. Managers have an incentive to hedge in order to reduce the variability of the firm's cash flows because even though a firm may be able to carry forward losses, there is the loss-of-time value.

Multiple-Choice Questions

Choose the correct answer(s).

1. The Modigliani–Miller theorem, as applied to the firm's hedging decision, states the following:

    (a) In perfect markets and for given cash flows from operations, hedging is irrelevant because by making private transactions in the money and foreign exchange markets, the shareholders can eliminate the risk of the cash flows.
    (b) Bankruptcy is not costly when capital markets are perfect.
    (c) A firm's value cannot be increased by changing the proportion of debt to equity used to finance the firm. Thus, the value of the tax shield from borrowing in home currency exactly equals the risk-adjusted expected tax shield from borrowing in foreign currency.
    (d) If the shareholders are equally able to reduce the risk from exchange-rate exposure as the firm, then hedging will not add to the value of the firm.
    (e) Markets are perfect, so hedging by the manager of the firm and the shareholders is irrelevant.

2. Hedging may reduce agency costs because

    (a) some of the uncertainty of a manager's lifetime income has been diversified away;
    (b) the shareholders will always prefer volatile projects while the debtholders will prefer nonvolatile ones;
    (c) risk-averse employees will demand a risk premium from a firm that is more likely to be in financial distress;
    (d) customers will think twice about purchasing goods from a company that may not be able to offer long-term customer service;
    (e) a reduction in the variability of the firm's cash flows may reduce the likelihood for conflicts between the debtholders and the shareholders.

3. Which of the following items represent capital market imperfections?

    (a) Agency costs.
    (b) The difference between half of the bid–ask spread between the spot and forward markets.
    (c) The potential costs from renegotiating a loan that has gone into default.
    (d) The time value lost from having to carry forward losses into a future tax year.
    (e) Fees for liquidators, lawyers, and courts in the event of bankruptcy.

Applications

1. Using the following data, compute the cost of hedging for each forward
   contract in terms of implicit commission and in terms of the extra spread
   as a percent of the midpoint spot rate.

Maturity	Rates	Bid–ask	Hedging cost	Extra spread
Spot	49.858–49.898	0.040		
Fwd 30 days	49.909–49.965	0.056		
Fwd 60 days	49.972–50.043	0.071		
Fwd 90 days	50.061–50.157	0.096		
Fwd 180 days	50.156–50.292	0.136		

2. In the wake of the North American Free Trade Agreement, the firm All-
   American Exports, Inc. has begun exporting baseball caps and gloves
   to Mexico. Suppose that All-American is subject to a tax of 30% when
   it earns profits less than or equal to USD 10 million and 40% on the
   part of profits that exceeds USD 10 million. The table below shows the
   company's profits in USD under three exchange-rate scenarios, when the
   firm has hedged its income and when it has left its income unhedged.
   The probability of each level of the exchange rate is also given.

	Hedged profits	Unhedged profits	Probability
S_{high}	15m	20m	25%
$S_{unchanged}$	10m	10m	50%
S_{low}	5m	0	25%

   (a) Compute the taxes that All-American must pay under each scenario.
   (b) What are All-American's expected taxes when it hedges its income?
   (c) What are All-American's expected taxes when it does not hedge its income?

3. In order to hedge its Mexican peso earnings, All-American is considering
   borrowing MXN 25 million, but is concerned about losing its USD interest
   tax shield. The exchange rate is USD/MXN 0.4, $r_{t,T} = 8\%$, and $r^*_{t,T} = 6\%$.
   The tax rate is 35%.

   (a) What is All-American's tax shield from borrowing in USD?
   (b) What is All-American's tax shield from borrowing in MXN?
   (c) What is the risk-adjusted expected tax shield from borrowing in MXN?

4. Graham Cage, the mayor of Atlantic Beach, in the United States, has
   received bids from three dredging companies for a beach renewal project.
   The work is carried out in three stages, with partial payment to be
   made at the completion of each stage. The current FC/USD spot rates

are NZD/USD 1.6, DKK/USD 5.5, and CAD/USD 1.3. The effective USD returns that correspond to the completion of each stage are the following: $r_{0,1} = 6.00\%$, $r_{0,2} = 6.25\%$, and $r_{0,3} = 6.50\%$. The companies' bids are shown below. Each forward rate corresponds to the expected completion date of each stage.

Company	Stage 1	Stage 2	Stage 3
Auckland Dredging	NZD 1,700,000	NZD 1,800,000	NZD 1,900,000
Forward rate NZD/USD	$F_{0,1} = 1.65$	$F_{0,2} = 1.70$	$F_{0,3} = 1.75$
Copenhagen Dredging	DKK 5,200,000	DKK 5,800,000	DKK 6,500,000
Forward rate DKK/USD	$F_{0,1} = 5.50$	$F_{0,2} = 5.45$	$F_{0,3} = 5.35$
Vancouver Dredging	CAD 1,300,000	CAD 1,400,000	CAD 1,500,000
Forward rate CAD/USD	$F_{0,1} = 1.35$	$F_{0,2} = 1.30$	$F_{0,3} = 1.25$

(a) Which offer should Mayor Cage accept?

(b) Was he wise to accept the bids in each company's own currency? Please explain.

13

Measuring Exposure to Exchange Rates

We have established three important facts about the effect of exchange-rate volatility on a firm's value. First, changes in the nominal exchange rate are not offset by corresponding changes in prices at home and abroad. That is, there are persistent and significant deviations from purchasing power parity, implying that there is real exchange-rate risk (chapter 3). Second, the forward rate is not successful in forecasting the exchange rate nor are other fundamental variables (chapter 10). Third, given the market imperfections in the real world, hedging exchange-rate risk can lead to an increase in the value of the firm (chapter 12). We may conclude, therefore, that at least some firms may want to hedge their exposure to the exchange rate at least some of the time. The issue that is still unsettled is how much should be hedged. Specifically, one issue is whether hedging of contractual exposure, as discussed in chapter 5, suffices: shouldn't we hedge all "expected" cash flows, whether contractual or not? And shouldn't we also think of the effect of exchange-rate changes on accounting values (as opposed to cash flows)?

In the first section of this chapter we distinguish between exchange-rate *risk* and *exposure to* the exchange rate. We next explain how one can classify the effects of exchange-rate changes into two categories. First, exchange-rate changes may have an impact on accounting values (known as *accounting exposure* or *translation exposure*). Second, the exchange rate may affect the firm's cash flows and market value (called *economic exposure*), either through its effect on existing contracts (labeled *contractual exposure* or *transaction exposure*) or through its impact on the future operating cash flows of the firm (known as *operating exposure*). Having already discussed the hedging of contractual exposures in chapter 5, our discussion of this item here focuses on what it achieves, and where it stops, rather than on the mechanics (section 13.2). The rest of the chapter then considers operating and translation exposure, in sections 13.3 and 13.4, respectively.

13.1 The Concepts of Risk and Exposure: A Brief Survey

In general, we need to distinguish between the terms exchange risk and exchange exposure. (Some people use them interchangeably, which is not a good idea.)

Risk. We interpret *exchange risk* as synonymous with uncertainty about the future spot rate. Possible measures of exchange risk include the standard deviation or the variance of the future spot rate change.

Exposure. A firm is said to be *exposed* to exchange risk if its financial position is affected by unexpected exchange-rate changes. A large exposure means that a given exchange-rate change has a large impact on the firm. That is, by *exposure* we mean a numerical measure of how sensitive the financial position of a firm is to changes in the exchange rate.

This concept has already been used in chapter 5, where we generally defined exposure as a number that tells us by what multiple the HC value of an asset or cash flow changes when the exchange rate moves by ΔS, everything else being the same. We denoted this multiple by $B_{t,T}$:

$$B_{t,T} = \frac{\Delta \tilde{V}_T}{\Delta \tilde{S}_T}. \tag{13.1}$$

Note again the "T" subscripts to V and S: we have in mind values at T, so the deltas must mean that we compare two possible situations at the same (future) moment T, not two observations made at different moments in time. (We are so wont to interpret Δ as a change over time that explicit notation is in order, here.) Another way of saying this is that we have in mind a kind of *partial* derivative with respect to the exchange rate, holding constant other items (including time). We used this concept to price and hedge options (chapter 9).

The above definition assumes that $\tilde{V}_T$ is an exact function of $\tilde{S}_T$. If the relation is known only up to noise or is otherwise imperfect—for instance because we willingly ignore nonlinearities in the relation—a related concept of exposure crops up: the variance-minimizing hedge instead of the exact, perfect hedge. We looked at the variance-minimizing hedge already, notably in chapter 6 on futures, and we'll use it again in this chapter. Recall that this hedge ratio is similar to the above exposure: a regression coefficient measures the sensitivity of $\tilde{V}_T$ to $\tilde{S}_T$, holding constant the regression residuals (which is "everything else," in a regression). So in that sense the general partial-derivative definition also covers the regression hedge-ratio measure of exposure.

We have already showed that B has the dimension of a number of FC units. But what is meant by $\tilde{V}_T$? In the literature one typically lists three alternative possible specifications of what could be covered by this symbol:

Contractual exposure. In the case of contractual exposure, $\tilde{V}_T$ is defined as the HC value, at maturity, of a net contractual cash flow denominated in

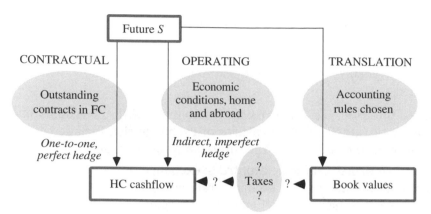

Figure 13.1. Exposure concepts: an overview. *Key:* Contractual inflows or outflows can be hedged peso-for-peso, if there really is no other risk. Operating exposures imply a noisy, convex relation between exchange rates and (HC-measured) cash flows, so the hedge is imperfect. Even getting a good idea of that relation is far from obvious: it requires a good understanding of the business and its environment. Translation exposure, lastly, primarily affects book values rather than cash flows—except indirectly if and when changed book values generate tax effects.

an FC that matures on that date. It includes, per currency and per date, all A/R, A/P, deposits, and loans denominated in a given FC, forward currency contracts, and contracts to buy or sell goods in future at known FC prices (chapter 5). (Note that not all required information is found in the accounting system: commodity contracts where no delivery has been made yet have not yet given rise to A/P or A/R, but they do generate contractual flows.) The exposure B is then the FC value, which is assumed to be risk free.

Operating exposure. In the case of operating exposure one looks at the firm not as a portfolio of FC contracts signed in the past and generating cash inflows or outflows in the future, but as a set of activities that require constant decisions by management, customers, and competitors. These future decisions depend, among other things, on future exchange rates, so that the cash flows are exposed in both FC and HC terms. (In the case of contractual exposure, in contrast, the FC amount is by assumption fixed, and only the HC value depends on the exchange rate.) In short, here $\tilde{V}_T$ is the cash flow from future operations rather than from past contracts, and the FC cash flow, C^*, is not a constant but depends on the future spot rate, $\tilde{S}_T$, and possibly other variables $\tilde{X}_T$: $\tilde{V}_T = C^*(\tilde{S}_T, \tilde{X}_T) \times \tilde{S}_T$.

Translation exposure (or, less aptly, *accounting* exposure) arises when a multinational company has to consolidate its financial statements. As all subsidiaries' balance sheets and income statements are originally drawn up in the local currency, they must be translated first, and the result of this inevitably depends on the exchange rate at the reporting date.

Note that in the case of translation exposure we are talking about accounting values, that is, numbers written into books rather than cash flows that enter or leave bank accounts. To stress the difference, contractual and operating exposures are often referred to as *economic* exposures, as opposed to translation exposure.

We provide a more in-depth discussion of each of these in the rest of this chapter. We start with a discussion of contractual exposure.

13.2 Contractual-Exposure Hedging and Its Limits

In chapter 5 we have already seen how one can close a contractual exposure, primarily by manipulating the financial items in the above list. We also saw how one can pool exposures for "similar" dates and hedge the aggregate net exposure, but too much grouping may create an interest-rate exposure problem. What we want to add now is a discussion of the limits and limitations of contractual-exposure hedging. First we consider the limitations: we show that hedging contractual exposure can achieve less than the uninitiated may have hoped. We then discuss the limits: how firm and certain should a cash flow be for it to be "contractual"; and what happens if we are less strict about this and include near-certain or even just "expected" cash flows?

13.2.1 What Does Management of Contractual Exposure Achieve?

You may remember the example of Slite, the shipping line that keeled over when the devaluation of the FIM had made its new ship unaffordable. This could have been avoided by buying forward DEM. But this example is rather specific in that it involved a one-shot, and huge, exposure. The situation for a committed exporter or importer is different: there is a steady stream of in- or outflows, each of which is relatively small. The message to take home from this subsection is that even if such a firm continuously hedges all its contractual exposures, the impact of the exchange rate will be far from completely eliminated. There will still be exposure to the exchange rate from two sources: (i) exposure to variations in the forward rate, and (ii) "operating" exposure through the effect of the exchange rate on the volume of sales. We explain these issues below.

Consider an Italian firm, Viticola, which exports its fine wines to the United States. Viticola can choose between at least two invoicing policies: (a) invoice in USD at (in the short run) constant U.S. prices, and hedge each invoice in the forward market; or (b) invoice in EUR at (in the short run) constant home currency prices. In either case, Viticola has zero contractual exposure. Still, the exchange rate affects its profits:

Invoicing constant USD prices and hedging forward. Assume that the Italian firm extends three months' credit to its U.S. customers. If the firm hedges its contractual exposure systematically every time a new invoice is sent, its EUR cash flows 90 days later will be proportional to the 90-day forward rate prevailing at the invoicing date. If, on the other hand, Viticola does not hedge its contractual exposure, its cash flows will be proportional to the spot rate prevailing when the invoice matures. In the long run, both series will have a similar variability, with the hedged version following the swings in the unhedged one with a three-month lag.

Example 13.1. Suppose that Viticola sets the price of a bottle of wine at USD 10. If Viticola does not hedge its transaction exposure, the revenue in EUR from U.S. sales is random, and depends on the EUR/USD spot rate prevailing in three months' time: USD $10 \times \tilde{S}_{t+3\text{mo}}$. If, on the other hand, Viticola hedges each contract, the EUR cash flows from the sale of each bottle is USD $10 \times F_{t,t+3\text{mo}}$. You should realize, however, that even though the forward rate for three months from now is known today, future forward rates are as uncertain as future spot rates. Thus, the revenue from future sales is an uncertain number, equal to USD $10 \times \tilde{F}_{T_i,T_i+3\text{mo}}$. Every decrease in the EUR/USD spot rate means a virtually identical decrease in the forward exchange rate, which is then reflected in lower revenue for Viticola three months later.

Thus, even perfect hedging of contractual exposure does not reduce the long-run variability of cash flows; it merely facilitates three-month budget projections.

Invoicing at constant EUR prices. This means we let the exchange rate determine the USD price. From a contractual exposure point of view, Viticola is perfectly hedged since the contract is denominated in its home currency. Clearly, however, a policy of holding constant the domestic currency price may create huge swings in the USD price of the product and, therefore, may result in huge changes in the volume of Viticola's sales and profits, as illustrated below.

Example 13.2. Suppose that Viticola decides to set the price of each bottle of wine it sells at EUR 10. At the current spot rate of EUR/USD 1, this implies a price of USD 10, a price at which Viticola can sell 10,000 bottles in the United States, and its total revenue from U.S. sales is EUR 100,000. Assume that next month the USD depreciates to EUR/USD 0.95. Given that Viticola does not change its EUR price, the U.S. price, translated at the new exchange rate, is now USD 10.53. At this new price, in the competitive wine market, Viticola can sell only 9,000 bottles. Thus, the export revenue of Viticola now declines to $9,000 \times 10 = 90,000$. True, the firm can now sell an extra 1,000 bottles at home, but exports were the preferred solution (at the old rate, at least) and extra domestic sales probably require extra discounts too. Clearly, the total revenue of Viticola is exposed to the exchange rate.

The second policy, with its constant EUR prices, guarantees a stable profit per bottle sold but may cause big swings in volume. So the exposure is there, even if contractually there is none. The first policy, with its constant USD price, should guarantee fairly stable volumes, everything else being the same, but it leads to volatile profit margins. It is not obvious which of the two is the riskier, even after hedging. Hedging the expected USD revenue, if pricing is in USD, merely postpones the effects of exchange-rate changes on EUR revenue. In statistical jargon, hedging reduces the *conditional* variance of the 90-day cash flow to zero: conditional on what we know today (including the 90-day forward), there is no exchange-rate-related uncertainty about the 90-day cash flow. But unconditionally there is not much of a change in the variability. In still other words, Viticola's three-month budgets are less uncertain, but the uncertainty is merely pushed back 90 days. We still have no idea how the next three-month budget will look.

The alert reader may already have concluded that, in the long run, the pricing policy is actually more important than the invoicing decision. For instance, the exporter may invoice in EUR but adjust the EUR prices every month to compensate for changes in the exchange rate so as to keep the USD price roughly constant. In terms of contractual exposure, there is no risk (as invoicing is in EUR), but the variability of the profit margins remains. At the other extreme, the exporter may invoice in USD and hedge forward, but also adjust the USD price every month in order to maintain roughly constant EUR prices. Again, there is no contractual exposure, but the variability of the USD price and, hence, of the sales volumes remains. Whatever the policy, or whatever combination of policies a firm uses, future profits will remain exposed to exchange-rate changes. Therefore, to hedge against changes in the exchange rate, one has to go beyond simply hedging contractual exposure.

13.2.2 How Certain Are Certain Cash Flows Anyway?

The other way to get to the same conclusion starts from the notion that the certainty seemingly implied by the word "contractual" is often illusory. There is always a nonzero probability of default on the counterpart's behalf, and occasionally the credit risk can be so big that one wonders whether hedging is even a good idea.

Example 13.3. You signed a big export contract some time ago (time t_0), but now you hear that the company is in deep trouble. In fact, you estimate your chances of seeing the promised money to be about even. The deal is hedged and this forward sale has a current market value of $(F_{t_0,T} - F_{t,T})/(1 + r_{t,T})$. What to do now?

- You could close out, "betting" on default by the customer. But if he survives and does pay, you have an open long spot position, the receivable.

- Alternatively, you could carry on, hoping for a happy end. The risk is then that there is default after all; and then you will find yourself saddled with an open short forward position, this time the hedge.

Clearly, it is not obvious which alternative is more attractive: you are potentially damned if you hedge and potentially damned if you don't. The only way to avoid dilemmas like this is to take out some form of credit insurance, which comes at a cost too.

While credit risk can be insured, other uncertainties about execution of a contract cannot. For instance, some contracts have built-in uncertainty, like cancellation clauses under certain conditions, or marked-to-market clauses if the exchange-rate change exceeds certain limits. In short, many contractual in- or outflows are not really certain.

On the other hand, some noncontractual positions are quite close to contracts, once one realizes that contracts offer no certainty anyway. What about a memorandum of understanding or a letter of intent? What about a verbal deal—legally a contract as there is consensus, but hard to prove and, therefore, hard to enforce? What about near-certainty about future sales contracts based on experience from the past? Many committed exporters or importers would be tempted to go beyond pure contractual positions, and hedge also near-certain forex revenue, hoping to thus postpone the impact of exchange-rate changes beyond the credit period.[1]

13.2.3 Hedging "Likely" Cash Flows: What Is New?

One should realize that the hedging of "likely" cash flows has two implications. First, noise creeps in, stemming from other variables than future exchange rates. Second, abstracting from noise, the relation between the HC cash flow and the exchange rate is likely to be convex. That is, we go from an exact linear relation (like $\tilde{V}_T = B_{t,T}\tilde{S}_T$) to a noisy and nonlinear one: $E(\tilde{V}_T \mid S_T) = f_{t,T}(\tilde{S}_T)$. How come?

The *noise* comes from the fact that the final decision is still to be taken by the customer (or the exporter), and this decision will inevitably depend on other variables than the exchange rate. A car exporter's foreign sales, for instance, will depend on other producers' prices and promotions, on interest rates for personal loans, the level of consumer confidence, etc. The *convexity*, on the other hand, stems from optimal reaction to exchange-rate changes. The exporter does have the option to sell at a constant FC price, in which case the translated revenue would rise or fall proportionally with the exchange rate, everything else being the same. But this passive policy will be abandoned if the exchange-rate change is sufficiently big and if reaction does improve the situation. Thus, in 1974 VW might have been exporting its Beetles to the United States at USD 2,000 apiece, but with a falling dollar and shrinking profit margins they would surely increase the USD price if that beats the passive policy. (This should probably have come with further changes in the marketing mix.) Even abandoning exports would be an option: zero cash flows are better than negative ones. In the case of a rising dollar, similarly, VW might have considered lowering its USD price below 2,000, giving up some profit margin in exchange for more market share. Again, this will be adopted if it beats the passive policy. The final picture is one of a piecewise-linear, convex relation

---

[1] Recall that pure A/P hedging just postpones the impact of shifts by the credit period, like three months in the Viticola example.

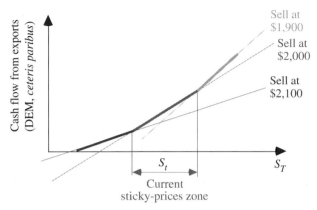

Figure 13.2. How convexity arises in operating exposure. *Key:* The lines show an exporter's HC cash flows for a given FC sales price, everything else being constant. The optimal price depends on the exchange rate. A policy of always choosing the best price leads to a convex relation between S and the expected cash flow.

(figure 13.2): passive sticky-prices policies for exchange rates close to the current level, but switching to new and better policies if the change has become sufficiently big.

In fact, in the above paragraph we have actually wandered from the realm of contractual exposure into that of short-term operating exposure. Before we proceed with this, let us point out one major implication of the fact that the effect of exchange-rate changes is now of a general nonlinear form, $E(\tilde{V}_T \mid S_T) = f_{t,T}(\tilde{S}_T)$, rather than a contractual-exposure-type relation $\tilde{V}_T = B_{t,T}\tilde{S}_T$. The implication is that exposure is no longer some number of FC units that can be found in the balance sheet or an FC cash flow as stated in a pro forma P&L. Rather, exposure has to be computed—notably from a comparison of two or more possible outcomes for the firm at time T, one outcome per possible exchange rate. As a colleague put it, "the idea is completely foreign to accounting-tied CFOs." Here's your chance to get ahead.

13.3 Measuring and Hedging of Operating Exposure

While contractual exposure focuses on the effect of the exchange rate on future cash flows whose value in foreign currency terms is contractually fixed in the past, operating exposure analyzes the impact of future exchange rates on *noncontractual* future cash flows. These FC cash flows that are likely to be random even in terms of the foreign currency, partly as a result of other factors than exchange rates and partly because of the exporter's endogenous response to the exchange-rate change. Thus, the complicating factors relative to contractual exposure are that the relation between the HC cash flow $\tilde{V}_T$ and the exchange rate $\tilde{S}_T$ has become noisy and nonlinear. Worse, the relation has become hard to identify, as it depends on the economic environment that the firm competes in, and on how the firm reacts to changes in the exchange rate, given its competitive environment.

13.3.1 Operating Exposure Comes in All Shapes and Sizes

There are at least two misconceptions about the source of operating exposure. The first misconception, already discarded in the previous section, is that if a firm denominates all of its sales and purchases in terms of its own currency, it faces no exposure to the exchange rate. We know better, now. The second misconception is that only those firms that have foreign operations are exposed to the exchange rate; that is, only those firms that buy or sell goods abroad or use imported inputs are exposed to the exchange rate, while firms that only have domestic operations are not exposed to the exchange rate. This is usually wrong too. For instance, a change in exchange rate can turn a potential foreign exporter into an active competitor.

Example 13.4. Consider a firm located in the United States. Assume that the firm's production is based in the United States, and that the firm uses only inputs that are produced in the United States and that the firm's entire sales are in the United States. The naive view would suggest that this firm's operations are not exposed to the exchange rate. This view is false if the firm faces competition from abroad. Every time the USD appreciates, the foreign competitors gain; they can lower their USD prices and still obtain the same amount of their own home currency. U.S. firms that faced this type of situation include Caterpillar, Kodak, General Motors, and Chrysler. In the early 1980s, when the USD appreciated against the JPY, all of these firms lost market share to their Japanese competitors, Komatsu, Fuji, Honda, and Toyota respectively. This erosion of market share led to large decreases in profits for the U.S. firms.

The second way an apparently noninternational player may be affected by exchange rates is indirectly, at one remove: the firm may buy from local firms that, in turn, do import, or it may sell to local firms that, in turn, do export. Or, even more indirectly, in an economy with a large open sector, the general level of economic activity may depend on the state of health of the export and the import-substituting industries.

Example 13.5. A U.K. firm has set up a subsidiary in our favorite country, Freedonia. Assume, for simplicity, that the subsidiary's cash flow, in terms of the Freedonian crown (FDK), can take on one of two (equally probable) values, FDK 150 or FDK 100, depending on whether the Freedonian economy is booming or in a recession. Let there also be two equally probable time T spot rates, GBP/FDK 1.2 and 0.8. Thus, measured in terms of the home currency, the GBP, there are four possible outcomes for the future cash flows, as shown in table 13.1. In each cell, we also show the joint probability of that particular combination of outcomes for the exchange rate and the state of the economy. When the FDK is expensive, a recession is more probable than a boom because an expensive currency means that Freedonia is not very

Table 13.1. Joint distribution of $\tilde{S}_T$ and $\tilde{CF}_T$ for the Freedonian subsidiary.

	Boom: CF* = 150	Bust: CF* = 100	$E(\tilde{V}_T \mid S_T)$
$S_T = 1.2$	$150 \times 1.2 = 180$	$100 \times 1.2 = 120$	$\dfrac{180 \times 0.15 + 120 \times 0.35}{0.15 + 0.35} = $ GBP 138
	$p = 0.15$	$p = 0.35$	$p = 0.50$
$S_T = 0.8$	$150 \times 0.8 = 120$	$100 \times 0.8 = 80$	$\dfrac{120 \times 0.35 + 80 \times 0.15}{0.35 + 0.15} = $ GBP 108
	$p = 0.35$	$p = 0.15$	$p = 0.50$
	$p = 0.50$	$p = 0.50$	

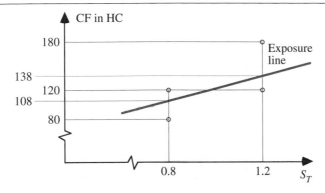

competitive. The inverse happens when the crown is trading at a low level. Thus, we assume that the probability of the exchange rate being high and the economy booming is fairly low: 0.15 not 0.25,[2] and likewise for the unexpected combination of a cheap krone and a slumping economy. The more expected outcomes get probabilities 0.35.

One step toward quantifying the impact of the exchange rate is to first compute the conditional expected cash flow for each level of the exchange rate—each row, in the table. These numbers are added in the right-most column of the table and amount to 138 when the rate is high and 108 when the rate is low. Thus, the expected impact of the change in exchange rate is 30 (million) pounds.

In the example, there is more risk than just the uncertainty about the exchange rate (with its differential impact of 30): here, there is no one-to-one relation between the state of the economy and the level of the exchange rate, so the firm's cash flow is not yet fully certain once you observe (or hedge) the exchange rate. In regression parlance, this would be called a residual uncertainty.

The example also illustrates how the relation between the HC cash flow (or the FC cash flow) and the exchange rate can be noisy. Below, we give a simple example where a convexity arises from the exporter's optimal reaction.

---

[2] If the health of the Freedonian economy had been independent of the level of the spot rate, the probability of each cell would be $0.5 \times 0.5 = 0.25$.

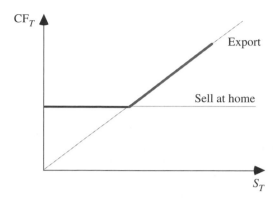

Figure 13.3. *Bourbonnaise des Eaux*'s option to export mineral water.

Example 13.6. A French niche producer of bottled mineral water can export its output to the United States, where it sells at USD 1.25 per bottle (the market price minus the shipment costs, etc.). But it can also sell at home, at EUR 1.00. Obviously, for $\tilde{S}_T < 0.80$, they would do better to sell at home, while for higher rates the wiser solution is to export:

$$\tilde{V}_T = \begin{cases} 1.00 & \text{if } \tilde{S}_T \leqslant 0.80, \\ 1.25 \times \tilde{S}_T & \text{if } \tilde{S}_T > 0.80. \end{cases} \qquad (13.2)$$

So the function is a piecewise linear one (figure 13.3).

The above examples are all about short-term exposures. By short term we mean, as in microeconomics, that the investments (P&E) are given; no major expansion or downsizing or relocation is being considered. Recall the example where VW was revising its marketing and pricing policies in light of the DEM/USD exchange rate. These were short-term reactions. But VW's reaction did become "long term" when it considered moving its production abroad. In the late 1970s, it effectively built factories in Brazil, Mexico, and the United States.

Thus, operating exposure comes in all kinds of shapes and sizes. How, then, can one still hedge it? What is the measure of exposure? This depends on the type of hedge instrument one has in mind. When hedging is done with a linear tool like a spot or forward position, we have to approximate the (noisy, nonlinear—remember?) relation by a linear one, using regression. If a nonlinear hedge is used, for instance, a portfolio of options, things are different. We begin with linear hedges.

13.3.2 The Minimum-Variance Approach to Measuring and Hedging Operating Exposure

Note from the definition of operating exposure given in equation (13.1) that exposure tells us by how much the cash flows of the firm change for a unit change in the exchange rate. Adler and Dumas (1983) suggest the use of simulations to compute the economic exposure. The simulation requires that we come up with a number of possible future values for the spot exchange rate and compute the value, in home currency, of the cash flows for each possible future exchange-rate value. The exposure of the firm to the exchange rate can then be computed by decomposing the HC value of the asset or cash flow, $\tilde{V}_{T,s}$ in scenario $s = 1, \ldots, n$, into a part linearly related to the spot rate in that scenario and a part uncorrelated with the spot rate—a technique commonly called linear regression:

$$
\begin{aligned}
\tilde{V}_{T,s} &= A_{t,T} + B_{t,T}\tilde{S}_{T,s} + \tilde{\epsilon}_{t,T,s} \\
&= \underbrace{A_{t,T} + \tilde{\epsilon}_{t,T,s}}_{\substack{\text{Uncorrelated} \\ \text{with } \tilde{S}}} + \underbrace{B_{t,T}\tilde{S}_{T,s}}_{\substack{\text{Exactly} \\ \text{linear in } \tilde{S}}} .
\end{aligned}
\tag{13.3}
$$

If $\tilde{V}$ were truly linear in $\tilde{S}$, we could have used the familiar conditional-expectation equation, $E(\tilde{V}_{T,s} \mid S_{T,s}) = A_{t,T} + B_{t,T}S_T$, but that is usually not appropriate: the above is just a linear approximation or linear decomposition or linear projection of something that is really nonlinear. But we need the linear approximation rather than the true relation because our hedge instrument is linear anyway. We start with a number of examples where the situation is so simple that the regression can almost be done with the naked eye. In the first illustration there isn't even any noise ($\tilde{\epsilon}$).

13.3.2.1 A Problem with Just Two Possible Exchange Rates, No Noise

Example 13.7. Belgium's Android MetaProducts NV/SA wishes to hedge its exposure to the exchange rate stemming from its ownership of a marketing affiliate located in the United Kingdom. This is 1992, and the GBP has just formally joined the ERM after maintaining a constant rate for two years. Still, there is risk: what worries Android is that, in the past few years, inflation has been substantially higher in the United Kingdom than on the continent, raising the question of whether the current exchange rate, BEF/GBP 60, is sustainable. After discussion with its bankers, Android ends up with two possible outcomes:

- The U.K. government may switch to a strongly deflationary policy and stabilize the exchange rate at 60. Such a deflationary policy is expected to depress sales and would decrease the net cash flow of the marketing affiliate to GBP 1.55m.

- Alternatively, the U.K. government may let the GBP depreciate and follow a moderately deflationary policy. In this case, the exchange rate would be BEF/GBP 55, and management expects a cash flow of GBP 1.8m.

How can we hedge this? Obviously, as we have an asset denominated in pounds, the exposure seems bound to be positive—but should we hedge the lower amount, or the higher one, or something in-between? The message below will be that the above "obvious" diagnosis is totally off the mark: the exposure

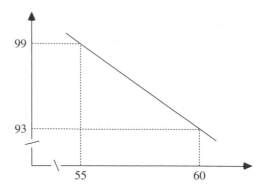

Figure 13.4. Android and the pound.

is nowhere near the 1.55–1.80m range. In fact, it is massively negative. We see this by computing the two possible HC values:

$$\text{(no devaluation):} \quad V_T = 1.55\text{m} \times 60 = \text{BEF 93m},$$

$$\text{(devaluation):} \quad V_T = 1.80\text{m} \times 55 = \text{BEF 99m}.$$

This tells us that we win if the pound loses value, which means the exposure is negative. Figure 13.4 illustrates this. It is quite easy to compute the slope of the line connecting the two possible outcome points:

$$\text{slope} = \frac{93\text{m} - 99\text{m}}{60 - 55} = \frac{-6\text{m}}{5} = -\text{GBP } 1.2\text{m}. \tag{13.4}$$

This slope is, of course, none other than our exposure, B: if there are just two possible points, the regression is the line through those two points. We now show that if Android takes a position in the forward market with the opposite sign—minus minus 1.2m, that is, buying forward 1.2m—it is hedged. Suppose that the forward rate is 58. The outcomes are analyzed as follows:

Case	Raw cash flow	Outcome of hedge	Hedged cash flow
$S = 60$	93m	$1.2\text{m} \times (60 - 58) = +2.4\text{m}$	$93\text{m} + 2.4\text{m} = \text{BEF } 95.4\text{m}$
$S = 55$	99m	$1.2\text{m} \times (55 - 58) = -3.6\text{m}$	$99\text{m} - 3.6\text{m} = \text{BEF } 95.4\text{m}$

DIY Problem 13.1. Verify that if the forward rate had been different, the level of the hedged cash flow would be affected but not the fact that the investment is hedged. For instance, with a forward rate of 57 instead of 58 the hedged asset would have been 1.2m higher, at 96.6m. Show it.

Remember two things from the example. First, exposure is computed from a comparison of alternative future outcomes, not from one single number found in a balance sheet or a pro forma cash-flow statement for next year. Second, the size and (here) even the sign of exposure can be very different from what gut feeling would suggest. Here, an accounting-tied CFO would have taken for granted that exposure is positive: we talk about a GBP asset, don't we? Wrong; the position behaves like a 1.2m liability.

DIY Problem 13.2. We have just showed that exposure defined as a slope of the line linking the two points does work: in this (overly simple) example, all risk is gone. Show that if you had followed your intuition and had hedged (sold forward) GBP 1.55m, or GBP 1.8m, or in fact any positive number, the uncertainty after such "hedging" would have been higher than before.

13.3.2.2 A Problem with Two Possible Exchange Rates and Noise

Let us generalize. The fact that the regression hedge always succeeds in taking away all exchange-related risk can be proved in just two lines:

$$\tilde{V}_T^{\text{Hedged}} = \underbrace{A_{t,T} + B_{t,T}\tilde{S}_T + \tilde{\epsilon}_{t,T}}_{\text{Value unhedged}} + \underbrace{[-B_{t,T}]}_{\substack{\text{Size of} \\ \text{hedge}}}\underbrace{[\tilde{S}_T - F_{t,T}]}_{\substack{\text{Expiry value} \\ \text{per GBP}}}$$

$$= \underbrace{A_{t,T} + \tilde{\epsilon}_{t,T}}_{\substack{\text{Uncorrelated} \\ \text{with } \tilde{S}}} + \underbrace{B_{t,T}F_{t,T}}_{\text{Risk free}}. \tag{13.5}$$

Thus, what regression-based hedging generally achieves is eliminating all uncertainty that is linearly related to the exchange rate: $B_{t,T}F_{t,T}$ has taken the place of $B_{t,T}\tilde{S}_T$. The uncertainty that is *not* correlated with the exchange rate, in contrast, cannot be picked up by the forward contract, so it remains there. It can be shown that this regression hedge ratio is also the one that reduces the variance of the remaining risk to the lowest possible level. This is why this section is called minimum–variance hedging and why ordinary regression is called least squares (= minimal residual variance).

In the Android example there was assumed to be no residual risk, which is hard to believe. Our earlier Freedonia example, in contrast, does have this feature: the state of the economy (and, therefore, the cash flow) is not fully known once the exchange rate is observed, so there is only an imperfect correlation between the HC cash flow and the exchange rate. Table 13.2 repeats the Freedonia data and then shows the hedged cash flows. To find the hedged cash flows we of course need the exposure. In the case with just two possible values of $\tilde{S}_T$, the regression line runs through the points representing the conditional expectations. We identified these expectations as 138 when $S_T = 1.20$ and 108 when $S_T = 0.80$. So the exposure now equals

$$B_{t,T} = \frac{138 - 108}{1.20 - 0.80} = \frac{30}{0.4} = \text{FDK 75.} \tag{13.6}$$

Note, in passing, that even though the cash flow, in FC, is either 150 or 100, the exposure is not even in the range [100, 150]: it equals 75. The only way to come with a meaningful exposure number again is to compare the two scenarios; neither scenario in itself gives you a reliable answer, nor does any accounting number. Let us show that our FC 75 does make sense. Assuming

Table 13.2. Joint distribution of $\tilde{S}_T$ and $\tilde{CF}_T$ for the Freedonian subsidiary.

	Unhedged cash flows		
	Boom: $CF^* = 150$	Bust: $CF^* = 100$	$E(\tilde{V}_T \mid S_T)$
$S_T = 1.2$	$150 \times 1.2 = 180$	$100 \times 1.2 = 120$	$\dfrac{180 \times 0.15 + 120 \times 0.35}{0.15 + 0.35} = \text{GBP } 138$
	$p = 0.15$	$p = 0.35$	$p = 0.50$
$S_T = 0.8$	$150 \times 0.8 = 120$	$100 \times 0.8 = 80$	$\dfrac{120 \times 0.35 + 80 \times 0.15}{0.35 + 0.15} = \text{GBP } 108$
	$p = 0.35$	$p = 0.15$	$p = 0.50$
	Hedged cash flows		
$S_T = 1.2$	$180 - 18 = 162$	$120 - 18 = 102$	$\dfrac{162 \times 0.15 + 102 \times 0.35}{0.15 + 0.35} = \text{GBP } 120$
$S_T = 0.8$	$120 + 12 = 132$	$80 + 12 = 92$	$\dfrac{132 \times 0.35 + 92 \times 0.15}{0.35 + 0.15} = \text{GBP } 120$

the forward rate is 0.96, the payoffs from the hedges would be

$$\text{when } S_T = 1.20: \quad -B_{t,T}(S_T - F_{t,T}) = -75 \times (1.20 - 0.96) = -18,$$
$$\text{when } S_T = 0.80: \quad -B_{t,T}(S_T - F_{t,T}) = -75 \times (0.80 - 0.96) = +12.$$

From the table, we see that now not all uncertainty is gone: the deviations between cash flow and conditional expectations remain as large as before. That is because these deviations are the $\tilde{\varepsilon}$s, about which nothing can be done—at least not with currency forwards. But the conditional expected cash flows have been equalized, and as a result total risk is down. Again, this is the best reduction in the variance one can achieve, with these data.

13.3.2.3 *General Minimum-Variance Hedging*

When, realistically, the exchange rate can assume many more values than just two, it is generally the case that all conditional expected values no longer lie on a line. In fact, on the basis of our optimal-response argument we would expect cash flows to be convex in the exchange rate. Table 13.3 gives an example. It shows eleven possible exchange rates, the corresponding expected cash flows (in HC), and the probabilities of each. The slope of the regression is 87 370,

Table 13.3. Data for a nonlinear exposure example.

S	0.80	0.82	0.84	0.86	0.88	0.90	0.92	0.94	0.96	0.98	1.00
V	42 181	42 821	43 607	44 572	45 754	47 203	48 977	51 148	53 805	57 054	61 026
p	0.02	0.04	0.06	0.10	0.16	0.24	0.16	0.10	0.06	0.04	0.02

and $R^2 = 0.92$. Figure 13.5 shows the original expectations for each exchange rate (the upward-sloping array of little squares), the regression line, and the hedged expected cash flows (the little triangles in a smile pattern).

Two remarks about these results, for the statistically initiated reader. First, note that since the data do not contain deviations from the conditional expectations, this is not the usual R^2: it tells you that the regression captures 92% of the variability of the conditional expected cash flows, not of the potential cash flows themselves. So this tells you that the nonlinearity is not terrible, but you cannot conclude that hedging reduces risk by 92% since the residual risk is being ignored, here. Second, you may be wondering how the hedged-expectations series, which shows quite some curvature, still only contains just 8% of the variability of the original data. The answer is that the data are probability-weighted. The "distant" ends of the hedged series contain low-probability events that have only a minor impact on the variance. We are not used to this: our typical regression data in other applications are never weighted this way, or rather, we always let the sample frequencies proxy for the probabilities. Thus, our eye is trained to see each dot on the graph as equally probable, whereas here the central dots represent many observations. (In fact, the low-tech way to weigh the data is to repeat the observations such that their frequencies in the data matrix become proportional to the probabilities.) The weighting also explains why the regression line looks like mostly "below" the data. This is just because the regression line is heavily attracted by the central data, where most of the probability mass is.

13.3.2.4 General Issues in Minimum-Variance Hedging

The above problems were kept simple, which is fine if the purpose is to explain the concept. Still, in fairness it must be added that the hedging of an operating exposure is a bit of a minefield once in the real world. Here is a list of the steps to be taken, and the issues to be solved.

Getting data. One can either go for data from the past or for numbers about possible future scenarios.

- *Past data.* One can proceed in the same way as one estimates a market beta: collect past data on stock prices and exchange rates, and regress. We see the following problems. (i) This allows you, at best, to estimate the risk of the firm as a whole, not a new project or a separate business. (ii) The assumption is that the future is like the past, which is often not true: PPP deviations come in long swings, for instance, and exposure

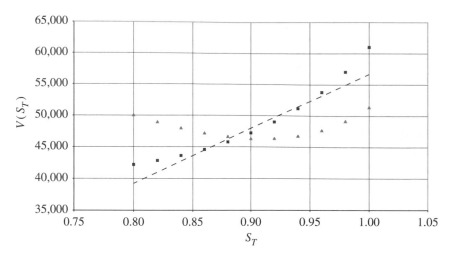

Figure 13.5.   Results for the nonlinear exposure example.

during a period of dollar overvaluation is a poor guide to exposure in the subsequent period of undervaluation. (iii) Even past exposure is estimated poorly because, for most firms, exchange risk is only a weak determinant of returns, which means that estimates are imprecise. (iv) If you nevertheless go for this data-mining approach, you should realize that, with time-series data, there is a problem of unit roots (ask your statistics teacher). This means that one has to use return data (percentage changes in values), not the value data themselves. The regression coefficient one gets from a returns regression is an elasticity (that is, $(\partial V/\partial S)(S/V)$), whereas the B we need is a partial derivative, $\partial V/\partial S$. So one would need an adjustment, multiplying the slope coefficient by V/S. Then a decision needs to be made whether this correction will be based on the time series means, or the most recent values, or something else. We have no good guide as to how to solve this issue.

- *Alternative scenarios for future cash flows.* The alternative to using time series of past data is to work with a cross section of alternative scenarios about the future. In principle this makes more sense. The only issue is the quality of these data in a real-world situation. The finance staff should know that the sales and cost data they get from marketing and operations, respectively, are crucial: if these are worthless, your hedge will be worthless too. Question them. Make sure the costs are not accounting COGS with markups for overheads, for instance, but truly marginal cash outlays. Ask the marketing people how they would change their four or five P's under what scenario, thus forcing them to actually *think*.

Identifying the distribution of the future spot rate(s). If you decide to work with scenarios, then you almost surely need to know how to weigh the possible pairs of possible future spot rates and associated expected cash flows. There are only three exceptions to this: weights are not needed if either it is reasonable to consider just two possible rates, as in the Android example, or if the expectations are linear in S, or if you go for a nonlinear hedge (see below). But a two-point situation is exceptional; and if you get expected-cash-flow data that are linear in S, that probably means the people who gave you the data were lazy: a priori, one expects convexity.

Option traders typically start from a lognormal and then thicken the tails somewhat. You could get a standard deviation from them: ask for the implied standard deviation (ISD). The mean, on the other hand, can be inferred from the forward rate: we know there is, in principle, a risk correction that intervenes between CEQs and expectations, but it is small, both empirically and theoretically, and the choice of the mean has little impact on the regression anyway. Using forwards and ISDs, your forecasts for different horizons will be mutually compatible too. If you use a more wet-finger approach, compatibility over time is not guaranteed.

Linear or nonlinear hedges? When, realistically, the exchange rate can assume many more values than just two, it is generally the case that all conditional expected values no longer lie on a line. You then need to make up your mind as to whether you are happy with a static, linear hedge as we have discussed so far or prefer to go for a nonlinear hedge. If, as in our example, the regression captures 92% of the expectations, you might be happy with the linear approximation and the associated hedge.

The alternative is to go for a portfolio of options. In that case you construct a piecewise linear approximation to the data, using either your common sense (helped by pencil and ruler) or a regression with linear splines.[3] You start with a forward hedge whose size is, for instance, equal to the slope in the first linear section. With options you then let the exposure of your hedge portfolio change wherever you want, mirroring the changing exposures of your expectations. Alternatively, you can use dynamic replication of the options, but this introduces model risk: the dynamic replication will not do as well as the option itself, and how badly it deviates depends on the adequacy of the model chosen. Dynamic hedging is described in chapter 9, on the binomial model.

The advantages of the nonlinear hedge are twofold. First, you do not need the probability distribution of S: you leave this to the market, which then builds its perceptions about the density into the option prices. Second, there is a better fit with the data. The drawbacks include higher complexity, higher transaction costs, and perhaps overreliance on expectations data that are more seat-of-the-pants than you may wish.

---

[3] First decide at what values of S you want a change of slope. These points are called knot points; for instance, in our example you may want a single change of slope, at $S = 0.90$ (right in the middle). Then make dummies $I_{k,j}$ indicating whether observation S_j is beyond the kth knot point K_k; for instance, with one knot at $S = 0.90$, all observations with $S_j \geqslant 0.90$ get $I_{1,j} = 1$, and all lower observations get $I_{1,j} = 0$. Then regress $V_j = A + B_0 S_j + D_1 [I_{1,j}(S_j - K_1)] + D_2 [I_{2,j}(S_j - K_2)] + \cdots$. The coefficient D_k tells you how much the slope changes in knot point K_k.

Hedging other risks? If cash flows depend on other variables beside the exchange rate, and if for these other variables one also has forward or futures contracts, then you have the option to hedge the other exposures too. For instance, the oil price could be such a variable. We denote the additional variable by X, and there could of course be more than one extra X. The mean–variance hedge now requires that you run a multiple regression, $V = A + B \cdot S + C \cdot X$. For this, you will need many more scenarios, and a joint probability distribution for X and S, which is not easy.[4]

13.3.3 Economic Exposure: CFO's Summary

Let us conclude this review of economic exposure by summarizing a few crucial results and integrating them with ideas mentioned in earlier chapters.

We can divide economic exposure into two categories—contractual exposure (also known as transaction exposure) and operating exposure. Managers typically focus on contractual exposure, which arises from accounts receivable, accounts payable, long-term sales or purchase contracts, or financial positions expressed in foreign currency. This is because if one's source of information is accounting data, as it typically is, then transaction exposure is very visible and easy to measure. In contrast, operating exposure is much harder to quantify than contractual exposure; it requires a good understanding of competitive forces and of the macroeconomic environment in which the firm operates. For many firms, however, operating exposure is more important than contractual exposure, and it is critical that you make an attempt to identify and measure the exposure of operations to exchange rates.

Also, it is incorrect to assume that a firm with no foreign operations is not exposed to the exchange rate. For example, if a firm's competitors are located abroad, then changes in exchange rates will affect that firm's competitive position and its cash flows. Another common fallacy is the presumption that a policy of systematic hedging of all transaction exposure suffices to protect the firm against all exchange rate effects. As explained above, even if a firm perfectly hedges all contractual exposure, its operations are still exposed to the exchange rate.

Whether one considers transaction or operating exposure, one can use a forward contract (or the equivalent money-market hedge) to hedge the corresponding uncertainty in the firm's cash flow. Recall, however, that a forward or spot hedge is a double-edged sword. It is true that bad news about future operations is offset by gains on the forward hedge. However, you would likewise

---

[4] Note that this makes sense only if you really want to hedge the additional risk with a linear hedge instrument, like oil futures or forwards. The econometrician's knee-jerk reaction is to add as many possible variables to a regression to improve the R^2 and isolate the contribution of S from that of other variables Z that are correlated with S. But if there is no hedge instrument for Z, sorting out the separate contributions of the two does not make sense. In fact, the difference between a multiple B and a simple-regression B is that the latter includes the effect of Z to the extent that Z resembles S. This is good, because then we at least do hedge the effect of Z (to the extent that Z resembles S).

lose on the forward hedge if the exchange-rate change improves the value of your operations. For example, in 1991, the Belgian group Acec Union Minière had hedged against a "further drop" of the USD. Instead, the USD rose, causing losses of no less than BEF 900m on the forward contracts. Four managers were fired. If you dislike this symmetry implicit in the payoff of a forward contract, you may consider hedging with options rather than forwards, to limit the downward risk without eliminating potential gains from exchange-rate changes. As one banker once put it, "with a forward hedge you could end in the first row of the class or in the last; with an option, at worst you end somewhat below the middle."

A second potential problem that a treasurer needs to be aware of, when using short-term forward contracts to hedge long-term exposure, is the possibility of ruin risk, that is, liquidity problems that arise when there is a mismatch between the maturity of the underlying position and the hedging instrument. These liquidity concerns already came up in our discussion about hedging with futures contracts that are marked to market, but they arise any time the hedge triggers cash flows that come ahead of the exposed cash flow itself, for instance if a five-year exposure is covered by five consecutive one-year contracts.

Third, remember that, unlike many contractual exposures, operating exposure cannot be obtained from a balance sheet or a pro forma P&L statement. It has to be deduced from a cross-sectional analysis of possible future outcomes—cash flows, typically. The level of the true exposure can be totally out of the ballpark of the sizes of the exposed cash flows themselves, and can even have a different sign: remember the Android example.

Fourth, it is important to keep in mind that the estimate of exposure that one calculates changes over time, and may not be very precise at any given moment. However, this measure is useful—even if it gives us only an approximate indication of the sign and size of a firm's exposure—because it forces us to think about the way exchange rates affect the firm's operations.

Finally, hedging is like an aspirin—quite useful for short-term headaches but not a long-run remedy for most serious diseases. It does provide you with a financial gain that is intended to offset operating losses, but it does not reduce the operating losses themselves. One can live with operating losses as long as they are temporary; and the point of hedging, in such a case, is that it does provide the cash that tides you over a bad patch. But if the problem is likely to be more than just temporary, you need strategic changes in operations—for example, revising the marketing mix, reallocating production, choosing new sourcing policies to reduce exposure, and so on. Again, financial hedging just provides cash that eases the pain and helps financing the adjustments; it does not solve the underlying problem.

In this respect, when making scenario projections about the possible future exchange rates, we should also make contingency plans for various possible future exchange rates, including less likely ones. One can win crucial time if the response has been talked through before; otherwise one wastes too much time deciding what exchange-rate changes are "big" and "structural" or not, what the available options are, not to mention who should be on the "task force" that ruminates on all this, and so on and so forth.

This finishes our discussion of economic exposures. We now turn to translation exposure.

13.4 Accounting Exposure

The $\tilde{V}_T$ entry in the exposure definition has been interpreted, thus far, as the portfolio of contractual FC-denominated undertakings inherited from the past, or a portfolio of activities that need continuous decisions influenced by, among other things, exchange rates. The third definition we discuss is the firm's accounting value. This accounting value may be affected by exchange rates in two ways. First, the firm may have contractual exposures which the firm is also *marking to market*, thus adjusting their book values to the rates that prevail on the valuation date. Second, the firm may have foreign subsidiaries, and the HC value of their *net worth*, in the accounting sense of the word, probably depends to some extent on the exchange rate that prevails on the consolidation date.

13.4.1 Accounting Exposure of Contractual Forex Positions

The issue of how to book contractual exposures has been brought up already in chapter 5, where we argued that translation at the then-prevailing forward rates makes more sense. Still, many firms use the spot rate. The issue here is different, though. Notably, if the firm has booked a contractual position in the past, should it adjust the book value on the reporting date, and, if so, how?

A/P, A/R, deposits, loans. For these items, both U.S. GAAP and the IFRS rules would agree, sensibly, that marking to market is recommended; in the case of IFRS, that is even the general rule. Our earlier logic would then imply that the current forward rate be used to translate the values of A/R, A/P, deposits, loans, etc., into HC. (Ideally, one would also correct for time value and changes therein by PV-ing all numbers, but this is still too rarely done even though IFRS supports this.) Any increase of the value of an asset would be balanced by an increased "liability," the unrealized capital gain that adds to the shareholders' net worth. (Similar statements can be made for losses, and for short positions, of course.) Being unrealized, many managers would prefer that the gain would not pass through P&L first, but IFRS begs to differ.

Futures. For futures hedges and the like, the same logic holds. Instead of mentioning a zero value off balance sheet for a futures contract, one can add a capital gain or loss $f_{t,T} - f_{t_0,T}$. This entry is the counterpart, on the liability side, of all net marked-to-market cash flows that have been received from the clearing corporation since the initial value date t_0 (or the beginning of the accounting period if there has been at least one earlier financial report, which presumably contains the gains/losses before that date) and, therefore, have already shown up in the "bank account," on the assets side of the balance sheet. If the marked-to-market cash flows have the character of a final payment rather than adjustments to security posted—the telltale symptom would be that there is no interest earned on outward payments, nor due on inward payments—then one could argue that the gain or loss is realized and, therefore, should be shown as part of P&L rather than just as an unrealized item among the shareholders' funds. This is the position of the Financial Accounting Standards Board (FASB). The position of the International Accounting Standards Committee (IASC), as reflected in IFRS, is that all gains or losses have to be shown, whether realized or not.

Note that if the firm has taken out a futures contract to hedge another position, if that other position is not being marked to market, and if the firm has to book its marked-to-market cash flows on the futures as a profit or loss, then realized profits become more volatile even though the hedging aims to reduce variability. In that case, the FASB would waive the requirement to book the gains and losses via P&L, provided the futures position was immediately designated as a hedge of a well-identified balance-sheet item. There is no such rule for forwards (where, by FASB rules, marking-to-market does not have to go through P&L) or cash hedges (where, presumably, the firm's marked-to-market rules for hedge and hedgee are always in agreement). But neither is there a similar rule for exposures that are not yet in the balance sheet, which is anomalous, economically. Also, while the rule says that "speculative" futures positions should be fully marked to market, there is no such requirement for speculative positions in forward or spot markets.

Forwards. For forwards there is no cash movement prior to expiry, so the accounting entries in case of a gain on a long position would be (i) a revaluation of an asset with original book value zero, and (ii) an upward adjustment in shareholders' funds, possibly as an unrealized and undistributable item. Again, almost surely the time value part that we showed in chapter 4 would be missing: only the un-PV-ed part $F_{t,T} - F_{T_0,T}$ would be reported.

IFRS prescribes that all forward positions be shown—initially at zero value, and later marked to market using the change in the forward rate (undiscounted). The A/R or A/P position is to be booked at the spot rate, and marked to market at the spot rate. So the marking to market of hedge and hedgee will roughly match but the difference between initial spot and forward is treated as a capital gain or loss—a bad idea, I argued in chapter 5, because laypersons will think it actually *means* something.

The rule that forwards need to be marked to market creates a problem if the hedge is undertaken before the invoice is written or received: then, pending the invoice, the forward contract would already trigger marked-to-market

Bonuses. In order to make performance measures comparable, foreign data need to be translated into a common currency. For example, many firms have bonus plans that link their managers' compensation to their performance. Decisions to promote or fire managers are also based on performance. To make such decisions, one needs to translate the financial statements of the foreign subsidiaries into the currency of the parent.

Valuation. To value the entire firm (as an outside investor or financial analyst), one needs far more than just accounting data. Still, valuation is often partially based on accounting values; or, at the very least, the accounting value serves as a benchmark. For instance, if the discounted cash flow value of the entire firm turns out to be four times its book value, one would surely take a closer look at both types of information. Again, the book value of the firm as a whole cannot be computed unless assets and liabilities of foreign subsidiaries are first translated into a common currency.

In the next section we first discuss the general objectives that any method used to translate the accounts of the subsidiary into the currency of the parent firm tries to accomplish, and then the details of the various methods that are used for translation.

13.4.3 The Choice of Different Translation Methods

Accounting exposure arises because the outcome of translating a subsidiary's balance sheet from foreign currency to home currency depends on the exchange rate at the date of consolidation, an exchange rate that is uncertain. Firms may like to hedge this exposure to reduce or eliminate the swings in reported profits that arise simply due to these translation effects. This exposure, of course, depends on the rules used to translate the accounts of the subsidiary into the currency of the parent firm. There is a variety of approaches that one can adopt to translate the income statement and balance-sheet items of the subsidiary into the currency of the parent firm.

Example 13.9. Suppose a Canadian firm buys a competitor in England for GBP 1m, when the exchange rate is CAD/GBP 2.0. A year later, the exchange rate is CAD/GBP 2.1. Thus, assuming that the subsidiary is still worth GBP 1m and translation is done at CAD/GBP 2.1, its translated value in terms of the currency of the parent is CAD 2.1m. One question is whether one *should* translate the GBP value at the new rate at all; and, if the answer is positive, the next question is how to report this increase in the value of the British subsidiary in the accounts of the parent firm. For example, should the exchange rate effect be shown as part of the reporting period's income, or should it just be mentioned on the balance sheet, as an unrealized gain?

If the decision is to translate at the historical exchange rate—the one prevailing when the asset was purchased—then there is no translation exposure. Otherwise there is, but its size depends on how one translates; for example, one could opine that real assets do not really lose value following a devaluation, etc.

Table 13.5. Translating the Australian balance sheet into MTL.

		C/N		M/N		Closing rate	
	Value in AUD	(at 0.333)	(at 0.3)	(at 0.333)	(at 0.3)	(at 0.333)	(at 0.3)
Assets							
Cash, securities	1,000	333	300	333	300	333	300
A/R	1,000	333	300	333	300	333	300
Inventory	1,000	333	300	*325*	*325*	333	300
Plant, equipment	5,000	*1,625*	*1,625*	*1,625*	*1,625*	1,665	1,500
Total assets (a)	8,000	2,624	2,525	2,616	2,550	2,664	2,400
Liabilities							
A/P	500	166.5	150	166.5	150	166.5	150
Short-term debt	2,000	666.0	600	666.0	600	666.0	600
Long-term debt	2,400	*780.0*	*780.0*	799.2	720.0	799.2	720.0
Total debt (b)	4,900	1,612.5	1,530	1,631.7	1,470	1,631.7	1,470
Net worth (a)–(b)	3,100	1,011.5	995.0	984.3	1,080.0	1,032.3	930.0
Of which:							
Retained	0	*0*	*0*	*0*	*0*	*0*	*0*
Equity	3,100	*1,002.0*	*1,002.0*	*1,002.0*	*1,002.0*	*1,002.0*	*1,002.0*
Equity adjustment	—	9.5	7.0	17.7	78.0	30.3	72.0

Exposure of net worth	$\dfrac{1{,}011.5 - 955.0}{0.333 - 0.300}$	$\dfrac{984.3 - 1{,}080.0}{0.333 - 0.300}$	$\dfrac{1{,}032.3 - 930.0}{0.333 - 0.300}$
	= AUD 500	= AUD − 2,900	= AUD 3.100
	= NWC	= NMA	= Net worth

Key: Items deemed to be nonexposed are printed in italics. C/N, current/noncurrent; M/N, monetary/nonmonetary; NWC, net working capital; NMA, net monetary assets.

The above example illustrates what the controversy between accountants is all about. Accountants do not agree which assets and liabilities should be translated at the historical exchange rate and which at the "current" or "closing" exchange rate, that is, at the rate prevailing at the date of consolidation. There is also some disagreement about whether and when exchange rate gains or losses should be recognized in income. A major criterion of accountants in devising the translation rules is whether these rules are consistent with the rules for domestic accounting. However, from a firm's point of view, the principal requirement is that the rules be such that they provide accurate information about the performance of the subsidiary. Lastly, firms also wish that the rules be such that they do not lead to wide swings in the figures reported in the financial statements.

In the rest of this section, we describe four different translation methods and the philosophy underlying each method. Each method has a set of rules for translating items in the balance sheet and the income statement. The rules for translating items in the income statement are quite similar across the different methods; hence, we will focus on the rules for items reported in the balance sheet. To illustrate the differences between these methods, we shall consider the example of an Australian subsidiary of a Maltese firm. A simplified balance sheet of the subsidiary is shown in the second column (value in AUD) of table 13.5. We shall explain the notion of accounting exposure by considering translation on December 31, 2007, at two different exchange rates, MTL/AUD 0.333 and MTL/AUD 0.300, and by seeing how the value of the subsidiary changes depending on the accounting method being used. Throughout this discussion, our focus will be on studying what the different translation methods imply for the firm's accounting exposure.

The four methods all share the following steps: (i) translate assets and debt, using the method's rules as to what items are exposed or not; (ii) compute net worth (assets minus debts, in HC); (iii) subtract equity at historic valuation (including past retained earnings, each at its own historic valuation) to identify the balancing item (equity adjustments).

13.4.3.1 The Current/Noncurrent Method

The current/noncurrent method for translating the financial statements of foreign subsidiaries is one that was commonly used in the United States until the mid 1970s. As its name suggests, whether an item is translated at the closing exchange rate or the historical rate depends on its time to maturity. Thus, according to this method, current (i.e., short-term) assets and liabilities in the balance sheet are translated at the closing exchange rate, while noncurrent items, such as long-term debt, are translated at the historical rate. The logic underlying this is that the value of short-term assets and liabilities is fixed, or at least quite sticky, in AUD terms, so that its HC value changes proportionally with the exchange rate. For example, the future value of an AUD T-bill is fixed in AUD nominal terms; and, in the short-term, goods prices are sticky and therefore quasi-fixed in AUD terms, too. Long-term assets and liabilities, in contrast, will not be realized in the short run—and by the time they are realized, the closing exchange-rate change may very well turn out to have been undone by later, opposite changes in the spot rate. That is, the effect of a closing exchange-rate change on the realization value of long-term assets and liabilities is very uncertain. As accountants hesitate to recognize gains or losses that are very uncertain, the current/noncurrent method simply prefers to classify the long-term assets and liabilities as unexposed.

Thus, under the current/noncurrent method, translation at the closing rate is restricted to only the short-term assets and liabilities. Thus, exposure is given by the difference in short-term assets and liabilities, that is, net working capital.

Example 13.10. In table 13.5, we assume that long-term debt was issued and long-term assets (plant and equipment) were bought in early 2007, at which time the exchange rate was MTL/AUD 0.325. Thus, these items are recorded at their historical values (indicated as italicized text) and are not affected by the exchange rate. It follows that net exposure equals short-term assets minus short-term liabilities, or net working capital: AUD 500. The effect of the exchange-rate change from 0.333 to 0.300 is a drop in net worth of AUD $500 \times (-0.033) = -$MTL 16.5.

Evaluation.

- The assumption underlying this method seems to be that there is mean reversion in exchange rates; that is, exchange-rate fluctuations tend to be undone in the medium run, which (if true) means that they affect short-term assets only. However, as discussed in chapter 11, there is little empirical support for this view (except for the small movements of exchange rates around a central parity): typically, changes in exchange rates are not undone in the medium term, and floating exchange rates behave like random walks.

- Most firms have positive net working capital and would therefore be deemed to be positively exposed (losing value, that is, following a devaluation of the host currency). Yet economic logic says that the true effect on economic value should be hard to predict in general, depending, for instance, on whether the firm is an exporter or an importer, a price taker or a price leader, in a small open economy or in a large, closed one, or competing against locals or versus foreign companies, etc. Thus, there is little hope that this method will capture the true value effect except by pure serendipity.

- The consolidated accounts are not compatible with the subsidiary's original accounts. The relative values of items differ according to whether one uses HC or FC numbers, and many of the standard ratios will be affected. This is not good news if, for example, performance analysis is based on ratios.

- The resulting translated balance sheet is a mixture of actual and historic rates and is therefore hard to interpret.

To translate the subsidiary's income statement, the current/noncurrent method uses an average exchange rate for the period, assuming that cash flows come evenly over the period—except for incomes or costs corresponding to nonrecurrent items (like depreciation of assets): these are translated at the same rate as the corresponding balance-sheet item. This creates another inconsistency between the AUD and MTL P&L figures, and between the translated P&L and A&L figures.

13.4.3.2   The Monetary/Nonmonetary Methods

The monetary/nonmonetary methods and their close kin, the temporal method, are said to be ideally suited if the foreign operation forms an integral part of the parent. The idea is that, accordingly, the translation should stay as close as possible to what would have happened if the operation had been run as a branch, that is, just a part of the main company that happens to be active abroad and has assets abroad but does not have a separate legal personality.

If the foreign business had indeed been a branch, without any separate accounting system, the translation issue would not have arisen: everything would have been in the parents' books already, in HC, except for monetary assets whose value by definition is fixed in FC terms and needs to be translated. For instance, if the parent firm held forex cash or other monetary assets expressed in forex, any value change would have been recorded and probably included in the parent's P&L; but its machines and buildings would have been unaffected, in terms of book value, by exchange-rate changes. Since by assumption the subsidiary is really a part of the parent, the subsidiary's monetary A&L are translated at the closing rate, and the nonmonetary items at the historic rate. Any resulting gains or losses are mentioned among the reserves, as unrealized gains or losses.

The above argument assumes that domestic assets are valued at historic cost—a principle that is becoming less and less popular. But there exists another angle to justify the rule. It is sometimes argued that, in the long run, inflation differentials should undo exchange-rate changes (PPP). So in the long run the real value of real assets will not be affected. Thus, according to this method, we should adjust only the monetary (not the real) assets and liabilities for changes in the exchange rate. It follows that only the net foreign-currency monetary position, financial assets minus debt, is exposed.

> **Example 13.11.** In table 13.5, the net worth figures under each of the two possible year-end exchange rates differ by MTL +95.7. The exposure was 2,000 − 4,900 = −2,900 (AUD) under this method.

Evaluation.

- The purchasing power parity view of the world has received little empirical support, except vaguely in the never-arriving long run.[5] Accountants do not usually rely on highly uncertain prospects.

- In addition, PPP just says that translated values of assets abroad tend to be equal to values at home. If true, this would mean that changes in values of foreign and domestic assets are equal to each other; but there is no claim that the value change at home is zero.

---

[5] Recall that all we know is that uncertainty about future real exchange rates does not grow proportionally with the length of the horizon, which is a far cry from uncertainty somehow disappearing entirely the longer one waits.

- Likewise, in the "closely related operations" versions of the story, the nonmonetary assets are treated as they would have been treated if they were at home and, therefore, left unchanged. But that is historic costing. In many cases, under replacement value or fair value the value of the foreign-based asset would differ from one at home, and the argument would break down.

- This measure of exposure, financial assets minus debts, is likely to be negative for most firms. Thus, under the monetary/nonmonetary method, a devaluation will typically lead to an accounting gain rather than to a loss. But, from our earlier discussion on a related point in the current/noncurrent method, economic reality should be very different for different firms, so the hope that this method produces the true number is, again, slim.

- Also, here, HC relative values differ from FC ones, affecting ratios; there is no consistency.

- Finally, the resulting mixture of actual and historic translations is again hard to interpret.

To translate the subsidiary's income statement, the monetary/nonmonetary method uses an average exchange rate for the period, except for incomes or costs corresponding from nonmonetary sources (like depreciation of assets). These are translated at the same rate as the corresponding balance-sheet item. This again creates an inconsistency between the AUD and MTL P&L figures, and between the translated P&L and A&L figures.

13.4.3.3 The Temporal Method

The temporal method of translating the financial statements of a foreign subsidiary is similar to the monetary/nonmonetary method. One difference between the two methods arises if "real" items have been marked to market in HC. As we saw, under the monetary system, inventory is always translated at the historical exchange rate, since it is a nonmonetary asset. Under the temporal method, in contrast, inventory may be translated at the current (i.e., closing) exchange rate if it is recorded in the balance sheet at current market prices. The advantage of this approach is that it is less inconsistent with the accounting rules used for the parent firm if the parent marks to market its domestic inventory too. Another aspect of the temporal method is that it makes translation effects part of reported income, which can lead to large swings in reported earnings. Thus, under this method CFOs tried to hedge exposures that were just arbitrary paper results, not real cash flows.

The U.S. accounting directive that was used from 1976 to 1981, FASB 8, was based on the temporal method. (Before that, the United States imposed the current/noncurrent method.) The closing-rate method, introduced by FASB 52 in the United States, is designed to overcome some of these problems.

13.4.3.4 The Current-Rate or Closing-Rate Method

This is the simplest approach for translating financial statements. According to the current-rate method or closing-rate method, all balance-sheet items are translated at the closing exchange rate. Typically, exchange gains are reported separately in a special equity account on the parent's balance sheet, thus avoiding large variations in reported earnings, and these unrealized exchange gains are not taxed.

Example 13.12. For the Australian subsidiary's simplified balance sheet, the exposed amount is net worth, AUD 3,100.

Evaluation.

- The main advantage is consistency between the parent's and the subsidiary's relative numbers. Likewise, using one rate produces a number that is easier to interpret than one resulting from mixtures of closing and historic translations.[6]

- Under this method, a 15% devaluation means a 15% decrease in the net value of the investment. Economically, one expects that a devaluation of, say, 15% leads to a value loss of 15% only if all subsequent cash flows are unaffected (in HC terms), which assumes a very closed economy. So, again, this method is unlikely to capture the true economic effect.

To translate the income statement, one translates all items at either the closing exchange rate or the average exchange rate of the reporting period. The first method is chosen for consistency with the balance-sheet translation. The second method is based on the argument that expenses that have been made gradually over the year should be translated at the average exchange rate. (Curiously, this argument does not seem to apply to expenses that end up capitalized into balance-sheet items.) Profits, the argument goes, are realized gradually over the year, and should be translated at an average rate. This, of course, contradicts the translation of the balance sheet at a single exchange rate.

13.4.4 Accounting Exposure: CFO's Summary

As we have seen, there are various methods for translating a subsidiary's balance sheet into the parent's currency. Many regulating bodies favor the closing-rate method. For example, the U.S. Financial Accounting Standards Board has essentially imposed this method (FASB 52, 1982) for most operations, and allows the old temporal method only for foreign operations closely integrated with the domestic headquarters. Similar rules were issued soon thereafter

---

[6] If the subsidiary's accounts themselves mix historic costs—some of them possibly very dated—with true(r) recent valuations, the result remains hard to interpret. But at least the translation procedure no longer adds to that problem.

in the United Kingdom and Canada. The International Accounting Standards Committee has likewise come out in favor of the closing-rate method (IASC 21, 1983—a text that, unlike FASB 52, is well-written, lucid, and short), again except for closely related operations, where the temporal method is imposed.

However, the IASC can only provide recommendations; it has no statutory power to impose accounting rules anywhere. In continental Europe there is no consensus as to what method is to be followed. For example, in many countries (including, until the early 1990s, Italy and Belgium), consolidation was not mandatory and, therefore, not regulated, while in other countries (including Germany), the obligation to consolidate was not extended to foreign subsidiaries. The EC 7th Directive, passed in 1983 and implemented in most member states by the early 1990s, imposes consolidation but does not prescribe any particular translation method. The only requirement is that the notes to the accounts should disclose the method that was used. Only under IFRS, the IAS rules do apply; but in the EU IFRS is mandatory only for listed companies and financials. Other companies can use traditional local GAAP, which typically leaves considerable discretion.

Given the wide choice that is offered in many cases, one could wonder which method is best. And even where one particular method is imposed, one could consider whether it is useful to adopt a different method for internal reporting purposes. Even more fundamentally, one could ask whether accounting exposure matters at all. Let us briefly dwell on this before we close this chapter.

From the discussion of the various translation methods, we see that the question of which translation method to choose is similar to the issue of whether the firm should use the method of last-in/first-out (LIFO), or first-in/first-out (FIFO), or some average cost, for the purpose of valuing its inventory. One could argue that the accounting method for inventory valuation does not matter, since a shift from, say, LIFO to FIFO will change neither the firm's physical inventory nor its cash flows (except possibly through an effect on taxes). Moreover, one could argue that neither LIFO nor FIFO nor average cost is correct; only replacement value is theoretically sound. In the same vein, one could argue that the choice of the translation method does not affect reality—except possibly through its effect on taxable profit—so that the whole issue is, basically, a nonissue. Furthermore, while in the case of inventory valuation, one could argue that LIFO, being generally closer to replacement value, is the least of all evils, it is not obvious which of the translation methods generally corresponds best to economic value. The whole issue is, perhaps, best settled on the basis of practical arguments. Accounting data are already complicated enough, so that the current-rate method is probably a good choice, given its simplicity and internal consistency.

In table 13.6 we compare economic and accounting exposures. Perusal of the list will reveal that economic and not accounting exposure is the one to watch. But although accounting exposure suffers from the limitations

Table 13.6. Economic versus translation exposure: summary.

1. Economic exposure relates to changes in genuine cash flows and their PV.	Accounting exposure focuses on book values with, usually, no cash-flow repercussions. (One possible exception is through taxes, if translation gains are taxed.)
2. Economic exposure is forward looking: it relates to future cash flows.	Accounting exposure is backward looking: it relates to past decisions on assets and liabilities as recorded on the balance sheet.
3. Economic exposure covers all cash flows, whether or not they can be found in the current financial statements.	Accounting exposure is confined to A&L and P&L items.
4. Economic exposure exists for virtually all firms.	Accounting exposure only exists when there are FC-denominated A&L items or subsidiaries whose accounts need to be consolidated.
5. Economic exposure depends on economic facts, like the contracts the firm signed or the economic environment it operates in.	Accounting exposure depends on the translation method chosen or prescribed, without reference to the economic framework.

described above, accounting data are often the only data that are readily available to a firm. Thus, it is important that treasurers and CFOs be aware of these limitations when using accounting data to make hedging decisions.

*   *   *

Let us recapitulate the results obtained thus far in the current part. We first argued that hedging adds value at least for some firms some of the time. We then discussed exposure, that is, the size of the forward hedge that should be added to minimize uncertainty. But the decision about whether or not to hedge was hitherto discussed in isolation from other risks the firm incurs, many of which are not hedgeable at all. So perhaps the question should be what the total risk of the company is, and by how much this total risk goes down if exchange risk is being hedged. Such a holistic, portfolio view is taken by Value-at-Risk (VaR), the issue of the next chapter.

TEST YOUR UNDERSTANDING

Contractual Exposure

Quiz Questions

True-False Questions

1. Exchange risk describes how volatile a firm's cash flows are with respect to a particular exchange rate.

2. Exchange exposure is a measure of the sensitivity of a firm's cash flows to a change in the spot exchange rate.

3. Hedging exposure means eliminating all risk from a net position in a foreign currency.

4. If you need to hedge a series of exposures with different maturities and you use duration hedging, it is best to hedge the negative exposures separately from the positive exposures.

5. Contractual exposure is the absolute change in the firm's cash flows for a unit change in the spot exchange rate.

6. Operating exposure is the exposure that results when the forward rate is at a discount with respect to the spot rate at the moment you sign a sales or purchase contract.

7. Contractual exposure is additive for one maturity and one currency.

8. Options are undoubtedly the best choice for hedging foreign currency exposure because the possibility of profiting from a favorable change in the exchange rate remains open without the losses from an unfavorable change in the exchange rate.

9. Reverse exchange risk is the risk that arises when you receive a foreign currency A/R that you left unhedged, and the exchange rate at the time of receipt is unexpectedly low.

10. When interest rates are zero, we can aggregate exposures of a given currency across time.

11. If interest rates are positive but certain, and exchange rates are uncertain, we can aggregate the exposure of one currency across time once we take time value into account.

12. By pooling the aggregate exposure of one currency across time, we can ignore time value, because we have arbitraged away interest-rate risk. The only risk that remains is exchange-rate risk. Duration is the average life of a loan.

Matching Questions

Suppose that you are a manager at a British firm, and you are responsible for managing exchange-rate exposure. Determine whether the following statements are related to accounting exposure, operating exposure, or contractual exposure.

1. Your German subsidiary has recently made new investments.

2. You bought a call option on EUR to hedge an EUR accounts payable.

3. You have just sold goods to an American customer. The customer has 90 days to pay in USD.

4. You have just developed an exciting new product. The success of this product depends on how it is priced in the local currencies of your export markets.

5. You have made a bid to deliver your exciting new product to schools in France during the next academic year. You will learn whether or not the bid has been accepted in three months.

6. You sell wool but face potential competition from Australia. If there are no imports, the price of your wool will be GBP 1. However, Australians enter your market once the exchange rate falls below GBP/AUD 2.

Applications

1. The American firm, American African Concepts, has a one-year EUR A/P totaling EUR 100,000 and a one-year Senegalese A/R totaling CFA 120,000,000. The CFA/EUR exchange rate is fixed at 655.957.
   (a) Can AAC offset its EUR A/P with its CFA A/R?
   (b) If so, how much exposure remains?

2. The Dutch manufacturer Cloghopper has the following JPY commitments:
   - A/R of JPY 1,000,000 for 30 days.
   - A/R of JPY 500,000 for 90 days.
   - A sales contract (twelve months) of JPY 30,000,000.
   - A forward sales contract of JPY 500,000 for 90 days.
   - A deposit that at maturity, in three months, pays JPY 500,000.
   - A loan for which Cloghopper will owe JPY 8,000,000 in six months.
   - A/P of JPY 1,000,000 for 30 days.
   - A forward sales contract for JPY 10,000,000 for twelve months.
   - A/P of JPY 3,000,000 for six months.

   (a) What is Cloghopper's net exposure for each maturity?

   (b) How would Cloghopper hedge the exposure for each maturity on the forward market?

   (c) Assume that the interest rate is 5% (compound, per annum) for all maturities and that this rate will remain 5% with certainty for the next twelve months. Also, ignore bid–ask spreads in the money market. How would the company hedge its exposure on the spot market and the JPY money market? Describe all money-market transactions in detail.

   (d) If the interest rate is 5% (compound, per annum) for all maturities and will remain 5% with certainty for the next twelve months, how would the company hedge its exposure on the forward market if only one forward contract is used?

   (e) Assume that Cloghopper prefers to use traded options rather than forward contracts. The option contracts are not divisible, have a life of either 90, 180, 270, or 360 days, and for each maturity the face value of a contract is JPY 1,000,000. How could Cloghopper hedge its exposure? Do the options offer a perfect hedge for each maturity?

   (f) Drop the assumption of a flat and constant term structure. If Cloghopper wants to hedge its exchange-rate exposure using one forward contract and its interest rate exposure using FRA contracts, how would the analysis of parts (c) and (d) be affected? A verbal discussion suffices.

   (g) The term structure is flat right now (at 5% p.a., compound), but is uncertain in the future. Consider the spot hedge of part (c). If, instead of FRAs, duration is used to eliminate the interest-rate risk, how should Cloghopper proceed?

Operating Exposure

Quiz Questions

True–False Questions

1. A firm that has no operations abroad does not face any operating exposure.

2. Only firms with exports, or firms that compete against foreign exporters, face operating exposure.

3. A firm that denominates all of its contracts in home currency, or hedges all of its foreign currency contracts, faces no operating exposure.

4. Almost every firm faces some operating exposure, although some firms are only exposed indirectly (through the country's general economic activity).

5. As large economies have a big impact on world economic activity, companies in such countries tend to be very exposed to exchange rates.

6. Small economies tend to fix their exchange rates relative to the currencies of larger economies, or tend to create currency zones (like the EMS). Therefore, companies in small economies tend to be less exposed to exchange rates.

7. The smaller a country, the more open the economy. Therefore, exposure is relevant for most of the country's firms.

8. Everything else being the same, the larger the monopolistic power of a firm, the smaller its exposure because such a firm has more degrees of freedom in adjusting its marketing policy.

9. Consider an exporting firm that has substantial monopolistic power in its product market. Everything else being the same, the more elastic foreign demand is, the more an exporting firm will profit from a devaluation of its own currency. Similarly, the less elastic foreign demand is, the less an exporting firm will be hurt by an appreciation of its own currency.

10. Most information needed to measure operating exposure can be inferred from the firm's past export and import contracts.

Multiple-Choice Questions

Choose the correct answer(s).

1. In a small, completely open economy:

   (a) PPP holds relative to the surrounding countries.
   (b) A 10% devaluation of the host currency will be offset by a 10% rise in the host country prices.
   (c) The value of a foreign subsidiary, in units of the foreign parent's home currency, is unaffected by exchange-rate changes.
   (d) The real value of a foreign subsidiary to an investor from the host country is unaffected by exchange-rate changes.
   (e) In the absence of contracts with a value fixed in the host currency, the real value of a foreign subsidiary to an investor from the parent's home country is unaffected by exchange-rate changes.
   (f) In the absence of contracts with a value that is fixed in foreign currency, the real value of a foreign subsidiary to an investor from the host country is unaffected by exchange-rate changes.
   (g) There is little or no advantage to having one's own currency: exchange rate policy has virtually no effects.

2. In a completely closed economy:

   (a) PPP holds relative to the surrounding countries.
   (b) A 10% devaluation of the host currency will be offset by a 10% rise in the host country prices.
   (c) The value of a foreign subsidiary, in units of the foreign parent's home currency, is unaffected by exchange-rate changes.
   (d) The real value of a foreign subsidiary to an investor from the host country is unaffected by exchange-rate changes.
   (e) In the absence of contracts with a value fixed in host currency, the real value of a foreign subsidiary to an investor from the parent's home country is unaffected by exchange-rate changes.

(f) In the absence of contracts with a value that is fixed in foreign currency, the real value of a foreign subsidiary to an investor from the host country is unaffected by exchange-rate changes.

(g) There is little or no advantage to having one's own currency: exchange rate policy has virtually no effects.

3. In an economy that is neither perfectly open nor completely closed:

   (a) Consider a company that produces and sells in this economy. Apart from contractual exposure effects, its value in terms of its own (local) currency is positively exposed to the value of other currencies.

   (b) The value of an importing firm located in this economy could either go up or go down when the local currency devalues: the effect depends on such factors as the elasticity of local demand and foreign supply.

   (c) Consider a company that produces and sells in this economy. Apart from contractual exposure effects, its value in terms of a foreign currency is positively exposed to the value of its currency expressed in terms of other currencies.

4. Suppose that the value of the firm, expressed in terms of the owner's currency, is a linear function of the exchange rate up to random noise.

   (a) The firm's exposure is the constant $a_{t,T}$ in $V_T(i) = a_{t,T} + b_{t,T}S_T(i) + e_{t,T}(i)$.

   (b) The exposure is hedged by buying forward $b_{t,T}$ units of foreign currency.

   (c) Hedging means that all risk is eliminated.

5. Suppose that the value of the firm, expressed in terms of the owner's currency, is a nonlinear function of the exchange rate up to random noise. Suppose that you fit a linear regression through this relationship, and you hedge with a forward sale with size equal to the regression coefficient.

   (a) All risk will be eliminated.

   (b) There is remaining risk, but it is entirely independent of the realized value of the exchange rate.

   (c) There is remaining risk, but it is uncorrelated to the realized value of the exchange rate.

   (d) There is no way to further reduce the variance of the firm's hedged value.

   (e) There is no way to further reduce the variance of the firm's hedged value if only exchange rate hedges can be used.

   (f) There is no way to further reduce the variance of the firm's hedged value if only linear exchange rate hedges can be used.

Applications

SynClear, of Seattle, Washington, produces equipment to clean polluted waters. It has a subsidiary in Canada that imports and markets its parent's products. The value of this subsidiary, in terms of CAD, has recently decreased to CAD 5m due to the depreciation of the CAD relative to the USD (from the traditional level of USD/CAD 0.85 to about 0.75). SynClear's analysts argue that the value of the CAD may very well return to its former level if, as seems reasonable, the uncertainty created by Canada's rising government deficit and Quebec's possible secession is resolved. If the CAD recovers, SynClear's products would be less expensive in terms of CAD, and the CAD value of the subsidiary would rise to about 6.5m.

1. From the parent's (USD) perspective, is the exposure of SynClear Canada to the USD/CAD exchange rate positive or negative? Explain the sign of the exposure.

2. Determine the exposure, and verify that the corresponding forward hedge eliminates this exposure. Use a forward rate of USD/CAD 0.80, and USD/CAD 0.75 and 0.85 as the possible future spot rates.

3. SynClear's chairman argues that, as the exposure is positive and the only possible exchange-rate change is an appreciation of the CAD, the only possible change is an increase in the value of the subsidiary. Therefore, he continues, the firm should not hedge: why give away the chance of gain? How do you evaluate this argument?

In the remainder of this series of exercises, SynClear Canada's cash flows and market values are assumed, more realistically, to depend on other factors than just the exchange rate. The Canadian economy can be in a recession, or booming, or somewhere in-between, and the state of the economy is a second determinant of the demand for SynClear's products. The table below summarizes the value of the firm in each state and the joint probability of each state:

State of the economy	Boom	Medium	Recession
$S_T = 0.85$: joint probability	0.075	0.175	0.25
Value$_T$ (USD)	5.25	4.75	4.50
$S_T = 0.75$: joint probability	0.25	0.175	0.075
Value$_T$ (USD)	4.25	3.857	3.50

1. What are the expected cash flows conditional on each value of the exchange rate?

2. Compute the exposure, the optimal forward hedge, and the value of the hedged firm in each state. The forward rate is USD/CAD 0.80.

14

Value-at-Risk: Quantifying Overall Net Market Risks

Not all risks are hedgeable or insurable, and even those that can be covered are often hedged only partially. To get a picture of the risks that remain after hedging (if any), one cannot just stare at the list of exposures: one would like to know how much can be lost if things go wrong. Elementary statistics will have taught you that this question is probably impossible to answer; rather, at best one might be able to say what the worst loss is that occurs with, for instance, 5% probability. For example, a company may calculate that, in 99 days out of 100, the worst loss will be less than 750,000 dollars, and equal or larger than that in only 1 day out of 100.

Elementary statistics will have taught you even more. First, such statements are only possible if we know the distribution of the risks, either in analytic form or via a large sample of past realized values. This means we need to specify not just a distribution, like normality, but also a horizon: the worst possible risk over a one-week interval must be larger than that over a one-day horizon. Second, if risks are imperfectly correlated with each other, it does not do to calculate risks separately per asset class. For example, a Canadian company may calculate that its maximum loss, at 1% probability, on EUR is CAD 200,000 and its 1% worst loss on GBP is 480,000; but this does not mean that, with 99% confidence, the combined worst risk is 680,000: this would be true only if there were an exact positive linear relation between the two exchange rates (perfect positive correlation). In reality, the worst 1% likely loss must be below 680,000 because part of it is diversified away: bad luck with the EUR and GBP are not one and the same event, with one of them occurring if and only if the other occurs. So we need to take into account to what extent pounds and euros move together. Come to think of it, we then also need to know to what extent our currencies move together with our bond portfolio, and our stocks, and our commodity positions.

This, then, is what Value-at-Risk (VaR) calculations are about. The purpose is to come to a maximum loss at a given confidence level, say 99%, for all the market risks present in the company as a whole and for a given time horizon, say one day. This can be done by computing a track record for the current portfolio over the last 500 days and looking at the fifth-worst day. It can also be done analytically, assuming, for example, normality and computing a standard deviation for the daily return. Most companies, if they do these calculations at all, do both. They also look at VaRs for various horizons and confidence levels.

Calculations like this were first made by a group of quants at JPMorgan, London. JPMorgan soon started providing this service to its customers under the copyrighted name RiskMetrics©. A whole cottage industry then sprang up doing similar things, and many banks made their own versions, occasionally even relying on the RiskMetrics© variance–covariance matrix. The whole idea received a big impetus under Basel II, the BIS-sponsored consensus recommendation on how banks should handle market risks.[1] Basel II recommends the use of a formal model or procedure, bought from outside or developed in-house. All banks in the EU and all big listed banks in the United States need to comply with Basel II. Nonfinancials are also often interested. So this chapter tries to explain the logic behind these efforts and, equally importantly, their limitations and pitfalls, some of which became very plain to see during the crisis that developed as of August 2007.

We first review, in section 14.1, the normality-based approach, and immediately continue with a long discussion of the limitations and pitfalls, and the corrections that can be administered (section 14.2). The nonparametric[2] "backtesting" procedure is presented and discussed in section 14.3, along with a second alternative, stress testing, and a third, Monte Carlo and its nonparametric twin, bootstrapping. We conclude in section 14.4 with the usual CFO's summary, followed by an epilogue on the roots of the 2007–8 financial meltdown.

14.1 Risk Budgeting: A Factor-Based, Linear Approach

In normality-based VaR calculations, the hard part is to compute the standard deviation of the value of the portfolio for a given horizon, e.g., one day for very liquid assets and up to two weeks for illiquid assets. Given this, and assuming that the distribution for the portfolio value is Gaussian, one can then compute, for instance, the 99%-worst outcome as 2.33 standard deviations below the expected value.

Example 14.1. Let us consider a portfolio with current value 100m, expected return 10% and standard deviation 30%, both per annum. All assets are liquid, so the horizon is one trading day, i.e., 1/260th year. In principle, we proceed as follows:

---

[1] Basel I, discussed briefly in chapter 5, dealt with credit risks on loans, which in those days were largely nontraded assets. Soon the awareness grew that unhedged interest-rate risks also matter, which then logically led to the idea that all market-value risks should be tracked too.

[2] Nonparametric means that no particular theoretical distribution is postulated.

- The portfolio's expected value tomorrow is $100m \times (1 + \frac{0.10}{260}) = 100.04m$.
- The portfolio's variance is assumed to be linear in the time horizon, so the variance over one day is 1/260th of the per annum variance; the standard deviation over one trading day then equals $100m \times 0.30 \times \sqrt{1/260} = 1.9m$.
- So the maximal loss below the expected value (with 99% confidence) would be calculated as $1.9m \times 2.33 = 4.427m$ over one day.

So the firm needs at least 4.43m in long-term capital. If this is not available, the portfolio risk must be lowered until new equity has been raised.

This, at any rate, is how a theoretical statistician might do it. Bankers and their overseers are more prudent. While 99% confidence sounds quite tough by statistical standards, it is unacceptable to financial risk managers. For one thing, if there were just enough capital to cover this, the firm would see its reserves wiped out in one day 2.5 times a year. So 99.75 or 99.99% certainty looks more like it, implying 2.8 or even 3.8 standard deviations. In addition, there are many reasons for not quite trusting the computed sigma and the normal distribution, as we shall see in this chapter. As a result, risk managers and overseers would actually use a margin of seven standard deviations, and even ten or more if backtesting does not confirm the diagnosis of the parametric approach.

Still, regardless of how many sigmas one uses, the calculation of the standard deviation is key. The first concepts to be mastered are those of factors and exposures.

14.1.1 Factors and Exposures: A Sneak Preview

In portfolio theory, the standard approach is to write a portfolio's value V_p as a sum of the prices of the component assets, weighted by how many of these assets you hold. The change in the value of the portfolio is then easily identified as a capital-weighted sum of the asset returns.

Example 14.2. You buy 1,000 certificates, at 13,000 JPY each, of a Nikkei Index Fund and 30,000 ounces of copper at 600 JPY per troy ounce. Below we show the initial capital amounts per asset and their total, at the original prices and the new prices one month later. The change in value of the portfolio can be computed directly, or indirectly as the sum of capital investment times rate of return:

Asset	(a) $n_{i,t}$	(b) $P_{i,t}$	(c) = (a) × (b) Initial capital	(d) $P_{i,t+1}$	(e) = (a) × (d) Final capital	(e) Return	(c) × (e) Cap × Ret
Nikkei	1,000	13,000	13,000,000	13,650	13,650,000	0.05	650,000
Copper	30,000	600	18,000,000	660	19,800,000	0.10	1,800,000
Total			31,000,000		33,450,000		2,450,000

So we can always write

$$\Delta V_{\mathrm{p}} = \sum_{i=1}^{N} n_{i,t}(P_{i,t+1} - P_{i,t}) = \sum_{i=1}^{N} \underbrace{n_{i,t}P_{i,t}}_{\substack{\text{Initial} \\ \text{capital} \\ \text{invested}}} \underbrace{\frac{P_{i,t+1} - P_{i,t}}{P_{i,t}}}_{\text{Return}}. \tag{14.1}$$

The variance of the total change in value can then be computed as a weighted average of the variances and covariances of the returns. Portfolio theory adopts this approach, as you may know or might discover in chapter 19. In the VaR context this is called the *full-covariance-matrix/normality approach*.

This approach works beautifully on paper, but a big bank or fund or an insurance company typically holds too many different assets to proceed like this. With, say, 20,000 assets you would need at least 20,000 observations to get a nonsingular estimated covariance matrix.[3] This is about 80 years of daily data. But very few assets are 80 years old; and for those that do date back that far, the old information is of doubtful relevance nowadays. Moreover, with daily returns one would miss comovements that are not complete within a 24-hour window. Going for weekly data would require an impossible 400 years of data. Clearly, this is a dead end.

There are two main tricks one typically adopts to reduce the dimension of the problem. First, investments in stocks are assumed to be well-diversified per country, so that one can work with, say, total French stock investments times the return on the French index. This way, one does not need to trace hundreds or thousands of individual shares per country. Second, instead of tracking scores of individual bonds, one tracks a limited number of yields (say, 7, 30, 90, and 180 days, and 1, 2, 3, 4, 5, 7, 10, 20, and 30 years), and one expresses bond-price changes as functions of shifts in interest rates. What is common to the two tricks is that the returns on (probably many) individual assets are viewed as generated by a much smaller number of underlying factors. This is the *factor-covariance/normality approach*.

Going for a database on interest rates means that some of the explanatory variables are no longer asset prices. But we can still get an expression quite close to equation (14.1). The bit of math below may look overly abstract to some readers, but it will be illustrated in later examples. At this stage, the objective is that you (dimly) grasp the idea that a change in the portfolio value can be traced to "factors" in an expression that is no more complicated than equation (14.1).

Let us generally define a *factor* as the unexpected percentage change in one of these X_js (the exchange rate, stock price index, interest rate, or commodity price) that affect the return on an asset. We assume a *short horizon*. Exactly

---

[3] If one has a database on 1,000 assets with 999 observations per asset, then the time series of any individual asset's 999 returns can be expressed as a linear combination of the 999 other assets' returns. So the covariance matrix would become singular. Even with 1,000 observations it would be nearly singular, giving the impression that nearly risk-free portfolios are possible.

at what time a horizon stops being short is of course impossible to say. To mathematicians, anything beyond the "instant," dt, is already long and "finite" (which, here, means "not infinitesimal" rather than "not infinite"). To us, pragmatically, the horizon is short when linear approximations work; and this is as much a matter of curvature in the relation $V(X)$ and volatility of the factors as one of calendar time.

So let us assume a short horizon in that sense. We can then express the change in the capital invested in an asset i, to a first-order approximation, as a total differential,[4] then divide and multiply each term by X_j and V_j, bringing out the factors (percentage changes), the initial capital, and an elasticity or sensitivity. The product of capital and sensitivity is denoted by $E_{i,j}$, asset i's exposure to factor j.[5] Lastly, we sum over the assets to get the portfolio's exposure to the factor:

$$dV_i \approx \sum_{j=1}^{n} \frac{\partial V_i}{\partial X_j} \, dX_j$$

$$= \sum_{j=1}^{n} \underbrace{\overbrace{V_i}^{\text{Init. cap.}} \times \overbrace{\frac{\partial V_i}{\partial X_j} \frac{X_j}{V_i}}^{\substack{\text{Elasticity} \\ \text{w.r.t. factor} \\ j}}}_{\text{Pseudo-capital } E_{i,j}} \times \underbrace{\frac{dX_j}{X_j}}_{j\text{th factor } f_j}$$

$$= \sum_{j=1}^{N} E_{i,j} \, \tilde{f}_j,$$

$$\implies \quad dV_{\mathrm{p}} = \sum_{i=1}^{n} dV_i = \sum_{j=1}^{n} \underbrace{\sum_{i=1}^{N} E_{i,j}}_{=E_{p,j}} \, \tilde{f}_j = \sum_{j=1}^{n} E_{p,j} \, \tilde{f}_j. \tag{14.2}$$

We conclude that the value change of the entire portfolio is still a weighted sum of random variables, except that the random variables are now factors (percentage changes in explanatory variables), and the weights are pseudo-capital amounts—a combination of initial capital values and elasticities or sensitivities to the factor. This remains as simple as the original expression, equation (14.1), except that, crucially, there are far fewer factors than assets. We have *mapped* all returns into a limited number of underlying factors.

One example is a stock option. From chapter 9, in the short run the option behaves like a portfolio of stocks and risk-free assets. So we could say that the relevant factors are the stock factor and an interest rate, and we then use theory to compute the elasticity of the option's price with respect to the stock

---

[4] We use standard calculus. In stochastic calculus a second-order term must be added which is first order in magnitude, but it is nonstochastic, so it adds nothing to the standard deviation.

[5] Note that the dimension of E is units of HC, not units of FC like the exposures we used in chapter 13.

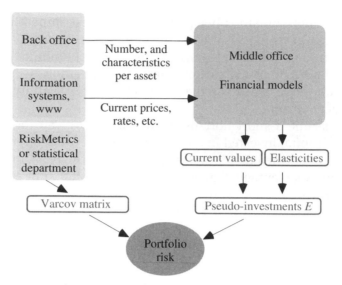

Figure 14.1. The Value-at-Risk process.

price and the interest rate. Next we take the portfolio perspective, and see what other assets also depend on this particular stock price and this particular interest rate. In this way we obtain the dependence of the entire portfolio on each of these factors. The final expression, (14.2), says we can think of the entire portfolio as consisting of pseudo-amounts E_j invested in pseudo-assets with returns $\tilde{f}_j$.

RiskMetrics© provides a covariance matrix for hundreds of these factors, and updates it regularly. The invested amounts are, of course, obtained from the back office and price providers. The elasticities are derived from theory—sometimes quite simple theory. Figure 14.1 summarizes this process.

We now turn to the implementation, starting with the toughest case: bonds.

14.1.2 Domestic Interest Risk

There are many ways in which one can handle bonds. We start by describing one possible approach below, and then sketch a few possible variants. The approach explained first works in three simple steps:

Step 1. Decompose every individual bond or loan into a replicating package of promissory notes.

Example 14.3. A three-year 6% bond paying out 1m with first coupon date in eight months boils down to:

- one promissory note (PN) of HC 60,000, eight months;
- one PN of HC 60,000, twenty months; and
- one PN of HC 1,060,000, thirty-two months.

Step 2. Relate, for each PN, the price change to the change of the corresponding interest rate. Not surprisingly, we discover duration here.[6]

Example 14.4. The promissory note (PN) of HC 60,000, 8 months, goes up or down with the eight-month interest rate. To a first-order approximation, the relation is

$$dV_{8mo} = \frac{\partial 60,000/(1 + R_{8mo})^{0.667}}{\partial R_{8mo}} dR_{8mo}$$

$$= -0.667 \frac{60,000}{(1 + R_{8mo})^{0.667+1}} dR_{8mo}$$

$$= -\underbrace{\frac{0.667}{1 + R_{8mo}}}_{\text{Duration}} \underbrace{\frac{60,000}{(1 + R_{8mo})^{0.667}}}_{\text{Current value } V} dR_{8mo}.$$

This is not yet ready for use as our database does not have the eight-month rate: we just have the six- and nine-month levels. Hence step 3.

Step 3. Express the interest rate and its change as functions of the six- and nine-month interest factors (or whatever the factors are that best resemble what you really want). Here, one can be quite fancy. The simplest approach is to interpolate:

$$R_{8mo} \approx \tfrac{1}{3} R_{6mo} + \tfrac{2}{3} R_{9mo},$$

$$\implies \quad dR_{8mo} \approx \tfrac{1}{3} dR_{6mo} + \tfrac{2}{3} dR_{9mo}$$

$$= \tfrac{1}{3} R_{6mo} \underbrace{\frac{dR_{6mo}}{R_{6mo}}}_{\text{Factor } j} + \tfrac{2}{3} R_{9mo} \underbrace{\frac{dR_{9mo}}{R_{9mo}}}_{\text{Factor } k}.$$

Example 14.5. Let the six- and nine-month compound interest rates be 3 and 3.06% p.a. Then

- the 8-month interest rate is about $R_{8mo} = \tfrac{1}{3} \times 0.03 + \tfrac{2}{3} \times 0.0306 = 0.0304$,
- the asset is worth $60,000/(1 + \tfrac{8}{12} \times 0.0304) = 58808.15$,
- duration is $\tfrac{8}{12}/1.0304 = 0.646\,997\,93$,
- the weights for the factors are $\tfrac{1}{3} \times 0.03 = 0.01$ and $\tfrac{2}{3} \times 0.0306 = 0.0204$.

So we can write

$$dV \approx -0.646\,997\,93 \times 58808.15 \times (0.01 \times f_{6mo} + 0.0204 \times f_{9mo})$$

$$= -380.48 \times f_{6mo} - 776.19 \times f_{9mo}. \tag{14.3}$$

The above gives a feel for what is going on. One can make the interpolation fancier by fitting a curve through the data points, for instance a polynomial

---

[6] You probably saw this in a basic finance course, but here is the definition just in case. The duration, $-\partial V(R)/\partial R \cdot 1/V(R)$, tells you how large, at the margin, the percentage loss is on a bond, per percentage point change in the yield. For a single-cash-flow bond, V equals $(1 + R)^{-n}$, so the derivative equals $-n(1+R)^{-n-1}$, and the duration becomes $n(1+R)^{-n-1}/(1+R)^{-n} = n/(1+R)$.

or something called a spline function or even a formal term-structure model. In the latter case one would work with far fewer factors than, say, thirteen different interest rates to describe the term structure.

DIY Problem 14.1. Look at a 10-year zero-coupon bond with face value 100,000. The per annum compound rate, 10 years, is 5%. Verify the following:

- investment (or capital) is 61,391;
- duration is 9.52;
- pseudo-capital E is $-29,222$.

14.1.3 Equity Investments

For stocks one typically adopts a top-down approach: the investment in country-A stocks is assumed to be a position in the country's index. For domestic stocks, things are then quite easy: the elasticity equals unity, the pseudo-capital is the actual capital, and the factor is the index return:

Domestic stocks:
$$\text{value change} = [\text{current HC value}] \times [\text{return on index}]. \qquad (14.4)$$

For foreign stocks, the approach is not much more complicated. If $\tilde{r}^*$ denotes the return on foreign stocks measured in FC, and $\tilde{s}$ the percentage change in the exchange rate, then the number of FC units we own grows by a factor $(1 + \tilde{r}^*)$ while the value of each currency unit grows by a factor $(1 + \tilde{s})$. So the combined net growth is $(1 + \tilde{r}^*)(1 + \tilde{s}) - 1$, which equals $\tilde{r}^* + \tilde{s} + \tilde{r}^*\tilde{s}$. This is then approximated as $\tilde{r}^* + \tilde{s}$, the sum of the local-currency return and the percentage change in the exchange rate.[7]

Example 14.6. We list a few possible stock returns and exchange-rate changes. Compare the exact and the approximate solutions:

Return on stock, FC	Change in S	Total HC return	1st-order approx.	Approx. error
-0.05	0.005	-0.04525	-0.045	-0.00025
-0.03	0.015	-0.01545	-0.015	-0.00045
-0.01	0.025	0.01475	0.015	-0.00025
0.01	0.025	0.03525	0.035	0.00025
0.03	0.015	0.04545	0.045	0.00045
0.05	0.005	0.05525	0.055	0.00025

---

[7] There is an inconsistency here: there should be a cross-term too, and that cross-term contains a covariance, so by ignoring the cross-term we ignore a covariance in the expected return. This would be crucial in portfolio theory, where expected returns are weighted against risks and where, accordingly, one should never drop covariances in expected returns while simultaneously retaining them in the portfolio-risk calculations. But here the focus is just on risk, where the cross-term has a minimal effect: while the covariance hidden inside a cross-term is nontrivial, covariances between two such cross-terms (or between a cross-term and other returns) are of second order of smalls. See chapter 19 for more on where and why the cross-term matters.

Since the FC stock-index return and the exchange-rate change are both considered to be factors, we notch up two pseudo-investments, one for each of the factors:

Foreign stocks:

$$\text{value change} = [\text{current HC value}] \times [\text{FC return on index}]$$
$$+ [\text{current HC value}] \times [\% \text{ change in } S]. \qquad (14.5)$$

Again, the elasticities are unity here, or the pseudo-capital amounts are genuine amounts.

14.1.4 Foreign Bonds; Currency Forwards and Swaps; Options

How to handle a foreign bond should be obvious, by now. Holding HC 1m worth of foreign bonds means that 1m is exposed to the currency factor, and 1m to the risk about the FC value. The FC value is then treated in the manner we described for domestic bonds: we cut up the bond into as many PNs as there are payments, and assign each of them to nearby benchmark interest factors.

A currency swap is decomposed into one bond held long and another one, in a different currency, held short. Each is then treated as if it were a bond of its own. The forward contract is simpler, as it immediately dissociates into two PNs. An interest swap, or the floating-rate leg of a circus swap, behaves just like a deposit or loan that expires at the first coupon date; so this one is also quite simple to handle.

We already mentioned the solution for an option: it is replicated by a portfolio of some forex PNs—or stocks, for options on equities—and some home-currency PNs. Each is then handled as a position on its own.

14.1.5 Aggregates for the Portfolio as a Whole

The total picture is then obtained by aggregating, factor per factor, all the pseudo-capitals that are exposed to a given factor, across all assets that share that factor. The end result is sometimes called the *risk budget*, a clever term but misleading in the sense that, here, the budget items cannot be added up.

The following simple example should make clear what the risk budget is and what it means.

Example 14.7. Suppose that your portfolio contains just three positions: (i) domestic stock worth HC 150; (ii) foreign stock worth HC 200; and (iii) a 10-year forward sale worth, in PV, HC 100 each leg (that is, zero net value). Let $R_{10} = 5\%$ and $R_{10}^* = 4\%$.

There is exposure to five factors: domestic stock, foreign stock, the exchange rate, the 10-year HC zero-coupon rate, and the 10-year FC zero-coupon rate. The elasticities are arrayed in the table below; the unit and zero cases should be obvious, and the only ones that are mildly difficult are the PNs implicit in the forward contract.

(Do not forget we need a regular elasticity; duration is (minus) a semi-elasticity so we need to multiply by the interest rate and flip the sign.)

			Factors		
Assets	Stock	Stock*	Xrate	R_{10}	R_{10}^*
			Elasticities		
Home stock	1	0	0	0	0
Foreign stock	0	1	1	0	0
Forward sale	0	0	−1	−0.476	0.385
			Pseudo-capital		
Home stock	150	0	0	0	0
Foreign stock	0	200	200	0	0
Forward sale	0	0	−100	−47.6	38.5
Portfolio	150	200	100	−47.6	38.5

To the untrained eye (or the very sleepy reader) this may look like a budget, but the true meaning of the numbers is that they can be used in the equation that links the capitals gain/loss to the factors, as follows:

$$dV_{\mathrm{p}} \approx 150\,\tilde{r}_{\mathrm{stock}} + 200\,\tilde{r}_{\mathrm{stock}*} + 100\frac{\mathrm{d}S}{S} - 47.8\frac{\mathrm{d}R_{10}}{R_{10}} + 38.5\frac{\mathrm{d}R_{10}^*}{R_{10}^*}. \quad (14.6)$$

Clearly, adding up the pseudo-capitals does not make sense because the various $\mathrm{d}X/X$s are all different from each other. Still, the table is a neat summary of the exposures, in a sense. Which brings us to a question that may have been nagging you for some time: aren't these pseudo-capitals just like the exposures as defined before?

DIY Problem 14.2. Q. Look at the "100" that precedes the exchange-rate return, $(\mathrm{d}S)/S$. Isn't this just the familiar currency exposure?

A. No, it has the wrong dimension. Here, the pseudo-capital is a number of ... units while our standard exposure is a number of ... units. So the pseudo-capital is the exposure multiplied by ....

14.2 The Linear/Normal VaR Model: Potential Flaws and Corrections

Once the risk budget is established, things should go smoothly, you might feel: compute the portfolio variance as a double-weighted average of all the variances and covariances; take a square root to get σ_{p}; and multiply by the adequate standard. It is true that all this is not very laborious. The problem is whether the resulting VaR number really measures what it is intended to measure.

In fact, we made a lot of assumptions to get to VaR. None of these was discussed properly, and many were not even made explicit. Yet assumptions are the most crucial part of any piece of math or calculation: barring mathematical or computational mistakes, you get out what you put in. One problem is that almost every conceivable assumption is a simplification of reality—if reality did not need simplification, there would be no models—and therefore a source of errors. Another problem is that we might not even be aware of the assumptions we made in, for instance, the previous section. Here is a list of assumptions or issues that we want to go through:

- Intertemporal independence of changes in the levels of prices or interest rates.
- Constant distribution of percentage changes in the levels of prices or interest rates.
- Constant linear relationships between the changes in the levels of prices or interest rates.
- Linearizations of links between underlying variables and between asset prices and factors.
- Choice of factors: in some respects too many, in other respects too few factors.
- Normality of the portfolio value.
- Liquidity.

14.2.1 A Zero-Drift ("Martingale") Process

Assumption 14.8. *The first postulate regards the expected value: the best predictor of the price or interest rate tomorrow is today's value of the variable, apart from a (negligible) constant long-run multiplicative "drift" or average return in stock prices, etc. Everything is lognormal, here. This assumption creeps in when factors are defined as percentage changes in variables and when there is no allowance for autocorrelation in changes or squared changes.*

Counterexamples. It is not difficult to think of counterexamples: in the medium to long run, there is mean reversion in many factors (interest rates, exchange rates, even stocks). There are also links between the levels of the variables. For instance, interest rates for five and seven years can never wander off very far from each other, but the basic model would ignore this: day-to-day changes are allowed to be correlated, of course, but in a martingale any realized increase in the distance between the two interest rates is assumed to remain uncorrected for ever, on average. One would need an *error-correction term* in the model to capture this mutual attraction in the levels.[8]

---

[8] A simple example would be $dR_7 = \kappa_7(R_5 - R_7 + \alpha) + \epsilon_7$, $0 < \kappa_7 < 1$, and similarly for the five-year rate R_5. α measures the normal difference between seven- and five-year yields. So when the seven-year rate is unusually low relative to the five-year one it tends to go up, and vice versa. κ is called the speed of adjustment, and the term $\kappa_7(R_5 - R_7)$ the error-correction term. More sophisticated models make κ a function of the size of the deviation.

Evaluation. Over a one-day or even one-week horizon, this kind of effect is trivial relative to the standard deviation. It would be a problem for longer horizons, but this is expressly not the purpose of this kind of exercise.

14.2.2 A Constant-Variance Process

Assumption 14.9. *Another feature is that variance is assumed to always be the same, so that the variance over N days is N times the one-day variance. Actually, the assumption extends not just to the variance, but to the entire distribution around the mean: the factors are postulated to follow a constant, one-regime process that can be estimated univariately from the past.*

Counterexamples. Again, it is not difficult to come up with violations:

- Changes in managed exchange rates are a mixture of (i) intra-band-changes (whose distributions depend on the position in the band), and (ii) "jumps" (realignments) whose chances are time-varying. Likewise, stock and bond prices usually behave "normally" but are also subject to jump risk (crashes, notably) with time-varying probabilities. So the distribution is a mixture of at least two more basic ones: a crash and an "everything as usual" distribution.

- While devaluations are distinct events, one could argue that a crash is just a day with a large uncertainty and, therefore, an extreme outcome. There are also extreme positive outcomes, like August 2–3, 1982, in New York or January–February, 1975, in the United Kingdom. So instead of crash days, one could argue in favor of days with unusual variances, and let the variance change all the time and on a continuous scale instead of allowing only two regimes.

By estimating variances from the past without much ado, basic implementations miss all this.

Evaluation. Estimating the standard deviation is the key issue in VaR, so any mistake here is directly relevant. Some days are *ex ante* high-risk days and some days are not. Also, such uncertainty comes in waves, and is also otherwise recognizable *ex ante*. Implicit standard deviations tell us that perceived risk over the next few months on an index can be as low as 10% p.a. (in much of 2005) and as high as 45% (around the LTCM crisis, for instance, and much worse in the fall of 2008). But by using the historic variance we act as if today were an average day, a random drawing from the sample period. In reality, at any moment the investors are well aware whether they are in a high-risk or low-risk day. Yet an "unconditional" variance acts as if the Great Dice-Roller in the Sky still has to decide on today's risk. That's wrong.

Correction step 1. Alternative (a): GARCH models. Generalized autoregressive conditional heteroskedasticity models try to capture two intuitive truths about how to model today's *ex ante* risk (the variance you perceive in the morning about the day to come). One strand is how about today's *ex ante* risk is affected by yesterday's *ex ante* risk, the other about how it is affected by the size of yesterday's *ex post* return:

Autoregressive (AR). When, yesterday morning, we felt that the day would be more risky than an average day, then today we typically feel the same way, albeit less so:

$$\text{var}_t = (1 - \phi)\, \overline{\text{var}} + \phi\, \text{var}_{t-1}, \quad 0 < \phi < 1,$$
$$= \overline{\text{var}} + \phi\, [\text{var}_{t-1} - \overline{\text{var}}]. \tag{14.7}$$

(The second line shows that a fraction ϕ of the unusual *ex ante* risk is carried over—if that wasn't already obvious from the first line.)

Moving average (MA). When, yesterday evening, we saw that the squared realized return was larger than we had expected in the morning, then we increase today's risk to some extent:

$$\text{var}_t = (1 - \psi)\, \text{var}_{t-1} + \psi\, \epsilon_{t-1}^2, \quad \epsilon_{t-1} := r_{t-1} - E_{t-2}(r_{t-1}), \, 0 < \psi < 1,$$
$$= \text{var}_{t-1} + \psi\, [\epsilon_{t-1}^2 - \text{var}_{t-1}], \tag{14.8}$$

which tells us that a fraction ψ of the unexpected jump size is built into the next risk forecast.

The combined AR–MA risk model is called GARCH:[9]

$$\text{var}_t = (1 - \phi - \psi)\, \overline{\text{var}} + \underbrace{\phi\, \text{var}_{t-1}}_{\text{Autoregressive}} + \underbrace{\psi\, \epsilon_{t-1}^2}_{\text{Mov. avg.}}, \quad \text{with} \begin{cases} 0 < \phi < 1, \\ 0 < \psi < 1, \\ 0 < \phi + \psi < 1. \end{cases}$$
$$\tag{14.9}$$

This is the "$(1, 1)$" variant, with one AR and one MA term. There could be risks echoing from earlier days too (the "(p, q)" model that goes back p days for *ex ante* risks and q days for *ex post* squared returns); one could have an asymmetric model where negative and positive surprises act differently, or, more generally, models where the feedback rule changes depending on certain thresholds (TGARCH); one could include other risk drivers into the variance equation; one could let the mean be driven by the variance and vice versa (M-GARCH) or use an exponential to make sure that the computed *ex ante* variance is always positive (E-GARCH), and so on and so forth.

GARCH models sound super, but they turn out to be occasionally hard to estimate,[10] to change disconcertingly depending on the sample, and they are rarely impressively successful out-of-sample. Moreover, they miss all changes

---

[9] For the *petite histoire*: the grandfather version had just AR terms, and was called ARCH. Later, when also MA items were brought in, the word "generalized" was added: GARCH sounds better than ARMACH.

[10] For example, $\phi + \psi$ is often uncannily close to unity, which counterintuitively would imply that variance does not reverse to a long-run mean, on average. The explanation is often that

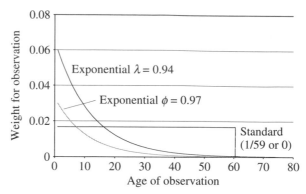

Figure 14.2. Weights in a GARCH(0,1) model *à la* RiskMetrics©.

in risk led by other variables than the factor itself or by Zs not taken into account by the model—let's face it: increases in uncertainty can come from anywhere.

RiskMetrics©, the JPMorgan VaR service, uses a GARCH(0,1) like equation (14.8). It boils down to variance computed with exponentially decaying weights for older and older observations, as can be seen by substituting the similar equation for var_{t-1} into the equation, and then var_{t-2} and so on:

$$\mathrm{var}_t = \underbrace{(1-\psi)^n}_{\to 0} \mathrm{var}_{t-n}$$
$$+ \psi \left[\epsilon_{t-1}^2 + (1-\psi)\epsilon_{t-2}^2 + (1-\psi)^2\epsilon_{t-3}^2 + \cdots + (1-\psi)^{n-1}\epsilon_{t-n}^2 \right].$$
$$(14.10)$$

RiskMetrics© sets $1-\psi$, the weight for the previous variance (see equation (14.8)), equal to 0.94 for daily and 0.97 for monthly. Stated the other way around, the most recent daily observation gets a weight of 0.06 or 0.03. This is much larger than what one does in a regular variance estimate: with a moving sample of sixty observations—and few people would even consider using fewer than that—a regular variance would attach a weight of $1/59 = 0.017$ to the most recent observation. Thus, the GARCH weights of 0.03 (monthly) or 0.06 (daily) are really large. Older observations get less and less weight (figure 14.2), as equation (14.10) shows. Note, in passing, that these RiskMetrics© numbers create more variability in daily variances than in monthly ones, reflecting the fact that waves of uncertainty die out the longer one waits.

Figure 14.3 shows you, in (a)-(c), time-series plots of estimated variances from a GARCH(1,0) model; the data are monthly, and $1-\psi$, the weight for the previous variance, is set equal to 0.97. Any number represents an estimated

---

there are other shifts in the variance that are not modeled well. For instance, a long-run regime change following a change of government policy will be very confusing to a GARCH computer program, which always looks for mean-reverting uncertainty; at the very least one needs to add a dummy for the regime change. In another example, ERM realignments are huge jumps that are *not* followed by similarly jumpy days, so they do not fit the standard GARCH logic and need dummies.

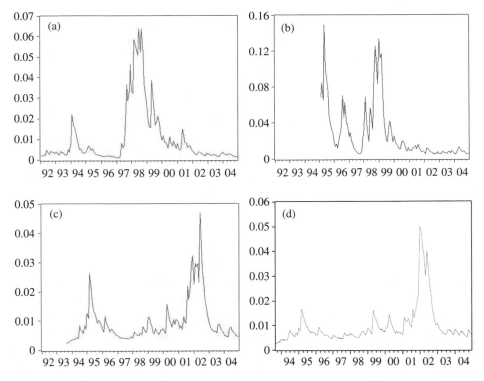

Figure 14.3. The plots show time series of variances, estimated as GARCH(0,1), for (a) Malaysia, (b) Russia, and (c) Argentina, and as TGARCH(1,1) for (d) Argentina. The graphs were kindly provided by Rosanne Vanpée.

one-month variance. Thus, the Russian peak of almost 0.16 means a standard deviation of $\sqrt{0.16} = 0.4$, that is, 40% over the next *month*. For your reference, a p.a. volatility for an OECD market typically is of order 0.2, implying a variance of order $0.2^2 = 0.04$ *per annum* or $0.04/12 = 0.0033$ (0.33%) per month. A line representing a variance of 0.0033 would be hardly visible on the graphs I show.

The countries are Malaysia, Russia, and Argentina. Note how unstable the variance looks, with gigantic peaks: around 1997–99 for Malaysia (the Asian and Russian crises, and President Mahathir's quarrel with Prime Minister Anwar Ibrahim); all of the 1990s for Russia (with the Russian default still looking not quite as bad as the earlier political and monetary uncertainties); and 2001–2 for Argentina (currency and banking crisis plus moratorium early 2002, followed by prolonged political turmoil). If one had just computed a regular variance, weighting all observations equally, one would have forced a flat line through the graph, underestimating the risk in the worst days and vastly overestimating it more recently.

Despite all the apparent sophistication you should not think that GARCH allows you to estimate risk with satisfactory precision. The estimates are very sample and model dependent. To show how different the results can be even if only small changes are administered, look at the output of this model and a variant, a TGARCH(1,1), for Argentina, whose time-series plot is shown in figure 14.3(d). The "T" in TGARCH stands for "threshold," which allows the feedback coefficients to change when the unexpected return exceeds a specified barrier. Here the barrier is set at 0; that is, the impact of a positive ϵ_{t-1} is not necessarily the same as that of a negative ϵ_{t-1}. To the uncritical eye, the graphs look similar. But the 1995 one-month variance is estimated to peak at 2.5% in the first model, against 1.7% in the second. The first model shows two pre-peaks before the 2002 crisis, the second of which is the larger one, while the second shows three pre-peaks, each smaller than the preceding one. The leftmost graph has the variance peak three times during the crisis, with the last one being the worst; no, says the other graph, there were two peaks, of which the first was the most vicious one. And also in 2003–4 there are differences: two mini-blips in the graph on the left, ending at 0.5%, while on the right there are four minor blips, and they end at 0.8%.

Which model is right? The T coefficient in the TGARCH model is significant; but it would be safe to bet that there must be even more complicated models out there that do even better in fitting the sample. And what the out-of-sample performances of the models are is anybody's guess. In short, a healthy dose of skepticism and agnosticism is in order. Try different models, and remember the uncertainties about the final result before making a final choice. An experiment run by the Federal Reserve showed that firms had "wildly different estimates for the risks of similar portfolios of investments. Someone somewhere is investing on flawed assumptions." (*Economist*, September 23, 2006, p. 9.)

Correction step 1. Alternative (b): implicit standard deviations (ISDs). GARCH is just one possible correction to the naive, constant-variance model. With luck, there is a useful and independent alternative. When there are options, we can use the implicit standard deviation, that is, the p.a. σ that makes an observed option price fit the Black–Merton–Scholes model. These are forward-looking rather than backward-looking, and should incorporate all information that the market thinks is relevant. Again, with a bit of luck one can even find a forecast that approximately matches the VaR horizon.

There are still problems. The lognormality assumed by BMS is not empirically correct: the tails are too thick. Probably to a large extent because of this, the ISD differs across options depending on moneyness ("the ISD smirk"): the impact of tail-thickness on the option price depends on whether the in-the-money area is just the tail or also contains more middle-of-the-road outcomes. So we really don't know what we are computing. The consensus is that around-the-money ISDs are most informative. Nowadays, you can find the numbers on the websites of many risk services.

Correction step 2. Covariances. If variances fluctuate, then so must covariances. GARCH models can be extended to cover covariances too, but estimation can be quite difficult unless one severely restricts the models. In the case of exponentially decaying weights, for instance, one can let the covariance depend on just the past cross-products of the two factors that are being studied, and weigh the same way one does for the variances. Another simple solution is to assume constant correlations, and then let the covariances be implied by the (constant) correlation and the (fluctuating) risks: $\text{cov}_t(\tilde{y}, \tilde{x}) = \rho(\tilde{x}, \tilde{y}) \, \text{std}_t(\tilde{x}) \, \text{std}_t(\tilde{y})$. This would also be used to compute changing covariances from ISDs.

Correction step 3. Add factors. Either way, var_t not only enters into the variance–covariance matrix, but should also become a factor: it directly affects option prices, for instance. Then the issue becomes how all these variances, in their role as factors, also covary with each other and how variable the variances are. One solution is to treat the squared factors as factors too, and estimate the variance of each squared change and its covariance with other squared returns. The sensitivity of the variance to the most recent squared return can be read off from equation (14.8), and the sensitivity of an option price can be found in textbooks that drill deeper into such issues; alternatively, type *vega of an option* or *greeks (finance)* into Google or Wikipedia or the like.

For bonds, *convexity*, a familiar concept in the fixed-interest literature, plays a similar role, measuring the price impact of the squared percentage change in the yield, $(\partial^2 V / \partial R^2)/V$.[11] Using second-order approximations is called *delta-gamma* analysis, with delta referring to the first partial derivative to the factor and gamma to the second.

14.2.3 Constant Linear Relationships between Factors

Assumption 14.10. *This assumption is that the interrelations between the factors are linear, and independent of the size of the change or the length of the period. We have not only constant variances but also constant correlations.*

Counterexamples.

- In the case of large changes, especially downward ones, correlations between stock returns turn out to be much larger than usual.

- There is an "intervalling" effect: over longer periods (e.g., from week to week), correlations turn out to be higher than from day to day.

Evaluation. The implications of the crash correlations are obvious: we would be underestimating the risks in crash circumstances—diversification largely breaks down under circumstances when we need it most. So the chance that

---

[11] So instead of using a linear approximation one uses quadratic approximations. In a two-factor case, for example,

$$dV(x, y) = \frac{\partial V}{\partial x}dx + \frac{\partial V}{\partial y}dy + \frac{1}{2}\left\{\frac{\partial^2 V}{\partial dx^2}(dx)^2 + 2\frac{\partial^2 V}{\partial x \partial y}dxdy + \frac{\partial^2 V}{\partial y^2}(dy)^2\right\}.$$

a portfolio has extremely negative returns would be way larger than that suggested by a standard textbook calculation. Consider a stock portfolio. Suppose that, under crash circumstances, all σs double and all ρs go from 0.2 to 0.8. Then the typical covariance goes up by a factor of 16, that is, the portfolio standard deviation roughly quadruples.

The intervalling effect is also active at short horizons. It is mainly a problem for assets that do not trade very often or get little attention from analysts. As a result, they react or seem to react to market-wide news with a lag. Since a basic VaR model only looks at contemporaneous changes, part of the longer-run relation between some variables is underestimated. Even mainstream currencies are subject to this: in the old EMS days, the DEM led the pack, and the other currencies needed up to two days to fully follow its movements against, for example, the USD. As a result, when one looks at two- or three-day holding periods instead of days, covariances go up faster than variances.

Correction. One implication again is that the variance of a market on its own is not constant, but goes up under crash circumstances, when all stocks move far more in unison (see above). But across markets we have the same effect. One solution is to work with two- or three-state correlation models, where the correlation can have, say, three regimes: one for moderate changes, one for big positive returns, and one for big negative ones. The determination of a VaR for the portfolio would become computationally heavier, but that's what computers are for.

There are corrections for the intervalling effect too (see, for example, Scholes and Williams 1977; Dimson 1979): compute covariances between the returns on asset j and k as $\text{cov}(\tilde{r}_j, \tilde{x}_k)$ with $\tilde{x}_k = \sum_{l=-L}^{+L} \tilde{r}_{k,t-l}$.

The above three issues are all related to the distribution of the factors. We now turn to the issue of linearity of the links between assets and factors.

14.2.4 Linearizations in the Mapping from Factors to Returns

Assumption 14.11. *Asset prices are linear in the factors, or, more fairly, nonlinearities are not very relevant.*

Counterexamples. We know that bond prices are nonlinear in the underlying rates and that option premia are nonlinear in the underlying prices.

Evaluation. This is not a problem in the infinitesimally short run ("dt") when changes are small ("dx"). But even with a one-day horizon big changes can occur in reality; a crash may take just a few hours and still be catastrophic. Thus, we again see the issue of crashes or changing variances popping up.

Correction. One alternative is to use stress testing instead of—or next to—VaR (see section 14.3). Within the VaR framework one can improve on the linearity assumption by adopting quadratic approximations, thus taking into account a bond's "convexity" or an option's "gamma" or "vega," and also introduce squared changes as factors, as we have discussed above. But this leads to a doubling in the number of factors, and potentially to degenerate covariance matrices when the number of factors exceeds the number of observations per time series.

The next issue is about the choice of factors.

14.2.5 The Choice of Factors

Standard menu. Standard software uses exchange rates, stock market indices, interest rates (up to thirteen per currency), and commodity prices. The assumption is that this is adequate, but the list is arguably too short in some respects and too long in others:

Counterexamples (1): missing factors. Volatility is a fluctuating parameter, not the constant one assumed in the basic models, but this factor is missing from the basic list. Idiosyncratic risk is also assumed to be absent, even though some portfolios may be far from perfectly diversified.

Counterexamples (2): excessive factors. It is hard to believe one needs as many as thirteen numbers to describe the term structure and its changes. Three factors already do a great job: shifts (up–down), slope (long versus short maturities), and curvature.

Corrective action. GARCH variances and quadratic approximations have already been discussed in connection with the distribution of the factors and their link to asset prices, but this would not suffice. For options, notably, the volatility should be treated as a factor on its own. For idiosyncratic risk in stock portfolios, one occasionally adds the average unexplained variance from the market model regression, divided by the number of assets in the portfolio, a correction that is OK for a randomly selected, equally weighted portfolio, as you will be asked to show yourself. To have a more parsimonious term-structure representation, one could adopt a formal closed-form model or even a purely empirics-driven curve.

> **DIY Problem 14.3.** Let us agree that $\tilde{r}_m$ denotes the stock market return, $\tilde{\epsilon}_j$ the idiosyncratic variance of stock j (as in $\tilde{r}_j = \alpha_j + \beta_j \tilde{r}_m + \tilde{\epsilon}_j$), and $\overline{\text{var}}$ an average across asset j. To get a portfolio variance $\text{var}(\tilde{r}_m) + \overline{\text{var}}(\tilde{\epsilon})/n$, what assumptions need to be made?
>
> - Consider an equally weighted portfolio of n assets?
> - Asset weights are not correlated with betas or idiosyncratic variances?
> - The "error" returns $\tilde{\epsilon}_j$ are idiosyncratic, i.e., uncorrelated across assets?
> - All asset betas are unity?
> - The portfolio has a unit beta?

(The above rule was once proposed by some U.K. academics, during Basel II hearings, as a simple correction to VaR: use $\sigma = \sigma_m\sqrt{1 + \zeta/n}$ with $\zeta =$

$\overline{\mathrm{var}}(\tilde{\epsilon})/\mathrm{var}(\tilde{r}_{\mathrm{m}})$. The proposal was voted down because a square root was deemed to be too complicated. This, admittedly, was a long time ago.)

14.2.6 Normality of Changes in the Portfolio Value

Assumption 14.12. *As we saw in the introductory example, the basic logic assumes that returns are normal. A sufficient condition for this is that each and every factor is normally distributed, and linearly related to the other factors via a network of regressions (multivariate normality). An alternative justification is that the portfolio is well-diversified, so that some central limit theorem (CLT) effect is at work.*

Counterexamples. Individual asset return distributions are too peaked in the center and too fat in the tails to be normal, in reality, so we can forget the first way to get Gaussian portfolio returns.

Example 14.13. "According to Goldman Sachs, the latest jump in the Vix (a measure of stockmarket volatility) took it eight standard deviations from its average. If conventional models are correct, such an event should not have happened in the history of the known universe. Then again, the move in energy prices that caused the collapse last year of Amaranth, the hedge fund, was a nine standard-deviation event. Perhaps modellers do not know the universe as well as they would like to think." (*Economist*, March 1, 2007.)[12]

Modelers as referred to in the above quote do not really exist: no sane risk manager believes in Gaussian distributions for speculative assets individually. The bottom line is that we cannot assume normality for individuals as a basis for normality for the portfolio as a whole. As Jorion (2003, p. 361) writes, "Every financial market experiences one or more daily price moves of 4 standard deviations or more each year. And in any year, there is usually at least one market that has a daily move greater than 10 standard deviations." During the early stages of the subprime crisis, Goldman Sachs suffered losses that, according to their computers, should occur only once every 100,000 years, 25 standard deviations down (*Economist*, August 18, 2007, pp. 9 and 60). In a talk held in Leuven in November 2008, my colleague Paul De Grauwe calculated that many of the S&P daily returns in October 2008 should not have happened in trillions, quadrillions, or even quintillions of years if one takes the unconditional standard deviation as the norm. Obviously, the conclusion is that one should *not* take the unconditional risk as the basis for risk management.

What about the CLT route? The CLT says that "the distribution of a (roughly equally weighted) average of returns on individual assets, randomly and independently drawn from a constant distribution, converges to a normal if the

---

[12] The energy price jump referred to was in natural-gas futures, August 2006. The volatility index (Vix) hike followed the Shanghai crash of March 2007.

number of assets becomes very large. So one should be cautious of using this logic for cases where the CLT story rings false:

- portfolios with few assets, especially assets that themselves have far-from-normal distributions, like options (except in the hyper-short run),
- specialized portfolios with highly correlated assets, or
- crash scenarios, when correlations go through the roof.

There is a more fundamental problem: the central limit theorem holds for the *center* of the distribution,[13] but we are interested in the tails—the extreme outcomes. For the tails, other limits are possible beside the exponential (e.g., Gaussian): tails may converge to a high-power law with thick tails, a bit like a low-df Student *t* distribution.

Evaluation. Often, distributions are fatter-tailed than the Gaussian. Extreme events are therefore more probable than the Gaussian law would predict.

Corrective action. Modeling the distribution more correctly is usually a slow and painful solution. One can work with thick-tailed distributions like a Student *t* with four to seven degrees of freedom, and abandon the analytical approach and work with Monte Carlo instead, or with bootstrapping—see below. Another (quite common and sensible) reaction is to set VaR at two or three times the level it would have been in a perfectly Gaussian world. While this would be a bit of an overkill reaction if the only problem were fat tails, the extra margin is also intended to cover crashes or surges in volatility (if this can be distinguished from fat tails at all) and, especially, liquidity issues. To which we now turn.

14.2.7 All Assets Can Be Liquidated in One Day

Assumption 14.14. *By calculating the maximum one-day loss, there is an assumption that if all equity gets eaten up in 24 hours one can stop the losses and sell out immediately, without extra price pressure.*

Evaluation. For portfolios that are tiny relative to the market as a whole this is no problem, in principle, but it is hard to imagine that every single position in stocks or bonds is tiny, relative to the daily turnover. In addition, under panic circumstances many players want to sell, so what matters is the aggregate amount of selling pressure, not the size of the individual portfolio. There can be problems at the buy side too: OTC-markets (swaps, forward, many options) can "dry up" in periods of high uncertainty because all major players have hit their credit limits. During the LTCM panic many hedge funds were scared into unwinding very similar currency positions all at once and made the dollar fall against the yen by a full percentage in a few hours and by a whopping 13% in

---

[13] Ever wondered why it is called the *central* limit theorem?

three days.[14] The same scenario was replayed at the onset of the "subprime" crisis: in August 2007, the unwinding of massive JPY/NZD carry trades sent the yen up by 10% against the New Zealand dollar in one week.

Even if the problem is largely confined to one player, as in the LTCM case, there can be substantial price pressure; that, at least, was the view of Federal Reserve Chairman Alan Greenspan when he bullied a few large banks into arranging a credit line which gave LTCM time to liquidate in a matter of months rather than days. Liquidating Leeson's portfolio of futures (panel 6.1 in chapter 6) came at a cost of over 50 million pounds. It is not publicly known, at the time of writing, how much of Kerviel's 5b loss (see panel 6.1) represents price pressure following speed liquidation, but Kerviel's colleagues were saying that liquidation stood for two thirds of the overall loss. The hasty super-sale is even rumored to have contributed greatly to the crashing markets in Asia and Europe which, in turn, convinced Bernanke, at the Federal Reserve, to lower USD interest rates by an uncommonly large 0.75% even though the U.S. stock market was closed that day.

Evaluation. This is generally taken to be a serious problem. If liquidation takes days, VaR should be doubled even if there is no price pressure. But nobody knows well what the extra contribution of price pressure would be in a massive crash. Thin markets and price pressure are hard to separate, conceptually, anyway. In fact, the whole 2007–8 meltdown illustrates how some assets cannot be liquidated at all at any reasonable price, not even in ten or twenty days, when there is extreme distrust. CDO markets simply disappeared, as described in the epilogue to this chapter (section 14.5).

Corrective action. The least one can do is to widen the horizon to a few days or a week for less liquid assets, and correspondingly increase the maximum losses for this class. The Basel rule, binding for banks (or at least the big international banks, in the United States), is to set the horizon to ten trading days, and nonfinancials go to up to one month.

How does one implement this? One simple way is to first estimate a daily VaR and then extrapolate it to a d-day VaR by multiplying it by $\sqrt{d}$. The logic is impeccable given the assumptions: a two-day return is (close to) the sum of two one-day returns, so when returns are i.i.d., a two-day variance is twice a one-day variance. So a two-day standard deviation is $\sqrt{2}$ times a one-day standard deviation, and the situation is similar for VaR.

---

[14] The yen reaction was due to the unwinding of the "carry trade" by hedge funds. A carry trade, remember, consists of borrowing at low interest rates (mostly yen, nowadays) and investing in high-rate currencies. As long as the yen does not appreciate (or, in accounting terms, as long as one can keep the yen debt at historic values), this produces a profit. The yen initially falls if enough players adopt this strategy: they all sell borrowed yen and buy, say, dollars. When a scare prompts the investors to rush for the exit, they all want to buy yen to pay off (or at least close out) their loans, which sends the yen through the roof. On days like this, the fabulous depth of currency markets is indeed a fable.

Of course, this impeccable logic becomes rather peccable once we realize that returns are autocorrelated, and their variances too. An alternative way to get a ten-day VaR would then be to abandon one-day data altogether and work with two-week returns. The obvious cost is that one has far fewer observations, and one may have to get very ancient data to avoid spurious nonsingularity in the variance–covariance matrix. For example, for 500 factors one needs substantially more than 500 observations, so substantially more than 10 years of two-weekly returns.

Either way, a complementary reaction is to simply set VaR at many more σs than the statistician would have done.

14.2.8 Parametric VaR: Summing Up

The strong point of this approach is that it takes an overall point of view and tells us what the maximum loss would be, on a not unusual day, at some given confidence level. But there are limitations.

First, the notion of "maximum loss on a regular day" is somewhat self-contradictory: on regular days, by definition, nothing major happens. Actually, this is just sloppy wording: in reality we would compute a VaR for a day with average risk, and then add a bit of a wet-finger correction for the fact that bad days are not average days. Also, you should abandon any hope that percentiles can be determined with any precision. At this point it should be obvious, I hope, that VaR is too much of an art to expect real scientific precision.

It should also be obvious, from the discussion above, that VaR can be a guide in, at most, the short run. For long horizons, indeed, nonlinearities can become quite important. For the same reason, VaR holds only for small changes in the factors. Problems are not confined to the modeling of $dV(f)$: the distribution of the factors is also a minefield. Densities are thick-tailed, risks change over time with a large random element in the time series process, and correlations change depending on what is going on.

Given these problems, you should understand why VaR is typically set at say nine σs rather than three. Overseers even insist on increasing the level even more if the parametric VaR does not agree with the backtesting results, to which we now turn.

14.3 Historical Backtesting, Bootstrapping, Monte Carlo, and Stress Testing

14.3.1 Backtesting

The idea behind *historical backtesting* is simple and sound: compute, for every day in the last two or four years, what the value would have been of the current portfolio, and then figure out the histogram of the percentage changes. The selected percentile change can then be applied to the current portfolio.

Example 14.15. Suppose you have a history of 500 daily values for the current portfolio. The first percentile then would be the fifth worst realized return. If this is −7.5% and the portfolio is currently valued at 100m, VaR would be set at 7.5m.

This has some strong aspects. It avoids all distributional restrictions or linear approximations: one simply works with the real-world pricing mechanism and the real-world distribution, including thick tails and changes in risks or correlations. Second, it is not necessarily top-down: in principle one can track the exact stock or bond portfolio rather than the index. Third, it avoids approximations: for every day you can compute the full model price of an option or a bond ("full valuation"), instead of relying on a first- or second-order approximation for the change in the price of the option or bond ("local valuation").

But there are weaknesses too. Upon reflection, one is not really working with the real-world distribution but with a relatively small sample taken from it. At the time of writing, there has not been any major crash recently or an LTCM-type scare in the last few years; in fact, implicit standard deviations have recently been uncannily low. Can we really use this as the standard?

Second, what we are now trying to construct is an unconditional distribution—some kind of average of high- and medium- and low-risk days, all thoroughly mixed together. That would be fine if we had no idea whether today is viewed as high- or medium- or low-risk; but in reality we do know that. That is, we really need a conditional distribution for today, not a "marginal" one for an average day randomly sampled from the past n years.

There is more. A 99% VaR is not good enough, as we saw, so one would like to get to, say, 99.75%, which is the worst loss out of 400 days or the second worst out of 800 days. But tails of distributions are hard to estimate because extreme events are thin on the ground. Ask yourself the question what would happen if you wanted an nth percentile. For $n = 50$, that is, if you wanted the median, not a lot would change if the crucial observation had been absent, or replaced by, say, the nearest (just above or below the candidate median, that is): in the middle of the distribution, observations are thick and close to each other. But in the tails, coincidences have a bigger impact. Without any distributional assumptions, one simply cannot precisely estimate a percentile unless the sample is huge.

The statistician's knee-jerk reaction to this objection would, of course, be to increase the sample size: go back twenty years rather than two or four. But in doing so one might hit data problems for individual stocks, where the birth-, death-, and takeover-rates are quite high. For bonds, the availability of, for instance, the longest-duration data is patchy because borrowers stop placing very long-term paper when rates are higher and vice versa. More philosophically, one can question the relevance of old data. For instance, how informative are yield-change data from the days when rates were 12% rather than 4%? How relevant are DEM fluctuations when its successor is a currency for twelve countries? As another example, overseers have learned from the 1987 crash, the LTCM scare, the Barings fraud case, and the 1999 accounting scandals; and investors should have learned, for a time, from the dotcom boom and bust—so should we still take these events into account in our plans for the future? Cynics would reply that maybe we did learn to partly deal with some events, but there are always new catastrophes that we have no experience with. Most catastrophes were never thought of beforehand.

Given that old data are probably not very useful and samples are therefore small, we cannot reliably estimate a 99.99% VaR. But we can still use backtesting for less extreme hurdles than a 99.99% reliable worst case. That is, one can test whether the parametric VaR for 5, 2.5, 1, and perhaps even 0.5% are in reasonable agreement with the sample. Thus, historical backtesting is often used as a complement to parametric VaR; overseers want to test the quality of the analytical VaR numbers against old data, for example. If the supposed 5% confidence bound gets violated substantially more often than 25 times out of 500 past daily realizations, the calculated VaR should be increased. Note that there is again a statistical problem here: with low-probability events in relatively small samples, when does one start panicking? If the chance of falling below a certain critical return really is 5%, one expects, in 500 trials, 25 worse days, but this number could easily be as high as 28, at the 95% confidence level.

DIY Problem 14.4. Explain the statement to your little brother: what *exactly* does that mean? While you're at it, explain to yourself how this number is calculated.

So, if in a backtest you observe twenty-eight losses worse than the predicted level, the problem is, is the model wrong or were you just unlucky? (The same question arises as well, of course, at twenty-seven and twenty-six.) How large should a sample be to narrow down the confidence interval from ±3 to ±1? The standard deviation would have to shrink by a factor of 3, so the number of observations should go up by a factor of 9, to eighteen years of data. This would surely raise the problem of data completeness and relevance we just brought up.

A last trick that is being used to—more or less—get around the problem of thinness in the tails is to estimate some percentiles that are not too far into the tails, say 1, 2.5, or 5% quantiles, and then extrapolate to more extreme cases. This, strictly speaking, requires some knowledge of the distribution, so in practice this becomes a kind of wet-finger exercise: just double or triple a 99% VaR instead of going for an estimate of a 99.75% or 99.90% VaR.

14.3.2 Bootstrapping and Monte Carlo Simulation

In a *bootstrapping* exercise, one samples from the sample. Suppose, for instance, that you have a time series of 500 daily returns. Instead of just considering this single motion picture of the past, you can sample, 500 times, a randomly chosen return from this series. In this way you have constructed one possible alternative course of events. The quantile(s) will be different from the original (unless you foolishly sample "without replacement"). In fact, nothing stops you from repeating the entire exercise 1,000 times; thus, you would have 1,000 numbers for each quantile. This would give you a feel for how much the VaR can vary just because of pure sampling coincidences.

The procedure can also be used to construct ten-day VaRs. From one two-year time series one can extract 52 nonoverlapping two-week returns, which just allows you to estimate, imprecisely, the 98th percentile as "probably between the worst and the second-worst return." It would even be utterly impossible to estimate a 99th or 99.5th percentile. But if one bootstraps, one can construct 520 possible 10-day sums of returns by sampling 5,200 times a daily return from the original 500 data and then computing 520 different 10-day sums.

This has all the advantages of historic backtesting, plus the boon that there is some experimentation with how different things could have been. But one should not overestimate the strong points. One does have more observations, but the original sample still provides a limited view of the total population: the future will be sampled from the true population distribution, not from the samples of past realizations. If the recent past contains no genuine crash, for example, bootstrapping will not generate you a crash. You should also realize that if one aggregates to 10-day returns by summing randomly sampled daily returns, one destroys the autocorrelation in the true returns and in the true squared returns—that is, one underestimates the variance of what can happen over 10 days. To preserve most of the waves in returns and risks one could, instead, randomly sample one of the 490 possible starting days in the original sample and pick the return from the 10-day period that follows. Such a *"block" bootstrap* does use far more information than the original 52 nonoverlapping observations and it does preserve the intertemporal structure, but at the cost of generating dependencies across returns because of the overlap between the episodes.

Monte Carlo simulation is a halfway house, mixing ideas used in bootstrapping with those from parametric VaR. First one chooses a distribution for returns, say a Student *t* for stocks and gamma for yields. One then gives each distribution the mean and the variance estimated as for parametric VaR, plus the autocorrelation and the GARCH effects if the VaR horizon exceeds the holding period in the data, plus the changing correlations for big moves in the market, and so on. In step 3, lastly, one estimates what could happen over, say, 10 days by generating returns not by sampling from the past but from the theoretical price-generating model. One can sample as often as one wants without creating dependencies. And one can create a crash, to some extent, even if the past had no such big event. Indeed, if there was no really bad episode in the sample, then the standard deviation (SD) computed from the past will probably underestimate the true risk, but the Monte Carlo computer program will still be generating the occasional 4SD return and, if you consider enough markets, even the odd 10SD one. Finally, when the asset is not the factor one can compute a full model price, taking into account all the nonlinearities one wants.

There must be some snag, you probably feel, otherwise the earlier alternatives would not even have been mentioned. Well, a truly large Monte Carlo takes a lot of time. It also forces you to make a lot of modeling choices—coming up with a distribution, modeling all the links across assets and over time—instead of just "letting the data speak." One never knows whether one made the right assumptions; in fact, the cure might be worse than the disease.

14.3.3 Stress Testing

Stress testing provides a last complement to the original VaR approach. One looks at some terrible days in the past, and computes how the portfolio would have done. In addition, one dreams up a few conceivable new catastrophe scenarios—for instance, China being tired of its ever-growing USD balances and selling off its bonds, sending the dollar down and dollar interest rates through the roof, thus tipping the financial markets into a tailspin; or a catastrophic bird-flu pandemic—you name it. The scenario could be that all stock markets are 20% down—too optimistic, the 2008 experience taught us—yields 3% up, index volatilities at 45%, and so on.

Example 14.16. Goldman Sachs, according to a 2007 review by Moody's, first replay the 1998 LTCM bond-market meltdown. The "supercrash" test for equities is a 50% fall in all markets. The "Armageddon" test assumes that, in each market, the worst outcomes over the last 30 years pop up again—simultaneously. (*Economist*, May 19, 2007, special report, p. 26.)

On the plus side, here you again compute exact option premia and bond prices for the scenario, so you do take into account nonlinearities. By studying worst-case scenarios you also correct for the fact that the two years may have been strangely uneventful, as they were, recently, except for the mild Shanghai crash that was immediately undone and forgotten. You can build-in qualitative insights like "a crash hits all stocks in very similar ways." But one could again question the relevance of old catastrophes ("we have learnt to prevent this and/or deal with this"). And "new" catastrophes are hard to think of. The above China story sounds very lame to me—especially if one remembers how surprising the old catastrophes were, if only because they arose from combinations of events. While it is already difficult to answer what the worst possible scenario is for each factor separately, the issue of naming the worst possible combinations of factors one could imagine is even thornier. Dreaming up combinations of unrelated catastrophes is not difficult, but neither is it convincing: a bird-flu pandemic may cause panic among the yen-carry-traders but it is unlikely that, simultaneously, the earth shakes wildly along the entire U.S. West coast and New York gets attacked by whales. It is the related and logical combinations that one should see coming in advance. One usually does not.

Example 14.17. The 1992 EMS crisis started with, of all things, the Finnish mark—not even an EMS member—dropping through its self-declared floor. Speculators, aghast that central banks' promises were worth less than they had thought, then started dumping their Swedish crowns, also a currency that was unilaterally fixed to the ECU. The Bank of Sweden raised short-term interest rates to a staggering 600 percent p.a. but then caved in. By noon, the GBP had also sunk below its EMS floor, with the Bank of England frantically denying a devaluation but Her Majesty's government not calling for the massive help from the BuBa it could have asked for—surprising behavior for a six-month ERM member. The pound then dropped out of the system, along with the lira (which did later rejoin). In the afternoon the Portuguese escudo and the Spanish peseta devalued, and Dublin reinstated strict capital controls. The EMS was in fact in tatters in a matter of five hours, two years after the eu(ro)phoria following the Maastricht Treaty.

So one never quite knows whether the stress tests are tough enough. For example, in October 2007, well into the "subprime" crisis, the United Kingdom overseer, the Financial Services Authority (FSA), found that Northern Rock[15] had not gone far enough in its stress tests—although the FSA simultaneously allowed the distressed bank to pay out a higher dividend (*Economist*, October 20, 2007, p. 86). The subsequent development of the crisis definitely illustrates that, with hindsight, nobody had gone far enough: events were more extreme and more unexpected in nature than anybody had thought possible, early 2007. At that time, people were still mumbling about flu scenarios, remember?

14.4 CFO's Summary

The official purpose of VaR computations is to find out how much can be lost in one day (or more, for less liquid assets) in, say, a 99.5%-worst case. One can do this parametrically, assuming normality and trying to get a good picture of the standard deviation of the entire portfolio. To that end one usually traces back changes in asset values to a few hundred underlying factors, and one then computes the total risk from the variance–covariance matrix of the factors and, of course, the exposures to each of the factors. The *mapping* works with *local valuation*, i.e., using a (linear or quadratic) approximation for the price changes implied by the factors. Alternatively, one can use the mapping (or risk budget) as the basis for a gigantic *Monte Carlo* exercise, where distributions can be much more complicated than the multivariate normal implied by the original model and where one can use *full valuation* instead of approximations. If the simulations use realized past data instead of computer-generated returns, the procedure is called *bootstrapping.* Using just one time series of realized past returns to simulate portfolio returns is

---

[15] The English bank that suffered a run in 2007 and was taken over, in the end, by the government. See chapter 2, especially figure 2.3.

called *backtesting*. Either can be complemented by *stress testing*, i.e., valuation under nightmare scenarios, either historical or dreamt-up by the VaR band.

Following up VaR (or the sigma that underlies it) over time does give a good idea about changes of short-term risk under normal circumstances. But the number could be misleading about worst possible losses (i) for longer horizons, (ii) for large changes in individual factors, (iii) under crash circumstances, and (iv) when there are sudden shifts in risks. Backtesting may provide additional information, either as a way to get a VaR number or as a way to verify parametric VaR calculations; but with reasonably recent data there is inevitably a zone of possible test outcomes where one is not sure whether the parametric calculations are to be rejected or not. In stress testing, one never knows quite what is the worst possible scenario for each factor separately, let alone what is the worst joint outcome. In fact, none of the approaches we discussed can answer that question.

In short, if we are realistic, we will admit that VaR for a given percentage cannot be determined with any decent precision. Basel II accordingly abandons the objective of precision and goes for a required level of capital as follows:

- assume 10 days for liquidation;
- start from 99% VaR numbers but multiply them by three or more (see below);
- use at least one year of daily data;
- update VaR at least every quarter.

The formula for the *market-risk charge* (MRC) would then be

$$MRC_t = \text{Max}\left(k \sum_{l=1}^{60} \frac{\text{VaR}_{t-l}}{60}, \text{VaR}_{t-1}\right) + SRC_t. \tag{14.11}$$

This tells you to take either yesterday's 99% VaR or k times the moving average 99% VaR over the last 60 days, whichever is the highest. The number k should be at least 3, but could be increased by a *plus-factor* of at least 1 if there is no agreement between backtests and a priori VaR computations. In practice this usually means that you take three or four times the moving-average VaR: today's VaR is rarely higher than that unless you massively rejig the portfolio. The ten-day VaR is $\sqrt{10}(= 3.16)$ times the one-day VaR. VaR can be computed from a program developed by a reputed service provider or developed in-house, provided that it satisfies the overseers as sufficiently professional. The specific risk charge (SRC) is an add-on for asset-specific risks in the case of underdiversification. For instance, if you hold lots of shares and bonds issued by a big reinsurer, then a bad earthquake will affect both your share and bond portfolios in a way that is not captured by calculations that assume diversified bond and stock positions. (SRC is a minefield on its own.) All this is rather ad hoc, and you probably understand that choices like that must be made anyhow. The purpose is not really to set a well-defined VaR; rather, the rule stipulates a

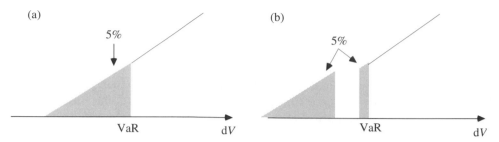

Figure 14.4. Two different risks with the same VaR measure.

minimum required level of equity plus long-term debt; and erring on the safe side is better than the other way around.

More fundamentally, however, one could question the whole idea of just considering a particular percentile. For instance, one might instead want to look at the expected loss given that one is in a bottom $n\%$ outcome, and to do this for many more values than just the fifth percentile. Two portfolios can have the same percentile but a very different distribution below that VaR number, as figure 14.4 shows. In (a) there is a stylized left tail of a distribution; the shaded area measures 0.05, so the fifth percentile is where the shaded area ends, at the right. In (b) we have exactly the same VaR, but the losses once one is below VaR can be much worse. A risk manager who just watches the VaR number would not notice, however. A related issue is the risk of "gaming," that is, exploiting the loopholes in a formal criterion. For example, if the 0.25% VaR is 10m, a perfidious trader might write a digital option saying that if his portfolio drops by 10.5m or more, he will pay out 5m. This type of contract would generate the change in the tail shown in the picture. If the only rule were the VaR, then this contract would be formally acceptable: it does not worsen the 0.25% VaR, it only aggravates events that have even lower probabilities.

A complement to VaR would accordingly be to also estimate the *conditional tail expectation*, that is, the expected payoff given that the return is among the $n\%$ worst. This is sometimes called conditional VaR (CVaR)—a bit of a misnomer since VaR is a single percentile and CVaR an expectation not a conditional percentile (whatever that is); other names are *expected shortfall* (really) or, better, *expected tail loss*. In principle, CVaR is computed from a list of all $n\%$ worst events, times their probability, rescaled by the chance that you get into the $n\%$ worst-event zone:

$$\mathrm{E}(\tilde{x} \mid x < \mathrm{VaR}(n)) = \frac{\int_{-\infty}^{\mathrm{VaR}(n)} x f(x)\, \mathrm{d}x}{\int_{-\infty}^{\mathrm{VaR}(n)} f(x)\, \mathrm{d}x}. \tag{14.12}$$

Conceptually this makes a lot of sense, but it will be clear that all practical problems that we encountered for VaR are present here too, with a vengeance.

The conclusion surely is VaR is no panacea. It is best calculated in various ways, and backtesting should be used not only to get one independent estimate for VaR and as a test of the parametric one, but also to provide information about the entire tail, with stress tests added to make one remember how much worse things could be. In the end, however, one will always need judgement on how much capital should be available as a cushion against market risks. Fortunately, many banks now take pride in their generous "equity" base, and flaunt it in their ads; this is an improvement relative to the beginning of the Basel discussions, when safety was still said to be expensive and a distraction thought up by bureaucrats.

For completeness, you might want to know that VaR and Basel II have also embraced the old Basel I issue, credit risk. This is like market risk except that loan values can only jump between full nominal value and zero; one estimates (co)variances for such events and adds these risks to market risk ("CreditMetrics"). This not being anywhere near a truly international issue, we just leave it at that.

Our discussion of Basel II has focused on VaR, which is the prescribed solution for stocks and other traded assets. For (nontraded) bank loans, the banks should get a rating from a rating agency, or develop their own in-house rating model, Basel says. But overseers do not necessarily like what they hear. Europe has agreed, by and large: all banks should have fully implemented it during the course of 2007–8. Still, the safety cushion is not allowed to fall too fast, at least over the first three years. Hong Kong similarly started in 2008. But the United States is lukewarm: only a few dozen big banks have to adopt Basel II, starting in 2009; their safety cushions are not allowed to fall by more than 15% over three years below the old Basel I levels; and another U.S. rule, the "leverage ratio," remains in place: a lender's safety cushion must amount to at least 3% of its total lending.

The most fundamental problem with the entire Basel approach, however, is that it considers a single bank that gets into trouble by an unusual return on an unusual portfolio. As we have now seen, it does not really help when many big players get into trouble with similar portfolios, or when all markets seem to crash simultaneously. Anyway, at the time, such a scenario was viewed as utterly unthinkable. My view on how this nevertheless came to happen is presented in the epilogue below.

Risk does not stop at price risks and default risks. There are also operational uncertainties, where calamities might occur. In September–October 2007, the U.S. government experimented with a simulated pandemic. Every week for three weeks in a row, 2,725 financial institutions were told by the government which of their employees were to stay home "because of the flu." (The government randomly drew some letters from the alphabet; anybody with a surname beginning with such a letter was deemed to be ill.) A similar experiment had taken place in the United Kingdom one year before. Firms discovered that having medicine is not enough; one also needs a policy about whom to treat if and when too many are ill. Firms also discovered they needed new holiday rules if one third of the staff are already down with flu, and so on and so forth.

Lastly, even default risk can be insured, as long as it does not happen on a systemic scale. In fact, there are various contracts that are specifically designed to reduce and/or shift (= insure) credit risks as they arise in international trade. Indeed, default is a much thornier issue when the players are from different judicial and legal systems. We look at this problem in the next chapter.

14.5 Epilogue: The Credit Crunch Blues

The subprime crisis and the ensuing credit crunch had many roots and causes. For this reason, this epilogue is like a meandering tale rather than a neatly structured analysis. Self-servingly, the financial sector tends to refer to the economic environment, but I prefer to heap much of the blame on the financial world itself. Many players all over the world did avoid the excesses I describe below, but enough of them did not.

Let's start with the banks. Traditionally, bankers were conservatively pin-striped nine-to-fivers who worked, not always hard, in the same local agency for decades and received a small share of their agency's net contribution to overall corporate profits. As of the 1980s (in Europe—the change must have come earlier in the United States), the incentives started shifting, and local managers' compensations became based on the deals' putative NPV rather than on the gradually realized profits. Such a faster remuneration meant stronger incentives, especially since bankers no longer stayed in one place for ages. The concomitant risk, of course, was that they might too myopically focus on accounting contribution (the margin between loan rate and funding rate, which determines the computed NPV), at the cost of ignoring the too-distant-looking and hard-to-model default issues; but this long-run perspective was supposedly taken care of by the credit committees at HQ and, sometimes, by claw-back clauses on bonuses in case the loans turn sour. Claw-back clauses, however, were rare, and their enforcement even rarer, and they fail to impress *ex ante* if deal makers are job-hopping all the time.

In short, too many deal makers cared less and less about loan quality. Simultaneously, even at HQs the credit committee's incentives started deteriorating when loans were no longer carried till maturity by the bank, as they traditionally had been. Instead, loans were increasingly often put into a portfolio, and claims against that portfolio were then flogged to the public. This started in New York in the 1980s, using, initially, the best mortgage loans (*mortgage-backed securities* or *mortgage-backed obligations*), following long-standing practice in Denmark and Germany (*Pfandbriefe*). Gradually, student loans, car loans, credit card loans, and, in the end, anything and everything, it seemed, was also repackaged and resold as collateralized debt obligations (CDOs)—including, crucially, low-quality contracts. Over the period 2000–6, the *Economist* reports, the fraction of non-investment-grade loans kept by banks fell from 90% to 60% in Europe, and from 60% to a mind-boggling 20% in the United States. In this way, bankers became too focused on deal making and the bonuses it brought, shrugging off default issues: these were supposed to be the concern of the buyer (*caveat emptor*—let the buyer beware) and of the rating agencies that vetted the CDOs.

Obviously, the buyers did not beware. They should have been familiar with the agency issues and adverse-selection problems that arise when a well-informed party (the bank that grants the loan) passes on a product to a less-informed one. Actually, many of the unbewaring buyers were non-U.S. banks that wanted to join the party, and hedge, pension, and mutual funds—institutions where the incentives were often as distorted as at the banks that issued the CDOs in the first place. Also, overseers should have lifted eyebrows sky-high; but instead of viewing this CDO fashion as a perversion of incentives—the Sodom and Gomorrah of banking—overseers regarded this innovation as the zenith of efficiency, a blessing to humanity (see Greenspan's ravings about "the cross-pollinating bees of Wall Street").

To tell the rest of the tale, I need to briefly digress about Basel I, the first and crude internationally coordinated attempt to instill common risk management standards into banks. As you know, the idea is that a typical unsecured loan of size 100 to a private party would need 8 in equity and retained earnings ("*tier-one capital*") plus long-term or junior debts. But the "risk weighting" was much reduced for loans to financial institutions and for loans that were insured against default risk. In a splendid illustration of the law of unintended consequences, banks started to wriggle around these well-intended and defensible principles. Instead of granting loans to individuals and corporations, they now lent to nonbank financial institutions (called *conduits* or *special investment vehicles*), which then re-lent to corporations or invested in CDOs issued by the bank itself or by other banks.

In this way, less capital was consumed, and risk was tucked away in balance sheets not subject to either Basel I or II. Also, in response to Basel I, banks started buying huge amounts of credit insurance from insurers, like American Insurance Group (AIG), one of the best-rated and biggest players until 2008, when it ignominiously collapsed and ended up in the reluctant arms of the U.S. government. Insurers were happy to guarantee loans—we all know that IBM will not default, don't we?—and then gradually got hooked on the easy money, again myopically closing their eyes to possible future problems. Banks even started buying insurance from the general public too: banks arranged *credit default swaps* that allowed them to exchange defaulting loans for risk-free income.

Soon the CDS-ensured volume amounted to three times the volume of underlying loans; that is, the average loan was ensured three times. This overinsurance phenomenon should actually have been viewed as a signal of underpricing of insurance contracts. But most CDSs were underwritten by unrelated parties who, unhindered by expertise, adequate information, or a good historical perspective, thought the insurance income was irresistibly high. Thus, once more, the unbewaring buyers did not smell a rat. Instead of seeing red lights flashing (asymmetric information + asymmetric expertise + divergent incentives = adverse selection = I lose), they loved the easy short-term money that the CDSs seemed to bring. And shareholders loved it: banks offered them returns on equity of 15%, financial profits amounted to 40% of all U.S.-listed-firm profits, and the stock market valuation rose in keeping.

Very few shareholders asked questions, and those who did were accused of wanting to slaughter the goose with the golden eggs. Greenspan, finally, just dreamed of bees. All the time, the rating agencies were supposed to shine their harsh, objective light on all this: they vetted the paper that was placed with other banks and institutional investors. But the raters were hired by the issuers, not by the investors in whose interests they were supposed to act. IKB, a medium-sized German bank that was one of the first to get into trouble in mid 2007, had paid about 200m euros a year in fees to raters and other intermediaries. Only a fool would believe that, faced with such fees, the rating agencies would remain objective. In reply to a worried email about the firm's willingness to rate a product, one analyst famously wrote "we rate any paper, even if it's written by a cow."

In a very partial defense of buyers and raters and overseers, the early 2000s were a period of unprecedentedly low default and low volatility as measured by, for example, implicit standard deviation or VIX. Also, after each hiccup—the Asian default (1997), the Russian default and the LTCM crisis (1998), the dotcom bust (2000–1), and 9/11 (2001)—the Fed duly flooded the market with money. Easy, cheap M0 and the recycling of loans via CDOs led to a frantic search for new investment opportunities and to a steady lowering of the quality of covenants imposed on the borrowers (*covenant-lite loans*). The flood of liquidity and the low interest rates also led to an unprecedented real-estate boom, which then started a new vicious circle of its own when banks started lending to low-quality lenders, betting that house prices would keep rising long enough to stave off problems in case of default.

Borrowers' claims about income were accepted without checking, and banks' *haircuts* on the security shrank and ultimately became negative: a house of estimated value 100 entitled one to a loan, not of, say, 75 (a haircut of 25% to cover liquidation price risk), but of 105 or more. Next, amortization was set to zero for a few years, and then even became negative: the initial service payments did not even cover interest and the shortfall was simply capitalized and added to the principal.

In short, beggars were bribed into taking up loans by brokers and deal makers who just thought of their commission or the next bonus. It was in this subprime segment, actually only a small part of the entire CDO market, where the rot first became visible when the real-estate bubble burst. Things were not helped by U.S. law, under which a mortgage borrower can walk away from a property, leaving the bank with value shortfall; in most other countries, the borrowers remain responsible for any gap between the realized liquidation value and the loan's face value.

So, as we have seen, rating agencies, buyers, and overseers all failed to be critical. Academics, too, were cheerleading, by and large: they had supported the wave of liberalization that had, ever since the 1980s, done wonders in so many sectors, like air transportation. Markets were deemed to be efficient, prices tautologically reflected true economic value because if they did not they would immediately be corrected, and marking to market therefore always made sense. Math was wonderful, as was greed, and VaR was a science not an art. Spreading risks all over the economy was regarded as almost tantamount to utterly eliminating the risk. Rating agencies had such a valuable reputation to lose that they would never even dream of lying. It all sounded so logical.

What about the banks themselves: shouldn't the middle-office staff have intervened? After all, Basel-II-inspired risk management was supposed to take care of excess risk taking. (CDOs were deemed to be traded securities, so the related risk management became a VaR-like issue, not a credit-risk one.) But Basel II was imposed too late. Worse, Basel II takes the point of view of a single bank that gets into trouble through a combination of unusual returns on an unusual portfolio. So this approach does not cover a systemic problem like the current one, where too many banks get in trouble simultaneously with the same products and where markets totally freeze owing to a sudden lack of trust.

Also, in fairness, risk managers often did sound the alarm; but it is difficult to keep up the role of Cassandra, the prophetess of doom, when the dealers' bonuses are at stake and when, period after period, actual losses stay way below the computed VaR. Top management was not critical either—how could they be, given their incentives? In addition, the CDOs became harder and harder to evaluate: it became standard to slice the loan portfolios into hard-to-verify risk classes, which were then vetted, repackaged and resliced and revetted, and so on.

Finally, there was the belief that the Fed would intervene (the "Greenspan put option," later the "Bernanke put," as Wall Street adoringly named it). This belief was so strong that when the Fed and the U.S. government actually did let Lehman Brothers implode, the markets went into total shock, destroying all trust between banks and other financials. Relending stopped, everybody started hoarding cash, and the credit crunch began in earnest. In hindsight, overseers were naive. The investment banks (Bear Sterns, Lehman, Merrill Lynch, Goldman Sachs, Morgan Stanley) were unregulated and hugely overlevered. (Now many nonbanks, like the last two investment banks and American Express) adopt a banking status for the safety cushion it brings.)

Central bankers balked at the idea that they had to stop bubbles in financial and real-estate markets, a position that may need reconsideration. The incentives for and remuneration of raters need to be reviewed. Reforms will surely involve limits on leverage, explicit and implicit, and hopefully also on the level and type of bonuses and on the unloading of risks on to innocent or naive bystanders.

TEST YOUR UNDERSTANDING

Quiz Questions

True–False Questions

1. VaR does not take into account the correlations and cross-hedging between various asset categories or risk factors and is therefore not comparable across different asset classes.

2. One of the main advantages of VaR is that it is sub-additive, i.e., $\rho(X + Y) \leqslant \rho(X) + \rho(Y)$.

3. VaR does not distinguish between the different liquidities of market positions and only captures short-term risks in normal circumstances.

4. VaR can be extended from a one-day horizon to a t-day horizon by multiplying by the square root of t if and only if the returns are i.i.d. and are normally distributed.

5. VaR should be complemented by stress testing for identifying potential losses under extreme market conditions.

Multiple-Choice Questions

1. The market risk department of Trustworthy Bank reports a $5 million overnight VaR figure with 99.5% confidence level. The bank
   (a) can be expected to lose at most $5 million in 1 out of the next 100 days;
   (b) can be expected to lose at least $5 million in 1 out of the next 200 days;
   (c) can be expected to lose at most $2.5 million in 1 out of the next 100 days;
   (d) can be expected to lose at most $5 million in 1 out of the next 200 days.

2. Given two portfolios, X and Y, whose returns are bivariate normal (implying that returns on portfolios of them are also normally distributed), do we have:
   (a) $\mathrm{VaR}(X) + \mathrm{VaR}(Y) \leqslant \mathrm{VaR}(X + Y)$?
   (b) $\mathrm{VaR}(X) + \mathrm{VaR}(Y) = \mathrm{VaR}(X + Y)$?
   (c) $\mathrm{VaR}(X) + \mathrm{VaR}(Y) \geqslant \mathrm{VaR}(X + Y)$?
   (d) None of the above?

3. Drop the normality from the preceding question. So, given two portfolios, X and Y, do we have:
   (a) $\mathrm{VaR}(X) + \mathrm{VaR}(Y) \leqslant \mathrm{VaR}(X + Y)$?
   (b) $\mathrm{VaR}(X) + \mathrm{VaR}(Y) = \mathrm{VaR}(X + Y)$?
   (c) $\mathrm{VaR}(X) + \mathrm{VaR}(Y) \geqslant \mathrm{VaR}(X + Y)$?
   (d) None of the above?

4. Which of the following portfolios is the most risky? Assume 240 trading days per year and 5 trading days a week (CI, confidence interval).

Portfolio	Horizon	VaR	CI
1	10	16	97.5
2	25	16	95
3	10	16	99
4	15	16	99
5	20	16	97.5

Applications

1. The Basel Accord requires that banks must meet, on a daily basis, a capital requirement based on the market risk charge, given by

$$MRC_t^{\text{IMA}} = \text{Max} \left(k \frac{1}{60} \sum_{i=1}^{60} \text{VaR}_{t-i}, \text{VaR}_{t-1} \right) + SRC_t$$

The multiplication factor, k, is based on the quality of the bank's risk management system, subject to an absolute minimum of 3. Chico Marx, the Governor of the Central Bank of Freedonia, decides one fine day that all banks in Freedonia will henceforth calculate the capital requirement based on a multiplication factor of 5 or above instead of 3 or above. What are the implications of such a move on Freedonian banks?

2. Graucho, Chico's brother and Freedonia's president, along with his Cabinet Ministers (Harpo, Gummo, and Zeppo Marx), wonder why k exceeds unity, whether there is a typo (the formula says Max instead of Marx), why VaR is for 99%, and what SRC means. Enlighten them.

3. Zeppo doubles as treasurer of Duck Soup Inc.—admittedly owing his position to the fact that he is from the ruling family. Duck Soup Inc. has an asset worth $25 million and he needs to know the 99% worst-case loss over a 1-day period. Assume that the daily price volatility is 2.7% and the FDK/USD exchange rate is 3.4567. Give Zeppo *an* answer and then add all caveats that you think are appropriate.

4. Harpo, the bright star in the Marx intellectual firmament, muses that a 99% VaR means 2.33 standard deviations, so the Basel number $k = 3$ stipulates a capital of just 7 standard deviations. Yet, Harpo wonders, Philippe Jorion writes that almost every year some market moves by 10 standard deviations. Thus, Basel is inadequate. Right?

5. Discuss the impact of the following factors on VaR:
   (a) options;
   (b) liquidity.

15

Managing Credit Risk in International Trade

In chapter 12, we argued that a firm could increase its value by reducing the variability of its cash flows and by hedging exchange-rate risk. In chapter 13 we described how firms could measure economic exposure to the exchange rate and how they could hedge this by using financial instruments. The impact on total market-related risk was studied in chapter 14. In this chapter, our focus is on how one can hedge other risks that arise in international trade—risks that are not related to the exchange rate or other market prices—and the related issue of how the exporter can obtain trade finance in an efficient manner.

Risks. Some of the risks that arise in international trade are the following:

- The exporter may not ship the goods he had agreed to send (a form of *default risk*).

- The goods shipped may not conform to the contract's specifications (*delivery risk*).

- The importer may not pay, or may pay too little or too late (*credit risk*).

- The importer's country may have run out of reserves by the time payment is due, so the central bank or the trade ministry may not allow the importer to buy hard currency and transfer these funds to the supplier of the goods (*transfer risk*).

Funding. The financing issue relates to the fact that the supplier usually has to buy the goods long before they are shipped. There is an interval between the time that the exporting trader (or producer) must pay for labor and other inputs and the time that the importer has agreed to pay for the goods, and this time interval must be bridged.

In this chapter, we describe various payment techniques that allow one to finance trade efficiently, reduce the buyer's incentive to default, and shift the risks (insofar as they are not already eliminated by the payment contract) toward parties that can better assess these risks or bear them at a lower cost. In section 15.1, we discuss payment modes and contract structures not backed by bank guarantees. In section 15.2, we consider payment structures involving bank guarantees. In section 15.3, we look at other standard ways of coping with default risk: factoring and credit insurance.

15.1 Payment Modes without Bank Participation

Initially, we ignore the issue of how to finance international trade, and focus on how instruments are designed so as to limit default and transfer risks. We consider two extreme contract structures: (i) trading on an open account with payment upon or after delivery, and (ii) payment before shipment. We then focus on the financing aspect of international trade, and present the case for the use of trade bills.

15.1.1 Cash Payment After Delivery

Within a country, a supplier usually sends goods *on open account*, that is, on the basis of a simple invoice. The customer pays either upon delivery—in cash, by bank transfer, or by check—or at an agreed-upon later date. The crucial characteristic of such a contract is that it allows the buyer to take possession of the goods and inspect them before payment is made.

The practice of shipping goods on open account is widespread in domestic business, but also in international trade it is often adopted, especially when the importer and exporter have a long-standing, positive business relationship and when transfer risk is negligible. If the foreign customer is new, if his or her credit standing deteriorates, or if the customer's country is short of foreign exchange reserves, the exporter faces default risk and transfer risk. Specifically:

(a.1) The customer might refuse to take possession of the goods.

(a.2) The customer may be unable (or simply unwilling) to pay for the goods.

(a.3) The importing firm may not be able to import the goods because it has no import license.

(a.4) The importer may be unable to buy foreign currency because its central bank has a shortage of foreign exchange.[1]

In table 15.1, the pros and cons of various techniques are summarized. The entries in the column "Payment after delivery" corresponding to risks (a.1) to (a.4) are marked with a minus, indicating that from the exporter's point of view,

---

[1] The lack of hard currency is a problem because in the case of trade with countries that restrict the convertibility of their currencies, the exporter typically requests payment in some hard (freely convertible) currency. In addition, a country with currency controls typically forbids payment in its own currency. The reason is that if payment in the importer's currency were allowed, the exporter would still have serious difficulties in converting this money into hard currency, and might therefore be willing to sell the blocked foreign-currency balances to another nonresident at a discount. As this would lead to a parallel exchange market beyond the control of the monetary authorities, it is typically forbidden to pay in the importer's currency.

Table 15.1. Exporter's and importer's risks for various payment forms.

		Pay after delivery	Pay before shipment	D/P	D/A	L/C	Confirmed L/C
		(a) Exporter's risks					
(a.1)	Importer refuses goods	−	+				
	Importer refuses documents	n.a.	n.a.				
(a.2)	Importer defaults	−	+				
	L/Cs issuing bank defaults	n.a.	n.a.				
(a.3)	No license to import goods	−	+				
(a.4)	No license to remit payment	−	+				
		(b) Importer's risks					
(b.1)	Exporter doesn't send goods	+	−				
(b.2)	Goods sent do not conform	+	−				
(b.3)	No license to ship the goods	+	−				

payment after delivery is rated poorly with respect to these risks. (The second lines for (a.1), (a.2), and (a.3) become relevant further on in this chapter.)

It should be clear that apart from transfer risks, these problems are not fundamentally different from the problems encountered in domestic trade. However, they acquire a special importance in the case of international trade because the importer and the exporter operate under different legal and judicial systems and the costs of transportation are much greater. For instance, in case (a.1) or (a.3), the exporter has not lost possession of the goods, but incurs ever-increasing warehousing costs. Thus, the exporter must choose to have the goods shipped back or to auction them off abroad, and both solutions are costly.

15.1.2 Cash Payment Before Shipping

If the exporter is in a very strong bargaining position relative to the importer and the latter is viewed as risky, we might see the opposite situation: the supplier ships the goods only after receiving payment from the foreign customer. In contrast to the case where goods are shipped on open account, the importer now bears all of the risk because:

(b.1) the supplier may not ship any goods at all;

(b.2) the supplier may ship the goods too late, the goods may be substandard, or the quantities may not conform with the contract;

(b.3) the supplier may not have obtained an export license, implying that the exporter is not allowed to ship the goods.

In table 15.1, the corresponding entries in the column "Payment before shipment" are marked with a minus, indicating that from the importer's point of view this payment technique is poorly rated as far as risks (b.1)–(b.3) are concerned. We also note that under "Payment before shipment" the exporter avoids the risks (a.1)–(a.4). This is reflected by the plus marks: with respect to risks (a.1)–(a.4), the exporter prefers payment before shipment. Likewise, the importer gives positive ratings to "Payment after delivery" as far as risks (b.1)–(b.3) are concerned.

Thus, the two payment modes discussed thus far represent the two extreme ways in which the risks can be shifted from the exporter to importer and vice versa. In section 15.2, we shall see how compromise solutions can be found. Before that, we shall consider the financing issue, and explain why trade bills are often used to facilitate financing.

15.1.3 Trade Bills

The second practical issue in international trade is the financing of working capital. In international trade, there can be a rather long period of time between the moment the producer/exporter has to pay for inputs and the moment the importer receives payment from his own customer. The mode of payment determines which party has to provide which part of the financing. For example, when payment takes place before the goods are shipped, most or all of the financing of incremental working capital has to be provided by the buyer/importer, while the seller/exporter has to come up with most or all of the financing when payment is after delivery. Obviously, it is in the exporter's and importer's joint interest to minimize the total financing cost. Unless one party can obtain financing at a cost below regular bank rates, the investment is usually financed through bank loans. Bank loans are easily obtained, and at attractive rates, if payment involves a *trade bill* (also known as a *draft*, in the sense of something that is *drawn*, or a *bill of exchange*).

15.1.3.1 What Is a Trade Bill?

As the word suggests, in many ways a trade bill is like a summary of an invoice. It refers to an underlying commercial transaction, and it states the amount to be paid, the date on which the payment is due, and the place and manner of payment. The supplier (the *drawer*) *draws* the bill on the customer (the *drawee*). Like an invoice, a trade bill is a "you owe me" document. Unlike an invoice, a trade bill is specifically designed to be negotiable; it can be passed on to a financial institution in return for cash.

However, a trade bill is not as reliable as an I.O.U. ("I owe you") document, such as a *promissory note* written and signed by the debtor. That is, the trade bill in itself contains no confirmation by the drawee that the debt actually exists. To give a trade bill the same credibility as a promissory note, the drawer typically sends it to the drawee with a request to *accept* it, that is, to add the drawee's signature and thus to acknowledge and confirm the existence of the underlying debt. A trade bill drawn on and accepted by the importer is called a *trade acceptance*; a bill drawn on and accepted by a bank is called a *banker's acceptance*. A banker's acceptance is like a cashier's check: it is usually safer for the exporter to hold a banker's promise to pay than one by the importer.

In many ways, an acceptance *payable on sight* is similar to a check: it can be cashed in at any moment. Very often, however, the bill is payable some time after delivery on a date explicitly stated on the bill, like on a postdated check, or at least on an ascertainable date, like "90 days after arrival of the goods in the port of delivery." In such a case, the exporter can still get immediate cash by borrowing against the discounted face value of the bill or acceptance, and ceding the acceptance to the lender (who will collect the debt from the drawee). Borrowing against the bill is called *discounting* the bill. Discounting is done by commercial banks or by specialized institutions (such as *discount houses*).

15.1.3.2   Advantages and Disadvantages of Trade Bills

Lending money by discounting a trade bill is comparatively safe from the bank's point of view—and therefore comparatively cheap for the exporter—for a number of reasons:

- Bills and acceptances are *negotiable*, that is, they can be sold and resold in the money market like any other form of commercial paper. For instance, a commercial bank that has discounted a bill can remobilize its funds by passing along the paper to another financial institution. This is known as rediscounting.[2]

- In some countries, banks can still *rediscount* export bills and acceptances at subsidized rates by dealing with a government agency that promotes exports. Within the EU and OECD this has been discontinued.

- Bills are *self-financing*. If a bank or discount house discounts a bill, the bank or discount house will receive the paper and collect the debt directly from the drawee. That is, no complicated provisions must be made to cover the risk of the exporter cashing in the accounts receivable and spending the money rather than paying back the bank loan.

- To increase the cost of defaulting on a bill, many countries officially publish lists of all *protested* bills, including the name of the person or firm that defaulted. Clearly, a company's name appearing on such a list would immediately ruin the company's credit standing throughout the country. Managers will, therefore, think twice about defaulting on a bill.

---

[2] In many countries, the central bank or an affiliated official institution extends or contracts credit to the private sector by increasing or reducing its holdings of bills and acceptances bought from banks. This is especially true for the European countries conquered by Napoleon; Napoleon was a great promoter of trade bills. The *code civil*, which he introduced and which still forms the basis of many continental legal systems, contains detailed legislation of bills. Thus, trade bills are quite popular in these countries.

- The discounting bank (or any other third holder of the bill) has *recourse* on the preceding holder of the bill in case of default—unless discounting is done explicitly on a no-recourse basis, which is rare. That is, from the exporter's point of view, discounting is really like obtaining an advance against the bill; the drawer, as the first holder of the bill, *backs*[3] the bill and, therefore, still bears the default risk and the transfer risk. Conversely, from the point of view of the bank, there is at least one additional signature (the exporter's) backing the acceptance, which makes it safer than a promissory note.

For all of these reasons, banks favor bills and are willing to discount them at attractive interest rates. However, from the point of view of credit risk and transfer risk, the instrument remains almost as risky as an invoice. For instance, the drawee might not even accept the bill, might default on it, or might not have a license to remit foreign exchange.

15.1.4 The Problems with Legal Redress

Although in a breach of contract (cases (a.1), (a.2) and (b.1), (b.2) on our checklist in table 15.1), legal redress can be sought, it is impossible to underestimate the difficulties of legal procedures in a foreign environment. First, the injured party might not speak the language, is unlikely to be familiar with the legal system, and, in many countries, has the general disadvantage of being viewed as "the foreigner." Second, although the contract typically stipulates which court will deal with any disputes (possibly even an international arbitration court such as the Chamber of Commerce in Paris or Stockholm), the next problem is how to enforce the court's ruling outside of its jurisdiction. Third, litigation is often time-consuming and costly. Finally, even if a court's ruling is enforced, the judgment may come too late. For instance, the prospect of financial compensation in lieu of the goods, or belated delivery of the goods, are imperfect alternatives for an importer who needs the goods now. Likewise, the exporter may go bankrupt if swift payment is not made for the goods shipped.

The exporter's position is even more precarious if default is due to a decision made by the importing company's government. If the foreign government is also the customer, the exporter can ask a court to seize the foreign government's assets located abroad. Usually, however, a government has only a few marketable foreign assets, and there may be many claims on these assets. In contrast, if the problem is simply one of a shortage of hard currency, a foreign government that blocks the payment is not acting as a party to a commercial contract and by international common law, a sovereign acting as a sovereign rather than as a contract party is beyond any court's power. In short, the exporter can achieve very little in court if his payment is blocked.

---

[3] The term backing (or *endorsing*) actually stems from the fact that the holder, when (re)discounting a bill, signs it on the back (*dorsum*, in Latin).

We conclude that legal redress in case of default by either the exporter or the importer is slow and costly; thus, compromise contracts are sought. We discuss how these compromise contracts work and how they can be combined with bank guarantees in the next section.

15.2 Documentary Payment Modes with Bank Participation

Given the inadequacy of legal redress, one often chooses a mode of payment in which the risks are shared (rather than borne entirely by either the exporter or the importer), and that reduces both the probability of as well as the cost of default. As we shall see, such contracts usually involve at least one financial institution, which acts as a kind of trustee for the main contracting parties. In addition, some of the risks of the transaction are often shifted to the intermediary. This is economically efficient if the intermediary is better placed to assess or bear these risks.

To get an idea of the generic solution, consider the following scenario. The exporter entrusts the goods to a go-between who inspects them; likewise, the importer sends payment to the same go-between/trustee. If both the goods and the payment conform to the contract, the trustee forwards the goods and the money to the normal recipients; if not, the goods and the money are returned to the original sender.

The role of banks is, as we shall see, similar to that of such a trustee. However, no regular bank would view the running of a big warehouse as part of its corporate mission. Thus, the arrangement is that the bank receives a set of documents rather than the goods themselves. The exporter and the importer have to agree on what documents will be required. These documents may serve many purposes. For example, the documents must give reasonable evidence that the goods have been shipped and conform with the contract. The documents should also represent title to the goods, so that the holder of the documents can claim them from the customs warehouse or from the shipping company's premises. Finally, the importer and exporter may agree to also include documents that guarantee that the goods will be cleared through customs. Thus, a very complete set of documents is (almost) as good as the goods. One task of the intermediary, then, is to check the documents instead of the goods. Any further responsibilities of the bank depend on the contract. The list of documents that are typically exchanged is summarized below.

Documents needed for the customs administration(s):

- A regular commercial invoice (an original and duplicates).
- A *customs invoice*—a form used to clear the goods through customs (for example, as a basis for customs duties and for statistical purposes).
- A *consular invoice*—a document certifying that there is an import license for the transaction at hand.

- A *certificate of origin* delivered by the exporter's government or the local chamber of commerce—this is necessary if the import duty depends on the country of origin or if there are country-by-country import quotas.

- *Phytosanitary certificates* for verification of compliance with local agricultural regulations.

Documents needed by the importer:

- The commercial invoice.

- An *inspection certificate*, that is, a report on the state and properties of the goods delivered for shipment.[4]

- An *insurance policy* for each individual transaction or, if the exporter's insurance policy covers many transactions, an insurance certificate. (Proof of insurance is essential for a cost, insurance, freight (CIF) contract.)

- A *mate's receipt*, which confirms that the goods have been loaded on board a vessel (vital for a CIF or free-on-board (FOB) contract, and useful whenever evidence of shipping is needed).

- A *shipping list*, describing the parcels, crates, or containers.

- A document that represents title to the goods—for transport by sea, the *bill of loading* or *bill of lading* (B/L), which simultaneously serves as the contract between the exporter and the shipping company.[5]

We now describe the simplest example of such a payment mechanism: *documents against payment* (D/P).

15.2.1 Documents against Payment

Under D/P, the bank checks whether all documents listed in the contract are present. If nothing is missing, the bank *remits* these documents to the importer against payment—that is, the importer receives the papers only if and when the agreed-upon price is paid. The importer, being in possession of the documents, can then claim the merchandise from the warehouse. Of course, the remitting bank will charge a small consideration for its effort, say 0.125%, capped at a few hundred dollars.[6]

In many instances, D/P is a reasonable solution to the problem of default risk. You are encouraged to verify this on the basis of our checklist of risks in table 15.2. We explain our rating of the D/P, given in table 15.2, as follows:

---

[4] Such a certificate is delivered by a specialized firm, for example, Switzerland's Société Générale de Surveillance, a company that is so well-regarded that it has actually been put in charge of some countries' customs administrations.

[5] The first mate, who receives the goods, adds his or her remarks to the B/L if there is visible damage to the packaging or if the number or nature of containers does not comply with the description given in the contract. Any such remarks make the B/L "*dirty*" and will prompt the bank to return the documents to the exporter. If everything seems to be perfect, the first mate gives a "*clean*" bill.

[6] An Anglo-Saxon variant would require the importer to sign a *trust receipt*, too. This document states that the goods remain the exporter's property as long as the bill is not paid, and that the importer sells them in the role of the exporter's agent only.

Table 15.2. Exporter's and importer's risks for various payment forms.

		Open invoice	Pay before shipment	D/P	D/A	L/C	Confirmed L/C
				(a) Exporter's risks			
(a.1)	Importer refuses goods	−	+	+	+	+	+
	Importer refuses documents	n.a.	n.a.	−	−	+	+
(a.2)	Importer defaults	−	+	+	−	+	+
	L/Cs issuing bank defaults	n.a.	n.a.	n.a.	n.a.	−	+
(a.3)	No license to import goods	−	+	+	+	+	+
(a.4)	No license to remit payment	−	+	−	−	−	+
				(b) Importer's risks			
(b.1)	Exporter doesn't send goods	+	−	+	+	+	+
(b.2)	Goods sent do not conform	+	−	+?	+?	+?	+?
(b.3)	No license to ship the goods	+	−	+	+	+	+

- Risk (a.1) (importer refusing the goods) is resolved, but now another risk arises: the importer may never bother to claim the documents or may refuse to accept them. In table 15.2, we give D/P a "plus" relative to the risk that the importer does not pick up the goods, but we immediately add a new line which rates D/P as "minus" with respect to the risk that the importer does not pick up the documents.

- Assume that the documents have been handed over, the goods have been paid for, and there is obviously no default risk (hence the "plus" for risk (a.2), that is, importer defaulting).

- If the importer's country requires import licenses, the exporter can insist on evidence that there is a license.

- Transfer risk is not covered by D/P: the importer's central bank can still refuse an exchange license.

- From the importer's point of view, the documents prove that the goods have been shipped, which explains the "plus" rating with respect to risks (b.1) and (b.3). That is, the importer has shipped the goods and has the license to ship them.

- While the documents can provide a lot of information about the quality of the goods, they can never guarantee 100% conformity—hence our qualified plus rating ("+?") with regard to risk (b.2). If there is no inspection certificate, even the "+?" may be overly optimistic.

In table 15.2, we see that the "D/P" column receives far more plus ratings than does either payment before or after shipment mechanisms, and that there are no unambiguously negative ratings left. Thus, this technique is an improvement over the two extreme solutions considered in section 15.1. From the pure financing side, a drawback of D/P is that it precludes the use of bills (which, as we saw in section 15.1.3, allow cheap financing). For that reason, a variant called *documents against acceptance* (D/A) is also available. This is discussed below. We will also see how D/P or D/A, suitably combined with bank guarantees, addresses the problems of the importer refusing goods or documents, or defaulting on the payment.

15.2.2 Documents against Acceptance

Under a D/A arrangement, the drawer obtains some degree of certainty about acceptance by stipulating the following:

(i) As under D/P, the documents will be sent to a remitting bank rather than directly to the customer. The set of documents now includes a bill drawn by the exporter on the importer.

(ii) If the set of documents is complete, the bank will remit the documents to the importer as soon as the latter has accepted (signed) the bill. The acceptance then goes back to the exporter, who may discount it.

The main difference between D/P and D/A is that, under D/A, the importer has accepted the bill but has not paid for the goods. Thus, under D/P, the importer can still default after taking possession of the goods. This is reflected by the "minus" for risk (a.2) in table 15.2. Still, exporters may be willing to bear this risk because of the swift and cheap financing provided by acceptances.

15.2.3 Obtaining a Guarantee from the Importer's Bank: The Letter of Credit

There is an obvious and simple way to reduce (or at least shift) the default risk in a D/A or D/P arrangement. The exporter can insist that the importer have the payment or bill guaranteed by his or her bank, which also acts as remitting bank. Of course, the exporter will insist on evidence of such a commitment before sending any documents. The letter issued by the importer's bank (issuing bank), ascertaining that such a guarantee exists, is called the *letter of credit* (L/C). If, as is usual, the bank's guarantee is conditional on receiving a set of *conformable* documents (see next paragraph), the arrangement is called a *documentary credit*.[7]

Note that, in contrast to D/P or D/A payments, the issuing bank is now responsible for the payment as soon as it accepts that the documents conform to the contract. Therefore, rather than simply checking whether all the documents are present (as in a D/P or D/A contract), the bank will now scrutinize the documents very carefully for conformity. The exporter should make sure that the documents are indeed conformable, that is, they in no way deviate

---

[7] Any credit arrangement is, in principle, revocable under certain conditions, or even at the issuing bank's will; thus, from the exporter's point of view, it is best to insist on an irrevocable L/C. Nowadays there are no more revocable LCs.

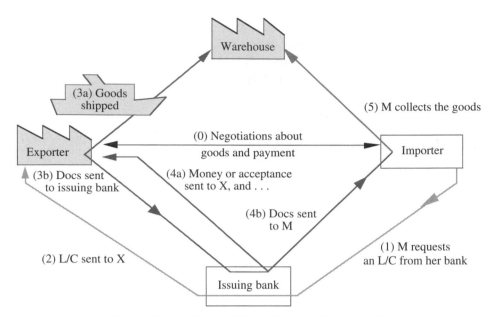

Figure 15.1. D/P or D/A with an L/C: the movie.

from anything stipulated in the contract. The least imperfection can and will be invoked by the bank to reject the documents, because any such imperfection can be invoked, in turn, by the importer.

If the documents are found to be conformable, then depending on the deal the bank's payment is either immediate (in cash or check or transfer or by nonrecourse discounting of a bill drawn on the importer) or by a banker's acceptance. The issuing bank is free to make its own arrangements with the importer, like insisting on up-front payment into an escrow account at one extreme and open unsecured credit at the other. A general credit arrangement can include a window for L/Cs, alongside credits for overdraft facilities, discounting of bills from customers, forward hedging, and so on.

The rules underlying L/Cs are standardized internationally, according to the *Uniform Rules and Usances of the International Chamber of Commerce* in Paris. An exporting firm can strengthen its legal position if the issuing bank actually signs a bill (as is the case with L/Cs that stipulate D/P); the bank's engagement then also falls under the local legislation on bills rather than just under the International Usances.

The entire process, from the initial agreement between buyer and seller to the final payment, is summarized in figure 15.1. Let us analyze the L/C arrangement from an economic point of view and see what it accomplishes. The first two arguments suggest the L/C lowers the cost of default. The next two have to do with the probability of default.

   (i) The L/C shifts the default risk to a party that is better placed to bear it: default may be crippling to a small exporting firm, while to a bank with a large portfolio of L/Cs the same risk is largely diversifiable. Such risk-shifting from weak to strong is the principle at the core of all insurance contracts.

(ii) The bank issuing the L/C is typically the importer's house bank. This implies that, in the case of default, the monetary and nonmonetary costs of legal proceedings are lower because the importer's house bank operates in the same legal environment as the defaulting party.

(iii) Being specialized in evaluating credit risks, and having privileged information about the importer, the issuing bank is in a better position to assess the importer's default risk than is the exporter.

(iv) The likelihood of default by the importer is reduced because, from the importer's point of view, it is more tempting to neglect her obligations toward an exporter in a distant country than toward the house bank.

Although the above L/C arrangement reduces the probability and cost of default, the L/C arrangement is still far from perfect. Occasionally, letters of credit turn out to be counterfeited or issued by banks that, judging by their name and logo, look like branches of major international banks but are, in fact, just minor local banks. Finally, even if the issuing bank is sound, transfer risk still exists. In managing all of these problems, the exporter's house bank can play a useful role, as described below.

15.2.4 Advised L/Cs and Confirmed L/Cs

There are several ways in which an exporter can further reduce the default risk, even after having obtained an L/C. First, the exporter can ask the issuing bank to send the L/C to a designated bank trusted by the exporter, called an *advisory* bank. The advisory bank receives the L/C from the issuing bank; its task is to check whether that issuing bank exists and is in good financial standing, whether the signatures seem to be legitimate, and whether the bank manager who signed the L/C actually has the power to do so. The advisory bank then forwards the L/C to the exporter, but without adding any guarantees. That is, the exporter still bears the risk that the issuing bank might go bankrupt or might not be able to obtain a foreign exchange license.[8]

The exporter can also ask the importer to have the L/C *confirmed* by a bank located in the exporter's country, or at least confirmed by a well-known bank trusted by the exporter. Under such an arrangement, the confirming bank will actually guarantee the payment; that is, it will pay the exporter if the original issuing bank defaults or if the transfer is blocked. Thus, a confirmed L/C also offers insurance against default on behalf of the issuing bank and against

---

[8] Very often, the advisory bank is also willing to give an advance to the exporter if the documents are remitted and found to conform with the terms of the agreement; and, if it does so, the advance is on a no-recourse basis. However, the advisory bank can always refuse to give such an advance if the issuing bank and/or its country seem too risky.

transfer risks. Moreover, the confirming bank is bound to pay out in cash (D/P) or to discount a banker's acceptance without recourse on the drawer (D/A) if its confirmation was requested by the bank that issued the original L/C.[9] In such a case, from the exporter's point of view, it is as if the L/C had been issued by the confirming bank.

The exporter could have the bank-backed bill or the issuing bank's acceptance discounted without recourse. This again shifts the transfer risk and the risk of default to the discount house and the issuing bank. This technique is called *forfeiting* and is used by specialized forfeiter companies (mainly in the United Kingdom, Switzerland, and traditionally Austria).[10] For exports to eastern Europe, where bills were uncommon in the old days, forfeiters are sometimes willing to discount regular commercial invoices on a no-recourse basis.

Confirmation offers advantages above and beyond pure risk shifting. These benefits are similar to those obtained from an L/C, as described in section 15.2.3:

(i) Insurance: risk-shifting from weak to strong.

(ii) The issuing bank is still in a better position relative to the importer (who needs the bank in its daily business), knows more about that firm, and operates in the same legal environment.

(iii) If there is any moral hazard from the issuing bank, then the confirming bank is in a better position relative to the issuing bank (which needs other banks in the network for its international business), and knows more about that bank than the exporter.

(iv) The confirming bank can also better assess transfer risk than the exporter. That's part of their job.

In the next section, we consider two other ways of shifting risks in the context of international trade, factoring, and credit insurance.

15.3 Other Standard Ways of Coping with Default Risk

The letter of credit is not the only way to insure against credit risks. Exporters can also use factor companies or they can buy insurance from specialized insurance companies. We describe these two alternative ways of shifting risk below.

---

[9] The rule is that the issuing bank should ask for confirmation. In continental Europe, banks also confirm at the exporter's request, which irritates Anglo-Saxon issuing banks.

[10] Forfeiting can also be used without an L/C. Then, however, the exporter still bears the risk of nonacceptance and, likewise, is not sure that the bill will be guaranteed by the importer's bank. Forfeiters, as a rule, do not discount paper without a bank guarantee.

15.3.1 Factoring

A factor company, whether domestic or international, can offer the following services:

Pure debt collection. Under such an arrangement, the seller cedes any claims to the factor company and receives payment if and when the customer pays, after the deduction of a fee of 0.125–0.5%. The factor does not guarantee payment, though. For international debts, the "*export factor*" will cooperate with a corresponding "*import factor*" to collect the debts.

Credit insurance. If the agreement also includes credit insurance, the factor guarantees the payment in case of default, sometimes up to 100%, for a fee of 0.5–2%. Note that credit insurance usually does not imply insurance against transfer risks.

Accounts receivable financing. The factor can also finance the invoices, for example, up to 85% for uninsured invoices, and up to 100% for insured invoices, after the deduction of interest (at the overdraft rate, the prime rate, or the rate on straight loans). Financing of insured invoices also eliminates exchange risks as of the date on which the exporter obtains the cash.

Thus, in its most complete form, factoring is similar to forfeiting or no-recourse discounting of bills. A major difference, however, is that factoring cannot be used on a transaction-by-transaction basis. A bank that issues an L/C is contacted by the importer and can vet this party (if still necessary) or arrange security deal by deal; a factor company, in contrast, works for the exporter and gets no chance to (re-)check the importer's quality each time goods are sold. Also, the bank issuing an L/C is in a stronger position than the factor: it is in the same legal environment and is often the house bank; a factor is not. So in order to avoid ending up with only those transactions that have a poor credit risk, a factor company therefore insists on handling all sales, or at least all sales for a given market. Very often the factor also first evaluates the importer and may impose credit limits per importer and/or per country. Thus, factoring is better suited for long-lasting repeat business, while documentary credits also serve for occasional export deals.

15.3.2 Credit Insurance

Virtually every country has a government agency that insures credit and/or transfer risks, like the export–import bank (Eximbank) in the United States, the Export Credit Guarantee Department in the United Kingdom, COFACE in France, and so on.[11] The biggest private companies in 2006 were Euler Hermes

---

[11] COFACE stands for Compagnie Française d'Assurance pour le Commerce Extérieur; other official agencies include Servizi Assicurativi del Commercio Estero (SACE SpA, Italy), Export Finance and Insurance Corporation (EFIC, Australia), Eximbank Hungary, ASHRA (the Israel Export Insurance Corporation), ÖKB Austria, CESCE Spain, EDC Canada, KUKE Poland, Finnvera Finland, EGAP Czechia, EKN Sweden, NDD/OND Belgium, ERG Switzerland, and NEXI Japan, plus Japan Bank for International Cooperation.

(headquartered in Germany) and Atradius (in the Netherlands, formerly known as Gerling NCM).

If the export contract is with a foreign government institution, credit risks and transfer risks are often not separate and one needs to insure both, while for contracts with private customers the exporter can usually insure either risk separately. Relative to private credit insurance companies, government agencies tend to insure large export contracts and trade with developing countries, and most of them are rumored to sell insurance at subsidized rates as part of the government's overall export promotion policy. Insurance can be bought on a transaction-by-transaction basis or for all contracts for a given market. The coverage is typically less than 100%. One risk covered by government insurance agencies, and not by L/Cs, private insurers, or forfeiters, is the risk of the contract being canceled before the goods are finished and shipped.

15.3.3 Export-Backed Financing

Suppose that a country has a temporary shortage of hard currency. Then firms in this country may find it difficult to import goods. In such a case, banks (or a group of banks) may grant advances to the firm against the firm's future exports. This is called export-backed financing. To ensure that the loan is safe, the lending bank typically adds two clauses to the loan contract. The first clause stipulates that the exporting firm must sell its output forward, and the second clause is that the buyer of the output should pay the bank rather than the exporting firm.[12] When this payment is received, the bank withholds the amount required to service its loan and pays out the balance to the exporting firm.

Example 15.1. Generale Bank extends a loan to Mexicana de Cananea, a copper-mining company. As part of the contract, Cananea sells copper forward to a commodity trader, Sogem. Sogem's payments for its copper purchases are to be made not to Cananea but rather to Generale. The balance (after withholding whatever was needed to service the loan) will then be paid by Generale to Cananea.

From the point of view of Cananea and Generale Bank, the forward contract with Sogem eliminates the price risk—assuming, of course, that Cananea can deliver the copper—while the arrangement also ensures that the proceeds of the forward sale will first go to Generale Bank. Thus, from Generale Bank's point of view, the only

---

[12] The forward transaction may be a standard forward contract, with fixed quantity and price or, alternatively, a commitment by the customer to buy at the (as yet unknown) future market price for a fixed overall value (topping-up clause: when prices are low the quantity is increased, and vice versa). The commitment by the buyer may also be a pure quantity commitment, that is, to buy a fixed quantity at the (as yet unknown) market price. With the first and second types of contracts, the exporting firm is sure of its hard-currency revenue if, at least, it can deliver enough of the goods. This delivery risk still means that the bank will never finance 100% of the (discounted) value of the contract. When there is only a quantity commitment without fixed price, there is greater uncertainty about the revenue, so the bank will finance only, say, 60 or 80% of the estimated future value of the exported output.

risk is the risk of nondelivery of the copper, which is considered to be a minor risk as Cananea is an open stripmine.

Let us consider another example.

Example 15.2. Two companies in Ghana are facing problems obtaining hard currency credit. Ghana Petroleum needs USD 30m to pay for its upcoming imports from British Oil, and Ghana Cocoa urgently needs hard currency: USD 20m to build a new processing plant and USD 10m to buy fertilizers and pesticides for the next planting season. Ghana's main source of export revenue is cocoa, but shipments will not start until October and will last only until January. In view of Ghana's balance-of-payments problems, unsecured loans from foreign banks would carry a hefty spread above Libor.

Ghana Cocoa turns to one of its standard customers, the British cocoa importer, BCI, which regularly buys 25% of Ghana Cocoa's output. Ghana Cocoa's next crop is estimated at 255,000 short tons,[13] or (at an expected price of USD/ton 1,600) about USD 408m. With the help of a syndicate led by its London bank, BCI assesses the risks and uncertainties: output variability, price volatility, compatibility with the export quota under the International Cocoa Agreement, availability of export licenses, and transportation contracts. BCI finally agrees to buy 64,000 tons of cocoa, about one quarter of the expected crop, in four equal lots from October to January, at 2% below the spot price prevailing in each month. The syndicate agrees to finance 60% of BCI's estimated purchases, that is, $0.6 \times [\text{USD } 408\text{m}/4] \times 0.98 = \text{USD } 60\text{m}$. The proceeds of this loan are distributed as follows:

- USD 20m is made available directly to Ghana Cocoa to finance purchases of equipment from various local and western suppliers.
- USD 10m is paid to Ghana Cocoa's Irish supplier of fertilizers. Implicitly, this replaces another loan to Ghana Cocoa, the proceeds of which are immediately used to pay for the fertilizer imports.
- USD 30m is paid to British Oil as payment for Ghana Petroleum's imports, while Ghana Petroleum pays the Ghanaian pound equivalent to Ghana Cocoa. These transactions implicitly replace (1) a loan of USD 30m to Ghana Cocoa, (2) an immediate spot sale of these USD 30m from Ghana Cocoa to Ghana Petroleum, and (3) a payment for the same amount by Ghana Petroleum to British Oil.

All in all, Ghana Cocoa has implicitly borrowed USD 60m, secured by its expected sales to BCI. As we saw, part of this USD 60m was implicitly re-lent to Ghana Petroleum; but Ghana Cocoa, being the earner of hard currency, has been made responsible for the service payments of this loan. When shipments start, BCI pays the going market price of cocoa minus 2% to the banking syndicate.

15.4 CFO's Summary

In this chapter, we have considered various payment mechanisms that may be used to reduce the default and transfer risks that are present in international trade. We first evaluated two extreme models of payment: cash payment before goods are shipped and payment after the goods are delivered. We saw that the first method of payment was extremely unfavorable from the importer's point of view and the second unfavorable from the exporter's point of view. We then discussed how banks can perform an important role by being intermediaries in trade transactions. One way the exporter can guarantee payment for goods shipped is to obtain a letter of credit from the importer's bank. We also discussed that an exporter could use a factor company to reduce default risk. Alternatively, an exporter can buy insurance against default risk and transfer risk. This insurance is often sold by government agencies that have been set up to promote distant and/or big-ticket exports, sometimes at subsidized rates. Both insurance and documentary credit can be arranged deal by deal. Factoring, in contrast, is for repeat business, and may include insurance and financing. Documentary credits work smoothly even though there is no codified law behind it and a fortiori no internationally homogeneous legislation. It is purely private law: the legislator is the International Chamber of Commerce of Paris, and the enforcer is the club: no bank wants to be kicked out of the network. And the neat idea behind it is to shift the credit risk to a party that is within the same judicial system as the importer and has a lot of leverage over her. Still, L/Cs are being used less and less, because trade increasingly happens between closely related parties or even within a group of companies.

This has brought us to the end of the risks' section of this book. We now proceed to that last big part, which bears on long-term financing and investment decisions: bond markets, stock markets, and various issues in capital budgeting or NPV analysis.

TEST YOUR UNDERSTANDING

Quiz Questions

True-False Questions

1. Trade on open account, with payment after or on delivery, is the standard way of doing business internationally among unrelated parties without an established business relationship because this method of payment has proved its value in domestic trade.

2. Under payment on or after delivery, most of the risks are borne by the exporter.

3. Under payment before shipment, the exporter bears only the risk of contract cancellation before shipment.

4. Suppose that, under payment upon delivery, the importer does not accept the goods. Then the exporter has no problem whatsoever, as he is still in possession of the goods.

5. In international trade, there is often a relatively large time gap between production outlays and payment by the final customer. However, it does not generally matter who provides this working capital. In addition, the issue of how to finance working capital is entirely separable from the issue of how the payment is structured.

6. Discounting a bill is similar to selling the bill for a price equal to the discounted value of the nominal (future) value.

7. Discounting a bill simply means giving an advance on the bill equal to the discounted value of the nominal (future) value. In addition, the discounter receives the bill as security for the payment.

8. Discounting a bill is like factoring with financing but without credit insurance, except that discounting of bills can be done transaction by transaction. Likewise, discounting without recourse is like factoring with financing and credit insurance.

9. Forfeiting, or discounting without recourse, is like factoring with financing and credit insurance, except that discounting of bills can be done transaction by transaction.

10. Under international law, a foreign government can never be judged by a court.

11. Under ordinary D/A and D/P (without an L/C) the intervening bank still guarantees the payment, and will therefore reject any set of documents that is not perfectly conformable with the contract.

12. A trust receipt is often used to reduce the seller's risks in a D/P arrangement.

13. A letter of credit is a statement by a bank that promises to extend a loan to the exporter if certain conditions are met.

14. An irrevocable L/C offers the same security as an acceptance signed by the importer and insured with a government agency against credit risks.

15. An irrevocable, confirmed L/C offers the same security as an acceptance signed by the importer and insured with a government agency against political and credit risks.

16. Under an L/C, the bank agrees to inspect the goods, and to pay the exporter or accept the bill if the goods are fully conformable with the contract.

Table 15.3.

	Pay after delivery	Pay before shipment	D/P	D/A	L/C	Confirmed L/C
			(a) Exporter's risks			
(a.1) Importer refuses goods						
Importer refuses documents						
(a.2) Importer defaults						
L/Cs issuing bank defaults						
(a.3) No license to import goods						
(a.4) No license to remit payment						
			(b) Importer's risks			
(b.1) Exporter doesn't send goods						
(b.2) Goods sent do not conform						
(b.3) No license to ship the goods						

Applications

1. What are the risks borne by the exporter and exporter, respectively, under payment before shipment and payment on delivery, respectively?

2. What characteristics of trade bills make these instruments well-suited to obtain low-cost financing?

3. Why is legal redress in international trade disputes more difficult than in domestic trade?

4. The writing and confirming of L/Cs must achieve more than just risk shifting without overall gains, otherwise these techniques would not exist. What are the advantages?

5. Some of the documents used in D/A, D/P, and documentary credits represent title to the goods. What purpose do the other documents serve?

6. Fill in the correct word from the following list: accept, the drawer, trade bill, promissory note, the drawee, You Owe Me, I Owe You, banker's acceptance, trade acceptance.

    As the word suggests, in many ways a (a) is like a summary of the invoice. The supplier (b) draws the bill on the customer (c). That is, like an invoice, a trade bill is a (d) document. In itself, a trade bill is not as trustworthy as an (e) document, such as a (f), which is written and signed by the debtor. To give a trade bill the same credibility as a (g), the drawer typically sends it to the drawee with a request to (h) it, that is, to add the drawee's signature and thus to acknowledge and confirm the existence of the underlying debt. A trade bill drawn on and accepted by the importer is called a (i); a bill drawn on and accepted by a bank is called a (j).

7. Complete table 15.3 by adding "+," "−," or "0" in each cell. A "+" rating means that the exporter (in part (a)) or the importer (in part (b)) is adequately covered against the risk described on the left-hand side of the corresponding line. A "−" rating reflects that the risk is uncovered. A "0" rating reflects a compromise.

8. (This is a tough one, for readers who actually studied the appendixes to chapter 9 on lognormal option pricing.) The Johannesburg branch of Shanghai Chartered Bank (SCB) is considering a three-month loan to Bechuana Coffee Plantations (BCP), to be backed by BCP's export receipts. The expected harvest is about 100 tons, and the expected world coffee price is about 7,000 crowns/ton.

   (a) SCB must decide how much it can lend if it can use BCP's entire export revenue as security. What precautions could SCB take to make sure that the export revenue is actually used to pay back the loan?

   (b) One of SCB's analysts is asked to estimate the worst-case export revenue. Unfortunately, both BCP and the coffee market have changed quite a lot since the company's founding twenty years ago, so that the analyst cannot simply use the history of BCP's export revenue to assess the risk.

   > The analyst assumes that the actual output ($\tilde{O}$) and the price ($\tilde{P}$) are lognormally distributed, because this distribution is more consistent with the nonnegativity of outputs and prices than a normal distribution and because then the revenue ($\tilde{O} \times \tilde{P}$) is also conveniently lognormal. On the basis of commodity option prices and output data from similar plantations, the analyst then estimates the parameters of output and prices separately. The plan is to compute the confidence intervals for the normally distributed variable $\ln(\tilde{O} \times \tilde{P}) = \ln(\tilde{O}) + \ln(\tilde{P})$, which has mean and variance equal to $[\mu_o + \mu_p]$ and $[\sigma_o^2 + 2\,\text{cov}_{o,p} + \sigma_p^2]$, respectively. From the lower bound on $\ln(\tilde{O} \times \tilde{P})$ the analyst can then infer the lower bound on ($\tilde{O} \times \tilde{P}$). From traded commodity option prices, SCB's analyst infers that the standard deviation of the log price is 10% over three months (20% p.a.). From past data on planted acreage and output for similar plantations, the standard deviation of BCP's output is estimated to be 15% over three months. Using the output and price expectations given above, what are μ_o and μ_p—the expected values of $\ln(\tilde{O})$ and $\ln(\tilde{P})$, rather than $\tilde{O}$ and the price $\tilde{P}$?

   (c) The analyst argues that, since Botswana has only a small share in the coffee market, the variance of the export revenue can be computed as if the covariance between local output and the world price is zero. Is this a conservative assumption or not? (*Hint.* What would be the sign of the covariance between the world output of coffee and the world price, and between BCP's output and the world price?)

   (d) How would SCB compute a 90% confidence interval for BCP's entire export revenue?

(e) It turns out that BCP needs far less than 500,000 crowns. BCP signs a contract with CEH Jouy-en-Josas, a well-known and solid French coffee trader, to deliver 40 tons at the forward price of 6,900 crowns/ton. When computing the maximum amount it can lend on the strength of this forward contract, should SCB take a similar safety margin relative to the expected revenue from this transaction as the one computed in part (e)?

(f) Suppose instead that CEH agrees to buy 50 tons at the (as yet unknown) future spot price for coffee. How should the analyst assess the risk in this case?

PART IV

Long-Term International Funding and Direct Investment

About This Part

The prime sources for long-term financing are the markets for fixed-interest instruments (bank loans, bonds) and stocks. We review the international aspects of these in chapters 16 and 17–18, respectively. Expected returns on stocks provide one key input of investment analysis, so in chapter 19 we consider the CAPM and the adjustments to be made to take into account real exchange risk. The other inputs into NPV computations are expected cash flows, and these are typically quite similar to what one would see in domestic projects. There is one special issue here: international taxes (chapter 20). In chapter 21, we see how to do the actual NPV, extending the usual two-step approach—NPV followed by adjusted NPV to take into account the aspects of financing, relevant in imperfect markets—to a three-step version to separately handle intra- and extra-company financial arrangements. We conclude with an analysis of joint-venture projects, where NPV is mixed with the issue of designing a fair profit-sharing contract (chapter 22).

A Joint Venture Project between Weltek, Antwerp, and Fusioneering, Jamspedpur

> This is based on a real-world case, but the names of the two main companies and their managers, as well as all dates and amounts, have been changed.

Mr. Dondeyn is the general manager of Weltek, a producer of welding electrodes and equipment. Over the last few years, he and his assistant general manager Ms. Dewulf have been negotiating a joint venture (JV) with three Indian partners, aiming at the local production of electrodes and possibly also the distribution of Weltek products imported into India.

The core business of Weltek is in "special" welding electrodes for maintenance and repair, not for plain-vanilla construction welding. Weltek belongs to the subtop in the industry and would like to grow. Founded in Belgium in the 1960s, it has subsidiaries in Italy, the Netherlands, the United Kingdom, Spain, the United States, and South Africa. All these are wholly owned. Production is concentrated in Belgium and Spain; the other subsidiaries are marketing and service companies.

Weltek has been interested in an Indian production unit for years. The internal market is huge, not only because of the size of the population, but more importantly also because repair is big business there. Like many developing countries, India is short of capital to import new equipment, and in the late

1990s the still-highish import tariffs made replacement very expensive; as a result, most equipment (industrial machinery, cars, appliances, etc.) is used for much longer than in most OECD countries. This implies an important maintenance and repair market, which in its turn induces a market for hand-welding fillers and equipment. India could also be a stepping-stone for exports toward other countries in the area, including CIS countries.

Weltek had in mind a production JV, not a wholly owned subsidiary nor a marketing JV. The JV option had to do not only with the local regulations—the investment code limited foreign ownership to 40%—but also with Weltek's financial capacity and its lack of knowledge of the local market. There was a transfer-risk issue too: in those days, there was free repatriation of capital brought in for direct investments, but there was still a bureaucratic delay, and the occasional nationalist noises by the then-ruling BJP party were not encouraging. (Restrictions on portfolio investments were even more restricted, whether inward or outward, in those days.) A JV meant a smaller investment, so smaller transfer risk. Local production, not just marketing of imported products, was preferred because even after India's liberalization of the 1990s its import tariffs were still high by Western standards. Therefore, exports to India are viable only for selected specialty products for which demand is too low to justify local production. A pure license contract wouldn't do either. One argument was control over the training and marketing effort. "We have a very intensive and well-developed formal training scheme for the sales force and for the engineers; an engineer, for instance, has to know literally everything about his or her products. So we were not willing to surrender control over training to an independent party," Mr. Dondeyn explains. Second, in view of government restrictions on the life of a license contract (five years) and on the size of the payments (at most 5%), a joint venture could be expected to be much more profitable than a stand-alone license contract.

Fusioneering, of Jamshedpur, was, among others things, in the arc-welding business, but given the youth of the company and its as yet limited expertise its managers felt that they needed more up-to-date know-how and technology. Thinking that the really big fish would not be interested in a small and as yet unprofitable business, they talked to mid-sized players like Weltek. A visit led to lengthy policy discussions, and ultimately to a memorandum of understanding. The parties agreed to live with low or negative profits for a couple of years, during which free samples would be distributed to build up credibility. The JV would buy the raw materials for production of ten Lastek electrodes, and sell the output. Still, it took almost two more years until all feasibility checks had been done and (especially) all investment licenses were obtained. During that time, Mr. Dondeyn was busy with other things. The Asian financial crisis and a misunderstanding about registration put the whole project on ice, but talks were reopened after a chance meeting at a trade fair. The tentative deal was as follows.

Pro forma P&L statements.

	Time (years)					
	0	1	2	3	4	5
Investments:						
Land	5					
Plant and equipment	10					
Training	5					
Up-front license	2					
P&L projections (1999 prices)						
Revenue:						
Gross sales	0	10	17	22	24	25
⟨Excise tax⟩	0	0.3	0.51	0.66	0.72	0.75
⟨Rebates⟩	0	0.5	0.85	1.1	1.2	1.25
⟨Provisions bad debt⟩	0	0.15	0.255	0.33	0.36	0.375
Net sales	0	9.05	15.385	19.91	21.72	22.625
Cost:						
Variable production costs	0	4	6	7	8	8.5
Depreciation P&E	2.5	2.5	2.5	2.5		
Depreciation training	2.5	2.5				
Overhead	1	2	2.5	3	3	3
License: up-front fee	2					
Royalties	0	0.46	0.782	1.012	1.104	1.15
Interest paid	1.6	1.6	1.28	0.96	0.64	0.32
Profit before tax	−9.6	−4.01	2.323	5.438	8.976	9.655
Tax computations:						
Cumulative profits	−9.6	−13.61	−11.287	−5.849	3.127	12.782
Losses carry back	−9.6	−13.61	−11.287	−5.849	0	0
Taxable income	0	0	0	0	3.127	9.655
Taxes	0	0	0	0	1.2508	3.862
Profit after tax	−9.6	−4.01	2.323	5.438	7.7252	5.793
Cash flows to shareholders						
Add back depreciation	5	5	2.5	2.5	0	0
⟨Amortization of loan⟩	0	4	4	4	4	4
Cash flow	−4.6	−3.01	0.823	3.938	3.7252	1.793

1. Investments are estimated and timed as follows:

   - Land is bought and paid for on 1/1/2000; cost: 5m rupees.
   - Construction (plant and equipment) starts on 1/4/2000 and lasts six months; cost: 10m.
   - Training of engineers starts on 1/7/2000; cost: 5m, including travel to and from Belgium.

   Total up-front investment is, therefore, 20m. Also to be financed are the initial cash drains, estimated at about 5m in year 0 and 3m in year 1 (see below).

The equity is set at 10m, 40% of which is provided by Weltek and 60% by Fusioneering. The equity is fully paid up on 1/1/2001 but lent back to the shareholders at zero cost with the proviso that they should finance, 40/60, any cash drains that might occur, as long as the cumulative drain remains below 10m. If cash drains exceed 10m, any shareholder has the option to sell his stake at book value to the other; and if both want to sell, the JV is to be liquidated. The investments themselves are financed by a loan (20m rupees at 8%), guaranteed entirely by Weltek and Weltek's house bank; the loan is to be taken up on 1/1/2000, and amortized in five equal annual tranches of 4m as of (the end of) 2001.

2. Production starts 1/10/2000. There is a three-month lead time (production, storage in Hyderabad, distribution, storage at the sales point) between the start of production and sales, so sales start on 1/1/2001. The contract also stipulates that Weltek receives an up-front license fee of 2m rupees, plus a five-year, 5% royalty on net sales payable early April after the reporting period.

3. Projected P&L are based on the following figures and comments:

   - Sales in the first year start as of 1/1/2001. "Gross sales" is computed as (volumes sold) × (list prices). The list prices include the excise tax (3%), which must be deducted for the purpose of profit calculations. Also deducted is an estimated 5% representing rebates for large orders, and a provision for nonperforming receivables estimated at 1.5%. The result is net sales income. Customers obtain a 30-day credit period.

   - Production costs (variable, depreciation, overhead) are as shown in the table. Training can be depreciated over two years, and equipment over four years, starting in year zero. Depreciation has to be linear.

   - Know-how and financial charges. There is an 2m up-front licensing fee and the 5% royalty on net sales. The interest on the bank loan is computed on a loan balance of 20m in January 2000 and 2001, 16m in January 2002, 12m in January 2003, 8m in January 2004, and 4m in January 2005. Interest is payable in four quarterly tranches (2% effective per quarter).

   - Taxable profit is the annual profit minus any tax shield from carried-over losses. Taxes (40%) are payable in the middle of the year following the reporting year; that is, taxes on 1994 profits are paid mid 1995, etc.

On the flight back to Belgium, Mr. Dondeyn types the projected P&L statement into his laptop, and runs a quick-and-dirty NPV. To compute the cash flows, Mr. Dondeyn notes that the net investment is zero (total investments are entirely financed by a loan); so he takes profits after taxes, adds back depreciation and subtracts the loan amortizations. The cost of capital is set at 14% (the 8% on the loan being the subsidized rate at which the JV would be able to borrow, plus a 6% risk premium assuming a unit beta). The NPV seems to be −0.71m rupee: not hugely negative, but negative nevertheless.

Issues

1. The NPV calculations do not seem to involve anything special: it all looks like domestic capital budgeting. Are there no special issues that arise when the project is international?

2. The quick-and-dirty calculation ascribed to Mr. Dondeyn ignores the fact that there are two shareholders, and is made as if this were a wholly owned project. Even so, these calculations are very flawed: I stuffed about every mistake into the spreadsheet one could possibly make. Read this part, identify the errors, and correct them.

3. Is there a way to judge the fairness of the proposed cash-splitting rules for the JV? What should one look at? If one finds a good measure of fairness, is there a straightforward way of achieving this fairness, or is it just a matter of trial and error?

16

International Fixed-Income Markets

In this chapter, we have a look at one source of financing for companies: international money, loan, and bond markets. Related short-term fixed-interest products, like deposits and short-term loans or commercial paper, are briefly touched upon. Other related instruments, notably interest forwards and futures, were introduced in the appendixes to chapters 4 and 6.

These international fixed-interest markets used to largely coincide with what was (and largely still is) called *euromoney* and *eurobond* markets, that is, markets for banking products or bonds denominated in a currency that is not the official money of the country where the loan was taken up or the bonds were issued. For example, a Norwegian investor may deposit USD not in the United States but with a bank located outside the United States, for example, in Oslo or in London. Or a Peruvian company may issue bonds in London and denominate them in JPY.

The prefix "euro" became misleading when such extra-territorial markets also emerged in, for example, Asia. One then began to hear of asiadollars, and so on. Since the advent of the euro as a currency, the prefix has also become ambiguous: are we talking about bonds expressed in EUR or bonds issued outside the home turf of the currency? Also, the term could lead to absurd combinations, like euro-euro for EUR bonds placed in London. There have been feeble attempts to find a new term; the *Economist* even invited suggestions from the public at large, and in the end backed the by no means new "xeno" proposal (from Greek ξενος, meaning foreign). But the entire prefix issue fizzled out of its own accord, since people no longer thought there was anything special about setting up deals in a particular currency outside its original territory. If ever the distinction is important to you, you can just add the adjective: everybody will catch your drift. In most of this text I prefer to use "international." The term "offshore" might have done well, too, if it weren't for the connotation with "having a special tax status," which is not what we have in mind right now.

In the sections that tell the tale of how the international markets emerged, we still use the euro prefix in its "international" meaning. For simplicity, when we say euro we also mean to include other international markets in the Middle

East and especially in the Far East (Tokyo, Hong Kong, Singapore). This largely conforms to standard practice in the Americas and Europe.

The earliest activity in the international markets was in the deposit and loan segments, the segments where banks act as intermediaries between investors and borrowers. The emergence and growth of the eurobanking business was mainly the result of low costs, which enable a more narrow bid–ask spread. The success of this unregulated, wholesale banking market was soon imitated in the bond section and in the short-term securities part of the capital market (eurobonds and eurocommercial paper, respectively).

This chapter is organized in the following way. In the first section, we describe the traditional eurobanking world: markets for short-term international deposits, bank loans, and credit lines. We then discuss the counterparts of these banking products in the securities markets, namely, the international bond and commercial paper (CP) markets (section 15.2). The final issue we bring up, in section 16.3, is how to compare one's fixed-financing alternatives across currencies and markets. We conclude in section 16.4.

16.1 "Euro" Deposits and Loans

The banking segment is the oldest segment of the international markets. Even before World War II, there was a small market for USD deposits and loans in London, then the world's financial heart. However, the market took off in earnest only in the 1960s. We start by explaining the reasons for its rapid growth since then. We distinguish between circumstances that facilitated the emergence of the market and reasons for its longer-term success. The proximate reasons had mostly to do with bad economic-policy decisions and regulations that had unexpected consequences.

16.1.1 Historic, Proximate Causes of Euromoney's Growth

Liberalization of trade and exchange. The eurodollar markets began to expand in the 1950s and 1960s, after the lifting of the widespread exchange controls. These controls had been imposed after World War II because of the scarcity of dollars (the only internationally accepted currency at the time, since even the GBP's international use had become heavily controlled and regulated).

Note, however, that while liberalization of the exchange market is a necessary condition for the emergence of euromoney markets, it is not an explanation of that emergence.

The U.S. trade deficit. The liberalization of the European exchange markets was possible only because the shortage of USD did not last long. Immediately after the war, the United States launched an international aid program (the Marshall Plan). In addition, the United States imported more goods and services than it exported, and U.S. corporations became important international investors, buying companies or building plants all over the world. But, tautologically, the balance of payments has to balance, remember. So the deficit on the current account, the "capital" (aid) account, and the FDI balance meant that there must be a surplus or a set of "source" deals elsewhere (see chapter 2). This offsetting surplus was realized by exporting U.S. government or corporate bonds and short-term assets, including sight money. Most countries cannot export sight money in any meaningful amounts, but the United States could since its money was also the closest one can get to world money: it was used everywhere for international transactions. Thus, the U.S. deficit on the current account and the aid and FDI accounts meant that more and more sight money ended up in the hands of foreign investors. Foreign central banks held some too, but preferred interest-bearing forms.

Note, again, that this is not a true explanation for the rise of euromoney markets. The fact that there were foreign-owned USD does not explain why part of these USD balances were held via European banks rather than directly with U.S. banks. The next three arguments relate to positive incentives for eurodollar transactions.

Political risks. Since the 1950s, the cold war created political risks for communist countries that wished to hold USD deposits: the U.S. government could seize Soviet deposits held in New York. For that reason, the Soviet Union and China shifted their dollar balances to London and Paris, out of reach of the U.S. government. This meant that there was a Western bank between them and the U.S. banking system (see, again, chapter 2).

U.K. capital controls and restrictions. In the nineteenth century, London had been the world's center for international financing and sterling the world's favorite currency. After World War II, however, the GBP was chronically overvalued, and the United Kingdom had serious balance-of-payments problems of its own.[1] Thus, the British government limited foreign borrowing in GBP.[2] As a result, U.K. banks borrowed USD (that is, accepted USD deposits), which were then used to extend USD loans instead of GBP loans.

U.S. capital controls and restrictions. In the United States, the disequilibrium on the merchandise and invisibles, aid, and direct-investment balances, combined with the growing overvaluation of the USD against the DEM and related

---

[1] The pound maintained its gold parity from the early 1700s until 1931, when it was devalued by 25%. By the end of World War II this rate had become totally unrealistic, and British exporters again had a hard time while imports boomed. The United Kingdom could no longer hope that sterling balances, sent abroad in payment for its net imports, would happily be held by traders all over the world; rather, outstanding pound balances were being returned and converted into dollars. All this put pressure on sterling. (The pound devalued by 40% in 1949 and by another 16% in 1967. Controls were lifted gradually, and only entirely went out of the window in the 1980s, under Margaret Thatcher.)

[2] A speculator, remember, would borrow a currency deemed weak, and sell the proceeds (hoping to be able to buy back later at a low cost), thus putting additional pressure on the spot rate. Until the 1980s–90s, governments often had the lamentable habit of forbidding the symptoms rather than curing the disease. So Her Majesty's government forbade pound loans to nonresidents.

currencies, pushed up U.S. interest rates. President Kennedy tried to alleviate the problem by imposing the *interest equalization tax* (1963–74) on foreign borrowing in the United States. This tax allowed internal U.S. interest rates to remain below USD interest rates offered in Europe. President Kennedy and later, President Johnson, also imposed *foreign credit restraints* (1965, 1968–74) that hindered borrowing by foreigners in the U.S. market. Simultaneously, *Regulation Q* (enacted in 1966, relaxed in 1974, and abolished in 1986) imposed interest ceilings on domestic USD deposits with U.S. commercial banks. The combined effect of all of this was that U.S. corporations and investors preferred to hold USD deposits in Europe (where they obtained better rates), and these dollars were then re-lent to non-U.S. borrowers who were no longer allowed to borrow USD in the United States. Finally, President Nixon's "voluntary" (and later, mandatory) *curbs on capital exports* had the unintended result that U.S. multinationals avoided depositing their funds in the United States lest these funds be blocked there. The money was deposited, instead, in the euromarkets.

16.1.2 Comparative Advantages in the Medium Term

The eurodollar markets did not collapse after all of the regulations described above were abolished. Nor can the above factors explain the subsequent emergence of international markets for other currencies, like the DEM, the JPY, or the ECU, and—to a lesser extent—the CHF, NZD, NLG, etc. The long-term explanation of the success of these international markets is their lower bid–offer spread (that is, the difference between interest rates on loans and interest rates on deposits), which in turn reflects the lower costs of international banking as compared with domestic banking. There are many reasons for the low operating costs.

A lean and mean machine. The international market is essentially a wholesale market, where large volumes of transactions allow narrow spreads. Eurobanks, unlike many domestic commercial banks a few decades ago, were not expected to offer politically or socially inspired subsidized loans to ailing companies or house-building families. Nor do they need an expensive retail network.

Low legal costs. Most euroborrowers are sovereign states or high-grade corporations. This means that there are hardly any costs of credit evaluation, bonding, and monitoring.

Lighter regulation. For eurodollar banking (as opposed to domestic banking) there is no compulsory deposit insurance, which means that there are no insurance costs. Nor are there any reserve requirements (which are, in fact, similar to taxes on deposits),[3] and local monetary authorities tended to be far

---

[3] A 5% reserve requirement would mean that a bank, when receiving a customer deposit for 100, has to redeposit 5 in a non-interest-earning account with the central bank. Thus, only 95 can be re-lent. This increases the effective cost of accepting the deposit.

more lenient as far as credit restraints are concerned when borrowing did not involve their home currency.[4]

Universal banking. In the United Kingdom, as in much of continental Europe, there was no equivalent of the U.S. Glass Steagall Act that separated commercial banking (sight and time deposits, overdrafts and loans) from investment banking (placing, underwriting, and holding securities). Although, by definition, you do not need universal banks for deposits and loans, companies still liked institutions that could both offer loans and help place their paper: both are very close substitutes. Nor was there anything, in the United Kingdom, like the U.S. ban on interstate banking, a rule that imposed a cap on U.S. banks' growth (except for a handful of international players).

Lower taxes. Eurobanks were often located in tax havens or are part of a financial network involving tax havens. Also in mainstream OECD countries, international transactions often received beneficial tax treatment when compared with domestic businesses (for example, a waiver of stamp duties or withholding taxes; in this respect, many OECD countries have now followed the lead of tax-haven countries).[5] Furthermore, many investors with undeclared income—the "Swiss dentist" or the "Belgian dentist," as the *Economist* or *Euromoney* fondly call them—appreciated the opportunities for tax avoidance or tax evasion available in euromoney markets. Foreign deposits were often fiscally anonymous (that is, the bank cannot be forced to reveal their identity to a foreign tax authority), or are often in the form of bearer securities.

16.1.3 Where We Are Now: A Truly International Market

As Merton Miller beautifully put it, silly regulation provided the grain of sand—the thing that starts as an irritant to an oyster but ultimately grows into a pearl.[6] The market survived the abolition of the currency controls and excessive regulation; these had speeded up the growth of the market, but even without them a similar market would have emerged sooner or later because there was a need for a fast, lightly regulated field for big, professional players. London and other centers provided just that.

Nowadays, however, the playing field has become much more even, and the "euro" markets' comparative advantage was eroding fast. Wholesale,

---

[4] It is true that eurobanks are subject, like any other banks, to the so-called Bank of International Settlements (BIS) rules. However, these are not reserve requirements. Rather, the BIS rules set the minimum amount of equity a bank should have, in light of its balance-sheet and off-balance-sheet positions.

[5] A stamp duty is a tax on transactions in securities. A withholding tax is a tax levied on interest or dividends, withheld when the interest or dividend is paid out (rather than collected afterward, on the basis of a tax return).

[6] Actually, pearls do not grow in oysters (*ostreida*) but in two species closer to mussels, *pterida* and *meleagrina* (also known as *pintada*); and they do not start from grains of sand but from indigestible food residues. But otherwise the image is accurate.

Table 16.1. Largest banking centers.

	Banking deposits Dec 05 (USD tr)	Number of banks Mar 05 (number)	Branches and subsidiaries of foreign banks Mar 05 (number)	Return on capital 2006 (%)	Cost/ income ratio 2006 (%)	Cross- border lending Mar 07 (%)	Cross- border borrowing Mar 07 (%)
JP	5.1	129	69	16.2	69.4	9	2
U.S.	5.2	7,540	228	22.2	59.9	20	12
U.K.	4.6	347	264	19.6	50.2	10	23
DE	3.1	**2,344	125	4.7	61.5	9	7
FR	1.5	**318	*217	15.7	63.9	8	9

*End 2004; **end 2005. *Source:* International Financial Services London. *International Financial Markets in the U.K.*, November 2007, www.ifsl.org.uk/research; based on Bank of England, KPMG, Banque de France, The Banker, Bank for International Settlements, European Banking Federation, Bank of Japan, FDIC, and the U.S. Federal Reserve.

simple deals with prime borrowers can be signed everywhere. "Regulatory arbitrage"—that is, borrowers and investors migrating away from the overly regulated markets—has forced countries everywhere to dump rules, taxes, and duties that did more harm than good. In the United States, Glass Stea-gall and the ban on interstate banking have been repealed. Currency controls have gone for most currencies, as have credit restraints and, in many countries, reserve requirements. Tax authorities cooperate internationally, and governments exchange information on foreign deposits and/or foreign investment income. Originally, this was just in cases where crime- and drugs-related money laundering was suspected or, later, terrorist activities; but cooperation for fiscal purposes is coming in too. Within the EU, information on nonresidents' income is already being shared; a few countries still impose withholding taxes instead but this will be phased out. Secret ("numbered") bank accounts, for a long time one of the attractions of, most notably, Swiss, Austrian, and Liechtenstein banks, are essentially a thing of the past: bankers must know their customers' identities. Tellingly, countries with a dark reputation are now being blacklisted by the OECD; when in the early 2000s a new government in Mauritius proposed setting up a "high-privacy" banking sector, the big countries were all over her and Mauritius hastily withdrew the proposal.

As a result, there is no longer much difference between domestic and international banking, certainly not for wholesale deals in OECD countries and the like. In that sense, in a large part of the world, markets nowadays are truly international, not just a collection of local markets with, on the fringe, an international corner for the big guys.

In the following sections, we review the products offered by international banks. The first product in our *tour d'horizon* is the deposit.

16.1.4 International Deposits

Initially, international deposits were typically *time deposits* (or *term deposits*), that is, nonnegotiable, registered instruments with a fixed life. A *certificate of deposit* (CD) is the tradable-security version of the traditional term deposit: it is negotiable (that is, can be sold to another investor at any time) and is often a bearer security.

The bulk of the deposits have a very short duration—for instance, overnight, one or two weeks, but mostly one, three, or six months. These short-term deposits or CDs pay no interim interest; there is a single payment, principal and interest, at expiration. For long-term CDs or long-term deposits (up to seven years), there is a fixed coupon or floating-rate coupon. For CDs with *floating-rate* coupons, the life of the CD is subdivided into subperiods of usually six months. The interest rate that applies for each period consists of a fixed spread laid down in the contract, and a risk-free market rate that is reset every period. Following the by-now familiar "spot" tradition, this resetting occurs two working days before the beginning of the period (the *reset date*). The market rate on the basis of which the rate is reset is usually the London Interbank Offer Rate (Libor) or the Interbank Offer Rate (IBOR) in the currency's domestic financial center. "The" Libor and similar IBORs[7] are computed as an average of the rates offered by an agreed-upon list of banks; the EBA has standard lists. The basis of the floating rate may also be the bid rate, or the mean (midpoint) rate, or, in the United States, the T-bill rate or the prime rate. If the basis rate is an ask rate (like IBOR or the prime rate[8]), the spread is usually negative: we are talking about deposits, here.

> **Example 16.1.** An investor buys an NZD 1,000,000 floating-rate CD with a life of two years, at NZD Libor minus 0.375%, reset every six months. The initial reference interest rate is 4% p.a., which implies that after six months the investor receives $1,000,000 \times (4 - 0.375)\%/2 = $ NZD 18,125. The reset date is two days before this interest is paid out, and the six-month Libor on this reset date may turn out to be, say, 3.5% p.a. This means that the second interest payment will be only $1,000,000 \times (3.5 - 0.375)\%/2 = $ NZD 15,625. There will be two more of these reset dates. At the end of the last period, the principal is also paid back.

You can view such a floating-rate CD as a series of short-term CDs that are automatically rolled over without reinvestment of the interest earned each period. Sometimes a floating-rate CD has a *cap* or a *floor*, that is, the interest rate that the investor actually receives has an upper or lower bound. We shall discuss caps and floors in the next section, which describes euroloans.

---

[7] The rule is to make the first letter refer to a city, like Aibor (Amsterdam), Bibor (Brussels), Pibor (Paris), Tibor (Tokyo), and so on. For the EUR one refers to Euribor; the old national IBORs have gone, including Frankfurt's Fibor.

[8] The prime rate was once the posted rate for unsecured loans to good-quality borrowers; nowadays it is, de facto, applied to rather mediocre borrowers.

16.1.5   International Credits and Loans

International banks offer essentially the same products as domestic banks: loans and credit lines. But there are a few interesting differences.

16.1.5.1   Consortia

One difference is that the loans tend to be extended by a group of banks (a *syndicate* or *consortium*) rather than by a single institution. The members of the consortium or syndicate can play very different roles.

- The *mandated arranger* (or, more traditionally, the *lead bank* or *lead manager*) negotiates with the borrower for tentative terms and conditions, obtains a mandate from him to get the loan together, and looks for other banks that are willing to provide the money or at least to act as a backup for the money. In the event that several banks unanimously agree to form a mandated arranger group, the title is assigned to all banks within such a group. *Bookrunner* status is then assigned to the bank that runs the book (i.e., solicits and records the commitments by other banks to participate in the funding) for a deal that is sent out into general syndication. The bookrunner often leads the consortium even if arranging is, formally, shared. Bookrunnership is now, in turn, getting shared among many banks; soon we will need a lead bookrunner, and a few years from now a coordinator of the lead bookrunners.

- The banks that provide the actual funding are called *participating banks*.

- Because the funding is not yet arranged at the time of the negotiations, the lead bank or the group of joint bookrunners often contacts a smaller number of *managing banks* to underwrite the loan, that is, guarantee to make up for the shortage of funds if there is a shortage. These banks are also called *underwriters, co-managers, co-leads,* or *co-arrangers.*

- The *paying agent* or *facility agent*, finally, is the bank that receives the service payments from the borrower and distributes them to the participating banks.

Any given bank can play multiple roles. For instance, the lead bank is almost invariably also the largest underwriter (hence, the name "lead manager") and usually provides some of the funding as well. The main objective of syndication is to spread the risks, but it also eliminates the moral hazard of the borrower paying off its bigger lenders and ignoring the small debtholders: because of the paying-agent system, the borrower either defaults toward all banks or toward none.

As in domestic banking, the borrower often signs promissory notes (that is, IOU documents), one for each payment. The advantage of receiving promissory notes is that they are easily negotiable. That is, if the lending bank needs funds, it can pass on the promissory note to another financial institution as security for a new loan or it can sell the promissory note. Regular loans are not so

---

$500m Turkish bank loan syndication for Vakifbank signed in Dubai
UAE Central Bank governor addresses signing ceremony

6 December 2004; Dubai, UAE: A US$500 million syndicated term loan agreement for Vakifbank (Türkiye Vakiflar Bankasi T.A.O.) one of the strongest banks in Turkey, was signed in Dubai today by a syndicate of 56 blue-chip regional and international banks. The loan was raised to pre-finance Turkish export contracts and has a margin of 60 basis points per annum. VakifBank is currently rated Bpi by S&P, B+ by Fitch, and B2 by Moody's. On 1st of November 2004 Fitch increased the National Long Term Rating of VakifBank by two notches to A-(tur).

Bookrunners: Citibank NA, Standard Bank London Limited and WestLB AG.

Documentation Agent: Standard Bank London Limited.

Facility Agent: Sumitomo Mitsui Banking Corporation Europe Limited.

Information Memorandum: WestLB AG.

Coordination, Publicity and Signing: Standard Bank London Limited.

Mandated Arrangers: ABN AMRO Bank N.V., Al Ahli Bank of Kuwait, Alpha Bank A.E., American Express Bank GmbH, Banque Saudi Fransi, The Bank of Tokyo-Mitsubishi, Ltd., Burgan Bank, Citibank N.A., Demir-Halk Bank (Nederland) N.V., Deutsche Bank AG London; Dresdner Kleinwort Wasserstein (acting through Dresdner Bank AG, Niederlassung Luxemburg), GarantiBank International N.V., Gulf Bank KSC, HVB Group (represented by members of HVB Group), ING, J.P. Morgan plc, Mashreqbank P.S.C., Natexis Banques Populaires, Raiffeisen Zentralbank Österreich AG, Standard Bank London Limited, Standard Chartered Bank, Sumitomo Mitsui Banking Corporation Europe Limited, UFJ Bank Limited; Wachovia Bank, National Association and WestLB AG, London Branch.

Co-Arrangers: Gulf International Bank B.S.C., HSH Nordbank AG, Samba Financial Group, Managers, Doha Bank, Arab African International Bank, Banque Misr – Overseas Branch, Erste Bank (Malta) Limited, Finansbank (Holland) N.V., Raiffeisenlandesbank Oberösterreich Aktiengesellschaft, The Bank of Nova Scotia, The Commercial Bank Of Qatar (Q.S.C.), The Saudi National Commercial Bank, Bahrain, UBAE Arab Italian Bank Spa

Participants: Bankmuscat S.A.O.G., Arab Bank plc, Baden-Württembergische Bank Aktiengesellschaft, Banca Nazionale del Lavoro S.p.A., London Branch, Banco Bilbao Vizcaya Argentaria S.A., Bank Hapoalim B.M., Bank of Ireland, Banque Internationale De Commerce – BRED, Credit Suisse, First Gulf Bank, Misr International Bank S.A.E., Sabanci Bank PLC, United Bank Limited, UAE, Zivnostenská Banka, a.s., Banca Monte Dei Paschi di Siena s.p.a., Habib Bank AG Zürich, London Forfaiting Company Limited, Tunis International Bank.

Figure 16.1. An international syndicated loan: Vakifbank. *Source:* www.international.standardbank.com/AboutUs/PressReleases.aspx?id=232.

easily traded: they need to be packed into special vehicles which then issue claims against the vehicle's assets (loan-backed securities, collateralized debt obligations, and the like).

Until well into the 1990s a big loan would show up in *Euromoney*, the *Economist*, or *Business Week* and the like as a "tombstone," that is, an austere-looking advertisement that trumpets the signing of a new deal. Sadly, these are now replaced by internet press releases. Figure 16.1 shows one by Turkey's Vakifbank.

16.1.5.2 *Revolving or Floating-Rate Loans*

Another difference between traditional bank loans and big international loans is that the latter tend to be of the floating-rate (FR) type, whereas many domestic loans still have an interest rate that is fixed over the entire life of the loan. The reason for this predilection for FR loans is the very short funding of banks (see above): banks do not like the risk that, after having lent long term at a fixed rate, they may have to refinance short term at unexpectedly high interest rates. The emergence of interest swaps, however, has made the hedging of an interest gap easier. International banks now lend longer and domestic banks resort to FR loans more often too.

Example 16.2. A bank accepts a three-month, DKK 100m deposit at 4% p.a. and extends a loan for six months at 4.5% p.a. For simplicity, assume that this deposit and this loan represent the bank's entire balance sheet. After the deposit has expired, the bank must pay DKK $100m \times (1 + 4\%/4)$ = DKK 101m to the original lender. Since there are no cash inflows yet from the loan, the bank must borrow this amount (that is, accept a new three-month deposit). If, at that time, the three-month rate has increased to 7% p.a., then after another three months the bank has to pay $101m \times (1 + 7\%/4)$ = DKK 102,767.5m, though it receives only $100m \times (1 + 4.5\%/2)$ = DKK 102,250m from the original six-month borrower. Thus, because of the increase in the short-term interest rate the bank lost DKK 517,500 rather than making money.

In the above example, the maturity mismatch is not large because the loan is assumed to be for only six months. However, borrowers often have long-term capital needs; and rolling over short-term loans (at interest rates revised at each rollover date) is awkward for the borrower: the bank can always refuse to extend a new loan or drastically increase the spread over Libor. The need to reconcile the banker's desire for a safe interest margin with the borrower's preference for long-term guaranteed funding gave rise to the *revolving loan* or *floating-rate loan*. This is a medium-term or long-term loan where the interest rate is reset every period on the basis of the then-prevailing money market rate plus a spread. For example, if interest is payable every six months, then, just as for FR deposits, two days before the beginning of each such period, the interest rate for the next half year is set equal to the then-prevailing six-month Libor rate, contractually increased with a spread of, say, $\frac{1}{2}$% p.a. Thus, the bank is protected against interest-rate risk, and the borrower's funding is guaranteed for an agreed-upon period at a preset risk-spread over the base rate. The basis of the interest rate in rolled-over loans is typically the Libor or a similar interbank rate. Occasionally, the U.S. prime rate or the U.S. T-bill rate is chosen.

16.1.5.3   Revolving Loans with Caps or Floors

Sometimes there is a *cap* and/or a *floor* to the effective interest rate. For instance, the contract may say that the interest rate will never exceed 6% p.a. (cap) or fall below 3% p.a. (floor). These caps or floors are like European-type options on T-bills or on eurodeposits or euroloans. You are, of course, thinking of calls as being relevant when prices are high, and puts when prices are

Table 16.2.   A revolving loan with a cap and a floor.

Rates (%)		Equivalent PN story			Mood		Option executed
Libor	Rate on loan	Face value	Fair PV	Proceeds	Bank	You	
3	3.5/2 = 1.75	101.75	100.25	100	☺	☹	Bank's call
3.5	3.5/2 = 1.75	101.75	100.00	100			(None)
4	4.0/2 = 2.00	102.00	100.00	100			(None)
4.5	4.5/2 = 2.25	102.25	100.00	100			(None)
5	4.5/2 = 2.25	102.25	99.76	100	☹	☺	Your put

Key: The loan is about 100m, at six-month Libor but with a floor at 3.5% p.a. and a cap at 4.5% p.a. Thus the six-monthly PN the borrower has to hand over has a face value of $100 \times (1 + \text{Libor})$, but no lower than 101.75m and no higher than 102.25. With very low Libors, when the fair value of a PN at 101.75 would be higher than 100, the borrower gets no more than 100: the bank exercises its call on the note. With very high Libors, when the fair value of a PN at 102.26 would be lower than 100, the borrower still gets 100: she exercises her put on the note.

low. But market values of loans are inversely related to interest rates. So a floor on the interest rate is a cap on the price and vice versa.

> **Example 16.3.** Suppose that you have a one-year, NZD 100m loan, with half-yearly interest payments capped at 4.5% *p.a.*, that is, 2.25% per half year. The interest rate for the period that starts immediately is already known, say, 4% p.a. The 2.25% cap on the next six-month effective return means that, after six months, you have the right to borrow NZD 100m at 2.25% (effective) for another six-month period. That is, six months from now you have the right to place (= sell) a new six-month promissory note with expiration value NZD 102.25m at a price of NZD 100m, a right that is valuable to you if at the reset date the six-month rate is above 4.5% p.a. and the normal market value of a six-month 102.25m note is therefore below 100m. In standard optionspeak, you hold a put option on an NZD 102.25m note at a strike price set at $X = \text{NZD } 100\text{m}$.

> **DIY Problem 16.1.** Suppose that you have a one-year, NZD 1m loan, with half-yearly interest payments with a floor at 3.5% *p.a.*, that is, 1.75% per half year. The interest rate for the period that starts immediately is already known; for instance, it may be 4% p.a. or 2% effective. Interpret the 3.5% floor as an option on a PN: who holds and who writes the option, what type of option is it, what exactly are the terms and conditions of the underlying PN?

Both the example and the DIY problem are summarized in table 16.2.

In short, the floor on the interest rate is a call option on a promissory note, and the option is held by the lender and written by the borrower. The cap on the interest rate is a put option on a promissory note, and the option is held by the borrower and written by the lender. The reason why it is useful to restate caps and floors as puts and calls on PNs is that a PN, unlike an interest rate, is an asset. So one can express a put–call parity in terms of option prices, an underlying PN price, and a discounted strike price. There is no similar direct link between option values and interest rates, except when prices are expressed as functions of interest rates.

DIY Problem 16.2. Buying a European-style call and selling a European-style put still means a forward purchase, and the forward purchase at strike X still has the same value as the underlying. So put–call parity still takes the form

$$\text{(Call premium)} - \text{(Put premium)} = \text{(Market value forward purchase)}$$

$$= \text{PV asset} - \frac{X}{1 + r_{t,T}}. \qquad (16.1)$$

Write the PV of the asset as a function of the limit rate (e.g., the 3% from the example) and the current market rate. Show that the right-hand side of the equation can be written as the *discounted* difference between the limit and market effective rates of return.

Hasty traders occasionally ignore the discounting, and express option prices as p.a. percentages so as to get a link with the p.a. interest rates in the formula.

16.1.5.4 Costs of a Loan

There are various costs associated with a euroloan. These include:

- An up-front *management fee* and *participation fee*, sometimes 0.25% and sometimes a few percentages (see below). The up-front feature means that this amount is deducted from the principal. That is, the borrower receives only 99–99.5% of the nominal value of the loan.

- A *paying agent's fee* of a few basis points to cover the administrative expenses.

- The *risk spread* above the risk-free rate (that is, above Libor in the case of a floating-rate loan or above the long-term fixed rate paid by a government of excellent credit standing). This spread depends on the quality of the borrower, the transfer risk of his or her country, the maturity and grace period, and the up-front fee. Also, the market situation affects the spread: there are strong cycles, with spreads widening when something bad happens, then competition gradually narrowing the spread until a new bad event happens and so on.[9]

In principle, the fees are compensation for the services of the intermediaries, while the spread is a compensation for default risk. However, one can trade a higher up-front fee for a lower spread, and vice versa. For instance, borrowers often accept a high up-front fee in return for a lower spread because the spread

---

[9] The famous hedge fund Long-Term Capital Management (LTCM) was betting on a shrinking spread when, instead, a very bad thing happened: Russia's default. Betting again on a falling spread, LTCM was again wrong-footed, notably by the Asian crises. That was the beginning of the end for LTCM.

is sometimes seen as a quality rating. One corollary of the trading of up-front fees for risk spreads is that the spread that country X pays may be a poor indicator of the creditworthiness of country X: an ostensibly reassuring spread may have been bought off by a large up-front fee. Another corollary is that reliable comparisons between offers from competing banks can be made only if there is a single, overall measure of cost. Thus, when comparing offers from competing syndicates, one should convert the up-front fees into equivalent spreads, or the spreads and paying-agent fees into equivalent up-front costs.

Example 16.4. Suppose that an up-front fee of USD 425,000 is asked on a five-year loan of USD 10,000,000 with an annual interest payment of 5% (including spreads) and one single amortization at the loan's maturity date. The effective proceeds of the loan are, therefore, USD 10,000,000 − 425,000 = USD 9,575,000. The effective interest rate can be estimated by computing the internal rate of return or yield, denoted by y, on the transaction:

$$\text{Find } y: \quad 9{,}575{,}000 = \frac{500{,}000}{1+y} + \frac{500{,}000}{(1+y)^2} + \cdots + \frac{10{,}500{,}000}{(1+y)^5}. \tag{16.2}$$

This equation can be solved on a spreadsheet or on a calculator. The solution is, approximately, $y = 6.0092\%$, which is about 1% above the stated rate. Conversely, the up-front fee is equivalent to adding 1% p.a. to the stated rate.

In the above example, the future payments are known because the loan had a fixed interest rate. If the loan has a floating rate, one can no longer compute the yield because the future cash flows are unknown. However, the up-front fee can still be translated into an equivalent annual payment or equivalent annuity, using the interest rate on a fixed-rate loan with the same life and the same default risk. (To get the required number, simply ask for a quote for a fixed-for-floating swap.) The equivalent annuity can then be converted into an equivalent percentage spread by dividing the annuity by the loan's nominal value.

Example 16.5. We use the same data as in the previous example except that the loan has a floating rate. If the normal all-in market rate on a fixed-rate loan with the same life and default risk as the floating-rate loan is 6%, the equivalent annuity (EqAn) of USD 425,000 up-front is determined as follows:

$$\text{EqAn:} \quad 425{,}000 = \frac{\text{EqAn}}{1+y} + \frac{\text{EqAn}}{(1+y)^2} + \cdots + \frac{\text{EqAn}}{(1+y)^5}$$

$$= \text{EqAn} \times 4.212\,367,$$

$$\implies \quad \text{EqAn} = \frac{425{,}000}{4.212\,367} = 100{,}893.47. \tag{16.3}$$

Thus, the up-front fee is equivalent to a spread of 100,893.47/10,000,000, that is, about 1% p.a.

If you ever have to do sums like this on a no-frills calculator, the shortcut to remember is

$$\frac{1}{1+y} + \frac{1}{(1+y)^2} + \cdots + \frac{1}{(1+y)^n} = \frac{1-(1+y)^{-n}}{y}. \tag{16.4}$$

DIY Problem 16.3. If you applied the approach of the last example to the one before, you would have found an equivalent spread of 1.0089%, not the 1.0092 of the earlier example. Why is there a difference? Which do you think is the best figure (assuming anybody would bother about differences as tiny as this one)?

16.1.5.5 Credit Lines

In addition to outright loans, eurobanks also offer standby credits. These come in two forms:

- A standard line of credit (or credit line) of, say, GBP 100m gives the beneficiary the right to borrow up to GBP 100m, at the prevailing interest rate plus a preset spread. The difference between a credit line and a loan is that with a credit line the company is not forced to actually borrow the money: money is *drawn down* only if and when it is needed, and paid back at any date before the expiry date. Interest (in the strict sense) is payable only on the portion actually used, while on the unused funds only a *commitment fee* of 0.125–1% p.a. needs to be paid.

  A credit line is, in principle, a short-term commitment—say, three months. In practice, a credit line tends to get extended, but this is not an automatic right to the creditor. Unless stated otherwise, the credit line can be revoked by the bank if there are substantial changes in the creditor's credit standing.

- Under a *revolving commitment*, the creditor has the irrevocable right to borrow up to a stated limit, at the then-prevailing rate plus a preset spread during an agreed-upon period of (usually) several years. For instance, a borrower may have the right to borrow up to GBP 50m at interest of six-month Libor plus 1.5% p.a. This is similar to a credit line, except that it cannot be revoked during its life.

A credit line is like a single, short-lived option on the preset spread, and the revolving commitment is like a series of such options (one expiring every six months, for instance). These contracts are options, not forward contracts, because the beneficiary can always borrow elsewhere if the market-required spread drops. The credit line and the revolving commitment differ from caps in the sense that the contract imposes a ceiling on the spread, not on the interest rate.

Example 16.6. A company has the right to borrow at 1% above Libor. If the company's credit rating deteriorates, or if average spreads in the market increase, the 1% spread has become a bargain relative to what would have to be paid on new borrowing, and the credit will be effectively used. If, on the other hand, the company's rating improves, or if average spreads in the market fall, the 1% spread may be very high.

If the company uses the credit line, it still has to pay the agreed-upon 1% spread. However, the company can also borrow elsewhere, at a spread that reflects its better standing or the lower average spreads. Thus, the company has a cap option on the 1% spread.

This finishes our review of international banking products. We now describe their counterparts in the securities markets.

16.2   International Bond and Commercial-Paper Markets

Almost simultaneously with the emergence of euromoney markets, firms and governments started issuing USD bonds outside the United States, and sold the bonds to non-U.S. residents. Such a bond was called a eurodollar bond. As of the 1960s, and particularly in the 1970s, some eurobonds were also denominated in currencies other than the USD. Even though the dollar has long preserved its dominant market share, the fraction of dollar-denominated bonds occasionally drops below the total for European currencies, nowadays. Also in the 1970s, corporations and governments started issuing short-term paper, although this short-term eurocommercial paper market did not really take off until the late 1980s.

The markets to be discussed in this section are the tradable-security versions of the banking products that we discussed in the preceding section. Table 16.3 matches the eurobanking products with the closest equivalent in the eurosecurities markets. You may want to check these correspondences as we proceed.

16.2.1   Why Eurobond Markets Exist

The explanations for the long-term success of international securities markets are largely similar to the ones cited for eurocurrency markets:

Lighter regulation for international public issues. A bond issue aimed at the general public of one particular country is subject to many rules and regulations (although less so now than in the 1950s and 1960s). There are usually all kinds of publication requirements, and the issue has to be examined and approved by one or more regulatory agencies. In many countries, there are or were also issuing calendars (and, hence, queues) because the local government does not want foreigners to affect the country's reserves, money supply, or exchange rate; nor does the government want foreigners to "crowd out"

Table 16.3. Relationships between international banking products and securities.

Banking	Securities
Short term	
Money market	Commercial paper (CP) market
Short-term loan	CP issue
Short-term credit line	CP program
Rolled-over credit line	Note-issuing facility (NIF)
Revolving commitment	Revolving underwritten facility (RUF)
FF, FRA	Interest-rate futures
Medium and long term	
Longer-term loans	Notes and bonds
Fixed-rate loans	Fixed-rate bond
Revolving or floating-rate (FR) loan	Floating-rate note (FRN)
FR loan with cap	HIBO (higher-bound) bond
FR loan with floor	LOBO (lower-bound) bond

local borrowers—especially not the government itself. By contrast, "international" transactions tend to be less regulated. For one thing, monetary authorities and capital market regulators are less concerned with issues that do not involve their own currencies and are targeting a few well-off and well-informed investors or (even better) foreign investors. This lack of regulation is especially true for tax-haven states that are often used as launching pads for international issues, but they also hold for *private issues* in mainstream countries.

Swift and efficient private placement. By traditional U.S. standards, publication requirements in Europe were never very stringent, and no rating is required for euro-issues. Even these comparatively lax requirements can be largely or entirely avoided if the issue is private rather than public. For loans privately placed with a limited number of professional investors, there is no queuing, and there are no (or almost no) disclosure requirements. In the EU, for instance, the telling feature is whether face values of EUR 50,000 or less are being offered; if so, the issue is deemed to be targeted at retail investors rather than professionals, and a prospectus must be published, approved by the local central bank. (Approval by one central bank suffices to sell anywhere in the Union—the so-called "passport.") But large-denomination bonds escape all this hassle.

Simple contracts. As borrowers are generally of good credit standing, euro-bonds tend to be unsecured; thus, legal costs, as well as the expenses of bonding and monitoring, are avoided. Since lenders have no control whatsoever over the borrower, only companies with a good reputation can play this game at a reasonable price; small players often find the risk spread they would have to offer unattractive.

Tax games. Eurobonds, being anonymous bearer bonds, traditionally make it easier to evade income taxes. Withholding taxes can be avoided by issuing the bonds in tax havens, and most OECD countries have recently waived withholding taxes for nonresidents.

Large issues. Issues below USD 100m are very rare, nowadays. Most issues are now 500–1,000m USD or EUR, but even 5b issues are placed in a day or two (not including the unofficial bookbuilding) and no longer raise eyebrows. In 2006, the largest issue was 22b. Such a big placement allows relatively low issuing costs.

Disintermediation. Since the mid 1970s, impetus for the growth of the eurosecurities market has come from the general *disintermediation* movement. Disintermediation means "cutting out the intermediary"; that is, corporations borrow directly from investors. This evolution was the result of two forces. First, in the 1980s, many banks lost their first-rate creditworthiness when parts of their loan portfolios turned sour (due to the international debt crisis[10] and the collapse of the real estate markets[11]). As a result, these banks were no longer able to fund at the AAA rate, which meant that top borrowers could borrow at a lower cost than banks could—by tapping the market directly. Second, as a response to the lower profits from lending and borrowing and to the stricter capital adequacy rules, banks preferred to earn fee income from bond placements or commercial paper issues. Unlike operations involving deposits and loans, this commission business creates immediate income (rather than income from bid–offer spreads, received later on) and does not inflate the balance sheet.

16.2.2   Institutional Aspects of the International Bond Market

We briefly describe some institutional aspects of the international bond market.

---

[10] Emerging-market debt ballooned after the oil price doubled in 1974 (which made many countries borrow heavily) and when a wave of inflation in the late 1970s had increased interest rates to unusual levels (much of the oil debt was at floating rates). Borrowers defaulted or renegotiated both their bank debt (in the "London Club") and their government-to-government debt (in the "Paris Club").

[11] One background item was that, in the early 1970s, the distinction between thrifts and banks was lifted. Thrifts (or Saving & Loans) were originally cooperatives where members made time deposits and got time loans, mostly mortgage loans. Unlike commercial banks, they could not take sight deposits and give overdraft facilities. When the distinction was lifted, the old S&L were left with far fewer controls than commercial banks. As a result they made many bad investments, contributing to a boom and bust in real estate. The mess took years, and trillions, to sort out. The real-estate bubble also spread to Europe and hurt the old commercial banks, most notably in the United States, the Nordic countries, and France.

Bearer securities. Eurobonds are bearer bonds, that is, anonymously held rather than held by investors listed in a register. In the old days, "bearer" actually meant "made out to bearer"—actual pieces of paper, with coupons that could be clipped off and cashed in by the holder. The principal of the bond was represented by the mantle, the main part of the paper (after the coupons have been clipped off). In many countries, an investor could cash in coupons and principal paid out by bearer securities without having to reveal his or her identity to the bank that acts as paying agent. In contrast, if the security had been a registered security, the issuer would know the identity of the current holder of each bond, and pay interest by mailing a check. U.S. domestic bonds are usually registered, nowadays. In the EU, even bearer bonds tend to be *non-deliverable* nowadays, that is, not physical pieces of paper; investors buy them electronically from intermediaries, but the issuer still does not keep a register.

Interest payments. Eurobonds originally carried (and to a large extent still carry) fixed coupons. Coupons are most often paid annually instead of every six months (the domestic U.S. pattern). Floating-rate notes (FRNs) gained popularity when interest rates rose, in the 1970s–80s, making many borrowers hesitant about long-term fixed-rate bonds; when interest rates are low, in contrast, investors tend to be the party that shuns fixed interest rates. In a floating-rate loan, the interest rate is periodically reset on the basis of the then-prevailing Libor for that horizon plus a preset spread. Sometimes, the FRN has a cap or floor on the floating interest rate. Capped FRNs are sometimes called *HIBO bonds* (*higher-bound bonds*) and floored FRNs *LOBO bonds. Perpetual FRNs* were briefly fashionable in the mid 1980s.

Amortization. Amortization of the bond's principal amount typically occurs at maturity. Such bonds are known as *bullet bonds.* Alternatively, the borrower may undertake to buy back predetermined amounts of bonds in the open market every year. This is called a *purchase-fund provision* or a *sinking-fund provision.* Under a variant provision, the borrower does not have to buy back the bonds if market prices are above par. Instead, the borrower has a right to call a predetermined part of the issue every year.

Currency of denomination. The currency of denomination of the bonds is most often a single currency (especially the USD, DEM, or, now, EUR, JPY, and CHF). Also the private ECU gained some popularity as a currency of denomination in the early-to-mid 1990s. Other currency baskets, such as the SDR or the European Unit of Account, have never really caught on. Some bonds have currency options attached to them. Such currency options bonds are discussed in chapter 8. Occasionally, you also see a dual currency bond, which pays out its coupons in one currency and the principal in another currency.

DIY Problem 16.4. Suppose that the holder of a five-year bond receives an annual coupon of USD 500 and can choose to receive at maturity either USD 10,000 or EUR

10,000. Taking the USD as home currency, you can describe this bond in two ways, one involving a put and one involving a call. Find these two descriptions, and link them via put–call parity.

Stripped bonds. Bond stripping essentially means that the coupons and the principal components of the bond are sold separately. If bonds are actual pieces of paper made out to the bearer, you can strip bonds at home with a pair of scissors: just clip off all of the remaining coupons, and sell them separately from the mantle, the piece that stands for the principal. On a larger scale, and especially when bonds are registered rather than bearer securities, stripping is done by buying coupon bonds, placing them into an incorporated mutual fund or a trust, and issuing separate claims against this portfolio, representing either the coupons or the principal.

The main consequence of stripping is that the principal can be sold separately, as a zero-coupon bond. One motivation for stripping is that immunization and asset/liability management are simplified if there are zero-coupon instruments for many maturities. Also, zero-coupon bonds, offering capital gains rather than interest, get favorable tax treatment in many countries. In some countries, including Japan and Italy, capital gains are often partially exempt from personal taxation. Thus, the principal is sold to, for example, Japanese or Italian investors, and the (taxable) coupons are sold to low-tax investors.

Issuing procedures (1): the consortium. Placement of eurobonds is most often through a syndicate of banks or security houses.

- The *bookrunner* (formerly called *lead bank* or *lead manager*) negotiates with the borrower, brings the syndicate together, makes a market (at least initially), and supports the price during and immediately after the selling period. Bookrunnership can be shared by a group.

- There are often, but not always, *managing banks* that underwrite the issue and often buy part of the bonds for their own account.

- The *placing agents* call their clients (institutional investors or individuals) and sell the bonds on a commission basis.

  Just as in the case of bonds, there is creeping title inflation. More and more often the underwriters are called lead managers, and the term co-managers then refers to firms that just distribute the paper (the placing agents of old).

- The *fiscal agent* takes care of withholding taxes, while the *trustee bank* monitors the bond contract (if any such contract exists; most bonds are unsecured and do not have bonding clauses).

The various players get their commission through the discount they get when they buy the paper. In the table below we start from a set of commission percentages and then work out their implications for the prices at which the players buy and resell the bonds. The paper is assumed to have a nominal value of 10,000 per unit.

	Commission specs (%)	The bank buys at	...and sells at	
Lead manager	0.5	9,750	9,800	(To underwriters)
Underwriters	1.0	9,800	9,900	(To selling agents)
Sellers	1.0	9,900	10,000	(To public or back to underwriters)

Prospective customers can find information about the issuing company and about the terms and conditions of the bond in a prospectus. Often, an unofficial version of the prospectus is already circulating before the actual prospectus is officially approved. This preliminary prospectus is called the *red herring* and is part of the *bookbuilding* stage, where the putative managing group is gauging the market's willingness to buy. Once the decision to issue has become final and the prospectus is official, investors can already buy forward the bonds in the few weeks before the actual issuing period starts. This period of unofficial trading is called the *gray-market period.*

The whole process typically takes up about a month or more—not exactly fast. For this reason, alternative issuing procedures have emerged.

Issuing procedures (2): alternatives to the consortium. One rarer solution is the *bought deal*: a bank single-handedly buys the entire issue, before building a book and finding co-underwriters. This is riskier to the bank, so typically the implied underwriting fee is larger and/or the issue smaller—one always pays some price for speed.

Other alternatives entirely omit underwriting. In a *fixed-price reoffer*, the price to be paid by the public is set, and sellers get a commission if and when they place paper, say 0.15%. The borrower bears the risk that the whole issue flops, but since the procedure is faster than the traditional consortium method, the risk is thought to be bearable, by some. Still, one rarely sees such deals. In a *yield pricing* issue the price is set at the very end, taking into account yields of comparable bonds in the secondary market. The issuer again buys speed, and there is far less risk that the paper is unsellable, relative to the case where the coupon is set weeks before the actual placement. But rates can still change after the selling starts, or the risk spread may not please the market, so there is obviously no certainty about quantity and price until the selling is over.

Another method is like the traditional *au robinet* (on tap) method, the way a bank traditionally issues its own retail CDs to the general public. This is best known as the *medium-term note* (MTN) method even though it is now used for paper of 9 months to up to 30 years. Here, the borrower mandates a bank to sell paper within certain guidelines, say "money in the 1–5 year range at 50 basis points or less over the relevant U.S. T-bill rate"; and the mandatee simply waits for queries from big investors with excess liquidities. A deal like this can be made quite fast, occasionally even within one hour, and costs are quite low. One reason is that there is no official soliciting, no prospectus, etc., is needed. In addition, the intermediary is not guaranteeing anything. But obviously the issuer has no idea how long it will take to raise the sum they had in mind, and may have to improve the terms after a while. Still, this issuing procedure has become a serious alternative to the consortium system.

Secondary market. The secondary market for eurobonds is not always very active. Many bonds are listed on the Luxembourg Bourse, but this is largely a matter of formality. A few hundred issues trade more or less actively on London's International Stock Exchange Automated Quotation (SEAQ International) computer system. Through SEAQ International, market makers post bid-and-ask prices for non-U.K. blue-chip stocks and for eurobonds. There is also an over-the-counter market, where (bored) bond dealers keep buying and selling to each other. Multilateral clearing institutions like Euroclear in Brussels, Clearstream (formerly Cedel) in Luxembourg, and the London Clearing House reduce the costs of physical delivery of the bond certificates themselves. (They also offer clearing services for trades of stocks listed on exchanges; Clearstream is now owned by Deutsche Börse.)

Figure 16.2 shows a press release by the European Bank of Reconstruction and Development on a ruble bond issue.

Eurobonds represent the long end of the eurosecurities market. We now turn to markets for securities with shorter times to maturity.

16.2.3 Commercial Paper

Commercial paper refers to short-term securities (from seven days to a few years) issued by private companies. Just as bonds are the disintermediated version of long-term bank loans, commercial paper (CP) forms the disintermediated counterpart of short-term bank loans. CP markets have existed in an embryonic form ever since banks drew promissory notes on their borrowers as a way to document loan agreements. However, the market became important only in the eighties when, as part of the general disintermediation movement, large corporations with excellent credit standing started issuing short- and medium-term paper, which then was (and is) placed directly with institutional investors. The volume of the market remains low relative to the bond and bank-loan market.

The market consists of notes, promissory notes, and certificates of deposits. *Notes* are medium-term paper with maturities from one to seven years, usually paying out coupons; many Europeans would simply call them bonds. *Promissory notes* have shorter lives (sometimes as short as seven days) and are issued on a discount basis, that is, without interim interest payments. Notes and promissory notes issued by banks are called *certificates of deposit* (CDs).

Nine banks underwrite new EBRD rouble bond

Rate on first quarterly coupon set at 5.56 percent

The EBRD has completed the placement of its second rouble bond, underwritten by a syndicate of nine international and Russian banks. The rate on the first coupon has been set at 5.56 percent.

This new 5-billion rouble (equivalent to €147 million) five-year floating rate instrument is being launched by the EBRD to meet the strong demand in Russia for the Bank's local currency loans. The EBRD raised its first rouble bond in May 2005 for exactly the same amount and with the same tenor.

The Russian subsidiaries of Citibank and Raiffeisenbank Austria are the Joint Lead Arrangers of the new issue – with JP Morgan Bank International, ABN Amro Bank AO, ING Bank (Eurasia) ZAO, Bank WestLB Vostok (ZAO) acting as senior co-lead managers. SAO Commerzbank(Eurasija) and Gazprombank are co-lead managers. Vneshtorgbank is the co-manager. ING will also act as the Calculation Agent for the issue.

The new EBRD bond's floating rate coupon is once again linked to MosPrime Rate, a money market index launched last year under the auspices of Russia's National Currency Association (NCA).

The MosPrime rate is calculated daily for 1-month, 2-months and 3-months deposits based on the quotes contributed by eight banks: ABN Amro, ZAO Citibank, Gazprombank, International Moscow Bank, Raiffeisenbank, Sberbank, Vneshtorgbank and WestLB.

The launch of the EBRD's second floating rate note underscores the development of the MosPrime Rate as a widely accepted money market benchmark in Russia since its launch in April 2005. Several public transactions have been linked to this index in the past year, the most recent, as well as the largest, being a 7.2 billion rouble (equivalent to €212 million) loan for Mosenergo.

The new issue was registered with the Federal Financial Markets Service (FFMS) on April 11. Just as with the first issue, the EBRD will apply for its bonds to be listed and traded on the Moscow Interbank Currency Exchange (MICEX) and for the Central Bank to include them in its Lombard list. This would make the bond available for repo transactions with the Central Bank.

The issue pays a quarterly coupon, with the coupon rate reset every three months in line with the then-prevailing MosPrime offered rates. The coupon rate for the bond will be published at Reuters page EBRDRUBFRNRATE.

The EBRD enjoys an AAA/Aaa rating from international rating agencies.

Press contact:
Richard Wallis, Moscow – Tel: +7495 787 1111; E-mail: wallisr@ebrd.com

Figure 16.2. EBRD ruble bond issue:
www.ebrd.com/new/pressrel/2006/40apr28.htm.

Although a CP issue can be a one-time affair, many issuers have a CP-program contract with a syndicate. A bare-bones CP program simply eliminates the bother of getting a syndicate together each time commercial paper needs to be placed, but many programs also offer some form of underwriting commitment (for issues up to a given amount and within a given period). Such a commitment can stipulate the following terms.

A fixed spread. An arrangement under which a borrower can issue CP at a fixed spread, e.g., 0.5% over Libor, is called a note-issuing facility (NIF). This

Kertih Terminals Signs RM500 Million Financing Agreement For Bulk Chemical Storage Project

Kertih Terminals Sdn Bhd (KTSB) has signed an agreement with RHB Sakura Merchant Bankers Bhd as Arranger and Agent for a RM500 million Revolving Underwritten Facility (RUF) with Term Loan Conversion to finance the development of its centralized liquid bulk chemical storage and handling facility in Kertih, Terengganu. The financing agreement was signed today in Kuala Lumpur between KTSB, RHB Sakura Merchant Bankers and a group of financial institutions as underwriters and tender panel members of the RUF.

Under the agreement, KTSB, taking advantage of the prevailing favourable interest rates, will issue short-term negotiable debt instruments directly to investors during the first five years of the RUF, after which the facility is convertible into a four-year Term Loan. Additional features of the RUF, which has been assigned a short-term rating of MARC-1 by Malaysian Rating Corporation Bhd, include the option to raise fixed rate debts via conventional borrowings, structured debts (bonds) instruments or Islamic financing instruments.

KTSB, a joint venture between PETRONAS (40 percent), GATX Terminals (Pte) Ltd (30 percent) and Dialog Equity Sdn Bhd (30 percent), is undertaking the centralized chemical storage project which forms an integral part of the Kertih Integrated Petrochemical Complex (IPC) currently being developed by PETRONAS. Phase one of the storage project is at an advanced stage of construction. When fully operational, the facility will have 37 tanks with a total storage capacity of 403,358 cubic metres to cater to a host of users and customers at the Kertih IPC. These include Vinyl Chloride (Malaysia) Sdn Bhd, PETRONAS Ammonia Sdn Bhd, BP PETRONAS Acetyls Sdn Bhd, Aromatics Malaysia Sdn Bhd and the Union Carbide Corporation-PETRONAS' derivatives joint venture.

Issued by:
Kertih Terminals Sdn Bhd
109 Block G, Phileo Damansara 1
No 9 Jalan 16/11
46350 PETALING JAYA
Tel: 03-7551199

Figure 16.3.   An RUF: Kertih terminals: www.petronas.com.my/internet/corp/news.nsf/2b372bb45ff1ab3a48256b42002b19a7/a09ff4bccca787b048256adf0049a50f?OpenDocument.

preset spread may become too high later on, notably if the borrower's rating improves or if the average spread in the market falls. In such cases, the borrower loses—he pays too much, in view of the changed circumstances—and the placing agent gains because he or she can place the paper above the initially anticipated price. In contrast, if the preset spread becomes too low, the borrower unambiguously wins; the cost is then borne by the underwriter, who has to buy the issue at a price that exceeds the fair market value.

Figure 16.3 refers to an RUF extended to Malaysia's Kertih.

The difference between an NIF and an RUF is less important than it may seem at first. Even an NIF is an option on a spread, not a forward contract on a spread, because the borrower is under no obligation to use the facility. That is, if spreads go down in the market, the borrower can simply forget about the NIF and issue paper through a new syndicate or under a new agreement. Under such circumstances, the advantage of the RUF to the borrower is that it avoids the cost and complications of setting up a new issuing program and, of course, that there is a cap on the risk spread.

16.3   How to Weigh Your Borrowing Alternatives

Companies can get tentative offers from more than one bank or group of banks, or offers in many currencies. How to compare them?

One of this book's fundamental tenets is that, in a perfect market, everything is priced correctly, and nothing is gained or lost by the mere switching from one borrowing alternative to another. NPVs on all financial transactions would be zero, in the sense that the PV of the future service flows is fully reflected in the price. Yet this does not mean that a real-world CEO can always relax and pick a loan at random from just any bank. Let us review a few arguments that have already come up in the preceding chapters and add a few new ones. We group the relevant items under two headings: interactions with operational cash flows and market imperfections.

Interactions with operations.   To a company, a financial contract may deliver more than the contract's very own cash flows; notably, as we saw in chapter 12, the choice of the denomination of one's assets or liabilities may interact with the operational cash flows in a wider sense, for instance, by affecting the probabilities of financial distress and the costs that come with it. If so, these interactions would affect the firm's market value.

Imperfections.   Many aspects of real-world markets could make the choice between borrowing alternatives relevant. Information asymmetries among lenders are likely to lead to inconsistent risk spreads across banks, for instance, or tax asymmetries may make high-interest or high-volatility currencies more attractive. An even more fundamental imperfection would be if prices in exchange and money markets are fixed by the government and/or if a license *raj* prevents arbitrageurs and speculators from doing their usual jobs: then even deals at the risk-free rate, assuming away any information or tax issues, are likely to come with nonzero NPVs. Nonzero NPVs could also arise from less glaring forms of market inefficiency, though, like herd behavior—anything that might lead to mispricing, which the astute speculator can then take advantage of. Lastly, there are the fees that banks charge, and the careful money manager has to check and recheck that the lenders are not trying to overcharge.

We start with the issues that should be the most likely cause of relevance in well-developed markets: costs and risk spreads. These are also easily quantified and summarized into one number. Having ranked the alternatives in terms of these items, we can then assess whether there is a good reason to deviate from that ranking. The easiest case is one where the home and foreign capital markets are both very open and developed. Agents can freely choose where to borrow, from whom and in what currency they want. There are, in addition, competitive swap markets where foreign-currency borrowing can be separated from borrowing abroad. In such a situation it is plausible that if there were no default risk and no information asymmetries, little value would be gained or lost by switching to another currency—whether we do so explicitly or via a swap. In such a setting we can focus on just the costs asked by competing banks over and above the risk-free rate, that is, the items reflecting default risk and information asymmetries.

16.3.1 Comparing All-In Costs of Alternatives in Open, Developed Markets

Let us work via an example. The issuer is a U.S. company that has a preference for USD borrowing; but there is an EUR offer too. The hoped-for proceeds would be USD 200m before costs, or, at the spot rate of USD/EUR 1.25, EUR 160m, and the CFO is going for a seven-year bullet loan. Table 16.4 shows the conditions, along with some other useful data and the computations. Please refer to them as the discussion proceeds.

16.3.1.1 Evaluation under Idealized Circumstances

We could look at the sum of discounted risk spreads and other costs, using the swap rate as the discount rate. This is similar to what we did in chapters 5 (on forward contracts) and 7 (on swaps), except, trivially, that now we add an up-front cost. But there we took the swap dealer's point of view, whose risk is not the same as those borne by a lender. So let us first tell a story that describes why a procedure like this also makes sense, subject to a caveat, for lenders and borrowers without right of offset.

We regard a bond issue or a bank loan as an NPV problem. To the borrower, the proceeds are immediate, and the costs are the subsequent service flows—just the reverse of what one sees in capital budgeting, but that is not important. Let us denote the swap rate, a risk-free yield-at-par, by s; the spread as asked by banker b over and above s by ρ_b; and the required discount rate by R. Finally, let V_{nom} denote the gross size of the loan, and U_b the up-front cost proposed by banker b.

The NPV of accepting b's proposal equals the net proceeds, $V_{\text{nom}} - U_b$, over and above the PV of the future service streams. We write this in line one, below. In line two, we just simplify and regroup, as follows:

$$\text{NPV}_b = \underbrace{V_{\text{nom}} - U_b}_{\text{Net IN}} - \underbrace{V_{\text{nom}} \times [1 + (s + \rho_b - R) \times a(R, \# \text{ years})]}_{\text{PV of subsequent outflows}}$$

$$= V_{\text{nom}} \times (s - R) \times a(R, \# \text{ years}) - \underbrace{[U_b + V_{\text{nom}} \times \rho_b \times a(R, \# \text{ years})]}_{\text{The bank-specific part}}.$$

(16.5)

Table 16.4. Appalachian Barracuda Corp.'s analysis of funding offers.

1. The competing offers

	(a) Swap rate	(b) Loan rate	(b) − (a) Spread	Up-front fee	7-year annuity factors At swap rate	At IRR
USD	4.50%	4.00%	0.50%	2.00%	6.002 054 67	5.819 282 33
EUR	4.35%	3.80%	0.55%	1.75%	6.046 667 84	5.860 778 76

Spot rate USD/EUR 1.25

2. Comparing the loans via swap-rate-based PVs

USD loan:

Risk spreads (PV)	$200\text{m} \times 0.005 \times \overbrace{6.002\,054\,67}^{a(7\text{yr,swap\$})} =$	USD	6,002,055
Up-front	$200\text{m} \times 0.02 =$		4,000,000
Total cost		USD	10,002,055

EUR loan:

Risk spreads (PV)	$160\text{m} \times 0.0055 \times \overbrace{6.046\,667\,843}^{a(7\text{yr,swap€})} =$	EUR	5,321,068
Up-front	$160\text{m} \times 0.0175 =$		2,800,000
Total cost		EUR	8,121,068
Id. in USD	$8,121,068 \times 1.25 =$	USD	10,151,335
Extra cost of EUR =	USD 10,151,335 − 10,002,055 =	USD	0.149m

3. Comparing the loans via IRR-based PVs

USD loan:

$\text{YIELD}(\overbrace{\text{"1/1/2001"}}^{\text{Some start date}}, \overbrace{\text{"12/31/2007"}}^{\text{7 years later}}, \overbrace{0.045}^{\text{Coupon}}, \overbrace{98}^{V_t}, \overbrace{100}^{V_T}, \overbrace{1,1}^{\text{Don't ask}}) =$ % 4.844

Swap rate	% 4.000
All-in spread	% 0.844

Cost in USD: $200\text{m} \times [0.008\,44 \times \underbrace{5.819\,282\,33}_{a(7\text{yr,IRR\$})}] =$ USD   9.823m

EUR loan:

YIELD("1/1/2001", "12/31/2007", 0.0435, 98.25, 100, 1, 1) =	% 4.649
Swap rate	% 3.800
All-in spread	% 0.849

Cost in EUR: $160\text{m} \times [0.008\,49 \times \overbrace{5.860\,778\,76}^{a(7\text{yr,IRR€})}] =$ EUR   7.961m

Cost in USD: $1.25 \times 7.961 =$	USD	9.951m
Extra cost of EUR loan = 9.951m − 9.823m =	USD	0.128m

Key: Method 1 computes the PV-ed spreads using the swap rate *s* and then adds the up-front. The resulting cost difference is USD 149,000. Method 2 computes an internal rate of return (IRR)—I show the spreadsheet command that does it for you—and finds the IRR is 0.844% above the swap rate for the dollar loan, and 0.849% for the euro loan. The cost above the swap rate is then PV-ed at the IRRs.

Offers may have been requested from various bankers, all for the same amount V_{nom}; and s and R are market-wide numbers. Thus, the first part in the NPV expression, equation (16.5), is common to all offers, and for that reason the competing offers from various banks can be ranked by looking at just the second part, the up-front cost plus the PV-ed spreads, labeled "The bank-specific part" in the equation. The spread asked consists of the "objective" risk premium one would see in perfect markets, plus, in realistic bond markets, a compensation for the investors' unfamiliarity with the borrower: unknown parties look more risky. The investment bank, in the case of a bond issue, tries to reduce the unfamiliarity premium by road shows, etc., but this increases U_b, the up-front cost. In addition, part of the bank's up-front expenses may be paid for not via the up-front fee U_b but by an extra interest spread instead; alternatively, as we have seen, the parties may agree to lower the very visible spread, and increase the less visible up-front fee U_b instead. That's why we should look at the whole package. Thus, we propose the PV criterion,

$$\text{PV-ed total bank-specific component} = U_b + V_{nom} \times \rho_b \times a(R, \# \text{ years}). \quad (16.6)$$

This is what we did when we compared risk spreads in the swaps chapter, except that we add the up-front cost and we use R not s. Using s was justified for a swap dealer, who benefits from the right of offset and the credit trigger. For a bank (or the counterpart, the lender), the uncertainties are usually greater, so very often one needs to be a bit more careful about default risk.

16.3.1.2 How Well Do We Know R, in Reality?

This looks like a cut-and-dried problem. The only hitch is that R, the required rate of return, is not easily observable. Only the Great Banker in the Sky knows it well. How come? Can't we just take the prior that the NPV is zero, which would allow us to infer R as the internal rate of return? In perfect markets, of course, NPVs from financial transactions must be zero. In reality we cannot bank on that, though, because acquisition of information is costly and time-consuming. This is especially an issue in the case of risky corporate borrowing, which is full of information asymmetries—either between banks and borrowers or among the banks that might compete to act as lenders. Let us look at each of these asymmetries.

- If the financiers know more about the market situation than you do, chances are that they make a gain and you a loss. Not *all* bankers are angels. There is court evidence how investment bankers have underpriced the IPOs they managed, so as to be able to dole out goodies to friends and cronies. You may also have heard how derivatives dealers openly mailed each other about the "rip-off factors" they had included in their contracts, and how during the dot.com bubble investment bankers made fun of the "fools" they sold to.

- These are, of course, just anecdotes; but there exists a respectable academic literature on "hold-up" behavior. House bankers have a bit of a monopoly position, so the argument goes, since they have built up long-term knowledge about the borrower. Breaking up the relation would be costly for the borrower, since it takes time and effort for another bank to just rediscover all the info and insights the incumbent already has. Thus, the house bank is in a position to exact a monopoly rent—not too much, of course, otherwise they lose the account. Empirical evidence shows that banks actually do so.

For these reasons, mildly negative NPVs are far from unlikely. The borrower might still go along with a negative-NPV bond deal if, as pointed out, the loss is not large enough to justify changing banks or consortia and if the loss is small relative to the NPV of the direct investment that is being financed. In a way, the bankers just grab a slice of the firm's business gains. But the bottom line surely is that you cannot just postulate that competition is perfect, that NPVs are therefore zero, and that R is visible as the IRR of the deal.

16.3.1.3 Evaluation under Realistic Circumstances

Bearing all this in mind, let us now critically review two feasible methods and see how they relate to the ideal solution we have just outlined.

PV the spreads at the swap rate; add up-fronts. This is close to our first criterion, equation (16.5), except that we use the swap rate s instead of the risk-adjusted rate R. In defense of this method, remember that we do not want to value a given loan; rather, we want to rank two loans on the basis of the difference of the cost components, over and above the swap rates. Thus, first, we only discount the bank-specific part; so most of the service streams are not considered, which also eliminates most of the valuation errors created by using s instead of R. In fact, the PV of the spreads ρ_b is mostly affected by the size of ρ_b, in the numerator, not so much by the discount rate. Second, we make the same mistake for all loan alternatives, so that the net impact on the calculated cost differential is even smaller.

Compute an IRR, subtract the swap rate, and PV the total cost at the IRR. The IRR, familiarly, is the stand-in discount rate that would equalize the discounted value of the future payments to the net value (after up-front costs). (This must be done numerically; the table shows a spreadsheet command that provides the answer.) So this method simply postulates that the deal's NPV in equation (16.5) is zero, which, if true, allows you to compute an estimate of R. This allows us to estimate a total-cost spread that can be discounted at the IRR.

Assuming a zero NPV is not a crazy idea: in the absence of asymmetries it would actually be quite natural that both lender and borrower made a breakeven deal. So this estimate of R must be close to the mark for big lenders with little information asymmetries. For smaller borrowers, negative NPVs are far more likely, in which case R is overestimated and the PV-ed cost underestimated.

> **Example 16.7.** Think of the one-period case where we easily see what is going on. The swap rate is 8%. Suppose the fair value of a 10% loan is 100 but you are ripped off and only get 99. The IRR would be $110/99 - 1 = 11.11\%$ while the true R is $110/100 - 1 = 10\%$. Using the IRR we would estimate the cost at $(11.11 - 8)/1.11 = 2.799$ while the true figure is $2/1.1 + 1 = 2.818$.

The reassuring finding, in table 16.4, is that the two measures of the differential cost are very similar. Using swap rates we would reckon the cost difference between the USD and the EUR offers is USD 149K in favor of the HC offer, while the estimate is USD 128K when we use IRRs. The disagreement is 21K, a tiny number relative to the face value, USD 200,000K. Even more important, both methods agree that the HC loan, USD, has the lower costs.

16.3.1.4 A Translated or Equivalent Spread for FC Loans

In the above, I recommend that you size up the whole package in PV terms, an amount of cash money. Bankers and CFOs often look at percentages, though. Why not PVsPVs instead? First, basic financial logic tells us to generally trust PVs, i.e., numbers in dollars or euros or pounds, not percentages: we pay for our shopping with money not percentages, and 1% extra on 1,000,000 means more money than 2% extra on 100. True, in this particular instance this is not an issue since the alternatives, by design, all have the same scale, USD 200m, implying that there is no harm in looking at the percentages here. But there is a second reason why PVs, in units of money, are better than spreads: amounts of money are easily understood and easily compared across currencies. In contrast, to many business people it would be hard to see whether a spread of 0.75% on top of a swap rate of 8% is better or worse than a spread of 0.30% on top of a swap rate of 2%.

Despite all this, some traditional finance *babu*s insist on percentage spreads. If your boss really presses you, here is how you could respond without giving up rigor.

The simple way to arrive at a p.a.-spread-type number is to divide the HC PV numbers by the HC annuity factor, which means that we compute the equivalent annuity of all costs, up-front or not. Then we express the equivalent annuity as a percentage. Table 16.5 shows the results. Note how, by always using the same number—HC annuity factor times HC face value—to rescale the PV-ed costs, we cannot possibly change the ranking of the alternatives. It is, in fact, easily shown that the FC costs are those of swapped FC loans, not of the original FC loans. Just hope that your boss does not raise the question; and if (s)he does, say that the numbers are adjusted for currency risk.

Table 16.5. Percentage total spreads of borrowing alternatives.

	USD loan	EUR loan	Difference
Using swap rates			
(a) PV-ed cost in USD	10.002	10.151	
(b) EqAn: PV/6.002 054 67	1.666	1.691	
(c) Id/200,000,000	0.833%	0.846%	0.012%
Using IRRs			
(a) PV-ed cost in USD	9.823	9.951	
(b) EqAn: PV/5.819 229 22	1.688	1.710	
(c) id/200,000,000	0.844%	0.855%	0.011%
Difference of % cost estimates	0.011%	0.009%	

The calculations show, first, that the estimated total spreads are not very much affected by whether you use swap rates or IRRs: these intra-column differences, shown in the bottom line, amount to one basis point only. The second conclusion is that both methods agree that the EUR and USD offers are very close, with a disadvantage of slightly over one basis point for the EUR loan. These differentials across columns are shown in the rightmost column of the table.

16.3.1.5 Making a Decision

If cost is the only consideration, then in this example the USD offer has the edge, but it is a very close race. What other considerations could have swayed the balance? Basically, anything that would imply a preference for EUR would do, given that costs are essentially the same.

One consideration that could interfere with this conclusion would be speculation, the way we defined it in earlier chapters. The calculations here would be very different: instead of comparing the USD loan to the swapped EUR loan, we would have to consider the unswapped version and see whether the difference of the IRRs is justified by the expected currency movements. In table 16.4 the IRR of the unswapped EUR loan was found to be 4.65%, against 4.84% for the USD offer. So if the EUR appreciates by less than 0.2% per year, on average, then in terms of expectations it would be less expensive than borrowing dollars. In early 2008, many may feel that the euro is actually overvalued and is expected to slide back to lower levels. If, in addition, the yield is lower, then we would have an argument for EUR borrowing. This logic is very different from the cost-based calculations, where any discrepancy between the differential swap rates and the expected rate of appreciation is postulated to be rational—for instance, reflecting risk considerations.

Speculation is not the only argument that might affect the final decision. There may be EUR-related assets that need to be hedged anyway. Bear in mind, though, that the existence of foreign assets does not necessarily mean that

Table 16.6. People's Bank of China interest rates, late 2006.

Lending rate		Savings rate	
		3 months	1.80%
6 months	5.58%	6 months	2.25%
6–12 months	6.12%	1 year	2.52%
1–3 years	6.30%	2 years	3.06%
3–5 years	6.48%	3 years	3.69%
>5 years	6.84%	5 years	4.14%

these assets come with a positive exposure; remember the Android example in chapter 13.

You will agree that weighing the speculative and hedging aspects is difficult, as neither is easily quantified. But things are even less satisfactory when the foreign currency under consideration lacks financial instruments like forwards and swaps or, even worse, the foreign money and exchange markets are plagued by controls.

16.3.2 Comparing All-In Costs of Alternatives in Regulated, Incomplete Markets

The alternative to the USD loan (200m, as before) is now a CNY one, as the investment is now in China. There are no long-term forwards or swaps. There is no liquid government-bond market, and if there were one there is still the problem that there are exchange controls. Neither Chinese investors nor foreigners can freely switch their funds from CNY to USD, so that one cannot just assume that yuan and dollar loans are correctly priced relative to each other in one international market.

The hoped-for proceeds of a possible yuan loan, at the spot rate of CNY/USD 8.00 (this is a rounded number to simplify the figures), would be CNY 1.600m. The CFO is still going for a 7-year bullet loan. The terms offered are a loan at 6.75% and total up-front fee of 1%. To see whether this is good or bad, you could look at the bids and asks of the People's Bank, the market leader, as shown in table 16.6. The lending rates are, in fact, the People's Bank's reference rates. The central bank is indeed the entity that decides on reference interest rates for loans, but it also sets a band within which local bank branches have some discretion in adjusting their lending rates. As of 1999, the band is 10% below and 30% above the reference rate and for loans to large enterprises, the upper limit is 10% above the reference rate. According to García-Herrero et al. (2006), due to the banks' lack of expertise in assessing borrowers' credit risk, most loans are just contracted at, or even below, the People's Bank's reference rate despite the additional flexibility provided by the liberalization of interest rates.

An uncritical spreadsheet-adept could calculate that the borrowing rate for the best-quality borrowers would be the rate at the bottom of the People's Bank's admissible range, i.e., $6.84\% \times 0.90 = 6.156\%$. The corresponding risk spread would then be $6.75\% - 6.156\% = 0.594\%$. Below, then, are shown the calculations using that stand-in for the risk-free rate; the corresponding annuity factor is $5.551\,560\,664$. I show the NPV and total-spread calculations.

Example 16.8 (CNY alternative).

Risk spreads (PV)	$(1,600 \times 0.005\,94 \times 5.551\,560\,664)/8.00 =$	USD	6,595,254
Up-front	$1,600 \times 0.01/8.00 =$		2,000,000
Total cost			8,595,254
Equivalent annuity	$8,595,254/5.551\,560\,664 =$		1,548,259
Same, in percent	$1,548,259/200\text{m} =$	%	0.774
YIELD("1/1/2001","12/31/2007",0.0575,99,100,1,1)		$=$	% 6.935
Risk-free proxy			% 6.156
All-in spread			% 0.779

So far so good—but what is the point of the calculations? We do not really have a risk-free rate: 6.156 is a possible lower bound that is, however, rarely applied. If we had worked with 6.5 as the risk-free proxy, the equivalent annuity would have been calculated as 0.25% above 6.5%, and the IRR at 0.435% above it, not 0.77–0.78%. We could even make a case for using the midpoint rate rather than a borrowing rate. That midpoint rate would be 5.49, implying all-in spreads of 1.44%, as you can calculate.

DIY Problem 16.5. Do calculate the equivalent annuity part. (The IRR part is, of course, trivial.)

As long as spreads are small and similar across countries, as in the USD–EUR case, these refinements hardly change the conclusions, but here we have a spread of 2.7% between bid and ask. We conclude that all calculations are, at best, tentative.

But lack of knowledge of the risk-free rate is not the only problem. Even if we had an active internal market for government bonds, the rate would still not be integrated with rates for other currencies because worldwide financial investors cannot freely switch between CNY and USD lending (or borrowing, for that matter). The mechanism that normally equalizes the values and wipes out nonzero NPVs is missing, and along with that we have lost all grounds to believe that the "risk-free" versions of the USD and CNY loans are truly equivalent. Remember that this last notion was the reason why only the PV-ed risk-spreads and costs need to be compared even for loans in different currencies. Conversely, without market integration the whole let's-just-compare-spreads approach is built on sand. Quicksand actually.

So all we can say is that, in terms of IRRs, USD borrowing would cost 4.84% while in CNY the figure is 6.94%. If the yuan were expected to depreciate by about 2% per year, the two loans would be expected to have the same cost:

Breakeven appreciation rate on FC, a:

$$\underbrace{(1 + a)(1 + R^*)}_{\text{Total return on FC}} = \underbrace{(1 + R)}_{\text{Return on HC}},$$

$$\Longrightarrow \quad a = \frac{1 + R}{1 + R^*}$$

$$= \frac{1.0484}{1.0694} - 1$$

$$= -1.96\%.$$

In the case of the yuan, at the time of writing the decision would be easy: the currency is undervalued by most standards; there is pressure from U.S. Congress to revalue it, and the People's Bank seems to have chosen a course of slow and gentle appreciation. In short, the smart money would bet on an appreciation not depreciation of the yuan against the U.S. dollar. Given the extra 2% cost, there is no case for yuan borrowing.

Of course, one is not always so lucky: with overvalued currencies (a policy often preferred by politicians in the past),[12] we would have to weigh the cost of a high yield against the boon of expected depreciation. Signs of overvaluation would be a hamburger-parity rate far above those of comparable countries, or PPP rates that are unusually high; exchange controls; and interest-rate ceilings. But all this generates only hints and directions, not precise expected values. To make things worse, expectations are only part of the story: we should think of a normal risk premium too.

16.4 CFO's Summary

The main differences between international ("euro-") and domestic transactions are that the former are often extraterritorial, and the market is a liquid and unregulated wholesale market. As a result, spreads and costs are quite low, and the international markets have become an increasingly important source of funding for medium or large corporations. Apart from this, the transactions one can make in these markets are not fundamentally different from the transactions in standard domestic markets: there are time deposits and term loans, credit lines, and markets for bonds and short-term paper.

A more recent instrument is the forward or futures contract on interest rates, which we discussed in the appendixes to chapters 4 and 6. Remember, from that discussion, that interest rates (spot and forward interest rates) and

---

[12] An overvalued home currency makes manufactured imports cheaper, which suits the city population and the political class; farmer exporters are hurt, but they often have less influence. An expensive currency rate is also regarded as adding prestige; devaluing would be an admission of defeat.

"yields at par" are all linked by arbitrage. Forward interest rates in various currencies are likewise linked through the forward markets.

Comparing loans is easy when markets are well developed and free. In that case, differences between risk-free rates should reflect the market's opinion about the currency, and switching between risk-free FC and HC lending would not affect value. The CFO's focus should therefore be on up-front costs and risk spreads. Using swaps, one can separate the currency of effective borrowing from the currency of effective exposure, for instance, by borrowing at home and swapping into FC. So the rule is *always* to borrow where it is cheap in terms of costs and spreads, whether you fancy the currency or not. You can change the denomination afterward via a swap, if you want. Hedging of operational exposure could be a consideration in the decision whether or not to swap the cheapest loan into another money. So could speculation, but bear in mind that the records of exchange-rate forecasters are patchy.

With less well-developed markets, the absence of a clear and market-set risk-free rate makes decisions much more difficult. One can compute total costs, but one often cannot separate out a risk-free component; and if a locally set risk-free rate proxy is available after all, it is still unlikely to reflect a currency's relative prospects as viewed by the international market. If currency and risk-free interest rates reflect some officials' opinion rather than the market's views, the usual prior that financial deals are zero-NPV transactions would not even hold as a first approximation.

A sensible general prior might be that, for reasonably respectable companies, borrowing in developed markets should be more attractive, for the simple reason that sophisticated markets are cheaper to operate and its players better informed. Selectively subsidized loans in the host country could offset that, but the WTO frowns on practices like that. Interest rates that are capped without discrimination, in contrast, would be acceptable to the WTO, and still exist in some places. Another item that could tilt the balance back to the host-country market is the exchange rate. Controlled exchange rates often imply one-way bets: it is usually obvious whether the currency is overvalued or the converse. But remember that getting the timing and size of the adjustment right remains difficult. There is no easy way out, here. For decisions like this, CFOs will not be replaced by computers any time soon.

TEST YOUR UNDERSTANDING

Quiz Questions

The questions also cover interest forwards and futures, which were discussed in the appendix to chapter 4.

True–False Questions

1. The abolition of the interest equalization tax, Regulation Q, the cold war, and the U.S. and U.K. foreign exchange controls have taken away most of the reasons why euromarkets exist. As a result, we can expect these markets to decline in the near future.

2. Without the U.S. trade deficit, the euromarkets would have developed more slowly.

3. With a floating-rate loan, the bank is free to adjust the interest rate at every reset date in light of the customer's creditworthiness.

4. One of the tasks of the lead bank under a syndicated bank loan is to make a market, at least initially.

5. The purpose of using a paying agent is to reduce exchange risk.

6. Caps and floors are options on interest rates. Because interest rates are not prices of assets, one cannot price caps and floors using an option-pricing model based on asset prices.

7. Because euroloans are unsecured, the spread over the risk-free rate is a very reliable indicator of the borrower's general creditworthiness.

8. FRAs are not really a good hedge against future interest rates because one does not actually make the deposit or take up the loan.

9. A note-issuing facility forces the borrowing company to borrow at a constant spread, while a revolving underwritten facility gives the borrower the benefit of decreasing spreads without the risk of increasing spreads.

10. The fact that eurobonds are bearer securities makes them less attractive to most investors.

11. Bond stripping is always done with a pair of scissors: you just clip off the coupons.

12. Disintermediation is the cause of the lower creditworthiness of banks, and has led to capital adequacy rules.

13. Ignoring the small effects of marking to market, the standard quote for a eurocurrency futures price is basically a forward price on a CD.

Multiple-Choice Questions

1. Eurocurrency and euroloan markets are attractive because:

   (a) the spread between the buy and ask exchange rates is lower than in the interbank exchange market;

   (b) the bid–ask spread between the lending and borrowing interest rates is lower;

   (c) eurobanks are not subject to reserve requirements;

   (d) eurobanks are not subject to capital adequacy rules (the so-called BIS rules).

2. Eurobanks borrow for short maturities and lend for longer maturities. They can reduce the interest-rate risk by:

   (a) extending fixed-rate loans;

   (b) extending floating-rate loans;

   (c) extending revolving loans;

   (d) shorting forward forwards (that is, getting a forward contract on a loan, not on a deposit);

   (e) shorting in FRAs;

   (f) going long eurocurrency futures;

   (g) buying forward the currency in question.

3. A cap on a floating-rate euroloan:

   (a) protects the borrower against high short-term interest rates;

   (b) protects the lender against high short-term interest rates on the funding side;

   (c) is similar to a call option on short-term paper with the cap rate, as nominal rate, and the borrower is the holder of the call option;

   (d) is similar to a put option on short-term paper with the cap rate, as nominal rate, and the borrower is the holder of the put option;

   (e) is similar to a put option on short-term paper with the cap rate, as nominal rate, and the lender is the holder of the put option.

4. Which of each pair best describes eurobanking?

   (a) retail/wholesale;

   (b) individual lender/bank consortium;

   (c) reserve requirements/limited or no reserve requirements;

   (d) unsecured/secured;

   (e) fixed-rate lending/floating-rate lending;

   (f) foreign exchange markets/money markets;

   (g) open to all companies/open to the better companies only

5. Matching questions. Choose from the following list of terms to complete the sentences below: paying agent, managing banks, trustee bank, placing agents, market, lead bank (or lead manager), participating banks, prospectus, gray market, fiscal agent, buy forward, underwrite, lead manager, red herring.

A consortium (or syndicate) that extends a euroloan consists of many banks that could play different functions. In a euroloan, the (a) negotiates with the borrower for tentative terms and conditions, obtains a mandate, and looks for banks to provide the money or undertake to provide the money if there is any shortfall in funds. The banks that provide the actual funding are called (b). Because at the time of the negotiations the funding is not yet arranged, the (c) often contacts a smaller number of (d) banks which (e) the loan, that is, guarantee to make up for the shortage of funds if there is any such shortfall. The (f), finally, is the bank that receives the service payments from the borrower and distributes them to the participating banks.

Placement of eurobonds is most often via a syndicate of banks or security houses. The lead bank or (g) negotiates with the borrower, brings the syndicate together, makes a (h) (at least initially), and supports the price during and immediately after the selling period. There are often, but not always, (i) that underwrite the issue and often buy part of the bonds for their own account. The (j) call their clients (institutional investors or individuals) and sell the bonds on a commission basis. The (k) takes care of withholding taxes, while the (l) monitors the bond contract. Prospective customers can find information about the issuing company and about the terms and conditions of the bond in the (m). Often an unofficial version of the prospectus is already circulating before the actual prospectus is officially approved; this preliminary prospectus is called the (n). On the basis of this document, investors can already (o) the bonds for a few weeks before the actual issuing period starts. This period of unofficial trading is called the (p) period.

Applications

1. You are an A-quality borrower, and you pay 10% on a five-year loan with one final amortization at the end and annual coupons. This is 1% above the spread paid by an AAA borrower. What will be the up-front fee for which your bank should be willing to lower the rate by 1%?

2. A bank offers you the following rates for a five-year loan with annual coupons: 10% fixed or (when you borrow floating-rate) Libor + 2%. You prefer to borrow floating-rate, as you expect a drop in interest rates. Another bank offers you Libor + 1.5%, but asks a substantial up-front fee. How can you compute which bank offers the better terms?

3. You bought an option that limits the interest rate on a future six-month loan to, at most, 10% p.a.

    (a) If, at the beginning of the six-month period, the interest rate is 11%, what is the expiration value of this option?

    (b) What is the option's expiration value if the interest rate turns out to be 8%?

4. You bought an option that limits the interest rate on a future six-month deposit to at least 10% p.a.

    (a) If, at the beginning of the six-month period, the interest rate is 11%, what is the market value of this option?

    (b) What is the option's value if the interest rate turns out to be 8%?

17

Segmentation and Integration in the World's Stock Exchanges

Suppose your CEO argues that, given the company's recent foreign acquisitions, it should start thinking in international style and raise some cash from the global equity market. How to react? First, you would need to sharply change your CEO's view: there is no such thing as a global equity market except, in a limited sense, for a few hundreds or thousands of giant companies. That is, relative to the fixed-income side of the international capital market—bonds and commercial paper—the international equity markets are somewhat underdeveloped and fragmented. The reasons include the following:

- Perhaps the biggest obstacle to international portfolio investment is the fact that valuing stocks requires more information than is required for high-quality bonds. Since investors are wary of buying stocks about which they know nothing, only a few thousand big companies are really traded internationally. The bulk of the listed stocks are held locally only, or perhaps in adjacent countries. Within the United States (and presumably in other large countries) there is even a documented preference for companies from the same state or region.

- Even for this subset of stocks, international dealing is made complicated by the substantial differences in the ways trading and price-setting are organized across the world. There is some convergence going on, but getting to one global exchange will remain a pipedream for many more years.

- Exchanges differ not just in the way they organize the trade process: there are also big deviations as to the listing requirements (at IPO time and afterward), the disclosure or corporate-governance requirements they impose on listed firms, the general legislation/regulation on securities markets, and so on. Some of these are the exchange's own choosing, others are imposed by the government(s). Unifying the regulation will simply remain impossible, in the foreseeable future.

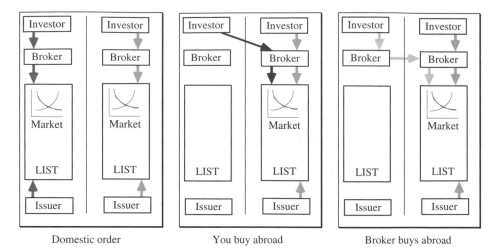

Figure 17.1.   International equity trading: the long way.

The implication of markets being separated is that international trading is more complicated. In segmented markets, brokers "get a seat"[1] in the local exchange, and local firms get listed on the local exchange. Domestic investors then buy these shares in the local markets via their brokers. But what if an investor wants to buy a foreign share? One solution is to buy abroad, via a foreign broker. But this can be a hassle: the investor needs to open an account with the foreign broker and typically has to buy forex; and international transfers are costly even without forex conversions. You need to be a semi-pro before this becomes worthwhile; Schwab, for instance, a big U.S. low-cost/no-frills internet broker, does not accept foreign accounts with less than USD 100,000 of margin. Alternatively, the investor's domestic broker places the order through a foreign colleague, thus sparing the customer the hassle but implying, instead, two brokerage fees rather than one. Figure 17.1 pictures these solutions

There are two other standard solutions (and a more radical one labeled "Euronext," in figure 17.2), and these are especially relevant when there is a lot of cross-border demand. First, the domestic broker may also get a seat on the other exchange. At the time of the Euronext–NYSE merger, for instance, about forty brokerage houses already had seats on both exchanges. This is less than 10% of the total, and the obvious reason is that it is costly too: the broker needs to put up capital twice, has to cough up two membership fees, and may have to buy the extra seat; again, the investor will pay, ultimately. Alternatively, the issuing firm may get listed on both exchanges rather than just at home. This obviously avoids extra hassle for brokers and investors;

---

[1] The "seat" is slang for the right to be a broker. Some exchanges have a fixed number of seats, and if a candidate wants to join, she has to buy a seat from another member. NYSE seats sell for a few million dollars. In other exchanges it suffices to meet the eligibility rules and pay a membership fee.

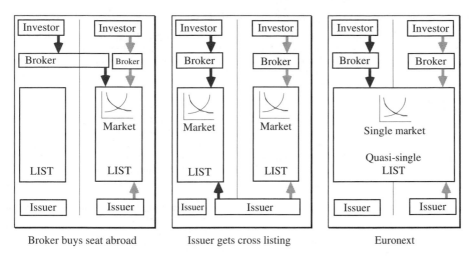

Figure 17.2. International equity trading: life made easier.

another advantage is that the firm can probably sell more shares, this way: the issuer can now actively promote its stock without running foul of investor-protection rules; and some investors, like pension funds, may even be barred from buying assets that are not listed. But again there is a cost: the firm has to make an IPO or SEO involving due diligence audits, consultants, a prospectus, road shows, fees for the banks that advise, run the book, subscribe and/or sell, and so on and so forth; pay listing fees twice; come up with two versions of the financial statements—different in terms of language, at best, but often also in terms of content because accounting rules are incompatible, and so on. Investors may pay too: the market is now spread across two exchanges, probably with one being liquid and the other not, or less so, resulting in higher spreads.

Instead of having the broker straddle the border by getting a second seat, or the firm by getting a second listing, one can let the list and the market straddle the border. This is what Euronext has done. The domestic and foreign lists get pooled: a company listed abroad can be bought directly by a broker who has only a domestic seat, and vice versa. Additional savings are generated as IT systems get unified and streamlined. Finally, pricing remains unified in one market (see panel 17.1).

All this is reviewed more thoroughly in this and the next chapter. In the present chapter we first provide some background material, notably some statistics on the valuation (market cap) and openness of various stock exchanges over the globe, and some information on the way(s) markets are organized. We then ask why these separate markets have not merged a long time ago, or whether any worldwide merger might be in the offing in the near future. The prime reasons, I think, why markets will not merge any time soon are that there is surprisingly little interest from investors in international diversification, and that officials' ideas about the ideal regulatory

The purpose of Euronext was to offer a cheaper and more efficient market that would, therefore, be more attractive to both investors and issuers. The question is how to set up an international market when each of the five countries involved has its own legislation and its own regulator. This is how they did it.

First, from the outside, many things look unchanged:

Issuers select their country, as before. A French firm is likely to choose the Paris list. This would mean that its IPOs/SEOs and its information policy should meet French legislation and regulation.

Brokers select their own country, as before. A broker opting for the Dutch section has to follow Dutch securities law, for instance.

Investors select the broker they like, as before.

What is different is the operations:

Brokers get a "single passport": a broker accepted in Portugal, for instance, automatically also qualifies for the four other markets. Thus, if a Portuguese broker receives an order to buy a Dutch stock, there is no longer any need to enlist a Dutch intermediary or (if it happens very often) get a seat on the Dutch exchange: from a broker's point of view, there is just one single list. As a result, most brokers no longer differentiate, fee-wise, between domestic and foreign stocks.

Trading system: there is a single trading system for cash stocks, NSC (*Nouveau Système de Cotation*)—much cheaper to buy and maintain than five separate systems. NSC, a joint product of Euronext and France's Atos Origin, is also running on thirteen other exchanges (as of February 2006) and has a few other prospective customers.

LIFFE, in London, likewise uses one system, *Connect*, to replace six old systems (one in BE, NL, PT, UK; two in FR: one for futures, one for options).

Single rule book. Behind the single passport is the fact that the Euronext admission rules for brokers are now identical across all four countries. So are the listing requirements (initial and ongoing) for issuers.

College of regulators. There are still five regulators and five sets of laws and rules, but when Euronext negotiates changes in its operations, for instance, the five chairs meet together and decide jointly.

Euronext has spun off *Clearnet*, its clearing house, which then merged with the London Clearing House. LCH.Clearnet also clears for the London Metal Exchange, for instance. Settlement and custody are also independent, and can, for example, be done by *Euroclear* or London's *Crest*, which also works for LSE, for instance.

Euronext does still own and run a clearing organization, *Bclear*, but that is for outside OTC deals. Thus, when bank X sells bonds, OTC, to company Y via Bclear, legally there is a sale from X to Bclear and a sale from Bclear to Y; Bclear thus guarantees execution. It also offers straight through processing (STP).

Euronext also has a "strategic alliance" with Tokyo, a "partnership" with Luxembourg (which runs NSC and lists 29,000 eurobonds (2007)), a 5% equity stake (the legal maximum) in India's National SE, and a Joint Venture with Borsa Italiana to run a popular government bond-trading platform, MTS.

Each member exchange has the same numbers of seats on the board and the management committees.

The achievements are, first, internationalization of deals. In the third quarter of 2005, 25% of the trades were cross-border, against 9% four years earlier. In Brussels, in June 2005 two thirds of the orders came from foreign brokers, against only 9% four years before, and the number of active brokers went from 80 (of which 55 were Belgian) to 120 (35 Belgian). As a result of higher efficiency and more competition, costs fell: between 2001 and 2005, the all-Euronext average cost per trade dropped from EUR 1.53 to EUR 0.98. Gajewski and Gresse (2003) conclude that, even in the early years, NSC was already cheaper than London's SETS (Stock Exchange Electronic Trading Service). (But, LSE replies, big orders fare better in London.) Between 2004 and 2006 volumes went up by 40%, spreads down by 20%, and volatility down by 10% (Pagano and Padilla 2005), but, here, outside factors must have helped too.

Panel 17.1.   Euronext.

and legal background are too different across countries. In fact, regulatory and legal differences may mean that an internationally traded stock actually has different aliases, like one for trading in European countries with bearer shares, one for European countries with registered shares, and one for the United States. Lastly, we ask the question of whether unification may not be achieved indirectly—with all quoted companies getting a listing in one important exchange (or one of a few important exchanges), and the other markets just dwindling away. That outcome, I think, is unlikely too.

17.1 Background Information on International Stock Markets

17.1.1 How Large and How International Are Stock Markets?

In December 2007, the market capitalization of all stocks traded on exchanges that are members of the international federation of stock exchanges, Fédération Internationale de Bourses de Valeurs (FIBV), was USD 60 trillion. In this total, all firms are counted only once, notably in their country of economic nationality or primary listing; so if a British firm has asked a U.S. financial institution to issue carbon copies of the British shares that are then traded in the United States, all that value is counted as British. (Grouping by the nationality of the issuer is far easier than by nationality of the holder: many countries either have no good information on the latter or it is not centralized.) The total number for the world also includes just the formally listed stocks, not the OTC-traded securities.

This USD 60 trillion total was 175% above the level in 1998, as you can see from table 17.1, and, despite the *subprime* gloom at the time, still one quarter above the 2005 level. U.S. companies, which for a long time represented about half of the global market cap, are now down to one third. The reason is not so much a bad return performance of the U.S. exchanges, but a combination of three trends. First, in the United States, more firms are being taken into private control, while in Central Europe and especially Asia more firms are getting listed, partly even in new exchanges. Second, of course, there is the weak dollar. Third, more (non-U.S.) exchanges have recently joined FIBV, most notably Mumbai (Bombay), Shanghai, and Shenzen, which together already represent almost 10% of the total. Europe somewhat increased its value weight, at about 28%, with London dramatically losing market share, the rest of "old" Europe marking pace, and "new" Europe winning. Asia, as one would expect, gained ground too: its market share shot up by over 12 percentage points, to end at 28%, on a par with Europe.

Table 17.3 shows the top ten exchanges, ranked by various criteria. In terms of market cap, the New York Stock Exchange (NYSE) maintains a very clear lead (15 trillion), followed by four exchanges with caps of about 4 trillion: Tokyo, Euronext, Nasdaq, and London. Deutsche Börse, itself the result of a 1990s merger of six regional exchanges inside Germany, is eager to grow and join the top league: in 2004–6 it made repeated purchase offers for London and

Table 17.1. Domestic market capitalization of world's stock exchanges.

	1998		2005		2007	
	b$	%	b$	%	b$	%
NYSE	8,880	40	13,311	30.0	15,421	25.4
Amex	125	0.6	86	0.2	282	0.5
Nasdaq	1,738	7.8	3,604	8.1	3,865	6.4
U.S.	10,742	48.3	17,001	38.4	19,568	32.2
Canada	997	4.5	1,482	3.3	2,186	3.6
U.S. and Canada	11,739	53	18,483	41.7	21,754	35.8
London	1,996	9	3,058	6.9	3,851	6.3
Amsterdam	469	2.1				0.0
Brussels	139	0.6				
Paris	676	3				
Euronext3	1,284	5.8				
Lisbon	39	0.2				
Euronext	1,323	6	2,707	6.1	4,223	7.0
Helsinki	73	0.3				
Stockholm	265	1.2				
Copenhagen	338	0.4				
OMX	338	1.5	803	1.8	1,243	2.0
Germany	825	3.7	1,221	2.8	2,105	3.5
Spain	290	1.3	960	2.2	1,781	2.9
Athens	34	0.2	145	0.3	265	0.4
Budapest			33	0.1	46	0.1
Cyprus			7	0.0	29	0.0
Irish SE	49	0.2	114	0.3	144	0.2
Istanbul	61	0.3	162	0.4	286	0.5
Italy	345	1.6	798	1.8	1,072	1.8
Ljubljana	2	0	8	0.0	29	0.0
Luxembourg	34	0.2	51	0.1	166	0.3
Malta	0	0	4	0.0	6	0.0
Oslo	67	0.3	191	0.4	353	0.6
Switzerland	575	2.6	935	2.1	1,271	2.1
Vienna	37	0.2	126	0.3	236	0.4
Warsaw	12	0.1	94	0.2	211	0.3
Europe	6,083	27.4	11,416	25.8	17,317	28.5
Mexico	157	0.7	239	0.5	397	0.7
Buenos Aries	59	0.3	48	0.1	57	0.1
Colombia	0	0	51	0.1	101	0.2
Lima	17	0.1	24	0.1	69	0.1
Brazil	255	1.1	475	1.1	1,370	2.3
Santiago	72	0.3	136	0.3	212	0.3
Bermuda				0.0	3	0.0
Latin America	561	2.5	972	2.2	2,209	3.6

Table 17.1. *Continued.*

	1998		2005		2007	
	b$	%	b$	%	b$	%
Cairo Alessandria	0	0	80	0.2	193	0.3
Mauritius	0	0	2	0.0	8	0.0
Tehran	11	0.1	36	0.1	44	0.1
Tel Aviv	44	0.2	123	0.3	235	0.4
Johannesburg	212	1	549	1.2	828	1.4
Africa and Middle East	267	1.2	790	1.8	1,308	2.2
Australian	295	1.3	804	1.8	1,095	1.8
Bombay	0	0	553	1.2	1,298	2.1
Colombo	0	0	6	0.0	8	0.0
Hong Kong	413	1.9	1,055	2.4	2,654	4.4
Jakarta	29	0.1	81	0.2	212	0.3
Japan	2,217	10	4,573	10.3	4,542	7.5
Korea	42	0.2	718	1.6	1,122	1.8
Kuala Lumpur	93	0.4	181	0.4	325	0.5
New Zealand	30	0.1	41	0.1	47	0.1
Philippines	31	0.1	40	0.1	103	0.2
Shanghai	0	0	286	0.6	3,694	6.1
Shenzhen	0	0	116	0.3	785	1.3
Singapore	106	0.5	257	0.6	539	0.9
Taiwan	297	1.3	476	1.1	664	1.1
Thailand	23	0.1	124	0.3	197	0.3
Asia, Pacific, Australia	3,577	16.1	9,310	21.0	17,285	28.5
FIBV all	22,226	101.2	44,315	100	60,692	100

Source: Computed from FIBV data, mid December. The columns headed by "%" show the exchange's market cap as a fraction of the world total. Foreign and cross listings are not included.

Euronext, only to be rebutted and, in the case of Euronext, defeated by NYSE.[2] But Deutsche has now been overtaken by Shanghai (a bubbly market), Hong Kong, and Canada.

The "cash" stock section of Euronext itself was set up by the old Amsterdam, Brussels, and Paris exchanges; Lisbon joined more recently. Euronext has also taken over LIFFE, the London derivatives exchange, and has concentrated all the former Amsterdam, Brussels, Paris, and Lisbon derivatives business there. Milan has also long been wooed by Euronext, but it ended up in the arms of LSE (2007). Another ambitious player is OMX. OM started off as a private options

---

[2] Euronext had been talking to London too, and London to the Nasdaq (which at one point even held almost 30% of LSE's stock). OMX had made a bid for LSE too. In the end, the Nasdaq seems to have ended up as the owner of OMX, with Dubai as co-owner; OMX is hot because of its software systems.

Table 17.2. Foreign and cross listings in the world's stock exchanges.

	1998		2005		2007	
	#	%	#	%	#	%
NYSE	355	13.5	452	19.9	421	18.5
Amex	63	8.9	100	16.8	104	17.4
Nasdaq	454	8.3	332	10.5	307	10.0
Chicago	0	0.0				
Toronto	58	4.1				
Vancouver	0	0.0				
Montreal	12	2.2				
Canada Toronto SE	70	2.1	39	1.0	70	1.8
London	467	18.6	334	10.8	719	21.7
Amsterdam	149	42.8				
Brussels	127	47.9				
Paris	184	19.9				
Euronext3		0.0				
Lisbon	0	0.0				
Euronext4		0.0	293	23.3	225	19.5
Helsinki	2	1.6				
Stockholm	16	6.1				
OMX	0.0	22	3.2	24	2.8	
Germany		0.0	166	20.4	105	12.1
Spain	9	0.9			39	1.1
Athens	0	0.0	2	0.7	3	1.1
Budapest			0	0.0	2	4.9
Copenhagen	12	4.8				
Cyprus			0	0.0	0	0.0
Irish SE	19	18.6	13	19.7	13	17.8
Istanbul	1	0.4	0	0.0	0	0.0
Italy	4	1.7	7	2.5	6	2.0
Ljubljana	0	0.0	0	0.0	0	0.0
Luxembourg	228	80.3	206	84.1	227	87.0
Malta			0	0.0	0	0.0
Oslo	21	9.7	28	12.8	40	16.1
Switzerland	212	49.5	116	29.0	84	24.6
Vienna	37	26.8	19	17.1	17	14.3
Warsaw	0	0.0	7	2.9	23	6.1

market (note the initials), in Stockholm, but now runs four of the five Nordic exchanges (Denmark, Finland, Iceland, Sweden), plus an "alternative" Nordic market (Nordic First AM), plus the three Baltic exchanges; it also owns a chunk of the Oslo Stock Exchange's stock.[3] The Vienna Stock Exchange is the main

---

[3] OMX sells a highly regarded trading "platform" (a trading software system), and had over sixty software customers at the time of writing (most of them not for entire trading platforms, though). Atos Origin, which developed Euronext's platform, runs its systems on at least thirteen exchanges. Montreal, which had provided the original electronic order-driven trading systems in Europe in the 1980s, has successfully sold its SOLA system in Asia; Boston's Options Exchange also uses it.

Table 17.2.   *Continued.*

	1998		2005		2007	
	#	%	#	%	#	%
Mexico	4	2.0	176	54.0	242	65.9
Buenos Aries	0	0.0	4	3.8	5	4.5
Colombia			0	0.0	0	0.0
Lima	3	1.2	31	13.8	38	16.8
Rio de Janeiro	1	0.2				
Santiago	0	0.0	1	0.4	3	1.2
Saõ Paulo	1	0.2	2	0.5	9	2.2
Cairo Aless			0	0.0		
Mauritius			0	0.0	3	4.3
Tehran	0	0.0			0	0.0
Tel Aviv	2	0.3				
Johannesburg	27	4.2	25	6.7	37	9.0
Australian	60	4.9	71	4.1	85	4.3
Bombay			0	0.0	0	0.0
National SE India			0	0.0	0	0.0
Colombo			0	0.0	0	0.0
Hong Kong	20	3.0	9	0.8	9	0.7
Jakarta	0	0.0	0	0.0	0	0.0
Korea	0	0.0	0	0.0	2	0.1
Kuala Lumpur	3	0.4	4	0.4	3	0.3
New Zealand	55	28.9	32	17.3	26	14.6
Osaka	1	0.1	1	0.1	1	0.2
Philippines	0	0.0	2	0.8	2	0.8
Shanghai			0	0.0	0	0.0
Shenzhen			0	0.0	0	0.0
Singapore	40	12.0	122	17.8	290	38.1
Taiwan	0	0.0	5	0.7	5	0.7
Thailand	0	0.0	0	0.0	0	0.0
Tokyo	60	3.2	28	1.2	25	1.0
FIBV all						
Foreign	3,649		3,533		3,214	
Local	44,975		42,041		40,900	
Ratio (%)	8.1		8.4		7.9	

Source: Computed from FIBV data, mid December. The columns "%" show the number of foreign listings as a percentage of the total (domestic + foreign). The ratio at the bottom shows the number of foreign listings divided by the number of listed companies, worldwide. SE, Stock Exchange.

sponsor and manager of the Budapest Stock Exchange and the two exchanges share an interlinked structure, exchange of stocks, and information. Similar cooperation is being set up for the Bucharest Stock Exchange and the Zagreb Stock Exchange.

Table 17.3. Leading exchanges, mid December 2007.

By size		By number of foreign companies		As a percentage of foreign companies	
NYSE	15,421	London	719	Luxembourg	87.0
Japan	4,542	NYSE	421	Mexico	65.9
Euronext	4,223	Nasdaq	307	Singapore	38.1
Nasdaq	3,865	Singapore	290	Switzerland	24.6
London	3,851	Mexico	242	London	21.7
Shanghai	3,694	Luxembourg	227	Euronext	19.5
Hong Kong	2,654	Euronext	225	NYSE	18.5
Canada	2,186	Germany	105	Irish SE	17.8
Germany	2,105	Amex	104	Amex	17.4
Spain	1,781	Australian	85	Lima	16.8

Source: Computed from FIBV data, mid December 2007.

Despite these efforts toward consolidation, the European markets remain hopelessly fragmented, as does much of Asia, Latin America, and Africa and the Middle East. Many of the stocks traded there are held only locally. The international companies from countries with smaller exchanges typically get an additional listing in one of the major centers: New York, London, Euronext, Luxembourg, Singapore, Deutsche Börse, or Zürich. Note again that table 17.1 reports the companies by original nationality; thus, the U.S. market cap does not include the foreign stocks that are "cross listed" in the United States as well as at home, and similarly for other markets.

Table 17.2 shows the numbers and percentages of foreign companies listed in the FIBV exchanges for selected years. London clearly leads, with over 700 listings by foreign stocks. NYSE and Nasdaq are distant second and third. Euronext still has a respectable score but the last of big five, Tokyo, is nowhere to be seen in this respect. Some mezzanine markets are surprisingly open, in terms of number of companies: Mexico, Singapore, and Luxembourg. Remember that these numbers do not include nonlisted securities that are traded over the counter (OTC) or privately; especially in the United States this form of trading is important. www.adr.com reports that, at the end of 2006, the total number of non-U.S. companies that are registered in the United States as being somehow traded there in some form exceeds 2,000. This implies that the number of OTC-traded or privately placed issues is larger than the number of formally listed foreign securities. The 2,000 total includes securities created in the United States as stand-ins for foreign securities and marketed by U.S. investment banks (see below for details); it does not include foreign shares bought directly by U.S. investors from non-U.S. exchanges. There is no good information on similar nonlisted presence in other countries, but one source mentions 4,000 as the world total of stand-in securities designed for trading outside their home country, of which 2,000 would be "global" (i.e., non-U.S.).

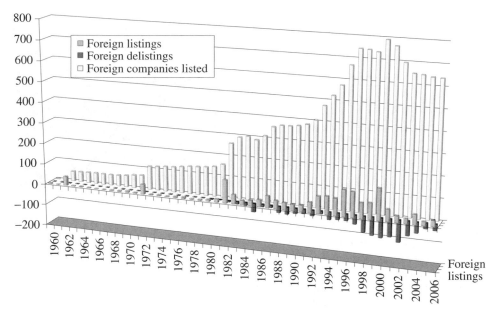

Figure 17.3. U.S. foreign listings, 1960–2004. *Source:* From listing to delisting, Working Paper, 2007; 2005–6 added from FIBV website.

The totals that I added at the bottom of table 17.2, on the right, show that foreign and cross listings remain a marginal affair, at about 8%. In addition, there is no evidence that the phenomenon is (still) on the rise.

In terms of percentages (number of foreign stocks versus total listed), many exchanges are more international than NYSE, but they are often smaller centers. Among the second-league players, Euronext is almost as international as London, by these relative numbers; in 2005 it was even more international, by percentage of foreign listings. Note that the Hong Kong tally of foreign stocks does not include Chinese ones, which under FIBV definitions are deemed to be local.

The rise of New York as an international market is recent by European standards: it all started in the 1980s (figure 17.3). The number of U.S. foreign listings has gone down recently, but so has the number of domestic U.S. listings. Much to the chagrin of New York—the stock exchange, city, and state—in 2006 London and Hong Kong briefly overtook the United States in terms of IPO volume. We will return to this later.

Why firms get second listings elsewhere is one of the big issues in long-term funding. In fact, we devote all of the next chapter to it. First let's look at how these markets work.

17.1.2 How Do Stock Markets Work?

We first discuss ways of matching supply and demand, and then the clearing and settlement. We end with what one might call semi-exchanges: crossing

(a)

Naam effect : ▼ KBC GROEP			
Laatste	**84.52 EUR**	Hoogste	89.80
Variatie (%)	**-5.56**	Laagste	83.96
Variatie (Pts)	**-4.98**		
Aantal	1229723		
Openingskoers	88.91	Hoogste koers/jaar	107.96
Slotkoers(d-1)	89.50	Laagste koers/jaar	74.77
Nat. ID	BE0003565737	Reuters-code	KBC.BR
Markt	BRU		

Aankoop		Verkoop	
Aantal	**Koers**	**Aantal**	**Koers**
882	84.53	200	84.64
2462	84.52	100	84.65
253	84.50	141	84.74
1575	84.49	872	84.76
128	84.48	853	84.87

☐ **Auto-refresh (/10sec)**

(b)

Figure 17.4. Public limit-order books. *Key:* (a) A customer version of Euronext's book for KBC Group, a Belgian banking company: five price levels each side, and numbers of shares offered or asked. (b) A broker's screen at the Hong Kong SE. Top left are the four most recent trades. Bottom left you see the order book itself, with the current best buy and sell prices (133.00 and 133.10), and then quantities asked/offered for five tick levels up or down, often in ,000s ("K"). Also shown, in parentheses, is the number of brokers behind aggregate supply and demand (e.g., 57 buyers at 133.00, 23 sellers at 133.10). Who exactly these 57 or 23 brokers are is revealed in the list of brokers' codes on the right. *Source:* (a) www.bolero.be. (b) Kindly provided by Jean-Claude Maswana, Kyoto University.

networks or matching engines that are now competing with the traditional exchanges.

17.1.2.1 Price- versus Order-Driven Markets

Stock markets across the world can have quite different approaches regarding the matching of supply and demand. One traditionally distinguishes order- and price- (or quote-) driven markets. Nowadays, hybrids seem to have become the norm.

Quote-driven markets. Some markets work with market makers, that is, financial institutions that post prices at which they are prepared to buy and sell. Examples include the London Stock Exchange, London's SEAQ, and America's Nasdaq.[4] The market makers provide bids and asks when prompted by customers, using electronic communication, nowadays. There is common software, and rules about trading and information provision by listed companies and so on, but until recently the contacts between customer and market maker traditionally remained purely bilateral.

Order-driven markets. In Canada and in many European countries investors enter their *limit orders* into a computer which aggregates them into market-wide supply and demand schedules. At the opening (*call*), the system crosses

---

[4] SEAQ stands for Stock Exchange Automated Quotation; Nasdaq stands for National Association of Security Dealers Automated Quotation.

supply and demand, which provides the opening price and already executes the highest possible volume of orders. Unmatched orders remain displayed in a *public limit-order book*—computer screens, really, these days—and remain there until they expire, are matched with a new order that came in later, or are withdrawn. The screens show quantities available for, for example, three or five different price levels at both sides of the *fork* or *inside quote* (the best buy and sell orders) (see figure 17.4). Brokers see the screens and can take some of the outstanding orders when a customer wants them; or they can add/cancel orders, or match new buy and sell orders internally (*in-house crossing*) if this is possible at a price within the fork or, for big trades, close to the fork; such in-house trades must traditionally be reported to the exchange, though. Nowadays also customers can see the book, at a price. In Japan, "intermediaries" keep the book; they change the price to balance supply and demand, but like the bookmakers of old in Europe or Canada they do not in principle buy and sell themselves.

The obvious advantage of market making is that an investors can always quickly buy and sell reasonably large packets of shares (*immediacy* and *liquidity*); in order-driven systems, liquidity and immediacy can be poor if there is little interest in a particular stock. On the other hand, in the case of bilateral market making, the aggregation of information is less perfect because—or, better perhaps, if—investors see only one market-maker's quote and market makers see only a small part of demand and supply. In addition, an order-driven market is very transparent since every move is recorded in the book. What we observe, nowadays, is a kind of convergence of the two systems, in an attempt to unite the best of the two systems.

Hybrid markets. NYSE and AMEX,[5] for instance, have market makers (called *specialists*) but also a limit-order book. It must be added that the market-making part has dwindled to next-to-nothing in recent years. Euronext is primarily organized as an order-driven market, but now has "liquidity providers" that undertake to continuously post bids and asks in the limit-order book so that investors can trade the securities at all times. Deutsche Börse's XETRA system is explicitly hybrid; tellingly, the version of XETRA run in Vienna is called EQOS (Electronic Quote and Order-Driven System). Also, London's SETS is hybrid.

In quote-driven systems increasingly often there is a common platform that continuously shows quotes for different market makers on one screen, or automatically picks/shows the best bids and asks only. For instance, Nasdaq's *Level I quote* shows, for each stock, the best bid and the best ask across all market makers; its Level II screen shows bids and asks for each and every market maker. These screen systems, originally called "supermontage," actually

---

[5] New York Stock Exchange; American Exchange (also located in New York, right next to ground zero). Amex and Nasdaq merged in 1998 but broke up again in 2004. Amex has the softest listing and disclosure requirements of all three. It now looks as if Amex will end up in NYSE's arms soon.

imitate what was emerging in the OTC market, as we shall see. Neither screen is a limit-order book: it still shows only one "order" per market maker—the best, presumably—and a fortiori no limit orders directly from customers; but it does represent a step in the direction of a limit-order book.

Despite these elements of convergence, the systems remain quite different. A broker who wants to directly trade in three markets needs three software systems, three sets of screens, and three memberships ("seats"), one for each exchange. Also, given these different operating principles, it is not easy to set up a world market for stocks. Euronext (Amsterdam, Brussels, Lisbon, Paris) groups exchanges that had similar systems at the outset, but attempts to cooperate/merge with Germany's Deutsche Börse or London's LSE have come to naught, at the time of writing. Euronext has teamed up with NYSE, but it is far from obvious, to say the least, whether NYSE and Euronext's operational integration will ever go as far as what was achieved within the old Euronext. Ownership of the existing exchanges is surely changing, and cross listing and after-hours trading will probably be facilitated, and all markets will ultimately use the same software and screens, but the SEC may never agree with "single passports" for brokers and issuers, and its cooperation with the other regulators remains unclear too. A common regulatory framework is unthinkable in the foreseeable future. (At the time LSE seemed close to a takeover by Nasdaq, the United Kingdom even hurriedly initiated legislation that would explicitly rule out LSE having to follow U.S. regulation.) Even the old (purely European) Euronext is to some extent a confederation of four exchanges rather than one exchange. In fact, there have been loud and clear whispers that Deutsche's bid for Euronext was doomed because it wanted a full and complete merger of the two (or is it five?) exchanges, while NYSE is more flexible—for the time being. Deutsche Börse also insists on its trading system, XETRA, and its "silo" model: the exchange doing the trading and pricing, and working with one clearing house for clearing and settlement, Clearstream, which is fully owned by the exchange. This has brought us to a second aspect in which exchanges differ, namely clearing and settlement.

17.1.2.2 *Clearing and Settlement*

Trading requires not just matching and pricing of orders, but also clearing and settlement (C&S).

- Clearing and the closely related function of *novation*—all contracts being run through a *central counterparty* (CCP), who takes over the counterparty default risk—are familiar from futures exchanges (chapter 6). In stock markets, CCPs are relatively new; the idea has been borrowed from the futures exchanges.

- Settlement requires the help of a *central security depository* (CSD), which holds the bearer shares, if any, and keeps a register of who currently

The *Markets in Financial Instruments Directive* contains the following provisions:

- First, the *single passport* idea — a license to deliver a particular financial service at home that is also automatically applicable in other member states—is being extended from commercial banking, collective investments, and insurance to all financial instruments, and to that end investor-protection regulation is also to be harmonized.

- Second, the remaining *monopolies* on equities trading, notably in France, Italy, and Spain, have to go, and interbank and OTC trading are to be facilitated. Similarly, the old rule that a broker must report in-house matches of customer orders to the national exchange has gone; other forms of making the deal public will do too (like Reuters or Bloomberg). Also OTC trades in unlisted securities must be made more public.

- Third, there is to be more *transparency*. For example, one should be able to see best quotes across all exchanges, and the broker should guarantee best execution (dealing at the best price across all exchanges or networks). A second transparency aspect is that fees for trading, clearing, and settlement should be clearly separated, and that

there best execution should also apply. So silos or other one-to-one relations between exchanges and C&S institutions are out: the investor should be able to choose the cheapest provider.

- A last provision is that every seller of retail financial products has to draw up a *risk profile* of the customer, and take that into account when recommending or even just executing trades or investments. The intermediary's excuse that the customer took the initiative herself, not the intermediary (an "execution only" deal), cannot be invoked for risky stuff like derivatives and hedge funds: the customer should be warned or informed if the order does not fit the profile. For professional customers all this is not required.

MiFID was issued in November 2006 and took effect in November 2007. Investment bankers were still wondering how to organize best execution in OTC markets. They and their overseers also point out that MiFID contains just principles, no details. So overseers will probably still come up with different implementations of "best execution," etc., unless they hammer out a consensus rulebook among themselves.

Panel 17.2. MiFID?

owns these shares, or which acts as letterbox for the issuer's registrar of shareholders. We met CSDs when we discussed eurobonds in chapter 16.

Sometimes order matching, novation/clearing, and settlement are all done by the same institution, or by institutions linked to each other and with no free choice for the investor; this is called the *silo model*.

Euronext Paris had its own CCP/clearing house, Clearnet, but has spun it off. Clearnet and LCH (London Clearing House, LIFFE's clearer) are now merged into, unimaginatively, LCH.Clearnet, which still works for Euronext but also, for example, for the London Metal Exchange. Settlement and custody is also by an independent entity at the customer's discretion, for instance Euroclear (Brussels) or Crest (London).

Before that, Brussels, Milan, and Lisbon also followed the silo model. The 2006–7 EU Directive, shortened to MiFID (see panel 17.2), prohibits silos and imposes that investors have more choice as far as clearing and settlement are concerned. Still, silos need not be expensive, as the panel shows: Deutsche Börse looks costly, but Lisbon and Italiana were quite cheap. (Deutsche Börse disputes the numbers shown in the panel.) The ECB has even threatened to set up an EU-wide C&S institution, the Target 2 Securities (TS2) system, if the

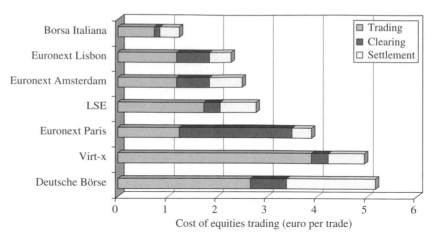

Figure 17.5. Trading costs in Europe: scope for improvement. *Source:* Based on numbers from the EU Commission, quoted in the *Economist*, September 7, 2006.

private sector does not get its act together soon, but some banks and existing settlement houses have expressed doubts about such a role for a central bank. Still, the ECB seems ready to forge ahead. In the United States, there is one central C&S institution, the Depository and Trust Corporation (DTC), and it easily beats the European counterparts on cost. Tellingly, the European trading network Turquoise, which is to be kickstarted in 2008, chose the DTC as its clearer,[6] not one of the local outfits. Trading costs surely diverge(d) weirdly across Europe's exchanges and, until recently, even within Euronext. Figure 17.5 shows that Paris was easily half as expensive again as Lisbon, with especially clearing being extravagantly costly. Even cheap Lisbon was twice as expensive as Milan. Costs should come down by cutting profit margins and by consolidation. Clearing is, in fact, still very profitable—insiders mention profit margins of 40% in 2007—so there is room for price cutting at constant costs. In addition, the many clearers all have their fixed costs (ITC, mainly), so consolidation would cut costs too. America's DTC handles over twice the volume of Euroclear, the world's second. In 2007–8, the costs of clearing and settlement were already coming down, because of MiFID and under pressure from the investment banks, which do a lot of custodian work themselves. To put the C&S cost differences in perspective, however, I should add that the numbers shown do not include the bid–ask spread, and that the latter is responsible for 80–90% of the cost of trading.

In short, exchanges differ in terms of trading systems and C&S. One cannot help thinking that debates about trading and C&S systems occasionally also hide antiquated nationalism—or self-preservation by the exchange's officers, perhaps: a small exchange opting for a merger is like turkeys voting for an early Christmas. There are unifying forces, however, even if exchanges will or cannot cooperate: trading networks and best-execution rules.

---

[6] Via DTC's subsidiary, the European Central Counterparty (EuroCCP).

17.1.2.3 ECNs, Crossing Networks, and Best-Execution Rules

One unifying force, in a way, has been the rise of international trading networks. Traditionally, big blocks were often traded outside the regular systems (e.g., the *"upstairs market"* in London; *secondary offerings* in New York) or migrated to OTC markets run from banks' *"block desks."* For bonds, this had already become the rule by the 1960s. OTC was originally a telephone market, like the currency markets of old, but computers have now taken over a lot of that trade. This has come in two forms: electronic communication networks and crossing networks.

The electronic communication networks (ECNs) set up electronic PLOBS for stocks that have a primary listing in an official exchange. That does not make them genuine exchanges: besides running an order-matching system (its PLOB), a genuine exchange has to evaluate listing applications from would-be listees; follow up the listing requirements and information provision by listees; provide price and volume information on the exchange; provide historic prices and so on. An exchange also needs a license to trade. The riposte of the ECNs (and the exchanges' customers) is that gathering and providing price and volume information comes at a zero cost and in fact used to be free. Nowadays, data provision stands for about half of the exchange's income—the other big bits are listing fees and trading fees—so that's not a burden, the critics say, it's a monopoly rent; the same holds for listing. In return, exchanges gripe that the platforms are free-riding on the quality-labeling and vetting done by exchanges. What exchanges surely dislike even more is the price competition. Setting up an off-the-shelf trading system costs a mere USD 7–8m (*Economist*, May 16, 2007, p. 76), and the marginal costs are low. Turquoise (see below) expects to offer trades at half Euronext's fees, which are about ten times New York's (ibid.).

Nasdaq was the oldest de facto ECN, but it became an official exchange in 1994, just before the SEC came up with rules on alternative trading systems (Reg ATS, 1994). Instinet followed, and Island, and Bloomberg's Tradebook. One newcomer is Chicago's BATS,[7] which is now itself applying for full exchange status. Italy's MTS is one of the oldest networks in Europe, originally set up for Italian government debt (of which there is plenty) but now handling bonds from anywhere. In stocks, Chi-X[8] is active, and London's Project Turquoise, backed by seven bulge-bracket investment banks, was due to start in late 2008 (but got delayed because of the credit crisis). Also BATS announced plans to come to Europe.

Even more informal than ECNs are the *crossing networks* and *(dark) pools* like Liquidnet, Pipeline, ITG's Posit, or Goldman Sachs's SIGMA X. Banks have

---

[7] The acronym modestly refers to a Better Alternative Trading System; the founder, Dave Cummings, loves to be pictured holding a baseball bat "to whack Nasdaq."

[8] The name alludes not to a sexist term for younger persons of the female gender, but to X, for eXchange, and to the Greek chi (χ), the "cross" that is meant to echo the notion of crossing.

long kept private limit-order books showing their own and their customers' orders. Crossing networks or pools (sometimes labeled "dark pools"), then, are peer-to-peer networks where members can browse each others' books to find a match. Prices are not made public, so these crossing networks do not contribute to price discovery. Actually, prices are mostly taken from the exchange where the stock has its primary listing.

Some successful networks have disappeared fast—not because their luck turned, but because they had awakened the appetite of the traditional exchanges. NYSE, for instance, which had gone on trading in the old floor-based "open-outcry" fashion for far too long, bought the Archipelago network for its electronic expertise and its low cost. Archipelago's ArcoEx had actually just acquired the status of an exchange and offered Nasdaq-style fees for NYSE stocks, a move soon imitated by other ECNs and Nasdaq itself. It now operates as NYSE Arca.[9] To some extent Arca cannibalizes NYSE big-board trade (10% of trade in shares listed there happens on Arca), but it also took 20% of Nasdaq listees' liquidity. Nasdaq similarly bought INET, a spin-off of Instinet.

Another unifying force, beside trading networks, is the *best-execution* rules that are being imposed. In the United States, brokers must offer the best price available on any exchange or network at that particular moment (Regulation National Market System—Reg NMS, implemented in 2007). In Europe, the MiFID directive that came into force a few months after NMS (see panel 17.2) has a similar provision. The best-execution principle is a substitute for the old *concentration rule*, which gave official exchanges a monopoly such that pricing and liquidity would be concentrated in one spot. With upstart exchanges and networks draining away part of the liquidity, markets got too fragmented—hence the new best-execution rule, forcing brokers to browse across all markets. The intermediaries are grumbling that, while getting prices from exchanges may not be too difficult, it is far less obvious to find the best possible OTC price and to prove that you did find it. There are trading networks, but to be sure about the best price one would have to be a member of all networks, or the networks would all have to merge into one single entity. Probably for that reason, MiFID's wording about what best execution actually means is left rather blurry.

To what extent the networks and the best-execution rules will unify markets without a full-scale merger of the traditional exchanges is far from obvious, at this stage. But there are fundamental issues, like different legislation on securities and corporate governance, that are much more difficult to solve than differences in trading and settlement systems. Before addressing this

---

[9] NYSE's interest in Archipelago was not just based on the latter's electronic know-how, but also in its ownership of a (young) derivatives exchange. Similarly, one of Euronext's attractions, to NYSE, was its ownership of LIFFE. The idea is that trading in stocks and derivatives should be better integrated, including the clearing and settlement. Deutsche Börse has similarly bought ICE to add to its existing high-flying derivatives exchange, Eurex—itself a merger of Deutsche termin Börse and Switzerland's SOFFEX. But this type of integration is across products, not across markets.

we consider a last technical issue: the feature that a stock that does trade internationally may actually be represented by different aliases in different markets.

17.1.3 Certificates, Receipts: Different Aliases for a Company's Stocks

Another technical feature illustrating the lack of internationalization is that one share is not always tradable as such in two or more places. In fact, theoretically, every place of trading could require its own version of the company's share. The origin could be securities law, notably whether shares are bearer or registered, or it could be the need to separate cross-listed shares into a domestic section and a foreign one, a need felt especially by the U.S. regulators.

17.1.3.1 Bearer/Anonymous versus Registered

Some countries have a tradition of *bearer* shares (anonymous pieces of paper, in principle),[10] whereas in most countries the stockholders are *registered* in the company's register of shareholders. Investors who are used to bearer shares often do not cherish the idea of giving up their anonymity. In countries where shares are traditionally made out to the bearer, foreign companies with registered shares face a hurdle: they must convert their shares into bearer shares. To that end, a *custodian* institution buys and holds registered shares, and then issues bearer *certificates* or *receipts* that represent *n* original shares. For instance, in Brussels, companies like Rio Tinto Zinc or Tanganjika were traded by means of certificates standing for 1, 10, 25, or 50 shares. The custodian does this, for a fee, at the request of a *depository* institution (a bank or a trust corporation), which acts as *transfer agent* between the custodian and the investors and as *fiscal agent*. For instance, the depository takes care of distributing the dividends (paying out cash in return for coupons clipped off from the share or certificate), paying the withholding taxes on dividends if any, distributing the periodic financial reports, making filings with the overseeing authorities, passing on requests for information from shareholders, announcing assembly general meetings, and so on. Similarly, companies with bearer shares can convert them into registered shares via a custodian, who holds the paper and acts as *registrar*—that is, keeps a register of owners of the (nondeliverable) receipts or certificates issued against the shares. The depository bank or trust can start the program at the request of the issuing company (*sponsored program*), but occasionally issues certificates on its own account if it sees a market for the securities.

---

[10] Nowadays, *deliverable* bearer shares are getting rare: instead of buying and receiving a piece of paper, the buyer is being recorded as being the new owner of a share that is physically residing with a clearing organization and custodian like Clearstream or Euroclear—this is still different from a registered share, where the issuing company is keeping the register; a *securities account* with a bank will also do. Deliverable bearer securities are set to disappear altogether, in Europe, by 2015.

17.1.3.2   United States: Separation of U.S. versus non-U.S. Slices of Cross-Listed Equity

But similar issues may arise even if no conversion from bearer to registered or vice versa is needed. Buying abroad is a hassle: one needs to do a forex trans-action and (often) pay two brokers or have an account with a foreign broker, and afterward there is the following-up of dividends, information, taxes, etc. Kind financial institutions then lovingly take this burden from your shoulders (in exchange for a fee): they buy foreign shares and issue, for example, depository receipts. This could be demand-driven (an unsponsored program); but since 1983 all U.S. depository receipts are supply driven, that is, sponsored and initiated by the firm that issued the original shares. The United Kingdom similarly got rid of unsponsored issues in the early 2000s.

But American depository receipts (ADRs) are not just about investors' convenience: there are major legal issues too. First, an issuer of shares, whether foreign or not, cannot usually "push" his securities in a big way unless they have been approved by a local overseer. This approval can be largely a formality if the placement is a private one and/or if the buyers are all knowledgeable pros, but it can be as demanding as what is required for a local IPO targeting retail investors. Regulators may also insist on seeing a local antenna which is responsible for the chores (dividends, taxes, reports, filings, and so on) and which is not likely to simply up sticks and disappear at short notice. In addition, many institutional investors like pension funds and retail-oriented mutual funds can only buy local, approved securities. This is all taken care of by (sponsored) receipts. The issuer of the receipts then registers the issue with the overseer, helps in getting the necessary approval, and acts as the locally responsible party for dividends, taxes, filings and reports, and so on; and the receipts are, legally, local securities rather than foreign ones—subject to local regulation and legislation, not the rules from the issuer's country.

The country that is most exacting in all this is the United States. If the securities to be sold are to be traded on an exchange or OTC rather than being solely available to qualified professionals, local carbon copies of the original shares have to be created for trade inside the United States. These U.S.-registered versions of the shares can be called shares too, or, alternatively, receipts, depending on the name the intermediary invented for the product. For example, the Dutch holding companies Royal Dutch and Unilever N.V. have *New York shares*—shares of the New York registry, representing equity ownership in a non-U.S. company, allowing for a part of the capital of the company to be outstanding in the United States and part in the home market. A New York share issued by a U.S. transfer agent and registrar on behalf of the company and—note the beautiful legalese—"created against the cancellation of the local share" by the local registrar.

A similar but more flexible version is that the issuer has *receipts* created for trading inside the United States, instead of New York shares. For example, in the case of both Royal Dutch and Unilever N.V., their respective U.K. incorporated sister companies, Shell Transport & Trading and Unilever plc, use receipts.[11] Below, we take a closer look at the American versions of these receipts. After all, the United States was for a long time the undisputed leading destination for cross listings, and nowadays many American receipts are actually traded in London, Paris, Frankfurt, and Hong Kong too. Lastly, you need to know the basics to understand the empirical research we review in the next chapter. A good guide is www.adr.com, from whose glossary I did a lot of cutting and pasting.

An *American depository receipt* is a dollar-denominated negotiable certificate that represents ownership of shares in a non-U.S. company. They were first invented by J. P. Morgan, a venerable but successful bank that is now part of a much wider group, JPMorgan Chase. (The Chase leg had already incorporated once proudly independent banks like Manufacturers Hanover ("Manny Hanny") and Chemical Bank.) The structure of an ADR includes a *ratio*, which tells us how many underlying shares are represented by one receipt; a nonunit ratio is primarily chosen to obtain a price in the USD 10–100 price range, the U.S. tradition. (In many other countries one adjusts the *lot size*, the number of shares in a normal order, if the share is too expensive or too cheap; in the United States one splits or regroups the shares.) An ADR can be canceled and exchanged for its underlying shares at anytime. An ADR program is usually sponsored by the issuer of the shares; unsponsored programs are getting rare. Again, the depository acts as transfer agent between the investors and the custodian. In the United States, the primary electronic safekeeping, clearing, and settlement organization is the *Depository Trust Corporation* (DTC). DTC uses electronic book-entry to facilitate settlement and custody rather than physical delivery of certificates. It is owned by U.S. banks and brokers, all of which have accounts in DTC. Its European counterparts are *Clearstream* and *Euroclear*.

The main difference between an ADR and a New York share is flexibility. ADRs come in three versions (called *levels*), which mainly differ in reporting requirements:

- The *Level I ADR* structure "provides issuers with a simple and efficient means of building a core group of U.S. investors with minimal regulatory and reporting requirements," a brochure informs us. The ADRs

---

[11] Both Unilever and Royal Dutch Shell were created by a merger between a Dutch and a British company. For tax reasons the new working company was, however, 50/50 owned by two holding companies, one Dutch and one British, and the listed shares were those of the holding companies. Similar structures exist, for example, for Fortis (Dutch and Belgian) or Dexia (French and Belgian). Nowadays, Shell Trading (United Kingdom) and Royal Dutch (NL) have merged into one share, Royal Dutch Shell.

are traded on the over-the-counter "*pink sheet*" market[12] and on some exchanges outside the United States. Generally, the establishment of a Level I program is considered a first step by issuers into the U.S. public equity market. Non-U.S. issuers of pink sheets need not register under Section 12 of the 1934 Exchange Act.

- *Level II ADR* structures are traded on an exchange (NYSE, Nasdaq, Amex). At the time of listing, the issuer did not register a public offering, unlike in a Level III program. Level II programs require a greater degree of SEC reporting than a Level I. Issuers must reconcile their accounting to U.S. GAAP and meet the listing requirements of a particular U.S. exchange.

- The *Level III ADR* structure is a simultaneous public offering[13] and listing of equity securities on a U.S. exchange. The issuer registers the offering under the 1933 Securities Act (F-1/F-3) and subsequently registers and reports under the 1934 Exchange Act. As under a Level II program, issuers must provide a full reconciliation of their accounting to U.S. GAAP, and meet exchange listing requirements. Unless an exemption is available, the Level III program requirements must be met where a non-U.S. issuer intends to publicly acquire a U.S. company using ADRs as the transaction currency and does not previously have a listed ADR program in existence.

The main difference between a Level III ADR and a New York share is that the ADR can have a ratio other than unity. Both types are typically issued by the same custodians and depositories because they are so similar.

You can easily spot the above differences, plus a few more, from table 17.4.

Besides these, there are also Rule-144 ADRs (RADRs) that are placed privately with *qualified institutional buyers* (QIBs).[14]

---

[12] *Pink Sheets LLC* is the leading provider of pricing and financial information for the OTC securities markets. Its centralized information network includes services designed to benefit market makers, issuers, brokers, and OTC investors. Quotations are entered by dealers acting as market makers in the individual securities. OTC pricing is carried live through OTCquote.com, a subscription service operated by Pink Sheets LLC. An electronic version of the pink sheets is updated once a day, and distributed to Internet financial portals and proprietary data vendors.

[13] An offering refers to shares being sold to the public by the issuing company (*primary offering*) or by major shareholders (*secondary offering*). So in a Level II issue the shares are already publicly traded and now merely cross the ocean, while in a Level III issue at least some of the shares have not yet been publicly traded.

[14] The 144A structure, adopted by the SEC in 1990, allows for private market capital raising by issuers and secondary trading among QIBs. QIBs are primarily institutions that manage at least USD 100 million in securities including banks, savings and loans, insurance companies, investment companies, public employee benefit plans, employee benefit plans under ERISA, or an entity owned entirely by qualified investors. Also included are registered broker-dealers owning and investing, on a discretionary basis, USD 10 million in securities of nonaffiliates. 144A ADRs are traded generally within the United States on the PORTAL system. PORTAL is an acronym for Private Offerings, Resales and Trading through Automated Linkages—a screen-based automated system that provides security descriptions and pricing information specifically for 144A issues. PORTAL was developed by the National Association of Securities Dealers (NASD) to support the distribution of private offerings and to facilitate liquidity in the secondary trading of Rule 144A securities.

Table 17.4. ADR programs by type.

| | Broadening shareholder base using existing shares | |
	Level I	Level II
Description	Unlisted in U.S.	Listed in major U.S. exchanges
Trading location	OTC pink sheet trading	NYSE, Amex, or Nasdaq
SEC registration	Yes	Yes
U.S. reporting required	Exempt	Yes, annual

| | Raising new capital with new share issue in U.S. or elsewhere—not in home basis | | |
	Level III	Rule 144a (RADR)	Global offering
Description	Offered and listed in major U.S. exchanges	Private placement to QIB	Global offer of securities in two or more markets, not in issuer home market
Trading location	NYSE, Amex, or Nasdaq	U.S. private placement using PORTAL	U.S. and non-U.S. exchanges
SEC registration	Yes, also for offering	No	Depends: (a) private placement: no; (b) new issue: yes, also for offer
U.S. reporting required	Yes, annual; also for subsequent offerings	Exempt	Depends: (a) private placement: exempt; (b) new issue: yes, annual; also for subsequent offerings

Source: Adapted from Karolyi (1998) and Citibank, Security Service Department, *An Information Guide to Depository Receipts*, 2005.

From the U.S. perspective, a *global registered share* (also known as a *global share* or *global depository receipt* (GDR)) is the reverse of an ADR: a U.S. share gets converted into a version traded outside the United States. GDRs lose their U.S.-security status; holders cannot invoke U.S. securities laws, and some pension funds may not be allowed to hold them as they are not U.S. listed, and so on. Nowadays the name GDR is also applied to non-U.S. shares that are offered in other places than the United States and the home land. Global registered shares carry a fixed 1:1 ratio, whereas the ADR to local share ratio can be packaged to be priced within its U.S. peer group. A GDR is primarily used to raise dollar-denominated capital either in the United States or in European private markets. The name GDR actually is a generic term describing Rule 144A or Reg S receipt structures deployed to raise capital either in dollars and/or euros.[15] (If the currency is euros, the instrument is often called an EDR, or

---

[15] A *Regulation S offering* is an offering made outside the U.S. to non-U.S. persons. Oftentimes, Reg S offerings are seen as a non-U.S. tranche of a Rule 144A offering. Regulation S sets forth the rules governing offers and sales made outside the United States which are not registered under the U.S. securities laws. Securities acquired under Reg S can only be resold in the United States if they are registered under the Securities Act, or an exemption therefrom is available.

European depository receipt.) For 144A depository receipts, settlement is by DTC, while Reg S depository receipts may be settled by both Euroclear and Clearstream.

All this is not to say that direct listing of a share in a second country is not possible. In Europe, direct listing of the foreign share is quite standard—although GDRs and EDRs are becoming popular too—and in the United States, Canadian shares can likewise be traded directly. London's SEAQ section even used to have an international section, SEAQ-I, where brokers made markets in foreign ordinaries at their (the brokers') own initiative, not at the company's. Thus, the issuer did not do any marketing, paperwork, and so on.[16] But it remains a fact that, in the country that, until recently, was the most important destination of cross listings—the United States—most foreign issuers have to appoint an intermediary and create a special U.S. version of their share. This situation represents another illustration that there is no such thing as a smoothly working global stock market.

17.2 Why Don't Exchanges Simply Merge?

We discuss, consecutively, home bias (the obvious preference, among investors, for local stocks), the corporate-governance and investor-protection regulation, and the resulting separation of lists and the technicalities it generates for cross-listed stocks.

17.2.1 Home Bias

The term home bias refers to the widespread phenomenon that investors have a (strange?) predilection for local stocks. This is easily documented internationally, but even within countries it exists. U.S. investors, for instance, who hold utility stocks of telecom shares, prefer the local electric-power producer or the regional phone company. We somehow prefer stocks that look familiar.

Academics call the phenomenon strange because there are theoretically compelling reasons for complete diversification. You probably know that in the CAPM world all investors hold the same portfolio of all stocks—the economy's market portfolio. The same holds in other models: maximal risk sharing is recommended. As these models assume perfect markets, it is likely that market imperfections explain why people disagree with theory. Yet it is far from clear exactly what makes the world so different from Markowitz's and Sharpe's setting; academics are puzzled (see panel 17.3).

Perhaps "familiarity" is just what the word says: one invests only in stocks one has heard of, and most people know only local companies plus a hundred world players. For this to be a good explanation, the benefits from international diversification must be perceived to be less than overwhelming, or foreign

---

[16] But the active support of the company may be vital: SEAQ-I closed down in 2004.

Recall that investors' portfolios everywhere exhibit pervasive *home bias*, massively over-weighting their home market. One likely reason for home bias is *familiarity*: we all are strangely reluctant to invest in companies we have never heard of. Local companies, or big international firms that have become household names everywhere, are therefore favored over other companies.

This familiarity effect may be stranger than it sounds: while it is true that we do know more about local companies—their products, their size, and perhaps some impression about their profitability and growth—we rarely know enough about them to be able to say whether their market price is fair or not. As long as this last question is not answered, a vague familiarity is not objectively helpful. In addition, as long as foreigners are doing a good job following-up and pricing their own companies, we need not reinvent the wheel and re-do the evaluation: we can free-ride on their work in the same way we free-ride on local analysts' work on our own local stocks. And while domestic companies do have the advantage that they appear in the local media, so that the local investor needs no explicit effort to hear about them, that is not a really good reason for limiting one's investments to local firms: one can indirectly buy into less well-known foreign companies through mutual funds (called "unit trusts" in the United Kingdom), whose managers are, presumably, well-informed about the stocks they pick.

Perhaps, then, familiarity does not primarily stand for information about the firm's fundamentals but about how the managers behave and how much faith we can put into a market price. There is a saying that subscribers to share issues are fools: they give money to people they don't know, they have no idea what these people will do with the money, and on top of that they still hope to be rewarded for their risk. There is surely an agency problem and a problem of trust. True, in countries where most companies have a dominant shareholder or a group of shareholders that jointly control the firm, the latter are likely to know more about what management did because the size of their stake justifies the effort or monitoring; but the new risk is then that they act in cahoots with the management, again at the expense of the small outside shareholders.

Again, this corporate-governance issue is a genuine problem, but not necessarily a good reason for home bias. If half of a company's cash gets stolen by insiders, that fact should be reflected in the stock price. So we again arrive at the conjecture that lack of trust in the price may be the true reason. But if perceived reliability of prices is the issue, most countries should overweight on U.S. stocks: no country has so many analysts and investment bankers per stock as them. Yet in individual portfolios American stocks are hardly less underweighted than, say, French ones.

Panel 17.3. Home bias, investor recognition, familiarity.

investments must be associated with vague, ill-specified risks. Whatever the reason, home bias surely means that there is no strong pressure from investors to get away with all the extra complications that arise when buying foreign stocks. Big companies with familiar names get a cross listing, and everybody seems happy enough.

But there is more. Regulators and legislators also violently disagree on how a putative world market should be organized. These opinions are revealed by looking at how the various mandarins have arranged things at home.

17.2.2 Differences in Corporate Governance and Legal/Regulatory Environment

The term *corporate governance* refers to the way the company has structured its relations with the stakeholders. Good governance systems contain checks and balances such as:

- separation of the jobs of chairman of the board of directors and CEO;
- a sufficient presence of independent directors on the board;
- an audit committee that closely watches the accounts;
- comprehensive information provision toward investors;
- a willingness, among the board members, to fire poorly performing CEOs, perhaps on the basis of preset performance criteria;
- a board that can be fired by the assembly general meeting in one shot (as opposed to staggered boards, where every year only one fifth comes up for (re)election, for example);
- an annual general meeting that can formulate binding instructions for the board and the CEO.

Protection of minority shareholders is not just a matter of corporate governance: it also has to do with the country's institutions. For instance, how well are new share issues scrutinized and vetted by independent experts, like investment bankers? Is the periodic evaluation of the company's financial health by its house bank(s), each time loans are rolled over or extended, a good substitute for outside scrutiny? Are minority shareholders well protected under corporate law, and are the laws enforced? Are there efficient ways to start legal action, for example, by equivalents of the U.S. "*class action*" or "*derivative actions*"?[17] How stringent are the disclosure requirements? Are there active large shareholders, like pension funds, that follow the company's performance and put pressure on management teams they are unhappy with? How many financial analysts are tracking the company and poring over its accounts and reports? Is there an active market for corporate officers, so that good managers get rewarded and vice versa? Is there an active acquisitions market where poorly performing companies get taken over and reorganized?

The investors' predilection for investments in big companies probably reflects, among other things, the corporate governance context. Specifically, large companies are followed-up by many analysts and reporters, so their managers can be expected to behave better, on average; and their market values are probably closer to fair valuations, by the same token. But there are important differences across countries too, with the United States scoring well on many (but by no means on all) of the above corporate governance issues and, say, many former Soviet countries doing quite poorly. So a Russian oil company would still have a smaller and different clientele than a similar-sized U.S. oil company.

---

[17] Class actions are court actions where a group of plaintives act together rather than each file separate claims or complaints. In a derivative action, a shareholder sues the management on behalf of the company (all shareholders together, if you want); any damages awarded accrue to the corporation, not the shareholder. You use a derivative action if you want the management to make up for damage done to the company; the company's normal representative, the management, obviously will not start such an action itself.

In table 17.5 I summarize an oft-quoted table of shareholder rights, creditor rights, rule of law, and ownership concentration, based on La Porta et al. (1998a). The original table contains entries for 49 individual countries; but the data are dated by now—some already were by the time of their publication, in fact—and not uniformly of excellent quality.[18] To hopefully reduce the problems I provide just averages for countries grouped by legal system: English-, French-, German- (i.e., Prussian-) based, or Scandinavian, and for the first three groups I also provide averages for the countries that belong to the generalized Western subgroup:

English. *West*: Australia, Canada, Ireland, Israel, New Zealand, United Kingdom, United States. *Other*: Hong Kong, India, Kenya, Malaysia, Nigeria, Pakistan, Singapore, South Africa, Sri Lanka, Thailand, Zimbabwe.

French. *West*: Belgium, France, Greece, Italy, Netherlands, Portugal, Spain. *Other*: Argentina, Brazil, Chile, Colombia, Ecuador, Egypt, Indonesia, Jordan, Mexico, Peru, the Philippines, Turkey, Uruguay, Venezuela.

German. *West*: Austria, Germany, Switzerland. *Other*: Japan, South Korea, Taiwan.

Scandinavian. Denmark, Finland, Norway, Sweden.

You should take the table with a spadeful of salt: some lawyers raise eyebrows about the classification of the countries, and the selection of criteria may reflect the conventional wisdom in the United States (La Porta et al. are Americans). For example, most of the issues raised toward the end of this chapter, taken from a survey in the *Economist* (a very British publication), are not even mentioned by La Porta et al. As mentioned, there are serious data problems. Also, La Porta et al. (try to) describe the rules, but reality could be very different. Black mentions how the new Russian corporate law code would be rated 12/13 in his own rating system, while U.S. law would probably not even manage a 3/13; yet nobody would think that, in reality, Russia is a legally safe environment.

Keeping all this in mind, here are La Porta et al.'s broad findings (the main conclusions would still be acceptable to most observers):

---

[18] When Spamann (2006), a Harvard law professor, wanted to replicate a similar table by La Porta et al. (1998a) from freshly collected data, he obtained a very different final result:

> I re-code the "Antidirector Rights Index" (ADRI) of shareholder protection rules from La Porta et al. 1998 for 46 countries in 1997 and 2005 with the help of local lawyers. My emphasis is on consistent coding; I do not change the original variable definitions. Consistently coded ADRI values are neither distributed with significant differences between Common and Civil Law countries, nor predictive of stock market outcomes. ... I ... review the other index components and conclude that the ADRI is unlikely to be a valid measure of shareholder protection. Results derived with the ADRI in the literature may have to be revisited.

The problems are not confined to the ADR index: Bernard Black, another law professor, calls LLSV "serial offenders."

Table 17.5. Stylized differences in legal environments.

Shareholders versus directors	Engl	Id, W	Fra	Id, W	Deu	Id, W	Scan	U.S.	U.K.
One share, one vote: each ordinary share has one and only one vote, and all votes can be used	0.17	0.00	0.29	0.00	0.33	0.00	0.00	0.00	0.00
Proxy voting by mail allowed:	0.39	1.00	0.05	0.14	0.00	0.00	0.25	1.00	1.00
Shares not blocked before AGM: no need to deposit shares for a number of days before AGM	1.00	1.00	0.57	0.14	0.17	0.17	1.00	1.00	1.00
Cumulative voting or proportional representation: shareholders can cast all their votes for one candidate director or minority shareholders may name a proportional number of directors	0.28	0.33	0.29	0.14	0.33	0.33	0.00	1.00	0.00
Oppressed minority protection: minority (10% of shares!) can challenge management decisions in court, or force company to buy them out in case of major changes	0.94	1.00	0.29	0.14	0.50	0.50	0.00	1.00	1.00
Preemptive rights: current shareholders have first right to buy new stock unless they vote otherwise	0.44	0.17	0.62	0.74	0.33	0.33	0.75	0.00	1.00
% of equity needed to call an extraordinary AGM	0.09	0.08	0.15	0.11	0.05	0.07	0.10	0.10	0.10
Total anti-director right: sum of the above	4.00	4.33	2.33	2.50	2.33	1.66	3.00	5.00	5.00
Mandatory dividends: percentage of net income that must be distributed to ordinary shareholders	—	—	0.11	0.05	—	—	—	—	—
Creditor protection									
No automatic stay on secured assets: reorganization does not suspend creditors' rights on assets pledged as security	0.72	0.50	0.26	0.14	0.67	1.00	0.25	0.00	1.00
Secured creditors first: secured creditors are paid first, even ahead of workers and government	0.89	1.00	0.65	0.71	1.00	1.00	1.00	1.00	1.00
Restriction for going into reorganization: reorganization is possible only subject to restrictions, like creditor consent	0.72	0.67	0.42	0.29	0.75	0.67	0.75	0.00	1.00
Management does not stay: court or creditors appoint person(s) in charge of reorganization, thus replacing management	0.78	0.67	0.26	0.14	0.33	0.33	0.00	0.00	1.00
Total anti-director right: sum of the above	3.11	2.50	1.58	1.43	2.33	3.00	2.00	1.00	4.00
Legal reserve: minimum percentage of share capital needed to avoid dissolution	0.01	0.00	0.21	0.16	0.41	0.23	0.16	0.00	0.00

Table 17.5. *Continued.*

Shareholders versus directors	Engl	Id, W	Fra	Id, W	Deu	Id, W	Scan	U.S.	U.K.
Rule of law									
Efficiency of legal system: Business International's (BI) assessment of investors' 1980–83 assessment of efficiency and integrity of legal environment as it affects [...] particularly foreign firms. 10 = best	8.15	9.71	6.56	7.14	8.54	9.50	10.00	10.00	10.00
Rule of law: International Country Risk's (ICR's) assessment of law and order tradition, 1983–95; 10 = best	6.46	8.74	6.05	8.57	8.68	9.75	10.00	10.00	8.57
Corruption: ICR's assessment of corruption in government; 10 = best	7.06	9.01	5.84	8.00	8.03	9.16	10.00	8.63	9.10
Risk of expropriation: ICR's assessment of risk of outright confiscation or forced nationalization, 1982–95; 10 = best	7.91	9.46	7.46	9.16	9.54	9.86	9.66	9.98	9.71
Repudiation of contract by government: risk of [...] repudiation postponement, scaling down of contract, 1982–95; 10 = best	7.41	8.87	6.84	8.68	9.47	9.78	9.44	9.00	9.63
Accounting standards, Center for International Accounting and Auditing Trends: checkboxing for presence of 90 items in balance sheets of "representative sample" of industrial (70%) and financial (30%) firms	69.62	72.00	51.17	58.71	62.67	61.33	74.00	71.00	78.00
Ownership concentration									
Ownership, ten largest private firms: average percentage of common shares owned by top-three shareholders in top-ten nonfinancial company with no government investors	0.43	0.29	0.54	0.49	0.34	0.49	0.37	0.20	0.19

Source: Adapted from La Porta et al. (1998a). *Key:* Engl, Fra, Deu, and Scan refer to legal systems; "Id, W" refers to Western countries within that legal group. Country entries in "Shareholders versus directors" are dummies (Yes = 1, No = 0), so 0.17 means that 17% of countries have a yes. "Rule of law" entries are on a scale of 10. The table shows averages per group or subgroup, plus raw data for the United States and the United Kingdom.

- English-based law is more shareholder-friendly, and French- and German-based codes less so; Scandinavia scores in-between.
- English-based law is also more creditor-friendly, French-based code less so; German-based and Scandinavian law scores in-between.
- Scandinavian and German-based codes do best on rule of law, followed by English-type law and, lastly, French-based code.

Do not forget that these are just averages: there are enormous heterogeneities across countries even when classified as "similar." Look at the difference between U.K. and U.S. scores on creditor protection, for instance. Similarly, in the original country-by-country tables, the Netherlands has Scandinavian-style scores on "law," despite its *Code Napoléon* basis. Or imagine the difference between rule of law between Zimbabwe and its former colonizer, the United Kingdom. Anyway, relative to what is available in the former Soviet Union, the differences between French and Scandinavian rules of law are minor variations in luxury.

In a series of related articles, La Porta et al. go on to show that there are correlations with general economic development, capital-market development, and valuation of companies. The strength of these relations should not be overrated. French-based Luxembourg is the richest per capita country of the West and has, all things considered, a big stock market, for instance. Similarly, until one decade ago it was still fashionable to ascribe the amazing post-war growth of Germany and Japan to their bank-based governance systems, where monitoring was deemed so much more hands-on than the market-based, indirect mechanisms of the United States and the United Kingdom, while the United Kingdom was called "the sick man of Europe" in those days, despite its now vaunted legal system; Ireland, now a topper, was even sicker. The heterogeneities within countries are equally amazing—unemployment within Belgium varies between 3 and 20% across provinces, for instance—again illustrating how differences between Western legal systems are but one of the many determinants. There are huge issues of simultaneity and causality in all studies of economic development, and statistical issues, like dependencies and common history or spurious correlations.

Let us return to our main story, though. The point to be remembered is that corporate governance matters, and that the legal and regulatory framework differs a lot across countries. To some extent, a company can improve the governance situation via its own charter and its own disclosure policies. Yukos, one Russian example, in the late 1990s acquired some fame (and a tenfold rise in its market value) for all of a sudden switching from an opaque, murky entity to one with lots of information and maximum transparency—only to be ignominiously taken over, in 2003, by a government puppet. Yet there seems to be little Yukos can—could—do about the institutional environment, in the short run: on its own, Yukos cannot change Russia's laws and institutions. Interestingly, though, a Russian company can "buy" some of the

benefits of, say, the U.S. environment by getting a listing in the United Kingdom or the United States. The company can even decide, to a large extent,
on the dosage of corporate governance it wants: NYSE rules are tougher than
Nasdaq rules which, in turn, beat Amex rules; and disclosure requirements are
very different, depending on under what alias (share, type of ADR, etc.) it is
sold abroad.

*   *   *

We have reviewed formal reasons why exchanges will not be merged into a
global exchange any time soon: home bias (lack of interest from investors)
and disagreement on how markets should be regulated. Thus, a company that
wants to issue shares internationally has to get a second listing (or a third listing, etc.) in the new market it wants to access. Given the hassle and costs, you
may wonder why companies bother; after all, it should be easier and cheaper
to make a *seasoned-equity offer* (SEO) at home, i.e., issue new stock of the same
type as that which is already outstanding. We look at this in the next chapter.
Here we first ask the question of whether a global stock market could not be
achieved via the back door, via a winner-takes-all effect, with all companies
ending up with a listing in the best exchange. This is the issue in section 17.3.

17.3 Can Unification Be Achieved by a Winner Taking All?

The two most important markets for foreign listings are New York and London. True, New York leads clearly in many ways, but London has gained much
ground in 2005 and 2006. And true, Euronext is big too, in numbers of foreign issues listed; but continental banks—even French ones—have nevertheless shifted a lot of equities trading and derivatives to London while British-
based banks never do the obverse; and London is simply gigantic in forex,
OTC, and legal too, which makes it a leading financial center. If there is to be
a main winner in terms of attracting the international equities business, then
the most promising candidates are surely New York and London.

The original basis of the City's strength—the cluster which until the 1970s
was essentially located in the one square mile where the Lord Mayor's writ ran,
within the Elizabethan city walls, but has now very much spread out—was its
role as the financial heart of the world's then-dominant economic and political
power, and a market-oriented power at that. Arguably as of World War I, and
certainly after World War II, that role should have been taken over by New
York, the money center of the new world power. But, as we saw in chapter 16,
the United States bungled its regulation and thus chased a good part of the
dollar banking business to London. New York did remain the undisputed stock-
market capital of the world, though. It liberalized brokerage commissions in
1976;[19] London waited ten years to follow suit. Partly because of this, London

---

[19] In most exchanges, brokers used to have one uniform schedule of brokerage fees, which
depended on the size of the order but otherwise did not allow any competition.

has remained smaller than New York as far as the listing and trading of equities is concerned. Also in private equity[20] and hedge funds,[21] New York—the east coast, really—leads unambiguously. In OTC derivatives, though, which began with products closely related to forex and fixed income, London dominates, as in a few related businesses like legal advice.

17.3.1 Centripetal versus Centrifugal Effects in Networks

Why is the business so concentrated in two or three centers, and should we expect even more concentration in future, with one winner taking all? This prospect might follow from the view that financial sectors are networks, which become increasingly more valuable the more members they have and thus might be like natural monopolies. If you ask bankers why they all want to move part of their business to a big financial center, the answer invariably is the network:

Finding employees. There is a huge pool of experienced professionals of any kind you might need. In (say) Madrid it is not so easy to quickly find twenty seasoned traders at short notice; but in London, for example, there is usually enough frictional unemployment, and if there isn't you simply buy a team from a competitor. Of course, the availability of challenging and rewarding jobs then also attracts gifted individuals from all over the globe, setting off one of the virtuous circles of a network.

Outside help and expertise. For many applications one needs not employees but outside experts, paid by the job. In the centers the financial firms can immediately call on excellent legal, tax, and accounting experts.

Contacts and visibility. To attract business from the network, informal contact during lunch hours and at other times can help a lot, as can copper plates next to the entrances and logos on the office towers. Out of sight out of mind.

Signaling. The mere presence in the metropolis acts as a signal that the company is ambitious, and successful enough to be able to afford the rent and the bonuses.

Cross-pollination. When people meet face to face, interaction is much faster and more intens, and new ideas often emerge: *du choc des idées jaillit la lumière*, as someone once beautifully put it ("the clash of ideas sparks

---

[20] The term covers various equity transactions of unlisted firms. For instance, large companies can go private (delist) with the help of private equity firms; large privately owned companies are being bought and sold; family businesses with a succession problem can go to them; venture capitalist help young firms, often in high-tech business; and new firms get start-up financing from them.

[21] Originally, the term covered short–long funds, that is, funds that hedge their long bets by short bets so as to remain market neutral and concentrate on making money from under- and overpricing. Later, the term was widened to funds that can use leverage, go short, and buy and sell derivatives. Nowadays it covers anything that is not classical stocks and bonds. A "macro" hedge fund, for instance, may speculate on currency movements.

enlightenment"). As the *New York Times* wrote in a March 13, 2007 editorial on Halliburton's move to Dubai, "when engineers and investors meet at a Happy Hour, something happens. Something starts to ferment. News spreads fast from person to person, and not just via MySpace." This holds for people from the same organization, but equally for cross-company contacts.

Outlets for risks. The presence of many players means that risks can be easily shifted by unloading them onto OTC markets (asset-backed securities, credit derivatives, and so on), or sharing them (syndicates) at acceptable costs. Without this, large deals would not be possible.

These virtuous-circle effects mean that business attracts business, and people attract people, and contracts attract contracts.

But all this does not mean that the logical final equilibrium is a winner-takes-all one. Increased concentration has costs too. There are obvious disadvantages in locating at the heart of a metropolis: property costs are outrageous, and transportation is a mess, which puts a limit to the amount of business a single center can attract. Already, London and New York have been exporting some of the work—from the back-office rather than the deal-making—to neighboring regions. Manchester has now become the United Kingdom's second financial center, much to the dismay of Edinburgh, and New York's business is spreading out to neighboring states in the northeast.

17.3.2 Clienteles for Regional and Niche Players?

Let us recapitulate. We saw that the centripetal forces from networking in the end fail to steer all business to one center since concentration adds to costs too, thus creating its own centrifugal counterforce. But this is not the only brake on concentration. You have to realize that the unanimous race to the top—with all stocks ending up in one place—is not the only possible equilibrium if and when the steady state ever arrives. Just as there are many types of cars to cater for people with different incomes and tastes, there is likely to be far more than one optimum *Finanzplatz*. The expensive information requirements of NYSE are bearable for large companies, but smaller players might think the costs prohibitive. That is why New York is not just the NYSE: there is Nasdaq too, for the smaller or less ambitious players. Likewise, a more minority-friendly corporate-governance environment probably sounds swell if you are a minority investor, but does not look quite that way if you are a dominant shareholder who enjoys nice perks and pickings on the side; and, to a large extent, it is these very blockholders that get to decide where the stock is listed. The distance traveled by the customer is a third reason why the world will probably not end with one single financial center: small bread-and-butter deals will naturally be made locally. Small companies also prefer to deal in their own language rather than in English, and in a legal framework that is familiar to them.

A last factor favoring local markets is home bias, a phenomenon have already referred to. Small local companies therefore stand a fair chance at home, and far less so abroad. But even when a mid-cap stock gets cross listed, a substantial part of the trading remains at home, and pricing remains largely a domestic affair. So for these companies also, the home market remains relevant.

All this explains why there is surely some life outside the two leading centers, and why this will remain true for the near future. Recall that right now *Tokyo* is purely local, as far as listed stocks are concerned. Japan's banks used to be very active in the international loan markets in the 1970s and 1980s; and in the 1980s the country's stock market bubble left the rest of the world staring in stunned disbelief. But Tokyo lost most of its glory in the 1990s. The stock market, which at its 1989 peak had stood for one third of the world market cap, crashed horrendously in December 1989 and January 1990. Real estate followed. Worse, the capital losses and the recession that followed made private investors very risk-averse and unwilling to spend. Companies stopped borrowing and investing too. And commercial banks got into deep trouble with nonperforming loans, both real-estate and industrial ones. Tokyo did not officially acknowledge the banks' problems, let alone start a liquidation program of the type the United States had adopted to solve its own 1980s' savings-and-loan debacle (see section 16.2.1). Instead, they decided to let the banks sit it out. In the end, this policy seems to have worked, but it took fifteen years and it did leave Japan's banks in no shape to remain world players, meanwhile. They might try a comeback now, their balance sheets being clean again. Still, right now four fifths of Tokyo's one-time foreign listings have been canceled, and many of the hedge funds active in Japan are based in Hong Kong. A recent report includes recommendations to strengthen trading and settlement systems,[22] establishing markets for professional players, IFRS, English-language disclosure, and more CFAs.

Switzerland is strong in private banking, mostly portfolio management and the like. In addition, its banks are world players in London, New York, and Hong Kong. So are a few German banks. *Frankfurt* has been a fast riser; but the euro has not drawn a lot of forex business away from London. *Hong Kong* seems set to become the London of (at least) China—Shanghai is fighting back, though—and possibly of the entire region. Korean stock brokers, fund managers and investment bankers now operate from Hong Kong in the same way as much of the European continent's equity and derivatives business is handled in London. The gargantuan share offering by ICBC, a Chinese bank, in October 2006 took place in Hong Kong (and, to a lesser extent, Shanghai) not

---

[22] In 2005, one trader inadvertently entered an order to sell one share for JPY 166,000 as 166,000 shares at JPY 1 each. Unforgivably, by standards from anywhere else, the system neither reported an error nor asked any questions. Since it was impossible to find so many shares, the poor trader had to settle in cash, paying 166,000 times JPY 180,000 in lieu of delivering the 166,000 shares.

New York or London; the placement was worth EUR 19b or USD 22b, thus beating NTT DoCoMo's longstanding 1998 record as the largest-ever issuer (USD 14b, placed in Japan and overseas). But, as already mentioned, Hong Kong is now suffering from China's efforts to get IPOs and even listings back home, to Shanghai and Shenzen. *Singapore* is a competitor to Hong Kong, but is not as well placed to conquer the China business. *Dubai*, lastly, is building a center from scratch, hoping to attract the oil money from the Middle East; but the lack of a solid base of domestic issuers is, comparatively, a handicap.

In short, there will always be regional or less exacting markets for small, local firms or for companies dominated by individuals who prefer a bit of shade over glaring daylight showing up every last imperfection. Yet the above does not preclude that, for large, value-oriented companies, there may still be one single place to be because its legal and corporate-governance framework is simply the best. But even that is probably not true either. While all agree that the United States does a very good job, many people add that the place is far from perfect. In the fall of 2006, the *Economist* published a number of articles on the London-versus-NY thing (*Economist*, London as a financial centre, October 19, 2006; Down on the street, November 23, 2006; In search of cheap money, July 20, 2006; The Stomeridge showdown, July 16, 2007). Here's the gist.

17.3.3 Even New York Is Not Perfect

17.3.3.1 The Narrowing Gap between London and Hong Kong

The United States is still well ahead of Europe in hedge-fund and mutual-fund assets, securitization, syndicated loans, and turnover in equities and exchange-traded derivatives. In all but one of these, however, the gap narrowed in 2005. Europe's corporate-debt market overtook America's in 2006 (see figure 17.6(a)), although America still leads in high-yield "junk" bonds—a distinction less dubious than it once was, the *Economist* adds. But according to Luigi Zingales, an economist who sits on the Committee on Capital Markets Regulation (CCMR), the best guide to the competitiveness of America's markets is the behavior of overseas firms that choose to list their shares at home and abroad. In this market for IPOs, America's value share has collapsed rather badly since the late 1990s (see figure 17.6(b)). Seven years ago, New York placed five times as much newly listed equity as London and Hong Kong taken together; in 2006 it was beaten by both. The 1999 peak does reflect the frenetic IPO activity on Nasdaq, but even if we look at the flagship exchanges only (NYSE and LSE, thus omitting Nasdaq and AIM), the conclusion remains valid. True, of the growing number of firms which are no longer cross listing in America, more than 90% still choose to market their shares to investors in the United States; but it is as "144A" private placements, which gives them access to the American market without the full registration and compliance costs.

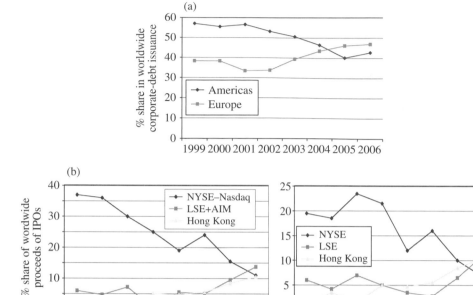

Figure 17.6.   Wall Street versus Threadneedle Street, 2006 (January–October only). *Source:* Data taken from the *Economist*, November 26, 2006.

It turned out that 2006 was a low point: New York did better in 2007, and Hong Kong suffered from China's gentle pressure on local companies to list in Shanghai or Shenzen instead of in Hong Kong. But the episode scared many, and the market share is still much down compared with eight years ago. The uneasiness led to much soul-searching and demands for reform. Some of the explanations for New York's loss of market share have to do with events happening outside the country, but other reasons are of the United States' own making. We review these in turn. Our main source is various reports written for the city or state of New York, as summarized in the *Economist*.

17.3.3.2   Exogenous Factors

Competitors clean up their act. Wall Street's rivals are now fighting harder for business. London is being seen as the preferred habitat for firms from emerging markets: big Russian companies, for instance, prefer to list there, echoing the old Soviet Union's predilection for European banks (chapter 16). Euronext likewise agrees that Chinese or Indian companies prefer London over New York (and adds that they want a share of that business (*De Standaard*, December 27, 2006)). Some Russian and Arab lenders, flush with oil dollars, also dislike the United States for political reasons (Israel, the alleged war on Islam, etc.) and now go for London. Hong Kong has benefited from the emergence of China. There is also fierce competition to lead regional financial markets, especially with an ambitious bid from Dubai to conquer the Middle East and its oil money.

One of the attractions of competitors is that they offer more than just equities business. True, New York is big in banking, both the commercial and investment varieties. But London dominates absolutely in banking, international bonds, and even corporate bonds *tout court.* It has a thriving derivatives exchange—owned by Euronext, it must be added—and so on. Also, Euronext and LSE went electronic much earlier than NYSE. In fact, Euronext's technological lead and product range were major reasons why NYSE was interested in a merger. A year before, it had already taken over a U.S. fledgling market that did electronic trading and derivatives.

Finance has become more footloose. U.S. firms have always been more inclined to go public than European or emerging-market ones, and until recently would regard a local listing as virtually the sole relevant option. But technological innovation has now made it easier for supply and demand of capital to go where the best deals are available. So more and more firms now consider London, for example, worthy of consideration.

Immigration controls. Problems also arose from tougher immigration controls imposed after 9/11. With work visas harder to obtain, it can be too much hassle for managers of a global firm to gather in the United States at short notice. Meeting in London is much easier. America's universities have similarly suffered in attracting foreign PhD students, thus reducing the supply of top graduates to Wall Street.

Beside these external issues, the *Economist*'s summary also enumerates important internal factors behind America's falling competitiveness. Notably, as Messrs Bloomberg and Schumer write, New York's "almost exquisite balance between regulation and entrepreneurial vigor" of old has recently been upset.

17.3.3.3 Legal and Regulatory Issues in the United States

SOX Section 404. This is the most visible and controversial part of Sarbanes–Oxley.[23] It requires an annual "internal control report," which must be certified by auditors and personally signed off by two executives. SOX-404 has forced management to review their procedures and accounting choices more carefully, but has raised costs considerably: auditors now spend far more time per customer.

---

[23] The Public Company Accounting Reform and Investor Protection Act of 2002 (commonly called SOX or Sarbox, after sponsors Senator Paul Sarbanes and Representative Michael Oxley) is a controversial United States federal law passed in response to a number of major corporate and accounting scandals (like Enron, Tyco, Peregrine, and WorldCom) that had damaged public trust in accounting and reporting practices (Wikipedia). The act, approved by Congress "by Soviet-style majorities," establishes new or enhanced standards for all U.S. public company boards, management, and public accounting firms.

It is true that firms have been learning fast, if one judges by the number of post-Enron court cases. The number of filings of class-action suits went down from about 180 in 2005 to about 120 in 2006, according to Cornerstone Research. Auditing costs have fallen, too, since the early years, accountants hasten to add. But, according to the *Economist*, these costs can still top several million dollars a year for a firm with a market capitalization of USD 1 billion. The rise in auditing costs has been harder to bear for smaller auditees, because many of the costs of compliance are fixed. Perhaps this explains why, in 2004–7, fifty young American firms headed for London's AIM and hundreds of others are said to be considering it.[24]

A related adverse evolution has been the decline in analyst coverage of smaller stocks since banks were forced by New York State's prosecutor, Mr. Spitzer, to tighten up their research procedures and be more objective.[25]

True, Sarbanes–Oxley is not necessarily just adding to costs. A priori, a higher standard of corporate governance should result in a higher valuation: listing in a well-regulated market shows a commitment from a company not to rip off the smaller investors. (We look at this argument, and similar ones, in the next chapter.) Any such value gain reduces the costs of compliance and may even leave the shareholders with a net gain. One study, reviewed in the next chapter, was conducted after Sarbanes–Oxley and estimates that the value to a firm of an emerging-market listing in New York is about 37% higher than its domestic value would have been. Preliminary research suggests the value of a London listing is not as high. But, again, these gains are weightier for big firms. Mr. Zingales's rough calculations suggest that the New York premium does not compensate for the extra costs for companies with a market value of less than USD 230m.

There has been rising pressure to review SOX, for instance, by keeping the goals largely the same but giving firms and their auditors more choice in how to achieve them. By the end of 2007, the Securities and Exchange Commission (SEC), America's chief market regulator, and the Public Company Accounting Oversight Board, which was created by Sarbanes–Oxley, had both announced reviews of Section 404, hinting strongly that the burden will be eased, especially for smaller firms.

Accounting rules. Some critics have long advocated a major review of accounting standards. The United States was surely ahead of other countries in terms of dropping historic-cost valuation of assets and adopting fair-value

---

[24] London's Alternative Investment Market caters for firms with smaller values and a shorter record than those traded on the main market. Most markets have such a "second (or third) board" nowadays, e.g., Alternext.

[25] After the 2000 crash, Mr. Spitzer went for the big New York banks, accusing them of biased investment advice during the dot-com craze. The banks got away with a modest out-of-court settlement, but the publicity was very bad.

principles, but IFRS has now done likewise.[26] While America continues to believe that its accounting rules are still better than internationally accepted standards, others point out that, on many issues, U.S. GAAP really is a collection of formal possible solutions in a shelf-filling manual; there is always one precedent that suits you, they object—box-ticking, in short, not true and fair representation. And every rule has so many exceptions with, in turn, second-layer exceptions and so on. Here's the opinion of Arthur Levitt Jr, a former chair of the U.S. SEC.

> **Example 17.1.** Intense interest-group lobbying has delayed action and severely compromised [various issues]. When the FASB falls prey to these compromises, the resulting standards can end up overly complex and confusing.
>
> FAS 133, for instance, deals with the accounting for derivatives. When it was first proposed, the standard was significantly simpler and easier to understand and—we expect—to apply. Yet, as many interests asked for exceptions to the rule, it metastasized into an 800-page treatise of rules and interpretations that continues to grow with each passing month.
>
> The cause of this complexity is rooted in the structure of the FASB.... Various constituencies in practice have board seats set aside for them.... Those who fill them, in turn, at times have lobbied for the groups that put them there. Exceptions are then thrown in to create a compromise that pleases every constituent group. The result is a regulatory sausage that is hard for companies and investors to swallow.
>
> *Wall Street Journal Europe*, March 9, 2007, p. 11.

But quite apart from the question of whether U.S. GAAP is clearly better, the fact was that the rest of the world was going for IFRS. Foreign firms would be keener to list their shares in New York if they did not have to reconcile their accounts. In 2007, the SEC did give firms the choice between IFRS and U.S. GAAP, but only in its true, original IAS version. In many countries, local lobbies have succeeded in adding exceptions and modifications to IFRS, meaning that there are now too many "dialects" around, so to speak.

> **Example 17.2.** In an interview, Mr. De Proft, CEO of Icos Vision Systems, a 1982 start-up, talks about (among other things) the delisting from Nasdaq. He brings up three of the above points: Europe's exchanges improving; accounting rules; and S-Ox:
>
> **Q:** Why? Wasn't [the Nasdaq listing] a nice business card?
>
> **A:** Yes, but there's no need to get sentimental about it. We went to the Nasdaq in 1997, when there was no Euronext and even no euro. In 1998 Easdaq followed, later relaunched as Nasdaq Europe, but it was a failure. In 2003 we then went

---

[26] IFRS is the International Accounting Standards Association's recommended set of principles. In Europe they became mandatory for listed companies in 2005, amid much wailing and gnashing of teeth. The most common objection among managers was that income smoothing would become impossible, in principle. Academics pointed out a major advantage: income smoothing would become impossible, in principle. Even China is going IFRS by 2008, despite a shortage of established accountants and markets for assets; other Asian countries are making up their minds.

to Euronext and saw that all our volume followed us there, which meant our Nasdaq listing became pointless.

Also, it was a complicated business card. At some point we had to comply with seven or eight accounting codes that occasionally contradicted each other. [Getting] a single listing was an enormous simplification. Add to that S-Ox 404. There have been virtually no public offers in the U.S. because S-Ox imposes an improbably heavy burden upon companies regarding their internal controls. As a result, the audit costs are doubled or tripled.

De Standaard, March 3, 2007, p. 23.

Since then, however, the SEC has largely come around: as of 2009, IFRS will become the norm for all U.S.-listed firms.

Litigation and tort law. Critics regard America's legal system, with its punitive jail terms and class-action "lotteries," even less favorably ("a jungle," a senior regulator said) than they view Sarbanes–Oxley, the *Economist* reports. Asian firms, for instance, are still hesitant about a New York listing after China Life, an insurer, fell victim to a shareholder lawsuit within days of going public. Most firms involved in mergers in America have to factor possible legal troubles into the costs of the deal, the *Economist* cites. "Many firms that choose to list their shares elsewhere point to America's 'litigation lottery' as the principal reason" (*Economist*, June 16, 2007, p. 76).

A radical recommendation—unlikely to make it in the foreseeable future—would be to limit prosecutions to individuals rather than companies. Under such a rule, Arthur Andersen would still be alive. Two equally bold suggestions are that damages should be agreed through arbitration or by professional judges rather than awarded by juries, and that contingency fees should go.[27] Early in 2007, the U.S. Supreme Court stopped juries from including damages done to third parties in the punitive damages, but this fell far short of limiting punitive damages themselves.[28]

In a splendid example of the triumph of legal fiction over economic reality, in the United States lawsuits can be brought because of falling share prices. This makes a mockery of the principle of *caveat emptor* (and also of the honorable New York tradition of never giving a sucker an even break, the *Economist* reminds us). Worse, while lawyers argue that the "legal person," the company, should be liable for its misdeeds, the economic reality is that the plaintiff is compensated by his fellow shareholders, who mostly suffered the same losses and are almost surely not responsible for that loss.

---

[27] Contingency fees are fees that are due to lawyers only if they win the case: then, depending on the contract, 10–40% of the spoils go to the law firm, while nothing is due if the case is lost. The system is widely seen as an incentive to sue even if odds are slim. Outside the United States, lawyers' fees tend to be independent of the outcome; and often the judge decides whether the guilty party, if any, has to pay the legal costs of the counterparty, or at least part of them.

[28] Punitive damages are compensations awarded over and above the damages actually suffered by the victim. The argument in favor of such extra damages is that if a firm has only a 5% chance of being caught and found guilty, then the fine should be twenty times the actual damage before the system becomes fair.

Shareholder rights. America's shareholders lack certain basic rights. For instance, they have only a limited say in electing company boards, unlike investors in Britain, and they have to contend with staggered boards (where only a fraction of the directors stands for re-election in a given year, making it impossible for a majority of shareholders to sack the board in one go). The assembly cannot even make binding recommendations to the CEO. Poison-pill takeover defenses are omnipresent. Boards, not shareholders, decide on executive pay (again, unlike in Britain).[29] Also, in two thirds of the listed companies the positions of CEO and Chairman of the Board are often held by a single person; in most countries this is frowned upon, and in the United Kingdom only one in ten boards accept it.

Regulation. Three main areas of concern are discussed in the *Economist*'s review: how financial supervisors interact with the private sector; how they arrive at their decisions; and the fragmented nature of the rules. The Securities and Exchange Commission (SEC) plays a key role, here. It used to be too slow, some complain, but nowadays it has become hyperactive—the "Spitzerization" of the agency.[30]

Of course, being active is what the SEC is for. It has unparalleled numbers of retail investors to protect and it does not want to be outflanked by aggressive state prosecutors. But the SEC should also think of the need for markets to be efficient as well as clean. Relative to Britain's Financial Services Authority (see the next subsection), far more of the SEC's energy goes into enforcing current regulation rather than searching for better rules. Harvey Pitt, a former SEC chairman, complains about the increasing dominance of enforcement lawyers. By one estimate, over 700 of them now earn more than their chairmen. Critics clamor for more economists and more evaluation, including better cost–benefit analysis of old and new regulations. This, some say, is what Britain's super-regulator, the Financial Services Authority, is much better at. The FSA employs far more economists relative to lawyers than does the SEC. It also prefers principles over hard rules, and nudging over bullying.

Lastly, the U.S. regulatory regime is much more fragmented than in Europe. Next to the SEC there is the Commission for Commodity Futures Trading (which incongruously also oversees financial futures), the Office of the Comptroller of the Currency, and then fifty-one state overseers for banking and insurance. Such fragmentation leads to conflicting regulation and turf wars. As boundaries between cash and derivatives markets are fading, a merger of

---

[29] The NYSE now requires that only independent board members have a say in the management's compensation. But this does not apply to unlisted firms or Nasdaq-listed companies. Increasingly often, shareholders raise a hue and cry about pay, and occasionally get away with it, but it remains an uphill struggle.

[30] Until the end of 2006, Spitzer was New York's State Attorney, that is, the chief prosecutor. Prosecutors in the United States are elected (and see the job as a step up to higher positions: Mr. Spitzer, for instance, became New York's governor in 2007, but had to step down under a cloud in 2008), so it would be only human if they occasionally feel tempted to seek high-profile campaigns to win votes.

Table 17.6. Market share of financial-services markets, latest as at end 2007.

% share	U.K.	U.S.	JP	FR	DE	SI	HK	Other
Cross-border bank lending (Mar 2007)	20	9	7	9	10	2	2	41
Foreign equities turnover (Jan–Sep 2007)	53	36	—	—	4	—	—	7
Foreign exchange turnover (Apr 2007)	34	17	6	3	3	6	4	27
OTC derivatives turnover (Apr 2007)	43	24	4	7	4	3	1	14
International bonds:								
secondary market (2006)	70	—	—	—	—	—	—	—
Fund management (end 2006)	8	52	7	6	3	—	1	23
Hedge funds assets (2006)	21	66	2	1	—	1	2	7
Private equity: investment value (2006)	14	60	2	4	1	1	—	18
IPOs (Jan–Sep 2007)	15	26	—	—	—	1	8	50
Securitization: issuance (2006)	6	79	2	—	1	—	—	12

Source: FIBV (number of foreign listed stocks); International Financial Services London, *International Financial Markets in the U.K.*, November 2007 (for other data).

the SEC and the Commodity Futures Trading Commission, for instance, would simplify life for all players.

17.3.4 London's Comeback

London had been the world's financial center in the nineteenth and early twentieth centuries, but lost its lead after two crippling world wars. Its reemergence as a banking center and bond market, in the 1960s–80s, has been described in chapter 16. By the early 1980s, London hosted far more foreign banks than any other financial center and had the biggest slice of the foreign-exchange market. There were so many U.S. banks that Moorgate, a street in the City, was nicknamed "the Avenue of the Americas"; and London's dollar business dwarfed its sterling dealings. The Square Mile hosts 255 banks. London even has offices of more Japanese banks than Tokyo.

Yet the stock market took no part in this. The reemergence of London as an equities center took another ten years. Behind this renaissance were the "Big Bang" reform of the exchange, London's openness to foreign players, and its light-touch regulation. You should notice these three aspects in the historical sketch that follows.

17.3.4.1 The Golden Eighties and Nineties

While London's growth in fixed-interest instruments was a slow and gradual affair, the equities business reemergence is commonly traced to one single day, October 27, 1986 (also known as *Big Bang* day), when very new rules for equities trading came into effect.

The London stock exchange used to be a closed shop, with "single capacity": brokers brought the business and *jobbers* made markets in shares. Brokers were paid a fixed minimum commission on shares and government bonds (*gilts*, short for gilt-edged securities), which ripped off big clients, and jobbers lacked the capital to deal in big amounts. Jobbing and broking were also separated from investment banking. The exchange had no incentive to change much. Being a cooperative or a mutual that was owned by the brokers, it was run in the interests of the brokers, not the customers or the economy. (This was the case all over the world. Most exchanges have now *demutualized* and become ordinary companies, listed on their own boards.)

By the 1980s, trading in top British shares was starting to move to New York, where investment banks were able to offer keener prices: they could combine broking and market making as well as underwriting new issues, and New York's fixed-commission cartel had been abolished since the mid 1970s. Thatcher's government did not like any of this one bit. Her Majesty's Office of Fair Trading in fact started a court case against the exchange, claiming the brokers acted as a cartel. In July 1983 the LSE signed a historic deal: the OFT dropped the case in return for a promise that the exchange would get rid of minimum commissions by the end of 1986. At the same time, the government would withdraw the regulations that had led to the old division of labor.

Clamoring that "the one-stop shop" was the way forward, domestic and international banks took stakes in virtually every broker and jobber. American commercial banks, at that time still banned from the U.S. securities business by the Glass Steagall Act, were eager to learn the trade in London and bought brokers, jobbers, and investment bankers. Nobody in the government seriously thought about stopping the foreigners, in sharp contrast to what is still the mindset of too many EU15 continental governments.[31]

The invasion by the Americans changed London forever. Gone were the nine-to-five, pinstripe-suited, and bowler-hatted bankers. Americans brought not just cash and contacts, but also meritocracy, long working hours, and exhilarating bonuses. Traders in financial futures at LIFFE, a market founded in 1982, even wore colored jackets. Minds boggled all over Albion.

Not everything went smoothly for the local players. The 1990s were especially bad. Britain's main initial frontrunners as investment banks—S. G. Warburg and Barclays de Zoete Webb—fell by the wayside, the first being bought by the Swiss, the second being wound down by its parent, Barclays Bank. Then Nick Leeson's rogue trading brought down Barings, a centuries-old merchant bank once called the sixth great power of Europe. Most of the financial firms are now foreign-owned—or, perhaps, again foreign-owned: already in the

---

[31] Italy tried to stop takeovers of some of its banks as late as 2006; only a slap on the wrist from the EU Commission and the ECB stopped them. No French bank has been beleaguered recently, but in view of France's reaction to takeover plans or rumors concerning Novartis, Suez (or even its Belgian subsidiary Electrabel), or Danone, there is little uncertainty over how France's ruling class thinks. Germany is hardly more open; see my comment, in the next chapter, on Mannesmann in discussing takeovers as a monitoring mechanism. Belgium is now quite liberal, like the Netherlands; but in the 1990s its king still granted an earlship to the CEO of Generale, then a major bank, for resisting a takeover by ABN Amro. Central European countries, in contrast, tend to be more sensible.

1800s, key investment bankers were originally German (like Warburg, Baring (no "s" in those days), Rothschild, Kleinwort, Schroders, or, in a related business, Reuters). Even the LSE—since 2001 a listed company itself—was under siege from Nasdaq. Tellingly, the government's only worry about the possible takeover of the LSE was that it could lead to a back-door introduction of American-style regulation—a threat that was quickly blocked through a change in the law.

"Light-touch" regulation has proved to be a third key factor behind London's success, the *Economist* thinks. In 1997 the new Labour government replaced the labyrinthine maze of statutory and self-regulatory bodies by one regulator, the Financial Services Authority (FSA). In 2004 the Authority set up separate divisions, and separate regulation, for wholesale and institutional markets. The FSA is now highlighting the need for regulation based on principles rather than detailed rules.

17.3.4.2 The Last Decade

After the slowdown of the mid 1990s, London has been swinging again. (This *epitheton ornans* used to refer to London's rock and pop music, pop art, and fashion scene. How the mighty have fallen.) Although Euronext took over LIFFE in 2002, in 2005, 98% of the value of the Paris-based exchange's trading in derivatives was done in London. The City simultaneously secured a vital commanding stake in over-the-counter (OTC) derivatives, where turnover is many times higher than that of exchange-traded derivatives. London's share of this booming market has risen from 27% of daily turnover in 1995 to 43% in 2004.

Some of the biggest customers for derivatives are hedge funds. The global value of assets in hedge funds has doubled since the end of 2002 to reach USD 1.2 trillion by the end of 2006. Here London has become the regional leader. Although the industry is still dominated by the east coast of America, investments managed out of London are worth a fifth of the world total, up from a tenth in 2002, and almost four fifths of those in Europe. And there has been a spectacular growth in legal services, which are vital in backing the work of a global financial center. Over 200 foreign law firms have offices in London, which is also headquarters for three of the four largest firms in the world. Exports from Britain generated by international law firms were three times higher, by 2005, than ten years before.

17.4 CFO's Summary

All over the world, bonds are often traded over the counter rather than in formally organized exchanges. In international bond markets this is even more the case: there are some emerging electronic trading platforms or networks, but their purpose is just that: to facilitate trading, not add regulation. The customers are mostly professionals, and the issues are often deemed to be private, implying simple, unregulated issues. Relative to this, the stock markets could not be more different.

Everywhere, public launching and trading of stocks is relatively more regulated because information asymmetries are much more severe and the scope for abuse correspondingly higher. In addition, there are vast differences in the degree of investor protection offered in various countries' legislation, with, broadly speaking, more developed countries or common-law countries scoring better in minority protection (and, usually, creditor protection); German- or Scandinavian-type legislation scoring in-between, and *Code Napoléon*-based systems doing somewhat worse. There is an inverse relation between minority protection and shareholding concentration: in countries with poor protection, controlling blockholders or coalitions are more prevalent, although the direction of causality is unclear.

Investor protection is not just a matter of corporate governance and company law, but also of securities and exchange regulation. In the United States, which in recent decades has been the most important market for cross listings, virtually all issuers use an intermediary who buys the original shares and issues U.S.-registered securities against them, which are sold and traded; even a private issue must be organized via an ADR-1 or RADR.

The bottom line of all this is that there is no global market for shares, not even for large companies. If you want to tap international investors, you have to choose a specific country, and possibly an exchange and a type of security. The costs are often higher than for a domestic issue. You may wonder, in light of this, why firms bother. The reason is that, basically, a security issued in, say, New York is different from one issued in, say, Moscow—precisely because the whole legal framework differs. As a result, some issuers can obtain better prices abroad, while others may prefer a local issue, despite the lower price, because they prefer the local legal and regulatory situation. We look at this in the next chapter.

TEST YOUR UNDERSTANDING

Quiz Questions

True–False Questions

1. In quote-driven markets, the exchange system provides the price for a stock by crossing demand and supply; while in order-driven markets, a market maker provides bid and ask prices.

2. Quote-driven markets are always preferred over order-driven markets because they stand out in immediacy and liquidity.

3. An ADR mostly comes with a nonunit ration, mainly because the stock price in the United States is preferred to be in the USD 10–100 range.

4. There will never be one unified financial center because investors are home-biased, they only want to invest in stocks that are familiar to them.

5. Sarbanes–Oxley is the main reason why New York is losing market share to London and Euronext in terms of IPO proceeds.

Multiple-Choice Questions

1. A market maker:

   (a) only works on quote-driven markets;
   (b) has a complete overview of the demand and the supply of a stock;
   (c) can always guarantee liquidity and immediacy;
   (d) provides bid and ask prices for a certain stock.

2. Indicate the correct statement(s):

   (a) English-based law is more shareholder-friendly.
   (b) The United Kingdom and the United States have similar standards for creditor protection.
   (c) Companies can compensate for weak regulatory institutions in their country.
   (d) The main advantages of a unified financial center result from network effects.
   (e) A Level I ADR requires more reporting than a Level III ADR.
   (f) A global registered share is a U.S. share that gets converted to a version traded outside the United States.

18

Why—or When—Should
We Cross List Our Shares?

In the last chapter's introduction your CEO argued that, given the company's recent foreign acquisitions, it should start thinking in an international manner and raise some cash from the global equity market. By now you have disabused him: there is no such thing as a global equity market. Perhaps around a thousand giant companies are held worldwide, but even these have to choose which exchange(s) they want to be listed on; and exchanges can differ vastly in terms of organization and corporate-governance context.

Given that there is a set of distinct markets instead of one global stock exchange, the first question your CFO would have to decide is whether the new shares should be launched at home or abroad. Things are not as simple here as they are for bonds and loans, where you could (in most cases) simply compare costs: here, an international listing can bring serious indirect benefits too. In fact, the choice of where to get listed is not so much a matter of the direct expenses (the costs of preparing, obtaining, and maintaining a listing; and the costs of trading the shares—spreads, commissions, price impact) but what tilts the balance in favor of an international issue is usually that you get a higher price for your stocks. One reason why you get a higher price may be that there is a lower international "cost of capital" (discount rate as applied by the market in setting the stock price), because some of the risks that are undiversifiable to your home-biased domestic shareholders become diversifiable to foreign investors. A second mechanism behind a higher price may be that the corporate-governance implications of your choice inspire more confidence in your investors—an influence that may work via both the expected cash flows and the discount rate. But there is more to an international issue than just the IPO price. A sample of additional issues that should interest any CEO worth his or her salt may include the following. What is the effect of being exposed to moods and fads from a new class of investors: is the beta relative to the home market affected? Is an estimate of our stock's beta versus the foreign market, as obtained from pre-IPO data, any good in predicting the post-IPO foreign beta? Is volatility typically up, afterward? Do bid–ask spreads go down, or are they up? Doesn't a foreign listing harm liquidity, if turnover gets spread over two exchanges instead of one?

We first list the possible reasons why corporations might like a foreign issue. We then treat the issue within a classical CAPM context, showing that investors should like foreign stocks better than local ones and that this may mean a big drop in discount rates. Section 18.3 reviews the empirical evidence from event studies and from value comparisons. Section 18.4 concludes.

18.1   Why Might Companies Want to List Shares Abroad?

First some terminology. A *cross listing* is a second listing, in a country other than that of the first listing. The term *foreign listing* often means the same as cross listing, but sometimes it means that the listing abroad is actually the company's first listing; you simply don't address the home exchange. Israeli firms, especially tech stocks, are fond of U.S. listings: about as many are listed only there as in Tel Aviv.

Both foreign and cross listings can be accompanied by a *primary offering* (new stocks are being issued); otherwise it is fully a *secondary offering*: the current shareholders sell part or all of their holdings. Often, the offer is part primary and part secondary. Don't mix this up with a primary/secondary listing. The *primary listing* is where the shares are primarily registered and where the receipts or global shares or certificates or even dually listed shares refer to. The place of primary listing need not be the economic center of the firm nor the most liquid market. In 1994, in light of the 1997 handover of Hong Kong to China, Jardine Matheson, a leading HK group, moved its primary listing from Hong Kong to London. Still, its headquarters had been in Bermuda since 1984, and it has a secondary listing in Singapore, where most of the liquidity is. The firm also delisted from Hong Kong, saying they wanted to remain under British law; China felt miffed. Hong Kong and Shanghai Bank, in contrast, maintained its Hong Kong listing but moved both its headquarters and its primary listing to London; it later obtained additional listings on NYSE and Euronext.

Don't mix up the primary and secondary offerings with first and second boards. The *first board*, often the traditional core market of the exchange, has relatively strict listing and information requirements. Often, a *second board* was added with more flexible rules, aiming at smaller and younger companies (New Market, *Neuer Markt*, *Nouveau Marché*), where less financial history, market cap, and traded volume are required to get listed and remain listed. Sometimes the second board is complemented by an "*alternative*" market (in established markets like Euronext or London (Alternative Investment Market (AIM)), but also in newer markets like the Baltic countries (OMX's "First North") and Thailand), where youngsters with absolutely no track record still get a chance.

In the subsections that follow, we discuss the potential pros and cons of cross and foreign listings. As foreign listings (in the strict sense of the term) are rarer than cross listings, we will not keep repeating them separately; most of what follows also holds for them.

18.1.1 Possible Gains from Foreign or Cross Listings

Below, we survey the potential pros of a cross listing. We mention all the aspects that make logical sense a priori, without adding whether they are empirically important or even statistically detectable. This exposition paves the way for Section 18.3, where we review the empirical literature, evaluate the validity of some of these claims, and expand on the corporate-governance aspects.

Broadening the shareholder base.

- In small local markets it can be difficult to raise large amounts fast. The U.S. and U.K. markets are comparatively well-organized and deep; investors are arguably less risk averse and have an equity culture.

- The issuer may also value increased dispersion that may come with a foreign listing. It reduces shareholder power and the threat of hostile takeovers or even expropriation.

- A cross listing helps overcome capital-market barriers:

  — Regulation may require that institutional investors only buy stocks that are listed in a local exchange. So a listing abroad would also enable institutional investors in that country to buy your stock.

  — It is usually also legally impossible to launch a large-scale selling drive for assets that are not approved by the overseer and listed or at least registered (e.g., for OTC trading). Without the investor recognition that comes with a listing or a registration, most investors will not even notice you.

- Investors dislike buying foreign stocks via a foreign exchange since that involves a forex transaction; they pay higher costs abroad, whereas spreads and settlement costs in the United States and the United Kingdom are quite good; and information is often less complete or more difficult to obtain.

Getting a better issue price.

- If your domestic market is a small local exchange, home-biased investors are likely to view your company as being exposed to similar factors as the stocks they already hold, implying that beta is high. To foreigners who already hold many assets, possibly including a fair dose of international stocks, these risks are to a larger extent diversifiable, which means a low beta to them. As a result, they are willing to pay a higher price.

Note that, for this to be an issue, there must be some unidentified invest-ment barriers; the foreign issue overcomes these by bringing shares to foreign investors who otherwise would not have bought them.

- If the corporate-governance environment in the foreign market is better than that in your company's home market, there would be value gains because investors would trust you more.

- In small local markets there may not be enough analysts and investment bankers who understand the business you are in. During the dot-com craze this was a popular reason for going to the Nasdaq rather than a local exchange.

Price discovery: more efficient pricing in the aftermarket.

- In active and well-developed capital markets, volumes are higher, which brings liquidity. Liquidity is valued per se by all investors; but it is also useful for informed traders, who prefer thick and deep markets in which to hide their trades and reduce price pressure.

- The activity of informed traders is reinforced by the activity of analysts. In emerging markets, stock prices are much more sensitive to the market factor[1] because not enough people follow up company-specific news. In the United States, the modal number of analysts per stock is 4; foreign-listed stocks even achieve 5.7 on average.

Visibility in the goods and factor markets.

- A listing not only brings investor recognition, but possibly also visibil-ity among consumers and potential employees. Especially in small coun-tries, the news that you go to the Nasdaq or (whisper it!) NYSE can change your public image drastically.

Diversification benefits for the home investors.

- The equity price gets exposed to no new sources of risk, and exposure to domestic sources of risk is lowered. Before cross listing, the market factor that most affects the share price is the local one; the sensitivity (beta) to the foreign market return is mostly indirect, via the local market. After a seizable foreign issue, sensitivity to the foreign market hardly changes and sensitivity to the original home market goes down—a bit of a puzzle, actually.

The bottom line, then, is that (largely nondiversified) local risk is traded in for (largely diversifiable) foreign risk, which is good. That, at least, is how an academic would see this. Less cold-hearted individuals might view the increased exposure to foreign factors as an extra risk. All of which has seamlessly brought us to the flip side, the costs of a cross listing.

---

[1] Not in terms of beta—this always equals unity, on average—but in terms of R^2.

18.1.2 Costs of a Cross Listing

- The costs of issuing are often higher, especially if the prospectus has to be more complete and the due-diligence audit more thorough. Costs of advertising and roadshows and so on tend to be higher too. A recent study even found small and medium Chinese firms willing to pay up-front costs that amount to 25% of the issue, on average, for a Hong Kong listing, and 16% for a listing in next-door Shenzhen's Second Board. (For large issues in major exchanges, 5% or less is a more normal figure.)

- Multiple listings create extra costs since each exchange tends to have its own information requirements and accounting rules. Several versions of the periodic accounts may be required (IFRS should reduce this problem) and translated, and more interim reports may be required. In Europe, for instance, twice-yearly reports are the rule, but in the United States quarterly statements are required by the major exchanges. Lastly, there are listing fees. For instance, the cost of maintaining a listing, including translation expenses, by a foreign company on the Tokyo Stock Exchange runs from USD 100,000 to USD 500,000 p.a.

- An indirect cost has to do with the cost of trading the shares in the aftermarket. This includes the broker's fees, the exchange's tax, the price impact—in order-driven markets, you might have to descend deep into the book to have a big order executed—and, for quote-driven markets, (half) the bid–ask spread for a given order size. The cost of trading is hard to calculate, as it changes over time and across stocks and depends on the order size. Arguably, an issuer should only care about the impact of these costs on the issue's proceeds, but this impact is even harder to quantify. So, at best, you can keep in mind any trading-cost information you have, to possibly tilt the balance between otherwise comparable alternatives; otherwise this information is hard to use.

The cost and hassle of U.S. information requirements have long been cited as a deterrent for a U.S. listing. Sarbanes–Oxley, Congress's reaction to the Enron et al. disasters, is now widely seen as too onerous, especially the requirement that top management sign, in its own blood, that the financial statements contain no misrepresentations. Audit costs have certainly soared.

In what follows, we flesh out two of the economically most interesting theories, the views that higher market values come from a lower discount rate (via diversification) as opposed to a superior corporate-governance framework. We start with the diversification argument, worked out in a standard CAPM context. The assumption is that you have a dim grasp of the efficient-set picture and the efficiency condition. If you feel the need, read about this at the beginning of chapter 19.

18.2   Shareholders' Likely Reaction to Diversification Opportunities

We proceed in two steps. First, theory says that investors should hold portfolios that are internationally well-diversified; under standard CAPM assumptions the prediction is actually that they all hold a world market portfolio of stocks. Second, it follows that when a country opens up, or at least one stock joins the world capital market, the expected return should drop—and drastically so, in many cases.

18.2.1   Why Would Investors Diversify Internationally?

We work with standard portfolio theory: investors hold portfolios that offer maximal expected returns for whatever level of variance risk they choose. In a plot that shows standard deviation on the x-axis and expected return on the y-axis, the feasible set of portfolio risks and returns is bound on the left by the minimum-risk bound or "minvar" bound, the upper half of which is the *efficient set*. (The lower half exhibits minimal not maximal return for the chosen level of risk, so it is not efficient.) In principle, international investment is useful when the mean–variance opportunity set constructed from international assets is wider than the feasible set constructed just from domestic assets. This must be the case in general unless, implausibly, the new assets offer returns that are all exact linear functions of already-available domestic assets.

To illustrate the existence of benefits and provide an impression of their size, we proceed as follows. The database, constructed by Lieven De Moor from DataStream files, consists of monthly stock returns from 1980 to 1999 for 39 countries[2] and 34 sectors.[3] The database is free from multiple listings as De Moor kept only the main listing of each company. This main listing is almost always the listing on the home exchange, i.e., the exchange of the company's nationality. Each stock is allocated to its appropriate country and sector index according to its DataStream nationality code and its DataStream sector index.

In constructing minvar sets we start from the U.S. market as the home market; if there are benefits when starting from this particular home base, then this must be a fortiori the case for home countries with much narrower asset

---

[2] The 39 countries are Argentina, Australia, Austria, Belgium, Brazil, Canada, Chile, China, Colombia, Denmark, Finland, France, Germany, Greece, Hong Kong, India, Indonesia, Ireland, Italy, Japan, Luxembourg, Malaysia, Mexico, the Netherlands, New Zealand, Norway, Peru, the Philippines, Portugal, Singapore, South Korea, South Africa, Spain, Sweden, Switzerland, Taiwan, Thailand, the United Kingdom, and the United States.

[3] The 34 sectors are aerospace and defense, automation and parts, banks, beverages, chemicals, construction materials, diversified sector, electricity, electro and electric, engineering and machinery, food and drug retailing, food producers, forestry and paper, household goods and textile, healthcare, IT hardware, insurance, leisure and hotels, life assurance, media and entertainment, mining, oil and gas, personal care and house, pharmaceuticals and biotech, real estate, retailer (general), software and services, specialty and financial, steel and other metals, support services, telecom services, tobacco, transport, and other utilities.

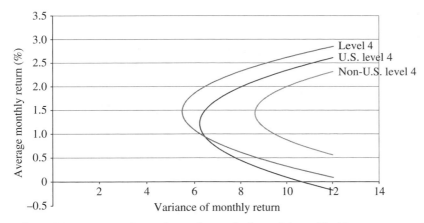

Figure 18.1. Minimum–variance bounds made from 34 worldwide sector portfolios, 34 U.S. sector portfolios, and 34 non-U.S. sector portfolios. *Key:* The vertical axis shows expected return (estimated from samples), the horizontal one shows variance. The curves show the estimated lower bounds on risk reduction for various levels of expected return. The outer minimum–variance bound is made from 34 worldwide sector portfolios, the middle one from 34 U.S. sector portfolios, and the inner one from 34 non-U.S. sector portfolios. Graph kindly provided by Lieven De Moor.

menus. Rather than working with all individual assets we work with the 34 sector portfolios. We estimate the means and covariances of the portfolio returns using 20 years of monthly data, 1981–2000, provided by DataStream. Working with 34 pre-packaged portfolios rather than, say, 7,000 individual assets means that we forgo some scope for diversification. But few individual shares survive 20 years; a 7,000 by 7,000 matrix inversion is not practical; estimation errors are less of a problem for portfolios; and for non-U.S. assets we use a similar pre-packaging so that the diversification handicap probably applies equally to both sets. The information from the 34 means and the 34×34 covariances allows us to compute the U.S. minimum–variance boundary as a simple quadratic function of the desired expected return. We then form 34 portfolios of both U.S. and non-U.S. assets and compute the new set. The result is shown as figure 18.1.

The figure shows the U.S. minvar set as the middle curve. The smaller one inside it is the set computed from 34 non-U.S. industry portfolios, and the best one, more to the left and higher up, is the fully international one. Thus, the maximum Sharpe ratio attainable from the U.S. sector indices is better than the maximum Sharpe ratio attainable from non-U.S. sector indices, so diversification across U.S. sector indices is a more effective tool to reduce risk than diversification across non-U.S. sector indices, even though the latter contain investments from so many countries. (I was surprised, frankly.) But the efficient set of risky assets is further improved when the menu is extended by using both U.S. and non-U.S. assets.

You could object that these are just estimates obtained from sample data; in the population, the situation may be different. But that is a red herring: to have no improvement whatsoever, the returns from non-U.S. assets would have to be exact linear functions of U.S. returns; and if in the population all the non-U.S. asset returns were exact functions of U.S. assets, then this would happen in any given sample too. So we are sure that the expanded menu generally widens the opportunities. I can even statistically prove, if challenged, that the two sets are not tangent to each other and have the same tangency portfolio. The conclusion is that international diversification pays in the sense of offering better risk–return combinations than what is feasible using just domestic assets—even with a domestic feasible set as extended as the U.S. one. The next step is that this should translate into a lower cost of capital.

18.2.2   Why Would Companies Prefer Global Investors? A Partial Equilibrium Exploration

18.2.2.1   The Karolyi–Stulz Litmus Test on the Risk Premium

If people do invest internationally, the multicountry tangency portfolio that they all hold is less risky than the old national tangency portfolio. If the risk is lower, the investors should be happy with lower expected returns too. But a falling world-market risk premium does not necessarily mean that all risk premia are falling, or even that the average premium from each country is falling. Might not some countries see a higher cost of capital?

A simple test is provided by Karolyi and Stulz (2002). It starts from the CAPM in its most basic form. This says that if people hold efficient portfolios, then the portfolio weights must be such that the covariances of asset returns with the overall portfolio return are proportional to the expected excess returns.[4] The factor of proportionality is called the investor's *relative risk aversion*; and if the efficient portfolio we consider is the market portfolio, the factor of proportionality is the market's relative risk aversion, which depends on individual risk aversions and invested wealth. Below, we denote this number by η (eta). (The relation is derived in chapter 19; you can take a quick look if you do not quite trust me.) The proportionality between risk premia and covariance risks also holds for linear combinations of assets, even including the efficient portfolio itself. Below, we apply the rule to the average stock of country k.

The average stock from country k is, almost by definition, represented by its local market index M_k, with the market being defined by the nationality of the issuing firm. The risk premium on M_k equals relative risk aversion times the covariance with the market return which, in turn, equals $\tilde{r}_{M_k}$ prior to integration and $\tilde{r}_w$ afterward (where the subscript "w" stands for the world market

---

[4] The excess return is the return in excess of the risk-free rate; the expected excess return is also called the risk premium.

portfolio). Thus

$$\text{Post:} \quad E(\tilde{r}_{M_k} - r_0)_{\text{post}} = \eta \, \text{cov}(\tilde{r}_{M_k}, \tilde{r}_w),$$

$$\text{Pre:} \quad E(\tilde{r}_{M_k} - r_0)_{\text{pre}} = \eta \, \text{var}(\tilde{r}_{M_k}),$$

$$\implies \quad \frac{E(\tilde{r}_{M_k} - r_0)_{\text{post}}}{E(\tilde{r}_{M_k} - r_0)_{\text{pre}}} < 1 \text{ if and only if } \frac{\text{cov}(\tilde{r}_{M_k}, \tilde{r}_w)}{\text{var}(\tilde{r}_{M_k})} < 1 \text{ and vice versa.}$$

$$(18.1)$$

This means that, for equal r_0 and η (and constant moments), the risk premium drops if we have a below-unity value for the (local) beta of the world market portfolio—the regression coefficient in

$$\tilde{r}_w = \alpha_w + \beta_w \tilde{r}_{M_k} + \tilde{\epsilon}_w. \tag{18.2}$$

Indeed, a simple regression coefficient is, generally, equal to $\text{cov}(y, x)/\text{var}(x)$; and, here, the y variable is the world market return while the x variable is the local market return.

In the standard beta regression that we use to estimate nondiversifiable risk, individual returns are regressed on the market return: x is the average of the ys. Here, in marked contrast, y is the average of the xs. Statistically gifted readers have already spotted that, because of this, the average beta here is below unity. Here's the proof for the more laid-back customers:

$$\frac{\text{cov}(\tilde{r}_{M_k}, \tilde{r}_w)}{\text{var}(\tilde{r}_{M_k})} = \frac{\text{cov}(\tilde{r}_{M_k}, \tilde{r}_w)}{\text{std}(\tilde{r}_{M_k})^2}$$

$$= \frac{\text{cov}(\tilde{r}_{M_k}, \tilde{r}_w)}{\text{std}(\tilde{r}_{M_k}) \, \text{std}(\tilde{r}_w)} \frac{\text{std}(\tilde{r}_w)}{\text{std}(\tilde{r}_{M_k})}$$

$$= \rho_{k,w} \frac{\text{std}(\tilde{r}_w)}{\text{std}(\tilde{r}_{M_k})}, \tag{18.3}$$

where $\text{std}(\cdot)$ denotes standard deviation and ρ the correlation coefficient. Correlations between country returns and world market returns are substantially below unity. In addition, the standard deviation of the world market is substantially below that of the country return. Thus, each of the two factors on the right-hand side is below unity. It follows that Stulz's betas are below unity, implying that expected excess returns of risk premia on country indices fall upon integration.

We can say more. Emerging markets have lower correlation coefficients with the world total than mature countries, and higher volatilities. Thus, for emerging markets each of the two factors on the right is even lower than for the typical country. It follows that emerging countries especially should benefit, in terms of falling risk premia.

Let us look at some empirical results. In table 18.1 we show for a number of countries the OLS-estimated betas, along with robust t-stats versus $H_0: \beta_w = 1$, and the estimated change in the country's average cost of capital assuming a 5% risk premium (a conservative number). All estimated betas are below

Table 18.1. Stulz test coefficients, t-tests, and risk premia avoided by integration.

	β_w	std(β_w)	t-stats versus $H_0 : \beta = 1$	p.a. diff. in $E(\tilde{r}_{M_k})$
Argentina	0.150	0.033	−25.38	4.25
Austria	0.480	0.087	−6.00	2.60
Belgium	0.554	0.068	−6.55	2.23
Brazil	0.142	0.026	−32.56	4.29
Canada	0.427	0.047	−12.14	2.87
Chile	0.357	0.047	−13.60	3.21
Colombia	0.129	0.051	−17.03	4.35
Denmark	0.610	0.067	−5.80	1.95
Finland	0.274	0.031	−23.64	3.63
France	0.654	0.049	−7.10	1.73
Germany	0.519	0.041	−11.78	2.41
Greece	0.180	0.038	−21.49	4.10
Hong Kong	0.310	0.036	−19.15	3.45
Indonesia	0.098	0.023	−39.88	4.51
Israel	0.306	0.040	−17.46	3.47
Italy	0.362	0.049	−13.14	3.19
Japan	0.452	0.049	−11.21	2.74
Korea	0.165	0.023	−36.54	4.18
Malaysia	0.115	0.032	−27.83	4.43
Mexico	0.289	0.036	−19.92	3.55
Netherlands	0.641	0.045	−8.04	1.79
Norway	0.533	0.049	−9.60	2.34
Philippines	0.172	0.033	−25.45	4.14
Poland	0.164	0.028	−29.77	4.18
Portugal	0.380	0.054	−11.38	3.10
Singapore	0.276	0.032	−22.48	3.62
South Africa	0.214	0.037	−21.14	3.93
Spain	0.537	0.044	−10.60	2.31
Sweden	0.488	0.037	−13.72	2.56
Switzerland	0.606	0.067	−5.87	1.97
Thailand	0.178	0.026	−31.19	4.11
Turkey	0.108	0.019	−47.16	4.46
U.K.	0.807	0.086	−2.25	0.96
U.S.	0.640	0.046	−7.78	1.80
Venezuela	0.088	0.025	−36.71	4.56
Average	0.354			3.23

Source: Table kindly provided by Rosanne Vanpée.

unity, suggesting that integration lowers the risk premium. The differences $\beta - 1$ are significant, too: the standard errors probably understate the true error margins, but with t-ratios as high as ours and with priors as strong as ours there can be little doubt that the typical beta is less than unity. If the risk premium is about 5% p.a., then the typical savings in risk premia would amount to more than 3% per year, ranging from 1% (e.g., the United Kingdom) to 4.5 (e.g., Venezuela).

The above results are almost surely too optimistic: they assume that expected returns are in fact proportional to covariance risk—which is debated—and, worse, that investors take the model so seriously that they actually hold the world market portfolio—which is patently untrue. Lastly, we assume that relative risk aversion is constant and identical across countries. In short, theoretically we are not on as strong ground as it might look to the untrained eye. On the other hand, the intuitive argument sounds very convincing: many risks that were undiversifiable to home-biased domestic shareholders should become diversifiable to international investors. The positive economist's reaction to such a conjecture is to go and test the prediction. There is indeed an impressive number of published articles on this hypothesis and, in fact, on many of the other predictions in our earlier list of possible advantages of getting a cross listing. We consider this literature in the next section.

18.3 Sifting through the Empirics on Cross-Listing Effects

Not surprisingly, research published in finance journals has focused on items on which we have accessible data: prices at the announcement, Tobin's Q ratios, liquidity, and spreads. In what follows, we will closely follow the excellent review article by Karolyi (2006), itself a major update of a 1998 forerunner. The facts mentioned here are all quantified and referenced there.

18.3.1 The Conventional Wisdom from 1980 to 2000

In many (but not all) studies, spreads fall upon the cross listing and total trading volume is up, often drastically. Volatility is not affected, or is hardly affected. This evidence is consistent with the hypothesis of improved liquidity. Regarding the domestic and foreign betas, there is an asymmetry depending on whether the cross listing was obtained in the United States (by a non-U.S. firm), or vice versa:

Non-U.S. firm listed in the U.S.:
Domestic beta falls, but sensitivity to U.S. market is not noticeably higher. The fall is strongest for Asian issuers, weaker for continental European ones, and weakest for the U.K. companies. Using the domestic beta as input into the CAPM, the cost of capital would fall by about 1.25% on average—ranging between 0.33% (Europe) and 2% (Asia).

U.S. firm listed elsewhere:
No change in either beta—or perhaps a slight rise in domestic beta.

Thus, there is risk-reduction to non-U.S. shareholders.

The picture regarding the price impact of a cross listing, upon announcement, is similarly asymmetric:

Non-U.S. firm listed in U.S.:
The announcement of a cross listing leads to an increase in share prices of about 1% on average, with up to 2% jumps for certain subsamples.

U.S. firm listed elsewhere:
The price change is barely noticeable, or is even absent.

In most studies mentioned in Karolyi's 1998 review, the price change is happily attributed to a falling cost of capital, itself the result of the cross listing overcoming investment barriers. The findings of constant betas and no price reaction for U.S. firms are surely consistent with each other, and suggest that the U.S. market is sufficiently complete in itself and has so much weight in the world total that a U.S. stock's risk does not look substantially diversifiable to non-U.S. investors. (Our own earlier evidence from the minvar sets would mildly disagree.) The fact that home bias among U.S. investors is stronger than in the United Kingdom or Europe fits in with this idea too. So all seems well. Only Stulz (1999) is not so sure, and his criticism has led to a debate and reinterpretation.

18.3.2 Puzzles with the Received Wisdom

Stulz lists five puzzling issues with the price-reaction results; I add a sixth:

1. The observed price reactions, upon announcing a cross listing, seem small against the estimated drop in the cost of capital. With an initial cost of capital of, say, 12%, Karolyi's average cost-of-capital fall by 1.25% should give a rise in the stock price of 12% or so.[5] Even for Europe, where Karolyi comes up with an estimated drop in the cost of capital by 0.33, prices should have jumped by roughly 3%; and a drop in the discount rate by 2% (Asia) should have sent up the price by about one fifth. In short, at 1–2%, the actually observed price reaction is quite subdued.[6]

---

[5] I calculated this assuming perpetuities. This is debatable, but the purpose is to check whether predicted and observed price changes are even roughly in the same ballpark.

[6] True, there also is a price run-up of 10% in the two years before the event, but most of that is undone by a slow post-event decline of, on average, 9%. Also, it is by no means clear that all of the run-up, or any of it, is in anticipation of a cross listing. The cross-listing decision may be a reaction to the run-up, as managers feel the price is overvalued and want to grasp the opportunity (market timing).

Karolyi reports a subsequent decline in post-cross-listing prices, which would surely be consistent with the opportunism story. It would also be consistent with a substantial drop in expected returns, though. But a recent working paper by Carpentier et al. (2008) finds that this reported post-IPO underperformance seems to be due to shoddy statistics: the phenomenon disappears when a value-weighted market index is used as the standard rather than an equally weighted one, or when the Fama–French CAPM is used instead of the basic one. (The FF CAPM looks at the book-to-market-value and size factors beside the market risk, and can resolve many anomalies that seem to arise from the basic model.)

Thus, the bottom line remains that there is a 10% pre-cross-listing price run-up followed by a small announcement effect.

2. If non-U.S. firms can increase their market value by overcoming investment barriers, how come only 10% of non-U.S. firms get a U.S. listing?

3. If the gain comes from overcoming investment barriers, how come Canadian firms gain as much as others, even though their market is the best
   integrated with the U.S. market?

4. With increasing integration through better information and disappearing
   capital restrictions, the number of foreign listings should have fallen over
   time. In reality it has not.

5. The rise is larger for exchange-traded instruments (2.6% instead of 1%!)
   and smaller for secondary offerings. Yet these distinctions have no
   obvious link with market segmentation.

6. How come U.S. stocks do not gain from a foreign listing, even though
   an international portfolio dominates a pure U.S. one and the stock's
   covariance versus the world should be below that versus the home
   market?

Stulz's explanation, later joined by Karolyi, is that corporate-governance issues
are at work too, and are perhaps more important than cost-of-capital effects.
Karolyi (2006) reviews old and new evidence and sums up the literature in five
themes.

18.3.3 Five Lessons from the Recent Literature

1. Corporate governance, agency conflicts, and "legal bonding."

> One important reason why firms may choose to cross list their shares on over-
> seas markets is that it represents an opportunity to improve a firm's corporate
> governance system. Cross listing is a vehicle through which a firm's manage-
> ment and/or its large, controlling shareholders can "bond" themselves to a
> legal system with more effective protection for minority shareholders against
> managerial self-dealing or excess consumption of private benefits of control.

Karolyi's verdict is based on the following evidence:

- Private and OTC placements, where there is less of a formal engagement
  about information and scrutiny, experience a smaller price jump, upon
  announcement, than do Levels II–III ADRs and shares.

- Companies from countries with poorer legal protection are more likely
  to list in the United States, and especially on the major exchanges. In
  addition, they are highly likely to come back with follow-up equity issues
  in their original home market, consistent with the bonding view rather
  than the overcoming-investment-barriers one.

- Tobin's Q premium[7] of cross-listed firms relative to similar firms from across the world is higher (i) when investor protection in the home country is poor, (ii) when the growth prospects are high and shareholder protection is poor (an interaction), and (iii) when the issue is exchange listed (37% extra value!) rather than a private or OTC-traded one.

- The value of control, as inferred from the voting premium in dual-class shares[8] is 43% lower for 137 firms cross listed in the United States than for 745 comparable domestic firms. This suggests lower private benefits extracted by the main shareholders. Likewise, for 37 dual-share firms that started their cross listing somewhere in the sample period, the value of the votes fell. Also, firms with dominant shareholders are less likely to seek a cross listing, *ceteris paribus*.

- Mexican firms without ADRs pre-react about 30 days before earnings announcements, suggesting widespread insider dealing. The problem is much reduced for firms that have a cross listing in the United States.

Still, the legal bonding view of why firms seek cross listings is not a perfect explanation. There is lots of evidence that does not fit:

- "Doubts about the 'bonding' hypothesis abound, especially in regards to the effectiveness of enforcement actions by regulatory authorities against such firms in these new markets," writes Karolyi. For instance, the SEC rarely goes for foreign companies; at best, there is an out-of-court settlement.

- The extra Tobin's Q premium for (Canadian) cross-listees is noticeable only for firms that list large fractions of their equity in the United States— but why would legal bonding be tied to the fraction of equity listed in the United States?

- Also, the voting premium inferred from dual-class stocks may depend on many other things than private benefits.

- Next, when a foreign firm with a listed ADR takes over a U.S. company, the probability that it uses equity as the means of payment, as opposed to cash, still depends on the home country's legal protection. Under the bonding view, the U.S. legal environment should be the sole determinant.

- Lastly, there is an extra Tobin's Q premium for cross-listees even if the U.S. issue is just a Rule 144a private placement, without any noteworthy legal bonding.

---

[7] Tobin proposed to measure "rents" by the ratio of the firm's market value over the replacement value of its assets. In empirical work, replacement value is often taken to be book value.

[8] A dual-class share structure means that there are two classes of equity, one of which has more voting rights relative to income rights than the other.

So legal bonding is not the sole answer and may not even be the primary answer. The last finding suggests that the premium may stem from, for example, voluntary information provision rather than legal bonding. This fits in with work by La Porta et al. (2006), who "find little evidence that public enforcement benefits stock markets, but strong evidence that laws mandating disclosure and facilitating private enforcement through liability rules benefit stock markets." Which brings us to the next theme from the recent literature.

2. Changes in the information environment through cross listing.

> When firms raise funds from public markets, they must not only provide extensive disclosure at the time of issuance, but also commit to furnish information on an ongoing basis. The more information they provide and the stronger the commitment to provide it continuously, the less costly it is for investors to monitor management and, hence, the more favorable the terms and conditions of financing. Cross listing on an exchange with extensive disclosure requirements is one credible way for companies from around the world to commit to extensive and continuous disclosure.

The information argument does not mean that all firms end up on the NYSE. The tougher boards are so costly in terms of information provision that only the larger and more international firms seek such a form of listing, an earlier study reported. Since then, various signaling models have been developed, showing what types of firms would go for what level of disclosure. There is also a literature on how exchanges would profile themselves, some racing for the top (low trading costs, high information standards), others choosing intermediate levels. Here is some evidence that supports the information theory:

- U.S. firms that cross list abroad experience no announcement effect, as opposed to non-U.S. firms that place a U.S. issue. The tentative reason is that information provision improves for the former group, not for the latter.

- Firms that cross list on the NYSE get more analysts and media coverage than firms that go for the (less expensive) LSE, suggesting that one of the objectives of the NYSE listing is better communication.

- The pre-cross-listing run-up and post-cross-listing decline is much stronger for firms that get a listing on the NYSE instead of the LSE. This suggests a stronger "visibility effect" in New York.

- Relative to comparable domestic firms, cross-listed companies have more analysts following them; the analysts provide more accurate earnings forecasts; market values are higher; and price reactions to earnings announcements are more pronounced. These effects get stronger the weaker the minority-protection rules are at home or the larger the holdings of dominant shareholders. For unknown reasons, these effects are also stronger for Rule 144a or OTC issues compared with exchange-listed issues.

Note that these effects may come from self-selection: companies that get a listing may be different from those that do not, and causality may come from that rather than from the mere fact of getting a listing. Econometrically, this is a tough issue.

- From reports on their stock holdings one can infer that U.S. institutional investors are keener on firms that report according to U.S. GAAP; and switching to U.S. GAAP attracts more such investors.

- European companies that cross list in the United States rather than on another European exchange are typically high-tech, high-growth ones, where information asymmetries are rife and the value of analysts' coverage is correspondingly high. Within Europe, though, firms tend to go to countries with similar cultures (German, Latin, Anglo) or to G5 countries or countries that are geographically close by. So intra-European cross listings may be chosen in light of minimal information-transmission costs.

3. Multi-market trading and liquidity, price discovery, and arbitrage.

> Cross listing shares of a company's stock allows for market-makers from more than one market to compete for order flow in those shares, which can enrich and, at the same time, complicate the price discovery process. The home market appears to continue to play a dominant role in price discovery, but evidence suggests that the foreign markets—often, the U.S. exchanges—are playing an increasingly important role. There is considerable cross-sectional variation across firms that researchers associate with the trading environment itself: the higher the fraction of global trading that takes place in the new market, the greater its contribution to price discovery.

One example is that non-U.S. stocks with dual listings react more strongly to earnings announcements than other companies, suggesting more active analysis and more news-related trading. Also the lower R^2 relative to the home market fits in: when news about companies is absent or goes unheeded, stocks merely follow the market; more analysis weakens the impact of general news. In the U.S. for instance, the market-model R^2 has dropped substantially relative to the pre-World War I situation, as the market got more sophisticated.

> However, there is still an open question as to the causality of the relationship and whether it is just a transitory effect around the listing or more permanent. Firm-specific factors related to the information environment of the firm, such as its size, ownership structure, and analyst coverage, as well as country-level factors, such as market-wide and exchange-rate volatility, investment restrictions, gross and net transaction costs, impact multi-market trading, liquidity, and the joint dynamics of stock dynamics in the competing markets.

4. The monitoring role of capital markets.

Increased access to capital in new markets is an important motivation for firms in pursuing international cross listings. Success, however, may be predicated on the roles played by various agents that facilitate access to the capital markets. One such important role is in monitoring the firms on behalf of public investors to help mitigate against potential agency conflicts and agency problems. Research has focused on the certification role of investment bankers who stake their reputations on marketing the securities of these newly listed firms to their investor clients. ... Large institutional investors, which can also serve an effective monitoring role, are significantly more likely to invest in non-U.S. equities that cross-list as ADRs. Finally, a more active takeover market—which can act as an external monitoring device for managers of poorly performing firms—develops for non-U.S. firms that cross list their shares in the United States.

Investment banks certify information about the company at the time cross listing starts, and stake their reputation on the reliability of this information. The higher the bank's reputation, the more credible the certificate because being caught lying would destroy a lot of value.

- Domestic SEO announcements tend to trigger price drops; but multi-market global equity offerings (GEOs) experience smaller price drops despite their higher costs to the company; the before-cost effect could even have been a price rise. The beneficial effect is ascribed to the involvement of more investment bankers.

- Domestic equity offerings tend to have a poor long-run post-issue performance, possibly reflecting market timing by managers. This also occurs for GEOs, but far less so when the issuer is from an emerging country or the issue is listed (Levels II and III)—cases where the certification is more important relative to the brief visibility/investor-recognition effect.

New, large, active shareholders. Large subscribers not only provide capital but, being large, might also act as monitors, an activity not worth the effort for small individual investors. Since, unlike the traditional dominant domestic shareholders, these large new institutional shareholders act at arm's length, their activity may be beneficial. There are no studies that directly look at actual monitoring, but a few papers do show that ADRs are better at attracting U.S. institutions as investors than non-cross-listed ("ordinary") foreign shares:

- Big U.S. investors' holdings of foreign firms with ADRs are roughly in proportion to their (float-adjusted) weight in world market cap; other ("ordinary") foreign shares are not held or held to a far lesser extent. For example, of U.S. cross-listees, 17% of the equity is on average held by Americans, against 3% for non-cross-listed foreign shares.

- Especially for countries with poor shareholder protection, low liquidity, high transaction costs, or low analyst coverage, mutual funds almost exclusively go for ADRs instead of ordinaries. (Incidentally, the ADR effect does not wipe out the negative effect from having a large domestic shareholder, which confirms that legal bonding via a U.S. cross listing is an imperfect solution.)

A critical comment on this is that it is about potential monitoring only. The above evidence might equally be invoked by traditionalists, in whose view foreign listings help overcome investment barriers.

The market for corporate control. The threat of a takeover can be a powerful deterrent against misappropriation of corporate cash flows when all internal mechanisms fail. In many countries, hostile takeovers are simply *not done.* For example, the 1999–2000 takeover of Germany's Mannesmann, a mobile operator, by Britain's Vodafone was then a totally unheard-of event, and has unexpectedly remained unheard-of since now. In 2005 Germany's vice-Chancellor Franz Müntefering famously described hostile bidders as "locusts." Type "Muntefering Locust" into your browser window to get a feeling for the shockwaves he created.

There are no studies, in Karolyi's 2006 review, that look at takeovers of foreign firms with versus without ADRs; but there are a number of papers that show that ADRees are better able to take over U.S. firms than are pure foreign firms, presumably because ADR-issuing new owners inspire more trust.

- The odds of being able to take over a U.S. firm improve the more control is relinquished by the original domestic controlling shareholder, notably when the first U.S. placement is all secondary, when a second U.S. placement has already followed, when the drop in the fraction of the erstwhile dominant shareholder's voting and income rights is more pronounced, and when the company initiates other corporate-governance improvements.

- Relative to acquisitions of U.S. firms by pure foreign companies, takeovers by ADRees need lower acquisitions premia when payment is in cash—even though these foreign firms still pay more than U.S. acquirers—and are more likely to be paid for with equity rather than with cash.

Whether listees benefit themselves from additional takeover "risk" remains untested.

5. Real effects of a cross listing.

If globalization expands a firm's opportunity set by widening the capital base it can access or by facilitating improvements in governance systems to lower its capital costs, the firm should realize gains not only in the capital market environment (greater liquidity, more analyst coverage, broader shareholder ownership, higher valuations), but also in its investment and operating performance. There could also be real consequences—both positive and negative—for the other firms competing with those pursuing cross listings and for the overall economy in which these firms are domiciled. Only preliminary evidence exists to date. The investment and operating performance of those firms cross listing on overseas markets do improve in a way that is consistent with favorable capital-market reactions to these events, but whether these improvements are transient or permanent is not known. There is mixed evidence on the consequences of these cross listings for competitor firms, but most of these studies focus only on the stock returns and trading volume of firms in the same home market or industry. Aggregate cross-listing activity does spur on cross-border portfolio investment activity, but there is some evidence of an adverse impact on overall trading activity, especially in emerging markets.

Under the "real effects" heading, Karolyi groups two themes. First, the fact that a firm gets a cross listing could have spillover effects at home on the firms that do not go overseas. Second, the company's own investments and operations may be affected.

Spillover effects at home. A priori, the effect on stay-at-homes could be positive: international investors start noticing the country and consider buying into similar firms, or local investors think that the home-alones will soon follow their more daring colleagues. Or the effect could be negative: domestic investors become painfully aware that the stay-at-homes do not much care about corporate governance or are unambitious losers. Interestingly, the first hypothesis is related to the view that cross-listing gains come from investment barriers being overcome, the second one is possibly about legal bonding or information provision.

- It turns out that, especially for less mature markets, the stocks that go international drain attention away from the stocks of firms that remain just locally listed. The first group becomes bigger relative to GDP in terms of market cap, capital inflows, and trading activity, but the home-alones lose out on all these counts.

- Many studies have also looked at the effect from a cross-listing announcement on the stock-market prices of one subgroup of stay-at-homes: competitor firms. A study that looks at the first ADR issue per issuer's country finds positive spillovers for competitors: stock prices are up, local betas down, foreign betas up, and volatilities down. This is what one would expect under the lower-barriers view. Two other studies consider all ADR issues, and find that competitor prices on average fall in line with the legal bonding view. Perhaps the result from the first study comes from a stronger lowered-barrier effect when the ADR issue is a country's first; or maybe such a restricted sample is just more prone to noise. The studies that find negative spillovers for competitors are surely consistent with those finding negative effects for stay-at-homes in general.

Effects on the issuer's numbers. Papers on the effect on the issuer's own behavior are surprisingly thin on the ground. One study finds that, after the foreign issue, quarterly corporate investments become less dependent on quarterly internal cash generation—but it is not clear whether this effect is stronger than for domestic share issues. The effect is noticeable only for emerging countries and markets with poor investor protection. Another study finds that performance is up (net income, operating income, capital investments, all scaled by total assets), but the link with the foreign issue is unclear: already a year before the cross listing, stock prices rise.

18.4   CFO's Summary

The main conclusion from this fascinating literature is that selling shares at home versus abroad is very different from, for example, selling cars at home versus abroad. By the mere fact of getting a listing abroad, the "product," a share, is often being changed, and the issuing company along with it.

Things are most momentous if a stock from a sleepy, old-fashioned exchange is being cross listed on the NYSE. The whole information policy of the issuer needs to change, new accounts need to be prepared for the future and the past, analysts are all over you, regulators watch your every step and frown on suspicious price movements, like big jumps prior to announcements, investors sue you because you did (not) announce item X or event Y, reporters pore over your statements looking for a juicy scandal. Tellingly, when L&H, a now-dead Flemish dot-com company, started reporting sales that later were found to be fictitious, it was *Wall Street Journal* reporters who wondered how South Korean companies could possibly be buying so many speech-to-text-to-speech licenses, not the local paparazzi; without their Nasdaq listing, L&H would not even have been noticed by the *Wall Street Journal*.

The rewards can be great. For high-tech companies, the U.S. market remains unparalleled because it has so many technology-savvy analysts and investment bankers. For companies that want to signal improved disclosure and corporate-governance policies, NYSE must be the most expensive option and, by that token, also the most convincing one. As a result, the offering gets a better valuation; in fact, even follow-up equity issues at home fetch better prices. There are also fringe benefits, like lower volatility; narrower spreads; higher analyst attention and (partly therefore) lower market sensitivity, which brings diversification benefits, and stronger reactions to company news.

Yet the costs are, in many cases, not trivial. Smaller companies tend to prefer Nasdaq or LSE, where information requirements are less severe; or the company might opt for an OTC or private placement. One noteworthy cost of a listing on one of the three major U.S. exchanges is Sarbanes Oxley's Article 404, which has been called "toxic" for New York and might be behind London's recent gains as the cross-listing place to be. But the benefits from cross listing can be smaller than you hoped, too. And remember: once listed on NYSE, Nasdaq, or AMEX you cannot simply delist if you think the benefits do not, or no longer, justify the cost. Voluntary delisting would leave U.S. investors in the lurch, the legislator opines, so they can veto a delisting.

A study looking at all 1,626 foreign listings[9] that have occurred since the 1960s in the United States found that 932 delisted within the sample period (1960–2005): 499 involuntarily because they failed to meet the continuing listing requirements,[10] 378 via a merger or acquisition, and 55 voluntarily. The average time of staying listed has fallen from 32 years for a 1970s entrant to 3 years for 1996–2000 entrants; or, while all of the 1970s entrants were still listed ten years later, only one third of the 1996–2000 entrants. (The U.S. domestic IPO record is even worse.) For the voluntary delistings the typical story is not costly regulation but failed investor recognition: low profits, a share price drop by 50% or more, falling stock exchange turnover and therefore falling analyst attention. But the number of involuntary delistings ("for cause") is perhaps the more disconcerting one. And their story is similar: poor profits, or falling markets, or adverse currency movements—anything that leads to poor performance and low prices. Thus, many of the once eager listees were overly optimistic.

Of course, the above is about averages for delisted firms; many firms do succeed, or get taken over without being distressed. Others quit voluntarily because the costs have increased or the benefits fallen. Recall the story by Mr. De Proft, CEO of Icos Vision Systems: "In 2003 we then went to Euronext and saw that all our volume went there, which meant our Nasdaq listing became pointless. Also, ... at some point we had to comply with seven or eight accounting codes that occasionally contradicted each other. [Getting] a single listing was an enormous simplification. Add to that S-Ox 404. ... As a result, the audit costs are doubled or tripled."

Most of this was about getting a U.S. listing. For a reverse cross listing, from the United States to overseas, the analysis is reversed. Getting, say, a London listing without delisting at home has almost no benefits, except access to retail investors. (All the pros outside the United States easily buy and sell directly in America.) Getting a non-U.S. listing instead of a U.S. one avoids S-Ox 404 and other costs, but may be viewed as a negative signal about openness and governance.

∗   ∗   ∗

This finishes our discussion of the long-term funding side of corporate finance. We now turn to the capital-budgeting part, and we start with an issue close to what we have just considered: the cost of capital in open or closed financial markets.

---

[9] No pink sheets or RADRs.

[10] The typical conditions include sufficiently high market cap, turnover, and sales revenue.

TEST YOUR UNDERSTANDING

Quiz Questions

True-False Questions

1. Cross listing is always more costly than a domestic listing.
2. The higher stock price after a cross listing is caused by a drop in the cost of capital (discount rate).
3. All firms that list abroad experience an announcement effect: the announcement of a cross listing leads to an increase in the share prices of about 1% on average.
4. Cross-listed companies have more analysts following them than domestic companies.
5. If your competitor cross lists its shares, this is favorable for you: international investors start noticing your country and your business and can create an extra demand for your shares.

Multiple-Choice Questions

1. Why can you possibly get a higher price for your shares if you opt for an international listing?
   (a) You can issue a larger amount of shares.
   (b) The costs of preparing and getting the listing are lower.
   (c) The foreign stock market is larger and thus more liquid than the domestic market.
   (d) The international cost of capital is lower due to more diversifiable risks for foreign investors.

2. The pre-cross-listing run-up and post-cross-listing decline is stronger for firms that list on the NYSE than on the LSE. This is probably because:
   (a) information provision in New York is better;
   (b) discount rates for stocks trading on the NYSE are lower;
   (c) the SEC primarily controls foreign firms;
   (d) the announcement effect only occurs for firms that list in the United States.

19

Setting the Cost of International Capital

This chapter deals with how to set the cost of capital, which is the discount rate used in capital budgeting. The chapter title adds one word: international. Note that what is said to be international is *capital*. The title does not say "the international cost of capital," as the 1994 book (and many others) did: such a title would have suggested that there is something like a national cost (for domestic projects, presumably) and, next to that, an international cost, for transborder investments. No, there is just one cost of capital, and that capital is international. Shares in large corporations are held by people everywhere; and, equally important, even shareholders of smaller, more locally held firms still invest part of their wealth in foreign stocks. This has two implications for the way the cost of capital is set. First, managers should ask how much risk this project adds to an internationally diversified portfolio instead of to a local market portfolio (the traditional method), and set a cost of capital that is commensurate with this international risk. Second, management has to take into account that the expected return differs depending on what currency the shareholder uses as the (quasi-)real numéraire; and so does the risk-free rate that serves as one benchmark item in the model. That is, when setting the cost of capital, the issue of exchange risk has to be taken into account too, in the sense of investors having different numéraires in which they are doing, or supposed to be doing, their optimum-portfolio calculations.

There is a second—and largely independent—issue related to exchange rates: how do we bring expected cash flows and cost of capital in line with one other? The issue arises because when, say, an Australian firm invests in India, the expected future cash flows are normally first expressed in rupees. Yet, the argument typically goes, the Australian owners care about Australian dollars only—we will make this argument more precise as we proceed—and the cost of capital we would estimate is probably expressed in AUD. One cannot discount INR cash flows using an AUD discount rate. So at some point we need to go from INR to AUD.

There seem to be two ways we could go about this, similar to what we did earlier for risk-free cash flows. As we saw, a risk-free claim on INR 1 can be

PV-ed in INR terms first, by discounting the INR cash flow (unity) at the INR risk-free rate and this value is then translated into AUD at the going spot rate. Alternatively, we can translate the future cash flow into AUD using the expected future spot rate, and then discount at an AUD rate that takes into account the risk. Both are linked via the forward rate as the risk-adjusted expectation and CIP:

$$\frac{E_t(\tilde{S}_T)}{1 + r_{t,T} + RP_{t,T}} = \frac{F_{t,T}}{1 + r_{t,T}} \qquad \text{(F = CEQ)}$$

$$= \frac{1}{1 + r_{t,T}^*}S_t \qquad \text{(CIP).} \qquad (19.1)$$

Similarly then, in the case of a risky FC cash flow, we could first translate the *future* INR cash flows into AUD using the expected future spot rate, and then PV these using an AUD discount rate, set, for example, on the basis of the standard capital asset pricing model (CAPM), the way Australians would value a domestic Australian project. Alternatively, we could argue that the Australian ownership hardly matters, and simply conduct the entire cost–benefit analysis in INR, the way an Indian owner would do: take INR cash flows, and discount at the rupee rate of return. Having found the value in INR, we then translate the *present* value into AUD. And if that second solution really works, exchange-rate forecasts and currency risk can be totally eliminated from the analysis, it would seem.

In this chapter we show that the above analysis is quite incomplete. The main lessons to be remembered from this chapter are the following.

Translation of FC cash flows requires more than just an expected exchange rate. Suppose we follow the first route and translate our rupee cash flows, $\tilde{C}_T^*$, into AUD. What we need are expected AUD cash flows; but the expectation of a product, $\mathrm{E}(\tilde{C}_T^*\tilde{S}_T)$, involves not just the expectations of $\tilde{C}_T^*$ and $\tilde{S}_T$, but also the covariance between the two.

This, at first sight, makes the first route even more difficult. All the more reason to go for the alternative one, then? Unfortunately, this alternative would not always work:

Host-currency versus home-currency valuation. Valuation in rupees, the way an Indian investor would do it—using the rupee risk-free rate and a premium for market risk measured in rupees—should produce the same result, after translation, as valuation *à l'Australienne* only if the Indian and Australian capital markets are well integrated. Indeed, if investors from each country can freely invest in each other's market (and possibly in other markets), arbitrage flows would occur if the value to Australians were different from the value to Indian investors (after translation into a common currency).

In the case of India, integration of the capital market into the mainstream work market is doubtful, for the time being. But even if it were true, the Indian rupee approach would still not exonerate us from thinking about expected exchange-rate changes and exchange covariance risk:

In open markets, exchange risk affects any cost of capital... In principle, exchange risk enters asset pricing as soon as the investor base for which we want to value the project is part of an international market. Thus, Australia being part of a nearly worldwide capital market, an international CAPM (InCAPM) should be used whether the project is situated at home or abroad. Intuitively, in an international capital market, asset prices result from the interaction of portfolio decisions by people from many different countries, each having their own currency. Exchange risk makes people disagree about expected returns and risk; for example, the AUD treasury bill is risk free to Australians, but not to Canadians or Japanese. This heterogeneity of perspectives does affect asset pricing, and introduces currency risk premia into the CAPM, in principle one for each currency area that is part of the international capital market.

Thus, in a way things are even more complicated than you might have thought possible: you need expected returns on *all* currencies in the international capital market, and covariances for your project with each of these currencies. In addition, exposures to exchange rates are even harder to estimate than betas. Fortunately:

...but currency risk premia are small. The literature on the forward rate as a predictor of futures spot rates shows that, while the currency risk premium is surely not a constant, it is small and seems to fluctuate around zero. So one could use a shortcut, omitting the forex items in the InCAPM formula, so that it looks rather like the familiar domestic CAPM. Two differences remain: the market portfolio is the world-market index rather than a domestic one, and the market beta is from a multiple regression with all exchange rates included.

The discussion can be summed up as follows.

(i) **Which CAPM?** You use a (possibly simplified) InCAPM when the *home* country is part of an international capital market; the domestic model works only for segmented home markets.

   Note, incidentally, that this holds for any investment, whether at home or abroad.

(ii) **Which currency?** If home and host are *both* part of the same international market, either currency will do for valuation purposes; otherwise, only the investors' HC can be used.

This chapter addresses these issues in the following order. First we discuss the effect of capital-market integration or segmentation on the capital-budgeting procedure (section 19.1), notably which should come first, translation from FC to HC or discounting. The bulk of the chapter then relates to the determination of the cost of capital. In the second section, we present the traditional single-country CAPM, starting from the efficient-portfolio problem familiar from basic finance courses. In section 19.3, we explain how to modify this model when assets are priced in an international market. The case that we discuss is one where capital markets are integrated across many countries, but where imperfections in the goods markets create real exchange risk. Section 19.4 concludes with a review of the implications of this chapter for capital budgeting.

19.1 The Link between Capital-Market Segmentation and the Sequencing of Discounting and Translation

To initiate our discussion of the effect of capital-market integration or segmentation on the capital-budgeting procedure, we explain why capital budgeting can be done in terms of foreign currency when the home- and host-country capital markets are integrated, and how the procedure is to be modified when the home- and host-country capital markets are segmented from each other.

Almost inevitably, capital budgeting starts with cash-flow projections expressed in host (foreign) currency. When one prepares cash-flow forecasts there is no real choice but to start from currently prevailing prices for similar products in foreign currency. On the basis of this you set your own price(s), taking into account the positioning of the product(s). Then you try to figure out production costs on the basis of data from similar plants and local wages and other input costs. (Don't forget the initial inefficiencies, i.e., the learning curve. And think of possible price drops later when competition catches up or the rich segment has been creamed off or excitement about your product wanes.) In this way you obtain cash-flow forecasts, all typically at current (i.e., constant) FC prices. Finally, you adjust the figures for expected foreign inflation. This practice stems from the empirical fact, noted in chapter 3, that prices in any given country are sticky (apart from general inflation) and to a large extent independent of exchange-rate changes.

DIY Problem 19.1. You could think of an alternative version of the final step: translate the constant-prices cash flow into HC and then adjust for inflation in the investor's home country. Show that this unattractively assumes relative PPP, at least as an expectation. For simplicity, assume risk-free cash flows at constant FC prices.

So we usually end up with expected cash flows in FC. However, the ultimate purpose of capital budgeting is to find out whether the project is valuable to the parent company's shareholders. The correct procedure is to see how *they* price similar existing projects. We can see that only by looking at their own capital market; that is, we use the shareholders' home capital market to get the risk-free rate and the estimated risk premium. But this delivers a cost of capital in HC units, which can only be used to discount HC expected future cash flows. For example, one would not use a low JPY-based discount rate to PV a stream of Zimbabwe dollar cash flows. In short, although the natural input data are cash-flow forecasts expressed in foreign currency, in principle we have to make the translation from foreign currency to home currency before we can discount. To what extent would it be acceptable, instead, to discount FC cash flows at an FC rate, and then to translate the FC PV into HC using just the current spot rate? After all, this is the way a local investor goes about the valuation.

This type of valuation in foreign currency, as if the owner were a host-country investor, is correct if the host- and home-country financial markets are integrated, that is, if there are no restrictions on cross-border portfolio investment between the two countries and if investors effectively hold many foreign assets. Indeed, the implication of market integration is that all investors, regardless of their place of residence, use the same cost of capital when they compute the price of any given asset (in some given common currency) from the expected cash flows of this asset (expressed in the same common currency). One way to explain this claim is by contradiction. If investors from countries A and B used a different cost of capital when computing the price of some given asset (in some given base currency) from the asset's expected cash flows (measured in the same base currency), then the price of the asset in country A would differ from the price of the same asset in country B. The resulting arbitrage opportunities would lead to international trading in the shares until the price difference disappeared. By equating prices across countries, international arbitrage also equates the costs of capital that various investors use when linking the asset's price to the expected cash flows paid out by the asset.[1] Thus, in integrated markets, a home-country investor and a host-country investor fully agree on the project's value.

In the perfect-markets approach of chapter 4, perfect integration was taken for granted. But in the case of FDI into emerging countries it is not always obvious that integration is a reasonable approximation, even though restrictions are gradually being abolished in many countries. The problem is that in segmented markets one cannot simply value a foreign cash flow as if it were owned by host-country investors. In the absence of free capital movements, there is no mechanism that equates prices and discount rates across the two markets. Thus, to the managers of the parent firm, the relevant question becomes: what price would home-country investors normally be prepared to pay for the project? As we saw, the way to proceed is to identify cash-flow patterns that have similar risks and that are already priced in the home-country capital market. Once we have identified a similar asset that is

---

[1] Investors who are not willing to pay a high price then sell to others who are. Portfolio rebalancing also modifies the risk: the risk of holding Samsung shares is very different depending on whether this company represents 90% of one's portfolio or just 0.1% of a well-diversified package of securities. So reducing the weight of one asset, and replacing it by others that offer more diversification, lowers required returns for that asset and increases the price one is willing to pay for it. In the end, when both domestic and foreign investors hold very similar portfolios, required returns would converge.

already priced in the home capital market, we can then use the same discount rate for the project we want to value as that for the traded assets. To implement this procedure, we need a theory, like CAPM, to tell us what types of risk are relevant, how these risks should be measured, and what return is expected in the home-country capital market in light of the project's risks. Since we use the home-country capital market as the yardstick, the discount rate is the required return in home currency—and if the cost of capital is expressed in home currency, we have to translate the expected cash flows and their risks from foreign currency into home currency before we discount.

For such a translation, we need expected values for the future spot rates for various maturities. In fact, we also need the covariance. If $\tilde{C}^*$ denotes the cash flow in FC and $\tilde{C}^*\tilde{S}$ the cash flow in HC, then

$$E(\tilde{C}^*\tilde{S}) = E(\tilde{C}^*) \times E(\tilde{S}) + \text{cov}(\tilde{C}^*, \tilde{S}). \qquad (19.2)$$

You may have noticed the covariance effect in the Freedonian crown exposure example in chapter 13, which we reproduce here.

Example 19.1. A British company is considering a project in Freedonia. Assume that the Freedonian crown (FDK) cash flow can take on either of two equally probable values, FDK 150 or FDK 100, depending on whether the Freedonian economy is booming or in a funk. Let there also be two equally probable time T spot rates, GBP/FDK 1.2 and 0.8. Thus, measured in GBP, there are four possible cash flows: $150 \times 1.2 = $ GBP 180, $150 \times 0.8 = $ GBP 120, $100 \times 1.2 = $ GBP 120, and $100 \times 0.8 = $ GBP 80. These numbers are shown in table 19.1. In each cell, we also show the joint probability of each particular combination. When the FDK is expensive, a recession is more probable than a boom because an expensive currency means that Freedonia is not very competitive. The inverse happens when the crown is trading at a low level; then it is more likely that the economy will be booming. These effects are reflected in the probabilities shown in each of the four cells in table 19.1.

The expectations of the exchange rate and the FDK cash flows are easily calculated as

$$E(\tilde{S}) = (0.50 \times 1.2) + (0.50 \times 0.8) = 1.00, \qquad (19.3)$$
$$E(\tilde{C}^*) = (0.50 \times 150) + (0.50 \times 100) = 125. \qquad (19.4)$$

But the expected cash flow is not $1.00 \times 125 = 125$:

$$E(\tilde{S}\tilde{C}^*) = (0.15 \times 180) + (0.35 \times 120) + (0.35 \times 120) + (0.15 \times 80) = 123. \quad (19.5)$$

The shortfall of 2 (= 125 − 123) is due to the fact that high FDK cash flows tend to go together with low exchange rates and vice versa. This effect is lost if one just multiplies through the two expectations, because that computation implicitly assigns probabilities 0.25 to each cell:

$$E(\tilde{S})E(\tilde{C}^*) = [(0.50 \times 1.2) + (0.50 \times 0.8)] \times [(0.50 \times 150) + (0.50 \times 100)]$$
$$= (0.25 \times 180) + (0.25 \times 120) + (0.25 \times 120) + (0.25 \times 80). \qquad (19.6)$$

Table 19.1. Cash flows for the Freedonian project.

| | State of the economy | | | |
	Boom: $C^* = 150$	Slump: $C^* = 100$	$\Pr(S)$	$\mathrm{E}(\tilde{C} \mid S)$
$S_T = 1.2$	$p = 0.15; C = 180$	$p = 0.35; C = 120$	0.50	138
$S_T = 0.8$	$p = 0.35; C = 120$	$p = 0.15; C = 80$	0.50	108
$\Pr(C^*)$	$p = 0.50$	$p = 0.50$		

So when we use the translate-first approach, the expected GBP cash flow is GBP 123 not 125.[2] This number is to be discounted at the appropriate home-currency discount rate, that is, the GBP risk-free rate plus a risk premium that reflects the risk of the GBP cash flows to the British investor.[3] CAPM, to be discussed in sections 19.2 and 19.3, provides a way to estimate the appropriate discount rate.

While the translate-first approach is very general, it requires explicit exchange-rate forecasts, and the covariance. These do not come in explicitly if we take the discount-first route, and compute a PV for the expected flow $\mathrm{E}(\tilde{C}^*) = 125$, using the FDK risk-free rate and risk premium. This would be all right if the Freedonian and British markets are well integrated.

We have seen how to obtain expected cash flows, but not how to obtain appropriate discount rates when cash flows are risky. This is the task in the remainder of this chapter. Section 19.2 reviews the single-country CAPM. Section 19.3 extends the model to a multi-country setting.

19.2 The Single-Country CAPM

Our discussion of the traditional (single-country) CAPM starts from asset demand theory. The key assumption of this theory is that investors rank portfolios on the basis of two numbers: the expected nominal portfolio return and the variance of the nominal portfolio return. Implicit in the use of nominal returns is an assumption that inflation is deterministic, or at least that inflation uncertainty has little impact on asset pricing. The theory of optimal portfolios, as developed by Markowitz (1952), can also be interpreted as a theory that tells us how expected returns are related to risk in an efficient portfolio. This relationship is due to Sharpe (1964), Lintner (1965), and Mossin (1966).

---

[2] In the above example, the covariance correction is relatively small. But the link between exchange rate and cash flow is weak too, in the above story: it just works via general economic activity. In reality, there is often a strong, direct link, for instance, if the firm is an exporter or importer, and then the covariance would be bigger.

[3] Recall that if capital markets within, say, the OECD are well integrated, the U.K. value would also be correct for any other investor from any other OECD country. (The OECD is just an example: the world market now counts many non-OECD members.)

19.2.1   How Asset Returns Determine the Portfolio Return

The model is typically derived in terms of returns rather than prices: academics use returns in empirical work, and practitioners want a formula for the expected return to be used for NPV applications. The key relation is that the realized return on the portfolio (subscript "p") can always be written as (i) the risk-free return over that period plus (ii), for all risky assets in the portfolio, the weighted average of the returns over and above the risk-free rate,

$$\tilde{r}_{\mathrm{p}} - r = \sum_{j=1}^{N} x_j (\tilde{r}_j - r), \tag{19.7}$$

with a weight x_j defined as the initial amount invested in asset j, divided by total initial investment. A return over the risk-free rate is called an *excess return*, and its expected value is called the *risk premium.*

Example 19.2. You have 1,000 to invest. Below, we show for three risky assets (denoted as 1, 2, 3) an initial price, the number of shares you buy, your total initial investment per asset, the asset weight, a possible time-1 price, the corresponding return, and the weighted return. The risky assets take up 900 of the money, so the balance, 100, is invested risk free at, say, 5%. In the table we see the weights[4] and how they sum to unity. We next compute the value of the portfolio at time 1, and see that it has gone up to 1,105, implying a (net rate of) return of 0.105, i.e., 10.5%. The excess return is $10.5 - 5 = 5.5\%$, and this is exactly what you get by summing the value-weighted "excess" returns on the three risky assets.

	j	$V_{j,0}$	n_j	$n_j V_{j,0}$	x_j	$V_{j,1}$	$n_j V_{j,1}$	r_j	$r_j - r$	$x_j(\tilde{r}_j - r)$
			Time-0 data and decisions			Time-1 result			(Excess) rates of return	
Risky:	1	100	4	400	0.40	120	480	0.20	0.15	0.060
	2	50	4	200	0.20	70	280	0.40	0.35	0.070
	3	25	12	300	0.30	20	240	−0.20	−0.25	−0.075
Subtotal				= 900	= 0.90					= 0.055
Risk free:	0			+100	+0.10		105			+0.05
Total				= 1,000	= 1.00		= 1,105			$r_{\mathrm{p}} = 0.105$

DIY Problem 19.2. Rework the example by changing the initial investment in asset 1 from 400 to 800, maintaining the other risky positions and adjusting the risk-free one. Check that the weighted excess-return formula still gives the right answer.

19.2.2   The Tangency Solution: Graphical Discussion

Consider the feasible combinations of expected return and standard deviation. The simplest case is one with a risk-free asset, subscripted "0," and a risky stock subscripted "s." We invest a fraction x into the risky stock portfolio

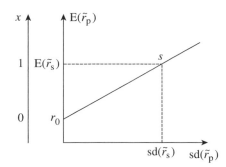

Figure 19.1. Combinations of risky stock portfolio s and asset 0.

with return $\tilde{r}_s$ while $1 - x$ is invested risk free. The portfolio return is

$$\tilde{r}_p = x\tilde{r}_s + (1 - x)r_0 = r_0 + x\,(\tilde{r}_s - r_0),$$

$$\implies \begin{cases} E(\tilde{r}_p) = r_0 + x\,E(\tilde{r}_s - r_0), \\ \text{sd}(\tilde{r}_p) = |x|\,\text{sd}(\tilde{r}_s). \end{cases} \tag{19.8}$$

So for nonnegative values of x, both expected return and standard deviation are linear functions of x. This will imply that all (E,sd) combinations achievable with the risk-free asset and the risky portfolio are found on a half line. To show this we use a trick that is often applied in thermometers, where heat is measured on two scales, say Celsius and Fahrenheit, that are linearly related. Same here: x and $E(\tilde{r}_p)$ are linearly related, so we can show them as two scales on one axis, as we do in figure 19.1. To link the x and E_p scales we calibrate them using any two known corresponding points: $x = 1$ means $E(\tilde{r}_p) = E(\tilde{r}_s)$ while $x = 0$ means $E(\tilde{r}_p) = r_0$. All this gives us the double-scaled axis shown in figure 19.1. If $\text{sd}(\tilde{r}_p)$ is linear in x_+, then looking at the other scale of the axis we must conclude it is linear in $E(\tilde{r}_p)_{>r_0}$ too. The sd values for the calibration points are 0 and $\text{sd}(\tilde{r}_s)$, respectively, and all risk–return combinations for intermediate or higher values of x or $E(\tilde{r}_p)$ are on one and the same (half) line. This gives us the total picture: all feasible combinations with $x \geqslant 0$ are on a half line from $(\text{sd}(\tilde{r}_p), E(\tilde{r}_p)) = (0, r_0)$ through $(\text{sd}(\tilde{r}_s), E(\tilde{r}_s))$. The slope of that half line is called the *Sharpe ratio*:

$$\forall x \geqslant 0: \quad \frac{E(\tilde{r}_p - r_0)}{\text{sd}(\tilde{r}_p)} = \frac{E(\tilde{r}_s - r_0)}{\text{sd}(\tilde{r}_s)} = s\text{'s Sharpe ratio.} \tag{19.9}$$

Now look at a second simple case, where the portfolio consists of two imperfectly correlated risky assets, subscripted "1" and "2." Now we have

$$\tilde{r}_p = x_1\tilde{r}_1 + (1 - x_1)\tilde{r}_2,$$

$$\implies \begin{cases} E(\tilde{r}_p) = E(\tilde{r}_1) + x_1\,[E(\tilde{r}_1) - E(\tilde{r}_2)], \\ \text{sd}(\tilde{r}_p) = \sqrt{x_1^2\,\text{var}(\tilde{r}_1) + 2x_1(1 - x_1)\,\text{cov}(\tilde{r}_1, \tilde{r}_2) + (1 - x_1)^2\,\text{var}(\tilde{r}_2)}. \end{cases} \tag{19.10}$$

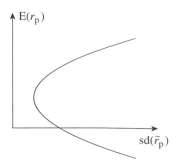

Figure 19.2.   The risk–return bound with just risky assets.

From the first equation we conclude that x_1 and the expected return are still two sides of the same thermometer. The sd function looks messier. But we immediately see that variance is quadratic in x_1 and, therefore, in $E(\tilde{r}_p)$ too. This means a rotated U-shaped graph opening toward the right. Warping the risk axis by taking square roots does not fundamentally change the shape of the relation, as you can check by using a spreadsheet. We end up with a feasible set as in figure 19.2. Basic textbooks will tell you that if there are more than two risky assets, the feasible combinations in a (std,E) space graph are still similar.

The last step is to look at N risky assets and a risk-free one. We return to figure 19.1 except that the risky part of the portfolio, s, must be chosen from a feasible set shaped as in figure 19.2. A risk-averse mean–variance investor wants to be leftward/upward in the graph: high return, low risk. So s will be chosen from the left-upper risky-asset bound. Among all such portfolios, the best one is the portfolio that rotates the half line from $(sd = 0, E = r_0)$ as far upward/leftward as is feasible—the one with the highest Sharpe ratio. It follows that the optimal choice is the *tangency portfolio*, the one where the half line from $(sd = 0, E = r_0)$ just touches the curve that bounds the risky-assets risk–return set. All portfolios on this half line are efficient. They all are combinations of the risk-free asset and the *tangency portfolio*, subscripted "t."

We now want to take a peek at the analytical solution and its implication. To understand how the tangency portfolio can be found we need to understand first how a small change in one of the portfolio weights affects the expected return and the variance of the portfolio return.

19.2.3   How Portfolio Choice Affects the Mean and the Variance of the Portfolio Return

We want to understand what happens if investors choose portfolios on the basis of the mean and the variance of the portfolio return. To figure out how these people think, we need to understand how portfolio choice affects the mean and the variance of the total return. The link is, of course, equation

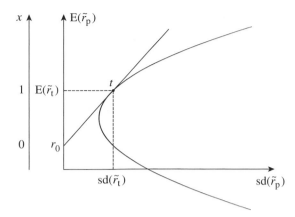

Figure 19.3. Efficient portfolios and the tangency portfolio.

(19.7): $\tilde{r}_p = r + \sum_{j=1}^{N} x_j (\tilde{r}_j - r)$. From this it follows that

$$E(\tilde{r}_p) = r + \sum_{j=1}^{N} x_j E(\tilde{r}_j - r), \qquad (19.11)$$

$$\text{var}(\tilde{r}_p) = \sum_{j=1}^{N} x_j \sum_{k=1}^{N} x_k \, \text{cov}(\tilde{r}_j, \tilde{r}_k). \qquad (19.12)$$

The first formula is pretty obvious. To interpret the second one, it helps to derive it in two steps, as follows:[5]

$$\text{var}(\tilde{r}_p) = \text{cov}(\tilde{r}_p, \tilde{r}_p) = \text{cov}\left(\sum_{j=1}^{N} x_j \tilde{r}_j, \tilde{r}_p \right) = \sum_{j=1}^{N} x_j \, \text{cov}(\tilde{r}_j, \tilde{r}_p), \qquad (19.13)$$

where

$$\text{cov}(\tilde{r}_j, \tilde{r}_p) = \text{cov}\left(\tilde{r}_j, \sum_{k=1}^{N} x_k \tilde{r}_k \right) = \sum_{k=1}^{N} x_k \, \text{cov}(\tilde{r}_j, \tilde{r}_k). \qquad (19.14)$$

This tells you that the portfolio variance is a weighted average of each asset's covariance with the entire portfolio; and each of these assets' portfolio covariances is, in turn, a weighted average of the asset's covariance with all components of the portfolio.

Example 19.3. We compute the portfolio expected excess return, the assets' covariances with the portfolio return, and the portfolio variance when the risky assets' weights are 0.50 and 0.40 (implying $x_0 = 0.10$):

	$E(\tilde{r}_j - r)$	$\text{cov}(\tilde{r}_j, \tilde{r}_1)$	$\text{cov}(\tilde{r}_j, \tilde{r}_2)$
1	0.200	0.16	0.05
2	0.122	0.05	0.09

---

[5] We use the fact that, inside a variance, risk-free returns added or subtracted play no role: $\text{var}(r + \sum x_j(\tilde{r}_j - r)) = \text{var}(\sum x_j \tilde{r}_j)$.

$$E(\tilde{r}_p - r) = 0.50 \times 0.200 + 0.40 \times 0.122 = 0.1488,$$
$$\mathrm{cov}(\tilde{r}_1, \tilde{r}_p) = 0.50 \times 0.160 + 0.40 \times 0.050 = 0.1000,$$
$$\mathrm{cov}(\tilde{r}_2, \tilde{r}_p) = 0.50 \times 0.050 + 0.40 \times 0.090 = 0.0610,$$
$$\implies \quad \mathrm{cov}(\tilde{r}_p, \tilde{r}_p) = 0.50 \times 0.100 + 0.40 \times 0.061 = 0.0744.$$

How do these numbers change when the portfolio weights are being tweaked? First look at an example involving two risky assets and see how mean and variance are affected by a small change in the weight of asset 1 (implicitly matched by a small offsetting change in the weight for the risk-free bond, asset zero):

$$E(\tilde{r}_p - r) = x_1 E(\tilde{r}_1 - r) + x_2 E(\tilde{r}_2 - r),$$
$$\implies \quad \frac{\partial E(\tilde{r}_p - r)}{\partial x_1} = E(\tilde{r}_1 - r), \tag{19.15}$$

and

$$\mathrm{var}(\tilde{r}_p) = x_1^2 \, \mathrm{var}(\tilde{r}_1) + 2 x_1 x_2 \, \mathrm{cov}(\tilde{r}_1, \tilde{r}_2) + x_2^2 \, \mathrm{var}(\tilde{r}_2),$$
$$\implies \quad \frac{\partial \, \mathrm{var}(\tilde{r}_p)}{\partial x_1} = 2 x_1 \, \mathrm{var}(\tilde{r}_1) + 2 x_2 \, \mathrm{cov}(\tilde{r}_1, \tilde{r}_2)$$
$$= 2[x_1 \, \mathrm{cov}(\tilde{r}_1, \tilde{r}_1) + x_2 \, \mathrm{cov}(\tilde{r}_1, \tilde{r}_2)]$$
$$= 2[\mathrm{cov}(\tilde{r}_1, x_1 \tilde{r}_1) + \mathrm{cov}(\tilde{r}_1, x_2 \tilde{r}_2)]$$
$$= 2 \, \mathrm{cov}(\tilde{r}_1, x_1 \tilde{r}_1 + x_2 \tilde{r}_2)$$
$$= 2 \, \mathrm{cov}(\tilde{r}_1, \tilde{r}_p). \tag{19.16}$$

Similarly,

$$\frac{\partial E(\tilde{r}_p - r_0)}{\partial x_2} = E(\tilde{r}_2 - r) \quad \text{and} \quad \frac{\partial \, \mathrm{var}(\tilde{r}_p)}{\partial x_2} = 2 \, \mathrm{cov}(\tilde{r}_2, \tilde{r}_p).$$

DIY Problem 19.3. Recompute the expected excess return and variance when, in the previous example, x_1 is increased from 0.50 to 0.51. Check how the scaled change in the mean, $\Delta E / \Delta x_1$, is exactly the first asset's own expected excess return. Likewise, check how the scaled change in the variance, $\Delta \mathrm{var} / \Delta x_1$, is about twice the first asset's own covariance with the portfolio return.[6]

DIY Problem 19.4. Consider a portfolio with, initially, $x_1 = 0.5$ and $x_2 = 0$ so that $\mathrm{var}(\tilde{r}_p) = \mathrm{var}(0.5 \, \tilde{r}_1) = 0.5^2 \, \mathrm{var}(\tilde{r}_1)$. Then increase the second weight to 0.001. Write out the change in the variance, and check whether it is far from $2 \, \mathrm{cov}(\tilde{r}_2, \tilde{r}_p) \times 0.001$.

---

[6] For the variance, the scaled difference is not perfectly the same as the partial derivative because the function is quadratic in the weights, not linear. (For nonlinear functions, obviously, $\Delta y / \Delta x \ne dx/dy$.) But note how the scaled change in fact equals the average of the original and the revised covariances (0.1000 when $x_1 = 0.50$ and 0.1016 when $x_1 = 0.51$). In the limit, the two covariances are so close that they become indistinguishable from their average.

19.2.4 Efficient Portfolios: A Review

Recall that a portfolio is efficient if it has the highest expected return among all conceivable portfolios with the same variance of return. We have just reviewed the probably familiar result that any efficient portfolio is a combination of two building blocks: the risk-free asset and the tangency portfolio of risky assets (figure 19.3). But what is perhaps less obvious is how the tangency portfolio must be constructed and what this implies for the risk–return relation. Let us consider this.

It is easily shown that if a portfolio is to be efficient, then for each and every asset the marginal risk–return ratio—the ratio of any asset's marginal "good" (its contribution to the portfolio's expected excess return) to the asset's marginal "bad" (its contribution to the portfolio's risk)—must be the same (see technical note 19.1). We have just identified the asset's contribution to the portfolio's expected excess return as the asset's own expected excess return, while the asset's contribution to the portfolio variance is twice the covariance between the asset's return and the portfolio return. Thus, the general efficiency condition can be written as follows:

$$\frac{\mathrm{E}(\tilde{r}_j - r)}{\mathrm{cov}(\tilde{r}_j, \tilde{r}_\mathrm{p})} = \lambda \quad \text{for all risky assets } j = 1, \ldots, N, \tag{19.17}$$

where r is the risk-free rate of return and $\tilde{r}_j$ the uncertain return on asset j. The common return/risk ratio, λ, depends on the investor's attitude toward risk, and is called the investor's *relative risk aversion*.

Example 19.4. Let there be two risky assets ($j = 1, 2$) with the following expected excess returns and covariances of return:

	$\mathrm{E}(\tilde{r}_j - r)$	(Co)variances	
Asset 1	0.092	$\mathrm{cov}(\tilde{r}_1, \tilde{r}_1) = 0.04$	$\mathrm{cov}(\tilde{r}_1, \tilde{r}_2) = 0.05$
Asset 2	0.148	$\mathrm{cov}(\tilde{r}_2, \tilde{r}_1) = 0.05$	$\mathrm{cov}(\tilde{r}_2, \tilde{r}_2) = 0.09$

Given these data, a portfolio p with weights ($x_1 = 0.4$, $x_2 = 0.6$) is efficient. We can verify the efficiency of this portfolio in two steps:

- First we compute the contribution of each asset to the total risk of portfolio p (covariance), as follows:[7]

$$\text{Asset 1:} \quad \mathrm{cov}(\tilde{r}_1, x_1\tilde{r}_1 + x_2\tilde{r}_2) = 0.4 \times 0.04 + 0.6 \times 0.05 = 0.046,$$
$$\text{Asset 2:} \quad \mathrm{cov}(\tilde{r}_2, x_1\tilde{r}_1 + x_2\tilde{r}_2) = 0.4 \times 0.05 + 0.6 \times 0.09 = 0.074.$$

- Next we compute, for each asset, the excess return/risk ratio and note that both ratios equal 2:

$$\frac{0.092}{0.046} = 2 = \frac{0.148}{0.074}, \tag{19.18}$$

which implies that the portfolio is efficient.

Moreover, this is not just any efficient portfolio: it is actually the tangency portfolio of risky assets. This is because (1) any efficient portfolio is a combination of the risk-free asset and the tangency portfolio of risky assets, and (2) this particular efficient portfolio contains no risk-free assets.

The portfolio in the example will be selected by an investor with relative risk aversion equal to $\lambda = 2$. One way to detect differences in risk aversion among mean–variance investors is to watch the proportions they invest in the risk-free asset. An investor with a higher relative risk aversion simply allocates more of his or her wealth to the risk-free asset, and less to the tangency portfolio of risky assets.

Example 19.5. Suppose that an investor invests half of his or her wealth in the tangency portfolio identified in the previous example, and the remainder in the risk-free asset. That is, the weights in portfolio p' are $x_0 = 0.5$ for the risk-free asset and ($x_1 = 0.2$, $x_2 = 0.3$) for the risky assets. We can easily verify that p' is still an efficient portfolio and that this investor has a relative risk aversion equal to 4.

- The risks of the assets in portfolio p' are computed as follows:

$$\text{Asset 1:} \quad \text{cov}(\tilde{r}_1, x_1\tilde{r}_1 + x_2\tilde{r}_2) = 0.2 \times 0.04 + 0.3 \times 0.05 = 0.023,$$
$$\text{Asset 2:} \quad \text{cov}(\tilde{r}_2, x_1\tilde{r}_1 + x_2\tilde{r}_2) = 0.2 \times 0.05 + 0.3 \times 0.09 = 0.037.$$

- The excess return/risk ratios now both equal 4:

$$\frac{0.092}{0.023} = \frac{0.148}{0.037} = 4, \tag{19.19}$$

which implies that the portfolio is also efficient.

Thus, the investor's relative risk aversion can be inferred from his or her portfolio choice. Relative to the tangency portfolio chosen by an investor with $\lambda = 2$, the more risk-averse investor with $\lambda = 4$ simply reduces the proportion invested in the risky assets by half. This, as we notice, also halves the (covariance) risks of each risky asset in the total portfolio. This stands to reason: if the total portfolio risk falls, assets' contributions to that total risk must fall too.

There is another, related, way to measure risk aversion: compute the excess-return-to-variance ratio for the entire portfolio. This ratio produces the same number as the previous ones since it takes the same linear combination of both numerators and denominators:[8]

$$\text{If} \quad \frac{0.092}{0.023} = \frac{0.148}{0.037} = 4, \quad \text{then} \quad \frac{0.2 \times 0.092 + 0.3 \times 0.148}{0.2 \times 0.023 + 0.3 \times 0.037} = 4. \tag{19.20}$$

---

[8] The general way to establish this is to write the efficiency condition as $\text{E}(\tilde{r}_j - r) = \lambda \, \text{cov}(\tilde{r}_j, \tilde{r}_p)$. This implies that $x_j\text{E}(\tilde{r}_j - r) = \lambda x_j \, \text{cov}(\tilde{r}_j, \tilde{r}_p)$ and therefore $\sum_j x_j\text{E}(\tilde{r}_j - r) = \lambda \sum_j x_j \, \text{cov}(\tilde{r}_j, \tilde{r}_p) = \lambda \, \text{cov}(\sum_j x_j\tilde{r}_j, \tilde{r}_p)$. Thus, $\text{E}(\tilde{r}_p - r) = \lambda \, \text{cov}(\tilde{r}_p, \tilde{r}_p) = \lambda \, \text{var}(\tilde{r}_p)$.

We conclude that, for efficient portfolios, the holder's relative risk aversion can be measured by the overall excess-return/risk ratio:

$$\text{Relative risk aversion} = \lambda = \frac{E(\tilde{r}_p - r)}{\text{var}(\tilde{r}_p)}, \tag{19.21}$$

a relation that stands us in good stead when deriving the CAPM in the next subsection.

Using a variety of proxies for the market portfolio and a variety of methodologies, (19.21) has been used to estimate the U.S. average risk aversion. The estimates vary, but the consensus in long-term tests is that λ exceeds unity. This result will also come in handy later.

19.2.5   The Market Portfolio as the Benchmark

Let us now go from an individual investor's portfolio to the market portfolio—defined as the aggregate asset holdings of all investors in a particular group. The group typically considered in the standard CAPM is composed of all investors in the economy. What exactly "the" economy corresponds to in practice—a country? a region?—is left vague, but, crucially, this set of investors is assumed to have *homogeneous opportunities*, that is, equal access to the same list of assets, and *homogeneous expectations*, that is, equal perceptions about the return characteristics of the assets.

The effect of these homogeneity assumptions is that all of the investors agree about the composition of the tangency portfolio. If each investor holds the risk-free asset plus the same tangency portfolio, then the aggregate portfolio must also be a combination of the risk-free asset plus that very same tangency portfolio. But any such combination is efficient. Therefore, for the market portfolio (denoted by subscript "m"), the efficiency condition equation (19.17) must hold, with λ_m now defined as the market's risk aversion (which can be shown to be a kind of weighted average of the individuals' risk aversions):

$$\frac{E(\tilde{r}_j - r)}{\text{cov}(\tilde{r}_j, \tilde{r}_m)} = \lambda_m \quad \text{for all risky assets } j = 1, \dots, N. \tag{19.22}$$

Although equation (19.22) is not yet written in the standard CAPM form, this equation is already an embryonic capital asset pricing model because it tells us what the expected excess return should be as a function of the asset's covariance risk in the market portfolio. To implement the model, we need to know the relative risk aversion for the average investor. But we have just found a way to infer this: simply use (19.21) to identify the market's relative risk aversion. This leads us straight to the CAPM:

$$\begin{aligned} E(\tilde{r}_j - r) = \lambda_m \, \text{cov}(\tilde{r}_j, \tilde{r}_m) &= \frac{E(\tilde{r}_m - r)}{\text{var}(\tilde{r}_m)} \, \text{cov}(\tilde{r}_j, \tilde{r}_m) \\ &= \beta_{j,m} \, E(\tilde{r}_m - r). \end{aligned} \tag{19.23}$$

In equation (19.23), $\beta_{j,m} = \text{cov}(\tilde{r}_j, \tilde{r}_m)/\text{var}(\tilde{r}_m)$ is the asset's rescaled co-variance risk, or the asset's beta. The advantage of rescaling the covariance risk is that $\beta_{j,m}$ is also the slope coefficient from the so-called *market model*, the regression of the return from asset j, on the return from the market portfolio, $\tilde{r}_j = \alpha_{j,m} + \beta_{j,m}\tilde{r}_m + \epsilon_{j,m}$. Thus, the rescaled risk (the asset's relative risk, or market sensitivity) in equation (19.23) can be estimated by using time-series data of past stock returns and market returns, assuming, at least, that beta risks and expected returns are constant. We can summarize this model as follows:

- The beta is a measure of the asset's relative risk—that is, the asset's market covariance risk $\text{cov}(\tilde{r}_j, \tilde{r}_m)$, rescaled by the portfolio's total risk, $\text{var}(\tilde{r}_m)$. Beta can be estimated from the market-model regression.

- A risky asset with beta equal to zero should have an expected return that is equal to the risk-free rate, even if the asset's return is uncertain. The reason is that the marginal contribution to the total market risk is zero.

- If an asset's beta or relative risk is nonzero, the asset's expected return should contain a risk premium. The additional return that can be expected per unit of beta is the market's expected excess return above the risk-free rate.

19.2.6 A Replication Interpretation of the CAPM

An enlightening joint interpretation of the market model regression and the CAPM is as follows. A regression $\tilde{y} = a + b\tilde{x} + \tilde{e}$ has the property that it offers the best possible fit between $\tilde{y}$ and $a + b\tilde{x}$, in the sense that no other numbers a and b produce a lower residual variance, $\text{var}(\tilde{e})$. Now suppose that you were asked to find a combination of investments in the risk-free asset and a market-index fund that best resembles a particular asset, say Apple Computers common stock. This best-replication portfolio can be identified by regressing Apple's return onto the market return.

Example 19.6. Suppose that $\beta_{\text{Apple}} = 0.75$. If we invest 75% in the market and 25% in the risk-free asset, we hold a portfolio that offers the best possible replication of Apple's return, among all portfolios that consist only of the market portfolio and the risk-free asset.

Since, in the best replication, a fraction β is invested in the market and $(1-\beta)$ in the risk-free asset, the expected return on such a best-replication portfolio is

$$\text{E}(\tilde{r}_{\text{Apple's replication}}) = \beta_{\text{Apple}}\,\text{E}(\tilde{r}_m) + (1 - \beta_{\text{Apple}})r$$
$$= r + \beta_{\text{Apple}}\text{E}(\tilde{r}_m - r). \tag{19.24}$$

But this is exactly the CAPM's prediction of the return on Apple itself. So the CAPM tells us that the expected return on stock j is equal to the expected return on its best-replication portfolio.

In that sense, the logic of the CAPM is to some extent similar to the logic of asset pricing by replication, as used in part II of this book, except that we now use the best possible replication rather than exact replication. Because the replication is not exact, we need the CAPM assumptions to justify why the expected return on an asset should still be the same as the expected return on its best-replication portfolio, and why the market portfolio is the only replication instrument that is to be considered. In the CAPM logic, investors do not care about the imperfections in the replication (that is, the part of Apple's return not "explained" by the market) because they all hold the market portfolio anyway; the part of Apple's return not correlated with $\tilde{r}_m$ is simply diversified away.

19.2.7 When to Use the Single-Country CAPM

The CAPM as derived in section 19.2 is routinely used in capital budgeting to determine the return that shareholders expect on investments with a given level of beta risk. For many countries, financial institutions provide estimates of the betas for various industries. Yet one ought to interpret these figures with some caution. The assumption that underlies many of these estimates is that the CAPM holds country by country, in the sense that the market portfolio is equated with the portfolio of all assets issued by firms from that country alone. For example, beta service companies in the United States tend to compute the beta of, say, the U.S. computer industry by regressing the returns from a portfolio of U.S. computer firms on the Vanguard index, which is an index of thousands of U.S. stocks traded on the New York Stock Exchange, Amex, and Nasdaq. Likewise, in France, one often estimates the risk of, say, the French steel industry by regressing the returns from a portfolio of steel companies on the index of French stocks. In the same vein, the expected excess return on the market would be estimated from past returns on the Vanguard index or on the index of French stocks traded on the Paris section of Euronext, respectively.

Is the market portfolio of assets held by a country's investors the same as the portfolio of assets issued by the country's corporations? This is only true if investors have access to local shares only *and* all local shares are held by residents of the country. That is, if one equates the market portfolio with the portfolio of locally issued shares, capital markets are assumed to be fully segmented. However, in most countries there are no rules against international share ownership; investors can easily diversify into foreign assets, and foreigners are allowed to buy domestic shares. Thus, the traditional interpretation that the market portfolio consists of the index of stocks issued by local companies is valid only in segmented markets.

Example 19.7. Until the late 1990s, the stock markets of India, South Korea, and Taiwan were almost perfectly segmented from the rest of the world in the sense that foreigners could buy only a small fraction of the local stocks, and local investors could not easily buy foreign assets. Thus, the Indian market portfolio was essentially the same as the portfolio of stocks issued by Indian firms, and the position was similar for Korea and Taiwan.

In the presence of market segmentation, the cost of capital to be used by, say, a North American or European firm is likely to be different from the cost of capital to be used by an Indian firm, even when these companies are evaluating similar investments. For the Indian case, we would have used a one-country CAPM. The question addressed in the next section is how, say, a Canadian firm should determine its cost of capital, knowing that its investors are part of a market that is much wider than just Canada. There are no rules that prevent Canadian investors from buying U.S. or European assets, nor are nonresidents barred from buying Canadian stocks. Under these circumstances the index of stocks issued by Canadian firms is likely to be a poor proxy for the portfolio held by the average Canadian investor. It follows that a Canadian firm cannot use the single-country CAPM to set the cost of capital for an investment project. Not only does the Canadian stock index miss foreign stocks held by residents, it also ignores the fact that many Canadian stocks are held by foreigners. Note also that this problem arises whether the project is domestic or foreign: it's not as if Canadians can still use a one-country CAPM for home investments and only have a problem if the project is foreign.

19.3   The International CAPM

As we have just stated, there are no rules preventing Canadian investors from buying U.S. or European assets, nor are there any regulations barring nonresidents from buying Canadian stocks. Still, this mere fact is not sufficient to lead to international diversification by investors. We have already argued, in chapter 18, that there are strong incentives for investors to diversify internationally. We have just pointed out why this causes a problem with the standard CAPM, at least in the version that uses the locally issued stock index rather than the locally held stock index. From this starting point we add four items: we explain the role of exchange risk for asset pricing in an internationally integrated capital market; we derive a two-country version of the international CAPM of Solnik (1974) and Sercu (1980, 1981); we generalize to the case with many countries and stochastic inflation; and we conclude with a review of empirical tests of the international CAPM.

19.3.1   International Diversification and the Traditional CAPM

International diversification is beneficial for the investor, and investors do use this added opportunity to reduce risks. Clearly, it is then no longer acceptable to use a CAPM equation with, as its benchmark portfolio, the local stock index (defined as the index of all securities issued by firms incorporated in the country). First, this benchmark omits foreign assets, which represent an important component of the local investor's asset holdings. Second, this benchmark ignores the fact that a substantial part of the stock issued by local corporations is, in fact, held by nonresidents.[9] All of this means that, in internationally integrated markets, the true stock market portfolio for any country is unobservable—and, with an unobservable national stock market portfolio, the standard CAPM is of no practical use to managers who, for instance, want to assess the cost of capital or evaluate the performance of their investment advisers.

19.3.2 Why Exchange Risk Pops Up in the International Asset Pricing Model

How can we get around this problem of an unobservable market portfolio? One could argue that, even if we do not know what shares are held by whom, we can still observe the *world* market portfolio. (For conciseness, we will refer to the countries that allow free capital movements as "the world," with an apology to residents of China and other unworldly countries.) Even if we do not know what stock is held by whom and where, we do know what stocks are listed somewhere in the world and how many shares are outstanding at what price. Thus, the world market portfolio contains all securities issued by all firms in the world, and it can be obtained by constructing a value-weighted sum of all member countries' local stock indices.[10] As investors do hold assets from all over the world, and as the world market portfolio is observable, a very simple approach to international asset pricing would be to interpret the world as one huge country, and use the world market portfolio as the benchmark in a unified-world CAPM.

There is, however, one important reason why international asset pricing in integrated capital markets cannot simply be reduced to an as-if-one-country CAPM. Even if international capital transactions are unrestricted and have low costs, transactions in the commodity markets are still difficult and costly. These imperfections in the goods market, as we saw in chapter 3, lead to substantial deviations from relative purchasing power parity and to real exchange risk. The (real) return on, say, IBM common stock as realized by a German investor differs from the (real) return realized by a Japanese investor on the same asset. As a result, the distributions of the real return from a given asset depend on the nationality of the investor. This then violates the homogeneous

---

[9] The same problem arises when one includes in the market portfolio all stocks—domestic or foreign—that are listed on the national stock exchange(s). Investors can (and do) buy foreign assets in foreign stock exchanges, or can (and do) buy foreign assets through mutual funds that are traded over-the-counter; and all of these investments are missing from the menu of locally listed stocks.

[10] A well-known proxy for such an international stock market index is the Morgan Stanley Capital International (MSCI) index, or DataStream's World Market Index. Both are biased toward large firms; but small firms are held locally, mostly, so that's not a huge problem.

expectations assumption of the CAPM, which states that all investors agree on the probability distribution of the (real) asset returns. In a sense, the investors' perceptions about real return distributions are segmented along country lines because goods prices differ across countries, implying that investors from various countries have different views on the distributions of real returns on any given asset or portfolio.

Example 19.8. A clear example is the return on the two countries' T-bills. Suppose that there is no inflation. While to a U.S. investor, the CAD T-bill is one of the available risky assets, it is risk free to a Canadian investor. On the other hand, the USD T-bill is a risky asset to a Canadian investor but risk free to a U.S. investor. Thus, the perceived distribution of (real) returns depends on the nationality of the investor.

Thus, we need to derive a CAPM that takes into account the heterogeneous viewpoints of investors from various countries. In keeping with our discussion of the standard CAPM, we initially ignore inflation. To simplify the analysis, we shall initially assume there are just two countries, the U.S. and Canada. Once you understand the two-country model, you can easily generalize to the case of many countries.

The problem is that the Canadian investor's portfolio choice is based on how each asset contributes to the variance and expected excess return on the portfolio measured in CAD, while the U.S. investor's portfolio choice is based on the assets' contributions to a portfolio whose risk and return are expressed in USD. As usual, the asterisk refers to the foreign country (say, the United States); p^* refers to the portfolio held by the U.S. investor; $\tilde{r}_j^*$ refers to a return in FC on stock j (whose nationality, if any, we do not really need to know); r^*, unsubscripted, as usual refers to the USD risk-free rate; and $\tilde{r}_{p*}^*$ denotes the return, in USD, on the U.S. market portfolio p^*. Then what we know about portfolio choice can be summarized as follows:[11]

$$\text{Canadians choose } p \text{ such that } E(\tilde{r}_j - r) = \lambda \, \text{cov}(\tilde{r}_j, \tilde{r}_p), \qquad (19.25)$$

$$\text{Americans choose } p^* \text{ such that } E(\tilde{r}_j^* - r^*) = \lambda \, \text{cov}(\tilde{r}_j^*, \tilde{r}_{p*}^*). \qquad (19.26)$$

What, then, is the relation between expected excess returns and the world market portfolio, which is the sum of p and p^*? To identify that link, we have to translate (19.26) into the same currency as (19.25), the CAD. Using a trick called Ito's lemma (see technical note 19.2), (19.26) can be translated into CAD as follows:

$$\text{Americans choose } p^* \text{ such that } E(\tilde{r}_j - r)$$
$$= \lambda \, \text{cov}(\tilde{r}_j, \tilde{r}_{p*}) + (1 - \lambda) \, \text{cov}(\tilde{r}_j, \tilde{s}), \qquad (19.27)$$

where $\tilde{s}$ is the percentage change in the exchange rate (CAD per USD). What is going on here is that U.S. investors really care about their wealth expressed

---

[11] It would not have been very painful to allow for different risk aversions across countries too, but little additional insight would have been gained, so we set $\lambda^* = \lambda$.

Table 19.2. Exchange rate exposure: good or bad?

	Example 1: covariance > 0		Example 2: covariance < 0		Comment
$W_{\text{U.S.}}$ (in CAD)	12,000	16,000	12,000	16,000	Same distribution for $W_{\text{U.S.}}$ ...
S (CAD/USD)	1.00	1.50	1.50	1.00	and same distribution for S
$W^*_{\text{U.S.}}$ (in USD)	12,000	10,667	8,000	16,000	but the positive-cov case has ...
$E(W^*_{\text{U.S.}})$		11,333		12,000	– a lower mean $W^*_{\text{U.S.}}$ ...
$\text{std}(W^*_{\text{U.S.}})$		667		4,000	– and a lower s.d. $W^*_{\text{U.S.}}$

in USD, $W^*_{\text{U.S.}}$, because the consumption prices relevant to them are (almost) constant in USD and far less so in CAD. We can always reexpress $W^*_{\text{U.S.}}$ as CAD-measured wealth divided by the CAD/USD exchange rate, $W^*_{\text{U.S.}} = W_{\text{U.S.}}/S$. So people who care about W^* will act as if they care about wealth in CAD sure enough—because, everything else being equal, the higher their CAD wealth, the higher also their wealth in USD. The fact that, holding constant the exchange rate, they care about CAD-expressed wealth then explains why the first half of the efficiency condition looks like the Canadian investor's condition. But U.S. investors will all the time also think of the exchange rate, because deep down they care about USD-measured wealth only. It is this concern about the exchange rate that induces a second item. But, as we shall see, it is less obvious whether the U.S. investor, thinking in CAD terms but caring about USD numbers, likes exchange-rate exposure or not.

Example 19.9. In table 19.2 we have picked two examples where, in each example, there are two equally probable scenarios for CAD wealth and the exchange rate. The means and variances are the same across the two examples, but the first one has a positive association between CAD wealth and the exchange rate while in the second example the correlation is negative. We see that a larger positive covariance is a mixed blessing: it lowers both the mean (bad!) and the variance (good!). So whether on balance the effect is preferred depends on your degree of risk aversion, notably whether you attach more weight to the rise in return than to the rise in risk.

It can, in fact, be shown that investors with risk aversion equal to 1 ignore covariance with S. More risk-averse investors ($\lambda > 1$) like it because they like the variance-reduction effect, while less risk-averse people dislike it: the drop in the mean is viewed as too high a price for the lower risk. But note that, among financial economists, the consensus probably is that lambda exceeds unity. (Macroeconomists are not so sure.) Thus, the modal investor probably prefers the hedging effect and is willing to accept a lower mean return on asset j if it does help as a hedge.

What assets would be especially attractive to U.S. investors from that perspective? One might guess that U.S. stocks may be more appealing than Canadian stocks. But such a view may be simplistic, as the next subsection argues.

19.3.3   Do Assets Have a Clear Nationality?

For a better understanding of the exchange-rate covariance risk of individual assets, it is convenient to scale the covariance risk by the exchange-rate variance. Consider the following regression equation:

$$\tilde{r}_j = \alpha_{j,s} + y_j \, \tilde{s}_{\text{CAD/USD}} + \epsilon_{j,s}. \tag{19.28}$$

The regression coefficient y_j equals $\text{cov}(\tilde{r}_j, \tilde{s}) / \text{var}(\tilde{s})$, which is the asset's exchange-rate covariance risk scaled by the variance of the exchange-rate change. In this sense, y_j measures the relative exchange risk of asset j or the relative exposure of asset j to the exchange rate, in the same way beta measures the relative exposure of a stock to market movements. We now consider the exchange-rate exposure of six types of assets: a domestic and foreign risk-free asset, a foreign exporter and importer, and a domestic exporter and importer.

- Consider the domestic T-bill, asset 0. Since this return is not stochastic, it has zero exposure to the exchange rate.
- The next asset we consider is the USD T-bill, asset 1. The return, measured in CAD, on the USD T-bill increases by 1% if the CAD/USD spot rate increases by 1%. This follows from

$$\tilde{r}_{\text{USD T-bill}} \approx r^* + \tilde{s}_{\text{CAD/USD}}. \tag{19.29}$$

  Clearly, if $\tilde{r}_j = r^* + \tilde{s}_{\text{CAD/USD}}$, then, in the relative exposure regression equation (19.28), we must have $y_{\text{USD T-bill}} = 1$ (and $\alpha_{\text{USD T-bill}} = r^*$). In this sense, the exposure regression (equation (19.28)) for the foreign T-bill will reveal a very clear nationality for that asset. In CAD terms, the USD T-bill is exposed one-to-one to its "own" exchange rate, CAD/USD.

Thus far, things are clear: the home T-bill has zero exposure and the foreign one has a unit exposure. For stocks, however, nationality is much more blurred:

- Let asset 2 be a Canadian importer. Typically, an appreciation of the USD relative to the CAD is bad news for such a firm, because its costs have gone up. Thus, for a Canadian importer, the relative exposure (y_j) is negative.
- Now consider as asset 3 a Canadian producer competing against U.S. producers in the U.S. and/or Canadian market. Typically, an appreciation of the USD relative to the CAD is good news for such a firm, because its competitive position has improved. Thus, for a Canadian exporter or import-substituter, the relative exposure (y_j) is positive.
- The next case we look at is a U.S. corporation that competes against Canadian firms in the U.S. and/or Canadian market. Holding constant the USD price of the stock, a 1% appreciation of the USD adds 1% to the return on that stock in CAD. However, an appreciation of the USD

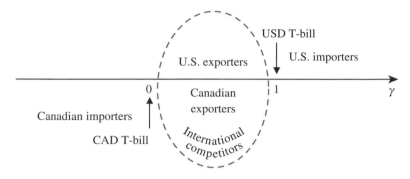

Figure 19.4. Relative exposures (γ) of various assets.

simultaneously is bad news for this company, because its competitive position has deteriorated. Thus, the price of the stock measured in USD typically drops when the USD appreciates. This drop in the USD value of the stock weakens the effect of the exchange rate itself, and will lead to a relative exposure that is below unity.

Example 19.10. Suppose that, empirically, the stock price in USD of a U.S. firm goes down by, on average, 0.25% for a 1% increase in the CAD/USD rate. This then implies that the return, in CAD, on the stock will go up by about 0.75% for a 1% rise in the CAD/USD rate. That is, the Canadian investor on average suffers a 0.25% capital loss in USD terms, which is to be subtracted from the 1% gain on the USD itself.

- Lastly, consider a U.S. importer. An appreciation of the USD relative to the CAD is good news for this U.S. firm, because its costs have gone down. Thus, for a U.S. importer, we would typically see a rise of the USD stock price, reinforcing the effect that the exchange rate itself has on the asset's CAD value. Thus, the gamma would exceed unity.

We conclude that exchange-rate covariance risks can be very different for different assets. The relative exposure of a foreign T-bill is unity, but the relative exposure of a foreign stock could be higher, or lower. Notably, there is a whole group of foreign firms with gammas below 1 and a bunch of domestic firms with gammas above 0. We'd probably better speak of all of these as internationally competing firms that do not fundamentally differ from each other. In short, unlike T-bills, their stocks have no clear-cut economic nationality.

19.3.4 The International CAPM

Let us again consider the two equations that determine the Canadian and U.S. market portfolios:

$$\text{CDN:} \quad \mathrm{E}(\tilde{r}_j - r) = \lambda \, \mathrm{cov}(\tilde{r}_j, \tilde{r}_\mathrm{p}), \tag{19.30}$$

$$\text{U.S.:} \quad \mathrm{E}(\tilde{r}_j - r) = \lambda \, \mathrm{cov}(\tilde{r}_j, \tilde{r}_{p*}) + (1 - \lambda) \, \mathrm{cov}(\tilde{r}_j, \tilde{s}). \tag{19.31}$$

In technical note 19.3 it is shown that these equations can be aggregated into the following:

$$E(\tilde{r}_j - r) = \lambda \, \text{cov}(\tilde{r}_j, \tilde{r}_w) + \kappa \, \text{cov}(\tilde{r}_j, \tilde{s}), \qquad (19.32)$$

with $\tilde{r}_w$ referring to the return on the world market portfolio and κ being a function of the national invested wealths and the national (unity minus) risk aversions. Compared with the country-by-country efficiency conditions, what we now have on the right-hand side is a covariance with the *world* market portfolio, which is more observable than the national portfolios, and a covariance with exchange rate, the result of taking into account the heterogeneous expectations induced by exchange-rate uncertainty.

This is, again, half a CAPM in the sense that it tells us what expected returns should be, taking into account the risks of the assets. As before, we need to know the prices of risk before this is of any use whatsoever to an investor or analyst. The approach is the same as before except that we now need two benchmarks. If we pick the world market portfolio and the USD treasury bill, a simple generalization of the one-country CAPM emerges, as shown in technical note 19.4,

$$E(\tilde{r}_j - r) = \beta_{j,w}E(\tilde{r}_w - r) + y_{j,s}E(\tilde{s} + r^* - r), \qquad (19.33)$$

where β and y are from the multiple regression that combines the market model and the exposure model we considered in the preceding subsection:

$$\tilde{r}_j = \alpha_{j;w,s} + \beta_{j,w;s}\tilde{r}_w + y_{j,s;w}\tilde{s} + \tilde{\epsilon}_{j;w,s}. \qquad (19.34)$$

The subscripts "j" and "s" to β should remind you that this is not the simple beta we are used to: we are now holding constant the exchange rate. Likewise, the subscripts "j" and "w" to gamma tell you we are now holding constant the world market return, unlike in the simple exposure regression we looked at a few pages ago.

To interpret the regression (19.34) and the international CAPM (19.33), note that the regression again identifies the best possible replication of asset j that one can achieve using the two benchmark portfolios, the world market portfolio and the foreign T-bill, along with the risk-free asset.

Example 19.11. Suppose that, for a U.S. stock, the coefficients in equation (19.34) are estimated as $\beta_{j,w;s} = 1.2$ and $y_{j,s;w} = 0.75$. Consider portfolios that consist of an investment in the world market portfolio (with weight x_w), an investment in the USD T-bill (with weight x_s), and weight $1 - x_w - x_s$ invested in the CAD risk-free asset. If $\beta_j = 1.2$ and $y_j = 0.75$, we invest $x_w = 1.2$ in the world market portfolio, $x_s = 0.75$ in the USD T-bill, and $1 - 1.20 - 0.75 = -0.95$ in the domestic risk-free asset. This portfolio provides the best possible replication of the return from asset j using just the two benchmark portfolios as replicating instruments.

The international CAPM then says that the expected return on a stock j is the same as the expected return on the stock's best replication portfolio (see technical note 19.5 for the details).

Example 19.12. Continue the same example ($\beta_{j,\mathrm{w;s}} = 1.2$ and $\gamma_{j,\mathrm{s;w}} = 0.75$). If the world market portfolio has an estimated risk premium of 0.05 and the currency of 0.01 p.a., then the expected risk premium on the stock is estimated as $1.2 \times 0.05 + 0.75 \times 0.01 = 0.0675$, or 6.75% (on top of the risk-free rate).

19.3.5 The *n*-Country CAPM

The "world" (in the sense of the integrated capital market) has far more than two countries. The generalization of the two-country model is obvious. First, there will be as many gammas as there are exchange rates in the world. Second, the beta and the gammas must be estimated from one regression containing r_w and all the $\tilde{s}_i$s,

$$E(\tilde{r}_j - r) = \beta_{j,\mathrm{w};..}E(\tilde{r}_\mathrm{w} - r) + \gamma_{j,s_1;..}E(\tilde{s}_1 + r_1^* - r)$$
$$+ \gamma_{j,s_2;..}E(\tilde{s}_2 + r_2^* - r) + \cdots + \gamma_{j,s_n;..}E(\tilde{s}_n + r_n^* - r), \quad (19.35)$$

where beta and the n gammas are from the multiple regression that combines the market model and n exposure models, one per currency, that we considered in the preceding subsection:[12]

$$r_j = \alpha_{j,\mathrm{w};\underline{s}} + \beta_{j,\mathrm{w};..}r_\mathrm{w} + \gamma_{j,s_1;..}\tilde{s}_1 + \gamma_{j,s_2;..}\tilde{s}_2 + \cdots + \gamma_{j,s_n;..}\tilde{s}_n + \epsilon_{j;\mathrm{w},\underline{s}}. \quad (19.36)$$

In practical applications, restraint is recommended, as Goethe would readily concur. A CAPM *cum* regression of 150 terms will not do: it would add more noise than information. One reason is that exchange-risk premia $E(\tilde{s} + r^* - r)$ are empirically small, have a long-run mean that is hard to statistically distinguish from zero, and are not easy to estimate with reasonable precision. Also, gammas are similarly difficult to estimate precisely. So my advice is to surely restrict, a priori, the list of countries to those where there is a good common-sense reason for expecting an exposure, and censor away the gammas with the wrong size or sign. Personally I would perhaps even entirely omit the exposure terms: given the uncertainties surrounding the risk premia and the exposures, one might just work with the world-market term in the InCAPM, and simply widen the scope of the sensitivity analysis that should be part and parcel of every capital-budgeting exercise:

$$E(\tilde{r}_j - r) \approx \beta_{j,\mathrm{w};..}E(\tilde{r}_\mathrm{w} - r). \quad (19.37)$$

The only surviving difference with the standard CAPM would then be the use of a world market as benchmark, and the multiple beta.[13]

---

[12] Apologies for the baroque subscripts. The semicolon usually initiates a list of variables that are held constant. Here the list would be too long, so we drop it. Still, you should remember that these are multiple-regression coefficients, measuring the impact of one variable holding constant the other ones.

[13] The need to still use a multivariate regression even in the truncated model follows from the fact that our basic model is equation (19.32), not equation (19.22). Equation (19.32) simplifies to the univariate equation, (19.22), only if either the prices of exchange covariance risk, η_k, are

19.3.6 Empirical Tests of the International CAPM

In this chapter, we are suggesting that you replace your familiar single-market CAPM equation by a more complicated version, equation (19.35) or (19.37). The first issue is whether one of the basic assumptions of the international model, the absence of controls on capital flows, is reasonable. Second, are the empirical data compatible with the international CAPM and, if so, can we also reject the single-country view of the world?

Let us first examine the effect of direct controls on foreign investment. The controls may either limit foreign investment into a country or restrict domestic residents from investing abroad. Restrictions on foreign investment into a country may be imposed in different ways, in the form of a limit on the fraction of equity that can be held by foreigners or a restriction on the types of industries in which foreigners can invest. Historical details on the type and magnitude of these restrictions can be found in Eun and Janakiramanan (1986, table 1). There may also be domestic controls on how much a resident can invest abroad. For example, Japanese insurance companies could not invest more than 30% of their portfolio in foreign assets at the time, and only 30% of Spanish pension funds could be invested abroad. Two questions need to be answered. One, if these restrictions exist, do they have a significant impact on the choice of the optimal portfolio and hence, potentially, on asset pricing? Two, how significant are these constraints today?

Bonser-Neal et al. (1990) examine whether the restrictions on investing abroad are binding. They look at closed-end country funds and find that these mutual funds trade at premia relative to their net asset values, indicating that the French, Japanese, Korean, and Mexican markets are at least partially segmented from the U.S. capital market. Hietala (1989) studies the effects of the Finnish law that prevented investors from investing in foreign securities and finds that there is a significant difference between the returns on domestic assets required by residents compared with foreigners. Gultekin et al. (1989) find strong evidence that the U.S. and Japanese markets were segmented prior to 1980. However, while there were substantial controls on capital flows before the 1980s, this is no longer true. Halliday (1989) was already reporting that even in those days there were few constraints on investing in foreign stock markets. This was and is especially true for investing in the markets of developed countries. For example, in the 1980s there were already no controls on international investment into or from Austria, Belgium, Denmark, Ireland, Italy, Japan, the Netherlands, the United Kingdom, the United States, and West

---

all zero, or the covariances between asset returns and exchange-rate changes themselves are zero. The first case requires very special utility functions (with $\lambda = 1$) and the second case cannot possibly be true for all assets and home currencies simultaneously. Thus, we do need the multivariate model. Moreover, although the risk premium for exchange risk can be small it is unlikely to be exactly zero. That is, we use the one-factor world model merely as an approximation. If we, in addition, used a univariate beta, we would be introducing another (unnecessary) error to the approximation.

Germany. The controls studied by Hietala (1989) and Gultekin et al. (1989) were removed in 1986 and 1980, respectively. Also, looking at restrictions that limit domestic residents from investing abroad, one sees that these constraints are often not binding. For example, Fairlamb (1989) reports that in 1988 only 8% of Spanish funds were actually invested in foreign assets, while the limit was 30%. Thus, while direct controls on foreign investment may have been important in the past, they are probably no longer an important determinant of portfolio choice and asset pricing in the main OECD countries.

Let us now discuss the more direct tests of international asset pricing models. Solnik (1974), who did the first theoretical and empirical work in international asset pricing, tests a special case of equation (19.35), where the world market risk premium and exposure risk premia could be merged into one single term. He concludes that the data are consistent with his international CAPM, although he does not test his model against the single-country alternative.

An early test that does compare an international asset pricing model against the single-country alternative was carried out by Stehle (1977). Specifically, Stehle tries to find out empirically whether U.S. stocks are priced in a national market or in a world market. He, too, uses a restricted version of equation (19.35), assuming that λ equals unity so that all currency risk premia disappear. The only remaining difference between the international model (equation (19.35)) and the national model is the definition of the market portfolio. Specifically, in equation (19.35), the benchmark portfolio is the world market portfolio, while in equation (19.23), it is the national market portfolio. Stehle's tests are not able to empirically reject one in favor of the other, and Stehle concludes that asset pricing is done in a single-market context. Dumas (1977), however, argues that when the data do not allow us to distinguish between single-country asset pricing and international asset pricing, then we ought to retain the simplest view, that is, we should conclude that there is one international market instead of the many separate national markets.

There have been many additional empirical investigations, with a large portion of them testing special restricted versions of equation (19.35). The conclusions tended to be ambiguous. But more recent work has come up with more definite answers. As already mentioned, Gultekin et al. (1989) provide strong evidence that the U.S. and Japanese markets were segmented prior to 1980. However, they also show that after the enactment of the Foreign Exchange and Foreign Trade Control law in 1980, there is no longer any significant evidence against the hypothesis that U.S. and Japanese stocks are priced in an integrated market. A careful, and more recent, test is by Dumas and Solnik (1995). They test the Solnik–Sercu international CAPM, allowing for changes in risks and risk premia over time. Using data from major OECD countries, they reject Stehle's hypothesis that the exposure risk premia, y_i, are zero, but they do not reject the full version (with nonzero risk premia for exchange-rate exposure). They also reject single-country asset pricing (with a purely local

Table 19.3. Rules for the capital-budgeting process: overview.

	CoCa model	Currency of calculations
1. Foreign investments:		
• Home and host financially integrated	InCAPM	FC and HC
• Home and host financially segmented		
• Home country part of larger financial market	InCAPM	HC only
• Home country totally isolated	CAPM	HC only
2. Domestic investments		
• Home country part of larger financial market	InCAPM	n.a.
• Home country totally isolated	CAPM	n.a.

benchmark). All of this lends support to the international CAPM, at least for the major OECD countries that do not impose explicit restrictions on capital movement. There are also a few papers by De Santis and Gérard (1997, 1998) that allow for autocorrelation in not just expected returns but also in variances and covariances, modeling the fact that risk comes in waves. Their work confirms that exchange-rate exposure is often nonzero and earns a statistically significant premium.

19.4 The CFO's Summary re Capital Budgeting

International asset pricing is potentially complicated by two extra issues: exchange risk and segmentation of capital markets. If the capital market of the home country and the host country are integrated, the cash flows of an investment project can be valued in any currency, including the host currency. This simplifies capital budgeting in the sense that no exchange-rate forecasts seem to be necessary for the translation. On the other hand, in integrated markets it becomes impossible to observe the portfolio of risky assets held by the average investor in any of the individual countries. Thus, the international CAPM has to be used, which means that, in principle, exchange-rate expectations and exposures still show up in the cost of capital. In short, forecasts and exposures can only be eliminated by cutting corners.

Thus, the first issue is whether or not there is integration. Having selected either the single-country CAPM or the international CAPM, the next issue is to obtain estimates of the model parameters. We need the stock market sensitivity or beta and, in the international CAPM, the exchange-rate exposures. We also need the expected return on the corresponding benchmark portfolios.

19.4.1 Determining the Relevant Model

If the capital market of the home country and the host country are segmented from each other, the investing firm should set the cost of capital equal to the return that is expected by its own shareholders. This means that a particular investment may be profitable for a foreign firm but not profitable for a local firm.

Example 19.13. At the time of writing, the Chilean stock market remains strongly segmented from the rest of the world. If a Chilean firm makes an investment in Chile, the firm will estimate the beta by regressing returns from a portfolio of stocks in the same industry on the Chilean stock market index. Note that the returns from this investment are likely to be strongly correlated with the Chilean market index because there are important common factors, like the business cycle or interest rates, that affect all Chilean firms in similar ways. Thus, the investment is relatively risky for a Chilean firm. But the same project may be low-risk from the point of view of, say, an Austrian firm. The reason is that, because the Chilean economy is only loosely connected to North America, Europe, and Asia, the returns from the Chilean project will not be highly correlated with the returns on the typical world investor's portfolio, which is strongly diversified internationally. So the investment adds little to the risk of an international portfolio, but much more to the risk of a purely Chilean portfolio.

Note that segmentation of the home-country and the host-country capital markets does not mean that each market is a single-country market. The shareholders of the Austrian firm are likely to live in many different countries, and they all have access to non-Austrian shares, too. Thus, it is appropriate for the Austrian firm to set its cost of capital using an international model, that is, using the "world" market portfolio as a proxy for the true benchmark relevant to its shareholders.

19.4.2 Estimating the Risk of a Project

The market risk and the exchange risk exposures are defined as the slope coefficients in the regression of j's return on the world market return and all relevant exchange-rate changes. Estimates obtained from time series of past data are subject to substantial estimation errors, stemming from pure sample-specific coincidences. A standard solution is to estimate the risks from returns on industry portfolios rather than from individual stock data. That is, one estimates returns on, typically, an equally weighted portfolio of all stocks in the same industry i: one then estimates the risks by regressing industry-portfolio returns rather than individual stock returns. The underlying idea is that, as portfolio returns are more diversified, there is less residual noise in the regression, which improves the quality of the estimates.

Example 19.14. Suppose that Toyota considers building a new plant in the United Kingdom, which would sell its output in the entire European Union. Then Toyota could estimate the beta and gammas of the European car industry as a whole, rather than estimating the risks using just a simple stock.

Still, the portfolio approach assumes that all firms in the index have the same risks. In practice, one would often have serious difficulties in identifying a sufficiently large number of firms that have the same exposure as the project at hand.

Example 19.15. Suppose that Oerlikon, a Swiss firm, wants to build a plant for the production and sale of maintenance welding electrodes in India. There may be a number of Indian firms active in the welding industry, but not one of them is priced in the OECD capital market. Hence, Oerlikon cannot directly measure the risk of the Indian welding industry relative to the world market portfolio.[14] Thus, when valuing the project, Oerlikon would have to use an indirect, forward-looking approach to assess the risk. For instance, Oerlikon could argue that (1) the maintenance welding industry is not very cyclical, (2) the Indian business cycle is still largely independent of economic cycles in the OECD, so that (3) the beta of this Indian project relative to the OECD market portfolio is bound to be low. In addition, Oerlikon could argue that the exposures of rupee cash flows to OECD exchange rates are small or zero because the Indian economy is still relatively closed. In short, beta is probably low, the rupee gamma is probably equal to unity or thereabouts (as cash flows are unexposed in rupee terms), and the other gammas must be close to zero.

Data availability is just one possible issue. The relevance of any available data is another. As pointed out in chapter 13, exchange risk exposure when you are at the top of a PPP-deviation cycle would be very different from an exposure when the currency is at a low, in real terms. In such case, rather than estimating a misleading gamma you could (i) work with forward-looking scenarios (see chapter 13) and then hedge the currency effect on the basis of the implied exposure, or (ii) ignore currency elements in the cost of capital, and widen the range of the sensitivity analyses.

19.4.3 Estimating the Risk Premia

Assuming that we have an approximate idea of the beta and gammas, we need estimates of the expected risk premia per unit of risk. The expected excess return on the world market portfolio is still rather hard to estimate, even though it is not quite as bad as a typical currency-risk premium. The sample averages of returns observed in the past differ substantially across sample periods, and it is also known that the expected return changes over time.[15] Still, we know that there is a positive risk premium on the world stock market, and variations over time in the expected excess return may not be overly important

---

[14] A procedure that consists of translating rupee returns on Indian stocks into an OECD currency and then estimating the risks is flawed because the prices of these Indian companies in the Bombay stock market are different from what they would have been if the assets had been priced internationally.

[15] The return is partially predictable on the basis of (1) the risk spread (the difference between low-grade bond yields and government bond yields), (2) the term spread (the difference between short-term and long-term bond yields), and (3) the dividend yield.

when the NPV evaluation horizon is, say, one decade rather than a month or two days.

Turning to the expected excess return on the various foreign T-bills, these risk premia also change over time, as we have seen in chapter 10, and, unlike for the world market risk premium, we are not even sure whether the long-run mean actually differs from zero. Since exchange risk premia are small in the short run and close to zero in the long run, for practical applications one might have to be content with an approach that ignores these and use the following simplified version of equation (19.35):

$$E(\tilde{r}_j - r) \approx \beta_{j,w;s} E(\tilde{r}_w - r), \tag{19.38}$$

where the beta is still estimated from a multivariate regression (equation (19.36)) rather than from a bivariate regression.

You should not be overly discouraged by these approximations. No model is perfect; and the international CAPM does work better than competing models. Still, the cost of capital is measured imperfectly, and NPV computations should always be undertaken for a whole range of reasonable discount rates, to see to what extent the accept/reject recommendation is sensitive to the estimate of the cost of capital.

19.5 Technical Notes

Technical note 19.1 (the efficiency condition). Let the desirability of the portfolio p be denoted by $V_p = V(E(\tilde{r}_p - r), \mathrm{var}(\tilde{r}_p))$. The optimum is found by setting, for each risky asset j, the derivative of V_p with respect to x_j equal to zero. The effect of a small change in x_j on V_p works through two channels—the expectation and the variance—so below we see x_js effect on V_p via the mean, and similarly x_js effect on V_p via the variance. In the second line we fill in the effect of x_j on mean and variance, equations (19.15) and (19.16):

$$\begin{aligned}
0 = \frac{\partial V}{\partial x_j} &= \frac{\partial V}{\partial E(\cdot)} \frac{\partial E(\cdot)}{\partial x_j} + \frac{\partial V}{\partial \mathrm{var}(\cdot)} \frac{\partial \mathrm{var}(\cdot)}{\partial x_j} \\
&= \frac{\partial V}{\partial E(\cdot)} E(\tilde{r}_j - r) + \frac{\partial V}{\partial \mathrm{var}(\cdot)} 2\, \mathrm{cov}(\tilde{r}_j, \tilde{r}_p), \\
\implies \quad 0 &= E(\tilde{r}_j - r) - \lambda_p \, \mathrm{cov}(\tilde{r}_j, \tilde{r}_p),
\end{aligned} \tag{19.39}$$

where

$$\lambda_p := -2 \frac{\partial V / \partial \mathrm{var}(\cdot)}{\partial V / \partial E(\cdot)}.$$

This is a positive number since a higher variance lowers the desirability V while a higher expected return increases it. Crypto-mathematicians recognize this ratio of partial derivatives as the implicit derivative (or marginal trade-off) of mean for variance in the chosen solution.

Technical note 19.2 (using Ito's lemma to transcribe the FC efficiency condition). Start by relating the CAD return on j to the USD return: $1 + \tilde{r}_j = (1 + \tilde{r}_j^*)(1 + \tilde{s})$, with $\tilde{s} = \Delta S/S$ and S is CAD/USD. Solve for $\tilde{r}_j^*$ and Taylor expand as follows:

$$\tilde{r}_j^* = \frac{1 + \tilde{r}_j}{1 + \tilde{s}} - 1 \approx \tilde{r}_j - \tilde{s} - [\tilde{r}_j\, \tilde{s}] + \tilde{s}^2. \tag{19.40}$$

A readily acceptable result of Ito's lemma is that, for shorter and shorter holding periods, products of three or more returns become too small to matter. This, firstly, justifies the above second-order expansion. It also means that if we consider covariances of two FC returns, we only need to look at first-order terms,

$$\begin{aligned} \mathrm{cov}(\tilde{r}_j^*, \tilde{r}_k^*) &\approx \mathrm{cov}(\tilde{r}_j - \tilde{s}, \tilde{r}_k - \tilde{s}) \\ &= \mathrm{cov}(\tilde{r}_j, \tilde{r}_k) - \mathrm{cov}(\tilde{r}_j, \tilde{s}) - \mathrm{cov}(\tilde{r}_k, \tilde{s}) + \mathrm{var}(\tilde{s}), \end{aligned} \tag{19.41}$$

because all the other terms would lead to products of three or four returns.

Also, one often reads that inside an expectation only the first-order terms matter, because products of returns are second order of smalls. But this is patently wrong. Indeed, variances and covariances of returns are averages of products of two returns, but this surely does not mean that they can be set equal to zero. Now the expectation of, say, the third term is

$$\mathrm{E}(\tilde{r}_j^*\, \tilde{s}) = \mathrm{E}(\tilde{r}_j^*)\, \mathrm{E}(\tilde{s}) + \mathrm{cov}(\tilde{r}_j^*, \tilde{s}). \tag{19.42}$$

If we let the periods over which one observes the return become shorter and shorter, all means and all (co)variances shrink roughly in proportion to the time interval Δt, so they preserve the same order of magnitude relative to each other. But this means that the product of two means, $\mathrm{E}(\tilde{r}_j^*)\, \mathrm{E}(\tilde{s})$, shrinks to zero much faster than the covariance. That is, the product of two means is second order of smalls but the covariance is not:

$$\mathrm{E}(\tilde{r}_j^*\, \tilde{s}) \approx \mathrm{cov}(\tilde{r}_j, \tilde{s}) \quad \text{and} \quad \mathrm{E}(\tilde{s}^2) \approx \mathrm{var}(\tilde{s}).$$

Using the above in equation (19.40), we get the following translated expected return:[16]

$$\mathrm{E}(\tilde{r}_j^*) \approx \mathrm{E}(\tilde{r}_j) - \mathrm{E}(\tilde{s}) - \mathrm{cov}(\tilde{r}_{p*}^*, \tilde{s}) + \mathrm{var}(\tilde{s}). \tag{19.43}$$

Our results (19.43) and (19.41) for the translated mean and variance imply that the efficiency condition (19.26) translates into the first equation below. We next write that equation for the special case where asset j is the HC risk-free asset,

---

[16] Note, in passing, how we recover our earlier numerical result that covariance between the CAD asset return and the CAD/USD exchange rate lowers the expected USD return. We also discover that exchange risk has its impact on the expected return too. So both the covariance and the variance have both "good" and "bad" aspects.

and lastly we perform the following subtraction:

$$E(\tilde{r}_j) - \quad E(\tilde{s}) \quad - \text{cov}(\tilde{r}_j, \tilde{s}) \quad + \text{var}(\tilde{s}) = \lambda\,[\text{cov}(\tilde{r}_j, \tilde{r}_{p*}) \quad - \text{cov}(\tilde{r}_j, \tilde{s})$$
$$\qquad\qquad\qquad\qquad\qquad\qquad\qquad\qquad\qquad\qquad - \text{cov}(\tilde{r}_{p*}, \tilde{s}) + \text{var}(\tilde{s})]$$
$$r - \qquad E(\tilde{s}) \quad - 0 \qquad\quad + \text{var}(\tilde{s}) = \lambda\,[0 \qquad\quad - 0$$
$$\qquad\qquad\qquad\qquad\qquad\qquad\qquad\qquad\qquad\qquad - \text{cov}(\tilde{r}_{p*}, \tilde{s}) + \text{var}(\tilde{s})]$$

$$E(\tilde{r}_j) - r \qquad - \text{cov}(\tilde{r}_j, \tilde{s}) \qquad\qquad = \lambda\,[\text{cov}(\tilde{r}_j, \tilde{r}_{p*}) \quad - \text{cov}(\tilde{r}_j, \tilde{s})]$$

which leads to (19.27) and (19.31).

Technical note 19.3 (aggregating the two efficiency conditions). We want to aggregate, and obtain the world-market return, which is defined as

$$\tilde{r}_{\text{w}} = \frac{W_{\text{Ca}}\tilde{r}_{\text{p}} + W_{\text{U.S.}}\tilde{r}_{p*}}{W_{\text{Ca}} + W_{\text{U.S.}}} \tag{19.44}$$

with W_{Ca} and $W_{\text{U.S.}}$ defined as the invested wealths, both measured in CAD, of Canada and the United States, respectively. To build this world return into the model we multiply both sides of (19.30) by W_{Ca}, and (19.31) by $W_{\text{U.S.}}$. On the right-hand sides of the equations below we have immediately put these factors inside the covariances. Next we sum the two equations, and lastly we divide by total world wealth and use (19.44):

$$W_{\text{Ca}}E(\tilde{r}_j - r) = \lambda\,\text{cov}(\tilde{r}_j, W_{\text{Ca}}\,\tilde{r}_{\text{p}})$$
$$W_{\text{U.S.}}E(\tilde{r}_j - r) = \lambda\,\text{cov}(\tilde{r}_j, W_{\text{U.S.}}\,\tilde{r}_{p*})$$
$$\qquad\qquad\qquad\qquad + W_{\text{U.S.}}(1 - \lambda)\,\text{cov}(\tilde{r}_j, s)$$

$$(W_{\text{Ca}} + W_{\text{U.S.}})E(\tilde{r}_j - r) = \lambda\,\text{cov}(\tilde{r}_j, (W_{\text{Ca}}\,\tilde{r}_{\text{p}} + W_{\text{U.S.}}\,\tilde{r}_{p*}))$$
$$\qquad\qquad\qquad\qquad + W_{\text{U.S.}}(1 - \lambda)\,\text{cov}(\tilde{r}_j, s)$$

$$\implies \quad E(\tilde{r}_j - r) = \lambda\,\text{cov}(\tilde{r}_j, \tilde{r}_{\text{w}}) + \frac{W_{\text{U.S.}}}{W_{\text{Ca}} + W_{\text{U.S.}}}(1 - \lambda)\,\text{cov}(\tilde{r}_j, s).$$

For ease of manipulation, in (19.32) we denote

$$\frac{W_{\text{U.S.}}}{W_{\text{Ca}} + W_{\text{U.S.}}}(1 - \lambda) = \kappa.$$

Technical note 19.4 (identifying λ and κ). Write the equation in matrix form:

$$E(\tilde{r}_j - r) = \begin{bmatrix} \text{cov}(\tilde{r}_j, r_{\text{w}}) & \text{cov}(\tilde{r}_j, \tilde{s}) \end{bmatrix} \begin{bmatrix} \lambda \\ \kappa \end{bmatrix}. \tag{19.45}$$

To identify λ and κ we write this for two benchmarks, the world market portfolio with return r_{w} and the USD T-bill with return $r^* + \tilde{s}$:

$$\begin{bmatrix} E(\tilde{r}_{\text{w}} - r) \\ r^* + E(\tilde{s}) - r \end{bmatrix} = \begin{bmatrix} \text{var}(\tilde{r}_{\text{w}}) & \text{cov}(\tilde{r}_{\text{w}}, \tilde{s}) \\ \text{cov}(\tilde{r}_{\text{w}}, \tilde{s}) & \text{var}(\tilde{s}) \end{bmatrix} \times \begin{bmatrix} \lambda \\ \kappa \end{bmatrix}, \tag{19.46}$$

$$\implies \quad \begin{bmatrix} \lambda \\ \kappa \end{bmatrix} = \begin{bmatrix} \text{var}(\tilde{r}_{\text{w}}) & \text{cov}(\tilde{r}_{\text{w}}, \tilde{s}) \\ \text{cov}(\tilde{r}_{\text{w}}, \tilde{s}) & \text{var}(\tilde{s}) \end{bmatrix}^{-1} \begin{bmatrix} E(\tilde{r}_{\text{w}} - r) \\ r^* + E(\tilde{s}) - r \end{bmatrix}. \tag{19.47}$$

This can be substituted back into (19.45). Now the covariance matrix of $(\tilde{r}_w, \tilde{s})$ premultiplied by the vector of covariances of r_j with these same variables $(\tilde{r}_w, \tilde{s})$ is the row vector of multiple regression coefficients of r_j onto $(\tilde{r}_w, \tilde{s})$—a generalization of $b = \text{cov}(\tilde{y}, \tilde{x}) \times \text{var}(\tilde{x})^{-1}$ in $\tilde{y} = a + b\tilde{x} + \tilde{e}$:

$$
\begin{aligned}
&\mathrm{E}(\tilde{r}_j - r) \\
&\quad = \begin{bmatrix} \text{cov}(\tilde{r}_j, r_w) & \text{cov}(\tilde{r}_j, \tilde{s}) \end{bmatrix} \begin{bmatrix} \text{var}(\tilde{r}_w) & \text{cov}(\tilde{r}_w, \tilde{s}) \\ \text{cov}(\tilde{r}_w, \tilde{s}) & \text{var}(\tilde{s}) \end{bmatrix}^{-1} \begin{bmatrix} \mathrm{E}(\tilde{r}_w - r) \\ r^* + \mathrm{E}(\tilde{s}) - r \end{bmatrix} \\
&\quad = \begin{bmatrix} \beta_{j,\text{w};\text{s}} & \gamma_{j,\text{s};\text{w}} \end{bmatrix} \begin{bmatrix} \mathrm{E}(\tilde{r}_w - r) \\ r^* + \mathrm{E}(\tilde{s}) - r \end{bmatrix}. \quad\quad\quad (19.48)
\end{aligned}
$$

Technical note 19.5 (the best-replication reading of the InCAPM). The claim can be shown as follows. In the first line, we write the return on a general portfolio with weights x_w and x_s for the world market and the foreign T-bill, and in the second line we group terms in x_w and x_s:

$$
\mathrm{E}(\tilde{r}_{j\text{'s replication}}) = x_w \mathrm{E}(\tilde{r}_w) + x_s(r^* + \tilde{s}) + (1 - x_w - x_s)r \quad\quad (19.49)
$$
$$
= r + x_w \mathrm{E}(\tilde{r}_w - r) + x_s(r^* + \mathrm{E}(\tilde{s}) - r). \quad\quad (19.50)
$$

For best replication, we have to set $x_w = \beta_{j,\text{w};\text{s}}$ and $x_s = \gamma_{j,\text{s};\text{w}}$. Thus,

$$
\mathrm{E}(\tilde{r}_{j\text{'s replication}} - r) = \beta_{j,\text{w};\text{s}} \mathrm{E}(\tilde{r}_w - r) + \gamma_{j,\text{s};\text{w}}(r^* + \mathrm{E}(\tilde{s}) - r). \quad\quad (19.51)
$$

TEST YOUR UNDERSTANDING

Basics of the CAPM

Quiz Questions

True–False Questions

1. The risk of a portfolio is measured by the standard deviation of its return.

2. The risk of an asset is measured by the standard deviation of its return.

3. Each asset's contribution to the total risk of a portfolio is measured by the asset's contribution to the total return on the portfolio.

4. A risk-averse investor always prefers the highest possible return for a given level of risk or the lowest risk for a given level of expected return.

5. The means and standard deviations of all optimal portfolios selected from a risk-free asset and a set of risky assets are found on the line that originates at r_0 and is tangent to the efficient portfolio of risky assets.

6. Relative risk aversion shows the price in currency units of a given amount of risk.

7. Relative risk aversion varies from asset to asset because some assets are riskier than others.

8. Portfolio theory assumes that all investors are equally risk averse.

Multiple-Choice Questions

1. When using portfolio theory, we must make a number of assumptions. Which of the following assumptions are made? Which are not?

   (a) The rates of inflation at home and abroad are equal.
   (b) There is no information or transaction costs.
   (c) There are no taxes.
   (d) Investors want to know the distribution of wealth at the end of the period.
   (e) Investors care about the future expected return on their portfolio and the variability of this return.

Applications

1. The country Prince Rupert's Land (PRL) has two companies, the Hudson Bay Company (HBC) and the Boston Tea Traders (BTT). In equilibrium, the returns of these two companies have the following distributions:

	Expected excess return	Covariances HBC	BTT
HBC	0.11	0.04	0.01
BTT	0.08	0.01	0.02

   (a) Vary the weight of HBC from 0 to 1 by increments of 0.1 and compute how the portfolio covariance risks of HBC and BTT change as a function of the weights x_{HBC} and $x_{BTT} = 1 - x_{HBC}$.
   (b) Find the optimal weights of x_{HBC} and $x_{BTT} = 1 - x_{HBC}$ and the average risk aversion.
   (c) If the total value of the PRL stock market portfolio is 1,000, what are the values of HBC and BTT?

2. Consider the following covariance matrix and expected return vector for assets 1, 2, and 3:

$$V = \begin{bmatrix} 0.0100 & 0.0020 & 0.0010 \\ 0.0020 & 0.0025 & 0.0030 \\ 0.0010 & 0.0030 & 0.0100 \end{bmatrix} \quad \text{and} \quad E(\tilde{r}_j) = \begin{bmatrix} 0.0330 \\ 0.0195 \\ 0.0250 \end{bmatrix}.$$

(a) Compute the expected return on a portfolio with weights for assets j = $0, \ldots, 3$ equal to $[0.2, 0.4, 0.2, 0.2]$, when the T-bill (asset 0) yields a return of 1%. Do so directly, and then via the excess returns.

(b) Compute the variance of the same portfolio.

(c) Compute the covariance of the return on each asset with the total portfolio return and verify that it is a weighted covariance.

(d) Is the above portfolio efficient?

(e) Are the following portfolios efficient?

  - Weights $(0.7, 0.1, 0.1, 0.1)$ for assets $j = 0, \ldots, 3$.
  - Weights $(0.6, 0.2, 0.1, 0.1)$ for assets $j = 0, \ldots, 3$.

(f) What is the portfolio held by an investor with risk-aversion measure $\lambda = 2.5$?

(g) Assume that there are no "outside" bills, that is, all risk-free lending and borrowing is among investors. Therefore, the average investor holds only risky assets. What is the portfolio composition? What is the average investor's risk-aversion measure λ?

International CAPM

Quiz Questions

True–False Questions

1. The entire NPV analysis can be conducted in terms of the host (foreign) currency if money markets and exchange markets are fully integrated with the home market.

2. The entire NPV analysis can be conducted in terms of the host currency if money markets, stock markets, and exchange markets are fully integrated with the home market.

3. Forward rates can be used as the risk-adjusted expected future spot rates to translate the host-currency cash flows into the home currency. The home-currency cash flows can then be discounted at the appropriate home-currency discount rate if money markets and exchange markets are fully integrated with the home market.

4. Regardless of the degree of market integration, the host-currency expected cash flows can always be translated into the home currency (by multiplying them by the expected spot rate), and then discounted at the home-currency discount rate.

5. Regardless of the degree of market integration, the host-currency expected cash flows can always be translated into expected cash flows expressed in home currency. The home-currency cash flows can then be discounted at the home-currency discount rate that takes into account all risks.

6. If you use the forward rate as the risk-adjusted expected spot rate, there is no need to worry about the dependence between the exchange rate and the host-currency cash flows.

7. If markets are integrated and you translate at the forward rate, the cost of capital need not include a risk premium for exchange-rate exposure.

8. If markets are integrated and you translate at the forward rate, the cost of capital need not include a risk premium for exposure to any currency.

9. If you discount expected cash flows that are already expressed in home currency, the cost of capital should include a risk premium for exposure to the host-currency exchange rate.

10. If you discount expected cash flows that are already expressed in home currency, the cost of capital should include a risk premium for exposure to all relevant exchange rates.

11. If you translate at the forward rate, you can entirely omit exchange-rate expectations from the NPV procedure.

12. Exchange rate risk premia are sizable. In fact, they are about as large as the (world) market risk premium.

13. A highly risk-averse investor will only accept variance risk if he or she is fully certain to be compensated for this risk.

14. A highly risk-averse investor will never select a high-variance portfolio.

15. A risk-averse investor will select a high-variance portfolio only if the expected excess return is sufficiently high.

16. A risk-averse investor will select a low-return portfolio only if the variance is sufficiently low.

17. A particularly risk-averse investor will always select a low-return portfolio. This is because low return means low risk, and because the investor does not want to bear a lot of risk.

For the next set of questions, assume that access to money markets and exchange markets is unrestricted and the host-currency cash flow is risk free. Are the following statements true or false?

1. You can translate at the expected spot rate and discount at a risk-adjusted home-currency cost of capital.

2. You can translate at the forward rate and discount at a home-currency rate that takes into account exchange risk.

3. You can translate at the forward rate and discount at the risk-free home-currency rate.

4. You can discount the host-currency cash flows at the foreign risk-free rate and then translate the result at the current spot exchange rate.

5. You can discount the host-currency cash flows at the foreign risk-free rate and then translate the result at the expected future spot exchange rate.

6. You can discount the host-currency cash flows at the foreign risk-free rate and then translate the result at the forward exchange rate.

7. If access to forward markets or foreign and domestic money markets is restricted, then the true value is always overstated if the foreign currency cash flow is translated at the forward exchange rate and then discounted at the domestic risk-free rate.

Additional Quiz Questions

1. Suppose that you observe an efficient portfolio. There are two methods with which you can infer the degree of risk aversion of the investor that selects this particular portfolio. What are these two methods?

2. What is wrong with the following statement: "The CAPM says that the expected return on a given stock j is equal to the best possible replication that one can obtain by using the risk-free assets and the set of all risky assets (other than stock j)."

3. Below, we reproduce some equations from the derivation of the CAPM. Equation (20.1) is the efficiency criterion. Equation (19.59) is the CAPM. Explain the equations:

$$\frac{E(\tilde{r}_j - r)}{\text{cov}(\tilde{r}_j - \tilde{r}_{\mathrm{m}})} = \theta \tag{19.52}$$

for all risky assets $j = 1, \ldots, N$;

$$E(\tilde{r}_j - r) = \theta \ \text{cov}(\tilde{r}_j, \tilde{r}_{\mathrm{m}}) \tag{19.53}$$

$$= [\theta \ \text{var}(\tilde{r}_{\mathrm{m}})] \frac{\text{cov}(\tilde{r}_j, \tilde{r}_{\mathrm{m}})}{\text{var}(\tilde{r}_{\mathrm{m}})} \tag{19.54}$$

$$= [\theta \ \text{var}(\tilde{r}_{\mathrm{m}})] \beta_j \tag{19.55}$$

$$\sum_{j=1}^{N} x_j E(\tilde{r}_j - r) = 0, \tag{19.56}$$

$$\sum_{j=1}^{N} x_j \, \text{cov}(\tilde{r}_j, \tilde{r}_{\mathrm{m}}) = \theta \ \text{cov} \left(\sum_{j=1}^{N} x_j \tilde{r}_j, \tilde{r}_{\mathrm{m}} \right) \tag{19.57}$$

$$= \theta \ \text{cov}(\tilde{r}_{\mathrm{m}}, \tilde{r}_{\mathrm{m}}), \tag{19.58}$$

$$E(\tilde{r})_j - r = \beta_j [E(\tilde{r}_{\mathrm{m}}) - r]. \tag{19.59}$$

4. Suppose that investors from a country have access to a large set of foreign stocks and that foreign investors can also buy stocks in that country. Which of the following statements is (are) correct?

(a) The single-market CAPM, where the market portfolio is measured by the index of all stocks issued by local companies, does not hold.

(b) The single-market CAPM, where the market portfolio is measured by the index of all stocks held by local investors, does not hold.

(c) The single-market CAPM, where the market portfolio is measured by the index of all stocks held by local investors, is formally correct but not fit for practical use, because the correct index is not readily observable.

(d) The single-market CAPM, where the market portfolio measured by the index of all stocks worldwide, is correct provided that there is a unified world market for all stocks.

(e) The single-market CAPM, where the market portfolio is measured by the index of all stocks worldwide, is correct provided that there is no (real) exchange risk.

Applications

1. Suppose that you have the following data. Asset 0 is the (domestic) risk-free asset, and asset weights in a portfolio are denoted as x_j, where $j = 0, \ldots, 2$. Which of the following portfolios is efficient, and if the portfolio is efficient, what is the investor's degree of risk aversion?

   (a) $x_0 = 0$, $x_1 = 0.4$, $x_2 = 0.6$.
   (b) $x_0 = 0$, $x_1 = 0.6$, $x_2 = 0.4$.
   (c) $x_0 = 0$, $x_1 = 0.5$, $x_2 = 0.5$.
   (d) $x_0 = 0.2$, $x_1 = 0.4$, $x_2 = 0.4$.
   (e) $x_0 = 0.5$, $x_1 = 0.25$, $x_2 = 0.25$.
   (f) $x_0 = -1$, $x_1 = 1$, $x_2 = 1$.
   (g) $x_0 = 1$, $x_1 = 0$, $x_2 = 0$.
   (h) $x_0 = 2$, $x_1 = -0.5$, $x_2 = -0.5$.

2. Suppose that the capital markets of the following three countries are well integrated: North America (with the dollar), Europe (with the EUR), and Japan (with the yen). Suppose that you choose the yen as the home currency.

   (a) Why does the average investor care about the JPY/USD and JPY/EUR exchange rates (beside how it relates to how his or her wealth is measured in JPY)?

   (b) What moments are needed in a mean-and-(co)variance framework, to summarize the joint distribution of asset returns? Which of these are affected by the portfolio choice?

3. Suppose that your assistant has run a market-model regression for a company that produces sophisticated drilling machines and finds the following results (t-statistic in parentheses):

$$\tilde{r}_j = \alpha + \beta \tilde{r}_m + \gamma s + \tilde{e}_j,$$
$$\tilde{r}_j = 0.002 + 0.56\tilde{r}_m + 4.25\tilde{s} + \tilde{e}_j.$$
$$(0.52) \quad (1.25) \quad (2.06)$$

Your assistant remarks that, as the estimated beta is insignificant, the true beta is zero. The exposure, in contrast, is significant, and must be equal to the estimated coefficient. How do you react?

4. Suppose that the world beta for a German stock (in euros) equals 1.5, and its exposures to the dollar, the yen, and the pound are 0.3, 0.2, and 0.1, respectively.

   (a) What is the best-replication portfolio if you can invest in a world-market index fund, as well as in dollars, yen, pounds, and euros?

   (b) What additional information is needed to identify the cost of capital?

5. Suppose that there are two countries: the United States (which is the foreign country) and Canada. The exposure of the company XUS, in terms of USD, is estimated as follows:

$$\tilde{r}^*_{XUS} = 0.12 + 0.30\tilde{s}_{USD/CAD} + \tilde{\varepsilon}.$$

What is the company's exposure in terms of CAD?

20

International Taxation of Foreign Investments

We have just reviewed how you can set the cost of capital, which is the discount rate to be used in NPV calculations. The second ingredient in investment analysis is the amounts to be discounted. These are similar to what you would see in domestic capital-budgeting applications. There is, however, one marked exception: international taxation is usually much more complex. We need to have some idea of how it works before we can move on to the NPV procedure.

In this chapter, we therefore explain how to compute the taxes to be paid on profits and how taxes can be minimized by transfer pricing or unbundling the cash flows in a particular way. Rather than going into the details of tax charters of specific countries, we shall focus on the basic principles of stylized, generic tax systems and tax treaties. The first issue, discussed in section 20.3, is whether or not the host country (or, in fiscal jargon, the *source country* for the income) has the right to tax the profits of this branch. We shall describe how and when this right to levy taxes can lead to double or triple taxation, and how legislators try to obtain a more neutral tax situation by reducing multiple taxation. The two main systems are the *credit system* and the *exclusion system*. In sections 20.3 and 20.4, we consider how each of these two (conflicting) tax systems is applied to a branch. Section 20.5 then looks at the wholly owned subsidiary (WOS) or joint venture (JV) and describes the various ways in which such a subsidiary can remit funds to its shareholders. Sections 20.6 and 20.7 discuss taxation of a subsidiary under the credit system and the exclusion system. We summarize our discussion in section 20.8.

20.1 Forms of Foreign Activity

In order to understand tax issues and other problems that arise when the NPV criterion is applied to international investment projects, we first need to understand the different ways in which a firm can generate and repatriate income from its foreign operations. This is relevant because the method of operations will affect the company's overall tax bills, as well as the transfer risk of its foreign cash flows. We first classify the forms of foreign involvement from a managerial or marketing point of view, then from a legal point of view, and lastly from a fiscal perspective.

20.1.1 Modes of Operation (1): A Managerial Perspective

When venturing abroad, or considering venturing abroad, there is a simple home truth you should bear in mind: you are at an intrinsic disadvantage relative to the locals, because you are less well informed about the cultural and legal frameworks, the customers' wants, the distribution channels, and so on, and you have no contacts and no network. So it is imperative that you first sit down and identify a competitive advantage that could, hopefully, overcome that handicap. This could be a product idea, production skills, know-how, a strong brand, or management skills. If you cannot find a convincing competitive advantage, try a comparative advantage—one that comes with your country rather than your company. If still unsuccessful, abandon your plan.

Assuming you have identified an advantage, how will you exploit it? We restrict ourselves to a brief taxonomy; a complete discussion of the operational advantages and disadvantages of these various forms can be found in an international marketing or international management textbook.

1. *Pure exports* are one way to do business abroad. Under this mode of operation, the firm's skills are used at home in order to produce goods that are then sold abroad. All activity takes place at home.

2. With *international product marketing*, the marketing of the firm's goods, and possibly also their production, is undertaken abroad. Most of the activities of multinational companies belong in this category.

3. In both of the above modes, the firm exploits its own competitive advantage (in production, marketing, or general management) by marketing a product abroad. Alternatively, the firm can sell its skills directly to another company, without first using them to create a product. This requires some form of cooperative agreement. *Licensing* consists of the transfer of intellectual property (a production process, technical know-how, or a brand name), often for a limited period and for a restricted market. *Franchising* transfers the firm's marketing know-how or a part of it. *Management contracts* transfer a general organizational or management skill. Under these forms of foreign involvement, the "seller" of the skill derives no revenue from product sales. Rather, for management contracts, a management fee is received and, for the transfer of know-how, the firm is compensated in the form of a royalty (that is, a periodic payment proportional to the volume of sales, the value of sales, or the level of production) and often also an initial lump sum and/or a yearly lump-sum license fee.

Management strategy gurus would now wheel out a two-by-two matrix, showing in one dimension the home country's comparative advantage (good, bad) and in the other the company's competitive strength (good, bad). Each cell then has at least one good strategy (exports, international production and marketing, becoming a licensor, etc.) or one of the negatives (imports, inward foreign investment, becoming a licensee, etc.).

DIY Problem 20.1. Try it.

		Home-country competitive advantage	
		Good	Bad
Company's competitive strength	Good		
	Bad		

However, exports, international product marketing, international technology transfers, and cooperative agreements are not mutually exclusive. In practice, they are often used simultaneously. For instance, a firm may set up a wholly owned subsidiary for production and marketing abroad, implying that there is international product marketing. In addition, there may be a licensing contract and a management contract between the parent and the affiliate, and there may also be exports of some products or components to its foreign business. One objective of such a mixed approach might be a reduction in the tax burden, by "unbundling" the cash transfers from subsidiary to parent, for example, paying out interest payments and royalties rather than just dividends. Another objective could be to reduce political risk. In the case of a joint venture, an additional consideration is that, by mixing the forms of foreign involvement, the risks and expected revenues can also be redistributed among the stakeholders.

20.1.2 Modes of Operation (2): A Legal Perspective

One alternative to the above classification is to classify foreign activities according to the legal form in which they are set up. In ascending order of foreign involvement, our list is as follows:

1. Exports may occur through *independent agents.* An independent agent is, by definition, an unrelated company or person who sells the firm's products abroad, so that there is no legal ownership link with the parent.

2. Exports may also occur through a *dependent agent* abroad. For instance, a French company may send one of its employees to Lima, Peru, to advertise its fine products. This employee is likely to rent an apartment there, and have a car, a phone, and a fax machine—all paid for by the French company. From the perspective of Peruvian law, however, the agent is

just a private person living in Lima. Legally, the French exporter is not present in Peru.

3. A higher form of foreign presence is obtained by *opening a foreign branch.* By fulfilling some legal requirements, like registering the firm, depositing a copy of the bylaws and specimens of relevant signatures with the Chamber of Commerce or Commercial Court, etc., the French company can establish a legal presence in Lima. The formal opening of a branch implies that the phone or the car in Lima will be recognized as the French company's property, not the agent's, and that the contracts signed by the agent (if she or he has the power to do so) bind the French company, and not just the agent as an individual.

Not being incorporated as a separate company, the branch remains essentially a part of the French company. It has no separate accounting system. All of its profits and losses are immediately and automatically part of the overall profits and losses of the company.

4. Finally, one may set up a *subsidiary,* that is, an entity that is incorporated as a separate company. The separate foreign company may be a wholly owned subsidiary with one parent, or a joint venture where there are two or more parents. A separate company can, for instance, pay out dividends, royalties, or interest to its parent(s), lend money to its owner(s), obtain loans, or subscribe to the parent's stock, and so on. This is, by definition, not possible with a branch: one cannot pay dividends to oneself, or lend money to oneself, etc.

20.1.3   Modes of Operation (3): A Fiscal Perspective

Fiscal laws in many countries claim the right to tax on two different principles:

The residence principle. All residents of the country (that is, private persons living in the country and incorporated companies established in the country) can be taxed on their worldwide income.

The source principle. All income earned inside the country, whether by residents or nonresidents, is taxable in this country. Earning, in this context, means that some income-generating activity is carried on inside the country, or that income has been received from abroad that stems from a property—real estate, financial assets, intellectual property—like rent, dividends, interest income, or royalties.

The two principles are in perfect agreement when the entire income of a resident is earned in the country of residence. In an international context, however, there is often no perfect overlap between the two principles. Consider an Icelandic academic who works one semester as a visiting professor in Paraguay. According to the source principle, he or she may have to pay taxes in Paraguay on labor income earned in Paraguay. According to the residence principle, however, the professor is also taxable at home, on worldwide income—including the Paraguayan income. This implies that the Paraguayan income can be taxed twice, unless some form of relief against double taxation is provided.

In our review of international taxation, we first consider two extreme modes of foreign operations: direct exports (without foreign representation), and the wholly owned subsidiary (WOS) or the joint venture company (JV). After this discussion, we cover the middle ground between these two extremes.

Direct exports. Under direct exports, all business transactions are made at home. Not only does production take place in the exporter's home country, but the decision to accept or not to accept export orders is also taken in the domestic headquarters. Thus, a pure exporter is not a resident of the foreign country. Nor does the pure exporter "earn" anything abroad; there is no foreign activity, and the company does not receive any dividends, license income, or interest income from the foreign country. Therefore, the foreign country can invoke neither the residence principle nor the source principle. Conversely, the resulting export profits are domestic income and are taxed in the firm's home country only. Thus, in this case, double taxation is not an issue.

Foreign subsidiary. At the other extreme, a WOS or a JV is legally a separate entity incorporated abroad. In this case, there is a proliferation of potential taxes:

- The WOS or JV is unambiguously a resident of the host country. Thus, the host country will invoke the residence principle and impose its normal corporate taxes on the profits of the WOS or JV.

- In principle, however, the parent is also subject to taxes on all dividend, interest, or license income, etc., it receives from the subsidiary. Such additional taxes may be levied by both countries.

  — The host country will note that the parent earns some income in the country, and that the source principle therefore applies. That is, the host country may levy a tax on the dividends, interest fees, or royalties paid out to the parent. This tax is called a *withholding tax.*[1]

---

[1] In accordance with the source principle, this withholding tax is levied only on the income earned by the parent in that particular host country, not on the parent's worldwide income. The withholding tax is flat (not progressive), and in most cases the rate is lower than the regular income tax rate. The tax is withheld immediately when the dividend is received, rather than being levied afterward on the basis of a tax return. The reason for withholding the tax at the source is that the foreign recipient of the dividend, not being a resident of the host country, cannot be forced by the host country to file a tax return or to pay taxes later on. Therefore, the host country collects its tax while the money is still in the host country, by withholding it from the dividend payment. In practice, the bank that pays out the dividend is instructed to withhold the tax and pay it to the tax authorities.

Table 20.1. Triple taxation of a WOS.

	Who taxes	Whom?	Basis?	Excuse?
WOS makes profit	Host? Yes Home? No	WOS	Local income	Both
WOS pays dividend	Host? Yes Home? Yes	Parent Parent	Dividend Dividend	Source Residence

— In addition, the parent's home country will, in principle, invoke the residence principle of taxation, and tax the parent on its worldwide incomes.

Example 20.1. A Greek subsidiary of a French company makes a profit of EUR 170,000 before taxes. Greek corporate taxes are EUR 70,000. The entire after-tax profit of EUR 100,000 is paid out as a dividend to the French parent company through KBΓ, a Greek bank. If the withholding tax is 25%, the bank will withhold EUR 25,000 from the ("gross") dividend and transfer this amount to the Greek tax administration. The balance, the "net" dividend of EUR 75,000, will be paid to the foreign shareholder. Finally, the French parent will have to declare its Greek income of EUR 75,000 in its French tax return and potentially pay taxes on it.

In short, when the foreign business unit is incorporated as a separate company, there is potential for double or triple taxation. This is in marked contrast with the pure exports case, where income is taxed only once, at the corporate level at home. What about the intermediate cases: the dependent agent or the branch? Where exactly between these two extremes does the source or residence principle kick in?

The permanent establishment. As we just saw, from a legal point of view there is a foreign presence if the enterprise formally opens a branch. The definition of presence from the fiscal point of view is subtly different. The host country can invoke the source principle as soon as an *activity* is conducted in the country. The tax terminology for conducting an activity in a given country is "having a *permanent establishment*" there. Under the influential OECD Model Treaty for the reduction of double taxation, such a permanent establishment (PE) is said to exist when two conditions are met simultaneously:

- There is a permanent physical presence (like an office or a warehouse).
- Some vital entrepreneurial activity takes place in the host country; that is, the foreign office does more than just render services (like storing goods, advertising, or centralizing orders).

Example 20.2. If the agent of a U.S. corporation in Peru simply faxes incoming orders to the company headquarters for acceptance or rejection there, there is no

Table 20.2. Where does the source principle apply?

	Activity in host country?	
Independent agent	Physical presence?	No (not by company)
	Key activity?	No (not by company)
Direct exports	Physical presence?	No
	Key activity?	No
Passive dependent agent	Physical presence?	Yes
	Key activity?	No
"Permanent establishment"	Physical presence?	Yes
	Key activity?	Yes
Full-monty WOS	Physical presence?	Yes*
in host country	Key activity?	Yes

*Residence principle applies too.

PE and, therefore, no taxation in Peru (table 20.2). However, if the agent ultimately decides whether or not the order is to be accepted, or if there is local production, then there is a PE, and the profits made on the Peruvian sales are taxable in Peru.

The double taxation issue also arises for the PE. Not being incorporated as a separate company, the PE's profit is also part of the overall company's profit and will be subject to taxes in the parent's country under the residence principle. Note that, unlike the case of an incorporated foreign unit, the host country can tax only the PE's profits. There are no dividend payments, interest fees, or license payments between the branch and the main office, implying that there cannot be any withholding tax.

20.2 Multiple Taxation versus Tax Neutrality

Even tax authorities concur—reluctantly—that full double or triple taxation is too much of a good thing, and thus they wish to provide relief against multiple taxation. In this section, we consider the alternative principles that can underlie such relief measures.

20.2.1 Tax Neutrality

Relief from double taxation can be provided by unilateral measures built into the host country's standard tax rules. It can also be provided by a bilateral tax treaty between two countries. If there is such an international treaty, it supersedes the national rules; that is, the national rules are the default options that hold if there is no tax treaty. Today, most tax treaties are based on the OECD Model Tax Treaty—even treaties signed with or between non-OECD countries. Such international tax agreements all have the same structure and use the same legal definitions. They may, however, differ from the model on the percentage of withholding taxes, or on the right to tax more or less special cases (like the wages of visiting professors). Thus, one should always check the bilateral treaty rather than assuming that it is identical to the OECD Model Tax Treaty.

20.2.1.1 Double Taxation: Our Base-Case Scenario

To understand the alternative principles that can underlie the measures that mitigate multiple taxation, let us consider an Icelandic company that establishes a business in Vanuatu in the form of a branch/permanent establishment. As we saw, the issue of double taxation arises because the tax authorities levy taxes on the basis of two principles. The residence criterion says that all residents of a country are taxable. Therefore, the Icelandic company, being a resident of Iceland, is taxable in Iceland, on the basis of its world income. The source principle says that the Vanuatuan branch, earning income in Vanuatu, can be taxed in that country on its Vanuatuan income. In the absence of any relief for double taxation, the Vanuatuan income would therefore be taxed both in Iceland and in Vanuatu.

> **Example 20.3.** Assume that the income of the Vanuatuan branch, after translation into ISK, is ISK 100, and suppose that the tax rate is 40% in Iceland and 35% in Vanuatu. In the "Double taxation" column in table 20.3, we show what happens when there is no relief against double taxation. The Vanuatuan income after Vanuatuan taxes, ISK $100 - 35 = 65$, is added to the Icelandic income and is taxed again at 40% in Iceland.[2] Thus, the total tax is ISK 61.

In the above example, under the double taxation scheme, the total corporate tax burden is 61, of which 35 is paid in Vanuatu and 26 in Iceland. This is high relative to two possible benchmarks. If the same ISK 100 had been earned in Iceland, taxes would have been only ISK 40 and, if the branch had been an independent Vanuatuan entity, taxes would have been only ISK 35. Whatever the benchmark chosen, taxes are not "neutral": rather, there is a fiscal penalty associated with the fact that ownership and operations straddle two countries.

Tax laws aim to reduce or possibly even eliminate the above discrimination between the foreign-owned branch and a purely Icelandic or purely Vanuatuan company. Tax neutrality (that is, the absence of tax penalties associated with international ownership) can be achieved on the basis of either of two, generally conflicting, approaches. One principle says that the Vanuatuan branch should be taxed the same way as a purely Vanuatuan entity (that is, at 35%). The

---

[2] The Icelandic parent is allowed to deduct the Vanuatuan taxes from its worldwide income as part of its expenses. For simplicity, we also assume, for the time being, that both tax authorities agree on the allocation of profits to the Vanuatuan branch.

Table 20.3. A branch: double taxation, and tax relief via exclusion or tax credit.

	Double taxation	Exclusion method	Credit method
Vanuatu			
Branch profit	100	100	100
(−) 35% tax (a)	(−) 35	(−) 35	(−) 35
Net profit 65	65	65	
Iceland			
Net Vanuatuan profit	65	65	65
Gross-up	n.a.	n.a.	(+) 35
Taxable income	65	65	100
Tax due (40%)	26	0	40
Tax credit	n.a.	n.a.	(−) 35
Tax really due (b)	26	0	5
Total taxes (a) + (b)	61	35	40

alternative principle says that the total tax burden should be the same whether the Icelandic firm earns its income at home or in Vanuatu (that is, at 40%).

20.2.1.2 Capital Import Neutrality and the Exclusion System

The first principle is based on the argument that there should be no penalty or advantage attached to the fact that the branch is foreign owned. This is called the *capital import neutrality* principle: a foreign-owned entity should be allowed to compete on an equal basis with a Vanuatuan-owned competitor. To achieve this, the Icelandic tax authorities would have to exempt foreign-source income from Icelandic taxes, that is, exclude foreign branch profits from taxable income. This is called the *exclusion method*.

Example 20.4. Assume that the income of the Vanuatuan branch, after translation into ISK, is still ISK 100, and suppose that the tax rate is 40% in Iceland and 35% in Vanuatu. In the "Exclusion method" column of table 20.3, we show the effect of the exclusion tax rule. The Vanuatuan income is simply excluded from the Icelandic taxable income, which of course means that there is no Icelandic tax on the Vanuatuan income. Thus, the overall tax is just the Vanuatuan tax (ISK 35).

20.2.1.3 Capital Export Neutrality and the Credit System

Under the alternative principle—which is called *capital export neutrality*—the Icelandic tax authorities do not want to create a tax incentive for firms to export capital and employment to a relatively low-tax country like Vanuatu. Thus, the principle is that the overall corporate tax should be the same as if the branch had been located in Iceland. Under this system, the Icelandic tax authorities first "gross up" the after-tax income with all foreign taxes, implying that they recompute the before-tax income; they then apply the home-country tax rules to that income, and give credit for foreign taxes already paid when they come up with the final reckoning.

Example 20.5. Under capital export neutrality, the Icelandic tax authorities want the Vanuatuan branch's before-tax income, ISK 100, to be taxed at 40%. The figures are shown under the column "Credit method" in table 20.3. The procedure consists of "grossing up" the net income (ISK 65) with all foreign taxes (ISK 35) that have been levied on that income. Thus, the tax basis in Iceland is ISK 65 + 35 = 100. On this grossed-up income, the Icelandic tax authorities then apply the Icelandic tax rate of 40%, which is the Icelandic norm. Thus, the total tax should be ISK 40. As foreign taxes are less than ISK 40, the Icelandic company must pay some taxes in Iceland to bring its total taxation up to the "normal" level. In other words, the total tax burden is 40, but the Icelandic main office obtains a credit for taxes paid abroad (ISK 35) and pays only the balance (ISK 5) in Iceland.

DIY Problem 20.2. An old tax lawyer in your firm mumbles that he's always "happy when the taxman announces that some domestic tax is due; it's the cases where no home tax is imposed that are the bad ones." Is this a symptom of *dementia precox* or of deep wisdom and insight?

20.2.1.4 Limitations to Tax Neutrality

Each of the alternative neutrality principles—capital import neutrality or capital export neutrality—reduces the overall tax burden to a level deemed to be "normal." However, the definition of what is normal clearly differs depending on the principle adopted. Thus, there will generally be no universal neutrality, in the sense of simultaneous capital import and export neutrality. Universal neutrality requires that the two tax rates be the same and that both countries use the same definition of taxable income. For instance, if in table 20.3 the Vanuatuan tax rate were also 40%, a credit system would, in principle, be indistinguishable from an exclusion system, as is easily verified.

In practice, there are other reasons why taxes are seldom neutral. A credit system, as it is applied in practice, never completely achieves its professed objective of capital export neutrality, and an exclusion rule rarely achieves complete capital export neutrality. Some of the practical problems in applying either system are discussed in the following sections. First, we consider the case of a branch and then a subsidiary, each time under either the credit or the exclusion system.

20.3 International Taxation of a Branch (1): The Credit System

We shall first describe some of the practical problems that can arise when the credit method applies to the income of a foreign branch; next, we discuss the meaning of tax planning under these circumstances. The problems we discuss are (1) disagreement between the two tax authorities about what the taxable income is, and (2) the problem of excess tax credits.

20.3.1 Disagreement on the Tax Basis

One of the practical problems in applying either the credit system or the exclusion system to branch income is that the company's worldwide profits have to be divided into the portion earned by the branch (or each of the branches, if there are many), and the portion earned by the main office. Allocating sales over the different entities does not usually create problems; however, the computation of the cost of goods sold is somewhat trickier, and the allocation of overhead to the various offices can be even more troublesome. The reason is that the overhead or the indirect cost, by definition, cannot be allocated in any practical, logical way; this then implies that rules of thumb have to be used. If the national tax authorities have different cost-allocation rules, taxes will not be neutral even if the tax rates in the two countries are equal. In fact, the company runs the risk that some of its indirect costs may not be tax deductible anywhere.

Example 20.6. Assume that sales are ISK 1,200 in Iceland and ISK 400 in Vanuatu, and that the corresponding direct costs of goods sold are ISK 700 and 300, respectively. Total indirect (overhead) costs are ISK 300 and have to be allocated to Iceland and Vanuatu using some rule of thumb.

- Assume that the Icelandic tax authorities allocate this overhead in proportion to direct cost. As the head office accounts for 70% of the direct costs, 70% of the ISK 300 overhead (that is, ISK 210) is assigned to the main office for the purpose of Icelandic tax computations.
- On the other hand, the host-country tax agency allocates overhead in proportion to sales. The Vanuatuan branch has 25% of overall sales, so the Vanuatuan tax authorities assign one quarter of the overhead, ISK 75, to the branch.

With ISK 210 deductible in Iceland and ISK 75 in Vanuatu, not all overhead (ISK 300) has been deducted worldwide. Stated differently, ISK 15 will be taxed twice, as shown in table 20.4.

20.3.2 The Problem of Excess Tax Credits

Another problem in attaining capital export neutrality is that a credit system is seldom fully neutral if foreign taxes exceed the domestic norm. In such a case, there is rarely a full refund of the excess taxes paid abroad.

Example 20.7. If the Vanuatuan tax rate in table 20.3 is 45%, the after-tax branch profit in Vanuatu is ISK 55. For the purpose of Icelandic taxation, this after-tax income will be grossed up, under the credit system, from ISK 55 to ISK 100. The

Table 20.4. Effect of different indirect-cost allocation rules on taxable income.

	Iceland	Vanuatu	Total
	Management accounting system		
Sales	1,200	400	1,600
(−) Direct cost	(−) 700	(−) 300	(−) 1,000
(=) Contribution	500	100	600
(−) Overhead cost	—	—	(−) 300
(=) Total gross income	—	—	300
	Tax returns		
Sales	1,200	400	1,600
(−) Direct cost	(−) 700	(−) 300	(−) 1,000
(−) Allocated overhead	$\frac{700}{700+300}300 =$ (−) 210	$\frac{400}{1,200+400}300 =$ (−) 75	(−) 285
(=) Taxable	290	25	315

Icelandic norm requires a total tax bill of ISK 40. As the Vanuatuan taxes already exceed this norm, there is no additional Icelandic tax. Instead, there is an *unused tax credit* or *excess tax credit* of ISK 5.

Now this excess tax credit is not necessarily fully lost. If foreign incomes from all countries are bundled together before the final tax computations are made, excess tax credits from one branch can be used to offset home-country taxes due on any income from branches in low-tax countries.[3]

Example 20.8. In table 20.5, we examine the case where the Vanuatuan tax is 50%. We work out two simple cases where, in addition to the Vanuatuan income, the parent also has branch income from Hong Kong (taxed at 25%). Note that the Vanuatuan tax exceeds the Icelandic norm, but the Hong Kong tax rate is below the 40% Icelandic tax rate. Depending on the size of the Hong Kong profits, there may or may not be excess tax credits left if Icelandic taxes are assessed on the basis of total foreign income rather than on a country-by-country basis.

We see that, in case 1 (where low-taxed Hong Kong profits are a large part of foreign income), the total foreign tax (50 in Vanuatu and 25 in Hong Kong) is less than the 40% due on the total foreign income, ISK 200 × 0.40 = ISK 80. That is, the excess Vanuatuan tax is used to offset some of the taxes due on the Hong Kong profits, and the head office actually has to pay additional taxes to bring the overall tax burden up to 40%.

In case 2, the Hong Kong sales and profits are so small that the total tax (50 in Vanuatu and 10 in Hong Kong) is still above the 40% due on total foreign income, ISK 140 × 0.40 = ISK 56. That is, the excess Vanuatuan taxes exceed

---

[3] If your home country is exceptionally generous, credits for foreign taxes can even be used against domestic income taxes, though this can still leave the firm with excess tax credits.

Table 20.5. Taxation of a branch: the credit system with pooling of foreign income.

	Case 1		Case 2	
Host country	Vanuatu	Hong Kong	Vanuatu	Hong Kong
	(tax 50%)	(tax 25%)	(tax 50%)	(tax 25%)
Sales	220	200	220	100
(−) Cost	(−) 120	(−) 100	(−) 120	(−) 60
(=) Branch profit	100	100	100	40
(−) Taxes	(−) 50	(−) 25	(−) 50	(−) 10
(=) Net profit	50	75	50	30
Iceland				
Net profit	50	75	50	30
Gross-up	50	25	50	10
Taxable, by branch	100	100	100	40
Total taxable foreign income	100 + 100 = 200		100 + 40 = 140	
Tax due	80		56	
(−) Credit	50 + 25 = (−) 75		50 + 10 = (−) 60	
Net tax due	5		0	
Unused tax credit	0		4	
Total taxes paid	80		60	
Total tax, as %	80/200 = 40%		60/140 = 43%	

the additional tax that is due on the Hong Kong profits. As a result, the Icelandic company still ends up with an unused tax credit—although less than if there had been no Hong Kong branch. The effective tax rate on the Vanuatuan income, in this case, decreases from 50% to 43%, but not all the way to 40%.

The net excess tax credit in case 2 of table 20.5, ISK 4, is not necessarily lost. The parent country's revenue service may use what is known as carry-forward or carry-back rules.

Carry-forward. If, in the near future, we have to pay additional home-country taxes, we shall be allowed to use this year's excess foreign taxes as a credit. Thus, there is a kind of refund, but it is delayed (implying a loss-of-time value), and it is limited to home-country taxes that would be payable within the next few years, for instance, five years if there is a five-year carry-forward.

Carry-back. If, in the recent past, we have paid more than ISK 4 in additional home-country taxes, we can now claim them back. Such a carry-back rule is a pure refund of excess tax credits, but the refund is limited to home-country taxes paid in the last few years, for instance, two years if there is a two-year carry-back.

If a carry-back rule applies, the parent would first carry back as much as possible. Any credits not recuperated in this way would then be carried forward up to the maximum allowed number of years.

Example 20.9. Suppose that there is a two-year carry-back and a three-year carry-forward rule in Iceland, and that the Icelandic company paid Icelandic taxes (on foreign income) worth ISK 1 two years ago, and ISK 1.5 last year. The current excess credit (ISK 4) is treated as follows:

- ISK 1 is carried back two years, resulting in a refund of ISK 1.
- ISK 1.5 is carried back one year, resulting in an additional refund of ISK 1.5.
- The balance, 4 − 1 − 1.5 = ISK 1.5, is carried forward, that is, it can be used within the next three years as a credit against possible Icelandic taxes on foreign income.

Carry-forward and carry-back rules imply that occasional excess tax credits can be recuperated (possibly with a delay). However, if a corporation systematically has excess tax credits, these excess taxes are lost forever, and thus, the credit system may not be fully capital-export neutral.

20.3.3 Tax Planning for a Branch under the Credit System

The general objective of corporate tax planning is to minimize taxes. The rule of the credit system is that taxes on foreign branch income are never lower than the foreign income times the standard home tax rate. One element of this rule is the determination of the foreign branch income. As we saw, there can be conflicts between the indirect cost allocation rules used by the company and the rules adopted by the tax authorities involved. Thus, a first implication is that it is important to know the rules used by tax authorities, and to minimize the risk that part of the expenses would be rejected for tax purposes in one of the countries involved.

The second element in the credit system says that, given the home country's assessment of the foreign branch income, the tax rate will never be less than the standard home tax rate. As we saw, the effective tax rate can be higher than this, notably when there are excess foreign tax credits and when these unused tax credits cannot be fully carried back or offset against other tax liabilities. Thus, given the assessment of foreign branch income, the implication is that one should minimize excess tax credits.

The only thing that can be done in this respect within the framework of a branch is the reallocation of profits from high-tax branches to low-tax branches, with the purpose of reducing total foreign taxes and, hence, also excess tax credits. One way to achieve this is to reallocate indirect expenses strategically; but, as we saw, the scope for indirect cost reallocation is limited. A second way to reallocate profits is to change the transfer prices, that is, the prices used to value goods and services transferred between the branches (or subsidiaries) of one company or group of companies. For instance, goods produced in Hong Kong are sold by the Vanuatuan branch, or experts from headquarters come over and help in the branches. There is some scope for using transfer pricing to reduce taxes because there is never an unambiguous

Table 20.6. Taxation of a branch under the credit system: using transfer pricing.

Host country	Before		After	
	Vanuatu	Hong Kong	Vanuatu	Hong Kong
	(tax 50%)	(tax 25%)	(tax 50%)	(tax 25%)
Sales	220	100	220	140
(−) Cost	(−) 120	(−) 60	(−) 160	(−) 60
(=) Branch profit	100	40	60	80
(−) Taxes	(−) 50	(−) 10	(−) 30	(−) 20
(=) Net profit	50	30	30	60
Iceland				
Net profit	50	75	50	30
Gross-up	50	10	30	20
Taxable, by branch	100	40	100	40
Total taxable foreign income	100 + 40 = 140		100 + 40 = 140	
Tax due	56		56	
(−) Credit	50 + 10= (−) 60		30 + 20 = (−) 50	
Net tax due	0		6	
Unused tax credit	4		0	
Total taxes paid	60		56	
Total tax, as %	60/140 = 42.86%		56/140 = 40%	

way to determine the true cost of items delivered, and because the concept of a normal profit margin is equally ill-defined.

Example 20.10. In table 20.6, we continue with case 2 of example 20.8 (Vanuatuan tax 50%, Hong Kong tax 25%, Icelandic tax 40%), with an ISK 4 excess foreign tax credit. The parent attempts to decrease the total foreign tax by increasing the transfer price for technical and management assistance rendered by the Hong Kong branch to the Vanuatuan branch by ISK 40. Thus, expenses in Vanuatu increase by ISK 40 and income in Hong Kong rises by the same amount. Total before-tax income for the branches remains the same, but ISK 40 worth of income has been transferred from high-tax Vanuatu to low-tax Hong Kong. The effect is that Vanuatuan income taxes decrease by ISK $40 \times 50\%$ = ISK 20 while Hong Kong income taxes increase by only ISK $40 \times 25\%$ = ISK 10. In short, total foreign taxes are lower by ISK 10, which eliminates the unused tax credit.

Two factors impose limits on what can be achieved by transfer pricing.

- First and foremost, the host-country tax authorities may reject part or all of the increased expenses, on the basis that these costs are above the *arm's-length* level that would have been paid if the buyer and the seller had been unrelated. Such a rejection of part of the declared costs would result in some expenses not being deductible anywhere, so that taxes would be higher than before the cost reallocation. Worse, there could be fines, too. The largest-ever tax settlement in the United States, at the time of writing, was about transfer pricing.

> **Example 20.11.** In September 2006, "America's taxman reached an agreement with GlaxoSmithKline, a British drugs company, in which it will pay $3.4 billion to resolve charges that it tried to minimise its tax bill by underreporting its American profits through a system of transfer pricing. GSK will also drop its claim that it is owed $1.8 billion by the IRS." (*Economist*, September 14, 2006). A few months later another drugs maker, Merck, disclosed that it might have to cough up USD 5.6m in back taxes and interest to U.S. and Canadian tax authorities, again for non-arm's-length transfer pricing (*Economist*, 24 February 2007, p. 10).

- Second, if profits are reallocated through a change in the prices charged for the delivery of goods rather than services, one side effect is that import taxes levied on the traded goods will increase. The issue is then whether the (certain) additional cost in terms of import duties is smaller than the hoped-for gain in terms of income taxes.

20.4 International Taxation of a Branch (2): The Exclusion System

We now discuss the exclusion system of taxation. As we saw, unused tax credits and disagreements about the tax basis are some of the reasons why a credit system is rarely perfectly capital-export neutral. We explain below that the exclusion system, as it is applied in reality, does not usually achieve its professed objective of capital-import neutrality either. We first discuss the problems with this tax system, and then summarize its implications for tax planning.

20.4.1 Partial Exclusion and Progressive Taxes

In practice, an exclusion system is rarely capital-import neutral in the sense that exclusion is often incomplete.

- First, in their unilateral legislation, many countries limit the exclusion privilege to a certain percentage (for example, to 50%, 75%, or 90% of the foreign branch income) rather than granting full exemption. The justification given is that some of the expenses deducted by the main office from its domestic income are really associated with the management of the foreign branch. Since these expenses are hard to identify precisely, they are assumed to be a given percentage of the foreign profits. Thus, if the domestic costs associated with running a foreign branch are deemed

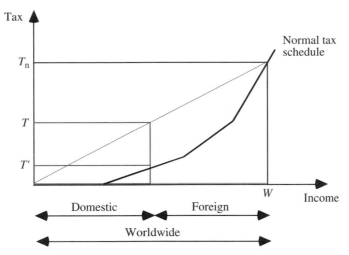

Figure 20.1. Preservation of tax progressiveness. *Key:* Worldwide income W is the sum of domestic income and foreign income. The tax authority first computes the total tax T_n that would have been due if the taxed income had been worldwide income W, then computes the average tax rate T_n/W (which is the slope of the ray through the origin), and applies this average tax rate to the taxable (i.e., domestic) income. The resulting tax is T. Under a truly import-neutral system the tax would have been T'.

to be 10% of the profits of the branch, the exclusion privilege for these profits is set at 90%.[4]

- Second, in bilateral tax treaties, many countries grant (nearly) complete exclusion only if the foreign tax rate is rather similar to the home tax rate. Otherwise, they argue, there is too much of an incentive to shift profits toward low-tax foreign countries. This, of course, belies the stated objective of the system, capital-import neutrality.

- Third, if taxes are progressive, the tax authorities first compute what the normal average tax rate would be on the company's worldwide income, and then apply this average tax rate to its taxable income (that is, domestic profits plus nonexcluded foreign income). If tax schedules are progressive, this procedure obviously increases the average tax rate. This rule is illustrated in figure 20.3.

20.4.2 Disagreement on the Tax Basis

As under the credit system, the exclusion system requires that the company's worldwide profits be divided into the portion earned by the foreign branch and

---

[4] The home country's right to tax part of the foreign income is recognized in the EU Parent–Subsidiary Directive on the taxation of intracompany dividends, but the exclusion percentage cannot be lower than 95% (for dividends paid between EU member countries). The United States has an 85% exclusion privilege for dividends received by U.S. corporations from other U.S. corporations. (For foreign dividends, the United States applies the credit system.)

the portion earned by the main office. Thus, conflicts can arise with respect to the allocation of indirect costs and with respect to transfer prices.

20.4.3   Tax Planning for a Branch under the Exclusion System

Under the exclusion system, tax planning consists of first identifying the country with the lowest overall tax burden, and then trying to allocate as much profit as possible to the corresponding branch. If the exclusion privilege is 100% (that is, if foreign profits are fully exempt from domestic taxes), we only have to compare the home and the foreign tax rates to identify the most tax-friendly country. If there is less than 100% exclusion, we have to take into account the home-country tax on the nonexcluded part of the foreign income.

> **Example 20.12.** An Italian company has a branch in France. We consider two scenarios:
>
> - Suppose that the French tax on branch profits is 30%, and the Italian corporate tax is 35%, with a 100% exclusion privilege for profits of the foreign branch. A French branch profit of EUR 100 before taxes will lead to a profit of EUR 70 after French taxes, with no additional taxes in Italy, while a similar profit in the head office will generate only EUR 65 after (Italian) tax. If, through transfer pricing or reallocation of overhead, we can reduce Italian income by EUR 100 and increase French income by EUR 100, EUR 5 can be saved in taxes. Thus, the objective in this case is to increase French profits and decrease Italian profits.
> - Suppose now that the (Italian) exclusion privilege for profits of the foreign branch is only 75%. A branch profit of EUR 100 leads to a profit of EUR 70 after French taxes, but one quarter of this, that is, EUR $70 \times 0.25 =$ EUR 17.5, is taxable in Italy at 35%. The total tax then equals EUR 30 (in France) plus $17.5 \times 0.35 =$ EUR 6.125 (in Italy), that is, EUR 36.125 altogether. In contrast, a similar profit in Italy is subject to a tax of only EUR 35. Thus, in this case, the firm should try to shift profits from France to Italy.

The limitations of such profit shifting are similar to the limitations discussed in connection with the credit system: the tax collector in the high-tax country may reject a portion of the declared costs, and import duties may be affected by the transfer pricing policy. However, although the tax planning rules look similar under the credit system and the exclusion system, their effects are different in one important respect. Under a full exclusion system, a company gets to keep all tax savings below the domestic tax rate while, under a credit system, any such savings have to be paid at home as additional domestic taxes.

> **Example 20.13.** Suppose that an Icelandic company has a total foreign income of ISK 140 and owes ISK 60 (that is, 42.86%) in foreign taxes. The Icelandic tax rate is 40%. Suppose that by transfer pricing between its foreign branches the company lowers its total foreign tax by ISK 10 to ISK 50. If the credit system applies in Iceland, an additional tax of ISK $(140 \times 40\%) - 50 =$ ISK 6 will be due, so that the net saving

Table 20.7. Tax planning for a branch PE under the exclusion system.

Origin of profits' exclusion	Italian	French	
		100%	75%
Profit	100.0	100.0	100.0
(−) French tax	n.a.	(−) 30.0	(−) 30.0
(=) After tax inc.	n.a.	(=) 70.0	(=) 70.0
French taxable	100.0	0.0	17.5
(−) French tax	35.0	0.0	6.1
All tax	35.0	30.0	36.1

Key: An Italian company has a French branch. French taxes on the branch's profits are 30% and the Italian corporate tax is 35% with a 100 or 75% exclusion privilege for profits of the foreign branch.

is only ISK 4. In contrast, if Iceland has an exclusion system, no additional tax will be levied, and the net saving equals ISK 10.

In the remainder of this chapter, we see how the two generic systems for the reduction of multiple taxation are applied in the case of subsidiaries. We shall see that the approach is similar to the branch case.

20.5 Remittances from a Subsidiary: An Overview

Our discussion so far has pertained to the simplest form of doing business abroad—the branch. Under this mode of operation, the firm is immediately and automatically the sole owner of all cash flows that arise from the foreign investment. Funds generated by one branch can be used to finance investments in another branch or in the main office, or they can be paid out by the company to its shareholders as dividends without any complication. In contrast, a foreign subsidiary must make explicit payments if ownership of the funds is to be transferred to the parent or to a related company. One may argue that, for a wholly owned subsidiary (WOS), the issue of who owns the cash—subsidiary or parent—is a legal concern without economic relevance. That is, it may seem that if the parent owns the subsidiary, it also owns its cash and can use this cash anywhere. The problem, however, is that if we want to transfer money from a subsidiary in one host country to the parent or to a subsidiary in another country, we have to respect the legal separation of the subsidiary from the rest of the group of companies. If the money is needed somewhere else, our WOS cannot just donate funds to the parent or to a sister company; it has to use an established, accepted way to transfer these funds—and such a transfer has tax repercussions. In this section, we review the various ways in which a subsidiary can transfer cash to other companies in the group. Sections 20.6 and 20.7 then discuss how dividends and other remittances are taxed under the credit and exclusion system, respectively.

20.5.1 Capital Transactions

Capital transactions between parent and subsidiary can be on equity or on loan accounts. As far as equity transactions are concerned, the subsidiary may buy back some of its own shares from the parent or it may buy stock issued by the parent or by sister companies. Alternatively, the subsidiary can lend funds to its parent or sister companies, or amortize outstanding loans prematurely, or agree to alter the credit periods on intracompany sales (which represents an implicit way to extend or reduce intracompany loans).

The advantage of capital transfers is that, in principle, they are not subject to immediate income taxes in either country.[5] Still, these transfers raise the issue of income taxes in later periods (when dividends or interest payments are received by the subsidiary). Also, regulatory agencies may dislike cross-participation, or the tax authorities of both countries may treat share repurchases or subscriptions to the parent company stock as disguised dividends, and tax them as such.

20.5.2 Dividends

Dividends are a simple way of transferring ownership of funds from a subsidiary to the parent company. There are some major differences between a WOS paying out dividends and a branch that transfers cash:

1. Unlike a branch, a subsidiary has a *timing option* as far as home-country taxation is concerned. A dividend can be declared more or less independently from the reporting period's income—and the parent, being a separate entity, cannot be taxed until it actually receives dividends (or interest payments and royalties, for that matter). This *deferral principle* implies that, under a credit system as well as a partial exclusion system, home-country taxation of foreign profits can be postponed by deferring the payout of dividends from the subsidiary to the parent.[6]

> **Example 20.14.** In the first seventy-five years of its existence, the Australian subsidiary of General Motors never paid out any dividend. Thus, as far as U.S. taxes were concerned, the existence of the Australian subsidiary did not

---

[5] There may be a registration tax on newly issued stock, though. Inside the EU this has now gone.

[6] There are exceptions to this deferral principle. For instance, under Subpart F, the United States levies a tax on the profits of wholly owned "base companies" as if these profits had been paid out as dividends. A base company is a kind of reinvoicing center and holding company which gathers profits from all over the world in a tax haven (within the leeway left by transfer pricing restrictions in the various host countries). Without the Subpart F rule, a U.S. multinational could postpone U.S. taxation (and redirect funds to other group companies) until the funds are actually needed within the United States.

matter. In contrast, if GM's Australian activities had been in the form of a branch, there would have been U.S. tax repercussions each year.

2. The amount that can be paid out as dividends by a subsidiary tends to be smaller than the subsidiary's total cash flow. The reason is that the dividends are paid out of profits, and profits are net of depreciation charges. Thus, a subsidiary can never transmit, as a dividend, the part of the cash flow that corresponds to depreciation allowances. In contrast, in the branch case, the entire cash flow—including depreciation—is (automatically) available to the main office.

3. The home tax shield on losses made by the branch is lost when the branch is converted into a subsidiary. This is because losses by a branch are part of the parent's income and are therefore automatically and fully tax deductible from the parent's home profits.[7] Losses of a subsidiary, in contrast, cannot be offset against the parent's profits since the subsidiary is a separate unit.[8]

4. As we have seen, the fact that the subsidiary's profits and the parent's dividends are incomes to different legal entities also leads to withholding taxes. The host-country tax authorities invoke the source principle and tax not only the subsidiary, but also the parent. In contrast, a branch does not pay any withholding taxes since it does not pay any dividends.[9]

The last two aspects in the above list show that there are tax disadvantages associated with a full-equity WOS. As we shall see, these disadvantages can be mitigated by *unbundling* the payout stream, that is, by remitting cash under forms other than just dividends.

20.5.3 Other Forms of Remittances (Unbundling)

Thus far, we have considered only capital transfers and dividends as ways in which the WOS can transfer funds to the parent or to related companies. In addition to dividends, the subsidiary can also pay out royalties, interest, or management fees for services rendered (or claimed to be rendered)—items that are, by definition, impossible for a branch to pay to the parent. In addition, the subsidiary can lease equipment from its parent, and remit both the principal and the interest on the implicit loan in the form of lease payments.[10]

---

[7] Depending on the two tax laws, the loss could even be deductible twice—once when it is taken over by the head office for home-country tax purposes, and once when the branch carries forward or backward its losses to different income periods for host-country tax purposes.

[8] This is true unless the parent's local tax authority can be convinced that the losses justify a permanent reduction in the value of the participation. This is not easy.

[9] Again, there are exceptions. For example, until the late 1980s France levied a deferred withholding tax when the foreign parent paid out dividends. The withholding tax was based on the French branch's share in the foreign company's overall profits.

[10] Under a capital lease contract, a leasing company or lessor buys a piece of equipment and lends it to a user, the lessee, for the entire normal life of the equipment. At the end of the

These alternative payment forms are tax-deductible expenses to the subsidiary and, therefore, reduce the subsidiary's tax bill. However, to complete the picture, we also have to think of the recipient's taxes, both in the host country (withholding taxes) and in the company's home base (corporate income taxes, hopefully with some relief for the withholding tax).

20.5.4 Transfer Pricing

A subsidiary can remit funds to a related company by agreeing to pay more for its purchases of goods and services from the other company, or by charging less for sales to the other company. This, we saw, is also possible with a branch, except that in the case of a subsidiary, the transactions are regular purchases and sales, with invoices and actual payments and change of legal ownership, rather than accounting entries that allocate profits to different branches within the same company.

After this review of the various ways in which a company can transfer funds, we now consider the tax treatment of dividends, royalties, and interest payments in the home country. Again, we have to distinguish between the exclusion rule and the credit system.

20.6 International Taxation of a Subsidiary (1): The Credit System

When a subsidiary remits dividends to its parent, or royalties or interest payments to a related company, the same principles apply as in the branch case. Under the credit system, each payment is grossed up with the foreign taxes that have been levied on the income, and these foreign taxes are used as a credit against the home-country tax that is normally payable on the recipient's total foreign income (or, in some countries, the recipient's worldwide income). The only complication that could arise is the tax credit that accompanies a dividend.

20.6.1 Direct and Indirect Tax Credits on Foreign Dividends

In a strict legal sense, the only tax paid by the parent on the dividend is the withholding tax (if any); the corporate tax on the subsidiary's profits is, legally speaking, paid by a separate entity. Economically, though, the parent and a WOS are one entity. Thus, if the parent received no credit for the corporate taxes paid by the subsidiary, there would be a substantial fiscal penalty

---

contract, the lessor has an option to buy the equipment at a price that corresponds to the initial estimate of the terminal value. The lessee's periodic lease payments compensate the lessor for the principal and the interest of the investment. Such a lease contract is very similar to the lessee buying the equipment with borrowed money and using the equipment as security for the loan. Note that, in some countries, the right to depreciate the equipment is with the legal owner (the lessor) while in other countries the depreciation is done by the user (the lessee). Thus, in the case of international leasing, a piece of equipment can sometimes be depreciated twice. Spoilsport OECD countries have taken measures against such double depreciation.

Table 20.8. Credit system: branch versus full-equity subsidiary.

	Branch	Full-equity WOS: 100% payout	Full-equity WOS: 50% payout
Vanuatu			
Branch profit	100	100	100
(−) Taxes	(−) 35	(−) 35	(−) 35
(=) Net profit	65	65	65
Gross dividend	. . .	65	32.5
(−) Withholding tax	. . .	(−) 11	(−) 5.5
(=) Net dividend	. . .	54	27.0
Iceland			
Net income	65	54	27.0
Gross-up (1): direct	35	11	5.5
Gross-up (2): indirect	. . .	35	17.5
Taxable	100	100	50.0
Tax due	40	40	20.0
Tax credit (1): direct	(−) 35	(−) 11	(−) 5.5
Tax credit (2): indirect	. . .	(−) 35	(−) 17.5
Net tax due	5	0	0.0
Unused tax credit	0	6	3.0

attached to the incorporation of a branch into a subsidiary. For this reason, the credit system uses a kind of look-through rule. It goes back all the way to the subsidiary's before-tax income (out of which the dividend was paid), and grants a credit for corporate taxes paid by the WOS. Thus, a dividend carries with it two tax credits: the *direct tax credit* for the withholding tax paid on the dividend, and the *indirect tax credit* for the corporate *taxes deemed paid* on the dividend. Apart from this, the logic is the same as in the branch case.

20.6.1.1 A 100%-Equity WOS: The Full-Payout Case

Consider the following example of a fully equity-financed subsidiary, which is owned by the parent firm.

Example 20.15. In table 20.8, we again consider an Icelandic-owned Vanuatuan operation with an income of ISK 100. The Vanuatuan corporate tax rate is 35% and the withholding tax on dividends is 17%. The first column repeats the tax computations for a branch under the "Credit method" that appeared in table 20.3. The middle column considers a WOS with the same income, which is paid out entirely as a dividend. Ignore the third column for the time being. In the middle column, the Vanuatuan corporate tax of ISK 35 leaves ISK 65 as the after-tax profit, which is, by assumption, fully paid out. The withholding tax on this gross dividend is ISK $65 \times 0.17 =$ ISK 11. The net dividend, therefore, is ISK $65 - 11 =$ ISK 54. In Iceland, this net dividend is grossed up with the direct credit for the withholding tax, ISK

11, and with the indirect credit for Vanuatuan corporate taxes, ISK 35. That is, one goes back to the before-tax Vanuatuan income, ISK 54 + 11 + 35 = ISK 100. If the Icelandic parent's tax rate is 40%, ISK 40 is due on this income, but Vanuatuan taxes were already ISK 35 + ISK 11 = ISK 46. Thus, the parent will potentially be left with an excess tax credit of 6.

The example illustrates how the credit system intends to avoid fiscal discrimination between the branch and a full-equity, full-payout WOS (which is, after all, very close to a branch). The only difference is the withholding tax, which in this example potentially creates an excess tax credit. If this excess tax credit cannot be absorbed elsewhere or carried back or forward, it might be advantageous to defer the dividend (and its withholding tax) to a year in which excess tax credits can be used against other income taxes. This is the timing option implicit in the deferral system. Another solution might be to "unbundle" the payout. Before we discuss unbundling, however, we discuss the rules that apply when the payout is less than 100% or when the foreign company is not 100% owned by the recipient.

20.6.1.2   The General Case

In many countries, the indirect tax credit is obtained only if the recipient company has a controlling interest in the foreign company that pays out the dividend. In the United States, for instance, the rule is that the recipient must own at least 25% of the foreign company, directly or indirectly. Thus, the indirect tax credit is lost when the participation is classified as a pure portfolio investment rather than as an active participation in the foreign company.

If the dividend is less than 100% of profits, then, in principle, the indirect tax credit is computed as

$$\text{Indirect tax credit} = \frac{[\text{Gross dividend (i.e., before withholding taxes)}]}{[\text{Corporate profit after corporate taxes}]}$$
$$\times [\text{Corporate tax paid}]. \quad (20.1)$$

In the full-payout case, the ratio in the first part of this formula equals unity. With a partial payout, the tax credit is reduced proportionally.

Example 20.16. The rule for indirect tax credits is illustrated in the last column of table 20.8. Since the dividend is only 50% of the profits after Vanuatuan taxes, the indirect tax credit is reduced proportionally:

$$\text{Indirect tax credit} = \frac{32.5}{65} \times 35 = 17.5. \quad (20.2)$$

Together with the withholding tax, this still creates a 46% total foreign tax rate, which leaves the parent with a 6% (that is, ISK 3) potential excess tax credit.

We finish our discussion of tax credits on dividends with some technical notes on equation (20.1). First, as in the branch case, the subsidiary's before-tax income as computed by the parent's tax authorities may differ from the one in the subsidiary's tax return, since the parent's home tax collector may reallocate expenses and reassess the foreign income. Thus, the corporate profits after corporate taxes in equation (20.1) are to be interpreted as the reassessed foreign profits minus the (effectively paid) foreign tax. The possibility of reassessments of foreign profits means that we cannot write equation (20.1) as [Indirect tax credit] = [Gross dividend] $\times \tau/(1 - \tau)$, where τ is the foreign corporate tax rate.[11]

Second, if the after-tax corporate profit in a given year is negative and there is a dividend, then equation (20.1) would imply a negative credit. One solution is to set the credit equal to zero if the formula yields a negative number. However, this means that there is no tax shield when a subsidiary pays a dividend out of retained earnings in a year where its earnings are negative, even though the retained earnings were taxed in the past. A related problem is associated with the fact that the effective foreign tax rate fluctuates over time, for instance, because of tax breaks received abroad or because of reassessments of foreign profits by the parent's tax authorities. If the subsidiary pays out its retained earnings in a year where the effective foreign tax rate happens to be low, then there would be a low tax credit even if the effective taxes in the past were high. To reduce these problems, the U.S. tax code bases the tax credits on the cumulative taxes and the cumulative after-tax profits since 1986 (the year of a major tax reform):

Indirect tax credit

$$= \text{Max} \left(\frac{[\text{Cumulative taxes since 1986}]}{[\text{Cumulative after-tax earnings since 1986}]} \times [\text{Gross dividend}], 0 \right).$$

(20.3)

If the host and home tax authorities always agreed on the taxable income and if the foreign tax rate were a constant, denoted by τ, then the ratio in equation (20.3) would be equal to $\tau/(1 - \tau)$. By cumulating the taxes and the net profits over time, this formula dampens the fluctuations in the indirect tax credit that could occur with formula (20.3) if, in a given year, the company receives a tax break or if there is a substantial upward reassessment of the subsidiary's profits.

---

[11] If the reassessed profits equal the profits declared and taxed in the host country, then host-country taxes in year t are equal to $\tau \times \text{Profits}_t$ and after-tax earnings for year t are equal to $(1 - \tau) \times \text{Profits}_t$. Thus, equation (20.1) would become

$$[\text{Gross dividend}] \times \frac{\tau \times \text{Profits}_t}{(1 - \tau) \times \text{Profits}_t} = [\text{Gross dividend}] \times \frac{\tau}{1 - \tau}.$$

Table 20.9.   Credit system: the effects of unbundling.

	Full equity	ISK 40 paid as interest to parent	
Vanuatu			
Branch profit	100	100	
(−) Interest paid to parent		(−) 40	
(=) Taxable	100	60	
(−) Taxes	(−) 35	(−) 21	
(=) Net profit	65	39	
		Dividend	Interest
Gross paid out	65	39.0	40
(−) Withholding tax	17% (−) 11	17% (−) 6.6	20% (−) 8
(=) Net paid out	54	32.4	32
Iceland			
Net received	54	32.4	32
Gross-up (1): direct	11	6.6	8
Gross-up (2): indirect	35	21.0	. . .
Taxable	100	60.0	40
Total taxable foreign income	100	100	
Tax due	40	40.0	
Tax credit (1): direct	11	14.6	
Tax credit (2): indirect	35	21.0	
Net tax due	0	4.4	
Unused tax credit	6	0	
Total taxes	46	40	

20.6.2   Tax Planning through Unbundling of the Intragroup Transfers

We saw, in table 20.8, that the compounding of host-country corporate taxes and withholding taxes increases the chance that the parent company ends up with excess foreign tax credits. In the branch case, the basic remedy against such unused foreign tax credits is to make sure that there is enough low-tax foreign income from elsewhere, so that the total foreign tax on the entire foreign income does not exceed the domestic norm. The same applies in the case of subsidiaries. The parent can combine dividends from high-tax host countries with dividends from low-tax host countries. But there is another remedy that does not require the existence of low-taxed sisters: the subsidiary from any given host country can unbundle the payments and remit low-taxed royalties, interest, and management fees next to a (high-taxed) residual dividend.

Example 20.17. In table 20.9, we modify the example presented in table 20.8 as follows: part of the equity is converted into an intracompany loan carrying an interest payment of ISK 40 subject to a 20% withholding tax. This has the following effects:

- The Vanuatuan profit, corporate tax, net profit, dividend, and withholding tax are all lowered. So is the grossed-up dividend, which is now ISK 60 rather than ISK 100.

- The decrease in the dividend is amply compensated by the interest income. The net interest payment carries its own tax credit and is grossed up to ISK 40.

- Total grossed-up foreign income, for the purpose of Icelandic taxation, is the sum of grossed-up dividend income and interest income. This amounts to ISK 100, exactly as before. However, total foreign taxes after unbundling (ISK 21+6.6+8 = ISK 35.6) are lower than before unbundling (ISK 35+11 = ISK 46). Thus, the original excess foreign tax credit is eliminated.

If foreign taxes can be used to offset taxes on worldwide income (including the parent's domestic income), it is less likely that the firm will be left with unused tax credits. However, most countries, including the United States, separate the taxation of domestic income from the taxation of foreign income. The natural temptation of U.S. corporations with excess foreign tax credits is then to transform domestic income into low-tax foreign income.

Example 20.18. Assume that a U.S. firm has an excess foreign tax credit, and that the firm holds domestic bonds. The strategy would be to sell these bonds, and buy foreign bonds, for instance, USD bonds issued by an offshore financing center of a big U.S. multinational corporation. Economically, nothing has changed, but the tax effect is that the erstwhile domestic interest income has been replaced by (low-taxed) "foreign" interest income. Excess foreign tax credits from foreign operations can then be used to avoid income taxes on the interest from the bonds.

To forestall such strategies, the U.S. tax authority divides foreign income into different so-called baskets, for example, active foreign income from subsidiaries in which the parent has a substantial equity participation, and passive foreign income from other sources. The foreign bonds in the above example would surely be passive income, the dividends from the WOS would not. Overall taxes would then be computed per basket, not allowing any transfer of excess tax credits from one basket to the other.

Our last comment concerns foreign tax breaks and tax holidays. As we saw, with a credit system, there is no way to pay less than the home tax rate; tax planning can achieve no more than a reduction or elimination of what you pay above the domestic tax rate. However, this means that tax holidays or rebates granted by the host country are effectively undone by additional taxation in the home country. Essentially, by their tax concessions, host-country tax authorities transfer money to the home-country tax authorities rather than to the investing company. This is especially offensive to developing countries, who see their tax incentives disappear into the treasuries of rich countries. Bilateral tax treaties signed with developing countries therefore sometimes contain *tax sparing clauses* which let the investing parent keep the tax benefit.

20.7 International Taxation of a Subsidiary (2): The Exclusion System

We now study the exclusion system as applied to subsidiaries in foreign countries. A home country that adopts the exclusion system will typically apply the exclusion privilege only to dividends received from abroad. The reason is that for other forms of remittances from the subsidiary to the parent—like royalties, interest payments, and lease payments—the foreign tax (if any) is a withholding tax; and because this tax is much lower than a typical corporate tax, it would be unreasonable to also exempt nondividend income from home-country taxation. Therefore, a credit system rather than an exclusion system often applies to nondividend remittances, or the exclusion percentage is much lower than that for dividends.

Under such an exclusion system, tax planning is easy. Compute the overall tax burden per form of remittance (dividends paid out of profits, royalties, interest payments, and lease payments), and remit as much as possible under the lowest-tax form. The total tax on dividends and on the underlying profits then consists of host-country corporate taxes and withholding taxes, plus possibly some home-country tax if the exclusion privilege is not 100%. Taxes on other remittances include withholding taxes and home taxation. The following example illustrates how one computes and compares the total tax burdens on each form of remittance.

Example 20.19. Suppose that 95% of the dividends received by a Belgian company from its foreign subsidiary are excluded from taxable income, while a standard credit system applies to nondividend income. Corporate taxes are 33% at home and 25% abroad, and there is a nondiscriminatory 25% withholding tax on dividends, interest payments, and royalties. In table 20.10, we compare the after-tax proceeds if EUR 100 is paid out as a royalty, and if EUR 100 is treated as part of the subsidiary's profit and then paid out as a dividend. We conclude that, in this example, profits (paid out as dividends) are beaten by royalties in spite of the low corporate tax on profits (25, abroad) versus on royalties (33, home). The key is that the dividend withholding tax does not bring a credit, in the exclusion method, while the one on royalties does.

A barebones exclusion system offers one glaring potential loophole. As we know, a firm can remit most of the subsidiary's gross earnings as nondividend income to escape corporate taxes in the host country. A gain will already result if home-country taxes are lower than host-country taxes, but we can even avoid most or all of the home-country taxes if the deductible remittances enter the home country in the form of tax-exempt dividends. To achieve this, the subsidiary's remittances are paid not to the parent but to an offshore holding company fully owned by the parent and located in a tax haven. The holding company receives this income, pays a minimal tax on it, and then transfers the income as dividends to the parent. Under an exclusion system, this eliminates virtually all taxation.

Table 20.10. Computation of total taxes on different remittances.

	Payout in the form of	
	profits and dividends	interest or royalties
Host country		
Branch profit	100	100
(−) Taxes	(−) 25	(−) · · ·
(=) After tax	75	100
Withholding tax 20%	(−) 15	(−) 20
(=) Net paid out	60	80
Home country		
Net income	60	80
Gross-up: direct	· · ·	20
Taxable	5% of 60 = 3	100
Tax due (33%)	1	33
Tax credit direct	· · ·	(−) 20
Net tax due	1	13
Total taxes	41	33

Example 20.20. If a U.S. subsidiary remits interest income to its Belgian parent, the taxes are (1) U.S. withholding taxes, and (2) Belgian corporate taxes (with only partial credit for the U.S. withholding tax). Alternatively, until a recent tax reform, the parent could create a wholly owned holding company in the Netherlands, which then sets up a wholly owned holding company in the Dutch Antilles that, in turn, lends money to the U.S. subsidiary. Interest paid by the U.S. subsidiary was free of U.S. withholding taxes to the Antilles holding company, which pays a minimal corporate tax (1.5–3%) on its interest income. The funds were then remitted as dividends (with zero withholding tax) to the Netherlands, where a minimal corporate tax applied provided a "one-sixteenth" ruling—don't ask—was obtained, and then to Belgium, where an exclusion system applied.[12] Thus, the Belgian corporate tax on interest income was replaced by a minimal Antilles and Dutch tax, with no further Belgian tax on the dividends.

Example 20.21. Corporations that have portfolio investments in domestic bonds pay taxes on the coupon income. Instead, the company (or a financial institution) can set up an incorporated mutual fund in, say, Luxembourg. The fund buys the bonds, escapes normal Luxembourg corporate taxation (since it is a mutual fund), and pays out the coupons in the form of dividends to its corporate investors. Again, taxable coupon income would be transformed into tax-free dividend income.

---

[12] The Dutch company was needed because, under Belgian law, a dividend from a tax haven like the Antilles does not benefit from the dividend exclusion privilege.

To close this loophole, countries often refuse to sign bilateral tax treaties with tax havens (or refuse to extend a treaty, if the special tax rule for off-shore companies became effective after the original treaty was signed). In the absence of such a treaty, then, there would be a unilateral rule offering partial rather than full exclusion. Another countermeasure could be a look-through rule. The holding company is ignored because it is a construct with, as its sole purpose, the avoidance of taxes. Under such a rule, taxes are based on economic substance rather than on legal form; that is, the dividends would be taxed as the underlying royalties or interest fees. A third possible countermeasure is to refuse exclusion of dividends from low-tax countries, from foreign companies that enjoy a special low-tax status, or from incorporated mutual funds.

20.8   CFO's Summary

This chapter provides an introduction to the broad principles of taxation of foreign income. To reduce double taxation, countries apply either the exclusion principle or the credit system. In principle, under the exclusion system, the only tax is the foreign tax, so that a foreign-owned company can compete with a purely local company (capital import neutrality). In principle, a credit system ensures that the total tax on foreign income is the same as on domestic income, so that there is no fiscal incentive for foreign investment (capital export neutrality). However, the actual application of either system usually falls short of the system's stated aim since, in practice, taxes are never fully capital-import or capital-export neutral. In addition, tax rates differ across countries, so that the exclusion system and the credit system would lead to different results even if each system were implemented in a perfect way. These considerations make tax planning a worthwhile exercise for the corporate treasurer.

Tax planning consists of determining where to allocate costs and profits (within the leeway offered by arm's-length rules) and how to remit the cash flows. Taxes depend on how much is remitted in the form of royalties, interest payments, lease payments, and management fees; taxes also depend on how indirect costs are allocated and on how transfer prices are set. Under a credit system, there is a preference for the form of remittance that attracts minimal foreign taxes. This rule minimizes the loss from unused tax credits but cannot reduce the total tax rate below the domestic rate. Under the exclusion system, the overall tax burden (home and foreign taxes) is computed for each type of remittance, and the lowest-tax form is preferred; total taxes can fall below the domestic rate. Next to actual financial remittances (such as dividends, royalties, and interest payments) and quasi-remittances (such as management fees, transfer pricing, and lease payments), one could also use equity transactions or intragroup loans to transfer funds from the subsidiary to the parent or to another related company.

Tax planning and "treaty shopping" are rather complex, and rules tend to change quickly in response to newly discovered loopholes. For these reasons, tax planning is better left to specialists, and no investment project should be accepted solely on the basis of hoped-for gains from tax planning. Stated differently, you should look at these gains as an extra sweetener, but not as a consideration that could actually tilt the balance in favor of adopting a project.

One final comment is about the merits of branches versus subsidiaries. From the discussion, we can get various pros and cons. The cons are the most obvious ones: (i) there is a withholding tax, raising the stakes from double taxation to triple taxation; and (ii) losses abroad cannot immediately be offset against the parent's overall income: the subsidiary can still carry them forward and (maybe) get tax rebates later, but the parent has to prove that the subsidiary's value is fundamentally impaired by the loss before a tax deduction would be possible at home. But there are pluses too: (iii) there is deferral—dividend payout can be timed; and, more importantly, (iv) under the credit system, unbundling of the subsidiary's payout offers much more scope for avoiding excess tax credits than does profit reallocation among branches.

TEST YOUR UNDERSTANDING

Quiz Questions

True-False Questions

1. The term "permanent establishment" (PE) is just tax-speak for "branch." That is, every branch is a PE and vice versa.

2. As soon as there is a permanent physical presence abroad, there is a PE.

3. A PE has a separate accounting system, while a branch does not.

4. If a person lives or earns income in more than one country, there may be double taxation.

5. The source principle says that any person earning money in a particular country is taxable in that country on his or her worldwide income.

6. Withholding taxes are levied by the host country on the taxpayer's worldwide income.

7. The legal basis for withholding taxes on nonlabor income paid to foreigners is the residence principle.

8. The capital import neutrality principle says that the foreign branch ought to be taxed as if it were a locally owned company.

9. The capital export neutrality principle says that the foreign branch ought to be taxed as if it were a locally owned company.

10. The capital export neutrality principle says that there should be no fiscal benefit or penalty associated with the fact that ownership and operations straddle two countries.

11. The deferral principle applies equally to the exclusion system and the credit system.

12. The disagreement on how to compute the income of a foreign branch arises only under the credit system.

13. The disagreement on how to compute the income of a foreign branch arises under both the credit system and the exclusion system.

14. The disagreement on how to compute the income of a foreign subsidiary arises only under the credit system.

15. The disagreement on how to compute the income of a foreign subsidiary arises under both the credit system and the exclusion system.

Below, a marginal tax rate is to be understood as the additional taxes you pay per cent or penny or öre of additional foreign income from one particular host country. The average tax rate is to be understood as the total tax paid on all foreign income as a percentage of the foreign income. For the questions that relate to the credit system, it is assumed that foreign income is taxed separately from domestic income. Verify whether the following statements are true or false.

16. Under a 100%-exclusion system, the marginal tax rate on foreign income is the foreign corporate tax rate (τ_c^*).

17. Under a 100%-exclusion system, the marginal tax rate on foreign income is the foreign corporate tax rate (τ_c^*) plus the foreign withholding tax (τ_w^*).

18. Under a 100%-exclusion system, the marginal tax rate on foreign income is given by
$$1 - (1 - \tau_c^*)(1 - \tau_w^*) = \tau_c^* + \tau_w^* - \tau_c^* \tau_w^*.$$

19. Under a credit system, the marginal tax rate on foreign income is the home-country corporate tax rate τ_c.

20. Under a credit system, the marginal tax rate on foreign income is the higher of either the home-country corporate tax rate τ_c or the marginal foreign tax.

21. Under a credit system, the marginal tax rate on foreign income is bounded from above and below by the home-country corporate tax rate τ_c and the marginal foreign tax.

22. Under a credit system, the average tax rate on foreign income is the home-country corporate tax rate τ_c.

23. Under a credit system, the average tax rate on foreign income is either the home-country corporate tax rate τ_c or the average foreign tax, whichever is higher.

24. Under a credit system, the average tax rate on foreign income is bounded from above and below by the home-country corporate tax rate τ_c and the average foreign tax.

Additional Quiz Questions

1. Suppose that foreign activity is conducted through a wholly owned subsidiary. Which assumptions are needed to achieve both capital import and capital export neutrality?

   (a) The home and host corporate tax rates are the same.
   (b) There is no withholding tax on dividends.
   (c) The tax basis is computed in exactly the same way in both countries.
   (d) There is full payout.
   (e) There are no interest payments, no license payments, no lease payments, and no management fees between WOS and parent.
   (f) A credit system applies to nondividend remittances from WOS to parent.
   (g) What does one mean by the residence principle and the source principle? What do these principles imply for the taxation of income on:
      • Pure (direct) exports?
      • Exports through a dependent agent?
      • Exports through a branch/PE?
      • Foreign activities through a subsidiary?

2. Explain, using a numerical example of your own, how differences between the host- and home-country rules for the allocation of overhead can impair the neutrality of a credit system or an exclusion system.

3. How do companies take advantage of the basic exclusion system for dividends? Which additional tax rules can be applied to prevent these unintended uses?

4. How can one reduce excess foreign tax credits by transforming domestic income into foreign income? Which additional tax rules can be applied to prevent such tactics?

5. Conventional wisdom says that tax planning means minimizing foreign taxes. Is this true under the exclusion system? Is it true under the credit system? If your answer was yes in both cases, is there no difference between these systems regarding the tax savings you make by tax planning?

6. The bartender at your favorite pub sneers that, by using transfer pricing, a company can always eliminate its excess foreign tax credits. Do you agree, or do you think that your friend is forgetting something? Why?

Applications

1. A foreign-owned company earns 100,000 in its host country. The host-country corporate tax is 50%, the withholding tax 20%, and the home-country tax is 40%.

   (a) What is the total tax if there is no relief from double taxation?

   (b) Still assuming full double taxation, what tax could have been avoided if the business had been conducted through a branch/PE?

   (c) Go back to the case of a WOS. What is the total tax burden if there is full payout and if the exclusion principle applies in the home country?

   (d) What is the total tax burden if there is full payout and if the exclusion privilege is only 80%?

   (e) What is the total tax burden if there is full payout and the home country uses a credit system?

   (f) In question (e), does it matter whether the home country taxes foreign income separately from domestic income?

2. Suppose that the corporate tax schedule in Finland is as follows:
   - 25% tax on income below EUR 50,000;
   - 30% tax on income between EUR 50,000 and EUR 100,000;
   - 35% tax on all income exceeding EUR 100,000.

   (a) What is the tax if a Finnish corporation's income is EUR 200,000, of which 100,000 is the profit on domestic sales and 100,000 is the profit on exports to Hong Kong (without PE in Hong Kong)?

   (b) Assume that Hong Kong levies a flat 15% corporate tax and no withholding tax on dividends, and that Finland applies a pure exclusion system. Is there any incentive to set up a branch/PE in Hong Kong? If so, what is the worldwide tax?

   (c) Add to question (b) a rule under which Finland preserves the progressiveness of the tax schedule (see figure 20.1). Is there still an incentive to set up a branch/PE in Hong Kong? If so, what is the worldwide tax?

   (d) Repeat question (c) and assume that Hong Kong's tax schedule is identical to Finland's and that Hong Kong also preserves progressiveness. Is there still an incentive to set up a branch/PE in Hong Kong? If so, what is the worldwide tax?

3. The company Think Tankards has a stable foreign income, which is taxed at a low rate abroad. In each of the three preceding income years, it effectively paid USD 50m in additional U.S. taxes on foreign income, and it expects to do the same for the years to come. For the current year, however, there is a USD 100m excess foreign tax credit. How is this excess credit treated under each of the following carry-forward/carry-back rules? What is the present value of the loss if future tax breaks are discounted at 15%?

    (a) No carry-back, one-year carry-forward.

    (b) No carry-back, two-year carry-forward.

    (c) One-year carry-back, two-year carry-forward.

    (d) Two-year carry-back, two-year carry-forward.

4. A Belgian bank holds EUR 10 billions' worth of seven-year EUR government bonds, with a direct yield of 10% (that is, its annual interest income is EUR 1 billion).

    (a) Until a tax reform in 1992, the bank could transform its interest income into dividend income, which enjoyed a 90% exclusion privilege. Specifically, the bank sold its bonds to a Dublin dock company (DDC), which was fully owned by an Irish holding company (IHC), which in turn was fully owned by the Belgian bank (BB). Interest income received by the DDC was taxed at 10% and then paid out as a dividend to IHC, which did not pay any taxes (100% exclusion within Ireland). IHC then paid the dividend to its owner, BB. Assume no withholding tax between Belgium and Ireland, and a 90% dividend exclusion and a 40% corporate tax rate in Belgium. What was the annual tax gain?

    (b) A tax consultant suggested that BB would gain even more by swapping its seven-year, 10% EUR bonds into NZD, which at that time yielded 20%. Thus, the consultant argued, the gains would be doubled. What crucial feature is overlooked in this argument? (*Hint.* You need an insight from chapter 4.)

5. Your two foreign outposts, a branch in Germany and one in Singapore, each have sales of 100. The host-country tax rates are 40% and 20%, respectively.

    (a) If your home country uses the credit system and has a 30% tax, how would you (try to) allocate total costs (120) over the two subsidiaries? Assuming an unlimited potential to shift costs, is there an incentive to allocate all costs to one branch?

    (b) Assume that your country uses a credit system, and that you have very little leeway in reallocating costs over the two branches. So you consider increasing the transfer price charged by Singapore to Germany. Imports into the European Union are taxed at 25%. Would you increase or decrease the transfer price?

    (c) In question (b), at what level of the import duty τ_m is the advantage wiped out?

    (d) Same question as (a), except that your home country applies a 90% exclusion rule?

6. Your only source of foreign income is a marketing WOS in Hong Kong, where the tax rate is 20%. At home you pay 35%. There is no withholding tax.

    (a) Under the 100% exclusion method, would you use a high transfer price or a low transfer price for sales to the subsidiary?

    (b) Same question as (a), except that the credit method applies.

    (c) Same question as (a), but there is a 10% import duty on sales to Hong Kong.

7. Suppose that the German parent has sales equaling 200, and the Tunisian branch, 100. Direct costs are 80 and 30, respectively. German tax authorities allocate overhead, which amounts to 120, on the basis of sales, while in Tunisia allocation is proportional to direct cost. German and Tunisian taxes are 40%. Are you vexed by or happy with this discrepancy between the rules? Consider both the credit system and the exclusion system.

8. A U.S. corporation has two foreign marketing branches, one in France and one in Hong Kong. The current situation is summarized as follows (all numbers in thousands of USD):

	Hong Kong	France	U.S. (domestic income)
Sales	1,000	5,000	10,000*
Costs:			
purchases from parent	500	2,500	n.a.
other expenses	100	500	6,000
depreciation	100	500	1,000
Profits	300	1,500	3,000
Corporate taxes	45 (15%)	600 (40%)	900 (30%)
Profits after taxes	255	900	2,100

*Including sales to subsidiaries.

(a) The U.S. tax rate is 30% and taxation of foreign and domestic income is separated, with the foreign tax credit applied to the tax on foreign income only. Is there still a U.S. tax due or is there an unused tax credit?

(b) The parent is currently making a profit on its "sales" to the branches but considers changing the profit allocation. The company thinks that it can increase or decrease the transfer price by up to 5% without creating any problems with the tax authorities, on the condition that the transfer price remains the same for both branches. Should the company increase the price or decrease it?

(c) Is your conclusion in (a) or (b) affected if domestic and foreign income is taxed together (that is, the tax is computed on worldwide income and then the tax credit is applied)?

9. Sales and costs are 200 and 100, respectively, for the Tunisian branch, and 100 and 60 for the Hong Kong branch. The tax rates are 50% in Tunisia and 25% in Hong Kong. The parent's home country, Germany, has a 40% tax rate and applies the credit system.

(a) Verify that there is an excess tax credit of 4.

(b) Verify that when the parent shifts costs worth 40 from Hong Kong to Tunisia, the original excess tax credit has been replaced by a foreign tax shortfall of 6.

(c) Suppose that the Tunisian tax authorities unexpectedly reject the additional costs (40), so that this part of the costs is not deductible anywhere. What is the total tax?

21

Putting It All Together: International Capital Budgeting

In this chapter, at long last, we consider how to apply standard capital-budgeting or investment analysis—where one computes the net present value (NPV), that is, the difference between the present value of the future cash flows and the initial outlay—when the project at hand is international. The basic rule in capital budgeting is to accept a stand-alone project if the NPV is positive; and when there are mutually exclusive alternatives—like starting immediately versus waiting and seeing—one goes for the alternative with the highest NPV. Many of the relevant ingredients in international NPV calculations have already been discussed, including how to set the discount rate or how to assess international taxes. What remains to be done is to present the main methodology into which these ingredients fit, and settle some remaining issues that do not warrant an entire chapter by themselves.

The structure of this chapter is as follows. In section 21.1, we review the basics of standard (domestic) investment analysis. In sections 21.2–21.5, we address the main issues that arise when capital budgeting is applied to international investment projects: how to handle the financing aspects, how to deal with exchange rates and exchange risk, what to do about political risk, and what incremental cash flows are most likely to be missed by the hasty analyst. We add, in section 21.6, a checklist of remaining loose ends you need to keep in mind when preparing an investment analysis report.

21.1 Domestic Capital Budgeting: A Quick Review

In this section, we review the concepts of NPV, adjusted NPV, and weighted average cost of capital (WACC). We argue that it is easier and typically more accurate to use the NPV rule as opposed to the WACC criterion for making capital-budgeting decisions.

21.1.1   Net Present Value (NPV)

The traditional approach to capital budgeting is to compute the net present value as the difference between the present value of the expected future cash flows (discounted at a constant cost of capital) and the initial outlay. The basic rule is to accept a project if its benefits exceed its cost, that is, if the NPV is positive. And if there are competing, mutually exclusive projects, one selects the alternative with the highest (positive) NPV. We shall briefly elaborate on the notions of cash flows and discounting, and then provide an example.

Discounted Cash Flows

Capital budgeting is about discounted cash flows not discounted profits. As you should know, profits and cash flows differ with respect to timing. First, the initial outlay associated with an investment is generally up-front, whereas the profit and loss (P&L) statements report these outlays over several years in the form of annual depreciation charges. Second, the projected P&L statements assign revenues and production expenditures to the reporting period during which the final product was sold. However, the actual production expenditures generally occur long before the moment when a good is sold, and the customer often pays months or occasionally years after the moment of sale. Since we are interested in cash flow not accounting profits, we should add back the depreciation charges to the projected profits, and recognize the investment outlays when they actually occur. Likewise, one has to correct for the leads in production outlays and lags in sales income (*investments in working capital*, in short) in order to correctly compute the present value of the cash flows. We discuss the various ways you can account for that in a separate subsection.

   We need to discount the expected cash flows to account for the fact that the cash flows are spread out over several years. If the risk of these cash flows is fairly stable over time, we can take uncertainty into account by discounting the expected cash flows at a risk-adjusted cost of capital, that is, the risk-free rate plus a (usually positive) risk premium. According to the capital asset pricing model (CAPM), the relevant risk to be taken into account is not the total uncertainty of the investment in itself, but the project's contribution to the total risk of the firm's cash flows, and ultimately to the risk of the shareholders' wealth. The InCAPM, in its full version, also takes into account the effects of international ownership, notably the fact that the investors' valuation units depend on where they live.

Accounting for Leading Outflows, Lagging Inflows

Workers and suppliers are traditionally paid before the moment of selling and customers pay afterward. The difference can amount to a few months, or even years in the case of big-ticket sales like passenger jets. There are two issues. First, this gap has to be bridged: we have to find the money to make the early payments. This means we need an idea of how much "net working capital" is needed. Second, in the NPV calculations we need to account for the leading of the outflows and the lagging of the inflows.

One convenient way to achieve both objectives simultaneously is to subtract the working-capital investments from the free cash flow. The usual approach is to estimate each year's NWC as a constant fraction of sales and to count any increase as an outflow and any decrease as an inflow. A related method shifts part of the outflows into the previous calendar year and part of the inflows into the next one. Alternatively, if NPV is all one is after, one can correct for leads and lags directly in the discounting procedure. For instance, if outlays take place three months before selling, on average, and customers pay one month later, the outflows can be discounted at $(1 + R)^{t-3/12}$ and the inflows at $(1 + R)^{t+1/12}$. The example hopefully makes all this less theoretical.

Example 21.1. We consider a one-year problem. In year 1, sales are budgeted at 180, and costs at 120. A/R will be cashed 30 days after the sale, while A/P and wages, etc., are paid 30 days before the sale. So the implied A/R at the end of the year amounts to the December sales, i.e., 15 units; and the prepayments in year 0 amount to the cost of the January sales, $120/12 = 10$ units. So NWC, in steady state, would be A/R + INV − A/P = $15 + 10 = 25$.

In method 1, below, we deduct the 25 NWC "investment" in year 1, and "recuperate" it the year after. In method 2 we push the prepayments (10) into year 0, and the lagged receipts (15) into year 2. In method 3 we recognize the lead and lag in the discounting operation:

$$\text{Method 1:} \quad PV = \frac{(180 - 120) - 25}{1.10} + \frac{25}{1.10^2} = 52.48;$$

$$\text{Method 2:} \quad PV = \frac{-10}{1.10^0} + \frac{(180 - 15) - (120 - 10)}{1.10^1} + \frac{15}{1.10^2} = 52.40;$$

$$\text{Method 3:} \quad PV = \frac{180}{1.10^{1+1/12}} - \frac{120}{1.10^{1-1/12}} = 52.38.$$

In the example, the choice hardly matters. In multiyear examples, more questions arise; and one can also consider ease of application:

▷ **Method 1 (NWC/sales).** This method assumes that [inventory + A/R] is a constant fraction of sales. This creates a problem if the profit margin changes considerably over time, for instance because of falling prices due to "market creaming" and increasing competition: then costs (and the investment in inventory) become a larger fraction of sales. Similarly, the method fails if there are falling costs (learning effects, economies of scale, etc.): falling costs relative to prices would make the true NWC/sales ratio fall, but our method would ignore this. For the same reason, in multiproduct examples where conditions differ, a problem arises if the product mix is shifting over time.

▷ **Method 2 (shift ▷ and ◁).** This method can handle changing profit margins, since adjustments at the cost and sale sides are separated. It can also handle many types of sales and costs, each having its own lead/lag. It does complicate the spreadsheets, arguably, but this is not a major issue.

▷ **Method 3 (build leading/lagging into discounting).** This method is very similar to method 2, except perhaps that it may be simpler to program. It also allows further refinement with timing.

Standard NPV, in effect, recognizes integer years only. (Kids have that limitation too.) It typically assumes that all investments are immediate (time 0) and all sales take place at times $1, 2, \ldots$, and so on. A better approximation to the reality of continuous sales and outlays is to put the timing in the middle of the year, and then correct for NWC effects. For the investment period one can likewise be more subtle, and the start-up year can be different with, sales starting in the middle of the year and being timed, accordingly, as occurring at 3/4 of the year on average. So in the above example, the timing would be $1.5 \pm 1/12$ instead of $1 \pm 1/12$, and investments could be timed for time 0.75 (the middle of the second semester), etc.

Base-Case NPV Computations: An Illustration

The following example illustrates the basic NPV procedure without any international ramifications. We need to be clear about this before we can discuss how such a base-case NPV must be adjusted to deal with the issues that arise when evaluating an international project.

Example 21.2. A Chinese family-owned company, GuoWeltek, currently produces heavy-duty equipment for construction welding. The company is considering a proposal to set up a new business unit, which would produce and market electrodes for maintenance and repair welding in China. For simplicity, assume that the life of the project is five years. The initial investment consists of the following items (all figures are in millions of CNY):

1. Land, worth CNY 100. This investment cannot be depreciated. The expected liquidation value after five years, reflecting expected inflation of 5% p.a., is CNY 130.

2. Plant and equipment (P&E), worth CNY 350. This investment is depreciated linearly over five years, and has no scrap value at the end of the project's life.

3. Entry costs: CNY 250, including training of the sales force, initial advertising, free samples, and so on. We assume that under local law, these expenditures are to be capitalized and depreciated linearly over five years rather than deducted immediately from initial profits.[1]

---

[1] If allowed, accelerated depreciation or, a fortiori, immediate expensing are, of course, more attractive: the sooner we get the tax rebate, the better.

Table 21.1. NPV of the cash flow generated in Weltek's new business unit.

Year	(a1) Sale of goods	(a2) Sale of land	(b) Variable costs	(c) Overheads	(d) Depreciation	(e) Taxable income	(f) Taxes
1	650	—	260	105	120	165	58
2	1,000	—	400	110	120	370	130
3	1,100	—	440	116	120	424	148
4	600	—	240	122	120	118	41
5	300	—	120	128	120	−68	−24
6	—	130	—	—	—	30	11
PV	1,991	40	872	312	—	—	198

Key: Sales, variable costs, and overheads forecasts for the proposed new business unit are provided by the marketing and operations divisions. Depreciation of the investment outlays is described in the beginning of the example. For years 1–5, (e) = (a1) − (b) − (c) − (d). For year 6, (e) is the liquidation value of the land minus initial value; (f) = (e) × 0.35. Taxes and present values are rounded to the nearest integer. PVs are computed using a 20% discount rate. See technical note 21.1 for further details.

Weltek is a 100%-equity-financed firm and it has the funds that are necessary for a new investment. Estimates of sales, variable production costs, overheads, depreciation charges, and corporate taxes (35%) are shown in table 21.1. All data take expected inflation (5% p.a.) into account. Negative taxes in year five correspond to the tax rebate the company gets from setting off the loss from this project against its other income. The figures for year six reflect the liquidation value of the land (130), and the tax bill in year six is calculated based on the accounting gain (liquidation value minus historic cost, or 130 − 100 = 30).

The sales revenue, variable costs, overheads, and taxes must be discounted back to time 0, taking into account investments in working capital. The shareholders use a 20% discount rate, which is probably not outrageous for under-diversified owners, especially since equipment is rather a cyclical business in general and since heavy-construction welding itself is already quite cyclical. In technical note 21.1 we do this and obtain an NPV of −13m yuan. The conclusion is that the cost exceeds the benefits and that, at least on the basis of the current data, the project should be rejected.

DIY Problem 21.1. Looking at the P&Ls in the table it seems that the project could be saved by the simple expedient of stopping one year earlier: the last year produces a loss of 68, whose discounted value, if dropped, would be enough to reverse the currently negative NPV. No?

Incremental Cash Flows

The principle to be kept in mind is that since NPV measures the change in the shareholders' wealth, the cash flows to be used in the analysis are the incremental cash flows, that is, the change in the company's overall expected cash flows when the project is added to the company's existing activities. In the above example, the determination of the cash flows started from the projected profit and loss (P&L) accounts of the proposed business unit. However, the incremental cash-flow principle means that one must often also consider cash flows that are not accounted for by the P&L of the proposed new business unit. For example, sales made by the new business unit may partly replace existing sales made by another unit within that company or group. Likewise, the new unit often buys from (or sells to) the parent or other units in the group, and these trades generate profits to the parent or sister company. Lastly, the project will trigger not just corporate taxes in the host country, but also withholding taxes as well as domestic corporate taxes. If some or all of these effects on the overall cash flows are omitted, the NPV computations are misleading.

Example 21.3. Consider the project analyzed in example 21.2. During a discussion of the investment proposal, a manager points out that the proposed unit will buy the coating for the electrodes from an existing business unit. Following a sound business principle, the transfer price used in the projected P&Ls is based on arm's-length prices for similar coatings. Obviously, this transfer price includes a normal profit of the supplying business unit. Although this profit is not included on the projected P&L statements for the proposed unit, it is nevertheless generated by the project and should be included in the evaluation of the new project.

Suppose that the intracompany transactions represent about one quarter of the project's variable costs and that each delivery valued at the arm's-length price of 100 yuan increases the profits of the unit that acts as the supplier by 50 yuan; that is, variable costs are half of the transfer price. The additional deliveries of coating material will not require any additional investment nor will they affect the company's overheads. We leave the valuation of the profits the parent makes on its intracompany sales as an exercise. Assume that the result of valuing the incremental cash flows is CNY 71m. Let us now evaluate the project. The true NPV (using the incremental cash flows) equals:

- NPV of the cash flows realized by the new business unit   −13m
- PV of the linked cash flows generated by the supplying unit   71m

Total (in CNY):	58m

Thus, once one accounts for the cash flows generated outside the proposed business unit, the project is profitable.

21.1.1.1 Sensitivity Analysis

Anybody who has ever had to provide, or at least evaluate, the estimations and assumptions that accompany an NPV analysis will appreciate how tenuous many of the input data are. It is therefore vital that you experiment with variants of the assumptions after you have solved the base case. For instance, you should do a sensitivity analysis where you lower the sales figures by 10%, or 20%, or perhaps even 50%, and see how sensitive the NPV is to the sales estimates. A similar procedure can be followed with respect to production and overhead costs, and the discount rate. The estimate of the required return is imprecise because our estimates of the project's risk and the expected risk premium per unit of risk are not very exact. Even the initial investment itself deserves a closer look. In practice, the projected outlays are frequently under-estimated and, more often than not, the construction and start-up phase also lasts longer than initially projected. Finally, for international NPV problems, exchange-rate forecasts may be necessary, and these forecasts should also be subject to a sensitivity analysis.

21.1.2 Adjusted Net Present Value (ANPV)

It has become standard practice to analyze domestic investment proposals in two steps. In the first stage, the analysis assumes that the whole investment is financed by equity and that the money is already available so that no new shares or bonds have to be issued. Accordingly, the cash flows do not take into account interest payments or loan amortizations; and the discount rate is based on the risk of the operating cash flows. In this stage of the valuation, the focus is on the inherent economic value of the project, not on the financing aspects. This is, in fact, what we did in examples 21.2 and 21.3.

The financing aspects of undertaking the project are then considered in the second stage of the analysis, and lead to adjustments in the first-stage NPV calculations. This second stage results in an *adjusted net present value* (ANPV). For instance, if new equity or bonds have to be issued, then the associated costs must be deducted from the NPV. Similarly, subsidies, in the form of capital grants or interest subsidies, are also taken into account in the second stage.

Example 21.4. Suppose that in order to implement the project we considered in example 21.3, the company has to raise new equity at a cost of CNY 5, and that it obtains a capital grant of CNY 40 from the government because the investment is made in a rural area. The ANPV is

$$\text{ANPV} = \text{NPV} - \text{Issuing costs} + \text{Subsidy} = \text{CNY } 58 - 5 + 40 = \text{CNY } 93. \qquad (21.1)$$

If there is borrowing, the NPV calculations still work with total investment (not the part coughed up by the shareholders), total future cash flows (not the part that accrues to shareholders after servicing debt), and a discount rate for unlevered equity (the asset beta, not the beta for levered equity). Under Miller–Modigliani assumptions, the NPV is independent of borrowing. But the NPV adjustments may also include tax savings created by corporate borrowing. This is discussed in the next section.

21.1.3 The Interest Tax Shield Controversy

Unlike dividends, interest payments are a tax-deductible expense for a corporation. Debt financing, therefore, typically reduces corporate taxes. The following example illustrates the potential advantage of the tax shield.

Example 21.5. Ms. Taikoon is the sole owner of a Finnish company that makes a perpetual profit of EUR 50m before interest and taxes. She now extends a perpetual 5% loan of EUR 500m to the company, with the instruction to use the money to repurchase part of her equity. Apart from taxes, nothing has changed: the 500m is back in her bank account, and Ms. Taikoon is still the sole owner and recipient of all payouts; but the company's taxable profits decrease by EUR 500m × 5% = EUR 25m. Given a corporate tax rate of 30%, this implies annual corporate tax savings of 25m × 30% = EUR 7.5m.

If a company undertakes an investment project, the firm's gross present value increases, which means that its borrowing capacity also goes up. One of the adjustments in ANPV might therefore be the present value of taxes saved if the firm uses the new borrowing capacity.

Example 21.6. Suppose the yield on perpetual debt is 5%, and that Ms. Taikoon initially considers to maintain the debt at 500m forever and a day. Without the tax break, the company would already be worth EUR 50m/0.05 = 1,000m. The annual savings are worth, in PV terms, an additional EUR 7.5m/0.05 = 150m.

Suppose there is a new project that would add EUR 10m p.a. to the annual cash flow and, therefore, 10m/0.05 = 200m to the value, not accounting for tax breaks from any additional borrowing. Since cash flows are up by 20%, she could let debt rise by 20% too without raising the leverage ratio. Thus

- she can lend an extra 100m to the company;
- this would add 100m × 0.05 × 0.30 = 1.5m in tax savings;
- the PV of this, 1.5m/0.05 = 30m, can be added to the NPV.

This is generalized in technical notes 21.2 and 21.3. However, this type of computation is likely to overestimate the tax savings. First, not all of the tax shields may be used effectively if the earnings before interest are not sufficiently large.

Example 21.7. Suppose that the profits of Ms. Taikoon's company are typically EUR 20m before interest and taxes, rather than EUR 50m. The EUR 25m in interest fees implies that annual profits will be systematically negative. Thus, the annual tax savings from interest payments are only 30% of the earnings before interest, that is, EUR 20m × 30% = EUR 6m, rather than the EUR 7.5m that we computed in example 21.5.

Even if the company expects to be able to use its interest tax shield in most years, there is still a loss in time value whenever, for a particular year, the profits after interest payments are negative and part of the tax subsidy has to be carried forward into a future tax year.

Moreover, the above analysis of the tax shield generated by corporate borrowing is incomplete because it considers only corporate taxes. To determine whether paying out interest is more attractive than paying out dividends, we have to look at the total tax burden including, for instance, the shareholders' and bondholders' personal taxes. Differential taxation at the personal level may partially or wholly offset the discrimination at the corporate level, namely if, at the personal level, interest income is taxed more heavily than income from shares. For instance, in many countries, capital gains (which form a substantial part of the total remuneration of equity) remain untaxed or are taxed at a rate below the standard rate. In some countries, individual investors can even obtain partial or full credit for corporate taxes when dividends are taxed at the personal level, in which case the tax advantage on debt at the corporate level is partially or fully undone at the personal level.[2]

Example 21.8. Suppose that the company's profits are again EUR 50m before interest and taxes. Ms. Taikoon pays no personal income taxes on dividends, but pays 30% tax on interest income. Then, the EUR 25m interest payments on the loan will still save EUR 7.5m in corporate taxes, but they will also lead to an additional EUR 7.5m personal income tax. Thus, on balance, there would be no tax gain from issuing debt in this case.

In view of the diversity of tax regulations with which your shareholders and bondholders may be confronted, it may be difficult to calculate the total tax subsidy, taking into account both corporate and personal taxes. For a firm whose shares and bonds are held internationally, this task is even more daunting.

But that's not the end of our problems yet. Even if we could establish that there is a subsidy and if we had an approximate idea of its size, it would still be very difficult to figure out what part of the assumed interest tax subsidy accrues to the shareholders and what part to the bondholders. We would generally expect that the tax subsidy (if any) is somehow shared among shareholders and bondholders. The reason is that if borrowing is subsidized, the company's lenders will be able to raise the interest rate because of the increased demand for debt financing. This means that at least part of the total subsidy will go to the lenders; that is, if we think that all of it goes to the shareholders, then the ANPV is overstated.

---

[2] In chapter 20, we discussed tax credit systems in international corporate tax, but it can also be applied within a country to prevent double taxation at the corporate and personal level. The essence is that corporate taxes are treated as an advance personal tax. For example, if Ms. Taikoon receives a dividend of EUR 70, the tax man computes that the underlying before-tax corporate profit was $70/(1 - 0.3) =$ EUR 100. Under a credit system, Ms. Taikoon then has to declare a dividend income of 100 before taxes. If her tax rate is 40%, the total tax due is $100 \times 40\% = 40$, but she obtains credit for the 30 paid by the corporation. Also interest income would be taxed at 40%, and Ms. Taikoon would not gain from her corporate borrowing.

Example 21.9. Suppose that there are two hotels in town, the Equity Hotel and the Bond Hotel. Hotel expenses are initially assumed not to be tax deductible and both hotels charge USD 100 per night, the breakeven price.

A change in the legislation now makes hotel bills from the Bond Hotel tax deductible, while the expenses incurred at Equity Hotel remain part of the taxable profit. If the tax rate is 33.33%, one of the many possible new equilibria is that the Bond Hotel increases its prices to USD 150 per night. Then, the after-tax cost for a night at the Bond is $150 \times (1 - 33.33\%)$ = USD 100, which is equal to the cost of staying at the Equity. There *is* a subsidy of USD 50 in this case, and the subsidy *is* related to the tax deductibility—but it ends up in the pockets of the Bond Hotel rather than with the company that deducts the Bond Hotel's bills from its profits.

Thus, the true beneficiary of a tax subsidy may be the supplier of the tax-deductible service (the Bond Hotel in the above example or, in the interest tax shield case, the bondholder) rather than the user (the company and, ultimately, the firm's shareholders). We need detailed information about supply and demand in order to be able to say exactly who gets what part of the subsidy.[3] In summary, if we are not sure whether there is a tax subsidy, and how much of it accrues to shareholders, we surely have a good reason for keeping it separate from the main NPV calculations.

21.1.4 Why We Use ANPV rather than the Weighted Average Cost of Capital

We conclude this section with a brief discussion of an alternative rule that is still occasionally used as a substitute for ANPV. In the weighted average cost of capital (WACC) approach, there is only one step: all cash flows are discounted at a rate that is the weighted average of the after-tax p.a. cost of debt, $R_D(1 - \tau)$, and the cost of equity, $E(\tilde{R}_{EQ})$. This cost of equity is the p.a. rate of return expected by the shareholders. Thus, the WACC is computed as follows:

$$\text{WACC} = \frac{D}{E + D} \times R_D(1 - \tau) + \frac{E}{E + D} \times E(\tilde{R}_{EQ}), \tag{21.2}$$

with D standing for borrowings for this project and E for equity, which is total value minus debt. Stated differently, $E + D$ stands for the project's gross present value, GPV = I_0 + ANPV.

One reason for quickly forgetting this formula (or producing a sad smile when colleagues bring it up) is that using WACC is unnecessarily convoluted. It is, in fact, far more complicated than the modal user realizes. The root of the problem is that WACC weights are based on market values, which we only have when we have finished the valuation. In addition, the expected return

---

[3] Miller (1977) develops a theory which implies that all of the tax subsidy goes to the bondholders. Of course, Miller is rather selective in his assumptions, but his main point is that it is naive to believe that all of the subsidy (if any) accrues to the shareholders.

on equity depends on leverage, with leverage again being defined in market-value terms—which we do not know until we have finished the valuation. This presents a nice chicken-and-egg problem.

The problem of $E(\tilde{R}_{EQ})$ depending on market-value weights can be avoided by restating the WACC in terms of the expected return on assets (subscript "a") for an unlevered firm (superscript "u"):

$$\text{WACC} = \underbrace{\frac{D}{E + D} \times R_D + \frac{E}{E + D} \times E(\tilde{R}_{EQ})}_{E(\tilde{R}_a^u)} - \frac{D}{E + D} \times R_D \times \tau$$

$$= E(\tilde{R}_a^u) - \frac{D}{E + D} \times R_D \times \tau. \qquad (21.3)$$

The underbraced group in the first line is the WACC if there is no tax advantage, for instance if the firm has so many loss carry-forwards or other deductible items, that the interest tax shield does not really add any tax savings anymore. In the absence of a tax effect, we know that the Miller–Modigliani cost of capital is invariant to leverage and can be interpreted as the expected return on equity of an unlevered firm, often called the expected total return on the assets. This is the discount rate we use in step 1 of ANPV. So WACC is this base rate corrected for a tax effect. It is simpler to work with that rate rather than with the expected return on equity: to compute the latter you again need market weights.[4]

While simpler, the new WACC formula still contains a weight that requires a market valuation. There are three ways people deal with the chicken-and-egg problem:

Let GPV dictate D rather than vice versa One option is that you do not fix D in light of the project's cost and the firm's liquidity situation, but let it be decided by the GPV and a target leverage ratio. For instance, if the cost is 1,000, the GPV 1,500, and the target leverage 1/3, then the firm borrows $1,500/3 = 500$; any excess or shortage of cash would then be solved by dividends or equity issues, respectively. This policy would allow you to use WACC since you know beforehand what the leverage ratio will be: 1/3.

Very few firms would actually behave like this. Some textbooks nevertheless recommend using a long-run target leverage ratio in the WACC, regardless of the amount D actually used for the project. This, it is argued, is approximately valid if there are many projects over time and across divisions and if the firm adjusts its dividend or share-issuing policies to remain close to, say, a 1/3 leverage ratio: then occasional under- or overshooting in

---

[4] If you have a naive trust in statistics, you can try and estimate the equity's beta and compute an expected return. But it is wiser to start from industry-expected returns, where firm-by-firm betas are corrected for leverage and then averaged across stocks. This is a zero-leverage number, the expected return on an all-equity firm. The averaging across firms eliminates estimation errors, so this is less unreliable.

the project-by-project leverage ratio would tend to cancel out. Many companies do actually follow a target-leverage rule—but in terms of book values rather than market values; in fact, such a capital-structure policy would be quite difficult if there are important fluctuations in the firm's market cap. And the it-all-averages-out approach may be unrealistic for small firms or in the case of huge projects. Below we see what you can do when D is dictated by the project's cost and the firm's cash situation rather than long-term policy.

Use accounting weights. Most people use D/I_0 as the ratio, not $D/(I_0 + \text{ANPV})$. Usually, this is because they don't even know that the proper interpretation is based on market values.

For some applications the error is not a problem, since we are still likely to get the sign right; we just exaggerate the magnitudes:

- if the true NPV is positive, this approach overestimates leverage, underestimates the required return, and thus overstates the NPV;
- when the true NPV is negative, leverage is underestimated, the cost of capital overestimated, and as a result the NPV picture looks even worse than it really is.

There is a serious problem, however, if we want to compare mutually exclusive projects: when we select the "best" among all positive-NPV proposals, then we need unbiased NPVs, not numbers with a positive but otherwise unknown bias.

Iterate. You can start by provisionally using the WACC-for-dummies approach using accounting weights, that is, assuming a zero NPV when computing the discount rate. Compute the NPV, and from this reestimate the WACC, and so on.

Very often, the iteration approach is relevant. True, this is not outrageously difficult—but why bother at all if ANPV gives you the answer in one shot? This argument becomes even more convincing once you take into account the additional shortcomings of WACC:

- Beside being cumbersome, the WACC method has the disadvantage that it merges the first-stage NPV computation with the second-stage computation of the tax advantage from borrowing. In doing so, the WACC assumes that (i) the tax shield is always fully used, (ii) the corporate tax savings are not offset by any fiscal discrimination at the personal level, and (iii) all of these savings end up with the shareholders. All this, as we have just argued, is overly optimistic.

- Second, the WACC method only works for constant leverage. In contrast, ANPV can handle any (deterministic) cash-flow pattern or capital structure.

*   *   *

We are now ready to look at the valuation issues in an international environment. There are two big issues that arise in international capital budgeting and that we have still not discussed. First, in international investment projects, the financing issues include not just outside financing (from banks or bondholders) but also intragroup deals, like loans from parent to subsidiary or management and license contracts, etc., which often are mainly tax-inspired. How should one handle this in the ANPV stage? Also, there are political risks. Foreign-earned funds may be blocked abroad, because the host country has insufficient reserves of hard currency (transfer risk). Another political risk is expropriation risk. How should one account for such risks? These issues are discussed in the next two sections. We also review our points relating to the sequencing of translation and discounting (HC, FC) and its relation to market segmentation and exchange risk; and we look again at the incremental-cash-flow principle, explicitly listing what items one is wont to overlook and why. The final sections cover a few remaining loose ends.

21.2 InNPV Issue #1: How to Deal with the Implications of Nonequity Financing

When valuing operations in a foreign country, we need to take into account the tax effects for the company as a whole. In an international context, taxation does not end with corporate taxes on the profits of the foreign subsidiary. The host country will tax not just the profits of the subsidiary, but also the parent when the subsidiary remits income to the parent. In addition, the parent's foreign income (dividends, interest income, royalties) is, in principle, taxable in its home country, as are the parent's profits from sales to the foreign subsidiary. This interaction and potential proliferation of various taxes then gives rise to the following issues:

- How should one set the transfer prices for intragroup sales of goods and services so as to minimize taxes? That is, how should one allocate profits between the parent and the subsidiary? Or, if the foreign presence is in the legal form of a branch, how should one divide the company's total profits into a foreign-earned part and a domestic part?

- How should the foreign subsidiary remit its cash flows to the parent? That is, what is the optimal remittance policy? As we have seen, the subsidiary can remit cash to its parent through equity transactions, loans, dividends, interest payments, royalties, or management fees, and each method has different tax implications. The financial manager must make optimal use of the intricacies, shortcomings, and loopholes in tax rules or tax treaties that reduce double taxation on branch profits and on remittances from a subsidiary. In addition, the manager must make optimal decisions with respect to the timing and size of the dividend remittances.

In short, one issue in international capital budgeting is tax planning—but tax planning, we argue, is best separated from the valuation of the cash flows from operations. Recall that the first stage in a domestic-investment analysis problem focuses on the economics; the cash flows associated with financial decisions are considered later. In an international setting, we likewise start by focusing on the operational cash flows, and reserve the financing issues and their tax implications for a later stage. Note, however, that in international projects, the financing issues have an extra dimension. As in a domestic project, one has to adjust the NPV of the operations for the costs and possible benefits associated with *external* financing, like borrowing from banks or unrelated bondholders or issuing new shares. In addition, and unlike in a domestic project, one has to account for the costs and benefits associated with the *intragroup* financial arrangements between parent and subsidiary, like intragroup loans or license contracts. Thus, we recommend a three-step process for valuing international projects:

Step 1 (branch stage). In the first stage, the focus is on the cash flows from operations. Accordingly, we ignore all financial arrangements between the parent company and the foreign subsidiary, by assuming that the foreign venture is just an (unincorporated) branch of the parent rather than a legally separate company.

Step 2 (unbundling stage). In the second round, the foreign venture is incorporated as a separate company that can choose a remittance policy. We analyze the costs and benefits of the intragroup financial arrangement by which the foreign entity unbundles its remittances into license fees and royalties, interest payments, and dividends. We call this stage the unbundling stage.

Step 3 (external financing). At the end, adjustments are made for the effects of external financing, like issue costs and subsidies.

Comparing the valuation procedure of an international project to the procedure used for a domestic investment, the change is the insertion of step 2.

21.2.1 Step 1: The Branch Scenario or Bundled Approach

In the first stage, we assume that the project is implemented as a branch of the company, not a subsidiary. Unlike a subsidiary, a branch has no remittance policy, and the scope for tax planning is very limited. All cash flows are automatically and immediately owned by the parent. Thus, the focus at this stage is on the economics of the project—sales, costs, differences between cash flows realized by the project and overall incremental cash flows, exchange risks, political risks, and so on.

The practical implication is that if the projected P&L accounts contain interest payments to outside lenders or to other companies in the group, and royalties paid to a related company, you should immediately remove these items and recalculate the taxes accordingly. So we go from the first version

Table 21.2. Projected P&L statements including royalties and interest.

	(a)	(b) Variable	(c)	(d)	(e)	(f)	(g) Taxable	(h)
Year	Sales	costs	Overheads	Depreciation	Royalty	Interest	income	Taxes
1	650	260	105	120	33	40	92	32
2	1,000	400	110	120	50	32	288	101
3	1,100	440	116	120	55	24	345	121
4	600	240	122	120	30	16	72	25
5	300	120	128	120	15	8	−91	−32

Key: Sales and costs are as in table 21.1. A royalty of 5% of annual sales is paid to Weltek U.K. The interest payments relate to a 16% five-year unsecured bank loan with an initial book value of CNY 250m, of which CNY 50m is amortized at the end of each year. (g) = (a) − (b) − (c) − (d) − (e) − (f). Figures are rounded to the nearest integer.

	(a1) Sale of	(a2) Sale of	(b) Variable	(c)	(d)	(e) Taxable	(f)
Year	goods	land	costs	Overheads	Depreciation	income	Taxes
1	650	—	260	105	120	165	58
2	1,000	—	400	110	120	370	130
3	1,100	—	440	116	120	424	148
4	600	—	240	122	120	118	41
5	300	—	120	128	120	−68	−24
6	—	130	—	—	—	30	11
PV	1,991	40	872	312	—	—	198

Key: For years 1–5, (e) = (a) − (b) − (c) − (d). For year 6, (e) is the liquidation value of the land minus initial value; (f) = (e) × 0.35. Taxes and present values are rounded to the nearest integer. PVs are computed using a 20% discount rate. See technical notes for further details.

of table 21.2 to the one shown in the second panel, the one we have already used. Note that this implies not just the deletion of a few columns, but also a reworking of the taxes column.

The main reason for doing so is that it helps us to avoid certain mistakes and pitfalls:

Pitfall #1. *Confusing out-of-pocket costs and left-pocket/right-pocket payments.* An NPV under "branch" assumptions steers clear of a common pitfall among novices (which probably includes you), namely to consider the royalties or interests on an intracompany loan as a "cost" to the subsidiary, while forgetting that these payments also represent an income to the parent. These are not out-of-pocket expenses but left-pocket/right-pocket operations. Leaving these payments out, in stage 1, is simpler than working with two worksheets, and patiently deducting the remittances in company A's table while adding them in company B's.

Pitfall #2. *Confusing tax savings and tax shifting.* The other pitfall is to focus on the reduction of corporate taxes in the host country created by payments of royalties or interest, while forgetting that the parent is taxed on this royalty or interest income at home. Usually, one does not avoid taxes, one replaces them by other taxes paid elsewhere, by the new recipient of the remittance. It is simpler to just compute, separately, the net change in taxes rather than to rework the entire spreadsheet of the project and add a table for the parent.

Pitfall #3. *Inconsistent discount rates.* We have no good methodology for incorporating a license contract into an NPV calculation. In the case of debt, as we saw, one can work out a cost of capital for levered cash flow under the assumption that leverage is constant. Specifically, one can argue that actual borrowing fluctuates randomly around the long-run borrowing capacity, which is proportional to GPV, and accordingly use a WACC based on potential debt rather than actual debt. As we saw, such a WACC-based computation probably provides too optimistic an answer. But for license contracts and so on there is not even an equivalent of a WACC in the first place. The royalties are almost surely of lower risk than the net cash flows,[5] but it is difficult to work out the beta of the cash flows net of royalties. One cannot use a constant-weight assumption since the GPV of the project and the PV of the royalties are not, in principle, proportional. Competition drives rents to zero, so an initially profitable project should have a falling GVP—but the sales can go on growing, and so would the royalties. Almost inevitably, the discount rates you use for royalties, net-of-royalty cash flows, and total cash flows will be mutually inconsistent.

Pitfall #4. *Getting too distracted by tax issues.* Starting with a branch scenario where tax games are ruled out, the managers can focus on the inherent merits of the project, without being unduly diverted by fiscal details. Tax planning is complex and technical, and is best left to fiscal experts and tax consultants. Simultaneously, to many people it is strangely exhilarating—so much so that it takes away too much attention from the economics. Last, when estimating the tax effects of incorporating a branch into a subsidiary, one needs to make tenuous assumptions about the size and timing of dividend payouts; and the hoped-for savings from fiscal planning may disappear when tax codes are changed. In fact, tax authorities feel a regrettable urge to close fiscal loopholes. Thus, the safer procedure is to accept a project on the basis of its economic merits, and consider any additional gains from tax planning as a welcome but nonessential boon, to be worked out by experts after the decision is taken.

---

[5] There is a leverage effect if the "out" element in cash flows, the production cost, has a lower beta than the sales, the "in" side. The existence of partly fixed costs is enough to generate this. As a result, one has $\beta_{\text{net flows}} > \beta_{\text{sales}} > \beta_{\text{costs}}$.

Pitfall #5. *Thinking that tax loopholes will persist forever.* Unfairly, authorities have a tendency to close loopholes. Thus, if you had let a hoped-for tax gain tilt the NPV from negative to positive, then any subsequent change in the rule would land you with a bad project.

Example 21.10. Example 20.20 described a rather convoluted way to get cash from the United States to Belgium at next-to-nothing cost, exploiting a tax treaty between the United States and the Dutch Antilles, and Belgium's 95% exclusion rule for dividends. It was hugely popular in the 1980s. A few years later, the U.S. revoked the tax treaty; and exclusion in Belgium was canceled for dividends from companies with special tax status or from a tax haven. The game was over.

Thus, it is safer to regard tax games as just a cherry on the cake, and make the decisions on the merits of the cake itself—the economic, step-1 value.

21.2.2 Step 2: The Unbundling Stage

The second step in the valuation process consists of analyzing the intracompany financial arrangements[6] that become possible as soon as we incorporate the branch into a wholly owned subsidiary.

The second stage of the calculations is to some extent similar to the second stage in a standard (one-country) NPV problem, in the sense that the project's financing is examined. The reason why we separate the costs and benefits of intragroup financing (step 2) from those of external financing (step 3) is that the former can be estimated in a more reliable way than the latter. With intragroup contracts, we know exactly who the beneficiaries are and how they are currently taxed; and the benefits clearly accrue to the group as a whole. In contrast, it is hard to quantify the overall tax benefit generated by outside borrowing, and it is even harder to find out who is the actual beneficiary of the tax subsidy.

The following example illustrates how to adjust the branch NPV calculations for the effects of a royalty or intracompany loan contract.

Example 21.11. Let us give an international flavor to the investment project discussed in table 21.1. The company that is considering setting up a company for the production and marketing of welding electrodes in China is now Weltek U.K. The value of the operations in the form of a branch is assumed to be unaffected by this change of ownership; that is, the cash flows realized in China still have an NPV of CNY −13m and the additional cash flows generated by profitable sales of inputs by Weltek U.K. to Weltek China increase the total NPV to CNY 58m. One of the managers points out that the corporate taxes paid by Weltek China will be substantially reduced if (1) Weltek China signs a license contract with Weltek U.K. and

---

[6] The term "intracompany" is a standard way to refer to transactions between related companies (for instance, between parent and subsidiary or between subsidiary A and subsidiary B of the same parent). From a legal point of view, the term is somewhat imprecise, since there is more than one company.

pays a royalty equal to 5% of its Chinese sales as a compensation for the use of the parent's know-how, and (2) Weltek China borrows funds from a Chinese bank. The manager proposes a five-year loan of CNY 250m. The principal is amortized in five equal payments of CNY 50m and the yearly interest charged is 16% on the amount outstanding at the beginning of the year. The tax savings become obvious, the manager argues, if one compares the revised P&L projections in table 21.2 with the projections in table 21.1 (where there were no royalties or interest payments).

We evaluate the loan part of this proposal as follows. First, it is not known what the total tax effect of the external loan actually is, nor is it known how much of the supposed benefit accrues to the shareholder, Weltek U.K. Thus, we should leave this financing aspect to step 3, if we wish to consider it at all. Second, if we really feel sure all the potential corporate-tax benefits will be realized and that they will all accrue to the shareholders, we should still never work with actual borrowing (as in the example), but with potential borrowing based on a long-term target leverage ratio and a time-varying GPV.

In evaluating the benefit of the license contract, we should also consider the taxes that Weltek U.K. will pay on the royalty. Suppose that Weltek U.K. pays no taxes on dividends received from Weltek China (this is the "exclusion" rule; the actual U.K. rules are different), and that income from licensing is taxed in the United Kingdom at 30%, 5% below China's corporate tax rate. Thus, if the subsidiary pays out royalties worth CNY 100, there is a saving of CNY 35 in Chinese corporate taxes but an additional cost of CNY 30 in U.K. taxes, implying a net tax saving of just 5% on the gross royalties. Weltek would, therefore, like to set the royalty as high as possible. Suppose that tax consultants tell Weltek that any royalty in excess of 6% would probably be rejected by the Chinese tax authorities as above normal.[7] In view of this information, Weltek U.K. decides to set the royalty at 6% rather than at 5% (as proposed in table 21.2). The present value of the benefits (the 5% tax saving on the 6% royalty on sales) is then[8]

$$\text{PV tax saving} = \sum_{t=1}^{5} \frac{\overbrace{0.06}^{\text{Royalty \%}} \times \text{Sales}_t}{1.18^{t+0.5}} \underbrace{\times 0.05}_{\text{\% tax saved}} = \text{CNY 6.6m.} \qquad (21.4)$$

---

[7] Recall that tax laws of most countries have a rule saying that payments for goods and services bought from related foreign companies should be based on arm's-length prices, that is, at prices that would be normal among independent parties. Thus, any part of an expense declared in China that exceeds the arm's-length level can be rejected as a cost, and would then be taxable in China as part of the subsidiary's profit. The U.K. taxes on the parent's income would still be based on the royalties as actually received, not on the arm's-length royalty. Thus, the rejected part of the royalties would be taxed twice.

[8] We assume that the royalties are paid every month on the basis of the sales (not on the basis of the actual payments from customers); that is, royalties are paid at times $1.5, 2.5, \ldots, 5.5$ on average. The present value of the tax saving is computed at a rate of 18% rather than the 20% cost of capital used for the entire cash flow because royalties are based on sales, which have a lower risk than the overall net cash flows. Recall the argument: net cash flows are like the payoffs from a portfolio of sales revenue (held long) and costs (held short). If the beta risk of costs is lower than the risk of sales revenue, then the beta of the net cash flow will be higher than that of either the sales or the costs. The effect is similar to the effect of financial leverage.

As we know, royalties are just one possible element in the company's tax-planning strategy. Tax planning was discussed in greater detail in chapter 20. From that chapter one should remember that it is by no means obvious that royalties generally save taxes (as they do in the above example).

21.2.3 Step 3: The Implications of External Financing

The third and final stage in the international capital-budgeting process pertains to the aspects of external financing. If the group has to raise equity, or if the parent or subsidiary issues bonds or borrows from banks, there are likely to be costs. Likewise, there might be tax subsidies on borrowing. However, it is hard to know what extra present value is created by interest tax shields, and it is even harder to know who receives what part of the subsidy.

If you believe that there are fiscal subsidies on external borrowing, and feel you have a pretty good idea of how much of the tax benefits you will receive, all kinds of interesting issues arise in the third step. Who should borrow, the parent or the subsidiary? And should one borrow in a high-interest currency or in a low-interest currency? For answers to these questions, one might feel tempted to go back to the traditional (domestic) capital-budgeting literature, where the well-known conclusion is that the present value of the corporate tax shield is a positive function of the corporate tax rate and of the interest rate. The message we want to get across is that these standard conclusions are not necessarily correct in an international setting.

21.2.3.1 Who Should Borrow?

One of the decisions to be made is whether the external loan should be taken out by the parent or by the subsidiary. On the basis of the standard (domestic) analysis one would conclude that it is optimal for the parent to borrow if the home-country corporate tax is higher than the host-country rate, and vice versa.

Example 21.12. Suppose that the corporate tax rate is 16% in Hong Kong, while in Belgium it is 33%. If the Hong Kong subsidiary deducts HKD 100 as interest payments, this saves HKD 16 in Hong Kong taxes. If, on the other hand, the Belgian parent borrows, Belgian taxes worth HKD 33 are avoided. Thus, the impression is that borrowing should be done in Belgium.

However, the above analysis is incomplete, as it only considers the borrower's corporate taxes. One should also take into account that if the Hong Kong subsidiary does not borrow, its profits will be higher, which means that (sooner or later) its dividends will be higher than they would have been if there had actually been a loan in Hong Kong. These higher dividends will trigger additional Hong Kong taxes on dividend remittances, and also higher Belgian taxes on dividend income from the Hong Kong subsidiary. Thus, the decision cannot be made just on the basis of the corporate tax rates.

Example 21.13. Suppose that the corporate tax rate is 16% in Hong Kong, while in Belgium it is 33%. Suppose also that dividends paid out by a Hong Kong company are taxed at 5% in Hong Kong and at 33% in Belgium, with a credit for foreign taxes. This, as we know, means that the Hong Kong dividends are normally taxed at 33% altogether, so that Hong Kong borrowing also saves 33% not 16% in (total) taxes—same as borrowing in Belgium. We conclude that an analysis of tax shields based purely on taxes on corporate profits (16% versus 33%) would have been misleading.

DIY Problem 21.2. What about the withholding tax that is paid on the interest and the corporate income taxes? Should they not be brought into the picture too?

21.2.3.2 In What Currency Should One Borrow?

The firm also needs to decide on the currency of borrowing; specifically, it has to decide whether borrowing should be in a high-interest currency or in a low-interest currency. On the basis of the standard (domestic) analysis, one may conclude that borrowing in high-interest currencies is beneficial in terms of tax subsidies. However, as we argued in chapter 5, this rule of thumb, when used to compare loans in different currencies, is wrong because it ignores the capital gains or losses due to changes in exchange rates. In terms of risk-adjusted expectations or PVs, the capital gains or losses are exactly offset by the difference between the interest rates. It follows that, in terms of risk-adjusted expectations, the taxes on the capital gains or losses are exactly offset by the taxes on the difference between the interest rates, as long as taxes do not discriminate between interest and capital gains. Thus, from an *ex ante* tax point of view, the currency of borrowing does not matter, even in the presence of taxes, as long as the spot and forward markets are in equilibrium and the capital gains tax is the same as the tax on ordinary income. Of course, the absence of *ex ante* tax considerations in choosing between currencies does not mean there could be no other reasons for favoring one currency, like PV-ed risk spreads, exposure, and contribution to financial distress risk.

21.3 InNPV Issue #2: How to Deal with Exchange Rates

From the preceding chapter, one almost invariably starts from FC cash-flow projections, while the investment analysts work with a cost of capital in home currency. One or the other has to change in order to proceed. Our earlier discussion, summarized in table 21.3, yielded the following rules, which depend on whether the home- and host-country's capital markets are integrated or not.

Integrated markets. In this case, valuation can be done in either currency. Note that the HC and FC procedures should use the same market portfolio; but this does not mean that expected returns and (co)variances are the same across the two currencies. Also, remember that, in integrated markets, one should

Table 21.3. Rules for the capital-budgeting process: overview.

	Discount rate is from...	Everything done in...
Are home and host country part of one integrated financial market?		
• Yes	InCAPM	FC or HC
• No		
• Home country part of wider capital market	InCAPM	HC only
• Home country totally isolated?	CAPM	HC only

use an InCAPM, in principle; so it would be wrong, in principle, to think that one can ignore exchange-rate exposure by working in FC.

Segmented markets. If home and host are not part of one integrated market, there is no reason to believe that foreign and home investors would value the project in the same way. The company's yardstick is, of course, the home valuation. There are two implications. First, the cost of capital should be set in HC, because one observes how assets are priced in that market and that currency. The model can be a one-country CAPM if *home* is cut off from the rest of the world; more likely, *home* is part of a wider market, and the InCAPM should be used, in principle. Second, the cash flow needs to be translated into HC. Remember that, in principle, a covariance is involved here; if you have imprecise priors about that, widen the range of sensitivity analyses correspondingly.

In the transition from our domestic Chinese project to an international investment by a U.K. corporation, we have so far left out one potentially huge effect: the impact on the cost of capital. We kept using 20%, a rate that is not unreasonably high for underdiversified family owners, and we kept using CNY cash flows throughout. But Weltek U.K.'s shareholders can diversify far more. Here's one possible story.

Example 21.14. Since China's economy is still relatively closed off from the Western ones, Weltek can argue that the project's beta would be below unity, say, 0.5.[9] So Weltek can work with a (GBP-based!) discount rate of 5% risk free plus a $1/2 \times 5\%$ risk premium. This must be applied to the CNY cash flows, so we need translation. Weltek's bankers reckon that, in view of the continuous pressure from U.S. Congress to let the yuan appreciate, the currency will drift upward by about 2% a year against the USD; and since moves in the USD/GBP rate are hard to predict, the yuan would then also appreciate by 2% against the pound. So a PV operation would now look

---

[9] Don't be shocked at how impressionistic this beta is. It's difficult to do anything more scientific here, as there are no share price histories for Western-owned Chinese welding-equipment shares on Western stock exchanges. Just add sensitivity calculations assuming betas of 0.25 or 0.75.

like discounting at 5.39% ($= 1.075/1.02 - 1$):

$$\frac{CF_t^* \times (S_0 \times (1.02)^t)}{1.075^t} = \frac{CF_t^* \times S_0}{(\frac{1.075}{1.020})^t} = \frac{CF_t^* \times S_0}{[1 + (\frac{1.075}{1.020} - 1)]^t} = \frac{CF_t^* \times S_0}{1.0539^t}. \qquad (21.5)$$

This will have a whopping effect on NPV.

DIY Problem 21.3.

- Try it.
- Work out an implied discount rate (like the 5.39%, above) in the following case: (i) the FC cash flows are in constant year-0 prices, (ii) foreign inflation is 4%, (iii) home inflation is 2%, and (iv) the real exchange rate is expected to appreciate by 3%. You should find an implied rate of 2.32%.
- Same assumptions, but the FC cash flows are already adjusted for foreign inflation. Show that the implied discount rate is 6.41%.

21.4   InNPV Issue #3: How to Deal with Political Risks

Beside issues arising from international taxation, one also must take into account transfer risks when valuing a foreign investment. Transfer risk refers to the possibility that when the reserves of hard currency in the host country are low, the cash generated abroad may be blocked by the host government. That is, the parent may not be able to repatriate the interest, dividends, or royalties it earned abroad, or the funds held in a bank account opened by our branch office. As part of the valuation of an international project, we discuss three issues with respect to transfer risks. First, how can the risks be minimized proactively, that is, before the problem actually arises? Second, what can be done once the parent's funds are effectively blocked? Lastly, how can transfer risks be incorporated into the NPV analysis?

21.4.1   Proactive Management of Transfer Risk

We have seen in step 2 of the capital-budgeting process how unbundled intra-company payments, such as royalties and interest, can be used to reduce the total tax liability. In this section, we argue that unbundling can also be used to manage transfer risk. The reason is that countries with foreign currency reserve problems will not suddenly forbid all remittances. Some forms of remittances are more likely to be blocked than others.

Transactions on the capital account, such as equity transfers and loans granted to other companies in a group, are generally the first type of transactions to be blocked. If the subsidiary is regularly buying goods or services from other companies in the group, then the subsidiary can still make a disguised loan to its supplier by speeding up ("leading") the payments for the goods it bought. In this way money can be taken out of the country without openly making a loan.

> **Example 21.15.** Every month, a subsidiary buys USD 1m worth of goods from its parent and pays 60 days later. Suppose that, after the imposition of currency controls in July, the parent shortens the credit period to 30 days. This means that the parent receives two payments in August—one for the deliveries made two months before and one for the previous month's deliveries.
>
> This is equivalent to keeping the credit period at 60 days and making an interest-free loan from the subsidiary to the parent for USD 1m without a stated expiration date.

The same effect is obtained by delaying ("lagging") payments from the parent to the subsidiary for sales of goods by the subsidiary to the parent. If you want to be able to use leading and lagging, you have to proactively establish a tradition of intragroup transactions. However, you should not expect too much. Governments with besieged currencies often impose limits on credit terms for exports and imports. Also, setting up such a "just in case" tradition of trade could be expensive in terms of transportation costs, delay risks, and export/import taxes.

Dividends are usually next on the list of transfers that are blocked (or at least limited).[10] However, even dividends are not always entirely blocked. Rather, as a first measure, a government will limit dividend payments (to 5% of equity, for example). Strategies that increase the capital base may be used to reduce the effect of such a dividend ceiling. For instance, one could increase the capital base by cheaply taking over a local company with a huge nominal capital but a low market value, or bringing in equipment as equity-in-kind, at a rather generous valuation. Another useful proactive defense against the risk of blocked dividends is to include the parent's own government, a government agency, or the International Finance Corporation (IFC)[11] as a minority shareholder of the subsidiary. From the host government's point of view, antagonizing the World Bank or a government is (somewhat) more embarrassing than blocking dividends due to a private foreign company.

Interest payments and license fees are next on the list of payments to be blocked by a foreign government that is short of hard currency. Interest on intracompany loans and royalties paid to the parent are blocked less often than dividends. Moreover, interest payments made to a foreign bank are blocked less often than similar payments on an intracompany loan. Therefore, a not-uncommon strategy is to use a bank as a front in a back-to-back loan: the parent lends funds to an international bank, which then relends these funds to the subsidiary. (The parent's deposit serves as a guarantee for the loan, so that the bank's risk is minimal.) Again, a host government

---

[10] If they have the choice, monetary authorities prefer to block dividends rather than interest or royalty payments because dividends are not contractually fixed.

[11] The IFC is a subsidiary of the World Bank that takes equity participations. Apart from bringing in capital (and official World Bank support), the IFC can also help by offering its expertise about countries, markets, and such, and by helping with feasibility and profitability studies—for a fee.

will think twice before it blocks interest payments to an international bank. A variant is the double back-to-back loan, involving a local bank: you lend to an international bank, which lends to a local bank, which lends to the project. Stopping the payments would now bring the local banking system into international disrepute, so governments may think thrice about doing that. In addition, the link between parent and subsidiary is now even better hidden. Finally, loans structured as bearer-bond issues are even less subject to sovereign risks than bank loans. For example, during the international-debt-crisis years in the eighties, there was no instance of rescheduling of eurobonds.[12]

Finally, **payments with a nonfinancial label** (management fees, payments for intracompany trade and for technical assistance) are blocked only in extreme circumstances. These payments are not viewed as financial transfers, but as payments for imports of goods and services. Of course, it would look suspicious if the parent suddenly increased its transfer prices after the imposition of exchange controls. The correct proactive defense, therefore, is to start charging high transfer prices long before the exchange controls are imposed.[13] In the same vein, the parent may create a management contract, or may "sell" technical assistance on a more or less regular basis, rather than taking these funds out of the country as dividends. Note, however, that most countries reserve the right to reject transfer prices that are deemed to be above the arm's-length value, that is, the normal market price paid between independent parties.

21.4.2 Management of Transfer Risk after the Imposition of Capital Controls

Once currency controls have been imposed, the firm can overcome these by leading the payments from subsidiary to parent and lagging the payments from parent to subsidiary. It can increase transfer prices and management fees or charge more for technical assistance. However, substantial changes in transfer pricing or credit terms will trigger reactions from the host country authorities. Thus, substantial amounts of money are likely to remain effectively blocked. Such blocked funds are not irrevocably lost.

---

[12] When bank debt is to be rescheduled, a government in distress knows which banks are involved; in contrast, renegotiating a bond issue is difficult if the securities are (or are said to be) held by many anonymous individual investors.

[13] Note that there may be various costs associated with intracompany trade at high transfer prices. First, import duties on the goods sold to the subsidiary will be higher. Second, if the corporate tax paid by the parent is higher than the rate paid by the subsidiary, high transfer prices may imply a higher overall tax burden for the group as a whole. Third, buying goods from the parent rather than producing them locally may be expensive in terms of direct production and transportation costs.

1. The parent may invest them in the local money or capital markets, new projects, or inventory. Internationally traded goods may be a comparatively good investment, since their value is less subject to devaluation risks. Still, there is likely to be some loss of value, since these "second-best" investments would otherwise not have been made.

2. Alternatively, the parent may try to spend the funds as wisely as possible, perhaps by buying local goods or services that would otherwise have been bought elsewhere, by organizing executive meetings and conferences in the host country, or by buying airline tickets from the local carrier. Again, there will almost certainly be a loss of value, since these purchases would normally have been undertaken elsewhere, at lower prices (since the host-country currency is likely to be overvalued and import restrictions make host-country prices artificially high).

21.4.3 How to Account for Transfer Risk in NPV Calculations

Three approaches can be used to quantify the impact of transfer risks on a project's value:

- First, we could add an extra risk premium (for transfer risk) to the project's discount rate. In general, this is not recommended because we have no idea how to determine this risk premium.[14]

- Second, if we have an idea about the probability of the funds being blocked and about how much value will be lost if the funds are actually blocked, we can take this into account when computing the expected cash flows. However, quantifying this information is not easy. Also, we do not know at what rate the (adjusted) expected cash flows are to be discounted.

- Fortunately, transfer risks can typically be insured by private insurance companies or government-run insurance agencies. This means that the present value of the (after-tax) insurance premia can be used to estimate the risk-adjusted expected value of the transfer risks. This approach is probably the best. It uses readily available market information and is a strategy that is easy to implement.

Example 21.16. Let us return to example 21.3. Our earlier NPV computation, CNY 58m, assumes that the funds generated in China are immediately and automatically available to the parent. This would be true if Weltek U.K. did not incorporate its foreign business as a separate company and if there is no risk that the funds

---

[14]If a company from the host country has internationally traded bonds outstanding that are denominated in hard currency, we can observe some kind of transfer risk premium by comparing the yield on these bonds to the yield on risk-free bonds in the same currency. However, the transfer risks of dividends are likely to be higher than the risks present in bearer bonds. Thus, the risk premium observed for eurobonds understates the risk premium required for other claims.

Table 21.4. Quantifying Weltek's transfer risk.

Reporting year	Book value assets	Insurance premium	$Id \times (1 - \tau)$, i.e., after taxes
0	700	7.0	4.55
1	580	5.8	3.77
2	460	4.6	2.99
3	340	3.4	2.21
4	220	2.2	1.43
5	100	1.0	0.65
PV			14.04

will be blocked in China. Worried about the latter contingency, Weltek contacts the U.K. Export Credit Guarantee Department and learns that it can buy insurance against transfer risks for dividends (up to 10% of the book value of equity) and for repatriation of the invested capital, at 1% p.a. of the book value of the foreign operations, payable at the beginning of each year. The cost of insurance is computed in table 21.4. Weltek will pay this fee as long as the subsidiary is not bankrupt or otherwise liquidated; that is, the risk of the insurance payments is the same as the risk of default by its subsidiary. In view of the low risk, Weltek discounts these amounts at the rate the subsidiary would pay on a bank loan, which is 7%. Because this fee is tax deductible, the true cost to Weltek is

$$PV = \left(4.55m + \frac{3.77m}{1.07^1} + \frac{2.99m}{1.07^2} + \frac{2.21m}{1.07^3} + \frac{1.43m}{1.07^4} + \frac{0.65m}{1.07^5}\right) = 14.04m. \quad (21.6)$$

We see that political risk reduces the NPV by CNY 14.04.

21.4.4 Other Political Risks

Other political risks, besides transfer risk, include the possible expropriation of a company, the "distress" sale of equity following the imposition of minimal local ownership rules, or the nationalization of entire economic sectors.

Again, one can often buy insurance against these forms of expropriation. One way to incorporate the expected cost of expropriation, therefore, is to use insurance premia as part of the cash flows. However, this approach does not work as well for expropriation risks as it does for transfer risks. This is because, first, compensation is too often still based on accounting values, which can deviate substantially from true values. One reason might be inflation: accounting numbers are based on historic nominal costs. At least equally important for modern firms, brand, brains, processes, and know-how are worth more than the bricks and steel you find on the balance sheet.

A second reason why insurance works very imperfectly here is that it usually takes some time before the damage is recognized and assessed; so there is the loss-of-time value. Finally, expropriation can take place covertly. A government can slowly strangle a company, for example, by refusing it investment licenses

Political risk insurance used to be dominated by government-owned institutions and the World Bank's Multilateral Investment Guarantee Agency (MIGA). Governments were better placed to shoulder the biggest risks, one heard in those days, and governments were also willing to subsidize their insurers so as to help the national industry. Often, insurance was (and is) also part and parcel of the country's foreign policy. Lastly, a government as insurer may have a stronger position than a private company, especially in emerging countries that depend on Western aid.

In most of the richer countries, however, subsidizing is no longer acceptable—Japan remains a notable exception—and private insurers are big enough to take on most risks. So the latter are back, nowadays, and have taken about half of the market. The list of big players includes AIG, Chubb, some syndicates at Lloyds, and a newcomer, the Bermuda-based Sovereign Insurance Group. Government companies are still relatively dominant in emerging markets, as part of the sponsor's development policy and because of their comparative strength re bargaining. This relative dominance in the "southern" markets is especially noticeable in insurance for expropriation risks and transfer risks and so on, but also for the humbler business of guaranteeing export credits (chapter 15).

Panel 21.1. Who insures against political risk?

or import licenses. In the end, such a company has no choice but to sell its operations to a local firm. In this case, there is no formal expropriation, and therefore no compensation from any insurance contract. Fortunately, unless the recent Chávez–Morales precedents develop into a real trend, expropriations and nationalizations are less fashionable and frequent than they used to be, so that when considering foreign investment, this risk is rather small for most host countries. Given the small risk, the imperfections in the insurance contract as a protection against expropriation risks are not a major concern in the NPV calculations.

21.5 Issue #4: Make Sure to Include All Incremental Cash Flows

The incremental cash flow principle means that one should consider not only the cash flows that can be inferred from the subsidiary's projected P&L accounts, but also the change in the cash flows elsewhere in the company. In international projects, interactions with other activities are the rule rather than the exception. For instance, foreign production usually comes as the sequel to a period of exports, and the net cash contribution from these exports would disappear if the foreign investment project were accepted. Likewise, there tends to be a lot of intracompany trade, and to the extent that such trade increases or decreases after the investment, we should trace the net cash contribution generated elsewhere in the group. Lastly, there are almost surely taxes to be paid by the parent, whether in the host country or at home. So don't forget the host-country corporate taxes and withholding taxes, and the home-country corporate taxes. These taxes are not found in the subsidiary's projected P&L statements.

The temptation to overlook these interactions is especially high in an international investment proposal. One reason is that foreign investments are usually implemented by legally separate companies, each with its own separate accounting systems, rather than business units within a single company where there is just one overall accounting system. Another reason is that the subsidiary's managers may be tempted to consider only their own company's profits if their bonus plans depend on the subsidiary's profits rather than on the subsidiary's contribution to the profits of the group as a whole.

21.6 Other Things to Do in Spreadsheets While You're There

The remaining points relate to the general procedure for international capital budgeting.

Separation of operating and financing issues. In order to separate the operating and financing issues, capital budgeting for international applications should be done in three steps. The first step assumes that the project is implemented in a branch, which ignores all gains that can be made by unbundling the payments. Thus, one should remove intragroup interest payments and royalties from the P&L statements and recompute the taxes to reflect the branch scenario.

Inflation. The projected P&L statements often start from a constant-price scenario. When including the effects of inflation, one can often do better than postulating a uniform percent inflation to all items in the cash-flow statement for all years. First, it is not necessary for the rate to be constant over time; if inflation is unusually high right now, one should expect it to be brought down to a lower, long-run level in the coming years, and vice versa. Second, the effect of inflation is not necessarily the same for all cash-flow items. In the long run, the prices of raw materials have tended to lag behind the prices of semi-finished goods, consumer goods, and services—in that order—despite occasional commodity booms as in the early 1970s and in 2005. (Whether we can still bet on this for the future is not obvious, though.) On top of these broad trends, a lot of thinking has to go into projects that involve new products in new markets. In such cases, sales prices typically fall over time as competition stiffens, but so do costs (learning effects). If the data that you get seem to assume constant sales prices and production costs, in many cases you should send back the spreadsheet and insist on more serious work.

Profits versus cash flows. Costs are typically disbursed months before the time of selling, while revenues are received months afterward, but this difference in timing is not reflected in the projected P&L statements. One simple way to handle these leads and lags is to build them into the discounting procedure, as explained in the appendix. Alternatively, you can try to quantify investments in working capital. If you use this alternative procedure, you should forecast accounts payable, inventory, and accounts receivable, count any change in working capital as a cash flow, and remember to cash in ("recover") the remaining working capital at the end of the evaluation horizon.

Terminal value. In most cases, it is unreasonable to assume that all fixed assets are worthless at the end of the evaluation horizon. This means that a terminal value has to be assessed. Three procedures are popular.

- First, the terminal value could be set equal to the book value. This has the merit of simplicity, and it is also likely to be conservative, implying that a positive NPV based on this assumption is on the safe side, everything else being the same.

- Second, the company can be valued as a going concern, using a long-term average price/cash flow ratio for comparable firms (same industry, country, and size).

- Third, an explicit forecast can be avoided by repeating the NPV computations for many different terminal values, until the critical liquidation value is found where the NPV switches from negative to positive. In fact, you can easily compute it analytically, or have your kids do that for you, once you have an NPV computed with a zero liquidation value. Often, one can tell whether this breakeven terminal value is above, below, or within the range of actual terminal values that can be reasonably expected.

Example 21.17. Suppose Weltek's NPV is calculated at -13m, as in the first round. Liquidation, if any, would take place at time 6.5, with a 35% capital-gains tax following at time 7.5. The total NPV would be zero if the PV-ed net liquidation value had a value of $+13$m. We take the 5.39% cost of capital derived in an earlier example, a rate for FC amounts that already include foreign inflation, derived from an HC discount rate of 7.5% "minus" 2% appreciation of the yuan. The breakeven liquidation value L can be found as follows:

$$L: \quad \frac{L}{1.0539^{6.5}} - \frac{L \times 0.35}{1.0539^{7.5}} = 13,$$
$$\implies \quad L \times 0.475 = 13,$$
$$\implies \quad L = 13/0.475 = 27.4.$$

(Note that this assumes that the book values are zero, which may need correction in many cases.) Thus, instead of coming up with a reliable estimate of the expected final value, Weltek's management just needs to be able to say whether that expected value is almost surely above CNY 27.4, including inflation.

Of course, you can use your spreadsheet's SOLVER instead, or just try many candidate values for L until you get close to a zero NPV.

Sensitivity analysis. The sales, costs, and exchange rate forecasts are probably as debatable as the estimates of the terminal value. Therefore, you should also experiment with a number of (optimistic and) pessimistic scenarios and see whether, and to what extent, reasonable variations in these estimates affect the sign of the NPV. Another item of uncertainty is the discount rate, because the cost of capital estimate is never very precise. Finally, even the investment outlays themselves, and the effective start-up date of operations, deserve some experimentation.

21.7 CFO's Summary

Capital budgeting in a domestic context best uses two-stage NPV, with a full-equity first version followed by a correction for issue costs, subsidies, and so on (adjusted NPV). The corporate tax advantage from borrowing is best left for stage 2, not for stage 1 via a WACC, because not all potential tax gains will be realized, some gains may be undone at the personal level, and bondholders and banks must be taking part of the gains too.

In international applications, an extra stage is best inserted for intracompany financial arrangements. These are different from external borrowing in that we do know the tax situation of the two players (parent and subsidiary) and because the division of the tax gains is not really an issue when the two parties are, economically, one. Also, doing a separate computation of the tax effects from royalties, etc., is far easier and safer than reworking two spreadsheets. Lastly, tax games should be regarded as the icing on the cake—nice, but not really essential. Leave tax planning to specialists, and focus on economics yourself.

Another potentially big issue is transfer risk. This is well accounted for by including the cost of insurance into the cash flows. Expropriation risk is less well covered via insurance because book values overlook many relevant items.

There is a risk that managers adopt the "project point of view," focusing on their own unit's balance-sheet and profit-and-loss statements. This is bad: it ignores operational cash flows and profits (or profits lost) elsewhere in the company, or it ignores the fact that parents are the recipients of intracompany royalties or must pay taxes on various kinds of remittances. It should also be kept in mind that the NPV calculations are done on behalf of the parent's shareholders. This also has implications as to the currency in which all the calculations must be done: the parent's HC, in principle. Only in well-integrated markets will a local-currency NPV do too.

Frequent mistakes may also come from working-capital or inflation adjustments (or the lack thereof), or from terminal value. NPV looks quite scientific, but the quality of the inputs is crucial. Given the uncertainty surrounding these, the sensitivity-analysis section of the NPV report should perhaps be as long as the main part.

There is another reason why NPV should be taken with a spoonful of salt. Almost tautologically, it works only with quantifiable aspects—expected cash flows. However, analysts understandably hesitate to quantify aspects of the project that have very diffuse cash-flow implications. For instance, a new project may lead to others that can be very profitable. In many cases, we have only very vague ideas about what type of extensions or spin-off businesses could result and what their cash-flow implications would be. Even if we have an idea about the nature of possible later extensions, it is often anybody's guess whether the probability of such an extension is 30%, 20%, or 10%. Equally hard to quantify are elements like the repercussions on the company's image or political risks. Yet nonquantifiability does not mean irrelevance. Therefore, you should at least think very hard about the qualitative considerations and include these in your decision-making process along with the NPV computations. There is no escape from genuine thinking.

A last risk you should be aware of is the rosy-glasses risk. The champions of a project are, almost tautologically, excited about it and may unwittingly be erring on the optimistic side in their assumptions. Causality can go either way. If forecasts are good, enthusiasm often follows, so the bigger the overestimation, the bigger the enthusiasm. Alternatively, the excitement may have come first: the new idea looks intrinsically fun and surely less boring than run-of-the-mill management, so the champion subliminally looks for assumptions that would justify the project. Brealey et al. (2007) tell the sobering tale of a company where a review of accepted projects shows a strong link between degree of overestimation of the benefits and the nature of the project, from boring (replacement NPV) to mildly interesting (expansion projects) and then to challenging (new products and/or new markets). What you should do is appoint a devil's advocate who does not believe any of the champion's claims, requests justification everywhere, and tries to disprove everything. Also, for macro figures like inflation or growth or exchange-rate changes, the champion should be forced to use official forecasts, or if there are many, some average of external forecasts.

Let us add one final word of wisdom, again borrowed from Brealey and Myers: don't get absorbed by the technicalities of investment analysis to the extent that you forget what basic economics has to say about competition and profits. If entry is cheap and fast, we know that competition drives monopoly "rents" to zero. Translated into capital-budgeting terms: if your calculations show a positive NPV but you cannot point out a competitive advantage or a barrier to entry, the reason for the positive result must have been overstated profit margins. And even if you can identify a competitive edge, bear in mind that it cannot last long: imitators will follow fast.

*   *   *

All the above is directly applicable to wholly owned subsidiaries. For joint ventures, one would think, there seems to be no choice but to split the cash flows into parts received by each of the partners. That, however, is too pessimistic. In the next chapter we show that a careful, systematic approach to JV problems requires nothing but as-if-wholly-owned NPVs, possibly with second-stage adjustments for tax savings as we have done in this chapter.

21.8   Technical Notes

Technical note 21.1 (an alternative to NWC corrections: directly accounting for the leads and lags in the discounting procedure). NWC investments are caused by the fact that most expenses are paid before the final good is sold, while most revenue comes in after the good is sold. P&L statements miss this because costs and revenues are grouped by the moment of sale. There are at least two ways to account for this.

The most direct way to account for the leads and lags in, respectively, production costs and sales revenue is to build these leads and lags directly into the discounting procedure. This is the approach we adopt in the text. The approach abandons the usual assumption that cash flows occur at the beginning of each year. Working on a continuous time line allows us to be more realistic about the timing of each cash-flow item, and provides a simple way to take into account investments in working capital. For instance, assume that the time frame in example 21.2 is as follows:

- The investment outlay (CNY 700) is paid for, on average, 0.5 years from the decision date.

- Sales start one year from now and are spread evenly over the year. That is, sales occur on average at times $1.5, 2.5, \ldots, 5.5$. But customers pay three months later; that is, cash actually comes in, on average, at times $1.75, 2.75, \ldots, 5.75$. And production costs are, on average, paid three months before the goods are sold; that is, on average, the costs are paid at times $1.25, 2.25, \ldots, 5.25$.

- Overheads are paid, on average, in the middle of the year (at times $1.5, 2.5, \ldots, 5.5$).

- Taxes are paid at the end of each year (at times $2, 3, \ldots, 6$ for ordinary income tax and time 7 for liquidation tax).

- The liquidation value is realized at time 6.5.

Discounting of the (risky) operating cash flows is done at a compound rate of 20% p.a. Discounting of the initial investment itself is at the short-term risk-free rate of 12% p.a. because there is no risk associated with the investment itself. Taking into account the timing of the cash flow as outlined above, we discount the cash flows given in table 21.1, and compute the NPV as follows:

$$\text{NPV} = \sum_{t=1}^{5} \frac{\text{Sales}_t}{1.2^{t+0.75}} + \sum_{t=1}^{5} \frac{\text{Variable costs}_t}{1.2^{t+0.25}} + \sum_{t=1}^{5} \frac{\text{Overheads}_t}{1.2^{t+0.5}}$$

$$+ \frac{\text{Land sale}_t}{1.2^{6.5}} + \sum_{t=1}^{6} \frac{\text{Taxes}_t}{1.2^{t+1}} - \frac{\text{Investment}_0}{1.12^{0.5}}$$

$$= 1{,}991 - 872 - 312 + 40 - 198 - 661 = -13. \tag{21.7}$$

Technical note 21.2 (adjusting the NPV for borrowing). In principle, the gain for the shareholders is the difference between what they receive (PV-ed, of course) and what they invest. Let X_u denote the after-tax cash flows of the unlevered firm and Y the after-tax debt service payments; D stands for the initial debt and I_0 for the initial investment. Below we use $\text{PV}(\cdot)$ as the present-value operator, that is, $\text{PV}(x) := \sum_{\forall t} x_t / (1 + R)^t$. Assuming that operations are not affected by borrowing, the levered firm can pay out $X_u - Y$ to the shareholders, so their gain is

$$\text{NPV} = \text{PV}(X_u - Y) - (I_0 - D)$$

$$= \underbrace{\text{PV}(X_u) - I_0}_{\text{NPV unlevered}} + \underbrace{D - \text{PV}(Y)}_{\substack{\text{NPV of pure} \\ \text{borrowing}}}. \tag{21.8}$$

The NPV from pure borrowing is zero under original MM assumptions, but is positive if there is a tax subsidy from borrowing. If so, we just need to amend the unlevered NPV; there is no real need to work with cash flows net of debt service, and suitably adjusted discount rates, as would have been required if we had directly worked with equation (21.8). Actually, it would be quite difficult, in general, to work with shareholders' flows only, since the leverage ratio is not constant and, moreover, needs to be defined in market-value terms. Instead, one proceeds as follows. Debt service Y consists of amortization, A, and interest payments after tax, $I \times (1 - \tau)$. The latter can be split into a tax part and a before-tax part. Before-tax interest plus amortization tautologically produce a PV equal to the face value of the loan, D: what we pay the banks is $I + A$ and what we plainly get for it is D up front,

$$D - \text{PV}(Y) = D - \text{PV}(I - \tau \times I + A)$$

$$= D - \text{PV}(I + A) + \tau \times \text{PV}(I)$$

$$= \tau \times \text{PV}(I). \tag{21.9}$$

The discount rate that fits our a priori knowledge that $D = \text{PV}(A + I)$ is the interest rate of the loan. So this is the rate we should also use for the tax savings, because they are as risky as the loan itself.

Technical note 21.3 (adjusting the NPV for tax subsidies under constant leverage). In general, the savings would be computed as follows, given the firm's long-run debt/assets ratio (δ), the gross present value (GPV) of the project, the corporate tax rate (τ), and the interest rate paid on the debt (R_D, a per annum rate):[15]

$$[\text{Additional borrowing capacity}]_t = \delta \times \text{GPV}_t, \tag{21.10}$$

$$[\text{Tax saving due to project}]_t = R_D \times \tau \times \delta \times \text{GPV}_t, \tag{21.11}$$

$$[\text{PV of tax savings}]_t = \sum_{s=t}^{T} \frac{R_D \times \tau \times \delta \times \text{GPV}_s}{(1 + R_D)^{s+1-t}}. \tag{21.12}$$

There is one extra layer, though: the GPV should include the tax saving. Let us denote the (time-varying) GPV of the unlevered project by GPV_t^{u} and the PV-ed tax saving for years t to T by TS_t. Equation (21.12) then says that at the beginning of the last year (T) the last tax saving is proportional to the levered GPV, with proportionality factor $k = \tau \delta R_D / (1 + R_D)$. This allows us to work out the levered GPV:

$$\text{GPV}_T = \text{GPV}_T^{\text{u}} + TS_T$$

$$= \text{GPV}_T^{\text{u}} + k\,\text{GPV}_T,$$

$$\implies \quad \text{GPV}_T \times (1 - k) = \text{GPV}_T^{\text{u}},$$

$$\implies \quad \text{GPV}_T = \frac{\text{GPV}_T^{\text{u}}}{1 - k}. \tag{21.13}$$

In the MM case of stationary, perpetual cash flows, this formula works for all years because GPV is a constant. When GPV_t^{u} is allowed to take any pattern over time, there is no such easy formula, and the solution must be found by recursive calculations, easily done in, for example, a spreadsheet:

$$\text{GPV}_{T-1} = \text{GPV}_{T-1}^{\text{u}} + TS_{T-1}$$

$$= \text{GPV}_{T-1}^{\text{u}} + k\left(\frac{\text{GPV}_T}{1 + R_D} + \text{GPV}_{T-1}\right),$$

$$\implies \quad \text{GPV}_{T-1}(1 - k) = \text{GPV}_{T-1}^{\text{u}} + k\frac{\text{GPV}_T}{1 + R_D},$$

$$\implies \quad \text{GPV}_{T-1} = \frac{\text{GPV}_{T-1}^{\text{u}}}{1 - k} + \frac{k}{1 - k}\frac{\text{GPV}_T}{1 + R_D}; \tag{21.14}$$

---

[15] The tax saving is assumed to be realized one year after the time counter, $s = t, \ldots, T$, and T marks the beginning of the last operating year in the calculations. The formulas are easily adjusted for other patterns.

$$GPV_{T-2} = GPV^u_{T-2} + k\left(\frac{GPV_T}{(1+R_D)^2} + \frac{GPV_{T-1}}{1+R_D} + GPV_{T-2}\right),$$

$$\implies GPV_{T-2} = \frac{GPV^u_{T-2}}{1-k} + \frac{k}{1-k}\left(\frac{GPV_T}{(1+R_D)^2} + \frac{GPV_{T-1}}{1+R_D}\right), \tag{21.15}$$

$$\implies GPV_t = \frac{GPV^u_t}{1-k}$$
$$+ \frac{k}{1-k}\left(\frac{GPV_T}{(1+R_D)^{T-t}} + \frac{GPV_{T-1}}{(1+R_D)^{T-t-1}} + \cdots + \frac{GPV_{t+1}}{1+R_D}\right). \tag{21.16}$$

So you start at the end, at period T, compute GPV^u_{N-1} and hence GPV_T; then you go backward one period and compute the new unlevered GPV, which gives you the levered version, and so on.

TEST YOUR UNDERSTANDING

Quiz Questions

True-False Questions

1. Net present value analysis assumes that the risk of the project is constant.

2. ANPV and WACC are essentially substitutes; neither is superior to the other.

3. The sum of a project's profits, when accumulated over time without taking time value into account, is identical to the sum of the project's cash flows.

4. The sum of a project's investments and disinvestments in working capital, when accumulated over time without taking time value into account, is zero.

5. When the firm has the choice between either gradually depreciating an investment or charging the investment off entirely to the year's profit-and-loss account, the first choice is generally recommended. It does not affect the total amount paid in taxes (over the project's entire life), and it avoids unnecessary fluctuations in profits.

6. When applying NPV, you should take great care in reallocating the firm's general overheads, and charge a fair portion of these overheads to the new project, for instance, proportionally with sales or direct costs.

7. When valuing a project, you should not include in the cash-flow estimates of the (arm's-length) profits made by other business units on their sales to the new unit. That is, the project should be viable even when it must pay normal (arm's-length) prices for the components it buys.

8. Adjusted NPV contains corrections for qualitative aspects that were ignored in the first-stage NPV calculations.

9. Since borrowing reduces corporate taxes, one should always compute the tax savings (borrowing capacity × interest rate × tax rate), and add their present value to the first-stage NPV.

10. The WACC correctly measures the gain to the shareholders from undertaking a project if and only if (1) the project is either a perpetuity or a one-period venture, (2) the tax shield is always fully used, and (3) all gains accrue to the shareholders.

11. Exports occur through a dependent agent or through a branch, while operating through a subsidiary falls into the category of international marketing.

12. A firm that is very good at marketing will often become a franchisee; likewise, a firm that is very good at developing a new technology or that possesses a valuable brand name will typically become a licensee.

13. The licensor or franchiser typically receives a stated fraction of the project's profits.

14. Having a foreign branch is like having a dependent agent abroad, except that the foreign operations are incorporated as a separate company.

15. The incremental value principle says that since the gains from tax planning and "tax-treaty shopping" are unambiguously related to the project, these gains should be considered in the decision to accept or reject.

16. When conducting an NPV analysis, one should be as realistic as possible, and subtract, for example, the license fees, interest payments and amortization of intracompany loans, and management fees from the project's cash flows.

17. Since the money paid to bank(s) to service loan(s) does not accrue to the shareholders, one should subtract these payments from the operational cash flows before computing the NPV.

18. A sound rule of thumb is that the company should borrow in a weak currency for two reasons. First, the firm can expect a capital gain when the loan is paid back. Second, the high interest payments mean that there is a large interest tax shield.

19. To account for expropriation risk, one simply deducts the insurance premium (after taxes) because this premium is equal to the market's risk-adjusted expected cost of expropriation.

20. The best way to account for transfer risk is to add a risk premium to the discount rate. The next best way is to subtract the expected losses on blocked funds from the operating cash flows.

21. Leading and lagging are ways to speculate on changes in transfer prices.

Additional Quiz Questions

1. What are the reasons why the tax saving from corporate borrowing is often smaller than the present value of (borrowing capacity × borrowing rate × tax rate)?

2. Why does a firm often combine, for example, exports, foreign marketing, and licensing, rather than choosing only one of the above methods of operations?

3. What are the main differences between an independent agent and a dependent agent? A dependent agent and a branch? A branch and a subsidiary? A subsidiary and a joint venture?

4. Why is it better to separate the analysis of intracompany financial arrangements from the analysis of the operations and the analysis of the effects of external financing?

5. Describe how the proactive and reactive management of transfer risk differ.

6. What cash flows are not shown in the projected profit-and-loss accounts for the project, but should nevertheless be taken into account when doing an NPV analysis?

Applications

1. Consider example 21.2. Suppose that intracompany transactions represent one quarter of the project's variable costs, and every delivery valued at the arm's-length price of 100 yuan increases the profits of the supplying unit by 50 yuan; that is, variable costs are half of the transfer price. Additional deliveries of coating material will not require any additional investment nor will they affect the company's overheads. Evaluate the profits that the parent makes on its intracompany sales and incorporate them into the NPV analysis.

2. To take into account leads and lags (investments in working capital), assume that:

   • The supplying unit ships the coating, on average, six months before the subsidiary sells its final product (that is, shipment occurs at times $1, 2, \ldots, 5$).

   • Production of the coating consists of grinding and mixing, and takes virtually no time; the supplying unit usually has about one month's worth of raw material in its inventory and pays its own suppliers 30 days after delivery.

Workers are paid every week. Thus, the supplying unit's cash outflows also take place at times $1, 2, \ldots, 5$.

- The new business unit pays 60 days after delivery; taking into account one month for the actual shipment, this means that the supplying unit is paid at times $1.25, 2.25, \ldots, 5.25$.

3. Again consider example 21.3. We add a second interaction. Specifically, assume that Weltek U.K. is currently exporting to China, via an independent agent. If Weltek chooses to continue exporting instead of setting up production in China, unit variable costs will be higher (due to transportation costs, tariffs, etc.), and sales will be lower than expected because the agent is not as interested in promoting Weltek's goods as Weltek itself. On the other hand, no investments in fixed assets and marketing organization are required if exporting remains the mode of operation, and exporting does not create any extra overheads. Weltek's profits from exporting, and the corresponding taxes, are presented below.

4. Due to shipping delays and the increased inventory levels needed in view of the distance, production for exports takes place six months before the moment of sale to the final Spanish customer (that is, at times $1, 2, \ldots, 5$). Production costs lead production by three months. Compute the PV of the export profits lost when the project is undertaken, and decide whether Weltek U.K. should still consider direct investment in Spain. Use a 20% cost of capital.

5. An Andorran company, Walden Inc., considers a proposal to produce and sell market inverters in Prisonia. The Prisonian dollar (PRD) is fully convertible into any OECD currency and the country's capital market is unrestricted and well-integrated with Western markets. The life of the project is three years. The initial investment consists of land (PRD 1,000) with an expected liquidation value of PRD 1,100; plant, equipment, and entry costs equal PRD 6,000 and are to be depreciated at 66% in year 1, 33% in year 2, and 1% in year 3. Estimated figures for sales, variable costs, and overheads are as follows.

Sales occur, on average, in the middle of the year; variable costs are disbursed one month earlier, and customers pay three months later. Overheads and taxes are paid in the middle of the year. The investment occurs in the middle of year 0 and liquidation occurs in the middle of the fourth year. The discount rate is 15% for the operating cash flows, and 10% for the investment itself. (The initial loss can be carried forward, but this is already reflected in year-2 taxes.) Is this a viable proposal?

22

Negotiating a Joint-Venture Contract: The NPV Perspective

Our discussion, in chapter 21, of international capital budgeting assumes that a project is implemented as a branch of the investing firm or as a wholly owned subsidiary. Yet many projects involve two or more parent companies that join forces to undertake a particular venture. The purpose of this chapter is to present a coherent and practical approach for the valuation, determination of profit-sharing rules, and tax planning of such international joint-venture projects.

NPV is an essential ingredient in the process of negotiating a joint venture in the sense that NPV allows any partner to verify whether the expected cash flows which that partner receives from a proposed joint-venture contract exceed the costs the partner has to incur. However, joint-venture negotiations are much more complicated than simple NPV calculations, because the prospective partners also have to determine the profit-sharing rules. From chapter 20, we know that there are many ways to share cash flows between two companies:

- The profit-sharing contract could be a straightforward proportional (pure-equity) contract, where the partners simply contribute part of the initial investment, and then distribute the operating cash flows in proportion to these relative initial investments.

- There could also be a license contract between the joint venture and a partner (or even two or more partners). Under such a contract, a lump-sum fee and/or royalties is first paid to the licensor. These license payments are subtracted from the operating income of the joint-venture company, and the residual cash flow, if any, then gets shared among the shareholders in proportion to their initial investments. Thus, the distribution of the (total) operating cash flows is nonproportional. The same happens when technical-assistance or management fees or other transfer prices are paid that contain a profit for the parent that sells the good or service.

- A third way to affect the distribution of the gains is to allow one partner to bring in an intangible asset at a negotiated value. The effect is that this partner's share in the equity and in the later cash flows exceeds his share in the initial cash investment. The same effect can be obtained by agreeing to overvalue a physical asset brought in by one of the partners.

The issue is how such a joint-venture contract should be negotiated, taking into account factors such as restrictions on foreign equity ownership in the host country, ceilings on royalty percentages, differences in taxes paid by the partners on their respective dividend incomes, differential tax treatment of dividends versus license income, etc., and capital market segmentation (which implies that the partners may use different discount rates).

It is difficult to value and negotiate such joint-venture contracts without the help of a systematic framework. The purpose of this chapter is to offer such a framework. One crucial issue is how to distribute the *synergy gains*, that is, the present value over and above the summed PVs that the joint-venture partners can realize on their own. Elementary bargaining theory provides us with a simple rule for the division of the synergy gains: give every partner an equal share in the gains. This is in fact the default option in practice too. The simplest way to implement an agreed-upon division of the gains is to set up a purely proportional joint venture. Likewise, any nonproportional contract can also be designed so that the expected synergy gains are still shared equally.

Thus, we suggest that the negotiation and valuation of a joint-venture contract start with the simplest possible contract, a simple pure-equity or proportional contract. In this first stage of the analysis, the focus is on the economics of the project rather than on tax planning and legal constraints, and the procedure is very similar to an NPV analysis for a wholly owned subsidiary. After this first-stage evaluation, two separate adjustments follow. The first adjustment to the pure-equity solution focuses on special intragroup arrangements (such as a license contract between one of the parents and the joint-venture company), while the second adjustment relates to extra-group financial arrangements (such as borrowing from third parties). The focus of this chapter is on the first stage (the proportional contract) and on the nonproportional elements in the joint-venture contract (the second-stage intragroup financial arrangements).

This chapter has a lot of impressive-looking (or scary) math, with complicated subscripts. Don't be fooled: it is all very simple, really. Even then, your attention should focus on the logic and intuition, not the math: once the set-up is clear, any problem is solvable in a spreadsheet without having to type in any of the formulas mentioned here. Once you tell your computer program how the cash-flow sharing depends on a candidate value for, say, the equity share for partner A, then it is easy to tell your computer to find a new value that achieves a fair distribution of the gains. There's really no need to solve anything analytically.

The chapter is structured as follows. In section 22.1, we present the case for the three-step evaluation procedure of international projects in general and for joint-venture proposals in particular. In section 22.2, we state the basic principle of bargaining theory that we use in this chapter. In section 22.3, we show how to apply this basic principle to the simplest possible case, the pure-equity joint branch with neutral taxes and integrated capital markets. In section 22.4, we explain how to adjust the joint-branch solution for differences in the tax rate or the cost of capital. Section 22.5 introduces the most common deviation from the pure-equity framework—a license contract or management contract. Section 22.6 discusses various ways in which the results presented here can be generalized, for example, to account for transfer pricing or for a contribution of equity in kind.[1]

22.1 The Three-Step Approach to Joint-Venture Capital Budgeting

The standard procedure for investment analysis is to evaluate the project in two steps. In the first stage, the project is assumed to be financed by equity, and the funds are assumed to be already available; accordingly, the focus is on the valuation of operating cash flows. In the second stage, this NPV is then adjusted for financing aspects. As we saw in the preceding chapters, valuing international projects gives rise to many additional issues, including political risk, the effects of the project on the operating cash flows of the parent company or other related companies, the effect of exchange risk and capital market segmentation on the cost of capital, and the impact of international taxation on the remittance policy. The remittance policy is important because most foreign ventures are carried out in the form of a separate company (a subsidiary). Domestic projects, in contrast, are typically assumed to be in-house projects so that the investing firm is immediately and automatically the full owner of the project's cash flows. International capital budgeting can, therefore, be implemented in three steps:

Step 1, the "bundled" valuation or "branch" version, where the project is assumed to be carried out in the form of a foreign branch and where the focus is on the economics of the project (for example, operational cash flows and exchange and political risks).

Step 2, the unbundling stage, where the tax implications of various intracompany financial arrangements are considered.

Step 3, the adjustments for the effects of external financing.

An additional complication in valuing international projects arises when the project takes the form of a joint venture. Joint ventures are useful when there

---

[1] An equity input in kind is an input which is not in the form of cash. Such a noncash input could be a tangible asset, such as land or equipment, or an intangible asset, such as a brand name, a distribution network, or production or marketing knowledge (know-how).

is a complementarity between the partners' assets or competitive advantages, or when the partners want to share the uncertainty. For a joint venture, we can essentially follow the three-step approach outlined above for a wholly owned subsidiary. That is, we can first do the NPV exercise, assuming the foreign business is conducted as a joint branch. We define a joint branch as an unincorporated entity with proportional sharing of all cash flows (that is, not only profits or losses, but also financing of working capital, and depreciation).[2] The valuation of a joint-branch version of the project is intrinsically interesting for at least two reasons:

- First, it separates tax planning issues from economic issues. All cash flows held by the branch are automatically the property of the owners of the branch. It is true that by considering the joint-branch case, we ignore potential tax advantages of a clever remittance policy—but anticipated tax gains from nonequity contracts may disappear when loopholes are closed, and assumptions about dividend payouts (and the corresponding advantage of tax deferral relative to a joint-branch structure) are inevitably shaky. For these reasons, it is helpful to know what part of the NPV is tax related and what part is based on the intrinsic economic merits of the project.

- The joint branch may, in fact, be the best way to structure the contract. Relative to a pure-equity, incorporated joint venture, the joint branch can avoid withholding taxes on dividends. Thus, by first valuing the branch mode of operating, the company can quantify the effects of incorporating the joint venture into a separate company, and estimate whether the cost in terms of withholding taxes is offset by fiscal advantages from royalties and other remittance techniques.

Once the joint-branch solution has been analyzed, it becomes relatively straightforward to adjust it for nonequity arrangements in the joint-venture contract (step 2), as we shall show in a number of examples. These adjustments are similar to the step-2 ANPV adjustments for tax effects of borrowing under Miller–Modigliani (MM) assumptions. The step-3 adjustments for external financing can be done in the standard way outlined in chapter 21, and will not be discussed in this chapter.

The three-step approach for joint ventures is similar to the approach recommended for wholly owned projects. However, there are complications in a joint-venture capital-budgeting problem that do not arise in wholly owned

---

[2] In practice, the joint branch's working capital needs can be financed through bank loans. However, as each parent implicitly guarantees the loans of the joint branch, outside borrowing by the joint branch is essentially the same as outside borrowing by the parents. If there are no costs or tax issues, such borrowing would not affect the NPV; and if there are borrowing costs and tax benefits, these should be considered in step 3. Likewise, the joint branch can invest free cash flows in the money market. However, in the absence of tax effects or transaction costs, this does not affect the NPV; and transaction costs or tax effects associated with outside lending should be analyzed in step 3.

projects. For one thing, NPV analysis is intertwined with the issue of profit sharing and is therefore hard to separate from the contract negotiations. To further complicate matters, the valuation of a project's cash flows by one partner may differ from the valuation by the other partner(s) because of different tax rules (chapter 20), or because of different required returns reflecting capital market segmentation (chapter 19). To come to grips with the issue of valuing and negotiating a complicated joint-venture project, we first introduce a simple rule for profit sharing.

22.2 A Framework for Profit Sharing

We adopt the standard bargaining model of Nash (1950), Rubinstein (1982), and Sutton (1986) to integrate NPV analysis with the joint-venture negotiations between two companies. Let us denote these two companies by A and B. One element in the negotiations is the value of the partners' alternatives, that is, the value that each of the prospective partners can realize if the joint-venture negotiations fail. For example, in the absence of a joint-venture agreement, the best alternative for company A may be to pursue a similar investment on its own, to work together with a third party, to go on exporting as before (if this was the case), or to abandon the project altogether. The value of each player's best alternative can be identified by standard NPV analysis. We denote the net present values of the players' best alternatives as NPV_A and NPV_B, respectively, and we initially assume that all parties agree on these values and other relevant data.

Obviously, no party will accept a joint-venture contract that gives it less than what it can realize without the joint venture. For this reason, the value of the best alternative is called the player's *threat point*. As each player wants at least the NPV it can get from its best alternative, positive synergy gains are a prerequisite for successful negotiations. Given the existence of positive synergy gains, the issue is then how to divide these gains. In practice, the usual rule of thumb is to split the difference equally. This equal-gains rule has received theoretical support on axiomatic grounds (Nash 1950) and has also been derived as approximately the outcome of a potentially multi-stage, time-consuming, bargaining game among players with equal patience (Rubinstein 1982; Sutton 1986).[3] Thus, we adopt the rule that A and B should make equal (and positive) gains:

$$\text{A's gain} = \text{B's gain} > 0, \tag{22.1}$$

$$\text{where A's gain} = [\text{NPV of A's cash flow from the JV}] - NPV_A, \tag{22.2}$$

$$\text{B's gain} = [\text{NPV of B's cash flow from the JV}] - NPV_B. \tag{22.3}$$

---

[3] If the cost of delaying the implementation is higher to one partner than to the other partner, the synergy gain will not be split equally. In what follows, we assume that the cost of delaying the implementation is equal for both partners. It is straightforward, following Sutton's (1986) analysis, to identify a different distribution rule and adjust our procedure accordingly.

Example 22.1. Suppose that firm A can realize a net present value of $NPV_A = 100$ on its own, while B can realize $NPV_B = 200$. Negotiations about a joint venture can be successful only if A obtains at least 100 and B at least 200 from the joint operation. That is, the threat points are 100 and 200, respectively. Suppose that, with a joint venture, a total NPV of 450 can be obtained. The synergy gain is then $450 - (100 + 200) = 150$. If A gets 175 and B receives 275, the synergy gain is split equally: A's gain is $175 - 100 = 75$, and this gain equals B's gain, $275 - 200 = 75$.

Thus, we have to devise a joint-venture contract that splits the gains according to equation (22.1). We start with the simplest possible case, a purely proportional contract in a context where taxes are neutral and capital markets are integrated. We then consider the effects of different tax rates and discount rates. Finally, we analyze licensing contracts and management fees. Whatever the contract, our approach is to express the cash flows received by A and by B as functions of the contract parameters (like the equity share or the royalty percentage), and then to choose these parameters so that the gains to the partners are equal.

22.3 Case I: A Simple Pro-Rata Joint Branch with Neutral Taxes and Integrated Capital Markets

Consider a joint-branch contract where both the initial investment and the later cash flows are shared on the basis of an initially agreed-upon percentage. We shall assume, for the time being, that the initial investment, I_0, brought in by A and B consists entirely of cash or physical assets with an easily ascertainable and verifiable market value. That is, we do not yet consider intangible assets (like know-how, brand name, or clientele), whose valuation is part of the negotiations. Similarly, for the time being, we ignore profits that A or B could make from sales to the subsidiary. Any such sales are assumed to be invoiced at cost. In this section, we also assume that the partners are subject to the same tax rules and use the same discount rate (that is, we assume integrated capital markets).[4] We use the following notation:

ϕ is A's share in the investment and the later cash flows.

τ is A and B's effective tax rate on branch profits.

Rev_t is the year-t sales revenue of the joint branch on a cash basis (that is, the effective cash receipts from the customers, not the amount invoiced).

$Opex_t$ is the year-t operating expenses of the branch on a cash basis (that is, the effective disbursements, not the cost of goods sold as shown in the profit-and-loss statements).

---

[4] In integrated capital markets, exchange rates are not an issue in the sense that cash flows expressed in A's currency, discounted at a currency-A cost of capital, must yield the same value as the cash flows expressed in B's currency, discounted at a currency-B cost of capital and converted at the spot rate into currency A. See chapter 19 for details.

Sales$_t$ is the year-t sales (the amount invoiced for the year as shown in the profit-and-loss statement).[5]

Cost$_t$ is the year-t costs (the cost of goods sold as shown in the profit-and-loss statement).[6]

I_0 is the value of cash and tangible assets invested in the joint venture at time 0.

$\text{PV}(CF) = \sum_{t=0}^{T} CF_t / (1 + R)^t$ is the present value operator for a series of cash flows CF_t, $t = T_1, \ldots, T_N$, measured relative to the valuation date, $t = 0$; for instance, CF could be the series of revenues or taxes.

R is a per annum compound discount rate that reflects the riskiness of the cash flow that is being discounted.

With homogeneous tax rates and discount rates, the NPV of the entire joint-venture project, NPV$_{JV}$, is well-defined. In fact, this NPV is computed in exactly the same way as the net present value of a wholly owned project:

$$\text{NPV}_{JV} = \text{PV}(\text{Rev} - \text{Opex} - \text{Taxes}) - I_0$$
$$= \text{PV}(\text{Rev} - \text{Opex} - (\text{Sales} - \text{Cost})\tau) - I_0. \qquad (22.4)$$

Shareholder A pays a fraction ϕ of the initial investment I_0 and receives a fraction ϕ of the subsequent cash flows $[\text{Rev}_t - \text{Opex}_t - (\text{Sales}_t - \text{Cost}_t)\tau]$. Likewise, B's share in the investment and the later cash flows is $1 - \phi$. Thus, A's and B's parts in the NPV of the joint project are as follows:

$$\text{NPV of A's cash flows from the joint venture} = \phi\text{NPV}_{JV}, \qquad (22.5)$$
$$\text{NPV of B's cash flows from the joint venture} = (1 - \phi)\text{NPV}_{JV}. \qquad (22.6)$$

We substitute these relationships into the equal-gains rule (equation (22.1)):

$$\text{A's gain} = \text{B's gain},$$

where A's gain equals [NPV of A's cash flows from the joint venture, as shown in (22.5)] minus NPV$_A$, and B's gain equals [NPV of B's cash flows from the joint venture, as shown in (22.6)] minus NPV$_B$. Thus, in the present application we can write equation (22.1) as follows:

$$\phi\text{NPV}_{JV} - \text{NPV}_A = (1 - \phi)\text{NPV}_{JV} - \text{NPV}_B. \qquad (22.7)$$

This is readily solved for ϕ:

$$\phi = \frac{1}{2} + \frac{\text{NPV}_A - \text{NPV}_B}{2\text{NPV}_{JV}}. \qquad (22.8)$$

Thus, company A will obtain an equity share greater than 50% if its threat point, NPV$_A$, is higher than B's threat point, NPV$_B$, that is, if A's best alternative is more valuable than B's best alternative.

---

[5] The main difference between Sales and Rev is the change in accounts receivable.

[6] The main differences between Opex and Cost are the change in accounts payable and inventory and the depreciation allowances.

Example 22.2. Assume that company A can proceed without B (that is, there is a positive NPV$_A$), but that B cannot proceed without A's help. For instance, partner A is the foreign parent and possesses, say, proprietary know-how, while the local parent, company B, has a well-established brand name and distribution network but lacks the technical skills that are needed to produce the new product. The complementarities in the partners' strengths and weaknesses lead to synergy gains. Assume the following data: NPV$_{JV}$ = 493; NPV$_A$ = 152; NPV$_B$ = 0. Then

$$\phi = \frac{1}{2} + \frac{152 - 0}{2 \times 493} = 0.654. \tag{22.9}$$

Thus, under the pure-equity solution with integrated markets and identical tax rules, A and B share the initial investment and all cash flows on a 65.4/34.6 basis. Partner A gets more of the equity because its alternative (NPV$_A$ = 152) is of more value than B's (NPV$_B$ = 0).

From a practical point of view we note that, in the case discussed here, a joint-venture negotiation and evaluation requires three NPV computations: NPV$_A$, NPV$_B$, and NPV$_{JV}$. Each of them—even NPV$_{JV}$—is computed in exactly the same way as in a wholly owned project. For a joint-venture contract to be rational, the difference between NPV$_{JV}$ and (NPV$_A$ + NPV$_B$) must be positive. If the synergy gain is positive, the fair equity share for partner A is given by equation (22.8).

This solution assumes neutral taxes and integrated markets. We now show how the pure-equity solution for ϕ needs to be adjusted when the tax rates or discount rates for the partners are different.

22.4 Case II: Valuing a Pro-Rata Joint Branch when Taxes Differ

In the case discussed in the previous section, we could unambiguously define NPV$_{JV}$ without knowing ϕ. This is no longer possible if A and B's tax rates differ. For instance, if the foreign parent A is taxed more heavily than B, the total value of the joint venture is higher the larger B's stake, since this reduces the overall tax burden. The one unit of before-tax cash flow has a different value depending on who receives the cash flow. So the PV also depends on which owner's perspective we take.

Let us use the following notation:

τ_A is A's effective tax rate on branch profits—host-country taxes as well as possible home-country taxes.

τ_B is B's effective tax rate on branch profits.

Recall that we are still considering a joint branch where the two partners share all cash flows according to an agreed-upon percentage ϕ. The NPV realized by firm A is the present value of its share in the before-tax operating cash flows, ϕ (Rev$_t$ − Opex$_t$), minus the present value of the taxes paid by A on its part of the joint-branch income, ϕ (Sales$_t$ − Cost$_t$)τ_A, and minus A's share in the initial investment, ϕI_0:

$$\text{NPV of A's cash flow} = PV[\phi \text{ (Rev − Opex)}] − PV[\phi \text{ (Sales − Cost)}\tau_A] − \phi I_0$$
$$= \phi [PV(\text{Rev − Opex}) − PV((\text{Sales − Cost})\tau_A) − I_0]$$
$$= \phi \, \text{NPV}_{JV,A}, \tag{22.10}$$

where $\text{NPV}_{JV,A} \equiv PV[\text{Rev − Opex}] − PV[(\text{Sales − Cost})\tau_A] − I_0$.

The second line of equation (22.10) says that A's share is just ϕ times the NPV of the joint venture computed as if the entire joint-branch cash flow would be paid to A (and, therefore, as if the tax rate applicable to the joint branch's entire income was τ_A). In equation (22.10), we have denoted this figure by $\text{NPV}_{JV,A}$. By a similar argument, B gets $(1 − \phi)$ times $\text{NPV}_{JV,B}$, where in $\text{NPV}_{JV,B}$ all taxes are computed using a tax rate τ_B, as if B received the entire cash flow. Finally, ϕ has to satisfy the equal-gains rule (equation (22.1)):

$$\text{A's gain = B's gain,}$$

where A's gain is [NPV of A's cash flows from the joint venture as shown in (22.10)] minus NPV_A, and B's gain is [NPV of B's cash flows from the joint venture analogous to equation (22.10)] minus NPV_B. Thus, the equal-gains rule is now specified as

$$\phi \, \text{NPV}_{JV,A} − \text{NPV}_A = (1 − \phi)\text{NPV}_{JV,B} − \text{NPV}_B. \tag{22.11}$$

The solution for ϕ is

$$\phi = \frac{\text{NPV}_{JV,B}}{\text{NPV}_{JV,B} + \text{NPV}_{JV,B}} + \frac{\text{NPV}_A − \text{NPV}_B}{\text{NPV}_{JV,B} + \text{NPV}_{JV,B}}. \tag{22.12}$$

Let us compare this with equation (22.8):

- We see that equation (22.8) is a special case of equation (22.12), because equation (22.8) assumes equal taxes and, therefore, $\text{NPV}_{JV,A} = \text{NPV}_{JV,B}$. Thus, when $\text{NPV}_{JV,A} = \text{NPV}_{JV,B}$ the first term simplifies to 1/2 and the denominator of the second term simplifies to 2NPV_{JV}, as in equation (22.8).

- The second term in equation (22.12) still implies that ϕ is a positive function of $\text{NPV}_A − \text{NPV}_B$: if A's best alternative is more valuable than B's, A should obtain a larger share of the before-tax cash flows of the joint venture.

- Equation (22.12) also says that if the partners' best alternatives are equally valuable, A's share will nevertheless exceed 1/2 if $\text{NPV}_{JV,B} > \text{NPV}_{JV,A}$. To understand this, note that the relationship $\text{NPV}_{JV,B} > \text{NPV}_{JV,A}$ means that B pays less in taxes than A. Thus, under the equal-gains rule, B has to give A a larger share in the joint-venture cash flows, as a compensation for the fact that A has to pay more taxes at home than B.

Example 22.3. Assume the following: $\tau_A = 40\%$; $\tau_B = 35\%$; $NPV_A = 135$; $NPV_B = 0$; $NPV_{JV,A} = 465$ (using A's 40% tax rate and a 20% discount rate); $NPV_{JV,B} = 493$ (using B's 35% tax rate and a 20% discount rate). From these data we can derive the solution:

$$\phi = \frac{493}{493 + 465} + \frac{135 - 0}{493 + 465} = 0.656. \tag{22.13}$$

Let us compare this with the base case considered in example 22.2, where ϕ was 65.4%. We see that the introduction of different taxes hardly affects the value of ϕ, at least with the data we used in this example. On the one hand, company A's position is weakened by its lowered NPV_A (which decreased from 152 in the previous example to 135, reflecting A's higher tax rate). On the other hand, A gets compensated from B for its higher tax burden. With the data in example 22.3, the latter effect dominates marginally.

From a practical point of view, we note that when taxes differ, a joint-venture negotiation and evaluation requires four NPV computations: NPV_A, NPV_B, $NPV_{JV,A}$, and $NPV_{JV,B}$. Each of them is computed in exactly the same way as in a wholly owned project, and the joint-venture cash flows are to be evaluated twice—once using A's tax rate and once using B's rate. These four numbers then allow us to set the equity share in a fair way.

The analysis can be repeated for the case where the discount rates differ, because of segmentation of capital markets. One then interprets NPV_X as the NPV computed as if X were the sole owner, using the discount rate relevant to that player. Of course, the formulas then also cover cases where both tax rates and discount rates differ across the two players.

As we argued in section 22.1, the pure-equity solution discussed thus far is interesting because it keeps us from getting lost in a maze of tax details from the onset. Also, such a purely proportional contract may make good sense because it avoids conflicts of interest that may arise with nonproportional sharing rules. However, the pure-equity solution may not be legally feasible (for instance, because the solution violates limits on foreign ownership), or it may not be optimal with respect to taxes. Then a license contract may be useful. This is the topic of the next section.

22.5   Case III: An Unbundled Joint Venture with a License Contract or a Management Contract

Thus far, we have considered only those contracts where profits and other cash flows are shared in proportion to the investments. In step 2 of the adjusted NPV procedure discussed in section 22.1, the joint operation becomes an incorporated business, and an "unbundled" remittance policy becomes possible. That is, in step 2, we continue to analyze the effect of cash flows from the joint-venture company to the parents, but we focus on nonproportional ways of sharing the cash flows.

One popular ingredient in nonproportional contracts is a licensing deal or a management contract, stipulating some or all of the following payments: (i) a royalty tied to sales, (ii) an up-front licensing fee, and (iii) periodic fixed payments.[7] Another contract that deviates from the strictly proportional approach is the contract in which one of the parent companies brings in its know-how as equity in kind, or where one of the parents is allowed to overvalue a tangible asset contributed as equity in kind. In such a nonproportional contract, there are now many decision variables. For instance, there is the profit share, the royalty percentage and the lump-sum payments from the license contract or management contract, the up-front payment for the know-how or another intangible asset, or the accounting valuation of noncash inputs. Thus, we can choose some of these parameters on the basis of other considerations (like restrictions on foreign-equity ownership, political risks, tax advantages, fiscal restrictions on royalty percentages, and so on) and use the remaining parameters to achieve the desired division of the synergy gains.[8]

In this section, we analyze a license contract. The analysis of a management contract is analogous. Contributions in kind are similar to an up-front payment, except for possible tax-related details, and are discussed in section 22.6.

22.5.1 Possible Motivations for a License Contract

License contracts provide for the payment of a *royalty*, typically computed as a percentage p of the sales over an agreed-upon period. Besides royalties, often there are also periodic lump-sum fees L_t. The time-t subscript to L reflects possible variations over time; for instance, there may be a substantial up-front payment and smaller subsequent payments. Almost invariably, the contract has a finite life, and contains stipulations whether the licensee can still use the intellectual property afterward or not. The contract should also state whether the licensee may add improvements and who owns these improvements. Some countries also impose an upper bound on the life of a license contract.

---

[7] The effect of the fixed payments is to increase the breakeven output to the user of the know-how or the brand name (the licensee). This creates an incentive for the licensee to work harder. Another nonproportional sharing rule can be obtained by arranging loans between a parent and the joint venture. A loan at the normal market rate of interest is not a way to transfer NPV, though; and "abnormal" interest rates are likely to be treated, for tax purposes, as disguised dividends. So licensing contracts, or other ways to compensate for a know-how, are the prime instruments we analyze in step 2. In addition, an incorporated joint venture can also borrow from outside sources, but this is considered in step 3.

[8] Ideally, an optimization approach should be adopted, but tax considerations, combined with legal restrictions, always lead to a priori obvious *corner solutions*: either zero royalties or else the maximum that is feasible within legal or other external constraints. (Corner solutions are solutions where a decision variable is set equal to its upper or lower limit. Examples of corner solutions are $\phi = 0$, $\phi = 1$, $L_t = 0$, $p = 0$, and so on. In linear problems we always get corner solutions.) Considerations like public relations or political risks may lead to what mathematicians call *interior solutions*, but such aspects are hard to model in a formal, quantitative way. In practice, one has little choice but to experiment, and possibly iterate, until a reasonable-looking solution is found.

There are many motivations for using a licensing contract alongside, or even instead of, an equity participation.

- Risk sharing may be one motivation for a license contract. For instance, if the licensor is closer to financial distress than is the other partner, licensing provides income with a low variance.

- Information asymmetries with respect to the size of the market or the quality of the local partner's inputs may be a second reason. The willingness of the better-informed partner to accept a big share of the risk then acts as a signal for the project's quality, and the shareholder with the information disadvantage obtains a license income that is less risky and easier to assess.

- Constraints on the equity that can be invested can be a third reason for a license contract. Royalty payments are a way of sharing the synergy gains when one partner cannot invest the amount of cash that would be necessary in a pure-equity contract. For instance, one partner may be short of cash, and unwilling to borrow (because of the costs of financial distress) or to issue equity (because of the loss of independence in a closely held corporation). Similarly, there may be legal restrictions on foreign-equity ownership imposed by the host country, public relations considerations (for instance, a desire for a local image), or political risks.

  Thus, when the fair pure-equity solution is $\phi = 0.45$ but the law restricts the equity share to 40%, then you can arrange a first payment via licensing and share the remaining 40/60. This way you get more than 40% of the NPV.

- Tax considerations, finally, may provide a powerful motivation for incorporating a licensing deal in a joint-venture contract. The license payments are tax-deductible expenses to the joint-venture company. If foreign dividends or branch profits are heavily taxed in the host country, the overall tax rate on branch profits or dividends is likely to exceed the effective tax rate on licensing income under any tax system.

Note that tax considerations do not always lead one to favor a license contract. For instance, suppose that A's home country grants an exclusion privilege for foreign dividends or foreign branch profits rather than a credit for foreign taxes. If the host-country's corporate taxes are low, overall taxes on A's dividend income can then be lower than the taxation of A's licensing income. In such a case, taxes would penalize a license contract relative to dividends or branch profits.

Example 22.4. Assume that a Hong Kong subsidiary pays 16% in corporate taxes, and there is no withholding tax on dividends. If the foreign investor is not taxed on foreign dividends (because the investor's home country applies the exclusion system), total taxes on profits and dividends are only 16%. Royalty payments, in contrast, are not taxed in Hong Kong because they are tax-deductible expenses, but they are taxed in the parent's home country at the standard rate, say 35%. Thus, from a tax point of view, a license contract is expensive here.

In themselves, tax considerations always lead to corner solutions: either the licensing income or the equity participation, ϕ, equals zero when taxes are the only criterion. Such corner solutions may be unacceptable or infeasible on other grounds, though. For instance, a zero-equity solution would give control of the joint venture to company B, which may be unacceptable to firm A—unless a massive deviation from one share/one vote is negotiated, which may look strange to outsiders. In other situations, a tax-driven zero-equity solution may necessitate a royalty percentage and/or lump-sum annual fee which would be deemed not "at arm's length" by the tax authorities; that is, the required royalty payments may be so high that the host tax authorities would treat part of the license payments as disguised dividends. Similarly, a solution without licensing income may lead to an equity share ϕ that is incompatible with, for example, explicit legal restrictions on foreign ownership or a desired local image. In short, in many cases, both the equity fraction ϕ and the licensing income will be positive, reflecting nontax considerations. For example, if there is a legal limit to ϕ and dividends are taxed at a lower rate than license income, one sets A's equity share equal to the legal limit and one then adds a license contract so as to give A enough of the synergy gains, and vice versa.

22.5.2 The Equal-Gains Principle with a License Contract

We use the following notation:

p is the royalty percentage (relative to sales) received by A.

L_t is the lump sum amount received by A in year t.

LP_t is the total license payments received by A in year t; $LP_t = p \times \text{Sales}_t + L_t$.

$\tau_{A,D}$ is A's effective total tax rate on dividends (including taxes on the underlying profits).

$\tau_{A,L}$ is A's effective total tax rate on licensing income.

$\tau_{B,D}$ is by B's effective tax rate on dividends (including taxes on the underlying profits).

In the remainder of this chapter, "Cost$_t$" remains defined as in sections 22.3 and 22.4, that is, as the cost of goods sold plus the depreciation of tangible assets, but not including license fees and so on.

Under a scheme with nonzero equity and nonzero royalties, B initially invests $1 - \phi$ of the required cash, while A invests ϕ of the cash needed.

From the yearly operating cash flows, the annual lump-sum fee L_t plus a royalty of $p\%$ on sales goes to A. The residual is then split between A (who gets the fraction ϕ) and B (who receives $1 - \phi$). We now have to choose a combination of L_t, p, and ϕ such that company A still gets half of the synergy gains. Using a conservative approach, we shall assume full dividend payout.[9]

We first consider A's annual cash flows, where company A is defined as the parent that receives the royalty. A's cash flows consist of the after-tax royalty, plus A's share in the residual cash flows, minus taxes paid by A on its share in the profits. In equation (22.14), we then rearrange the terms to determine the differences between this contract and the pure-equity case:

Cash flow from the joint venture accruing to A at time t

$$
= LP_t(1 - \tau_{A,L}) + \phi(\text{Rev}_t - \text{Opex}_t - LP_t) - \phi(\text{Sales}_t - \text{Cost}_t - LP_t)\tau_{A,D}
$$
$$
= LP_t[(1 - \tau_{A,L}) - \phi(1 - \tau_{A,D})] + \phi[\text{Rev}_t - \text{Opex}_t - (\text{Sales}_t - \text{Cost}_t)\tau_{A,D}]. \tag{22.14}
$$

The last term in the square brackets, $\text{Rev}_t - \text{Opex}_t - (\text{Sales}_t - \text{Cost}_t)\tau_{A,D}$, is a joint-venture cash flow as if A were the sole owner of an all-equity project. Bearing in mind that A also pays a fraction ϕ of the initial investment, it follows that A's share in the NPV of the joint venture can be written as

NPV of A's cash flow from the joint venture

$$
= \text{PV}_A(LP)[(1 - \tau_{A,L}) - \phi(1 - \tau_{A,D})]
$$
$$
+ \phi\{\text{PV}_A[\text{Rev} - \text{Opex} - (\text{Sales} - \text{Cost})\tau_{A,D}] - I_0\}
$$
$$
= \text{PV}_A(LP)[(1 - \tau_{A,L}) - \phi(1 - \tau_{A,D})] + \phi\text{NPV}_{JV,A}, \tag{22.15}
$$

where $\text{PV}_A(LP) = p\,\text{PV}_A(\text{Sales}) + \text{PV}_A(L)$; $\text{PV}_A(\text{Sales})$ is the present value of the sales, discounted at a rate that reflects the riskiness of the sales from A's shareholders' point of view, and $\text{PV}_A(L)$ is the present value of the before-tax lump-sum payments, discounted at a rate that reflects the risk of these lump-sum payments to A's shareholders. The rate used to discount sales or the lump-sum payments L is probably lower than the rate used in $\text{NPV}_{JV,A}$, because sales and a fortiori lump-sum payments are likely to be less risky than the entire (all-equity) cash flows in $\text{NPV}_{JV,A}$.[10] One could use the JV's borrowing rate as a first approximation for the discount rate for L.

Equation (22.15) shows us how A's NPV in a pure-equity problem is to be adjusted for royalty payments. Analogously, we derive B's adjusted NPV by

---

[9] This assumption ignores the possible tax advantage of deferring the payout, but the advantage is often small and can be quantified only after making arbitrary and tenuous assumptions about future payouts.

[10] Recall from chapter 21 that this holds if the beta risk of costs is lower than the beta risk of sales, which sounds fine, as costs are partly fixed and therefore partly insensitive to demand fluctuations. The lower beta on the short side then creates a leverage-like effect in the net cash flow, lifting its beta above that of the long side of the cash flow.

considering B's annual cash flows:

Cash flow$_t$ from the joint venture accruing to B

$$= (1 - \phi)(\text{Rev}_t - \text{Opex}_t - LP_t - (\text{Sales}_t - \text{Cost}_t - LP_t)\tau_{\text{B,D}})$$

$$= (1 - \phi)(\text{Rev}_t - \text{Opex}_t - (\text{Sales}_t - \text{Cost}_t)\tau_{\text{B,D}}) - (1 - \phi)LP_t(1 - \tau_{\text{B,D}}).$$

$$(22.16)$$

This implies the following:

NPV of B's cash flow from the joint venture

$$= (1 - \phi)\text{NPV}_{\text{JV,B}} - (1 - \phi)\text{PV}_{\text{B}}(LP)(1 - \tau_{\text{B,D}}).$$

$$(22.17)$$

The equal-gains rule (equation (22.1)) is implemented as before:

A's gain = B's gain,

where A's gain equals the NPV of A's cash flows from the joint venture, as shown in (22.15), minus NPV$_{\text{A}}$, and B's gain equals the NPV of B's cash flows from the joint venture as in equation (22.17), minus NPV$_{\text{B}}$. Below, we consider two specific applications among the many possible ones.

22.5.3 Finding the Fair Equity Share when the Terms of the License Contract Are Given

In one possible illustration, assume that tax considerations or other factors induce the joint-venture partners to fix p and L at an exogenous bound. For instance, if license income is taxed at a lower rate than profits and dividends, we set the license fees at the highest level that is still acceptable to the tax authorities. If, due to constraints on the terms of the contract, the license income fails to give partner A a sufficient share in the synergy gains, some equity is needed to achieve balance. We can then solve as follows for the equity fraction, ϕ, that A requires:

$$\phi = \frac{[\text{NPV}_{\text{JV,B}} - (1 - \tau_{\text{B,D}})\text{PV}_{\text{B}}(LP)]}{[\text{NPV}_{\text{JV,A}} - (1 - \tau_{\text{A,D}})\text{PV}_{\text{A}}(LP)] + [\text{NPV}_{\text{JV,B}} - (1 - \tau_{\text{B,D}})\text{PV}_{\text{B}}(LP)]}$$

$$+ \frac{[\text{NPV}_{\text{A}} - \text{NPV}_{\text{B}}] - (1 - \tau_{\text{A,L}})\text{PV}_{\text{A}}(LP)}{[\text{NPV}_{\text{JV,A}} - (1 - \tau_{\text{A,D}})\text{PV}_{\text{A}}(LP)] + [\text{NPV}_{\text{JV,B}} - (1 - \tau_{\text{B,D}})\text{PV}_{\text{B}}(LP)]}.$$

$$(22.18)$$

The two terms can be easily combined (as they share the same denominator) but the above version facilitates the interpretation of this expression:

- Consider the first term. If the total tax rates on dividends and the underlying profits are identical to A and B, we can drop the A or B subscripts in this expression. Each of the three terms in square brackets then measures the same thing—the NPV of the project net of the license payments. Thus, in a world with equal taxes the first term simplifies to a half and the denominator of equation (22.18) becomes twice the NPV of the project net of license payments. That is, if $\tau_{A,D} = \tau_{B,D} = \tau_D$, equation (22.18) simplifies to

$$\phi = \frac{1}{2} + \frac{[\text{NPV}_A - \text{NPV}_B] - (1 - \tau_{A,L})\text{PV}(LP)}{2[\text{NPV}_{JV} - (1 - \tau_D)\text{PV}(LP)]}. \tag{22.19}$$

- If tax rates do differ, a lower tax rate for B still increases the first term of equation (22.18) above a half. As in section 22.4, the explanation is that this comparative advantage must be shared with A, by giving A a higher share in the cash flows of the joint branch.

- The second term in equation (22.18) reflects the now-familiar effect of each player's alternatives. If A has better outside alternatives than B, A should obtain a larger fraction of the equity. However, the difference between the threat points is now reduced by A's license income after taxes, $(1 - \tau_{A,L})\text{PV}(LP)$. Thus, the license income can be viewed as a side payment that partly compensates for the difference in the value of the players' best alternatives. The imbalance between the threat points not yet compensated for by license payments is then reflected in the equity fraction ϕ.

Example 22.5. Return to our equal-tax, integrated-markets situation from example 22.2, with $\text{NPV}_A = 152$, $\text{NPV}_B = 0$, $\text{NPV}_{JV,A} = \text{NPV}_{JV,B} = 493$, $\tau_{A,D} = \tau_{B,D} = 0.35$, and $\tau_{A,L} = 0.30$. With these tax rates, there is a tax incentive to maximize the license income because royalty income is taxed at 30% while the tax on profits and dividends is 35%. Assume that, to satisfy legal or fiscal limits, p is set at 0.05 and that $L_t = 0$. If $\text{PV}(\text{Sales}) = 2{,}962$, the present value of after-tax license income is $0.70 \times 0.05 \times 2{,}962 = 103.67$. With these inputs, the fair equity percentage is to be set at

$$\phi = \frac{1}{2} + \frac{[152 - 0] - 103.67}{2[493 - 103.67]} = 0.562. \tag{22.20}$$

This is much closer to 1/2 than A's equity share in the absence of a license contract (65%) because the license payments greatly reduce the imbalance between the threat points. If the license payments had been worth 152 rather than 103.67, the outcome would have been a 50/50 equity share.

22.5.4 Finding the Fair Royalty for a Given Equity Share

In the preceding section, the royalty percentage p was set at an upper bound (5%), and we computed the equity share ϕ that is necessary to obtain a fair share of the synergy gains. In other situations, the contract parameter that is already determined may be ϕ, and the terms and conditions of the license contract are then to be set so as to satisfy the equal-gains principle. For instance, a desire for maximal control within government-set limits on foreign ownership may suggest that we set ϕ equal to the legal bound. Or, perhaps, higher taxes on dividend income may suggest that we set $\phi = 0$. For a given choice of ϕ, the remaining decision variables are L_t and p. Then, for any given value of L_t, you can solve the equal-gains condition for p, with A and B's PV-ed income from the JV defined as in equations (22.15) and (22.17). The analytical solution is not hard to derive, but long and not particularly enlightening. The mathematically rusty reader can always use, for instance, the SOLVER tool in a spreadsheet to find the solution, or ask his or her kids to solve the problem.

Example 22.6. We consider example 22.5, except that we remove the tax advantage for royalties: $NPV_A = 152$, $NPV_B = 0$, $NPV_{JV,A} = NPV_{JV,A} = 493$, $\tau_{A,D} = \tau_{B,D} = \tau_{A,L} = 0.35$. Company A prefers maximum control, subject to the legal limit $\phi \leqslant 0.49$, so ϕ is set at 0.49.

- Let us see how far we get when $L_t = 0$. The present value of sales is still 2,962. With these inputs, the royalty percentage over the five years should be $p = 8.24\%$ to achieve equal sharing of the synergy gains.

- If tax lawyers say this seems suspiciously high, the firm may have to look for another way to cash in, for instance by selling know-how to the JV for up-front cash (L_0). A very similar ploy is to receive shares for a brand name brought in as equity in kind, or make transfer-pricing gains on sales to the JV, etc.

An important message from this section is that license payments and equity shares are substitutes for each other, and should be analyzed simultaneously. For instance, Veugelers and Kesteloot (1996) finds that 52% of the 221 international production joint ventures in her sample are 50/50 companies and that, in only 8% of the cases, one of the shareholders owns less than 25% of the shares. If one is not aware of the existence of side payments like license income, one would tend to infer that, in most cases, the players have comparable alternatives NPV_A and NPV_B. However, in light of our analysis, a more careful conclusion is that the partners tend to prefer balanced equity holdings, and then use side payments to settle most of the difference between their threat points.

22.6 CFO's Summary and Extensions

In this last section we first review the key concepts, then discuss ways to extend the analysis, and close with a general comment on JVs.

Relative to the valuation of domestic investment projects, international capital budgeting is more complicated because there are often political risks, international taxation issues, and interactions with other parts of a firm's business. Analogously to our recommendation regarding WOS projects in chapter 21, we propose to evaluate JV projects in three steps. First, value the project assuming an all-equity branch mode of operating; then, value the tax effects of creating a subsidiary and unbundling the remittances; and, finally, add the effects of external financing. For JV projects, the NPV analysis is intimately related to the issue of how the total NPV is to be shared between the partners. An additional problem is that with heterogeneous taxes the project's total value depends on the profit-sharing rule. In this chapter, we show how, once there is agreement on sales and cost projections with and without the joint venture, the solution follows almost mechanically from the equal-gains principle.

The principle applied in our analysis allows one to tackle problems even when there are many departures from the simple, proportional contract. The approach is to start from each partner's after-tax cash flows under a proposed contract, compute present values, and insert these into the equal-gains equation. We illustrated this approach by starting from a purely proportional joint-venture contract with equal tax rates. Next, we showed how differential tax rates can be taken into account. As an interim result, we note that the step-one (joint-branch) part of any JV project can be analyzed by solving the problem as if the whole project were a wholly owned subsidiary. Partner A analyzes the problem using her own tax rate on the entire cash flow, while B does the same, using his tax rate. If each of these NPVs is positive, we can then find the fair sharing rule by combining the NPVs with the threat points. After this analysis of the proportional JV, we considered license payments or management fees.

The approach proposed in this chapter can be generalized in many ways.

1. First, we have assumed symmetric information: A and B fully share all relevant data and agree on their implications. If the partners do not agree on the values, the above approach can still be used to formulate and evaluate proposals. Each negotiating team can use its own estimates of the relevant data and compute the implications for JV proposals as a starting point in the bargaining.

2. Second, we have assumed that there are only two partners. If there are three or more, the equal-gains rule still applies. For instance, when three partners with equal bargaining strengths are involved, each should get one third of the synergy gains.

3. Third, we have assumed that the synergy gains were shared equally. However, one could easily adjust the formulas for any other division of the incremental value among the partners. For a 40/60 share, for instance, the sharing rule is

$$\text{B's gain} = 1.5 \times [\text{A's gain}]$$

and the gains are still quantified as before. A SOLVER-like tool in a spreadsheet will solve this for you if you have lost the patience or ambition for analytical solutions.

4. Fourth, we have assumed that all sales of goods and services between the joint venture and the parents are done at cost. This ensures that all benefits from the venture are included in the negotiations. In practice, transfer prices will usually include a profit margin: most tax authorities would not accept zero-profit sales to a related company. In addition, strategic transfer pricing may be used to shift profits and cash flows from

high-tax to low-tax locations, or to obtain a fair share of the synergy gains that would otherwise be unattainable due to host-country regulations on equity ownership, dividend payments, license fees, and so on.

From an NPV perspective, the extra flows transferred in this way to A or B are very similar to license payments because they are deductible expenses for the joint venture and taxable income for the supplier/parent. Thus, transfer-pricing profits can be added to the formulas in essentially the same way as royalties. Just come up with a variable, call it TPP (short for transfer pricing profits), and handle it in the same way we did with license payments. Note that profits should be interpreted as net cash contribution after taxes, not accounting profits.

5. Fifth, we have assumed that all equity contributions are in the form of cash or tangible assets with an objective market value. In practice, one partner often contributes an intangible asset, whose valuation is a matter of negotiation. Similarly, the partners may agree to overstate the value of a tangible asset brought in. Receiving equity rights on the basis of an intangible asset or through overvaluation of an intangible asset is very similar to receiving an up-front fee, L_0, as the following example shows.

Example 22.7. Assume that a project requires an initial cash investment of GBP 120 and that there are no taxes. Suppose also that the value of the best alternative decision for the foreign partner, A, is higher than B's threat point by GBP 80. In a purely proportional contract, this means that A's share, ϕ, must exceed 0.50. Suppose, however, that foreign investors are not allowed to own more than 50% of the equity of the joint venture. To agree to a contract that gives A only 50% of the future cash flows, A needs a side payment that compensates for the difference in the threat points. For instance, if despite the 50/50 rule for the sharing of the future cash flows, A and B agree that A contributes 20 in cash and B contributes 100, then the difference between the threat points is compensated for by the difference between the cash inputs. This can be achieved in two ways:

(a) To make the unequal cash inputs legally compatible with $\phi = 0.50$, A and B can agree that A is also contributing some intangible asset that is valued, for the purpose of the contract, at 80. Thus, A has an equity share of

$$\phi = \frac{\text{Book value of A's input}}{\text{Book value of all input}} = \frac{20 + 80}{20 + 100 + 80} = 0.50,$$

even though the effective cash input of A is only 20 out of a total of 120.

(b) Alternatively, A may formally pay 100 in cash and receive from the joint venture an up-front license payment $L_0 = $ GBP 80 in return for its know-how. A's share in the equity is still $100/200 = 50\%$ and its effective cash injection is still GBP $100 - 80 = 20$. Thus, receiving an up-front license payment, which is then ploughed back as equity, is similar to receiving shares for an intangible asset.

There may be subtle tax differences between receiving license income and being allowed to contribute an intangible asset as equity. Apart from these tax complications, however, we can adopt the approach used in section 22.5 to identify the value of L_0 that is compatible with some royalty percentage, p, some equity-sharing rule, ϕ, and an equal sharing of the synergy gains.

6. Lastly, we have often assumed integrated markets, in the sense that both parties agree on the PV of any given cash flow (apart from, perhaps, taxes). There is an issue as to how one could implement Nash's equal-utility approach when agents are not free to trade with each other. Having said that, nothing stops us from interpreting terms like $\text{NPV}_{\text{JV,A}}$ as "the NPV of the entire cash flow computed using A's tax rate *and discount rate*; likewise, NPV_{A} would have been computed using the tax and discount rate relevant to A, etc.

To conclude, our proposed approach can be applied to the very different circumstances that frequently arise in practice, and can help the financial manager in analyzing the profit-sharing problem rigorously and systematically.

As a last comment, there is much more to JVs than the rather technical issues tackled here—how to simultaneously evaluate and negotiate them. The economics of the JV are, of course, relevant too, and even though these issues may be more appropriate for an international-management or -strategy course, I cannot remain totally silent on them. The main pro of the joint operations is, as was stressed throughout this chapter, the synergy. But the main con may be equally important: the partners need to agree on so many things, and so much can go wrong. Sources of conflict of interest arise in all aspects of business, and often relate to the risk of favoring one partner's related firms or own people:

- on the input side: where and from whom to buy materials, etc.; whom to hire, promote, fire;

- on the production side: where to produce; where to expand or downsize;

- on the sales side: where to sell how much and at what prices, via what channels;

- on the funding size: what financing mix, in light of the players' own financial strengths and tax status; what if a major expansion seems necessary and one partner cannot fork out enough cash to subscribe to the new equity;

- on the remitment side: pay out or reinvest? how to remit, in light of the players' own financial needs and tax status.

Many of these issues come up in the following report by the *Economist*:

Robert Dudley, the boss of TNK-BP, ... blames BP's recent troubles on its Russian partners. They are Mikhail Fridman, the head of Alfa Group, and his partners Viktor Vekselberg and Leonard Blavatnik, who are collectively known as the AlfaAccessRenova consortium. In an interview with Vedomosti, a Russian business daily, Mr Dudley said there were disagreements between TNK-BP's shareholders, and that managers had deliberately filed incorrect visa applications for 150 of TNK-BP's foreign staff. Separately, an obscure Moscow brokerage, called Tetlis, filed a lawsuit in Siberia claiming that TNK-BP's payments to BP contractors amounted to extra dividends, and secured an injunction barring BP staff from TNK-BP. According to Tetlis's website, two of its three top managers used to work for Mr Fridman's Alfa Group. ... what is behind the hostility? People close to BP say the Russian oligarchs are up to their old tricks again, and are trying to exploit Russia's weak institutions and take control. ... But the Russian shareholders claim to have a genuine grievance. They say BP treats TNK-BP as a subsidiary, rather than an independent company run for the benefit of all shareholders. They say BP cares more about its oil reserves than costs or profits. TNK-BP provides 40% of BP's replacement reserves and 25% of its oil production. The Russians would like TNK-BP to expand abroad, but that would turn it into a rival to BP. A recent memo from Mr Dudley, seen by the *Economist*, bars managers from discussing deals in countries blacklisted by America's state department, including Cuba, Iran and Syria. "TNK-BP is an independent Russian company and should be subject to Russian laws," says Mr Fridman. Russian shareholders also object to TNK-BP's payment of hundreds of millions of dollars to BP contractors, citing a conflict of interest. "There is certainly room for cost cutting in TNK-BP," says Ivan Mazalov, a fund manager at Prosperity Capital Management, a minority shareholder.

Food for thought, I'd say.

TEST YOUR UNDERSTANDING

Quiz Questions

Suppose that company A can realize an NPV of 200 from doing the project on its own, while company B can realize 100. The NPV from joint operations is 400. There are no taxes.

True–False Questions

1. In a pure-equity contract, A will get two thirds of the equity of the JV, while B will get one third.

2. In a pure-equity contract, A will get two thirds of the synergy gain from the JV, while B will earn one third.

3. A's bargaining position is stronger than B's (because of its higher threat point), so A will get more than half of the synergy gain.

4. In a pure-equity contract, A will usually receive half of the synergy gain from the JV unless A's bargaining position is stronger or weaker than B's, that is, unless A is less impatient or more impatient than B.

5. In a nonproportional contract, A will not usually agree to receive only one half of the synergy gain of the JV.

6. In order to agree to a 50/50 joint venture, A will expect an additional payment of 100 from B.

7. In order to agree to a 50/50 joint venture, A will need a side payment of 100 from the joint venture.

Additional Quiz Questions

1. Why does the investment analysis of a JV comprise more than just an NPV analysis?

2. What additional assumptions are needed to make the following statement true: "In a joint venture where neither partner can achieve anything without the other's help, the ownership should be divided 50/50."

3. In negotiating a license contract, one should consider the opportunity cost, that is, money that could have been earned by signing a license contract with another company. How is this accounted for in our approach?

4. Why might a company prefer licensing over direct investment?

5. Tax rules, in themselves, favor corner solutions where either equity or licensing income is not used. Still, we often observe that both are used. Give some reasons why a contract may include both equity and nonequity features.

Applications

The exercises below focus on the logic used in this chapter rather than on number crunching. You should try to solve them without using any of the analytical solutions from the text.

1. Suppose that company A's project has an NPV of 200 on its own, while company B can realize 100. The synergy gain is 200. There are no taxes, the financial markets are integrated, and A and B have equal bargaining strengths.

   (a) How much of the total NPV (500) should go to A and how much to B?
   (b) To achieve this, what should the equity holdings be in a pure-equity JV?
   (c) Suppose that A and B agree that A will receive licensing fees from the JV worth 80 (in present value).

      (i) How much of the total NPV (500) is left to be shared in proportion to the original cash inputs?

      (ii) Write down the equal-gains principle, and solve for ϕ.

      (iii) Verify whether the synergy gains are shared equally.

  (d) Suppose, instead, that A and B agree on a 50/50 joint venture. What is the present value of the licensing income or management fees that A must receive in order to accept this equity structure?

2. Suppose that company A's project has an NPV of 200 on its own, while company B can realize 100. The synergy gain is 200. There are no taxes, and the financial markets are integrated. Assume, however, that B has a better bargaining position, and is able to obtain 45% of the equity in the first-pass negotiations (the pure-equity joint venture).

  (a) What part of the synergy gains goes to A, what part to B?

  (b) Suppose that, in the second-stage negotiations, A asks for a license contract worth 80 (in present-value terms). How should the equity shares be adjusted to preserve the division of the synergy gains (that is, to make both parties equally well-off as in the pure-equity solution)?

  (c) Which licensing contract is compatible with a 50/50 joint venture and the bargaining strengths used in part (a) of this question?

3. In Freedonia and Prisonia there are no taxes, and the capital markets are well-integrated across the two countries. Two multinational utility firms, FreeCorp and PriCorp, have WOSs that compete in the Prisonian market for electric power. Right now, the aggregate annual revenue of both producers is 1,050m, without any growth prospects. The current market value of FreeCorp's WOS is 200m, while PriCorp's WOS is worth 100m. Both companies are fully equity-financed. FreeCorp and PriCorp are negotiating a merger of their Prisonian subsidiaries. This would stop competition and would allow the producers to increase the price of electric power by 10%. Total sales would drop slightly, to 1,000m per year, but the higher profit margin would lead to a JV with a market value of 400m.

  (a) Assume initially that the newly formed JV would be a fully equity-financed firm (no bonds, royalties, management fees, etc.). The merchant bank that acts as the adviser proposes that, as FreeCorp's assets are currently worth 200m and PriCorp's assets 100m, FreeCorp should get two thirds of the shares.

      (i) Evaluate this proposal: who gets how much of the synergy gains?

      (ii) Formulate a counterproposal if you disagree.

  (b) The Prisonian Foreign Investment Act restricts the equity share of foreign owners to 50% at most.

      (i) How much of the synergy gain accrues to each parent if $\phi = 50\%$ and if there is no other contract (like a license contract, for instance)?

      (ii) As a result of the above contract, what is the side payment that PriCorp must make to FreeCorp, one way or another, so that the gains are fairly shared?

(c) PriCorp proposes that FreeCorp receive an annual management fee of 0.5% of annual sales as payment for the accounting software contributed by FreeCorp. Given perpetual sales of 1,000m per year and a yield on perpetual bonds equal to 10%, the present value of this perpetual management fee is

$$\frac{0.5\% \times 1,000m}{10\%} = 50m.$$

(d) However, the proposal is vague about whether the management fee is paid out by the JV or by PriCorp.

   (i) From FreeCorp's point of view, does it make a difference whether the management fee is paid out by the JV or by PriCorp?
   (ii) If it makes a difference, evaluate the proposed management fee for each case, and formulate a counterproposal.

Further Reading

In this age of the World Wide Web there is no longer a problem finding articles on any subject. A few seminal papers have been mentioned already in the appropriate chapters and their references are provided in the general list that follows this chapter, so this (brief) chapter itself is intended for readers with a more catholic interest.

Books

Here are a few classics on macroeconomics, including international finance and going much further than my chapters 2 and 10–11:

Wyplosz, M., and C. Burda. 1997. *Macroeconomics: A European Text*. Oxford University Press.
Heijdra, B. J., and F. van der Ploeg. 2002. *The Foundations of Modern Macroeconomics*. Oxford University Press.

For the more adventurous:

Wickens, M. 2008. *Macroeconomic Theory: A Dynamic General Equilibrium Approach*. Princeton University Press.
Obstfeld, M., and K. Rogoff. 1996. *Foundations of International Macroeconomics*. Cambridge, MA: MIT Press.

Descriptions of currency markets (chapters 3–8) and so on are provided in all textbooks that directly compete with this one and which, of course, will not be listed here. A very different discussion is provided in Lyon's book on spot currency markets, which takes a market-microstructure point of view and sees how players behave and interact:

Lyons, R. K. 2001. *The Microstructure Approach to Exchange Rates*. Cambridge, MA: MIT Press.

Forwards, futures, options, and swaps—uses and pricing—are discussed in great depth, including the continuous-time math versions, in:

Hull, J. C. 2005. Options. In *Futures and Other Derivatives*. Prentice Hall Series in Finance. Upper Saddle River, NJ: Prentice Hall International.

The classic on Value-at-Risk is:

Jorion, P. 2006. *Value at Risk: The New Benchmark for Managing Financial Risk*, 3rd edn. New York: McGraw-Hill.

For (one-country) CAPMs (and a good introduction to many other fundamental issues), I still like:

Fama, E. F. 1977. *Fundamentals of Finance*. New York: Basic Books.

A more up-to-date (and advanced) book, with a good dose of econometrics, is:

Cochrane, J. 2005. *Asset Pricing*. Princeton University Press.

Articles

The articles mentioned in the body of this book are referenced in the main list of references, which follows this chapter. If you want more, look at the great collection of selected articles on, specifically, international finance that was put together in:

Karolyi, A., and R. Stulz. 2003. *International Capital Markets*, 3 volumes. Edward Elgar.

I will not even attempt to indicate which ones I like best (beside mine). Just read them all. An excellent review paper on cross listings, too recent to be in that collection, is:

Karolyi, A. 2006. The world of cross-listings and cross-listings of the world: challenging conventional wisdom. *Review of Finance* 10(1):99–152.

References

Abuaf, N., and P. Jorion. 1990. Purchasing power parity in the long run. *Journal of Finance* 45:155-74.

Adler, M., and B. Dumas. 1983. International portfolio choice and corporation finance: a synthesis. *Journal of Finance* 38:925-84.

Adler, M., and B. Lehman. 1983. Deviations from PPP in the long run. *Journal of Finance* 38:1471-87.

Alexander, S. S. 1961. Price movements in speculative markets: trends or random walks. *Industrial Management Review* 2:7-26.

Altavilla, C., and P. De Grauwe. 2006. Forecasting and combining competing models of exchange rate determination. CESIFO Working Paper 1747.

Ammer, J., and A. D. Brunner. 1997. Are banks market timers or market makers? Explaining foreign exchange trading profits. *Journal of International Financial Markets, Institutions & Money* 7:43-60.

Apte, P., M. Kane, and P. Sercu. 1994. Relative PPP in the medium run. *Journal of International Money and Finance* 13:602-22.

Apte, P., P. Sercu, and R. Uppal. 2004. The exchange rate and purchasing power parity: extending the theory and tests. *Journal of International Money and Finance* 23(4): 553-71.

Backus, D., and G. Smith. 1993. Consumption and real exchange rates in dynamic economies with non-traded goods. *Journal of International Economics* 35:297-316.

Backus, D., S. Foresi, and C. Telmer. 2001. Affine term structure models and the forward premium anomaly. *Journal of Finance* 56:279-304.

Balassa, B. 1964. The purchasing power parity doctrine: a reappraisal. *Journal of Political Economy* 72:584-96.

Bansal, R. 1997. An exploration of the forward premium puzzle in currency markets. *Review of Financial Studies* 10:369-403.

Bansal, R., and M. Dahlquist. 2000. The forward premium puzzle: different tales from developed and emerging economies. *Journal of International Economics* 5(1):115-44.

Baum, C. F., J. T. Barkoulas, and M. Caglayan. 2001. Non-linear adjustment to purchasing power parity in the post-Bretton Woods era. *Journal of International Money and Finance* 20:379-99.

Bekaert, G., and R. J. Hodrick. 2001. Expectations hypotheses tests. *Journal of Finance* 56:1357-94.

Bell, S., and B. Kettell. 1983. *Foreign Exchange Handbook*. Graham and Trotman.

Berkowitz, J., and L. Giorgianni. 2001. Long-horizon exchange rate predictability? *Review of Economics and Statistics* 83(1):81-91.

Black, F., and M. Scholes. 1973. The pricing of options and corporate liabilities. *Journal of Political Economy* 3:637-54.

Blomberg, S. B., and G. D. Hess. 1997. Politics and exchange rate forecasts. *Journal of International Economics* 43:189-205.

Bonser-Neal, C., G. Brauer, R. Neal, and S. Wheatley. 1990. International investment restrictions and closed-end country fund prices. *Journal of Finance* 45:523-47.

Brealey, R. A., S. C. Myers, and F. Allen 2007. *Principles of Corporate Finance with S&P Bind-in Card*. McGraw-Hill Higher Education.

Brennan, M. 1979. The pricing of contingent claims in discrete time models. *Journal of Finance* 34:53–68.

Breuer, J. B. 1994. An assessment of the evidence of purchasing power parity. In *Estimating Equilibrium Exchange Rates* (ed. J. Williamson). Washington, DC: Institute for International Economics.

Carpentier, C., J.-F. L'Her, and J.-M. Suret. 2008. Does cross-listing reduce the cost of equity? Working Paper, Laval University, Québec.

Chang, P. H. K., and C. L. Osler. 1999. Methodical madness: technical analysis and the irrationality of exchange-rate forecasts. *Economic Journal* 109:636–61.

Cheung, Y.-W., and M. D. Chinn. 1998. Integration, cointegration and the forecast consistency of structural exchange rate models. *Journal of International Money and Finance* 17(5):813–30.

Cheung, Y.-W., M. D. Chinn, and A. G. Pascual. 2005. Empirical exchange rate models of the nineties: are any fit to survive? *Journal of International Money and Finance* 24(7): 1150–75.

Chinn, M., and J. Frankel. 2002. Survey data on exchange rate expectations: more currencies, more horizons, more tests. In *Monetary Policy, Capital Flows and Financial Market Developments in the Era of Financial Globalizsation: Essays in Honour of Max Fry*, pp. 145–67. London: Routledge.

Clarida, R. H., L. Sarno, M. P. Taylor, and G. Valente. 2003. The out-of-sample success of term structure models as exchange rate predictors: a step beyond. *Journal of International Economics* 60(1):61–83.

Cornell, B., and M. R. Reinganum. 1981. Forward and futures prices: evidence from the foreign exchange markets. *Journal of Finance* 36:1035–45.

Cox, J., S. Ross, and M. Rubinstein. 1979. Option pricing: a simplified approach. *Journal of Financial Economics* 7:229–63.

Cumby, R. E. 1987. Is it risk? Explaining deviations from uncovered interest parity. *Journal of Monetary Economics* 22:279–300.

Cumby, R. E., and M. Obstfeld. 1984. International interest rate and price level linkages under flexible exchange rates: a review of recent evidence. In *Exchange Rate Theory and Practice* (ed. J. Bilson and R. Marston). University of Chicago Press.

Curcio, R., and C. Goodhart. 1991. Chartism: a controlled experiment. LSE Financial Markets Group Discussion Paper 124 (October).

Darby, M. R. 1983. Movements in purchasing power parity: the short and long runs. In *The International Transmission of Information* (ed. M. R. Darby and J. R. Lothian). University of Chicago Press.

Deardorff, A. V. 1979. One-way arbitrage and its implications for the foreign exchange markets. *Journal of Political Economy* 87:351–65.

De Grauwe, P., and M. Grimaldi. 2001. Exchange rates, prices and money: a long-run perspective. *International Journal of Finance and Economics* 6(4):289–313.

De Santis, G., and B. Gérard. 1997. International asset pricing and portfolio diversification with time-varying risk. *Journal of Finance* 52:1881–912.

———. 1998. How big is the premium for currency risk? *Journal of Financial Economics* 49:375–412.

Diebold, F. X., S. Husted, and M. Rush. 1991. Real exchange rates under the gold standard. *Journal of Political Economy* 99:1252–71.

Dimson, E. 1979. Risk measurement when shares are subject to infrequent trading. *Journal of Financial Economics* 7:197–226.

Domowitz, I., and C. S. Hakkio. 1985. Conditional variance and the risk premium in the foreign exchange market. *Journal of International Economics* 19:47–66.

Dooley, M. P., and J. Schafer. 1983. Analysis of short-run exchange rate behavior: March 1973 to November 1981. In *Exchange Rate Instability: Causes, Consequences and Remedies* (ed. D. Bigman and T. Taya). Cambridge, MA: Ballinger.

Dumas, B. 1977. Testing international asset pricing: discussion. *Journal of Finance* 32: 512–16.

———. 1992. Dynamic equilibrium and the real exchange rate in a spatially separated world. *Review of Financial Studies* 5:153–80.

Dumas, B., and B. Solnik. 1995. The world price of foreign exchange risk. *Journal of Finance* 50:445–79.

Edison, H. J. 1985. Purchasing power parity: a quantitative reassessment of the 1920s experience. *Journal of International Money and Finance* 4(3):361–72.

Eldridge, R. M., and R. Maltby. 1992. On the existence and implied cost of carry in a medieval English forward/futures market. *Review of Futures Markets* 11(1):36–47.

Engel, C. 1995. Why is the forward exchange rate forecast biased? A survey of recent evidence. *Federal Reserve Bank of Kansas City* Research Working Paper 95-06.

Engel, C., and K. D. West. 2005. Exchange rates and fundamentals. *Journal of Political Economy* 113:485–517.

Eun, C., and S. Janakiramanan. 1986. A model of international asset pricing with a constraint on the foreign equity ownership. *Journal of Finance* 41:897–914.

Evans, M. D. D. 2002. FX trading and exchange rate dynamics. *Journal of Finance* 57: 2405–47.

Evans, M. D. D., and R. K. Lyons. 2005. Meese–Rogoff redux: micro-based exchange rate forecasting. Working Paper, Haas School, Berkeley and Georgetown University.

Fairlamb, D. 1989. The elusive El Dorado of Spanish pensions. *Institutional Investor* (April), pp. 177–84.

Fama, E. 1984. Forward and spot exchange rates. *Journal of Monetary Economics* 14: 319–38.

Fase, M. M. G., and A. P. Huijser. 1989. The profitability of official foreign exchange market intervention: a case study for the Netherlands 1974–1989. Research Memorandum 8821, De Nederlandsche Bank.

Faust, J., and J. H. Rogers. 2003. Monetary policy's role in exchange rate behavior. *Journal of Monetary Economics* 50:1403–24.

Faust, J., J. H. Rogers, and J. H. Wright. 2003. Exchange rate forecasting: the errors we've really made. *Journal of International Economics* 60(1):35–59.

Fischer, A. M. 2003. Measurement error and the profitability of interventions: a closer look at SNB transactions data. *Economics Letters* 81(1):137–42.

Frankel, J. A. 1979. On the mark: a theory of floating exchange rates based on real interest differentials? *American Economic Review* 69:610–22.

Frankel, J. A., and C. Engel. 1984. Do asset-demand functions opitimize over the mean and variance of real return? A six-currency test. *Journal of International Economics* 17(3–4):309–23.

Frankel, J. A., and A. K. Rose. 1994. A survey of empirical research on nominal exchange rates. National Bureau of Economic Research Working Paper W4865.

———. 1996. A panel project on purchasing power parity: mean reversion within and between countries. *Journal of International Economics* 40(1–2):209–24.

French, K. 1983. A comparison of futures and forward prices. *Journal of Financial Economics* 12:311–42.

Froot, K., and R. Thaler. 1990. Anomalies: foreign exchange. *Journal of Economic Perspectives* 4:179–92.

Gajewski, J. F., and C. Gresse. 2003. Trading cost analysis: a comparison of Euronext Paris and the London Stock Exchange. Mimeo, Université Paris XII and Université Paris X.

García-Herrero, A., S. Gavilá, and D. Santabárbara. 2006. China's banking reform: an assessment of its evolution and possible impact. *CESIFO Economic Studies* 52:304–63.

Garman, M. B., and S. W. Kohlhagen. 1983. Foreign currency options values. *Journal of International Money and Finance* 2:231–37.

Gençay, R. 1999. Linear, non-linear and essential foreign exchange rate prediction with simple technical trading rules. *Journal of International Economics* 47(1):91–107.

Gernaey, K. 1988. *Technische Trading Rules: Een Empirische Onderzoek op de Belgische Vrije Wisselmarkt voor de Periode 20/02n6 tot 20/08/87.* S. N. Leuven.

Glen, J. D. 1992. Real exchange rates in the short, medium, and long run. *Journal of International Economics* 33(1–2):147–66.

Goodman, S. H. 1979. Foreign exchange rate forecasting techniques: implications for business and policy. *Journal of Finance* 34:415–27.

Grabbe, O. 1983. The pricing of put and call options on foreign exchange. *Journal of International Money and Finance* 2:239–53.

——. 1995. *International Financial Markets*, 3rd edn. New York: Elsevier.

Green, P. 1992. Is currency trading profitable? Exploiting deviations from uncovered interest rate parity. *Financial Analysts Journal* 48:82–86.

Grossman, S. J., and J. E. Stiglitz. 1980. On the impossibility of informationally efficient markets. *American Economic Review* 70:393–408.

Gultekin, M., B. Gultekin, and A. Penati. 1989. Capital controls and international capital market segmentation: the evidence from the Japanese and American stock markets. *Journal of Finance* 44:849–69.

Hansen, L. P., and R. J. Hodrick. 1980. Forward exchange rates as optimal predictors of future spot rates: an econometric analysis. *Journal of Political Economy* 88:829–53.

Halliday, L. 1989. The international stock exchange directory. *Institutional Investor* March, pp. 197–204.

Hietala, P. 1989. Asset pricing in partially segmented markets: evidence from the Finnish market. *Journal of Finance* 44:697–718.

Hodrick, R. J. 1988. The empirical evidence on the efficiency of forward and futures foreign exchange market. *Journal of International Economics* 25(3–4):387–90.

——. 1989. Risk, uncertainty and exchange rates. *Journal of Monetary Economics* 23: 433–59.

Hodrick, R. J., and S. Srivastava. 1984. An investigation of risk and return in forward foreign exchange. *Journal of International Money and Finance* 3:1–29.

——. 1986. The covariation of risk premiums and expected future spot exchange rates. *Journal of International Money and Finance* 5:5–22.

Hollifield, B., and R. Uppal. 1997. An examination of uncovered interest parity in segmented international commodity markets. *Journal of Finance* 52:2145–70.

Hopper, G. P. 1997. What determines the exchange rate: economic factors or market sentiment? *Federal Reserve Bank of Philadelphia Business Review* 1997:17–29.

Huisman, R., K. Koedijk, C. Kool, and F. Nissen. 1998. Extreme support for uncovered interest parity. *Journal for International Money and Finance* 17:211–28.

Ikenberry, D., J. Lakonishok, and T. Vermaelen. 1995. Market underreaction to open market share repurchases. *Journal of Financial Economics* 39:181–208.

Jensen, M. C. 1986. Agency cost of free cash flow, corporate finance, and takeovers. *American Economic Review* 76:323–29.

Jensen, M. C., and W. H. Meckling. 1976. Theory of the firm: managerial behavior, agency costs and ownership structure. *Journal of Financial Economics* 3:305–60.

Jorion, P. 2003. *Value at Risk: The New Benchmark for Managing Financial Risk*, 2nd edn. New York: McGraw-Hill.

Jorion, P., and R. J. Sweeney. 1996. Mean reversion in real exchange rates: evidence and implications for forecasting. *Journal of International Money and Finance* 15(4): 535–50.

Karolyi, G. A. 1998. Why do companies list shares abroad? A survey of the evidence and its managerial implications. *Financial Markets, Institutions & Instruments* 7(1):1–60.

———. 2006. The world of cross-listings and cross-listings of the world: challenging conventional wisdom. *Review of Finance* 10(1):99–152.

Karolyi, G. A., and R. M. Stulz. 2002. Are financial assets priced locally or globally? NBER Working Paper 8994. (Appeared in 2003 in *Handbook of the Economics of Finance* (ed. G. M. Constantinides, M. Harris and R. M. Stulz), 1st edn, volume 1, pp. 975–1020. Elsevier.)

Kho, V. 1996. Time varying risk premia, volatility, and technical trading profits. *Journal of Financial Economics* 41:249–90.

Kilian, L., and M. P. Taylor. 2003. Why is it so difficult to beat the random walk forecast of exchange rates? *Journal of International Economics* 60:85–107.

Kim, S., and N. Roubini. 2000. Exchange rate anomalies in the industrial countries: a solution with a structural VAR approach. *Journal of Monetary Economics* 45:561–86.

Kroner, K. F., and J. Sultan. 1993. Time-varying distributions and dynamic hedging with foreign currencies. *Journal of Financial and Quantitative Analysis* 28:535–51.

Krugman, P. R. 1989. *Exchange-Rate Instability.* Cambridge, MA: MIT Press.

La Porta, R., F. Lopez-de-Silanes, A. Shleifer, and R. W. Vishny. 1998a. Law and finance. *Journal of Political Economy* 106:1113–54.

———. 1998b. Legal determinants of external finance. *Journal of Finance* 52:1131–1150.

La Porta, R., F. Lopez-de-Silanes, and A. Shleifer. 2006. What works in securities laws? *Journal of Finance* 61:1–32.

Leahy, M. P. 1995. The profitability of U.S. intervention in the foreign exchange markets. *Journal of International Money and Finance* 14:823–44.

LeBaron, B. 1996. Technical trading rule profitability and foreign exchange intervention. Working Paper, University of Wisconsin at Madison.

———. 1998. A dynamic trading strategy approach to deviations from uncovered interest parity. Working Paper, University of Wisconsin at Madison.

Levich, R. M. 1980a. Analyzing the accuracy of foreign exchange advisory services: theory and evidence. In *Exchange Risk and Exposure: Current Developments in International Financial Management* (ed. R. M. Levich and C. G. Wihlborg), chapter 5. Lanham, MD: Rowman & Littlefield.

———. 1980b. Use and evaluation of foreign exchange forecasts. In *Currency Risk and the Corporation* (ed. B. Antl). London: Euromoney Publications.

———. 1982. Evaluating the performance of the forecasters. In *The Management of Foreign Exchange Risk* (ed. R. Ensor). London: Euromoney Publications.

———. 1983. Exchange rate forecasting. In *International Finance Handbook* (ed. I. Giddy and A. George), chapter 8. John Wiley.

Levich, R. M., and L. R. Thomas. 1993. The significance of technical trading-rule profits on the forex market. *Journal of International Money and Finance* 12:451–74.

Lewis, K. 1989. Changing beliefs and systematic forecast errors. *American Economic Review* 79:621–36.

Lintner, J. 1965. The valuation of risk assets and the selection of risky investments in stock portfolios and capital budgets. *Review of Economics and Statistics* 47(1):13–37.

Lisi, F., and A. Medio. 1997. Is a random walk the best exchange rate predictor? *International Journal of Forecasting* 13(2):255–67.

Liu, F., and P. Sercu. 2008. The forward puzzle: the roles of exchange-rate regime and base-currency strength. K. U. Leuven FEB-AFI Working Paper.

Lothian, J. R. 1997. Multi-country evidence on the behavior of purchasing power parity under the current float. *Journal of International Money and Finance* 16(1):19–35.

Lothian, J. R., and M. P. Taylor. 1996. Real exchange rate behavior: the recent float from the perspective of the past two centuries. *Journal of Political Economy* 104:488–509.

Lui, Y.-H., and D. Mole. 1998. The use of fundamental and technical analyses by foreign exchange dealers: Hong Kong evidence. *Journal of International Money and Finance* 17(3):535–45.

Lustig, H., and A. Verdelhan. 2007. The cross section of foreign currency risk premia and consumption growth risk. *American Economic Review* 97:89–117.

Lyons, R. J. 1998. Profits and position control: a week of FX dealing. *Journal of International Money and Finance* 17(1):97–115.

Mark, N. C. 1988, Time-varying betas and risk premia in the pricing of forward foreign exchange contracts. *Journal of Financial Economics* 22:335–54.

——. 1995. Exchange rates and fundamentals: evidence on long-horizon predictability. *American Economic Review* 85:201–18.

Mark, N. C., and D. Y. Choi. 1997. Real exchange-rate prediction over long horizons. *Journal of International Economics* 43:29–60.

Mark, N. C., and Y. Wu. 1997. Risk, policy rules, and noise: rethinking deviations from uncovered interest parity. Tinbergen Institute Discussion Papers 97-041/2.

Markowitz, H. M. 1952. Portfolio selection. *Journal of Finance* 7:77–91.

Meese, R. A., and K. S. Rogoff. 1983. Empirical exchange rate models of the seventies: do they fit out of sample? *Journal of International Economics* 14(1–2):3–24.

——. 1988. Was it real? The exchange-rate interest differential relation over the modern floating-rate period. *Journal of Finance* 43:933–48.

Meese, R. A., and A. K. Rose. 1991. An empirical assessment of non-linearities in models of exchange rate determination. *Review of Economic Studies* 58(3):603–19.

Merton, R. 1973. Theory of rational option pricing. *Bell Journal of Economics and Management Science* 4(1):141–83.

Michael, P., A. Robert Nobay, and D. A. Peel. 1997. Transactions costs and nonlinear adjustment in real exchange rates: an empirical investigation. *Journal of Political Economy* 105:862–79.

Miller, M. H. 1977. Debt and taxes. *Journal of Finance* 32:261–75.

Miller, M., and F. Modigliani. 1958. The cost of capital, corporation finance, and the theory of investment. *American Economic Review* 48:261–97.

Mossin, J. 1966. Equilibrium in a capital asset market. *Econometrica* 34(4):768–83.

Murray, C. J., and D. H. Papell. 2002. The purchasing power parity persistence paradigm. *Journal of International Economics* 56:1–19.

Murray, J., M. Zelmer, and S. Williamson. 1990. Measuring the profitability and effectiveness of foreign exchange market intervention: some Canadian evidence. Technical Report 53, Bank of Canada.

Mussa, M. 1986. Nominal exchange rate regimes and the behavior of real exchange rates: evidence and implications. *Carnegie-Rochester Conference Series on Public Policy* 25: 117–213.

Myers, S. C. 1977. Determinants of corporate borrowing. *Journal of Financial Economics* 5:147–75.

Myers, S. C., and N. Majluf. 1984. Corporate financing and investment decisions when firms have information that investors do not have. *Journal of Financial Economics* 13: 187–221.

Nash, J. F. 1950. The bargaining problem. *Econometrica* 1950:1552–62.

Neely, C. J. 1998. Technical analysis and the profitability of U.S. foreign exchange intervention. *Federal Reserve Bank of St Louis Review*, pp. 3–17.

Neely, C. J., and P. Weller. 2003. Intraday technical trading in the foreign exchange market. *Journal of International Money and Finance* 22(2):223–37.

Neely, C. J., P. Weller, and R. Dittmar. 1997. Is technical trading profitable in foreign exchange markets? A genetic programming approach. *Journal of Financial and Quantitative Analysis* 32:405–26.

Obstfeld, M., and A. M. Taylor. 1997. Nonlinear aspects of goods-market arbitrage and adjustment: Heckscher's commodity points revisited. *Journal of the Japanese and International Economies* 11:441–79.

Okunev, J., and D. White. 2003. Do momentum-based strategies still work in foreign currency markets? *Journal of Financial and Quantitative Analysis* 38:425–48.

Pagano, M., and A. J. Padilla 2005. Efficiency gains from the integration of exchanges: lessons from the Euronext "natural experiment". Report for Euronext, Nonconfidential version, LECG, 4 May.

Pesaran, M. H., and R. Smith. 1995. Estimating long-run relationships from dynamic heterogeneous panels. *Journal of Econometrics* 68:79–113.

Raj, M. 2000. Transaction data tests of efficiency in the Singapore futures markets. *Journal of Futures Markets* 20:687–704.

Rawls, S. W. III, and C. W. Smithson. 1990. Strategic risk management. *Journal of Applied Corporate Finance* 2:6–18.

Rendleman, R., and B. Bartter. 1980. The pricing of options on debt securities. *Journal of Financial and Quantitative Analysis* 15:11–24.

Robinson, B., and P. Warburton. 1980. Managing currency holdings: lessons from the floating period. *London Business School Economic Outlook* February, pp. 18–27.

Rogoff, K. S. 1996. The purchasing power parity puzzle. *Journal of Economic Literature* 34:647–68.

Roll, R. 1979. Violations of purchasing power parity and their implications for efficient international commodity markets. In *International Finance and Trade* (ed. M. Sarnat and G. P. Szegö). Cambridge, MA: Ballinger.

Roll, R., and S. Yan. 2000. An explanation of the forward premium "puzzle". *European Financial Management* 6(2):121–48.

Rubinstein, A. 1982. Perfect equilibrium in a bargaining model. *Econometrica* 50:97–109.

Rubinstein, M. 1976. The valuation of uncertain income streams and the pricing of options. *Bell Journal of Economics and Management Science* 7:407–25.

Samuelson, P. A. 1964. Theoretical notes on trade problems. *Review of Economics and Statistics* 46:145–54.

Samuelson, P. A., and R. C. Merton. 1969. A complete model of warrant pricing that maximizes utility. *Industrial Management Review* 10:818–41.

Sarantis, N. 1999. Modeling non-linearities in real effective exchange rates. *Journal of International Money and Finance* 18:27–45.

Sarno, L. 2005. Viewpoint: towards a solution to the puzzles in exchange rate economics: where do we stand? *Canadian Journal of Economics/Revue Canadienne d'Économique* 38(3):673–708.

Scholes, M., and J. Williams. 1977. Estimating betas from non-synchronous data. *Journal of Financial Economics* 5:308–28.

Schotman, P., S. Straetmans, and C. de Vries. 1997. Big news in small samples. Discussion Paper 97-083/2, Tinbergen Institute.

Sercu, P. 1980. A generalisation of the international capital asset pricing model. *Revue de l'Association Française de Finance* 1(1):91–135.

———. 1981. Mean–variance asset pricing with deviations from PPP. FETEW Doctoral Dissertation Series 40, K. U. Leuven.

Sercu, P. 1983. De ideale basisperiode in de koopkrachtpariteitstheory (The ideal basis period in PPP theory). *Tijdschrift voor Economie en Management* 27(3):315-35.

Sercu, P., and R. Uppal. 1995. *International Financial Markets and the Firm.* Mason, OH: South-Western Publishing Co.

Sercu, P., and M. Vandebroek. 2005. What UIP tests on extreme samples reveal about the missing variable. *Journal of International Money and Finance* 24(8):1237-60.

Sercu, P., and T. Vinaimont. 2006. The forward bias in the ECU: peso risks vs. fads and fashions. *Journal of Banking & Finance* 30(8):2409-32.

Sercu, P., and X. Wu. 2000. Cross- and delta-hedges: regression- versus price-based hedge ratios. *Journal of Banking & Finance* 24(5):735-57.

Sercu, P., M. Vandebroek, and X. P. Wu. Forthcoming. Is the forward bias economically small? Evidence from intra-ERM rates. *Journal of International Money and Finance.*

Sercu, P., M. Vandebroek, and T. Vinaimont. 2008. Thin-trading effects in beta: bias v. estimation error. *Journal of Business Finance and Accounting* 35:1196-219.

Sharpe, W. F. 1964. Capital asset prices: a theory of market equilibrium under conditions of risk. *Journal of Finance* 19:425-42.

———. 1978. *Investments.* Upper Saddle River, NJ: Prentice Hall International.

Sjöö, B., and R. J. Sweeney. 2000. Time-varying foreign-exchange risk and central bank intervention: estimating profits from intervention and speculation. *Journal of International Financial Markets, Institutions & Money* 10(3-4):275-86.

———. 2001. The foreign-exchange costs of central bank intervention: evidence from Sweden. *Journal of International Money and Finance* 20:219-47.

Solnik, B. H. 1974. The international pricing of risk: an empirical investigation of the world capital market structure. *Journal of Finance* 29:365-78.

———. 1977. Testing international asset pricing: some pessimistic views. *Journal of Finance* 32:503-12.

Spamann, H. 2006. On the insignificance and/or endogeneity of La Porta et al.'s "Anti-director rights index" under consistent coding. Discussion Paper 7, Harvard Law School/John M. Olin Center.

Stehle, R. 1977. An empirical test of alternative hypotheses of national and international pricing of risky assets. *Journal of Finance* 32:493-502.

Stulz, R. M. 1999. Globalization of equity markets and the cost of capital. *Journal of Applied Corporate Finance* 12(3):8-25.

Surajaras, P., and R. J. Sweeney. 1992. *Profit-Making Speculation in Foreign Exchange Markets.* Boulder, CO: Westview Press.

Sutton, J. 1986. Non-cooperative bargaining theory: an introduction. *Review of Economic Studies* 53:709-24.

Sweeney, R. J. 1986. Beating the foreign exchange market. *Journal of Finance* 41:163-82.

———. 1988. Some new filter rule tests: methods and results. *Journal of Financial and Quantitative Analysis* 23:285-300.

———. 1997. Do central banks lose on foreign-exchange intervention? A review article. *Journal of Banking and Finance* 21:1667-84.

———. 2000. Does the Fed beat the foreign-exchange market? *Journal of Banking and Finance* 24:665-94.

———. 2006. Mean reversion in G-10 nominal exchange rates. *Journal of Financial and Quantitative Analysis* 42:685-708.

Taylor, D. 1982. Official intervention in the foreign exchange market, or bet against the central bank. *Journal of Political Economy* 90:256-68.

Taylor, J. B. 1993. Discretion versus policy rules in practice? *Carnegie-Rochester Conference Series on Public Policy* 39:195-214.

Taylor, M. P. 1988. An empirical examination of long-run purchasing power parity using cointegration techniques. *Applied Economics* 20(10):1369-81.

Taylor, M. P., and D. A. Peel. 2000. Nonlinear adjustment, long-run equilibrium and exchange rate fundamentals. *Journal of International Money and Finance* 19:33-53.

Taylor, M. P., D. A. Peel, and L. Sarno. 2001. Nonlinear mean-reversion in real exchange rates: toward a solution to the purchasing power parity puzzles. *International Economic Review* 42(4):1015-42.

Taylor, S. J. 1992. Rewards available to currency futures speculators: compensation for risk or inefficient pricing? *Economic Record* 68(Supplement):105-16

———. 1994. Trading futures using a channel rule: a study of the predictive power of technical analysis with currency examples. *Journal of Futures Markets* 14:215-35.

Taylor, S. J., and H. Allen. 1992. The use of technical analysis in the foreign exchange market. *Journal of International Money and Finance* 11:304-14.

Thomas, L. R. 1986. Random walk profits in currency futures trading. *Journal of Futures Markets* 6:109-26.

Uppal, R. 1993. A general equilibrium model of international portfolio choice. *Journal of Finance* 48:529-53.

Veugelers, R., and K. Kesteloot. 1996. Bargained shares in joint ventures among asymmetric partners: is the Matthew effect catalyzing? *Journal of Economics* 64(1): 23-51.

Villanueva, M. 2002. Forecasting currency returns: can we exploit the forward bias. Working Paper, Brandeis University.

Wu, Y. 1996. Are real exchange rates nonstationary: evidence from a panel-data test. *Journal of Money, Credit, and Banking* 28(1):54-63.

Xu, Z. 2003. Purchasing power parity, price indices, and exchange rate forcasts. *Journal of International Money and Finance* 22:105-30.

Index